The Princeton Review®

PrincetonReview.com

THE BEST VALUE COLLEGES

2012 Edition

By Robert Franek, Laura Braswell,
David Soto, Seamus Mullarkey, and
The Staff of The Princeton Review

Random House, Inc., New York
2012 Edition

The Princeton Review, Inc.
111 Speen Street, Suite 550
Framingham, MA 01701
E-mail: editorialsupport@review.com

Published in the United States by Random House, Inc., New York, and simultaneously in Canada by Random House of Canada Limited, Toronto. This is a revised edition of a book first published in 1992.

ISBN 978-0-375-42760-2

Senior VP—Publisher: Robert Franek
Editors: Seamus Mullarkey, Laura Braswell
Production: John Wujcik, Ryan Tozzi, Aaron DeLand and Vanessa Han
Data Collection: David Soto

Printed in the United States of America on partially recycled paper.

9 8 7 6 5 4 3 2 1

2012 Edition

CONTENTS

PART 1: INTRODUCTION 1

Introduction 1
How to Use This Book 10
Getting into the Best Value Colleges 19
Top 10 Private Colleges 19
Top 10 Public Colleges 22
Tuition-Free Schools 25
Best Value Private Schools 28
Best Value Public Schools 42
Start Your College Search Here 57
Schools by Region 58
Schools by Price 70
Lists by Interests 89

PART 2: SCHOOL PROFILES 129

Top 10 Private Colleges 129
Top 10 Public Colleges 171
Tuition-Free Schools 213
Best Value Private Schools 235
Best Value Public Schools 367

PART 3: INDEXES 499

Index by Name 499
Index by State 501

INTRODUCTION

Obviously, you want to find a college that has the educational and social environment you're looking for, and where you will be well suited to flourish as a full-blown college student. You should begin with a thorough self-examination or personal inventory. Once you identify the things that are most important to you, make a chart to help keep your research organized. When you visit a school or as you navigate through school websites, note how well these schools fit into your ideal situation. The best colleges for you will gradually begin to stand out.

The Importance of Cost in the Overall Scheme of Things

You might have noticed in your research of colleges that the cost of college is getting more and more expensive, and at a steeper rate than most other things. Some people think a school's cost is a pretty good indicator of the quality of the academics it offers. Otherwise, why would a perfectly reasonable person shell out so much cash to go to one school over another that charges significantly less? But there are many schools offering outstanding academics at far lower costs than their academically competitive counterparts. Some schools—like the ones in this book—are, for one reason or another, exceptionally good deals. There's a really good chance that you will find happiness and a great education (at a price that won't hurt your future) at one of the schools in this book. As for the schools that aren't in this book: Our best advice is to use common sense. A good deal is a good deal, and we're sure you know one when you see it. Finding the best fit school for you is a personal journey; this book is to highlight schools that we know are great deals for a large majority of students.

You should also keep in mind that many factors will probably influence your decision about which colleges you apply to, and where you ultimately decide to go. In addition to cost, there's location, size, and your intended major. Intangible qualities are important, too. What's the school's reputation? Does the campus look like a little slice of paradise or a cross between Legoland and the seventh ring of Hell? Will you have the chance to learn almost anything, such as underwater basket weaving? Will you have anything remotely resembling a good time during your four years? Will you make connections with people that will help you build a successful business future?

In a nutshell, our advice about how you should choose a best college for you is to take the best deal you can get at a school where you think you'll get a great education while having a good time. Attending a school just because it is affordable makes no sense if you are going to be miserable for (at least) four years. College should be fun. On the other hand, it makes no sense to pay out the nose at some swanky private school if you can go to a school that's less expensive, just as good, and able to provide equally bright prospects for your future. The truth is that you need to think long and hard before signing up for a college—and perhaps a major—that may not set you up for a high-paying job after graduation. We're not against it, but if you are going to assume significant student loan debt in order to finance it, you will likely have a hard time making ends meet once it's time to start repaying those loans.

Nonmonetary Factors to Consider When Choosing a College

Ultimately, every school in this book offers a fabulous education. Only a few schools, however, offer world-renowned cooperative education programs, student housing on a beach, a broad core curriculum, the opportunity to be a fighter pilot, or classes in that obscure language that you have set your sights on learning.

As you get information from your parents, friends, guidance counselor, mailed brochures, and guidebooks like this one, you'll form some ideas about your college options. The more research you do, the better. Remember that brochures from and websites built by the school are not going to be completely objective because they are trying to lure you to those schools. In the best of this material, you can get a decent idea of the academic offerings and the basic admissions requirements. You will see some of the best-looking students and the most appealing architecture on campus, and you won't hear anything about anything that is remotely unpleasant. Look this stuff over, but don't make any decisions based solely on what you read and see in these fancy, glossy materials. There is a ton of information out there. Keep your information organized and go to many different sources for information. Naturally, we're pretty sure that our tools are the most useful and best designed, but we know that we're not the only game in town, so look around and compare your findings against one another. If at all financially possible, visit all the schools to which you are seriously considering applying. Try to arrange through the Admissions Office to stay on campus with a current student who can show you the real ins and outs of the school.

Here are some things to consider as you embark upon your college search.

Public Versus Private

Public post-secondary schools are usually operated by a state or local government (or both) and supported by money collected through taxes. Private post-secondary schools are operated as nonprofit organizations. They generally need to receive more money from their students in order to operate, though not all of their students pay full price. "State" colleges and universities are public schools that offer a relatively low-cost education to residents of the state in which they are located. You're probably well-acquainted with your state's big universities. A catch with these schools is that they're only a lower-cost option for state residents. If you're from out of state, these schools will charge much more money for you to attend, sometimes as much as the full price of a private college or university. Another public post-secondary school with which you're likely to be familiar is your local community college (see below). It would cost you even less to attend a community college than it would to attend a "state" school in your home state. Private colleges and universities include some of the most well-known and difficult-to-get-into schools in the country. Harvard College, Massachusetts Institute of Technology (MIT), and Stanford University are some private institutions of which you may have heard.

School's Acceptance Rate

Knowing the percentage of applicants who are admitted each year is helpful, but it can be deceiving. Why? Because many schools have self-selecting applicant pools. Brigham Young University, for instance has a very high acceptance rate, but don't even try waltzing in there with a B-average and middle-range ACT scores. Despite its relatively high acceptance rate, BYU remains exceptionally difficult to get into because virtually every applicant belongs to The Church of Jesus Christ of Latter-day Saints and has very strong academic credentials. Another obvious example is state schools. You will likely face a notably more selective evaluation as a nonresident (out-of-state) applicant than applicant to the same school who is a resident, though at some schools the reverse is true

Student/Faculty Ratio

At almost every college, the average class size—particularly for first- and second-year students—is larger than its student/faculty ratio appears to indicate, and it's even larger at many big universities. Keep your eye on this statistic, but what matters most is whether students at a school actually like their teachers and their classes. Visit the school and ask the students how happy they are with their courses and whether they think their professors are accessible. Better yet, sit in on a few core curriculum courses or general education courses to see firsthand how you're likely to spend much of your freshman year.

Standardized Test Scores

It's important to remember that average does not mean the same thing as minimum. Some students look at colleges in college guides like this one and eliminate schools where the average range for SAT or ACT scores is higher than their own. Don't do that! An average is not a cutoff. Don't exclude schools with combined SAT average that are 150 points over—or under—your own.

Location, Location, Location

Hopping urban nightlife or rural serenity? Weekends at the beach, or strapping on snowshoes? Close to home or as far away from home as possible? Remember that you're selecting not only a school, but also a place to live for the next few years. If you just can't decide between a college in Maine and a college in California and you're not so keen on cold weather, think about the weather! There's also a really good chance that many of the employers who recruit on campus will be from the area. And, speaking of work, a big city (or a big-time college town) will offer more employment opportunities if you're going to have to work your way through school. It will be easier to find jobs that won't bring you into constant contact with your schoolmates, too, if the prospect of them seeing you waiting tables in a shirt and silly bowtie bothers you.

School Size

Big schools have more diverse student populations, a ton of extracurricular activities, and massive libraries. Though classes might be huge and impersonal, there are a lot more of them to choose from. Often, big schools are full of annoying red tape, but life is not as overwhelming as you might think because the university is divided into smaller colleges. Big schools are often located in big cities or college towns, where a wealth of cultural and social activities are constantly available. There will probably be a 24-hour grocery store within walking distance of where you live. Sporting events are exhilarating, nationally televised, and larger than life. (That also breeds an atmosphere for lots of distractions, so keep that in mind as well!) Small schools, in contrast, have smaller classes—and fewer of them. Students are generally taught by real professors (not by graduate teaching assistants) in intimate classroom settings. If you want to ask questions in class, you can do so without feeling foolish. You'll meet most of the people in your class and much of the administration. You are likely to develop more friendships at a smaller school, but you will have to choose your friends, your boyfriends, your girlfriends, and your enemies all from the same small group of people. If you're a good athlete but not all-state, you'll get the chance to play intercollegiate sports at a smaller school. And if you are into theater but not plotting a gilded path to Broadway, you'll have a better chance of landing parts in your school's productions. There will be fewer extracurricular activities overall, but more opportunities to be deeply involved in a particular pursuit and to secure leadership roles.

Social Life

Some schools have a really active social atmosphere, while others are filled with students who study ALL the time. Most schools are a mix of both—mostly depending on which crowd you choose to hang out with. Do you picture the base camp of your social life to be on campus or off campus? Does a huge fraternity scene excite or alarm you? Do you want a school where the football (or basketball or hockey) team is the main focus of social life? These are just a few of the things you want to consider. How important will intramural sports be to you? Do you want to be published in the literary magazine on campus?

Fellow Students

At some schools, every student does his or her own thing, and many different ethnicities, nationalities, religions, and cultures are represented. At other schools, everybody looks and acts pretty much the same. Some schools settle in between these two extremes. Make sure you choose a school where you'll be able to get along with and feel comfortable with your peers for (at least) four years.

No one knows colleges and universities better than the students who currently attend them. Seek out any and all personal friends, sons and daughters of family friends, and recent graduates of your high school who attend college, especially those who attend colleges that you are considering. Call them. Send them an e-mail. Stop by their houses. See if you can visit them at school. Pick their brains about everything they know and about their experience. You simply won't find any information that is more direct and honest.

Percentage of Students who go on to Graduate or Professional School

High percentages mean either that the college is an intellectual enclave of incubating professors or that it is a bastion of future lawyers and doctors. Low percentages mean graduates are going out and getting real jobs. These outcomes are neither good nor bad. Also know that virtually every college in the country can boast of high acceptance rates into medical school because premed programs are designed to weed out those who will not be strong candidates even before they apply. If you're thinking about medical school, ask the colleges how many of their students apply to medical school each year.

Getting In

As selective as you'll be about choosing the right college for you, know that many of the colleges we profile will be selective in choosing the right students for their college. While some of the schools might admit upwards of 80 percent of their applicants, some schools admit less than 10 percent of their applicants, and so you might find yourself competing for a seat at a school that has many more applicants that there are seats. You're likely going to have to put quite a bit of effort into getting in. High grades and challenging courses are just the beginning!

If you're at all like the more than 2 million high school students who apply to college each year, you're probably wondering what college admissions officers are really looking for in an applicant. What exactly does it take to get into a great college? What can I do to make my application stand out? Once I get accepted, how do I know which college is best for me?

> We have some basic advice for you here, but we have lots more advice on **PrincetonReview.com**, so make sure you take some time to explore not only college profiles, but standardized test prep help and financial aid advice.

Timing

The most important thing to remember is that waiting until the last minute is not a good idea at all. It takes time to fill out applications and to write essays. A lot of colleges—especially selective ones—require supplemental essays, and you'll need recommendation letters. You'll want to give teachers and counselors plenty of time to write the letters so they can write a thorough and supportive recommendation. They'll probably be writing letters for lots of students, so don't wait until the last minute to gather all of these materials together. You'll also have to leave time to request official transcripts. So you'll have to look at school application deadlines and plan to be finished at least a few weeks before that date.

Criteria

When colleges describe their ideal candidates, they all describe more or less the same person. This ideal candidate has top-notch grades, high standardized test scores, exemplary extracurricular activities, a fascinating after-school job, terrific hobbies, and a shelf filled with awards. Real college applicants sometimes feel defeated before they even begin because they try to compare themselves to this invisible ideal candidate. Don't discount your changes simply because you don't feel like you measure up to the ideal candidate. You are an individual with wonderful experiences; you just have to make sure that your application shows those experiences. And if, even after a lot of self-reflection, you don't feel like you've done anything amazing, then spend some time venturing into new activities, such as volunteer work or a community service to build out that application.

Additionally, even those students who come frighteningly close to the ideal picture we've painted don't always get into the school of their dreams. There are lots of perfect scores and 4.0-plus GPAs. But even extremely selective schools will turn those people down and instead invite someone who seems more "interesting" in the name of diversity. It takes all kinds of students to create an enriching campus atmosphere. No matter who you are, nobody's application is "perfect." But if you show that you work hard for good grades in challenging classes and that you spend time outside of class doing activities you are passionate about and that are enriching, then you'll be on the right track. If you study hard for those standardized tests and spend some time reading and writing, and you'll have an even better chance.

When colleges are looking at your transcripts, these are things they will notice:

All A's Are NOT Created Equal—That A you earned in media studies or archery is not going to shine as brightly on your transcript as the A you earned in AP chemistry. Anybody can inflate their grade point average by taking a lot of easy courses that don't require much thought or academic muscle, so take as many challenging English, foreign language, math, history, and science classes as you can while still consistently making A's and perhaps a few B's.

B's in Hard Course are Better than an A in an Easy Course—If you can handle the work in honors, AP, or other accelerated courses, you should be taking at least a few of them if they are offered at your school. If it is obvious from your transcript that you are taking a lighter load than you can handle, Admissions Officers at selective colleges are going to wonder about your motivation.

Class Rank—It matters. Many colleges say that class rank is more revealing than grade point average, though most colleges are interested in both. This isn't rocket science: Students who end up near the bottom of their high school classes tend to end up near the bottom of their college classes. So, start getting higher grades if you want to move up in the world.

Junior and Senior Grades Versus Freshman and Sophomore Grades—Your grades later in high school matter more than your freshman and sophomore grades. This is not an excuse to slack off in early years because your overall GPA for all four years of high school will inhabit a very prominent position in every college application. But if you are reading this book at the beginning of your junior year and your grades are only mediocre, all hope is definitely not lost. Students who show steady improvement in their grades the closer they get to graduation—and in harder classes—prove they are maturing and developing their potential. That means that a senior year decline conveys the opposite of "maturing and developing" to Admissions Officers. It may also indicate laziness, which is worse. Colleges really do care about your senior grades, so don't coast through. They expect you to take challenging academic courses and to keep your grades up throughout your high school career.

Extracurricular Activities—They're important. They aren't nearly as important as grades and test scores, but Admissions Officers want to know how you fill up your time when you aren't studying—and you shouldn't be studying all of the time. Extracurricular activities aren't limited to sports and leadership roles. Community service, part-time employment, band, Boy Scouts Girl Scouts, (and other activities) can give some insight into what experiences you will be able to share with your fellow college classmates. One thing to avoid is having a laundry list of activities. Nobody can really dedicate themselves to twenty-three organizations. Colleges want to see that you stuck with a few activities that mattered to you and that you assumed a leadership role in at least one of them.

Paying for College Tips

When it comes to actually paying for college, there is a lot of information out there. A great resource is the book *Paying for College Without Going Broke* by Kal Chany. Here, we have some tips from Kal for applying for financial aid and ways to trim the costs of college.

1. **Get the best score possible on the ACT or SAT**. Colleges don't just consider your standardized test score(s) in their admissions decisions—they consider them in their financial aid decisions as well. Even a 10-point increase in your SAT score, for example, could save your family thousands of dollars. Simply put, colleges want students with high test scores and they give better aid packages to these students. You should enroll in a test preparation course or, at the very least, buy a book with practice tests or sample questions.

2. **Be a smart shopper.** Check schools' financial aid statistics on PrincetonReview.com. Your chances of getting significant aid will be better at schools that give generous financial aid packages. Make sure you pay attention to our Financial Aid Rating for each school.

3. **Don't immediately rule out a college because you think it's too expensive.** The higher the cost, the more aid you may receive. Many colleges—especially the private ones—have increased their aid budgets to attract applicants whose families are now more cost-conscious given the state of the economy. A generous aid award from a pricey private school can make it less costly than a public school with a lower sticker price. But have some back-up schools in case you don't receive enough aid to attend the pricier schools.

4. **Apply to "financial aid safety schools."** You should purposely apply to some schools where your test scores and academic record exceed the school's admission standards. These schools, in addition to being "safety schools" in the traditional sense, are much more likely to give you merit-based aid or a better need-based aid package (i.e. one with more scholarships or grants and fewer loans). You should also apply to schools that you can afford without much—or any—aid. Most likely this will mean applying to a public institution in your home state as well as a nearby school

that would allow you to live at home and skip the cost of room and board.

5. **Consider attending a community college for two years.** After two years, you can transfer to a pricier school to finish your bachelor's degree. The diploma won't say "transfer student" on it but it will be identical to the one earned by a student who paid high tuition for all four years. Just plan ahead and be sure that the college to which you expect to transfer will accept the community college's credits.

6. **Be realistic about outside scholarships.** These scholarships account for less than five percent of all aid awarded. Research them at PrincetonReview.com or other free sites. Steer clear of scholarship search firms that charge fees and "promise" scholarships.

7. **Earn college credits while still in high school.** You should take AP classes as many colleges award credits for high AP exam scores. Also take "dual enrollment" classes if they are offered at your high school. Dual enrollment classes are special classes at your school that will earn you credit at a nearby college. You'll be able to take these credits with you when you start college. If your high school doesn't offer dual enrollment, consider taking CLEP (College-Level Examination Program) exams in the subjects you take in high school. Depending on the college, a qualifying score on any of the 33 CLEP exams can earn students 3 to 12 college credits. Some students have cut a year off their college tuition through AP classes, dual enrollment, and/or CLEP.

8. **Explore whether "cooperative education" (co-op) programs are offered at the colleges on your list.** More than 900 colleges allow students to combine their college education with a job. It can take longer to complete a degree this way, but graduates generally owe less in student loans and have a better chance of getting hired after graduation.

9. **Talk to your parents about maximizing your family's aid eligibility.** Financial aid awards for your first year of college will be based in part on your family's income for the calendar year beginning Jan. 1 of your junior year and ending Dec. 31 of your senior year of high school. For this reason, it is not too early to begin planning when you are in the 9th or 10th grade. Your family should consider making the appropriate adjustments to its assets, debts, and retirement funds. If your family has a complicated financial situation, it may be beneficial for your parents to hire an independent financial aid consultant.

10. **Apply for financial aid regardless of your family's financial situation.** There is no automatic cut-off if your family makes a certain amount of money; you should assume that you're eligible. Even if you don't end up being eligible for need-based aid, some merit-based aid (for academic ability, athletic ability, etc.) may only be awarded if you have submitted financial aid applications.

11. **Don't wait until you've been accepted to a school to apply for financial aid there.** Meet each school's financial aid deadlines. A school's financial aid office website is the best place to find its filing requirements and deadlines. Most schools have deadlines between January 31st and March 15th. If you submit your forms after a school's priority filing deadline(s), the amount of aid you are awarded may be reduced.

12. **Complete all of the required aid forms.** All students seeking aid must submit the Free Application for Federal Student Aid (FAFSA). However additional forms, including special-state aid forms, the College Board's CSS PROFILE, or the school's own forms may be required. Check with each school for specifics. For the FAFSA and, if applicable, the CSS PROFILE you will need to meet the earliest deadline for that form among the schools to which you are applying.

13. **Don't fear the PROFILE.** While this form requests more information than the FAFSA does, don't be dismayed if a school requests it. This form can actually lead to more aid in many circumstances as schools that require the PROFILE generally have more of their own aid to give out in addition to state and federal assistance.

14. **If your parents' or your own tax returns cannot be completed prior to the deadline for a financial aid form, estimate income and other tax information.** Aid applications ask for tax return information for those who file or will file taxes. If your parents' or your own taxes (if applicable) won't be done in time to meet a deadline, you can put estimated numbers on your aid forms; it is more important that you submit each aid form by the appropriate deadline than it is to be 100% accurate with income and expense figures. You will be able to provide the final numbers later, after taxes have been done. But don't forget this last step—many schools will request a copy of tax returns or non-filer statements to verify the information on your aid applications.

15. **Don't rush.** Financial aid forms are like the SAT—you get the most credit for being right and on-time, not "first in line." To get the most aid possible, you should have some understanding of how each question on each form will impact your aid eligibility. As this information is not provided on the aid forms themselves, you should refer to a consumer-friendly publication for assistance. (Paying for College Without Going Broke, for example, provides line-by-line strategies for completing the FAFSA and PROFILE to your best advantage.) If your financial situation is complicated, you might consider hiring a financial aid consultant to assist you.

16. **If you don't already have your U.S. Department of Education PIN (Personal Identification Number), apply for it now.** A PIN allows one to sign the FAFSA electronically, which reduces processing time. You can either go to the PIN web site (www.pin.ed.gov) or request a PIN as you complete the FAFSA on the Web. Note: students who are required to provide parental information on the FAFSA will need to have their parent(s) (or custodial stepparent, if applicable) sign the FAFSA. Each person who wants to sign the FAFSA electronically must have for their own PIN.

17. **Frequently check your email and log onto school websites to track the status of your financial aid applications.** Once the schools have received your financial aid forms, they may require additional info (e.g., your parents' tax returns) that they haven't already mentioned. Be on the lookout for updates regarding your status.

18. **Know that the schools are the ones in charge**—the FAFSA and PROFILE processors just give a school's financial aid office the information it needs to make their financial aid decisions. The financial aid office will determine the types and dollar amounts of the aid you will receive; it can override the analysis done by the form processors. If your family's circumstances have a taken a turn for the worse since last year, you can request additional aid directly from schools' financial aid office. But expect that supporting documentation will be required

19. **Learn as much as you can about how the aid process works.** In theory, financial aid funds are supposed to go to those who need the money the most. The reality, however, is that financial aid funds flow to those who know how to navigate the aid process to their best advantage. The more you know about the process, the more confident you can be that you will get the most aid possible!

The Princeton Review and USA TODAY

With college costs continually increasing, we know students and parents are extremely concerned about paying for college. We also know that it's become tougher for families to save for college. Bottom line: Families need to make every education dollar count, get all the aid they can, and be savvy college shoppers. It's not easy doing all that, so we've done much of the research and pulled it together in this book to help families identify the colleges most generous with aid and/or with lower sticker prices

.

For several years, we've reported our picks of "best value" colleges in various formats. What started in 2003 as a "Best Academic Bang for Your Buck" ranking list has been printed in many iterations, including book form and as an online entity with a publishing partner, USA TODAY. For the past few years, our annual list has appeared both on our website, www.PrincetonReview.com and on USA TODAY's site in a dedicated area—bestvaluecolleges.usatoday.com where users can click on an interactive map and access a database with stats and facts about each school and a report on why The Princeton Review considers it a Best Value College.

With the publication of this book, The Princeton Review's Best Value Colleges project and our affiliation with USA TODAY move to a broader level in two ways. First, we have increased the number of schools we identify as "best values." Our list for 2012 identifies 150 schools we've chosen as the "Best Value" colleges—75 four-year private colleges/universities, 75 four-year public colleges/universities, plus 10 tuition-free schools. The schools listed provide high-quality academics at a reasonable price, either by controlling costs or offsetting them with stellar financial aid packages. Second, we present in-depth profiles of these schools, plus information on what it takes to get in to them, in this book. Our narrative profiles enable us to give families even more insight into the schools on this year's list.

We are delighted to have worked together with USA TODAY to bring this valuable information about these "best value" colleges to an increasingly wider range of parents and students and to have it be available in different formats. We salute USA TODAY for its continuing commitment to this project and to its many readers and site visitors. Our annual list, along with statistics and analysis about students, admissions, academics, and financial aid information continues to be available on our website, at www.PrincetonReview.com and on the unique Best Value Colleges area at USA TODAY's site—bestvaluecolleges.usatoday.com—as a free, online, and interactive database.

For more information about how we selected our Best Value Colleges for 2012 as well as details about our criteria and our methodology, see page 16.

Our annual list, along with statistics and analysis about students, admissions, academics, and financial aid information continues to be available on our website, at www.PrincetonReview.com and on the unique Best Value Colleges area at USA TODAY's site—bestvaluecolleges.usatoday.com—as a free, online, and interactive database.

HOW TO USE THIS BOOK

It's pretty self-explanatory. We have done our best to include lots of helpful information about choosing colleges and getting admitted into them. The profiles we have written contain the same basic information for each school (though we expanded that information for the top 10 public schools and the top 10 private schools) and follow the same basic format. The Princeton Review collects all of the data you see in the sidebars of each school. As is customary with college guides, our numbers usually reflect the figures for the academic year prior to publication. Since college offerings and demographics significantly vary from one institution to another and some colleges report data more thoroughly than others, some entries will not include all of the individual data described. Please know that we take our data collection process seriously. We reach out to schools numerous times through the process to ensure we can present you with the most accurate and up-to-date facts, figures, and deadlines. Even so, a book is dated from the moment it hits the printing press. If a school changes its policies, procedures, requirements, or application deadline once our book is already on the shelves, it is too late for us to change it. Be sure to double-check with any schools to which you plan to apply to make sure you are able to get them everything they need in order to meet their deadlines.

Profiles

Each of the colleges and universities in this book has its own profile. The top 10 public schools and top 10 private schools have 4-page profiles, and the other schools including tuition free schools have 2-page profiles. To make it easier to find and compare information about the schools, we've used the same profile format for every school. We have included student quotes, information from administrators, and collected data to give you insight into each college.

Sidebars

The sidebars contain various statistics culled from our surveys of students attending the school and from questionnaires that school administrators complete at our request in the fall of each year. Keep in mind that not every category will appear for every school—in some cases the information is not reported or not applicable. We compile the eight ratings—Quality of Life, Fire Safety, Green Rating, Academic, Profs Interesting, Profs Acces¬sible, Admissions Selectivity, and Financial Aid—listed in the sidebars based on the results from our student surveys and/or institutional data we collect from school administrators. These ratings are on a scale of 60–99. If a 60* (60 with an asterisk) appears as any rating for any school, it means that the school reported so few of the rating's underlying data points by our deadline that we were unable to calculate an accurate rating for it. (These measures are outlined in the ratings explanation below.) Be advised that because the Admissions Selectivity Rating is a factor in the computation that produces the Academic Rating, a school that has 60* (60 with an asterisk) as its Admissions Selectivity Rating will have an Academic Rating that is lower than it should be. Also bear in mind that each rat¬ing places each college on a continuum for purposes of comparing colleges within this edition only. Since our ratings computations may change from year to year, it is invalid to compare the ratings in this edition to those that appear in any prior or future edition.

Quality of Life Rating:

On a scale of 60–99, this rating is a measure of how happy students are with their campus experiences outside the classroom. To compile this rating, we weighed several factors, all based on students' answers to questions on our survey. They included the students' assessments of: their overall happiness; the beauty, safety, and location of the campus; comfort of dorms; quality of food; ease of getting around campus and dealing with administrators; friendliness of fellow students; and the interaction of different student types on campus and within the greater community.

Fire Safety Rating:

On a scale of 60–99, this rating measures how well prepared a school is to prevent or respond to campus fires, specifically in residence halls. We asked schools several questions about their efforts to ensure fire safety for campus residents. We developed the questions in consultation with the Center for Campus Fire Safety (www.campusfiresafety.org). Each school's responses to eight questions were considered when calculating its Fire Safety Rating.

They cover:

1. The percentage of student housing sleeping rooms protected by an automatic fire sprinkler system with a fire sprinkler head located in the individual sleeping rooms.
2. The percentage of student housing sleeping rooms equipped with a smoke detector connected to a supervised fire alarm system.
3. The number of malicious fire alarms that occur in student housing per year.
4. The number of unwanted fire alarms that occur in student housing per year.
5. The banning of certain hazardous items and activities in residence halls, like candles, smoking, halogen lamps, etc.
6. The percentage of student housing fire alarm systems that, if activated, result in a signal being transmitted to a monitored location, where security investigates before notifying the fire department.
7. The percentage of student housing fire alarm systems that, if activated, result in a signal being transmitted immediately to a continuously monitored location, which can then immediately notify the fire department to initiate a response.
8. How often fire safety rules-compliance inspections are conducted each year. Schools that did not report answers to a sufficient number of questions receive a Fire Safety Rating of 60* (60 with an asterisk). You can also find Fire Safety Ratings for the *Best Value Colleges* (and several additional schools) in our *Best 376 Colleges* book and our *Complete Book of Colleges* book.

Green Rating:

We asked all the schools we collect data from annually to answer a number of questions that evaluate the comprehensive measure of their performance as an environmentally aware and responsible institution. The questions were developed in consultation with ecoAmerica, a research and partnership-based environmental nonprofit that convened an expert committee to design this comprehensive rating system, and cover: 1) whether students have a campus quality of life that is both healthy and sustainable; 2) how well a school is preparing students not only for employment in the clean energy economy of the twenty-first century, but also for citizenship in a world now defined by environmental challenges; and 3) how environmentally responsible a school's policies are. Each school's responses to ten questions were considered when calculating its Green Rating.

The Green Rating questions cover:

1. The percentage of food expenditures that go toward local, organic, or otherwise environmentally preferable food.
2. Whether the school offers programs including free bus passes, universal access transit passes, bike sharing/renting, car sharing, carpool parking, vanpooling, or guaranteed rides home to encourage alternatives to single-passenger automobile use for students.
3. Whether the school has a formal committee with participation from students that is devoted to advancing sustainability on campus.
4. Whether new buildings are required to be LEED Silver certified or comparable.
5. The schools overall waste diversion rate.
6. Whether the school has an environmental studies major, minor or concentration.
7. Whether the school has an 'environmental literacy' requirement.
8. Whether a school has produced a publicly available greenhouse gas emissions inventory and adopted a climate action plan consistent with eighty percent greenhouse gas reductions by 2050 targets.
9. What percentage of the school's energy consumption, including heating/cooling and electrical, is derived from renewable resources (this definition included 'green tags' but not nuclear or large scale hydro power).
10. Whether the school employs a dedicated full-time (or full-time equivalent) sustainability officer. Colleges that did not supply answers to a sufficient number of the green campus questions for us to fairly compare them to other colleges receive a Green Rating of 60*.

Type of school: Whether the school is public or private.

Affiliation: Any religious order with which the school is affiliated.

Environment: Whether the campus is located in an urban, suburban, or rural setting.

Total undergrad enrollment: The total number of degree-seeking undergraduates who attend the school.

% male/female through # countries represented: Demographic information about the full-time undergraduate student body, including male to female ratio, ethnicity, and the number of countries represented by the student body. Also included are the percentages of the student body who are from out of state, attended a public high school, live on campus, and belong to Greek organizations.

Academic rating: On a scale of 60–99, this rating is a measure of how hard students work at the school and how much they get back for their efforts. The rating is based on results from our surveys of students and data we collect from administrators. Factors weighed included how many hours students reported that they study each day outside of class, students' assessments of their professors' teaching abilities and of their accessibility outside the classroom and the quality of students the school attracts as measured by admissions statistics.

4-year graduation rate: The percentage of degree-seeking undergraduate students graduating in four years or less.

6-year graduation rate: The percentage of degree-seeking undergraduate students graduating within six years.

Calendar: The school's schedule of academic terms. A "semester" schedule has two long terms, usually starting in September and January. A "trimester" schedule has three terms, one usually beginning before Christmas and two after. A "quarterly" schedule has four terms, which go by very quickly: the entire term, including exams, usually lasts only nine or ten weeks. A "4-1-4" schedule is like a semester schedule, but with a month-long term in between the fall and spring semesters. (Similarly, a 4-4-1 has a short term following two longer semesters.) It is always best to call the admissions office for details.

Student/faculty ratio: The ratio of full-time undergraduate instructional faculty members to all undergraduates.

Profs interesting rating: On a scale of 60–99, this rating is based on levels of surveyed students' agreement or disagreement with the statement: "Your instructors are good teachers."

Profs accessible rating: On a scale of 60–99, this rating is based on levels of surveyed students' agreement or disagreement with the statement: "Your instructors are accessible outside the classroom."

Most common regular class size; Most common lab size: The most commonly occurring class size for regular courses and for labs/discussion sections.

Most popular majors: The majors with the highest enrollments at the school.

Admissions selectivity rating: On a scale of 60–99, this rating is a measure of how competitive admission is at the school. This rating is determined by several factors, including the class rank of entering freshmen, test scores, and percentage of applicants accepted.

% of applicants accepted: The percentage of applicants to whom the school offered admission.

% of acceptees attending: The percentage of accepted students who eventually enrolled at the school.

 # accepting a place on wait list: The number of students who decided to take a place on the wait list when offered this option.

% admitted from wait list: The percentage of applicants who opted to take a place on the wait list and were subsequently offered admission. These figures will vary tremendously from college to college, and should be a consideration when deciding whether to accept a place on a college's wait list.

# of early decision applicants: The number of students who applied under the college's early decision or early action plan.

% accepted early decision: The percentage of early decision or early action applicants who were admitted under this plan. By the nature of these plans, the vast majority who are admitted ultimately enroll.

Range SAT critical reading, range SAT math, Range SAT writing, Range ACT composite: The average and the middle fifty percent range of test scores for entering freshmen. Don't be discouraged from applying to the school of your choice even if your combined SAT scores are 80 or even 120 points below the average, because you may still have a chance of getting in. Remember that many schools value other aspects of your application (e.g., your grades, how good a match you make with the school) more heavily than test scores.

Average HS GPA: The average grade point average of entering freshman. We report this on a scale of 1.0–4.0 (occasionally colleges report averages on a 100 scale, in which case we report those figures). This is one of the key factors in college admissions.

% graduated top 10%, top 25%, top 50% of class: Of those students for whom class rank was reported, the percentage of entering freshmen who ranked in the top tenth, quarter, and half of their high school classes.

Early decision, early action, priority, and regular admission deadlines: The dates by which all materials must be postmarked (we'd suggest "received in the office") in order to be considered for admission under each particular admissions option/cycle for matriculation in the fall term.

Early decision, early action, priority, and regular admission notification: The dates by which you can expect a decision on your application under each admissions option/cycle.

Nonfall registration: Some schools will allow incoming students to register and begin attending classes at times other than the fall term, which is the traditional beginning of the academic calendar year. Other schools will allow you to register for classes only if you can begin in the fall term. A simple "yes" or "no" in this category indicates the school's policy on nonfall registration.

Financial aid rating: On a scale of 60–99, this rating is a measure of the financial aid the school awards and how satisfied students are with the aid they receive. It is based on school-reported data on financial aid and students' responses to the survey question, "If you receive financial aid, how satisfied are you with your financial aid package?"

Annual in-state tuition: For public colleges, the cost of tuition for a resident of the school's state. Usually much lower than out-of-state tuition for state-supported public schools.

Annual out-of-state tuition: For public colleges, the tuition for a nonresident of the school's state. This entry appears only for public colleges, since tuition at private colleges is generally the same regardless of state of residence.

Required fees: Any additional costs students must pay beyond tuition in order to attend the school. These often include fitness center fees and the like. A few state schools may not officially charge in-state students tuition, but those students are still responsible for hefty fees.

Tuition and fees: In cases when schools do not report separate figures for tuition and required fees, we offer this total of the two.

Comprehensive fee: A few schools report one overall fee that reflects the total cost of tuition, room and board, and required fees. If you'd like to see how this figure breaks down, we recommend contacting the school.

Room and board: Estimated annual room and board costs.

Books and supplies: Estimated annual cost of necessary textbooks and/or supplies.

% frosh receiving need-based aid: The percentage of all degree-seeking freshmen who applied for financial aid, were determined to have financial need, and received any sort of aid, need-based or otherwise.

% UG receiving need-based aid: The percentage of all degree-seeking undergrads who applied for financial aid, were determined to have financial need, and received any sort of aid, need-based or otherwise.

% receiving non-need-based aid: The percentage of all degree-seeking undergrads who received any non-need-based scholarship or grant aid.

% receiving need-based self-help aid: The percentage of all degree-seeking undergrads who received any need-based self-help aid.

% receiving any financial aid: The percentage of all degree-seeking undergrads receiving any financial aid (need-based, merit-based, gift aid).

Avg indebtedness: The average per-borrower cumulative undergraduate indebtedness of those who borrowed at any time through any loan programs (institutional, state, Federal Perkins, Federal Stafford Subsidized and Unsubsidized, private loans that were certified by your institution, etc.; exclude parent loans).

Nota Bene: *The statistical data reported in this book, unless otherwise noted, was collected from the profiled colleges from through the fall of 2011. In some cases, we were unable to publish the most recent data because schools did not report the necessary statistics to us in time, despite our repeated outreach efforts. Because the enrollment and financial statistics, as well as application and financial aid deadlines, fluctuate from one year to another, we recommend that you check with the schools to make sure you have the most current information before applying.*

Methodology

The Princeton Review chose the 150 schools on its Best Value Colleges list for 2012 based on institutional data and student opinion surveys collected from 650 colleges and universities the company regards as the nation's academically best undergraduate institutions. The institutional data was collected from fall 2010 through fall 2011. All cost and financial aid data came from fall 2011 surveys. The list has 75 public and 75 private colleges with the top 10 schools in each category reported in rank order and the remaining 65 unranked.

The selection process took into account a range of data that covered more than 30 factors in three areas: academics, cost of attendance, and financial aid. Academic factors included the quality of students the schools attract as measured by admissions credentials as well as how students rated their academic experiences. Cost of attendance factors included tuition, room and board, and required fees. Financial aid factors included the average gift aid (grants and scholarships, or free money) awarded to students, the percentage of graduating students who took out loans to pay for school, and the average debt of those students. Also included was survey data on how satisfied students were with the financial aid packages they received.

THE PRINCETON REVIEW'S 150 BEST VALUE COLLEGES FOR 2012

The Princeton Review and USA TODAY have collaborated to bring you this list of 150 Best Value Colleges. We selected the 150 schools (75 private and 75 public) based on 30 factors covering academics, costs, and financial aid. For information about each school and an exclusive analysis in an interactive database and map, go to www.bestvaluecolleges.usatoday.com

Top 10 Private Schools

1. Williams College
2. Swarthmore College
3. Princeton University
4. Harvard College
5. Rice University
6. Pomona College
7. Washington University in St. Louis
8. Yale University
9. California Institute of Technology
10. Hamilton College

Tuition-Free Schools

Berea College
College of the Ozarks
Deep Springs College
The Cooper Union for the Advancement of Science and Art
United States Air Force Academy
United States Coast Guard Academy
United States Merchant Marine Academy
United States Military Academy—Westpoint
United States Naval Academy
Webb Institute

Top 10 Public Schools

1. The University of North Carolina at Chapel Hill
2. University of Virginia
3. New College of Florida
4. State University of New York at Binghamton
5. University of Wisconsin—Madison
6. College of William & Mary
7. University of Florida
8. University of Georgia
9. University of Washington
10. The University of Texas at Austin

Best Value Private Schools

Agnes Scott College
Amherst College
Barnard College
Bates College
Beloit College
Boston College
Bowdoin College
Brandeis University
Brown University
Bryn Mawr College
Bucknell University
Carleton College
Centenary College of Louisiana
Centre College
Claremont McKenna College
Colby College
Colgate University
College of the Atlantic
College of the Holy Cross
Colorado College
Columbia University
Cornell College
Cornell University
Dartmouth College
Davidson College
DePauw University
Duke University
Emory University
Franklin W. Olin College of Engineering
Georgetown University
Gettysburg College
Grinnell College
Hanover College
Harvey Mudd College
Haverford College
Hillsdale College
The Johns Hopkins University
Lafayette College
Macalester College
Massachusetts Institute of Technology
Middlebury College
Mount Holyoke College

Northwestern University
Occidental College
Randolph College
Reed College
Scripps College
Sewanee—The University of the South
Stanford University
Thomas Aquinas College
University of Chicago
University of Notre Dame
University of Pennsylvania
University of Redlands
University of Richmond
Vanderbilt University
Vassar College
Wabash College
Wake Forest University
Wellesley College
Wesleyan College
Wesleyan University
Wheaton College (IL)
Whitman College
Wofford College

Best Value Public Schools

Appalachian State University*
California Polytechnic State University, San Luis Obispo*
California State University—Long Beach*
Christopher Newport University
City University of New York—Brooklyn College
City University of New York—Hunter College
Clemson University
College of Charleston
The College of New Jersey
The Evergreen State College
Florida State University
Georgia Institute of Technology
Indiana University—Bloomington
Iowa State University
James Madison University
Kansas State University
Longwood University*
Missouri University of Science and Technology
New Mexico Institute of Mining & Technology*
North Carolina State University
The Ohio State University—Columbus
Purdue University—West Lafayette
Southern Utah University*
St. Mary's College of Maryland
State University of New York at Geneseo
State University of New York at New Paltz*
State University of New York—College of Environmental Science and Forestry*
State University of New York—Oswego*
State University of New York—Stony Brook University
State University of New York—University at Buffalo
Truman State University
University of California—Berkeley
University of California—Davis
University of California—Irvine*
University of California—Los Angeles
University of California—Riverside
University of California—San Diego
University of California—Santa Barbara
University of California—Santa Cruz
University of Central Florida
University of Colorado—Boulder
University of Delaware
University of Houston
University of Illinois at Urbana-Champaign
University of Kansas
University of Mary Washington
University of Maryland, College Park
University of Massachusetts Boston*
University of Michigan—Ann Arbor
University of Minnesota, Crookston*
University of Minnesota—Twin Cities
University of Missouri—Kansas City*
University of North Carolina at Asheville
University of North Carolina—Wilmington*
University of North Florida*
University of Oklahoma
University of Pittsburgh at Bradford*
University of Pittsburgh—Pittsburgh Campus
University of South Carolina—Columbia
The University of South Dakota
University of Tennessee
University of Tennessee at Martin*
University of Wisconsin—Eau Claire*
Utah State University*
Virginia Tech

WE WANT TO HEAR FROM YOU

To all of our readers, we welcome your feedback on how we can continue to improve this guide.
We hope you will share with us your comments, questions, and suggestions.
Please contact us at **editorialsupport@review.com**.

GETTING INTO THE BEST VALUE COLLEGES

We get lots of questions from parents and students about how to actually get in to the Best Value Colleges. We've done our best to give you a little bit of insight into the typical student who is admitted into these colleges. You'll notice that some of the schools are highly selective, and other schools have more self-selecting applicant pools. The thing to remember is that even if the average scores listed here aren't exactly your scores, these are ranges; for instance, if you're within about 150 SAT points under or over, you should still consider applying. Also remember that smaller schools may be able to spend a little more time with your application assessing the parts of the application that truly make you an individual candidate, such as your essay and interview. All of the schools in this book will offer you amazing academic opportunities, so spend some time checking into and researching colleges you might never have heard of; you might be surprised at what you find.

TOP 10 PRIVATE

#1

Williams College 130

Williamstown, Massachusetts

Williams is admittedly much more than the sum of its statistics, and so high grades and test scores work more as qualifiers than to determine admissibility, and the standards are rigorous. The entire admissions staff discusses each candidate in comparison to the entire applicant pool, working in rounds to weed out weak candidates in comparison to the entire pool. Admission decisions must be confirmed by the agreement of a plurality of the committee. The basic formula for undergraduate academics, according to the school, is "get outstanding grades in tough courses"; fitting for a school in which 88 percent of the 2014 incoming class was in the top 10 percent of their high school class. Williams asks prospective students to show what they would bring to the table outside of just the GPA and test score box, and the office is extremely interested in hearing about non-academic involvements and jobs held.

Total undergrad enrollment	1,996
# of applicants	6,631
Range SAT Critical Reading	660–770
Range SAT Math	650–760
Range ACT Composite	29–34
percent graduated top 25% of class	98

#2

Swarthmore College 134

Swarthmore, Pennsylvania

Competition for admission to Swarthmore remains fierce, as the school receives more than enough applications from top students across the country. There is no rigid emphasis on any one factor, and admissions officers look for evidence of intellectually curious, highly motivated, and creative-minded candidates in high school grades and ranking, standardized tests, activities, essays, and three separate recommendations. Still, you can bet that grades play a huge part in the decision: 90 percent of Swarthmore graduates go on to graduate school or professional school.

Total undergrad enrollment	1,509
# of applicants	6,041
Range SAT Critical Reading	670–760
Range SAT Math	670–770
Range SAT Writing	670–770
Range ACT Composite	29–33
percent graduated top 10% of class	84
percent graduated top 25% of class	96

#3

Princeton University 138

Princeton, New Jersey

If you can make it there, you can make it almost anywhere: Princeton typically admits 10 percent or less of its applicants (it admitted just 8.5 percent for the Class of 2015, out of more than 27,000 applications). Of these lucky few, 14 percent had a perfect 4.0 average, and 21 percent had an SAT score above 2300. The school holds high standards for previous academic experience and looks for students who have challenged themselves with their coursework and extracurriculars, but given its socioeconomic reach, it is particularly understanding the context of a student's past, and the opportunities that were available. Two personal essays are required and carefully reviewed; off-campus alumni interviews are usually offered, but not required. Admission to Princeton comes with a great deal of prestige, and to make the deal even sweeter, Princeton's remarkable no-loan financial aid program means that every student has 100 percent of financial need met, without student loans; the school expects to award grants totaling nearly $110 million to more than 3,100 undergraduates for the 2011–2012 school year.

Total undergrad enrollment	5,142
# of applicants	26,247
Range SAT Critical Reading	690–790
Range SAT Math	710–790
Range SAT Writing	700–790
Range ACT Composite	31–35
Average HS GPA	3.89
percent graduated top 10% of class	99
percent graduated top 25% of class	100

#4
Harvard College 142
Cambridge, Massachusetts

It just doesn't get any tougher than this. Harvard denies admission to the vast majority, and virtually all of them are top students. Rather than being as detailed and direct as possible about the selection process and criteria, Harvard keeps things close to the vest—before, during, and after. Though it does use the Common Application, the school also requires a lengthy supplement, and the guidelines it offers prospective students (beyond seeking out the "creative and reflective") tend to hinge on vague holistic questions like "Has the candidate reached her maximum growth?" Hey, it worked for 6.1 percent of this fall's incoming class.

Total undergrad enrollment	6641
# of applicants	30,489
Range SAT Critical Reading	690–800
Range SAT Math	700–790
Range SAT Writing	710–800
Range ACT Composite	31–34

#5
Rice University 146
Houston, Texas

Last year, only about 20 percent of regular decision applicants were offered a spot in the incoming class. (For a variety of reasons, early decision applicants are accepted at a higher rate.) The middle range of SAT scores for Critical Reading and Math was 1420–1540 (18 percent of incoming class were National Merit Finalists), and for the ACTs it was 31–34. Applicants must specify which of the school's six academic divisions they are applying to: architecture, engineering, humanities, music, natural sciences, or social sciences. Although this is not a binding choice, the decision should not be made lightly, as the school strongly reads into the thought put into the reasoning behind the choice. Students applying to the school of architecture must accompany their application with a portfolio of creative work, while music students must audition on the Rice campus.

Total undergrad enrollment	3,529
# of applicants	13,804
Range SAT Critical Reading	650–750
Range SAT Math	690–790
Range SAT Writing	660–760
Range ACT Composite	31–34
percent graduated top 10% of class	85
percent graduated top 25% of class	96

#6
Pomona College 150
Claremont, California

Admissions officials thoroughly evaluate a student's academic record, and extra weight is given to honors, IB, and AP classes, so rigor of coursework is an absolute necessity in order to apply here (and yet still, 90 percent of admitted students graduated in the top 10 percent of their high school class). Quality of thought in essays and recommendations from the school are also of great significance. If you live in Southern California, Pomona expects you to interview on campus; students in other regions are strongly encouraged to do an alumni interview and to visit campus.

Total undergrad enrollment	1,546
# of applicants	6,764
Range SAT Critical Reading	690–780
Range SAT Math	700–780
Range SAT Writing	690–770
Range ACT Composite	31–34
Average HS GPA	NR

percent graduated top 10% of class	91
percent graduated top 25% of class	100

#7
Washington University in St. Louis 154
St. Louis, Missouri

Lack of instant name recognition might affect Wash U's admission rate, but students with above-average academic records who aren't quite Ivy material are the big winners at this top-notch but underrated school. Marginal candidates with high financial need may find difficulty; the admissions process at Wash U isn't need-blind and may take into account candidates' ability to pay if they're not strong applicants. Applicants must select one of Wash U.'s five undergraduate schools as a "primary point of interest" at the time of application.

Total undergrad enrollment	6,542
# of applicants	24,939
Range SAT Critical Reading	680–750
Range SAT Math	710–790
Range ACT Composite	32–34
percent graduated top 10% of class	96
percent graduated top 25% of class	100

#8
Yale University 158
New Haven, Connecticut

Yale looks to build a class more than it does admit one student. With so many qualified applicants to choose from (almost 26,000 for the Class of 2014), Yale can afford to winnow the ranks down to a balanced one, in terms of income level, racial/ethnic background, geographic origin, and academic interest. The school estimates that more than three-quarters of all its applicants are qualified to attend the university, but less than 10 percent get in. 93 percent of the Class of 2014's students were in the top 5 percent of their high school classes, with 45 percent logging SAT Critical Reading scores of 760–800, and more than 50 percent doing the same for Math and Writing. 13 percent of all students are legacies, while 12.5 percent are the first in their families to attend a four-year college. The Admissions Committee gives greatest weight to the documents required of all applicants, but in cases of special (and substantial) talent, it will accept supplementary submissions of audio recordings, musical scores, art samples, writing samples, scientific research papers, and links to personal websites.

Total undergrad enrollment	5,279
# of applicants	25,869
Range SAT Critical Reading	700–800
Range SAT Math	700–780
Range SAT Writing	700–790
Range ACT Composite	30–34
percent graduated top 10% of class	96
percent graduated top 25% of class	100

#9
California Institute of Technology 162
Pasadena, California

There are a lot of numbers and formulas at Caltech—but not in the admissions office. Each Caltech application receives three independent reads before it's presented to the admissions committee (which includes undergraduate students). A heavy math and science background is required, as well as SAT or ACT scores, SAT Mathematics Level 2, and one SAT Subject Test in Biology (Ecological), Biology (Molecular), Chemistry, or Physics. Admissions rates hover around 8 percent, and (unsurprisingly) 99 percent of students were in the top 10 percent of their high school class. The mid-50 percent range for the SATs is 2200–2340, while the same range for the ACTs (composite) is 33–35.

Total undergrad enrollment	967
# of applicants	4,859
Range SAT Critical Reading	700–780
Range SAT Math	770–800
Range SAT Writing	710–780
Range ACT Composite	34–35
percent graduated top 10% of class	96
percent graduated top 25% of class	100

#10
Hamilton College 166
Clinton, New York

Hamilton relies heavily on academic achievement and intellectual promise—the mid-50 percent SAT range for the Class of 2015 (Critical Reading and Math) is 1300–1470—but the school also factors in overall personality and drive. 41 percent of those students who were in the top decile of their class were admitted, as compared to a 27 percent overall admittance rate from the gen pop. The admissions team at Hamilton is adamant about interviews either on or off campus with alumni volunteers.

Total undergrad enrollment	1,843
# of applicants	4,857
Range SAT Critical Reading	650–740
Range SAT Math	650–730
Range SAT Writing	650–730
Range ACT Composite	27–31
percent graduated top 10% of class	73
percent graduated top 25% of class	97

TOP 10 PUBLIC

#1
The University of North Carolina at Chapel Hill 172
Chapel Hill, North Carolina

As one of the strongest state university systems in the country, UNC's admissions process is highly selective, and the school seeks excellence in all area's of a student's life. For this year's entering class, North Carolina students competed against other students from across the state for 52 percent of admissions offers; out-of-state students competed for the rest. 90 percent of the same classes reported a GPA of 4.0 or higher. State residents will find the admissions standards high, and out-of-state applicants will find that it's one of the hardest offers of admission to come by in the country.

Total undergrad enrollment	17,943
# of applicants	23,272
Range SAT Critical Reading	590–700
Range SAT Math	610–710
Range SAT Writing	590–690
Range ACT Composite	27–31
Average HS GPA	4.47
percent graduated top 10% of class	78
percent graduated top 25% of class	99

#2
University of Virginia 176
Charlottesville, Virginia

As one of the premier public universities in the country, UVA holds its applicants to high standards. The high school course requirements for the school may look standard, but most successful applicants exceed them, so take the most rigorous academic program available at your school, honors and AP included. The school does not use interviews in the application process, so shine on paper. 93.5 percent of students entering in fall of 2010 were in the top percentile of their high school class, and the middle 50 percent of SAT scores were 610–720 for Critical Reading, 630–740 for Math, and 620–720 for Writing. Applicants should be aware that geographical location holds significant weight, as Virginia residents are given preference.

Total undergrad enrollment	14,232
# of applicants	22,124
Range SAT Critical Reading	600–710
Range SAT Math	620–740
Range SAT Writing	610–720
Range ACT Composite	28–32
Average HS GPA	4.17
percent graduated top 10% of class	90
percent graduated top 25% of class	97

#3
New College of Florida 180
Sarasota, Florida

New College isn't your typical public school. The tiny student body allows admissions officers here to review each application carefully; expect a thorough going over of your essays, recommendations, and extracurricular activities. Iconoclastic students tend to thrive here, and the admissions staff knows that. Free spirits abound, and with no rigid core curriculum, the admissions committee does not place as much emphasis on high school grades as other schools (though good ones certainly don't hurt). The middle 50 percent range for SATs for the incoming class in 2010 was 1230–1390 (Critical Reading + Math), and 27–31 for the ACTs.

Total undergrad enrollment	801
# of applicants	1,414
Range SAT Critical Reading	640–740
Range SAT Math	580–760
Range SAT Writing	600–690
Range ACT Composite	27–31
Average HS GPA	4.03
percent graduated top 10% of class	50
percent graduated top 25% of class	94

#4
State University of New York at Binghamton 184
Binghamton, New York

SUNY Binghamton is one of the premiere public institutions on the East Coast, and one of the most selective in the SUNY system. There's no magic formula for gaining entrance here; you'll need to have taken a rigorous course load in high school and demonstrated academic success within advanced placement or honors courses, not to mention extracurriculars. Last year, more than 28,000 people applied for just more than 2,400 spots, so if you're hoping to secure a coveted spot, don't slack in any area.

Total undergrad enrollment	11,745
# of applicants	27,248
Range SAT Critical Reading	580–670
Range SAT Math	620–700
Range SAT Writing	570–660
Range ACT Composite	26–30
Average HS GPA	3.6
percent graduated top 10% of class	50
percent graduated top 25% of class	86

#5
University of Wisconsin—Madison 188
Madison, Wisconsin

Though it's not at the top tier of selectivity, Wisconsin has high expectations of its candidates. Admissions officers are most concerned with the high school transcript (course selection and grades); test scores are important, and the school typically sees GPAs between a 3.5 and a 3.9, a class rank in the 85–96 percentile, and a score between 1860–2090 on the SAT. Though not required, students are encouraged to submit two letters of recommendation and two personal statements.

Total undergrad enrollment	28,897
# of applicants	25,522
Range SAT Critical Reading	530–670
Range SAT Math	620–750
Range SAT Writing	580–680
Range ACT Composite	26–30
Average HS GPA	3.69
percent graduated top 10% of class	86
percent graduated top 25% of class	93

#6
College of William and Mary 192
Williamsburg, Virginia

There probably isn't a tougher public college admissions committee in the country—that's why W&M is one of only eight "Public Ivies" in the nation. The volume of applications at W&M is extremely high; thus, admission is ultra-competitive. Only very strong students from out of state should apply; approximately 80 percent of admitted students are in the top 10 percent of their high school graduating class, and the middle 50 percent SAT range (Critical Reading and Math) is 1240–1450.

Total undergrad enrollment	5,836
# of applicants	12,539
Range SAT Critical Reading	640–730
Range SAT Math	620–710
Range SAT Writing	620–720
Range ACT Composite	28–32
Average HS GPA	4.05
percent graduated top 10% of class	79
percent graduated top 25% of class	96

#7
University of Florida 196
Gainesville, Florida

Few students are admitted purely on academic merit. While this is the primary consideration, UF's application review process also considers personal essays, academic awards, extracurricular activities, family background, and home community. The middle 50 percent of the 2011 freshman class had an SAT score in the 1830–2090 range and a high school GPA of 4.1–4.4. First-generation college students from disadvantaged backgrounds qualify for the Florida Opportunity Scholars program, which fully covers four years of educational costs.

Total undergrad enrollment	32,660
# of applicants	26,513
Range SAT Critical Reading	570–670
Range SAT Math	600–690
Range ACT Composite	26–30
Average HS GPA	3.90

#8

University of Georgia 200

Athens, Georgia

A school as large as UGA must start winnowing applicants by the numbers, though its acceptance rate is higher than many of the other schools in the top 10. The school makes no bones about the importance of grades; GPA and rigor of curriculum weigh roughly three to two to standardized tests in predicting academic success at UGA, so students with lower standardized test scores (but consistently high grades) may just get in. The mid-50 percent range of SAT scores for the incoming fall class in 2011 was 1750–2020. George state residents who earn at least a 3.0 in high school will also have a large portion of their tuition paid.

Total undergrad enrollment	25,709
# of applicants	17,408
Range SAT Critical Reading	560–660
Range SAT Math	560–670
Range SAT Writing	560–660
Range ACT Composite	25–29
Average HS GPA	3.82
percent graduated top 10% of class	83
percent graduated top 25% of class	90

#9

University of Washington 204

Seattle, Washington

In recent years, UW abandoned the previous process by which a formula was used to rank applicants according to high school GPA and standardized test scores, and now the school uses an individualized application review more typically found at smaller private universities and colleges. The admissions office looks at both academic performance and the ambition of the coursework taken, as well personal achievements and character.

Total undergrad enrollment	27,647
# of applicants	22,843
Range SAT Critical Reading	530–650
Range SAT Math	570–690
Range SAT Writing	520–640
Range ACT Composite	24–30
percent graduated top 10% of class	85
percent graduated top 25% of class	95

#10

The University of Texas at Austin 208

Austin, Texas

It's quite competitive to become a Longhorn. The university is required to automatically admit enough Texas applicants to fill seventy-five percent of available spaces set aside for students from Texas, automatically admitting those Texas residents who are in the top 9 percent of their high school class (for the summer/fall 2012 and the spring 2013 entering freshman class; new cutoffs are released each September). Space for out-of-state students is limited, meaning they'll have even higher hurdles to clear.

Total undergrad enrollment	36,711
# of applicants	29,501
Range SAT Critical Reading	540–660
Range SAT Math	570–690
Range SAT Writing	540–670
Range ACT Composite	24–30
percent graduated top 10% of class	75
percent graduated top 25% of class	95

TUITION-FREE SCHOOLS

Berea College 214

Berea, Kentucky

The full-tuition scholarship that every student receives understandably attracts a lot of applicants. Competition among candidates is intense, and the personal interview really does matter. To make matters worse, you may be too wealthy to get admitted here, as Berea won't admit students whose parents can afford to send them elsewhere. Most Berea students score between 20 and 30 on the ACT (1410–1980 SAT) and have a cumulative high school GPA of at least 3.0 in a strong college prep curriculum.

Total undergrad enrollment	1,552
# of applicants	3,264
Range SAT Critical Reading	520–650
Range SAT Math	500–630
Range SAT Writing	480–615
Range ACT Composite	21–26
Average HS GPA	3.42
percent graduated top 10% of class	31
percent graduated top 25% of class	71

College of the Ozarks 216

Point Lookout, Missouri

The unusual nature of the C of O translates directly into its admissions process. Because a significant aspect of the school's mission statement is to provide educational opportunities to those in need of financial aid, candidates for admission must demonstrate that need. The school receives more than 3,000 applications for just 300 or so slots, so students should be in the top half of their graduating class (with above-average grades in English classes, and give a good interview. That said, it's more important to be a good fit with the school philosophically and financially than to have a sky-high GPA or standardized test scores (you only need to score a 20 on the ACT or a 950 on the SAT Math and Critical Reading sections (no writing component is required). Oh yeah, a serious work ethic is a must!

Total undergrad enrollment	1,376
# of applicants	2,975
Range ACT Composite	20–25
Average HS GPA	3.53
percent graduated top 10% of class	30
percent graduated top 25% of class	64

Deep Springs College 220

Dyer, Nevada

Well, with a school of 26 students, suffice it to say that the admissions committee looks pretty deep; this isn't just about grades. Students will be hard-pressed to find a school with a more personal or thorough application process than Deep Springs. Given the intimate and collegial atmosphere of the school, matchmaking is the top priority, and the essays and interview weigh in far more heavily than grades (still, SAT scores of accepted students generally average in the upper 700 range for Critical Reading and about 700 for Math). Candidates are evaluated by a body composed of students, faculty, and staff members, and those who make it through the first round must schedule a 3- or 4-day visit with the school. The application is writing intensive; finalists are expected to spend several days on campus, during which they will undergo a lengthy interview.

Total undergrad enrollment	26
# of applicants	170
Range SAT Critical Reading	750–800
Range SAT Math	700–800
percent graduated top 10% of class	86
percent graduated top 25% of class	93

The Cooper Union for the Advancement of Science and Art 218

New York, New York

The admission rate to Cooper Union is extremely competitive. In recent years, only about 8 percent of applicants have been accepted to the undergraduate program. The fine arts (BFA) program is usually the most competitive of Cooper's three schools (art, architecture, and engineering), though all admits must be academically accomplished and at the top of their high school class. Depending on if you plan to pursue engineering, art, or architecture, admissions requirements and applications deadlines vary; for example, students applying to the art or architecture school must complete a "home test," which consists of a number of visual projects to be completed in approximately 3 to 4 weeks and returned to The Cooper Union for review.

Total undergrad enrollment	910
# of applicants	3,354

Range SAT Critical Reading	610–730
Range SAT Math	610–780
Range SAT Writing	620–640
Range ACT Composite	29–33
Average HS GPA	3.60
percent graduated top 10% of class	93
percent graduated top 25% of class	98

United States Air Force Academy 222

Colorado Springs, Colorado

The Air Force Academy promises a demanding four years, and the faint-hearted need not apply. Due to the arduous nature of the school, it's no wonder that applicants face stringent requirements right at the outset: The school even suggests applying to Air Force ROTC and a participating college at the same time. Aside from an excellent academic record, successful candidates need to be physically fit. They also must win a nomination from their congressperson. Honor is a valued quality at the academy, and admissions officers will accept only those with the strength of character and determination necessary to succeed at one of the country's most elite institutions. Most students will hear whether or not they are accepted in March.

Total undergrad enrollment	4,619
# of applicants	11,627
Range SAT Critical Reading	570–680
Range SAT Math	620–700
Range SAT Writing	570–650
Range ACT Composite	29–32
Average HS GPA	3.86
percent graduated top 10% of class	51
percent graduated top 25% of class	80

United States Coast Guard Academy 224

New London, Connecticut

Gaining acceptance into the Coast Guard Academy is a highly competitive process. The admissions committee is looking not only for outstanding academic achievement but also for applicants who demonstrate leadership ability and strong moral character; a thorough, holistic review is conducted by the Cadet Candidate Evaluation Board for each candidate. In addition, unlike other colleges, you'll also need a physical fitness examination and evaluation, and you will need to provide evaluations from a math and English instructor, as well as a coach/ PE instructor evaluation. Successful candidates usually score at least 1100 combined Critical Reading and Math on the SAT or have an ACT Composite of at least 24.

Total undergrad enrollment	1,017
# of applicants	2,223
Range SAT Critical Reading	550–670
Range SAT Math	600–690
Range SAT Writing	530–650
Range ACT Composite	25–30
Average HS GPA	3.70
percent graduated top 10% of class	51
percent graduated top 25% of class	87

United States Merchant Marine Academy 226

Kings Point, New York

Prospective midshipmen face demanding admission requirements. The USMMA assesses scholastic achievement, strength of character, and stamina (applicants must meet specific physical standards). Candidates must also be nominated by a proper nominating authority, typically a state representative or senator. The current minimum qualifying scores for the SAT Reasoning Test are 520 for Critical Reading and 560 for Math; for the ACT, the current minimum qualifying scores for the ACT are 22 for English and 24 for Math. Students must be U.S. citizens to gain admission, aside from a limited number of international midshipmen specially authorized by Congress.

Total undergrad enrollment	985
# of applicants	1,734
Range SAT Critical Reading	540–640
Range SAT Math	600–660
Range ACT Composite	25–29
Average HS GPA	3.60
percent graduated top 10% of class	18
percent graduated top 25% of class	23

United States Military Academy—West Point 228

West Point, New York

The fact that you must be nominated by your Congressional representative in order to apply to West Point tells you all you need to know about the school's selectivity. Contact your district's Congressional representative to learn the deadline for nomination requests; typically these are made in the spring of your junior year. Successful candidates must demonstrate excellence in academics, physical conditioning, extracurricular involvement, and leadership. They must also be willing to commit to five years of active duty and three years of reserve duty upon graduation. Almost 13,000 applied for the 1,375 available slots for the entering class of 2014, who had average SAT scores of 625 on Verbal (Critical Reasoning) and 642 on Math. More so than most schools, athletic participation helps in the admissions decision.

Total undergrad enrollment	4,686
# of applicants	12,264
Range SAT Critical Reading	560–670
Range SAT Math	580–650
Range SAT Writing	540–650
Range ACT Composite	25–30
Average HS GPA	3.80
percent graduated top 10% of class	47
percent graduated top 25% of class	77

United States Naval Academy 230

Annapolis, Maryland

USNA is an intensely rigorous and demanding program that requires, expects, and receives the best possible candidates. The most important non-academic criteria are the personal interview, the applicant's character, and the desire of the applicant to attend the academy. It's the perfect program for anyone wanting to both serve in the U.S. Navy or Marines and receive a first-class education. Candidates must pass a medical and fitness assessment test; 52 percent of the Class of 2015 were in the top 10 percent of their class. As soon as all of the candidate packet forms are received, the admissions boards will determine the applicant's scholastic "whole person" qualification. If the record of achievement is truly outstanding, the student could receive an early offer called a Letter of Assurance that indicates intent to offer admission; those who do not receive the letter will continue to compete against other applicants following the normal timeline.

Total undergrad enrollment	4,603
# of applicants	17,419
Range SAT Critical Reading	550–670
Range SAT Math	590–690
percent graduated top 10% of class	56
percent graduated top 25% of class	81

Webb Institute 232

Glen Cove, New York

Let's not mince words; admission to Webb is mega-tough. Webb's admissions counselors are out to find the right student for their curriculum—one who can survive the school's rigorous academics. The applicant pool is highly self-selected because of the focused program of study: naval architecture and marine engineering. It is recommended that applicants take calculus and mechanical drawing and have a B average in physics, chemistry, and mathematics. Also, all applicants must be physically and mentally capable of performing all work required in the academic courses and in the annual practical work periods.

Total undergrad enrollment	80
# of applicants	72
Range SAT Critical Reading	640–700
Range SAT Math	700–740
Range SAT Writing	620–720
Average HS GPA	3.90
percent graduated top 10% of class	63
percent graduated top 25% of class	88

Agnes Scott College 236

Decatur, Georgia

Take the time to craft a solid application if you want to be considered seriously, because this is a very competitive school where admissions officers give each candidate a very careful look. Undergraduate academic performance is the biggest factor that the school takes into consideration (including two years of a foreign language), and SAT/ACT scores are optional (though suggested); those who decline to submit scores must provide an analytically or critically graded writing sample or submit to an admissions interview. The school is looking for high-achieving women who are active in a variety of clubs, classes, and groups. Agnes Scott waives the application fee for those who apply online.

Total undergrad enrollment	892
# of applicants	2,117
Range SAT Critical Reading	540–670
Range SAT Math	530–650
Range SAT Writing	550–650
Range ACT Composite	24–29
Average HS GPA	3.60
percent graduated top 10% of class	34
percent graduated top 25% of class	69

Amherst College 238

Amherst, Massachusetts

When reviewing your application, the admission committee gives the greatest weight to your academic transcript but also uses standardized test scores to compare you to other applicants. Students must submit SAT scores along with two Subject Tests, or ACT scores with a recommended essay. Only 15 percent of applicants were admitted to the Class of 2014, 87 percent of which were in the top 10 percent of their high school class.

Total undergrad enrollment	1,795
# of applicants	8,099
Range SAT Critical Reading	670–770
Range SAT Math	670–770
Range SAT Writing	680–770
Range ACT Composite	30–34
percent graduated top 10% of class	87
percent graduated top 25% of class	97

Barnard College 240

New York, New York

The school looks for women with proven academic strength, looking at school records, recommendations, writing, and test scores; the candidates' talents, abilities, interests, and history are also given careful consideration. The average GPA of the Class of 2015 was 3.78, with a median combined SAT of 2050; applicants should also have completed three or four years of a foreign language.

Total undergrad enrollment	2,456
# of applicants	4,618
Range SAT Critical Reading	630–730
Range SAT Math	620–710
Range SAT Writing	650–750
Range ACT Composite	28–32
percent graduated top 10% of class	81
percent graduated top 25% of class	95

Bates College 242

Lewiston, Maine

While holding its applicants to lofty standards, Bates strives to adopt a personal approach to the admissions process. Officers favor qualitative information and focus more on academic rigor, essays, and recommendations than GPA and test scores. The school recently completed a "triple crown" of admissions achievements: a record number of applications, one of the lowest acceptance rates in the college's history (26.9 percent), and the highest acceptance of offers in six years.

Total undergrad enrollment	1,725
# of applicants	4,517
Range SAT Critical Reading	620–710
Range SAT Math	620–700
Range SAT Writing	638–713
Range ACT Composite	29–32
percent graduated top 10% of class	66
percent graduated top 25% of class	92

Beloit College 244

Beloit, Wisconsin

Realizing that applicants are more than statistics on a page, the college works diligently to assess the the whole person. While most weight is given to a candidate's secondary school transcript, significant attention is also paid to essays and recommendations, as well as passions and aspirations, talents and concerns, involvement and achievements.

Total undergrad enrollment	1,308
# of applicants	2,003
Range SAT Critical Reading	570–700
Range SAT Math	620–680
Range ACT Composite	24–30
Average HS GPA	3.42
percent graduated top 10% of class	42
percent graduated top 25% of class	71

Boston College 246

Boston, Massachusetts

Nearly 30,000 candidates applied for 2,250 openings, and only 30 percent were admitted; highly competitive standardized test scores definitely improved the chances of admission (the mean SAT score for the Class of 2013 was 2030, and the mid-50 percent range of scores was 1920–2130). The school looks for strong academics, but it also relies heavily on recommendations and signs of serious commitment, leadership, and earned recognition from peers or adults.

Total undergrad enrollment	9,099
# of applicants	29,933
Range SAT Critical Reading	610–700
Range SAT Math	640–730
Range SAT Writing	630–720
Range ACT Composite	29–32
percent graduated top 10% of class	79
percent graduated top 25% of class	91

Bowdoin College 248

Brunswick, Maine

This highly selective liberal arts college admitted just 16 percent of applicants last year, and the school very much looks at the whole package. Though the student's academic record is the most important factor, standardized test scores are optional at Bowdoin, and approximately 15–18 percent of students choose not to submit them. Still, for those members of the Class of 2015 who did, the median score in Critical Reasoning was an impressive 710, and for Math, 700.

Total undergrad enrollment	1,751
# of applicants	6,018
Range SAT Critical Reading	650–750
Range SAT Math	660–750
Range SAT Writing	660–750
Range ACT Composite	30–33
Average HS GPA	3.80
percent graduated top 10% of class	83
percent graduated top 25% of class	97

Brandeis University 250

Waltham, Massachusetts

Admissions standards have risen at all top schools, and Brandeis is no exception: If you expect to get in here, you've got your work cut out for you. The acceptance rate is about 32 percent, and 71 percent of freshman were in the top decile of their high school graduating class.

Total undergrad enrollment	3,341
# of applicants	7,753
Range SAT Critical Reading	630–730
Range SAT Math	640–730
Range SAT Writing	640–730
Range ACT Composite	28–32
Average HS GPA	3.77
percent graduated top 10% of class	84
percent graduated top 25% of class	97

Brown University 252

Providence, Rhode Island

The majority of applicants are qualified for admission to Brown, so the school has the "humbling luxury" of choosing candidates who stand out for special abilities, backgrounds, and yes, academics. Coasting by on good grades isn't going to be enough—only 21 percent of valedictorians were accepted to the Class of 2014—so find a way to stand out otherwise, particularly if you come from a state (such as New York) or high school that is overrepresented in the applicant pool.

Total undergrad enrollment	6,318
# of applicants	30,946
Range SAT Critical Reading	660–760
Range SAT Math	670–760
Range SAT Writing	670–760
Range ACT Composite	29–33
percent graduated top 10% of class	93
percent graduated top 25% of class	99

Bryn Mawr College 254

Bryn Mawr, Pennsylvania

Outstanding preparation for graduate study draws an applicant pool that's well-prepared and intellectually curious. Interviews are strongly recommended but not required, and there are two rounds of binding Early Decision (which account for 25–30 percent of all admitted students). The school's "test flexible" policy allows applicants to select the standardized tests that they believe best represent their academic potential; the mid-50 percent range of the Class of 2014 scored 1170–1400 on the Critical Reasoning and Math sections of the SAT.

Total undergrad enrollment	1,287
# of applicants	2,271
Range SAT Critical Reading	590–720
Range SAT Math	580–700
Range SAT Writing	600–700
Range ACT Composite	26–30
percent graduated top 10% of class	64
percent graduated top 25% of class	92

Bucknell University 256

Lewisburg, Pennsylvania

Admission to Bucknell is competitive (about 27 percent), and admissions officers will cast a keen eye on the quality of your application, including your performance in a hopefully rigorous secondary school curriculum (the average GPA of those admitted to the Class of 2015 was 3.62), as well as your SAT or ACT test scores. In particular, the school places high importance on the quality of writing and content of the supplemental essays that accompany the Common Application.

Total undergrad enrollment	3,487
# of applicants	7,178
Range SAT Critical Reading	590–670
Range SAT Math	630–710
Range SAT Writing	600–690
Range ACT Composite	27–31
Average HS GPA	3.50
percent graduated top 10% of class	65
percent graduated top 25% of class	89

Carleton College 258

Northfield, Minnesota

Competitive though it is, it's possible to get in without stellar grades and test scores if you have some exceptional talent, but most successful applicants have all of these qualities. High school record is most important here and the admissions committee is attracted to students who do honors or advanced placement work (the more classes on your transcript, the better). 60 of the 518 students entering in fall of 2010 were National Merit scholars, and 78 percent were ranked in the top 10 percent of their class.

Total undergrad enrollment	1,991
# of applicants	4,856
Range SAT Critical Reading	650–750
Range SAT Math	650–750
Range SAT Writing	650–740
Range ACT Composite	29–33
percent graduated top 10% of class	76
percent graduated top 25% of class	93

Centenary College of Louisiana 260

Shreveport, Louisiana

Centenary's applicant pool has grown substantially over the past decade, allowing the school to become more selective in its admissions process. The school's reputation, though regional, is quite solid, and the college does a good job of enrolling those it admits. The mean SAT for the Class of 2014 was 1110, and the average ACT score was 24.

Total undergrad enrollment	891
# of applicants	1,076
Range SAT Critical Reading	520–630
Range SAT Math	520–620
Range ACT Composite	24–28
percent graduated top 10% of class	33
percent graduated top 25% of class	63

Centre College 262

Danville, Kentucky

If you're ranked in the top quarter of your graduating class and have taken challenging courses throughout your high school career, you should have smooth sailing through the admissions process. The mid-50 percent range of SAT scores for those admitted recently was 1,140–1,350; the school will take the applicant's best scores.

Total undergrad enrollment	1,214
# of applicants	2,056
Range SAT Critical Reading	550–670
Range SAT Math	570–670
Range SAT Writing	530–670
Range ACT Composite	26–30
Average HS GPA	3.58
percent graduated top 10% of class	59
percent graduated top 25% of class	89

Claremont McKenna College 264

Claremont, California

Colleges of such small size and selectivity devote much more energy to determining whether the candidate as an individual fits instead of analyzing test scores (still, the middle 50 percent SAT range of the freshman class in Critical Reading and Math is 1300–1500). That being said, competitive candidates for admission pursue the most demanding course work possible and receive strong grades: CMC admission officers can spot a "cake" class on a high school transcript from a mile away.

Total undergrad enrollment	1,210
# of applicants	3,856

Range SAT Critical Reading	630–730
Range SAT Math	660–750
percent graduated top 10% of class	85
percent graduated top 25% of class	98

Colby College 266

Waterville, Maine

Currently, only 29 percent of applicants are accepted; 60 percent were in the top 5 percent of their high school class, so hit the books, and the median SAT Critical Reading/Math/Writing scores were 700/700/710. More than 40 percent of the Class of 2015 came via Early Decision. One thing that could set you apart from the pack? An interest in travel. Two-thirds of Colby students study abroad—in fact, for some degrees it's required.

Total undergrad enrollment	1,825
# of applicants	4,213
Range SAT Critical Reading	630–710
Range SAT Math	620–710
Range SAT Writing	620–715
Range ACT Composite	28–31
percent graduated top 10% of class	70
percent graduated top 25% of class	91

Colgate University 268

Hamilton, New York

Colgate's selective admissions policy is designed to identify individuals of intellectual and cultural diversity, academic skill, and wide-ranging interests and backgrounds. The breadth and depth of a student's interests, both in and out of the classroom, help to distinguish among the majority of applicants who have outstanding grades and scores. Admitted students boast an average GPA of 3.75 and an average combined SAT of 1397 (Critical Reading and Math.)

Total undergrad enrollment	2,868
# of applicants	7,872
Range SAT Critical Reading	630–720
Range SAT Math	640–740
Range ACT Composite	29–32
Average HS GPA	3.60
percent graduated top 10% of class	64
percent graduated top 25% of class	90

College of the Atlantic 270

Bar Harbor, Maine

As applicants might expect, admissions standards at COA are somewhat atypical, and the application process is a personal and highly individualized process. Interviews and personal statements (the college even suggests some Thoreauvian topics) are where you can make your mark beyond the standard good grades and (optional) test scores—idealism and intellectual curiosity are key. Candidates should also demonstrate a kinship with the philosophy of human ecology.

Total undergrad enrollment	353
# of applicants	390
Range SAT Critical Reading	57–690
Range SAT Math	520–650
Range SAT Writing	570–670
Range ACT Composite	24–29
Average HS GPA	3.56
percent graduated top 10% of class	43
percent graduated top 25% of class	65

College of the Holy Cross 272

Worcester, Maine

Admission to Holy Cross is competitive; therefore, a demanding high school course load is required to be a viable candidate, including four years of classes in all five core areas (yes, even your senior year). Visits and interviews are not mandatory, but they are strongly encouraged; standardized test scores are truly optional. Students who graduate from a Jesuit high school might find themselves at a slight advantage.

Total undergrad enrollment	2,862
# of applicants	6,911
Range SAT Critical Reading	590–680
Range SAT Math	600–690
Range SAT Writing	600–690
Range ACT Composite	27–31
Average HS GPA	3.77
percent graduated top 10% of class	64
percent graduated top 25% of class	91

Colorado College 274

Colorado Springs, Colorado

Colorado College works to identify those students who will most benefit from its distinct academic environment, looking for "nerds at heart." Unique quirks and achievements make an applicant stand out, and the review process is truly holistic, looking at the entire student. All candidates should take the application essay seriously—strong writing skills are seen as critical to success at CC.

Total undergrad enrollment	2,040
# of applicants	9,466
Range SAT Critical Reading	610–710
Range SAT Math	610–710
Range SAT Writing	620–700
Range ACT Composite	28–32
percent graduated top 10% of class	59
percent graduated top 25% of class	89

Columbia University 276

New York, New York

Earning an acceptance letter from Columbia is no easy feat (there was a 6.9 percent acceptance rate last year). The school has received more than 35,000 applications for just 1,400 full-time spots in recent years, and each application is read in its entirety by at least two admissions officers before a final decision is rendered. Sure, stellar grades are great, but you're going to need more to stand out. The mid-50 percent SAT range of the Class of 2015 was 2150 and 2320 (all three sections); 98 percent of students were in the top 10 percent of their class.

Total undergrad enrollment	5,888
# of applicants	26,179
Range SAT Critical Reading	690–780
Range SAT Math	700–790
Range SAT Writing	690–780
Range ACT Composite	31–34
percent graduated top 10% of class	97

Cornell College 278

Mount Vernon, Iowa

It's no surprise that the admissions committee here focuses attention on both academic and personal strengths. Students are encouraged to submit a pre-application before the process even begins, and the tiny (and one-at-a-time) classes mean that the school is more interested in "fit" than straight numbers (64 percent of students rank within the top 25 percent of their high school classes, considered low for a selective school). Strong writers can do much for themselves under admissions circumstances such as these.

Total undergrad enrollment	1,183
# of applicants	3,791
Range SAT Critical Reading	540–680
Range SAT Math	530–680
Range SAT Writing	530–640
Range ACT Composite	24–29
Average HS GPA	3.50
percent graduated top 10% of class	62
percent graduated top 25% of class	88

Cornell University 280

Ithaca, New York

Some of the university's seven schools are more competitive than others. If you're thinking of trying to "backdoor" your way into one of the most competitive schools—by gaining admission to a less competitive one, then transferring after one year—be aware that you will have to resubmit the entire application and provide a statement outlining your academic plans, and the school is on high alert for this sort of gaming of the system. Exceptionally strong students may apply to one primary and one alternate school, but you must complete the application process (and crucial essays) for both.

Total undergrad enrollment	13,935
# of applicants	36,392
Range SAT Critical Reading	640–730
Range SAT Math	670–770
Range ACT Composite	29–33
percent graduated top 10% of class	90
percent graduated top 25% of class	99

Dartmouth College 282

Hanover, New Hampshire

Many students who meet all the qualifications are turned away because there simply isn't room for them (90 percent of the Class of 2014 was in the top 10 percent of their high school). Dartmouth reviews applications holistically, meaning your best shot is to compile an application that paints a compelling portrait; the personal essay and required peer evaluation should back this up. Some special talent, life experience, or personal trait may be your ticket in, if Dartmouth thinks it will enhance the education of your classmates.

Total undergrad enrollment	4,135
# of applicants	18,778
Range SAT Critical Reading	670–780
Range SAT Math	690–790
Range SAT Writing	690–790
Range ACT Composite	30–34
percent graduated top 10% of class	79
percent graduated top 25% of class	90

Davidson College 284

Davidson, North Carolina

Prospective applicants beware: Securing admission at this prestigious school is no easy feat. The school places importance on both the success and rigor of an applicant's high school courses, as well as writing ability, personal impact (as judged by recommendations), the depth and breadth of extracurricular pursuits, and standardized test scores. The college actively assembles a diverse incoming class each year, and the school accepted just ore than 25 percent of applicants this year, 85 percent of whom were in the top 10 percent of their class. Candidates with leadership experience generally garner the favor of admissions officers. The college takes its honor code seriously (exams are self-scheduled and unproctored) and, as a result, seeks out students of demonstrated reputable character.

Total undergrad enrollment	1,738
# of applicants	4,088
Range SAT Critical Reading	630–720
Range SAT Math	630–710
Range SAT Writing	620–720
Range ACT Composite	28–32
Average HS GPA	4.00
percent graduated top 10% of class	78
percent graduated top 25% of class	95

DePauw University 286

Greencastle, Indiana

Prospective applicants should not be deceived by DePauw's high acceptance rate (57 percent for the current year). The students who are accepted and choose to enroll here have the academic goods to justify their admission. The mid-50 percent range for the Class of 2015's SAT scores (Critical Reading and Math) is 1100–1340; for GPAs, it is 3.33–3.85. DePauw's generous merit scholarships have a lot to do with students' choice to enroll.

Total undergrad enrollment	2,362
# of applicants	5,206
Range SAT Critical Reading	530–640
Range SAT Math	550–670
Range SAT Writing	530–640
Range ACT Composite	24–29
Average HS GPA	3.56
percent graduated top 10% of class	53
percent graduated top 25% of class	83

Duke University 288

Durham, North Carolina

Duke is an extremely selective undergraduate institution (13 percent acceptance for last year), means the admissions office looks for multi-faceted, multi-talented students who excel in not just academics and outside activities, but are willing to make "interesting mistakes." For admission into either the College of Arts & Sciences or the School of Engineering, students must take either the ACT with writing exam or the SATs with two subject tests; you'll also have to present an exceptional record just to be considered.

Total undergrad enrollment	6,066
# of applicants	18,090
Range SAT Critical Reading	690–770
Range SAT Math	690–800
Range ACT Composite	29–34
percent graduated top 10% of class	90
percent graduated top 25% of class	98

Emory University 290

Atlanta, Georgia

Early Decision applications to Emory have risen drastically over the past few years, and there is a statistical advantage to applying Early Decision, though the profiles of students who apply early and regular are nearly the same. The middle 50 percent of the entering class in 2011 had an SAT range (Critical Reading and Math) of 1320–1510; writing is also heavily weighted, in that the school both requires the writing portion of the SATs or ACTs and closely looks at essays and short-answer responses on the application.

Total undergrad enrollment	7,140
# of applicants	15,550
Range SAT Critical Reading	640–740
Range SAT Math	670–760
Range SAT Writing	650–750
Range ACT Composite	30–33
Average HS GPA	3.84
percent graduated top 10% of class	84
percent graduated top 25% of class	98

Franklin W. Olin College of Engineering 292

Needham, Massachusetts

Not many colleges can boast that they are filled with students who turned down offers from the likes of MIT, Cal Tech, and Carnegie Mellon, but Olin can. This relatively new school is unique among engineering schools in that the admissions office really looks for more than just brains and places importance on "personal character" and "risk-taking." The school even encourages students to consider asking a non-math/science teacher for the second letter of recommendation. Of the 92 students in the Class of 2014, 12 were valedictorians, and the middle 50 percent SAT range was 2060–2240. Once the initial applications (Common, with supplement) are reviewed, the school selects approximately 210 top applicants as "candidates," who are then invited to campus to participate in Candidates' Weekends, which includes a design project, individual interviews, and team exercises. The final cut is made following these weekends in February and March.

Total undergrad enrollment	346
# of applicants	567
Range SAT Critical Reading	670–750
Range SAT Math	710–780
Range SAT Writing	650–730

Range ACT Composite	33–35
Average HS GPA	3.90
percent graduated top 10% of class	95
percent graduated top 25% of class	99

Georgetown University 294

Washington, D.C.

GU gets almost ten applications for every space in the entering class, and the academic strength of the pool is impressive: the mid-50 percent SAT range (Critical Reading and Math) of students accepted this past year was 1330–1540. Virtually fifty percent of the entire student body took AP courses in high school. Candidates who are wait-listed should hold little hope for an offer of admission, as the school takes very few off their lists.

Total undergrad enrollment	7,092
# of applicants	18,916
Range SAT Critical Reading	650–750
Range SAT Math	660–750
Range ACT Composite	27–33

Gettysburg College 296

Gettysburg, Pennsylvania

This competitive liberal arts school wants to see that students have made the most of the academic offerings at their high school (86 percent of the Class of 2014 were in the top quarter of their high school class) and that there was in-depth involvement with community and outside activities; no resume padding allowed. Early Decision applicants account for about 44 percent of the class. To really get a feel for Gettysburg, however, many students say a campus visit is a must.

Total undergrad enrollment	2,484
# of applicants	5,392
Range SAT Critical Reading	610–690
Range SAT Math	620–680
percent graduated top 10% of class	68
percent graduated top 25% of class	86

Grinnell College 298

Grinnell, Iowa

Grinnell is extremely selective for its 450 seats, so you'll have to give it your all. High school academics, involvement, and standardized test scores all play a role in admittance, as does the school's assessment of each candidate's potential contributions in the classroom and to the Grinnell campus community. An interview isn't required here for regular admissions (though it is for Early Decision), but do it anyway.

Total undergrad enrollment	1,603
# of applicants	2,845
Range SAT Critical Reading	610–740
Range SAT Math	610–730
Range ACT Composite	28–32
percent graduated top 10% of class	62
percent graduated top 25% of class	88

Hanover College 300

Hanover, Indiana

There are five main criteria that the Hanover admissions committee uses to evaluate applicants: academic record, personal excellence, respect for others, community responsibility, and accountability. Hanover expects 90 percent of its students to have an "off-campus experience" (i.e. a semester studying abroad or three weeks abroad during May term), so demonstrating an interest in the larger world can be helpful.

Total undergrad enrollment	1,004
# of applicants	2,964
Range SAT Critical Reading	510–610
Range SAT Math	500–600
Range SAT Writing	480–590
Range ACT Composite	22–28
Average HS GPA	3.64
percent graduated top 10% of class	31
percent graduated top 25% of class	65

Harvey Mudd College 302

Claremont, California

Like most top-tier science, math, and engineering schools, Harvey Mudd considers far more qualified applicants than it can accommodate in its incoming class. If your school offers honors, AP or IB courses, take 'em, and not just in math and science; you can stand out here by demonstrating an ability to appreciate the humanities. 89 percent of the Class of 2015 ranked in the top 10 percent of their high school classes, and 30 percent were National Merit Scholars, so accept the fact that being perfectly qualified to attend this school is no guarantee of admission.

Total undergrad enrollment	773
# of applicants	2,508
Range SAT Critical Reading	670–760
Range SAT Math	740–800
Range SAT Writing	668–760
Range ACT Composite	32–35
percent graduated top 10% of class	89
percent graduated top 25% of class	99

Haverford College 304

Haverford, Pennsylvania

Haverford's applicant pool is an impressive and competitive lot. Intellectual curiosity is paramount, and the greatest weight is placed on your academic transcript: Nearly 94 percent of the Class of 2015 placed within the top 10 percent of their high school class. The middle 50 percent range for SAT scores on Critical Reasoning and Math was 1300–1500. Additionally, the college places a high value on ethics, as evidenced by its honor code, and the admissions office seeks students who will reflect and promote Haverford's ideals (which is why an interview is recommended).

Total undergrad enrollment	1,177
# of applicants	3,312
Range SAT Critical Reading	650–740
Range SAT Math	650–750
Range SAT Writing	660–750
percent graduated top 10% of class	94
percent graduated top 25% of class	99

Hillsdale College 306

Hillsdale, Michigan

Don't be fooled by Hillsdale's high acceptance rate. Only serious, solid candidates who have taken aggressive college prep courses candidates bother applying here, and the average SAT score for incoming freshmen was 1970, with 48 percent having been in the top 10 percent of their graduating classes (and an average incoming GPA of 3.75). While you don't have to be politically oriented to get in, the school's rigorously enforced honor code challenges Hillsdale students to self-government.

Total undergrad enrollment	1,326
# of applicants	1,865
Range SAT Critical Reading	630–740
Range SAT Math	570–700
Range SAT Writing	590–720
Range ACT Composite	26–31
Average HS GPA	3.75
percent graduated top 10% of class	77
percent graduated top 25% of class	98

Johns Hopkins University 308

Baltimore, Maryland

Top schools like Hopkins receive more and more applications every year and, as a result, grow harder and harder to get into. With more than 18,000 applicants, Hopkins has to reject numerous applicants who are thoroughly qualified. The admissions office tries to help students put their best foot forward—they even provide examples of "Essays That Worked" for current students—but you have to take your own initiative.

Total undergrad enrollment	4,980
# of applicants	18,459
Range SAT Critical Reading	630–740
Range SAT Math	660–770
Range SAT Writing	640–740
Range ACT Composite	29–33
Average HS GPA	3.72
percent graduated top 10% of class	87
percent graduated top 25% of class	98

Lafayette College 310

Easton, Pennsylvania

With an acceptance rate hovering around 40 percent, applications must be strong. Emphasis is placed on an applicant's performance in secondary school, the quality of that education, and the class standing. The admissions committee also values a demonstration of personal character, as well as evidence of significant talent. The results of standardized tests are recommended but not required for admission (some academic departments use them for placement purposes); for those who submitted in the Class of 2014, the middle 50 percent SAT score range for Critical Reading and Math was 1230–1430.

Total undergrad enrollment	2,375
# of applicants	5,822
Range SAT Critical Reading	570–670
Range SAT Math	610–700
Range SAT Writing	590–680
Range ACT Composite	26–30
Average HS GPA	3.41
percent graduated top 10% of class	57
percent graduated top 25% of class	86

Macalester College 312

St. Paul, Minnesota

To say that Macalester's star is on the rise is to put it very mildly. The number of applicants to the school continues to increase, and it has grown substantially more difficult to gain admission here within a very short period of time (it accepted 32 percent for the Class of 2015, a 9 percent drop from the previous year). 76 percent of those admitted were in the top 10 percent of their high school class, and the median SAT score (Critical Reading and Mat) was 1410; for the ACTs, it was 31.

Total undergrad enrollment	2,005
# of applicants	4,317

Range SAT Critical Reading	640–740
Range SAT Math	620–720
Range SAT Writing	630–730
Range ACT Composite	28–32
percent graduated top 10% of class	69
percent graduated top 25% of class	92

Massachusetts Institute of Technology 314

Cambridge, Massachusetts

MIT has one of the nation's most competitive admissions processes; your best chance to get an edge is to stand out (and keep in mind that most applicants' GPAs and standardized test scores are all going to be top-notch). Make sure to schedule an interview, even if it is optional. Last year, the school admitted 12.4 percent of eligible applicants who had an interview (or who had their interview waived), but only 1.4 percent of those who chose not to interview. Most importantly, find ways to stress your creativity; students who have a special talent or skill may send in a portfolio or other relevant supplemental information.

Total undergrad enrollment	4,285
# of applicants	16,632
Range SAT Critical Reading	670–760
Range SAT Math	740–800
Range SAT Writing	670–770
Range ACT Composite	32–35
percent graduated top 10% of class	98
percent graduated top 25% of class	100

Middlebury College 316

Middlebury, Vermont

The highly selective (18 percent) Middlebury gives you options in standardized testing. The school will accept either the SAT or the ACT or three different SAT Subject Tests. Improve your chances of admission by crafting a standardized test profile that shows you in the best possible light; as a reference, the middle 50 percent SAT range for the Class of 2015 was 1950–2240, and for the ACTs, it was 30–33.

Total undergrad enrollment	2,502
# of applicants	7,984
Range SAT Critical Reading	640–740
Range SAT Math	650–740
Range SAT Writing	650–750
Range ACT Composite	30–33
percent graduated top 10% of class	86
percent graduated top 25% of class	09

Mount Holyoke College 318

South Hadley, Massachusetts

Mount Holyoke follows traditional admissions requirements (nearly three-quarters of recent admitees were in the top 20 percent of their class) but encourages applicants to submit supplemental materials exhibiting artistic or athletic talents. The school reviews applications in this order: transcript, essay/short answers, activities/involvement and letters of recommendation, and then the interview, which is optional but recommended.

Total undergrad enrollment	2,287
# of applicants	3,359
Range SAT Critical Reading	610–700
Range SAT Math	580–690
Range SAT Writing	620–710
Range ACT Composite	27–31
Average HS GPA	3.70
percent graduated top 10% of class	58
percent graduated top 25% of class	82

Northwestern University 320

Evanston, Illinois

Each application is carefully reviewed by several members of the admission committee, and all factors are taken into account. Applicants may submit either SAT or ACT scores, and the school recommends that students take at least two SAT Subject Tests. Applicants who choose Early Decision send a strong, positive message to Northwestern and enjoy a higher rate of admission. The school is also working to attract more low-income applicants by increasing the number of full scholarships available for students from low-income families.

Total undergrad enrollment	8,364
# of applicants	25,013
Range SAT Critical Reading	670–750
Range SAT Math	690–780
Range SAT Writing	670–750
Range ACT Composite	30–33
percent graduated top 10% of class	85
percent graduated top 25% of class	96

Occidental College 322

Los Angeles, California

The admissions team at Occidental is adamant about not adhering to formulas. Though admissions staff will carefully pore over your high school grades and offerings (a demanding course load is essential), your Admission will rely heavily on essays and recommendations. Successful applicants tend to be creative and academically motivated: 43 percent of admitted students to the Class of 2014 were in the top 5 percent of their high school class, and 61 percent were involved with competitive sports.

Total undergrad enrollment	2,073
# of applicants	5,882
Range SAT Critical Reading	600–690
Range SAT Math	600–690
Range SAT Writing	610–690
Range ACT Composite	26–30
Average HS GPA	3.60
percent graduated top 10% of class	62
percent graduated top 25% of class	93

Randolph College 324

Lynchburg, Virginia

Admitting highly qualified and well-matched students is a top priority at Randolph, and applicants can rest assured that their applications will be given due consideration (something guaranteed by the school's small size). There's no minimum GPA or standardized test score requirements, but the middle 50 percent scored between 1050–1250 on the Critical Reading and Math portions of the SAT and had a GPA between 3.2 and 3.7.

Total undergrad enrollment	517
# of applicants	734
Range SAT Critical Reading	500–600
Range SAT Math	500–610
Range ACT Composite	23–27
Average HS GPA	3.40
percent graduated top 10% of class	20
percent graduated top 25% of class	60

Reed College 326

Portland, Oregon

Reed admissions officers know exactly what type of student will thrive here, and that's who they seek. Reedies are fiercely intellectual (with high school grades to back it up) and more concerned with independent thought and self-motivated learning than simply getting a degree. Applicants may contact current Reed students interning in the Admissions Office with any questions they may have.

Total undergrad enrollment	1,418
# of applicants	3,075
Range SAT Critical Reading	670–750
Range SAT Math	640–710
Range SAT Writing	660–730
Range ACT Composite	30–33
Average HS GPA	3.90
percent graduated top 10% of class	63
percent graduated top 25% of class	90

Scripps College 328

Claremont, California

Though academic excellence is a prerequisite, when it comes to applying to Scripps, admissions is based on more than just the usual suspects. In lieu of formulas or standardized test minimums, admissions officers aim to establish a diverse and talented first-year class and do so by evaluating a variety of factors holistically. For the Class of 2015, the mid-50 percent SAT score range (Critical Reading and Math) was 1280–1450, and 56 percent received some sort of financial aid.

Total undergrad enrollment	946
# of applicants	2,097
Range SAT Critical Reading	640–740
Range SAT Math	630–710
Range SAT Writing	640–740
Range ACT Composite	28–32
Average HS GPA	4.10
percent graduated top 10% of class	37
percent graduated top 25% of class	62

Sewanee—The University of the South 330

Sewanee, Tennessee

The admissions office at Sewanee is very personable and accessible to students: Interviews may be required, but they can be conducted via Skype when necessary. Applicant evaluation is too personal for a lackadaisical approach to succeed, so all aspects of the application must be strong, from high school coursework to recommendations. The Class of 2014 had an average GPA of 3.6 and a middle 50 percent SAT range (Critical Reading and Math) of 1140–1340.

Total undergrad enrollment	1,455
# of applicants	2,765
Range SAT Critical Reading	580–690
Range SAT Math	580–670
Range SAT Writing	570–680
Range ACT Composite	26–30
Average HS GPA	3.62
percent graduated top 10% of class	50
percent graduated top 25% of class	77

Stanford University 332

Stanford, California

With record application numbers, open spots in this renowned institution are incredibly tight. Impressive grades in demanding courses and high standardized test scores will be given strong consideration, and essays should reflect the individual voice of the candidate. Optional alumni interviews are granted to students in some ZIP codes, but all applications are considered complete without an interview.

Total undergrad enrollment	6,889
# of applicants	32,022
Range SAT Critical Reading	670–760
Range SAT Math	690–790
Range SAT Writing	680–780
Range ACT Composite	30–36
percent graduated top 10% of class	90

Thomas Aquinas College 334

Santa Paula, California

A unique academic institution, TAC values students who are a good fit above all else. Academic prowess is a must, and candidates should also demonstrate intellectual curiosity and a love of reading. The rolling admissions policy means that getting in line at the starting gate is a good idea (though sometimes spots open up the summer before school starts), and the process is deliberately broad so as to allow students greater latitude in expressing their academic interests and strengths. Essays and letters of recommendation are closely read over by the admissions committee, and though there is no firm cutoff, the school does say that SAT scores below the 510–550 range for Math and the 570–600 range for Critical Reading (as well as ACT scores lower than 20 for Math or 24 for English) will often "raise concerns."

Total undergrad enrollment	355
# of applicants	168
Range SAT Critical Reading	630–730
Range SAT Math	570–670
Range SAT Writing	580–680
Range ACT Composite	27–31
Average HS GPA	3.79
percent graduated top 10% of class	44
percent graduated top 25% of class	78

University of Chicago, The 336

Chicago, Illinois

Terrific grades and scores are an absolute, but people here dwell more on deep thoughts and big ideas. Essay topics are legendarily of the thought-provoking "uncommon" type—last year, one option asked applicants to map a connection between Plato and Play-Doh™—so you need to demonstrate that you're capable of fitting in with a bunch of thinkers. Regional counselors with specific knowledge of their territory read all applications first, and qualifying applications are all reviewed multiple times before being passed to the admissions committee.

Total undergrad enrollment	5225
# of applicants	19,340
Range SAT Critical Reading	700–780
Range SAT Math	700–780
Range SAT Writing	690–770
Range ACT Composite	30–34
Average HS GPA	3.79
percent graduated top 10% of class	89
percent graduated top 25% of class	98

University of Notre Dame 338

South Bend, Indiana

Almost everyone who enrolls is in the top 10 percent of their graduating class and possesses test scores in the highest percentiles. However, strong academic ability isn't enough to get you in here; the school looks for students with other talents and seems to have a predilection for athletic achievement (75 percent of students in the 2011 freshman class participated in varsity athletics). Competitive applicants should reveal themselves and their personalities through well-written personal statements rather than straight facts.

Total undergrad enrollment	8,367
# of applicants	14,351
Range SAT Critical Reading	650–750
Range SAT Math	680–760
Range SAT Writing	640–730
Range ACT Composite	31–34

University of Pennsylvania 340

Philadelphia, Pennsylvania

With more than 31,000 applications for this Ivy League school, the competition in the applicant pool is formidable. The mid-50 percent SAT range (Critical Reading and Math) for the Class of 2015 was 1360–1530, and for the ACT, it was 31–34. Applicants can safely assume that they need to be one of the strongest students in their graduating class in order to be successful.

Total undergrad enrollment	9,865
# of applicants	26,941
Range SAT Critical Reading	660–750
Range SAT Math	690–780
Range SAT Writing	680–770
Range ACT Composite	30–34
Average HS GPA	3.89
percent graduated top 10% of class	96
percent graduated top 25% of class	99

University of Redlands 342

Redlands, California

The admit rate here is reasonably high and students with above-average high school records and respectable standardized test scores should see the school as a target (this year's entering freshman class had an average GPA of 3.52). Candidates who are interested in pursuing the self-designed programs available through the Johnston Center will find the admissions process to be distinctly more personal. Redlands does not offer an early admission program; the school treats every application as Early Action.

Total undergrad enrollment	2,335
# of applicants	3,587
Range SAT Critical Reading	520–620
Range SAT Math	520–620
Range ACT Composite	22–27
Average HS GPA	3.58
percent graduated top 10% of class	30
percent graduated top 25% of class	67

University of Richmond 344

Richmond, Virginia

The standardized test scores and grades of incoming students at Richmond are solid. The admitted Class of 2015 had a middle 50 percent SAT range (Critical Reading and Math) of 1260–1450, and most had some banner extracurricular achievement (i.e.: class presidents, athletic team captains, newspaper editors). Note the pile of financial aid (about $8 million) that's available here to students with exceptional credentials.

Total undergrad enrollment	2,945
# of applicants	8,661
Range SAT Critical Reading	580–680
Range SAT Math	600–700
Range SAT Writing	600–690
Range ACT Composite	27–31
percent graduated top 10% of class	54
percent graduated top 25% of class	86

Vanderbilt University 346

Nashville, Tennessee

Vanderbilt is a lot of students' first choices, and the admission statistics reflect as much. 85 percent of the students entering in the fall of 2010 were in the top 10 percent of their class, and 13 percent were National Merit Scholars. The middle 50 percent SAT range for Critical Reading and Math was 1360–1530. Every application is read by at least two readers who are only looking for positive factors that will put you above the rest of the pool.

Total undergrad enrollment	6,879
# of applicants	21,811
Range SAT Critical Reading	670–760
Range SAT Math	690–770
Range ACT Composite	30–34
Average HS GPA	3.70
percent graduated top 10% of class	85
percent graduated top 25% of class	96

Vassar College 348

Poughkeepsie, New York

The applicant pool is at an all-time high, and the acceptance rate is at an all-time low. Stellar academics are a must (the average combined SAT score hit a record high of 2092 for the Class of 2015), but more importantly, the school wants to get interesting students who will add to the vitality of the classic liberal arts school. Once admissions officers see you meet their rigorous scholastic standards, they'll closely assess your personal essay, recommendations, and extracurricular activities.

Total undergrad enrollment	2,408
# of applicants	7,822
Range SAT Critical Reading	670–740
Range SAT Math	670–720
Range SAT Writing	660–750
Range ACT Composite	29–32
Average HS GPA	3.77
percent graduated top 10% of class	65
percent graduated top 25% of class	96

Wabash College 350

Crawfordsville, Indiana

Wabash is one of the few remaining all-male colleges in the country, so the small applicant pool is highly self-selected, and the academic standards for admission, while selective, aren't especially demanding (the school places more importance on the course selection of students throughout high school). Graduating is a whole other matter. Don't consider applying if you're not ready to do the grueling work required for success here.

Total undergrad enrollment	872
# of applicants	1,535
Range SAT Critical Reading	510–615
Range SAT Math	540–660
Range SAT Writing	490–610
Range ACT Composite	22–28
Average HS GPA	3.58
percent graduated top 10% of class	43
percent graduated top 25% of class	67

Wake Forest University 351

Winston-Salem, North Carolina

Admittance rates (recently, around 38 percent) are not as daunting as they might seem, considering Wake Forest's considerable applicant pool. In particular, admissions officers remain diligent in their matchmaking efforts—finding students who are good fits for the school—and their hard work is rewarded by a high graduation rate. Wake Forest famously has an optional SAT/ACT policy, and students do not need to submit scores to be considered for admission (though accepted students will need to submit them eventually).

Total undergrad enrollment	4,560
# of applicants	10,553
Range SAT Critical Reading	580–690
Range SAT Math	600–700
Range ACT Composite	27–31
percent graduated top 10% of class	75
percent graduated top 25% of class	89

Wellesley College 354

Wellesley, Massachusetts

Wellesley considers a broad range of factors, including a student's academic record, the difficulty of her high school curriculum, participation in extracurricular activities, class rank, recommendations, personal essay, standardized test scores, leadership, and special talents. Writing ability is also a necessary strength, and three separate letters of recommendation are required. For the Class of 2014, the mean SAT Critical Reading score was 684, the mean SAT Writing score was 697, and the mean Math score was 681.

Total undergrad enrollment	2,296
# of applicants	4,267
Range SAT Critical Reading	640–740
Range SAT Math	630–740
Range SAT Writing	650–750
Range ACT Composite	28–31
percent graduated top 10% of class	78
percent graduated top 25% of class	95

Wesleyan College 356

Macon, Georgia

To evaluate a student's qualitative characteristics, Wesleyan recommends that applicants submit a teacher recommendation and have a personal interview with the admissions staff (though neither is required.) Students are also encouraged to submit samples of their creative work, such as poetry, music, or research projects. Of first-year students entering fall 2010 semester, the average SAT was 1090 (Critical Reading and Math), and the average high school GPA was 3.5.

Total undergrad enrollment	630
# of applicants	516
Range SAT Critical Reading	420–660
Range SAT Math	400–610
Range ACT Composite	18–25

Wesleyan University 360

Middletown, Connecticut

When Wesleyan says holistic evaluation, they *mean* holistic evaluation: The school won't even calculate an average GPA for recently admitted students. For a more detailed look behind the Wesleyan admissions process (and a good idea of the process for other highly selective schools), read *The Gatekeepers: Inside the Admissions Process at a Premier College,* by Jacques Steinberg, who spent an entire admissions season at the Wesleyan admissions office.

Total undergrad enrollment	2,837
# of applicants	10,657
Range SAT Critical Reading	635–740
Range SAT Math	660–740
Range SAT Writing	650–750
Range ACT Composite	30–33
Average HS GPA	3.77
percent graduated top 10% of class	68
percent graduated top 25% of class	91

Wheaton College 360

Wheaton, Illinois

Although Wheaton College looks for students who are strong academically, the college doesn't have any minimum requirements for GPA, class rank, or standardized test scores (though either the SAT or the ACT must be submitted, including the writing section). The school does look for evidence of Christian faith when making its decision, and proof of Christian commitment is necessary for admission. Only about 2,000 people apply for freshman admission, so the school is able to assign admissions counselors to each applicant to help guide them through the process.

Total undergrad enrollment	2,406
# of applicants	2,010
Range SAT Critical Reading	600–730
Range SAT Math	610–700
Range SAT Writing	590–710
Range ACT Composite	26–32
Average HS GPA	3.73
percent graduated top 10% of class	58
percent graduated top 25% of class	82

Whitman College 362

Walla Walla, Washington

Whitman is a mega-sleeper in terms of quality of education and loyalty of alumni. Educators all over the country know it as an excellent institution; high school students should note that it also admits more than half of students who apply. Whitman's admissions committee emphasizes essays and extracurriculars more than SAT scores; that being said, the middle 50 percent range of SAT scores for the Class of 2015 is 1230–1430 (Critical Reading and Math).

Total undergrad enrollment	1,535
# of applicants	3,164
Range SAT Critical Reading	610–720
Range SAT Math	610–720
Range SAT Writing	610–710
Average HS GPA	3.80
percent graduated top 10% of class	62
percent graduated top 25% of class	94

Wofford College 364

Spartanburg, South Carolina

Wofford carefully considers all of the applications it receives. Requirements are not that strict (65 percent gained admission last year), but students who have earned decent grades in challenging courses should find themselves with an opportunity to attend a school that is gaining a reputation as one of the South's premier liberal arts colleges. 74 percent of students in the Class of 2015 were in the top 20 percent of their class.

Total undergrad enrollment	1,525
# of applicants	2,595
Range SAT Critical Reading	560–675
Range SAT Math	590–680
Range SAT Writing	545–650
Range ACT Composite	25–28
Average HS GPA	3.56
percent graduated top 10% of class	56
percent graduated top 25% of class	80

Appalachian State University 368

Boone, North Carolina

Unsurprisingly, the vast majority of the 17,000 or so people at this North Carolina regional school come from in-state. Admission decisions are based on a combination of high school achievement and SAT or ACT score; the Class of 2014 had an average SAT score of 1136 (Math and Critical Reading) and an average ACT score of 26.

Total undergrad enrollment	15,137
# of applicants	12,434
Range SAT Critical Reading	510–610
Range SAT Math	530–610
Range SAT Writing	490–590
Range ACT Composite	22–26
Average HS GPA	3.92
percent graduated top 10% of class	19
percent graduated top 25% of class	57

California Polytechnic State University, San Luis Obispo 370

San Luis Obispo, California

Cal Poly requires applicants to declare a major on the application, so be sure to thoroughly educate yourself on your intended major's offerings and requirements: Some are more selective than others. SAT or ACT scores must be submitted; the ACT is the preferred score for Cal Poly.

Total undergrad enrollment	17,332
# of applicants	33,627
Range SAT Critical Reading	540–640
Range SAT Math	580–680
Range ACT Composite	24–29
Average HS GPA	3.84
percent graduated top 10% of class	52
percent graduated top 25% of class	86

California State University—Long Beach 372

Long Beach, California

Admission to Cal State schools is as straightforward as it comes: the CSU eligibility index uses the result of a formula that combines your achievement in high school courses (college prep, tenth through twelfth grade) with the results of the SAT or ACT. Applicants to CSULB must have a C grade point average or higher in order to be considered for competitive admission.

Total undergrad enrollment	27,436
# of applicants	47,673
Range SAT Critical Reading	450–570
Range SAT Math	470–590
Range ACT Composite	18–24
Average HS GPA	3.44
percent graduated top 25% of class	84

Christopher Newport University 374

Newport New, Virginia

As universities go in Virginia, CNU is right up there in selectivity. The admissions people definitely play close attention to your academic success in high school, especially the strength of the curriculum and any honors or AP courses. The middle 50 percent range for the Class of 2014 was 3.3–3.9, and the mid-50 percent SAT range (Math and Critical Reading) was 1140–1260.

Total undergrad enrollment	4,768
# of applicants	8,010
Range SAT Critical Reading	560–640
Range SAT Math	560–640
Range ACT Composite	22–27
Average HS GPA	3.69
percent graduated top 10% of class	19
percent graduated top 25% of class	57

City University of New York—Brooklyn College 376

Brooklyn, New York

Brooklyn College doesn't set the bar inordinately high; students with less-than-stellar high school records can receive a chance to prove themselves here. A minimum CAA (College Admissions Average) of 81 and a minimum combined SAT score of 1000 in Critical Reading and Math is required; the ACT is not accepted. Getting into Brooklyn College is one thing; surviving its academic challenges is a whole other thing entirely.

Total undergrad enrollment	11,740
# of applicants	18,455
Range SAT Critical Reading	490–580
Range SAT Math	520–610
Average HS GPA	3.30
percent graduated top 10% of class	18
percent graduated top 25% of class	52

City University of New York—Hunter College 378

New York, New York

Rolling admissions mean early application is pretty much a must here. Hunter admissions officers are inundated with more than 30,000 applications each year, which means cutoffs and formulas must be used. Although these aren't made public, freshmen who enrolled at Hunter in fall 2010 had an average SAT score (Critical Reading and Math) of 1198.

Total undergrad enrollment	14,609
# of applicants	30,256
Range SAT Critical Reading	520–620
Range SAT Math	530–630

Clemson University 380

Clemson, South Carolina

Don't just automatically think that Clemson's sports reputation means it doesn't take its academics seriously. It's one of the top public universities in the country; admissions are competitive, and a good GPA and test scores will be needed for all who apply. The middle 50 percent of recently admitted students had SAT test scores (Critical Reading and Math) ranging from 1160–1310. For the ACT, the middle 50 percent composite score range was 26–30.

Total undergrad enrollment	15,459
# of applicants	16,865
Range SAT Critical Reading	550–600
Range SAT Math	590–680
Range SAT Writing	540–640
Range ACT Composite	26–30
Average HS GPA	4.16
percent graduated top 10% of class	51
percent graduated top 25% of class	83

College of Charleston 382

Charleston, South Carolina

The College of Charleston is the thirteenth oldest university in the country, and its solid academics, combined with gorgeous beaches, weather, and city, mean that the applicant pool continues to grow every year. Leadership, extra-curricular activities, and other achievements play a role in admission, but the school states that high school curriculum, GPA, rank and test scores are far more important. Out-of-state students who get admitted here tend to have stronger test scores.

Total undergrad enrollment	9,771
# of applicants	11,280
Range SAT Critical Reading	570–650
Range SAT Math	570–640
Range ACT Composite	23–27
Average HS GPA	3.87
percent graduated top 10% of class	51
percent graduated top 25% of class	68

The College of New Jersey 384

Ewing, New Jersey

Admissions are as competitive as you would expect at a school that offers state residents a small-college experience and a highly respected degree for bargain-basement prices. Recently admitted students have an average SAT score around 1300 (Critical Reading and Math) and rank in the top 15 percent of their graduating classes. Competition among biology applicants has grown especially fierce.

Total undergrad enrollment	6,410
# of applicants	9,956
Range SAT Critical Reading	560–670
Range SAT Math	590–680
Range SAT Writing	560–670
percent graduated top 10% of class	60
percent graduated top 25% of class	91

The Evergreen State College 386

Olympia, Washington

Evergreen places a lot of credence in character and personal qualities when making admissions decisions, as the school wants to make sure the fit is right. Though admissions is not terribly selective, the student body is fairly strong; the average GPA for those admitted to the fall quarter 2010 was 3.08, the average SAT (Critical Reading and Math) score was 1100, and the average ACT composite score was 24.

Total undergrad enrollment	4,314
# of applicants	1,965
Range SAT Critical Reading	510–640
Range SAT Math	460–590
Range SAT Writing	480–590
Range ACT Composite	21–27
Average HS GPA	3.08
percent graduated top 10% of class	12
percent graduated top 25% of class	27

Florida State University 388

Tallahassee, Florida

With more than 30,000 applications to process annually, FSU must rely on a formula-driven approach to triage its applicant pool—no letters of recommendation will be necessary. Students are either clearly in or clearly out based on grades, curriculum, and test scores. Applicants should take both the SAT and ACT more than once, as the school uses the best composite/total score for admission and scholarship purposes.

Total undergrad enrollment	30,830
# of applicants	26,037
Range SAT Critical Reading	550–640
Range SAT Math	560–650
Range SAT Writing	550–630
Range ACT Composite	24–28
Average HS GPA	3.76
percent graduated top 10% of class	39
percent graduated top 25% of class	76

Georgia Institute of Technology 390

Atlanta, Georgia

Students considering Georgia Tech shouldn't be deceived by the relatively high acceptance rate (51 percent for 2011). Georgia Tech is a demanding school, and its applicant pool is largely self-selecting. Requirements vary depending on the school one applies to at Georgia Tech—applicants are advised to inquire in advance (though this choice does not affect admission). The mid-50 percent SAT range for the past year's freshman class is 1940–2160.

Total undergrad enrollment	13,160
# of applicants	13,495
Range SAT Critical Reading	590–690
Range SAT Math	650–740
Range SAT Writing	590–690
Range ACT Composite	27–32
Average HS GPA	3.87
percent graduated top 10% of class	89
percent graduated top 25% of class	98

Indiana University—Bloomington 392

Bloomington, Indiana

Above-average high school performers (defined by both a GPA of B or better and test scores above the state average for residents and the national average for non-residents) should meet little resistance from the IU admissions office. Preference is given to Indiana residents in the top 40 percent of their graduating class and out-of-state residents in the top 30 percent of their class.

Total undergrad enrollment	31,892
# of applicants	36,719
Range SAT Critical Reading	520–630
Range SAT Math	540–630
Range ACT Composite	24–29
Average HS GPA	3.61
percent graduated top 10% of class	38
percent graduated top 25% of class	74

Iowa State University 394

Ames, Iowa

Admission to ISU is based on a straight formula known as the Regent Admission Index (RAI), which takes into account your ACT composite score, class rank, high school GPA, and the number of years of high school courses completed in the core subject areas. Applicants who make the cutoff will automatically be offered admission; those who fall below will be considered on an individual basis.

Total undergrad enrollment	23,104
# of applicants	15,066
Range SAT Critical Reading	460–640
Range SAT Math	530–670
Range ACT Composite	22–28
Average HS GPA	3.54
percent graduated top 10% of class	29
percent graduated top 25% of class	61

James Madison University 396

Harrisonburg, Virginia

At JMU admissions are competitive, but the admissions staff insists that they're not searching for a "magic combination" of test scores and GPA. That being said, the majority of admitted students were in the top third of their high school with A's and B's in core classes. No interviews are granted, so the personal statement is a vehicle for conveying information an applicant deems important.

Total undergrad enrollment	17,306
# of applicants	22,221
Range SAT Critical Reading	540–640
Range SAT Math	550–650
Range SAT Writing	540–690
Range ACT Composite	23–27
Average HS GPA	3.84
percent graduated top 10% of class	27
percent graduated top 25% of class	72

Kansas State University 398

Manhattan, Kansas

Though K-State has plenty of strong students, admission is less than. Basically, get a 21 on the ACT (or a 980 or higher on the SAT Critical Reading and Math), or graduate in the top third of your high school class, and you're in. If you're a Kansas resident, a third way to get accepted is to complete the Kansas precollege curriculum with a 2.0 GPA. Non-residents need at least a 2.5.

Total undergrad enrollment	18,753
# of applicants	8,268
Range ACT Composite	21–27
Average HS GPA	3.45
percent graduated top 10% of class	20
percent graduated top 25% of class	45

Longwood University 400

Farmville, Virginia

Admission is based almost solely on academic performance in high school, which considers academic units completed (college preparatory), GPA, SAT or ACT scores, and class rank. Recent regularly admitted students have an average cumulative GPA of 3.4 and an average SAT of 1095 with Reading and Math only. Personal statements and participation in school and community activities are also considered, though not as strongly as academics.

Total undergrad enrollment	4,125
# of applicants	4,402
Range SAT Critical Reading	480–560
Range SAT Math	470–510
Range ACT Composite	20–23
Average HS GPA	3.34
percent graduated top 10% of class	11
percent graduated top 25% of class	38

Missouri University of Science and Technology 402

Rolla, Missouri

In line with other leading public universities, gaining entrance to Missouri S&T is largely a numbers game. Applicants are evaluated on a combination of standardized examination percentile (ACT or SAT test), class rank, and grade point average (GPA). The university draws a competitive, self-selecting pool of applicants, meaning the earlier you apply, the better the advantage you'll have.

Total undergrad enrollment	5,145
# of applicants	2,620
Range SAT Critical Reading	550–670
Range SAT Math	610–700
Range ACT Composite	25–31
Average HS GPA	3.63
percent graduated top 10% of class	43
percent graduated top 25% of class	71

New Mexico Institute of Mining & Technology 404

Socorro, New Mexico

Needless to say, NMT's applicant pool pretty much selects itself, so acceptance rates are not the best indicator of what you need to get in here. Students must submit a high school transcript, senior year class schedule, and SAT/ACT scores to be considered (admissions are rolling). For the Class of 2014, the middle 50 percent of students receive SAT scores ranging from 1110–1370 (Critical Reading and Math).

Total undergrad enrollment	1,385
# of applicants	1,178
Range SAT Critical Reading	530–690
Range SAT Math	580–680
Range ACT Composite	24–29
Average HS GPA	3.60
percent graduated top 10% of class	33
percent graduated top 25% of class	65

North Carolina State University 406

Raleigh, North Carolina

At North Carolina State University, the most important factor in the admissions decision is a student's high school record. Competitive applicants will have at least a B-plus average in a rigorous college prep curriculum. SAT or ACT scores are also considered (the school takes the highest SAT score), though the school puts more emphasis on a student's coursework, grade point average, and extracurricular/community service activities. More than 70 percent of students entering freshman year in the fall of 2011 are from in-state, and 45 percent of all students were ranked within the top 10 percent of their class. The mid-50 percent range of unweighted GPAs was 3.43–3.82.

Total undergrad enrollment	23,500
# of applicants	19,503
Range SAT Critical Reading	530–620
Range SAT Math	560–660
Range SAT Writing	510–610
Range ACT Composite	23–28
percent graduated top 10% of class	42
percent graduated top 25% of class	81

The Ohio State University—Columbus 408

Columbus Ohio

The sheer number of applicants to OSU each year is sizeable, so the school has a competitive admission process in which students are considered for admission based largely on their academic performance and credentials. 89 percent of students enrolled in the fall of 2010 were in the top 25 percent of their high school class, and the mid-50 percent SAT range (Critical Reading and Math) was 1160–1310.

The writing portion of the ACT or SAT is required and used as part of a holistic application review.

Total undergrad enrollment	40,851
# of applicants	24,302
Range SAT Critical Reading	540–650
Range SAT Math	590–700
Range SAT Writing	540–640
Range ACT Composite	26–30
percent graduated top 10% of class	54
percent graduated top 25% of class	89

Purdue University—West Lafayette 410

West Lafayette, Indiana

Purdue will consider your class rank within the context of your high school courses when reviewing your application (along with your grades, test scores, and application essay). The essay is a response to one of three questions provided by Purdue (including one option in which you write the title and introduction to your own hypothetical autobiography later in life). Students must select a single major or school when applying to Purdue, and admission can hinge upon how much space is left in that program, so apply early.

Total undergrad enrollment	30,836
# of applicants	30,707
Range SAT Critical Reading	500–610
Range SAT Math	540–680
Range SAT Writing	490–610
Range ACT Composite	23–29
Average HS GPA	3.60
percent graduated top 10% of class	37
percent graduated top 25% of class	71

Southern Utah University 412

Cedar City, Utah

It's as straightforward as it comes: First-time students are admitted to SUU using an admission index, which is where the GPA and test scores intersect (the full index is available on the school's website). Students with an admission index of 90 or higher will be admitted to Southern Utah University; basically, if you had a B average or higher in high school and you didn't completely bomb the SATs or ACTs, you shouldn't have trouble gaining admission.

Total undergrad enrollment	7,236
# of applicants	3,876
Range SAT Critical Reading	450–570
Range SAT Math	440–550
Range ACT Composite	19–25
Average HS GPA	3.49
percent graduated top 10% of class	31
percent graduated top 25% of class	56

St. Mary's College of Maryland 414

St. Mary's City, Maryland

As Maryland's public honors college, gaining admissions to St. Mary's is competitive. Admissions officers here really strive to get to know the applicant as an individual; one of the essay options even allows students to send in a video or DVD that acts as a "casting tape" for the upcoming class. While academic rigor definitely holds the most weight, extracurriculars are also extremely important. The middle 50 percent range for accepted students in the incoming class in the fall of 2010 was 1770–2040.

Total undergrad enrollment	1,943
# of applicants	2,133
Range SAT Critical Reading	568–680
Range SAT Math	550–650
Range SAT Writing	558–660
Range ACT Composite	25–29
Average HS GPA	3.58
percent graduated top 10% of class	33
percent graduated top 25% of class	71

State University of New York at Geneseo 416

Geneseo, New York

SUNY Geneseo increasingly receives applications from a strong candidate pool, and it accepted just 43 percent of applicants for the Class of 2015 (more than half were in the top 10 percent of their high school class). The middle 50 percent range for SATs (Critical Reading and Math) was 1290–1370; for ACTs, it was 27–30. Applicants who have excelled in honors, IB, or advanced placement courses will have a leg up. Geneseo also maintains a select wait list called "Guaranteed Admissions." These stronger applicants who do not make the cut are automatically given admission to the next spring or fall term.

Total undergrad enrollment	5,988
# of applicants	9,885
Range SAT Critical Reading	600–690
Range SAT Math	600–700
Range ACT Composite	27–30
Average HS GPA	3.75
percent graduated top 10% of class	52
percent graduated top 25% of class	87

State University of New York at New Paltz 418

New Paltz, New York

The "artsy" focus of New Paltz makes it one of the more selective SUNY schools. For freshmen accepted to the fall of 2011 class, the mean high school average was 92.0, and the mean SAT was 1190 (Critical Reading and Math). You will need to show a little personality in your essay, and you must include one teacher recommendation.

Total undergrad enrollment	6,582
# of applicants	15,204
Range SAT Critical Reading	520–610
Range SAT Math	520–610
Range ACT Composite	23–27
Average HS GPA	3.5
percent graduated top 10% of class	26
percent graduated top 25% of class	66

State University of New York—College of Environmental Science and Forestry 420

Syracuse, New York

With such a specialized focus, admission to SUNY—ESF is competitive, but the admissions process is a personal one. Strong grades in college prep courses are obviously expected, and students are encouraged to visit the school to make sure it's a fit. Approximately 20 percent of entering freshmen come from outside New York State—the third highest percentage in SUNY.

Total undergrad enrollment	1,728
# of applicants	1,706
Range SAT Critical Reading	520–640
Range SAT Math	550–640
Range ACT Composite	24–28
percent graduated top 10% of class	29
percent graduated top 25% of class	63

State University of New York—Oswego 422

Oswego, New York

The admissions process is relatively selective (48 percent for the past year), and the school makes it known that everything counts! SAT/ACT scores (no writing needed) are just one of the things the school looks at, and the Class of 2015 had a mid-50 percent range (Critical Reading and Math) of 1035–1185. Oswego admits a percentage of freshman on the basis of promise demonstrated by means other than traditional academic criteria, so having (and demonstrating) a "special talent" can help those students who don't have the highest of GPAs.

Total undergrad enrollment	7,377
# of applicants	10,594
Range SAT Critical Reading	530–600
Range SAT Math	530–600
Range ACT Composite	21–25
Average HS GPA	3.50
percent graduated top 10% of class	13
percent graduated top 25% of class	54

State University of New York—Stony Brook University 424

Stony Brook, New York

Known as one of the most academically rigorous SUNY schools, admission to Stony Brook University is competitive. Students with a particularly strong academic record may be considered for the university's special programs, including the Honors Program, the University Scholars program, and the Scholars in Medicine program, and those who demonstrate some sort of special talent or flair for extracurriculars/leadership receive special consideration. The mid-50 percent range of SAT scores for the Class of 2014 was 1130–1320 (Critical Reading and Math).

Total undergrad enrollment	16,045
# of applicants	27,822
Range SAT Critical Reading	530–630
Range SAT Math	580–680
Range SAT Writing	520–630
Range ACT Composite	25–29
Average HS GPA	3.60
percent graduated top 10% of class	38
percent graduated top 25% of class	72

State University of New York—University at Buffalo 426

Buffalo, New York

As students point out, UB "is famous for its architecture, nursing, and pharmacy schools," making those majors harder to get into. Admissions standards at UB have grown more demanding across all programs in recent years, and the school looks at GPA, rank-in-class, SAT (Critical reading and Math) or ACT score, and strength of the high school academic program, as well as essays, recommendations, documented evidence of exceptional creative talent, demonstrated leadership, and community service when making its decision.

Total undergrad enrollment	19,199

# of applicants	21,985
Range SAT Critical Reading	500–610
Range SAT Math	550–650
Range ACT Composite	23–28
Average HS GPA	3.30
percent graduated top 10% of class	28
percent graduated top 25% of class	65

Truman State University 328
Kirksville, Missouri

Those interested in studying at Truman State had better get to work; the school places a large emphasis on GPA, class rank, and academic rigor. Students who receive the strongest consideration for admission to Truman will have a 140 combined ability according to state board guidelines, which is determined by adding the high school class rank percent to the national percentile on the ACT or SAT college entrance exam (the school combines the two highest SAT scores from the math and verbal sections, and recognizes the highest ACT composite score.) Although early application has no bearing on admission, greatest scholarship consideration is given to those who apply before December 1.

Total undergrad enrollment	5,675
# of applicants	4,702
Range SAT Critical Reading	570–710
Range SAT Math	560–680
Range ACT Composite	25–30
Average HS GPA	3.76
percent graduated top 10% of class	47
percent graduated top 25% of class	77

University of California—Berkeley 430
Berkeley, California

UC Berkeley is a top-notch public university. Importance is placed on the totality of a student's application with a joint focus on the personal essay and academic excellence as noted by a student's GPA. Class rank isn't considered, and preference is given to California residents. All applications are read in their entirety by trained readers, and they are given a comprehensive score that is the basis upon which the student is ultimately admitted or denied, so don't slack on a single part of the application.

Total undergrad enrollment	35,838
# of applicants	52,945
Range SAT Critical Reading	620–740
Range SAT Math	660–770
Range SAT Writing	650–750
Average HS GPA	3.88
percent graduated top 10% of class	90
percent graduated top 25% of class	97

University of California—Davis 432
Davis, California

Admission to UC Davis is considerably easier than, say, admission to Berkeley (the acceptance rate for the fall of 2011 was 46 percent). Nevertheless the UC system in general is geared toward the best and brightest of California's high school students, and the school considers a broad range of criteria in deciding who to admit, from traditional academic factors to extracurricular achievement and responses to life challenges. The middle 50 percent SAT range (Critical Reading and Math) for the Class of 2015 was 1160–1430, and for the ACT, it was 26–32.

Total undergrad enrollment	24,497
# of applicants	43,295
Range SAT Critical Reading	530–650
Range SAT Math	570–640
Range SAT Writing	540–660
Range ACT Composite	24–30
Average HS GPA	3.90

University of California—Irvine 434
Irvine, California

This being the UC system and all, it's a good idea to go as far above the state requirements as possible to make yourself competitive with other applicants. UC Irvine requires students to submit SAT or ACT scores (including the writing section), as well as two SAT Subject tests. The middle 50 percent of the admitted freshman class in 2010 had scores ranging from 1130–1380 (Critical Reading and Math), and 97.5 percent of all admitted students completed at least four years of mathematics.

Total undergrad enrollment	21,976
# of applicants	45,742
Range SAT Critical Reading	520–640
Range SAT Math	570–680
Range SAT Writing	530–640
Average HS GPA	3.88
percent graduated top 10% of class	96
percent graduated top 25% of class	100

University of California—Los Angeles 436
Los Angeles, California

Competition is fierce to secure admittance to one of the nation's top public universities, which received 57,000 applications last year. Grades and test scores only tell part of the story, so you'll need to really stand out in terms of your personal interests, strengths, and passions. Each application is read twice by professional readers, who assign a comprehensive score that acts as the make-or-break number. It's a process that relies heavily on human judgment and appeal, so be sure to shine.

Total undergrad enrollment	26,162
# of applicants	57,670
Range SAT Critical Reading	570–680
Range SAT Math	600–740
Range SAT Writing	580–710
Range ACT Composite	25–31
Average HS GPA	4.25
percent graduated top 10% of class	97
percent graduated top 25% of class	100

University of California—Riverside 438

Riverside, California

The UC—Riverside admissions process is based heavily on quantitative factors. Applicants who have strong GPAs and standardized test scores should have no problem gaining acceptance. Extra points are awarded for each honors level and advanced placement courses taken (so long as you score a C or better).

Total undergrad enrollment	18,242
# of applicants	26,478
Range SAT Critical Reading	450–560
Range SAT Math	480–610
Range SAT Writing	460–570
Range ACT Composite	19–24
Average HS GPA	3.50
percent graduated top 10% of class	94
percent graduated top 25% of class	100

University of California—San Diego 440

San Diego, California

While not as lauded as Berkeley or UCLA, UCSD is quickly earning its place as one of the gems of the UC system, and the school received more than 53,000 freshman applications for fall 2011. The school continues to distinguish itself in a number of ways, including its individualized approach to admissions, in which weight is given to personal achievements and likely contributions to the campus if admitted.

Total undergrad enrollment	23,663
# of applicants	48,043
Range SAT Critical Reading	540–670
Range SAT Math	610–720
Range SAT Writing	560–640
Range ACT Composite	25–31
Average HS GPA	3.98

University of California—Santa Barbara 442

Santa Barbara, California

To be considered for admission to UC—Santa Barbara, students must succeed in both the academic preparation review and the academic promise review. The academic preparation review is more formulaic and takes into account test scores and GPA, and the academic promise review incorporates extracurriculars, personal achievements, and challenges overcome. The average SAT score (Critical Reading and Math) was 1216 for the incoming class in fall 2010.

Total undergrad enrollment	19,184
# of applicants	46,671
Range SAT Critical Reading	540–650
Range SAT Math	560–680
Range SAT Writing	540–660
Range ACT Composite	25–30
Average HS GPA	3.85

University of California—Santa Cruz 444

Santa Cruz, California

UC—Santa Cruz scores all applicants on a 9,200-point scale encompassing 14 criteria, including GPA, test scores, achievement in special projects, and geographic area. UCSC's acceptance rate (68 percent this past year) belies the high caliber of applicants it regularly receives; the average GPA of the incoming class in fall 2011 was 3.73, and the average SAT score was 1776.

Total undergrad enrollment	15,666
# of applicants	27,658
Range SAT Critical Reading	500–630
Range SAT Math	520–640
Range SAT Writing	510–620
Range ACT Composite	22–27
Average HS GPA	3.61
percent graduated top 10% of class	96
percent graduated top 25% of class	100

University of Central Florida 446

Orlando, Florida

As is the case at many state schools, it's all a numbers game here; students aren't required to interview or submit essays (though they should). When calculating your GPA, the admissions committee gives extra weight to honors, AP, dual enrollment, and International Baccalaureate academic classes more heavily than regular classes. The middle 50 percent of students admitted for the entering class in fall 2011 had a score range (Critical Reading and Math) of 1180–1310, and an ACT range of 25–29.

Total undergrad enrollment	47,652
# of applicants	32,876
Range SAT Critical Reading	520–650
Range SAT Math	590–670
Range SAT Writing	530–620
Range ACT Composite	25–28
Average HS GPA	3.80
percent graduated top 10% of class	33
percent graduated top 25% of class	72

University of Colorado—Boulder 448

Boulder, Colorado

With nearly one-third of the student body from out of state, CU boasts far more geographic diversity than most state schools. Applicants must indicate the school within CU to which they wish to be admitted, with Engineering and Applied Science being most competitive, and the College of Arts and Sciences the least (as well as the automatic fallback for those not admitted into their first- choice school). The middle 50 percent range of SAT scores (Critical Reading and Math) for freshmen admitted into this school in the fall of 2011 was 1070–1270.

Total undergrad enrollment	25,782
# of applicants	21,145
Range SAT Critical Reading	530–630
Range SAT Math	540–660
Range ACT Composite	23–28
Average HS GPA	3.55
percent graduated top 10% of class	26
percent graduated top 25% of class	59

University of Delaware 450

Newark, Delaware

Although UD is run by the state of Delaware, out-of-state students also benefit from the school's excellent academic and social offerings at a reasonable tuition, and about 50 percent of out-of-state applicants are usually admitted. The middle 50 percent of admitted freshmen last year had a HS GPA of 3.37–3.92 and an SAT range of 1780–2000; the admissions standards for the school's esteemed Honors Program are much higher. Essays are an important part of UD's admissions process.

Total undergrad enrollment	15,757
# of applicants	24,744
Range SAT Critical Reading	520–630
Range SAT Math	540–650
Range SAT Writing	520–640
Range ACT Composite	24–28
Average HS GPA	3.50
percent graduated top 10% of class	37
percent graduated top 25% of class	74

University of Houston 452

Houston, Texas

The school's 37,000 strong student body means that acceptance is easier to achieve than at some smaller schools. Students who meet the State of Texas Uniform Admission Policy, have a minimum SAT score of 1500 (or ACT score of 24), and are in the top half of their high school class are automatically guaranteed admission. Even if you don't meet one or all of these cutoffs, your application will still be submitted to an individual holistic review.

Total undergrad enrollment	29,378
# of applicants	12,571
Range SAT Critical Reading	470–580
Range SAT Math	510–620
Range ACT Composite	20–25
Average HS GPA	2.7
percent graduated top 10% of class	59
percent graduated top 25% of class	86

University of Illinois at Urbana-Champaign 454

Urbana, Illinois

You can ignore Illinois' relatively high acceptance rate; the school's excellent reputation means that those who aren't strong students usually don't bother to apply. There's no set formula for admission, but each application is individually reviewed (typically at least twice) and ranked based on a combination of all the factors. Prospective students have the opportunity to apply directly into a college and major, and so the applicant's strengths and experiences as they relate to their intended program of study are taken into consideration.

Total undergrad enrollment	31,540
# of applicants	27,273
Range SAT Critical Reading	530–660
Range SAT Math	680–770
percent graduated top 10% of class	56
percent graduated top 25% of class	93

University of Kansas 456

Lawrence, Kansas

There's very little personal touch to admissions at this large state school, which is formula-driven. Average and above-average students are shoo-ins, and even if you underperform in a certain category—test scores, class rank, or GPA—you can compensate in another. Requirements at the School of Engineering are considerably more rigorous (at least 3.0 GPA just to be considered).

Total undergrad enrollment	19,983
# of applicants	10,157
Range ACT Composite	22–28
Average HS GPA	3.50
percent graduated top 10% of class	2
percent graduated top 25% of class	55

University of Mary Washington 458

Fredericksburg, Virginia

UMW looks for the right fit above all else, and its admission process looks to compile a well-rounded student body. The admissions team gives each application a focused review, and successful candidates present records of sound preparation for study in the liberal arts and sciences, particularly in honors and advanced courses. The most recently admitted group (which admitted more than 75 percent of applicants) had a mid-50 percent SAT range of 1630–1890.

Total undergrad enrollment	4,271
# of applicants	4,766
Range SAT Critical Reading	530–640
Range SAT Math	520–610
Range SAT Writing	520–620
Range ACT Composite	23–27
Average HS GPA	3.58

University of Maryland, College Park 460

College Park, Maryland

Even with more than 26,000 applications a year, the school considers 25 different factors when determining who's in and who's out and gives each application a comprehensive review. Essays, recommendations, extracurricular activities, talents and skills, and demographic factors all figure into the mix along with the usual academic and standardized test stuff. Last year, the middle 50 percent of admitted students scored between a 1240–1380 on the SAT (Critical Reading and Math), and between 28–31 on the ACT.

Total undergrad enrollment	26,194
# of applicants	26,358
Range SAT Critical Reading	580–680
Range SAT Math	610–710
Average HS GPA	3.98
percent graduated top 10% of class	71
percent graduated top 25% of class	91

University of Massachusetts Boston 462

Boston, Massachusetts

UMass Boston isn't as selective as UMass Amherst, but you still have to put up a decent academic front to get in. All UMass Boston applicants are asked to submit a personal essay, which gives you the opportunity to present yourself in a way that grades and test scores cannot, and it is also used in consideration for admission to the honors program or scholarship opportunities for qualified applicants.

Total undergrad enrollment	11,568
# of applicants	6,748
Range SAT Critical Reading	460–560
Range SAT Math	480–580
Average HS GPA	3.0

University of Michigan—Ann Arbor 464

Ann Arbor, Michigan

Michigan admits on a rolling basis, a process that favors those who apply early. Though the admissions office doesn't just plug your stats into a calculator, it does make decisions based mainly on academics, including class rank, GPA, and quality/variety of academic interests. The average high school GPA for the freshman class of 2010 was 3.8, and the mid-50 percentile for the SATs was 1960–2200; the school does look at whether standardized test scores and GPA match up, as they're looking for strong overall academic performances. Though each successful application receives three rounds of review, the volume of applications—Michigan receives nearly 30,000 applications—means the admissions office must rely heavily on numbers to make its decision in the early rounds.

Total undergrad enrollment	26,830
# of applicants	31,613
Range SAT Critical Reading	590–690
Range SAT Math	640–750
Range SAT Writing	610–710
Range ACT Composite	27–31
Average HS GPA	3.76
percent graduated top 10% of class	84
percent graduated top 25% of class	97

University of Minnesota, Crookston — 466

Crookston, Minnesota

Getting accepted to UMC isn't all that tough; average and above-average students should have no problem. Once the school has received your application, including a transcript and SAT or ACT scores, you'll find out if you got in within just two weeks.

Total undergrad enrollment	2,528
# of applicants	787
Range SAT Critical Reading	420–540
Range SAT Math	410–520
Range SAT Writing	430–540
Range ACT Composite	19–24
Average HS GPA	3.1
percent graduated top 10% of class	11
percent graduated top 25% of class	34

University of Minnesota—Twin Cities — 468

Twin Cities, Minnesota

Despite what looks to be a fairly choosy admissions rate, it's the sheer volume of applicants that creates a selective situation at Minnesota. Students apply to one of the school's different colleges or majors and compete against the other applicants from that pool. Applicants will find out if they are admitted within two weeks of completing the process.

Total undergrad enrollment	33,607
# of applicants	36,853
Range SAT Critical Reading	530–690
Range SAT Math	600–720
Range SAT Writing	550–670
Range ACT Composite	25–30
percent graduated top 10% of class	43
percent graduated top 25% of class	83

University of Missouri—Kansas City — 470

Kansas City, Missouri

Admission to UMKC is based on the high school curriculum and a combination of ACT or SAT and class rank. For students attending high schools that do not rank, GPA will be used in admission decisions. Students that score above a 20 on their ACTs (or above a 970 on their SAT Critical Reading and Math) and are in the top third of their class are automatically guaranteed admission. Students who do not meet the automatic admission requirements will be reviewed individually for possible admission on a trial basis.

Total undergrad enrollment	9,863
# of applicants	3,997
Range SAT Critical Reading	500–640
Range SAT Math	500–650
Range ACT Composite	21–27
Average HS GPA	3.29
percent graduated top 10% of class	27
percent graduated top 25% of class	57

The University of North Carolina at Asheville — 472

Asheville, North Carolina

UNC—Asheville provides a sound public education in a small campus atmosphere, and an increasing number of students are setting their sights on it each year. The application process isn't difficult, but it is thorough; most students that have success have a strong B+ average in high school (including AP and honors classes), an average SAT score of 1180 (in Critical Reading and Math) or 26 on the ACT, and a healthy mix of extracurricular activities, awards, and athletics.

Total undergrad enrollment	3,418
# of applicants	2,362
Range SAT Critical Reading	540–650
Range SAT Math	520–620
Range SAT Writing	510–620
Range ACT Composite	22–27
Average HS GPA	3.91
percent graduated top 10% of class	22
percent graduated top 25% of class	58

University of North Carolina—Wilmington — 464

Wilmington, North Carolina

Admissions at any UNC school are competitive, and when reviewing a first-year application for admission, the admissions committee will look carefully at your academic rigor and coursework, standardized test scores, and personal qualities, and try to get a feel for you off paper. The mid-50 percent SAT range for students admitted to enter in fall 2011 was 1130–1250 (Critical Reading and Math).

Total undergrad enrollment	11,770
# of applicants	9,759
Range SAT Critical Reading	540–620
Range SAT Math	550–620
Range SAT Writing	520–600
Range ACT Composite	22–26
Average HS GPA	3.8
percent graduated top 10% of class	23
percent graduated top 25% of class	64

University of North Florida 476

Jacksonville, Florida

This up-and-coming school grows more selective by the year, admitting just 42 percent of applicants to the Class of 2014. The average GPA of admitted students for that year was 3.79, and the average SAT score (Critical Reading and Math) was 1204. The admissions process is not terribly personal here; do well in school and on standardized tests to set yourself apart.

Total undergrad enrollment	14,258
# of applicants	11,743
Range SAT Critical Reading	530–620
Range SAT Math	530–610
Range ACT Composite	22–25
Average HS GPA	3.64
percent graduated top 10% of class	22
percent graduated top 25% of class	52

University of Oklahoma 478

Norman, Oklahoma

Like at a lot of large public schools, the admissions process at the University of Oklahoma is a fairly standardized affair that favors state residents—well, above-average state residents. Students who graduate in the top half of their high school class and have a B average in college prep courses, as well as solid standardized test scores, stand a good chance at admission. Also worth noting: National Merit Scholars get a lot of perks here including a sweet scholarship package.

Total undergrad enrollment	20,498
# of applicants	9,996
Range SAT Critical Reading	510–650
Range SAT Math	530–660
Range ACT Composite	23–29
Average HS GPA	3.60
percent graduated top 10% of class	35
percent graduated top 25% of class	67

University of Pittsburgh at Bradford 480

Bradford, Pennsylvania

Admissions at Pitt—Bradford are pretty straightforward. The Admissions committee primarily looks at three factors in evaluating applicants: the applicant's record of high school achievement; standardized test results (SAT or ACT), and letters of recommendation from teachers or counselor. Class rank, extracurricular activities, personal qualifications, and potential role in the school community are also considered. Requirements for the nursing school are a little more competitive.

Total undergrad enrollment	1,627
# of applicants	926
Range SAT Critical Reading	430–550
Range SAT Math	440–560
Range SAT Writing	430–550
Range ACT Composite	18–24
Average HS GPA	3.18
percent graduated top 10% of class	9
percent graduated top 25% of class	28

University of Pittsburgh—Pittsburgh Campus 482

Pittsburgh, Pennsylvania

Despite receiving more than 22,000 applications a year, the school remains committed to the individual review of each and every application with a holistic perspective. Strong secondary school records and test scores rank high on the admit list. Applicants with honors classes, AP classes, and solid grades have the best chance of admission. A personal essay and letters of recommendation are not required, though you should give them some serious thought.

Total undergrad enrollment	17,994
# of applicants	22,616
Range SAT Critical Reading	570–680
Range SAT Math	600–690
Range SAT Writing	560–660
Range ACT Composite	25–30
Average HS GPA	3.91
percent graduated top 10% of class	51
percent graduated top 25% of class	85

University of South Carolina—Columbia 484

Columbia, South Carolina

Though the university is raising its academic profile, it's still not terribly hard to get in. Students with at least a B average in a college prep curriculum who score 1200 (Critical Reading and Math) on the SAT or 26 on the ACT will normally be considered for admission.

Total undergrad enrollment	20,031
# of applicants	18,485
Range SAT Critical Reading	530–630
Range SAT Math	560–650
Range ACT Composite	24–29
Average HS GPA	3.89
percent graduated top 10% of class	28
percent graduated top 25% of class	60

The University of South Dakota 486
Vermillion, South Dakota

Admission to USD is far from difficult; to be a candidate for general admission to USD, you simply must meet one of three general requirements: rank in the top fifty percent of your graduating class or obtain an ACT/SAT composite score of 21/990 or higher or have a minimum grade point average of at least 2.6 in high school courses meeting the curriculum requirements.

Total undergrad enrollmen	6,103
# of applicants	3,452
Range SAT Critical Reading	440–630
Range SAT Math	450–610
Range ACT Composite	20–25
Average HS GPA	3.25
percent graduated top 10% of class	13
percent graduated top 25% of class	34

University of Tennessee 488
Knoxville, Tennessee

The volume of applications UT receives each year doesn't allow for nuance. Students with above-average high school GPAs (in a reasonable college prep curriculum) and above-average standardized test scores pretty much all make the cut. The average enrolled freshman (weighted) GPA is 3.78, and the middle 50 percent of the fall 2010 admitted class had score ranges of 1110–1300 (Critical Reading and Math).

Total undergrad enrollment	20,849
# of applicants	3,452
Range SAT Critical Reading	440–630
Range SAT Math	450–610
Range ACT Composite	20–25
Average HS GPA	3.25
percent graduated top 10% of class	13
percent graduated top 25% of class	34

University of Tennessee at Martin 490
Martin, Tennessee

No secrets here: Graduates of an accredited high school gain admission if they get a composite score of 21 or above on the ACT and a cumulative high school grade point average of 2.5 or above, or an 18 on the ACT and a GPA above 2.85.

Total undergrad enrollment	7,947
# of applicants	3,402
Average HS GPA	3.4
percent graduated top 10% of class	23
percent graduated top 25% of class	53

University of Wisconsin—Eau Claire 492
Eau Claire, Wisconsin

Getting the go-ahead here requires some work. For the fall 2010 semester, approximately 7,100 applications were received for a freshman class of 2,070 students. The average admitted student was in the 78th percentile of his or her high school class, and the mid-50 percent ACT score range was 23–27. The ACT is the preferred standardized test of UW—Eau Claire.

Total undergrad enrollment	7,947
# of applicants	3,402
Range ACT Composite	20–24
Average HS GPA	3.4
percent graduated top 10% of class	23
percent graduated top 25% of class	53

Utah State University 494
Logan, Utah

Residents hoping to gain admission to this large state school must have a 2.5 high school GPA, an ACT score of 18 or an SAT score of 860 (Critical Reading and Math), and an index score of 90 (which represents the intersection of GPA and test scores, and the description of this index can be found on the school's website). Those who do not meet these requirements may still be considered under individual review.

Total undergrad enrollment	14,646
# of applicants	7,374
Range SAT Critical Reading	470–610
Range SAT Math	480–610
Range ACT Composite	21–27
Average HS GPA	3.54
percent graduated top 10% of class	24
percent graduated top 25% of class	50

Virginia Polytechnic Institute

496

Blacksburg, Virginia

It's a numbers game at Virginia Tech, a byproduct of the almost 20,000 applications that flood into the admissions office each year. High school grades and curriculum figure most prominently into the admissions decision (an A/B+ average is preferred), followed by standardized test scores. The middle 50 percent of admitted students had a (weighted) GPA of 3.81–4.24, and an SAT score of 1160–1340 (Critical Reading and Math). Majors such as engineering and architecture have additional requirements and stricter standards.

Total undergrad enrollment	23,600
# of applicants	19,981
Range SAT Critical Reading	540–640
Range SAT Math	580–680
Range SAT Writing	540–630
Average HS GPA	3.96
percent graduated top 10% of class	45
percent graduated top 25% of class	85

START YOUR COLLEGE SEARCH HERE:

Schools Organized by Region 58

Schools Organized by Tuition 70

Lists by Interest 89

Northeast

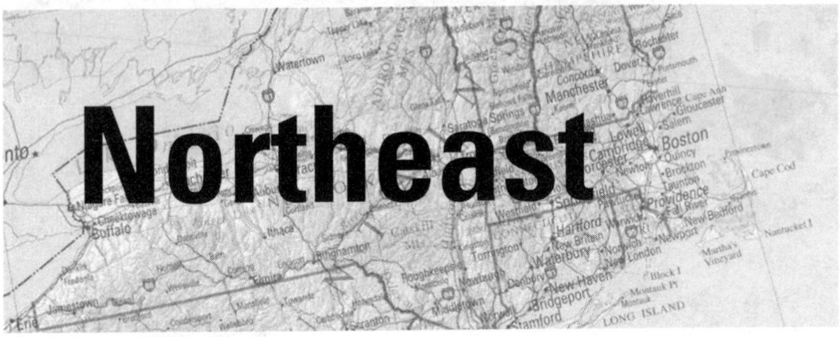

Connecticut

United States Coast Guard Academy 224
New London, Connecticut
At the small, challenging, and free United States Coast Guard Academy, you'll find a highly regimented environment, amazing camaraderie among Cadets, a host of excellent programs, especially engineering, and, of course, all manner of seafaring opportunities.

Wesleyan University 356
Middletown, Connecticut
Wesleyan University is a dynamic bastion of the liberal arts that provides a highly flexible curriculum, an immensely rewarding academic environment, and an extracurricular scene that absolutely runs the social gamut.

Yale University 158
New Haven, Connecticut
Yale is basically the platonic form of the prestigious, prominent research university, offering amazing academics and extensive resources and providing a phenomenal and incomparable education in pretty much every respect.

Delaware

University of Delaware 450
Newark, Delaware
On the very pretty campus of the University of Delaware, the large undergraduate population enjoys a diverse array of programs, a vibrant social scene, and a generally well-rounded college experience.

District of Columbia

Georgetown University 294
Washington, D.C.
Moderately sized Georgetown University in Washington, D.C., offers a great selection of very knowledgeable professors as well as a notable School of Foreign Service, a constant stream of high-profile guest speakers, and plenty of opportunities to pad your resume with big-time political and government internships.

Maine

Bates College 242
Lewiston, Maine
This quintessential New England liberal arts college in Maine boasts unique first-year seminars, mandatory senior theses, service-learning, a range of interdisciplinary majors, and a very impressive study abroad program.

Bowdoin College 248
Brunswick, Maine
At small, prestigious Bowdoin College, you'll find discussion-oriented classes, some of the best undergraduate research opportunities liberal arts schools have to offer, a beautiful Maine setting, and even quality cafeteria food.

Colby College 266
Waterville, Maine
On the picturesque campus of small, close-knit Colby College, devoted professors routinely go the extra mile for students and the "Jan Plan" allows students to pursue focused course work, independent study, or internships during an intensive four-week term between semesters.

College of the Atlantic 270
Bar Harbor, Maine
The College of the Atlantic in the nether reaches of Maine is a close-knit place full of tree-hugging, outdoorsy students that offers one major—human ecology—and an interdisciplinary approach to environmental and social issues.

Maryland

The Johns Hopkins University 308
Baltimore, Maryland
Johns Hopkins is a demanding academic powerhouse full of approachable professors (even in large classes) that is best known for producing scientists, doctors, and engineers.

St. Mary's College of Maryland 414
St. Mary's City, Maryland
Small St. Mary's College of Maryland is a public, secular honors college (the only one in the state) that offers a rigorous curriculum, passionate and approachable professors, intimate classes, and a remarkable sense of community.

United States Naval Academy 230
Annapolis, Maryland
The academic atmosphere is hellacious and life is very structured and regimented at the United States Naval Academy in Maryland, where Midshipmen are molded

over four years into the world's best naval officers.

University of Maryland, College Park 460
College Park, Maryland
The University of Maryland's flagship is large (in terms of both the number of students and sheer geographical size), and students have access to a vast multitude of opportunities including cutting-edge facilities and a nationally recognized business program.

Massachusetts

Amherst College 238
Amherst, Massachusetts
Small Amherst College is an academic powerhouse that offers a strong sense of community, a world-class faculty, a truly stellar reputation, and perks beyond belief.

Boston College 246
Chestnut Hill, Massachusetts
Medium-sized, Jesuit Boston College offers a strong core curriculum, a phenomenal faculty, big-time sports, a prestigious national reputation, and arguably the best metropolitan area for undergrads in the country.

Brandeis University 250
Waltham, Massachusetts
Brandeis University—the only nonsectarian Jewish-sponsored undergrad school in the country —boasts very strong academics, topnotch research opportunities, and a quirky and politically active student population.

College of the Holy Cross 272
Worcester, Massachusetts
The College of the Holy Cross is a smallish, rigorous Jesuit school where every student completes a broad liberal arts curriculum, where internship and study abroad opportunities are abundant, and where students have ample opportunities to network with ever-loyal alumni.

Franklin W. Olin College of Engineering 292
Needham, Massachusetts
It's pretty much all engineering, all the time at the super-small, super-intense, and super-innovative Franklin W. Olin College of Engineering, and all students receive a half-tuition scholarship regardless of their financial situations.

Harvard College 142
Cambridge, Massachusetts
It's Harvard and it's all you've heard and more; everything is competitive and everything is beyond awesome. The level of achievement among students and professors is mind-boggling.

Massachusetts Institute of Technology 314
Cambridge, Massachusetts
The workload definitely pushes beyond your comfort level and the resources are beyond extraordinary at MIT, the East Coast mecca of engineering, science, and mathematics, and home to enough Nobel laureates to fill a jury box.

Mount Holyoke College 318
South Hadley, Massachusetts
Small, all-female Mount Holyoke College is a supportive, highly student-focused bastion of the liberal arts (and a member of the prestigious Five Colleges Consortium) with a strong history of producing remarkable women who go on to achieve great things.

University of Massachusetts Boston 462
Boston, Massachusetts
The University of Massachusetts Boston is a largish school that offers unparalleled cultural diversity and engaging professors who bring a lot of real-world experience to their classes.

Wellesley College 354
Wellesley, Massachusetts
Small, eminent Wellesley College is widely considered to be the top women's college in the nation and it grooms its students to be strong leaders through a very broad and rigorous academic program, an intense intellectual environment, and a fierce commitment to social change.

Williams College 130
Williamstown, Massachusetts
Small, intense, and nationally renowned Williams College boasts an absolutely incomparable academic atmosphere, amazing facilities, plentiful research opportunities, and a one-month January term full of unique pass/fail courses that are a college student's dream come true.

New Hampshire

Dartmouth University 282
Hanover, New Hampshire
The campus at Dartmouth University looks exactly the way a campus should, and the fast-paced, interdisciplinary, and intense academic environment approaches Nirvana for students with the stomach for it.

New Jersey

Princeton University 138
Princeton, New Jersey
Princeton University has the wonderful, captivating professors, the preposterously qualified student body, and the massive resources that you'd expect from your standard Ivy; what sets it apart from its peers is its distinctive focus on the undergraduate experience.

The College of New Jersey 384
Ewing, New Jersey
The College of New Jersey, The Garden State's public liberal arts school, boasts a nicely diverse student population in just about every way, an amazing library, and professors who clearly have their students' best interests in mind.

New York

Barnard College 240
New York, New York
At all-women's Barnard College in the Morningside Heights neighborhood of Manhattan, students have the nurturing environment of a small liberal arts college and—thanks to its extensive partnership with Columbia University across the street—all the resources of an Ivy League school.

Colgate University 268
Hamilton, New York
Colgate University is known for a rigorous academic curriculum and plenty of faculty-student interaction as well as an invaluable alumni network.

Columbia University 276
New York, New York
Columbia University on Manhattan's Upper West Side is an intellectual oasis in the capital of the world that ranks among the world's great research universities, and it's also justly famous for its rich, historic core curriculum.

The Cooper Union for the Advancement of Science and Art 218
New York, New York
Full-tuition scholarships for everyone lucky enough to be admitted and a narrow focus on fine arts, architecture, and engineering are the main selling points of The Cooper Union, an immensely reputable school in Manhattan's East Village.

Cornell University 280
Ithaca, New York
Demanding, prestigious Cornell University in rural, cold upstate New York is by far the largest school in the Ivy League and it offers a correspondingly large number of excellent and challenging majors.

CUNY Brooklyn College 376
Brooklyn, New York
Brooklyn College is an academically challenging and rigorous school public school that offers tremendous honors programs and one of the most gorgeous campuses in the country.

CUNY Hunter College 378
New York, New York
Hunter College on Manhattan's Upper East Side boasts a superb learning environment and an astoundingly diverse population of independent and self-motivated students.

Hamilton College 166
Clinton, New York
A distinct open curriculum and close relationships between students and a slew of committed and genuinely caring professors are the hallmarks of Hamilton College, a small liberal arts school in upstate New York.

State University of New York at Binghamton 184
Binghamton, New York
SUNY Binghamton is a larger school where perks include top-tier academics, an impressive array of majors, and a very good variety of extracurricular activities.

State University of New York at Geneseo 416
Geneseo, New York
Smallish SUNY Geneseo in western New York offers challenging classes, very engaging professors, and a close-knit community complete with a snug, small-town feel.

State University of New York at New Paltz 418
New Paltz, New York
Small classes, a multitude of majors and minors, and renowned fine arts and performing arts programs are on offer at SUNY New Paltz, a smaller school located in a historic little town midway between Albany and New York City.

State University of New York—College of Environmental Science and Forestry 420
Syracuse, New York
Small, personal, and academically tough SUNY—ESF offers a couple dozen programs including environmental science and a bunch of different specialties in areas such as forestry, fisheries science, landscape architecture, construction management, paper engineering, and wildlife science.

State University of New York—Oswego 422
Oswego, New York
Excellent programs in business, a personal and comfortable learning environment, and truly awesome winter activities are a few of the highlights at SUNY—Oswego, a midsize school in a small town on Lake Ontario in north central New York.

State University of New York—Stony Brook University 424
Stony Brook, New York
Stony Brook University on New York's Long Island has more than 150 academic programs on offer but it's best known as a science powerhouse and a leader in premedical preparation.

State University of New York—University at Buffalo 426
Buffalo, New York
The research-intensive University at Buffalo—don't call it SUNY—is the largest public university in New York and, in fact, all of New England, and it offers a staggering number of excellent degree programs.

United States Merchant Marine Academy 226
Kings Point, New York
The Merchant Marine Academy on New York's Long Island is a small, prestigious, demanding, and tuition-free school that produces officers who go on to serve the economic and defense interests of the United States on commercial shipping vessels and in the armed forces.

United States Military Academy—West Point 228
West Point, New York
Illustrious, tuition-free, and ultra-demanding West Point is a seriously regimented place that transforms regular American high school students into intellectually and physically awesome military officers.

Vassar College 348
Poughkeepsie, New York
Small Vassar College provides an unusual amount of academic freedom (because there's basically no core curriculum), the kinds of research opportunities you'd expect to find at mammoth universities, excellent visual and performing arts programs, and a world-class, caring faculty.

Webb Institute 232
Glen Cove, New York
Webb Institute on Long Island is a tiny, tuition-free, and very competitive school that focuses exclusively on naval architecture and marine engineering and typically boasts a 100 percent placement rate in grad schools and careers.

Pennsylvania

Bryn Mawr College 254
Bryn Mawr, Pennsylvania
Bryn Mawr is an all-women's bastion where academics are interactive, stimulating, and very challenging, and where students can take a vast multitude of courses at nearby fellow powerhouses Haverford and Swarthmore.

Bucknell University 256
Lewisburg, Pennsylvania
Bucknell University delivers the classic East Coast college experience, with a balanced combination of a fabulous liberal arts education, a gorgeous campus, a sterling reputation, and a great social scene.

Gettysburg College 296
Gettysburg, Pennsylvania
Gettysburg College in south central Pennsylvania is home to friendly, community-oriented students, professors (and administrators) who know your name, and an amazing study abroad program.

Haverford College 304
Haverford, Pennsylvania
The classroom experience is routinely incredible, the academic experience is nothing less than stellar, and the honor code is serious at Haverford College, where students can also take courses at nearby Bryn Mawr, Penn, and Swarthmore.

Lafayette College 310
Easton, Pennsylvania
Lafayette College is a smaller, prestigious liberal arts and engineering school that offers a welcoming community and very well-respected programs across the board.

Swarthmore College 134
Swarthmore, Pennsylvania
On the lovely, resource-laden campus of small, distinguished Swarthmore College, classes are difficult, the academic atmosphere is tremendously stressful, and extracurricular activities are plentiful and popular.

University of Pittsburgh at Bradford 480
Bradford, Pennsylvania
Small, cozy, career-oriented Pitt-Bradford is a bit of a suitcase school but it's also an academic gem that provides students with small classes, plenty of personal attention from faculty members, and virtually no administrative hassle.

University of Pittsburgh—Pittsburgh Campus 482
Pittsburg, Pennsylvania
Pitt is a large university where research opportunities abound, professors are brilliant and passionate, and the lively social scene and surrounding city offer an infinite buffet of activities for pretty much every taste.

University of Pennsylvania 340
Philadelphia, Pennsylvania
The University of Pennsylvania is an academic paradise where very passionate and intellectually curious students from all over the country get access to incredibly well-versed professors, mind-blowing resources, and a library for pretty much any topic.

Rhode Island

Brown University 252
Providence, Rhode Island
As you'd expect from any Ivy, facilities are simply phenomenal and there are amazing professors in every department at Brown University.

Vermont

Middlebury College 316

Middlebury, Vermont

Small Middlebury College is a consummate liberal arts school in mountainous Vermont with standout offerings in pretty much everything, endless resources, and a challenging yet laidback environment.

Southeast

Florida

Florida State University 388

Tallahassee, Florida

Florida State University is a gargantuan, research-intensive, and football-crazy school in the Sunshine State's capital that offers a vast array of majors, a niche for everybody, and unbeatable weather.

New College of Florida 180

Sarasota, Florida

New College in sunny southwestern Florida is a uniquely small and unconventional public honors college that provides students with a ton of intellectual freedom (there are even narrative evaluations instead of grades) and a virtually beachside location.

University of Central Florida 446

Orlando, Florida

The University of Central Florida in Orlando is a huge research university that offers a vast array of majors and awesome technology all over campus.

University of Florida 196

Gainesville, Florida

The University of Florida is a tremendously large school with first-class amenities, majors and programs galore, and a football-crazed student population.

University of North Florida 476

Jacksonville, Florida

The University of North Florida possesses many of the aspects of a huge state college yet manages to maintain a more laidback feel than your standard larger state school.

Georgia

Agnes Scott College 236

Decatur, Georgia

Agnes Scott College is a small all-women's school located a stone's throw from Atlanta with a caring and attentive faculty and administration, heavy academics, and a seriously prized honor code.

Emory University 290

Atlanta, Georgia

Midsize Emory University, easily one of the South's premier undergraduate schools, offers demanding coursework, passionate and accessible professors, and a very active social scene.

Georgia Institute of Technology 390

Atlanta, Georgia

Georgia Tech is nationally renowned and ridiculously tough bastion of engineering and science that offers a great spirit of camaraderie—in no small part because of the level of academic difficulty—and a thriving social atmosphere.

University of Georgia 200

Athens, Georgia

The Peach State's flagship university provides students with tons of majors and programs, an amazing array of extracurricular options, and quite possibly the best off-campus social scene in the country.

Wesleyan College 356

Macon, Georgia

Tiny Wesleyan College, the first college in the world chartered to grant degrees to women, is an all-female bastion of the liberal arts and sciences that offers tough and intimate classes, impressive facilities, and a seriously a strong focus on sisterhood.

Kentucky

Berea College 214

Berea, Kentucky

Tuition is free and they even throw in a laptop at Berea College, a small school in central Kentucky with a career-oriented bent and a labor program that requires all students to work 10 to 15 hours each week.

Centre College 262
Danville, Kentucky
At small Centre College in Kentucky, you'll find exceptionally challenging coursework across a host of disciplines, hugely popular study abroad programs, and a dedicated faculty that provides oodles of one-on-one assistance.

Louisiana

Centenary College of Louisiana 260
Shreveport, Louisiana
Tiny Centenary College in the Pelican State's third-largest city fosters a congenial community atmosphere and gives students the opportunity to receive tons of individual attention from professors.

North Carolina

Appalachian State University 238
Boone, North Carolina
This midsize public university in the Blue Ridge Mountains of western North Carolina boasts challenging courses, administrators and professors who pride themselves on being available to students, and outdoor activities galore.

Davidson College 284
Davidson, North Carolina
Davidson College is a rigorous small school not too far from Charlotte where you'll receive a rewarding classic liberal arts education from devoted, approachable professors who are notoriously tough graders.

Duke University 288
Durham, North Carolina
Duke University is a pretty small school but it's a national academic powerhouse where students enjoy an amazing academic atmosphere and a bevy of extracurricular activities.

North Carolina State University 406
Raleigh, North Carolina
North Carolina State University is a big school that offers a vast range of academic options including cutting-edge programs in engineering and agriculture and an active social scene both on campus in the lively city of Raleigh.

The University of North Carolina at Asheville 472
Asheville, North Carolina
UNC Asheville is a public liberal arts university nestled in the Blue Ridge Mountain that offers passionate and accessible professors, a crunchy campus social feel, and fabulous options off campus for outdoors enthusiasts.

The University of North Carolina at Chapel Hill 172
Chapel Hill, North Carolina
UNC Chapel Hill boasts rigorous coursework, all the amenities of a large and nationally renowned school, and the perfect mixture of academics, sports, and social life.

University of North Carolina—Wilmington 474
Wilmington, North Carolina
UNC Wilmington is a midsize, beautiful public school with a dedicated faculty, a laidback social atmosphere, and excellent beaches nearby.

Wake Forest University 351
Winston-Salem, North Carolina
Wake Forest University is a smaller, private school that offers a big university's resources along with a small liberal arts college's strong sense of community, a devoted alumni network, and fabulous technology (including a school-issued laptop upon enrollment).

South Carolina

Clemson University 380
Clemson, South Carolina
Clemson University provides the full big-school experience to its students: challenging academics, a beautiful campus, a great sports atmosphere, and a thriving Greek system.

College of Charleston 382
Charleston, South Carolina
The College of Charleston is a midsize public school located in the heart of an historic and vibrant city that offers modern facilities and a wide-ranging liberal arts and sciences curriculum.

University of South Carolina—Columbia 484
Columbia, South Carolina
The Palmetto State's flagship university boasts a fantastic honors college, a stellar array of majors and programs, and an ample dose of deeply Southern tradition.

Wofford College 364
Spartanburg, South Carolina
Small, extremely challenging Wofford College boasts professors who genuinely care and clearly love to teach, a popular and highly visible administration, and a rollicking Greek scene.

Tennessee

Sewanee—The University of the South 330
Sewanee, Tennessee
The University of the South is a small, very demanding school atop a mountain in the middle of rural Tennessee with a very well-rounded core curriculum, a heaping helping of proud Southern tradition, and an

absolutely massive Greek scene.

University of Tennessee—Knoxville 488
Knoxville, Tennessee
The Volunteer State's flagship university is a major public research school that boasts a thriving academic atmosphere, amazing school spirit, and a really awesome surrounding city dripping with every kind of culture.

University of Tennessee at Martin 490
Martin, Tennessee
UT Martin is a regional school with smaller classes, a significant selection of online courses, a career-oriented bent, and a small-town, down-home atmosphere.

Vanderbilt University 346
Nashville, Tennessee
Challenging and intense Vanderbilt University is a school where everyone lucky enough to be admitted has countless opportunities at their fingertips and students are encouraged to excel academically, extracurricularly and socially.

Virginia

Christopher Newport University 374
Newport News, Virginia
Christopher Newport University in the Hampton Roads metropolitan area of Virginia is a public liberal arts college with a smallish enrollment, modern facilities, and a fabulous faculty.

College of William & Mary 192
Williamsburg, Virginia
The College of William & Mary provides its undergrads with endless and amazing academic opportunities and achieves a remarkable balance between the dynamic, progressive academics of a liberal arts college and the strong sense of history and tradition one would expect from America's second-oldest school.

James Madison University 396
Harrisonburg, Virginia
James Madison University in Virginia's breathtakingly beautiful Shenandoah Valley is a fairly large public school with up-to-date facilities, accessible professors, and a lot of school pride.

Longwood University 400
Farmville, Virginia
Medium-sized Longwood University is a public school in aptly named Farmville, Virginia offers small classes, professors who genuinely care about students, and a gorgeous campus dripping with immense history and tradition.

Randolph College 324
Lynchburg, Virginia
Small Randolph College in the foothills of the Blue Ridge Mountains boasts small classes, excellent professors, a beautiful campus, and plenty of wacky traditions.

University of Mary Washington 458
Fredericksburg, Virginia
The University of Mary Washington, location half-way between Virginia's capital and Washington, D.C., is as a smaller state university that boasts approachable professors and a lot of the amenities you'd expect to find at a private school.

University of Richmond 344
Richmond, Virginia
The University of Richmond in Virginia's state capital offers the resources of a large university with the personal attention of a small college, tremendous summer internships and study abroad programs, and just a hint of Southern charm.

University of Virginia 176
Charlottesville, Virginia
On the gorgeous, stately, and very historic campus of the University of Virginia (which was founded by none other than Thomas Jefferson), you'll find programs that routinely rank among the world's best, engaging and inspiring professors, and seriously hallowed traditions.

Virginia Tech 496
Blacksburg, Virginia
Large, research-oriented Virginia Tech offers great science programs, strong engineering programs, and a well-rounded, high quality of life that is not typically available at tech-heavy schools.

West

California

California Institute of Technology 162
Pasadena, California
Brilliant students, world-renowned professors, and a crippling academic workload are the hallmarks of tiny Caltech, arguably the greatest school in the world for math, science, and engineering.

California Polytechnic State University, San Luis Obispo 370
San Luis Obispo, California
Cal Poly, located midway between San Francisco and Los Angeles, is a bigger school with a focus on science and agriculture and it boasts one of the few programs in the country in winemaking.

California State University—Long Beach 372
Long Beach, California
California State University Long Beach—the largest among the schools with the California State moniker—offers a broad array of majors and programs, tremendous ethnic diversity, and all the perks of sunny Southern California.

Claremont McKenna College 264
Claremont, California
Small Claremont McKenna, one of the five schools in the Claremont Consortium, offers phenomenal academics including a justly famous economics program, incredibly accessible professors, and a completely pampering social environment.

Deep Springs College 220
Big Pine, California
Miniscule, all-male, and ultra-unique Deep Springs College, located in California's High Desert, is a free school where students take intense seminar classes and also run a a cattle ranch and alfalfa farm for two years, and then go on to graduate from ultra-elite colleges around the United States.

Harvey Mudd College 302
Claremont, California

Small, quirky, and rigorous Harvey Mudd in sunny Southern California is the science- and engineering-heavy school in the five-school Claremont Consortium.

Occidental College 322
Los Angeles, California
On the lush and exceptionally gorgeous of small Occidental College, just over the hill from the bustle of Los Angeles, you'll find accessible and caring professors, copious extracurricular activities, and happy, outgoing students.

Pomona College 150
Claremont, California
Small, prestigious Pomona College, one of the five colleges in the Claremont Consortium, offers engaging professors, great class discussions, extracurricular activities galore, and amazingly happy students.

Scripps College 328
Claremont, California
Tiny, all-female Scripps College in Southern California offers the best of all worlds: the small classes and intimacy of a small school and, thanks to membership in the five-college Claremont Consortium, the resources and atmosphere of a university.

Stanford University 332
Palo Alto, California
Stanford University is a world-renowned academic powerhouse that boasts a stunning campus, massive resources, an unrivaled academic atmosphere, and a lavish array of social options.

Thomas Aquinas College 334
Santa Paula, California
Very tiny Thomas Aquinas College in the Citrus Capital of the World boasts a strenuous intellectual atmosphere, a strong Catholic identity, and an academic program focused exclusively on the Great Books of Western Civilization.

University of California—Berkeley 430
Berkeley, California
UC Berkeley is among the best public universities in the world and it boasts an all-star faculty, amazing resources, fabulous extracurriculars, and one of a great, quirky surrounding town.

University of California—Davis 432
Davis, California
UC Davis is a huge research university in a cozy, rural, and relaxed college town in northern California with especially excellent programs in agricultural and food sciences programs and abundant research opportunities for undergrads.

University of California—Irvine 434
Irvine, California
UC Irvine is a large, serious public school in sunny Orange County that is a good fit for studious undergrads looking to benefit from the University of California's famous faculty, crazy resources, and ample undergraduate research opportunities.

University of California—Los Angeles 436
Los Angeles, California
UCLA is a large, highly esteemed school that boasts endless academic possibilities, unparalleled resources, and all manner of social hustle and bustle both on and off campus.

University of California—Riverside 438
Riverside, California
UC Riverside, located about 60 miles east of Los Angeles, is large research-oriented school with heaps of very up-to-date technology, a host of strong science programs, and a beautiful, tree-filled campus.

University of California—San Diego 440
La Jolla, California
UCSD is one of the world's premier research institutions and it offers a host of excellent majors and tremendous facilities as well as perfect weather and the distraction of amazing beaches only a few blocks away.

University of California—Santa Barbara 442
Santa Barbara, California
Large, prestigious UC Santa Barbara provides a fabulous array of cutting-edge research opportunities and a laidback, idyllic campus that is pretty much right on the beach.

University of California—Santa Cruz 444
Santa Cruz, California
UC Santa Cruz boasts world-class academic programs, approachable professors, a beautiful forest-like setting, and quite possible the coolest athletic team name on earth—the Banana Slugs.

University of Redlands 342
Redlands, California
The University of Redlands is a smallish, demanding liberal arts college in Southern California that emphasizes a balanced, broad education and boasts small classes, friendly and helpful professors, and a unique May Term, an intensive four-week period when students focus on one class (fairly frequently in some exotic locale).

Colorado

Colorado College 274
Colorado Springs, Colorado
Colorado College is an intimate and intensive bastion of the liberal arts and sciences where student take one course at a time over three-and-a-half-week chunks of time that boasts a resort-like social atmosphere and a fabled men's hockey team that perennially contends at the Division I level.

University of Colorado—Boulder 448
Boulder, Colorado
The flagship school of the University of Colorado offers excellent academics and a great social atmosphere as well as a truly incredible surrounding town and an endless abundance of easily reachable outdoor activities.

United States Air Force Academy 222
Colorado Springs, Colorado
The United States Air Force Academy is a hardcore, strenuous leadership laboratory and an incredibly prestigious institution that provides rigorous academic and military training for future Air Force officers.

New Mexico

New Mexico Institute of Mining & Technology 404
Socorro, New Mexico
New Mexico Tech is a rigorous school that specializes in science, engineering, and technology and offers a mother lode of opportunities to participate in cutting-edge research.

Oklahoma

University of Oklahoma 478
Norman, Oklahoma
The University of Oklahoma is a dynamic, very research-oriented, big-time school that is home to gorgeous and cutting-edge facilities, a slew of national merit scholars, rampant school spirit, and a storied football team.

Oregon

Reed College 326
Portland, Oregon
Seriously intellectually rigorous Reed College offers a challenging liberal-arts education in a small, creative community for self-admittedly weird kids.

Texas

Rice University 146
Houston, Texas
Houston's version of the Ivy League, prestigious Rice University boasts a stellar faculty, a vibrant research program, and an impressively vast selection of courses and departments.

University of Houston 452
Houston, Texas
The University of Houston offers state-of-the art facilities, an abundance of caring and accessible professors, an impressible diverse student population, and every major under the sun.

The University of Texas at Austin 208
Austin, Texas
The University of Texas at Austin has everything you want in a college: nationally renowned academics, big-time athletics, a social niche for virtually whatever you are into, and a fun, vibrant quirky surrounding city.

Utah

Southern Utah University 412
Cedar City, Utah
At Southern Utah University, you'll find passionate professors, helpful administrators, and a host of academic options including some notable programs in the fine and visual arts.

Utah State University 494
Logan, Utah
Utah State University, located in is small town in the middle of the mountains, boasts more than 200 majors including notable programs in engineering and education as well as some great skiing and snowboarding nearby.

Washington

The Evergreen State College 386
Olympia, Washington
The Evergreen State College is a smaller public school in the capital of Washington that provides small classes, an ultra- interdisciplinary academic approach, and narrative evaluations instead of letter grades.

University of Washington 204
Seattle, Washington
The University of Washington offers a great combination of high-powered academics, an excellent and varied social life, and a huge assortment of courses, all in the midst of always happening Seattle.

Whitman College 362
Walla Walla, Washington
Whitman College is a small bastion of the liberal arts and science in southeastern Washington where you'll find brilliant and interesting professors and a close-knit, relaxed social scene.

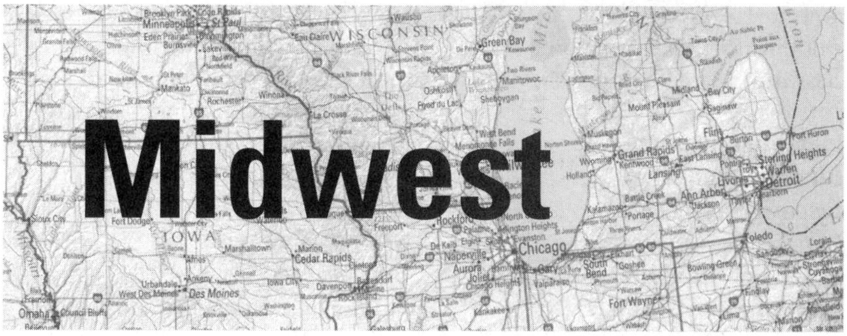

Illinois

Northwestern University 320
Evanston, Illinois
Northwestern University in a suburb just north of Chicago offers nationally acclaimed programs for almost anything you could be interested in, a Big 10 sports atmosphere, and very healthy social scene.

University of Chicago 336
Chicago, Illinois
The legendary and incomparable University of Chicago offers an intense and wonderfully interdisciplinary core curriculum, a faculty brimming with international celebrities, and one of the best (and ugliest) main libraries on the planet.

University of Illinois at Urbana-Champaign 353
Champaign, Illinois
The epically large flagship campus of the University of Illinois offers more than 150 undergraduate programs and the freedom to take your education and your social life in pretty much any conceivable direction.

Wheaton College 360
Wheaton, Illinois
Wheaton College is an academically rigorous and deeply religious liberal arts school in the suburbs of Chicago where you'll find very accessible professors, good cafeteria food, and serious integration of faith and learning.

Indiana

DePauw University 286
Greencastle, Indiana
DePauw University is a small liberal arts school in a small Indiana town that offers plenty of individual academic attention, extraordinary study abroad opportunities, a stellar alumni network, and a massively popular Greek system.

Hanover College 300
Hanover, Indiana
Tiny, extremely challenging Hanover College, located right on the Ohio River in southeastern Indiana, boasts small and engaging classes, professors take a personal interest in your education and interests, and a unique 4-4-1 calendar, which allows students to concentrate on a single class during the spring.

Indiana University—Bloomington 392
Bloomington, Indiana
Indiana University is a Big Ten research behemoth in a classic college town that offers a huge variety of majors—including a notable business school—and a very lively social scene.

Purdue University—West Lafayette 410
West Lafayette, Indiana
What usually comes to mind when people think of Purdue University are its outstanding engineering and agricultural programs but there are tons of excellent liberal arts and pre-professional programs at this very large school.

University of Notre Dame 338
South Bend, Indiana
The University Notre Dame is a strongly Catholic school that boasts enthusiastic professors who are invested in their students, a vibrant residential campus, and, of course, a legendary football team that students devoutly support every weekend in the fall.

Wabash College 350
Crawfordsville, Indiana
Tiny Wabash College in west central Indiana is a personalized, rigorous, and very unique school with a world-class faculty, a supportive administration, a very prominent Greek system, and an amazingly devoted alumni network.

Iowa

Cornell College 278
Mount Vernon, Iowa
Cornell College, a small liberal arts school in a postcard-perfect little Iowa town, boasts miniscule classes, professors who know how to motivate and encourage students, and a unique one-course-at-a-time program which students to focus on a single class each month.

Grinnell College 298
Grinnell, Iowa
Grinnell College amid the cornfields of Iowa is a small, academically rigorous, crazily eclectic bastion of the liberal arts and sciences with tremendously accessible professors and an astronomical endowment per student.

Iowa State University 394
Ames, Iowa
Big, Iowa State University is a large research-oriented school with a small-town feel, a strong support network for undergrads, and a great reputation for programs in engineering and agriculture.

Kansas

Kansas State University 398
Manhattan, Kansas
Kansas State University is a big school with a small-school feel that offers more than 250 majors and academic options including world-class programs in agriculture, architecture, and engineering.

University of Kansas 456
Lawrence, Kansas
The University of Kansas, in the surprisingly hilly and generally phenomenal college town of Lawrence, offers the broad range of majors you'd expect from a nationally respected public school, stellar facilities, and, of course, a legendary basketball team.

Michigan

Hillsdale College 306
Hillsdale, Michigan
Hillsdale College is a small, private, notoriously difficult school that provides a truly classical liberal arts education deeply rooted in the timeless concepts of Western Civilization and Christianity.

University of Michigan—Ann Arbor 464
Ann Arbor, Michigan
The University of Michigan is undeniably among the most prestigious public schools in the country and students have access to every kind of academic opportunity at all times as well as a spectacular social scene.

Minnesota

Carleton College 258
Northfield, Minnesota
Carleton College in Minnesota is a small and extremely rigorous school full of intense and passionate undergrads that offers a host of very strong programs in the liberal arts and sciences and a unique a trimester calendar.

Macalester College 312

St. Paul, Minnesota

Macalester College, located in a charming neighborhood in Minnesota's Twin Cities, is a small liberal arts school where students take academics and much else very seriously and good grades are pretty hard to come by.

University of Minnesota, Crookston 466

Crookston, Minnesota

The University of Minnesota, Crookston is a small public school in the northernmost reaches of the North Star State where you'll find excellent, hands-on programs in agriculture and the sciences as well as a host of programs with a career-oriented bent.

University of Minnesota—Twin Cities 468

Minneapolis, Minnesota

The flagship campus of the University of Minnesota is a big, busy place that offers academic programs in virtually anything you can imagine, a lively and hugely varied social scene, and a surrounding metropolitan area that is by all accounts one completely awesome.

Missouri

College of the Ozarks 216

Point Lookout, Missouri

This definitively Christian college tucked away in the southwest corner of Missouri offers small classes, amazing professors in a host of largely career-oriented majors, and free tuition thanks to a nationally renowned work study program.

Missouri University of Science and Technology 402

Rolla, Missouri

Missouri University of Science and Technology (known until pretty recently as University of Missouri—Rolla) is a seriously tough school in the sticks of the Show Me State with a very strong reputation in engineering.

Truman State University 428

Kirksville, Missouri

Highly regarded Truman State University is Missouri's public bastion of the liberal arts and sciences university the only highly selective public institution in the Show Me State.

University of Missouri—Kansas City 470

Kansas City, Missouri

UMKC is an extremely diverse school that offers a slew of notable majors including an outstanding business and fine arts programs and a unique six-year program provides a fast track to a medical degree.

Washington University in St. Louis 154

St. Louis, Missouri

Washington University in St. Louis is a top-tier university that offers a host of impressive majors, particularly in the sciences, and a warm, vibrant social environment.

Ohio

The Ohio State University—Columbus 408

Columbus, Ohio

Ohio State University in Columbus is a gargantuan research school—one of the largest universities in the country—and it offers every resource you could possibly need as well as unlimited academic and social opportunities.

South Dakota

The University of South Dakota 486

Vermillion, South Dakota

The University of South Dakota is a midsize public school that boasts professors who are routinely willing to go the extra mile for students and a solid array of excellent liberal arts and pre-professional programs.

Wisconsin

Beloit College 244

Beloit, Wisconsin

The academic experience at Beloit is very personal and friendly at Beloit College, a little school in Wisconsin with a wonderfully eclectic student population

University of Wisconsin—Eau Claire 492

Eau Claire, Wisconsin

The University of Wisconsin—Eau Claire boasts a close-knit campus, outstanding course offerings across a host of majors, and professors who are dedicated and very accessible outside of class.

University of Wisconsin—Madison 188

Madison, Wisconsin

The University of Wisconsin—Madison is a nationally renowned research institution where you can pursue any academic or creative feat, savor flourishing socioeconomic diversity, soak up epic party and sports scenes, and partake in an absolute slew of extracurricular activities.

Best Value Colleges: By Price

Nowadays, in addition to working hard to get into college, a lot of students and families worry about how to pay for it. And it doesn't help that the price of tuition ranges drastically from college to college, or that not everyone pays the same price for a given college. In fact, going to college is a bit like traveling on an airplane. If you ask the person across the aisle what fare she paid, it may be completely different from your own. Some people may be paying the full fare for college while others pay far less, so you should never initially rule out a school based on "sticker price."

What you may not know is that it may not cost any more to go to a school with a higher tuition than it would to attend one with a relatively inexpensive stated price. While it is true that on average the cost of attending a state institution is less than that of attending a private college or university, depending on a family's income and a college's available aid funds, the cost paid by the family for attending even the most expensive Ivy League schools may be less than the cost of attending an in-state public university.

The key is to focus not on the "sticker price," but on how much you as a family can pay, how much the student has to borrow, and what other kinds of tuition help are available. Investigate the financial aid options at each institution of interest and get a rough idea of your chances of receiving aid. Of course, a dose of pragmatism isn't a bad idea. Every student should apply to at least one school that will be affordable with little or no aid. There is a great deal of financial aid available—and we are talking billions of dollars—and almost every family now qualifies for some form of assistance. In fact, you may be surprised to find out that with the financial aid package some schools can put together for you, it may cost less to attend an "expensive" private school than it would to go to a "cheap" state school.

So while we've organized schools here by price range, keep in mind that the "sticker prices" of these schools probably won't be what you'll pay. Also know that for this section, "average need-based award" denotes free money, not loans, and tuition numbers always or almost always include tuition and fees.

Tuition Less than $10,000

Appalachian State University

Boone, North Carolina

Public 238

Students at this midsize university in the Blue Ridge Mountains enjoy an incredibly paltry annual in-state tuition rate of about $6,000. If you can't demonstrate North Carolina residency, you'll pay quite a bit more (about $18,000) but the cost of living on campus and in the surrounding town is pleasantly low. The average indebtedness once students graduate is about $16,000.

Berea College

Berea, Kentucky

Private 214

Small, career-oriented Berea College in Kentucky is a school where tuition is free and they even throw in a laptop. In exchange, all students participate in a labor program that requires them to work 10 to 15 hours each week. The cost for room, board, and fees is about $7,000 each year. Average indebtedness at graduation is a mere $6,000 or so.

California Polytechnic State University, San Luis Obispo

San Luis Obispo, California

Private 370

Cal Poly, a bigger school with a focus on science and agriculture, offers very attractive in-state tuition and a fairly reasonable cost of living. The cost for Golden State residents is only about $8,000 annually. If you can't claim California residency, expect to pay closer to $20,000. The average need-based award is about $2,400.

California State University—Long Beach
Long Beach, California
Public 372
California State University Long Beach is the largest among the schools with the California State brand and it's also a great bargain. The cost for state residents is not much more than $6,000 annually. Residents of other states pay around $18,000. The average need-based award is about $2,600. Graduates end up with an average of roughly $11,000 of loan debt.

City University of New York – Brooklyn College
Brooklyn, New York
Public 376
Cal Poly, a bigger school with a It's really expensive to live in or anywhere near New York City but tuition at Brooklyn College is incredibly affordable. Residents of the Empire State pay a paltry $5,500 per year. If you can't claim New York residency, expect to pay over $14,000. The average need-based award is around $3,600. Average indebtedness at graduation is close to $10,000.

City University of New York – Hunter College
New York, New York
Public 378
You'll spend quite a bit of money if you live anywhere near Hunter College on Manhattan's ritzy Upper East Side but tuition is really a bargain. New York residents pay about $5,500 per year. Nonresidents pay a little over $14,000. The average need-based award is around $6,000. Average indebtedness at graduation is less than $8,000.

College of Charleston
Charleston, South Carolina
Public 382
The midsize College of Charleston, in the heart of the historic, lively Southern city of the same name, offers residents of South Carolina an attractive annual tuition rate of approximately $9,000. If you can't finagle residency in the Palmetto State, you'll pay roughly $24,000. The average need-based award is about $3,000. Average indebtedness at graduation is nearly $21,000.

College of the Ozarks
Point Lookout, Missouri
Private 216
Definitively Christian College of the Ozarks, which bills itself as "Hard Work U," is a small school tucked away in the southwest corner of Missouri where tuition is free thanks to a nationally renowned work study program. In exchange for 15 hours per week and two 40-hour weeks in the on-campus work program (and various state and federal grants), students don't pay a dime for tuition and they get a laptop to boot. The one caveat here is that you might need to borrow money to pay for non-tuition costs.

The Cooper Union for the Advancement of Science and Art
New York, New York
Private 218
The very small and very prestigious Cooper Union focuses exclusively on fine arts, architecture, and engineering and every student gets a full-tuition scholarship. Keep in mind that living in Manhattan's East Village doesn't come cheap, though. The cost for room, board, supplies, and generally surviving will run you about $20,000 each year. Still, this place is an amazing deal. Average indebtedness at graduation is about $11,000.

Deep Springs College
Big Pine, California
Private 220
Tuition, room, and board are all totally free at Deep Springs College, a miniscule, all-male, and ultra-unique enclave located in California's High Desert. Moreover, incidentals will only cost you about $3,000. The catch in this very sweet deal is that all students work every day running a cattle ranch and alfalfa farm. Also, Deep Springs is only a two-year school. Graduates typically go on to elite colleges around the United States to complete their bachelor's degrees.

The Evergreen State College
Olympia, Washington
Public 386
The Evergreen State College is a smaller public school that takes an ultra-interdisciplinary academic approach to academics and provides narrative evaluations instead of letter grades. In-state tuition runs about $7500 while residents of states other than Washington pay approximately $19,000. The average need-based award is roughly $8,000. Average indebtedness at graduation is around $16,000.

Florida State University
Tallahassee, Florida
Public 388
Huge, research-intensive, and football-crazy Florida State University is a terrific bargain, at least for inhabitants of the Sunshine State. If you can claim state residency, you'll pay about $6,000 per year for tuition. Everybody else pays $21,000 or so. The average need-based award at FSU is approximately $4,500.

Georgia Institute of Technology
Atlanta, Georgia
Public 390
Nationally renowned and ridiculously tough Georgia Tech offers provides its undergrads with more than $100 million in merit-based and need-based aid per year. On top of that, tuition is relatively

cheap in the first place. Georgia residents pay a little more than $7,000 per year. Students who can't claim state residency pay quite a bit more—close to $26,000. The average need-based award is a little over $11,000 per year. Graduates end up with an average of roughly $22,000 of loan debt.

Iowa State University
Ames, Iowa

Public 394

Iowa State University is a big school that specializes in engineering and agriculture in a city where the cost of living is nicely reasonable. In-state tuition runs about $8,000 annually. If you can't convince the school that you are a resident of Iowa, expect to pay $20,000 or so. The average need-based award at ISU is roughly $7,500. Average indebtedness at graduation is pretty high—more than $30,000.

James Madison University
Harrisonburg, Virginia

Public 396

Fairly large James Madison University in Virginia's very pretty Shenandoah Valley offers a tuition rate of approximately $8,000 per year for Virginia residents. For out-of-state students, it's about $21,000. The average need-based award is $7,000 or so. Average indebtedness at graduation is about $20,000.

Kansas State University
Manhattan, Kansas

Public 398

Kansas State University is a tremendously affordable school with in an inexpensive college town. Tuition for residents of the Sunflower State is less than $8,000. For students who can't claim state residency, tuition is around $19,000. The average need award is a little more than $4,000. Students who borrow money to attend Colby can expect to graduate with an average debt of approximately $22,000.

Missouri University of Science and Technology
Rolla, Missouri

Public 402

Missouri S&T is a seriously tough school with a very strong reputation in engineering in an affordable, rural Missouri town. Tuition for Show Me State residents is in the $9,000 range. If you can't claim Missouri residency, you'll pay closer to $21,000. The average need-based award is about $4,000. Average indebtedness at graduation is more than $24,000.

New College of Florida
Sarasota, Florida

Public 180

Uniquely small and unconventional New College offers considerable intellectual freedom, narrative evaluations instead of grades, and a fabulous bargain for inhabitants of the Sunshine State. For Florida residents, tuition is only about $6,000 per year. Out-of-staters can expect to pay a great deal more, though—a whopping $30,000. The average need-based award is about $10,000 annually. Average indebtedness at graduation runs roughly $11,000.

New Mexico Institute of Mining & Technology
Socorro, New Mexico

Public 404

Science, engineering, and technology are the house specialties at New Mexico Tech, a haven of cutting-edge research in an affordable location where tuition for in-state students is an unbelievably low $5,000 or so per year. Students who aren't residents of the Land of Enchantment pay around $16,000, which is not bad relative to your typical of-of-state rate. The average need-based award is approximately $6,000. Average indebtedness at graduation is about $16,000.

North Carolina State University
Raleigh, North Carolina

Public 406

North Carolina State University is a big school that offers a vast range of majors including nationally recognized programs in engineering and agriculture. Tuition for North Carolina residents is a very impressive $7,000 or so. If you can't demonstrate state residency, you'll pay roughly $19,000. The average need-based award is in the $10,000 range. Average indebtedness at graduation is close to $20,000.

Ohio State University—Columbus
Columbus, Ohio

Public 408

The Ohio State University in Columbus is a massive research school where residents of the Buckeye State pay just less than $10,000 for tuition. The rate for students from other states is about $25,000. The average need-based award is $8,000 or so. Students who borrow money to attend Colby can expect to graduate with an average debt of approximately $22,000.

Purdue University—West Lafayette
West Lafayette, Indiana

Public 410

Purdue University, a Big 10 school famous for its outstanding engineering and agricultural programs, boasts a tuition rate barely under $10,000 for Indiana residents. If you hail from somewhere else, you'll pay almost three times more—about $28,000. The average need-based award approaches $10,000 per year. Average indebtedness at graduation is a little more than $26,000.

Southern Utah University
Cedar City, Utah
Public 412
Southern Utah University is located in a very affordable and charming little town and tuition is cheap. Residents of Utah pay the bargain-basement price of $5,000 or so per year. If you can't claim state residency, you'll pay about $16,000. The average need-based award is nearly $6,000 annually. Graduates who borrow money leave campus with their degrees and a debt of about $11,000.

State University of New York at Geneseo
Geneseo, New York
Public 416
Smallish SUNY Geneseo in in the upstate Finger Lakes region of New York is a public liberal arts college with a sticker price where tuition is less than $7,000 for New York residents and about $16,000 if you can't finagle residency in the Empire State. The average need-based award is about $4,000. Students who borrow money to pay for school can expect to graduate with an average debt close to $21,000.

State University of New York at New Paltz
New Paltz, New York
Publi 418
SUNY New Paltz is a smaller school located in a historic and moderately priced little town. Tuition for Empire Strate residents is comfortably less than $7,000. If you can't claim New York residency, you'll pay closer to $16,000. The average need-based award is about $5,000. Average indebtedness at graduation is more than $26,000.

State University of New York at Oswego
Oswego, New York
Public 422
SUNY Oswego is a midsize school in a small town on Lake Ontario that offers some solid merit scholarships and an attractive sticker price, particularly for in-state students. Tuition for residents of New York is substantially less than $7,000. For everyone else, tuition is closer to $16,000. The average need-based aid award is more than $6,000. Average indebtedness at graduation is a steep $26,000 or so.

State University of New York—Binghamton University
Binghamton, New York
Public 184
Binghamton University is a good-sized school with an excellent academic reputation. Tuition for residents of New York is a little more than $7,000 per year. If you can't demonstrate residency in the state of New York, expect to pay closer to $17,000. The average need-based aid award is pretty close to $7000. Average indebtedness at graduation is about $21,000.

State University of New York—College of Environmental Science and Forestry
Syracuse, New York
Public 430
SUNY-ESF offers a mouthful of an acronym and programs in environmental science, forestry, paper engineering, and the like. Residents of New York don't pay much of $6,000 annually to attend. For everyone else, the cost is about $15,000. The average need-based aid award is approximately $5,000. There are a fair number of merit scholarships on offer as well. Average indebtedness at graduation is pretty high—about $27,000.

State University of New York—Stony Brook University
Stony Brook, New York
Public 424
As far as science powerhouses go, Stony Brook University on Long Island is very affordable. For residents of New York, tuition is about $7,000 per year. If you can't convince the school that you are an inhabitant of the Empire State, expect to pay a little more than $16,000. The average need-based aid award is approximately $7,000. Average indebtedness at graduation is about $20,000.

State University of New York-University at Buffalo
Buffalo, New York
Public 426
The research-intensive University at Buffalo is the largest public university in all of New England and a great value. Tuition for New York residents isn't much over $7,000. For residents of other states, tuition is about $17,000. The average need-based aid award is about $7,000. Merit scholarships are also fairly abundant. Average indebtedness at graduation is pretty close to $17,000.

Truman State University
Kirksville, Missouri
Public 428
Truman State University is Show Me State's public bastion liberal arts college. Tuition for Missouri residents is about $7,000. If you can't finagle state residency, you'll pay close to $13,000, which is still pretty reasonable. Also, the cost of living in the surrounding town of Kirksville is cheap. The average need-based aid award is $4,000 or so. Average indebtedness at graduation approaches $22,000.

United States Air Force Academy
Colorado Springs, Colorado
Public 222
The prestigious, hardcore United States Air Force Academy provides military training for future Air Force officers. According to the school, the total cost to produce an Air Force officer is well more than $400,000, but you don't have to pay a cent. In fact, you get a stipend

of more than $900 a month to pay for books, uniforms, supplies, and the like. You also get free medical and dental care. The catch is that you are required to serve in the Air Force for at least eight years after graduation, five of which must be active duty.

United States Coast Guard Academy

New London, Connecticut

Public 224

The United States Coast Guard Academy is small, rigorous, and free. In addition to not paying anything, you'll receive a stipend of more than $900 a month to pay for uniforms, equipment, books, and other expenses. Upon graduation, cadets are required to serve as Coast Guard officers for five years.

United States Merchant Marine Academy

Kings Point, New York

Public 226

The small and demanding Merchant Marine Academy produces officers who go on to serve on commercial shipping vessels and in the armed forces. There is no cost for tuition, room, and board. There are some pretty minimal costs of attending, though. You have to buy a computer, for example, and you have to pay a very minimal amount for healthcare. Once they get their degrees, graduates are obligated to serve for at least five years as merchant marine officers, in the Navy, or in a United States maritime-related industry.

United States Military Academy

West Point, New York

Public 228

The United States Military Academy—West Point—is a regimented, difficult, and storied proving ground for American military officers. Tuition is totally free after an initial fee of $2,000. Medical care and dental care are also gratis. You also get more than $900 (and the amount goes up each year) to pay for uniforms, books, a computer, dry cleaning, and the like. After graduation, cadets must serve for at least five years as active-duty officers in the U.S. Army.

United States Naval Academy

Annapolis, Maryland

Public 230

The extremely regimented and academically demanding United States Naval Academy produces world-class naval officers. Tuition, room, board, and medical and dental care are all free. Other perks include a monthly stipend starting at more than $900 to pay a multitude of various fees and the ability to fly space-available in military aircraft around the world. After graduation, midshipmen must serve as officers in the Navy or the Marine Corps for at least five years.

University of Central Florida

Orlando, Florida

Public 446

The gargantuan University of Central Florida in Orlando offers a vast array of majors and it's very inexpensive. Tuition for residents of the Sunshine State can be had at a bargain-basement price—well under $6,000. On top of that, the average need-based aid award is more than $6,000. Average indebtedness at graduation is about $19,000.

University of Colorado—Boulder

Boulder, Colorado

Public 448

Tuition at CU is around $9,000 for state residents and an eye-popping $30,000 or so for everyone else. The surrounding city of Boulder, while breathtaking and a lot of fun, is not particularly affordable as far as college towns go but the average need-based aid award is more than $7,000. Average indebtedness at graduation is about $19,000.

University of Florida

Gainesville, Florida

Public 196

The tremendously large University of Florida is an excellent school academically one of the best deals around. Tuition for in-state residents is a mere $6,000 or so. If you can't finagle residency in the Sunshine State, expect to pay substantially more—about $28,000. The average need-based aid award runs in the neighborhood of $7,000. Average indebtedness at graduation is approximately $16,000.

University of Georgia

Athens, Georgia

Public 200

The University of Georgia provides students with top-notch academics, a rollicking social scene, and a wealth of scholarships. Tuition for Georgia residents is not much more than $9,000 annually. If you can't claim Georgia residency, the cost is closer to $28,000. The average need-based aid award is nearly $11,000. Average indebtedness at graduation is $16,000 or so.

University of Houston

Houston, Texas

Public 452

The University of Houston offers every major under the sun and a sticker price about $9,000 per year for residents of the Lone Star State. If you can't convince the school that you are from Texas, you'll be charged closer to $19,000. The average need-based award is about the same amount as in-state tuition—$9000 or so—and average indebtedness at graduation is approximately $15,000.

University of Kansas

Lawrence, Kansas

Public 456

Tuition at the University of Kansas is comfortably less than $10,000 for residents of the Sunflower State and about $23,000 for everyone else. KU also offers a four-year tuition compact which guarantees that you'll pay a fixed rate of tuition for four full years. The average need-based aid award is in the $5,500 range and average indebtedness at graduation runs approximately $23,000.

University of Mary Washington
Fredericksburg, Virginia
Public 458
The University of Mary Washington is as a smaller state university with a lot of sweet amenities. Tuition is about $9,000 for residents of Virginia and pretty close to $21,000 for out-of-staters. The average need-based award is a little more than $7,000 and scholarships include a smattering of full rides as well as the awards given to every student member of the school orchestra. Average indebtedness at graduation is in the ballpark of $16,000.

University of Maryland—College Park
College Park, Maryland
Public 460
The large University of Maryland offers a great academic atmosphere at a reasonable price. Tuition for residents of the Old Line State is less than $9,000. Nonresidents pay quite a bit more—about $26,000. The average need-based award is almost $8,000. Students graduate from this geographically immense campus with their degrees and an average loan debt of almost $23,000.

University of Michigan—Ann Arbor
Ann Arbor, Michigan
Public 464
Arguably the most prestigious public undergraduate school in the country, the University of Michigan offers a sticker price of about $12,000 per year for residents of the Great Lakes State. If you aren't from Michigan, tuition is far steeper—almost $38,000. The average need-based aid award is in the neighborhood of $7,000. Average indebtedness at graduation is close to $28,000.

University of Missouri—Kansas City
Kansas City, Missouri
Public 470
The sticker price for tuition at UMKC for residents of the Show Me State is right around $9,000 per year. For out-of-state students, the cost is about $21,000. Note, though, that residents of several Midwestern states are eligible for a steep discount thanks to the UMKC's participation in the Midwest Student Exchange Program. Also, residents of several Kansas counties close to Missouri pay in-state tuition. The average need-based aid award is close to $7,000. Average indebtedness at graduation is approximately $22,000.

University of North Carolina at Asheville
Asheville, North Carolina
Public 472
UNC Asheville, a crunchy public liberal arts university, offers a bargain-basement tuition rate of about $5,000 annually for North Carolina residents. If you can't claim state residency, you'll pay about four times that amount. The average need-based aid award is comfortably more than $6,000 per year. Students leave this school nestled in the Blue Ridge Mountains with an average loan debt of around $15,000.

University of North Carolina at Chapel Hill
Chapel Hill, North Carolina
Public 172
Large and nationally renowned school UNC Chapel Hill boasts all the academic resources most anyone is likely to need and very attractive in-state tuition. If you can claim residency in the Tar Hell State, your sticker price will be about $7,000 per year. If you are from another state, expect to pay about $27,000. Also worth noting is the Carolina Covenant, which makes it possible for many students from low-income families to graduate debt-free if they work on campus about 12 hours each week. The average need-based aid award is in the $12,000 range. Average indebtedness at graduation is about $15,000.

University of North Carolina at Wilmington
Wilmington, North Carolina
Public 474
Midsize UNC Wilmington offers a variety of scholarships and tuition comfortably less than $6,000 for state residents. If you can't convince the school you are an inhabitant of North Carolina, tuition is in the $17,000 range. The average need-based aid award is pretty close to $7,000. Average indebtedness at graduation is about $19,000.

University of North Florida
Jacksonville, Florida
Public 476
The University of North Florida offers a host of scholarships and, for Florida residents, annual tuition that won't break the bank. If you can claim residency in the Sunshine State, you'll only pay about $5,500 to attend. Students from other states face a cost of about $19,000. The average need-based aid award is roughly $6,500. Average indebtedness at graduation is in the ballpark of $15,000.

University of Oklahoma
Norman, Oklahoma
Public 478
Tuition at the University of

Oklahoma is about $8,000 per year for residents of the Sooner State and about $19,000 for everyone else. The average need-based aid award is a little more than $6,000 and scholarships are plentiful. If you happen to be a national merit scholar finalist, note that you can get a full ride and then some at OU regardless of your state residency. Average indebtedness at graduation is slightly high—$24,000 or so.

University of South Dakota

Vermillion, South Dakota

Public 486

The midsize University of South Dakota boasts a solid array of excellent academic programs and a surrounding town that, while often frigid, won't bust your budget. The tuition structure is sort of complicated. Yearly tuition for residents of the Mount Rushmore State is approximately $8000 and it's only a pittance more if you are from Minnesota. If you are from somewhere else, the cost is still comfortably less than $10,000, which is tremendously affordable for out-of-state tuition. About three-fourths of the undergrads at USD receive some kind of financial aid and the average need-based aid award is roughly $4,500. Average indebtedness at graduation is in the range of $21,000.

University of Tennessee—Knoxville

Knoxville, Tennessee

Public 488

The Volunteer State's flagship university is a major public research school and it's located in one of the greatest college towns on the planet. Tuition for Tennessee residents isn't much over $8000 per year. If you can't convince the school that you are from Tennessee, expect to a sticker price of about $25,000. The average need-based aid award is on the lower side—about $3,000 but there are more than 4,000 available each year. Average indebtedness at graduation is just less than $20,000.

University of Tennessee at Martin

Martin, Tennessee

Public 490

UT Martin is a regional school with a career-oriented bent in a fantastically affordable area. Tuition for Tennessee residents is less than $7,000 and about $19,000 for residents of other states. The average need-based aid award is about $6,000. Students leave UT Martin with an average debt of roughly $19,000.

University of Texas at Austin

Austin, Texas

Public 208

The University of Texas at Austin has every major, every resource, and every social scene. Tuition is just less than $10,000 for residents of the Lone Star State. Prepare for sticker shock if you come from another state, though, as tuition for everyone else runs about $32,000. The average need-based aid award is approximately $9,000. Average indebtedness at graduation is close to $25,000.

University of Wisconsin—Eau Claire

Eau Claire, Wisconsin

Public 492

Tuition at UW—Eau Claire is right about $8,000 for in-state residents and, under a reciprocity agreement, only a few hundred dollars if you are a resident of Minnesota. There are also sweet discounts for students from a host of other Midwestern states thanks to UW—Eau Claire's participation in the Midwest Student Exchange Program. If you can't demonstrate that you are an inhabitant of any of these states, expect a sticker price pretty close to $16,000. The average need-based aid award is in the $5,500 range. Average indebtedness at graduation is approximately $21,000.

University of Wisconsin—Madison

Madison, Wisconsin

Public 188

UW—Madison is an awesome, nationally renowned research institution that offers pretty much anything you could ever want academically and socially including an utterly fabulous college town. Tuition for residents of the Badger State is just a scintilla under $10,000 per year. For everyone else, it's in the $25,000 range. The average need-based aid award is approximately $6,000. Students leave Madison with a world-class degree and an average debt of close to $23,000.

Utah State University

Logan, Utah

Public 494

Utah State University is a fairly large agricultural and engineering school located in a small, affordable town in the middle of the mountains. Tuition is comfortably less than $6,000 for residents of Utah and about $16,000 for everyone else (which is pretty good as far as out-of-state tuition goes). The average need-based aid award is just about exactly $4,000 per year. Average indebtedness at graduation is about $15,000.

Tuition between $10,000 and $25,000

Centenary College of Louisiana
Shreveport, Louisiana
Private 260
To begin with, tiny Centenary College is quite a bargain, relatively, for an excellent private school. The cost of tuition for a year is about $23,000, and the cost of living in Shreveport is pretty cheap. Additionally, the average need-based award at Centenary is close to $18,000. Coincidentally, average indebtedness at graduation totals about $18,000 as well.

Christopher Newport University
Newport News, Virginia
Public 374
Christopher Newport University is a public liberal arts college with a sticker price just more than $10,000 per year for Virginia residents and just over $19,000 for everybody else. The average need-based award is $5,000 or so. Students who borrow money to pay for school can expect to graduate with an average debt close to $21,000.

Clemson University
Clemson, South Carolina
Public 380
Clemson University is a big school where annual tuition for state residents is roughly $13,000 and about $29,000 for people who can't claim residency in the Palmetto State. There is a plethora of merit scholarships available and the average need-based award is approximately $5,000. Average indebtedness at graduation is not too much more than $18,000.

The College of New Jersey
Ewing, New Jersey
Public 384
Yearly tuition at The College of New Jersey, The Garden State's public liberal arts school, is about $14,000 for residents of New Jersey. For everyone else, it's about $24,000. The average need-based award is right about $11,000. Students who borrow money to pay for school leave with an average debt of almost $25,000.

College of William & Mary
Williamsburg, Virginia
Public 192
The very old and historic College of William & Mary provides its undergrads with an awesome array of academic opportunities. Tuition for Virginia residents is approximately $12,000. Out-of-state students can expect to pay just about double that amount. The average need-based award is nearly $12,000 annually. Average indebtedness at graduation is nearly $22,000.

Franklin W. Olin College of Engineering
Needham, Massachusetts
Private 292
Franklin W. Olin College of Engineering is a tiny, incredibly intense, and super-innovative engineering school where all students receive a half-tuition scholarship regardless of their financial situations. Net tuition after the discount is about $20,000 annually. The total cost for everything—and we mean everything, including food and a laptop—is just less than $40,000. Average indebtedness at graduation is 13,000 or so.

Hillsdale College
Hillsdale, Michigan
Private 306
Small, infamously demanding Hillsdale College offers a truly classical liberal arts education at a wonderfully low price relative to other private schools of its caliber. Hillsdale also steers completely clear of all government subsidized loans, choosing instead to finance students on its own to the tune of about $14 million annually in scholarships, grants, and loans. Tuition is about $21,000 and the average need-based award is $7300. Average indebtedness at graduation is approximately $16,000.

Indiana University—Bloomington
Bloomington, Indiana
Public 392
IU Bloomington, a Big Ten school in a classic college town, provides Hoosier State residents with a tuition rate of about $11,000 per year. If you can't claim state residency, expect to pay substantially more—about $31,000. The average need-based award is just less than $10,000. Newly-minted graduates walk away from campus with a debt load of close to $28,000.

Longwood University
Farmville, Virginia
Public 400
Tuition on the gorgeous campus of medium-sized Longwood University is about $11,000 per year for Virginia residents and about $21,000 for everyone else. The average need-based award is $6,000 or so. Also, you are unlikely to break the bank for room and board anywhere in or near a town called Farmville. Average indebtedness at graduation is close to $23,000.

St. Mary's College of Maryland

St. Mary's City, Maryland

Public 414

Small St. Mary's College of Maryland is a public, secular honors college where about two-thirds of the students receive either a grant or a scholarship from the school Tuition for Maryland residents is around $14,000 per year. If you can't claim residency in the Old Line State, you'll pay approximately $26,000. The average need-based award is a little more than $8,000. Average indebtedness at graduation is about $18,000.

Thomas Aquinas College

Santa Paula, California

Private 334

Very tiny and very Catholic Thomas Aquinas College is home to an academic program focused exclusively on the Great Books of Western Civilization. At only $23,000 or so, tuition is a fantastic bargain for a private school. On top of that, the average need-based aid award is about $15,000. Average indebtedness at graduation is about $16,000.

Wesleyan College

Macon, Georgia

Private 356

Tiny, all-female Wesleyan College is an awesome bargain. At a measly $18,000 or so, the sticker price for tuition is competitive with a handful of state schools and absolutely blows away most private schools of its caliber, or any caliber. On top of the low price, merit-based scholarships are ample, the average need-based award is nearly $16,000, and the cost of living in the surrounding area is fairly inexpensive. Average indebtedness at graduation is on the high side, though—about $27,000.

University of California Berkeley

Berkeley, California

Public 430

UC Berkeley is the crown jewel of California's public universities and it's among the best public universities in the world. Some three-quarters of undergrads at Cal receive financial aid and the bulk of it is need-based. In-state tuition is a relatively steep $13,000, while the cost for out-of-staters is a downright expensive $36,000 or so. However, the average need-based aid award is more than $17,000. Average indebtedness at graduation is about $16,000.

University of California Davis

Davis, California

Public 432

UC Davis is a huge research university in a cozy, rural, and relatively inexpensive college town. Tuition for residents of the Golden State is nearly $14,000. For residents of other states, it's almost $37,000. The average need-based aid award is over $16,000, though, and some 4,500 students receive scholarships. Average indebtedness at graduation is roughly $17,000.

University of California Irvine

Irvine, California

Public 434

The studious undergrads at UC Irvine in sunny Orange County face tuition costs of around $13,000 provided they are California residents. If you aren't a California resident, expect to pay some $36,000. While those prices aren't cheap, the average need-based aid award is comfortably more than $12,000 per year. Students leave UCI with their degrees and an average debt of approximately $16,000.

University of California Los Angeles

Los Angeles, California

Public 436

UCLA is nationally renowned school that offers pretty much any academic program you can dream up. Tuition for California residents approaches $13,000 and it's almost $36,000 if you can't claim residency in the Golden State. Also, the cost of living in Los Angeles isn't cheap. However, scholarships are quite copious and the average need-based aid award is just over $16,000. Average indebtedness at graduation is approximately $18,000.

University of California Riverside

Riverside, California

Public 438

UC Riverside is large research-oriented school that is mostly famous strong science programs. Tuition for Californians is a stout $13,000 or so. For residents of other states, the cost is almost $36,000. Scholarships are widely available, though, and the average need-based aid award is just more than $17,000 per year. Average indebtedness at graduation is roughly $18,000.

University of California San Diego

La Jolla, California

Public 440

UCSD offers tremendous facilities, fabulous weather, and amazing beaches very close to campus. Tuition runs about $13,000 if you can say you are a California resident and a bit more than $36,000 if you can't. The average need-based aid award is about $12,000. Newly-minted graduates leave UCSD with their degrees and an average debt of approximately $19,000.

University of California Santa Barbara
Santa Barbara, California
Public 442

Pretty much right on the beach, UC Santa Barbara offers a tremendous array of academic resources and a bevy of scholarships. The sticker price for tuition is about $13,000 for California residents and more than $36,000. The average need-based aid award is close to $16,000. Average indebtedness at graduation is pretty close to $18,000.

University of California Santa Cruz
Santa Cruz, California
Public 444

Like at each of the other schools in the University of California system tuition at UC Santa Cruz is roughly $13,000 for residents of the Golden State and $36,000 or so for everyone else. The average award is approximately $15,000. Average indebtedness at graduation is right around $16,000.

University of Delaware
Newark, Delaware
Public 450

Tuition at the University of Delaware is about $11,000 for residents of the First State (that's Delaware) and some $27,000 for everyone else. The average need-based aid award is comfortably more than $7,000. Students leave UD with their degrees and average loan debt of roughly $17,000.

University of Illinois at Urbana-Champaign
Champaign, Illinois
Public 454

The University of Illinois offers more than 150 undergraduate programs and the biggest of big-time college atmospheres. If you can claim residency in the Land of Lincoln, tuition is in the neighborhood of $14,000 annually. For residents of other states, it's about $28,000. The average need-based aid award is almost $12,000. Average indebtedness at graduation is around $22,000.

University of Massachusetts Boston
Boston, Massachusetts
Public 462

A multitude of programs and diversity of every kind is on offer at the UMass Boston. While the surrounding city isn't particularly affordable, tuition for residents of the Bay State is a reasonable $11,000 or so per year. If you are from somewhere else, expect to pay close to $25,000. The average need-based aid award is around $7,000. Average indebtedness at graduation is approximately $22,000.

University of Minnesota, Crookston
Crookston, Minnesota
Public 466

The University of Minnesota, Crookston is a small, largely career-oriented school in the nether reaches of the state. The cool thing about this school is that all students are charged the standard in-state tuition rate, regardless of residency status. Regardless of where you live, you'll pay about $11,000 for tuition. The average need-based aid award is in the $9,000 range. Average indebtedness at graduation is on the higher end—pretty close to $26,000.

University of Minnesota—Twin Cities
Minneapolis, Minnesota
Public 468

Tuition at the big, busy, and hugely varied University of Minnesota is about $13,000 for residents of the North Star State and reciprocity agreements allow students from Wisconsin, North Dakota, and South Dakota (as well as the province of Manitoba, Canada) to enroll at discount rates. If you aren't from any of those places, tuition is about $18,000, which isn't chump change but as far as out-of-state tuition goes, it's a ridiculous bargain. The average need-based aid award is about $8000 and there are also quite a few scholarships. Average indebtedness at graduation is on the expensive end—roughly $28,000.

University of Pittsburgh
Pittsburg, Pennsylvania
Public 482

World-class opportunities abound at Pitt. Tuition is pretty pricey for a state school—about $16,000 for residents of Pennsylvania and about $25,000 for students from other states. However, the average need-based aid award is around $9500 and, as far as big cities go, the Steel City is reasonably affordable. Average indebtedness at graduation is more than $26,000.

University of Pittsburgh at Bradford
Bradford, Pennsylvania
Public 480

Small, cozy, career-oriented Pitt-Bradford is small school with something of career-oriented bent in an affordable town. Annual tuition for Pennsylvania residents is in the $12,000 range. For out-of-staters, the cost is closer to $23,000. The average need-based aid award is about $5,500 and there is also a plethora of scholarships on offer. Average indebtedness at graduation is approximately $22,000.

University of South Carolina—Columbia
Columbia, South Carolina
Public 484

South Carolina's flagship university offers a stellar array of majors and programs and oodles of Southern charm. Tuition is barely more than $10,000 for residents of the Palmetto State and about $26,000 for students who hail from elsewhere. The average need-based aid award is about $5,500. Students leave the lovely college town of Columbia with their degrees and an average loan debt approaching $22,000.

University of Virginia
Charlottesville, Virginia
Public 176
Students on the stately and historic campus of the University of Virginia enjoy world-class academic runs about $10,500 for residents of Virginia and a little more than $24,000 if you can't cook up a way to gain state residency. More than 60 percent of the students at Virginia Tech receive some kind of financial aid and the average need-based aid award is approximately $7,000. Average indebtedness at graduation is about $23,000.

University of Washington
Seattle, Washington
Public 204
The University of Washington is a high-powered bastion of research that distributes over $250 million in financial aid to undergrads each year. Also worth noting is the Husky Promise, which makes it possible for many students from low-income families to attend without having to borrow much money. Tuition for state residents is about $11,000 and about $28,000 for everyone else. The average need-based aid award is pretty close to $9,000. Average indebtedness at graduation is about $17,000.

Virginia Tech
Blacksburg, Virginia
Public 496
Virginia Tech is a large school that is especially known for its strong engineering programs. Tuition runs about $10,500 for residents of Virginia and a little more than $24,000 if you can't cook up a way to gain state residency. More than 60 percent of the students at Virginia Tech receive some kind of financial aid and the average need-based aid award is approximately $7,000. Average indebtedness at graduation is about $23,000.

Tuition more than $25,000

Agnes Scott College
Decatur, Georgia
Private 236
Tuition at Agnes Scott College, a small all-women's school near Atlanta, clocks in at about $33,000 per year but financial aid flows freely. Qualified students receive $15,000 per year for four years plus a separate $3,000 award for study abroad, an internship, or on-campus research. The average need-based financial aid award totals more than $25,000 annually and average indebtedness at graduation is about $27,000.

Amherst College
Amherst, Massachusetts
Private 238
Small Amherst College is a very prestigious academic powerhouse that boasts one of the country's best financial aid programs. The average aid award tops $40,000 and Amherst meets the full financial need of every admitted student—period—with no loans. If you have the credentials to get in, you'll graduate completely free of debt with a world-class education.

Barnard College
New York, New York
Private 240
All-female Barnard College on the Upper West Side of Manhattan provides its students with extensive resources of its own and many more thanks to an extensive partnership with Columbia University across the street. Tuition is about $40,000 per year and the cost of living and breathing in New York City is pretty high but Barnard is very generous with its aid. The average need-based financial aid award is about $37,000. Average indebtedness at graduation is around $15,000.

Bates College
Lewiston, Maine
Private 242
Bates College, a quintessential bastion of the liberal arts and sciences in New England, has a pretty staggering comprehensive fee of more than $55,000 per year for tuition, room, board, and fees. However, need-based financial aid packages average nearly $34,000. Average indebtedness at graduation is about $18,000.

Beloit College
Beloit, Wisconsin
Private 244
Beloit College is a highly eclectic little school in Wisconsin where the tuition cost of about $37,000 is offset by an average need-based award of more than $24,000. Also, the cost of living on and around campus is pretty reasonably.

Average indebtedness at graduation is about $18,000.

Boston College
Chestnut Hill, Massachusetts
Private 246
Students at medium-sized, prestigious, Jesuit Boston College face tuition costs of about $42,000 per year and receive an average need-based award of approximately $28,000. The city of Boston offers one of the best and most exciting metropolitan areas for undergrads in the country, but it's also pretty pricey. Average indebtedness at graduation approaches $20,000.

Bowdoin College
Brunswick, Maine
Private 248
Tuition at small, prestigious Bowdoin College is about $42,000 per year. Need-based financial aid packages average about $35,000, though, and the cost of living in the area once you arrive is pretty reasonable. Average indebtedness at graduation is about $18,000.

Brandeis University
Waltham, Massachusetts
Private 250
More than 70 percent of all undergraduates at nonsectarian Jewish-sponsored Brandeis University receive some form of need-based financial aid each year is about $30,000. Tuition is about $41,000 annually. Average indebtedness at graduation is more than $21,000.

Brown University
Providence, Rhode Island
Private 252
Brown University is an Ivy League school with all the resources of an Ivy League school including extraordinary financial aid. About 60 percent of the undergrads who receive need-based financial aid end up with no loans. Tuition runs about $42,000 per year. Need-based financial aid packages average about $35,000. Average indebtedness at graduation, if you have loans, is more than $22,000.

Bryn Mawr College
Bryn Mawr, Pennsylvania
Private 254
All-female academic powerhouse Bryn Mawr College shells out some over $23 million in grant assistance from its own resources to more than 60 percent of BMC undergrads. Tuition is about $40,000 a year and suburban Philadelphia is far from the cheapest place to live but need-based financial aid packages approach $30,000 per student annually. Average indebtedness at graduation is more than $23,000.

Bucknell University
Lewisburg, Pennsylvania
Private 256
In addition to providing the classic East Coast college experience, Bucknell University offers solid financial aid. While tuition is nearly $44,000 per year, the average need-based award approaches $24,000. About 50 percent of students receive aid directly from Bucknell. Average indebtedness at graduation is about $19,000.

California Institute of Technology
Pasadena, California
Private 162
If you are brilliant enough to get admitted to Caltech and to pass the classes there, the financial aid resources are as phenomenal as all the other resources. To begin with, tuition is a relative bargain at about $36,000. On top of that, the average need-based award is more than $31,000. Average indebtedness at graduation is about $11,000.

Carleton College
Northfield, Minnesota
Private 258
While tuition at small and extremely rigorous Carleton College is close to $43,000, the average need-based award is over $30,000. The average grant from Carleton alone is worth more than $26,000. Students who borrow money to pay for college leave Carleton with an average debt close to $20,000.

Centre College
Danville, Kentucky
Private 262
While the comprehensive fee for tuition and room and board at small, challenging Centre College in Kentucky is about $43,000, the average need-based award is more than $24,000. Also, Centre guarantees that you'll graduate in four years (and study abroad or revel in an internship) or you'll get up to an extra year tuition-free. Average indebtedness at graduation is about $20,000.

Claremont McKenna College
Claremont, California
Private 264
The sticker price at small Claremont McKenna, one of the five schools in the Claremont Consortium is pretty steep at more than $42,000. However, the average need-based award approaches $27,000, and CMC makes a very valiant effort to avoid saddling students or parents with loans. Financial aid packages consist of grants, scholarships, and work-study.

Colby College
Waterville, Maine
Private 266
The yearly comprehensive fee for tuition, room, and board at small, picturesque Colby College is a hefty $52,000 or so. At the same time, the average need-based award is nearly $35,000. Students who borrow money to attend Colby can expect to graduate with an average debt close to $25,000.

Average indebtedness at graduation is about $18,000.

Boston College
Chestnut Hill, Massachusetts
Private 246
Students at medium-sized, prestigious, Jesuit Boston College face tuition costs of about $42,000 per year and receive an average need-based award of approximately $28,000. The city of Boston offers one of the best and most exciting metropolitan areas for undergrads in the country, but it's also pretty pricey. Average indebtedness at graduation approaches $20,000.

Bowdoin College
Brunswick, Maine
Private 248
Tuition at small, prestigious Bowdoin College is about $42,000 per year. Need-based financial aid packages average about $35,000, though, and the cost of living in the area once you arrive is pretty reasonable. Average indebtedness at graduation is about $18,000.

Brandeis University
Waltham, Massachusetts
Private 250
More than 70 percent of all undergraduates at nonsectarian Jewish-sponsored Brandeis University receive some form of need-based financial aid each year is about $30,000. Tuition is about $41,000 annually. Average indebtedness at graduation is more than $21,000.

Brown University
Providence, Rhode Island
Private 252
Brown University is an Ivy League school with all the resources of an Ivy League school including extraordinary financial aid. About 60 percent of the undergrads who receive need-based financial aid end up with no loans. Tuition runs about $42,000 per year. Need-based financial aid packages average about $35,000. Average indebtedness at graduation, if you have loans, is more than $22,000.

Bryn Mawr College
Bryn Mawr, Pennsylvania
Private 254
All-female academic powerhouse Bryn Mawr College shells out some over $23 million in grant assistance from its own resources to more than 60 percent of BMC undergrads. Tuition is about $40,000 a year and suburban Philadelphia is far from the cheapest place to live but need-based financial aid packages approach $30,000 per student annually. Average indebtedness at graduation is more than $23,000.

Bucknell University
Lewisburg, Pennsylvania
Private 256
In addition to providing the classic East Coast college experience, Bucknell University offers solid financial aid. While tuition is nearly $44,000 per year, the average need-based award approaches $24,000. About 50 percent of students receive aid directly from Bucknell. Average indebtedness at graduation is about $19,000.

California Institute of Technology
Pasadena, California
Private 162
If you are brilliant enough to get admitted to Caltech and to pass the classes there, the financial aid resources are as phenomenal as all the other resources. To begin with, tuition is a relative bargain at about $36,000. On top of that, the average need-based award is more than $31,000. Average indebtedness at graduation is about $11,000.

Carleton College
Northfield, Minnesota
Private 258
While tuition at small and extremely rigorous Carleton College is close to $43,000, the average need-based award is over $30,000. The average grant from Carleton alone is worth more than $26,000. Students who borrow money to pay for college leave Carleton with an average debt close to $20,000.

Centre College
Danville, Kentucky
Private 262
While the comprehensive fee for tuition and room and board at small, challenging Centre College in Kentucky is about $43,000, the average need-based award is more than $24,000. Also, Centre guarantees that you'll graduate in four years (and study abroad or revel in an internship) or you'll get up to an extra year tuition-free. Average indebtedness at graduation is about $20,000.

Claremont McKenna College
Claremont, California
Private 264
The sticker price at small Claremont McKenna, one of the five schools in the Claremont Consortium is pretty steep at more than $42,000. However, the average need-based award approaches $27,000, and CMC makes a very valiant effort to avoid saddling students or parents with loans. Financial aid packages consist of grants, scholarships, and work-study.

Colby College
Waterville, Maine
Private 266
The yearly comprehensive fee for tuition, room, and board at small, picturesque Colby College is a hefty $52,000 or so. At the same time, the average need-based award is nearly $35,000. Students who borrow money to attend Colby can expect to graduate with an average debt close to $25,000.

Colgate University
Hamilton, New York
Private 268
Colgate University is a prestigious, rigorous, smaller school in central New York where the price tag for a year of tuition is about $43,000 and the average need-based award is more than $37,000. Average indebtedness at graduation is about $19,000.

College of the Atlantic
Bar Harbor, Maine
Private 270
There is one major at tiny College of the Atlantic—human ecology—and some 85 percent of the students receive some kind of financial aid. Tuition is about $36,000 annually but the average need-based award is more than $28,000. Average indebtedness at graduation is around $20,000.

College of the Holy Cross
Worcester, Massachusetts
Private 272
The College of the Holy Cross is a Jesuit school with a broad core curriculum and terrific financial aid. While tuition is about $41,000, the average need-based award is close to $30,000. Also, nearly half the students at Holy Cross receive scholarships and the average award is more than $26,000. Average indebtedness at graduation is close to $24,000.

Colorado College
Colorado Springs, Colorado
Private 274
At intimate, intensive Colorado College, students take one course at a time over three-and-a-half-weeks and they also receive ample financial aid. Tuition clocks in at about $40,000 per year but the average need-based aid award is some $32,000. Also, scholarships are pretty ample. Average indebtedness at graduation is approximately $18,000.

Columbia University
New York, New York
Private 276
Columbia University on Manhattan's Upper West Side ranks among the world's great research universities. Tuition is more than $45,000 annually but financial aid flows like water. The average need-based award tops $38,000 and the average financial aid award (including loans) for entering first-year students is more than $30,000.

Cornell College
Mount Vernon, Iowa
Private 278
Cornell College is a small liberal arts school in an affordable Iowa town, boasts miniscule classes, a unique one-course-at-a-time academic program, and fabulous financial aid. Tuition is about $32,000, which is obviously quite a bit of money but it's a bargain relative to most of Cornell's peer schools. The average need-based award is close to $25,000. Average indebtedness at graduation is approximately $22,000.

Cornell University
Ithaca, New York
Private 280
Cornell University is a pretty large Ivy League bastion in rural, cold upstate New York where financial aid is very abundant. For example, parents make no yearly contribution if your total family income is less than $60,000 (and your family's assets are less than $100,000). Also, if your family income doesn't exceed $75,000, you won't have to deal with any loans. The average need-based award at Cornell approaches $34,000 per year. Average indebtedness at graduation is approximately $21,000.

Dartmouth University
Hanover, New Hampshire
Private 282
Fast-paced, interdisciplinary Dartmouth University is an Ivy League school that meets 100 percent of every student's financial need. The sticker price for tuition is a hefty $43,000 or so but the average need-based award is close to $37,000. Average indebtedness at graduation is approximately $19,000, but for students who have family incomes less than $45,000 it's closer to $6,000.

Davidson College
Davidson, North Carolina
Private 284
Davidson College is a rigorous small school not too far from Charlotte where grading is notoriously stingy but financial aid is munificent. While tuition is a fairly stout $39,000 or so annually, some 40 percent of all students receive need-based financial aid and the average need-based award is more than $27,000. Average indebtedness at graduation is more than $23,000.

DePauw University
Greencastle, Indiana
Private 286
At DePauw University, a small liberal arts school in a small and inexpensive Indiana town, tuition is about $37,000 annually and the average need-based award is close to $26,000. Also, merit scholarships are ample. Students who borrow money to pay for college leave DePauw with an average debt close to $24,000.

Duke University
Durham, North Carolina
Private 288
The formidable sticker price for tuition at Duke University is close to $42,000 per year, but financial aid at this national academic powerhouse is equally impressive. Parents make no yearly contribution if your total family income is less than $60,000 and you don't have to deal with loans if your family

income is less than $40,000. The average need-based award is around $32,000. Average indebtedness at graduation is roughly $21,000.

Emory University
Atlanta, Georgia
Private 290
Midsize Emory University is among the South's premier undergraduate schools and it offers a relatively attractive tuition rate of about $35,000 as well as a bounty of financial aid. The average need-based award is more than $20,000. For students with family incomes of $50,000 or less, Emory eliminates loans altogether for tuition, room, and board. Also, Emory caps cumulative loan debt at $15,000 for undergrads with total family incomes between $50,000 and $100,000. Consequently, average indebtedness at graduation is nicely low—about $8,000.

Georgetown University
Washington, DC
Private 294
Tuition at moderately sized Georgetown University in fairly expensive Washington, D.C. is about $41,000 per year and the average need-based award is almost $27,000. Students who borrow money to pay for college leave Georgetown with an average debt around $25,000.

Gettysburg College
Gettysburg, Pennsylvania
Private 296
Gettysburg College is a small bastion of the liberal arts and sciences where tuition is over $42,000 but the average need-based award is more than $28,000. Over two-thirds of all students receive scholarships and grants to the tune of about $43 million each year. Average indebtedness at graduation is nearly $25,000.

Grinnell College
Grinnell, Iowa
Private 298
Academically awesome and wonderfully weird Grinnell College in rural Iowa boasts a sky-high endowment of approximately $750,000 per student and, consequently, some serious financial aid. While tuition is about $40,000 annually, Grinnell gives away some $38 million in gift aid every year, and the average need-based award is close to $31,000. Average indebtedness at graduation is close $19,000.

Hamilton College
Clinton, New York
Private 166
At Hamilton College, a small and prestigious liberal arts school in upstate New York, tuition is nearly $43,000 per year but the average need-based award is nearly $35,000 and endowed scholarships—funded by loyal alumni—account for roughly 43 percent of a scholarship budget of over $26 million. Average indebtedness at graduation is about $17,000.

Hanover College
Hanover, Indiana
Private 300
At less than $29,000, tuition at tiny, challenging Hanover College is a tremendous bargain and financial aid is ample on top of the low sticker price. The average need-based award is nearly $22,000. Also, the cost of living in the surrounding town is splendidly low. Average indebtedness at graduation is about $28,000 or so.

Harvard College
Cambridge, Massachusetts
Private 142
Both the academic atmosphere and the financial aid situation at Harvard are mind-bogglingly awesome. If your family income is less than $65,000, you won't have to pay one dime to attend and many students—not just stinking rich ones, either—are able to graduate with a Harvard degree and absolutely no debt. Also, unlike a whole lot of schools, Harvard doesn't consider home equity in determining your family contribution. Average indebtedness at graduation is about $10,000.

Harvey Mudd College
Claremont, California
Private 302
Harvey Mudd College is the science- and engineering-heavy school in the five-school Claremont Consortium. Tuition is more than $42,000 but more than 80 percent of students receive financial aid and some 40 percent qualify for our merit-based awards. The average need-based award approaches $30,000 per year. Average indebtedness at graduation is close to $22,000.

Haverford College
Haverford, Pennsylvania
Private 304
Haverford College offers fabulous amounts of financial aid. Tuition is a steep $42,000 but the average need-based award is close to $35,000 per year and Haverford typically replaces in financial aid packages with additional grants. Average indebtedness at graduation is about $16,000.

The Johns Hopkins University
Baltimore, Maryland
Private 308
Johns Hopkins is a demanding academic powerhouse with a sticker price of about $43,000 per year and an average need-based award of approximately $31,000. Students walk away from JHU with an average debt of about $24,000.

Lafayette College
Easton, Pennsylvania
Private 310
Lafayette College is a liberal arts and engineering school that ranks very, very highly in the all-important category of starting and mid-career salaries. Also, Lafayette offers purely grants instead of loans to most students with family incomes less than $50,000 and limits loans to $3,500 per year for students with family incomes between $50,000 and $100,000. Tuition is roughly $41,000 annually and the average need-based award is around $28,000. Average indebtedness at graduation is around $20,000.

Macalester College
St. Paul, Minnesota
Private 312
Macalester College is a small, prestigious liberal arts school where tuition runs about $42,000 and the average need-based aid award is more than $30,000. About three-fourths of all students at Macalester receive some kind of financial aid. Average indebtedness at graduation is about $18,000, and students leave Macalester with one of the lightest debt burdens in the North Star State.

Massachusetts Institute of Technology
Cambridge, Massachusetts
Private 314
MIT is the mecca of engineering, science, and mathematics on the East Coast and financial aid is nothing if not magnanimous. Basically, if you are good enough to get admitted, you'll be able to afford it. While tuition is about $41,000 per year, MIT gives away more than $85 million each year in scholarships and the average need-based award is $36,000. Also worth noting is the fact that a typical MIT grad makes a starting salary of more than $60,000 a year. Average indebtedness at graduation is about $15,000.

Middlebury College
Middlebury, Vermont
Private 316
Middlebury College is a consummate liberal arts school with endless resources in pretty much everything including financial aid. The comprehensive fee for tuition, room, and board is more than $55,000 but the average need-based award is about $33,000. Also, loans are limited at Middlebury. If your family income is less than $50,000, for example, your loan amount won't be more than $1,000 per year. Average indebtedness at graduation is about $22,000.

Mount Holyoke College
South Hadley, Massachusetts
Private 318
Small, all-female Mount Holyoke College is a member of the prestigious Five Colleges Consortium and financial aid is generous. While tuition is more than $41,000 annually, the average need-based award is almost $33,000. Also, scholarships are ample. Average indebtedness at graduation is about $23,000.

Northwestern University
Evanston, Illinois
Private 320
Northwestern University is a national powerhouse in both academics and financial aid. Tuition is a robust $42,000 or so per year but the average need-based award is close to $14,000. Also, Northwestern awards more than $100 million in aid out of its own pocket each year and pretty close to 50 percent of all undergrads receive a Northwestern scholarship. Average indebtedness at graduation is roughly $21,000.

Occidental College
Los Angeles, California
Private 322
Occidental College boasts a lush and gorgeous campus and exceptional financial aid. Though annual tuition approaches $43,000, the average need-based award offsets about $28,000 of that amount. Average indebtedness at graduation is less than $18,000.

Pomona College
Claremont, California
Private 150
Pomona College, one of the five colleges in the Claremont Consortium, boasts one of the most generous financial aid programs in the country. It has a sticker price at about $40,000 and an average need-based aid award of approximately $36,000. Students walk away from Pomona after graduation with an excellent degree and a debt of only $12,000.

Princeton University
Princeton, New Jersey
Private 138
Princeton University is an Ivy League school with a distinctive focus on the undergraduate experience and massive resources. Those resources most definitely include financial aid. Tuition is $37,000 a year, which is a lot but it's less than a lot of schools with lesser reputations charge and Princeton covers 100 percent of every student's demonstrated financial need with no loans. That's zip, zilch, zero, nada. The average need-based award is close to $36,000 and most students leave owing nothing after graduation.

Randolph College
Lynchburg, Virginia
Private 324
Small Randolph College is an affordable school located in a pretty affordable town in the foothills of the Blue Ridge Mountains. Tuition

is about $30,000—pretty low for a private school of Randolph's caliber—and the average need-based award is close to $19,000. Average indebtedness at graduation is in the high side—approximately $26,000.

Reed College

Portland, Oregon

Private 326

Reed College is an extremely intellectually rigorous school where tuition is close to $43,000 per year and the average need-based award approaches $35,000. About half the students at Reed receive some kind of financial aid. Average indebtedness at graduation is less than $17,000.

Rice University

Houston, Texas

Private 146

Prestigious, vibrant, and nationally known Rice University offers a very attractive sticker price of less than $36,000. On top of that, the average need-based award is close to $27,000. Graduates of Rice leave school with an excellent degree and an average student loan debt less than $17,000.

Scripps College

Claremont, California

Private 328

Tiny, all-female Scripps College is one of the Claremont schools and, like the other four schools in the Claremont Consortium, it offers tremendous financial aid. Tuition is a pretty steep $42,000 or so but merit-based scholarships are abundant at Scripps and the average need-based award is more than $33,000. Average indebtedness at graduation is less than $10,000.

Sewanee—The University of the South

Sewanee, Tennessee

Private 330

The small and demanding University of the South sits atop a mountain in a rural and very affordable area of Tennessee. At only $32,000 or so, the sticker price for tuition is an excellent bargain. In addition, about half of all students receive some kind of need-based aid and the average amount is close to $28,000 per year. Average indebtedness at graduation is about $19,000.

Stanford University

Palo Alto, California

Private 332

World-renowned Stanford University boasts a stunning campus, massive academic resources, and stellar financial aid. While tuition is about $40,000, the average need-based award is an impressive $38,000 or so and average indebtedness at graduation is fairly moderate—about $14,000.

Swarthmore College

Swarthmore, Pennsylvania

Private 134

At small, distinguished Swarthmore College, tuition is around $41,000 per year but the average need-based award is more than $35,000. About 50 percent of all Swatties receive need-based aid and, best of all, Swarthmore's aid packages are loan free (although some students and their parents borrow to pay their family contribution). Average indebtedness at graduation is about $19,000.

University of Chicago

Chicago, Illinois

Private 336

While tuition at the intense, interdisciplinary, and incomparable University of Chicago is about $43,000 per year, the average need-based award is close to $36,000. Also, the U of C is among a pretty small number of ridiculously selective schools to award merit-based scholarships and most students from low- and middle-income families don't have to borrow a dime to attend. For students who do have to borrow, average indebtedness at graduation is about $22,000.

University of Notre Dame

South Bend, Indiana

Private 338

Tuition at the strongly Catholic University Notre Dame is roughly $41,000 per year but the average need-based aid award is pretty close to $28,000. Students who borrow money leave Notre Dame with their degrees and average debt of about $24,000.

University of Pennsylvania

Philadelphia, Pennsylvania

Private 340

At the University of Pennsylvania, tuition is a pretty stiff $42,000 or so but financial aid is as Ivy League-caliber as the academic atmosphere. Some 80 percent of students who apply for financial aid receive need-based money and the average need-based award is nearly $34,000. Average indebtedness at graduation is about $17,000.

University of Redlands

Redlands, California

Private 342

At the smallish, demanding University of Redlands in Southern California, tuition is about $37,000 and the average need-based award is around $27,000. Some 80 percent of all students receive some kind of financial aid. Average indebtedness at graduation is approximately $20,000.

University of Richmond

Richmond, Virginia

Private 344

Tuition at the University of Richmond is a hefty $43,000 or so but the average need-based award is pretty close to $34,000. Students from Virginia with family incomes of $40,000 or less typically pay nothing for tuition, room, and board and walk away from campus after graduation owing nothing. Average indebtedness at graduation for everyone else is approximately $23,000.

Vanderbilt University
Nashville, Tennessee
Private 346

Vanderbilt University is a challenging, academically intense school where financial aid is ample. Tuition is nearly $42,000 but the average need-based award is more than $37,000 and Vanderbilt replaces a substantial percentage of need-based undergraduate student loans with grant and scholarship assistance. Students who choose to borrow money, anyway, leave with one of the premier degrees in the South and a debt of approximately $18,000.

Vassar College
Poughkeepsie, New York
Private 348

Small Vassar College provides an unusual amount of academic freedom, excellent visual and performing arts programs, and tremendous financial aid. While tuition is quite high—nearly $45,000—almost 60 percent of all students receive need-based aid and the average need-based award is almost $38,000. Average indebtedness at graduation is about $18,000.

Wabash College
Crawfordsville, Indiana
Private 350

At about $32,000, tuition at tiny, rigorous, and all-male Wabash College is a whale of a bargain compared to similarly elite schools. On top of the attractive sticker price, merit-based aid is ample and the average need-based award is around $18,000. Average indebtedness at graduation is on the high end, though—more than $29,000.

Wake Forest University
Winston-Salem, North Carolina
Private 252

At Wake Forest University, a smaller school with all the resources of a huge university, tuition is pretty close to $42,000 and the average need-based aid award is more than $29,000. Merit-based scholarships are also abundant. Average indebtedness can be pretty acute, however—about $30,000.

Washington University in St. Louis
St. Louis, Missouri
Private 154

Washington University in St. Louis is a top-tier university that offers a host of impressive academic programs and impressive financial aid. Merit-based scholarships are copious and the average need-based aid award is about $29,000. Also, as far as big cities go, the cost of living in St. Louis is pretty reasonable. About 40 percent of all undergrads take out loans.

Webb Institute
Glen Cove, New York
Private 232

Tuition is totally free at tiny Webb Institute a tiny, a very competitive school that focuses exclusively on naval architecture and marine engineering. While the cost for room, board, supplies, and general expenses will run you about $20,000 each year, Webb is still a great bargain if you can get in and keep up the frenetic academic pace. Also, graduates are in high demand; the placement rate is typically 100 percent in grad schools and jobs that pay quite well.

Wellesley College
Wellesley, Massachusetts
Private 354

Small, eminent, all-female Wellesley College is awash in financial aid. While tuition approaches $41,000 annually, the average need-based award is not too far from $37,000 and, importantly, the average student loans of Wellesley graduates are among the nation's lowest. Students leave Wellesley with a world-class degree and an average loan debt of about $12,000.

Wesleyan University
Middletown, Connecticut
Private 356

Wesleyan University is a nationally recognized bastion of the liberal arts and sciences with pretty steep tuition—about $44,000 per year—and an average need-based award close to $35,000. Also, if your family income is less than $40,000, you won't have to borrow any money to attend Wesleyan. For students who do take out loans, the average indebtedness at graduation is pretty steep—close to $30,000.

Wheaton College
Wheaton, Illinois
Private 360

Academically rigorous and definitively Christian Wheaton College in the suburbs of Chicago offers a relatively inexpensive tuition of $29,000 or so and a great deal of financial aid to boot. Scholarships are plentiful and the average need-based aid award is nearly $18,000 per year. Average indebtedness at graduation is about $21,000.

Whitman College
Walla Walla, Washington
Private 362

Whitman College is a small bastion of the liberal arts and science in southeastern Washington where tuition is close to $41,000 per year and the average need-based aid award is almost $25,000. Also, merit-based scholarships are widely available. Students leave Whitman with a degree and a relatively low average loan debt of about $14,000.

Williams College
Williamstown, Massachusetts
Private 130

Financial aid flows like water at small, intense, and nationally renowned Williams College. At about $43,000, tuition is definitely expensive but the average need-based aid award is a staggering $40,000 or so. There are loans at Williams, but they don't amount to much. Average indebtedness at graduation is roughly $8,000—a paltry sum for such a world-class degree.

Wofford College
Spartanburg, South Carolina
Private 364

Small Wofford College is located in an affordable town and, at about $34,000, a tuition price that is very affordable relative to many peer schools. Scholarships are abundant and the average need-based award is more than $28,000. Average indebtedness at graduation is approximately $23,000.

Yale University
New Haven, Connecticut
Private 158

Ultra-prestigious Yale University offers amazing academics and amazing financial aid. Tuition is about $41,000 but the average need-based aid award is more than $38,000 and, more importantly, there are no loans. Yale meets 100 percent of every student's demonstrated need with a financial aid package consisting of need-based scholarships, term-time employment, and a student income contribution (with a sweet wage of at least $11.75 an hour). For students who choose to borrow money, anyway, the average loan debt at graduation is about $11,000.

Lists by Interests

Oldest schools (year established) 93
Schools with the highest enrollments 93
Schools with the lowest enrollments 93
Schools with the largest campuses (acreage) 93
Schools with the smallest campuses (acreage) 93
Schools that don't require the SAT/ACT for admission 94
Schools whose incoming freshmen have high SAT scores 94
Schools whose incoming freshmen have high ACT scores 94
Schools with high admissions selectivity ratings 94
Schools with more women 95
Schools with more men 95
Schools with lots of international students 95
Schools with high out-of-state student populations 95
Schools with a high sticker price—private 96
Schools with a high sticker price—public, in-state 96
Schools with a high sticker price—public, out-of-state 96
Highest percentage of students receiving financial aid 97
Schools that offer free tuition to all students 97
Schools from which the greatest proportion of students graduate within 4 years 97
Schools from which the most number of students go to grad school within 1 year 97
Schools with 4-4-1 or 4-1-4 academic calendars: 97
Schools that don't give grades 98
Great schools for designing your own major 98
Schools that offer unusual/unconventional majors 98
Schools with active alumni associations 98
Schools with the most extensive library collections 98
Schools with the best on-campus museums 98
Schools with recording studios on campus 99
Schools with the largest stadiums 99
Schools with higher student-to-faculty ratios 99
Schools with lower student-to-faculty ratios 99
Schools that do not have a general foreign language requirement 100
Schools that require internships 100
Schools that require a thesis 100
Schools with great grant programs for independent study 100
Great opportunities to conduct research with professors 100
Schools that have a track record of publishing undergraduate papers 100
Schools with eco-conscious or eco-friendly campuses 101
Schools with the most vegetarian/vegan-friendly options 101
Schools with organic farms 101
Schools with great on-campus arboreta 101
Schools with botanical gardens 101
Schools with on-campus nuclear reactors 101
Schools with observatories 101
Schools with planetariums 102

Great technical colleges 102
Schools with great study abroad programs 102
Schools with the greatest proportion of students who study abroad 102
Schools with highest biology enrollments 103
Schools with highest computer/information science enrollments 103
Schools with highest economics enrollments 103
Schools with highest education enrollments 103
Schools with highest English enrollments 104
Schools with highest history enrollments 104
Schools with highest physics enrollments 104
Schools with highest poli-sci/gov't enrollments 104
Schools with highest psychology enrollments 105
Schools with terrific undergraduate film programs 105
Schools with great acting/theater programs 105
Schools with great graphic design programs 106
Schools with great interior design programs 106
Schools with great music composition programs 106
Schools with great music education programs 106
Schools with great music performance programs 106
Schools with great photography programs 106
Schools with great studio art programs 106
Schools with great mathematics programs 106
Schools with great applied mathematics programs 107
Schools with great business/finance programs 107
Schools with great international business studies programs 107
Schools with great marketing and sales programs 107
Schools with great accounting programs 107
Schools with great architecture programs 107
Schools with great tourism and hotel management programs 107
Schools with great aviation programs 108
Schools with great biology programs 108
Schools with great biochemistry programs....108
Schools with great biomedical engineering programs 108
Schools with great chemistry programs 108
Schools with great engineering programs 108
Schools with great computer engineering programs 109
Schools with great electrical engineering programs 109
Schools with great mechanical engineering programs 109
Schools with great environmental engineering programs 109
Schools with great entomology programs 109
Schools with great forensic science programs 110
Schools with great forestry programs 110
Schools with great geology programs 110
Schools with great marine biology programs 110
Schools with great medical technology programs 110
Schools with great nursing programs 110
Schools with great nutrition programs 110
Schools with great occupational therapy programs 110
Schools with great pharmacy programs 111
Schools with great physics programs 111
Schools with great psychology programs....111
Schools with great communications programs 111
Schools with great journalism programs 111

Schools with great broadcast journalism programs 111
Schools with great video game design programs 111
Schools with great education programs 112
Schools with great anthropology programs 112
Schools with great archeology programs 112
Schools with great criminology programs 112
Schools with great general studies programs 112
Schools with great history programs 112
Schools with great English literature/language programs 113
Schools with great creative writing programs 113
Schools with great international relation s..113
Schools with great philosophy programs 113
Schools with great political science programs 113
Schools with great social work programs 114
Schools with great theology programs 114
Schools with great actuarial science programs 114
Schools with great athletic training programs 114
Schools with great equine studies programs 114
Schools with great farming/agriculture programs 114
Schools with great turf grass science programs 114
Schools with great outdoor leadership/adventure education programs 114
Schools with great sports management/sports entertainment programs 114
Schools with great prelaw advising (outside of a pre-law program) 114
Schools with great pre-med advising (outside of a pre-med program) 114
Schools with great pre-vet programs 115
Schools with great pre-med programs 115
Schools that encourage entrepreneurial endeavors 115
Schools that have great co-op programs 115
Schools with great ROTC programs 115
Schools with great fellowship opportunities 115
Schools with great opportunities for off-campus employment 115
Schools that offer subsidies to students who use public transportation 116
Schools that spend a good percentage of their federal work-study funds on community service 116
Schools with largest endowments 116
Schools that attract the largest proportion of recruiters 116
Colleges where the State Department typically recruits 117
Schools from which the highest proportion of graduates join the Peace Corps. 117
Great job markets in the cities where these schools are located 117
Schools with lots of on-campus organizations 117
Top sports universities 118
Schools with greatest number of professionally drafted players 118
Schools with unusual mascots 118
Schools with famous/infamous rivalries 118
Schools with great football programs 118
Schools with great baseball programs 118
Schools with great basketball programs 118
Schools with great soccer programs 119
Schools with great hockey programs 119
Schools with great golf programs 119
Top-notch on-campus golf courses 119
Schools with on-campus rock-climbing walls 119
Schools with great archery programs 119
Schools with great badminton programs 119

Schools with great boxing programs 119
Schools with great cheerleading programs 119
Schools with great crew/rowing programs 119
Schools with great flag football teams 120
Schools with great gymnastics programs 120
Schools with great lacrosse programs 120
Schools with great polo programs 120
Schools with great sailing programs 120
Schools with great softball programs 120
Schools with great swimming/diving programs 120
Schools with great tennis programs 120
Schools with great indoor track and field programs 121
Schools with great outdoor track and field programs 121
Schools with great cross-country programs 121
Schools with great volleyball programs 121
Schools with great water polo programs 121
Schools with great wrestling programs 121
Schools with great juggling clubs 121
Schools with great outdoor adventure clubs 121
Schools with great rock-climbing clubs 121
Schools with great skiing/snowboarding opportunities 122
Schools with great surfing opportunities 122
Schools with rodeo programs 122
Schools with great ultimate Frisbee clubs 122
Schools with active community service programs/student volunteer work 122
Schools with great literary magazines 122
Schools with great choral ensembles 122
Schools with great a capella programs 122
Schools with unusual musical groups (e.g., steel pan groups, gamelan groups) 123
Schools with majority of students living in university housing 123
Strict Campuses 123
Relaxed campuses 123
Schools with great Greek life participation 123
Politically active schools 124
Most politically conservative schools 124
Politically liberal schools 124
Schools with exciting freshman orientations 124
Schools with great college radio stations 124
Schools with warm weather campuses 125
Schools with cold weather campuses 125
Schools with religious affiliation 125
Schools with the highest fire safety ratings 125
Schools with secret societies 125
Schools with wacky college traditions 126
Schools with a history of amazing pranks 126
Schools with haunted campuses 127

WHEN I WAS YOUR AGE

Oldest schools (Year Established)

Bowdoin College (1794)	248
Brown University (1764)	252
College of Charleston (1770)	382
College of William and Mary (1693)	192
Columbia University (1754)	276
Dartmouth University (1769)	282
Georgetown University (1789)	294
Harvard University (1636)	142
Middlebury College (1800)	316
Princeton University (1746)	138
United States Military Academy (1802)	228
University of Delaware (1743)	450
University of Georgia (1785)	200
University of North Carolina at Chapel Hill (1795)	172
University of Pennsylvania (1757)	340
University of Pittsburgh—Pittsburgh Campus (1787)	482
University of South Carolina Columbia (1801)	484
University of Tennessee—Knoxville (1794)	488
Williams College (1793)	130
Yale University (1701)	158

STUDENTS A-PLENTY

Schools with the highest enrollments

California State University—Long Beach	372
Florida State University	388
Indiana University—Bloomington	392
Iowa State University	394
North Carolina State University	406
Ohio State University—Columbus	408
Purdue University—West Lafayette	410
The University of Texas at Austin	208
University of California—Berkeley	430
University of California—Davis	432
University of California—Los Angeles	436
University of California—San Diego	440
University of Central Florida	446
University of Colorado, Boulder	448
University of Florida	196
University of Georgia	200
University of Houston	452
University of Illinois at Urbana-Champaign	454
University of Kansas	456
University of Maryland—College Park	460
University of Michigan—Ann Arbor	464
University of Minnesota, Twin Cities	468
University of Oklahoma	478
University of Washington	204
University of Wisconsin—Madison	188
Virginia Tech	496

WHERE EVERYBODY KNOWS YOUR NAME

Schools with the lowest enrollments

Deep Springs College	220
Webb Institute	232

SIZE MATTERS

Schools with the largest campuses

California Polytechnic State University—San Luis Obispo	370
Deep Springs College	220
Duke University	288
Indiana University—Bloomington	392
Iowa State University	394
North Carolina State University	406
Ohio State University—Columbus	408
Sewanee—The University of the South	330
Stanford University	332
United States Air Force Academy	222
United States Military Academy	228
University of California–Davis	432
University of California—San Diego	440
University of California-Santa Cruz	444
University of Florida	196
University of Illinois at Urbana-Champaign	454
University of Michigan—Ann Arbor	464
University of Minnesota, Twin Cities	468
University of Oklahoma	478
Virginia Tech	496

GOOD THINGS COME IN SMALL PACKAGES

Schools with the smallest campuses

Barnard College	240
CUNY—Hunter College	378

TEST FREE ADMISSIONS

Schools that don't require the SAT/ACT for admission

Bates College	242
Bowdoin College	248
College of the Atlantic	270
College of the Holy Cross	272
Hamilton College	166

2400, HERE THEY COME!

Schools whose incoming freshmen have high SAT scores

Amherst College	238
Brown University	252
California Institute of Technology	162
Carleton College	258
Columbia University—Columbia College	276
Dartmouth University	282
Deep Springs College	220
Duke University	288
Franklin W. Olin College of Engineering	292
Harvard College	142
Harvey Mudd College	302
Johns Hopkins University	308
Massachusetts Institute of Technology	314
Northwestern University	320
Pomona College	150
Princeton University	138
Rice University	146
Stanford University	332
Swarthmore College	134
University of Chicago	336
University of Pennsylvania	340
Washington University in St. Louis	154
Williams College	130
Yale University	158

36 NEVER SOUNDED SO GOOD

Schools whose incoming freshmen have high ACT scores

Amherst College	238
Brandeis University	250
Brown University	252
Carleton College	258
Claremont McKenna College	264
Colby College	266
Colgate University	268
College of William and Mary	192
Colorado College	274
Columbia University—Columbia College	276
Cornell University	280
Dartmouth University	282
Davidson College	284
Duke University	288
Emory University	290
Franklin W. Olin College of Engineering	292
Georgetown University	294
Grinnell College	298
Harvard College	142
Johns Hopkins University	308
Macalester College	312
Massachusetts Institute of Technology	314
Middlebury College	316
Northwestern University	320
Pomona College	150
Reed College	326
Rice University	146
Scripps College	328
Stanford University	332
United States Merchant Marine Academy	226
University of Chicago	336
University of Illinois at Urbana-Champaign	454
University of Michigan—Ann Arbor	464
University of North Carolina at Chapel Hill	172
University of Notre Dame	338
University of Pennsylvania	340
Vanderbilt University	346
Vassar College	348
Washington University in St. Louis	154
Wellesley College	354
Wesleyan University	358
Wheaton College (IL)	360
Whitman College	362
Williams College	130
Yale University	158

FEEL LIKE ONE IN A MILLION

Schools with high admissions selectivity ratings

Amherst College	238
Barnard College	240
Bates College	242
Boston College	246
Bowdoin College	248
Brandeis University	250
Brown University	252
Bryn Mawr College	254
Bucknell University	256
California Institute of Technology	162
Carleton College	258
Claremont McKenna College	264

Colby College	266
Colgate University	268
College of William and Mary	192
Columbia University—Columbia College	276
Cooper Union	218
Cornell University	280
Dartmouth University	282
Davidson College	284
Deep Springs College	220
Duke University	288
Emory University	290
Franklin W. Olin College of Engineering	292
Georgetown University	294
Grinnell College	298
Hamilton College	166
Harvard College	142
Harvey Mudd College	302
Haverford College	304
Johns Hopkins University	308
Lafayette College	310
Macalester College	312
Massachusetts Institute of Technology	314
Middlebury College	316
Northwestern University	320
Pomona College	150
Princeton University	138
Reed College	326
Rice University	146
Scripps College	328
Stanford University	332
Swarthmore College	134
United States Air Force Academy	222
United States Coast Guard Academy	224
United States Military Academy	228
United States Naval Academy	230
University of California, Berkeley	430
University of California—Davis	432
University of California—Irvine	434
University of California—Los Angeles	436
University of California—San Diego	440
University of Chicago	336
University of Michigan—Ann Arbor	464
University of North Carolina at Chapel Hill	172
University of Notre Dame	338
University of Pennsylvania	340
University of Richmond	344
University of Virginia	176
Vassar College	348
Wake Forest University	352
Washington University in St. Louis	154
Webb Institute	232
Wellesley College	354
Wesleyan University	358
Whitman College	362
Williams College	130
Yale University	158

DOUBLE X (CHROMOSOMES, THAT IS)

Schools with more women

Agnes Scott College	236
Barnard College	240
Bryn Mawr College	254
Mount Holyoke College	318
Scripps College	328
Wellesley College	354
Wesleyan College	356

XY HAVENS

Schools with more men

Deep Springs College	220
United States Air Force Academy	222
United States Merchant Marine Academy	226
United States Military Academy	228
United States Naval Academy	230
Missouri University of Science and Technology	402
Wabash College	350
Webb Institute	232

GLOBAL COMMUNITES

Schools with lots of international students

College of the Atlantic	270
Grinnell College	298
Macalester College	312
Mount Holyoke College	318
Wesleyan College	356

IN A DIFFERENT STATE

Schools with high out-of-state student populations

Amherst College	238
Bates College	242
Beloit College	244
Bowdoin College	248
Brown University	252
Bryn Mawr College	254
Colby College	266
Colorado College	274
Columbia University	276
Dartmouth University	282
Davidson College	284

Deep Springs College	220
Duke University	288
Franklin W. Olin College of Engineering	292
Georgetown University	294
Harvard College	142
Haverford College	304
Johns Hopkins University	308
Massachusetts Institute of Technology	314
Middlebury College	316
Princeton University	138
Reed College	326
Swarthmore College	134
United States Air Force Academy	222
United States Coast Guard Academy	224
United States Merchant Marine Academy	226
United States Military Academy	228
United States Naval Academy	230
University of Notre Dame	338
University of Pennsylvania	340
University of Richmond	344
University of Washington	204
Vanderbilt University	346
Washington University in St. Louis	154
Wellesley College	354
Wesleyan University	356
Williams College	130
Yale University	158

CHA-CHING!

Schools with a high sticker price—private

Amherst College	238
Barnard College	240
Boston College	246
Bowdoin College	248
Brown University	252
Bryn Mawr College	254
Bucknell University	256
Carleton College	258
Claremont McKenna College	264
College of the Holy Cross	272
Columbia University	276
Cornell University	280
Dartmouth University	282
Duke University	288
Emory University	290
Georgetown University	294
Hamilton College	166
Haverford College	304
Lafayette College	310
Massachusetts Institute of Technology	314
Mount Holyoke College	318
Northwestern University	320
Reed College	326
Scripps College	328
Swarthmore College	134
University of Chicago	336
University of Notre Dame	338
University of Pennsylvania	340
Vanderbilt University	346
Vassar College	348
Wake Forest University	352
Washington University in St. Louis	154
Wellesley College	354
Wesleyan University	358
Williams College	130

CHA-CHING, PART 2

Schools with a high sticker price—public, in-state

Ohio State University—Columbus	408
St. Mary's College of Maryland	414
SUNY College of Environmental Science and Forestry	420
The College of New Jersey	384
University of California—Davis	432
University of California—Los Angeles	436
University of California—Riverside	438
University of California—San Diego	440
University of California—Santa Cruz	444
University of Illinois at Urbana-Champaign	454
University of Maryland—College Park	460
University of Michigan—Ann Arbor	464
University of Pittsburgh at Bradford	480

CHA-CHING, PART 3

Schools with a high sticker price—public, out-of-state

Indiana University—Bloomington	392
Ohio State University—Columbus	408
St. Mary's College of Maryland	414
University of California—Davis	432
University of California—Los Angeles	436
University of California—Riverside	438
University of California—San Diego	440
University of California—Santa Barbara	442
University of California—Santa Cruz	444
University of Colorado, Boulder	448
University of Illinois at Urbana-Champaign	454
University of Maryland—College Park	460
University of Michigan—Ann Arbor	464
University of Pittsburgh at Bradford	480
University of South Carolina Columbia	484
University of Virginia	176
University of Washington	204
University of Wisconsin—Madison	188

AID ME!

Highest percentage of students receiving financial aid

Berea College	214
College of the Ozarks	216
Deep Springs College	220
DePauw University	286
Franklin W. Olin College of Engineering	292
University of Virginia	176
University of Washington	204
University of Wisconsin—Madison	188

CHA-BLING!

Schools that offer free tuition to all students

Berea College	214
College of the Ozarks	216
Franklin W. Olin College of Engineering	292
United States Air Force Academy	222
United States Coast Guard Academy	224
United States Merchant Marine Academy	226
United States Military Academy	228
United States Naval Academy	230
Webb Institute	232

EXPRESS LANE TO COLLEGE

Schools from which the greatest proportion of students graduate within 4 years

Amherst College	238
Barnard College	240
Bates College	242
Bowdoin College	248
Brandeis University	250
Brown University	252
Bucknell University	256
California Institute of Technology	162
Carleton College	258
Claremont McKenna College	264
Colby College	266
Colgate University	268
College of the Holy Cross	272
College of William and Mary	192
Columbia University—Columbia College	276
Cornell University	280
Dartmouth University	282
Davidson College	284
Duke University	288
Emory University	290
Georgetown University	294
Grinnell College	298
Hamilton College	166
Harvard College	142
Haverford College	304
Johns Hopkins University	308
Lafayette College	310
Massachusetts Institute of Technology	314
Middlebury College	316
Pomona College	150
Princeton University	138
Scripps College	328
Swarthmore College	134
Thomas Aquinas College	334
United States Air Force Academy	222
United States Naval Academy	230
University of Pennsylvania	340
University of Virginia	176
Vanderbilt University	346
Vassar College	348
Wellesley College	354
Wesleyan University	358
Williams College	130

HIGHER (AND HIGHER) LEARNING

Schools from which the most number of students go to grad school within 1 year

California Institute of Technology	162
Centenary College of Louisiana	260
Deep Springs College	220
Emory University	290
Reed College	326
United States Military Academy	228

NOT YOUR USUAL SCHEDULE

Schools with 4-4-1 or 4-1-4 academic calendars:

Berea College	214
Centre College	262
Colby College	266
DePauw University	286
Johns Hopkins University	308
Massachusetts Institute of Technology	314
Middlebury College	316
New College of Florida	180
Thomas Aquinas College	334
University of Delaware	450
Williams College	130
Wofford College	364

SCHOOLS THAT DON'T GIVE GRADES

Brown University	252
Evergreen State College	386
Middlebury College	316
New College of Florida	180
University of California—Santa Cruz	444

YOU'RE THE BOSS

Great schools for designing your own major

Brown University	252
Rice University	146
Stanford University	332
University of California—Santa Cruz	444
University of Chicago	336

THE UNDISCOVERED MAJOR

Schools that offer unusual/unconventional majors

Brown University	252
Columbia University	276
Cornell University	280
Massachusetts Institute of Technology	314
University of California—Berkeley	430
University of California—Riverside	438
University of California—Santa Cruz	444

GIVING BACK

Schools with active alumni associations

Clemson University	380
Columbia University	276
Duke University	288
Florida State University	388
Massachusetts Institute of Technology	314
Northwestern University	320
Ohio State University	408
Princeton University	138
Stanford University	332
University of California—Berkeley	430
University of California—Los Angeles	436
University of California—Santa Cruz	444
University of California—Riverside	438
University of Houston	452
University of Michigan	464
University of Notre Dame	338
Yale University	158

BOOKS, BOOKS, EVERYWHERE

Schools with the most extensive library collections

Columbia University (10.4 million volumes)	276
Cornell University (8 million volumes)	280
Duke University (5.5 million volumes)	288
Northwestern University (4.6 million volumes)	320
Ohio State University (5.5 million volumes)	408
Princeton University (7.2 million volumes)	138
Stanford University (9 million volumes)	332
University of California—Berkeley (10 million volumes)	430
University of California—Los Angeles (8 million volumes)	436
University of Chicago (8.5 million volumes)	336
University of Florida (5.3 million volumes)	196
University of Georgia (4 million volumes)	200
University of Illinois—Urbana-Champaign (10 million volumes)	454
University of Kansas (3.8 million volumes)	456
University of Michigan (9.5 million volumes)	464
University of North Carolina—Chapel Hill (5.8 million volumes)	172
University of Oklahoma (4.7 million volumes)	478
University of Pennsylvania (5.8 million volumes)	340
University of Pittsburgh (5.8 million volumes)	482
University of Texas at Austin (9 million volumes)	208
University of Virginia (5 million volumes)	176
University of Washington (6.2 million volumes)	204
University of Wisconsin—Madison (6.1 million volumes)	188
Yale University (12.5 million volumes)	158

ON EXHIBIT

Schools with the best on-campus museums

Colby College (Colby College Museum of Art)	266
Florida State University (Florida State Museum of Fine Arts, John and Mable Ringling Museum of Art)	388
Iowa State University (Brunnier Art Museum, Farm House Museum, Art on Campus Collection, Christian Petersen	

Art Museum) 394
Stanford University (Cantor Arts Center)
University of California—Berkeley (Berkeley Art Museum and Pacific Film Archive, Berkeley Natural History Museums, Lawrence Hall of Science) 332
University of California—Los Angeles (Hammer Museum, Fowler Museum) 436
University of Delaware (University Gallery Collection, Paul R. Jones Collection, Mineralogical Museum) 450
University of Michigan (Exhibit Museum of Natural History, Kelsey Museum of Archaeology, Museum of Art, Museum of Anthropology,Museum of Paleontology, Museum of Zoology) 464
University of North Carolina—Chapel Hill (Ackland Art Museum) 172
University of Pennsylvania (University of Pennsylvania Museum of Archaeology and Anthropology) 340
University of Richmond (Joel and Lila Harnett Museum of Art, Joel and Lila Harnett Print Study Center, Lora Robins Gallery of Design from Nature) 344
Wellesley College (Davis Museum and Cultural Center) 354

PUT IT ON WAX

Schools with recording studios on campus

Columbia University 276
Duke University 288
Johns Hopkins University 308
State University of New York at Buffalo 426
University of California—Berkeley 430
University of California—Irvine 434
University of California—San Diego 440
University of Illinois—Urbana-Champaign 454
University of Michigan 464
University of Missouri—Kansas City 470
University of Texas at Austin 208
University of Washington 204
Wesleyan University 358

AMERICAN GLADIATORS

Schools with the largest stadiums

University of Michigan (Michigan Stadium: 109,901 capacity) 464
University of Tennessee —Knoxville (Neyland Stadium: 102,455 capacity) 488
Ohio State University (Ohio Stadium: 102,329 capacity) 408
University of California—Los Angeles (Rose Bowl: 94,118 capacity) 436
University of Georgia (Sanford Stadium: 92,746) 200
University of Florida (Ben Hill Griffin Stadium: 88,548 capacity) 196
University of Oklahoma (Gaylord Family-Memorial Stadium: 82,112 capacity) 478
Florida State University (Doak Campbell Stadium: 82,000 capacity) 388
Clemson University (Memorial Stadium: 80,301 capacity) 380
University of Notre Dame (Notre Dame Stadium: 80,795 capacity) 338

E PLURIBUS UNUM

Schools with higher student-to-faculty ratios

Florida State University 388
University of Central Florida 446
University of Florida 196
University of North Florida 476
University of Oklahoma 478

CLOSER TO EQUAL

Schools with lower student-to-faculty ratios

California Institute of Technology 162
Columbia University—Columbia College 276
Deep Springs College 220
Emory University 290
Northwestern University 320
Princeton University 138
Rice University 146
Stanford University 332
United States Military Academy 228
United States Naval Academy 230
University of Chicago 336
University of Pennsylvania 340
Washington University in St. Louis 154
Williams College 130
Yale University 158

NO FOREIGN TONGUES NECESSARY

Schools that do not have a general foreign language requirement

Brown University 252
Kansas State University 398
University of Kansas 456

INTERNS NOT OPTIONAL

Schools that require internships

University of Pennsylvania	340
Utah State University	494

THESIS = DIPLOMA

Schools that require a thesis

Bates College	242
California State University—Long Beach	372
Claremont McKenna College	264
Haverford College	304
Massachusetts Institute of Technology	314
Occidental College	322
Princeton University	138
Reed College	326
Rice University	146
University of Chicago	336
University of Virginia (Engineering)	176

A PENNY FOR YOUR THOUGHTS

Schools with great grant programs for independent study

Columbia University	276
Duke University	288
Georgetown University	294
Johns Hopkins University	308
Princeton University	138
Stanford University	332
University of California—Berkeley	430
University of California—Irvine	434
University of Michigan	464
University of Minnesota	468
University of Pennsylvania	340
University of Wisconsin—Madison	188
Yale University	158

BUILDING RAPPORT

Great opportunities to conduct research with professors

Amherst College	238
Brandeis University	250
California Institute of Technology	162
Carleton College	258
College of the Atlantic	270
Cornell College	278
Cornell University	280
Davidson College	284
Franklin W. Olin College of Engineering	292
Harvey Mudd College	302
Haverford College	304
Johns Hopkins University	308
Massachusetts Institute of Technology	314
Northwestern University	320
Sewanee—The University of the South	330
United States Air Force Academy	222
United States Military Academy	228
United States Naval Academy	230
University of California—San Diego	440
University of Chicago	336
University of Texas—Austin	208
University of Wisconsin—Eau Claire	492
University of Wisconsin—Madison	188
Wabash College	350
Webb Institute	232
Wellesley College	354
Yale University	158

APPEARING SOON IN PRINT

Schools that have a track record of publishing undergraduate papers

California Institute of Technology	162
Colby College	266
Dartmouth University	282
Johns Hopkins University	308
Princeton University	138
Sewanee—The University of the South	330
Stanford University	332
University of California—Berkeley	430
University of California—Davis	432
University of California—Los Angeles	436
University of Florida	196
University of Michigan	464
University of Pennsylvania	340
University of Pittsburgh	482
University of South Carolina	484
Yale University	158

IT'S EASY BEING GREEN

Schools with eco-conscious or eco-friendly campuses

College of the Atlantic	270
Georgia Tech	390
University of California—Santa Cruz	444
Harvard	142
SUNY–Binghamton	194
Virginia Tech	496

HERBIVORE'S DELIGHT

Schools with the most vegetarian/vegan-friendly options

Bowdoin College	248
Columbia University	276
Cornell University	280
Stanford University	332
University of California—Berkeley	430
University of California—Santa Cruz	444
University of Maryland—College Park	460
University of Pennsylvania	340
University of Texas at Austin	208
Virginia Tech	496
Vassar College	348
Wesleyan University	358

EY-YI-EY-YI-YO

Schools with organic farms

Carleton College	258
College of the Atlantic	270
College of the Ozarks	216
Cornell University	280
Dartmouth University	282
Iowa State University	394
Middlebury College	316
North Carolina State University	406
Pomona College	150
Stanford University	332
University of California—Davis	432
University of California—Santa Cruz	444
University of Minnesota—Twin Cities	468
University of Wisconsin—Madison	188
Vassar College	348
Yale University	158

THE NATURAL WORLD

Schools with great on-campus arboreta

Cornell University	280
Haverford College	304
North Carolina State University	406
State University of New York at Geneseo	416
Swarthmore College	134
University of California—Davis	432
University of California—Santa Cruz	444
University of Central Florida	446
University of Michigan	464
University of Pennsylvania	340
University of Virginia	176
James Madison University	396
University of Washington	204
University of Wisconsin—Madison	188

THE LIFE BOTANICA

Schools with botanical gardens

Iowa State University	394
Mount Holyoke College	318
University of California—Berkeley	430
University of Delaware	450
University of Georgia	200
University of Michigan	464
University of Tennessee at Knoxville	488
Utah State University	494
Virginia Tech	496

SPLITTING THE ATOM

Schools with on-campus nuclear reactors

Georgia Institute of Technology	390
Kansas State University	398
Massachusetts Institute of Technology	314
North Carolina State University	406
Ohio State University	408
Reed College	326
University of California—Berkeley	430
University of California—Irvine	434
University of Florida	196
University of Maryland—College Park	460
University of Michigan—Ann Arbor	464
University of Tennessee—Knoxville	488
University of Wisconsin—Madison	188

KELLY, WATCH THE STARS

Schools with observatories

Amherst College	238
Brown University	252
California Institute of Technology	162
Colgate University	268
Cornell University	280
Gettysburg College	296
Grinnell College	298
Iowa State University	394
Macalester College	312
Massachusetts Institute of Technology	314
Mount Holyoke College	318
Sewanee—The University of the South	330
Swarthmore College	134
University of California—Berkeley	430
University of California—Santa Cruz	444
University of Central Florida	446
University of Colorado—Boulder	448
University of Delaware	450
University of Oklahoma	478
University of Texas—Austin	208
University of Virginia	176
University of Wisconsin—Eau Claire	492

Vanderbilt University	346
Vassar College	348
Wellesley College	354
Wesleyan University	358
Williams College	130
Yale University	158

QUIET NIGHTS OF QUIET STARS

Schools with planetariums

Amherst College	238
Bates College	242
Berea College	214
Florida State University	388
Gettysburg College	296
Ohio State University	408
State University of New York—New Paltz	418
United States Air Force Academy	222
University of California—Berkeley	430
University of California—Los Angeles	436
University of Georgia	200
University of Michigan—Ann Arbor	464
University of North Carolina—Chapel Hill	172
Williams College	130

TECHNICALLY SPEAKING

Great technical colleges

Franklin W. Olin College of Engineering	292
Webb Institute	232

THE WORLD IS YOURS

Schools with great study abroad programs

Agnes Scott College	236
Bates College	242
Boston College	246
Brandeis University	250
Carleton College	258
Centre College	262
Claremont McKenna College	264
Colby College	266
Duke University	288
Emory University	290
Georgetown University	294
Macalester College	312
Middlebury College	316
Pomona College	150
University of California (All campuses have the UC EAP program)	430
University of Delaware	450
University of Notre Dame	338
University of Texas at Austin	208
Vanderbilt University	346
Wofford College	364

LEAVING ON A JETPLANE

Schools with the greatest proportion of students who study abroad

Source: The Chronicle of Higher Education

Colby College	266
Colgate University	268
DePauw University	286
Duke University	288
Emory University	290
Georgetown University	294
Indiana University—Bloomington	392
Middlebury College	316
Ohio State University	408
University of Georgia	200
University of Illinois—Urbana-Champaign	454
University of Minnesota—Twin Cities	468
University of North Carolina—Chapel Hill	172
University of Notre Dame	338
University of Pennsylvania	340
University of Texas—Austin	208
University of Wisconsin—Madison	188
Vanderbilt University	346

BIOLOGY

Schools with highest biology enrollments

Agnes Scott College	236
Brandeis University	250
Bucknell University	256
Centenary College of Louisiana	260
Colby College	266
College of Charleston	382
Colorado College	274
Cornell University	280
Hanover College	300
Haverford College	304
Hillsdale College	306
Indiana University—Bloomington	392
Mount Holyoke College	318
North Carolina State University	406
Ohio State University—Columbus	408
Pomona College	150
Reed College	326
Rice University	146
Stanford University	332
SUNY at Stony Brook	424
SUNY College at Geneseo	416
Swarthmore College	134
Truman State University	428

University of California—Davis	432
University of California—Irvine	434
University of California—Riverside	438
University of Chicago	336
University of Delaware	450
University of Georgia	200
University of Illinois at Urbana-Champaign	454
University of Kansas	456
University of North Carolina at Chapel Hill	172
University of Tennessee at Martin	490
Virginia Tech	496
Washington University in St. Louis	154
Wofford College	364

COMPUTER/INFORMATION

Schools with highest computer/ information science enrollments

Harvey Mudd College	302
New Mexico Institute of Mining & Technology	404
Stanford University	332
University of California–Irvine	434
University of Maryland–College Park	460

ECONOMICS

Schools with highest economics enrollments

Amherst College	238
Bates College	242
Bowdoin College	248
Brandeis University	250
Carleton College	258
Centre College	262
Claremont McKenna College	264
Colby College	266
Colgate University	268
College of the Holy Cross	272
Colorado College	274
Columbia University—School of General Studies	276
Cornell College	278
Dartmouth University	282
DePauw University	286
Duke University	288
Emory University	290
Grinnell College	298
Hamilton College	166
Harvard College	142
Johns Hopkins University	308
Macalester College	312
Middlebury College	316
Northwestern University	320
Occidental College	322
Pomona College	150
Rice University	146
St. Mary's College of Maryland	414
Swarthmore College	134
The University of Texas at Austin	208
United States Naval Academy	230
University of California—Davis	432
University of California—Irvine	434
University of California—Los Angeles	436
University of California—Santa Barbara	442
University of Chicago	336
University of Michigan—Ann Arbor	464
University of Pennsylvania	340
University of Virginia	176
University of Washington	204
Wellesley College	354
Williams College	130
Yale University	158

EDUCATION

Schools with highest education enrollments

Cornell College	278
CUNY—Brooklyn College	376
SUNY College at New Paltz	418

ENGLISH

Schools with highest English enrollments

Agnes Scott College	236
Amherst College	238
Barnard College	240
Boston College	246
Bryn Mawr College	254
Centre College	262
Christopher Newport University	374
Colby College	266
Colgate University	268
Colorado College	274
Columbia University—Columbia College	276
CUNY—Hunter College	378
Davidson College	284
Georgetown University	294
Haverford College	304
Macalester College	312
Middlebury College	316
Mount Holyoke College	318
Occidental College	322
Pomona College	150
Princeton University	138
Reed College	326
Rice University	146
SUNY at Binghamton	184
The College of New Jersey	384
University of California, Berkeley	430
University of Chicago	336

University of Colorado, Boulder	448
University of Mary Washington	458
University of Michigan—Ann Arbor	464
University of North Carolina at Asheville	472
University of North Carolina—Wilmington	474
University of Richmond	344
University of Tennessee—Knoxville	488
University of Wisconsin—Madison	188
Vassar College	348
Wabash College	350
Wellesley College	354
Wheaton College (IL)	360
Whitman College	362

HISTORY

Schools with highest history enrollments

Bowdoin College	248
Brown University	252
Centre College	262
Colgate University	268
College of the Holy Cross	272
Columbia University—Columbia College	276
Grinnell College	298
Haverford College	304
Hillsdale College	306
Princeton University	138
Wabash College	350
Yale University	158

PHYSICS

Schools with highest physics enrollments

California Institute of Technology	162
Harvey Mudd College	302
New Mexico Institute of Mining & Technology	404

POLITICAL SCIENCE/ GOVERNMENT

Schools with highest poli-sci/ gov't enrollments

Amherst College	238
Bates College	242
Bowdoin College	248
Bryn Mawr College	254
Carleton College	258
Claremont McKenna College	264
College of the Holy Cross	272
College of William and Mary	192
Columbia University—Columbia College	276
Davidson College	284
Georgetown University	294
Gettysburg College	296
Hamilton College	166
Harvard College	142
Macalester College	312
Ohio State University—Columbus	408
Princeton University	138
Scripps College	328
St. Mary's College of Maryland	414
Swarthmore College	134
The University of Texas at Austin	208
United States Coast Guard Academy	224
United States Naval Academy	230
University of California, Berkeley	430
University of California—Los Angeles	436
University of Maryland—CollegePark	460
University of Richmond	344
University of Washington	204
University of Wisconsin—Madison	188
Vassar College	348
Wabash College	350
Wake Forest University	352
Whitman College	362
Williams College	130
Wofford College	364
Yale University	158

PSYCHOLOGY

Schools with highest psychology enrollments

Agnes Scott College	236
Appalachian State University	238
Barnard College	240
Bates College	242
Beloit College	244
Brandeis University	250
Bucknell University	256
California Polytechnic State University—San Luis Obispo	370
Christopher Newport University	374
College of William and Mary	192
Cornell College	278
CUNY—Brooklyn College	376
CUNY—Hunter College	378
Dartmouth University	282
Duke University	288
Emory University	290
Florida State University	388
Gettysburg College	296
Hamilton College	166
Hanover College	300
Harvard College	142
James Madison University	396
Longwood University	400
Middlebury College	316

Mount Holyoke College	318
New College of Florida	180
Ohio State University—Columbus	408
Purdue University—West Lafayette	410
Scripps College	328
St. Mary's College of Maryland	414
SUNY at Binghamton	184
SUNY at Buffalo	426
SUNY at Stony Brook	424
SUNY College at New Paltz	418
The University of South Dakota	486
Truman State University	428
University of California—Davis	432
University of California—Los Angeles	436
University of California—Riverside	438
University of California—Santa Barbara	442
University of California—Santa Cruz	444
University of Central Florida	446
University of Colorado, Boulder	448
University of Delaware	450
University of Florida	186
University of Georgia	200
University of Houston	452
University of Illinois at Urbana-Champaign	454
University of Kansas	456
University of Mary Washington	458
University of North Carolina at Asheville	472
University of North Carolina at Chapel Hill	172
University of North Carolina—Wilmington	474
University of Oklahoma	478
University of Pittsburgh—Pittsburgh Campus	482
University of Redlands	342
University of Tennessee—Knoxville	488
University of Virginia	176
University of Washington	204
University of Wisconsin—Madison	188
Vanderbilt University	346
Vassar College	348
Washington University in St. Louis	154
Wellesley College	354
Wesleyan College	356
Wheaton College (IL)	360
Whitman College	362

LIGHTS, CAMERA, ACTION!

Schools with terrific undergraduate film programs

Brooklyn College	376
California State University—Long Beach	372
Florida State University	388
James Madison University	396
State University of New York at Buffalo	426
University of California—Berkeley	430
University of California—Irvine	434
University of California—Los Angeles	436
University of California—Santa Barbara	442
University of California—Santa Cruz	444
University of Colorado at Boulder	448
University of Chicago	336
University of Florida	196
University of Texas at Austin	208
Wesleyan University	358

YOU TALKIN' TO ME?

Schools with great acting/theater programs

Agnes Scott College	236
Amherst College	238
California State University—Long Beach	372
Florida State University	388
Northwestern University	320
Occidental College	322
University of California—Los Angeles	436
University of California—San Diego	440
University of Chicago	336
Yale University	158

DESIGNS ON YOU

Schools with great graphic design programs

Florida State University	388
North Carolina State University	406

EXTREME MAKEOVER

Schools with great interior design programs

Florida State University	388
University of Florida	196
University of Texas—Austin	208

MAINTAIN YOUR COMPOSURE

Schools with great music composition programs

California State University—Long Beach	372
College of Charleston	382
Florida State University	388
Stanford University	332
University of California—Santa Barbara	442
University of Michigan	464
University of Tennessee	488
Vanderbilt University	346

MUSIC APPRECIATION 101

Schools with great music education programs

Appalachian State University	238
Boston College	246
Florida State University	388
University of North Carolina—Chapel Hill	172

SYMPHONY SPACE

Schools with great music performance programs

Appalachian State University	238
Northwestern University	320
University of California—Berkeley	430
University of California—Los Angeles	436
University of North Carolina—Chapel Hill	172

LENS OF THE BEHOLDER

Schools with great photography programs

College of the Atlantic	270
Harvard College	142
University of Delaware	450
University of Georgia	200
University of Illinois—Urbana-Champaign	454
University of Michigan—Ann Arbor	464

BRING YOUR ART ALIVE

Schools with great studio art programs

Binghamton University	184
University of Texas—Austin	208
University of Wisconsin—Madison	188

INTERESTED IN INTEGERS?

Schools with great mathematics programs

Amherst College	238
Boston College	246
Brown University	252
California Institute of Technology	162
Columbia University	276
Cornell University	280
Duke University	288
Georgetown University	294
Massachusetts Institute of Technology	314
Middlebury College	316
Northwestern University	320
Princeton University	138
Reed College	326
Rice University	146
Stanford University	332
University of California—Berkeley	430
University of Chicago	336
University of Texas—Austin	208

THE REAL WORLD

Schools with great applied mathematics programs

Barnard College	240
Brown University	252
California Institute of Technology	162
College of the Atlantic	270
Columbia University	276
Georgia Institute of Technology	390
Gettysburg College	296
Harvard College	142
Iowa State University	394
North Carolina State University	406
Northwestern University	320
Rice University	146
University of Texas—Austin	208
University of California—Berkeley	430
University of California—Los Angeles	436
University of California—Riverside	438
University of California—San Diego	440
University of California—Santa Cruz	444
Yale University	158

THEY MEAN BUSINESS

Schools with great business/finance programs

Boston College	246
Florida State University	388
Iowa State University	394
Massachusetts Institute of Technology	314
Rice University	146
University of California—Berkeley	430
University of California—Los Angeles	436
University of Florida	196
University of Michigan	464
University of Pennsylvania	340

BUSINESS, THE UNIVERSAL LANGUAGE

Schools with great international business studies programs

Clemson University	380
College of Charleston	382
Cornell College	278

Florida State University	388
Georgetown University	294
Gettysburg College	296
Iowa State University	394
James Madison University	396
University of Maryland—College Park	460
University of Pennsylvania	340
Wofford College	364

KNOW YOUR CUSTOMER

Schools with great marketing and sales programs

Indiana University—Bloomington	392
Iowa State University	394
James Madison University	396
University of Central Florida	446

SO LONG, ABACUS

Schools with great accounting programs

Boston College	246
Bucknell University	256
Claremont McKenna College	264
Clemson University	380
College of Charleston	382
Emory University	290
Georgetown University	294
Indiana University—Bloomington	392
Iowa State University	394
James Madison University	396

FROM BLUEPRINT TO FLYING BUTTRESS

Schools with great architecture programs

California Polytechnic State University—San Luis Obispo	370
Cornell University	280
North Carolina State University	406
University of California—Berkeley	430
University of California—Los Angeles	436
University of Michigan	464
University of Pennsylvania	340
University of Texas—Austin	208
University of Wisconsin—Madison	188
Yale University	158

DO NOT DISTURB

Schools with great tourism and hotel management programs

College of Charleston	382
Cornell University	280
Florida State University	388
James Madison University	396
Ohio State University—Columbus	408
University of Central Florida	446
University of Delaware	450
University of Illinois—Urbana-Champaign	454
University of South Carolina—Columbia	484

TAKE FLIGHT

Schools with great aviation programs

Ohio State University—Columbus	408
United States Air Force Academy	222

BIOLOGICAL IMPULSE

Schools with great biology programs

Agnes Scott College	236
Brandeis University	250
Colby College	266
Cornell University	280
Haverford College	304
Indiana University—Bloomington	392
Mount Holyoke College	318
Ohio State University—Columbus	408
Pomona College	150
Reed College	326
Rice University	146
Swarthmore College	134
University of California—Davis	432
University of Chicago	336
University of Delaware	450
Wofford College	364

BETTER LIVING THROUGH BIOCHEMISTRY

Schools with great biochemistry programs

Bates College	242
Claremont McKenna College	264
Cornell University	280
Florida State University	388
Georgetown University	294
Gettysburg College	296
Iowa State University	394
Pomona College	150
Rice University	146

Swarthmore College	134
University of Texas—Austin	208
University of California—Los Angeles	436
University of California—Riverside	438
University of California—San Diego	440
University of California—Santa Barbara	442
University of Georgia	200

AND NOW FOR SOMETHING MORE COMPLICATED...

Schools with great biomedical engineering programs

Brown University	252
Bucknell University	256
Duke University	288
Georgia Institute of Technology	390
Harvard College	142
Johns Hopkins University	308
Lafayette College	310
Northwestern University	320
Ohio State University—Columbus	408
Rice University	146
University of California—Berkeley	430
University of California—Los Angeles	436
University of California—Riverside	438
University of California—Santa Cruz	444
University of Washington	204
Yale University	158

ALL ABOUT THE CHEMISTRY

Schools with great chemistry programs

California Institute of Technology	162
Columbia University	276
Cornell University	280
Indiana University—Bloomington	392
Johns Hopkins University	308
Massachusetts Institute of Technology	314
Northwestern University	320
Ohio State University	408
Purdue University—West Lafayette	410
Princeton University	138
Rice University	146
University of California—Irvine	434
University of California—Berkeley	430
University of California—Los Angeles	436
University of California—San Diego	440
University of California—Santa Barbara	442
University of Chicago	336
University of Michigan—Ann Arbor	464
University of Minnesota—Twin Cities	468
University of North Carolina—Chapel Hill	172
University of Pennsylvania	340
University of Texas—Austin	208
University of Washington	204
University of Wisconsin—Madison	188
Yale University	158

ENGINEERING YOUR FUTURE

Schools with great engineering programs

California Institute of Technology	162
Columbia University	276
Cornell University	280
Duke University	288
Georgia Institute of Technology	390
Johns Hopkins University	308
Massachusetts Institute of Technology	314
Princeton University	138
Purdue University—West Lafayette	410
Stanford University	352
University of California—Berkeley	430
University of California—Los Angeles	436
University of California—San Diego	440
University of California—Santa Barbara	442
University of Colorado—Boulder	448
University of Illinois—Urbana-Champaign	454
University of Michigan—Ann Arbor	464

BUILDING THE NEXT HAL 9000

Schools with great computer engineering programs

Brown University	252
California Institute of Technology	162
Clemson University	380
Florida State University	388
Georgia Institute of Technology	390
Iowa State University	394
Johns Hopkins University	308
Massachusetts Institute of Technology	314
Northwestern University	320
Princeton University	138
Rice University	146
State University of New York—Binghamton	184
State University of New York—Buffalo	426
United States Air Force Academy	222
University of California—Berkeley	430
University of California—Los Angeles	436
University of California—Riverside	438

I SING THE BODY ELECTRIC

Schools with great electrical engineering programs

Brown University	252
Bucknell University	256
California Institute of Technology	162

Clemson University	380
Cornell University	280
Duke University	288
Florida State University	388
Georgia Institute of Technology	390
Harvard College	142
Iowa State University	394
Massachusetts Institute of Technology	314
Northwestern University	320
Princeton University	138
Rice University	146
University of California—Irvine	434
University of California—Berkeley	430
University of California—Los Angeles	436
University of California—San Diego	440
University of California—Santa Barbara	442
University of California—Santa Cruz	444
University of Delaware	450
Yale University	158

A QUESTION OF MECHANICS

Schools with great mechanical engineering programs

California Institute of Technology	162
Franklin W. Olin College of Engineering	292
Georgia Institute of Technology	390
Iowa State University	394
Massachusetts Institute of Technology	314
North Carolina State University	406
State University of New York—Buffalo	426
United States Military Academy	228
University of Michigan—Ann Arbor	464

SAVE THE WORLD

Schools with great environmental engineering programs

California Institute of Technology	162
Cornell University	280
Dartmouth University	282
Johns Hopkins University	308
Massachusetts Institute of Technology	314
Rice University	146
State University of New York—Buffalo	426
United States Military Academy	228
University of California—Riverside	438
University of Pennsylvania	340
Yale University	158

A BUG'S LIFE

Schools with great entomology programs

College of the Atlantic	270
Cornell University	280
Iowa State University	394
Ohio State University—Columbus	408
Purdue University—West Lafayette	410
University of California—Riverside	438
University of Delaware	450
University of Florida	196
University of Georgia	200
University of Illinois—Urbana-Champaign	454
University of Maryland—College Park	460
University of Wisconsin—Madison	188

CSI UNIVERSITY

Schools with great forensic science programs

College of the Ozarks	216
University of Central Florida	446

TIMBER!

Schools with great forestry programs

Clemson University	380
Cornell College	278
Gettysburg College	296
Iowa State University	394
Ohio State University—Columbus	408
Purdue University—West Lafayette	410
Sewanee—The University of the South	330
University of California—Berkeley	430
University of Florida	196
University of Georgia	200
University of Maryland—College Park	460
University of Michigan—Ann Arbor	464
University of Tennessee—Knoxville	488
University of Washington	204
Wake Forest University	352

SOLID AS A ROCK

Schools with great geology programs

Brown University	252
California Institute of Technology	162
College of Charleston	382
Columbia University	276
Cornell University	280
Duke University	288
Florida State University	388
Iowa State University	394

James Madison University	396
Johns Hopkins University	308
Massachusetts Institute of Technology	314
Pomona College	150
State University of New York—Binghamton	184
State University of New York—Buffalo	426
University of California—Los Angeles	436
University of California—Riverside	438
University of Pennsylvania	340
Yale University	158

THE LIFE AQUATIC

Schools with great marine biology programs

University of California—Los Angeles	436

IN THE LABORATORY

Schools with great medical technology programs

Clemson University	380
College of the Ozarks	216
City University of New York—Hunter College	378
Lafayette College	310
North Carolina State University	406
Ohio State University—Columbus	408
State University of New York—Buffalo	426
State University of New York—Stony Brook	424
University of Texas—Austin	208
University of Central Florida	446
University of Delaware	450

FUTURE FLORENCE NIGHTINGALES

Schools with great nursing programs

University of Pennsylvania	340

EAT YOUR VEGETABLES

Schools with great nutrition programs

Cornell University	280
City University of New York—Brooklyn College	376
City University of New York—Hunter College	378
Florida State University	388
Iowa State University	394
James Madison University	396
Ohio State University—Columbus	408
Purdue University—West Lafayette	410
University of Texas—Austin	208
University of Delaware	450
University of Georgia	200
University of Maryland—College Park	460
University of North Carolina—Chapel Hill	172

SET YOUR CAGED BIRD FREE

Schools with great occupational therapy programs

Lafayette College	310
Ohio State University—Columbus	408
State University of New York—Buffalo	426
University of South Dakota	486
University of Florida	196
University of Tennessee—Knoxville	488

CHECK YOUR PRESCRIPTION

Schools with great pharmacy programs

Ohio State University—Columbus	408
Purdue University—West Lafayette	410
University of Texas—Austin	208

LAWS YOU DON'T WANT TO BREAK

Schools with great physics programs

California Institute of Technology	162
Columbia University	276
Cornell University	280
Harvey Mudd College	302
Indiana University—Bloomington	392
Johns Hopkins University	308
Massachusetts Institute of Technology	314
Northwestern University	320
Ohio State University	408
Purdue University—West Lafayette	410
Princeton University	138
Rice University	146
University of California—Irvine	434
University of California—Berkeley	430
University of California—Los Angeles	436
University of California—San Diego	440
University of California—Santa Barbara	442
University of Chicago	336
University of Michigan—Ann Arbor	464
University of Minnesota—Twin Cities	468
University of North Carolina—Chapel Hill	172
University of Pennsylvania	340
University of Texas—Austin	208
University of Washington	204
University of Wisconsin—Madison	188
Yale University	158

EXPLORING THE MIND
Schools with great psychology programs

Bates College	242
Columbia University	276
Cornell University	280
Dartmouth University	282
Duke University	288
Gettysburg College	296
James Madison University	396
Princeton University	138
University of California—Davis	432
University of California—Los Angeles	436
University of California—Riverside	438
University of California—Santa Barbara	442
University of California—Santa Cruz	444
Yale University	158

HELLO, HELLO?
Schools with great communications programs

Clemson University	380
College of Charleston	382
Cornell University	280
City University of New York—Hunter College	378
Indiana University—Bloomington	392
Iowa State University	394
Northwestern University	320
University of Texas—Austin	208
University of California—San Diego	440
University of California—Santa Barbara	442

INVESTIGATIVE UNDERGRADUATE
Schools with great journalism programs

Northwestern University	320
University of Florida	196
University of North Carolina—Chapel Hill	172
University of Texas—Austin	208
University of Wisconsin—Madison	188

GOODNIGHT AND GOOD LUCK
Schools with great broadcast journalism programs

California State University—Long Beach	372
College of the Ozarks	216
Northwestern University	320
University of California—Los Angeles	436
University of Georgia	200
University of Oklahoma	478

IT'S A LONG WAY FROM ATARI
Schools with great video game design programs

Georgia Institute of Technology	390
Massachusetts Institute of Technology	314
University of Pennsylvania	340
University of California—Irvine	434
University of Central Florida	446
University of Washington	204

TO TEACH OR NOT TO TEACH
Schools with great education programs

Boston College (Lynch)	246
Columbia University (Teachers College)	276
Cornell University	280
Indiana University—Bloomington	392
Johns Hopkins University	308
Ohio State University	408
Stanford University	332
University of California—Berkeley	430
University of Illinois—Urbana-Champaign	454
University of Kansas	456
University of Maryland—College Park	460
University of Michigan—Ann Arbor	464
University of Minnesota—Twin Cities	468
University of Pennsylvania	340
University of Texas—Austin	208
University of Virginia	176
University of Washington	204
University of Wisconsin—Madison	188
Utah State University	494
Vanderbilt University	346

KNOW YOUR FELLOW HUMANS
Schools with great anthropology programs

Amherst College	238
Beloit College	244
Colby College	266
Colgate University	268
College of Charleston	382
Columbia University	276
Cornell University	280
Davidson College	284
Dartmouth University	282
DePauw University	286
Duke University	288
Emory University	290

Florida State University	388
Georgetown University	294
Indiana University—Bloomington	392
Iowa State University	394
James Madison University	396
Johns Hopkins University	308
Mount Holyoke College	318
Northwestern University	320
Princeton University	138
Reed College	326
Rice University	146
Stanford University	332
University of California—Berkeley	430
University of California—Irvine	434
University of California—Los Angeles	436
University of California—Riverside	438
University of California—San Diego	440
University of California—Santa Cruz	444

PAGING DR. JONES...

Schools with great archeology programs

Bowdoin College	248
Brown University	252
Bryn Mawr College	254
Columbia University	276
Cornell University	280
City University of New York—Brooklyn College	376
City University of New York—Hunter College	378
Harvard College	142
Stanford University	332
University of Texas—Austin	208
University of California—Los Angeles	436
University of California—San Diego	440
University of Michigan—Ann Arbor	464
Wesleyan University	358
Wheaton College	360
Yale University	158

LIFTING THE PRINTS

Schools with great criminology programs

North Carolina State University	406
Ohio State University—Columbus	408
University of Delaware	450
University of Maryland—College Park	460

SPEAKING IN GENERAL TERMS

Schools with great general studies programs

Columbia University	276
Stanford University	332
University of California—San Diego	440
University of Pennsylvania	340

AN EYE ON THE PAST

Schools with great history programs

Bowdoin College	248
Brown University	252
Centre College	262
Colgate University	268
College of the Holy Cross	272
Columbia University	276
Grinnell College	298
Haverford College	304
Hillsdale College	306
Princeton University	138
Wabash College	350
Yale University	158

THE COMPANY OF A THOUSAND GOOD BOOKS

Schools with great English literature/ language programs

Amherst College	238
Barnard College	240
Boston College	246
Brown University	252
Claremont McKenna College	264
Clemson University	380
City University of New York—Hunter College	378
Colby College	266
Colgate University	268
Columbia University	276
Cornell University	280
Dartmouth University	282
Duke University	288
Emory University	290
Gettysburg College	296
Princeton University	138
Rice University	146
Stanford University	332
University of California—Berkeley	430
University of Chicago	336
University of Michigan—Ann Arbor	464
Vassar College	348
Wellesley College	354
Yale University	158

VERSE 'TIL THE HEARSE

Schools with great creative writing programs

Brown University	252
Columbia University	276
Princeton University	138
University of California—Riverside	438
University of Florida	196
University of North Carolina—Chapel Hill	172
University of Wisconsin—Madison	188
University of Virginia	176
Vanderbilt University	346
Vassar College	348
Yale University	158

BE A JETSETTER

Schools with great international relations

Brown University	252
Claremont McKenna College	264
Georgetown University	294
Johns Hopkins University	308
University of California—Los Angeles	436

YOUR PAL SOCRATES

Schools with great philosophy programs

Bates College	242
Brown University	252
Columbia University	276
Claremont McKenna College	264
Gettysburg College	296
Princeton University	138
Rice University	146
University of California—Berkeley	430
University of Chicago	336
University of Pennsylvania	340
Yale University	158

POLITICKING

Schools with great political science programs

Amherst College	238
Bates College	242
Bowdoin College	248
Bryn Mawr College	254
Carleton College	258
Claremont McKenna College	264
College of the Holy Cross	272
Columbia University	276
Davidson College	284
Georgetown University	294
Gettysburg College	296
Macalester College	312
Princeton University	138
Stanford University	332
University of California—Berkeley	430
University of California—Los Angeles	436
University of Washington	204
Vassar College	348
Yale University	158

THE SOCIAL LIFE

Schools with great social work programs

Columbia University	276
University of California—Berkeley	430
University of California—Los Angeles	436
University of Michigan	464
University of North Carolina—Chapel Hill	172

IN GOD WE TRUST

Schools with great theology programs

Boston College	246
University of Notre Dame	338

RISK ASSESSMENT

Schools with great actuarial science programs

Florida State University	388
Ohio State University—Columbus	408
University of Central Florida	446
University of Illinois—Urbana-Champaign	454
University of Pennsylvania	340
University of Wisconsin—Madison	188

THE SCIENCE OF SPORTS

Schools with great athletic training programs

Iowa State University	394
University of Florida	196
University of Georgia	200
University of Michigan	464

WHOA, NELLY

Schools with great equine studies programs

Truman State University	428
University of Maryland—College Park	460
University of Minnesota—Crookston	466

GREEN ACRES

Schools with great farming/agriculture programs

Cornell University	280
Iowa State University	394
North Carolina State University	406
University of Delaware	450
University of Tennessee—Knoxville	488

LAYING DOWN THE LAWN

Schools with great turf grass science programs

Clemson University	380
North Carolina State University	406
Ohio State University—Columbus	408
University of Georgia	200
University of Maryland—College Park	460

SAFARI-BOUND

Schools with great outdoor leadership/adventure education programs

Bowdoin College	248
Bucknell University	256

COURTSIDE EVERY NIGHT

Schools with great sports management/sports entertainment programs

Gettysburg College	296
North Carolina State University	406
University of Texas—Austin	208
University of Central Florida	446
University of Delaware	450
University of Georgia	200
University of Michigan—Ann Arbor	464
University of South Carolina—Columbia	484
University of Tennessee—Knoxville	488

PETITION THE COURT

Schools with great prelaw advising (outside of a pre-law program)

Columbia University	276
Duke University	288
Georgetown University	294
Rice University	146
Stanford University	332
University of Chicago	336
University of Illinois—Urbana-Champaign	454
Washington University in St. Louis	154
Wesleyan University	356

WHAT'S THE PROGNOSIS?

Schools with great pre-med advising (outside of a pre-med program)

Brandeis University	250
California Institute of Technology	162
Cornell University	280
Georgia Institute of Technology	390
Haverford College	304
Johns Hopkins University	308
Massachusetts Institute of Technology	314
Northwestern University	320
Princeton University	138
Stanford University	332
University of California—Berkeley	430
University of Chicago	336
Washington University in St. Louis	154
Yale University	158

FLUFFY WILL THANK YOU

Schools with great pre-vet programs

Cornell University	280
North Carolina State University	406
Reed College	326
University of Florida	196
University of Georgia	200

A VIEW TO MED SCHOOL

Schools with great pre-med programs

Cornell University	280
Duke University	288
Johns Hopkins University	308
Stanford University	332
University of California—Los Angeles	436
University of Michigan	464
University of Pennsylvania	340
University of Wisconsin—Madison	188
Yale University	158

GREED IS GOOD
Schools that encourage entrepreneurial endeavors

Boston College	246
Columbia University	276
Georgia Institute of Technology	390
Harvey Mudd College	302
Massachusetts Institute of Technology	314
Princeton University	138
Rice University	146
Stanford University	332
University of California—Los Angeles	436
University of Illinois—Urbana-Champaign	454
University of Maryland—College Park	460
University of North Carolina—Chapel Hill	172
University of Notre Dame	338
Yale University	158
Washington University in St. Louis	154

A COOPERATIVE MANNER
Schools that have great co-op programs

California Polytechnic State University—San Luis Obispo	370
Cornell University	280
Georgia Institute of Technology	390
State University of New York—Buffalo	426
University of Houston	452
University of Texas—Austin	208
University of Washington	204

ENLISTED SERVICE
Schools with great ROTC programs

Boston College	246
College of the Holy Cross	272
Georgetown University	294
Massachusetts Institute of Technology	314
University of California—Berkeley	430
University of California—Davis	432
University of Illinois—Urbana-Champaign	454
University of Notre Dame	338
University of Pennsylvania	340
University of South Carolina	484
University of Washington	204
Virginia Tech	496

GET REAL PAID
Schools with great fellowship opportunities

Amherst College	238
Bates College	242
Boston College	246
Brown University	252
Bryn Mawr College	254
Massachusetts Institute of Technology	314
Stanford University	332
Swarthmore College	134
University of Chicago	336
University of Pittsburgh	482
University of Washington	204
Yale University	158

APPLY HERE
Schools with great opportunities for off-campus employment

Columbia University	276
Rice University	146
University of California—Berkeley	430
University of California—Los Angeles	436
University of California—San Diego	440
University of Central Florida	446
University of Chicago	336
University of Houston	452
University of Pennsylvania	340
University of Texas—Austin	208
University of Washington	204

ALL ABOARD!
Schools that offer subsidies to students who use public transportation

Brown University	252
California Institute of Technology	162
California Polytechnic State University—San Luis Obispo	370
Emory University	290
Massachusetts Institute of Technology	314
Rice University	146
Stanford University	332
University of California—Berkeley	430
University of California—Davis	432
University of North Carolina—Chapel Hill	172
Williams College	130

ENRICHING WHILE LEARNING
Schools that spend a good percentage of their federal work-study funds on community service

Source: The Washington Post/U.S. News and World

Brown University	252
California Institute of Technology	162

Columbia University	276
Cornell University	280
Duke University	288
Emory University	290
Johns Hopkins University	308
Massachusetts Institute of Technology	314
Northwestern University	320
Princeton University	138
Rice University	146
Stanford University	332
University of California—Berkeley	430
University of Chicago	336
University of Notre Dame	338
University of Pennsylvania	340
University of Washington	204
Yale University	158

MO' MONEY, MO' OPPORTUNITES

Schools with largest endowments

Amherst College	238
Boston College	246
Brown University	252
California Institute of Technology	162
Columbia University	276
Cornell University	280
Dartmouth University	282
Duke University	288
Emory University	290
Grinnell College	298
Massachusetts Institute of Technology	314
Northwestern University	320
Ohio State University	408
Princeton University	138
Rice University	146
Stanford University	332
Swarthmore College	134
University of Chicago	336
University of Delaware	450
University of Michigan	464
University of North Carolina—Chapel Hill	172
University of Notre Dame	338
University of Pennsylvania	340
University of Pittsburgh	482
University of Richmond	344
University of Virginia	176
University of Washington	204
Vanderbilt University	346
Wellesley College	354
Williams College	130

ACTIVELY EMPLOYING

Schools that attract the largest proportion of recruiters

Source: Wall Street Journal

College of William and Mary	192
Dartmouth University	282
Emory University	290
University of Michigan	464
Northwestern University	320
Ohio State University	408
Princeton University	138
Stanford University	332
University of California—Berkeley	430
University of Chicago	336
University of Michigan	464
University of North Carolina—Chapel Hill	172
University of Notre Dame	338
University of Texas—Austin	208
Vanderbilt University	346
Wake Forest University	352
Yale University	158

BIG BROTHER IS WATCHING

Colleges where the State Department typically recruits

Georgetown University	294
University of Texas—Austin	208

PEACE INCORPORATED

Schools from which the highest proportion of graduates join the Peace Corps.

Source: Peace Corps.

Boston College	246
Brown University	252
College of William and Mary	192
Colorado College	274
Cornell University	280
Dartmouth University	282
Evergreen State College	386
Georgetown University	294
Grinnell College	298
Indiana University—Bloomington	392
James Madison University	396
Middlebury College	316
Mount Holyoke College	318
Northwestern University	320
University of California—Berkeley	430
University of California—Los Angeles	436
University of California—Santa Cruz	444
University of Chicago	336
University of Colorado—Boulder	448

University of Mary Washington	458
University of Michigan—Ann Arbor	464
University of Minnesota—Twin Cities	468
University of North Carolina—Chapel Hill	172
University of Pennsylvania	340
University of Texas—Austin	208
University of Virginia	176
University of Washington	204
University of Wisconsin—Madison	188
Wake Forest University	352
Wellesley College	354
Wesleyan University	356

COME FOR THE SCHOOL, STAY FOR THE CITY

Great job markets in the cities where these schools are located

Source: Inc. (According to a recent report, these cities have great job markets)

Colorado College (Colorado Springs, Colorado)	274
Duke University (Durham, North Carolina)	288
Emory University (Atlanta, Georgia)	290
New College of Florida (Sarasota, Florida)	180
North Carolina State University (Raleigh, North Carolina)	406
United States Air Force Academy (Colorado Springs, Colorado)	222
University of Central Florida (Orlando, Florida)	446
University of North Carolina—Chapel Hill (Chapel Hill, North Carolina)	172
University of Texas—Austin (Austin, Texas)	208

SOMETHING FOR EVERYONE

Schools with lots of on-campus organizations

California Polytechnic State University—San Luis Obispo	370
College of William and Mary	192
Columbia University	276
Cornell University	280
Dartmouth University	282
Florida State University	388
Georgia Institute of Technology	390
Indiana University—Bloomington	392
Iowa State University	394
Kansas State University	398
Massachusetts Institute of Technology	314
North Carolina State University	406
Northwestern University	320
Ohio State University—Columbus	408
Purdue University—West Lafayette	410
Stanford University	332
SUNY at Buffalo	426
The University of Texas at Austin	208
University of California, Berkeley	430
University of California—Davis	432
University of California—Irvine	434
University of California—Los Angeles	436
University of California—Santa Barbara	442
University of Central Florida	446
University of Colorado, Boulder	448
University of Florida	196
University of Georgia	200
University of Houston	452
University of Illinois at Urbana-Champaign	454
University of Kansas	456
University of Maryland—College Park	460
University of Michigan—Ann Arbor	464
University of Minnesota, Twin Cities	468
University of North Carolina at Chapel Hill	172
University of Oklahoma	478
University of Pennsylvania	340
University of Pittsburgh—Pittsburgh Campus	482
University of South Carolina Columbia	484
University of Tennessee—Knoxville	488
University of Virginia	176
University of Wisconsin—Madison	188
Vanderbilt University	346
Virginia Tech	496

THE SPORTING LIFE

Top sports universities

University of California—Los Angeles	436
University of Florida	196
University of Georgia	200
University of Tennessee	488
University of Texas—Austin	208
University of Wisconsin—Madison	188

NEXT STOP: THE BIG LEAGUES

Schools with greatest number of professionally drafted players

Duke University	288
Florida State University	388
University of Michigan	464
University of Notre Dame	338

YOUR MASCOT IS WHAT!?

Schools with unusual mascots

University of California—Irvine (Anteater)	434
University of California—	

Santa Cruz (Banana Slug)	444
University of Richmond (Spider)	344
University of South Carolina—Columbia (Gamecock)	484

THEM VERSUS U.

Schools with famous/infamous rivalries

California Institute of Technology vs. Massachusetts Institute of Technology	314
Columbia University vs. Princeton University	138
Cornell University vs. University of Pennsylvania	280
Duke University vs. University of North Carolina—Chapel Hill	288
Florida State University vs. University of Miami	388
Georgetown University vs. Syracuse University	294
Harvard University vs. Yale University	158
Ohio State University vs. University of Michigan	408
Oklahoma State University vs. University of Oklahoma	478
Stanford University vs. University of California—Berkeley	332
Texas State University vs. University of Oklahoma	478
United States Military Academy vs. United States Naval Academy	228
University of California—Los Angeles vs. University of Southern California	436
University of Connecticut vs. University of Pittsburgh	482
University of Florida vs. University of Tennessee	196
University of Kansas vs. University of Missouri—Columbia	45
University of Notre Dame vs. University of Southern California	338
University of Oregon vs. University of Washington	204

GRIDIRON GLORY

Schools with great football programs

Boston College	246
Clemson University	380
Northwestern University	320
Ohio State University	408
University of California—Los Angeles	436
University of Florida	196
University of Georgia	200
University of Notre Dame	338
University of Oklahoma	478

DIAMOND DAYS

Schools with great baseball programs

Clemson University	380
Florida State University	388
Rice University	146
Stanford University	332
University of Florida	196
University of Kansas	456
University of South Carolina	484
University of Tennessee	488

SLAM DUNK

Schools with great basketball programs

Duke University	288
Stanford University	332
University of California—Los Angeles	436
University of Notre Dame	338
University of Tennessee	488

GOAL!!!

Schools with great soccer programs

Boston College	246
Duke University	288
Florida State University	388
University of California—Los Angeles	436
University of Notre Dame	338
University of Virginia	176

CHECK YOURSELF

Schools with great hockey programs

Boston College	246
Colgate University	268
Colorado College	274
Cornell University	280
Dartmouth University	282
Princeton University	138
University of Michigan	464

PAR FOR THE COURSE

Schools with great golf programs

Duke University	288
Emory University	290
Florida State University	388
Georgetown University	294
Georgia Institute of Technology	390
Northwestern University	320
Princeton University	138
Stanford University	332
University of California—Davis	432
University of California—Irvine	434
University of California—Los Angeles	436

University of California—Riverside	438
University of California—San Diego	440
University of Florida	198
University of Georgia	200
University of Michigan	464
University of Virginia	176
University of Washington	204
Vanderbilt University	346
Wake Forest University	352
Yale University	158

FIELD OF GREENS

Top-notch on-campus golf courses

Cornell University	280
Middlebury College	316
Ohio State University	408
Stanford University	332
University of Florida	196
Vassar College	348

ARTIFICAL MOUNTAIN

Schools with on-campus rock-climbing walls

Stanford University	332
University of California—Riverside	438
University of California—Santa Cruz	444

BULLSEYE!

Schools with great archery programs

Columbia University	276
James Madison University	396
Stanford University	332
University of California—Los Angeles	436

THE WORLD'S FASTEST RACQUET SPORT

Schools with great badminton programs

Bates College	242
Bryn Mawr College	254
Cornell University	280
Swarthmore College	134
University of California—Los Angeles	436

PUGILISTS UNITE!

Schools with great boxing programs

United States Air Force Academy	222
United States Military Academy	228
United States Naval Academy	230

GIVE ME A C-H-E-E-R

Schools with great cheerleading programs

College of Charleston	382
Duke University	288
North Carolina State University	406
University of Florida	196
University of Kansas	456
University of Oklahoma	478
University of Tennessee	488

ROW YOUR BOAT

Schools with great crew/ rowing programs

Brown University	252
Columbia University	276
Cornell University	280
Dartmouth University	282
Georgetown University	294
Massachusetts Institute of Technology	314
Mount Holyoke College	318
Princeton University	138
United States Naval Academy	230
University of California—Berkeley	430
University of Pennsylvania	340
University of Washington	204
Yale University	158

A KINDER, GENTLER GAME

Schools with great flag football teams

Florida State University	388
University of Central Florida	446
University of Florida	196

GYMNAST UTOPIA

Schools with great gymnastics programs

College of William and Mary	192
Ohio State University	408
Stanford University	332
United States Military Academy	228
United States Naval Academy	230
University of California—Los Angeles	436
University of Georgia	200
University of Michigan	464
University of Oklahoma	478

WE CAME LACROSSE THESE...

Schools with great lacrosse programs

Bucknell University	256
Cornell University	280
Duke University	288
Georgetown University	294
Johns Hopkins University	308
Northwestern University	320
Princeton University	138
University of Virginia	176

HORSE & MALLET

Schools with great polo programs

Cornell University	280
Ohio State University	408
Stanford University	332
University of California—Davis	432
University of Georgia	200
University of Texas—Austin	208
University of Virginia	176
Vassar College	348
Yale University	158

CALL ME ISHMAEL

Schools with great sailing programs

Boston College	246
College of Charleston	382
Stanford University	332
United States Naval Academy	230
Yale University	158

A KINDER, GENTLER BASEBALL

Schools with great softball programs

Northwestern University	320
Stanford University	332
University of California—Los Angeles	436
University of Georgia	200
University of Michigan	464
University of Oklahoma	478
University of Tennessee	488
University of Washington	204

FROM THE HIGH DIVE YOU CAN SEE FOR MILES

Schools with great swimming/ diving programs

Dartmouth University	282
Emory University	290
Ohio State University	408
Stanford University	332
University of Michigan	464
Yale University	158

YOU GOT SERVED

Schools with great tennis programs

Duke University	288
Northwestern University	320
Rice University	146
Stanford University	332
University of California—Los Angeles	436
University of Florida	196
University of Georgia	200
University of Illinois—Urbana-Champaign	454
University of Notre Dame	338
University of Texas—Austin	208
Vanderbilt University	346

INDOOR DECATHALON

Schools with great indoor track and field programs

Stanford University	332
University of California—Los Angeles	436
University of Tennessee	488

OUTDOOR DECATHALON

Schools with great outdoor track and field programs

Stanford University	332
University of California—Los Angeles	436
University of South Carolina	484
University of Tennessee	488

OVER THE RIVER AND THROUGH THE WOODS

Schools with great cross-country programs

College of William and Mary	192
Dartmouth University	282
Florida State University	388
Georgetown University	294
Ohio State University	408
Stanford University	332
University of Florida	196
University of Kansas	456
University of Notre Dame	338
University of Tennessee	488

University of Virginia	176

SIDEOUT

Schools with great volleyball programs

Ohio State University	408
Princeton University	138
Stanford University	332
University of California—Los Angeles	436
University of California—Santa Barbara	442
University of Wisconsin—Madison	188

REMEMBER YOUR SPEEDO

Schools with great water polo programs

Princeton University	138
Stanford University	332
University of California—Berkeley	430
University of California—Davis	432
University of California—Irvine	434
University of California—Los Angeles	436
University of California—San Diego	440
University of California—Santa Barbara	442
University of Michigan	464
University of Redlands	342

NO HOLDS BARRED

Schools with great wrestling programs

Iowa State University	394
University of Central Florida	446
University of Florida	196

FOUR BALLS UP IN THE AIR

Schools with great juggling clubs

Brown University	252
California Institute of Technology	162
Massachusetts Institute of Technology	314
Stanford University	332
University of California—Berkeley	430
University of Georgia	200
University of Illinois—Urbana-Champaign	454
University of Notre Dame	338
University of Texas—Austin	208
Whitman College	362
Yale University	158

THE GREAT OUTDOORS

Schools with great outdoor adventure clubs

Amherst College	238
Bates College	242
Binghamton University	184
Boston College	246
Brandeis University	250
Massachusetts Institute of Technology	314
University of California—Riverside	438
University of California—Santa Cruz	444
Whitman College	362

CLIFFHANGING

Schools with great rock-climbing clubs

Colby College	266
Ohio State University	408
University of California—Riverside	438

HIT THE SLOPES

Schools with great skiing/ snowboarding opportunities

Colby College	266
Colorado College	274
Middlebury College	316
University of Colorado—Boulder	448

SURFS UP!

Schools with great surfing opportunities

University of California—San Diego	440
University of California—Santa Barbara	442
University of California—Santa Cruz	444
University of Central Florida	446

8 SECONDS TO GLORY

Schools with rodeo programs

California Polytechnic State University—San Luis Obispo	370
Iowa State University	394
Kansas State University	398
University of Georgia	200
University of Tennessee—Martin	490

SOME FOLKS CALL IT FLATBALL

Schools with great ultimate Frisbee clubs

Brown University	252
Bucknell University	256
Carleton College	258
College of William and Mary	192
Stanford University	332
University of California—Berkeley	430
University of California—Davis	432
University of California—San Diego	440
University of California—Santa Barbara	442
University of California—Santa Cruz	444
University of Chicago	336
University of Georgia	200

LEND A HAND

Schools with active community service programs/student volunteer work

College of William and Mary	192
Stanford University	332
University of California—Los Angeles	436
University of California—Santa Cruz	444
University of Wisconsin—Eau Claire	492
Vassar College	348
Wesleyan University	358

LITERARY LANDMARKS

Schools with great literary magazines

Columbia University (Columbia Review)	276
Gettysburg College (Gettysburg Review)	296
Massachusetts Institute of Technology (Boston Review)	314
University of California—Irvine (Faultline)	434
University of California—Riverside (Crate)	438
University of Houston (Gulf Coast)	452
University of Georgia (Georgia Review)	200
University of Virginia (Meridian)	176

BACH 'TIL YOU DROP

Schools with great choral ensembles

Columbia University	276
Cornell University	280
Gettysburg College	296
Iowa State University	394
Princeton University	138
University of California—Berkeley	430
University of Michigan	464
University of North Carolina—Chapel Hill	172
University of Pennsylvania	340
Yale University	158

JUST DOO IT

Schools with great a capella programs

Amherst College	238
Brown University	252
College of William and Mary	192
Columbia University	276
Cornell University	280
Duke University	288
Northwestern University	320
Princeton University	138
Stanford University	332
Swarthmore College	134
University of Maryland—College Park	460
University of Michigan	464
University of North Carolina—Chapel Hill	172
University of Pennsylvania	340
University of Virginia	176
Washington University in St. Louis	154
Yale University	158

WORLD MUSIC

Schools with unusual musical groups (e.g., steel pan groups, gamelan groups)

Bates College (Steelpan, Gamelan)	242
Cornell College (Steelpan)	278
Massachusetts Institute of Technology (Gamelan)	314
Pomona College (Gamelan)	150
Swarthmore College (Gamelan)	134
University of California—Los Angeles (Gamelan)	436
University of California—Riverside (Gamelan)	438
University of California—Santa Cruz (African Drums)	444
University of Maryland—College Park (Gamelan)	460
Wesleyan University (Gamelan)	358

DORM ME UP, SCOTTY!

Schools with majority of students living in university housing

Agnes Scott College	236
Amherst College	238
Bates College	242
Beloit College	244
Bowdoin College	248

Bryn Mawr College	254
California Institute of Technology	162
Carleton College	258
Centre College	262
Claremont McKenna College	264
Colby College	266
Columbia University—Columbia College	276
Cornell College	278
Davidson College	284
Deep Springs College	220
DePauw University	286
Emory University , Oxford College	290
Franklin W. Olin College of Engineering	292
Gettysburg College	296
Hamilton College	166
Hanover College	300
Harvard College	142
Harvey Mudd College	302
Haverford College	304
Lafayette College	310
Massachusetts Institute of Technology	314
Middlebury College	316
Mount Holyoke College	318
Pomona College	150
Princeton University	138
Scripps College	328
Sewanee—The University of the South	330
Stanford University	332
Swarthmore College	134
Thomas Aquinas College	334
United States Air Force Academy	222
United States Coast Guard Academy	224
United States Merchant Marine Academy	226
United States Military Academy	228
United States Naval Academy	230
University of Richmond	344
Vassar College	348
Webb Institute	232
Wellesley College	354
Wesleyan University	358
Wheaton College (IL)	360
Williams College	130
Wofford College	364

CAMPUS LOCKDOWN

Strict Campuses

(Source: College Prowler)

Colby College	266
United States Military Academy	228
United States Naval Academy	230
University of Central Florida	446
University of Notre Dame	338

CAMPUS FREEDOM

Relaxed campuses

(Source: College Prowler)

Beloit College	244
Bryn Mawr College	254
Carleton College	258
Colgate University	268
Columbia University	276
Harvey Mudd College	302
Haverford College	304
Macalester College	312
Swarthmore College	134
University of Georgia	200
University of Pennsylvania	340
University of Virginia	176
Vanderbilt University	346
Yale University	158

CWANT PSIS WITH THAT?

Schools with great Greek life participation

Bucknell University	256
Centenary College of Louisiana	260
Centre College	262
Colgate University	268
College of William and Mary	192
Cornell College	278
Cornell University	280
Dartmouth University	282
DePauw University	286
Duke University	288
Emory University	290
Gettysburg College	296
Hanover College	300
Hillsdale College	306
Lafayette College	310
Massachusetts Institute of Technology	314
Northwestern University	320
Sewanee—The University of the South	330
Truman State University	428
University of Richmond	344
University of Virginia	176
Vanderbilt University	346
Wabash College	350
Wake Forest University	352
Washington University in St. Louis	154
Whitman College	362
Wofford College	364

THE MAN GOT YOU DOWN?

Politically active schools

Claremont McKenna College	264

Columbia University	276
Georgetown University	294
Harvard College	142
Macalester College	312
New College of Florida	180
Princeton University	138
United States Air Force Academy	222
United States Naval Academy	230
University of California—Berkeley	430
University of California—San Diego	440
University of Chicago	336
University of Delaware	450
University of Mary Washington	458
University of South Carolina—Columbia	484
University of Washington	204
University of Wisconsin—Madison	188
Wesleyan University	358

CONSERVATIVELY INCLINED

Most politically conservative schools

Clemson University	280
College of the Ozarks	216
Hillsdale College	306
James Madison University	396
Thomas Aquinas College	334
United States Air Force Academy	222
United States Merchant Marine Academy	226
United States Military Academy	228
Wheaton College	360
Wofford College	364

LIBERALLY INCLINED

Politically liberal schools

College of the Atlantic	270
Columbia University	276
The Evergreen State College	386
Grinnell College	298
Macalester College	312
New College of Florida	180
Reed College	326
University of California—Berkeley	430
University of California—Santa Barbara	442
University of California—Santa Cruz	444
Vassar College	348
Wesleyan University	358

WELCOME TO COLLEGE

Schools with exciting freshman orientations

Bucknell University	256
Columbia University	276
Rice University	146
University of California—Riverside	438
University of Chicago	336

TUNE IN

Schools with great college radio stations

Bates College	242
Brown University	252
Carleton College	258
DePauw University	286
Evergreen State College	386
Grinnell College	298
Reed College	326
University of California—Riverside	438
Washington University in St. Louis	154
Whitman College	362

BRING YOUR FLIP-FLOPS

Schools with warm weather campuses

California Institute of Technology	162
Florida State University	388
Occidental College	322
University of California—Irvine	434
University of California—Los Angeles	436
University of California—Riverside	438
University of California—San Diego	440
University of California—Santa Barbara	442
University of Central Florida	446
University of Florida	196

BRING YOUR MITTENS

Schools with cold weather campuses

Beloit College	244
Cornell University	280
Middlebury College	316
Northwestern University	320
State College of New York—Buffalo	426
University of Chicago	336
University of Michigan	464
University of Notre Dame	338

GOODNESS GRACIOUS

Schools with religious affiliation

Episcopal

Sewanee—The University of the South	330

Lutheran

Gettysburg College	296

Methodist

Centenary College of Louisiana	260
Cornell College	278
DePauw University	286
Duke University	288
Emory University	290
Emory University , Oxford College	290
Wesleyan College	356
Wofford College	364

Presbyterian

Agnes Scott College	236
Centre College	262
College of the Ozarks	216
Davidson College	284
Hanover College	300
Lafayette College	310
Macalester College	312

Roman Catholic

Boston College	246
College of the Holy Cross	272
Georgetown University	294
Thomas Aquinas College	344
University of Notre Dame	338

WHERE THERE'S SMOKE...

Schools with the highest fire safety ratings (Based on student residence hall fire prevention practices and policies)

Boston College	246
CUNY—Hunter College	378
Franklin W. Olin College of Engineering	292
University of California—Santa Barbara	442
University of Colorado, Boulder	448
University of Minnesota—Crookston	466
University of North Carolina at Asheville	472
University of Notre Dame	338
University of Washington	204
Wake Forest University	352
Williams College	130

SHHHHH...IT'S A SECRET

Schools with secret societies

College of William & Mary
(Bishop James Madison Society, Flat Hat Club) 192

Cornell University
(Quill and Dagger, Sphinx Head Society) 280

Dartmouth University
(Sphinx Senior Society) 282

Georgetown University
(Cloak and Dagger) 294

Georgia Institute of Technology
(Anak Society) 390

Northwestern University
(DERU) 320

University of Georgia
(Order of the Acropolis, Order of the Greek Horsemen) 200

University of Michigan —Ann Arbor
(Michigamua) 464

University of North Carolina—Chapel Hill
(Order of Gimghoul) 172

University of Pennsylvania
(Owl Society) 340

University of Texas—Austin
(The Eyes of Texas) 208

University of Virginia
(IMP Society, Seven Society, Skull and Bones, Z Society) 176

Wesleyan University
(Mystical 7) 356

Yale University
(Berzelius, Book and Snake, Elihu, Scroll and Key, Wolf's Head) 158

IN THE NAME OF TRADITION

Schools with wacky college traditions

Bates College
(Each St. Patrick's Day, come for the "Puddle Jump," stay for the hypothermia) 242

Brown University
(Too many to mention, but includes a gate you don't want to go through twice, a naked donut run, and various sundry activities in the science library) 252

Carleton College
(Exorcise your pent up anger the night before finals with a campus-wide primal scream) 258

Cornell University
(Celebrate the first day of school by skipping class and relaxing with your fellow students on "Slope Day") 280

Mount Holyoke College
(Each weeknight at 9:30pm, the cafeterias open to serve milk and cookies to students in need) 318

Pomona College
(Join the mysterious Muftis in their campus-papering exploits) 150

Princeton University
(Beware the administrators and elements when partaking in the naked run through campus during the first snowfall of the year) 138

Sewanee:
The University of the South (Know how to spot the smartest kids in class? They're the ones in the gowns. Get similar grades and you too can join the "Order of the Gownsmen") 134

Vassar College
(Each year both students and faculty unite to witness freshmen serenade seniors, and seniors assault freshmen with water balloons, shaving cream, and flour. Ah, academia...) 348

AN EDUCATED JOKE

Schools with a history of amazing pranks

California Institute of Technology
(Altering the "Hollywood" sign to read "Caltech," exploiting a lucrative loophole in a McDonald's promotion, and asserting their dominance over MIT on the scoreboard at the Rose Bowl) 162

Carleton College
(The disappearing reappearing bust of Schiller and the Goodhue Daylight Savings Time phenomenon) 258

Cornell University
(A lion in the gym, a pumpkin and disco ball impaled upon the McGraw tower's spire, and the 1930 appearance of Hugo N. Frye, much to the Republican Party's embarrassment) 280

DePauw University
(A high-story stunt during class) 286

Harvey Mudd College
(From relocating the dean's office to turning a student's room into an aquarium, entertaining yet reversible pranks are king on this campus) 302

Haverford College
(It's quite simple: Chevy Chase went here) 304

Johns Hopkins University
(Every spoon in the cafeteria "planted" on the lawn) 308

Massachusetts Institute of Technology
(Besides introducing the word "hack," students have turned the Great Dome into R2-D2's head, disguised the university president's door as a bulletin board, and inflated a massive balloon on the playing field during a Harvard-Yale game) 314

Ohio State University
(Students here formed the "Arm the Homeless Coalition," proving that just because you don't have a home doesn't mean you don't need protection) 408

Princeton University
(The creation of the "Veterans of Future Wars," a sarcastic league of gentlemen looking for their eventual wartime bonus) 138

Rice University
(An entire campus showed up at the student health care center with cups of urine after they received forged doctor's notes—what happened after wasn't pretty) 146

Stanford University
(After losing the game to Berkeley , the printing of a fake newspaper led their rivals to believe the referees' ruling had been overturned) 332

University of California—Berkeley
(Holding Stanford's mascot "The Tree" for ransom and the duping of USC's starting guard via instant messenger and a girl named Victoria) 430

University of Wisconsin—Madison
(Successfully brought the Statue of Liberty to Madison , even if it was only plywood) 188

Wabash College
(Stealing the Monon Bell from DePauw University) 350

Yale University
(Managed to have the Harvard crowd raise signs that read WE SUCK instead of GO HARVARD) 158

WHO YOU GONNA CALL?

Schools with haunted campuses

Bucknell University
(At Hunt Hall, a woman in a red raincoat is said to appear and play tricks on students) 256

University of Notre Dame
(Washington Hall can count the "Gipper"—of the "Win one for the Gipper" fame—as one of its otherworldly tenants) 338

WE WANT TO HEAR FROM YOU

To all of our readers, we welcome your feedback on how we can continue to improve this guide.
We hope you will share with us your comments, questions, and suggestions.
Please contact us at **editorialsupport@review.com**.

Our annual list, along with statistics and analysis about students, admissions, academics, and financial aid information continues to be available on our website, at www.PrincetonReview.com and on the unique Best Value Colleges area at USA TODAY's site—bestvaluecolleges.usatoday.com—as a free, online, and interactive database.

Top 10
Private Colleges

#1

Williams College

Williamstown, MA

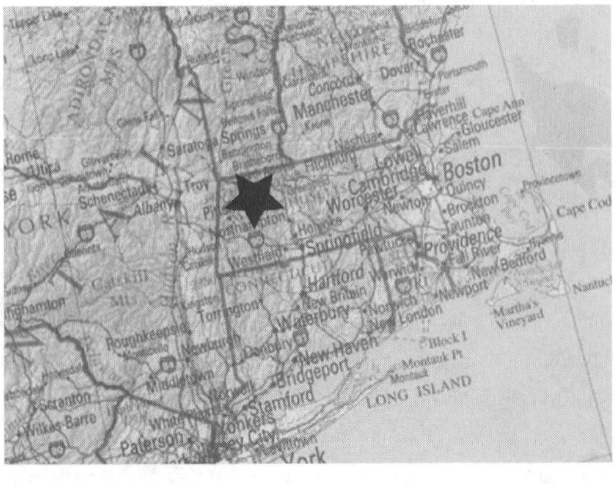

STUDENTS

1,996 undergrad enrollment

49% Male

51% Female

ADMISSIONS

6,631 applicants	→ **19%** admitted	**44%** enrolled	**EARLY ADMISSIONS**	→ **NR** applicants	**NR** accepted

NR avg. high school gpa

ACT range (0–36): 29–34

SAT range (200–800): reading **660–770**, math **650–760**

90% graduated top 10% of class

98% graduated top 25% of class

FINANCIAL INFO

$42,938 annual tuition	**$11,370** room & board	**$800** avg. book expenses	**$252** required fees

$8,369 avg. indebtedness

ACADEMICS

7:1 student to faculty ratio

0% classes taught by TAs

GRADUATION RATES

91% of students graduating within 4 years

95% of students graduating within 6 years

* NR = Not reported

Why Williams College is No. 1

Williams College is a small bastion of the liberal arts with a fantastic academic reputation. The school's location in the middle of the mountains fosters a campus-centric intimacy that's only furthered by its unique first-year living program (which dates back to 1925), which creates small, comfortable groups (called entries) who live alongside two Junior Advisors who serve as nurturing mentors. Classes are small, and utilize conventions such as tutorials and experiential learning to encourage students to learn together through osmosis. Professors jump at the chance to interact with students, and research opportunities are plentiful, with hundreds of students a year receiving support in funded summer research or internship projects.

If you can get into Williams, you can afford to attend; the school has increased financial aid in recent years, and now more than half of its students receive it in some form. Tucked away in the mountains, students happily enter into a little liberal arts bubble, where they learn to take their studies, not themselves, seriously. The school's mascot of a Purple Cow—derived from a 19th-century nonsense poem –is a good metaphor for the irreverent an enlightened individuals that comprise the Williams community.

ABOUT THE SCHOOL

Williams College emphasizes the learning that takes place in the creation of a functioning community: life in the residence halls, expression through the arts, debates on political issues, leadership in campus governance, exploration of personal identity, pursuit of spiritual and religious impulses, the challenge of athletics, and direct engagement with human needs. The school is an "amalgamation of the most thoughtful, quirky, and smart people that you will ever meet as an undergraduate." The rigorous academic experience "is truly excellent," and students say they "feel like I am learning thoroughly." Professors are accessible and dedicated. Distinctive academic programs include Oxford-style tutorials between two students and a faculty member that call for intense research and weekly debates. These tutorial programs offer students a distinctive opportunity to take a heightened form of responsibility for their own intellectual development. In January, a four-week Winter Study term allows students to take unique, hands-on pass/fail classes.

About 2,000 students inhabit this insanely gorgeous and cozy campus hidden away in the picturesque Berkshires of Massachusetts. Williams students are preppy, athletic, down-to-earth, enormously talented, and academically driven—even when they choose to pretend otherwise. There's a real sense of community and caring here, which is a good thing because students see nothing but one another all the time. You won't find frats at Williams, but "intercollegiate sports are "a huge part of the social scene," as are the various varsity teams, which "are the basic social blocks at Williams." A thriving party scene at Williams in addition to clubs, student organizations, and well-attended lectures and concerts keep campus life interesting, and "there is a variety of activities available that are definitely not found in the city," including sledding and

Why Students Love Williams College

"There is a variety of activities available that are definitely not found in the city."

Contact Info:

33 Stetson Court
Williamstown, MA 01267
Admissions: 413-597-2211
Financial Aid: 413-597-4181
E-mail: admission@williams.edu
Fax: 413-597-4052
Website: www.williams.edu

Fun Facts

- Williams College is the site of the Hopkins Observatory, the oldest extant astronomical observatory in the United States. Erected in 1836–1838, it now contains the Mehlin Museum of Astronomy, including Alvan Clark's first telescope (from 1852), as well as the Milham Planetarium, which uses a Zeiss Skymaster ZKP3/B optomechanical projector and an Ansible digital projector, both installed in 2005. The Hopkins Observatory's 0.6-m DFM reflecting telescope (1991) is installed elsewhere on the campus.
- The most famous items in the library's collection include first printings of the Declaration of Independence, Articles of Confederation, United States Constitution, and Bill of Rights, as well as George Washington's personal copy of the Federalist Papers.
- The Chapin Library's science collection includes a first edition of Nicolaus Copernicus's De revolutionibus orbium coelestium, as well as first editions of books by Tycho Brahe, Johannes Kepler, Galileo, Isaac Newton, and other major figures.
- On one of the first three Fridays in October, the president of the college cancels classes and declares it Mountain Day. The bells ring, announcing the event, members of the Outing Club unfurl a banner from the roof of Chapin Hall and students hike up Stony Ledge. At Stony Ledge, they celebrate with donuts, cider, and a cappella performances.

Williams College

CAMPUS LIFE

Quality of life Rating	82
Fire Safety Rating	74
Green rating	90
Type of School	Private
Environment	Village

STUDENTS

Total undergrad enrolllment	1,996
% Male to Female	49/51
% From out of state	87
% From public high school	57
% Live on Campus	93
% African American	8
% Asian	11
% Caucasian	60
% Hispanic	10
% International	7
# Of Countries Represented	73

ACADEMICS

Academic Rating	99
% Of students graduating within 4 years	91
% Of students graduating within 6 years	95
Calendar	4-1-4
Profs interesting rating	94
Profs accessible rating	99
Most common reg class size	fewer than 10 students
Most common lab size	10–19 students

MOST POPULAR MAJORS

Economics, English language and literature, visual and performing arts

SPECIAL STUDY OPTIONS

Cross-registration, double major, independent study, internships, student-designed major, study abroad.

broomball. The school has an "extensive alumni network," and graduates get plum jobs all over, and the school is a perennial feeder school to the top business, graduate, law, and medical schools in the nation.

BANG FOR YOUR BUCK

The outrageous endowment at Williams approaches $2 billion. That's substantially more than the annual gross domestic product of most countries. This colossal stash bountifully subsidizes costs for all students, including costs to study all over the world. The fact that Williams is simply awash in money also enables the school to maintain a 100 percent need-blind admission policy. Merit-based scholarships are an historical artifact here. So are loans. All financial aid is free, and it is based purely on need. Williams also offers a generous financial aid program for international students. Convincing this school that you belong here is the difficult part. If you can just get admitted, Williams guarantees that it will meet 100 percent of your financial need for four years. You will walk away with a degree from one of the best schools in the country without owing a single red cent.

Why Students Love Williams College

> "The most thoughtful, quirky, and smart people that you will ever meet as an undergraduate."

STUDENT BODY

Students describe their peers as "interesting and beautiful" "geniuses of varying interests." They're "athletically awesome." They're "freakishly unique" and at the same time "cookie-cutter amazing." Ethnic diversity is stellar and you'll find all kinds of students including "the goth students," "nerdier students," "a ladle of environmentally conscious pseudo-vegetarians," and a few "West Coast hippies." Sporty students abound. "There definitely is segregation between the artsy kids and the athlete types but there is also a significant amount of crossover." "Williams is a place where normal social labels tend not to apply," reports a junior. "Everyone here got in for a reason. So that football player in your theater class has amazing insight on Chekhov, and that outspoken environmental activist also specializes in improv comedy."

WHY STUDENTS LOVE WILLIAMS

"I went on a visit, and I just got 'that feeling'" is a common refrain of happy Williams students, who permeate the campus with a feeling of "general agreeableness." From the moment students set foot on campus, they begin "meeting talented and intelligent people and sharing in the beautiful aesthetic of the Berkshires." "My life is great. I'm surrounded by really smart people who are diligent in their studying during the week, but still like partying on the weekend," says a student. The entry system also makes the transition to campus easy, and acts as "an ultimate haven and safe zone."

Williams College

GENERAL INFO

Activities: Choral groups, dance, drama/theater, literary magazine, music ensembles, radio station, student government, student newspaper, student-run film society, symphony orchestra, yearbook, international student organization. **Organizations:** 110 registered organizations, 3 honor societies, 8 religious organizations. **Athletics (Intercollegiate):** *Men*: Baseball, basketball, crew/rowing, cross-country, diving, football, golf, ice hockey, lacrosse, skiing (downhill/alpine), skiing (nordic/cross-country), soccer, squash, swimming, tennis, track/field (outdoor), track/field (indoor), wrestling. *Women*: Basketball, crew/rowing, cross-country, diving, field hockey, golf, ice hockey, lacrosse, skiing (downhill/alpine), skiing (nordic/cross-country), soccer, softball, squash, swimming, tennis, track/field (outdoor), track/field (indoor), volleyball. **On-Campus Highlights:** Paresky Student Center, Schow Science Library, Williams College Museum of Art, Center for Theatre and Dance, Chandler Gymnasium. **Environmental Initiatives:** *Renewable Energy*: 26.7 kW photovoltaic array installed on the library shelving building. *Infrastructure Improvements*: Undertaking $1.5 million in energy conservation projects—lighting, motors, lab hood improvements, etc. Installed real-time electricity meters in almost all campus buildings. *Buildings*: LEED certification of new academic buildings.

THE BOTTOM LINE

Williams College is very similar to an Ivy League school. It has boundless, state-of-the-art resources in everything; a diploma with the Williams brand name on it will kick down doors for the rest of your life; and it's absurdly expensive. The total retail price here for tuition, room and board, and everything else comes to about $52,000 per year. Financial aid here is beyond generous, though, and you'd be insane to choose a lesser school instead because of the sticker price.

Why Students Love Williams College

"That football player in your theater class has amazing insight on Chekhov, and that outspoken environmental activist also specializes in improv comedy."

SELECTIVITY

Admissions Rating	**99**
# of applicants	6,631
% of applicants accepted	19
% of acceptees attending	44
# accepting a place on wait list	494
% admitted from wait list	7

FRESHMAN PROFILE

Range SAT Critical Reading	**660–770**
Range SAT Math	**650–760**
Range ACT Composite	**29–34**
% graduated top 10% of class	**90**
% graduated top 25% of class	**98**
% graduated top 50% of class	**100**

DEADLINES

Regular Deadline	**1/1**
Normal registration	**no**

FACILITIES

Housing: Coed dorms, cooperative housing. *Special Academic Facilities/Equipment*: Hopkins Observatory; Williams College Museum of Art; Adams Memorial Theatre; Chapin Rare Books Library; Spencer Studio Art Building, Center for Theatre and Dance, Hopkins Experimental Forest. *Computers*: 100% of classrooms, 100% of dorms, 100% of libraries, 100% of dining areas, 100% of student union, 100% of common outdoor areas have wireless network access. Students can register for classes online. Administrative functions (other than registration) can be performed online.

FINANCIAL FACTS

Financial Aid Rating	**96**
Annual tuition	$42,938
Room and Board	$11,370
Required Fees	$252
Books and supplies	$800
% frosh rec. need-based scholarship or grant aid	53
% UG rec.need-based scholarship or grant aid	54
% frosh rec. need-based self-help aid	53
% UG rec. need-based self-help aid	54
% frosh rec. any financial aid	53
% UG rec. any financial aid	53
% UG borrow to pay for school	41
Average cumulative indebtedness	$8,369

#2

Swarthmore College

Swarthmore, PA

STUDENTS

1,509 undergrad enrollment

49% Male

51% Female

ADMISSIONS

6,041 →	16%	40%	EARLY →	NR	NR
applicants	admitted	enrolled	ADMISSIONS	applicants	accepted

NR avg. high school gpa

ACT range: 29–33 (0–36)

SAT range (200–800):

reading	670–760
math	670–770
writing	680–770

84% graduated top 10% of class

96% graduated top 25% of class

FINANCIAL INFO

$40,816	$12,100	$1,150	$334
annual tuition	room & board	avg. book expenses	required fees

$19,016 avg. indebtedness

ACADEMICS

8:1 student to faculty ratio

0% classes taught by TAs

GRADUATION RATES

89% of students graduating within 4 years

93% of students graduating within 6 years

** NR = Not reported*

Why Swarthmore College is No. 2

A lot of schools claim a "work hard, play hard" mentality, but most probably don't even come close to what Swarthmore students (happily) consider hard. Swatties eat up the tough love that their four years here teaches them; the academics may be downright harrowing, and the pressure to excel in something else is omnipresent, but the students wouldn't have it any other way. There are tons of resources available to help any struggling student along the way, from professors and mentors to writing associates and psychological counselors, and the school's flexibility means that students can change their classes and correct course as often as they need to in order to succeed.

Students here are first and foremost busy, and you half expect to hear a buzzing when you set foot on the campus. They'd rather read than sleep; they'd rather join a club than sleep; they'd rather start a club than sleep. Career Services is an important part of student life at Swarthmore, and the office pairs nearly 200 students with alumni for externships each year, which provide one-week job shadowing experiences designed for career exploration. Academia is a common destination for Swatties, and within five years of graduation, 87 percent of alumni begin graduate or professional school. The school also instills in its students a sense of civic responsibility, and students will proudly admit that as cheesy as it sounds, they really are just a bunch of smart students who care about the world and want to make it better.

ABOUT THE COLLEGE

Swarthmore College is among the most prestigious liberal arts schools in the country. The locus of Swarthmore's greatness lies in the quality and passion of its faculty ("some of my professors have knocked me to the floor with their brilliance"). A student/faculty ratio of 8:1 ensures that students have close, meaningful engagement with their professors. "It's where to go for a real education—for learning for the sake of truly learning, rather than just for grades," says a student. The college's Honors Program features small groups of dedicated and accomplished students working closely with faculty, with an emphasis on independent learning, and helps further the school's reputation as "a community where everyone pushes each other toward success." With that intensity comes a certain measure of stress and anxiety; at the same time, Swatties are a bright and creative lot "who don't get enough sleep because they're too busy doing all they want to do in their time here." Professors and administrators are extremely supportive, and "view the students as responsible adults, and thus leave them to their own devices when they are out of class." Students also enjoy an expansive curriculum—about 600 course offerings each year. Swarthmore is part of the Tri-College Consortium (along with Bryn Mawr and Haverford), which means that students can take courses at those schools and use their facilities.

Swarthmore's small size combined with its vast number of clubs and organizations provide opportunities to participate in pretty much whatever you want. "There are so many organizations and clubs on campus that you'd be pressed to find none of the activities

Why Students Love Swarthmore College

"Some of my professors have knocked me to the floor with their brilliance."

Contact Info:

500 College Avenue
Swarthmore, PA 19081
Admissions: 610-328-8300
Financial Aid: 610-328-8358
E-mail: admissions@swarthmore.edu
Fax: 610-328-8580
Website: www.swarthmore.edu

Fun Facts

- Swarthmore's alumni include five Nobel Prize winners (second highest number of Nobel Prize winners per graduate in the U.S.), including the 2006 Physics laureate John C. Mather (1968), the 2004 Economics laureate Edward Prescott (1962) and the 1972 Chemistry laureate Christian B. Anfinsen (1937). Swarthmore also has 8 MacArthur Foundation fellows and hundreds of prominent figures in law, art, science, business, politics, and other fields.
- Suffragist and National Women's Party founder, Alice Paul belonged to the class of 1905.
- Nancy Roman NASA's first Chief of Astronomy in the Office of Space Science, "mother of the Hubble telescope."
- Michael Dukakis (1955) was the Democratic nominee in the 1988 presidential election.
- Novelist James A. Michener (1929) left his entire $10 million estate (including the copyrights to his works) to Swarthmore.
- Robert Zoellick (1976), current president of the World Bank.
- John C. Mather (1968), American astrophysicist, cosmologist, and Nobel Prize in Physics laureate for his work on COBE with George Smoot.
- David K. Lewis (1962), ground-breaking philosopher known for his work in Analytic Metaphysics, rated by fellow academics as one of the fifteen most important philosophers in the past 200 years.

Swarthmore College

CAMPUS LIFE

Quality of life Rating	83
Fire Safety Rating	89
Green rating	80
Type of School	Private
Environment	Village

STUDENTS

Total undergrad enrolllment	1,509
% Male to Female	49/51
% From out of state	88
% From public high school	59
% Live on Campus	94
# of Fraternities	2
% African American	6
% Asian	14
% Caucasian	45
% Hispanic	12
% International	7
# Of Countries Represented	58

ACADEMICS

Academic Rating	98
% Of students graduating within 4 years	89
% Of students graduating within 6 years	93
Calendar	semester
Profs interesting rating	97
Profs accessible rating	96
Most common reg class size	10–19 students
Most common lab size	fewer than 10 students

MOST POPULAR MAJORS

Biology, economics, political science

HONORS PROGRAMS

Swarthmore's Honors Program.

SPECIAL STUDY OPTIONS

Accelerated program, cross-registration, double major, exchange student program (domestic), honors program, independent study, internships, student-designed major, study abroad, teacher certification program, Swarthmore offers cooperative exchange programs with Rice and Tufts universities and Harvey Mudd, Pomona, Mills, and Middlebury colleges.

interesting," as well as dozens of community service groups, 22 varsity athletic teams, and lectures and performances occurring daily, so Swarthmore students are rarely idle. "The college wants to foster student life," and there are all kinds of school-sponsored events throughout the week. A student activity fee, paid annually with tuition, covers admittance to all on-campus events for the year. When they can spare a couple of hours, many Swatties like to blow off steam in nearby Philadelphia, which is easily accessible by public transportation.

BANG FOR YOUR BUCK

Swarthmore College maintains a need-blind admission policy. Admission here is not contingent on your economic situation, and financial aid awards meet 100 percent of admitted students' demonstrated need. Best of all, all Swarthmore financial aid awards are loan-free. Financial aid is even available for some international students. In most cases, Swarthmore students may apply their financial aid toward the cost of participation in a study abroad program.

Merit-based awards are copious. They include the National McCabe Scholarship, which meets the full demonstrated financial need of recipients. The Philip Evans Scholarship Program also meets the full demonstrated financial need of its beneficiaries while also providing recipients with a free computer and grants to do things like study abroad and independent research. Another unique possibility is the Eugene Lang Opportunity Grant, which provides up to $10,000 to sophomores to design and carry out social service projects. Also noteworthy is Swarthmore's extensive externship program. It matches students with alumni volunteers for job-shadowing experiences in laboratories, museums, publishing companies, labor unions, leading think-tanks, and other places where you might like to work someday.

Why Students Love Swarthmore College

"There are so many organizations and clubs on campus that you'd be pressed to find none of the activities interesting."

STUDENT BODY

Students are "not sure if there is a typical Swattie" but suspect that "the defining feature among us is that each person is brilliant at something: maybe dance, maybe quantum physics, maybe philosophy. Each person here has at least one thing that [he or she does] extraordinarily well." A Swattie "is [typically] liberal, involved in some kind of activism group or multicultural group, talks about classes all the time, was labeled a nerd by people in high school, and is really smart—one of those people where you just have to wonder, how do they get all their homework done and manage their extracurriculars and still have time for parties?" The campus "is very diverse racially but not in terms of thought—in other words, pretty much everyone's liberal, you don't get many different points of view. Multicultural and queer issues are big here, but you don't have to be involved in that to enjoy Swarthmore. You just have to accept it."

Swarthmore College

#2 Private

WHY STUDENTS LOVE SWARTHMORE

The school is truly challenging—"it teaches its students touch lessons not only about classes but about LIFE"—and "though it may be extremely, almost unbearably difficult sometimes, it's totally worth it." The school has a lovely campus, filled with "insightful, intelligent, and intense people" people that "are almost unbelievably friendly" and are "100 percent invested in their studies without coming off as total nerds because they choose to study what they are passionate about." Swat is academically rigorous "not because the kids have a pathological need to succeed, but because they truly love to do what they do." "We can do anything we want as long as nothing or no one is permanently damaged, we are safe, and we don't mess around with the arboretum plants," says a student.

GENERAL INFO

Activities: Choral groups, dance, drama/theater, jazz band, literary magazine, music ensembles, opera, student government, student newspaper, student-run film society, symphony orchestra, yearbook, campus ministries, international student organization. **Organizations:** 138 registered organizations, 3 honor societies, 12 religious organizations. 2 fraternities. **Athletics (Intercollegiate):** *Men*: Baseball, basketball, cross-country, golf, lacrosse, soccer, swimming, tennis, track/field (outdoor), track/field (indoor). *Women*: Badminton, basketball, cross-country, field hockey, lacrosse, soccer, softball, swimming, tennis, track/field (outdoor), track/field (indoor), volleyball. **On-Campus Highlights:** Kohlberg & Eldridge Commons Coffee Bars, Parrish Beach (the central campus lawn), Scott Outdoor Amphitheater, Mullan Tennis & Fitness Center, Paces (student-run cafe), War News Radio (www.warnewsradio.org), the Lang Center for Civic and Social Responsibility. **Environmental Initiatives:** 40% of the college's electrical demands are met by renewable wind power. The college has approximately 14,300 square feet of green roof. The college's Sustainability Committee is comprised of faculty, staff, and students and is charged with making recommendations to improve environmental sustainability on campus.

THE BOTTOM LINE

The cost of tuition for a year at Swarthmore is nearly $40,000. However, Swarthmore has staggeringly generous financial aid resources, and it will meet 100 percent of your demonstrated need without loans. The average financial aid award here is more than $35,000. Don't assume you won't receive aid because your family is too wealthy and definitely—please!—don't assume you can't afford Swarthmore because your family isn't wealthy enough.

Why Students Love Swarthmore College

"The defining feature among us is that each person is brilliant at something: maybe dance, maybe quantum physics, maybe philosophy."

SELECTIVITY

Admissions Rating	**98**
# of applicants	6,041
% of applicants accepted	16
% of acceptees attending	40

FRESHMAN PROFILE

Range SAT Critical Reading	**670–760**
Range SAT Math	**670–770**
Range SAT Writing	**680–770**
Range ACT Composite	**29–33**
% graduated top 10% of class	**84**
% graduated top 25% of class	**96**
% graduated top 50% of class	**100**

DEADLINES

Regular Deadline	**1/1**
Normal registration	**no**

FACILITIES

Housing: Coed dorms, men's dorms, women's dorms, Gender Neutral housing (students of any gender may share rooms and/or share bathrooms). *Special Academic Facilities/ Equipment*: The campus is a 399-acre, nationally registered arboretum. The Lang Performing Arts Center's resources include an art gallery, dance studios, cinema, and theater performance space. The athletics facilities include a lighted stadium complex, a 400-meter dual durometer track, and synthetic grass playing field, state-of-the-art fitness center, and three indoor tennis courts with Rebound Ace surface. *Computers*: 100% of classrooms, 100% of dorms, 100% of libraries, 100% of dining areas, 100% of student union, 100% of common outdoor areas have wireless network access.

FINANCIAL FACTS

Financial Aid Rating	**99**
Annual tuition	$40,816
Room and Board	$12,100
Required Fees	$334
Books and supplies	$1,150
% frosh rec. need-based scholarship or grant aid	53
% UG rec.need-based scholarship or grant aid	50
% frosh rec. need-based self-help aid	52
% UG rec. need-based self-help aid	48
% frosh rec. any financial aid	53
% UG rec. any financial aid	52

#3

Princeton University

Princeton, NJ

PRINCETON UNIVERSITY

STUDENTS

5,142 undergrad enrollment

51% Male ♂♂♂♂♂♂♂♂♂♂♂

49% Female ♀♀♀♀♀♀♀♀♀♀♀

ADMISSIONS

26,247 applicants	9% admitted	57% enrolled	EARLY ADMISSIONS	NR applicants	NR accepted

3.89 avg. high school gpa

ACT range (0–36): 31–35

SAT range (200–800): reading 640–790, math 710–790, writing 700–790

99% graduated top 10% of class

100% graduated top 25% of class

FINANCIAL INFO

$37,000	$12,069	$1,200	$5,225
annual tuition	room & board	avg. book expenses	avg. indebtedness

ACADEMICS

6:1 student to faculty ratio

19% classes taught by TAs

GRADUATION RATES

90% of students graduating within 4 years

96% of students graduating within 6 years

* NR = Not reported

Why Princeton University is No. 3

Located in a quaint little bubble of a New Jersey town, where the gothic spires reach the sky and the leaves turn impossible colors of autumn, Princeton offers one of the country's finest educations while being steeped in history so deep you half expect to see Woodrow Wilson strolling around campus. Best of all, thanks for its non-loan financial aid policy built on grants (it was the first in the country to do so, back in 2001), the school covers 100 percent of each admitted student's need, meaning no loans ever have to be repaid.

Princetonians are ardent boosters of all things Princeton; whether it's the campus' numerous traditions (some dating back hundreds of years) or the sheer love of the professors, the school builds a loyalty that extends far out beyond graduation and into alumnidom (you should see the campus during its annual reunion). Classes are demanding but absolutely top notch, and students don't mind forgoing sleep for four years in the name of their education. The school's focus on undergraduates (there are no business, law, or medical schools) and its status as a major research institution means that the opportunities that come to Princeton students are copious; whether it's a visit from a sitting president, the chance to study under the author of your textbook, or the numerous internships in the U.S. and abroad, students have more than enough chances to get their money's worth during their time at the school. Not to mention that when you graduate, you get to say—to employers, friends, and anyone who'll listen—that you went to Princeton.

No one said that getting in was easy; with benefits such as these, the applicant pool for Princeton grows (in size and strength) every year, but once you're in, you're in for life.

ABOUT THE SCHOOL

Princeton offers its 5,000 undergraduate students a top-notch liberal arts education, taught by some of the best minds in the world. The university is committed to undergraduate teaching, and all faculty, including the president, teach undergraduates. "You get the attention you deserve—if you seek it," says a student. Supporting these efforts are exceptional academic and research resources, including the world-class Firestone Library, the new Frick Chemistry Laboratory that emphasizes hands-on learning in teaching labs, a genomics institute, the Woodrow Wilson School of Public and International Affairs that trains leaders in public service, and an engineering school that enrolls more than 900 undergraduates. Freshman seminars take students into a variety of settings, such as to theaters on Broadway, geological sites in the West, art museums, and more. Princeton students can choose between more than 75 fields of concentration (majors) and interdisciplinary certificate programs, of which history, political science, economics, and international affairs are among the most popular. The school's excellent faculty-student ratio of 5:1 means that many classes are discussion-based, giving students a direct line to their brilliant professors, and "once you take upper level courses, you'll have a lot of chances to work closely with professors and study what you are most interested in."

Why Students love Princeton University

> "To meet and take classes from some of the most brilliant academic minds in the world."

Contact Info:

PO Box 430
Admission Office
Princeton, NJ 08544-0430
Admissions: 609-258-3060
Financial Aid: 609-258-3330
Fax: 609-258-6743
Website: www.princeton.edu

Fun Facts

- Founded: 1746, in Elizabeth, New Jersey, moved to Princeton in 1756.
- Original name: The College of New Jersey; changed in 1896.
- Official motto: Dei Sub Numine Viget (Under God's Power She Flourishes).
- Informal motto: Princeton in the Nation's Service and in the Service of All Nations.
- Colors: Orange and black; formally adopted in 1896.
- Mascot: Tiger; emerged around 1882.
- Insignia: The shield, which derives from the official seal, is designated for more common use. It includes an open Bible with Vet Nov Testamentum, signifying both Old and New Testaments. In its lower part is a chevron, signifying the rafters of a building. The official motto is sometimes displayed on a ribbon under the shield.
- Alma mater: "Old Nassau," since 1859. Modern first verse: "Tune ev'ry heart and ev'ry voice, Bid ev'ry care withdraw; Let all with one accord rejoice, In praise of Old Nassau. In praise of Old Nassau, we sing, Hurrah! Hurrah! Hurrah! Our hearts will give, while we shall live, Three cheers for Old Nassau."
- Alumni U.S. presidents: James Madison, Class of 1771; Woodrow Wilson, Class of 1879.

Princeton University

CAMPUS LIFE

Quality of life Rating	94
Fire Safety Rating	98
Green rating	96
Type of School	Private
Environment	Town

STUDENTS

Total undergrad enrolllment	5,142
% Male to Female	51/49
% From out of state	84
% From public high school	58
% Live on Campus	97
% African American	8
% Asian	17
% Caucasian	49
% Hispanic	8
% International	11
# Of Countries Represented	112

ACADEMICS

Academic Rating	95
% Of students graduating within 4 years	90
% Of students graduating within 6 years	96
Calendar	semester
Profs interesting rating	84
Profs accessible rating	90
Most common reg class size	10–19 students
Most common lab size	10–19 students

MOST POPULAR MAJORS
History, political science

SPECIAL STUDY OPTIONS

Cross-registration, exchange student program (domestic), independent study, student-designed major, study abroad, teacher certification program Special programs offered to physically disabled students include note-taking services, reader services, voice recorders.

All "unfailingly brilliant, open, and inspirational" faculty members also work closely with undergraduates in the supervision of junior-year independent work and senior theses. "Professors love teaching, and there are many fantastic lecturers," giving students a chance "to meet and take classes from some of the most brilliant academic minds in the world." Even before they start taking Princeton classes, select students each year are chosen for the Bridge Year Program, which provides funding for students to engage in public service opportunities in one of four countries: India, Peru, Ghana, or Serbia. There are "pools of resources available for students for all sorts of non-academic or extra-curricular pursuits."

The vast majority of Princeton undergraduates live on campus; within the residence halls, students not only become part of a social community (the school "places significant emphasis on creating a social and cohesive student body"), they also are supported by academic advisers within the residential colleges, each of which is overseen by a faculty master. "A student always has access to an administrator at some level," says one. In addition to academics, public service is a major focus of the university's mission. Undergraduates also may choose to do a public service internship through the Pace Center for Civic Engagement, or pursue internships overseas through the International Internship Program. "By gathering us, Princeton makes us wonder what world we want to contribute to create, and gives us the means we need to do so." Princeton is a powerhouse for men's and women's crew, men's lacrosse, and field hockey. If you find yourself needing a big city fix, Princeton is located equidistant from New York City and Philadelphia, an easy hour's drive from each.

BANG FOR YOUR BUCK

Princeton operates need-blind admissions, as well as one of the strongest need-based financial programs in the country. Once a student is admitted, Princeton meets 100 percent of each student's demonstrated financial need. One of the first schools in the country to do so, Princeton has eliminated all loans for students who qualify for aid—it is possible to graduate from this Ivy League school without debt. Financial awards come in the form of grants, which do not need to be repaid. More than 60 percent of Princeton students receive financial aid with an average grant of about $36,000 (more than Princeton's tuition.) No need to pinch yourself, you're not dreaming. In recent years, the amount of grant aid available at Princeton has outpaced the annual increase in school fees. Good news for international students: financial aid packages extend to international admits as well.

STUDENT BODY

It's not surprising that most undergraduates are "driven, competitive, and obsessed with perfection." "Academics come first," and Princeton students are typified by dedication to their studies and "a tendency to overwork." "Almost everyone at Princeton is involved with something other than school about which they are extremely passionate," and most have "at least one distinct, remarkable talent." "It's fairly easy for most people to find a good group of friends with whom they have something in common," and many students get involved in one of the "infinite number of clubs" on campus. Superficially, "The preppy Ivy League stereotype" is reflected in the student population, and many students are "well-spoken," "dress nicely," and stay in shape. A student jokes, "Going to Princeton is like being in a contest to see who can be the biggest nerd while simultaneously appearing the least nerdy."

WHY STUDENTS LOVE PRINCETON

"I'm being taught from people who are leading scholars in their field, and surrounded by intelligent and hard-working students," says a student. At a school where "the academics are impeccable, the student body is happy, and the alumni keep on giving and giving," everyone is proud to wear orange, and because Princeton has so many prestigious alumni, "there are so many chances to meet writers, performers, and professionals you admire."

The school's "virtually unlimited" resources are showered upon its students, and they cannot help but feel spoiled by the care lavished upon them. "It is the little things that the school does, like taking out your trash for you or not charging for laundry, etc. that make you feel really cared for," says a student. There are also "no financial restraints for research or service projects." The stunningly beautiful campus—as well as its location separate from, but close to, a large city—"provides an intimate campus setting where the professors and students interact on a level not seen on many other college campuses." All in all, "Princeton is a place that prepares you for anything and everything, providing you with a strong network every step of the way."

Why Students love Princeton University

"Academics come first."

GENERAL INFO

Activities: Choral groups, concert band, dance, drama/theater, jazz band, literary magazine, marching band, music ensembles, musical theater, opera, pep band, radio station, student government, student newspaper, student-run film society, symphony orchestra, yearbook, campus ministries, international student organization. **Organizations:** 250 registered organizations, 30 honor societies, 28 religious organizations. **Athletics (Intercollegiate):** *Men*: Baseball, basketball, crew/rowing, cross-country, diving, fencing, football, golf, ice hockey, lacrosse, light weight football, soccer, squash, swimming, tennis, track/field (outdoor), track/field (indoor), volleyball, water polo, wrestling. *Women*: Basketball, crew/rowing, cross-country, diving, fencing, field hockey, golf, ice hockey, lacrosse, soccer, softball, squash, swimming, tennis, track/field (outdoor), track/field (indoor), volleyball, water polo. **On-Campus Highlights:** Nassau Hall, Firestone Library, McCarter Theater, Princeton U. Art Museum, University Chapel, Frist Campus Center. **Environmental Initiatives:** Greenhouse Gas reduction goal: 1990 levels by 2020 through local verifiable action, while adding more than 1 million gross square feet of built area without the purchase of offsets. Sustainable Building Guidelines: requiring all new buildings and major renovations to be 50% more energy efficient than code requires, 95% demolition and construction debris recycling, and use of sustainable materials. Implementation of transportation demand management program to reduce by 10% the number of cars coming to campus by 2020.

THE BOTTOM LINE

If you can afford it, Princeton is far from cheap. A year's tuition is more than $36,000, plus about $12,000 in room and board. You'll pay another $1,200 in fees. Not to mention personal and academic expenses each year. These figures are nothing to scoff at. However, if you qualify for aid, you'll be granted the amount you need, without loans.

SELECTIVITY

Admissions Rating	**99**
# of applicants	26,247
% of applicants accepted	9
% of acceptees attending	57
# accepting a place on wait list	1,002
% admitted from wait list	16

FRESHMAN PROFILE

Range SAT Critical Reading	**690–790**
Range SAT Math	**710–790**
Range SAT Writing	**700–790**
Range ACT Composite	**31–35**
Average HS GPA	**3.89**
% graduated top 10% of class	**99**
% graduated top 25% of class	**100**
% graduated top 50% of class	**100**

DEADLINES

Regular Deadline	**1/1**
Normal registration	**no**

FACILITIES

Housing: Coed dorms, special housing for disabled students, apartments for married students, *Special Academic Facilities/Equipment*: Art museum, natural history museum, energy and environmental studies center, plasma physics lab, Center for Jewish Life, Center for Human Values, Woodrow WIlson School of Public and International Affairs, etc. *Computers*: 100% of classrooms, 100% of dorms, 70% of libraries, 100% of dining areas, 100% of student union, 20% of common outdoor areas have wireless network access.

FINANCIAL FACTS

Financial Aid Rating	**99**
Annual tuition	$37,00
Room and Board	$12,069
Books and supplies	$1,200
% frosh rec. need-based scholarship or grant aid	60
% UG rec.need-based scholarship or grant aid	60
% frosh rec. need-based self-help aid	60
% UG rec. need-based self-help aid	60
% frosh rec. any financial aid	60
% UG rec. any financial aid	60
% UG borrow to pay for school	23
Average cumulative indebtedness	$5,225

#4

Harvard College

Cambridge, MA

STUDENTS

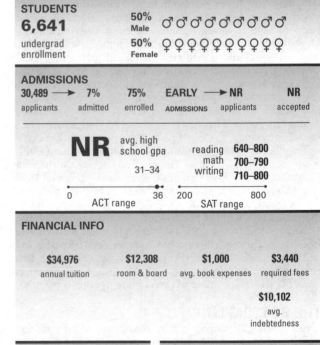

6,641 undergrad enrollment

50% Male

50% Female

ADMISSIONS

30,489 →	7%	75%	EARLY ADMISSIONS →	NR	NR
applicants	admitted	enrolled		applicants	accepted

NR avg. high school gpa

ACT range (0–36): 31–34

SAT range (200–800): reading 640–800, math 700–790, writing 710–800

FINANCIAL INFO

$34,976	$12,308	$1,000	$3,440
annual tuition	room & board	avg. book expenses	required fees

$10,102 avg. indebtedness

ACADEMICS

7:1 student to faculty ratio

0% classes taught by TAs

GRADUATION RATES

87% of students graduating within 4 years

97% of students graduating within 6 years

** NR = Not reported*

Why Harvard College is No. 4

It's a world of superlatives when it comes to Harvard University. Superb academics; world-famous professors; unbelievably talented students; notoriously expensive. Makes you wonder what a school like this is doing on a "Best Values Colleges" list, doesn't it? Well, the answer is simple. Harvard has found a way to make one of the best college educations available in the world today accessible to any student smart enough to get in, regardless of their financial circumstances. (Its multibillion-dollar endowment helps.) Simply put, you're getting your money's worth at Harvard—and then some.

Every top high school student and their brother put Harvard as a long (or close) shot in their applications, and for good reason. The faculty is composed of world-class scholars, the classes are rock solid, and in enrolling, you instantly become part of a centuries-old tradition, an honor you share with presidents, CEOs, and literary legends. Students come from all over the world and gather in the freshmen dining hall to pour out ideas and riffs, and then stroll back into the classroom to listen to their professors do the same on a higher level. Work hard for four years and internships and employers will take notice, and then, congrats: you graduated from Harvard. Rolls off the tongue, doesn't it?

Why Students Love Harvard College

"There is a lot of tolerance and acceptance at Harvard for individuals of all races, religions, socioeconomic backgrounds, life styles, etc."

ABOUT THE SCHOOL

Bully to those who get the chance to be a part of the "dynamic universe" that is Harvard College. Here you will find a faculty of academic rock stars, intimate classes, a cosmically vast curriculum, world-class facilities (including what is arguably the best college library in the United States), a diverse student body from across the country and around the world ("The level of achievement is unbelievable"), and a large endowment that allows the college to support undergraduate and faculty research projects. When you graduate, you'll have unlimited bragging rights and the full force and prestige of the Harvard brand working for you for the rest of your life.

All first-year students live on campus, and Harvard guarantees housing to its students for all four years. All freshmen also eat in the same place, Annenberg Hall, and there are adult residential advisers living in the halls to help students learn their way around the vast resources of this "beautiful, fun, historic, and academically alive place." Social and extracurricular activities at Harvard are pretty much unlimited: "Basically, if you want to do it, Harvard either has it or has the money to give to you so you can start it." With more than 400 student organizations on campus, whatever you are looking for, you can find it here. The off-campus scene is hopping, too. Believe it or not, Harvard kids do party, and "there is a vibrant social atmosphere on campus and between students and the local community," with Cambridge offering art and music, not to mention a couple of great bars. Downtown Boston and all of its attractions is just a short ride across the Charles River by the "T" (subway).

Contact Info:

86 Brattle Street
Cambridge, MA 02138
Admissions: 617-495-1551
Financial Aid: 617-495-1581
E-mail: college@fas.harvard.edu
Fax: 617-495-8821
Website: www.college.harvard.edu

Fun Facts

- Harvard's first instructor, schoolmaster Nathaniel Eaton, was also its first instructor to be dismissed—in 1639 for overstrict discipline.
- Harvard and Yale enjoy the oldest intercollegiate athletic rivalry in the United States, the Harvard-Yale Regatta, dating back to 1852, when rowing crews from each institution first met on Lake Winnipesaukee, New Hampshire. Harvard won that contest by two boat lengths. Since 1859, the crews have met nearly every year (except during major wars). The race is typically held in early June in New London, Connecticut.
- Every spring there is an "Arts First week," founded by John Lithgow during which arts and culture organizations show off performances, cook meals, or present other work.
- Eight U.S. presidents have been graduates, and 75 Nobel Laureates have been student, faculty, or staff affiliates.
- Harvard is also the alma mater of sixty-two living billionaires.
- The Harvard University Library is the largest academic library in the United States and one of the largest in the world.

Harvard College

CAMPUS LIFE

Quality of life Rating	82
Fire Safety Rating	60*
Green rating	99
Type of School	Private
Environment	City

STUDENTS

Total undergrad enrolllment	6,641
% Male to Female	50/50
% From out of state	74
% African American	7
% Asian	16
% Caucasian	43
% Hispanic	8
% International	10
# Of Countries Represented	110

ACADEMICS

Academic Rating	99
% Of students graduating within 4 years	87
% Of students graduating within 6 years	97
Calendar	semester
Profs interesting rating	71
Profs accessible rating	69
Most common reg class size	fewer than 10 students

MOST POPULAR MAJORS
Political science, sociology

SPECIAL STUDY OPTIONS

Accelerated program, cross-registration, double major, exchange student program (domestic), honors program, independent study, internships, student-designed major, study abroad, teacher certification program.

BANG FOR YOUR BUCK

Harvard is swimming in cash, and financial need simply isn't a barrier to admission. In fact, the admissions staff here often looks especially favorably upon applicants who have stellar academic and extracurricular records despite having to overcome considerable financial obstacles. About 90 percent of the students who request financial aid qualify for it. If you qualify, 100 percent of your financial need will be met. Just so we're clear: by aid, we mean free money—not loans. Harvard doesn't do loans. Instead, Harvard asks families that qualify for financial aid to contribute somewhere between zero and 10 percent of their annual income each year. If your family income is less than $60,000, the odds are very good that you and your family won't pay a dime for you to attend. It's also worth noting that Harvard extends its commitment to full financial aid for all four undergraduate years. Families with higher incomes facing unusual financial challenges may also qualify for need–based scholarship assistance. Home equity is no longer considered in Harvard's assessment of the expected parent contribution.

STUDENT BODY

Much as you might expect, ambition and achievement are the ties that bind at Harvard, and "Everyone is great for one reason or another," says a student. Most every student can be summed up with the same statement: "Works really hard. Doesn't sleep. Involved in a million extracurriculars." Diversity is found in all aspects of life, from ethnicities to religion to ideology, and "there is a lot of tolerance and acceptance at Harvard for individuals of all races, religions, socioeconomic backgrounds, life styles, etc."

Why Students Love Harvard College

"Basically, if you want to do it, Harvard either has it or has the money to give to you so you can start it."

"The brightest minds in the world."

WHY STUDENTS LOVE HARVARD

"It is impossible to 'get the most out of Harvard' because Harvard offers so much," says one student. "And who can argue? "The brightest minds in the world" gather on a gorgeous campus on the Charles to share their smarts, and between the books, activities, and city, "boredom does not exist here. There are endless opportunities and endless passionate people to do them with." There is a pub on campus that provides "an excellent venue to hang out and play a game of pool or have a reasonably priced drink," and parties happen on weekends at Harvard's finals clubs, though there's no real pressure for students to partake if they're not interested.

Harvard College

#4 Private

GENERAL INFO

Activities: Choral groups, concert band, dance, drama/theater, jazz band, literary magazine, marching band, music ensembles, musical theater, opera, pep band, radio station, student government, student newspaper, student-run film society, symphony orchestra, television station, yearbook, campus ministries, international student organization. **Organizations:** 393 registered organizations, 1 honor societies, 28 religious organizations. **Athletics (Intercollegiate):** *Men*: Baseball, basketball, crew/rowing, cross-country, diving, fencing, football, golf, ice hockey, lacrosse, sailing, skiing (downhill/alpine), skiing (nordic & cross-country), soccer, squash, swimming, tennis, track/field (outdoor), track/field (indoor), volleyball. *Women*: Basketball, crew/rowing, cross-country, diving, fencing, field hockey, golf, ice hockey, lacrosse, sailing, skiing (downhill/alpine), skiing (nordic & cross-country), soccer, softball, squash, swimming, tennis, track/field (outdoor), track/field (indoor), volleyball. **On-Campus Highlights:** Widener Library, Harvard Yard, Fogg Museum, Annenburg/Memorial Hall, Science Center. **Environmental Initiatives:** 1. Establishing a university-wide Office for Sustainability. 2. Adopting Campus wide Sustainability Principles and Green Building Standards. 3. Committing to a 30 percent greenhouse gas reduction by FY16, inclusive of growth.

THE BOTTOM LINE

The sticker price to attend Harvard is as exorbitant as its opportunities. Tuition, fees, room and board, and expenses costs between $53,000 and $56,000 a year. However, financial aid here is so unbelievably ample and generous that you just shouldn't worry about that. The hard part about going to Harvard is getting in. If you can accomplish that, Harvard will help you find a way to finance your education. Period.

Why Students Love Harvard College

"It's impossible to get the most out of Harvard because Harvard offers so much."

SELECTIVITY

Admissions Rating	**99**
# of applicants	30,489
% of applicants accepted	7
% of acceptees attending	75

FRESHMAN PROFILE

Range SAT Critical Reading	**690–800**
Range SAT Math	**700–790**
Range SAT Writing	**710–800**
Range ACT Composite	**31–34**

DEADLINES

Regular Deadline	**2/1**
Normal registration	**no**

FACILITIES

Housing: Coed dorms, special housing for disabled students, apartments for married students, cooperative housing. *Special Academic Facilities/Equipment*: Museums (University Arts Museums, Museums of Cultural History, many others), language labs, observatory, many science and research laboratories and facilities, new state-of-the-art computer science facility. *Computers*: 98% of classrooms, 100% of dorms, 100% of libraries, have wireless network access. Students can register for classes online. Administrative functions (other than registration) can be performed online.

FINANCIAL FACTS

Financial Aid Rating	**96**
Annual tuition	$34,976
Room and Board	$12,308
Required Fees	$3,440
Books and supplies	$1,000
% frosh rec. need-based scholarship or grant aid	63
% UG rec.need-based scholarship or grant aid	61
% frosh rec. need-based self-help aid	38
% UG rec. need-based self-help aid	50
% UG borrow to pay for school	34
Average cumulative indebtedness	$10,102

#5

Rice University

Houston, TX

RICE

STUDENTS

3,529 undergrad enrollment

52% Male

48% Female

ADMISSIONS

13,804 applicants	19% admitted	36% enrolled	EARLY ADMISSIONS	NR applicants	NR accepted

NR avg. high school gpa

ACT range: 31–34 (0–36)

SAT range (200–800):

reading	650–750
math	690–790
writing	660–760

85% graduated top 10% of class

96% graduated top 25% of class

FINANCIAL INFO

$34,900	$12,270	$800	$651
annual tuition	room & board	avg. book expenses	required fees

$13,944 avg. indebtedness

ACADEMICS

6:1 student to faculty ratio

4% classes taught by TAs

GRADUATION RATES

79% of students graduating within 4 years

92% of students graduating within 6 years

* NR = Not reported

Why Rice University is No. 5

A sunny and social place to get a prestigious degree, Rice University is Houston's answer to the Ivy League. One of the top universities of the nation, Rice maintains a stellar faculty and a diverse selection of courses and departments. With about 3,500 undergrads, the school offers students the opportunity to develop a strong rapport with their professors, and the tier-one research institution offers robust and extensive opportunities for research and internships. Students are urged to take advantage of outside the classroom experiential opportunities, and are even encouraged to propose and (with approval) to teach classes on subjects of their choosing.

Outside of the classroom, the atmosphere is unmatched. Orientation week offerings dive right in to getting students situated, and students become affiliated with the Residential College in which they live not for four years, but for life. Rice has a very accepting and caring culture in which students, faculty, and staff all assume responsibility for new undergraduates, and from the minute one walks onto Rice's campus, there are upperclassmen advisors, peer academic advisors, Rice health advisors, Residential College Masters, resident associates, and many more campus groups that help them navigate their way through freshman year.

Why Students love Rice University

> "There is something unique about every Rice student."

ABOUT THE SCHOOL

The culture at Rice is uniquely student-focused. The 11 colleges in the school's Residential College system— "the greatest thing ever"—each have their own history and traditions and their own system of self (student) governance, and the "super-strong sense of community" created by the system affords students a greater than usual amount of influence regarding University policies and academic offerings. With students taking such a unique hand in shaping their experience ("the amount of trust and responsibilities put in the hands of students is unparalleled"), you can imagine that the level of school pride positively soars here: "Rice is a place where everyone is smart, the professors are accessible, the community is strong, and you'll always feel like you belong somewhere and that people care about you."

Academics are well-integrated into student culture, making the environment feel "open and welcome socially, and not cutthroat." "We all help each other out academically and as a result, we all become great friends," says a student. The premed program, located next to the largest medical center in the world, is one of the country's finest, and the engineering program is beyond excellent (to single out a couple of strengths among many). With so many research opportunities (including mentored lab work, independent projects, and social science internships), students often develop a strong rapport with their instructors. One details, "Most Rice professors love what they're doing, and you can tell that they are truly passionate about the material." They may show this "by literally dancing around in the front of the classroom or by simply being available at any time to help students."

Contact Info:

MS 17 PO Box 1892

Houston, TX 77251-1892

Admissions: 713-348-7423

Financial Aid: 713-348-4958

E-mail: admi@rice.edu

Fax: 713-348-5952

Website: www.rice.edu

Fun Facts

- Rice has been ranked No. 1 for best quality of life by Princeton Review three years in a row and is also currently ranked No. 1 for happiest students.
- Just a couple of miles from the downtown of Houston, the country's fourth largest city, the Rice campus is an arboretum with nearly 5,000 trees and almost as many squirrels.
- Known for its "unconventional wisdom," Rice will celebrate its centennial in 2012.
- Rice is the second smallest university in the Association of American Universities, which makes it the fitting place for the discovery of the new science of nanotechnology.
- Two Rice alumni helped bring the Johnson Space Center to Houston, and Rice has produced 14 of the country's astronauts.
- Rice alumni currently serve as the mayor of Houston, the county judge/chief executive of Harris County and the president and CEO of the Metropolitan Transit Authority of Harris County, Houston, Texas.
- Just a couple of miles from the downtown of Houston, the country's fourth largest city, the Rice campus is an arboretum with nearly 5,000 trees and almost as many squirrels.

Top Ten Private Schools

Rice University

CAMPUS LIFE

Quality of life Rating	99
Fire Safety Rating	88
Green rating	79
Type of School	Private
Environment	Metropolis

STUDENTS

Total undergrad enrolllment	3,529
% Male to Female	52/48
% From out of state	55
% From public high school	70
% Live on Campus	77
% African American	7
% Asian	21
% Caucasian	43
% Hispanic	11
% International	10
# Of Countries Represented	47

ACADEMICS

Academic Rating	93
% Of students graduating within 4 years	79
% Of students graduating within 6 years	92
Calendar	semester
Profs interesting rating	84
Profs accessible rating	90
Most common reg class size	fewer than 10 students

MOST POPULAR MAJORS

Economics, English language and literature, visual and performing arts

HONORS PROGRAMS

Honors programs through individual departments. *Combined degree programs*: medical school program with Baylor College of Med. Special programs offered to physically disabled students include note-taking services, reader services, voice recorders.

SPECIAL STUDY OPTIONS

Cross-registration, double major, dual enrollment, English as a Second Language (ESL), honors program, independent study, internships, liberal arts/career combination, student-designed major, study abroad, teacher certification program, 8-year guaranteed medical school program with The Baylor College of Medicine.

BANG FOR YOUR BUCK

In addition to their terrific financial aid policy, Rice offers a number of merit scholarships to incoming students. No additional application is required, and students are selected for merit scholarships based on their admission applications, meaning that when the big envelope comes, it can sometimes offer double the fun. In addition to the monetary value, some scholarships include the opportunity to do individual research under the direction of a faculty member, adding even greater value to the Rice experience.

Even for students who receive no financial assistance, Rice remains one of the best values in higher education. With tuition set at thousands of dollars lower than Ivy League and other peer institutions, Rice walks the walk of keeping the highest caliber of education affordable for all.

STUDENT BODY

While they look like a bunch of "outgoing, down-to-earth kids," students reveal, "Everyone at Rice is, in some way, a nerd." At this "geek chic" school, "Regardless of your interest and no matter how nerdy it might be now, you'll definitely find someone else who shares your passion." "There is something unique about every Rice student," and career goals and intellectual interests run the gamut. A current undergraduate details, "Among my best friends, I have one who is working for Google next year, one who will be training for the Olympic trials over summer, and one who is currently working at a station in Antarctica." "Rice genuinely has a diverse community that accepts people of all backgrounds." Nonetheless, Rice students do share some common traits, generally described as "liberal for Texas," low-key, and "good natured." While most undergraduates are "studious," they're not overly serious. The typical student "rolls out of bed in a t-shirt" and is "willing to help you out in times of need."

Why Students love Rice University

> "Rice has an amazing atmosphere, and it makes me really happy to be here."

WHY STUDENTS LOVE RICE

"Rice has an amazing atmosphere, and it makes me really happy to be here," says a student. Students love that the college system " gives everyone a home away from home and also a way to get noticed and participate in events that would otherwise be inaccessible to students elsewhere," and Houston is "an amazing city with great resources, internships, cultural activities, and weather!!'" "The reputation of Rice and Rice students is like wow in Houston," says a student of town gown (and employer) relations. Accessibility reigns supreme at Rice, and scheduling a lunch with the Dean of Undergraduates or talking with our Athletic Director 'is as easy as walking into their office and introducing yourself." "Even today, I'm stunned by the level to which all of the members of our university interact," says a student.

Rice University

GENERAL INFO

Activities: Choral groups, concert band, dance, drama/theater, jazz band, literary magazine, marching band, music ensembles, musical theater, opera, pep band, radio station, student government, student newspaper, student-run film society, symphony orchestra, television station, yearbook, campus ministries, international student organization. **Organizations:** 215 registered organizations, 11 honor societies, 14 religious organizations. **Athletics (Intercollegiate):** *Men*: Baseball, basketball, cross-country, football, golf, tennis, track/field (outdoor), track/field (indoor). *Women*: Basketball, cross-country, soccer, swimming, tennis, track/ field (outdoor), track/ field (indoor), volleyball. **On-Campus Highlights:** Rice Memorial Center, Baker Institute for Public Policy, Brochstein Pavilion (cafe), Shepherd School of Music, Reckling Park—baseball stadium. **Environmental Initiatives:** 1. Green Building. At present, we have roughly 1,000,000 square feet of facilities on campus that are under construction that will receive some level of LEED certification, including the student dormitory Duncan College, which is targeted for LEED-Gold. In addition, an off-campus child-care center is pursuing LEED certification. Construction waste recycling, with diversion rates of 85–90% recycling. 2. Energy Consumption and Prediction Reporting Application. 3. Green Cleaning.

Why Students love Rice University

"We all help each other out academically and as a result, we all become great friends."

THE BOTTOM LINE

Tuition runs $34,900 a year, with an additional $15,000 or so in fees, room and board, and expenses. But, Rice meets 100% of demonstrated need for all admitted students. As of 2009, Rice eliminated loans to students whose family income is below $80,000, instead meeting their need through a combination of grants, work-study, merit aid (if qualified) and institutional funds. For students with need eligibility whose family income is above $80,000, Rice will award a small subsidized loan in combination with grants, work study, merit aid (if qualified) and institutional funds to cover 100% of the student's unmet need. The subsidized loan cap for students who show need is $2,500 each year, significantly limiting the debt at graduation for the small number of students in this category.

SELECTIVITY

Admissions Rating	**97**
# of applicants	13,804
% of applicants accepted	19
% of acceptees attending	36
# accepting a place on wait list	1,444
% admitted from wait list	9

FRESHMAN PROFILE

Range SAT Critical Reading	**650–750**
Range SAT Math	**690–790**
Range SAT Writing	**660–760**
Range ACT Composite	**31–34**
% graduated top 10% of class	**85**
% graduated top 25% of class	**96**
% graduated top 50% of class	**99**

DEADLINES

Regular Deadline	**1/1**
Normal registration	**no**

FACILITIES

Housing: Coed dorms, special housing for disabled students. All undergraduate students are automatically assigned to one of nine (coed) residential colleges and keep affiliation regardless of whether they live on campus or not. Special *Academic Facilities/Equipment*: Art gallery, museum, media center, language labs, computer labs, civil engineering lab, observatory. *Computers*: 100% of classrooms, 100% of dorms, 100% of libraries, 100% of dining areas, 100% of student union, 5% of common outdoor areas have wireless network access.

FINANCIAL FACTS

Financial Aid Rating	**98**
Annual tuition	$34,900
Room and Board	$12,270
Required Fees	$651
Books and supplies	$800
% frosh rec. need-based scholarship or grant aid	42
% UG rec. need-based scholarship or grant aid	40
% frosh rec. non-need-based scholarship or grant aid	7
% UG rec. non-need-based scholarship or grant aid	5
% frosh rec. need-based self-help aid	42
% UG rec. need-based self-help aid	36
% frosh rec. any financial aid	53
% UG rec. any financial aid	62
% UG borrow to pay for school	26
Average cumulative indebtedness	$13,944

#6

Pomona College

Claremont, CA

POMONA COLLEGE

STUDENTS

1,546 undergrad enrollment

49% Male

51% Female

ADMISSIONS

6,764 applicants →	15% admitted	40% enrolled	EARLY ADMISSIONS →	NR applicants	NR accepted

NR avg. high school gpa

ACT range: 27 (scale 0–36)

SAT range (scale 200–800):
- reading **690–780**
- math **700–780**
- writing **690–770**

91% graduated top 10% of class

100% graduated top 25% of class

FINANCIAL INFO

$39,572	$13,227	$900	$311
annual tuition	room & board	avg. book expenses	required fees

$8,776 avg. indebtedness

ACADEMICS

7:1 student to faculty ratio

19% classes taught by TAs

GRADUATION RATES

91% of students graduating within 4 years

94% of students graduating within 6 years

** NR = Not reported*

Why Pomona College is No. 6

ABOUT THE SCHOOL

Pomona College is the founding member of the Claremont Colleges consortium. This collaboration allows Pomona to offer the richly personal experience of a small, academically superb liberal arts college, and the breadth of resources normally associated with a major university. More than 2,000 courses are offered through the consortium each year. To students, this means that Pomona "is about getting the individual attention every student deserves and providing endless opportunities and resources." Professors are phenomenal and accessible. It's not uncommon to see faculty having lunch with students, or for faculty to invite students or a whole class to their homes. Students say that professors at Pomona "really take the time to meet students, learn names, and get to know them personally…between department barbecues, parties and weekend retreats, by the time you're an upperclassman you will know most of the professors in your major department quite well." Students regularly work side-by-side with professors in the classroom and in the lab as part of the curriculum, and on year-round and summer research projects.

Why Students love Pomona College

> "Underneath our sundresses and rainbow flip-flops we're all closet nerds—everybody is really passionate about something or other."

The Summer Undergraduate Research Program enables students to conduct extended, focused research in close cooperation with a Pomona faculty member. One English major says of the program, "the summer undergraduate research opportunities through Pomona are great! You get paid to either assist with a professor's research or pursue your own project. It's the most rewarding summer job imaginable." Students conduct research on campus, throughout Southern California and in locations that ranged from Oregon, Maine, Colorado, and Illinois, to Botswana, Ghana, Russia, Tanzania, Egypt, Pakistan, France, and the Cook Islands. The Pomona College Internship Program (PCIP) places about 150 students each year in internships in a wide-range of public, for-profit, and non-profit organizations. The best part of this program? "Getting paid by Pomona for unpaid internships," says one student.

Students here are among the most happy and comfortable in the nation. To help ease the transition to college life, first-year students are assigned to sponsor groups of 10 to 20 fellow first-years who live in adjacent rooms with two sophomore sponsors who help them learn the ropes of college life. Students rave that the sponsor program is "the single best living situation for freshmen." It "makes you feel welcome the second you step on campus as a new student," and is "amazing at integrating the freshmen into the community smoothly." Greek life is almost nonexistent, but you'll never hear a complaint about a lack of (usually free and awesome) things to do. There's virtually always an event or a party happening either on campus or just a short walk away on one of the other Claremont campuses (Scripps, Pitzer, Claremont McKenna, and Harvey Mudd). Students say that the Claremont Consortium offers "an abundance of nightlife that you wouldn't expect at a small elite liberal arts school." There are also quite a few quirky traditions here throughout the academic year. If you find yourself craving some big-city life, Los Angeles is just a short train ride away.

Contact Info:

Pomona College
333 N. College Way,
Claremont, CA 91711-6312
Admissions: 909-621-8134
Financial Aid: 909-621-8205
E-mail: admissions@pomona.edu
Fax: 909-621-8952
Website: www.pomona.edu

Fun Facts

- In 1964, a tongue-in-cheek student project "determined" that the number 47 appeared more often in nature than other random number. Ever since, 47 has retained special significance for Pomona College. Today, the Smith Memorial Clock Tower chimes on the 47th minute after the hour from 9:47 a.m. Tp 5:47 p.m., Monday through Friday.
- The campus in Claremont originally began with the donation of an incomplete hotel—what would become Sumner Hall. It is thought that Gwendolyn Rose (the campus ghost) haunts the basement of Sumner Hall. Students, housekeepers, and deans believe that she can be seen during late hours wearing a long, white dress.
- Pomona has a long tradition of student-run a cappella singing groups: Men's Blue and White, Women's Blue and White, the Claremont Shades, Midnight Echo, and Mood Swing.
- Near the San Gabriel Mountains and within driving distance of the Pacific Ocean, Pomona College takes advantage of its location to host an annual "Ski-Beach Day" each spring, which has been happening for at least twenty years. Students board a bus in the morning and are driven to a local ski resort where they ski or snowboard in the morning. After lunch, they are bused down to an Orange County or Los Angeles County beach for the rest of the day.

Pomona College

CAMPUS LIFE

Quality of life Rating	97
Fire Safety Rating	90
Green rating	94
Type of School	Private
Environment	Town

STUDENTS

Total undergrad enrolllment	1,546
% Male to Female	49/51
% From out of state	68
% From public high school	75
% Live on Campus	98
% African American	7
% Asian	11
% Caucasian	46
% Hispanic	11
% International	6
# Of Countries Represented	73

ACADEMICS

Academic Rating	97
% Of students graduating within 4 years	91
% Of students graduating within 6 years	94
Calendar	semester
Profs interesting rating	93
Profs accessible rating	97
Most common reg class size	10–19 students
Most common lab size	10–19 students

MOST POPULAR MAJORS

Economics, English language and literature, visual and performing arts

SPECIAL STUDY OPTIONS

Cross-registration, double major, exchange student program (domestic), independent study, internships, student-designed major, study abroad, The college has a 3-2 combined Bachelors (BA & BS) in Engineering with Washington University in St. Louis and the California Institute of Technology.

BANG FOR YOUR BUCK

The financial aid program here is exceedingly generous and goes beyond just covering tuition, room and board, and fees, for which Pomona can, and does meet, 100 percent of students' demonstrated financial need. The financial aid packages consist wholly of grants and scholarships, probably along with a campus job that you work maybe 10 hours a week. For students on financial aid who wish to participate in study abroad, Pomona ensures that cost is not a barrier. All programs carry academic credit and no extra cost for tuition or room and board. To ensure that all Pomona students are able to participate in the college's internship program, funding is provided in the form of an hourly wage for semester-long internships, making it possible for students to take unpaid positions. The Career Development Office (CDO) also subsidizes transportation to and from internships. In addition, the college offers funding, based on need, to students with job interviews on the East Coast during Winter Break Recruiting Days program.

Why Students love Pomona College

"You can't beat the climate, the community, or the classroom experience here."

STUDENT BODY

At Pomona, "Only a third or so of students are from California," yet the California attitude reigns supreme. Here, you'll find a number of "tree-hugging, rock-climbing, Tom's shoes–wearing" undergraduates, with most students generally falling within the "liberal, upper-middle-class, hipster-athlete" continuum. Students report a "decent level of diversity and a strong international community." Studious and talented, Pomona undergraduates "excel in the classroom and usually have some sort of passion that they pursue outside of the classroom." "Underneath our sundresses and rainbow flip-flops, we're all closet nerds—everybody is really passionate about something or other." At Pomona, "You will meet the football player who got a perfect score on his SAT or the dreadlocked hippie who took multivariable calculus when he was sixteen." Dress code is uniformly casual, and "flip-flops, polo, or tank tops and shorts" are the unofficial uniform.

WHY STUDENTS LOVE POMONA COLLEGE

"As far as liberal arts colleges go," says one psychology major, "you can't beat the climate, the community, or the classroom experience here." Others simply insist that it is "as close to paradise as a student will ever get!" Students here are "ridiculously happy" and agree that the "excellent professors and engaged students, along with the perfect weather, make the learning environment at Pomona second to none." Pomona's greatest strength, it seems, aside from the beautiful campus and pristine Southern Californian weather, is the perfect balance the school has achieved in most aspects of student life. To students, it exemplifies "the perfect balance between academic rigor and laid-back fun" with a California attitude; it is a small liberal arts college with the resources and social opportunities of a much larger university; and it is filled with "driven students in a non-competitive environment." Students love the "high level of camaraderie" and strong sense of community at Pomona, where "everyone knows and respects everyone else." They also value the small, intimate class sizes and the "accessibility, enthusiasm, and friendliness of its professors," who are a highlight of the Pomona experience. "Amazing opportunities for undergraduate research," "incredible" food, and 80-degree weather in the middle of January are just icing on top of the cake. To sum Pomona up, one student affirms that "it is one of the most rigorous and prestigious colleges in the country, but it is also one of the happiest."

GENERAL INFO

Activities: Choral groups, concert band, dance, drama/theater, jazz band, literary magazine, music ensembles, musical theater, pep band, radio station, student government, student newspaper, student-run film society, symphony orchestra, television station, yearbook, campus ministries, international student organization. **Organizations:** 280 registered organizations, 3 honor societies, 5 religious organizations. 3 fraternities. **Athletics (Intercollegiate):** *Men*: Baseball, basketball, cross-country, diving, football, golf, soccer, swimming, tennis, track/field (outdoor), water polo. *Women*: Basketball, cross-country, diving, golf, lacrosse, soccer, softball, swimming, tennis, track/field (outdoor), volleyball, water polo. **On-Campus Highlights:** Smith Campus Center, Sontag Greek Theater, Rains Center for Sports and Recreation, Brackett Observatory.

Why Students love Pomona College

"You will meet the football player who got a perfect score on his SAT or the dreadlocked hippie who took multivariable calculus when he was sixteen."

"The perfect balance between academic rigor and laid-back fun."

THE BOTTOM LINE

Tuition, fees, and room and board at Pomona run about $50,000 for a year. At the same time, the mantra here is that no one should hesitate to apply because of the cost. Pomona College has need-blind admissions and meets the full, demonstrated financial aid need of every accepted student with scholarships and work-study. Students say that Pomona "has a reputation of providing great financial aid packages."

SELECTIVITY

Admissions Rating	**98**
# of applicants	6,764
% of applicants accepted	15
% of acceptees attending	40
# accepting a place on wait list	300

FRESHMAN PROFILE

Range SAT Critical Reading	**690–780**
Range SAT Math	**700–780**
Range SAT Writing	**690–770**
Range ACT Composite	**31–34**
% graduated top 10% of class	**91**
% graduated top 25% of class	**100**
% graduated top 50% of class	**100**

DEADLINES

Regular Deadline	**1/2**
Normal registration	**yes**

FACILITIES

Housing: Coed dorms, theme housing. Language Residence Hall. 85% of campus accessible to physically disabled. *Special Academic Facilities/Equipment*: Oldenborg Center for Foreign Languages, Musuem of Art, Brackett Observatory. Computers: 75% of classrooms, 50% of dorms, 100% of libraries, 100% of dining areas, 100% of student union, 100% of common outdoor areas have wireless network access. Administrative functions (other than registration) can be performed online.

FINANCIAL FACTS

Financial Aid Rating	**99**
Annual tuition	$39,572
Room and Board	$13,227
Required Fees	$311
Books and supplies	$900
% frosh rec. need-based scholarship or grant aid	51
% UG rec.need-based scholarship or grant aid	52
% frosh rec. need-based self-help aid	51
% UG rec. need-based self-help aid	52
% frosh rec. any financial aid	50
% UG rec. any financial aid	53
% UG borrow to pay for school	47
Average cumulative indebtedness	$8,776

#7

Washington University in St. Louis

St. Louis, MO

Washington University in St. Louis

STUDENTS

13,869 undergrad enrollment

51% Male

49% Female

ADMISSIONS

24,939 applicants	21% admitted	31% enrolled	EARLY ADMISSIONS	NR applicants	NR accepted

NR avg. high school gpa

ACT range (0–36): 27

SAT range (200–800): reading 680–750; math 710–790

96% graduated top 10% of class

100% graduated top 25% of class

FINANCIAL INFO

$40,950	$13,119	$1,390	$1,042
annual tuition	room & board	avg. book expenses	required fees

ACADEMICS

7:1 student to faculty ratio

19% classes taught by TAs

GRADUATION RATES

86% of students graduating within 4 years

94% of students graduating within 6 years

** NR = Not reported*

Why Washington University in St. Louis is No. 7

Washington University in St. Louis is a hidden gem that offers students an opportunity to explore interests in a number of areas both academically and extracurricularly, all while maintaining core Midwestern values. Undergraduates truly have the flexibility to study what they want, and students can take any class offered in any college, double major or minor across colleges, or even get dual degrees. The strenuous academics are buttressed by an incredible faculty that will help a student out in any way, and even students will go out of their way to be helpful. Combined with a stellar reputation in the Midwest (and to a certain extent, nationally), and the university can't help but make people fall in love with the campus, people, and location.

Community is probably Washington University's greatest asset, and the Midwestern charm of the school creates a positive, vibrant environment for all who work and study there. The school has a beautiful campus and an active and friendly student body that is genuinely concerned about the city surrounding it, and who actively participate in social justice measures. The warm friendliness of the gorgeous campus and the surplus of resources fosters the antithesis cutthroat competition, and gives students the best opportunities and tools to succeed socially and academically.

Why Students Love Washington University in St. Louis

"The education of an Ivy League university with the atmosphere and warmth of home."

ABOUT THE SCHOOL

Washington University in St. Louis provides its students with a total educational experience designed not only to prepare each student to find success in whatever career path he or she chooses, but also to make a contribution to society. The school is "rich with great people, amazing extracurricular opportunities, an underrated city just down the street, and an education that will challenge you." Academic flexibility allows students to study across academic disciplines in the university's five undergraduate schools, and these co-curricular programs "are flexible enough to allow students to pursue academic interests in business, arts and sciences, art and architecture, and engineering all at once." Students at Washington University have the benefit of working alongside some of the brightest students in the world as they learn from world-renowned faculty who love to work with undergraduates. Professors "are engaged and lively," and faculty interactions can include research and mentoring, not only in the natural sciences, but in all fields, including through freshman programs. "You can tell everyone just loves to be here," says a student.

With the university's emphasis on exploration, advising is a key part of the process, and the administration "cares for the students immensely and provides an exemplary education." Students have advisors in all aspects of campus life, including residential advisers, academic advisers, peer advisers, pre-professional advisers, and career advisers. Approximately 400 businesses and non-profit organizations visit campus each year. Additionally, the Career

Contact Info:

Campus Box 1089,
One Brookings Drive,
St. Louis, MO 63130-4899
Admissions: 314-935-6000
Financial Aid: 888-547-6670
E-mail: admissions@wustl.edu
Fax: 314-935-4290
Website: wustl.edu

Fun Facts

- Washington University was conceived by seventeen St. Louis business, political, and religious leaders concerned by the lack of institutions of higher learning in the Midwest. Missouri State Senator Wayman Crow and Unitarian minister William Greenleaf Eliot, grandfather of the poet T.S. Eliot, led the effort.
- Washington University has been selected by the Commission on Presidential Debates to host more presidential and vice presidential debates than any other institution in history. The University has been selected to host a presidential or vice presidential debate in every United States presidential election since 1992.
- Washington University counts more than 114,000 living alumni, 26 Rhodes Scholars, and 22 Nobel laureates affiliated with the university as faculty or students.
- Famous students who dropped out: Charles Eames (who was expelled for defending modernist architecture); Tennessee Williams (who left in protest of not winning the poetry prize); Enterprise Rent-a-Car founder Jack C. Taylor (who withdrew to fight in World War II); actor Robert Guillaume (who withdrew to study opera); Pulitzer Prize winner Bill Dedman (who left to become a newspaper reporter); and IQ-record holder Marilyn vos Savant (who says she withdrew because she was bored).

Top Ten Private Schools

Washington University in St. Louis

CAMPUS LIFE

Quality of life Rating	98
Fire Safety Rating	86
Green rating	60*
Type of School	Private
Environment	City

STUDENTS

Total undergrad enrolllment	6,542
% Male to Female	51/49
% From out of state	91
% From public high school	60
% Live on Campus	79
# of Fraternities	12
# of Sororities	6
% African American	6
% Asian	15
% Caucasian	57
% Hispanic	5
% International	6
# Of Countries Represented	87

ACADEMICS

Academic Rating	96
% Of students graduating within 4 years	86
% Of students graduating within 6 years	94
Calendar	semester
Profs interesting rating	85
Profs accessible rating	88
Most common reg class size	10–19 students
Most common lab size	10–19 students

MOST POPULAR MAJORS

Economics, English language and literature, visual and performing arts

SPECIAL STUDY OPTIONS

Accelerated program, cooperative education program, cross-registration, double major, dual enrollment, English as a Second Language (ESL), exchange student program (domestic), independent study, internships, and the University Scholars Program.

Center sponsors trips to New York, Washington, D.C., Chicago, and Los Angeles for career exploration and networking. "There are so many opportunities for advising and additional help if you choose to utilize them. The university does an excellent job of making the student body aware of these resources and helping us make the most of them." Outside of the classroom, students contribute to the campus community and the St. Louis area through community service projects such as Each One Teach One and Dance Marathon, which has raised more than one million dollars for children's charities. Be it "an intramural sport, organizing a charity event, Greek life, the radio station, or the new live sketch comedy show, every student takes part in non-academic activities that build friendships and make college life far more colorful." "I was impressed by students' abilities to pursue academically rigorous classes, balance numerous activities, and still find time to spend at various campus events with friends," says a student.

WHY STUDENTS LOVE WASHINGTON UNIVERSITY IN ST. LOUIS

"Collaboration" over competition here "is key," as the school "provides the education of an Ivy League university with the atmosphere and warmth of home." "People here are incredibly considerate and easy to work with," says a student. The professors' "passion for the subject is contagious for the student body," and both "students and faculty go out of their way to help you without asking for anything in return."

The school "does a great job of allowing students the best resources for both work and play." The food "is delicious," the dorms "are beautiful," and students "are happy." St. Louis itself is well-beloved, and the popular Delmar Loop is "just a ten-minute walk from main campus." Loaded with restaurants and small storefronts, "It's an extremely popular place for students to walk around, shop at small boutiques, and grab a bite to eat." An "incredibly welcoming atmosphere" means that "you will always see smiles everywhere you go on campus."

BANG FOR YOUR BUCK

WUSTL offers a personalized approach to financial assistance. The university's financial aid office takes the time to understand each family's individual financial circumstances and award financial assistance that is tailored to a particular family's unique situation. (This works out particularly well for middle-income families with mitigating factors affecting their ability to pay.) In addition, WUSTL is committed to ensuring that no student is forced to leave school due to a change in his or her family's financial circumstances. A simple one-page application makes applying for financial assistance simple, and awards range up to the full cost of attendance. In addition to generous academic scholarships and need-based aid, WUSTL strives to reduce the amount of student loans being borrowed by students. Many students qualify for financial assistance awards which meet their demonstrated need without the use of student loans. Merit-based scholarships are plentiful. The John B. Ervin Scholars Program and Annika Rodriguez Scholars Program cover up to the full cost of tuition plus a stipend, and focus on leadership, service, and commitment to diversity and are open to applications in all academic areas.

Washington University in St. Louis

STUDENT BODY

Students here quickly fall captive to the "positive atmosphere." "Everyone here is happy! Seriously, you'll always see smiles everywhere you go on campus." Students say there's not "a 'typical' student at Wash U...I guess the best way to describe students here is that they defy the typical stereotypes. You'll have a fraternity brother who's a dancer [or] a premed student who's minoring in architecture, etc." Students "embrace that their fellow classmates have their own interests, even picking up new hobbies from their friends." Wash U provides the backdrop for "a diverse set of social circles." "There are the suburban East-Coasters, the liberal Texans, the local kids from St. Louis, the California jocks, etc." "The typical Wash U student graduated in the top two percent of her high school class, participated in at least four different clubs with an office in at least one (but probably two), was homecoming queen, and volunteered at an animal shelter on the weekends." Students here are "very involved and take both academics and extracurriculars (particularly community service) very seriously."

Why Students Love Washington University in St. Louis

"Everyone here is happy! Seriously, you'll always see smiles everywhere you go on campus."

"Flexible enough to allow students to pursue academic interests in business, arts and sciences, art and architecture, and engineering all at once."

GENERAL INFO

Activities: Choral groups, concert band, dance, drama/theater, jazz band, literary magazine, music ensembles, musical theater, opera, pep band, radio station, student government, student newspaper, student-run film society, symphony orchestra, television station, campus ministries, international student organization. **Organizations:** 200 registered organizations, 18 honor societies, 19 religious organizations. 12 fraternities, 6 sororities. **Athletics (Intercollegiate):** *Men*: Baseball, basketball, cross-country, diving, football, soccer, swimming, tennis, track/field (outdoor), track/field (indoor). *Women*: Basketball, cross-country, diving, golf, soccer, softball, swimming, tennis, track/field (outdoor), track/field (indoor), volleyball. **On-Campus Highlights:** Gallery of Art, Edison Theatre, Ursa's Cafe, Francis Gymnasium and Francis Field, Residence Halls.

BOTTOM LINE

Undergraduate tuition and fees ring in at about $40,400 annually. Add another $13,000 for room and board, and you're looking at a $53,400 baseline price tag, not including books, supplies, personal expenses, or transportation. Don't fret: Financial aid is generous and merit-based aid is available as well.

SELECTIVITY

Admissions Rating	**98**
# of applicants	24,939
% of applicants accepted	21
% of acceptees attending	31

FRESHMAN PROFILE

Range SAT Critical Reading	**680–750**
Range SAT Math	**710–790**
Range ACT Composite	**32–34**
% graduated top 10% of class	**96**
% graduated top 25% of class	**100**
% graduated top 50% of class	**100**

DEADLINES

Regular Deadline	**1/15**
Normal registration	**no**

FACILITIES

Housing: Coed dorms, fraternity/sorority housing, apartments for married students, cooperative housing, apartments for single students, wellness housing, special interest suites, upper-class housing, single sex floors in coed buildings, on-campus transfer-specific housing, and small-group housing for students who share common interests and goals. *Special Academic Facilities/Equipment*: Art gallery, business/economics experimental lab, botanical garden, NASA planetary imaging facility, TAP reactor system, triple monochromator, Computer Automated Radioactive Particle Tracking and gamma ray Computed Tomography, Observatory, EADS learning center, Student Enterprise Zone, Edison Theatre, lab science building, outdoor Tyson Research Center.

FINANCIAL FACTS

Financial Aid Rating	**97**
Annual tuition	$40,950
Room and Board	$13,119
Required Fees	$1,042
Books and supplies	$1,390
% frosh rec. need-based scholarship or grant aid	35
% UG rec.need-based scholarship or grant aid	40
% frosh rec. need-based self-help aid	28
% UG rec. need-based self-help aid	29
% frosh rec. any financial aid	37
% UG rec. any financial aid	41
% UG borrow to pay for school	38

#8

Yale University

New Haven, CT

STUDENTS

5,279 undergrad enrollment

49% Male ♂♂♂♂♂♂♂♂

51% Female ♀♀♀♀♀♀♀♀♀♀

ADMISSIONS

25,869 →	8%	67%	EARLY →	NR	NR
applicants	admitted	enrolled	ADMISSIONS	applicants	accepted

NR avg. high school gpa

30–34 ACT range (0–36)

reading	700–800
math	700–780
writing	700–790

SAT range (200–800)

96% graduated top 10% of class

100% graduated top 25% of class

FINANCIAL INFO

$40,500	$12,200	$1,000	$10,717
annual tuition	room & board	avg. book expenses	avg. indebtedness

ACADEMICS

6:1 student to faculty ratio

3% classes taught by TAs

GRADUATION RATES

90% of students graduating within 4 years

98% of students graduating within 6 years

** NR = Not reported*

Why Yale University is No. 8

Yale students are known to gaze into the distance and wax poetic about their school, and for good reason: the place is a gem, haven't you heard? Yale places unparalleled focus on undergraduate education, placing its world-class faculty front and center of the classrooms (all Yale faculty must teach at least one undergrad course per year). The school's academics mean that no matter the field that students may choose, they will receive excellent preparation for their next step. This freedom of academic exploration with guaranteed quality makes for a perfect combination of a liberal arts college and a big university with seemingly limitless resources, from the range of undergraduate research opportunities to the 12 million volumes in the Yale libraries.

Where students find something lacking, they create: Yale students are famous for forming and shaping their own clubs and organizations. The abounding Yale traditions help students feel connected to the University's rich history, and a residential college system further personalizes the experience and offers student support. Colleges have a Dean and a Master, each of which is only responsible for 300 to 500 students, so administrative attention is highly specialized and widely available. Diversity is easy when you can attract the best students in every demographic, and Yale exploits its advantage (and its ability to offer generous financial aid) to compile a student body drawn from all racial, ethnic, and socioeconomic backgrounds.

Why Students Love Yale University

"Everyone has many activities that they are a part of, which in turn fosters the closely connected feel of the campus."

ABOUT THE SCHOOL

As one of the triple towers of the Ivy League, when you say you attend "Yale" you don't really have to say much else—those four letters say it all. Beyond the gothic spires ("It reminds me of Hogwarts," says a student) and ivy-clad residence halls, Yale University truly lives up to its reputation as one of the preeminent undergraduate schools in the nation. At this world-class research institution, 5,000-plus undergraduates students (who are "are passionate about everything") benefit not only from "amazing academics and extensive resources" that provide "phenomenal in- and out-of-class education," but also from participation in "a student body that is committed to learning and to each other." Cutting-edge research is commonplace and great teaching the norm, and three quarters of courses enroll fewer than 20 students. A popular test-the-waters registration system allows students to sample classes for up to two weeks before they commit to their schedule, and the school "encourages its students to take a range of courses." "The wealth of opportunities in and out of the classroom made the choice very clear to me," says a student. The education they're getting prepares them for leadership on a massive scale. Case in point: Yale alumni were represented on the Democratic or Republican ticket in every U.S. Presidential election between 1972 and 2004. Still, no matter the end result, it's clear that "the people at Yale are genuinely interested in learning for learning's sake, not so that they can get a job on Wall Street."

Contact Info:

PO Box 208234

New Haven, CT 06520-8234

Admissions: 203-432-9300

Financial Aid: 203-432-2700

E-mail: student.questions@yale.edu

Fax: 203-432-9392

Website: www.yale.edu

Fun Facts

- Prestigious Yale University was founded in 1701 in, what was known at that time, as the Colony of Connecticut.
- It is the third oldest university in the country and is part of the elite Ivy League with schools like Harvard, Princeton, and Brown.
- Yale was originally founded as the Collegiate School at New Haven. Various clergymen in the colony wanted to establish a college to train clergy and political leaders for service to the colony. The founders were alumni from another prestigious school, Harvard, which was founded more than 60 years prior.
- The Collegiate School officially changed their name to Yale University in 1701. This was to honor Elihu Yale, the governor of the East India Company out of Great Britain. He donated a crate of goods to help the struggling school continue to operate.
- The *Yale Daily News* is the oldest collegiate daily newspaper still in existence. It has been printed five days a week since January 28, 1878. The school also has the oldest and best known a cappella group. The Wiffenpoos have been singing on Monday nights since 1909. They typically perform at Mory's, the famous, members only tavern on the Yale campus.

Yale University

Top Ten Private Schools

CAMPUS LIFE

Quality of life Rating	95
Fire Safety Rating	60*
Green rating	94
Type of School	Private
Environment	City

STUDENTS

Total undergrad enrolllment	5,279
% Male to Female	49/51
% From out of state	93
% From public high school	56
% Live on Campus	88
% African American	6
% Asian	14
% Caucasian	17
% Hispanic	9
% N.A.	1
% International	10
# Of Countries Represented	108

ACADEMICS

Academic Rating	96
% Of students graduating within 4 years	90
% Of students graduating within 6 years	98
Calendar	semester
Profs interesting rating	87
Profs accessible rating	87
Most common reg class size	10–19 students

MOST POPULAR MAJORS

Economics, biology, political science

SPECIAL STUDY OPTIONS

Accelerated program, distance learning, double major, English as a Second Language (ESL), honors program, independent study, internships, liberal arts/career combination, student-designed major, study abroad, teacher certification program.

At Yale, education extends well beyond the classroom. The widely diverse Yalies are some of the country's most motivated, brilliant students, and their "energy and Yale pride is evident the moment you step foot on campus." Residential colleges form the backbone of the school's social structure, and "become an incredibly close, smaller community within the larger university sphere." "Aside from the stress of midterms and finals, life at Yale is relatively carefree." Extracurricular activities are as diverse as the student body; there are more than 300 student groups on campus, from a cappella groups to anime marathons. Many students are politically active, and "a very large number of students either volunteer or try to get involved in some sort of organization to make a difference in the world." In their downtime, Yalies also venture into New Haven for world-class pizza and occasionally jump the commuter train down to New York City. "Instead of figuring out what to do with my free time, I have to figure out what not to do during my free time," says a student. Does life at Yale sound too good to be true? The school's incredible 99 percent freshman to sophomore retention rate says that life at Yale might really be that good.

BANG FOR YOUR BUCK

Here's a shocker: you don't have to be wealthy to have access to a Yale education. Thanks to a multibillion-dollar endowment, Yale operates a need-blind admissions policy and guarantees to meet 100 percent of each applicant's demonstrated need. In fact, Yale's annual expected financial aid budget is larger than many schools' endowments. Yale spends more than $100 million dollars on student financial annually. The average scholarship award is around $35,000, and it's entirely need-based—no athletic or merit scholarships are available. Seven hundred and fifty Yale undergraduates will have a $0 expected parent contribution next year—that's more than 10 percent of its student body. Yale even provides undergraduates on financial aid with grant support for summer study and unpaid internships abroad.

Why Students Love Yale University

"The spontaneity of the students."

STUDENT BODY

A typical Yalie is "tough to define because so much of what makes Yale special is the unique convergence of different students to form one cohesive entity. Nonetheless, the one common characteristic of Yale students is passion—each Yalie is driven and dedicated to what he or she loves most, and it creates a palpable atmosphere of enthusiasm on campus." True enough, the student body represents a wide variety of ethnic, religious, economic, and academic backgrounds, but they all "thrive on learning, whether in a class, from a book, or from a conversation with a new friend." Students here also "tend to do a lot." "Everyone has many activities that they are a part of, which in turn fosters the closely connected feel of the campus." Undergrads tend to lean to the left politically, but for "those whose political views aren't as liberal as the rest of the campus…there are several campus organizations that cater to them."

Yale University

WHY STUDENTS LOVE YALE

One of the great things about Yale is "the spontaneity of the students." A conversation is just as likely to be "about serious issues like what to do in the Middle East as something completely random as Pokemon." Students spend four years figuring out what it is that they love, and then pursue it the nth degree. "Here, people who get wacky ideas don't just sit on them, but try to do something with them," says a student. Students here are serious about enjoying their youths and studies, and "having the time of your life while still achieving what you want in life." This is easy enough when you live in "a magical place with incredible people, professors, and extracurriculars." "Everyone loves it here—why would someone go anywhere else?" asks one of the many happy Elis.

Why Students Love Yale University

"A student body that is committed to learning and to each other."

"The people at Yale are genuinely interested in learning for learning's sake, not so that they can get a job on Wall Street."

GENERAL INFO

Activities: Choral groups, concert band, dance, drama/theater, jazz band, literary magazine, marching band, music ensembles, musical theater, opera, pep band, radio station, student government, student newspaper, student-run film society, symphony orchestra, television station, yearbook, campus ministries, international student organization. **Organizations:** 350 registered organizations. **Athletics (Intercollegiate):** *Men*: Baseball, basketball, crew/rowing, cross-country, diving, fencing, football, golf, ice hockey, lacrosse, sailing, soccer, squash, swimming, tennis, track/field (outdoor), track/field (indoor). *Women*: Basketball, crew/rowing, cross-country, diving, fencing, field hockey, golf, gymnastics, ice hockey, lacrosse, sailing, soccer, softball, squash, swimming, tennis, track/field (outdoor), track/field (indoor), volleyball. **On-Campus Highlights:** Old Campus, Sterling Memorial Library, Yale British Art Center, Beinecke Rare Book and Manuscript Library, Payne-Whitney Gymnasium. **Environmental Initiatives:** Greenhouse gas commitment of 43% below 2005 levels by 2020, 40% of food served in the dining halls is local/organic, LEED Silver certification for all new construction.

THE BOTTOM LINE

Annual tuition to Yale is $38,300. Room and board in one of Yale's residential colleges is $11,500 per year bringing the total cost to about $50,000 annually, not to mention costs of books, supplies, health insurance, and personal expenses. Yale guarantees to meet 100 percent of all students' demonstrated financial need; as a result, the cost of Yale education is often considerably lower than the sticker price.

SELECTIVITY

Admissions Rating	**99**
# of applicants	25,869
% of applicants accepted	8
% of acceptees attending	67
# accepting a place on wait list	727
% admitted from wait list	11

FRESHMAN PROFILE

Range SAT Critical Reading	**700–800**
Range SAT Math	**700–780**
Range SAT Writing	**700–790**
Range ACT Composite	**30–34**
% graduated top 10% of class	**96**
% graduated top 25% of class	**100**
% graduated top 50% of class	**100**

DEADLINES

Regular Deadline	**12/31**
Normal registration	**no**

FACILITIES

Housing: Coed dorms, special housing for disabled students, Students are randomly assigned to 1 of 12 residential colleges where they live, eat, socialize, and pursue various academic and extracurricular activities. All undergraduate housing is provided through residential college system. *Special Academic Facilities/Equipment*: Art and history museums, observatory, electron microscopes, nuclear accelerators, center for international and areas studies, child study center, marsh botanical gardens, center for parallel supercomputing. *Computers*: 100% of classrooms, 100% of dorms, 100% of libraries, 100% of dining areas, 100% of student union, 100% of common outdoor areas have wireless network access.

FINANCIAL FACTS

Financial Aid Rating	**99**
Annual tuition	$40,500
Room and Board	$12,200
Required Fees	$0
Books and supplies	$1,000
% frosh rec. need-based scholarship or grant aid	60
% UG rec.need-based scholarship or grant aid	54
% frosh rec. need-based self-help aid	42
% UG rec. need-based self-help aid	45
% frosh rec. any financial aid	60
% UG rec. any financial aid	54
% UG borrow to pay for school	28
Average cumulative indebtedness	$10,717

#9

California Institute of Technology

Pasadena, CA

Caltech

STUDENTS

967 undergrad enrollment

60% Male ♂♂♂♂♂♂♂♂♂♂♂♂

40% Female ♀♀♀♀♀♀♀♀

ADMISSIONS

4,859 →	17%	36%	EARLY →	NR	NR
applicants	admitted	enrolled	ADMISSIONS	applicants	accepted

NR avg. high school gpa

ACT range: 34–35 (0–36)

SAT range (200–800): reading 700–780; math 770–800; writing 710–780

96% graduated top 10% of class

100% graduated top 25% of class

FINANCIAL INFO

$34,989	$10,755	$1,290	$3,660
annual tuition	room & board	avg. book expenses	required fees

$10,760 avg. indebtedness

ACADEMICS

3:1 student to faculty ratio

0% classes taught by TAs

GRADUATION RATES

81% of students graduating within 4 years

90% of students graduating within 6 years

* NR = Not reported

Why California Institute of Technology is No. 9

Caltech is pretty much one of, if not the, greatest research university out there. The math, science, and engineering programs are indisputably first-rate, and the school is a magnet for the world's brightest minds, and the corporations and organizations that want to fund them (it earned about $330 million in sponsored research in 2010 alone). Whatever path you choose (almost a third of the school's course offerings are in the humanities and social science division), the resources are plentiful. The chance to do real, hands-on research as an undergraduate is one of the things that makes Caltech such an extraordinary place, and the opportunities to interact with intellectual greatness (whether in the form of professors, grad students, or even fellow students) abound. Even outside of the school year, Caltech is looking out for its students, and every year the Career Development Office hosts 150-200 companies on campus (including Microsoft, the USPTO, and Oracle) with the goal of matching new graduates with future employment. The school also has a Summer Undergraduate Research Fellowships (SURF) program, which introduces students to research under the guidance of seasoned research mentors at Caltech and JPL.

Though the academic atmosphere is intense, to say the least, clubs and extracurricular activities run the gamut, and students that leave their rooms find it very easy to get involved . Even for those who might have found themselves on the awkward end of the social spectrum in high school are welcomed here, and Caltech's unique housing system (in which first-year students are required to live on campus, in one of eight houses) helps provide students with a support system and social community from the start. Nearby beaches, mountains, and desert are all within two hours, not to mention the cultural hub that is Los Angeles. Best of all, Caltech is interested in students' minds, not their wallets, and graduates of this need-blind university graduate with one of the lowest average indebtedness rates for four year private universities (as well as some of the highest starting salaries).

Why Students love California Institute of Technology

> "Where else do you have beaches, mountains and desert all within a 2-hour drive?"

ABOUT THE SCHOOL

The California Institute of Technology's swagger is completely out of proportion with its small size of fewer than 1,000 students. Thirty-one Caltech alumni and faculty have won the Nobel Prize; 65 have won the National Medal of Science or Technology; and 112 have been elected to the National Academies. To say that this science and engineering powerhouse is world-class is an understatement. Located in the suburbs of Los Angeles ("Where else do you have beaches, mountains and desert all within a 2-hour drive?"), Caltech boasts a long history of excellence with a list of major research achievements that read like a textbook in the history of science. It goes without saying that academics are highly rigorous and competitive; if you are used to getting straight A's, Caltech may be a shock to the system. "If you were the top student all your life,

Contact Info:

1200 East California Boulevard

Mail Code 1-94

Pasadena, CA 91125

Admissions: 626-395-6341

Financial Aid: 626-395-6280

E-mail: ugadmissions@caltech.edu

Fax: 626-683-3026

Website: admissions.caltech.edu

Fun Facts

- Two times a day, Sandra Tsing Loh, a Caltech alumnus, presents for 6 minutes the various Caltech discoveries. Some of them are really surprising and out of the ordinary.
- Find and meet your "new family" once here. There are various ethnic clubs at Caltech which organize events and leisure according to their native traditions. You can find also a club that matches with your favorite hobby or sport. If this club would not be active any more, maybe it would be an opportunity for you to make it live again.
- Numb3rs was a popular TV show that was filmed at Caltech.
- *Caltech Today* is the daily web newsletter of the various events happening on the campus and around the town (seminars, social events, athletics competitions, academic awards, outings, theatres, etc.).
- The Caltech Public Events is very active in organizing circus, musical, dance, theatre, singers events, seminars, conferences, documentaries and movies for all kind of publics (from family public to qualified and experts) for a nominal fee when it's not free for the Caltech community.

California Institute of Technology

CAMPUS LIFE

Quality of life Rating	76
Fire Safety Rating	65
Green rating	65
Type of School	Private
Environment	Metropolis

STUDENTS

Total undergrad enrolllment	967
% Male to Female	60/40
% From out of state	65
% From public high school	70
% Live on Campus	95
% African American	1
% Asian	39
% Caucasian	37
% Hispanic	6
% International	12
# Of Countries Represented	32

ACADEMICS

Academic Rating	93
% Of students graduating within 4 years	81
% Of students graduating within 6 years	90
Calendar	quarter
Profs interesting rating	61
Profs accessible rating	66
Most common reg class size	fewer than 10 students
Most common lab size	20–29 students

MOST POPULAR MAJORS

Mathematics, mechanical engineering, physics

SPECIAL STUDY OPTIONS

Cooperative education program, cross-registration, double major, English as a Second Language (ESL), exchange student program (domestic), independent study, liberal arts/career combination, student-designed major, study abroad, "remedial services" are not formally offered. However, remediation is available for students who are deficient in basic scientific knowledge or technical skills.

prepare to experience a big dose of humility because you'll have to work hard just to stay in the middle of the pack," says a student. Techers say working here is "like trying to drink from a firehose," which is 'as accurate a statement as can be made, given the breadth, intensity, and amount of coursework required."

Every undergraduate is required to complete Caltech's comprehensive core curriculum, which includes challenging coursework in math, physics, and chemistry. Unlike many research-focused universities, Caltech undergraduates are able to roll up their sleeves and dive into some serious research, even in the first year. Undergraduates are welcomed in graduate-level coursework, and even Nobel laureates occasionally teach first-year courses. Professors "tend to be very passionate about their subjects." And with its small student enrollment, the majority of classes are composed of just 10 to 20 students. As for students, there are plenty of Caltech students who spend their days (and nights) with their noses in some thick books. Still, Caltech isn't the nerdy Mecca you might expect. Sports, student clubs, and even humanities courses are popular, and there is a healthy sense of mischief; students seem to have a notorious reputation for "amusing" and generally harmless pranks.

Why Students love California Institute of Technology

"Every student is brilliant."

BANG FOR YOUR BUCK

Caltech is extremely affordable, while the school's immense reputation and plethora of opportunities ensure a bright future in research or academia for Caltech graduates. Caltech operates need-blind admissions for all U.S. citizens and permanent residents. Every year, financial aid awards meet 100 percent of demonstrated student need. Of particular note, the school makes every effort to limit a student's debt, awarding aid packages with little work-study or loans. Across the board, the maximum loan expectation for Caltech students is just $3,500 annually, and the average loan debt for Caltech students is less than $10,000 for all four years. The school also offers substantial need-based packages for international students, a rarity among private institutions. Caltech Scholarships are awarded based on demonstrated financial need.

STUDENT BODY

Caltech is home to "lots of whites and Asians," and the student population is overwhelmingly male. "Your typical student here was the math team/science team/quiz bowl type in high school." "This is nerd heaven." "Everyone's a scientist," and "every student is brilliant." Students also describe themselves as "hardworking," "quirky," and "slightly eccentric." You'll find a wide variety, though, "from cool party types, to scary hardcore nerds, to cool party types who build massive railguns in their spare time." Some students are "terribly creative." Ultimately, it's a hard group to pigeonhole. "You will meet someone who you might think is a total jock if you saw him or her on the street, but [he or she] works late at night on homework and aces exams," promises one student. "If you come here with stereotypes in mind, they will be broken."

California Institute of Technology

WHY STUDENTS LOVE CALTECH

Aside from the small size and the "location, location, location," students especially love the school's housing system, which provides an instant structure and social calendar. "The houses combine the feel and purpose of a dorm with the pride and spirit of a fraternity." When Caltech students throw a party, "it's a major operation," and "people go to incredible lengths for fun and parties." "Most parties here involve two weeks of prior planning and construction," and the end result is "usually pretty epic." This is also the place to go to blissfully geek out about anything you want, as "everyone is interested in math and science."

Why Students love California Institute of Technology

"The houses combine the feel and purpose of a dorm with the pride and spirit of a fraternity."

"If you come here with stereotypes in mind, they will be broken."

GENERAL INFO

Activities: Choral groups, concert band, dance, drama/theater, jazz band, literary magazine, music ensembles, musical theater, opera, pep band, student government, student newspaper, student-run film society, symphony orchestra, yearbook. **Organizations:** 148 registered organizations, 2 honor societies, 6 religious organizations. **Athletics (Intercollegiate):** *Men*: Baseball, basketball, cross-country, diving, fencing, soccer, swimming, tennis, track/field (outdoor), water polo. *Women*: Basketball, cross-country, diving, fencing, swimming, tennis, track/field (outdoor), volleyball, water polo. **On-Campus Highlights:** Caltech Bookstore, Moore Laboratory, Mead Chemistry Laboratory, Broad Center for the Biological Sciences, Red Door Cafe.

THE BOTTOM LINE

In 2010 Caltech's endowment was $1.55 billion. It's no wonder generous financial aid and scholarship packages are commonplace here. Tuition at Caltech is almost $35,000 annually, plus another $3,000-plus in student fees. Once you factor in $11,000 for room and board and several thousand more for supplies, personal expenses, and books, the estimated annual cost is more than $52,000 per year. Few students pay the full cost, while everyone benefits from the world-class education, making this school a best buy. Financial aid packages for freshman include a $26,000 grant on average.

SELECTIVITY

Admissions Rating	**98**
# of applicants	4,859
% of applicants accepted	12
% of acceptees attending	36
# accepting a place on wait list	337
% admitted from wait list	7

FRESHMAN PROFILE

Range SAT Critical Reading	**700–780**
Range SAT Math	**770–800**
Range SAT Writing	**710–780**
Range ACT Composite	**34–35**
% graduated top 10% of class	**96**
% graduated top 25% of class	**100**

DEADLINES

Regular Deadline	**1/3**
Normal registration	**no**

FACILITIES

Housing: Coed dorms, special housing for disabled students, apartments for married students, single-unit houses. *Special Academic Facilities/Equipment*: Jet Propulsion Laboratory, Palomar Observatory, Seismological Laboratory, Beckman Institute for Fundamental Research in Biology and Chemistry, Mead Chemistry Laboratory, Moore Laboratory. *Computers*: 50% of classrooms, 50% of dorms, 100% of libraries, 50% of dining areas, 100% of student union, 50% of common outdoor areas have wireless network access.

FINANCIAL FACTS

Financial Aid Rating	**97**
Annual tuition	$34,989
Room and Board	$10,755
Required Fees	$3,660
Books and supplies	$1,290
% frosh rec. need-based scholarship or grant aid	53
% UG rec. need-based scholarship or grant aid	53
% UG rec. non-need-based scholarship or grant aid	2
% frosh rec. need-based self-help aid	39
% UG rec. need-based self-help aid	49
% frosh rec. any financial aid	53
% UG rec. any financial aid	85
% UG borrow to pay for school	43
Average cumulative indebtedness	$10,760

Hamilton College

Clinton, NY

Hamilton

STUDENTS

1,843 undergrad enrollment

47% Male ♂♂♂♂♂♂♂♂♂♂

53% Female ♀♀♀♀♀♀♀♀♀♀♀

ADMISSIONS

4,857 →	29%	33%	EARLY →	NR	NR
applicants	admitted	enrolled	ADMISSIONS	applicants	accepted

NR avg. high school gpa

ACT range (0–36): 27–31

SAT range (200–800): reading 650–740, math 650–720, writing 650–720

73% graduated top 10% of class

97% graduated top 25% of class

FINANCIAL INFO

$42,220	$10,830	$1,300	$420
annual tuition	room & board	avg. book expenses	required fees

$16,982 avg. indebtedness

ACADEMICS

10:1 student to faculty ratio

NR% classes taught by TAs

GRADUATION RATES

91% of students graduating within 4 years

95% of students graduating within 6 years

* NR = Not reported

Why Hamilton College is No. 10

ABOUT THE SCHOOL

Three characteristics define a Hamilton College education: the open curriculum, the sense of community, and learning to write and express yourself well. In other words, "Hamilton is the quintessential liberal arts college." Hamilton is one of a select few U.S. colleges with an open curriculum, meaning there are no distribution requirements. One college freshman says: "I chose Hamilton because of the freedom to choose your classes." Imagine being in a course where all your classmates are there because they're interested in the subject, not because they have to fulfill some requirement. Sound nice? Well, that's the norm at Hamilton. The college's close sense of community translates into a supportive environment as a student and great networking opportunities as an alumnus: "the vast network of alumni...help the students both while they are at Hamilton and after, in the job search." You won't encounter cutthroat competition here. No matter their major, all Hamilton students learn to express themselves clearly and persuasively as "the English and writing department is excellent." Hamilton's writing-intensive curriculum produces graduates who are routinely seen as the best writers in their office; "Hamilton places a strong emphasis on developing students' writing and speaking skills." No matter what your major is, writing will be central to the work that you do. A strong science program also attracts students, as Hamilton boasts a "recently built state-of-the-art science center."

Why Students love Hamilton College

> "I am amazed by the incredible resources—especially for the sciences, and couldn't believe all of the opportunities and grants they offer to students who are passionate about pursuing their studies outside of the classroom."

Hamilton provides about 100 research opportunities for students to work closely with science and non-science faculty mentors each summer. Many students choice of college depend on the strength of the school's academic department, most relevant to their major: "I am amazed by the incredible resources—especially for the sciences, and couldn't believe all of the opportunities and grants they offer to students who are passionate about pursuing their studies outside of the classroom," says one sophomore. Oftentimes, the work leads to a paper published in a professional journal and gives the student a leg-up when competing for national post-graduate fellowships and grants. The college also provides about 25–30 stipends each summer so students can get career-related experience pursuing internships that are otherwise unpaid. A student contends that "the school has a lot of active alumni, so the networking opportunities are great. Many students find internships or jobs just through the alumni connections."

Contact Info:

Office of Admission, 198 College Hill Road, Clinton, NY 13323

Admissions: 315-859-4421

Financial Aid: 800-859-4413

E-mail: admission@hamilton.edu

Fax: 315-859-4457

Website: www.hamilton.edu

Fun Facts

- Hamilton is celebrating its bicentennial this year, but we were actually founded 19 years earlier as the Hamilton-Oneida Academy, "a school for the children of the Oneidas [Native Americans] and of the white settlers," according to the missionary-founder's plan
- Hamilton is named named for Alexander Hamilton, the nation's first Secretary of the Treasury, who was also one of the college's first trustees, but he never foot on campus.
- Hamilton is the only undergraduate college with a "study abroad" program in Antarctica.
- We have been host to the last two U.S. National Korfball tournaments.
- The great Oneida Indian chief Skenandoa is buried in the college cemetery next to Samuel Kirkland, who founded the academy, so that he could hold on to the hem of Kirkland and ascend to heaven with him.
- There is a mountain in California named for Hamilton College.
- The largest Norway Spruce in the nation is on Hamilton's campus

Hamilton College

CAMPUS LIFE

Quality of life Rating	85
Fire Safety Rating	85
Green rating	90
Type of School	Private
Environment	Rural

STUDENTS

Total undergrad enrolllment	1,843
% Male to Female	47/53
% From out of state	67
% From public high school	64
% Live on Campus	98
# of Fraternities	9
# of Sororities	7
% African American	4
% Asian	8
% Caucasian	67
% Hispanic	5
% Native American	1
% International	5
# Of Countries Represented	37

ACADEMICS

Academic Rating	96
% Of students graduating within 4 years	84
% Of students graduating within 6 years	88
Calendar	semester
Profs interesting rating	98
Profs accessible rating	96
Most common reg class size	10–19 students
Most common lab size	10–19 students

MOST POPULAR MAJORS
Political science, psychology

SPECIAL STUDY OPTIONS

Accelerated program, cross-registration, double major, English as a Second Language (ESL), independent study, internships, student-designed major, study abroad, 3-2 program in Engineering with Columbia University, Rensselaer Polytechnic Institute, and Washington University (St. Louis); 3-3 program in Law with Columbia University

During the week, students' focus is on navigating Hamilton's tough academics, but they definitely know how to cut loose on the weekends. Several students mention Hamilton has "good coffee shops, [that] people play a lot of sports, and there are many clubs, organizations, and musical groups." Greek life is a popular choice, as are organized trips to New York City. Overall, the consensus seems to be the following: "people are focused on getting their work done to the best of their ability during the week, but when it comes to the weekend people are focused on having as much fun as possible." Hockey lovers will appreciate Hamilton's on-campus rink, the second oldest indoor collegiate rink in the country. Winters are long here, and it's not uncommon for students to spend a Saturday night curled up in their dorm rooms if the weather is too inhospitable. One student warns, however: "it's nice that you don't really need a car—though if NONE of your friends have a car, you're basically stuck on campus, which can drive you crazy in the dead of winter."

Why Students love Hamilton College

"The school offered me a generous amount of financial aid."

BANG FOR YOUR BUCK

Once you are accepted, the Financial Aid Office will make your Hamilton education affordable through a comprehensive program of scholarships, loans, and campus jobs. The financial aid budget is approximately $26.2 million annually, enabling the school to make good on its commitment to meet 100 percent of students' demonstrated need. One student says, "The school offered me a generous amount of financial aid." The average financial aid package for students is $34,750. The average Hamilton College grant is $30,050 and does not have to be repaid.

WHY STUDENTS LOVE HAMILTON

One student describes Hamilton as "a liberal arts college in the middle of farmlands where professors offer plenty of opportunities for research and interaction." Another mentions that "my social life at Hamilton is stimulating and comforting." "People often think that just because Hamilton is in the middle of nowhere that there is nothing to do—but that's far from the truth. Different clubs and societies brings great acts on campus (comedy troupes, bands, public speakers, etc.). Greek life if popular but not threatening, and doesn't necessarily dominate the social scene." "Life at Hamilton is much like life anywhere else, only it takes place pretty much exclusively on top of a hill. We talk about the 'Hamilton bubble' a lot, and how we are pretty disconnected with our immediate surroundings, but I still think that students here have a heightened awareness and interest in the larger world."

In actuality, "life at Hamilton is fun [and] intellectually and artistically challenging." What's more, the "professors at Hamilton, though extremely demanding, know when to recognize success and hard work." In fact, "the ratio of faculty to students provides a lot of opportunities to get to know professors...because the campus is in a rural area, but still close to a city, there are less distractions."

The close-knit community can be somewhat insular, however, as one Junior writes: "I love that everyone lives on campus. Very few people don't live on the hill. That makes it really easy to visit people, to make friends, and to get around. It takes about 10 minutes to walk from one side of campus to the other in heavy snow." Picture this: "rolling hills, beautiful wooded areas, impressive buildings" and an "emphasis on writing...sets it apart from all other small, liberal arts schools."

GENERAL INFO

Activities: Choral groups, concert band, dance, drama/theater, jazz band, literary magazine, music ensembles, musical theater, radio station, student government, student newspaper, student-run film society, symphony orchestra, yearbook, campus ministries, international student organization. **Organizations:** 117 registered organizations, 8 honor societies, 4 religious organizations. 11 fraternities, 7 sororities. **Athletics (Intercollegiate):** *Men*: Baseball, basketball, crew/rowing, cross-country, diving, football, golf, ice hockey, lacrosse, soccer, squash, swimming, tennis, track/field (outdoor), track/field (indoor). *Women*: Basketball, crew/rowing, cross-country, diving, field hockey, ice hockey, lacrosse, soccer, softball, squash, swimming, tennis, track/field (outdoor), track/field (indoor), volleyball. **On-Campus Highlights:** Blood Fitness and Dance Center, Kirner-Johnson Commons, Outdoor Leadership Center/Root Glen, Science Center, Cafe Opus.

Why Students love Hamilton College

"Professors at Hamilton, though extremely demanding, know when to recognize success and hard work."

"Rolling hills, beautiful wooded areas, impressive buildings."

THE BOTTOM LINE

Hamilton College is one of the nation's top liberal arts colleges, and you certainly get what you pay for here. The total cost of tuition, room and board, and everything else adds up to about $52,000 per year. Hamilton pledges to meet 100 percent of students' demonstrated need.

SELECTIVITY

Admissions Rating	**96**
# of applicants	4,857
% of applicants accepted	29
% of acceptees attending	33
# accepting a place on wait list	532
% admitted from wait list	5

FRESHMAN PROFILE

Range SAT Critical Reading	**650–740**
Range SAT Math	**650–730**
Range SAT Writing	**650–730**
Range ACT Composite	**27–31**
% graduated top 10% of class	**73**
% graduated top 25% of class	**97**
% graduated top 50% of class	**99**

DEADLINES

Regular Deadline	**1/1**
Normal registration	**yes**

FACILITIES

Housing: Coed dorms, special housing for disabled students, apartments for married students, cooperative housing, apartments for single students, wellness housing. *Special Academic Facilities/Equipment*: Art gallery, language lab, fitness center, observatory, two electron microscopes. Arthur Levitt Public Affairs Center. *Computers*: 100% of classrooms, 100% of dorms, 100% of libraries, 100% of dining areas, 100% of student union, 100% of common outdoor areas have wireless network access.

FINANCIAL FACTS

Financial Aid Rating	**97**
Annual tuition	$42,220
Room and Board	$10,830
Required Fees	$420
Books and supplies	$1,300
% frosh rec. need-based scholarship or grant aid	51
% UG rec.need-based scholarship or grant aid	42
% frosh rec. need-based self-help aid	45
% UG rec. need-based self-help aid	37
% frosh rec. any financial aid	62
% UG rec. any financial aid	53
% UG borrow to pay for school	41
Average cumulative indebtedness	$16,982

Top 10
Public Colleges

#1

University of North Carolina—Chapel Hill

Chapel Hill, NC

THE UNIVERSITY
of NORTH CAROLINA
at CHAPEL HILL

STUDENTS

17,943 undergrad enrollment

41% Male ♂♂♂♂♂♂♂

59% Female ♀♀♀♀♀♀♀♀♀♀

ADMISSIONS

23,272 applicants	→ 32% admitted	52% enrolled	EARLY ADMISSIONS → NR applicants	NR accepted

4.47 avg. high school gpa

27–31 ACT range (0–36)

SAT range (200–800): reading 590–700, math 610–710, writing 590–690

78% graduated top 10% of class

99% graduated top 25% of class

FINANCIAL INFO

in-state $5,128	out-of-state $24,954	$9,470	$1,150	$1,880
annual tuition		room & board	avg. book expenses	required fees

$19,016 avg indebtedness

ACADEMICS

14:1 student to faculty ratio

21% classes taught by TAs

GRADUATION RATES

76% of students graduating within 4 years

90% of students graduating within 6 years

** NR = Not reported*

Why University of North Carolina—Chapel Hill is No. 1

The University of North Carolina system's flagship school has a long-standing place among leaders in higher education. Tar Heels are legendary for their devotion to their school, and with around 18,000 undergrads enrolled at a time, there sure are a lot of them. Somehow, the school finds a way to form a community (and smaller communities). Whether through majors, departments, sports, Greek life, or any of the other resources to which the school offers access, Carolina students are a happy and proud bunch.

Academic rigor doesn't certainly doesn't take a back seat to value here, and the vast majority of students say it's one of the main reasons they chose the school. The education at UNC is top notch, and all of its schools and departments consistently demand (and produce) the best from their students across the board. So long as students are willing to put in the time and effort and ask for help when they need it, Carolina will provide them with the tools to succeed. Accessibility is a hallmark of the school, and the University is committed to making certain that no admitted undergraduate student who qualifies for need-based aid will be barred from attendance because of lack of financial resources. Its Carolina Covenant program (an aid program for truly low-income students who remain dependent upon their families for support) is now in its eighth year, and recently welcomed its largest class. The school provides a breeding ground for anything you could think of, and if it doesn't exist, a student can make it happen.

Why Students Love UNC—Chapel Hill

"People think about getting their work done for classes and then having fun."

ABOUT THE SCHOOL

The University of North Carolina—Chapel Hill has a reputation for top academics, top athletics, and great overall value. Established in 1789 as the first public university in America, UNC Chapel Hill has a long legacy of excellence. Although its relative low cost makes Carolina a great bargain in higher education, the school is all about "top-notch academics while having the ultimate college experience." Professors are at the top of their fields and "will work with you above and beyond the normal scope of their position to help you with any concerns or interests you could possibly have." The chancellor even "holds meetings for students to meet with him to discuss school issues." The journalism, business, and nursing programs are ranked among the best in the country, and study abroad programs are available in more than 70 countries.

The student body is composed of students from every state and more than 100 countries, and the university has produced more Rhodes Scholars over the past 25 years than any other public research university. There are "many opportunities to gain experience for a future career," and just by applying to Carolina, students are considered for opportunities such as the school's First-Year Fellows Program, Carolina Research Scholars Program, Global Gap Year Fellowship, and assured enrollment in the university's business and journalism programs. The university's comprehensive career center assists students throughout their entire undergraduate education, and students are "at ease knowing that their hard work pays off." There are clubs for anyone of any interest, "from ballroom dancing to sky diving to paintball to religious groups." Even with so many activities beckoning (and downtown Chapel Hill just out the door), "people think about getting their work done for classes and then having fun."

Contact Info:

Office of Undergraduate Admissions
Jackson Hall
Chapel Hill, NC 27599-2200
Admissions: 919-966-3621
Financial Aid: 919-962-8396
E-mail: unchelp@admissions.unc.edu
Fax: 919-962-3045
Website: www.unc.edu

Fun Facts

- Chapel Hill derives it name from the highest point where a church (of England) was located in the late 1700s. Called New Hope Chapel hill (where The Carolina Inn stands today), the name was shortened to Chapel Hill.
- Chapel Hill has been referred to as the "Southern Part of Heaven," after the title of the book by William Meade Prince, which was published in 1950.
- Franklin Street, the main street through downtown Chapel Hill was named after Benjamin Franklin. Rosemary Street, a parallel street, was named after residents who lived at its opposite ends—Rose and Mary.
- Franklin Street's Carolina Coffee Shop was established in 1922 as the Carolina Confectionery, making it one of the oldest original restaurants in the area.
- Traditionally, fire engines are red. In Chapel Hill, however, the fire trucks are Carolina blue, like the color of the Carolina Tar Heel sports teams. In Chapel Hill, the Carolina Blue fire truck tradition began in 1996 to commemorate the joint purchase of Engine 32 by the Town of Chapel Hill, UNC and UNC Hospital. Since then there have been several joint purchases of trucks and since the Carolina Blue truck was so well liked it was decided to convert the entire fleet.

University of North Carolina—Chapel Hill

CAMPUS LIFE

Quality of life Rating	94
Fire Safety Rating	84
Green rating	95
Type of School	Public
Environment	Town

STUDENTS

Total undergrad enrolllment	17,943
% Male to Female	41/59
% From out of state	18
% From public high school	80
% Live on Campus	46
# of Fraternities	33
# of Sororities	21
% African American	9
% Asian	6
% Caucasian	66
% Hispanic	11
% Native American	1
% International	2
# Of Countries Represented	63

ACADEMICS

Academic Rating	80
% Of students graduating within 4 years	76
% Of students graduating within 6 years	90
Calendar	semester
Profs interesting rating	81
Profs accessable rating	77
Most common reg class size	10–19 students
Most common lab size	10–19 students

MOST POPULAR MAJORS

Biology, mass communication/media studies, psychology

HONORS PROGRAMS

Honors Carolina courses. Honors study abroad and Burch Research Seminars.

SPECIAL STUDY OPTIONS

Cross-registration, distance learning, double major, dual enrollment, honors program, independent study, internships, student-designed major, study abroad, teacher certification program.

BANG FOR YOUR BUCK

Carolina meets 100 percent of students' need, regardless of whether they are North Carolinians or out-of-state residents. Aid packages generally contain at least 65 percent in grant and scholarship assistance, with the remaining 35 percent in work study and loans. Low-income students who are 200 percent below the federal poverty standard, do not have to borrow at all to pay for their education—these students are designated Carolina Covenant Scholars and receive packages of grants, scholarships, and student employment. The university awards about 250 merit scholarships each year to students in the first-year class. These scholarships range in value from $2,500 to a full ride. Best of all, there is no separate application for merit scholarships; students are awarded scholarships on a need-blind basis based on information provided in the regular admissions application.

STUDENT BODY

One student after another comments about the feeling of generosity that pervades UNC—"the epitome of Southern hospitality"—and how it extends beyond mere school spirit and the wearing of Carolina blue and white on game days. "Carolina is family," one student says. "Most of us here are crazy about sports, but most will do anything at all to help a fellow UNC student." "Although the student body is very diverse, a commonality among students is the desire to serve others and work for humanitarian efforts." One reason for the closeness is that the vast majority of students hail from the Tar Heel state. So there are "lots of down-home, North Carolina types who excelled in their rural high schools." Students and faculty are viewed as leaning liberal politically, which makes for some interesting exchanges. "Political activism is huge here," a student says. But even though it's a vast school, "it has a place for everyone." "There are really only two common denominators: commitment to some kind of excellence (academic, extracurricular, etc.) and rooting against Duke."

WHY STUDENTS LOVE UNC—CHAPEL HILL

Carolina is unique in that "every person who attends or works with the university is in love with it." "UNC Chapel Hill is my Narnia," says one student. Basketball and football games at UNC are always "charged with energy," and student organizations dole out free t-shirts, food, and pompoms to get the crowd going. "There are few experiences that can top being in the risers at a UNC basketball game, or rushing famous Franklin Street when UNC beats Duke," says a student. Students do all sorts of things for fun, and "there are hundreds of active clubs and student organizations in which you can meet people with the same interests, or different interests." No student should be able to say that he or she incapable of understanding a concept, "because there are always people there to help." Professors genuinely want students to succeed, and "it is quite common to look at a book list for a class and have three texts written by your teacher." "I just wonder why anyone would go anywhere else," says a student.

University of North Carolina—Chapel Hill

Why Students Love UNC—Chapel Hill

"There are few experiences that can top being in the risers at a UNC basketball game, or rushing famous Franklin Street when UNC beats Duke."

"Most of us here are crazy about sports, but most will do anything at all to help a fellow UNC student."

GENERAL INFO

Activities: Choral groups, concert band, dance, drama/theater, jazz band, literary magazine, marching band, music ensembles, musical theater, opera, pep band, radio station, student government, student newspaper, student-run film society, symphony orchestra, television station, yearbook, campus ministries, international student organization. **Organizations:** 635 registered organizations, 19 honor societies, 42 religious organizations. 35 fraternities, 23 sororities. **Athletics (Intercollegiate):** *Men*: Baseball, basketball, cross-country, diving, fencing, football, golf, lacrosse, soccer, swimming, tennis, track/field (outdoor), track/field (indoor), wrestling. *Women*: Basketball, crew/rowing, cross-country, diving, fencing, field hockey, golf, gymnastics, lacrosse, soccer, softball, swimming, tennis, track/field (outdoor), track/field (indoor), volleyball. **On-Campus Highlights:** The Pit, McCorkle Place, Polk Place, Dean Smith Center, Student Union, Old Well, Coker Arboretum, Morehead Planetarium, Ackland Art Museum, Kenan Stadium. **Environmental Initiatives:** Partnered with Orange (County) Water and Sewer Authority (OWASA) to install a water reclamation and reuse system that replaces more than 210 million gallons of potable water annually. Fare Free Transit and Commuter Alternatives Program.

THE BOTTOM LINE

The cost of attending Carolina is a real bargain—especially if your home state is North Carolina. In-state students can expect to pay about $6,000 in tuition and fees. Out-of-state students have it pretty good too; they can expect to cough up about $24,000 for the cost of tuition and fees for one year. Cost of living in Chapel Hill is pretty cheap too—you can expect room and board to run you just over $9,000 per year.

Why Students Love UNC—Chapel Hill

"Top-notch academics while having the ultimate college experience."

SELECTIVITY

Admissions Rating	**98**
# of applicants	23,272
% of applicants accepted	32
% of acceptees attending	52
# accepting a place on wait list	1,114
% admitted from wait list	44

FRESHMAN PROFILE

Range SAT Critical Reading	**590–700**
Range SAT Math	**610–710**
Range SAT Writing	**590–690**
Range ACT Composite	**27–31**
Average HS GPA	**4.47**
% graduated top 10% of class	**78**
% graduated top 25% of class	**95**
% graduated top 50% of class	**99**

DEADLINES

Regular Deadline	**1/15**
Normal registration	**no**

FACILITIES

Housing: Coed dorms, special housing for disabled students, men's dorms, special housing for international students, women's dorms, fraternity/sorority housing. *Computers*: 75% of classrooms, 15% of dorms, 100% of libraries, 100% of dining areas, 100% of student union, 50% of common outdoor areas have wireless network access.

FINANCIAL FACTS

Financial Aid Rating	**94**
Annual in-state tuition	$5,128
Annual out-of-state tuition	$24,954
Room and Board	$9,470
Required Fees	$1,880
Books and supplies	$1,150
% frosh rec. need-based scholarship or grant aid	39
% UG rec. need-based scholarship or grant aid	36
% frosh rec. non-need-based scholarship or grant aid	18
% UG rec. non-need-based scholarship or grant aid	11
% frosh rec. need-based self-help aid	17
% UG rec. need-based self-help aid	19
% frosh rec. any financial aid	69
% UG rec. any financial aid	63

#2

University of Virginia

Charlottesville, VA

UNIVERSITY of VIRGINIA

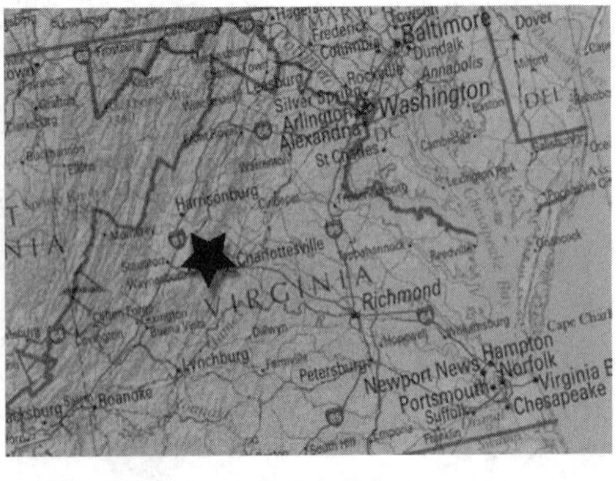

STUDENTS

14,232 undergrad enrollment

44% Male

56% Female

ADMISSIONS

22,124 applicants	→ 33% admitted	45% enrolled	EARLY ADMISSIONS	→ NR applicants	NR accepted

4.17 avg. high school gpa

ACT range (0–36): 28–32

SAT range (200–800): reading 600–710; math 620–742; writing 610–720

90% graduated top 10% of class

97% graduated top 25% of class

FINANCIAL INFO

annual tuition: in-state	annual tuition: out-of-state	room & board	avg. book expenses	required fees
$9,240	$33,562	$8,866	$1,184	$2,546

$19,384 avg. indebtedness

ACADEMICS

16:1 student to faculty ratio

10% classes taught by TAs

GRADUATION RATES

85% of students graduating within 4 years

93% of students graduating within 6 years

** NR = Not reported*

Why University of Virginia is No. 2

You want history? The University of Virginia's got history. Founded by none other than Thomas Jefferson, rectored by James Madison, and the former residence of James Monroe, UVA has a long tradition of attracting the nation's best and brightest minds to its campus, whose stunning beauty and architecture befit its pedigree. Made up of eleven schools in Charlottesville, plus the College at Wise in southwest Virginia, UVA offers rigorous but straightforward academics in the midst of the quintessential college town. Sticking to Jefferson's original goal—"to educate the public citizenry as a basis for participating in a democratic republic"—students receive a solid education based upon the highest of ideals.

While livin' and lovin' life in the South, UVA's 14,000 undergraduates strike a balance between work and fun, and walk away with one of the school's 51 different degrees. The sense of pride that dawns upon Wahoos pretty much the second they matriculate is only furthered by the school's legendary athletics; teams or individuals in 21 of Virginia's 25 sports advanced to postseason competition in 2010-11. In addition, one of the benefits of the strong alumni base (which includes Tina Fey, Woodrow Wilson, and Bobby Kennedy, to name a random few) is the Career Assistance Network, a database of alumni who have agreed to mentor students thinking about various career fields.

Why Students Love UVA

"Everyone here loves it—you can't find a school with more enthusiastic and dedicated students."

ABOUT THE SCHOOL

The University of Virginia's offerings live up to the school's presidential legacy. UVA seamlessly blends the academic advantages of the Ivy League with the social life and the price tag of a large state school. The wealth of academic and extracurricular activities available here is paralleled at just a handful of schools around the country, and the school "values academia while fostering an enjoyable atmosphere for students." While class sizes can be large, and getting into the courses you want can be difficult, students rave about their engaging and inspiring professors, "who care and keep students from being 'numbers.'" Graduation rates are among the highest in the country and the university has one of the highest graduation rates for African-American students. UVA also takes its history and traditions very seriously. The student-administered honor code is a case in point; sanctions can be harsh, but only for those who disrespect it. "Students claim full responsibility for their grades and actions while being engaged and challenged in all aspects of life," says a student.

UVA is the only university in the United States to be designated a World Heritage Site and students "are all champions at balancing work and play." Social life has a big-school vibe. Greek life is very prominent but "not all-consuming," and you can virtually always find someone, somewhere who is throwing a party. If that's not your scene, though, don't worry; most activities turn into social networks, and "most clubs have a pseudo-fraternity/sorority feel in the sense that they involve camaraderie, selectivity, dedication, and, of course, partying." Also, Charlottesville is a tremendous college town, and it's surrounded by opportunities for outdoor adventure.

Contact Info:

Office of Admission

PO Box 400160

Charlottesville, VA 22906

Admissions: 434-982-3200

Financial Aid: 434-982-6000

E-mail: undergradadmission@virginia.edu

Fax: 434-924-3587

Website: www.virginia.edu

Fun Facts

- The University of Virginia is in Charlottesville near Monticello—home of its founder Thomas Jefferson.
- Thomas Jefferson founded the university in 1819 in Charlottesville. The first class entered in 1825. Under Jefferson's guidance the university offered more specializations to students than many other universities at the time.
- The official mascot of the university are the Cavaliers, but the Wahoos are its unofficial mascot. A wahoo is a fish that, as some believe, is able to drink twice its body weight.
- Edgar Allan Poe lived in the room no. 13 before dropping out in 1826 because of substantial gambling debts. However, after leaving the university, Poe went on to write many famous works of American literature including the poem "The Raven."
- The Corner (where students hang out) isn't really a "corner", but rather an area along the main street with many bars, restaurants, and shops.
- Rugby Road is the road where most fraternity houses are and hence where many first-year students would go if they were interested in joining.

University of Virginia

CAMPUS LIFE

Quality of life Rating	88
Fire Safety Rating	73
Green rating	92
Type of School	Public
Environment	City

STUDENTS

Total undergrad enrolllment	14,232
% Male to Female	44/56
% From out of state	26
% From public high school	74
% Live on Campus	42
# of Fraternities	29
# of Sororities	16
% African American	8
% Asian	12
% Caucasian	59
% Hispanic	5
% International	5
# Of Countries Represented	136

ACADEMICS

Academic Rating	85
% Of students graduating within 4 years	85
% Of students graduating within 6 years	95
Calendar	semester
Profs interesting rating	82
Profs accessable rating	78
Most common reg class size	10–19 students
Most common lab size	20–19 students

MOST POPULAR MAJORS

Business/commerce, economics
international relations

HONORS PROGRAMS

Accelerated program, cooperative education program, double major.

SPECIAL STUDY OPTIONS

Jefferson Scholars. Echols Scholars-School of Arts and Sciences.

BANG FOR YOUR BUCK

UVA has one of the largest per-capita endowments of any public schools in the country and exerts a tremendous effort to ensure that its undergraduates have access to an affordable education regardless of economic circumstances. Around half of undergraduates receive some form of financial aid, and the university aims to meet 100 percent of every student's need for financial aid. There are loan-free financial aid packages for low-income students. There are caps on need-based loans for middle-income families. By limiting debt—or eliminating it altogether, in the case of students with the most need—UVA ensures that you can afford to attend the university as long as you can get admitted and maintain decent grades. Scholarships abound for Virginia residents, including the Virginia Commonwealth Award, which gives recipients up to $3,000 per academic year. There are plenty of other scholarships, too, available based upon need, academic achievement, and specific donor criteria. Take the John Allen Love Scholarship, which is for students from Missouri. Or maybe you are looking to become a minister in the Protestant Episcopal Church—the Skinner Scholarship is for you.

STUDENT BODY

Students here "often get typecast as homogeneous and preppy." While this type certainly exists on campus, "there is a place for everyone at UVA. There are a lot of preppy kids, but there are also tomboys, Goths, skaters, and I even know of one kid who wears a kilt on a regular basis." People here are "incredibly friendly" and the school is "a bastion of Southern gentility." The student body is a happy group: "Everyone here loves it—you can't find a school with more enthusiastic and dedicated students." In accordance with its Jeffersonian roots, UVA students "care about their community and their world, and are always looking for ways to make an impact." They "are really serious about succeeding, but they want to get all they can out of every part of college, too." They're apt to "party Thursday through Saturday" and spend the rest of the week hitting the books and participating in the many clubs and organizations on campus. Generally, the students here "are very engaged with current events and intellectual discourse," but "they also know the importance of mental down time and humor."

WHY STUDENTS LOVE UVA

Cavaliers say that "UVA is the ultimate mix of social and academic life where students know how to balance the two." "The Academics...are rigorous, the sports are competitive, the campus is amazing, Charlottesville is a perfect mix of art culture, shopping, and dining. There is nothing wrong," sums up a student. The school is "about exploring every pocket of interest within yourself," and those that are happiest (and it's a tough contest) are "social in [their] involvement." "It's really amazing to be able to hang out with people who think the same way as you, and at the same time be able to hang out with people who think so differently," says a student. The campus is, of course, "breathtakingly beautiful," and "it's just an overall relaxing place to be in, with a lot of people you can meet and a lot of resources you can make use of."

University of Virginia

#2 Public

GENERAL INFO

Activities: Choral groups, concert band, dance, drama/theater, jazz band, literary magazine, marching band, music ensembles, musical theater, opera, pep band, radio station, student government, student newspaper, student-run film society, symphony orchestra, television station, campus ministries, international student organization. **Organizations:** 7 honor societies, 44 religious organizations. 28 fraternities, 15 sororities. **Athletics (Intercollegiate):** *Men*: Baseball, basketball, cross-country, diving, football, golf, lacrosse, soccer, swimming, tennis, track/field (outdoor), track/field (indoor), wrestling. *Women*: Basketball, crew/rowing, cross-country, diving, field hockey, golf, lacrosse, soccer, softball, swimming, tennis, track/field (outdoor), track/field (indoor), volleyball. **On-Campus Highlights:** Rotunda/Academical Village (orig campus), Alderman and Clemons Libraries, John Paul Jones Arena, Football and Soccer Stadiums, Aquatic and Fitness Center, Location of the future "arts precinct"; new library housing original rare and early American manuscripts; Birdwood Golf Course; Observatory; Old Cabell Hall (music performances); Culbreth Theatre (drama); Newcomb Hall (student services building); University of Virginia Bookstore. **Environmental Initiatives:** *Academics*: The University of Virginia offers 70-plus courses in 8 different schools with significant focus on sustainability. *Sustainable Design and Construction*: The University's policy to achieve LEED certification on all new buildings and major renovations has led to 30 projects registered with the U.S. Green Building Council, with 2 of these complete and certified (1 Gold, 1 Silver). *Ongoing efficiency and conservation efforts*: award-winning recycling and stormwater management program, extensive building retro-commissioning team, Environmental Management System implementation, and Green Dining that include composting, reusable to-go containers, and local farm relationships.

Why Students Love UVA

"Students claim full responsibility for their grades and actions while being engaged and challenged in all aspects of life."

"There is a place for everyone at UVA."

BOTTOM LINE

There is a large disparity here between tuition and fees for in-state versus out-of-state students. That's not unusual, just something to note. It's also important to keep in mind that 100 percent of applicants with financial need have their needs met. The sticker price for tuition, fees, room and board, and personal expenses for Virginia residents is somewhere in the neighborhood of $22,000 per year. For residents of other states, it's more than twice as much. Financial aid packages for freshmen include an $11,000 grant on average.

SELECTIVITY

Admissions Rating	**99**
# of applicants	22,124
% of applicants accepted	33
% of acceptees attending	45
# accepting a place on wait list	2,112
% admitted from wait list	14

FRESHMAN PROFILE

Range SAT Critical Reading	**600–710**
Range SAT Math	**620–740**
Range SAT Writing	**610–720**
Range ACT Composite	**28–32**
Average HS GPA	**4.17**
% graduated top 10% of class	**90**
% graduated top 25% of class	**97**
% graduated top 50% of class	**99**

DEADLINES

Regular Deadline	**1/1**
Normal registration	**no**

FACILITIES

Housing: Coed dorms, special housing for international students, fraternity/sorority housing, apartments for married students, apartments for single students, theme housing. *Computers*: 100% of classrooms, 100% of dorms, 100% of libraries, 100% of dining areas, 100% of student union, 26%–50% of common outdoor areas have wireless network access.

FINANCIAL FACTS

Financial Aid Rating	**94**
Annual in-state tuition	$9,240
Annual out-of-state tuition	$33,562
Room and Board	$8,866
Required Fees	$2,546
Books and supplies	$1,184
% frosh rec. need-based scholarship or grant aid	31
% UG rec. need-based scholarship or grant aid	28
% frosh rec. non-need-based scholarship or grant aid	4
% UG rec. non-need-based scholarship or grant aid	3
% frosh rec. need-based self-help aid	20
% UG rec. need-based self-help aid	19
% frosh rec. any financial aid	59
% UG rec. any financial aid	50
% UG borrow to pay for school	32
Average cumulative indebtedness	$19,384

New College of Florida

Sarasota, FL

New College THE HONORS COLLEGE of Florida

STUDENTS

801 undergrad enrollment

40% Male ♂♂♂♂♂♂

60% Female ♀♀♀♀♀♀♀♀♀♀

ADMISSIONS

1,414 →	53%	24%	EARLY →	NR	NR
applicants	admitted	enrolled	ADMISSIONS	applicants	accepted

4.03 avg. high school gpa

ACT range (0–36): 27–31

SAT range (200–800): reading 640–740; math 580–760; writing 600–690

50% graduated top 10% of class

80% graduated top 25% of class

FINANCIAL INFO

in-state	out-of-state			
$6,032	$28,949	$8,472	$800	$0
annual tuition		room & board	avg. book expenses	required fees

$11,458 avg. indebtedness

ACADEMICS

10:1 student to faculty ratio

0% classes taught by TAs

GRADUATION RATES

57% of students graduating within 4 years

68% of students graduating within 6 years

** NR = Not reported*

Why New College of Florida is No. 3

As the official Honors College for Florida, New College of Florida gets the cream of the state's intellectual crop and has carved out a distinctive niche in Florida's public higher education system. The free-spirited academic program, in which students choose what they want to study, is designed to promote depth in thinking, open exchange of ideas and highly individualized interaction with faculty. All students receive guaranteed scholarship funding to attend New College if they are applying as a freshman, complete their application by February 15, and are U.S. Citizens, permanent residents, or eligible non-citizens; all you've got to do is get in.

Independence suits the independent spirits that go to New College, and the smart, creative, open-minded, and most definitely left-leaning students of NCF's 140-acre, bay-front campus are as non-conformist as the school they attend. Students live in dormitories with individual entrances, private baths, and central air-conditioning, and they enjoy a pretty hopping campus party scene on weekends. They are also able to study outdoors almost all year-round, a fact that shows in the overwhelming number of students that go on to academic greatness, whether in graduate and professional school, fellowships, and scholarships. School pride and freedom inspires each class to abide by the campfire rule—leave the school better than you found it—and the fervent alumni continue to sing the praises of the school long after they've left.

Why Students Love New College of Florida

"It is on one of the most beautiful beaches in the world."

"Dedicated and wise professors."

ABOUT THE SCHOOL

New College of Florida distinguishes itself from other elite colleges and universities through its unique collaborative curriculum, emphasis on independent learning, and "deep and stimulating academics." With a total enrollment of fewer than 1,000 students, New College offers a "small, intimate atmosphere" in which faculty and students engage collaboratively in in-depth exploration of ideas and subject matter, all at a public college price. "It [feels] like a family," says a student. With no graduate students on campus, undergraduates receive the full attention of their professors and work one-on-one with them to map their own intellectual journey, which culminates in a senior thesis. There is no rigid core curriculum required of all students ("Our school has been tailored to us"). The cornerstone of the New College experience is that in addition to traditional course offerings, the student has the ability to work with "dedicated and wise professors" to design their own independent study and research projects during the month of January, which is set aside for independent projects.

Contact Info:

5800 Bay Shore Rd

ROB 101

Sarasota, FL 34243-2109

Admisions: 941-487-5000

Financial Aid: 941-487-5000

E-mail: admissions@ncf.edu

Fax: 941-487-5010

Website: www.ncf.edu

Fun Facts

- The New College of Florida historic bay-front campus sits on the former estate of circus magnate Charles Edward Ringling, one of the five brothers who owned the Ringling Brothers and Barnum & Bailey Circus. College Hall was the main house built as a winter retreat. Cook Hall was built for Charles Ringling's daughter.
- The Four Winds Café is a student-owned and operated gourmet coffeehouse and vegetarian and vegan eatery on campus. It began as a thesis project of a New College economics student. It is also affectionately referred to as "The Barn" due to its previous use on the Ringling estate.
- Many New College of Florida students walk around barefoot regularly.
- At the Annual Spring Commencement, students embrace the long-standing tradition of not having to wear cap and gown. The assemblage of dressy outfits, costumes and casual wear is as creative, colorful, and individual as the students themselves.
- The campus is also home to several examples of high modernist architecture designed by I.M. Pei. These buildings include a complex of student residences known as "Pei,"a cafeteria, and a student center.

New College of Florida

CAMPUS LIFE

Quality of life Rating	80
Fire Safety Rating	82
Green rating	74
Type of School	Public
Environment	Town

STUDENTS

Total undergrad enrolllment	801
% Male to Female	40/60
% From out of state	20
% From public high school	80
% Live on Campus	76
% African American	1
% Asian	3
% Caucasian	76
% Hispanic	13
# Of Countries Represented	22

ACADEMICS

Academic Rating	94
% Of students graduating within 4 years	57
% Of students graduating within 6 years	68
Calendar	4–1–4
Profs interesting rating	98
Profs accessable rating	89
Most common reg class size	10–19 students

MOST POPULAR MAJORS

Biology, economics, psychology

HONORS PROGRAMS

New College of Florida is the state's officially designated "honors college for the liberal arts." Special programs offered to physically disabled students include note-taking services, reader services, voice recorders.

SPECIAL STUDY OPTIONS

Cross-registration, double major, exchange student program (domestic), honors program, independent study, internships, student-designed major, study abroad, academic contract, January interterm (independent study), narrative evaluation/pass-fail, senior thesis, tutorials, undergraduate research. Special and unique academic programs available.

Course work at NCF is intense and can be stressful. However, with fewer than 1000 students on campus, all students are guaranteed to receive plenty of personal attention from passionate and accessible professors. The student body takes "active participation in the running of the school," and The Center for Career Education and Off-Campus Studies helps students coordinate internships, make career decisions, conduct job searches, apply to graduate and professional schools, and network with New College alumni. This leads to impressive outcomes, as evidenced by the 44 Fulbright Scholarships that have been awarded to NSF students since 2001 (there were eight in 2011 alone).

BANG FOR YOUR BUCK

The combination of NCF's incredibly low tuition and rigorous, individualized academic program make it a tremendous value for both in-state and out-of-state students. Students and their families can take advantage of many funding opportunities, including grants, loans, book advances, and work-study. Scholarships are guaranteed to all admitted applicants meeting the February 15 application deadline. Additional scholarship opportunities may be available to students based upon their specialized high-school curriculum. In addition to an academic scholarship, gift assistance is available for qualifying students who submit the FAFSA by the February 15 priority deadline.

STUDENT BODY

New College students share "a few things in common: Most... are friendly, passionate about the things they believe in, very hard workers, liberal, and most of all, try to be open to new experiences." They're "largely middle-class, white, and liberal. There are of course exceptions, but the school is rather small,'" there is "a fairly strong queer community here, and many transgendered people who have decided to make New College their coming-out grounds. The student body is generally aware of gender issues and respectful of queer people of all types."

Why Students Love New College of Florida

"New College is a bunch of incredibly intelligent hippies exploring every facet of existence."

WHY STUDENTS LOVE NEW COLLEGE OF FLORIDA

Students sign on for the ability to perform "close work with professors [in the] pursuit of knowledge," not to mention the incredible academic autonomy that comes with being an NCF student. The lack of core curriculum, "ease of choosing and changing courses [and] options for independent, and off-campus study" make the school all about "freedom, intelligence, creativity, and challenging yourself." "We're a small school but we have a great student government and an open mindset that helps us get things done," says a student. It also doesn't hurt "that it is on one of the most beautiful beaches in the world." On weekends it is not uncommon to see "The Wall," which are the parties to which the entire school is invited, "where kids dance all night long." Students also applaud the realistic drug/alcohol policy "which keeps the student body safer by making it okay for them to ask for help when it becomes necessary rather than driving inevitable activity under the rug."

New College of Florida

GENERAL INFO

Activities: Choral groups, dance, drama/theater, literary magazine, music ensembles, musical theater, radio station, student government, student newspaper, student-run film society, campus ministries. **Organizations:** 90 registered organizations, 5 religious organizations. **Athletics (Intercollegiate):** *Men*: Sailing. *Women*: Sailing. **On-Campus Highlights:** The R.V. Heiser Natural Sciences Complex, Pritzker Marine Biology Research Center, The Caples Fine Arts Complex, Four Winds Cafe (Student owned and operated), Jane Bancroft Cook Library, Historic bayfront mansions. **Environmental Initiatives:** Waste Management efforts—recycling of all paper, newsprint, cardboard, phone books, magazines, junk mail, soft-cover books, cotton goods, cans (all types), glass and plastic, jars and bottles, auto batteries, used oil and filters, used antifreeze, toner cartridges, chemicals and solvents, white goods, scrap metal, precious metals, wastewater solids, used pallets, yard debris, masonry and concrete, fluorescent tubes, used lumber, etc. Purchasing efforts—all new appliances are EnergyStar. Facility design—construction and renovation efforts. New buildings are typically being made LEED-compliant.

Why Students Love New College of Florida

"Small, intimate atmosphere."

"Our school has been tailored to us."

THE BOTTOM LINE

Even in the era of rising higher education costs, tuition at New College of Florida is still incredibly low as evidenced by the comparatively low average debt for graduating students: just under $15,000. The sticker price is further offset by loans, grants, and scholarships. The average grant for freshman is just north of $10,000 and the average freshman loan is $4,110. The school estimates that books and supplies, personal necessities, and transportation may run another $4,500 per year. Independent study projects and senior theses may involve additional costs for travel, research expenses, and equipment.

SELECTIVITY

Admissions Rating	**94**
# of applicants	1,414
% of applicants accepted	53
% of acceptees attending	24
# accepting a place on wait list	56
% admitted from wait list	39

FRESHMAN PROFILE

Range SAT Critical Reading	**640–740**
Range SAT Math	**580–760**
Range SAT Writing	**600–690**
Range ACT Composite	**27–31**
Average HS GPA	**4.03**
% graduated top 10% of class	**50**
% graduated top 25% of class	**80**
% graduated top 50% of class	**94**

DEADLINES

Regular Deadline	**4/15**
Normal registration	**yes**

FACILITIES

Housing: Coed dorms, special housing for disabled students, apartments for single students. *Special Academic Facilities/Equipment*: Anthropology and psychology labs. Electronic music lab. Individual studio space for senior art students. *Computers*: 95% of classrooms, 100% of dorms, 100% of libraries, 100% of dining areas, 100% of student union, 20% of common outdoor areas have wireless network access.

FINANCIAL FACTS

Financial Aid Rating	**92**
Annual in-state tuition	$6,032
Annual out-of-state tuition	$28,949
Room and Board	$8,472
Books and supplies	$800
% frosh rec. need-based scholarship or grant aid	51
% UG rec. need-based scholarship or grant aid	51
% frosh rec. non-need-based scholarship or grant aid	8
% UG rec. non-need-based scholarship or grant aid	4
% frosh rec. need-based self-help aid	43
% UG rec. need-based self-help aid	45
% frosh rec. any financial aid	100
% UG rec. any financial aid	97
% UG borrow to pay for school	36
Average cumulative indebtedness	$11,458

#4

State University of New York at Binghamton

Binghamton, NY

BINGHAMTON
UNIVERSITY
STATE UNIVERSITY OF NEW YORK

STUDENTS

11,745 undergrad enrollment

53% Male	♂♂♂♂♂♂♂♂♂
47% Female	♀♀♀♀♀♀♀♀♀

ADMISSIONS

27,248 applicants	39% admitted	21% enrolled	EARLY ADMISSIONS	NR applicants	NR accepted

3.60 avg. high school gpa

ACT range (0–36): 26–30

SAT range (200–800):

reading	580–670
math	620–700
writing	570–660

50% graduated top 10% of class

86% graduated top 25% of class

FINANCIAL INFO

in-state annual tuition	out-of-state annual tuition	room & board	avg. book expenses	required fees
$5,270	$13,380	$11,810	$1,000	$1,946

$21,110 avg. indebtedness

ACADEMICS

21:1 student to faculty ratio

6% classes taught by TAs

GRADUATION RATES

66% of students graduating within 4 years

78% of students graduating within 6 years

* NR = Not reported

Why SUNY Binghamton is No. 4

One of the top public universities of the region, Binghamton University's top-tier academics and palatable sticker price attracts very talented and motivated students from all walks of life. Students have the opportunity to study nearly any subject that piques their interest (many choose multiple), and professors lend a sense of intimacy to even the larger classes. The school's beyond-reasonable in-state tuition benefits nearly 90 percent of residents who attend, and the school puts the vast majority of its institutional, alumni and donor-funded scholarships primarily toward those students who would not be able to attend college without financial assistance.

It's an even-keeled bunch that choose to go to (and get accepted into) Binghamton, and when the time comes to unwind, the school does a great job of making sure that there is something to do for every type of student. The university sponsors a number of fun events like hot dog eating competitions and a Battle of the Bands, and students actively participate in—and lead—more than 250 student clubs and organizations on campus, ranging from intramurals to cultural events to residential community competitions. Essentially, the doors are wide open for anything that students want to pursue and accomplish at Binghamton University.

Why Students love SUNY Binghamton

"The resources of a larger university, while also having the feel of a smaller school."

ABOUT THE SCHOOL

Binghamton University (a State University of New York institution) offers its students a true value: This medium-sized university is more competitive than many of the Northeast's private schools, yet its top-notch education is available for a low state-school price. Undergraduate students choose Binghamton because of its value, but also because every semester they experience a great return on their investment. Binghamton students aspire to more than bachelor's degrees, often earning dual degrees or double majors and minors from the "great range of course offerings." Binghamton's Career Development Center (CDC) reaches out to students, parents, alumni, faculty and campus administrators to provide information and advice about the realities of the job market as well as strategies for becoming competitive candidates for employment or graduate school. "I feel like I am learning things that I will be using in further education as well as in a future career," says a student.

Although the quality of a Binghamton education depends upon which school within the university you attend, top-notch departments include a good management program, a strong science department (especially in biology, premed, and psychology), stellar political science and philosophy programs, and a law program that yields high law school acceptance rates. Engineering and nursing programs provide good real-world prep. Professors run the gamut from research-minded to student-focused, and are "very accommodating and [try] to make their classes as engaging as possible." "I feel like my teachers genuinely care about me and my future," says a student. By most reports, the town of Binghamton doesn't provide many recreational activities; most students frequent the same bars, frats, and other hangouts, and "there's always something fun and exciting going on on-campus so boredom

Contact Info:

State University of New York at Binghamton
PO Box 6001
Binghamton, NY 13902-6001
Admissions: 607-777-2171
Financial Aid: 607-777-2428
E-mail: admit@binghamton.edu
Fax: 607-777-4445
Website: www.binghamton.edu

Fun Facts

- Nearly 70% of Binghamton University's 930–acre campus is in its natural state. The core of this undeveloped land is officially designated the Nature Preserve, encompassing 182 acres of land, which includes a 20-acre wetland. Binghamton uses this large, valuable resource for teaching and learning, research, ecology, arts, literature, and outdoor recreation. (http://naturepreserve.binghamton.edu)
- Laundry is free to all students living in on-campus housing.
- Binghamton has its own airport—BGM.
- Binghamton has an on-campus greenhouse that houses about 6,000 exotic plants.
- Students built small ramps for the salamanders in university's 190-acre nature preserve so the salamanders could easily and safely reach breeding grounds.

SUNY Binghamton

CAMPUS LIFE

Quality of life Rating	61
Fire Safety Rating	81
Green rating	99
Type of School	Public
Environment	City

STUDENTS

Total undergrad enrolllment	11,745
% Male to Female	53/47
% From out of state	11
% From public high school	89
% Live on Campus	59
# of Fraternities	34
# of Sororities	20
% African American	5
% Asian	12
% Caucasian	98
% Hispanic	8
% International	10
# Of Countries Represented	100

ACADEMICS

Academic Rating	73
% Of students graduating within 4 years	66
% Of students graduating within 6 years	78
Calendar	semester
Profs interesting rating	69
Profs accessable rating	72
Most common reg class size	10–19 students
Most common lab size	20–29 students

MOST POPULAR MAJORS

Biology, business administration and management, engineering

HONORS PROGRAMS

Each academic department offers an honors program. Binghamton also has a PricewaterhouseCoopers Scholars program for students in the School of Management.

SPECIAL STUDY OPTIONS

Accelerated program, cross-registration, distance learning, double major, dual enrollment, English as a Second Language (ESL), exchange student program (domestic), honors program, independent study, internships, liberal arts/career combination, student-designed major, study abroad, teacher certification program, Teacher Certification Program is graduate only.

isn't an option." This includes the school's Division I sports teams, residential communities, and 200-plus student clubs and organizations.

BANG FOR YOUR BUCK

When all is said and done, a Binghamton degree will cost a student literally one-third of what they can expect to pay at other comparable schools. The school also offers a plethora of student opportunities for experiential education through research, study abroad, and internships, along with the third highest four-year graduation rate in the nation for public institutions. In addition to the low price, the school further assists students through need-based financial aid and grant/scholarship packages. Binghamton targets the vast majority of its institutional, alumni and donor-funded scholarships primarily toward those students who would not be able to attend college without financial assistance. In most cases, new and current undergraduate students are required to complete only the Free Application for Financial Student Aid (FAFSA) to assist in determining financial need and scholarship eligibility. If you receive an award, the school makes every effort to offer you a similar financial aid package in subsequent years as long as your ability to pay remains unchanged. Binghamton students find numerous opportunities for on- and off-campus employment as well. The Binghamton Scholars Program is a selective, all-university, four-year honors program for students displaying exceptional merit and financial need.

STUDENT BODY

It might seem that the typical SUNY Binghamton student "looks as if they walked out of the Hollister catalogue." However, if you scratch the surface, you'll quickly find "many different types of students," and most undergrads find the campus "very diverse in terms of interests, cultures, religions, etc." Of course, geographically speaking, it often feels like "a large percentage of the school is from Long Island and Westchester." Fortunately, "Everyone here just goes out of their way to be friendly and to make you feel like part of the community." Most people "usually find their niche within their residential communities, or based on similar interests and student organizations." Many undergrads define their peers as "intelligent," and nearly everyone "takes their classes very seriously, which provides an intellectually stimulating environment." Further, Binghamton students are "always on the move. If not in class or studying, they will be off to some sort of club or team meeting, volunteer project, athletic training, or even heading out to a party whether it is a small dorm party or a bar bash." As this junior sums up, "From poor to rich, Canadian to Indian, stuck-up to completely relaxed, everyone fits in."

WHY STUDENTS LOVE STATE UNIVERSITY OF NEW YORK AT BINGHAMTON

Binghamton is one of the best public universities in the Northeast, not to mention "the tuition can't be beat." "I am saving money while also getting an amazing education," says a student. The (very green) campus is "distinctive and beautiful," and is surrounded by mountains and a nature preserve for easy hiking and skiing; there is also "a vast amount of clubs and social events to attend so it's easy to get out there and have fun and meet new people." Professors make a strong attempt to know their students outside of class, and "attending professors' office hours is merely one of many ways students can receive help in academics." All in all, it "has the resources of a larger university, while also having the feel of a smaller school, through the community building that takes place in the residential communities."

Why Students love SUNY Binghamton

"I feel like I am learning things that I will be using in further education as well as in a future career."

"I am saving money while also getting an amazing education."

GENERAL INFO

Activities: Choral groups, concert band, dance, drama/theater, jazz band, literary magazine, music ensembles, musical theater, opera, pep band, radio station, student government, student newspaper, student-run film society, symphony orchestra, television station, yearbook, campus ministries, international student organization. **Organizations:** 23 honor societies, 15 religious organizations. 23 fraternities, 23 sororities. **Athletics (Intercollegiate):** *Men*: Baseball, basketball, cross-country, diving, golf, lacrosse, soccer, swimming, tennis, track/field (outdoor), track/field (indoor), wrestling. *Women*: Basketball, cross-country, diving, lacrosse, soccer, softball, swimming, tennis, track/field (outdoor), track/field (indoor), volleyball. **On-Campus Highlights:** University Union, Fitspace, Nature Preserve, Events Center, Anderson Center for the Arts, Rosefsky Art Gallery, Libraries. **Environmental Initiatives:** Binghamton University's goal is to design, construct, operate and maintain all new buildings following guidelines set forth by the U.S. Green Building Council's LEED rating system. Binghamton University has invested more than $1 million dollars in energy conservation projects such as installation of efficient lighting, occupancy sensors, variable speed drives on motors, free-cooling devices to take advantage of cooler outdoor temperature, solar hot water heater and constant improvement to our energy management system. Environmental Management Program has also made a tremendous progress in areas such as recycling, waste reduction, composting, and community outreach. Binghamton University currently provides a student bus system operated jointly by students and the University serving residential student and other needs. Electric vehicle program on campus. HOV carpool program for vehicles coming to campus.

THE BOTTOM LINE

At this reasonably priced public school, in-state tuition is less than $5,000, while out-of-state and international students pay roughly $13,000. Tuition aside, students are required to pay an additional $2,000 in mandatory fees and about $1000 for books. For students who live on campus, the school charges approximately $11,000 for room and board, though these expenses can be reduced if the student chooses to live at home. It is important to note that, unlike undergraduates at many state schools, the vast majority of Binghamton students graduate in four years; therefore, they are not saddled with an additional year of tuition and fees.

SELECTIVITY

Admissions Rating	**94**
# of applicants	27,248
% of applicants accepted	39
% of acceptees attending	21
# accepting a place on wait list	500
% admitted from wait list	6

FRESHMAN PROFILE

Range SAT Critical Reading	**580–670**
Range SAT Math	**620–700**
Range SAT Writing	**570–660**
Range ACT Composite	**26–30**
Average HS GPA	**3.60**
% graduated top 10% of class	**50**
% graduated top 25% of class	**86**
% graduated top 50% of class	**98**

DEADLINES

Regular Deadline	**1/15**
Normal registration	**yes**

FACILITIES

Housing: Coed dorms, special housing for disabled students, apartments for single students, wellness housing, theme housing. *Special Academic Facilities/Equipment*: Art gallery, performing arts center, indoor/outdoor theater. *Computers*: 95% of classrooms, 100% of dorms, 100% of libraries, 100% of dining areas, 100% of student union, 60% of common outdoor areas have wireless network access.

FINANCIAL FACTS

Financial Aid Rating	**76**
Annual in-state tuition	$5,270
Annual out-of-state tuition	$13,380
Room and Board	$11,810
Required Fees	$1,946
Books and supplies	$1000
% frosh rec. need-based scholarship or grant aid	37
% UG rec. need-based scholarship or grant aid	39
% frosh rec. non-need-based scholarship or grant aid	1
% UG rec. non-need-based scholarship or grant aid	2
% frosh rec. need-based self-help aid	45
% UG rec. need-based self-help aid	46
% frosh rec. any financial aid	78
% UG rec. any financial aid	69
% UG borrow to pay for school	50
Average cumulative indebtedness	$21,110

#5

University of Wisconsin—Madison

Madison, WI

WISCONSIN
UNIVERSITY OF WISCONSIN–MADISON

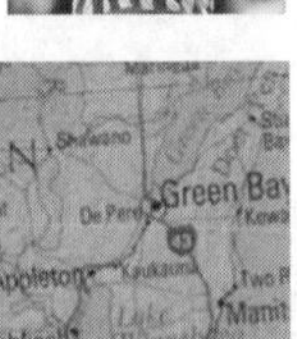

STUDENTS
28,897 undergrad enrollment
48% Male ♂♂♂♂♂♂♂
52% Female ♀♀♀♀♀♀♀♀♀♀

ADMISSIONS

6,631 →	19%	44%	EARLY →	NR	NR
applicants	admitted	enrolled	ADMISSIONS	applicants	accepted

3.69 avg. high school gpa

ACT range: 26–30 (0–36)

SAT range (200–800):

reading	530–670
math	620–750
writing	580–680

56% graduated top 10% of class
93% graduated top 25% of class

FINANCIAL INFO

in-state	out-of-state			
$9,672	$25,421	$7,780	$1,140	$3,180
annual tuition		room & board	avg. book expenses	required fees

$22,837 avg. indebtedness

ACADEMICS
17:1 student to faculty ratio
NR% classes taught by TAs

GRADUATION RATES
81% of students graduating within 4 years
84% of students graduating within 6 years

** NR = Not reported*

Why University of Wisconsin—Madison is No. 5

Phenomenal resources, prestige, and beautiful new buildings that seem to go up every other year are just some of the draws of the UW system's flagship school in Madison. This Big 10 school offers great academics and athletics, boundless research opportunities, hundreds of clubs and organizations, and a school spirit unlike any other, all at a reasonable in-state tuition. For such a large institution (not to mention major research university), the school smoothly channels and guides its students through their education, allowing for the development of personal interests through research and internships. Once a student moves away from larger intro courses and begins to specialize, the class sizes plummet, and there is an excellent Honors program that provides unique challenges for those who qualify.

The student body is active to say the least, and many people run walk and bike around either to get from place to place or to exercise. The places students go are numerous, from class to lakeside hangouts to lab work to filled-to-the-brim hockey arenas, and weekends at Madison practically require their own weekend to recover. School spirit is perhaps the greatest strength of the community at Madison; on home game days, it's practically impossible not to identify a Badger, even off-campus. This fun-loving yet involved student body is given an endless amount of opportunities of which to take advantage.

Why Students Love University of Wisconsin—Madison

> "Many people are passionate about many things, and it provides a great opportunity to see things from others' points of view."

ABOUT THE SCHOOL

Mostly known as "an amazing research institution," the University of Wisconsin—Madison offers 157 majors and abundant opportunities in study abroad, internships, research, and service learning, all of which operate under the Wisconsin Idea: the principle that education should influence and improve people's lives beyond the university classroom. "If you are proactive, you basically have the means and resources to pursue any academic or creative feat," promises a student. The "challenging" academic atmosphere "definitely makes you earn your grades," but academic advising is readily available, and students know when to hunker down and hit the books. "At UW, the students who are out partying Saturday night are the same ones you will see in the library Sunday morning," says a student.

Even within the large school, there are plenty of chances for a student to create a smaller world. The university residence halls feature seven learning communities that give students the chance to live and learn with other students who share their interests, and provide a more seamless experience that blends residential and academic life on campus. There are also First-Year Interest Groups, which are twenty students who live in the same residence hall or

Contact Info:

Armory and Gymnasium
716 Langdon Street,
Madison, WI 53706-1481
Admissions: 608-262-3961
Financial Aid: 608-262-3060
E-mail: onwisconsin@admissions.wisc.edu
Fax: 608-262-7706
Website: www.wisc.edu

Fun Facts

- 1913: Discovery of vitamin A
- 1916: Discovery of Vitamin B
- 1919: Oldest educational radio station
- 1926: First university dance program
- 1936: First artist-in-residence program at a university
- 1968: First bone marrow transplant
- 1970: Creation of the first synthetic gene
- 1998: First cultivation of embryonic stem cells in a lab

Notable Alumni
(*=Indicates attendance without receiving degree)

- Charles Lindbergh (1924)*: Trans-Atlantic aviator
- Jim Lovell (1950): Astronaut
- Dick Cheney (1968)*: U.S. Vice President
- Dale Chihuly (MS 1967): Glass artist
- Walter Mirisch (1942): film producer
- Allan "Bud" Selig (1956): Commissioner, Major League Baseball
- Frank Lloyd Wright (1890)*: Architect

University of Wisconsin—Madison

CAMPUS LIFE

Quality of life Rating	88
Fire Safety Rating	66
Green rating	87
Type of School	Public
Environment	City

STUDENTS

Total undergrad enrollment	28,897
% Male to Female	48/52
% From out of state	32
% Live on Campus	25
# of Fraternities	26
# of Sororities	11
% African American	2
% Asian	5
% Caucasian	78
% Hispanic	4
% International	6
# Of Countries Represented	132

ACADEMICS

Academic Rating	76
% Of students graduating within 4 years	51
% Of students graduating within 6 years	84
Calendar	Semester
Profs interesting rating	71
Profs accessable rating	70
Most common reg class size	fewer than 10 students
Most common lab size	10–19 students

MOST POPULAR MAJORS

Biology, economics, political science

SPECIAL STUDY OPTIONS

Accelerated program, cooperative education program, distance learning, double major, dual-enrollment, English as a Second Language (ESL), exchange student program (domestic), honors program, independent study, internships, liberal arts/career combination, student-designed major, study abroad, teacher certification program.

residential neighborhood and enroll in a cluster of three classes together. "No one's going to hold your hand and point you to what it is you want," but whoever you are, "there is a group for you and a ton of activities for you." Madison has "such a beautiful campus with so many different scenes." You "can spend part of your day walking downtown and enjoying the city, followed by a relaxing afternoon by the lake and trails," and then by night, "just being at a football, basketball or hockey game makes your adrenaline pump and the heart race!"

WHY STUDENTS LOVE UNIVERSITY OF WISCONSIN—MADISON

Besides the "beautiful campus and great campus activities," Madison is a "large, fun school that is also intellectually stimulating." Though the hard sciences and engineering programs get most of the pub, the school of business is "excellent" and boasts "some of the best facilities on campus," and "the liberal arts majors are fantastic." As one student says, "the school has an incredible amount of prestige, as far as academics go, and to me, it's more valuable to have this school on my resume than any other college in Wisconsin." The UW is "fun and friendly," whether it be at a house party, game day, a mass snow ball fight in the streets, or in class, and the whole of the school is "energetic" and likes "to get out and play just as much" as they like to study.

Why Students Love University of Wisconsin—Madison

"The school has an incredible amountof prestige, as far as academics go, and to me, it's more valuable to have this school on my resume than any other college in Wisconsin."

BANG FOR YOUR BUCK

No matter whether you're paying in-state or out-of-state tuition, think of the (reasonable) cost as granting access to a complete jackpot of resources. From intangibles (such as access to some of the state's brightest minds) to more easily defined benefits (research opportunities and internships galore), students can take their time here and make anything they want of it. Also, a UW grad is a Badger for life, and the alumni connection will serve you well for the rest of yours.

University of Wisconsin—Madison

STUDENT BODY

Ethnic diversity at Madison is in the eye of the beholder. "If you're from a big city, it's pretty white," proposes a sophomore. "But, then again, I've met people here who had one black person in their high school and had never met a Jewish person." Without question, socioeconomic diversity flourishes. "There is a prevalent rivalry between [Wisconsin] students (sconnies) and the coasties who are generally wealthier and from the East or West Coast." Beyond that, it's impossible to generalize. "All types of people make up the student body here, ranging from the peace-preaching grass-root activist, to the protein-shake-a-day jock, to the overly privileged coastie, to the studious bookworm, to the computer geek," explains a first-year student. "There is a niche for everyone." "There are a lot of atypical students, but that is what makes UW—Madison so special," adds a senior. "Normal doesn't exist on this campus." Politically, "Madison is a hotbed for political and social debate." "Many people are passionate about many things, and it provides a great opportunity to see things from others' points of view."

Why Students Love University of Wisconsin—Madison

> "All types of people make up the student body here, ranging from the peace-preaching grass-root activist, to the protein-shake-a-day jock, to the overly privileged coastie, to the studious bookworm, to the computer geek."

GENERAL INFO

Activities: Choral groups, concert band, dance, drama/theater, jazz band, literary magazine, marching band, music ensembles, musical theater, opera, pep band, radio station, student government, student newspaper, student-run film society, symphony orchestra, television station, yearbook, international student organization. **Organizations:** 685 registered organizations, 27 honor societies, 26 fraternities, 11 sororities. **Athletics (Intercollegiate):** *Men*: Basketball, cheerleading, crew/rowing, cross-country, football, golf, ice hockey, soccer, swimming, tennis, track/field (outdoor), wrestling. *Women*: Basketball, cheerleading, crew/rowing, cross-country, golf, ice hockey, soccer, softball, swimming, tennis, track/field (outdoor), volleyball. **On-Campus Highlights:** Allen Centennial Gardens, Kohl Center, Memorial Union Terrace, Chazen Museum of Art, Babcock Hall Dairy Plant and Store.

BOTTOM LINE

Tuition and room and board varies depending on which state you're from. Wisconsin residents can expect to pay around $22,542 for year (including room and board), Minnesota residents $26,060, and non-residents of either state are looking at about $39,201. About 22.5 percent of freshman students receive some sort of grant that does not have to be repaid, and additional scholarships, work study, and federal and campus loans are available.

SELECTIVITY

Admissions Rating	**93**
# of applicants	25,522
% of applicants accepted	57
% of acceptees attending	41

FRESHMAN PROFILE

Range SAT Critical Reading	**530–670**
Range SAT Math	**620–750**
Range SAT Writing	**580–680**
Range ACT Composite	**29–34**
Average HS GPA	**3.69**
% graduated top 10% of class	**56**
% graduated top 25% of class	**93**
% graduated top 50% of class	**99**

DEADLINES

Regular Deadline	**2/1**
Normal registration	**yes**

FACILITIES

Housing: Coed dorms, men's dorms, special housing for international students, women's dorms, fraternity/sorority housing, apartments for married students, cooperative housing, apartments for single students, theme housing. *Computers*: 100% of classrooms, 25% of dorms, 100% of libraries, 100% of dining areas, 100% of student union, 100% of common outdoor areas have wireless network access.

FINANCIAL FACTS

Financial Aid Rating	**74**
Annual in-state tuition	$9,672
Annual out-of-state tuition	$25,421
Room and Board	$7,780
Required Fees	$3,180
Books and supplies	$1,140
% frosh rec. need-based scholarship or grant aid	21
% UG rec. need-based scholarship or grant aid	23
% frosh rec. non-need-based scholarship or grant aid	28
% UG rec. non-need-based scholarship or grant aid	27
% frosh rec. need-based self-help aid	29
% UG rec. need-based self-help aid	31
% frosh rec. any financial aid	47
% UG rec. any financial aid	46
% UG borrow to pay for school	48
Average cumulative indebtedness	$22,837

#6

College of William & Mary

Williamsburg, VA

WILLIAM & MARY

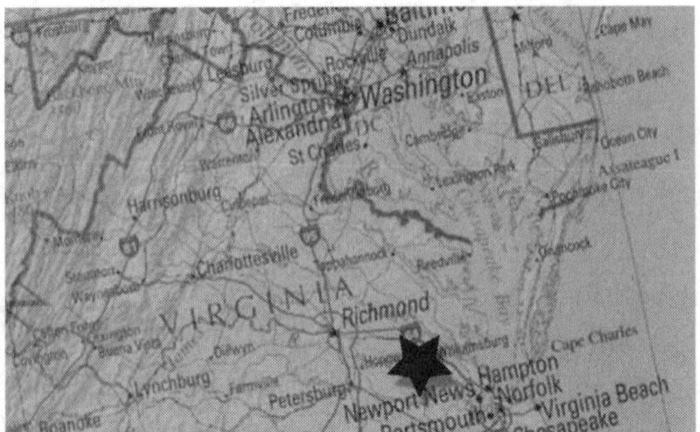

STUDENTS

5,836 undergrad enrollment

45% Male ♂♂♂♂♂♂♂

55% Female ♀♀♀♀♀♀♀♀♀♀

ADMISSIONS

12,539 applicants → 32% admitted

35% enrolled

EARLY ADMISSIONS → NR applicants

NR accepted

4.05 avg. high school gpa

ACT range (0–36): 28–32

SAT range (200–800): reading 640–730, math 620–710, writing 620–720

79% graduated top 10% of class

96% graduated top 25% of class

FINANCIAL INFO

in-state	out-of-state			
$8,270	$30,547	$8,772	$1,150	$4,862
annual tuition		room & board	avg. book expenses	required fees

$19,016 avg. indebtedness

ACADEMICS

11:1 student to faculty ratio

NR% classes taught by TAs

GRADUATION RATES

83% of students graduating within 4 years

91% of students graduating within 6 years

** NR = Not reported*

Why the College of William & Mary is No. 6

William & Mary achieves a remarkable balance between the dynamic, progressive academics of a liberal arts college and the strong sense of history and tradition one would expect from America's second-oldest school. As one of only eight "Public Ivies" in the nation, it offers an incredibly high level of academics for low in-state tuition. The school attracts the type of student who's itching to explore a topic beyond the textbook, and students here are smart, passionate, and serious about bringing good into the world, while still knowing how to have a good time. Campus activities and programming are plentiful and well attended, and off campus, students enjoy the charms of Colonial Williamsburg, the theme park Busch Gardens, and Jamestown Beach.

The school believes that original, hands-on research is something that's missing from most liberal arts educations, so there are endless and amazing opportunities here. From the start of a student's very first class, they are given unprecedented opportunities to work with peers and experienced faculty mentors on projects that inspire them. Professors even engage students outside of the classroom and give them the opportunity to conduct their own research projects; they are well aware what makes college students tick and are not afraid to make students challenge themselves.

Why Students love College of William & Mary

"Everyone at William & Mary cares about each other. People are competitive, but by no means cut-throat."

"From emailing to texting students with concerns, the professors at William & Mary are invested in the success of their students."

ABOUT THE SCHOOL

The College of William & Mary was founded in 1693 by a couple of English monarchs, King William III and Queen Mary II (hence the name). It's the second-oldest college in the United States. "I absolutely loved the feeling of community on campus," one student says. Another contends that "the traditions at William & Mary really ground students in campus life." The long list of prominent alumni who have graced the hallowed halls of this stately southern campus runs the gamut from Thomas Jefferson to Jon Stewart. The academic atmosphere here is intense and occasionally daunting. However, one student argues, "everyone at William & Mary care about each other. People are competitive, but by no means cut-throat." At the same time, the faculty is tremendous pretty much across the board, and professors are widely available outside of class "as they generally care about the students," says one sophomore. "From emailing to texting students with concerns, the professors

Contact Info:

College of William & Mary
Office of Admissions
P.O. Box 8795
Williamsburg, VA 23187-8795
Admissions: 757-221-4223 Financial Aid: 757-221-2420
E-mail: admission@wm.edu
Fax: 757-221-1242
Website: www.wm.edu

Fun Facts

- First and ONLY American college to receive a coat of arms from the College of Heralds (1694).
- Alumni include three Presidents of the United States (Thomas Jefferson, James Monroe and John Tyler), former Secretary of Defense Bob Gates, Pittsburgh Steelers Head Coach Mike Tomlin and comedian Jon Stewart.
- First college to establish an intercollegiate fraternity, Phi Beta Kappa (Dec. 5, 1776).
- George Washington was William & Mary's first American Chancellor.
- William & Mary is home to the Nation's oldest Law School.
- At the heart of our campus is the Sir Christopher Wren Building. Completed in 1699, the Wren Building is the oldest academic building in continuous use in the United States, and classes are still taught within its walls today.
- William & Mary has a number of traditions, including the Yule Log Ceremony, at which the president dresses as Santa Claus and reads a rendition of "How the Grinch Stole Christmas,"the Vice-President of Student Affairs reads "Twas the Night Before Finals," and The Gentlemen of the College sing the song "The Twelve Days of Christmas."
- William and Mary has eleven collegiate a cappella groups.

College of William & Mary

CAMPUS LIFE

Quality of life Rating	89
Fire Safety Rating	78
Green rating	92
Type of School	Public
Environment	Village

STUDENTS

Total undergrad enrolllment	5,836
% Male to Female	45/55
% From out of state	32
% From public high school	79
% Live on Campus	75
# of Fraternities	20
# of Sororities	11
% African American	7
% Asian	8
% Caucasian	55
% Hispanic	7
% International	3
# Of Countries Represented	47

ACADEMICS

Academic Rating	90
% Of students graduating within 4 years	93
% Of students graduating within 6 years	91
Calendar	semester
Profs interesting rating	93
Profs interesting rating	92
Most common reg class size	10–19 students
Most common lab size	10–19 students

MOST POPULAR MAJORS

Business, English, government, history, biology

HONORS PROGRAMS

Monroe Scholars, Sharpe Scholars, Murray Scholars, William & Mary Scholar Award, Alpha Lambda Delta and Phi Eta Sigma Honor Societies for freshmen.

SPECIAL STUDY OPTIONS

Accelerated program, double major, dual enrollment, honors program, independent study, internships, student-designed major, study abroad, teacher certification program.

Why Students love College of William & Mary

> "When you arrive at William & Mary, you instantly feel connected to a greater family."

at William & Mary are invested in the success of their students." One student says, "Even in my lecture class of over 200, the professor knows me by name. I think that speaks volumes about the atmosphere and expectations of William & Mary." A student describes her experience: "professors actively involve undergraduates in their research—I even got to co-write and present a paper at an academic conference last year!" Social life is strong. One senior explains that "I was excited about the prospect of entering an atmosphere where intellectualism and levity are considered compatible. While [William & Mary] students are intelligent hard-workers, they aren't obnoxious or über-competitive (grades are rarely discussed), and even if their brows are often furrowed, their lips are often smiling." "There's a certain intensity here: People are world-aware, involved, hard-working, motivated, and genuinely caring."

BANG FOR YOUR BUCK

William & Mary does a stellar job of meeting the financial need of its students: 100 percent of demonstrated financial need is met for Virginian residents and approximately 80 percent of demonstrated need is met for non-residents. In addition, for Virginia families whose income is $40,000 and below, grants replace the loan portion of the aid award. In addition to need-based aid, William & Mary offers merit-based scholarships. The Murray Scholarship provides the equivalent of in-state tuition and general fees, room and board, and a $5,000 stipend for research. In addition, the William & Mary Scholar Award is presented each year to a select group of students who have overcome unusual adversity and/or would add to the diversity of the campus community. This award provides the equivalent of in-state tuition and general fees. The Howard Hughes Medical Institute offers support through "Mentored Research Experiences" where students receive real-world experience.

STUDENT BODY

Students are quick to note that there's a generalization that the "T.W.A.M.P., or Typical William & Mary Person...is the person [who] does all their reading, shows up to class every day, and is a nerd," but most are equally quick to cast this stereotype aside. The real T.W.A.M.P., they tell us, is "open-minded, outgoing, charismatic, driven, dedicated, caring, and unique." The school is full of "well-rounded people who are in touch with their inner nerd," and "intellectual people who care about the world find the zaniest ways to have fun." "Students fit in many social circles," and students credit the close bonding that happens in freshmen dorms for this inclusivity. "You will often see the members of the football team in the library as much as any other student," and "everyone is involved with at least one other thing outside of class, and often... about ten other things." "Students are an eclectic bunch united by our thirst for knowledge and overwhelming Tribe Pride." "The workload at William & Mary is intense, and sometimes it seems overwhelming, but the students who are admitted are usually of sufficient capability and confidence to complete their work successfully."

WHY STUDENTS LOVE WILLIAM & MARY

"I'm humbled by my peers on a daily basis," confesses one junior attending William & Mary. "Whether at Yule Log, Convocation, or ringing the Wren Bell, by participating in these beloved rituals at W&M, you start to realize you've become a part of something much bigger than yourself...and that you will always remain a part of the College." Another student realized that "the professors not only care about your academic performance but also how you're doing personally. They check in on you constantly and make sure that you are doing well in all aspects of your life." "Freshmen and transfer orientation is also an incredible strength," says one sophomore student, "when you arrive at William & Mary, you instantly feel connected to a greater family." Another student says "along with the perfect campus size, opportunities, amazing professors [and] beautiful campus...the main reason I chose William & Mary would be the people; I can't think of a more genuine, down to earth group of people I would want to spend my next four years with." One student recalls: "I've been to a professor's houses for brunch, gone on picnics with a class, jammed with my professor, gone camping, and gotten cell phone numbers to call if I have a question." In the end, contends one graduating senior, William & Mary was "the kind of college experience I wanted: rigorous academics, caring and safe community, fascinating student body, vibrant campus life, a beautiful location, and dedicated and interesting professors."

GENERAL INFO

Activities: Choral groups, concert band, dance, drama/theater, jazz band, literary magazine, music ensembles, musical theater, opera, pep band, radio station, student government, student newspaper, student-run film society, symphony orchestra, television station, yearbook, campus ministries, international student organization. **Organizations:** 375 registered organizations, 32 honor societies, 32 religious organizations. 18 fraternities, 11 sorority. **Athletics (Intercollegiate):** *Men*: Baseball, basketball, cheerleading, cross-country, diving, football, golf, gymnastics, soccer, swimming, tennis, track/field (outdoor), track/field (indoor). *Women*: Basketball, cheerleading, cross-country, diving, field hockey, golf, gymnastics, lacrosse, soccer, swimming, tennis, track/field (outdoor), track/field (indoor), volleyball. **On-Campus Highlights:** Wren Building (oldest academic building), Muscarelle Museum of Art, Lake Matoaka/College Woods, Crim Dell Bridge, Sunken Garden.

BOTTOM LINE

William & Mary is a truly a steal for Virginia residents. The cost of in-state tuition, room and board, and fees is about $22,000 per year. Students from outside Virginia pay about double that amount. Financial aid is ample.

SELECTIVITY

Admissions Rating	**97**
# of applicants	12,539
% of applicants accepted	32
% of acceptees attending	35
# accepting a place on wait list	1,446
% admitted from wait list	17

FRESHMAN PROFILE

Range SAT Critical Reading	**640–730**
Range SAT Math	**620–710**
Range SAT Writing	**620–720**
Range ACT Composite	**28–32**
Average HS GPA	**4.05**
% graduated top 10% of class	**79**
% graduated top 25% of class	**96**
% graduated top 50% of class	**99**

DEADLINES

Regular Deadline	**1/1**
Normal registration	**no**

FACILITIES

Housing: Coed dorms, special housing for disabled students, special housing for international students, fraternity/sorority housing, apartments for single students, wellness housing, theme housing. *Special Academic Facilities/Equipment*: Observatory, continuous beam accelerator. *Computers*: 100% of classrooms, 100% of dorms, 100% of libraries, 100% of dining areas, 100% of student union, 33% of common outdoor areas have wireless network access.

FINANCIAL FACTS

Financial Aid Rating	**76**
Annual in-state tuition	$8,270
Annual out-of-state tuition	$30,547
Room and Board	$8,772
Required Fees	$4,862
Books and supplies	$1,150
% frosh rec. need-based scholarship or grant aid	23
% UG rec. need-based scholarship or grant aid	25
% frosh rec. non-need-based scholarship or grant aid	14
% UG rec. non-need-based scholarship or grant aid	12
% frosh rec. need-based self-help aid	20
% UG rec. need-based self-help aid	21
% frosh rec. any financial aid	67
% UG rec. any financial aid	60
% UG borrow to pay for school	38
Average cumulative indebtedness	$18,410

#7

University of Florida

Gainesville, FL

UNIVERSITY of FLORIDA

STUDENTS

32,660 undergrad enrollment

45% Male

55% Female

ADMISSIONS

26,513 applicants	→ 44% admitted	56% enrolled	EARLY ADMISSIONS	→ NR applicants	NR accepted

3.90 avg. high school gpa

reading	570–670
math	600–690

ACT range: 26–30 (0–36)

SAT range: (200–800)

NR graduated top 10% of class

NR graduated top 25% of class

FINANCIAL INFO

in-state	out-of-state		
$5,656	$27,933	$8,800	$1,070
annual tuition		room & board	avg. book expenses

$16,013 avg. indebtedness

ACADEMICS

20:1 student to faculty ratio

33% classes taught by TAs

GRADUATION RATES

64% of students graduating within 4 years

84% of students graduating within 6 years

* NR = Not reported

Why the University of Florida is No. 7

A top-tier research institute that is full of bright students who still know how to have fun (and sure know how to play football), the University of Florida is known for its consistently excellent academic programs all across the board. While the business and engineering programs are popular, the school is also known for journalism, premed (there is a strong teaching hospital on campus), and, well, a lot of things. While in-state tuition and numerous scholarship opportunities (such as the Florida Opportunity Scholarship for first-generation-in-college freshmen) make it a bargain, even out-of-state students will find the tuition far lower than most private colleges. There are plenty of on-campus jobs for students to earn some money and gain experience, and most every UF student has an opportunity to engage in an internship opportunity, volunteer or participate in an organized student group.

Every day is a weekend in Gainesville, and you will always find something going on Sunday through Saturday. The ease with which students are able to blend academic and social life provides the quintessential college experience, and school spirit is at a maximum here. The Gator bond is unfazed by time, geography, or even football losses; once you get beyond the school's huge campus, it doesn't matter where you are in the world, UF students and alumni are everywhere and ready to greet you with open arms and a hearty "Go Gators!"

Why Students Love University of Florida

"A beautiful school full of bright students who still know how to have fun, and you never feel alone."

ABOUT THE SCHOOL

The University of Florida is the prototypical large, state school that "provides its students with a well-rounded experience: an excellent education coated in incomparable school camaraderie." With a total enrollment of 50,000-plus, this school is among the five largest universities in the nation, proffering "first class amenities, athletics, academics, campus, and students." Those students hail from all 50 states and more than 100 countries, all of whom are looking for more than your standard academic fare. UF certainly doesn't disappoint, as the school has "a great reputation and…great academic programs for the tuition price." The campus is home to more than 100 undergraduate degree programs, and undergraduates interested in conducting research with faculty can participate in UF's University Scholars Program. The Career Resource Center (CRC) is a major centralized service that helps students prepare for their post-graduation experiences—UF "seeks to graduate academically ahead and 'real-world-prepared' alumni"—and organized career fairs are conducted regularly and the university is very successful in attracting top employers nationally to recruit on campus.

Nine hundred student organizations on campus, ranging from Quidditch and Underwater Hockey to the Neuroscience Club and Engineers Without Borders, ensure that students are kept equally busy outside of class. Those in search of a social life have come

Contact Info:

201 Criser Hall, Box 114000,
Gainesville, FL 32611-4000
Phone: 352-392-1365
Financial Aid Phone: 352-392-1271
Fax: 904-392-3987
Website: www.ufl.edu

Fun Facts

- Florida's largest university—and the nation's fourth-largest—traces its beginnings to a small seminary in 1853.

  Enrolling approximately 50,000 students annually, UF is home to 16 colleges and more than 150 research centers and institutes.

  Since 1985, UF has been a member of the Association of American Universities, the prestigious higher-education organization comprised of the top 62 public and private institutions in North America.

- The freshmen retention rate of 94 percent is among the highest in the United States.

- Royalty and licensing income includes the glaucoma drug Trusopt, the sports drink Gatorade, and the Sentricon termite elimination system.

- UF became the first university in the world to be designated a "Certified Audubon Cooperative Sanctuary."

University of Florida

CAMPUS LIFE

Quality of life Rating	85
Fire Safety Rating	60*
Green rating	96
Type of School	Public
Environment	City

STUDENTS

Total undergrad enrolllment	32,660
% Male to Female	45/55
% From out of state	5
% From public high school	84
% Live on Campus	23
# of Fraternities	38
# of Sororities	26
% African American	9
% Asian	8
% Caucasian	58
% Hispanic	16
% International	1
# Of Countries Represented	132

ACADEMICS

Academic Rating	68
% Of students graduating within 4 years	64
% Of students graduating within 6 years	84
Calendar	semester
Profs interesting rating	64
Profs accessable rating	73
Most common reg class size	10–19 students
Most common lab size	10–19 students

MOST POPULAR MAJORS

Finance, political science, psychology

HONORS PROGRAMS

University of Florida Honors Program

SPECIAL STUDY OPTIONS

Accelerated program, cooperative education program, cross-registration, distance learning, double major, dual enrollment, English as a Second Language (ESL), exchange student program (domestic), external degree program, honors program, independent study, internships, liberal arts/career combination, student-designed major, study abroad, teacher certification program, weekend college, Adult/Continuing Education, TV-delivered credit-bearing courses, Honors Program, and distance learning courses.

to the right place. Whether looking for a party or a Gators game, students show up with a passion in staggering numbers. "There are hardly any people who aren't proud of Gator athletes, and they are always ready to sport the orange and blue." There's a hefty club scene downtown and fraternity/sorority scene on campus, with about 30 percent of both men and women choosing to go Greek. About 7,500 students live in dorms, with thousands more living in nearby apartments. "UF satisfies what I hoped for in a good college experience," says a student. The campus has a major art museum, "wonderful libraries," radio and television stations, and one of the largest national history museums in the Southeast. There's also an on-campus lake with recreational equipment available and dozens of social organizations, religious groups, and other activities. Hometown Gainesville is a medium-sized town that houses "more [than enough] bars, clubs, and restaurants and shopping to keep you busy throughout the entire semester."

BANG FOR YOUR BUCK

The cost of attending University of Florida is well below the national average for four-year public universities. Annual tuition and fees hover around $5,044 (based on a typical schedule of 30 credit hours per year), while campus room and board will run you another $8,000-plus. Overall, Florida residents are the main benefactors of this great value. Out-of-state undergraduates pay almost $20,000 more in tuition and fees and must also factor in higher transportation costs.

STUDENT BODY

The typical UF student "has a popular major like engineering or business," "is witty, loves Gator football, and likes to party. An atypical student may be someone who doesn't party or may deviate from mainstream beliefs, practices, or political parties, but for the most part, any student is accepted as a member of the Gator nation," and most "seem to maintain a well-balanced life of studying and socializing." While "the sorority/fraternity people are the most dominant group on campus," there's also "a really strong indie scene (the two never interact)." In fact, "There are people all over the spectrum," although the place is so big that "half of them you may never meet." "We are one of the most diverse campuses in the nation," one student explains, "and we are all Gators at heart, first and foremost."

WHY STUDENTS LOVE THE UNIVERSITY OF FLORIDA

UF is "a beautiful school full of bright students who still know how to have fun, and you never feel alone." Add to the mix "great weather, great sports, great Greek system, great academics, [and] great fun in 70-degree weather year round," and "the morale of the students is high." While here, you can party to your heart's content; the university "certainly lives up to its role of number one party school," but "there is much more to UF than that." Gainesville is definitely a college town, and it "is perfect for anyone looking for the true college experience." "The town is completely devoted to the school, so students feel catered to no matter where you go." As one content student sums it up: "The University of Florida is about being a Gator, and that means that you're of above average intelligence, may like to party, and love football."

Why Students Love University of Florida

"We are one of the most diverse campuses in the nation."

"There are hardly any people who aren't proud of Gator athletes."

GENERAL INFO

Activities: Choral groups, concert band, dance, drama/theater, jazz band, literary magazine, marching band, music ensembles, musical theater, pep band, radio station, student government, student newspaper, student-run film society, symphony orchestra, television station, yearbook. **Organizations:** 853 registered organizations. **Athletics (Intercollegiate):** *Men*: Baseball, basketball, cross-country, diving, football, golf, swimming, tennis, track/field (outdoor), track/field (indoor). *Women*: Basketball, cross-country, diving, golf, gymnastics, lacrosse, soccer, softball, swimming, tennis, track/field (outdoor), track/field (indoor), volleyball. **On-Campus Highlights:** Center for Performing Arts, Florida Museum of Natural History, Cancer & Genetic Research Complex, Brain Institute, Lake Alice Wildlife Reserve. **Environmental Initiatives:** Zero Waste by 2015. UF recycles more than 6,500 tons of material annually, nearly 40% of the waste stream. Additionally, UF strives to recycle at least 75% of its deconstruction debris and has instituted an Electronics Reuse/Recycling Policy. Carbon Neutrality by 2025. LEED Gold certification for all new construction. UF built its first green roof atop the Charles R. Perry Construction Yard building. The roof, which contains soil and live plants, helps reduce storm water runoff and insulates the building against heat and sound.

THE BOTTOM LINE

With relatively low tuition and a strong scholarship program for in-state students, UF is an especially good value for Florida residents. The Florida Opportunity Scholarship (FOS) is a scholarship program for first-generation college freshmen from economically disadvantaged backgrounds. The scholarship provides a full grant scholarship aid package for up to four years of undergraduate education. Approximately 41 percent of UF students receive financial assistance through loans. Upon graduating from UF, student loan indebtedness is $15,932. Out-of-state students pay about five times as much to attend UF as their Florida counterparts. On the bright side, out-of-state students still receive all the benefits and resources of a major academic institution, and they may apply for financial aid to offset the costs.

SELECTIVITY

Admissions Rating	**92**
# of applicants	26,513
% of applicants accepted	44
% of acceptees attending	56

FRESHMAN PROFILE

Range SAT Critical Reading	**570–670**
Range SAT Math	**600–690**
Range ACT Composite	**26–30**
Average HS GPA	**3.90**

DEADLINES

Regular Deadline	**11/1**
Normal registration	**yes**

FACILITIES

Housing: Coed dorms, special housing for disabled students, special housing for international students, fraternity/sorority housing, apartments for married students, apartments for single students. *Special Academic Facilities/Equipment*: Natural history museum, art museum, art gallery, center for the performing arts, Aeolian Skinner organ, cast-bell carillon, citrus research center, coastal engineering wave tank, 100–kilowatt training and research reactor, academic computing center, microkelvin lab, self-contained intensive care hyperbaric chamber. *Computers*: 80% of classrooms, 100% of dorms, 100% of libraries, 100% of dining areas, 100% of student union, 100% of common outdoor areas have wireless network access.

FINANCIAL FACTS

Financial Aid Rating	**85**
Annual in-state tuition	$5,656
Annual out-of-state tuition	$27,933
Room and Board	$8,800
Books and supplies	$1,070
% frosh rec. need-based scholarship or grant aid	31
% UG rec. need-based scholarship or grant aid	31
% frosh rec. non-need-based scholarship or grant aid	47
% UG rec. non-need-based scholarship or grant aid	36
% frosh rec. need-based self-help aid	18
% UG rec. need-based self-help aid	22
% frosh rec. any financial aid	99
% UG rec. any financial aid	90
% UG borrow to pay for school	40
Average cumulative indebtedness	$16,013

#8

GEORGIA
1776
UNIVERSITY OF GEORGIA
Endowed with 40,000 acres of land in 1784 and chartered in 1785, the charter was the first granted by a state for a government controlled university. After Louisville and then Greensboro were first selected, the current site was chosen.
The first president, and author of the school's charter, Abraham Baldwin, resigned when the doors opened, and was succeeded by Josiah Meigs. The University first began to thrive under Moses Waddel, who became president in 1819. Alonzo Church was president in 1829-1859.
During the War for Southern Independence, most of the students entered the Confederate Army. The University closed its doors in 1864, and did not open again until January 1866. After the war, many Confederate veterans became students.
Famous pre-war professors were John and Joseph LeConte and Charles F. McCay, while famous students were Robert Toombs, Alexander H. Stephens, Howell Cobb, and Crawford W. Long.
Plans for a modern university were first developed by Walter B. Hill and realized under Harmon W. Caldwell. The best known of the post-war presidents (now chancellors) was David C. Barrow. The builder of the modern plant was Chancellor Steadman V. Sanford.
GEORGIA HISTORIC MARKER
1981

University of Georgia

Athens, GA

STUDENTS
25,709 undergrad enrollment
42% Male
58% Female

ADMISSIONS
17,408 applicants → **59%** admitted | **45%** enrolled
EARLY ADMISSIONS **NR** applicants → **NR** accepted

3.82 avg. high school gpa

ACT range (0–36): 25–29

SAT range (200–800):
reading 560–660
math 560–670
writing 560–660

83% graduated top 10% of class
90% graduated top 25% of class

FINANCIAL INFO
annual tuition: in-state **$7,282**; out-of-state **$25,492**
$8,708 room & board
$1,079 avg. book expenses
$2,190 required fees
$15,938 avg. indebtedness

ACADEMICS
19:1 student to faculty ratio
1% classes taught by TAs

GRADUATION RATES
54% of students graduating within 4 years
82% of students graduating within 6 years

** NR = Not reported*

Why University of Georgia is No. 8

The University of Georgia is the state's oldest, most comprehensive, and most diversified institution of higher education. The school is as broad and encompassing as it is eclectic, offering bachelor's degrees in more than 140 fields, as well as a lauded Honors Program, which encompasses nearly 10 percent of undergraduates. Bulldog pride certainly covers the school's football team, but it extends to the numerous academic and cultural distinctions that students, faculty, and researchers achieve under the UGA name. Top students consistently compete and win prominent national scholarships (including seven Rhodes scholars since 1996), receive acceptance into top graduate programs, and make lasting contributions to academia; the school's Grady College of Journalism and Mass Communication even administers the Peabody Awards.

When you think about how long the school's been around—it was founded in 1785—it's much easier to grasp the scope its existence, from the size of its grounds, to the reach of its alumni, to the impact of the sizeable research conducted here. The humming campus somehow manages to house and serve tens of thousands of people each day, each on their own personal path of study and play, and caters to almost every interest under the sun. The school combines Southern hospitality with a prestigious education system and terrific financial aid and surrounds it with perfectly pleasant weather.

Why Students Love University of Georgia

"I never tire of meeting new people and UGA has so many people to offer. It's incredible."

ABOUT THE SCHOOL

The University of Georgia's star is rising in academic circles, as a result of notice from the popular press and the prestigious awards and grants bestowed on faculty and students. "Academic rigor at UGA is one to be modeled after," and programs in journalism, science, agriculture, and literature, among others, are the backbone of the UGA's increasingly attractive profile as a world-class research institution that draws top faculty and students. "Everyone in Georgia strives to go to UGA," says a student. Students make note of the stellar, "experienced professors and research participation" opportunities, pointing out many of the classes—especially in the first two years—are large, and that it is to a student's advantage to go beyond just showing up. Smaller student-faculty ratios are available in honors program classes.

UGA students are educated on a beautiful, 759-acre main campus located in Athens, Ga., a quintessential college town known for its vibrant music and arts scene. "When classes are over and your studying is done, there is fun to be had all around Athens," including a full slate of on-campus, and out-of-class activities on offer. Students can choose from more than 600 extracurricular organizations ranging from sororities and fraternities to pre-professional ("a great way to meet people"), environmental, and civic groups. There's an "incomparable" music scene, a hippie scene, and a jock scene—to name just a few—and all 34,000 students on campus have an easy time finding a group where they feel welcome. "I never tire of meeting new people and UGA has so

Contact Info:

Terrell Hall

Athens, GA 30602

Admissions: 706-542-8776

Financial Aid: 706-542-6147

E-mail: undergrad@admissions.uga.edu

Fax: 706-542-1466

Website: www.uga.edu

Fun Facts

- "The Arch," an iron gate found on everything from the UGA logo to t-shirts is representative of the Arch on campus which was an original gateway to the school. Legend has it that if a freshman walks under The Arch during his first year, he will never graduate.
- When the UGA Bulldogs have won a home football game, the school's Chapel Bell traditionally rings until midnight. Except when Georgia beats Georgia Tech, one of their biggest rivals—then the bell rings the entire night! In the old days, it was the job of freshmen to do the hard work of ringing the bell—today, fans, students, and alumni all take turns.
- During the 2007 Season, the bell was ringing after UGA's defeat over the University of Florida, when the 877-pound bell fell. It has since been returned to the platform.
- The Bulldogs like to get their opponents 'Between the Hedges.' This is a reference to the hedges that grow all the way around the playing field of Sanford Stadium, and dates back to the 1930s, when a sports writer made the reference.
- In 1939, Coach Wally Butts decided silver pants would pair well with red jerseys—thus began the start of the Bulldog's 'silver britches.' Although Coach Vince Dooley changed the pants to white for several years, the silver britches were brought back in 1980, and were worn during the school's National Championship season.

University of Georgia

CAMPUS LIFE

Quality of life Rating	92
Fire Safety Rating	77
Green rating	92
Type of School	Public
Environment	City

STUDENTS

Total undergrad enrolllment	25,709
% Male to Female	42/58
% From out of state	9
% From public high school	78
% Live on Campus	28
# of Fraternities	32
# of Sororities	26
% African American	7
% Asian	7
% Caucasian	77
% Hispanic	4
% International	1
# Of Countries Represented	126

ACADEMICS

Academic Rating	72
% Of students graduating within 4 years	54
% Of students graduating within 6 years	82
Calendar	semester
Profs interesting rating	77
Profs accessable rating	71
Most common reg class size	20–29 students

MOST POPULAR MAJORS
Biology, English language and literature, psychology

HONORS PROGRAMS

General Honors Program (university-wide), Foundation Fellows, Center for Undergraduate Research Summer Research Fellows, CURO Apprentice Program Special programs offered to physically disabled students include note-taking services, reader services, voice recorders, tutors.

SPECIAL STUDY OPTIONS

Accelerated program, cooperative education program, cross-registration, distance learning, double major, dual enrollment, exchange student program (domestic), external degree program, honors program, independent study, internships, liberal arts/career combination, student-designed major, study abroad, teacher certification program.

many people to offer. It's incredible," says a student. Students often gather around that other constant of UGA, the Georgia Bulldogs. "There are so many choices here it's difficult to manage your time between studying and getting involved in all UGA has to offer," says a student. The University of Georgia Career Center provides centralized career services for students and is among the first in the nation to develop iPhone apps that connect students with potential employers. The university also offers an innovative Career Boot Camp, a day-long, intensive program that brings representatives of Fortune 100 companies to the campus to conduct exercises such as mock interviews.

BANG FOR YOUR BUCK

Georgia's merit-based HOPE Scholarship provides high school graduates who have a minimum 3.0 grade point average with a scholarship to cover the cost of tuition and a percentage of student fees and books. Ninety seven percent of Georgia-resident freshmen at UGA receive the scholarship. UGA also offers the prestigious Foundation Fellowship, which provides an annual stipend of approximately $9,000 for in-state students (in addition to the HOPE Scholarship) and $15,700 for out-of-state students (plus an out-of-state tuition waiver). The Fellowship provides numerous opportunities for national and international travel-study, faculty-directed academic research, and participation in academic conferences.

WHY STUDENTS LOVE UNIVERSITY OF GEORGIA

The school "has a history of breeding successful individuals," and in-state (and some out-of-state) students grow up wanting to come here. A degree from Georgia is "highly respected," and "when people here that you are a student of alum of the University of Georgia, that really says something about yourself." There "is nothing like walking on a campus that has so much history and tradition," and "students, professors, even other employees love where they are at." Most people are "working for the weekend," when "there's always some place to hang out with friends and enjoy each others' company." College sports also play a large part in the strengths of UGA, and the school's teams are "national champions in many sports and have one of the most widely recognized college football teams." There is "a wholly proud diversity of students all eager to chant 'Glory, Glory to Old Georgia.'"

STUDENT BODY

"Students are generally white, upper-middle-class, smart, [and] involved, and [they] have a good time," "seem to be predominantly conservative," and "are usually involved in at least one organization whether it be Greek, a club, or sports." "The typical student at UGA is one who knows how and when to study but allows himself or herself to have a very active social life." The majority are Southerners, with many students from within Georgia. "The stereotype is Southern, Republican, football-loving, and beer-drinking. While many, many of UGA's students do not fit this description, there is no lack of the above," and "there is a social scene for everyone in Athens." "There are a great number of atypical students in the liberal arts," which "creates a unique and exciting student body with greatly contrasting opinions."

University of Georgia

Why Students Love University of Georgia

"The typical student at UGA is one who knows how and when to study but allows himself or herself to have a very active social life."

"Academic rigor at UGA is one to be modeled after."

GENERAL INFO

Activities: Choral groups, concert band, dance, drama/theater, jazz band, literary magazine, marching band, music ensembles, musical theater, opera, pep band, radio station, student government, student newspaper, student-run film society, symphony orchestra, television station, yearbook, campus ministries, international student organization. **Organizations:** 597 registered organizations, 22 honor societies, 35 religious organizations. 34 fraternities, 25 sororities. **Athletics (Intercollegiate):** *Men*: Baseball, basketball, cross-country, diving, football, golf, swimming, tennis, track/field (outdoor), track/field (indoor). *Women*: Basketball, cross-country, diving, equestrian sports, golf, gymnastics, soccer, softball, swimming, tennis, track/field (outdoor), track/field (indoor), volleyball. **On-Campus Highlights:** Zell B. Miller Learning Center, Sanford Stadium, Ramsey Student Center for Physical Activity, Performing and Visual Arts Complex, Tate Student Center. **Environmental Initiatives:** Office of Sustainability. Eugene Odom School of Ecology. Academy of the Environment. UGA currently has more than 50 rain gardens and 14 cisterns installed or under construction totaling over 530,000 gallons storage capacity for continuous reuse.

THE BOTTOM LINE

The average in-state Georgia freshman pays $5,623 in tuition, while those from out of state cough up more than $22,000 a year. On-campus room and board costs just more than $8,000. Recent graduates left UGA with approximately $15,000 in cumulative debt, on average.

SELECTIVITY

Admissions Rating	**93**
# of applicants	17,408
% of applicants accepted	59
% of acceptees attending	45
# accepting a place on wait list	709
% admitted from wait list	7

FRESHMAN PROFILE

Range SAT Critical Reading	**560–660**
Range SAT Math	**560–670**
Range SAT Writing	**560–660**
Range ACT Composite	**25–29**
Average HS GPA	**3.82**
% graduated top 10% of class	**83**
% graduated top 25% of class	**90**
% graduated top 50% of class	**98**

DEADLINES

Regular Deadline	**1/15**
Normal registration	**yes**

FACILITIES

Housing: Coed dorms, special housing for disabled students, special housing for international students, women's dorms, fraternity/sorority housing, apartments for married students. *Special Academic Facilities/Equipment*: Miller Learning Center, Georgia Museum of Art, Georgia Museum of Natural History. *Computers*: 90% of classrooms, 15% of dorms, 100% of libraries, 100% of dining areas, 100% of student union, 100% of common outdoor areas have wireless network access.

FINANCIAL FACTS

Financial Aid Rating	**78**
Annual in-state tuition	$7,282
Annual out-of-state tuition	$25,492
Room and Board	$8,708
Required Fees	$2,190
Books and supplies	$1,078
% frosh rec. need-based scholarship or grant aid	40
% UG rec. need-based scholarship or grant aid	34
% frosh rec. non-need-based scholarship or grant aid	11
% UG rec. non-need-based scholarship or grant aid	6
% frosh rec. need-based self-help aid	19
% UG rec. need-based self-help aid	23
% frosh rec. any financial aid	48
% UG rec. any financial aid	43
% UG borrow to pay for school	45
Average cumulative indebtedness	$15,938

#9

University of Washington

Seattle, WA

UNIVERSITY *of* WASHINGTON

STUDENTS

27,647 undergrad enrollment

48% Male ♂♂♂♂♂♂♂

52% Female ♀♀♀♀♀♀♀♀♀♀

ADMISSIONS

22,843 →	57%	42%	EARLY ADMISSIONS →	NR	NR
applicants	admitted	enrolled		applicants	accepted

NR avg. high school gpa

24–30 ACT range (0–36)

SAT range (200–800)	
reading	530–650
math	570–690
writing	520–690

85% graduated top 10% of class

95% graduated top 25% of class

FINANCIAL INFO

in-state	out-of-state			
$8,701	$25,329	$8,169	$1,008	$272
annual tuition		room & board	avg. book expenses	required fees

$16,800 avg. indebtedness

ACADEMICS

11:1 student to faculty ratio

NR% classes taught by TAs

GRADUATION RATES

NR% of students graduating within 4 years

NR% of students graduating within 6 years

** NR = Not reported*

Why University of Washington is No. 9

Students find a great combination of high-powered academics, an excellent social life, and a wide variety of courses, all in the midst of exciting Seattle at the University of Washington. Research defines the UW experience, and it is the largest recipient of federal research funding among public universities and second among all public and private universities in the country—the university passed its billion dollar research budget milestone in 2006. Science programs in particular are incredible, and students have access to cutting-edge research and the leaders of biomedical sciences, stem cell research, and more. Even outside of the sciences, the breadth of the courses of study available is staggering, and an aimless student that comes to UW is sure to find a major that interests them by the time they leave. Pre-professional programs in business, law, nursing, medicine and engineering are all well-regarded, and for those fortunate enough to get in, the Honors Program creates a smaller community of highly motivated students.

The DIY aesthetic of Seattle plays heavily in the daily lives of students, who can take advantage of all the dynamic city has to offer, including a famous music scene, dining and shopping on the Ave, the lake, and, of course, coffee. The school's endless supply of students means and endless supply of clubs, organizations, and opportunities, and whether you are looking for abstract clubs like the peanut butter and jelly club, or want to study abroad in Russia, there is always something available. Essentially, the University of Washington provides every resource and opportunity for its students to succeed, so long as students take advantage of them.

Why Students Love University of Washington

"A great blend of thoughts, opinions, interests, and passions nestled in a progressive city with opportunities for everyone."

ABOUT THE SCHOOL

Known as "U-Dub," the University of Washington's flagship campus in Seattle is the largest university on the West Coast, providing excellent "course options, location, and a good price range." Its resources are truly astonishing, creating a "diverse student body with an aim to learn about diverse subjects." This "great, BIG institution for a reasonable tuition" is also the host university of the Research Channel program, the only TV channel in the United States dedicated solely for the dissemination of research from academic institutions and research organizations. The school's "great libraries and huge online databases…make researching for papers (almost) a snap!" The Career Center at UW ensures that students have access to a myriad of internship and other experiential learning opportunities. UW International Programs and Exchanges (IPE) provides hundreds of study abroad and internship options to UW students, and the school "boasts a great level of awareness of international issues." UW offers more than 70 student exchanges with universities around the world that are available to undergraduates from most fields. Students pay their regular UW tuition and fees and are able to attend classes at the partner university for a semester or an academic year.

Contact Info:

1410 NE Campus Parkway
UW Box 355852
Seattle, WA 98195-5852
Admissions: 206-543-9686
Financial Aid: 206-543-6101
Fax: 206-685-3655
Website: www.washington.edu

Fun Facts

- Clara McCarty of Puyallup became the first student to receive a bachelor's degree, which was based on the "scientific course." She became a teacher, the usual career for an educated woman at the time. In 1879, she was elected superintendent of schools in Pierce County. McCarty Hall, a UW student dormitory, is named in her honor.
- The process that brought us color television was invented by UW alumnus Willard Geer, a 1927 physics graduate.
- The University of Washington football team played its first collegiate opponent—Stanford—on Dec. 29, 1893, losing 40-0 before 600 spectators in West Seattle. Thirty years later, Washington's team was good enough for its first Rose Bowl appearance, which ended in a tie against Navy: 14-14.
- Bubble gum, vinyl, synthetic rubber and the color TV tube were all invented at the UW.
- Washington's athletic teams had been called the Sun Dodgers since 1919, but a lot of people thought that didn't do much for the school's—or the region's—image. An attempt to adopt the nickname Vikings in 1921 was met with protest by the students, and a joint committee of students, coaches, faculty, alumni and businessmen proposed new names. The Huskies nickname for athletic teams was officially adopted on Feb. 3, 1922.

University of Washington

CAMPUS LIFE

Quality of life Rating	81
Fire Safety Rating	94
Green rating	99
Type of School	Public
Environment	Metropolis

STUDENTS

Total undergrad enrolllment	27,647
% Male to Female	48/52
% From out of state	12
% Live on Campus	25
# of Fraternities	32
# of Sororities	16
% African American	3
% Asian	28
% Caucasian	49
% Hispanic	6
% International	7
# Of Countries Represented	107

ACADEMICS

Academic Rating	99
Calendar	Quarter
Profs interesting rating	70
Profs interesting rating	71
Most common reg class size	fewer than 20–29 students
Most common lab size	10–19 students

MOST POPULAR MAJORS
Economics, Political Science

HONORS PROGRAMS

We have a University Honors Program, as well as departmental honors options.

SPECIAL STUDY OPTIONS

Cooperative education program, distance learning, double major, English as a Second Language (ESL), exchange student program (domestic), honors program, independent study, internships, student-designed major, study abroad, teacher certification program, Friday Harbor Labs.

The "magnificent student body" here enjoys a balanced life with a "nice study environment." Hometown Seattle offers great food, shopping, or just people-watching, and the school's presence makes for "a great blend of thoughts, opinions, interests, and passions nestled in a progressive city with opportunities for everyone." Intramural sports are big. Husky athletics always draw huge crowds, and the school "has an electric campus" even on non-game days. More than 770 student clubs and organizations are on offer. The Greek community is big without being overwhelming. The campus is situated on a beautiful lake, so when the weather is nice students enjoy renting a canoe and paddling across the water. "Since everyone lives fairly close together there is always some way to group up for fun," says a student.

WHY STUDENTS LOVE UNIVERSITY OF WASHINGTON

"I think the University of Washington is about giving students the opportunity to study and excel in a diverse variety of fields," says a student. The berth of majors available to students is a plus for those who know they want to go to college, but are not sure of what they want to study. "I had no idea what I wanted to do when I came to college I knew that U.W. would be able to offer a program in whatever I chose," says a student. Because of the "small campus and smaller classroom sizes," students are "able to have easy access to…professors," and students mix "Top-notch education [with] top-notch fun!" The "vibrancy of the surrounding community" means that "if you like to party you can definitely go to frat parties and hang out with others who like to party, but if you don't, there are so many other fun things to do," such as "volunteer, watch independent films, go to concerts, [and] study at a café."

Why Students Love University of Washington

"I think the University of Washington is about giving students the opportunity to study and excel in a diverse variety of fields."

BANG FOR YOUR BUCK

The University of Washington is committed to making students' education affordable by providing financial assistance in a number of areas—from grants and loans to scholarships and work-study opportunities. The University of Washington offers a full range of grant opportunities for students who qualify. More than $117 million in grants were received by UW undergraduates in 2010–11. The average freshman grant was $5,600. Both merit- and need-based scholarship awards are also available, and the university provided $15 million in scholarships to about 2,700 undergraduates last year. UW's Husky Promise program guarantees full tuition and standard fees will be covered via grant or scholarship support for eligible Washington State students. The cut-off income level that UW has set for eligibility is the highest in the nation for comparable programs.

University of Washington

STUDENT BODY

"At such a large university, there is no 'typical' student," undergrads tell us, observing "one can find just about any demographic here and there is a huge variety in personalities." There "are quite a lot of yuppies, but then again, it's Seattle," and by and large "the campus is ultraliberal. Most students care about the environment, are not religious, and are generally accepting of other diverse individuals." Otherwise, "You've got your stereotypes: the Greeks, the street fashion pioneers, the various ethnic communities, the Oxford-looking grad students, etc." In terms of demographics, "The typical student at UW is white, middle-class, and is from the Seattle area," but "There are a lot of African American students and a very large number of Asian students." All groups "seem to socialize with each other."

GENERAL INFO

Activities: Choral groups, concert band, dance, drama/theater, jazz band, literary magazine, marching band, music ensembles, musical theater, opera, pep band, radio station, student government, student newspaper, student-run film society, symphony orchestra, television station, campus ministries, international student organization. **Organizations:** 711 registered organizations, 13 honor societies, 52 religious organizations. 31 fraternities, 16 sororities. **Athletics (Intercollegiate):** *Men*: Baseball, basketball, crew/rowing, cross-country, football, golf, soccer, tennis, track/field (outdoor). *Women*: Basketball, crew/rowing, cross-country, golf, gymnastics, soccer, softball, tennis, track/field (outdoor), volleyball. **On-Campus Highlights:** Henry Art Gallery, Burke Museum, Meany Hall for Performing Arts, football games at Husky Stadium, Waterfront Activities Center (WAC). **Environmental Initiatives:** College of the Environment. Environmental Stewardship and Sustainability Office; Strategy Management Finance and Facilities. This office supports the Environmental Stewardship Advisory Committee (ESAC). Charter signatory of the American College & University Presidents Climate Commitment (ACUPCC); development and submission of a Climate Action Plan.

Why Students Love University of Washington

"Since everyone lives fairly close together there is always some way to group up for fun."

BOTTOM LINE

In-state tuition at the University of Washington is about $8,700 annually, and out-of-state tuition is in the ballpark of $25,000. Room and board can be as much as an additional $9,000. Students graduate with about $16,800 in debt on average.

SELECTIVITY

Admissions Rating	**91**
# of applicants	22,843
% of applicants accepted	57
% of acceptees attending	42
# accepting a place on wait list	1,308
% admitted from wait list	30

FRESHMAN PROFILE

Range SAT Critical Reading	**530–650**
Range SAT Math	**570–690**
Range SAT Writing	**520–640**
Range ACT Composite	**24–30**
Average HS GPA	**4.47**
% graduated top 10% of class	**85**
% graduated top 25% of class	**95**
% graduated top 50% of class	**100**

DEADLINES

Regular Deadline	**12/1**
Normal registration	**yes**

FACILITIES

Housing: Coed dorms, special housing for disabled students, special housing for international students, fraternity/sorority housing, apartments for married students, apartments for single students. *Special Academic Facilities/Equipment*: Multiple art galleries, an anthropology and natural history museum, arboretum, closed-circuit TV studio. *Computers*: 100% of dorms, 100% of libraries, 100% of student union, have wireless network access.

FINANCIAL FACTS

Financial Aid Rating	**74**
Annual in-state tuition	$8,701
Annual out-of-state tuition	$23,329
Room and Board	$8,169
Required Fees	$272
Books and supplies	$1008
% frosh rec. need-based scholarship or grant aid	29
% UG rec. need-based scholarship or grant aid	29
% frosh rec. non-need-based scholarship or grant aid	7
% UG rec. non-need-based scholarship or grant aid	4
% frosh rec. need-based self-help aid	21
% UG rec. need-based self-help aid	24
% frosh rec. any financial aid	50
% UG rec. any financial aid	50
% UG borrow to pay for school	50
Average cumulative indebtedness	$16,800

Top Ten Public Schools

University of Texas at Austin

Austin, TX

THE UNIVERSITY OF TEXAS AT AUSTIN

WHAT STARTS HERE CHANGES THE WORLD

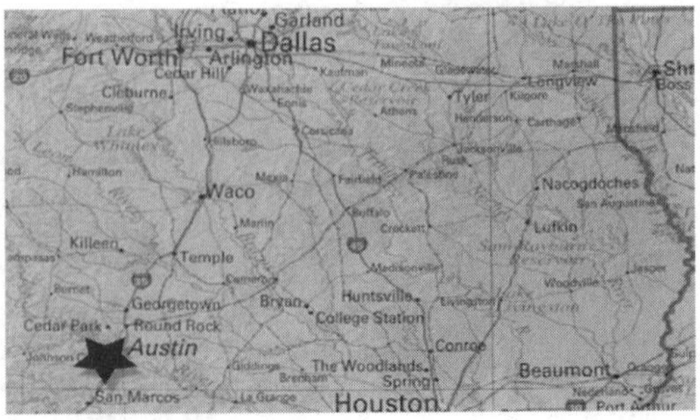

STUDENTS

36,711 undergrad enrollment

44% Male ♂♂♂♂♂♂♂

56% Female ♀♀♀♀♀♀♀♀♀

ADMISSIONS

29,501 →	44%	52%	EARLY ADMISSIONS	→ NR	NR
applicants	admitted	enrolled		applicants	accepted

NR avg. high school gpa

ACT range (0–36): 27

SAT range (200–800): reading 540–660, math 570–690, writing 540–670

75% graduated top 10% of class

95% graduated top 25% of class

FINANCIAL INFO

in-state	out-of-state			
$9,794	$32,506	$10,422	$874	$0
annual tuition		room & board	avg. book expenses	required fees

$17,000 avg. indebtedness

ACADEMICS

17:1 student to faculty ratio

NR% classes taught by TAs

GRADUATION RATES

48% of students graduating within 4 years

78% of students graduating within 6 years

* NR = Not reported

Why University of Texas at Austin is No. 10

You can feel the Longhorn love that emanates from this large, respected institution from clear across the state (not to mention country). And well-founded that love is, as UT—Austin has everything a student could want in a college: academics, athletics, social life, and location. The school and surrounding city offers its students infinite possibilities, and students can do what they please with them, grabbing a degree from the one hundred available majors, or developing their own niche through the school's plentiful research opportunities. As big a school as it is, students are given plenty of support, and anyone who wants to can join a First-year Interest Group (FIG) of 25 first-year students that take two to four classes together in order to develop a smaller sense of community before they become upperclassmen.

Everything is bigger in Texas, and this certainly includes the school spirit, which has never had an off year. Town-gown relations are some of the best in the country—no one is prouder of the university than the city of Austin—and within the plethora of music venues, coffeehouses, bars, and parks—and there are many—left brainers, right brainers, liberals, and conservatives all meld into one giant booster for the school. Surrounded by the UT embrace both on-campus and off, a college student newly out on his own is easily able to acclimate and thrive.

Why Students Love University of Texas—Austin

"The campus is crawling with experts in every field."

ABOUT THE SCHOOL

Some students at The University of Texas at Austin (UT—Austin) boldly make the claim that their school is considered the "Harvard of the South" and they would probably be able to make a strong case for it. Considered one of the best public schools in Texas, the massive UT—Austin campus offers a world-class education through its wide array of programs in the sciences and humanities as well as state-of-the-art laboratories. Despite the large size of some of the classes, the students find their professors to be supportive. According to one student, "They are always willing to meet you outside of class and they try their best to encourage students to speak up during class." Students flock to this research university not only for its robust academics but also for its famed athletic offerings. One student raves, "I think the greatest strengths are the level of education we receive and the athletics program. The classes here are very difficult and will prepare students very well for graduate schools or careers. The athletics program here is awesome." The football team (Go Longhorns!) certainly helps inspire the school's contagious school spirit.

The school's 350-acre campus serves as home to a student body of 50,000 and offers boundless opportunities for students to get a rich and diverse social education. With over 900 student organizations, the campus is bustling with activities such as sports games, festivals, movie screenings, concerts, and cultural events. For those who need the rush of city life, the campus is just a few blocks away from downtown Austin where students often frequent the numerous restaurants, bars, clubs, and live music venues especially those on 6th

Contact Info:

P.O. Box 8058

Austin, TX 78713-8058

Admissions: 512-475-7440

Financial Aid: 512-475-6282

E-mail: Fax: 512-475-7475

Website: www.utexas.edu

Fun Facts

- The University of Texas is located at Austin, Texas in the heart of the Texas Hill Country a city with more than 450,000 people and the hub of the state government.
- UT was founded in 1883 on 40 acres of land near the state capitol. It had one building, eight teachers, two departments and 221 students. It now has on its main campus of 357 acres and 120 buildings, home to more than 2,332 faculty, 15,000 staff members and close to 50,000 students.
- UT is now in it's 115th year. UT has awarded more than 350,000 degrees.
- Among the alumni are: Lady Bird Johnson, Walter Cronkite, Lloyd Bentsen, Bill Moyers, Federico Pena, Earl Campbell, and Tom Landry.
- In 1997, Texas Memorial Stadium was renamed the "Darrell K. Royal Texas Memorial Stadium" but, to most it will always be Memorial Stadium.
- The Longhorn Band was founded in 1900 by chemistry professor E. P. Schoch. The band has grown to 340 outstanding musicians. Only 15% are music majors, the other 85% represent virtually every academic discipline on UT.
- The UT Band is called "The Show Band of the Southwest" a term that was developed in the 1950s during the tenure of director Vincent R. DiNino.

University of Texas at Austin

CAMPUS LIFE

Quality of life Rating	92
Fire Safety Rating	75
Green rating	60
Type of School	Public
Environment	Metropolis

STUDENTS

Total undergrad enrolllment	36,711
% Male to Female	48/52
% From out of state	4
# of Fraternities	26
# of Sororities	22
% African American	5
% Asian	18
% Caucasian	54
% Hispanic	18
% International	4
# Of Countries Represented	125

ACADEMICS

Academic Rating	71
% Of students graduating within 4 years	48
% Of students graduating within 6 years	78
Calendar	Semester
Profs interesting rating	70
Profs accessable rating	62
Most common reg class size	10–19 students
Most common lab size	10–19 students

MOST POPULAR MAJORS

Biology, business/commerce, liberal arts and sciences

SPECIAL STUDY OPTIONS

Accelerated program, cooperative education program, distance learning, double major, dual enrollment, English as a Second Language (ESL), honors program, independent study, internships, liberal arts/career combination, student-designed major, study abroad, teacher certification program Special programs offered to physically disabled students include note-taking services, reader services.

Street, a major hotspot. Competitive academic programs, legendary athletics, a huge sprawling campus, the eclectic allure of Austin, a strong sense of Texas pride and an unabashed love of a good party are the hallmarks of an education at University of Texas at Austin.

BANG FOR YOUR BUCK

To apply for need-based financial aid, students must submit the FAFSA. Over half of UT—Austin undergrads receive some form of financial aid. The school has a "gift aid policy" which distributes need-based grant and scholarship funds to students based on various levels of need. The university also provides the President's Achievement Scholarship (PAS), which awards $2,500 to $5,000 per year up to four years to high school scholars who have overcome adversity to achieve high academic performance levels. The university provides a whopping 17 different career services offices. Another of UT—Austin's unique resources is its Office of Student Financial Services, which runs Bevonomics, a personal money management education program for university students.

Why Students Love University of Texas—Austin

"The athletics program here is awesome."

STUDENT BODY

"Because of the huge Greek life at UT, a 'typical student' would be a sorority girl or fraternity boy," but—and it's a big but—such students "are hardly the majority, since UT is actually made of more 'atypical' people than most other schools. Everyone here has his own niche, and I could not think of any type of individual who would not be able to find one of his own." Indeed, "Everyone at Texas is different! When you walk across campus, you see every type of ethnicity. There are a lot of minorities at Texas. Also, I see many disabled people, whom the school accommodates well. Everyone seems to get along. The different types of students just blend in together." Especially by Texas standards, "Austin is known for being 'weird.' If you see someone dressed in a way you've never seen before, you just shrug it off and say 'That's Austin!'"

WHY STUDENTS LOVE UNIVERSITY OF TEXAS

The combination of Texas pride and school spirit is intoxicating. "It's a place where everyone bleeds burnt orange," says one student referring to the school's trademark color. Students also love the diversity found at their school. One student explains, "I think the diversity allows us to learn about other people and cultures. Most everyone has a strong view on politics and the environment. We think not only of events not only happening domestically, but often discussions stem from international events."

University of Texas at Austin

Why Students Love University of Texas—Austin

"Life in Austin is amazing. 300 days of sunshine a year and full of lakes, hills and rivers."

"Everyone seems to get along. The different types of students just blend in together."

The school sets up its students for success with its wealth of resources. According to a student, "In my first year, I did not realize how much was available to me just as an enrolled student. There is free tutoring, gym membership, professional counseling, doctors visits, legal help, career advising, and many distinguished outside speakers. The campus is crawling with experts in every field you can imagine." Another of the school's resources is the surround city of Austin itself. In a description worthy of a tourist brochure, one student raves, "Life in Austin is amazing. 300 days of sunshine a year and full of lakes, hills and rivers. There are tons of great restaurants and a street full of bars. Austin has everything that a big city could have to offer, but at the same time it is located in the middle of the beautiful Texas hill country."

GENERAL INFO

Environment: Metropolis. **Activities:** Choral groups, concert band, dance, drama/theater, jazz band, literary magazine, marching band, music ensembles, musical theater, opera, pep band, radio station, student government, student newspaper, student-run film society, symphony orchestra, television station, yearbook, campus ministries, international student organization. **Organizations:** 900 registered organizations, 15 honor societies, 95 religious organizations. 26 fraternities, 22 sororities. **Athletics (Intercollegiate):** *Men:* Baseball, basketball, cross-country, diving, football, golf, swimming, tennis, track/field (outdoor). *Women:* Basketball, crew/rowing, cross-country, diving, golf, soc cer, softball, swimming, tennis, track/field (outdoor), volleyball. **On-Campus Highlights:** Texas Union, Frank Erwin Special Events Center, Performing Arts Center, Harry Ransom Humanities Research Center, Blanton Museum of Art.

THE BOTTOM LINE

For students who are Texas residents, the cost of tuition is a little under $9000 which makes the school very affordable for many. For any out-of-state students, the price tag jumps to around $31,218 plus another $10,100 for room and board. Whether you're an in-state or out-of-state student, do not forget to factor in the additional cost of books and supplies, which add up to a little less than $900.

SELECTIVITY

Admissions Rating	**91**
# of applicants	29,501
% of applicants accepted	44
% of acceptees attending	52

FRESHMAN PROFILE

Range SAT Critical Reading	**540–660**
Range SAT Math	**570–690**
Range SAT Writing	**540–670**
Range ACT Composite	**29–34**
% graduated top 10% of class	**75**
% graduated top 25% of class	**95**
% graduated top 50% of class	**99**

DEADLINES

Regular Deadline	**12/15**
Normal registration	**yes**

FACILITIES

Housing: Coed dorms, men's dorms, women's dorms, apartments for married students, apartments for single students. *Special Academic Facilities/Equipment*: Blanton Museum of Art, Lyndon Baines Johnson Presidential Library/Museum, Performing Arts Center, Texas Memorial Museum, Harry Ransom Humanities Research Center.

FINANCIAL FACTS

Financial Aid Rating	**90**
Annual in-state tuition	$9,794
Annual out-of-state tuition	$32,506
Room and Board	$10,422
Required Fees	$0
Books and supplies	$874
% frosh rec. need-based scholarship or grant aid	57
% UG rec. need-based scholarship or grant aid	44
% frosh rec. need-based self-help aid	60
% UG rec. need-based self-help aid	51
% frosh rec. any financial aid	60
% UG rec. any financial aid	54
% UG borrow to pay for school	42
Average cumulative indebtedness	$17,000

Tuition-Free Schools

Berea College

CPO 2220, Berea, KY 40404 • Admissions: 859-985-3500 • Fax: 859-985-3512

CAMPUS LIFE

Quality of life Rating	70
Fire Safety Rating	86
Green rating	81
Type of School	Private
Environment	Village

STUDENTS

Total undergrad enrolllment	1,552
% Male to Female	41/56
% From out of state	56
% Live on Campus	86
% African American	17
% Asian	1
% Caucasian	66
% Hispanic	2
% International	7
# Of Countries Represented	58

ACADEMICS

Academic Rating	85
% Of students graduating within 4 years	50
% Of students graduating within 6 years	64
Calendar	semester
Profs interesting rating	83
Profs accessible rating	81
Most common reg class size	10–19 students

MOST POPULAR MAJORS

Biology, business/commerce, family and consumer sciences/human sciences

SPECIAL STUDY OPTIONS

Double major, English as a Second Language (ESL), exchange student program (domestic), honors program, independent study, internships, student-designed major, study abroad, teacher certification program, 3-2 engineering program with Washington University, St. Louis, and University of Kentucky.

ABOUT THE SCHOOL

Perhaps best known for its tuition-free, four-year education, Berea has a whole lot more goin' on. At this predominantly Appalachian school in Kentucky, students can select from a curriculum that includes undergraduate research, service learning, and numerous study abroad opportunities, and expect to receive the full support of the school along the way. Since Berea's objective is to provide an education to students of limited economic resources, the school makes it clear that there is no slacking off; your spot here is an opportunity that could have gone to someone else. Academics are rigorous, classroom attendance is mandatory, and students are happy to be given an opportunity.

With such a distinct and regional mission, students here are not just another face in the crowd. All classes are taught by full professors, and everyone has access to the Learning Center, math and language labs, and tutors for assistance with papers, presentations, and homework. Service is also a way of life here, and Berea is one of the top schools in the nation for service learning. When students do need a rest from their studies, do-gooding, and work, there are more than 50 clubs and organizations available, as well as performing arts programs, theaters, and plenty of nature nearby.

Berea College is "about bringing underprivileged high school graduates from the Appalachian region and beyond together for a chance at a higher education, a career, and a better life." Thanks to a labor program that requires all students to work ten to fifteen hours each week (not to mention a ton of donated cash), tuition is entirely covered for each students, with a laptop thrown in for the duration of the school year to boot. In addition to a decent range of liberal arts and sciences majors, there are several career-oriented programs, all of which combines to make "a comfortable place for students to learn and grow."

BANG FOR YOUR BUCK

The school doesn't think your income should dictate your outcome, which is why it only admits students who have financial need. The school's endowment is what allows it to be so generous in awarding full scholarships to deserving students, and these scholarships works in conjunction with any other grants or scholarships students receive to completely cover the cost of tuition (as well as that laptop). In many cases, the school can even offer additional financial aid to assist with room, board, and other fees–not loans–according to each student's need. Simply put, students at Berea College pay what they can afford.

STUDENTS

1,552 undergrad enrollment

41% Male ♂♂♂♂♂♂♂

59% Female ♀♀♀♀♀♀♀♀♀♀

ADMISSIONS

3,264 applicants → 17% admitted — 76% enrolled

EARLY ADMISSIONS → NR applicants — NR accepted

3.42 avg. high school gpa

ACT range (0–36): 21 – 26

SAT range (200–800): reading 520 – 650; math 500 – 620; writing 450 – 615

GRADUATION RATES

50% of students graduating within 4 yrs

64% of students graduating within 6 yrs

Berea College

FINANCIAL AID: 859-985-3310 • E-MAIL: ADMISSIONS@BEREA.EDU • WEBSITE: WWW.BEREA.EDU

STUDENT BODY

"The typical student at Berea College is broke" but "has big dreams." "Most people are from working-class families." They were "raised in backwoods hollows" around "the Appalachian area." "We are all here because we have no money but are equipped with the hope for a bright future and a desire to learn," declares a senior. Students at Berea are "sleep deprived" and "too busy to really have the time to slack off (though there are some that still manage it)." They're "bright, hardworking," and "studious." "Most of us are nerds," admits a senior. There are "quite a few Bible thumpers." At the same time, Berea is "probably more liberal than conservative," and this is something of "a hippie school." "People are really big about recycling, sustainability, and the environment." Students tell us that Berea has "more diversity than most schools."

Why Students love Berea College

"We are all here because we have no money but are equipped with the hope for a bright future and a desire to learn."

WHY STUDENTS LOVE BEREA COLLEGE

"I would say that the academics are the greatest strength of Berea. Academics, and the financial aid that the students receive," says a student, echoing the obvious sentiment of many students. Many Bereans may not have had another shot at such a high quality education, and all of the students here are grateful and ambitious. The professors are equally as excited for their students to take this shot, and are willing and available for whatever needs may arise. "Students are able to get so much more one-on-one time than at larger colleges."

GENERAL INFO

Activities: Choral groups, dance, drama/theater, jazz band, literary magazine, music ensembles, pep band, student government, student newspaper, yearbook, campus ministries, international student organization. Organizations: 75 registered organizations, 14 honor societies, 5 religious organizations. Athletics (Intercollegiate): Men: Baseball, basketball, cross-country, golf, soccer, swimming, tennis, track/field (outdoor). Women: Basketball, cross-country, soccer, softball, swimming, tennis, track/field (outdoor), volleyball. On-Campus Highlights: Carillon (in Draper building tower), EcoVillage (married and single parent housing), Alumni Building (cafeteria, lounge, gameroom), Woods-Penn Complex (post office, cafe, etc.), Seabury Center (gym). Environmental Initiatives: 1. Sustainability and Environmental Studies academic program; 2. Ecological Renovations (including 1st LEED-certified building in Kentucky and the Ecovillage residential complex for student families); 3. Local Food Initiative.

BOTTOM LINE

Tuition costs are quite simple: every admitted student is provided with a 4-year tuition scholarship, knocking the $24,100 tuition down to zero. No tuition does not mean a full ride, however, and extra costs such as technology fees, insurance, food plans, etc., add up quickly (room, board, and fees run around $7,300 a year). However, about two-thirds of the students receive additional financial aid to help offset these costs. Each student is required to take an on-campus job for a certain number of hours per week as part of the school's Work Program, giving them valuable experience that translates into real world skills, as well as a salary (about $1,200 in the first year) to assist with living expenses.

SELECTIVITY

Admissions Rating	**93**
# of applicants	3,264
% of applicants accepted	17
% of acceptees attending	76

FRESHMAN PROFILE

Range SAT Critical Reading	**520–650**
Range SAT Math	**500–620**
Range SAT Writing	**480–615**
Range ACT Composite	**21–26**
Average HS GPA	**3.42**
% graduated top 10% of class	**31**
% graduated top 25% of class	**71**
% graduated top 50% of class	**96**

DEADLINES

Regular Deadline	**11/1**
Normal registration	**no**

FACILITIES

Housing: Men's dorms, women's dorms, apartments for married students, apartments for single parents and married students at our Ecovillage. *Special Academic Facilities/Equipment:* Appalachian Gallery, Special Collections and Sound Archives in the Hutchins Library, Planetarium and Observatory, Geology Museum, The Ecovillage, the Child Development Laboratory, and the Monty Saulmon Early Technology Lab. *Computers:* 33% of classrooms, 100% of libraries, 100% of dining areas, 100% of student union, 33% of common outdoor areas have wireless network access. Undergraduates are required to own a computer.

FINANCIAL FACTS

Financial Aid Rating	**91**
Annual tuition	$0
Room and Board	$5,792
Required Fees	$910
Books and supplies	$700
% frosh rec. need-based scholarship or grant aid	100
% UG rec.need-based scholarship or grant aid	100
% frosh rec. need-based self-help aid	100
% UG rec. need-based self-help aid	100
% frosh rec. any financial aid	100
% UG rec. any financial aid	100
% UG borrow to pay for school	100
Average cumulative indebtedness	$5,836

College of the Ozarks

Office of Admissions, P.O. Box 17, Point Lookout, MO 65726 • Admissions: 417-690-2636 • Fax: 417-335-2618

CAMPUS LIFE

Quality of life Rating	88
Fire Safety Rating	80
Green rating	75
Type of School	Private
Environment	Rural

STUDENTS

Total undergrad enrolllment	1,367
% Male to Female	43/57
% From out of state	18
% From public high school	88
% Live on Campus	80
% African American	1
% Caucasian	92
% Hispanic	2
% International	1
# Of Countries Represented	14

ACADEMICS

Academic Rating	80
Calendar	semester
Profs interesting rating	81
Profs accessible rating	83
Most common reg class size	10–19 students
Most common lab size	10–19 students

MOST POPULAR MAJORS

Business administration and management, elementary education and teaching, speech communication and rhetoric

SPECIAL STUDY OPTIONS

Accelerated program, double major, dual enrollment, independent study, internships, student-designed major, teacher certification program.

ABOUT THE SCHOOL

Welcome to Hard Work U, where students don't pay tuition, work for an education, graduate without debt, develop character, and value God and country. Debt is openly discouraged, and instead of paying tuition, all full-time students work campus jobs to defray the cost of education. Opportunities for gaining life and career skills abound through this program, ranging from landscaping to operating a four-star restaurant, and students learn to show up on time, finish the job right, and be a team player–skills that translate well into any profession. Students are graded by their work supervisors each semester and their work grades become a part of their permanent transcript, so good students have a great track record to provide to prospective employers.

The school is one of the most difficult private schools to gain acceptance to in the Midwest, and not just because it's free. While there are almost too many singular aspects of this small Christian college to name, one popular program in particular stands out: the Patriotic Education Travel Program, which offers students the opportunity to accompany WWII Veterans to Pacific and European battle sites. It's this type of unique educational experience that makes College of the Ozarks unique and an outstanding value in higher education.

Christian values and character, hard work, and financial responsibility comprise the fundamental building blocks of the "Hard Work U" experience. C of O is committed to its founding mission of providing a quality, Christian education to those who are found worthy, but who are without sufficient means to obtain such training. "My family didn't have enough money to send me to any other college, and I'm not afraid of a little hard work!" says a student.

BANG FOR YOUR BUCK

Generous donors who believe in what College of the Ozarks represents enable the College to provide tuition scholarships in exchange for work on campus (if you paid cash for instructional expenses at C of O, it would cost you $17,600 per year!). The Christian atmosphere keeps students away from the more party-heavy aspects of college life, so students stay focused on school and work. Whereas a lot of students approach prospective employers without much in the way of demonstrated work ethic; this is obviously not the case for College of the Ozarks alumni. Even during the economic downturn, 82 percent of graduates found employment upon graduation, and 13 percent pursued graduate school.

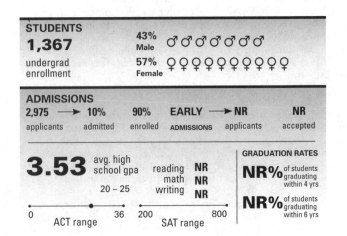

STUDENTS

1,367 undergrad enrollment

43% Male ♂♂♂♂♂♂♂

57% Female ♀♀♀♀♀♀♀♀♀♀

ADMISSIONS

2,975 applicants → **10%** admitted **90%** enrolled

EARLY ADMISSIONS → **NR** applicants **NR** accepted

3.53 avg. high school gpa

ACT range: 0 — 20 – 25 — 36

SAT range: 200 — 800; reading NR, math NR, writing NR

GRADUATION RATES

NR% of students graduating within 4 yrs

NR% of students graduating within 6 yrs

FINANCIAL AID: 417-690-3292 • E-MAIL: E-MAIL: ADMISS4@COFO.EDU • WEBSITE: WWW.COFO.EDU

STUDENT BODY

C of O students describe themselves as "friendly," "hardworking," "down-to-earth," and "very religious, but not pushy." The nature of the school places a strong emphasis on community, and first-year students bond during a week- long orientation called Character Camp. Most students are from Christian backgrounds, and they're "somewhat conservative." Many "are from the local Ozark region." Despite the similarities, students describe their school as "very diverse" and say that everyone is "welcomed into the community" and "always eager to help and support you in any type of situation." "There are the 'aggies,' the 'jocks,' the 'nerds,' and other types of students," like "the prep, the homeschooler...the indie...[and] the geek," but many students happily note the lack of exclusive cliques and say "social barriers are easily crossed."

Why Students love College of the Ozarks

"My professors are amazing. I know that I can go up to any of them and they are more than willing to help me with my academic pursuits and personal issues as well."

WHY STUDENTS LOVE COLLEGE OF THE OZARKS

Students praise their faculty as "amazing," "second-to-none," and most often as "passionate." "My professors are amazing. I know that I can go up to any of them and they are more than willing to help me with my academic pursuits and personal issues as well," says a student. Small class sizes provide for "easy one-on-one interaction with the professors" and encourage students to "become involved in active classroom learning." "There are groups and organizations for everyone," and "various organizations hold events for the whole campus like Senate Movie Night, and there are plenty of interesting speakers for convocations." Off campus, "there is always something to do in this area," "whether you hang out with your friends, go to shows in Branson, go to campus-sponsored events, or just go play ping-pong."

GENERAL INFO

Activities: Choral groups, concert band, drama/theater, jazz band, literary magazine, music ensembles, musical theater, pep band, radio station, student government, student newspaper, student-run film society, yearbook, campus ministries. **Organizations:** 45 registered organizations, 6 honor societies, 10 religious organizations. **Athletics (Intercollegiate):** *Men:* Baseball, basketball, cheerleading. *Women:* Basketball, cheerleading, volleyball. **On-Campus Highlights:** Memorial Fieldhouse and Keeter Gymnasium, Ralph Foster Museum, Williams Memorial Chapel, The Keeter Center, Agriculture, Edwards Mill, Fruitcake and Jelly Kitchen.

BOTTOM LINE

College of the Ozarks students do not pay a penny of tuition. Each student participates in the on-campus Work Education Program 15 hours each week and two forty-hour work weeks. Upon full completion of the Work Education Program, the College guarantees to meet the remaining balance through a combination of private scholarships and grants. Room and board still runs $5600 a year, as well as $300-400 in additional fees, but there are additional scholarships available for students unable to pay these costs.

SELECTIVITY

Admissions Rating	**91**
# of applicants	2,975
% of applicants accepted	10
% of acceptees attending	90
# accepting a place on wait list	800
% admitted from wait list	7

FRESHMAN PROFILE

Range ACT Composite	**20–25**
Average HS GPA	**3.53**
% graduated top 10% of class	**30**
% graduated top 25% of class	**64**
% graduated top 50% of class	**94**

DEADLINES

Regular Deadline	**2/15**
Normal registration	**no**

FACILITIES

Housing: Men's dorms, women's dorms, wellness housing. All full-time students must live in residence halls unless they meet one of the following criteria: 21 years of age or older, married, living with parents, or veteran of the armed forces. *Special Academic Facilities/Equipment:* Ralph Foster Museum, Edwards Mill, The Keeter Center, Fruitcake and Jelly Kitchen Greenhouses. *Computers:* 100% of dorms, 100% of libraries, 100% of dining areas, 100% of student union, have wireless network access.

FINANCIAL FACTS

Financial Aid Rating	**89**
Annual tuition	$0
Room and Board	$5,600
Required Fees	$430
Books and supplies	$800
% frosh rec. need-based scholarship or grant aid	86
% UG rec.need-based scholarship or grant aid	93
% frosh rec. non-need-based scholarship or grant aid	8
% UG rec. non-need-based scholarship or grant aid	13
% frosh rec. need-based self-help aid	78
% UG rec. need-based self-help aid	79
% frosh rec. any financial aid	100
% UG rec. any financial aid	100
% UG borrow to pay for school	11
Average cumulative indebtedness	$5,389

The Cooper Union for the Advancement of Science and Art

30 Cooper Square, Office of Admission, New York, NY 10003 • Admissions: 212-353-4120 • Fax: 212-353-4342

CAMPUS LIFE

Quality of life Rating	79
Fire Safety Rating	98
Green rating	82
Type of School	Private
Environment	Metropolis

STUDENTS

Total undergrad enrolllment	910
% Male to Female	62/38
% From out of state	40
% From public high school	65
% Live on Campus	20
# of Fraternities	2
# of Sororities	1
% African American	6
% Asian	25
% Caucasian	38
% Hispanic	9
% Native American	10
% International	6
# Of Countries Represented	6

ACADEMICS

Academic Rating	94
% Of students graduating within 4 years	68
% Of students graduating within 6 years	85
Calendar	semester
Profs interesting rating	72
Profs accessible rating	70
Most common reg class size	10–19 students
Most common lab size	more than 100 students

MOST POPULAR MAJORS

Electrical and electronics engineering, fine arts and art studies, mechanical engineering

HONORS PROGRAMS

Cooper Union is an all-honors college.

SPECIAL STUDY OPTIONS

Cross-registration, exchange student program (domestic), independent study, internships, student-designed major, study abroad. Research opportunities available. Students may take up to one year off during their studies with us to pursue other interests.

ABOUT THE SCHOOL

Believe it or not, free tuition isn't the only reason gifted students clamor for a spot at The Cooper Union for the Advancement of Science and Art. Though the college admits undergraduates solely on merit (giving full scholarships to all enrolled students), the school's reputable, rigorous academics and location in the heart of New York's East Village are equally as big draws. The school accepts just seven percent of students into its undergraduate student body of one thousand, and once in, students must handle a highly demanding workload.

The small nature of the school allows for very close relationships between the professors and the students, and the faculty is the intellectual pulse of the institution. Most come to Cooper Union while continuing their own personal research and work at various points in their academic careers, giving students frontline access to real world experience and insight, from professors that want to teach. Group projects are a major part of the curriculum, regardless of degree sought, and further the school's problem-solving philosophy of education. A Cooper Union degree is instant street cred in the job market, and many graduates become world-class leaders in the disciplines of architecture, fine arts, design, and engineering.

Through outstanding academic programs in architecture, art and engineering, and a Faculty of Humanities and Social Sciences, The Cooper Union for the Advancement of Science and Art is an all-honors private college that offers talented students rigorous, humanistic learning that is enhanced by the process of design and augmented by the urban setting. "An institution of the highest caliber," the school has a narrow academic focus, conferring degrees only in fine arts, architecture, and engineering, with "plenty of opportunities for independent study in your field." All students take a core curriculum of required courses in the humanities and social sciences in their first two years, and those that go on to the Fine Arts school have easy "access to established and interesting artists."

BANG FOR YOUR BUCK

The school's founder, Peter Cooper, believed that an "education of the first rank" should be "as free as air and water," and that is exactly the mission that his namesake institution is carrying out nearly a century and a half later. The engineering program is considered one of the best in the nation, and a degree from Cooper Union is a ticket into an excellent professional career. Forty percent of graduates go on to top-tier graduate programs, and the small school has produced three Fulbright scholars in just the last ten years.

STUDENTS

910 undergrad enrollment

62% Male ♂♂♂♂♂♂♂

38% Female ♀♀♀♀♀♀♀♀♀♀

ADMISSIONS

3,354 applicants →	8% admitted	76% enrolled	EARLY ADMISSIONS →	NR applicants	NR accepted

3.60 avg. high school gpa

ACT range (0–36): 29 – 33

SAT range (200–800):

reading	610 – 730
math	610 – 780
writing	620 – 640

GRADUATION RATES

68% of students graduating within 4 yrs

85% of students graduating within 6 yrs

The Cooper Union for the Advancement of Science and Art

FINANCIAL AID: 212-353-4130 • E-MAIL: ADMISSIONS@COOPER.EDU • WEBSITE: WWW.COOPER.EDU

STUDENT BODY

Cooper Union's campus is largely comprised of "three distinct types of students," each delineated by major field: art, architecture, and engineering. Typical art students are "alternative kids" with the "just-rolled-out-of-bed look" while future architects are "very sleek" and fashionable, but "never leave their studio." The more "socially awkward" engineers are also largely like minds. One says, "If you have some obscure technological passion, someone in the engineering school is guaranteed to be as passionate." According to some, "Artists hang out with artists, engineers with engineers, architects with architects." However, most Cooper Union students laugh off stereotypes, telling us the school is filled with "very unique, interesting people," eager to learn and cross-pollinate between departments. A current student reassures us, "Of course, the odds are high that a group of electrical engineers will end up talking about video games, but there seems to be a broad spectrum of personalities present here." Across the board, students in every major are serious about their studies, and most of Cooper's selective admits are "super intelligent, super creative, and/or just super hardworking."

Why Students love The Cooper Union

"Free tuition and a rigorous, stimulating curriculum."

WHY STUDENTS LOVE THE COOPER UNION

"Free tuition and a rigorous, stimulating curriculum" are the main sells, but the City That Never Sleeps is right up there. The school's location offers "an opportunity to live in one of the most energetic and dynamic cities in the world." Cooper Union will "push you to your limits, push you to succeed, and this common goal unites all the students as well." Professors are "very accessible, friendly, [and] expect a high level of quality for work," and "are devoted to the education of the youth." Together with students, a "close-knit community" is formed.

GENERAL INFO

Activities: Choral groups, concert band, dance, drama/theater, jazz band, literary magazine, music ensembles, student government, student newspaper, student-run film society, symphony orchestra, yearbook. **Organizations:** 90 registered organizations, 18 honor societies, 8 religious organizations. 2 fraternities, 1 sorority. **Athletics (Intercollegiate):** *Men:* Baseball, basketball, cross-country, soccer, tennis, volleyball. *Women:* Basketball, cross-country, soccer, tennis, volleyball. **On-Campus Highlights:** Great Hall, 41 Cooper Square, Foundation Building, Houghton Gallery. **Environmental Initiatives:** New academic building.

BOTTOM LINE

Students are accepted on the basis of merit alone, and every student receives a full-tuition scholarship currently valued at $35,000 annually. Students must still pay a number of fees, including room and board for dorm residents (available to underclassmen only), and which vary based on school. For the Art and Architecture schools, a commuter will pay around $6,445, and on-campus and off-campus residents will pay around $20,000, depending on rent. For the engineering school, a commuter will pay about $7,245, and on-campus and off-campus residents will pay around $20,000, depending on rent. Health insurance adds an additional $1,275 for those that require it. Financial Aid is available to assist with payment of all fees.

SELECTIVITY

Admissions Rating	**99**
# of applicants	3,354
% of applicants accepted	8
% of acceptees attending	76
# accepting a place on wait list	70
% admitted from wait list	7

FRESHMAN PROFILE

Range SAT Critical Reading	**610–730**
Range SAT Math	**610–780**
Range SAT Writing	**620–640**
Range ACT Composite	**29–33**
Average HS GPA	**3.60**
% graduated top 10% of class	**93**
% graduated top 25% of class	**98**
% graduated top 50% of class	**99**

DEADLINES

Regular Deadline	**1/1**
Normal registration	**no**

FACILITIES

Housing: Coed dorms. *Special Academic Facilities/Equipment:* The Great Hall; Houghton Gallery; The Brooks Lab, Prototyping Lab, Bio-Medical Engineering Lab, Tissue Engineering Lab, Center for Sustainable Design, Center for Infrastructure and Urban Systems, Center for Signal Processing Communications and Computer Engineering Research. *Computers:* 85% of classrooms, have wireless network access.

FINANCIAL FACTS

Financial Aid Rating	**91**
Annual tuition	$37,500
Room and Board	$13,700
Required Fees	$1,650
Books and supplies	$1,800
% frosh rec. need-based scholarship or grant aid	25
% UG rec.need-based scholarship or grant aid	27
% frosh rec. non-need-based scholarship or grant aid	100
% UG rec. non-need-based scholarship or grant aid	100
% frosh rec. need-based self-help aid	16
% UG rec. need-based self-help aid	20
% frosh rec. any financial aid	100
% UG rec. any financial aid	100
% UG borrow to pay for school	27
Average cumulative indebtedness	$11,414

Deep Springs College

Applications Committee, HC 72 Box 45001, Dyer, NV 89010 • Admissions: 760-872-2000 • Fax: 760-872-4466

CAMPUS LIFE

Quality of life Rating	93
Fire Safety Rating	82
Green rating	60
Type of School	Private
Environment	Rural

STUDENTS

Total undergrad enrolllment	26
% Male to Female	100/0
% From out of state	80
% From public high school	50
% Live on Campus	100
# Of Countries Represented	3

ACADEMICS

Academic Rating	99
Calendar	semester
Profs interesting rating	93
Profs accessible rating	99
Most common reg class size	fewer than 10 students

MOST POPULAR MAJORS

Liberal arts and sciences

SPECIAL STUDY OPTIONS

Independent study, internships.

ABOUT THE SCHOOL

You know the feeling you get when you look back at your second grade class picture and you can remember every single person's name, no matter how long ago that was? That is the level of camaraderie that is achieved at Deep Springs College, a teeny tiny, uber-selective, all-male school in the middle of the California desert. The school operates on the belief that manual labor and political deliberation are integral parts of a comprehensive liberal arts education, and every student must also work on the school's ranch and farm, which helps drive home the school's unique mission of service. After two years at Deep Springs (with full scholarship), the school's 26 students go on to complete a four year degree at the world's most prestigious universities.

Whereas at some colleges, professors' doors are always open, at Deep Springs, professors' porch lights are always on. Classes are intense and bleed into activities around the clock, and are sometimes also held in unconventional locations, like professors' homes or the irrigation ditch. Some students must wake up early to feed the cattle; some must stay up late to mend fences on the alfalfa farm. At every hour of the day, there are at least a few people awake and discussing Heidegger, playing chess, or strumming guitars. There is no other school like it, and students receive an education that transcends simply learning from books, as well as an unprecedented education in citizenship.

Deep Springs is an all-male liberal arts college located on a cattle-ranch and alfalfa farm in California's High Desert. Founded in 1917, the curriculum is based on the three pillars of academics, labor, and self-governance, offering "a unique liberal arts education that gives you very much freedom and requires a lot of responsibility for your classmates and environment." To say that the school's 26 students (along with its staff and faculty) form a close community would be an understatement. Everyone is on a first-name basis and knows each other like the back of their own hand.

BANG FOR YOUR BUCK

Deep Springs is one of the best educations a student can receive after high school, and though you may not have heard of the school before, the nation's top universities certainly have. Although percentages are somewhat moot for a school that has only 26 students over two class years, in the past five years, nearly 45% of students have gone on to Harvard, Yale, Brown, and the University of Chicago, as well as winning numerous prestigious scholarships and fellowships.

STUDENTS

26 undergrad enrollment

100% Male ♂♂♂♂♂♂♂

0% Female

ADMISSIONS

170 applicants →	7% admitted	92% enrolled	EARLY ADMISSIONS →	NR applicants	NR accepted

NR avg. high school gpa

NR — ACT range 0–36

reading 750 – 800
math 700 – 800 — SAT range 200–800

GRADUATION RATES

NR of students graduating within 4 yrs

NR of students graduating within 6 yrs

Deep Springs College

E-MAIL: APCOM@DEEPSPRINGS.EDU • WEBSITE: WWW.DEEPSPRINGS.EDU

STUDENT BODY

"Having only 26 students makes it even harder to characterize the 'typical' Deep Springer," students understandably warn, but they add that "we're all very able and driven, but in our own ways, not in the way that most Ivy League students are. Deep Springs isn't a stepping stone to the world of white-collar work but an end in itself that we all pursue with all our hearts. So I guess the typical student has a healthy disgust for the pedagogy of most other universities." Undergrads are also predictably "intelligent, motivated, and responsible," as they "must demonstrate depth of thought to be accepted" to the school. As one student puts it, "The typical student at Deep Springs is committed to the life of the intellect and committed to finding education in our labor program. Most of the students here believe that a life of service, informed by discourse and labor, is a necessary notion to understand in today's world."

Why Students love Deep Springs College

"From fixing a hay baler in the middle of the night, to puzzling over a particularly difficult passage of Hegel, Deep Springs has not disappointed."

WHY STUDENTS LOVE DEEP SPRINGS COLLEGE

"I chose Deep Springs College for the unparalleled challenges that if offers. From fixing a hay baler in the middle of the night, to puzzling over a particularly difficult passage of Hegel, Deep Springs has not disappointed," says a student (that's 4% of the undergrad population!). Deep Springs is "about obligation to community," and students "hold ourselves to a high level of excellence in all facets of life." "Each day I fail, whether it be in academics, labor or self-governance, and each day I am humbled." The school is structured in such a way that forces students "to take initiative, to teach others, and to feel responsible for something other than themselves. In other words, its greatest strength is that isn't like going to college."

GENERAL INFO

Activities: Student government. **Organizations:** 1 registered organizations. **On-Campus Highlights:** Boarding House, Dairy Barn, Horse Stables, The Upper Reservoir, The Druid.

BOTTOM LINE

Tuition, fees, and room and board at Pomona run about $50,000 for a year. That's steep. At the same time, the mantra here is that no one should hesitate to apply because of the cost. Pomona College is one of only a handful of schools that has need-blind admissions and meets the full, demonstrated financial aid need of every accepted student with scholarships and work-study

SELECTIVITY

Admissions Rating	**99**
# of applicants	170
% of applicants accepted	7
% of acceptees attending	92
# accepting a place on wait list	3
% admitted from wait list	0

FRESHMAN PROFILE

Range SAT Critical Reading	**750–800**
Range SAT Math	**700–800**
% graduated top 10% of class	**86**
% graduated top 25% of class	**93**
% graduated top 50% of class	**100**

DEADLINES

Regular Deadline	**11/15**
Normal registration	**no**

FACILITIES

Housing: Men's dorms. *Special Academic Facilities/Equipment:* Ranch–300 cattle, 20 horses, organic farm growing hay and produce; thousands of acres of wilderness surround the college.

FINANCIAL FACTS

Financial Aid Rating	**60**
Annual in-state tuition	$0
Room and Board	$0
Books and supplies	$1,200
% frosh rec. any financial aid	100
% UG rec. any financial aid	100

United States Air Force Academy

HQ USAFA/ RRS, 2304 Cadet Drive, Suite 2300, USAF Academy, CO 80840-5025 • Admissions: 719-333-2520

CAMPUS LIFE

Quality of life Rating	79
Fire Safety Rating	78
Green rating	76
Type of School	Public
Environment	Metropolis

STUDENTS

Total undergrad enrolllment	4,619
% Male to Female	79/21
% From out of state	93
% From public high school	79
% Live on Campus	100
% African American	6
% Asian	8
% Caucasian	73
% Hispanic	8
% International	1
# Of Countries Represented	36

ACADEMICS

Academic Rating	96
% Of students graduating within 4 years	78
% Of students graduating within 6 years	78
Calendar	semester
Profs interesting rating	88
Profs accessible rating	89
Most common reg class size	10–19 students
Most common lab size	10–19 students

MOST POPULAR MAJORS

Aerospace, aeronautical and astronautical/space engineering

SPECIAL STUDY OPTIONS

Double major, English as a Second Language (ESL), exchange student program (domestic), honors program, in- dependent study, internships, student-designed major, study abroad, Academically At-Risk Program Hospital Instruction Program Extra Instruction Program Summer Programs.

ABOUT THE SCHOOL

As you might expect, most of those who attend this prestigious military academy have designs on becoming officers in the Air Force and/or becoming pilots one day, and are willing to devote years and years of their life to receive top training. Not only are graduates guaranteed employment when they leave (each cadet will owe at least five years of service as an active-duty officer upon graduation), they leave with what amounts to a really cool skill set, between military free-fall parachute training, combat survival, skydiving, internships at national labs, and, of course, the best flying programs in the solar system. The Academy has one of the greatest locations of all of the U.S. service academies, and it offers extensive recreational facilities and a wide range of seasonal programs to help make Colorado and its seasons enjoyable for not just the cadets, but the entire base community.

The unyielding dedication to student success and character development is felt in every class, activity, and tradition. Constant professionalism is the minimum standard, and nothing is easy, but cadets are happy to rise to the challenge, and bring their brothers in planes along. Everyone is a leader, and all are working towards a common cause and belief regardless of ranking or position. If you can get in to the USAFA, the tools are here to help you stay.

BANG FOR YOUR BUCK

The Air Force puts a high premium on leaders with vision, dedication and ability, and the pay and allowances of a new officer compare favorably with starting salaries in business, industry and the professions. All career officers are eligible to apply for further education through AFIT at civilian colleges and universities, and selected officers attend on a full-time basis, receive pay and allowances, have their tuition and fixed fees paid and receive some reimbursement for books and thesis expenses, among other benefits. A certain percentage of students can become eligible for medical, law, or dental school upon graduation (law school requires two years of service first), and a few graduates will receive scholarships to attend civilian graduate schools immediately after graduation. Graduates in the top 15 percent of their class on overall performance average will normally be assured of future graduate education for a Master's degree if they meet two important criteria: they must perform well as officers, and the Air Force must need people from the degree program they wish to pursue.

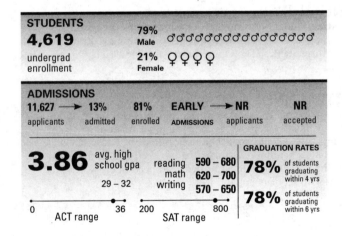

STUDENTS

4,619 undergrad enrollment

79% Male ♂♂♂♂♂♂♂♂♂♂♂♂♂♂♂

21% Female ♀♀♀♀

ADMISSIONS

11,627 →	13%	81%	EARLY →	NR	NR
applicants	admitted	enrolled	ADMISSIONS	applicants	accepted

3.86 avg. high school gpa

ACT range (0–36): 29 – 32

SAT range (200–800):

reading	590 – 680
math	620 – 700
writing	570 – 650

GRADUATION RATES

78% of students graduating within 4 yrs

78% of students graduating within 6 yrs

United States Air Force Academy

FAX: 719-333-3012 • E-MAIL: RR_WEBMAIL@USAFA.EDU • WEBSITE: WWW.ACADEMYADMISSIONS.COM

STUDENT BODY

"We are all a bunch of college kids in a very different environment," explains one cadet. "This school forces you to grow up and obtain a more mature outlook on life, yet, at the same time, the kids are normal kids who know when and how to have fun." The population at Air Force is overwhelmingly male. It's a "tight-knit community," and people tend to be "similar in beliefs and backgrounds." The military aspect limits how "atypical" anyone can really be. "You probably will not do well here" if you don't fit the mold. Cadets describe themselves as "hardworking and motivated," "fairly conservative," and "very patriotic." "The sense of pride and duty that comes from serving your country is something that you cannot explain to a civilian," one student says. They're "inventive," "studious," "physically fit," and "smart as a whip."

Why Students love U.S. Air Force Academy

"Once I graduate and am commissioned as an officer, I will have the opportunity to travel the world making a difference in lives and in history as I do."

WHY STUDENTS LOVE UNITED STATES AIR FORCE ACADEMY

Falcons come to the Academy for the noblest of causes: "the opportunity provided to serve my country after graduation." "Once I graduate and am commissioned as an officer, I will have the opportunity to travel the world making a difference in lives and in history as I do," says a student. Or, simpler motivations abound: "It's free and I can fly planes when I graduate." Life is strict, "but you find ways to have a good time." The "tight knit community of so many different people" form unbreakable bonds, and "snowboarding and skiing are very popular in the winter." Faculty members "rival those of any of the top schools in the country," and "professors and officers who teach classes go the extra mile to make themselves available."

GENERAL INFO

Activities: Choral groups, dance, drama/theater, marching band, musical theater, pep band, radio station, yearbook, campus ministries. **Organizations:** 77 registered organizations, 2 honor societies, 14 religious organizations. **Athletics (Intercollegiate):** *Men:* Baseball, basketball, boxing, cheerleading, cross-country, diving, fencing, football, golf, gymnastics, ice hockey, lacrosse, riflery, soccer, swimming, tennis, track/field (outdoor), track/field (indoor), water polo, wrestling. *Women:* Basketball, cheer- leading, cross-country, diving, fencing, gymnastics, riflery, soccer, swimming, tennis, track/field (outdoor), track/field (indoor), volleyball. **On-Campus Highlights:** USAF Academy Chapel, Thunderbird Lookout and Air Field, Falcon Stadium, Cadet Sports Complex, Visitor Center.

BOTTOM LINE

Aside from the free tuition, students receive a nominal monthly stipend. Each cadet will owe at least five years of service as an active-duty officer upon graduation, though additional programs (such as attending higher education, or becoming a pilot) can add to the commitment. The current law enables an officer to retire after completing 20 years of active service.

SELECTIVITY

Admissions Rating	**98**
# of applicants	11,627
% of applicants accepted	13
% of acceptees attending	81

FRESHMAN PROFILE

Range SAT Critical Reading	**590–680**
Range SAT Math	**620–700**
Range SAT Writing	**570–650**
Range ACT Composite	**29–32**
Average HS GPA	**3.86**
% graduated top 10% of class	**51**
% graduated top 25% of class	**80**
% graduated top 50% of class	**98**

DEADLINES

Regular Deadline	**1/31**
Normal registration	**no**

FACILITIES

Housing: Coed dorms. All students are required to live on campus all four years. *Special Academic Facilities/Equipment:* Language learning center, laser and optics research center, USAFA observatory, Dept. of Engineering Mechanics Lab, U.S. Air Force Academy visitor's center, consolidated educational training facility, Air Force Academy cadet chapel, American Legion Memorial Tower, Clune area athletic and speaking events (seats 6,000), air garden, Falcon Stadium, Aeronautics Lab, Meterology Lab, Arnold Hall Broadway Theater, ballroom and conference rooms, and historical displays. *Computers:* 100% of classrooms, 100% of libraries, 100% of student union, have wireless network access.

FINANCIAL FACTS

Financial Aid Rating	**60***
Annual in-state tuition	$0
Annual out-of-state tuition	$0
Room and Board	$0
Required Fees	$0
Books and supplies	$0

United States Coast Guard Academy

31 Mohegan Avenue, New London, CT 06320-8103 • Admissions: 860-444-8503 • Fax: 860-701-6700

CAMPUS LIFE

Quality of life Rating	66
Fire Safety Rating	77
Green rating	81
Type of School	Public
Environment	City

STUDENTS

Total undergrad enrolllment	1,017
% Male to Female	71/29
% From out of state	95
% From public high school	81
% Live on Campus	100
% African American	3
% Asian	4
% Caucasian	80
% Hispanic	8
% International	2
# Of Countries Represented	10

ACADEMICS

Academic Rating	90
% Of students graduating within 4 years	76
% Of students graduating within 6 years	79
Calendar	semester
Profs interesting rating	76
Profs accessible rating	98
Most common reg class size	10–19 students
Most common lab size	fewer than 10 students

MOST POPULAR MAJORS

Political science,
mechanical engineering,
oceanography–chemical and physical

SPECIAL STUDY OPTIONS

Double major, exchange student program (domestic), honors program, independent study, internships.

ABOUT THE SCHOOL

There is a special sense of pride at the Coast Guard Academy–pride in America, service, each class, each company, and in one's accomplishments. With a student body of less than 1,000, it's easy to see why graduates of the Coast Guard Academy form such a lifelong dedication to the school and each other. The USCGA graduates young men and women with "sound bodies, stout hearts and alert minds, [and] with a liking for the sea and its lore," not to mention a four-year Bachelor of Science degree. The curriculum is heavily oriented toward math, science and engineering, with a nationally recognized engineering program, as well as other programs in government, management, marine and environmental sciences, and more.

Given the intensity of Academy life, most cadets are eager for the opportunity to participate in extracurricular activities, and social events and organized activities are an integral part of the cadet experience. There are a number of long-standing traditions that cement the Coast Guard bond, from organized dress white formals to playful hazing between classes. While the opportunities afforded by a degree from this highly selective institution are impressive enough, top performers spend their senior summer traveling on exciting internships around the nation and overseas, and graduates have unmatched opportunities to attend flight school and graduate school.

BANG FOR YOUR BUCK

All graduates go on to become commissioned officers in the U.S. Coast Guard, and every junior officer in the Coast Guard can apply for the opportunity to obtain advanced education at Coast Guard expense (and additional service obligation). While in school, officers continue to receive full pay and benefits–their only job is to study and earn a degree. While acceptance into these programs is based on job performance and academic potential, there is such a broad range of opportunities offered that any Academy graduate has a good chance of being selected for one of the programs. In the last 10 years, every Academy engineering graduate who has applied for an engineering post-graduate program has been accepted and has gone on to complete a master's degree. Also of interest: up to ten percent (approximately 20 cadets) of the graduating class may attend flight training immediately upon completion of the four year Academy program.

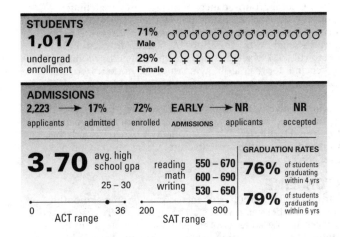

STUDENTS

1,017 undergrad enrollment

71% Male ♂♂♂♂♂♂♂♂♂♂♂♂♂♂

29% Female ♀♀♀♀♀♀

ADMISSIONS

2,223 →	17%	72%	EARLY ADMISSIONS →	NR	NR
applicants	admitted	enrolled		applicants	accepted

3.70 avg. high school gpa

ACT range (0–36): 25 – 30

SAT range (200–800): reading 550 – 670, math 600 – 690, writing 530 – 650

GRADUATION RATES

76% of students graduating within 4 yrs

79% of students graduating within 6 yrs

United States Coast Guard Academy

WEBSITE: WWW.USCGA.EDU

STUDENT BODY

Coast Guard cadets admit, "Despite the academy's best efforts," the campus can appear fairly homogenous. Indeed, "The typical student is still an upper-middle-class, white, Christian from a coastal state, most likely the Northeast." Luckily, a civil engineering major assures us, "Those students of different back- grounds easily fit in with everyone else." Not surprisingly, the academy seems to attract "highly motivated [people] with a strong desire to serve in the Coast Guard." Certainly, another hallmark of Coast Guard cadets is that they're "smart, hardworking, and eager to work with each other." A naval architecture and marine engineering major adds, "Type-A personalities are most common among the Corps." A first-year cadet is quick to say that "everyone is very welcoming." He goes on to attribute this to the "lasting bonds and friendship" we all form "because of going through boot camp together."

Why Students love U.S. Coast Guard Academy

"Truly unique in its ability to provide an environment where classmates become shipmates, friends, and eventually family."

WHY STUDENTS LOVE U.S. COAST GUARD ACADEMY

Many appreciate the "regimented environment," which, according to one management major, "gives me a standard to live up to and hold myself to, even when I am away from here." Still, there is time to relax on weekends, and "golf and outdoor activities are popular in the spring, and trips to Boston or NYC are often planned." With small class sizes and a clearly regimented way of life, the Coast Guard Academy "is truly unique in its ability to provide an environment where classmates become shipmates, friends, and eventually family." Professors are "willing to give up their time and stay after hours to help students succeed." As one impressed freshman proudly states, "You become a better person for going there."

GENERAL INFO

Activities: Choral groups, concert band, dance, drama/theater, jazz band, marching band, pep band, yearbook, campus ministries. **Organizations:** 2 honor societies, 7 religious organizations. Athletics (In-tercollegiate): *Men:* Baseball, basketball, crew/rowing, cross-country, diving, football, pistol, riflery, sailing, soccer, swimming, tennis, track/field (outdoor), track/field (indoor), wrestling. *Women:* Basketball, cheerleading, crew/rowing, cross-country, diving, pistol, riflery, sailing, soccer, softball, swimming, track/ field (outdoor), track/field (indoor), volleyball.

BOTTOM LINE

Tuition, room and board at the Coast Guard Academy are all paid for by the government. All candidates who accept an appointment to the Coast Guard Academy must submit $3,000 to purchase uniforms, a laptop computer, school supplies and other necessary items. Other than this initial deposit, there are no additional fees, and all cadets receive pay totaling $11,530 per year. Students have a 5-year service commitment after graduation, but that can be lengthened by the many available post-graduate degrees and training made available to USCGA alum. Approximately 80 percent of Academy graduates go to sea after graduation, and the other 20 percent of Academy graduates go to marine safety offices, ashore operations or flight training.

SELECTIVITY

Admissions Rating	**96**
# of applicants	2,223
% of applicants accepted	17
% of acceptees attending	72

FRESHMAN PROFILE

Range SAT Critical Reading	**550–670**
Range SAT Math	**600–690**
Range SAT Writing	**530–650**
Range ACT Composite	**25–30**
Average HS GPA	**3.70**
% graduated top 10% of class	**51**
% graduated top 25% of class	**87**
% graduated top 50% of class	**99**

DEADLINES

Regular Deadline	**12/15**
Normal registration	**no**

FACILITIES

Housing: Coed dorms 95% of campus accessible to physically disabled. *Special Academic Facilities/Equipment:* CG Museum; Library; Visitors Center; Alumni Center. *Computers:* 100% of classrooms, 65% of dorms, 100% of libraries, 50% of dining areas, 100% of student union, 50% of common outdoor areas have wireless network access. Students can register for classes online. Administrative functions (other than registration) can be performed online. Undergraduates are required to own a computer.

FINANCIAL FACTS

Financial Aid Rating	**60***
Annual in-state tuition	$0
Annual out-of-state tuition	$0
Room and Board	$0
Required Fees	$0
Books and supplies	$0

United States Merchant Marine Academy

Office of Admissions, Kings Point, NY 11024-1699 • Admissions: 516-773-5391 • Fax: 516-773-5390

CAMPUS LIFE

Quality of life Rating	61
Fire Safety Rating	60*
Green rating	60*
Type of School	Public
Environment	Village

STUDENTS

Total undergrad enrolllment	985
% Male to Female	88/12
% From out of state	86
% From public high school	71
% Live on Campus	100
% African American	3
% Asian	5
% Caucasian	84
% Hispanic	5
% Native American	1
% International	3
# Of Countries Represented	5

ACADEMICS

Academic Rating	62
Calendar	trimester
Profs interesting rating	61
Profs accessible rating	69
Most common reg class size	10–19 students
Most common lab size	10–19 students

MOST POPULAR MAJORS

Engineering, naval architecture and marine engineering, transportation and materials moving

SPECIAL STUDY OPTIONS

Honors program, independent study, internships. Career services: Alumni network, alumni services, career/job search classes, career assessment, internships.

ABOUT THE SCHOOL

Known for having the hardest academics out of all the military academies, the United States Merchant Marine Academy offers students free tuition, rigorous academics, and the widest range of career options available to graduates of U.S. service academies following graduation (including officers in any branch of the armed forces, or a number of civilian occupations). Professors are undoubtedly more than qualified in their fields of study, ranging from former NASA scientists to highly decorated and accomplished officers in the military.

The notorious freshman year is spent inducting students into a completely new way of life, in which they learn new terms, the quality of endurance, how to perform under pressure, and the definition of a wakeup call at "0-dark-thirty." The "sea year "spent studying on merchant vessels gives students a hands-on perspective that not many other engineering schools offer, and students typically visit 10 to 15 countries in the course of the school year. When liberty time is allowed, students have access to New York City, as well as a multimillion-dollar waterfront packed with power-boats (not to mention the know-how to use them). At the end of it all, students graduate with a bachelor of science degree, as well as the specialized training for licensing as a merchant marine officer, the military knowledge for commissioning in a reserve component of the Armed Forces, and a strong network of alumni that know how capable a USMMA graduate really is.

The United States is a maritime nation, and every hour of every day, ships of all types ply the waters in and around it. It's a dangerous and lucrative business, and that's why the country relies on graduates of the United States Merchant Marine Academy in Kings Point, New York, to serve the economic and defense interests of the United States through the maritime industry and armed forces. This "prestigious academy, paid for by the federal government" offers "opportunities upon graduation [that] are endless."

BANG FOR YOUR BUCK

After graduation, students are automatically qualified to enter any branch of the armed forces as an officer, including Army, Navy, Air Force, Marines, Coast Guard, or NOAA. Virtually 100 percent of graduates obtain well-paying employment within six months of commencement, with the majority at work within three months, and most with offers of employment before graduation day. Most students that attend the USMMA have their sights set on a solid job that only requires them to work six months out of the year.
The Academy's four-year program centers on a regimental system that turns its students–called midshipmen (a term used for both men and women)–into "top notch officers who are not only capable at sea, but have the ability to work under stress in any situation."

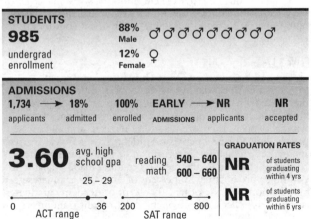

STUDENTS
985 undergrad enrollment

88% Male ♂♂♂♂♂♂♂♂♂
12% Female ♀

ADMISSIONS

1,734 applicants	→ 18% admitted	100% enrolled	EARLY ADMISSIONS	→ NR applicants	NR accepted

3.60 avg. high school gpa

reading	540 – 640
math	600 – 660

ACT range (0–36): 25 – 29

SAT range (200–800)

GRADUATION RATES

NR of students graduating within 4 yrs

NR of students graduating within 6 yrs

United States Merchant Marine Academy

FINANCIAL AID: 516-773-5295 • E-MAIL: ADMISSIONS@USMMA.EDU • WEBSITE: WWW.USMMA.EDU

STUDENT BODY

Students are quick to form a "mutual bond with one another" and "get along very well." "Outgoing and focused," "Everyone is strong-willed and generally respectful." The vast majority of students describe themselves as "white, male, intelligent, athletic, conservative, and competitive." Students are bonded by a fraternal patriotism and a strong work ethic. Regiments inspire an "esprit d'corps." "We are tight. We know everybody, and we are dedicated to everyone's success." Freshman year "is tough, both regimentally and academically." "As a plebe, a freshmen, you are an outcast from the rest of the regiment in order to build unity among their class. [Plebes] must complete a long series of steps before they become recognized."

Why Students love US Merchant Marine

"It provides a great all around experience. It's awesome."

"it's the best college in the West Coast. West Coast Best Coast.

WHY STUDENTS LOVE UNITED STATES MERCHANT MARINE ACADEMY

With "strong alumni support," and "100 percent job placement," the "academically challenging" USMMA "will push you far beyond what you thought you could do; it will also train you to assume a leadership role in any company." Many students cite "the ability to do whatever you want after graduation" as a huge draw of the school, as well as "the bond the students have with each other." Not to mention the fact that "they put us on a boat for months at a time and let us sail around the world learning in real life." With each midshipman carrying a specific responsibility, 'the regiment is primarily run by the students. All life revolves around going to sea." On weekends (well, once you're past your first year), students can engage in a more traditional college experience, and because "New York City is sixteen miles east of school...students take frequent trips on the weekends and enjoy the city life."

GENERAL INFO

Activities: Choral groups, concert band, drama/theater, marching band, student government, student newspaper, yearbook, campus ministries. **Organizations:** 3 religious organizations. **Athletics (Intercollegiate):** *Men:* Baseball, basketball, crew/rowing, cross-country, diving, football, golf, lacrosse, riflery, sailing, soccer, swimming, tennis, track/field (outdoor), volleyball, water polo, wrestling. *Women:* Basketball, crew/rowing, cross-country, diving, golf, riflery, sailing, softball, swimming, tennis, track/field (outdoor), volleyball.

BOTTOM LINE

The federal government pays for all of a student's education, room and board, uniforms, and books; however, midshipmen are responsible for the payment of fees for mandatory educational supplies not provided by the government, such as the prescribed personal computer, activity fees (athletic, cultural events, health services, student newspaper, yearbook, etc.), and personal fees. These fees range from $755 to $2530, depending on class year (loans are available). The service commitment for each student is determined by their choice of career following graduation.

SELECTIVITY

Admissions Rating	**90**
# of applicants	1,734
% of applicants accepted	18
% of acceptees attending	100

FRESHMAN PROFILE

Range SAT Critical Reading	**540–640**
Range SAT Math	**600–660**
Range ACT Composite	**25–29**
Average HS GPA	**3.60**
% graduated top 10% of class	**18**
% graduated top 25% of class	**23**
% graduated top 50% of class	**85**

DEADLINES

Regular Deadline	**3/1**
Normal registration	**no**

FACILITIES

Housing: Coed dorms, all students required to live on campus in dormitories provided. *Special Academic Facilities/Equipment:* American Merchant Marine Museum. *Computers:* Students can register for classes online. Administrative functions (other than registration) can be performed online. Undergraduates are required to own a computer.

FINANCIAL FACTS

Financial Aid Rating	**90**
Annual tuition	$0
Room and Board	$0
Required Fees	$2,905
Books and supplies	$0

United States Military Academy–West Point

646 Swift Road, West Point, NY 10996-1905 • Admissions: 845-938-4041 • Fax: 845-938-3021

CAMPUS LIFE

Quality of life Rating	80
Fire Safety Rating	87
Green rating	60*
Type of School	Public
Environment	Village

STUDENTS

Total undergrad enrolllment	4,686
% Male to Female	84/16
% From out of state	93
% From public high school	74
% Live on Campus	100
% African American	6
% Asian	5
% Caucasian	72
% Hispanic	9
% Native American	1
% International	1
# Of Countries Represented	35

ACADEMICS

Academic Rating	99
% Of students graduating within 4 years	77
% Of students graduating within 6 years	80
Calendar	semester
Profs interesting rating	97
Profs accessible rating	99
Most common reg class size	10–19 students
Most common lab size	10–19 students

MOST POPULAR MAJORS

Mechanical engineering, engineering management, economics

SPECIAL STUDY OPTIONS

Double major, exchange student program (domestic), honors program, independent study, internships, study abroad, opportunities to attend Army Schools (Airborne, Air Assault, etc.) to learn special skills.

ABOUT THE SCHOOL

There's just a little history behind this one, you see. Founded in 1802, the United States Military Academy–West Point is integral to the military and political history of the United States of America, having produced Generals Grant, Lee, Pershing, MacArthur, Eisenhower, Patton, Schwarzkopf and Petraeus. The school is all about transforming regular citizens into intellectual soldiers with unparalleled skills of leadership, who will be fit to lead America into battle. If it sounds like a tall order, that's because it is, and one that West Point has fulfilled time and time again over three centuries.

USMA is all about the leadership, and the school is very open about the grueling process involved in producing West Point-grade leaders that can make it to the front lines and back. The large core curriculum ensures that cadets are at the very least jacks of all trades, and mandatory sports events keep cadets in peak performance shape. Ethical, social, and spiritual development are also on the docket, and the school's staff and faculty role models and a vigorous guest speaker program helps to provide living proof of the values the school wishes to impart. These jam-packed schedules produce well-rounded students who are able to apply a wide range of analytical skills to life as a military officer, as well as a decision maker in all contexts.

Renowned as one of the world's preeminent leader development institutions, West Point's mission is to educate, train, and inspire the student body (called the Corps of Cadets) through a "strenuous schedule that requires hard work and sacrifice." Luckily, there "are absolutely excellent" instructors who "put an incredible amount of effort and work into making sure the students succeed." All cadets receive a Bachelor of Science degree, and each year, approximately 1,000 cadets who make it through all four years "join the Long Gray Line" as they graduate and are commissioned as second lieutenants in the U.S. Army.

BANG FOR YOUR BUCK

The doors West Point opens are innumerable, and those doors don't just lead to military careers. Joining "The Long Gray Line" of West Point graduates is a mark of distinction, and one that can carry over into civilian life. Training for a future career outside of the military can begin during the service obligation, as during senior year, cadets find out which specialized field, or "branch," they will enter (options include combat branches, support branches and intelligence, and even the Medical Service Corps). Both the needs of the Army and cadet preferences will be considered.

STUDENTS

4,686 undergrad enrollment

84% Male ♂♂♂♂♂♂♂♂

16% Female ♀♀

ADMISSIONS

12,264 applicants → 13% admitted — 82% enrolled — EARLY ADMISSIONS → NR applicants — NR accepted

3.80 avg. high school gpa

ACT range (0–36): 25 – 30

SAT range (200–800): reading 560 – 670; math 580 – 680; writing 540 – 650

GRADUATION RATES

77% of students graduating within 4 yrs

80% of students graduating within 6 yrs

United States Military Academy–West Point

E-MAIL: ADMISSIONS@USMA.EDU • WEBSITE: WWW.WESTPOINT.EDU

STUDENT BODY

"Physically fit," "type-A" "workaholics" fill the ranks at West Point, where "due to Army regulations, many people look the same in regards to facial hair and hair cuts. The uniform does not help either." There are a lot of "high school hero," "Captain America–type people" here. Not too many students stray from that prototype. One student warns, "Most people that do not eventually mold into the typical student do not make it through all four years. Cooperate and graduate." Although all students are "very competitive," there is a "great sense of duty to help out your classmates. Most students are very intelligent, polite, and professional."

Why Students love West Point

"Most students are very intelligent, polite, and professional."

WHY STUDENTS LOVE U.S. MILITARY ACADEMY–WEST POINT

"Free education, leadership opportunities, [and] unlimited resources" top the list of West Point pluses. In "developing a total student," West Point eliminates all distractions, and things like "laundry, food, utilities, etc. are all taken care of by outside institutions." Though the academics are "very difficult" to say the least, the professors are always at the ready, and "one-on-one tutoring from instructors is available on a daily basis," one grateful cadet reports. For fun, there are "lots of athletic activities available and a surprisingly wide range of student clubs (ranging from a Korean American relations seminar to the fly-fishing club)," and New York City is a short trip away for those who are granted leave. "It is an experience that can be unmatched by any other school," sums up a cadet. "Completing four years at West Point is an accomplishment I will hold with me for all my life," says another.

GENERAL INFO

Activities: Choral groups, drama/theater, jazz band, music ensembles, pep band, radio station, student government, student newspaper, television station, yearbook, campus ministries, international student organization. **Organizations:** 105 registered organizations, 7 honor societies, 13 religious organizations. **Athletics (Intercollegiate):** *Men:* Baseball, basketball, cross-country, football, golf, gymnastics, ice hockey, lacrosse, riflery, soccer, swimming, tennis, track/field (outdoor), track/field (indoor), wrestling. *Women:* Basketball, cross-country, riflery, soccer, softball, swimming, tennis, track/field (outdoor), track/field (indoor), volleyball. **On-Campus Highlights:** Cadet Chapel, West Point Museum, Eisenhower Hall, Michie Stadium, Trophy Point, Fort Putnam, West Point Cemetery.

BOTTOM LINE

Tuition is free, and all cadets receive a monthly stipend of approximately $10,000 a year. All graduates must serve at least five years of active duty (beginning as a second lieutenant in the Army) and three years in a Reserve Component, a total of eight years, after graduation. Cadets are expected to pay a fee upon admission to the Academy. This $2000 is not only a commitment to attend, but will be used to defray the costs of uniforms, books, and a computer–essential items for every cadet. The active duty obligation is the nation's return on a West Point graduate's fully funded, four-year college education that is valued in excess of $225,000.

SELECTIVITY

Admissions Rating	**97**
# of applicants	12,264
% of applicants accepted	13
% of acceptees attending	82

FRESHMAN PROFILE

Range SAT Critical Reading	**560–670**
Range SAT Math	**580–680**
Range SAT Writing	**540–650**
Range ACT Composite	**25–30**
Average HS GPA	**3.80**
% graduated top 10% of class	**47**
% graduated top 25% of class	**77**
% graduated top 50% of class	**99**

DEADLINES

Regular Deadline	**2/28**
Normal registration	**no**

FACILITIES

Housing: Coed dorms, coed dorms are called barracks. *Special Academic Facilities/ Equipment:* West Point Museum (oldest of U.S. army museums. Arvin gymnasium, featuring swimming pools, wrestling, squash, racquetball, handball, and volleyball. courts has undergone a major renovation to modernize and improve its contribution to the physical development of the corps of cadets. Michie Stadium. Holleder Center houses Tate Rink for the Army hockey team and Christl Arena is the home of the Army men and women's basketball teams. Eisenhower Hall, the modern "student union," contains a 4,500-seat auditorium, a 1,000-seat snack bar and cafeteria, a large ballroom, and other social and recreational rooms.

FINANCIAL FACTS

Financial Aid Rating	**60***
Annual tuition	$0
Books and supplies	$0

United States Naval Academy

117 Decatur Road, Annapolis, MD 21402 • Admissions: 410-293-1914 • Fax: 410-293-4348

CAMPUS LIFE

Quality of life Rating	80
Fire Safety Rating	70
Green rating	60*
Type of School	Public
Environment	Town

STUDENTS

Total undergrad enrolllment	4,603
% Male to Female	80/20
% From out of state	96
% From public high school	60
% Live on Campus	100
% African American	6
% Asian	4
% Caucasian	68
% Hispanic	12
% International	1
# Of Countries Represented	28

ACADEMICS

Academic Rating	91
% Of students graduating within 4 years	88
% Of students graduating within 6 years	89
Calendar	semester
Profs interesting rating	81
Profs accessible rating	97
Most common reg class size	10–19 students

MOST POPULAR MAJORS

Economics, history, political science

HONORS PROGRAMS

Voluntary Graduate Education Program–second semester seniors may enroll in graduate school at a nearby college or university.

SPECIAL STUDY OPTIONS

Double major, exchange student program (domestic), honors program, independent study, Voluntary Graduate Education Program

ABOUT THE SCHOOL

The deeply historic United States Naval Academy is one of the few colleges in the world that prepares students morally, mentally, and physically. There's an intense focus not only on regimentation, but also on the shaping of students moral character, and students here thrive on the academic and militaristic discipline required to make it as a midshipman. Those that decide to apply here–and receive the necessary Congressional recommendation to do so–are looking for more than a college degree, and so this self-selecting pool of the best and the brightest young men and women are ready to become the next military leaders of the world from the second they set foot in the Yard.

Through the school's well-worn system, students learn to take orders from practically everyone (Plebe Summer Training certainly provides and introduction to this), but before long, acquire the responsibility for making decisions that can affect hundreds of other midshipmen. Small class sizes, protected study time, academic advising, and a sponsor program for newly-arrived midshipmen all help ensure that students are given the tools to succeed at this tough school. After four years at the Naval Academy, the life and customs of the naval service become second nature, and most midshipmen go on to careers as officers in the Navy or Marines.

The scenic Naval Academy campus, known as the Yard, is located in historic Annapolis, Maryland, and has been the home to some of the country's foremost leaders, astronauts, scholars, and military heroes. With its combination of early 20th-century and modern buildings ("the facilities are unmatched"), the USNA is a blend of tradition and state-of-the-art technology, and the school's history is felt even in the most high tech of classrooms.

BANG FOR YOUR BUCK

All graduates go on to become an ensign in the Navy or a second lieutenant in the Marine Corps, and serve five years as an officer, followed by reserve commissions. Many also go on for additional training, including nuclear power, aviation, submarine warfare, and special operations. Especially capable and highly motivated students are able to enroll in the school's challenging honors programs, which provide opportunities to start work on postgraduate degrees while still at the Academy. Graduates of USNA tend to spread themselves beyond the military, and the school has produced one president, numerous astronauts, and more than 990 noted scholars in a variety of academic fields are Academy graduates, including 46 Rhodes Scholars and 24 Marshall Scholars.

STUDENTS

4,603 undergrad enrollment

80% Male ♂♂♂♂♂♂♂♂

20% Female ♀♀

ADMISSIONS

17,419 applicants → **8%** admitted | **85%** enrolled | **EARLY ADMISSIONS** → **NR** applicants | **NR** accepted

NR avg. high school gpa

NR

reading 550 – 670

math 590 – 690

0 — 36 ACT range

200 — 800 SAT range

GRADUATION RATES

88% of students graduating within 4 yrs

89% of students graduating within 6 yrs

United States Naval Academy

FINANCIAL AID: 909-621-8205 • E-MAIL: STROOP@USNA.EDU • WEBSITE: WWW.USNA.EDU

STUDENT BODY

At USNA, the average student is a "type-A personality that works hard to uphold the standards of the academy and to ultimately receive the service selection of their choice." There's an intense camaraderie among the midshipmen here; "the initial summer training really brings students together into a good group that works well together for the remainder of their four years." The typical student is "a pretty well-rounded blend of academic, athletic, and cultural values."

Why Students love U.S. Naval Academy

"The initial summer training really brings students together into a good group that works well together for the remainder of their four years."

WHY STUDENTS LOVE U.S. NAVAL ACADEMY

"Not only am I preparing my leadership skills so I can lead our nation's sailors and Marines, I am also earning a quality education," sums up a student. Midshipmen receive this "superior education" for free, with the added benefit of a guaranteed job and a "high caliber of people…to meet and befriend." The opportunities at the Naval Academy are "unlike any other institution of higher learning in the world," and "you get more face time with your professors and actually get to know them better than you would at any other college." The overall academic experience is "outstanding," and "there are numerous resources for academic assistance." The school is "the epitome of structure and routine due to its military atmosphere and its mandatory obligations," and so "standards are enforced, people are safe, and we are learning."

GENERAL INFO

Activities: Choral groups, concert band, drama/theater, jazz band, literary magazine, marching band, musical theater, pep band, radio station, student government, yearbook, campus ministries, international student organization. **Organizations:** 70 registered organizations, 10 honor societies, 8 religious organizations. **Athletics (Intercollegiate):** *Men:* Baseball, basketball, crew/rowing, cross-country, diving, football, golf, gymnastics, lacrosse, light weight football, riflery, sailing, soccer, squash, swimming, tennis, track/field (outdoor), track/field (indoor), water polo, wrestling. *Women:* Basketball, crew/ rowing, cross-country, diving, lacrosse, riflery, sailing, soccer, swimming, tennis, track/field (outdoor), track/field (indoor), volleyball. **On-Campus Highlights:** Bancroft Hall, U.S. Naval Academy Museum, Armel-Leftwich Visitor Center, U.S. Naval Academy Chapel, Lejeune Hall.

BOTTOM LINE

The Navy pays for the tuition, room and board, and medical and dental care of Naval Academy midshipmen. They also enjoy regular active-duty benefits including access to military commissaries and exchanges, commercial transportation and lodging discounts and the ability to fly space-available in military aircraft around the world. Midshipmen are also given a monthly salary of $864, from which laundry, barber, cobbler, activities fees, yearbook and other service charges are deducted. Actual cash pay is less than $100 per month your first year, increasing each year to $400 per month in your fourth year.

SELECTIVITY

Admissions Rating	**95**
# of applicants	17,419
% of applicants accepted	8
% of acceptees attending	85
# accepting a place on wait list	130
% admitted from wait list	12

FRESHMAN PROFILE

Range SAT Critical Reading	**550–670**
Range SAT Math	**590–690**
% graduated top 10% of class	**56**
% graduated top 25% of class	**81**
% graduated top 50% of class	**96**

DEADLINES

Regular Deadline	**1/31**
Normal registration	**no**

FACILITIES

Housing: Coed dorms. All midshipmen live in same dormitory. *Special Academic Facilities/Equipment:* Naval history museum, Naval Institute Proceedings, propulsion lab, wind tunnels, flight simulator, ship tow tanks, satellite dish, coastal chamber facilities, fleet of small training craft (power and sail), oceanographic research vessel. *Computers:* Students can register for classes online. Administrative functions (other than registration) can be performed online. Undergraduates are required to own a computer.

FINANCIAL FACTS

Financial Aid Rating	**60***
Annual in-state tuition	$0
Annual out-of-state tuition	$0
Room and Board	$0
Required Fees	$0
Books and supplies	$0

Webb Institute

298 Crescent Beach Road, Glen Cove, NY 11542 • Admissions: 516-674-9838 • Fax: 516-674-9838

CAMPUS LIFE

Quality of life Rating	93
Fire Safety Rating	72
Green rating	60*
Type of School	Private
Environment	Village

STUDENTS

Total undergrad enrolllment	80
% Male to Female	85/15
% From out of state	70
% From public high school	83
% Live on Campus	100
% Asian	8
% Caucasian	85
% Hispanic	2

ACADEMICS

Academic Rating	95
% Of students graduating within 4 years	88
% Of students graduating within 6 years	85
Calendar	semester
Profs interesting rating	89
Profs accessible rating	99
Most common reg class size	20–29 students
Most common lab size	20–29 students

MOST POPULAR MAJORS

Business/commerce, economics international relations

SPECIAL STUDY OPTIONS

Double major, independent study, internships.

ABOUT THE SCHOOL

Ever wondered what goes into designing an America's Cup yacht, U.S. Navy destroyer, or a cruise liner? That's the exact sort of curiosity that brings students to Webb Institute, an engineering college that has produced the nation's leading ship designers for more than a century. Imagine a tiny student body living, eating, sleeping, and learning ship design in a mansion in a residential area overlooking the beautiful Long Island Sound. Then imagine that when that tiny student body leaves their manse, they find a 100 percent placement rate in careers and graduate schools. That's Webb Institute.

As the only school of its kind in the country, Webb enjoys an unrivalled reputation within the marine industry, which is also where students (happily) complete their mandatory two-month internships each January and February. Life–and that includes study, work, and play–on a 26-acre beachfront estate with just 100 students and 11 full-time professors is a rare combination of challenge, focus, and adventure, so in a sense, every day at Webb is a beach day.

Webb Institute is a four-year, fully accredited engineering college that has specialized in naval architecture and marine engineering for the last 123 years. Founded in 1889 by prominent New York shipbuilder William H. Webb, the school's rigorous curriculum couples seamlessly with a total immersion in real world experience. The school's curriculum goes beyond mechanical, electrical, and civil engineering, taking a systems engineering approach to problem solving, meaning Webb graduates are capable of working across engineering disciplines. "If you're passionate about architecture and engineering, you cannot hope for a better learning environment." Everyone majors in naval architecture and marine engineering, although non-engineering electives are available to juniors and seniors, and Webbies are exposed to a smattering of the liberal arts and a ton of advanced math and physics.

BANG FOR YOUR BUCK

Webb's full-tuition scholarship creates the lowest average student loan indebtedness of any four-year college in the nation besides the military academies. Job prospects are phenomenal; every Webb student goes to work in the marine industry for two months every year, creating a professional network and resume content of eight 8 months or more industry experience. In part due to this experience, as well as the school's specialized nature and excellent reputation, every graduate has a job at graduation or within two months after.

STUDENTS

80 undergrad enrollment

85% Male ♂♂♂♂♂♂♂♂♂♂

15% Female ♀

ADMISSIONS

72 applicants → 44% admitted | 56% enrolled | EARLY ADMISSIONS → NR applicants | NR accepted

3.90 avg. high school gpa

ACT range (0–36): NR

SAT range (200–800):

reading	640 – 700
math	700 – 740
writing	620 – 720

GRADUATION RATES

88% of students graduating within 4 yrs

85% of students graduating within 6 yrs

Webb Institute

FINANCIAL AID: 516-671-2213 • E-MAIL: ADMISSIONS@WEBB-INSTITUTE.EDU • WEBSITE: WWW.WEBB-INSTITUTE.EDU

STUDENT BODY

The average Webbie is a "middle-class, white male who enjoys engineering and sciences." "Everyone is motivated and works hard." Basically, you have your bookworms who "don't socialize as much" and your more social students who get their work done but also play sports and "have a good time." Camaraderie is reportedly easy due to the academic stress and Webb's small size. Everyone interacts with everyone else, regardless of background. With fewer than 100 students, it's "impossible to completely isolate yourself." "There are no social cliques, and everyone is included in anything they'd like to be included in." As at most engineering schools, the ratio between males and females is pretty severely lopsided here. "We want more women!" plead many students.

Why Students love Webb Institute

"There are no social cliques, and everyone is included in anything they'd like to be included in."

WHY STUDENTS LOVE WEBB INSTITUTE

Understandably, "you're not just another number" at Webb, where "America's future ship designers and engineers" get their start. "The administration, professors, and students all work in the same building every day, every week." Faculty is "approachable," "always accessible," and "very dedicated to the school and students." "Though people generally think about homework and spend most of their time discussing class assignments," when students find some down time, movies and unorganized sports are common. Not surprisingly, "many people turn to the water" for amusement as well. "Sailing is popular." "The school has a skiff and sailboats, which are frequently used during the warm months," says a sophomore.

GENERAL INFO

Activities: Choral groups, drama/theater, music ensembles, student government, yearbook. **Organizations:** 2 registered organizations. **Athletics (Intercollegiate):** *Men:* Basketball, cross-country, sailing, soccer, tennis, volleyball. *Women:* Basketball, cross-country, sailing, soccer, tennis, volleyball. **On-Campus Highlights:** Stevenson Taylor Hall, Brockett Pub, Waterfront Facility.

BOTTOM LINE

Every Webb student receives a full-tuition scholarship founded by Mr. Webb, and continued by the generous contributions of alumni/ae, friends of Webb, parents, corporations, and the U.S. Government. All admitted students also get paid for two months of internships every year. The only costs are fees, books and supplies, room and board, and personal expenses (including transportation and a laptop), which come to around $21,150 each year. There are some additional scholarships available to deserving students to help defray these costs, and if a student needs additional financial assistance, the school recommends pursuing federal grants and loans (and they'll help you do so).

SELECTIVITY

Admissions Rating	**97**
# of applicants	72
% of applicants accepted	44
% of acceptees attending	56

FRESHMAN PROFILE

Range SAT Critical Reading	**640–700**
Range SAT Math	**700–740**
Range SAT Writing	**620–720**
Average HS GPA	**3.90**
% graduated top 10% of class	**63**
% graduated top 25% of class	**88**
% graduated top 50% of class	**100**

DEADLINES

Regular Deadline	**2/15**
Normal registration	**no**

FACILITIES

Housing: Coed dorms, men's dorms, women's dorms. 70% of campus accessible to physically disabled. *Special Academic Facilities/Equipment:* Towing tank for model testing, marine engineering lab. *Computers:* 100% of classrooms, 100% of dorms, 100% of libraries, 100% of dining areas, 100% of student union, 100% of common outdoor areas have wireless network access.

FINANCIAL FACTS

Financial Aid Rating	**83**
Annual in-state tuition	$0
Annual out-of-state tuition	$0
Room and Board	$12,480
Required Fees	$0
Books and supplies	$950
% frosh rec. need-based scholarship or grant aid	11
% UG rec.need-based scholarship or grant aid	8
% frosh rec. need-based self-help aid	16
% UG rec. need-based self-help aid	21
% frosh rec. any financial aid	25
% UG rec. any financial aid	20
% UG borrow to pay for school	33
Average cumulative indebtedness	$8,545

Best Value Private Schools

Agnes Scott College

141 East College Avenue, Atlanta/Decatur, GA 30030-3797 • Admissions: 404-471-6285 • Financial Aid: 404-471-6395

CAMPUS LIFE

Quality of life Rating	98
Fire Safety Rating	95
Green rating	94
Type of School	Private
Environment	Metropolis

STUDENTS

Total undergrad enrolllment	892
% Male to Female	0/100
% From out of state	39
% From public high school	77
% Live on Campus	86
% African American	28
% Asian	3
% Caucasian	43
% Hispanic	6
% International	10
# Of Countries Represented	37

ACADEMICS

Academic Rating	90
% Of students graduating within 4 years	59
% Of students graduating within 6 years	68
Calendar	semester
Profs interesting rating	95
Profs accessible rating	96
Most common reg class size	10–19 students
Most common lab size	10–19 students

MOST POPULAR MAJORS
Political science, psychology

SPECIAL STUDY OPTIONS

Accelerated program, cross-registration, double major, dual enrollment, independent study, internships, student-designed major, study abroad, teacher certification program, Presidential International Scholar program; "Success Initiative, Bonner Scholars, Community of Scholars, Learning Communities and Creative Writing Concentration.

ABOUT THE SCHOOL

Advertised as "the world for women," Agnes Scott College is a high-value option for students considering the Atlanta, Georgia area. The small campus and student focus make this an easy choice for many young women. "ASC is like the prep school I could never afford to go to! The classes are a huge strength—they are small in size, with the largest being around 30 students. Everyone is required to take a lot of distributional courses, so even with the small class sizes you tend to meet a lot of people across all the majors," says a current student. Another undergrad adds, "Classes are, for the most part, discussion-based even when they're officially listed as lectures. This means that class is rarely boring, but it does mean you have to be prepared to participate and learn something."

For a university experience with a small school heart, Agnes Scott has a very empowering environment. Students gain hands-on experience using a multi-faceted approach, and with the small campus and class sizes, all voices are heard. "Everyone on campus is on a mission and has the ability to succeed in whatever she chooses to do," shares a current student. She continues, "I really feel at home here. It is very easy to get comfortable and it becomes a second home." A recent graduate tells us why she chose ASC: "The academics are wonderful in every way and every department. The professors make you want to work hard and take pride in your work. As a new freshman explains, "I did not want to follow my high school classmates to an oversized state school. I wanted to meet new people, and the small class sizes help everyone be involved."

BANG FOR YOUR BUCK

Agnes Scott College boasts small class sizes, a student-faculty ratio of 9 to 1, and many opportunities for students to undertake research projects independently or in collaboration with faculty. The college has a hundred-year-old, student-run Honor System, and undergraduates have frequent opportunities to develop the leadership skills that its graduates are known for. Very important at the school is "the cultivation of intelligent women for the real world," according to one student. Other undergrads add that "Agnes Scott is a challenging school, both socially and academically that teaches women to claim their education, and have their voices heard." "A women's college with a central focus on academics and leadership."

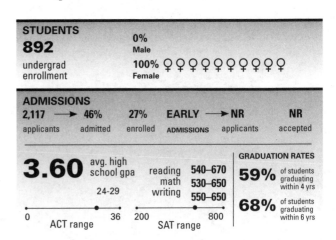

STUDENTS
892 undergrad enrollment
0% Male
100% Female ♀♀♀♀♀♀♀♀♀♀

ADMISSIONS
2,117 applicants → 46% admitted — 27% enrolled
EARLY ADMISSIONS → NR applicants — NR accepted

3.60 avg. high school gpa

ACT range: 0–36; 24-29

SAT range: 200–800
reading 540–670
math 530–650
writing 550–650

GRADUATION RATES
59% of students graduating within 4 yrs
68% of students graduating within 6 yrs

Agnes Scott College

E-MAIL: ADMISSION@AGNESSCOTT.EDU • FAX: 404-471-6414 • WEBSITE: WWW.AGNESSCOTT.EDU

STUDENT BODY

"It's almost impossible to describe a typical student" at Agnes Scott, where "you'll find everyone from preppy, Southern Baptist, Republican, in-state student debutantes to radical, vegan, communist lesbians, and everyone in between." As one student puts it, "We vary from women in pearls and plaid skirts to women in black parachute pants and metal in their noses." "Diversity is definitely one of Agnes Scott's strong points," students here agree. These "ambitious high-achievers" "not only consistently attend classes, but they are also involved in so many things–clubs, student government, taking more than the standard number of classes, work-study, etc.–that they barely have time to get everything done."

Why Students love Agnes Scott College

"The school's personality is elastic and intriguing."

WHY STUDENTS LOVE WOFFORD COLLEGE

Members of the student body find that "the school's personality is elastic and intriguing," as well as Agnes Scott being "a very 'Cheers' sort of place—everyone knows everyone else. Scotties volunteer and get involved way beyond the classroom." There is a "great alumnae network," and a "beautiful green campus," other undergrads inform us. Political awareness and sustainability are of importance to students at the college, too. Undergrads are pleased to find "the school is very socially conscious…there are a lot of groups on campus rallying for social change;" it's "common for more than one campus organization to be soliciting funds for charity in the dining hall at lunch time and it is even more common that people pitch in to help with almost every cause." Students looking to do things on the weekend often visit other campuses like Georgia Tech, Morehouse, and Emory.

GENERAL INFO

Activities: Choral groups, dance, drama/theater, literary magazine, marching band, music ensembles, musical theater, pep band, student government, student newspaper, symphony orchestra, television station, yearbook, campus ministries, international student organization. **Organizations:** 80 registered organizations, 12 honor societies, 12 religious organizations. **Athletics (Intercollegiate):** Basketball, lacrosse, soccer, softball, tennis, volleyball. **On-Campus Highlights:** New $36.5 million Science Center, Alston Campus Center, newly renovated Bradley Observatory, McCain Library, Several residence halls are on the National Register of Historical Places.

BOTTOM LINE

Agnes Scott College, while providing an exceptional education, is not inexpensive. Fortunately, scholarships and grants are plentiful, and the financial aid packages substantial. Annual tuition is $32,000, with room and board adding another $10,000. And while 70 percent of undergrads borrow in order to attend Agnes Scott, 100 percent of freshmen receive financial aid, and 75 percent benefit from need-based scholarships or grants. The average cumulative indebtedness for students upon graduating is $26,493.

SELECTIVITY

Admissions Rating	**90**
# of applicants	2,117
% of applicants accepted	46
% of acceptees attending	27
# accepting a place on wait list	0

FRESHMAN PROFILE

Range SAT Critical Reading	**540–670**
Range SAT Math	**530–680**
Range SAT Writing	**550–650**
Range ACT Composite	**24–29**
Average HS GPA	**3.60**
% graduated top 10% of class	**34**
% graduated top 25% of class	**69**
% graduated top 50% of class	**92**

DEADLINES

Normal registration	**no**

FACILITIES

Housing: Women's dorms, apartments for single students, theme housing. *Special Academic Facilities/Equipment:* Art galleries, state-of-the-art science building opened in January 2003, collaborative learning centers, language lab, electron microscope, observatory, instructional technology center, multi media production facility. *Computers:* 50% of classrooms, 100% of libraries, 100% of student union, 10% of common outdoor areas have wireless network access.

FINANCIAL FACTS

Financial Aid Rating	**94**
Annual tuition	$31,980
Room and Board	$10,150
Required Fees	$215
Books and supplies	$1,000
% frosh rec. need-based scholarship or grant aid	75
% UG rec.need-based scholarship or grant aid	73
% frosh rec. non-need-based scholarship or grant aid	25
% UG rec. non-need-based scholarship or grant aid	27
% frosh rec. need-based self-help aid	63
% UG rec. need-based self-help aid	64
% frosh rec. any financial aid	100
% UG rec. any financial aid	99
% UG borrow to pay for school	69
Average cumulative indebtedness	$26,493

Amherst College

Campus Box 2231, PO Box 5000, Amherst, MA 01002 • Admissions: 413-542-2328 • Fax: 413-542-2040

CAMPUS LIFE

Quality of life Rating	90
Fire Safety Rating	72
Green rating	66
Type of School	Private
Environment	Town

STUDENTS

Total undergrad enrolllment	1,795
% Male to Female	49/51
% From out of state	89
% From public high school	58
% Live on Campus	99
% African American	11
% Asian	11
% Caucasian	39
% Hispanic	11
% International	9
# Of Countries Represented	28

ACADEMICS

Academic Rating	98
% Of students graduating within 4 years	89
% Of students graduating within 6 years	94
Calendar	4-1-4
Profs interesting rating	87
Profs accessible rating	93
Most common reg class size	10–19 students

MOST POPULAR MAJORS

Economics, history, English, biology

HONORS PROGRAMS

Senior Honors Thesis–an opportunity to engage in extensive research with a professor as the student's advisor.

SPECIAL STUDY OPTIONS

Special programs offered to physically disabled students include note-taking services, reader services, voice recorders, tutors. Cross-registration, double major, exchange student program (domestic), honors program, independent study, student-designed major, study abroad, teacher certification program.

ABOUT THE SCHOOL

Situated on a lush 1,000-acre campus bordering Amherst, Massachusetts, Amherst College offers students an intellectual atmosphere fostered by friendly and supportive faculty members. Amherst College has an exploratory vibe with a virtually requirement-free curriculum that gives students unprecedented academic freedom. There are no core or general requirements. Beyond the first-year seminar and major coursework, students can choose what they want to study. One student told us, "I love the open curriculum and that you can do whatever you want here." Students can also receive credit for courses at neighboring colleges Smith, Mount Holyoke, Hampshire, and the University of Massachusetts–Amherst for a total selection of more than 6,000 courses. Students say that they love the "abundant academic and social opportunities" provided by the consortium. Almost half of Amherst students also pack their bags during junior year to study abroad. Students say that professors "are always available, and they want to spend time with us outside of the classroom." The school is also surprisingly diverse; minorities make up almost a third of the student body. Whether in a classroom, coffee shop, or sports arena, you'll find students engaged in lively (and sometimes heated) discussions concerning politics, environmental issues, ethics, and philosophy. According to one student, people at Amherst "think and talk about a wide variety of subjects and the student body is fairly intellectual and politically involved." Amherst provides students with real-world opportunities such as jobs and internships through its career center and Center for Community Engagement. The college also offers workshops on campus and recruiting events for students interested in different fields. Whether through academics, student organizations, or experiential learning opportunities, Amherst promotes choice in every way.

BANG FOR YOUR BUCK

Amherst College is a no-loan institution, which means the college does not include loans in its financial aid packages but focuses on providing grant and scholarship aid instead. It is possible to graduate from Amherst with no debt. In addition to a need-blind admissions policy, Amherst meets 100 percent of a students' demonstrated need, be they international or domestic. Every year, Amherst awards grants and scholarships to roughly half the student body. All students who apply for financial aid are automatically considered for grant and scholarship funds. The average freshman grant size is more than $34,000.

STUDENTS

1,795 undergrad enrollment

49% Male ♂♂♂♂♂♂♂♂♂♂

51% Female ♀♀♀♀♀♀♀♀♀♀

ADMISSIONS

8,099 applicants	→ 15% admitted	39% enrolled	EARLY ADMISSIONS	→ NR applicants	NR accepted

NR avg. high school gpa

ACT range (0–36): 30–34

SAT range (200–800): reading 670–770; math 670–770; writing 680–770

GRADUATION RATES

89% of students graduating within 4 yrs

94% of students graduating within 6 yrs

Amherst College

FINANCIAL AID: 413-542-2296 • E-MAIL: ADMISSION@AMHERST.EDU • WEBSITE: WWW.AMHERST.EDU

STUDENT BODY

Traditionally, the student body at Amherst has been known by the "stereotype of the preppy, upper-middle-class, white student," but many here note that the school is "at least as racially diverse as the country and more economically diverse than people think." That's not to say that the college doesn't have "a sizeable preppy population fresh from East Coast boarding schools," but overall students here report, "diversity–racial, ethnic, geographic, socioeconomic–is more than a buzzword here." The campus is also "a politically and environmentally conscious" place, as well as a "highly athletic one." The school's small size "means that no group is isolated, and everyone interacts and more or less gets along." The school is filled with "open-minded, intellectually passionate and socially conscious critical thinkers."

Why Students love Amherst College

"The school does its best to make sure everyone is happy and has a good time."

WHY STUDENTS LOVE AMHERST COLLEGE

Students love Amherst because it is a "community that values academics but doesn't forget the social side of college." At Amherst, students receive "individualized attention from top-notch professors who are here because they enjoy teaching students," but there are also "tons of discussions, colloquia, and speaker events on campus" for students to engage in. In their spare time, "Amherst students love to get involved in extracurriculars. It seems like everyone plays a sport, is a member of an a capella group, and has joined an affinity group." Students say that "there is a club or organization for every interest, and if there isn't, the school will find the money for it." First year dorms are described as "spacious, well-maintained, and luxurious as many five-star hotels"; they are also designed specifically "to facilitate social interaction, and the school does its best to make sure everyone is happy and has a good time." The town of Amherst and the surrounding areas are "incredibly intellectual," and students say that there are many "great restaurants" where they can dine and socialize. In general, students agree that "Amherst has a strong sense of community."

GENERAL INFO

Activities: Choral groups, concert band, dance, drama/theater, jazz band, literary magazine, music ensembles, musical theater, opera, radio station, student government, student newspaper, student-run film society, symphony orchestra, yearbook, international student organization. **Organizations:** 100 registered organizations, 2 honor societies, 7 religious organizations. **Athletics (Intercollegiate):** *Men:* Baseball, basketball, cross-country, diving, football, golf, ice hockey, lacrosse, soccer, squash, swimming, tennis, track/field (outdoor), track/field (indoor). *Women:* Basketball, cross-country, diving, field hockey, golf, ice hockey, lacrosse, soccer, softball, squash, swimming, tennis, track/field (outdoor), track/field (indoor), volleyball. **On-Campus Highlights:** Mead Art Museum, Pratt Museum of Natural History, Russian Cultural Center, Japanese Peace Garden, Observatory.

BOTTOM LINE

Annual tuition, fees, and room and board cost roughly $53,000 at Amherst. Once you consider books, supplies, personal expenses, and transportation, you can expect to spend anywhere from $58,000 to $60,000 per year. In the end, you'll get much more than what you pay for. The school meets 100 percent of its student body's demonstrated need. Students feel it is "hard to find somewhere better" and believe Amherst is "the best of the small, elite, New England colleges."

SELECTIVITY

Admissions Rating	**99**
# of applicants	8,099
% of applicants accepted	15
% of acceptees attending	39
# accepting a place on wait list	471
% admitted from wait list	3

FRESHMAN PROFILE

Range SAT Critical Reading	**670–770**
Range SAT Math	**670–770**
Range SAT Writing	**680–770**
Range ACT Composite	**30–34**
% graduated top 10% of class	**87**
% graduated top 25% of class	**97**
% graduated top 50% of class	**100**

DEADLINES

Regular Deadline	**1/1**
Normal registration	**no**

FACILITIES

Housing: Coed dorms, cooperative housing, French/Spanish language house, German/Russian language house, Latino culture house, African American culture house, health and wellness house, arts house, food cooperative house, and single-sex floors for men and women within specific dorms. *Special Academic Facilities/Equipment:* Art, natural history, geology museums, language labs, observatory, planetarium, The Amherst Center for Russian Culture, The Dickinson Homestead.

FINANCIAL FACTS

Financial Aid Rating	**96**
Annual tuition	$42,170
Room and Board	$11,200
Required Fees	$5,702
Books and supplies	$1,000
% frosh rec. need-based scholarship or grant aid	39
% UG rec.need-based scholarship or grant aid	55
% frosh rec. need-based self-help aid	50
% UG rec. need-based self-help aid	50
% frosh rec. any financial aid	60
% UG rec. any financial aid	57
% UG borrow to pay for school	42
Average cumulative indebtedness	$12,843

Barnard College

3009 Broadway, New York, NY 10027 • Admissions: 212-854-2014 • Financial Aid: 212-854-2154

CAMPUS LIFE

Quality of life Rating	99
Fire Safety Rating	71
Green rating	81
Type of School	Private
Environment	Metropolis

STUDENTS

Total undergrad enrollment	2,456
% Male to Female	0/100
% From out of state	68
% From public high school	53
% Live on Campus	90
% African American	4
% Asian	16
% Caucasian	65
% Hispanic	9
% International	5
# Of Countries Represented	39

ACADEMICS

Academic Rating	94
Calendar	semester
Profs interesting rating	94
Profs accessible rating	91
Most common reg class size	10–19 students
Most common lab size	10–19 students

MOST POPULAR MAJORS

English, economics, psychology, political science

HONOR PROGRAMS

The Barnard Centennial Scholars Program.

SPECIAL STUDY OPTIONS

Accelerated program, cross-registration, double major, dual enrollment, exchange student program (domestic), honors program, independent study, internships, liberal arts/career combination, student-designed major, study abroad, teacher certification program, independent scholars program, BA/BS in engineering and applied science.

ABOUT THE SCHOOL

Students of Barnard College say wonderful things about the school, such as "I loved the idea of a small liberal arts college in New York City." "Barnard is a school where students are challenged and given countless opportunities, but are given support and guidance from professors, advisors, administrators, and other students to achieve their goals." When asked about her choice, another student tells us, "I wanted to attend a school that had very small classes (two-thirds have 19 or fewer students), a community, and was still in the heart of New York City, specifically Manhattan, a wonderful island of activity."

The academic environment is one where all students are able to find something of value. A sophomore mentions, "Barnard is all about educating young women in the most effective ways to help create the future leaders of the world." A student in her senior year adds, "At Barnard, you are not a face in the crowd. Professors want to get to know their students, even if the class is a larger lecture. The professors are extremely passionate about their specialties and go out of their way to make sure students benefit from their classes. Another added benefit is having access to all of Columbia University's classes."

BANG FOR YOUR BUCK

The value of the school is in the people, the location, and the satisfaction found throughout the years by successful Barnard graduates. One recent graduate tells us, "The school has a strong faculty, outstanding students, fabulous career development services, a great alumnae network, and an important mission." Barnard College practices 'need-blind' admissions, which means that admissions officers are unaware of a student's financial circumstances when evaluating an application or debating an application in committee. Financial need is not considered when considering the qualifications of potential Barnard students. Once accepted, undergraduates have access to many financial assistance options; also included are study-abroad opportunities for qualified students.

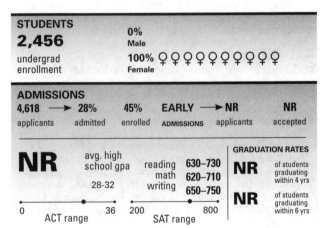

STUDENTS

2,456 undergrad enrollment

0% Male

100% Female ♀♀♀♀♀♀♀♀♀♀

ADMISSIONS

4,618 applicants	→ 28% admitted	45% enrolled	EARLY ADMISSIONS	→ NR applicants	NR accepted

NR avg. high school gpa

ACT range (0–36): 28-32

SAT range (200–800): reading 630–730, math 620–710, writing 650–750

GRADUATION RATES

NR of students graduating within 4 yrs

NR of students graduating within 6 yrs

E-MAIL: ADMISSIONS@BARNARD.EDU 2038 • FAX: 212-854-6220 • WEBSITE: WWW.BARNARD.EDU

STUDENT BODY

Even though it's all women here, Barnard is "the anti-women's college," as "very, very few students are here for the single-sex education"–they're here for the academics and New York. There's a definite liberal slant on campus, and these "usually politically savvy," "very cultured," "energetic and motivated" women are "ambitious and opinionated," with career and leadership goals at the top of their agenda. "Barnard students are not lazy" and have no problems booking their days full of study and activities. Most here learn to "fit into the mad rush" very quickly and take advantage of their four short years.

Why Students love Barnard College

"It is the best of both worlds: small community feel under a huge university in the greatest city in the world!"

WHY STUDENTS LOVE BARNARD COLLEGE

"Barnard is the perfect mixture of all the things you could want in a college," according to one satisfied student body member. When asked if she would recommend Barnard to others, a current student says, "The greatest strengths of the school are all of the people that comprise it. Both the professors and the administration take an invested interest in the students to ensure that she gets the most out of her classes. The girls who choose to attend Barnard tend to be passionate and incredibly interesting people. Being surrounding by these types of people helps motivate you to pursue your own passions and think for yourself." Another student tells us, "It is the best of both worlds: small community feel under a huge university in the greatest city in the world!"Those who hang around campus usually spend many hours in the dining hall or at Mollie's, the café, talking with friends.

GENERAL INFO

Activities: Choral groups, concert band, dance, drama/theater, jazz band, literary magazine, marching band, music ensembles, musical theater, opera, pep band, radio station, student government, student newspaper, student-run film society, symphony orchestra, television station, yearbook, campus ministries. **Organizations:** 100 registered organizations, 1 honor society. **Athletics (Intercollegiate):** Archery, basketball, crew/rowing, cross-country, diving, fencing, field hockey, golf, lacrosse, soccer, softball, swimming, tennis, track/field (outdoor), volleyball. **On-Campus Highlights:** Diana Center, Arthur Ross Greenhouse, Held Auditorium, Smart Media Classrooms, Liz's Place Cafe.

BOTTOM LINE

An education as valuable as one from Barnard College does not come without its costs; yearly tuition is $39,000. With room and board, as well as books, supplies, and fees being an additional $16,000, students are making a substantial investment. Freshmen, as well as upperclassmen, are pleased to find need-based scholarships and grants being provided to more than 40 percent of the student population. Also, more than 50 percent of all students benefit from financial aid. Just under half of enrollees do need to borrow to pay for school, and can expect an average indebtedness upon graduating from Barnard of $14,000; extremely reasonable given the cost of attending the college.

SELECTIVITY

Admissions Rating	**96**
# of applicants	4,618
% of applicants accepted	28
% of acceptees attending	45
# accepting a place on wait list	555
% admitted from wait list	9

FRESHMAN PROFILE

Range SAT Critical Reading	**630–730**
Range SAT Math	**620–710**
Range SAT Writing	**650–750**
Range ACT Composite	**28–32**
% graduated top 10% of class	**81**
% graduated top 25% of class	**95**
% graduated top 50% of class	**98**

DEADLINES

Regular Deadline	**1/1**
Normal registration	**no**

FACILITIES

Housing: Coed dorms, special housing for disabled students, women's dorms, apartments for single students. *Special Academic Facilities/Equipment:* Black Box Theater, infant toddler center, greenhouse, academic computer center, advanced architecture labs. *Computers:* 60% of classrooms, 80% of dorms, 80% of libraries, 100% of dining areas, 100% of student union, 100% of common outdoor areas have wireless network access.

FINANCIAL FACTS

Financial Aid Rating	**96**
Annual tuition	$40,422
Room and Board	$13,382
Required Fees	$1,762
Books and supplies	$1,146
% frosh rec. need-based scholarship or grant aid	41
% UG rec.need-based scholarship or grant aid	40
% frosh rec. need-based self-help aid	42
% UG rec. need-based self-help aid	42
% frosh rec. any financial aid	55
% UG rec. any financial aid	51
% UG borrow to pay for school	48
Average cumulative indebtedness	$14,142

Bates College

23 Campus Avenue, Lindholm House, Lewiston, ME 04240 • Admissions: 207-786-6000 • Fax: 207-786-6025

CAMPUS LIFE

Quality of life Rating	82
Fire Safety Rating	96
Green rating	94
Type of School	Private
Environment	Town

STUDENTS

Total undergrad enrollment	1,725
% Male to Female	46/54
% From out of state	90
% From public high school	54
% Live on Campus	93
% African American	5
% Asian	5
% Caucasian	75
% Hispanic	5
% International	6
# Of Countries Represented	67

ACADEMICS

Academic Rating	95
% Of students graduating within 4 years	85
% Of students graduating within 6 years	88
Calendar	4-4-1
Profs interesting rating	89
Profs accessible rating	95
Most common reg class size	fewer than 10 students
Most common lab size	10–19 students

MOST POPULAR MAJORS

Economics, political science, psychology

HONORS PROGRAMS

The Honors Program Special programs offered to physically disabled students include note-taking services, reader services, voice recorders, tutors.

SPECIAL STUDY OPTIONS

Accelerated program, cooperative education program, double major, honors program, independent study, internships, liberal arts/career combination, student-designed major, study abroad, teacher certification program.

ABOUT THE SCHOOL

Bates was founded in 1855, more than 150 years ago, by people who believed strongly in freedom, civil rights, and the importance of a higher education for all who could benefit from it. Bates is devoted to undergraduate in the arts and science, and commitment to teaching excellence is central to the College's mission. The College is recognized for its inclusive social character; there are no fraternities or sororities, and student organizations are open to all. Bates College has stood firmly for the ideals of academic rigor, intellectual curiosity, egalitarianism, social justice and freedom since its founding just before the Civil War. "The willingness of everyone to hear differing viewpoints and opinions even if they disagree" is very attractive to one student. Another is impressed that "Bates is an institution that challenges me to critically think in a way I never have before."

"Weaving together academics with real-world experience" is what one contented student likes best about Bates. Students who can demonstrate the intellectual soundness and potential value of an initiative–whether it's for a senior thesis project, a performance or an independent study–will receive every possible backing from the College. And one enrollee is very pleased to find that "you will not find it hard to gain access to resources." Bates has long understood that the privilege of education carries with it responsibility to others. Commitment to social action and the environment is something students here take seriously. Learning at Bates is connected to action and to others beyond the self. Bates faculty routinely incorporate service-learning into their courses, and about half of students take part in community-based projects in the Lewiston-Auburn region.

BANG FOR YOUR BUCK

With only 200 instructors at the school, those students fortunate enough to actually enroll can expect to find an outstanding student-to-faculty ratio of 10:1. More than 90 percent of freshmen return as sophomores and just a few percent less graduate within four years. Diversity is paramount at Bates; 90 percent of students are from out-of-state, and 65 different countries are represented on campus–extremely impressive for such a small institution. Internships and experiential learning opportunities are heavily encouraged, and more than two-thirds of alumni enroll in graduate study within ten years. Bates highly values its study abroad programs, unique calendar (4-4-1), and the many opportunities available for one-on-one collaboration with faculty. "The size of the student body allows for a relationship beyond that of typical professor-student and creates a sense of academic equality that produces incredible levels of scholarship at the undergraduate level."

STUDENTS

1,725 undergrad enrollment

46% Male ♂♂♂♂♂♂♂♂♂♂

54% Female ♀♀♀♀♀♀♀♀♀♀♀♀

ADMISSIONS

4,517 applicants → **32%** admitted | **34%** enrolled | EARLY ADMISSIONS → **NR** applicants | **NR** accepted

NR avg. high school gpa

ACT range (0–36): 29–32

SAT range (200–800): reading 620–710, math 620–700, writing 638–713

GRADUATION RATES

85% of students graduating within 4 yrs

88% of students graduating within 6 yrs

FINANCIAL AID: 207-786-6096 • WEBSITE: WWW.BATES.EDU

STUDENT BODY

"Your typical Batesie owns at least two flannel shirts" and "likes to have fun on the weekends." There are "a lot of jocks," and some "take the sports teams here way too seriously." Students here call themselves "down-to-earth" yet "intellectually driven." They enjoy "participating in academics, sports, and clubs." They "love the outdoors." However, this campus is "eclectic," and "Bates students are by no means monolithic in character." "We have everyone from the prep-school spoiled brat to the hippie environmentalist, from people with all different gender and sexual preferences and orientations to the former or current goth," observes a junior.

Why Students love Bates College

"I have never met so many professors who are willing to dedicate endless time outside of class to their students."

WHY STUDENTS LOVE BATES COLLEGE

Bates College "tries to be unique in the homogeneous world of New England's small liberal arts colleges by weaving together academics with real-world experience." First-year seminars, mandatory senior theses, service-learning, and a range of interdisciplinary majors are part of the academic experience. About two-thirds of the students here study abroad at some point before graduation. "Research and internship opportunities" are absurdly abundant. A fairly unusual calendar includes two traditional semesters and an "incredible" five-week spring term that provides really cool opportunities. Examples include studying marine biology on the Maine coast, Shakespearean drama in England, or economics in China and Taiwan. The "brilliant, accessible, and friendly" faculty does "whatever it takes to actually teach you the material instead of just lecturing and leaving." "The professors at Bates are here because they are passionate about their field and want to be teaching," explains a politics major.

GENERAL INFO

Activities: Choral groups, dance, drama/theater, jazz band, literary magazine, music ensembles, pep band, radio station, student government, student newspaper, student-run film society, symphony orchestra, yearbook, campus ministries, international student organization. **Organizations:** 99 registered organizations, 3 honor societies, 9 religious organizations. **Athletics (Intercollegiate):** *Men:* Baseball, basketball, crew/rowing, cross-country, diving, football, golf, lacrosse, skiing (downhill/alpine), skiing (nordic/cross-country), soccer, squash, swimming, tennis, track/field (outdoor). *Women:* Basketball, crew/rowing, cross-country, diving, field hockey, golf, lacrosse, skiing (downhill/alpine), skiing (nordic/cross-country), soccer, softball, squash, swimming, tennis, track/field (outdoor), volleyball.

BOTTOM LINE

The education that one receives at an institution like Bates College does not come without a price. When all costs are totaled–tuition, room, board, fees…a figure of $55,000 is arrived at. But, have no fear, students and parents; Bates College also meets 100 percent of average need. The total financial aid package is a whopping $35,000, on average, and the total need-based gift aid is only a few thousand less. Nearly half of all undergrads receive financial aid. The average graduate can expect to leave school with about $19,000 of loan debt. Additionally, scholarships and grants are plentiful, for international as well as domestic students. One student was excited that Bates "provided me the greatest amount of financial aid. It was very generous."

SELECTIVITY

Admissions Rating	**94**
# of applicants	4,517
% of applicants accepted	32
% of acceptees attending	34
# accepting a place on wait list	265
% admitted from wait list	12

FRESHMAN PROFILE

Range SAT Critical Reading	**620–710**
Range SAT Math	**620–700**
Range SAT Writing	**638–713**
Range ACT Composite	**29–32**
% graduated top 10% of class	**66**
% graduated top 25% of class	**92**
% graduated top 50% of class	**100**

DEADLINES

Regular Deadline	**1/1**
Normal registration	**yes**

FACILITIES

Housing: Coed dorms, men's dorms, women's dorms, theme houses, quiet/study houses and halls, chem-free and low chem houses and halls. *Special Academic Facilities/Equipment:* Art gallery, Edmund S. Muskie Archives, language labs, planetarium, 600-acre conservation area on seacoast for environmental studies, scanning electron microscope, Imaging Center. *Computers:* 40% of classrooms, 100% of dorms, 100% of libraries, 100% of dining areas, 100% of student union, 10% of common outdoor areas have wireless network access.

FINANCIAL FACTS

Financial Aid Rating	**95**
Annual tuition	$53,300
% frosh rec. need-based scholarship or grant aid	41
% UG rec.need-based scholarship or grant aid	42
% frosh rec. need-based self-help aid	40
% UG rec. need-based self-help aid	43
% frosh rec. any financial aid	43
% UG rec. any financial aid	45
% UG borrow to pay for school	36
Average cumulative indebtedness	$18,699

Beloit College

700 College Street, Beloit, WI 53511 • Admissions: 608-363-2500 • Financial Aid: 608-363-2663

CAMPUS LIFE

Quality of life Rating	82
Fire Safety Rating	71
Green rating	68
Type of School	Private
Environment	Town

STUDENTS

Total undergrad enrolllment	1,308
% Male to Female	43/57
% From out of state	77
% From public high school	79
% Live on Campus	99
# of Fraternities	3
# of Sororities	3
% African American	3
% Asian	2
% Caucasian	73
% Hispanic	7
% International	9
# Of Countries Represented	45

ACADEMICS

Academic Rating	89
% Of students graduating within 4 years	67
% Of students graduating within 6 years	77
Calendar	semester
Profs interesting rating	91
Profs accessible rating	95
Most common reg class size	10–19 students
Most common lab size	10–15 students

MOST POPULAR MAJORS

Anthropology, international relations, politcal science

SPECIAL STUDY OPTIONS

Double major, English as a Second Language (ESL), exchange student program (domestic), independent study, internships, liberal arts/career combination, student-designed major, study abroad, teacher certification program, 3-2 Programs in Engineering and Forestry. Over half of our graduates earn credit off-campus for at least a semester through our comprehensive study abroad and "field term" programs.

ABOUT THE SCHOOL

A recent graduate tells us that Beloit University allows students to "spend four years challenged to explore their passions, excel in their studies, and apply the lessons of the classroom to the larger world, in their careers, and in service to others. That focus–putting the liberal arts into practice–has long set this college and its graduates apart." This Wisconsin liberal arts school stands out for the value and opportunity it presents students. College admissions staff members tell us, "Study abroad, intern¬ships, research, service, and work opportunities are typical examples of the ways the Beloit experience extends beyond the classroom. Beloit students are more apt to value learning for its own sake and at the same time, understand the connec¬tion between college and the rest of their lives as citizens of the world."

Students have a similar feeling about their alma mater. When asked what drew them to Beloit, one student explained, "I love the fact that so many Beloit students study abroad." Other undergraduates are equally effusive, saying "the academic experience at Beloit…is very personal and friendly," placing the emphasis "on cooperating while at the same time developing each unique individual however his/her potential/interest leads." Another student adds, "Even though professors have a range of teaching styles, classes are very interdisciplinary and often work well in conjunction with other courses, even if the professors didn't really plan for that to happen!"

BANG FOR YOUR BUCK

Beloit takes a well-rounded approach to the admission process. The college works diligently to assess the students' total background. While most weight is given to a candidate's secondary school transcript, which is evaluated not only for grades but also for academic rigor, significant attention is also paid to essays and recommendations. Counselors strive to find students who not only demonstrate success in the classroom but also display strong character and leadership skills. An advisor says that "This allows Beloit students to explore social, academic, and occupational aspects of life in an experimental, hands-on manner and provides equal opportunities for all disciplines." An undergraduate adds, "Beloit is about classes which teach the student to look at topics in a broad sense and is also a school that shows kids how to prepare for their future."

STUDENTS

1,308 undergrad enrollment

43% Male ♂♂♂♂♂♂♂♂♂♂

57% Female ♀♀♀♀♀♀♀♀♀♀♀♀

ADMISSIONS

2,003 applicants → 73% admitted — 23% enrolled

EARLY ADMISSIONS → NR applicants — NR accepted

3.42 avg. high school gpa

reading 570–700

math 620–680

24-30

ACT range 0–36

SAT range 200–800

GRADUATION RATES

67% of students graduating within 4 yrs

77% of students graduating within 6 yrs

E-MAIL: ADMISS@BELOIT.EDU • FAX: 608-363-2075 • WEBSITE: WWW.BELOIT.EDU

STUDENT BODY

"Everybody has a niche at Beloit, whether you're interested in Greek life or LARPing on Saturday nights, and everything in between," and students "are really friendly, even (if not especially) with others who have wildly different interests" because "Beloit students are generally very curious about and accepting of the unfamiliar, with the single exception of religion. Christians at Beloit sometimes feel they need to hide their faith or risk being judged as conservative, judgmental, or uptight." Indeed, most here are "very liberal," which can make "discussion hard sometimes because so many people have the same ideas. Those with more conservative ideas either don't talk about their political views or are very bad at it."

WHY STUDENTS LOVE BELOIT COLLEGE

Beloit students care about making their college experience the best that it can be, and the college puts that within reach. "The value is placed on the people who comprise our school, not the money or the numbers," explains a sophomore. Another undergrad mentions that "I mostly chose Beloit because of the excellent financial aid, wide range of majors, and the eclectic student body." Beloit College is unique in all senses of the word. "Beloit is about having a diverse college experience, inside and out of the classroom." Most weeknights are spent doing homework, attending meetings and clubs, and some socializing. Although later in the week, that does tend to change a bit. As one student explains, "Most weekends I attend events of campus, watch movies with friends, and go to some of the crazy theme parties they have here."

Why Students love Beloit College

"The school is VERY generous with scholarships/financial aid."

GENERAL INFO

Activities: Choral groups, dance, drama/theater, jazz band, literary magazine, music ensembles, musical theater, radio station, student government, student newspaper, student-run film society, symphony orchestra, television station, yearbook, international student organization. **Organizations:** 95 registered organizations, 6 honor societies, 3 religious organizations. 3 fraternities, 3 sororities. **Athletics (Intercollegiate):** *Men:* Baseball, basketball, cross-country, football, golf, soccer, swimming, tennis, track/field (outdoor), track/field (indoor). *Women:* Basketball, cross-country, soccer, softball, swimming, tennis, track/field (outdoor), track/field (indoor), volleyball. **On-Campus Highlights:** Logan Museum of Anthropology, Wright Museum of Art, Center for the Sciences, Alfred S. Thompson Observatory, Laura H. Idrich Neese Theatre Complex. Other popular spaces include the Poetry Garden, the Java Joint, Morse Library, and Sports Center.

BOTTOM LINE

Annual tuition at Beloit College is just more than $36,000; room, board, and books will increase the total amount by $8,000. Generously, more than 70 percent of freshmen receive need-based scholarship or grant aid. Also, a very high number of students receive financial assistance packages–more than 90 percent, in fact. With an average cumulative indebtedness upon graduation being approximately $20,000, more than 70 percent of students do need to borrow in order to attend Beloit. However, as one student notes admiringly, "The school is VERY generous with scholarships/financial aid."

SELECTIVITY

Admissions Rating	**90**
# of applicants	2,003
% of applicants accepted	72
% of acceptees attending	23
# accepting a place on wait list	23
% admitted from wait list	43

FRESHMAN PROFILE

Range SAT Critical Reading	**570–700**
Range SAT Math	**620–680**
Range ACT Composite	**24–30**
Average HS GPA	**3.42**
% graduated top 10% of class	**42**
% graduated top 25% of class	**71**
% graduated top 50% of class	**94**

DEADLINES

Regular Deadline	**1/1**
Normal registration	**yes**

FACILITIES

Housing: Coed dorms, women's dorms, fraternity/sorority housing, cooperative housing, apartments for single students, theme housing. *Special Academic Facilities/Equipment:* Wright Museum of Art, Logan Museum of Anthropology, Center for Language Study. *Computers:* 80% of classrooms, 10% of dorms, 100% of libraries, 100% of dining areas, 80% of student union, 4% of common outdoor areas have wireless network access.

FINANCIAL FACTS

Financial Aid Rating	**94**
Annual tuition	$36,444
Room and Board	$7,502
Required Fees	$230
Books and supplies	$600
% frosh rec. need-based scholarship or grant aid	70
% UG rec.need-based scholarship or grant aid	66
% frosh rec. non-need-based scholarship or grant aid	28
% UG rec. non-need-based scholarship or grant aid	25
% frosh rec. need-based self-help aid	70
% UG rec. need-based self-help aid	66
% frosh rec. any financial aid	94
% UG rec. any financial aid	90
% UG borrow to pay for school	69
Average cumulative indebtedness	$19,564

Boston College

140 Commonwealth Avenue, Devlin Hall 208, Chestnut Hill, MA 02467-3809 • Admissions: 617-552-3100

CAMPUS LIFE

Quality of life Rating	89
Fire Safety Rating	91
Green rating	85
Type of School	Private
Environment	City

STUDENTS

Total undergrad enrolllment	9,099
% Male to Female	48/52
% From out of state	72
% From public high school	51
% Live on Campus	83
% African American	5
% Asian	10
% Caucasian	65
% Hispanic	9
% International	3
# Of Countries Represented	91

ACADEMICS

Academic Rating	84
% Of students graduating within 4 years	85
Calendar	semester
Profs interesting rating	83
Profs accessible rating	85
Most common reg class size	10–19 students

MOST POPULAR MAJORS

Communication studies, English language and literature, finance

HONORS PROGRAMS

Multiple Honors Programs in various schools and departments, along with a Presidential Scholars Program.

SPECIAL STUDY OPTIONS

Accelerated program, cross-registration, distance learning, double major, English as a Second Language (ESL), exchange student program (domestic), honors program, independent study, internships, liberal arts/career combination, student-designed major, study abroad, teacher certification program

ABOUT THE SCHOOL

Boston, one of the finest college towns in the United States, is home to some of the most prestigious institutions of higher learning around. Boston College shoulders this pedigree effortlessly. Within a rich and challenging environment, while promoting "Jesuit ideals in the modern age," the school offers a rigorous and enlightening education. A student says, "Upon my first visit I knew this was the place for me." Students benefit greatly from Boston College's location just outside of downtown Boston, which affords them internship, service-learning, and career opportunities that give them world-class, real-world experiences before they graduate. In addition, Boston College has an excellent career services office that works in concert with BC's renowned network of more than 150,000 alumni to assist students in career placement. Unique Jesuit-inspired service and academic reflection in core courses develop teamwork and analytical thinking skills. Many students are amazed at their own development: "I have never been so challenged and motivated to learn in my life." "I leave virtually every class with useful knowledge and new opinions."

BANG FOR YOUR BUCK

Boston College is one of a very few elite private universities that is strongly committed to admitting students without regard to their family's finances and that also guarantees to meet a student's full demonstrated financial need through to graduation. (That means your aid won't dry up after the heady generosity of freshman year.) For the 2010–2011 school year, Boston College awarded $128.4 million in student financial aid, including $80 million in need-based undergraduate financial aid. In addition, BC offers a highly selective program of merit-based aid that supports selected students from among the top one or two percent of high school achievers in the country. While Boston College is committed to helping superior students attend with need-based financial aid, it is also highly selective. The college's Presidential Scholars Program, in existence since 1995, selects candidates who are academically exceptional and who exhibit through personal interviews the leadership potential for high achievement at a Jesuit university. In addition to offering four-year, full-tuition scholarships to students, the program offers built-in supports for a wide range of co-curricular opportunities, including summer placements for advanced internships and independent study. The Office of International Programs is extremely helpful in getting students interested in and ready for studying abroad and "encourages a 'citizen of the world' mindset."

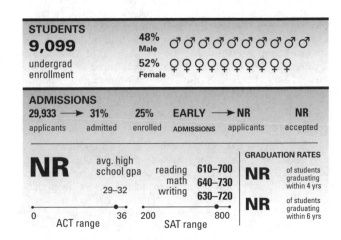

STUDENTS

9,099 undergrad enrollment

48% Male ♂♂♂♂♂♂♂♂♂♂

52% Female ♀♀♀♀♀♀♀♀♀♀

ADMISSIONS

29,933 applicants → **31%** admitted | **25%** enrolled

EARLY ADMISSIONS → **NR** applicants | **NR** accepted

NR avg. high school gpa

ACT range (0–36): 29–32

SAT range (200–800): reading 610–700, math 640–730, writing 630–720

GRADUATION RATES

NR of students graduating within 4 yrs

NR of students graduating within 6 yrs

Fax: 617-552-0798 • Financial Aid: 617-552-3300 • Website: www.bc.edu

STUDENT BODY

Boston College has gotten some flak for its "preppy," "white," and "homogenous" student body, and a communication student admits, "The school's nick- name as 'J. Crew U.' isn't entirely unwarranted," but one student says that each year "the student body becomes more and more diverse." One student says, "Once you've settled in you'll find that it's not at all difficult to find a group of friends" no matter who you are. "There is a large religious/spiritual community," because of the school's Jesuit affiliation, but "it is only one group of many." Boston College's Division I ranking means there are plenty of athletes and sports fans. Students warn that Boston College is "not the place to go to class in your pajamas." People, particularly women, are "very well-dressed" and "stylish." Students say their peers are "really ambitious" and "hardworking."

Why Students love Boston College

"There is just so much school spirit and love for the university!"

WHY STUDENTS LOVE BOSTON COLLEGE

Students benefit in numerous ways from the prime location of the college. "The transportation around campus is very helpful and allows us to get to downtown Boston quickly and efficiently," one student says. There is a new student center and recreation complex, and the campus "is always kept clean and easy to navigate." Students note that "friends at other schools often tell me how jealous they are of the programs that are put on, both in terms of guest lecturers and social functions," and that the social scene is "lively and fun, especially during football season." There's a strong sense of tradition at BC, coupled with its long history of athletic excellence, and "winning sports teams who make attending athletic events and fostering a BC community much more enjoyable." One student observes, "There is just so much school spirit and love for the university!"

GENERAL INFO

Activities: Choral groups, concert band, dance, drama/theater, jazz band, literary magazine, marching band, music ensembles, musical theater, pep band, radio station, student government, student newspaper, student-run film society, symphony orchestra, television station, yearbook, campus ministries, international student organization. **Organizations:** 225 registered organizations, 12 honor societies, 14 religious organizations. **Athletics (Intercollegiate):** *Men:* Baseball, basketball, cross-country, diving, fencing, football, golf, ice hockey, lacrosse, sailing, skiing (downhill/alpine), soccer, swimming, tennis, track/field (outdoor), track/field (indoor). *Women:* Basketball, crew/rowing, cross-country, diving, fencing, field hockey, golf, ice hockey, lacrosse, sailing, skiing (downhill/alpine), soccer, softball, swimming, tennis, track/field (outdoor), track/field (indoor), volleyball.

BOTTOM LINE

The sticker price for tuition, fees, room and board, and everything else at Boston College comes to about $55,000 per year. But you don't have to be an old guard Bostonian to be able to afford to go here. The average need-based financial aid package is $31,000 and includes a $19,000 grant, on average. "Their stellar academics and their generous financial aid were a combination that I couldn't find anywhere else," one grateful student exclaims.

SELECTIVITY

Admissions Rating	**96**
# of applicants	29,933
% of applicants accepted	31
% of acceptees attending	25
# accepting a place on wait list	2,686
% admitted from wait list	4

FRESHMAN PROFILE

Range SAT Critical Reading	**610–700**
Range SAT Math	**640–730**
Range SAT Writing	**630–720**
Range ACT Composite	**29–32**
% graduated top 10% of class	**79**
% graduated top 25% of class	**95**
% graduated top 50% of class	**100**

DEADLINES

Regular Deadline	**1/1**
Normal registration	**yes**

FACILITIES

Housing: Coed dorms, special housing for disabled students, women's dorms, Greycliff Honors House, multicultural and intercultural floors, a quiet floor, social justice floor, a community living floor, and a leadership house. *Special Academic Facilities/Equipment:* Art museum, theatre arts center, on-campus school for multi-handicapped students, athletic facility, state-of-the-art science facilities. *Computers:* 100% of classrooms, 100% of dorms, 100% of libraries, 100% of dining areas, 100% of student union, 100% of common outdoor areas have wireless network access.

FINANCIAL FACTS

Financial Aid Rating	**94**
Annual tuition	$41,480
Room and Board	$12,324
Required Fees	$1,174
Books and supplies	$900
% frosh rec. need-based scholarship or grant aid	39
% UG rec.need-based scholarship or grant aid	37
% frosh rec. non-need-based scholarship or grant aid	1
% UG rec. non-need-based scholarship or grant aid	1
% frosh rec. need-based self-help aid	39
% UG rec. need-based self-help aid	37
% frosh rec. any financial aid	61
% UG rec. any financial aid	66
% UG borrow to pay for school	49
Average cumulative indebtedness	$19,514

Bowdoin College

5000 College Station, Bowdoin College, Brunswick, ME 04011-8441 • Admissions: 207-725-3100

CAMPUS LIFE

Quality of life Rating	99
Fire Safety Rating	94
Green rating	96
Type of School	Private
Environment	Village

STUDENTS

Total undergrad enrollment	1,751
% Male to Female	50/50
% From out of state	88
% From public high school	58
% Live on Campus	93
% African American	5
% Asian	7
% Caucasian	65
% Hispanic	12
% International	3
# Of Countries Represented	31

ACADEMICS

Academic Rating	99
% Of students graduating within 4 years	90
% Of students graduating within 6 years	93
Calendar	semester
Profs interesting rating	96
Profs accessible rating	97
Most common reg class size	10–19 students
Most common lab size	10–19 students

MOST POPULAR MAJORS

Biology, economics
political science

SPECIAL STUDY OPTIONS

Accelerated program, double major, exchange student program (domestic), independent study, liberal arts/career combination, student-designed major, study abroad, teacher certification program, 3-2 or 4-2 Engineering Degree Programs with Dartmouth College, California Institute of Technology, Columbia University and the University of Maine; and 3-3 Legal Studies Degree Program with Columbia University Law School.

ABOUT THE SCHOOL

Bowdoin College has a lot to offer its happy students, including rigorous and varied academic offerings, a picturesque setting, and a vibrant community of faculty and fellow students. It even has great food; Bowdoin is particularly well-known for its dining services. The college has two major dining halls, and every academic year Bowdoin welcomes students back to campus with a lobster bake, "a venerable Bowdoin institution in and of itself." Small, discussion-oriented classes are the norm; professors are accessible and genuinely invested in student's success, often making time to meet with students one-on-one. Students say that "between the professors, students, deans, and other faculty, we have a really great support system."

Campus life is pretty cushy at Bowdoin. Dorms are beautiful. Dining services are top-notch. Hometown Brunswick is lovely, and students say they "love how Bowdoin is integrated in the community." Most of the students here hail from New England. Initially, they might come across as a little preppy, but dig a little deeper and you'll see the diversity lying just beneath the surface. Here, you'll find your jocks and frat boys, but you'll also find skaters, rockers, artsy types, and everything else in between. Students here are very athletic, and almost three-quarters are involved in some kind of sport. One student athlete says that the relationship between academics and athletics is ideal because students are "able to get a phenomenal education while having an amazing athletic experience, neither at the expense of the other." Bowdoin's outdoorsy student body loves to get outside and explore its surrounding environs through the popular Outing Club, which "goes out on numerous trips every week" to explore the countryside.

BANG FOR YOUR BUCK

Bowdoin meets students' demonstrated need with grant money from federal, state and institutional sources. The vast majority of students who apply for financial aid at Bowdoin receive it, and more than 40 percent of enrolled students receive some amount of grant assistance to help pay for college costs. Several students have said that the school gave them "more financial aid than I even thought I'd qualify for," and others say that Bowdoin gave them as much as "$10,000 a year more than any other school" they applied to. Eligibility for Bowdoin grant assistance is "need-based." If necessary, first-year students may elect to borrow up to $5,500 in low interest, federal Stafford loan money. Students graduate with $18,000 in loan debt on average.

STUDENTS

1,751 undergrad enrollment

50% Male ♂♂♂♂♂♂♂♂♂♂

50% Female ♀♀♀♀♀♀♀♀♀♀

ADMISSIONS

6,018 applicants	→ 20% admitted	43% enrolled	EARLY ADMISSIONS	→ NR applicants	NR accepted

3.80 avg. high school gpa

ACT range (0–36): 30–33

SAT range (200–800): reading 650–750, math 660–750, writing 660–750

GRADUATION RATES

90% of students graduating within 4 yrs

93% of students graduating within 6 yrs

FAX: 207-725-3101 • FINANCIAL AID: 207-725-3273 • E-MAIL: ADMISSIONS@BOWDOIN.EDU • WEBSITE: WWW.BOWDOIN.EDU

STUDENT BODY

You'll meet a lot of "wealthy, athletic, New Englanders" at Bowdoin College. In fact, students joke, "Everyone seems to be from a small town right outside Boston." Those outside the dominant demographic admit that there seems to be "a divide between the typical New England kid and the 'diverse' kids, who come from other states are less well-off, or are racially diverse." However, "Students here work really hard to create a community that is open and accepting," and the majority of students have "no trouble fitting in." On that note, "Bowdoin students truly are nice. We often marvel at how there do not seem to be mean or unfriendly people here." Student athletes are common, and "around seventy percent of the campus is involved in some kind of sport," from intramurals to the outing club.

Why Students love Bowdoin

"The dorms are spectacular, the food is awesome, and the campus is just beautiful in general."

WHY STUDENTS LOVE BOWDOIN

Most students agree that it is the people who attend here that set Bowdoin apart from other comparable, prestigious small liberal arts schools. Bowdoin students are "incredibly bright and motivated," but distinguish themselves through "collaboration rather than competition." Students love that their peers are "intensely genuine" and "so willing to help each other." The resulting close-knit community is composed of "enthusiastic, involved students who want to learn and be involved in the extracurricular community." Bowdoin students also love to take advantage of the school's pristine location "within hours of ski areas, national parks, and a bike ride away from the ocean." On top of all this, Bowdoin is known for its "fantastic quality of student life." One student elaborates: "The dorms are spectacular, the food is awesome, and the campus is just beautiful in general. It keeps people in a good mood, which makes the campus such a friendly place."

GENERAL INFO

Activities: Choral groups, concert band, dance, drama/theater, jazz band, literary magazine, music ensembles, musical theater, radio station, student government, student newspaper, student-run film society, symphony orchestra, television station, yearbook, international student organization. **Organizations:** 109 registered organizations, 1 honor societies, 4 religious organizations. **Athletics (Intercollegiate):** *Men:* Baseball, basketball, cross-country, diving, football, golf, ice hockey, lacrosse, sailing, skiing (nordic/cross-country), soccer, squash, swimming, tennis, track/field (outdoor), track/field (indoor). *Women:* Basketball, cross-country, diving, field hockey, golf, ice hockey, lacrosse, rugby, sailing, skiing (nordic/cross-country), soccer, softball, squash, swimming, tennis, track/field (outdoor), track/field (indoor), volleyball.

BOTTOM LINE

Incoming freshmen at Bowdoin can expect to pay about $42,000 in tuition and roughly another $400 in required fees. On-campus room and board totals more than $11,000. When you factor in other costs like, books, personal expenses, and travel, that brings the total sticker price to more than $55,000.

SELECTIVITY

Admissions Rating	**98**
# of applicants	6,018
% of applicants accepted	20
% of acceptees attending	43

FRESHMAN PROFILE

Range SAT Critical Reading	**650–750**
Range SAT Math	**660–750**
Range SAT Writing	**660–750**
Range ACT Composite	**30–33**
Average HS GPA	**3.80**
% graduated top 10% of class	**83**
% graduated top 25% of class	**97**
% graduated top 50% of class	**100**

DEADLINES

Regular Deadline	**1/1**
Normal registration	**no**

FACILITIES

Housing: Coed dorms, special housing for disabled students, apartments for single students, wellness housing, 3 small college houses, and 8 college house system houses. *Special Academic Facilities/Equipment:* Art museum; Arctic Museum; Arctic Studies Center; coastal marine biology and ornithology research facility on Orr's Island; scientific station on Kent Island; black box theater; Pickard Theater; Baldwin Center for Learning and Teaching; Outdoor Leadership Center.

FINANCIAL FACTS

Financial Aid Rating	**97**
Annual tuition	$42,386
Room and Board	$11,654
Required Fees	$430
Books and supplies	$820
% frosh rec. need-based scholarship or grant aid	47
% UG rec.need-based scholarship or grant aid	43
% frosh rec. non-need-based scholarship or grant aid	46
% UG rec. non-need-based scholarship or grant aid	40
% frosh rec. need-based self-help aid	35
% UG rec. need-based self-help aid	34
% frosh rec. any financial aid	44
% UG rec. any financial aid	47
% UG borrow to pay for school	43
Average cumulative indebtedness	$18,229

Brandeis University

415 South St, MS003, Waltham, MA 02454-9110 • Admissions: 781-736-3500 • Financial Aid: 781-736-3700

CAMPUS LIFE

Quality of life Rating	81
Fire Safety Rating	91
Green rating	90
Type of School	Private
Environment	City

STUDENTS

Total undergrad enrolllment	3,341
% Male to Female	44/56
% From out of state	73
% From public high school	70
% Live on Campus	77
% African American	9
% Asian	12
% Caucasian	48
% Hispanic	6
% International	12
# Of Countries Represented	59

ACADEMICS

Academic Rating	87
% Of students graduating within 4 years	86
% Of students graduating within 6 years	91
Calendar	semester
Profs interesting rating	83
Profs accessible rating	82
Most common reg class size	10–19 students

MOST POPULAR MAJORS

Biology, economics

SPECIAL STUDY OPTIONS

Cross-registration, double major, independent study, internships, student-designed major, study abroad.

ABOUT THE SCHOOL

The distinctive elements of a Brandeis University education are the intense intellectual engagement students share with faculty who are at the cutting-edge of their disciplines, in addition to the interdisciplinary connections and perspectives that unite teachers and students in such majors as International and Global Studies, Health and Science, Society and Policy, Film, Television and Interactive Media. "Attending classes at Brandeis is only part of my education," shares one sophomore, "because the students and faculty are interested and involved in social issues and we relate our education to the world around us. The focus is on producing globally and socially aware members of society." Another undergraduate tells us that "Brandeis cares–about learning both inside and outside the classroom, about other people, and about the world around us." A new student adds, "I was impressed by…the many opportunities for experiential learning. There is more to my education than sitting in a classroom, and Brandeis opens many doors for hands-on learning."

Why Students love Brandeis University

"My professors are incredibly talented individuals, and the fact that I can have such close contact with them on a daily basis is really something."

BANG FOR YOUR BUCK

When considering costs, Brandeis has many benefits. This New England campus has financial aid awards that meet the full demonstrated need for all admitted undergraduate students. Additionally, Brandeis has a policy for the treatment of outside scholarships that allows recipients to replace loans and work first, before any adjustment is made to Brandeis need-based scholarship. Most Brandeis students participate in internships connected with their liberal arts interests, either for credit or not. By graduation students have participated, on average, in three internships and have the experiences sought by top graduate schools and employers.

STUDENTS

3,341 undergrad enrollment

44% Male ♂♂♂♂♂♂♂♂♂

56% Female ♀♀♀♀♀♀♀♀♀♀♀

ADMISSIONS

7,753 applicants	→ 35% admitted	25% enrolled	EARLY ADMISSIONS	→ NR applicants	NR accepted

3.77 avg. high school gpa

ACT range (0–36): 28-32

SAT range (200–800): reading 630–730, math 640–730, writing 640–730

GRADUATION RATES

86% of students graduating within 4 yrs

91% of students graduating within 6 yrs

Brandeis University

E-MAIL: ADMISSIONS@BRANDEIS.EDU • FAX: 781-736-3536 • WEBSITE: WWW.BRANDEIS.EDU

STUDENT BODY

"There is no 'typical student' except that generally people are driven and creative," Brandeis undergrads tell us. Most here "are passionate about some thing and have many interests, though those interests are varied." Students tend to be "involved in a variety of activities" that include "community service or a peace group of some sort." Most are "probably double-majoring;" are "into dance, singing, or a musical band of some sort;" and have "frequent contact with leaders, administrators, and faculty." They're also likely to be "quirky... the reason they come to Brandeis is because they're drawn to these qualities... What other university would host a silent dance in their Campus Center where everyone's listening to their own iPod?" As one student sums up, "The typical student is studious, liberal, and passionate. Also Jewish. But not everyone is Jewish. There are atypical students, but the great thing about Brandeis is that we don't care if you're different."

WHY STUDENTS LOVE BRANDEIS COLLEGE

"The variety of options for students in terms of events, classes, etc. motivated me to select Brandeis," states one undergrad, continuing that "the main reason I chose to attend was the academics, hands down. My professors are incredibly talented individuals, and the fact that I can have such close contact with them on a daily basis is really something." Professor accessibility is something admired throughout the student body,, and teachers are very dedicated to student success. Instructors here "know your name, which in the end is important for things like recommendations," mentions a satisfied undergrad. "You are just not going to get that kind of contact at larger schools. College is a personal investment, and Brandeis invests in its people."

GENERAL INFO

Activities: Choral groups, concert band, dance, drama/ theater, jazz band, literary magazine, music ensembles, musical theater, radio station, student government, student newspaper, student-run film society, symphony orchestra, television station, yearbook, campus ministries, international student organization. **Organizations:** 253 registered organizations, 4 honor societies, 19 religious organizations. **Athletics (Intercollegiate):** *Men:* Baseball, basketball, cross-country, diving, fencing, soccer, tennis, track/ field (outdoor), track/field (indoor), wrestling. *Women:* Basketball, cheerleading, cross-country, diving, fencing, soccer, softball, tennis, track/field (outdoor), track/field (indoor), volleyball, wrestling. **On-Campus Highlights:** Shapiro Science Center, Spingold Theater, Usen Castle, Shapiro Campus Center, Rapaporte Treasure Hall. **Environmental Initiatives:** The Brandeis University Climate Action Plan has aggressive goals for future energy and climate impact reductions. Brandeis has invested significantly in energy reduction efforts.

BOTTOM LINE

Brandeis University, while providing a diverse curriculum and fantastic educational experience, has a yearly tuition of nearly $39,000. After including another $13,000 for room, board, books, and fees, one becomes quickly aware that financial support is essential for many students. Fortunately, need-based scholarships and grants are provided to nearly 60 percent of freshman, with the same percentage of the student body being recipients of financial aid. Approximately two-thirds of undergrads will borrow to pay for school; their average total debt will be more than $21,000 upon leaving Brandeis.

SELECTIVITY

Admissions Rating	**78**
# of applicants	7,753
% of applicants accepted	35
% of acceptees attending	25
# accepting a place on wait list	469
% admitted from wait list	38

FRESHMAN PROFILE

Range SAT Critical Reading	**630–730**
Range SAT Math	**640–730**
Range SAT Writing	**640–730**
Range ACT Composite	**28–32**
Average HS GPA	**3.77**
% graduated top 10% of class	**84**
% graduated top 25% of class	**97**
% graduated top 50% of class	**100**

DEADLINES

Regular Deadline	**1/1**
Normal registration	**yes**

FACILITIES

Housing: Coed dorms, men's dorms, women's dorms, apartments for single students, Thematic Learning Communities. *Special Academic Facilities/Equipment:* Art museum, multicultural library, intercultural center, theater arts complex, language lab, spatial orientation lab, research centers on aging, *Computers:* 100% of classrooms, 100% of dorms, 100% of libraries, 100% of dining areas, 100% of student union, 100% of common outdoor areas have wireless network access.

FINANCIAL FACTS

Financial Aid Rating	**82**
Annual tuition	$40,514
Room and Board	$11,894
Required Fees	$1,546
Books and supplies	$1,000
% frosh rec. need-based scholarship or grant aid	57
% UG rec.need-based scholarship or grant aid	45
% frosh rec. non-need-based scholarship or grant aid	6
% UG rec. non-need-based scholarship or grant aid	3
% frosh rec. need-based self-help aid	51
% UG rec. need-based self-help aid	41
% frosh rec. any financial aid	55
% UG rec. any financial aid	58
% UG borrow to pay for school	70
Average cumulative indebtedness	$21,351

Brown University

Box 1876, 45 Prospect St, Providence, RI 02912 • Admissions: 401-863-2378 • Fax: 401-863-9300

CAMPUS LIFE

Quality of life Rating	98
Fire Safety Rating	79
Green rating	92
Type of School	Private
Environment	City

STUDENTS

Total undergrad enrollment	6,318
% Male to Female	48/52
% From out of state	96
% From public high school	56
% Live on Campus	79
% African American	10
% Asian	15
% Caucasian	44
% Hispanic	9
% Native American	1
% International	10
# Of Countries Represented	110

ACADEMICS

Academic Rating	95
% Of students graduating within 4 years	86
% Of students graduating within 6 years	96
Calendar	semester
Profs interesting rating	88
Profs accessible rating	89
Most common reg class size	10–19 students

MOST POPULAR MAJORS

Biology, economics
international relations

SPECIAL STUDY OPTIONS

Cross-registration, double major, exchange student program (domestic), honors program, independent study, internships, student-designed major, study abroad, teacher certification program, 8-year medical program (AB or SCB plus MD) 5-year degree program (AB and SCB).

ABOUT THE SCHOOL

Located in historic Providence, Rhode Island and founded in 1764, Brown University is the seventh-oldest college in the United States. Brown is an independent, coeducational Ivy League institution. With its talented and motivated student body and accomplished faculty, Brown is a leading research university that maintains a particular commitment to exceptional undergraduate instruction. Known for its somewhat unconventional (but still highly regarded) approaches to life and learning, Brown University remains the slightly odd man out of the Ivy League, and the school wouldn't have it any other way. The school's willingness to employ and support different, methods such as the shopping period, the first two weeks of the semester where anyone can drop into any class to "find out if it's something they're interested in enrolling in," or the Critical Review, a student publication that produces reviews of courses based on evaluations from students who have completed the course, is designed to treat students "like an adult" through "freedom and choice." This open-minded environment allows them "to practice passion without shame or fear of judgment," the hallmark of a Brown education. Even if students do find themselves exploring the wrong off-the-beaten path, "there are multitudes of built-in support measures to help you succeed despite any odds." Other students tell us, "I have always considered the goal of college to teach students how to think, and Brown does exactly that;" "Brown, among all else, values knowledge and the independent pursuit of it."

BANG FOR YOUR BUCK

The Brown community forges an original relationship with the world and makes a distinctive contribution to global research, service and education. Brown's global reach extends beyond the gates of campus to establish the university's place as a positive force in a complex and interconnected world. Brown students, staff, and faculty are engaged in local schools, religious groups, charities and social justice organizations. Students are encouraged to get involved in the diverse and dynamic communities beyond the campus gates. The independent nature of the school in general "is one of the things that makes it such a strong institution," according to a student here. Because of the Open Curriculum, "we have the freedom to study what we want to study, unhindered by a core curriculum, with the connections and resources that an Ivy provides." Another undergrad is pleased that "it allows me to truly figure out what I would love to study and pursue." "It may seem intimidating because there is not much of a guide as to what a student should take, but it depends on the student to pave his or her own way."

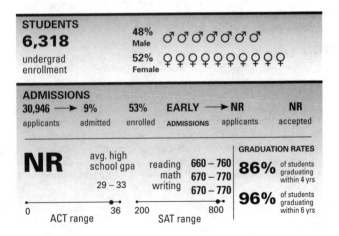

STUDENTS

6,318 undergrad enrollment

48% Male ♂♂♂♂♂♂♂

52% Female ♀♀♀♀♀♀♀♀♀♀

ADMISSIONS

30,946 applicants → 9% admitted | 53% enrolled | EARLY ADMISSIONS → NR applicants | NR accepted

NR avg. high school gpa

ACT range (0–36): 29 – 33

SAT range (200–800): reading 660 – 760; math 670 – 770; writing 670 – 770

GRADUATION RATES

86% of students graduating within 4 yrs

96% of students graduating within 6 yrs

Brown University

FINANCIAL AID: 401-863-2721 • E-MAIL: ADMISSION_UNDERGRADUATE@BROWN.EDU • WEBSITE: WWW.BROWN.EDU

STUDENT BODY

Students are diligent in their academic pursuits and feel assured they're "getting a wonderful education with the professors," most agree that their education is "really more about the unique student body and learning through active participation in other activities." It's a pretty unique crowd here, where "athletes, preps, nerds, and everyone in between come together" because they "love learning for the sake of learning, and [they] love Brown equally as much." "The 'mainstream' is full of people who are atypical in sense of fashion, taste in music, and academic interests," says a junior. Unsurprisingly, everyone here's "very smart," as well as "very quirky and often funny," and "a great amount are brilliant and passionate about their interests;" "most have interesting stories to tell." People here are "curious and open about many things," which is perhaps why sexual diversity is a "strong theme" among Brown interactions and events. The overall culture "is pretty laid-back and casual," and "most of the students are friendly and mesh well with everyone."

Why Students love Brown University

"Athletes, preps, nerds, and everyone in between come together."

WHY STUDENTS LOVE BROWN UNIVERSITY

Brown's location on College Hill is beautiful–"quintessential New England architecture with hidden cobblestone streets and enchanting historic homes." Thinking–yes, thinking–and discussing take up a great deal of time at Brown. "People think about life, politics, society at large, global affairs, the state of the economy, developing countries, animals, plants, rocket science, math, poker, each other, sex, sexuality, the human experience, gender studies, what to do with our lives, etc.," says a senior anthropology major. "Most people here don't go home that often," and like any school, "There are people who go out five nights a week and people who go out five nights a semester," but partying "never gets in the way of academics or friendship. If you don't drink/smoke, that's totally cool." There's also plenty of cultural activities, such as indie bands, student performances, jazz, swing dancing, and speakers. Themed housing (art house, tech house, interfaith house) and co-ops are also popular social mediators. There is a lot to do in the city of Providence, too, and Brown students get free public transportation privileges.

GENERAL INFO

Activities: Choral groups, concert band, dance, drama/theater, jazz band, literary magazine, marching band, music ensembles, musical theater, opera, pep band, radio station, student government, student newspaper, student-run film society, symphony orchestra, television station, yearbook, campus ministries, international student organization. **Organizations:** 400 registered organizations, 3 honor societies, 20 religious organizations. 8 fraternities, 2 sororities.

BOTTOM LINE

Obviously, the stellar education and overall academic experience a student receives from such an impressive institution as Brown University does not come without a cost. Tuition is over $40,000 per year, with room and board adding another $11,000. With $2,200 more for books, supplies, and fees, total costs are approximately $55,000. However, Brown University generously meets 100% of all need; more than 40% of undergrads receive financial aid, with the average being well more than $35,000.

SELECTIVITY

Admissions Rating	**98**
# of applicants	30,946
% of applicants accepted	9
% of acceptees attending	53
# accepting a place on wait list	600
% admitted from wait list	5

FRESHMAN PROFILE

Range SAT Critical Reading	**660–760**
Range SAT Math	**670–770**
Range SAT Writing	**670–770**
Range ACT Composite	**29–33**
% graduated top 10% of class	**93**
% graduated top 25% of class	**99**
% graduated top 50% of class	**100**

DEADLINES

Regular Deadline	**1/1**
Normal registration	**no**

FACILITIES

Housing: Coed dorms, special housing for disabled students, fraternity/sorority housing, cooperative housing, apartments for single students, wellness housing, theme housing. *Special Academic Facilities/Equipment:* Art gallery, anthropology museum, language lab, information technology center, NASA research center, center for modern culture/media. *Computers:* 50% of classrooms, 100% of dorms, 100% of libraries, 100% of dining areas, 100% of student union, 50% of common outdoor areas have wireless network access. Students can register for classes online. Administrative functions (other than registration) can be performed online.

FINANCIAL FACTS

Financial Aid Rating	**93**
Annual tuition	$41,328
Room and Board	$10,906
Required Fees	$902
Books and supplies	$1,358
% frosh rec. need-based scholarship or grant aid	48
% UG rec.need-based scholarship or grant aid	40
% frosh rec. need-based self-help aid	39
% UG rec. need-based self-help aid	40
% frosh rec. any financial aid	49
% UG rec. any financial aid	46
Average cumulative indebtedness	$20,836

Bryn Mawr College

101 North Merion Avenue, Bryn Mawr, PA 19010-2859 • Admissions: 610-526-5152 • Fax: 610-526-7471

CAMPUS LIFE

Quality of life Rating	94
Fire Safety Rating	76
Green rating	79
Type of School	Private
Environment	Metropolis

STUDENTS

Total undergrad enrollment	1,287
% Male to Female	0/100
% From out of state	88
% From public high school	65
% Live on Campus	95
% African American	6
% Asian	12
% Caucasian	39
% Hispanic	9
% International	12
# Of Countries Represented	63

ACADEMICS

Academic Rating	94
% Of students graduating within 4 years	80
% Of students graduating within 6 years	87
Calendar	semester
Profs interesting rating	90
Profs accessible rating	92
Most common reg class size	10–19 students

MOST POPULAR MAJORS

Biology, English language and literature, mathematics

SPECIAL STUDY OPTIONS

Double major, dual enrollment, honors program, independent study, internships, liberal arts/career combination, student-designed major, study abroad, teacher certification program.

ABOUT THE SCHOOL

An intellectually rigorous college like Bryn Mawr delivers an invaluable experience. This all-women's college delivers professors that "are not only passionate about their respective fields, but are also incredibly accessible," and many are on a first-name basis with the students. Labs and facilities are state-of-the-art. Classes here are intense and small, and students emphasize that "the social science and hard science departments are very strong." Stress is a way of life, especially when midterms and finals roll around, but the "passionate" women here say they "manage to find time to form a tight community, despite mounds of schoolwork." The administration is well-liked, not least because it gives students all manner of support in their academic endeavors. Bryn Mawr has a bi-college relationship with Haverford College, meaning that students from either school can live, study, and even major at both schools. They also share career services resources. Bryn Mawr and Haverford are also part of the Tri-College Consortium with Swarthmore College, which allows students from all three schools to use libraries and attend social functions, performances, and lectures on any campus. Cross-registration with Haverford, Swarthmore, and the University of Pennsylvania gives students access to more than 5,000 courses. Students praise the "vast resources offered through the Tri-Co," as well as the opportunities this system provides to "to grow culturally, academically, socially, and politically." Upon graduation, Mawrers can take advantage of a loyal network of successful alumnae who maintain a strong connection to the school.

BANG FOR YOUR BUCK

Bryn Mawr College is deeply committed to enrolling outstanding scholars. To eliminate financial barriers to attendance, the college meets 100 percent of the demonstrated financial need of enrolling students. In 2009–2010 alone, the college awarded $20.4 million dollars in grant assistance to 62 percent of undergraduate students. The average grant is approximately $33,000. If you are a veteran–or will soon be one–Bryn Mawr offers very generous benefits.
In addition, graduates of Bryn Mawr are very competitive when the time comes to find a job. Bryn Mawr provides a tremendous amount of funding for summer internships all over the country and abroad. The Career Development Office works really hard for students, bringing tons of employers to campus each year. There is a multitude of networking opportunities with faithful alumnae as well. Seniors even get free business cards.

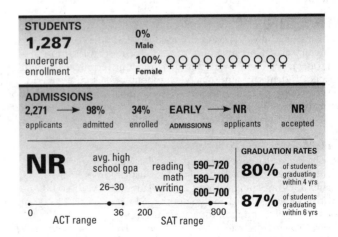

STUDENTS

1,287 undergrad enrollment

0% Male

100% Female ♀♀♀♀♀♀♀♀♀♀

ADMISSIONS

2,271 →	98%	34%	EARLY ADMISSIONS →	NR	NR
applicants	admitted	enrolled		applicants	accepted

NR avg. high school gpa

ACT range (0–36): 26–30

SAT range (200–800): reading 590–720, math 580–700, writing 600–700

GRADUATION RATES

80% of students graduating within 4 yrs

87% of students graduating within 6 yrs

Bryn Mawr College

FINANCIAL AID: 610-526-5245 • E-MAIL: ADMISSIONS@BRYNMAWR.EDU • WEBSITE: WWW.BRYNMAWR.EDU

STUDENT BODY

"There is no typical student," at Bryn Mawr, "aside from women with a passion for learning and a commitment to excellence." A German student reports, "The variety of people here is enormous," and this "creates the...uniqueness that Bryn Mawr prides itself on." People's thoughts on racial diversity, however, "are kind of conflicting." One student explains, "Coming from a big city...Bryn Mawr did not seem very diverse, but my roommate came from a very small town and thought Bryn Mawr was extremely diverse." What students do agree on is that they're "friendly and welcoming," "creative," and "a little quirky." Though the intense workload means students are "very interested in...academics and work hard to get good grades," they "are also social" and "take time to build up strong friendships with other students."

Why Students love Bryn Mawr

"It is a privilege to be surrounded by such knowledgeable, opinionated, and passionate women who want to be at Bryn Mawr and excel in life."

WHY STUDENTS LOVE BRYN MAWR

What many students feel sets Bryn Mawr apart from other top-notch schools is its "incredibly supportive, close community," which is built on an extremely "trusting atmosphere" among the women who go here. This trust is due in large part to the Bryn Mawr Honor Code, a unique and central feature of the university that students love and respect. Students' faithful adherence to this code promotes so much trust in this community of scholars that one student says she "feel[s] safe if I don't lock my door, and professors are comfortable with giving take home exams, knowing that students won't cheat." Bryn Mawr students also love the sense of empowerment that the administration gives them through the student government, which students say is "very strong and powerful on campus." According to one psychology and chemistry major, "the honor code and student government really gives everyone a chance to step up and make a difference in their school."

GENERAL INFO

Environment: Metropolis. **Activities:** Choral groups, dance, drama/theater, jazz band, literary magazine, marching band, music ensembles, musical theater, radio station, student government, student newspaper, student-run film society, yearbook. **Organizations:** 94 registered organizations, 10 religious organizations. **Athletics (Intercollegiate):** Badminton, basketball, crew/rowing, cross-country, field hockey, lacrosse, soccer, swimming, tennis, track/field (outdoor), track/field (indoor), volleyball. **On-Campus Highlights:** Thomas Hall (on National Historic Landma, Erdman Hall (designed by famed architect, The Cloister and Great Hall, Taft Garden, Rhys Carpenter Library, Goodhart Theater.

BOTTOM LINE

Tuition, fees, room and board, and everything else costs a little more than $50,000 each year. While that may seem like a lot, the college's need-based financial aid programs are among the most generous in the country.

SELECTIVITY

Admissions Rating	**92**
# of applicants	2,271
% of applicants accepted	48
% of acceptees attending	34
# accepting a place on wait list	392
% admitted from wait list	5

FRESHMAN PROFILE

Range SAT Critical Reading	**590–720**
Range SAT Math	**580–700**
Range SAT Writing	**600–700**
Range ACT Composite	**26–30**
% graduated top 10% of class	**69**
% graduated top 25% of class	**92**
% graduated top 50% of class	**100**

DEADLINES

Regular Deadline	**1/1**
Normal registration	**no**

FACILITIES

Housing: Coed dorms, women's dorms, cooperative housing, apartments for single students, students may live at Haverford. Foreign language houses available to students studying Chinese, French, German, Hebrew, Italian, Russsian or Spanish. Coed housing is available. *Special Academic Facilities/Equipment:* Museum of classical and Near Eastern archaeology, mineral collection, Child Study Institute, on-campus nursery school, Newfeld Collection of African Art, Language Learning Center.

FINANCIAL FACTS

Financial Aid Rating	**97**
Annual tuition	$39,860
Room and Board	$12,890
Required Fees	$964
Books and supplies	$1,000
% frosh rec. need-based scholarship or grant aid	65
% UG rec.need-based scholarship or grant aid	59
% frosh rec. non-need-based scholarship or grant aid	50
% UG rec. non-need-based scholarship or grant aid	50
% frosh rec. need-based self-help aid	63
% UG rec. need-based self-help aid	54
% frosh rec. any financial aid	79
% UG rec. any financial aid	69
% UG borrow to pay for school	59
Average cumulative indebtedness	$23,809

Bucknell University

Freas Hall, Bucknell University, Lewisburg, PA 17837 • Admissions: 570-577-1101 • Financial Aid: 570-577-1331

CAMPUS LIFE

Quality of life Rating	81
Fire Safety Rating	85
Green rating	87
Type of School	Private
Environment	Village

STUDENTS

Total undergrad enrolllment	3,487
% Male to Female	49/51
% From out of state	76
% From public high school	66
% Live on Campus	88
# of Fraternities	12
# of Sororities	8
% African American	3
% Asian	3
% Caucasian	81
% Hispanic	4
% International	4
# Of Countries Represented	52

ACADEMICS

Academic Rating	94
% Of students graduating within 4 years	89
% Of students graduating within 6 years	91
Calendar	semester
Profs interesting rating	90
Profs accessible rating	92
Most common reg class size	10–19 students
Most common lab size	10–19 students

MOST POPULAR MAJORS

Biology, business administration and managment, economics

SPECIAL STUDY OPTIONS

Double major, dual enrollment, honors program, independent study, internships, liberal arts/career combination, student-designed major, study abroad, teacher certification program.

ABOUT THE SCHOOL

Bucknell University delivers the quintessential East Coast college experience, and one student says it offers a balanced combination of "great academics, a liberal arts education, sterling reputation, and a great social scene." Lewisburg is located in central Pennsylvania and the campus is described as both beautiful and safe. Another student shares his experience, saying "Bucknell was the perfect next step from my high school; it is small enough that your teachers know your name but big enough that you don't know every person on campus. I felt the most comfortable at Bucknell, and I felt that the school actually cared about me as a person, compared to some of the larger state schools to which I applied."

Overall, Bucknell balances reputation with accessibility in a neat package. "It's extremely prestigious, beautiful, and the perfect size," shares one junior. A recent graduate sums up by saying, "Bucknell University is small enough to affect change, but big enough to attract national attention. It is a school where academics are amazing, school spirit is everywhere, and the people genuinely care." Another new student is excited that "Campus pride is obvious, and as a large liberal arts college there are a myriad of opportunities but I don't have to compete with a ton of people to take advantage of them."

BANG FOR YOUR BUCK

Bucknell pride extends into the community, and students become involved socially in many area projects and activities. One student relates, "Bucknell just felt like home. It is big enough where alumni and community connections are a huge benefit, but the campus is small enough that I'm not just a number. Professors take time to know me, and being included in class discussions is not a challenge." Another resident "wanted a small school where I could form close relationships with faculty and have the opportunity to do undergraduate research. So far it has exceeded my expectations, and the faculty and administration have made sure opportunities are within my reach." As another student notes appreciatively, "I also received a scholarship that allowed me to have an internship on campus, giving me work experience on top of my education."

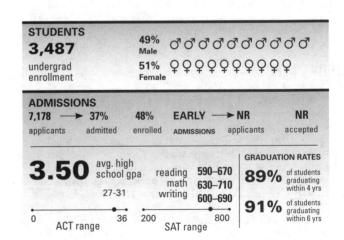

STUDENTS

3,487 undergrad enrollment

49% Male ♂♂♂♂♂♂♂♂♂♂

51% Female ♀♀♀♀♀♀♀♀♀♀

ADMISSIONS

7,178 applicants → 37% admitted | 48% enrolled | EARLY ADMISSIONS → NR applicants | NR accepted

3.50 avg. high school gpa

27-31 — ACT range (0–36)

reading 590–670
math 630–710
writing 600–690 — SAT range (200–800)

GRADUATION RATES

89% of students graduating within 4 yrs

91% of students graduating within 6 yrs

E-MAIL: ADMISSIONS@BUCKNELL.EDU • FAX: 570-577-3538 • WEBSITE: WWW.BUCKNELL.EDU

STUDENT BODY

While there are exceptions to any rule, Bucknell students are predominantly "white, upper-middle class, and from the Northeast." Attracting many likeminded recruits, Bucknellians are "rich but never flashy, classic preppy, intellectual, driven, friendly, social, and very active." Bucknell undergraduates also claim to be a particularly attractive set. Says one, "Our school seems to defy nature with the number of beautiful people on campus." On the whole, most Bucknell undergraduates "find a good balance between school and social life, and they are often dedicated to extracurriculars."

Why Students love Bucknell University

"Bucknell is small enough to know a lot of people, but big enough to be diverse in so many ways."

WHY STUDENTS LOVE BUCKNELL UNIVERSITY

Many students appreciate the value of the prestige of this established college, with its many years of academic success and campus traditions. Students say, "Bucknell is small enough to know a lot of people, but big enough to be diverse in so many ways. Every student is involved in at least some sort of student activity or group, and new student organizations are easily formed." One sophomore told us, "Even though we are in a rural location, there have been very few weekends where I have felt there is nothing to do. There's always plenty of school sponsored activities to keep students entertained in this small town." And as one sophomore explains, "Because it is a small Division 1 school the student body is generally very active and spirited."

GENERAL INFO

Activities: Choral groups, concert band, dance, drama/theater, jazz band, literary magazine, music ensembles, musical theater, opera, pep band, radio station, student government, student newspaper, student-run film society, symphony orchestra, yearbook, campus ministries, international student organization. **Organizations:** 150 registered organizations, 23 honor societies, 13 religious organizations. 12 fraternities, 8 sororities. **Athletics (Intercollegiate):** *Men:* Baseball, basketball, cross-country, diving, football, golf, lacrosse, soccer, swimming, tennis, track/field, water polo, wrestling. *Women:* Basketball, crew/rowing, cross-country, diving, field hockey, golf, lacrosse, soccer, softball, swimming, tennis, track/field, volleyball, water polo.

BOTTOM LINE

Bucknell University provides students with a fine educational experience. The yearly tuition does reflect that monetarily, at more than $40,000 a year. With room, board, and books adding another $11,000, students are making a large but wise investment in their future. The school does provide a variety of options to offset the cost of attending here, with 45 percent of freshmen receiving need-based scholarships or grants. 60 percent of students borrow to pay for school, although the same percentage also receives financial aid packages. Overall, upon graduating, students can expect to have amassed $19,000 in debt. "The school has been generous and fair in financial assistance, and easy to work with," relates a satisfied undergraduate.

SELECTIVITY

Admissions Rating	**96**
# of applicants	7,178
% of applicants accepted	31
% of acceptees attending	41
# accepting a place on wait list	621
% admitted from wait list	13

FRESHMAN PROFILE

Range SAT Critical Reading	**590–670**
Range SAT Math	**620–710**
Range SAT Writing	**600–690**
Range ACT Composite	**27–31**
Average HS GPA	**3.50**
% graduated top 10% of class	**65**
% graduated top 25% of class	**89**
% graduated top 50% of class	**100**

DEADLINES

Regular Deadline	**1/15**
Normal registration	**no**

FACILITIES

Housing: Coed dorms, special housing for disabled students, men's dorms, special housing for international students, women's dorms, fraternity/sorority housing, cooperative housing, apartments for single students, wellness housing, theme housing. *Special Academic Facilities/Equipment:* Art gallery, center for performing arts, poetry center, photography lab, observatory, 63-acre nature site, greenhouse, primate facility, electron microscope, herbarium, nuclear magnetic resonance spectrometer, high ropes course. *Computers:* 100% of classrooms, dorms, libraries, dining areas, student union, 95% of common outdoor areas have wireless network access.

FINANCIAL FACTS

Financial Aid Rating	**93**
Annual tuition	$43,268
Room and Board	$10,374
Required Fees	$238
Books and supplies	$900
% frosh rec. need-based scholarship or grant aid	45
% UG rec.need-based scholarship or grant aid	43
% frosh rec. non-need-based scholarship or grant aid	6
% UG rec. non-need-based scholarship or grant aid	6
% frosh rec. need-based self-help aid	45
% UG rec. need-based self-help aid	46
% frosh rec. any financial aid	62
% UG rec. any financial aid	62
% UG borrow to pay for school	61
Average cumulative indebtedness	$18,900

Carleton College

100 SOUTH COLLEGE STREET, NORTHFIELD, MN 55057 • ADMISSIONS: 507-222-4190 • FAX: 507-222-4526

CAMPUS LIFE

Quality of life Rating	89
Fire Safety Rating	67
Green rating	92
Type of School	Private
Environment	Village

STUDENTS

Total undergrad enrollment	1,991
% Male to Female	49/51
% From out of state	80
% From public high school	60
% Live on Campus	94
% African American	3
% Asian	6
% Caucasian	69
% Hispanic	6
% International	8
# Of Countries Represented	44

ACADEMICS

Academic Rating	95
% Of students graduating within 4 years	89
% Of students graduating within 6 years	93
Calendar	trimester
Profs interesting rating	98
Profs accessible rating	97
Most common reg class size	10–19 students
Most common lab size	10–19 students

MOST POPULAR MAJORS

Biology, political science/international relations, psychology

SPECIAL STUDY OPTIONS

Accelerated program, cross-registration, double major, dual enrollment, independent study, internships, student-designed major, study abroad, teacher certification program.

ABOUT THE SCHOOL

Carleton College emphasizes rigor and intellectual growth, without competition or hubris. Students attracted to Carleton's campus seek meaningful collaboration without the distraction of divisive academic one-upping. And the opportunities to work with bright and engaged students and professors are plentiful. One student explains that "Carleton is not a research college, so while professors do some research, they are much more focused on students." Carleton operates on a trimester calendar, which many students enjoy, saying that "it's nice to be only taking three classes, though more intensely, rather than spreading yourself over four or five." An endless array of social and co-curricular activities is on offer at Carleton, as well as numerous programs for off-campus studies. These opportunities combine rural and urban experiences in a friendly Midwestern environment; students can master Chinese, Japanese, Arabic, and modern Hebrew; they can study in the shadow of a wind turbine generating electricity for the campus; they can choose to live in an environmentally conscious way from their dorm arrangements to the food they eat. Students love the "great study abroad office," which provides students here with "opportunities to travel to China, Thailand, Spain, and Africa."

Experiential learning opportunities are immense here. Carleton Scholars is Carleton's highest-visibility experiential learning program and consists of taste-of-industry tours that introduce a variety of organizations in a particular field of interest, through site visits, panel discussions, receptions, and social activities. The 30 Minutes initiative provides students with access to one-on-one time, group discussion, and candid interviews with Carleton alumni luminaries in many fields. Carleton's Mentor Externships program connects students with alumni for one-four-week short internships, most with a focus project, and generally including home-stays with their alumni hosts.

BANG FOR YOUR BUCK

Carleton's financial aid program is primarily need-based, and the college commits to meeting the need of admitted students fully. This means that a student's aid award will include grants and scholarships from Carleton, applicable government grants, on-campus work, and a reasonable amount of loan. Students graduate with about $18,000 in loan debt on average. Carleton's financial aid program helps support the unique culture and character of this college through its goal of enrolling diverse students regardless of their ability to pay for college. With nearly three-fifths of the student body receiving need-based grant aid, there is a broad socioeconomic representa¬tion across the student body, and students laud Carleton for its "generous financial aid."

STUDENTS
1,991 undergrad enrollment
49% Male ♂♂♂♂♂♂♂♂♂♂
51% Female ♀♀♀♀♀♀♀♀♀♀

ADMISSIONS
4,856 applicants → 30% admitted — 34% enrolled
EARLY ADMISSIONS → NR applicants — NR accepted

NR avg. high school gpa

ACT range (0–36): 27–33

SAT range (200–800): reading 650–750, math 650–750, writing 650–740

GRADUATION RATES
89% of students graduating within 4 yrs
93% of students graduating within 6 yrs

FINANCIAL AID: 507-222-4138 • E-MAIL: ADMISSIONS@CARLETON.EDU • WEBSITE: WWW.CARLETON.EDU

STUDENT BODY

The "creative, warm, compassionate, and helpful" undergrads of Carleton are "quirky," but "Everyone is accepting of these little eccentricities." "Everyone's surprising," writes one student, "and that can be a little exhausting at times," but mostly students embrace the challenges their peers present. They "don't form cliques based on [conventional] criteria" such as "socioeconomic background, race, gender, [or] sexual orientation." An upbeat studio-art major writes, "We have a wonderful mix of people that reaches from nerds to jocks, people who dye their hair to [those] who swear by Abercrombie, people who are Republican to those who are Democrat to those who are Independent to those who don't care; we have vegetarians, and we have people who would live on steak if you let them.

Why Students love Carleton College

"The winters are fun because there's a uniting element in the fact that it's negative 50 degrees outside."

WHY STUDENTS LOVE CARLETON COLLEGE

Students love Carleton College because it provides a "great education with a personal touch and a fun social scene" on a beautiful campus nestled within a small and quaint community in the Midwest. The strong academic environment is a big draw here, and particularly the sciences; one student says that "no other school I found, or have heard of since, is so strongly liberal arts oriented with such serious science departments. I could truly explore what I wanted to do without feeling as though I would have to have a sub-par education in science, if that was what I chose to major in." Professors are "incredibly knowledgeable and accessible" and are able to give students their full attention.

GENERAL INFO

Activities: Choral groups, concert band, dance, drama/theater, jazz band, literary magazine, music ensembles, musical theater, radio station, student government, student newspaper, student-run film society, symphony orchestra, yearbook, campus ministries, international student organization. **Organizations:** 132 registered organizations, 3 honor societies, 17 religious organizations. **Athletics (Intercollegiate):** *Men:* Baseball, basketball, cross-country, diving, football, golf, soccer, swimming, tennis, track/field (outdoor), track/field (indoor). *Women:* Basketball, cross-country, diving, golf, soccer, softball, swimming, synchronized swimming, tennis, track/field (outdoor), track/field (indoor), volleyball. **On-Campus Highlights:** Cowling Arboretum, Art Gallery, Historic Goodsell Observatory, Japanese Garden, Recreation Center, Sayles Campus Center, Library.

BOTTOM LINE

At Carleton College, the total cost for tuition and fees and room and board comes to about $52,000 annually. Fortunately, the folks writing the checks at Carleton believe that cost should not be an obstacle to achieving a Carleton education. The average financial aid package for freshman includes a grant totaling $25,000–that gets you halfway there. When you factor in Carleton's other financial aid offerings in the form of scholarships, work-study, and loans, the dollar amount will seem much more manageable.

SELECTIVITY

Admissions Rating	**96**
# of applicants	4,856
% of applicants accepted	30
% of acceptees attending	34
# accepting a place on wait list	368
% admitted from wait list	14

FRESHMAN PROFILE

Range SAT Critical Reading	**650–750**
Range SAT Math	**650–750**
Range SAT Writing	**650–740**
Range ACT Composite	**29–33**
% graduated top 10% of class	**76**
% graduated top 25% of class	**93**
% graduated top 50% of class	**100**

DEADLINES

Regular Deadline	**1/15**
Normal registration	**no**

FACILITIES

Housing: Coed dorms, special housing for disabled students, apartments for single students. *Special Academic Facilities/Equipment:* Arboretum, greenhouse, observatory, scanning and transmission electron microscopes, refractor and reflector telescopes, nuclear magnetic resonance spectrometer, art gallery. *Computers:* 45% of classrooms, 15% of dorms, 85% of libraries, 50% of dining areas, 100% of student union, 15% of common outdoor areas have wireless network access.

FINANCIAL FACTS

Financial Aid Rating	**99**
Annual tuition	$42,690
Room and Board	$11,328
Required Fees	$252
Books and supplies	$1,460
% frosh rec. need-based scholarship or grant aid	52
% UG rec.need-based scholarship or grant aid	55
% frosh rec. non-need-based scholarship or grant aid	5
% UG rec. non-need-based scholarship or grant aid	10
% frosh rec. need-based self-help aid	50
% UG rec. need-based self-help aid	54
% frosh rec. any financial aid	57
% UG rec. any financial aid	62
% UG borrow to pay for school	44
Average cumulative indebtedness	$19,436

Centenary College of Louisiana

P.O. Box 41188, 2911 Centenary Boulevard, Shreveport, LA 71134-1188 • Admissions: 318-869-5131

CAMPUS LIFE

Quality of life Rating	68
Fire Safety Rating	82
Green rating	60*
Type of School	Private
Environment	Metropolis

STUDENTS

Total undergrad enrolllment	891
% Male to Female	41/59
% From out of state	93
% From public high school	70
% Live on Campus	66
# of Fraternities	5
# of Sororities	2
% African American	8
% Asian	2
% Caucasian	82
% Hispanic	4
% International	2
# Of Countries Represented	12

ACADEMICS

Academic Rating	83
% Of students graduating within 4 years	43
% Of students graduating within 6 years	57
Calendar	semester
Profs interesting rating	89
Profs accessible rating	87
Most common reg class size	10–19 students

MOST POPULAR MAJORS

Biology, business/commerce, mass communication/media studies

SPECIAL STUDY OPTIONS

Cross-registration, double major, dual enrollment, exchange student program (domestic), honors program, independent study, internships, liberal arts/career combination, student-designed major, study abroad, teacher certification program, weekend college, 3/2 Dual Degree (Liberal Arts/Engineering) program in cooperation with Case Western Reserve University, Columbia University, Texas A&M University, University of Southern California, and Washington University in St. Louis; Mathematics/Computer Science double degree program with Southern Methodist University; Semester in Washington, DC; British Studies at Oxford summer program.

ABOUT THE SCHOOL

With fewer than 1,000 undergraduates, Centenary College of Louisiana certainly qualifies as a small school. In fact, there are only a handful of elite undergraduate institutions smaller. That said, smallness has its virtues. As one student notes, "The small size of the student body gives students the opportunity to receive individual attention in class, be involved in many organizations and hold leadership positions outside of class." It also fosters "a community atmosphere" in which "professors really care about you emotionally and academically," along with providing "a lot of one-on-one help and projects." Premedical sciences are said to be excellent (nearly twenty percent of all students major in life sciences), as are business studies, music, and communications. Academics are "extremely rigorous and thorough," so much so that "no one graduates without expanding their knowledge base." As at many small schools, "the professors are absolutely wonderful. They're engaging, knowledgeable, and really care about what they're teaching and about their students." The school places a premium on such high-caliber teaching skill. "Bad teachers do not last long around here," one undergrad assures us. The downside of a small school, of course, is that certain limitations are an unavoidable fact of life. Some "miss the perks a bigger school [has to offer] like more classes and a better cafeteria."

BANG FOR YOUR BUCK

Centenary's applicant pool has grown substantially over the past decade, allowing the school to become more selective in its admissions process. The school's reputation is very solid, and they do a nice job of enrolling those it admits. Centenary takes great pride in treating each applicant as an individual; the application process is very personalized, and the school encourages all interested students to visit. Academics are "extremely rigorous and thorough," with a very competitive curriculum. Professors teach every class, and two-thirds of faculty members have their PhD's. Three-quarters of freshmen return for their sophomore years, and about half go on to pursue graduate studies.

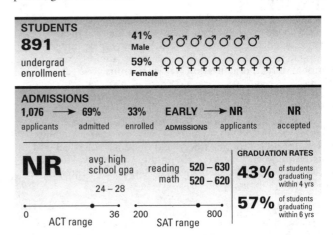

STUDENTS

891 undergrad enrollment

41% Male ♂♂♂♂♂♂♂

59% Female ♀♀♀♀♀♀♀♀♀♀

ADMISSIONS

1,076 applicants → 69% admitted — 33% enrolled

EARLY ADMISSIONS → NR applicants — NR accepted

NR avg. high school gpa

ACT range (0–36): 24 – 28

SAT range (200–800): reading 520 – 630, math 520 – 620

GRADUATION RATES

43% of students graduating within 4 yrs

57% of students graduating within 6 yrs

FAX: 318-869-5005 • FINANCIAL AID: 318-869-5137 • E-MAIL: ADMISSIONS@CENTENARY.EDU • WEBSITE: WWW.CENTENARY.EDU

STUDENT BODY

For such a small school, Centenary does a good job of drawing a diverse mix of interests and backgrounds. Here "You can find everything from far right-wing ministry majors to highly liberal individuals actively involved in campus organizations promoting gay rights" as well as "a large and diverse number of international students, most notably from Europe and Hong Kong." Most students here "are overachievers or hard workers, whether it is in an academic sense or in an extracurricular sense." Though many note that the student body is "generally white, middle-class, and religious," they are also quick to point out that it also accommodates "a lot of gay and lesbian students, and overall, the campus is very accepting and supportive of these students."

Why Students love Centenary College of LA

"You can find everything from far right-wing ministry majors to highly liberal individuals actively involved in campus organizations."

WHY STUDENTS LOVE CENTENARY COLLEGE OF LOUISIANA

Campus life centers around athletics, clubs, and Greek life at Centenary, where "the real trick is finding that one thing that you love (be it sororities, radio, theater, whatever) and excelling at it. The school has a lot of opportunities for responsible individuals." There's the "awesome" radio station, for one, and lots of lectures, internships, and mentoring opportunities. And while "There are occasional events on weekdays, including sports games," when it comes time for fun "life at Centenary revolves around the weekend" and "includes going to some of the local attractions, to a movie, to dinner, or to either one of the sport teams' house or a fraternity house."

GENERAL INFO

Activities: Choral groups, concert band, dance, drama/theater, jazz band, literary magazine, music ensembles, musical theater, opera, radio station, student government, student newspaper, student-run film society, yearbook, campus ministries, international student organization. **Organizations:** 58 registered organizations, 15 honor societies, 8 religious organizations. 5 fraternities, 2 sororities. **Athletics (Intercollegiate):** *Men:* Baseball, basketball, cross-country, golf, soccer, swimming, tennis. *Women:* Basketball, cross-country, golf, gymnastics, soccer, softball, swimming, tennis, volleyball.

BOTTOM LINE

Financial assistance is so astoundingly plentiful at Centenary College, it would seemingly be within just about anyone's budget. Tuition is right around $23,000; with room, board, books, and supplies amounting to roughly $9,000 and another $3,000 for fees and expenses, students are looking at a grand total of $35,000. And now, back to the aid–incredibly, 98% of freshman receive some form of assistance, and 93% of students overall. Nearly 85% of average need is met, with the total financial aid package being in the neighborhood of $19,000, in general. Centenary College of Louisiana certainly makes an admirable effort to provide the opportunity for a quality education to just about everyone.

SELECTIVITY

Admissions Rating	**79**
# of applicants	1,076
% of applicants accepted	69
% of acceptees attending	33

FRESHMAN PROFILE

Range SAT Critical Reading	**520–630**
Range SAT Math	**520–620**
Range ACT Composite	**24–28**
% graduated top 10% of class	**33**
% graduated top 25% of class	**63**
% graduated top 50% of class	**85**

DEADLINES

Regular Deadline	**2/15**
Normal registration	**yes**

FACILITIES

Housing: Coed dorms, women's dorms, fraternity/sorority housing. *Special Academic Facilities/Equipment:* Art museum, Art Center, art studios, theatre, performance and practice organs, piano lab, language lab, School of Music recording studio, Science Hall multimedia auditorium. *Computers:* 50% of classrooms, 25% of dorms, 50% of libraries, 100% of dining areas, 50% of student union, 10% of common outdoor areas have wireless network access.

FINANCIAL FACTS

Financial Aid Rating	**85**
Annual tuition	$22,880
Room and Board	$7,590
Required Fees	$1,200
Books and supplies	$1,200
% frosh rec. need-based scholarship or grant aid	67
% UG rec.need-based scholarship or grant aid	56
% frosh rec. non-need-based scholarship or grant aid	15
% UG rec. non-need-based scholarship or grant aid	16
% frosh rec. need-based self-help aid	46
% UG rec. need-based self-help aid	34
% frosh rec. any financial aid	98
% UG rec. any financial aid	93
% UG borrow to pay for school	64
Average cumulative indebtedness	$19,206

Centre College

600 West Walnut Street, 600 West Walnut, Danville, KY 40422 • Admissions: 859-238-5350 • Fax: 859-238-5373

CAMPUS LIFE

Quality of life Rating	85
Fire Safety Rating	60*
Green rating	82
Type of School	Private
Environment	Village

STUDENTS

Total undergrad enrolllment	1,214
% Male to Female	44/55
% From out of state	39
% From public high school	79
% Live on Campus	99
# of Fraternities	4
# of Sororities	4
% African American	4
% Asian	3
% Caucasian	88
% Hispanic	2
% International	2
# Of Countries Represented	12

ACADEMICS

Academic Rating	94
% Of students graduating within 4 years	79
% Of students graduating within 6 years	81
Calendar	4-1-4
Profs interesting rating	97
Profs accessible rating	98
Most common reg class size	10–19 students
Most common lab size	10–19 students

MOST POPULAR MAJORS

Economics, English language and literature, history

SPECIAL STUDY OPTIONS

Cross-registration, double major, honors program, independent study, internships, student-designed major, study abroad, teacher certification program. Special programs offered to physically disabled students include note-taking services, reader services, voice recorders, tutors.

ABOUT THE SCHOOL

Centre College provides its students with a personal education that enables them to achieve extraordinary success in advanced study and their careers, "bringing a worldwide cultural intellect and perspective to a small town in Kentucky," according to a grateful undergraduate. Professors challenge their students and give them the individual attention and sup¬port they need. Courses are "pertinent to modern issues and thought," says a student. This results in graduates with a can-do attitude and the ability to accomplish their goals. "Preparing students to be actively engaged global citizens" is important here, one student tells us. Academics are of course paramount, but Centre also puts emphasis on community involvement and the social development of its students; there is "a big movement on getting out of the classroom with the community-based learning." "If a professor doesn't require that kind of learning," a student explains, "then they almost always will still make connections outside the classroom whether to real life or to other classes." While Centre is in a small town in rural Kentucky, "there is never a dull moment. " Centre College has an active campus life. Fraternities and sororities have a big presence, but one student says, "There are a lot of students who are involved in Greek life, but there are a fair amount who are not involved in any way."

BANG FOR YOUR BUCK

Centre offers a multitude of advantages, such as a recognized academic reputation, a plethora of majors to choose from, and exposure to internationally known artists and scholars; benefits like these produce extraordinary success. For example, entrance to top graduate and professional schools; the most prestigious postgraduate scholarships (Rhodes, Fulbright, Goldwater); interesting, rewarding jobs (ninety-seven percent of graduates are either employed or engaged in advance study within ten months of graduation). Centre has an impressively strong study abroad program, and about eighty-five percent of their students take advantage; it "allows every student the chance to study abroad, regardless of major or financial situation," reports one student. Another undergrad states proudly that Centre "looks toward the future…of our world and the need for students to be pre¬pared for it." Just about everyone gets a job or accepted into some sort of graduate school after graduation. "They took a chance by letting me attend. I had a below average ACT score than the college accepted. They offered me a great scholarship that allowed attending their school financially feasible. I honor their decision by doing my best, which has led me not only to good grades but also a life changing experience.

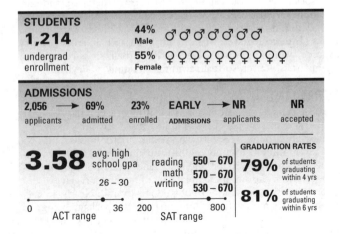

STUDENTS

1,214 undergrad enrollment

44% Male ♂♂♂♂♂♂♂

55% Female ♀♀♀♀♀♀♀♀♀♀

ADMISSIONS

2,056 applicants → **69%** admitted — **23%** enrolled

EARLY ADMISSIONS → **NR** applicants — **NR** accepted

3.58 avg. high school gpa

reading	550 – 670
math	570 – 670
writing	530 – 670

ACT range: 26 – 30 (scale 0–36)

SAT range (scale 200–800)

GRADUATION RATES

79% of students graduating within 4 yrs

81% of students graduating within 6 yrs

Centre College

FINANCIAL AID: 909-621-8205 • E-MAIL: ADMISSION@CENTRE.EDU • WEBSITE: WWW.CENTRE.EDU

STUDENT BODY

Centre College's small student body and rural setting lend it a "welcoming atmosphere" and help create a "close-knit community." Students are "kind, respectful, and friendly to peers, professors, and administrators alike." Students are "hyper-involved," either in athletics, Greek life, the many "clubs and organizations," or all three. Students may "work hard all week," but they still find time to "attend club meetings, support their friends in sporting events, relax in the campus center...attend sorority/fraternity activities, and attend events." The stereotype of the Centre student is one who is "white," "Southern," and "middle or upper-class," but many insist that Centre's student body has "changed dramatically." One student says, "I believe that Centre has lived up to its mission of improving racial diversity on campus."

Why Students love Centre College

"I find myself working harder than I ever thought possible…I feel so accomplished at the end of each semester."

WHY STUDENTS LOVE CENTRE COLLEGE

Centre College offers "a genuine, personal, practical education in all areas of life." Its "small classes" are focused and challenging. An international studies student comments, "I find myself working harder than I ever thought possible…I feel so accomplished at the end of each semester." Students are taught by "extremely passionate and dedicated professors." Teachers are "kind, supportive, caring, and are always available for help outside the classroom," and they make "an effort to work one-on-one with you if necessary." Students love this combination of global, local, and personal learning.

GENERAL INFO

Environment: Village. **Activities:** Choral groups, dance, drama/ theater, jazz band, literary magazine, music ensembles, musical theater, opera, pep band, radio station, student government, student newspaper, symphony orchestra, television station, campus ministries, international student organization. **Organizations:** 70 registered organizations, 12 honor societies, 6 religious organizations. 4 fraternities, 4 sororities.

BOTTOM LINE

Centre's small but capable student body reflects solid academic preparation from high school. If you're ranked in the top quarter of your graduating class and have taken challenging courses throughout high school, you should have no difficulties with the admissions process. Tuition, room, board, books, supplies, and fees will come to $40,000 at Centre College. Although, by meeting 85 percent of student need, an education of the caliber provided by the school is still within reach for most applicants. The average financial aid package is substantial, at around $25,000. Centre College provided one undergraduate with a "good financial aid package and made it possible for a student with little financial means to study abroad." Upon graduation, student loan debt is a very reasonable $17,000.

SELECTIVITY

Admissions Rating	**92**
# of applicants	2,056
% of applicants accepted	69
% of acceptees attending	23
# accepting a place on wait list	69
% admitted from wait list	41

FRESHMAN PROFILE

Range SAT Critical Reading	**550–670**
Range SAT Math	**570–670**
Range SAT Writing	**530–670**
Range ACT Composite	**26–30**
Average HS GPA	**3.58**
% graduated top 10% of class	**59**
% graduated top 25% of class	**84**
% graduated top 50% of class	**98**

DEADLINES

Regular Deadline	**1/15**
Normal registration	**no**

FACILITIES

Housing: Coed dorms, special housing for disabled students, men's dorms, fraternity/ sorority housing, apartments for single students, wellness housing, theme housing. *Special Academic Facilities/Equipment:* Arts center, physical science and math facility, electron microscope, visible and infrared mass spectroscopy equipment, visual arts center.

FINANCIAL FACTS

Financial Aid Rating	**85**
Annual comprehensive tuition	$39,000
Books and supplies	$1,200
% frosh rec. need-based scholarship or grant aid	64
% UG rec.need-based scholarship or grant aid	59
% frosh rec. need-based self-help aid	39
% UG rec. need-based self-help aid	42
% UG borrow to pay for school	53
Average cumulative indebtedness	$17,190

Claremont McKenna College

890 Columbia Avenue, Claremont, CA 91711 • Admissions: 909-621-8088 • Fax: 909-621-8516

CAMPUS LIFE

Quality of life Rating	99
Fire Safety Rating	92
Green rating	84
Type of School	Private
Environment	Town

STUDENTS

Total undergrad enrolllment	1,210
% Male to Female	55/45
% From out of state	56
% From public high school	70
% Live on Campus	98
% African American	3
% Asian	12
% Caucasian	49
% Hispanic	9
% International	6
# Of Countries Represented	24

ACADEMICS

Academic Rating	97
% Of students graduating within 4 years	87
% Of students graduating within 6 years	93
Calendar	semester
Profs interesting rating	99
Profs accessible rating	99
Most common reg class size	10–19 students

MOST POPULAR MAJORS

Economics, international relations, political science

SPECIAL STUDY OPTIONS

Cross-registration, double major, English as a Second Language (ESL), exchange student program (domestic), independent study, internships, student-designed major, study abroad.

ABOUT THE SCHOOL

Part of a new generation of liberal arts colleges, Claremont McKenna College was founded in 1946–more than a century later than many of its East Coast counterparts–but it has steadily built a reputation as one of the nation's best small schools. With a total enrollment of just 1,200 students, the average class size is under 20, making it easy for students to work directly with the school's talented faculty. One literature and government major gushes that her "academic experience has been so rich–full of dinners with Professors outside of class and conversations that make me a better scholar and person. I have been doing research on Robert Frost's letters that would usually be reserved for graduate students." Despite the comfortable environment, academics are surprisingly rigorous and varied. Offering a pragmatic approach to the liberal arts, the college is divided into 12 academic departments offering major programs in fields like biochemistry and history, as well as minor programs or "sequences" in unusual areas such as Asian-American studies and leadership. The most popular majors are economics, accounting, finance, government, and international relations. A psychology major relates that "the campus environment is extremely friendly, open, and career-focused. Students at CMC are motivated to make something of themselves in the world." As a part of the five Claremont colleges, Claremont McKenna offers students the intimacy of a small college with the variety of a larger system. Jointly, the colleges offer more than 2,500 courses, and cross-registration is encouraged (as is eating in neighboring colleges' dining halls.)

BANG FOR YOUR BUCK

Not only is CMC need-blind in its admission policies, but the college is committed to meeting every student's financial need through a combination of merit-based scholarships and need-based awards. There is a no-packaged-loan policy. In addition to state and federal grants, the school offers a number of merit-based scholarship awards derived from gifts and endowments given to the college. Army ROTC Scholarships are also available. The school's website offers detailed information about the amount of aid granted to incoming students in recent years based on their family's income level. Furthermore, for students interested in an unpaid internship with a public or nonprofit organization, the Sponsored Internship Program will provide funding for students to pursue internships anywhere in the world.

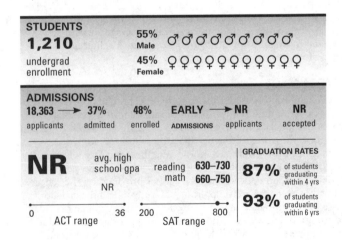

STUDENTS

1,210 undergrad enrollment

55% Male ♂♂♂♂♂♂♂♂♂♂

45% Female ♀♀♀♀♀♀♀♀♀♀♀♀

ADMISSIONS

18,363 →	37%	48%	EARLY →	NR	NR
applicants	admitted	enrolled	ADMISSIONS	applicants	accepted

NR avg. high school gpa NR

reading 630–730
math 660–750

0 — 36 ACT range

200 — 800 SAT range

GRADUATION RATES

87% of students graduating within 4 yrs

93% of students graduating within 6 yrs

Claremont McKenna College

FINANCIAL AID: : 909-621-8356 • E-MAIL: ADMISSION@CLAREMONTMCKENNA.EDU • WEBSITE: WWW.CLAREMONTMCKENNA.EDU

STUDENT BODY

"Claremont McKenna doesn't accept students who aren't amazing." "Amazing" means a "really smart and very physically fit," person who's "incredibly motivated and career-driven." It's "a tight-knit community of driven, competitive, and intelligent people who know how to be successful and have a great time." "A lot of kids are political and well-informed"; most are "active on campus," very into sports, and involved with internships or clubs. But even though the environment is "academically strict, the students...rarely fit the 'nerdy' stereotype." Students are extremely well-rounded; they "know how to lead a discussion...clock hours in the library, play a varsity or club sport, and hold a leadership position in a club or organization," and they also know how to throw "a great party on Saturday night."

Why Students love Claremont McKenna

"CMC is preparing us for the real world through internship opportunities, research with professors, study abroad, and class room discussion."

WHY STUDENTS LOVE CLAREMONT MCKENNA

Students say that "the focus on leadership at CMC is evident in the student body," who love CMC's "concentration on the practical applications of academia that permeate classes and extracurriculars" and value the school's heavy emphasis on success beyond college. "We aren't learning for the sake of learning," says one International Relations major, "but learning for the sake of doing. CMC is preparing us for the real world through internship opportunities, research with professors, study abroad, and class room discussion." To that end, "many professors have invaluable 'real world' experience from years in industry as opposed to a purely academic background," and students say that they "all truly care about our success and always make themselves available for extra help outside of the classroom."

GENERAL INFO

Activities: Choral groups, dance, drama/theater, music ensembles, pep band, radio station, student government, student newspaper, symphony orchestra, yearbook, campus ministries, international student organization. **Organizations:** 280 registered organizations, 7 honor societies, 5 religious organizations. **Athletics (Intercollegiate):** *Men:* Baseball, basketball, cross-country, diving, football, golf, soccer, swimming, tennis, track/ field (outdoor), water polo. *Women:* Basketball, cross-country, diving, golf, lacrosse, soccer, softball, swimming, tennis, track/field (outdoor), volleyball, water polo.

BOTTOM LINE

Full-time tuition at Claremont McKenna College is more than $21,000 per semester, or $42,000 annually. To live in the campus residence halls, students should expect to pay between $3,200 and $4,000 per semester, depending on the living arrangement they choose (single or double room, residence hall or campus apartments.) Meal plans also range in price, but they generally run between $2,800 and $3,200 per semester. As at any private school, the annual cost to attend CMC can be a bit pricey; however, the school meets 100 percent of a student's financial need, offering aid to students in a wide range of financial situations.

SELECTIVITY

Admissions Rating	**96**
# of applicants	3,856
% of applicants accepted	18
% of acceptees attending	40
# accepting a place on wait list	303
% admitted from wait list	8

FRESHMAN PROFILE

Range SAT Critical Reading	**630–730**
Range SAT Math	**660–750**
% graduated top 10% of class	**85**
% graduated top 25% of class	**98**
% graduated top 50% of class	**100**

DEADLINES

Regular Deadline	**1/2**
Normal registration	**no**

FACILITIES

Housing: Coed dorms, special housing for disabled students, apartments for single students. *Special Academic Facilities/ Equipment:* Art galleries, athenaeum complex, centers for Black and Chicano studies, computer lab, leadership lab, science center. *Computers:* 100% of classrooms, 100% of dorms, 100% of libraries, 100% of dining areas, 100% of student union, 100% of common outdoor areas have wireless network access.

FINANCIAL FACTS

Financial Aid Rating	**99**
Annual tuition	$41,995
Room and Board	$13,625
Required Fees	$245
Books and supplies	$2,000
% frosh rec. need-based scholarship or grant aid	92
% UG rec.need-based scholarship or grant aid	44
% frosh rec. non-need-based scholarship or grant aid	6
% UG rec. non-need-based scholarship or grant aid	15
% frosh rec. need-based self-help aid	42
% UG rec. need-based self-help aid	44
% frosh rec. any financial aid	45
% UG rec. any financial aid	51
% UG borrow to pay for school	30
Average cumulative indebtedness	$9,779

Colby College

4000 Mayflower Hill, Waterville, ME 04901-8848 • Admissions: 207-859-4800 • Fax: 207-859-4828

CAMPUS LIFE

Quality of life Rating	86
Fire Safety Rating	90
Green rating	84
Type of School	Private
Environment	Village

STUDENTS

Total undergrad enrollment	1,825
% Male to Female	46/54
% From out of state	88
% From public high school	54
% Live on Campus	93
% African American	4
% Asian	8
% Caucasian	57
% Hispanic	4
% Native American	1
% International	5
# Of Countries Represented	62

ACADEMICS

Academic Rating	96
% Of students graduating within 4 years	86
% Of students graduating within 6 years	90
Calendar	4-1-4
Profs interesting rating	92
Profs accessible rating	88
Most common reg class size	10–19 students
Most common lab size	10–19 students

MOST POPULAR MAJORS

Biology, economics, international/global studies

SPECIAL STUDY OPTIONS

Cross-registration, double major, exchange student program (domestic), honors program, independent study, internships, student-designed major, study abroad, teacher certification program, Summer research assistantships; Colby has coordinated 3-2 engineering programs with Dart- mouth; Colby offers junior-year abroad programs in France, Spain, and Russia. Special programs offered to physically disabled students include note-taking services, reader services, voice recorders, tutors.

ABOUT THE SCHOOL

Challenging academics and professors who work closely with students are the backbone of Colby College's reputation as a small but desirable liberal arts college. The school's location in Waterville, Maine may have some applicants asking, "Where?" But what that means is that students and professors alike, those who go to Colby do so because they want to be there. Academics are the focus here, so the work is rarely less than challenging. Incoming students should be prepared to deal with a hefty workload, but those who are aiming high will find that Colby is "Heaven for students who excel at everything." Studying abroad is also a major part of most Colby programs.

The school is also rarely less than diverse, with an eclectic, international student body. Some two-thirds of students here spend time studying abroad. It is that mix of people that makes Colby the school it is. "Colby's greatest strengths lie in its people," one student notes. "From the administrators to the faculty, staff, students, and alumni, Colby's community is one that is genuinely caring, genuinely smart, and genuinely engaging." The dorms are mixed-class, and most activities at Colby center around the self-contained campus, so that sense of community is essential for student contentment.

Night life here isn't necessarily thriving or hectic, with outdoor activities such as skiing and hiking the focus of much off-campus entertainment. Students who don't enjoy the outdoors or extra study time–a major pastime among Colby students–may find the campus "suffocating." Colby lacks a big Greek scene, so partying life tends to be limited to small dorm parties or, even more rarely due to their scarcity, drinking at local pubs. Colby does offer a wide array of school-sponsored events, though, a natural extension of the community feeling fostered here. Most students find the intimacy of the campus to be a positive, not a negative.

BANG FOR YOUR BUCK

Colby College has a highly selective admissions process that sees just a third of applicants accepted. However, Colby will meet the financial needs of students they accept, and they do so via grants rather than loans so as to alleviate the burden of loan debt. The school also sponsors National Merit Scholarships. Loan aid is available in the form of Direct Subsidized Stafford, Direct Unsubsidized Stafford, Direct PLUS, Federal Perkins, state loans, university loans from institutional funds, and Colby-funded student employment.

STUDENTS

1,825 undergrad enrollment

46% Male

54% Female

ADMISSIONS

4,213 applicants → **34%** admitted | **34%** enrolled | **EARLY ADMISSIONS** → **NR** applicants | **NR** accepted

NR avg. high school gpa

ACT range (0–36): 28–31

SAT range (200–800): reading 630–710, math 620–710, writing 620–715

GRADUATION RATES

86% of students graduating within 4 yrs

90% of students graduating within 6 yrs

Colby College

Financial Aid: 207-859-4832 • E-mail: admissions@colby.edu • Website: www.colby.edu

STUDENT BODY

While the prototypical Colby student may be "white and from twenty minutes outside of Boston," undergrads are quick to point out that "campus is very open to diversity and ready to embrace it." Students single out the administration for "doing a great job of bringing in a more diverse student population." One student explains, "More and more international students and urban kids are coming through programs like the Posse Scholarship." A junior adds, "We have students here that dress in business suits and bowties while others walk around in capes." Most students, however, settle for the more general description of "preppy students who enjoy the outdoors and enjoy having a good time." That said, students report, "There's pretty much a place for everyone somewhere at Colby; chances are you'll find people both very similar to you in interests, background, etc. and people who are completely the opposite."

Why Students love Colby College

"From the administrators to the faculty, staff, students, and alumni, Colby's community is one that is genuinely caring, genuinely smart, and genuinely engaging."

WHY STUDENTS LOVE COLBY COLLEGE

Colby's tough admissions standards and education-focused student body results in a community of people who love the school because it is a place where learning is a shared passion. Meeting "interesting, intelligent people...while receiving a world class education" is a key draw for those who go here. Because academics are such an essential part of the school's culture, students love that Colby "has one of the most dedicated and intelligent group of faculty out of any college," a group who are "truly in a class of their own." Despite this, the campus isn't one of fierce competition among students. Students here are "competitive with themselves, but not with each other."

GENERAL INFO

Activities: Choral groups, concert band, dance, drama/theater, jazz band, literary magazine, music ensembles, musical theater, radio station, student government, student newspaper, student-run film society, symphony orchestra, yearbook, international student organization. **Organizations:** 91 registered organizations, 9 honor societies, 6 religious organizations. **Athletics (Intercollegiate):** *Men:* Baseball, basketball, crew/rowing, cross-country, diving, football, golf, ice hockey, lacrosse, skiing (downhill/alpine), skiing (nordic/cross-country), soccer, squash, swimming, tennis, track/field (outdoor), track/field (indoor). *Women:* Basketball, crew/rowing, cross-country, diving, field hockey, golf, ice hockey, lacrosse, skiing (downhill/alpine), skiing (nordic/cross-country), soccer, softball, squash, swimming, tennis, track/field (outdoor), track/field (indoor), volleyball.

BOTTOM LINE

Yearly comprehensive tuition at Colby College nears $54,000, plus another $700 for books, though officials there say, "We don't want any student not to come to Colby because of concerns about paying off student loans." The college meets all calculated need with grants and scholarships. Weak off-campus job opportunities mean many students will look toward aid/scholarships. Students graduate with an average debt of $24,600.

SELECTIVITY

Admissions Rating	**94**
# of applicants	4,213
% of applicants accepted	34
% of acceptees attending	34
# accepting a place on wait list	507
% admitted from wait list	2

FRESHMAN PROFILE

Range SAT Critical Reading	**630–710**
Range SAT Math	**620–710**
Range SAT Writing	**620–715**
Range ACT Composite	**28–31**
% graduated top 10% of class	**70**
% graduated top 25% of class	**91**
% graduated top 50% of class	**98**

DEADLINES

Regular Deadline	**1/1**
Normal registration	**yes**

FACILITIES

Housing: Coed dorms, wellness housing, theme housing. Quiet halls, chem-free halls, apartments for seniors only, student interest halls. *Special Academic Facilities/Equipment:* 28,000 square foot art museum, arboretum, electronic microscopes, greenhouse, astronomical observatory, writer's center. *Computers:* 100% of classrooms, 100% of dorms, 100% of libraries, 100% of dining areas, 100% of student union, 10% of common outdoor areas have wireless network access.

FINANCIAL FACTS

Financial Aid Rating	**97**
Annual comprehensive tuition	$53,800
Books and supplies	$700
% frosh rec. need-based scholarship or grant aid	40
% UG rec.need-based scholarship or grant aid	42
% frosh rec. non-need-based scholarship or grant aid	1
% UG rec. non-need-based scholarship or grant aid	1
% frosh rec. need-based self-help aid	30
% UG rec. need-based self-help aid	33
% frosh rec. any financial aid	46
% UG rec. any financial aid	47
% UG borrow to pay for school	37
Average cumulative indebtedness	$24,600

Colgate University

13 Oak Drive, Hamilton, NY 13346 • Admissions: 315-228-7401 • Fax: 315-228-7544

CAMPUS LIFE

Quality of life Rating	84
Fire Safety Rating	78
Green rating	85
Type of School	Private
Environment	Rural

STUDENTS

Total undergrad enrolllment	2,868
% Male to Female	47/53
% From out of state	74
% From public high school	61
% Live on Campus	91
# of Fraternities	6
# of Sororities	3
% African American	7
% Asian	4
% Caucasian	72
% Hispanic	7
% International	6
# Of Countries Represented	36

ACADEMICS

Academic Rating	96
% Of students graduating within 4 years	83
% Of students graduating within 6 years	88
Calendar	semester
Profs interesting rating	91
Profs accessible rating	95
Most common reg class size	10–19 students
Most common lab size	10–19 students

MOST POPULAR MAJORS

English language and literature, sociology and anthropology

HONORS PROGRAMS

Cross-registration, double major, honors program

ABOUT COLGATE UNIVERSITY

Since 1819, Hamilton, New York, has hosted Colgate University, a small liberal arts college that has a "very rigorous academic curriculum" and that will prove challenging to students–gratifyingly so, since those who choose Colgate tend to be looking for a focus on "high intensity" academics. The science, medicine and health, music, and other programs at this "prestigious institution" win praise from those who attend. Students will be taught by professors who "love being at Colgate as much as the students do." Incoming students should expect small classrooms and hands-on teaching by professors, with class sizes that "allow for personal attention and a higher level of learning."

Yet it's not all academics at Colgate. Those attending will also enjoy "strong division 1 athletics, a wide variety of extracurricular activities, and a very special community." Football, baseball, softball, tennis, and other sports give students challenges to overcome outside the classroom. Students say Colgate offers "the perfect balance between academics and extracurricular activities." A strong sense of community helps. Success both in school and beyond is attributed to the "Colgate connection," a bond among the school's 2,800 students that lasts beyond their years here.

The school's philosophical core, and by extension its student body, is career-minded. This is reflected in an extensive set of career-development programs and services. Among others, these include shadowing programs, internship recruiting and off-campus recruiting, and the innovative Colgate on the Cuyahoga program, which gives those accepted an unprecedented opportunity to network with executives, politicians, and business owners. According to the school administration, "These programs offer many dynamic opportunities for students to connect with alumni, staff, faculty, and others to learn about and discuss interests and goals."

BANG FOR YOUR BUCK

Financial aid packages can be sizable at Colgate, averaging just more than $40,000 for the Class of 2015. The list of available grants and scholarships is extensive; graduating students call it "strong" and "generous." Over the next several years, school administration aims to lower the average debt for exiting students–and even that may be washed away easily for many students. Nearly three quarters of Colgate graduates are employed within a year of leaving school, and just less than 20 percent are attending graduate school.

STUDENTS

2,868 undergrad enrollment

47% Male ♂♂♂♂♂♂♂♂♂♂

53% Female ♀♀♀♀♀♀♀♀♀♀♀

ADMISSIONS

7,872 applicants → 33% admitted — 33% enrolled — EARLY ADMISSIONS → NR applicants — NR accepted

3.60 avg. high school gpa

reading 630–720
math 640–740

ACT range 0 — 29–32 — 36

SAT range 200 — 800

GRADUATION RATES

83% of students graduating within 4 yrs

88% of students graduating within 6 yrs

Colgate University

FINANCIAL AID: : 315-228-7431 • E-MAIL: ADMISSION@MAIL.COLGATE.EDU• WEBSITE: WWW.COLGATE.EDU

STUDENT BODY

Colgate boasts a "happy and enthusiastic student body" that "follows the motto 'work hard, play hard.'" A sophomore says, "Imagine J. Crew models. Now give them brains, and that is who is walking around Colgate's campus." Fraternities and sororities are popular: "Greek life does have a huge presence in the social life at Colgate," but "it is not exclusive to just those who are members." However, despite the "country club atmosphere," a computer science major says, "When you're stranded in Hamilton, New York, for four years you'll inevitably end up fitting in regardless whether you are the typical student or not."

Why Students love Colgate University

"People actually care about your goals and aspirations."

WHY STUDENTS LOVE COLGATE UNIVERSITY

Two words: "Colgate connection." Students adore the "incredible sense of community" fostered here. "It is a place where you can receive an Ivy education," one student reports, "without the cut-throatedness." Students say that at Colgate, "people actually care about your goals and aspirations. "The campus is breath-taking," one student enthuses, "and the people are brilliant and as beautiful as the campus." The location is one of the "most scenic, beautiful parts of the country"–it "looks like the Garden of Eden," according to one student–while the people here are "genuinely always happy and friendly." Professors "are always accessible, often giving students their home phone number."

GENERAL INFO

Activities: Choral groups, concert band, dance, drama/theater, jazz band, literary magazine, music ensembles, musical theater, pep band, radio station, student government, student newspaper, student-run film society, symphony orchestra, television station, yearbook, campus ministries, international student organization. **Organizations:** 280 registered organizations, 3 honor societies, 5 religious organizations. 3 fraternities. **Athletics (Intercollegiate):** *Men:* Baseball, basketball, cross-country, diving, football, golf, soccer, swimming, tennis, track/field (outdoor), water polo. *Women:* Basketball, cross-country, diving, golf, lacrosse, soccer, softball, swimming, tennis, track/field (outdoor), volleyball, water polo. **On-Campus Highlights:** Smith Campus Center, Sontag Greek Theater, Rains Center for Sports and Recreation, Brackett Observatory.

BOTTOM LINE

If the $42,000 annual tuition seems daunting, it should be offset by the fact that the school's generous need-based financial aid programs help carry a large share of that burden. About one third of students receive scholarship or grant aid, and a quarter receive self-help aid. Graduates leave Colgate with an average accumulated indebtedness of $18,600.

SELECTIVITY

Admissions Rating	**97**
# of applicants	7,872
% of applicants accepted	33
% of acceptees attending	33
# accepting a place on wait list	671
% admitted from wait list	0

FRESHMAN PROFILE

Range SAT Critical Reading	**630–720**
Range SAT Math	**640–740**
Range ACT Composite	**29–32**
Average HS GPA	**3.60**
% graduated top 10% of class	**64**
% graduated top 25% of class	**90**
% graduated top 50% of class	**98**

DEADLINES

Regular Deadline	**1/15**
Normal registration	**no**

FACILITIES

Housing: Coed dorms, special housing for disabled students, fraternity/sorority housing, cooperative housing, apartments for single students, wellness housing, theme housing. *Special Academic Facilities/ Equipment:* Art galleries, anthropology museum, language lab, cable TV station, life sciences complex, geology/fossil collection, observatory, electron microscopes, laser lab, weather lab.

FINANCIAL FACTS

Financial Aid Rating	**98**
Annual tuition	$42,625
Room and Board	$10,650
Required Fees	$295
Books and supplies	$1,010
% frosh rec. need-based scholarship or grant aid	32
% UG rec.need-based scholarship or grant aid	33
% frosh rec. need-based self-help aid	25
% UG rec. need-based self-help aid	26
% frosh rec. any financial aid	33
% UG rec. any financial aid	34
% UG borrow to pay for school	33
Average cumulative indebtedness	$18,629

College of the Atlantic

105 Eden Street, Admission Office, Bar Harbor, ME 04609 • Admissions: 207-288-5015 • Financial Aid: 207-288-5015

CAMPUS LIFE

Quality of life Rating	93
Fire Safety Rating	97
Green rating	99
Type of School	Private
Environment	Rural

STUDENTS

Total undergrad enrolllment	353
% Male to Female	30/70
% From out of state	74
% From public high school	61
% Live on Campus	43
% African American	1
% Asian	1
% Caucasian	67
% Hispanic	2
% International	16
# Of Countries Represented	34

ACADEMICS

Academic Rating	93
% Of students graduating within 4 years	59
% Of students graduating within 6 years	69
Calendar	semester
Profs interesting rating	95
Profs accessible rating	98
Most common reg class size	10–9 students

MOST POPULAR MAJORS

Field ecology, international relations, the arts

HONORS PROGRAMS

COA considers all students capable of honors work, which is why all students finish their time at COA with a term-long capstone, or senior project.

SPECIAL STUDY OPTIONS

Cross-registration, exchange student program (domestic), independent study, internships, liberal arts/career combination, student-designed major, study abroad, teacher certification program, Winter term program in Yucatan, Mexico. EcoLeague–consortium agreement with five other colleges for student exchanges (Alaska Pacific University, Antioch College, Green Mountain College, Northland College, Prescott College. Exchange program with Olin College of Engineering and University of Maine at Orono.

ABOUT THE SCHOOL

Those expecting a traditional roster of classes and majors will be thrown for a loop by Maine's College of the Atlantic, a school at which all undergrads major in "Human Ecology." What is Human Ecology? It is an interdisciplinary philosophy focused on social and environmental issues, one that "encourages students to participate in their community" and keeps students "focused on creating positive change in the world today." More important than the unique philosophy behind this universal major is the fact that it puts students "completely in charge" of their education, allowing them to choose their courses, direction, and areas of focused study.This slightly offbeat approach "allows for freedom and rigorous learning" and means that here, "students define their education" and have "the opportunity to develop a personalized program not available in the mainstream." It may seem unusual at first, but "classes that seem completely unrelated…all fit together." The classroom environment is a little offbeat, too. The style of education here is "more exploratory and hands-on than lecture-based." The "small class sizes and close community" here are "essential to its success." Students say they have "very close relationships with their professors." The College of the Atlantic wants students who are "trying to save the world with limited resources," and that means a large degree of self-motivation is key to succeeding here. That can be an uphill challenge for some, but "anyone who is self- motivated can do well at COA." Workload varies, but never veers towards light. Students are often "swamped with reading and homework."

Why Students Love the College of the Atlantic

"Acadia National Park is in my backyard and the Atlantic Ocean is in my front yard."

BANG FOR YOUR BUCK

The usual grants and scholarships such as Federal Pell, SEOG, Federal Perkins, and state, private and school grants and scholarships apply. Beyond that, College of the Atlantic offers an "excellent financial aid program" to applicants who "share an ideological affinity" with the school. Because of the off-beat admissions process, which seeks to identify students who will fit with the school's philosophical goals, the majority of students receive some kind of aid. Beyond money concerns, students should be ready for admissions standards that are as atypical as the school itself. Standardized testing is not required. Be prepared to lace essays and interviews with strong doses of your philosophy and personality.

STUDENT BODY

Undergrads at the COA readily acknowledge that many people assume they're "all tree-hugging hippies" who always wear "Birkenstocks and tie dye." And while there are plenty of "outdoorsy" types, students are quick to assert that many of their peers shatter this stereotype. Though the majority might categorize themselves as "atypical," most everyone is "compassionate, kind, and aware." One freshman gushes, "Everyone is incredibly cool and into something, whether it be poetry, fighting climate change, dance, whales [or] organic farming...everyone wants to improve the lives of others." With such a politically aware student body, COA is a bastion for liberal, left-leaning undergrads.

College of the Atlantic

E-MAIL: INQUIRY@COA.EDU • FAX: 207-288-4126 • WEBSITE: WWW.COA.EDU

WHY STUDENTS LOVE THE COLLEGE OF THE ATLANTIC

Many students at the College of the Atlantic are "attracted by a magical location," a "magic place" that is "located on the ocean near a fun town." Just how magic is it? "Acadia National Park is in my backyard and the Atlantic Ocean is in my front yard," one students notes. Another puts it more succinctly: "This island is beautiful." The gorgeous location provides recreational opportunities students in larger, urban schools often don't get, including "lots of bicycles, community gardens, kayaking, rock climbing, being outside, the fall colors and the beautiful Maine Coast." Couple that with a close-knit community and students say this is "an enriching way to live." The "small classes, accessible professors, and the promise of a unique education" are a big draw for students. "I really prefer small classes and I like to know everyone," one student said, while another noted, "The president, the dean of students, the academic dean, they all know my name." These factors mean that for some, the College of the Atlantic "is much more than a university, it's a preparation for life." The school is "all about taking responsibility over your studies. You have the freedom to become what you want."

GENERAL INFO

Activities: Choral groups, dance, drama/theater, jazz band, literary magazine, music ensembles, student government, student newspaper, yearbook. **On-Campus Highlights:** George B. Dorr Museum of Natural History, Blum Art Gallery, the pier, Turrets, Take-A-Break. College of the Atlantic has recently completed state-of-the-art sustainable dorms and a creative restoration of an historic building into a similarly sustainable campus center. **Environmental Initiatives:** COA has been carbon net zero since 2007, and COA's new student dorms have space heating and hot water provided by wood pellet boilers, have triple-pane windows, and composting toilets. COA has its own organic farm and hosts an organic community garden on its campus. Both sites helps supply the college cafeteria with local, organic food when possible given the northern growing season.

BOTTOM LINE

Attending the College of the Atlantic will cost students $44,913 annually between tuition ($35,532), room and board ($8,250), books and supplies ($600), and other required fees ($531). Students graduate with an average indebtedness of $20,125. Some 87 percent of incoming Freshmen receive need-based grants or scholarships.

STUDENTS

353 undergrad enrollment

30% Male ♂♂♂♂♂♂

70% Female ♀♀♀♀♀♀♀♀♀♀♀♀♀♀

ADMISSIONS

390 applicants → 69% admitted; 39% enrolled

EARLY ADMISSIONS → NR applicants; NR accepted

3.56 avg. high school gpa

ACT range (0–36): 24–29

SAT range (200–800): reading 570–690; math 520–650; writing 570–670

GRADUATION RATES

59% of students graduating within 4 yrs

69% of students graduating within 6 yrs

SELECTIVITY

Admissions Rating	**89**
# of applicants	390
% of applicants accepted	64
% of acceptees attending	34
# accepting a place on wait list	17
% admitted from wait list	35

FRESHMAN PROFILE

Range SAT Critical Reading	**570–690**
Range SAT Math	**520–650**
Range SAT Writing	**570–670**
Range ACT Composite	**24–29**
Average HS GPA	**3.56**
% graduated top 10% of class	**43**
% graduated top 25% of class	**65**
% graduated top 50% of class	**92**

DEADLINES

Regular Deadline	**2/15**
Normal registration	**yes**

Facilities

Housing: Coed dorms, special housing for disabled students, Substance-free housing; green (environmentally conscious) housing. *Special Academic Facilities/Equipment:* Natural history museum, pottery studio, greenhouse, Geographic Information Systems lab, Green Graphics Studio, Deering Common Campus Center, organic community garden. *Computers:* 100% of classrooms, 100% of dorms, 100% of libraries, 100% of dining areas, 100% of student union, 25% of common outdoor areas have wireless network access.

FINANCIAL FACTS

Financial Aid Rating	**90**
Annual tuition	$35,532
Room and Board	$8,250
Required Fees	$531
Books and supplies	$600
% frosh rec. need-based scholarship or grant aid	87
% UG rec.need-based scholarship or grant aid	84
% frosh rec. need-based self-help aid	82
% UG rec. need-based self-help aid	82
% frosh rec. any financial aid	88
% UG rec. any financial aid	85
% UG borrow to pay for school	66
Average cumulative indebtedness	$20, 125

College of the Holy Cross

Admissions Office, 1 College Street, Worcester, MA 01610-2395 • Admissions: 508-793-2443 • Fax: 508-793-3888

CAMPUS LIFE

Quality of life Rating	65
Fire Safety Rating	95
Green rating	93
Type of School	Private
Environment	City

STUDENTS

Total undergrad enrolllment	2,862
% Male to Female	46/54
% From out of state	63
% From public high school	50
% Live on Campus	89
% African American	5
% Asian	5
% Caucasian	66
% Hispanic	9
% International	1
# Of Countries Represented	19

ACADEMICS

Academic Rating	95
% Of students graduating within 4 years	90
% Of students graduating within 6 years	93
Calendar	semester
Profs interesting rating	93
Profs accessible rating	93
Most common reg class size	10–19 students
Most common lab size	fewer than 10 students

MOST POPULAR MAJORS

Economics, English language and literature, political science

HONORS PROGRAMS

Fenwick Scholar Program.

SPECIAL STUDY OPTIONS

Accelerated program, cross-registration, double major, dual enrollment, exchange student program (domestic), honors program, independent study, internships, liberal arts/career combination, student-designed major, study abroad, teacher certification program, first-year integrated living and learning program (Montserrat).

ABOUT THE SCHOOL

The College of the Holy Cross is a small, liberal arts college of fewer than 3,000 students offering rigorous academic preparation in more than 30 degree programs. Students are thrilled to discover the value of a Holy Cross education. "I realized with a degree from here, I can get a job almost anywhere," and the "large and strong" alumni network provides further professional connections. Students say that College of the Holy Cross "does an incredible job of giving its students a very broad education [and] preparing them with the tools for the real world."

But it's the professors that make students' four years at Holy Cross an extraordinary value. "The emphasis here is on teaching and learning, not research," enthused a freshman. All first-year students take part in full-year seminars that are heavy on intellectual development, and the college values effective communication skills. Faculty is accessible in and out of the classrooms. "At Holy Cross, the professors will keep you busy throughout the week." "Classes are hard," warns a biology major. Good grades are hard to come by. "You have to work your tail off to just get an A–." At the same time, students love their "caring" and "amazing" professors.

Holy Cross's has a top-notch Career Planning Center and Summer Internship Program that connects students with alumni working in business, government, media, medicine, law, public policy, research, and many other fields. In fact, the alumni network at Holy Cross is legendary for its willingness to mentor and assist students and graduates throughout their careers. Opportunities such as academic internships, community-based learning course, a prestigious Washington Semester, and experiences through study abroad and immersion trips also provide students with invaluable "real-world" experience. Holy Cross has extensive summer internship and study abroad opportunities.

BANG FOR YOUR BUCK

No student or family should be dissuaded from applying to Holy Cross because of the price tag. Holy Cross is need-blind in its admissions policy, which means the decision to admit students to this highly selective liberal arts college is made without regard to a student's ability to pay. Additionally, Holy Cross meets 100 percent of a student's demonstrated financial need with a combination of scholarship grants, loans, and work-study.

STUDENTS

2,862 undergrad enrollment

46% Male ♂♂♂♂♂♂♂♂♂

54% Female ♀♀♀♀♀♀♀♀♀♀♀

ADMISSIONS

6,911 applicants → 35% admitted — 30% enrolled

EARLY ADMISSIONS → NR applicants — NR accepted

3.77 avg. high school gpa

ACT range (0–36): 27–31

SAT range (200–800): reading 590–680, math 600–690, writing 600–690

GRADUATION RATES

90% of students graduating within 4 yrs

93% of students graduating within 6 yrs

College of the Holy Cross

FINANCIAL AID: 508-793-2265 • E-MAIL: ADMISSIONS@HOLYCROSS.EDU • WEBSITE: WWW.HOLYCROSS.EDU

STUDENT BODY

Holy Cross is a "remarkably" welcoming campus. "This is the most friendly campus you will ever step foot on," claims a senior. You can find students from just about every state, but the majority tends to come from New England and the mid-Atlantic states. Students tend to be Catholic, though there are certainly plenty of people with different religions and with no religion at all. "Religion is not a major issue" here, really. Atypical students exist, and they "fit in just fine," but most of the undergraduate population at Holy Cross does kind of fit a certain mold. "The typical student is upper-middle-class, white, somewhat preppy, and athletic." That student is "smart," "hardworking," and probably "from the suburbs." "If you dress really preppy all the time, party hard on the weekends, and study in the rest of your remaining time, this is the school for you."

Why Students love College of Holy Cross

"This is the most friendly campus you will ever step foot on."

WHY STUDENTS LOVE COLLEGE OF HOLY CROSS

When they're not studying, Holy Cross students enjoy a robust social scene, although "frats and sororities are unpopular or nonexistent." Satisfied undergrads report that "there are plenty of options for BC undergrads to become involved with," and that "intramurals, student government, clubs, the newspaper, theater, or music" are all fantastic options. With more than 100 student clubs and organizations on campus, there's always something going on, and hometown Worcester is only a short drive away from the bright lights of Boston. The majority of students tend to come from New England and the Mid-Atlantic states, and one undergrad finds that "students tend to be Catholic, though there are certainly plenty of people with different religions and with no religion at all." Another student observes, "Holy Cross is an outstanding school that wants the best for its students and to prepare them for the future."

GENERAL INFO

Activities: Choral groups, concert band, dance, drama/theater, jazz band, literary magazine, marching band, music ensembles, musical theater, pep band, radio station, student government, student newspaper, yearbook, campus ministries, international student organization. **Organizations:** 105 registered organizations, 20 honor societies, 4 religious organizations. **Athletics (Intercollegiate):** *Men:* Baseball, basketball, crew/rowing, cross-country, diving, football, golf, ice hockey, lacrosse, soccer, swimming, tennis, track/field (outdoor), track/field (indoor). *Women:* Basketball, crew/rowing, cross-country, diving, field hockey, golf, ice hockey, lacrosse, soccer, softball, swimming, tennis, track/field (outdoor), track/field (indoor), volleyball. **On-Campus Highlights:** Library, Smith Hall, St. Joseph Chapel, Hart Recreation Center, Hogan Campus Center.

BOTTOM LINE

At Holy Cross, the total cost for tuition and fees and room and board comes to about $50,000 annually. Don't fret; financial aid is generous here. The average financial aid package for freshman includes a grant totaling $26,000. Additional aid is available in the form of scholarships, work-study, and loans.

SELECTIVITY

Admissions Rating	**96**
# of applicants	6,911
% of applicants accepted	35
% of acceptees attending	30
# accepting a place on wait list	538
% admitted from wait list	4

FRESHMAN PROFILE

Range SAT Critical Reading	**590–680**
Range SAT Math	**600–690**
Range SAT Writing	**600–690**
Range ACT Composite	**27–31**
Average HS GPA	**3.77**
% graduated top 10% of class	**64**
% graduated top 25% of class	**91**
% graduated top 50% of class	**100**

DEADLINES

Regular Deadline	**1/15**
Normal registration	**no**

FACILITIES

Housing: Coed dorms, special housing for disabled students, apartments for single students, suites on campus available for juniors and seniors. Substance-free housing also available. *Special Academic Facilities/Equipment:* Art gallery, Concert Hall, Taylor and Boody tracker organ, O'Callahan Science Library, Rehm Library, Multimedia Resource Center, Wellness Center. *Computers:* 100% of classrooms, 100% of dorms, 100% of libraries, 100% of dining areas, 100% of student union, 60% of common outdoor areas have wireless network access.

FINANCIAL FACTS

Financial Aid Rating	**92**
Annual tuition	$40,910
Room and Board	$11,270
Required Fees	$578
Books and supplies	$700
% frosh rec. need-based scholarship or grant aid	47
% UG rec.need-based scholarship or grant aid	44
% frosh rec. non-need-based scholarship or grant aid	1
% UG rec. non-need-based scholarship or grant aid	2
% frosh rec. need-based self-help aid	43
% UG rec. need-based self-help aid	45
% frosh rec. any financial aid	58
% UG rec. any financial aid	55
% UG borrow to pay for school	58
Average cumulative indebtedness	$23,662

Colorado College

14 East Cache la Poudre Street, Colorado Springs, CO 80903 • Phone: 719-389-6344 • Financial Aid Phone: 719-389-6651

CAMPUS LIFE

Quality of Life Rating	78
Fire Safety Rating	81
Green Rating	98
Type of school	private
Environment	metropolis

STUDENTS

Total undergrad enrollment	2,040
% male/female	47/53
% from out of state	78
% from public high school	55
% live on campus	75
# of fraternities	2
# of sororities	3
% African American	1
% Asian	5
% Caucasian	76
% Hispanic	7
% International	5
# of countries represented	48

ACADEMICS

Academic Rating	94
% students graduating within 4 years	81
% students graduating within 6 years	87
Calendar	eight 3.5-week sessions 1 class each
Profs interesting rating	97
Profs accessible rating	96
Most common reg class size	10–19 students
Most common lab size	10–19 students

MOST POPULAR MAJORS

Biology, economics, political science

SPECIAL STUDY OPTIONS

Double major, English as a Second Language (ESL), independent study, internships, liberal arts/career combination, student-designed major, study abroad, teacher licensure program; Cooperative 3/2 program.

ABOUT THE SCHOOL

Colorado College provides an education without boundaries. With an average class size of 16 students and a 9:1 student/faculty ratio, students have access to an intimate learning experience where the focus is on immersion and independence. Pair a Liberal Arts education with the college's signature feature, the "Block Plan" (students take, and professors teach, one course at a time in intensive three-and-a-half week segments), locate the school in Colorado Springs, and you create unparalleled opportunities for field studies and experiential learning, as well as total subject immersion. "Taking one class at a time allows you to devote all of your time to it. It is definitely nice when you are in a class that you love, because you don't have to sacrifice any time for another class that you may like less, or that you have a harder time with."

On average there are 750 independent study blocks completed by students each year. Colorado College also offers $100,000 annually in Venture Grants, enabling students to pursue original research or an academic project of their choosing. "CC students care about the world. They are idealists and dreamers [who] want to change the world for the better. CC fosters an arena where dreams can grow and students can learn how to go about pursuing them." A Public Interest Fellowship Program awards more than 80 students paid summer and year-long postgraduate fellowships annually, a number of which have evolved into permanent positions.

BANG FOR YOUR BUCK

Overall, Colorado College provides a non-traditional learning opportunity where young adults can develop their passions in a beautiful and supportive environment. Not only is the educational opportunity perfect for individual learners, it is attainable. Great financial aid is a major selling point. The school is committed to the philosophy that cost should not deter a student from considering Colorado College. "The staff is very nice. If you go into to any office to ask anything they are very helpful. Financial Aid has been exceptionally helpful." Once Colorado College determines a student's eligibility for CC grant and scholarship funds, the school will make a four-year commitment to the family (except in limited circumstances) and renew the CC funds automatically each year at the same level. Funds have been specially designated to assist families who have been adversely impacted by the downturn in the economy.

STUDENTS

2,040 undergrad enrollment

47% Male ♂♂♂♂♂♂♂♂♂♂

53% Female ♀♀♀♀♀♀♀♀♀♀

ADMISSIONS

4,466 applicants → 34% admitted | 36% enrolled | EARLY ADMISSIONS → NR applicants | NR accepted

NR avg. high school gpa

28–32 ACT range (0–36)

SAT range (200–800)	
reading	610–710
math	610–700
writing	620–700

GRADUATION RATES

81% of students graduating within 4 yrs

87% of students graduating within 6 yrs

E-MAIL: ADMISSION@COLORADOCOLLEGE.EDU • FAX: 719-389-6816 • WEBSITE: WWW.COLORADOCOLLEGE.EDU

STUDENT BODY

"The population is not so diverse" at Colorado College according to some students. "Most students are white" and "from affluent families." Otherwise, students describe themselves as "intellectual, easygoing, and active." They're "environmentally aware," "idealistic," and "enthusiastic about trying new things." They have "many creative interests." They are "very liberal," too. "It is rare to find a conservative on campus." Other students tell us that Colorado College is "eclectic" and filled with every sort of student. There are two main groups: "hippies and preps." There are also plenty of "outdoor enthusiasts" "dressed in fancy outdoor gear." However, CC is small enough and students are open enough that there is quite a bit of overlap among cliques.

Why Students love Colorado College

"Taking one class at a time allows you to devote all of your time to it."

WHY STUDENTS LOVE COLORADO COLLEGE

From the beginning, you'll be told to "get out there" right away and make the most of your CC experience, if only to take advantage of the variety of people you meet while you're here. "During my first semester, I knew I should "get out there," but I didn't believe I could. I wish I had. When I finally auditioned and was cast for a play during seventh block of freshman year, it was like the last piece of the college puzzle clicked into place." "My favorite thing about CC is that there is always something going on. From readings by famous poets to porn debates, internationally known advocates to lacrosse games, protests to plays, music festivals to dances, techno raves to campus political debates, and fencing club to midnight pancake breakfasts... there is always something to do, an experience to have, a door to open, and an inspiration waiting to happen.

GENERAL INFO

Activities: Choral groups, concert band, dance, drama/theater, jazz band, literary magazine, music ensembles, musical theater, radio station, student government, student newspaper, student-run film society, yearbook, campus ministries, international student organization. **Organizations:** 147 registered organizations, 13 honor societies, 20 religious organizations. 1 fraternities, 3 sororities. **Athletics (Intercollegiate):** *Men:* Basketball, cross-country, ice hockey, lacrosse, soccer, swimming, tennis, track/field (outdoor). *Women:* Basketball, cross-country, lacrosse, soccer, swimming, tennis, track/field (outdoor), track/field (indoor), volleyball. **On-Campus Highlights:** Worner Student Center, Palmer Hall, Shove Chapel, Cutler Hall–Admission, View of Pikes Peak. **Environmental Initiatives:** Campus-wide, semester-long resource conservation and waste reduction campaign, "aCClimate14," which challenges campus community to adapt to shifting environmental and economic conditions.

BOTTOM LINE

Students are attracted to Colorado College for more than its stunning landscape. "Life at Colorado College is intense–everything from class to social life to long-weekend vacations–I have yet to meet someone who doesn't meet every opportunity with enthusiastic energy."

SELECTIVITY

Admissions Rating	**93**
# of applicants	4,466
% of applicants accepted	34
% of acceptees attending	36
# accepting a place on wait list	248
% admitted from wait list	0

FRESHMAN PROFILE

Range SAT Critical Reading	**610–710**
Range SAT Math	**610–700**
Range SAT Writing	**620–700**
Range ACT Composite	**28–32**
% graduated top 10% of class	**59**
% graduated top 25% of class	**89**
% graduated top 50% of class	**98**

DEADLINES

Regular Deadline	**1/15**
Normal registration	**yes**

FACILITIES

Housing: Coed dorms, men's dorms, women's dorms, fraternity/sorority housing, apartments for single students, theme housing. *Special Academic Facilities/Equipment:* Electronic music studio; telescope dome; multimedia computer laboratory; Balinese orchestras; the Colorado Electronic music studio; observatory; extensive herbarium collection. *Computers:* 100% of classrooms, 100% of dorms, 100% of libraries, 100% of dining areas, 100% of student union, 80% of common outdoor areas have wireless network access.

FINANCIAL FACTS

Financial Aid Rating	**89**
Annual tuition	$39,900
Room and board	$9,416
Books and supplies	$1,182
% frosh rec. need-based scholarship or grant aid	33
% UG rec. need-based scholarship or grant aid	36
% frosh rec. non-need-based scholarship or grant aid	10
% UG rec. non-need-based scholarship or grant aid	11
% frosh rec. need-based self-help aid	23
% UG rec. need-based self-help aid	24
% frosh rec. any financial aid	52
% UG rec. any financial aid	56
% UG borrow to pay for school	35
Average cumulative indebtedness	$16,172

Columbia University

212 Hamilton Hall MC 2807, 1130 Amsterdam A, New York, NY 10027 • Phone: 212-854-2522

CAMPUS LIFE

Quality of Life Rating	98
Fire Safety Rating	60*
Green Rating	60*
Type of school	private
Environment	metropolis

STUDENTS

Total undergrad enrollment	5,888
% male/female	52/48
% from out of state	72
% from public high school	57
% live on campus	95
# of fraternities	17
# of sororities	11
% African American	12
% Asian	17
% Caucasian	35
% Hispanic	14
% Native American	1
% international	11
# of countries represented	136

ACADEMICS

Academic Rating	96
% students graduating within 4 years	88
% students graduating within 6 years	96
Calendar	semester
Profs interesting rating	77
Profs accessible rating	74
Most common reg class size	10–19 students

MOST POPULAR MAJORS

Engineering, English, political science, biology

ABOUT THE SCHOOL

Columbia University provides prestigious academics and top-of-the-line resources for an Ivy League education with a Liberal Arts college feel in the heart of one of the greatest cities in the world. Nestled on the upper west side of New York City, one student tells us that the campus itself is, "an inspiration and a motivation to push and excel academically." The core curriculum is a large draw, providing students with a solid liberal arts education on which to base their future studies. Pair this with a location that provides unparalleled access to internship, community service, and research opportunities and you have a recipe for a melting pot of possibility.

Columbia undergraduates represent every socioeconomic, racial, and ethnic background, and hail from all fifty states and all over the world. Students' distinct interests and talents are reflected by their diverse academic pursuits: undergraduates study in more than ninety different academic fields. Engagement within the global community is central to the Columbia experience, and being in the heart of the city is like holding a passport to opportunity with a side of arts, culture, and entertainment.

Why Students love Columbia University

"It had the strong academic base I was looking for but lacked that catty competitiveness that creates stress."

BANG FOR YOUR BUCK

With nearly all undergraduate students living on campus, students are active participants in campus life through participation in hundreds of student clubs, community service organizations, and athletic teams. One student tells us, "The opportunities Columbia has to offer, not only on campus but also throughout New York City, attracted me to its gates. The dichotomy of a self-contained campus in the largest city in the U.S. is truly unique and cannot be surpassed by any other American University." Another student adds, "I am big on the sciences, and I knew that if I did not attend a school that had a Core Curriculum (required set of classes that surveys the humanities and the sciences), all I would take are science classes. With Columbia's core, I am able to have a more holistic education. Also, the location of Columbia is perfect–the university still has a campus feel even though it is in the middle of New York City!"

STUDENTS

5,888 undergrad enrollment

52% Male ♂♂♂♂♂♂♂♂♂♂

48% Female ♀♀♀♀♀♀♀♀♀♀

ADMISSIONS

26,179 applicants	→ 9% admitted	59% enrolled	EARLY ADMISSIONS	→ NR applicants	NR accepted

NR avg. high school gpa

ACT range (0–36): 31-34

SAT range (200–800): reading 690–780; math 700–790; writing 690–780

GRADUATION RATES

88% of students graduating within 4 yrs

96% of students graduating within 6 yrs

FAX: 212-894-1209 • WEBSITE: STUDENTAFFAIRS.COLUMBIA.EDU/ADMISSIONS

STUDENT BODY

A "diverse community of serious thinkers who also know how to have fun," Columbia students describe themselves as "bookworms" who are "cynical but enthusiastic" as well as "very politically active and liberal." With "driven" people "from distinct backgrounds, distinct ideologies, distinct everything," Columbia students list the school's diversity as one of its strengths, but one student cautions that "the diversity could use less of a leftist bias." "Extremely smart and interested in learning for its own sake," a "typical" Columbia student "has strong views but is willing to discuss and change them." Columbia students are also "more intense than those you might find at other schools," points out one student. Indeed, during exam season it's not uncommon to see students "bring sleeping bags and cases of Red Bull to the library."

WHY STUDENTS LOVE COLUMBIA UNIVERSITY

A recent graduate tells us, "Columbia took really good care of me financially, such that we pay what we can pay and the rest is taken care of quite generously. Another factor that tilted my decision in favor of Columbia is the core curriculum. I was always a fan of a diverse education and Columbia would let me do just that." Columbia offers a well-rounded opportunity. One student tells us, "As a liberal arts school, Columbia College offered a good balance and combination of the aspects I was looking for in a school. With a historical core curriculum, it assured a commitment to the liberal arts and having each of its students become as well-rounded as possible. However it simultaneously grants students with amazing resources in fields of networking, research and internships."

With a campus that "caters to every single person that comes through its doors," Columbia is "like being in a really rich agar" where students can pursue whatever they are interested in from "engaging in intellectual conversation" to "getting involved in politics through student groups on campus to continuing (or discovering) a love for the arts by being a part of a musical ensemble."

GENERAL INFO

Activities: Choral groups, concert band, dance, drama/theater, jazz band, literary magazine, marching band, music ensembles, musical theater, opera, pep band, radio station, student government, student newspaper, student-run film society, symphony orchestra, television station, yearbook, campus ministries, international student organization. **Organizations:** 300 registered organizations, 17 religious organizations. 17 fraternities, 11 sorority. **Athletics (Intercollegiate):** *Men:* Baseball, basketball, crew/rowing, cross-country, diving, fencing, football, golf, soccer, swimming, tennis, track/field (outdoor), track/field (indoor), wrestling. *Women:* Archery, basketball, crew/rowing, cross-country, diving, fencing, field hockey, golf, lacrosse, soccer, softball, swimming, tennis, track/field (outdoor), track/field (indoor), volleyball.

BOTTOM LINE

Earning an acceptance letter from Columbia is no easy feat. Admissions officers are looking to build a diverse class that will greatly contribute to the university. It's the Ivy League folks, and it's New York City, and there is a price tag that goes with both. A year's tuition is more than $41,000. Additionally, count on $10,000 in room and board (such a deal for NYC!). Columbia's New York City campus means that every manner of distraction is literally at your fingertips, so you'll want to factor in another nice chunk of change for things like transportation, personal expenses, outings, etc. These figures are nothing to sneeze at. Take heart: If you get over the first hurdle and manage to gain admittance to this prestigious university, you can be confident that the university will help you pay for it.

SELECTIVITY

Admissions Rating	**99**
# of applicants	26,179
% of applicants accepted	9
% of acceptees attending	59

FRESHMAN PROFILE

Range SAT Critical Reading	**690–780**
Range SAT Math	**700–790**
Range SAT Writing	**690–780**
Range ACT Composite	**31–34**
% graduated top 10% of class	**97**

DEADLINES

Regular Deadline	**1/1**
Normal registration	**yes**

FACILITIES

Housing: Coed dorms, special housing for disabled students, apartments for single students, suites on campus available for juniors and seniors. Substance-free housing also available. *Special Academic Facilities/Equipment:* Art gallery, Concert Hall, Taylor and Boody tracker organ, O'Callahan Science Library, Rehm Library, Multimedia Resource Center, Wellness Center. *Computers:* 100% of classrooms, 100% of dorms, 100% of libraries, 100% of dining areas, 100% of student union, 60% of common outdoor areas have wireless network access.

FINANCIAL FACTS

Financial Aid Rating	**99**
Annual tuition	$43,088
Room and board	$11,020
Required fees	$2,713
Books and supplies	$1,040
% frosh rec. need-based scholarship or grant aid	52
% UG rec. need-based scholarship or grant aid	50
% frosh rec. need-based self-help aid	40
% UG rec. need-based self-help aid	43
% frosh rec. any financial aid	54
% UG rec. any financial aid	60

Cornell College

600 First Street South West, Mount Vernon, IA 52314-1098 • Admissions: 319-895-4477 • Fax: 319-895-4451

CAMPUS LIFE

Quality of life Rating	74
Fire Safety Rating	74
Green rating	76
Type of School	Private
Environment	Rural

STUDENTS

Total undergrad enrollment	1,183
% Male to Female	46/54
% From out of state	81
% From public high school	79
% Live on Campus	92
# of Fraternities	8
# of Sororities	7
% African American	4
% Asian	3
% Caucasian	75
% Hispanic	6
% Native American	1
% International	5
# Of Countries Represented	19

ACADEMICS

Academic Rating	89
% Of students graduating within 4 years	62
% Of students graduating within 6 years	66
Calendar	semester
Profs interesting rating	93
Profs accessible rating	94
Most common reg class size	10–19 students
Most common lab size	20–29 students

MOST POPULAR MAJORS

Economics, history, psychology

SPECIAL STUDY OPTIONS

Accelerated program, double major, English as a Second Language (ESL), exchange student program (domestic), independent study, internships, liberal arts/career combination, student-designed major, study abroad, teacher certification program

ABOUT THE SCHOOL

Cornell College may be "a small private school in a quaint Iowa town," but this liberal arts school has something that makes it stand out from the crowd: A unique one-course-at-a-time program which affords students an opportunity to focus on just one course, or "block," at a time. This means during any given semester students will be wholly immersed in one focus of study. For at least one student, the "very appealing" one-course-at-a-time block plan "was my final decision-making factor," a plan that "makes it easier to try off-campus opportunities" and which "offers great advantages for humanities students."

Why Students love Cornell College

> "I feel that I'm learning a great deal while simultaneously learning how to apply that knowledge productively."

When it comes to the people delivering that education, the professors here "run the gamut from incredibly accessible and passionate to complete space-cadets who aren't that invested in the process." No matter the professor, relatively small class sizes make it easier to face each new course, and because of those small class sizes, "it's very easy to develop strong relationships with classmates." The work here is "difficult but rewarding." Cornell College will "will give you every opportunity for success," students say, but "it's up to you to make the most of it." That kind of reliance on individual spirit extends to the makeup of the student population. There is "oddness and diversity" on display among the student body, a "small community" with "a lot of unique people." It is, one student says, "all about being different and not giving a damn what others think of you." "It's easy to find a million things to do on any given day," even without leaving campus. Students say there are "always bands, theater, comedians, hypnotists, and a ton of other things right on campus." Off campus, down time takes place at dorm parties or town bars. Students also visit two nearby cities for a taste of a more urban-centric nightlife.

BANG FOR YOUR BUCK

A generous 75 percent of incoming freshmen receive need-based grants or scholarships, and a whopping 95 percent of undergraduates overall receive financial aid in one form or another. This aid comes in the form of Federal Pell grants, state, school and private scholarships and grants, Stafford loans, and others. There are modest off-campus job opportunities.

STUDENTS

1,183 undergrad enrollment

46% Male ♂♂♂♂♂♂♂♂♂

54% Female ♀♀♀♀♀♀♀♀♀♀♀

ADMISSIONS

3,791 →	39%	24%	EARLY ADMISSIONS →	NR	NR
applicants	admitted	enrolled		applicants	accepted

3.50 avg. high school gpa

ACT range (0–36): 24–29

SAT range (200–800): reading 540–680, math 530–680, writing 530–640

GRADUATION RATES

62% of students graduating within 4 yrs

66% of students graduating within 6 yrs

Cornell College

FINANCIAL AID: 319-895-4216 • E-MAIL: ADMISSIONS@CORNELLCOLLEGE.EDU • WEBSITE: WWW.CORNELLCOLLEGE.EDU

STUDENT BODY

There's "a great diversity of interests" in people who attend Cornell, and the "super busy" students have a hard time defining a more common characteristic than the fact that almost all are driven and involved. Some division into typical groups does occur–"the cafeteria design and Greek life are very conducive to this problem"–but "even group to group there is always mingling because you never know who will be in your next class." Since the classes are so small and "you see the same people four hours a day for three and a half weeks," people are generally accepting, and "You have to be really, really strange here to stick out." As one freshman says, "The only intolerance I've seen is toward the consistently indolent."

WHY STUDENTS LOVE CORNELL COLLEGE

Cornell College provides a unique education that makes students fall in love with the school. Those who embrace it say the block program "allows for some incredible and intense academic experiences." Overachievers love the system. However, be wary, because "if you don't fully commit, you feel terrible on the block plan." Overall, many students rank the one-course-at-a-time program as among "the greatest strengths of the school." None of this could be delivered without good teachers–and Cornell has them, students say. The "dedication and enthusiasm of the professors" offers students "a more personalized learning experience," something important to them. They appreciate "the opportunity to get to know faculty and staff on a personal level." Students here boast that their "absolutely amazing" professors have had "a huge impact on my academic, personal, and professional goals." They are "tough," another student says, "and make me work hard, but also know how to motivate and encourage their students." Those "wonderful professors" are "experts in their fields of study" who are "always available and work hard to work one-on-one with students."

GENERAL INFO

Activities: Choral groups, concert band, dance, drama/theater, jazz band, literary magazine, music ensembles, musical theater, opera, radio station, student government, student newspaper, symphony orchestra, yearbook, campus ministries, international student organization. **Organizations:** 90 registered organizations, 11 honor societies, 11 religious organizations. 8 fraternities, 7 sororities. **Athletics (Intercollegiate):** *Men:* Baseball, basketball, cross-country, football, golf, soccer, tennis, track/field (outdoor), track/field (indoor), wrestling. *Women:* Basketball, cross-country, golf, soccer, softball, tennis, track/field (outdoor), track/field (indoor), volleyball. **On-Campus Highlights:** Commons–Orange Carpet–student center, Cole Library, small multi-sports center, Kimmel Theatre, McWethy Hall–newly renovated art building. Most predominant features on campus are our beautiful King Chapel. A newly renovated Armstrong Hall of fine arts. A new pedestrian mall (with outdoor ampitheatre) that connects the entire campus. **Environmental Initiatives:** Engineering study on costs of replacing current campus-side steam heat network, including specific costs and energy savings payback times for each building. Currently spec'ing biodiesel refinery to convert food service discarded oils into fuel for college equipment.

BOTTOM LINE

Students accepted to Cornell College will pay an annual tuition of $32,720. Add to that $7,730 for room and board, $810 for books and supplies, and $200 for other fees, and costs go to $41,450 annually. Students leave Cornell with an average accumulated debt of $22,455.

SELECTIVITY

Admissions Rating	**92**
# of applicants	3,791
% of applicants accepted	39
% of acceptees attending	24
# accepting a place on wait list	75
% admitted from wait list	55

FRESHMAN PROFILE

Range SAT Critical Reading	**540–680**
Range SAT Math	**530–680**
Range SAT Writing	**530–640**
Range ACT Composite	**24–29**
Average HS GPA	**3.50**
% graduated top 10% of class	**33**
% graduated top 25% of class	**62**
% graduated top 50% of class	**88**

DEADLINES

Regular Deadline	**2/1**
Normal registration	**yes**

FACILITIES

Housing: Coed dorms, men's dorms, women's dorms, apartments for single students. Our first year students live on first-year only floors and/or in first-year only residence halls. *Special Academic Facilities/Equipment:* Geology center and museum, MNR machine in West Sc. Building, Luce Art Gallery. *Computers:* 100% of classrooms, 20% of dorms, 100% of libraries, 100% of dining areas, 100% of student union, 10% of common outdoor areas have wireless network access.

FINANCIAL FACTS

Financial Aid Rating	**90**
Annual tuition	$32,720
Room and Board	$7,730
Required Fees	$200
Books and supplies	$810
% frosh rec. need-based scholarship or grant aid	75
% UG rec.need-based scholarship or grant aid	74
% frosh rec. non-need-based scholarship or grant aid	67
% UG rec. non-need-based scholarship or grant aid	63
% frosh rec. need-based self-help aid	63
% UG rec. need-based self-help aid	62
% frosh rec. any financial aid	94
% UG rec. any financial aid	95
% UG borrow to pay for school	73
Average cumulative indebtedness	$22,455

Cornell University

Undergraduate Admissions, 410 Thurston Ave, Ithaca, NY 14850 • Admissions: 607-255-5241 • Fax: 607-255-0659

CAMPUS LIFE

Quality of life Rating	90
Fire Safety Rating	78
Green rating	97
Type of School	Private
Environment	Town

STUDENTS

Total undergrad enrolllment	13,935
% Male to Female	50/50
% From out of state	64
% From public high school	70
% Live on Campus	57
# of Fraternities	47
# of Sororities	19
% African American	5
% Asian	16
% Caucasian	46
% Hispanic	8
% International	9
# Of Countries Represented	120

ACADEMICS

Academic Rating	92
% Of students graduating within 4 years	86
% Of students graduating within 6 years	93
Calendar	semester
Profs interesting rating	77
Profs accessible rating	77
Most common reg class size	10–19 students
Most common lab size	10–19 students

MOST POPULAR MAJORS

Engineering, business/marketing, biology, agriculture, social sciences

SPECIAL STUDY OPTIONS

Accelerated program, cooperative education program, cross-registration, distance learning, double major, English as a Second Language (ESL), exchange student program (domestic), honors program, independent study, internships, liberal arts/career combination, student-designed major, study abroad, teacher certification program. Special programs offered to physically disabled students include note-taking services, reader services, voice recorders, tutors.

ABOUT THE SCHOOL

"Any person, any study." Perhaps no motto does a better job of summing up the spirit of a school than Ithaca, New York's Cornell University, an Ivy League school in upstate New York consisting of seven undergraduate colleges. Cornell University is not just Ivy League, it's the largest of the Ivy League schools–and it has a curriculum to match. The "unbelievably broad curriculum" at Cornell offers "large variety of academic programs" and "a plethora of classes to chose from," giving credence to the school's famous motto. There are more than 40 different majors at the College of Arts and Sciences alone. Factor in six other schools and it's clear that students have a wealth of options before them. Specializations in science, agriculture, and environmental studies are especially popular here, though engineering, pre-med and other studies receive just as much attention by attendees. "The research opportunities have been incredible," one student says. Another notes that thanks to the hard work it demands of students and the school's great reputation, Cornell is a "difficult school with great job placement after." With all the educational opportunities Cornell has to offer, it should come as no surprise that the campus features an "intellectually mature student body" who are intent on focusing on the school's "rigorous" academics. "The intellectual caliber of the student body here is really unmatched."

When study time ends, students exploring the "bustling student life" will see that "diversity here is definitely apparent…I love the fact that you can be surrounded by dairy farmers and wall-street wannabes all in the same quad." About the only thing tying Cornell's student population together is the fact that everyone is "very focused on performing well in the classroom." Outside the classroom, recreation is just as diverse as the classes. Being in Ithaca, New York, opportunities for outdoor adventure abound, and Greek life thrives. Sports are as popular here as partying–basketball, track, and hockey are the school's top sports–and students note that "if I want to go study in a library at 3 a.m. on Saturday night I will find a busy library full of other eager students, but if I want to go to a hockey game on a Saturday afternoon I will find just as many screaming fans to share the fun."

BANG FOR YOUR BUCK

Needs-based Federal Pell, SEOG, state scholarships/grants, private scholarships, school scholarship or grant aid from institutional funds are all available to prospective students. Loan aid is also available in the form of Direct Subsidized Stafford loans, Direct Unsubsidized Stafford, Direct PLUS, Federal Perkins, and university loans from institutional funds.

STUDENTS

13,935 undergrad enrollment

50% Male ♂♂♂♂♂♂♂♂♂♂

50% Female ♀♀♀♀♀♀♀♀♀♀

ADMISSIONS

36,392 →	18%	48%	EARLY →	NR	NR
applicants	admitted	enrolled	ADMISSIONS	applicants	accepted

4.09 avg. high school gpa

29–33

0 — 36 ACT range

reading 640–730

math 670–770

200 — 800 SAT range

GRADUATION RATES

86% of students graduating within 4 yrs

93% of students graduating within 6 yrs

FINANCIAL AID: 607-255-5147 • E-MAIL: ADMISSIONS@CORNELL.EDU • WEBSITE: WWW.CORNELL.EDU

STUDENT BODY

With such a large student body, "there is always a niche that any individual can fall into." Sure enough, the school's size and Ivy League status make it "a largely diverse and exciting bubble" where there is an abundance of "athletes or frat/sorority people," but at the same time, "you have a large group of students who do other activities." "We have our nerdy engineers, our outgoing hoteliers, our hipster art students, [and] our hardcore dairy farmers," brags one proud student. A "strong work ethic" seems to be the unifying thread among Cornell's diverse student body, as all students are "very focused on performing well in the classroom." "Most everyone has a secret nerdiness inside them that actually adds to their 'coolness,'" explains one. The different schools tend to naturally group together more frequently, so that each quad "has its own vibe," but "everyone is very friendly and approachable." Basically, "when you come here, you become the typical Cornellian."

Why Students love Cornell University

"The intellectual caliber of the student body here is really unmatched."

WHY STUDENTS LOVE CORNELL UNIVERSITY

"I wouldn't have been able to have an all expenses paid trip to Italy to go on an archaeological dig at a small liberal arts college!" And that's why students love Cornell University. Because it offers them opportunities they hadn't previously imagined. Yes, the university is in a "beautiful location" and "the campus is stunningly beautiful." Yes, it is a "big university [with] a small town feel" and is considered "a leader among colleges and universities." But many schools have a lovely campus and small town feel, and many are well-respected. What draws students to Cornell is the diversity in education it has to offer. Students enjoy that the curriculum "not only allowed but encouraged me to take courses in other fields." One student offered as a compliment that at Cornell you'll find "every kind of person, every kind of class, and everything about it is hard." Yet for many that will translate to "most incredible experience of their life."

GENERAL INFO

Environment: Town. **Activities:** Choral groups, concert band, dance, drama/theater, jazz band, literary magazine, marching band, music ensembles, musical theater, pep band, radio station, student government, student newspaper, student-run film society, symphony orchestra, television station, yearbook, cam- pus ministries, international student organization. **Organizations**: 841 registered organizations, 22 honor societies, 61 religious organizations. 50 fraternities, 19 sororities. **Athletics (Intercollegiate):** *Men:* Baseball, basketball, crew/rowing, cross-country, diving, football, golf, ice hockey, lacrosse, polo, soccer, squash, swimming, tennis, track/field (outdoor), track/field (indoor), wrestling. *Women:* Basketball, crew/rowing, cross-country, diving, equestrian sports.

BOTTOM LINE

An Ivy League education at Cornell University will cost attendees just more than $41,000 per year in tuition. Add to that $13,000 for room and board, and another $1,000 for books, fees, and supplies, and costs hover at about the $55,000 mark annually. Students are graduating from Cornell with an average accumulated debt of $20,000.

SELECTIVITY

Admissions Rating	**96**
# of applicants	36,392
% of applicants accepted	18
% of acceptees attending	48
# accepting a place on wait list	1,483
% admitted from wait list	0

FRESHMAN PROFILE

Range SAT Critical Reading	**640–730**
Range SAT Math	**670–770**
Range ACT Composite	**29–33**
% graduated top 10% of class	**90**
% graduated top 25% of class	**99**
% graduated top 50% of class	**100**

DEADLINES

Regular Deadline	**1/3**
Normal registration	**no**

FACILITIES

Housing: Coed dorms, special housing for disabled students, men's dorms, special housing for international students, women's dorms, fraternity/sorority housing, apartments for married students, cooperative housing, apartments for single students, theme housing. *Special Academic Facilities/Equipment:* Biotechnology institute, a woods sanctuary, 4 designated national resource centers, Africana studies and research center, arboretum, particle accelerator, supercomputer, national research centers. *Computers:* 20% of classrooms, 100% of dorms, 100% of libraries, 100% of dining areas, 75% of student union, 20% of common outdoor areas have wireless network access.

FINANCIAL FACTS

Financial Aid Rating	**95**
Annual in-state tuition	$41,325
Room and Board	$13,160
Required Fees	$216
Books and supplies	$800
% frosh rec. need-based scholarship or grant aid	50
% UG rec.need-based scholarship or grant aid	48
% frosh rec. need-based self-help aid	44
% UG rec. need-based self-help aid	44
% UG borrow to pay for school	52
Average cumulative indebtedness	$20,648

Dartmouth University

6016 McNutt Hall, Hanover, NH 03755 • Admissions: 603-646-2875 • Fax: 603-646-1216

CAMPUS LIFE

Quality of Life Rating	98
Fire Safety Rating	60*
Green Rating	94
Type of school	private
Environment	village

STUDENTS

Total undergrad enrollment	4,135
% male/female	50/50
% from out of state	95
% from public high school	62
% live on campus	87
# of fraternities	14
# of sororities	6
% African American	8
% Asian	15
% Caucasian	50
% Hispanic	8
% Native American	3
% international	7
# of countries represented	78

ACADEMICS

Academic Rating	96
% students graduating within 4 years	88
% students graduating within 6 years	95
Calendar	quarter
Profs interesting rating	86
Profs accessible rating	90
Most common reg class size	10–19 students

MOST POPULAR MAJORS

Economics, political science, psychology

HONOR PROGRAMS

Presidential Scholarship Research Program; Senior Honors Thesis; Senior Fellowship.

SPECIAL STUDY OPTIONS

Double major, exchange student program (domestic), honors program, independent study, intern- ships, student-designed major, study abroad, teacher certification program.

ABOUT THE SCHOOL

A member of the Ivy League, Dartmouth is a small, student-centered, undergraduate and graduate College, with three leading professional schools–Dartmouth Medical School, Thayer School of Engineering, and the Tuck School of Business. It is known for its commitment to excellence in undergraduate education, and has a reputation as a place where intellectual rigor and creativity collide. This comes from a flexible academic curriculum that emphasizes an interdisciplinary approach.

The campus community is generally relaxed, accepting, a bit outdoorsy, and usually bundled up under eight layers of clothing to get through the New Hampshire winters. What students learn outside the classroom is often as meaningful as what they learn inside. All incoming freshmen live in residential housing clusters located throughout the campus, and more than 80 percent of upperclassmen choose to do so as well. Almost all of the student body comes from outside the college's New Hampshire base. Greek groups add to the social mix because everyone is welcome to attend fraternity and sorority parties and events. Intramural athletics are insanely popular on campus as well.

Why Students love Darthmouth University

"Campus was gorgeous and all the students are remarkably welcoming of first years."

BANG FOR YOUR BUCK

Dartmouth's approximately 4,100 undergraduate students enjoy the college's strong reputation as a member of the Ivy League, as well as its high-quality academics through 29 departments and 10 multidisciplinary programs. Academics at New Hampshire's preeminent college, comparable with other Ivy League schools, are demanding, but Dartmouth students feel they are up to the challenge. Unlike many of the other Ivies, though, the student-faculty ratio of 8:1 favors the undergrads, who find graduate assistants in their classes to have the same open willingness to help them learn as the regular professors do.

STUDENTS

4,135 undergrad enrollment

50% Male ♂♂♂♂♂♂♂♂♂♂

50% Female ♀♀♀♀♀♀♀♀♀♀

ADMISSIONS

18,778 applicants → 12% admitted; 52% enrolled

EARLY ADMISSIONS → NR applicants; NR accepted

NR avg. high school gpa

reading 670–780
math 690–790
690–790

30-34 — ACT range (0–36)

SAT range (200–800)

GRADUATION RATES

88% of students graduating within 4 yrs

95% of students graduating within 6 yrs

Dartmouth University

FINANCIAL AID: 603-646-2451 • E-MAIL: ADMISSIONS.OFFICE @DARTMOUTH.EDU • WEBSITE: WWW.DARTMOUTH.EDU

STUDENT BODY

The quintessential Dartmouth undergraduate is "athletic, sociable, and very active within the community inside and outside of Dartmouth." "The binding element of the typical Dartmouth student is passion," one student tells us. "Whether it is academics or the environment, students are committed to an area of interest and try to contribute to that field." "There is a ton of diversity," one undergrad reports. "Through my friends I can interact and get a taste of Ghana, Trinidad, and Japan; what it means to be a Sikh, Jew, Buddhist, or Christian; how it feels to be a homosexual or transsexual; what it's like to live below the poverty line or miles above it." Wonder what they all share in common? "Everyone here is exceptional."

WHY STUDENTS LOVE DARTMOUTH

The attraction goes beyond the New England Ivy League tradition. One student explains, "Dartmouth has a flexible calendar (The D Plan) that made studying abroad possible. Besides its outstanding academic reputation, Dartmouth students know how to have fun. The work hard, party hard reputation was attractive to me." Another student shares, "Dartmouth produces future leaders and lifetime learners by constantly challenging students of every discipline to think critically, challenge conventional wisdom, and engage in hands-on learning, but does so without losing sight of the traditional, fun college experience." One alumna sums it up by commenting, "Dartmouth had the best of everything for me–name recognition but not too much pressure; wildly intelligent people who also know how to have fun; and a strangely inclusive Greek system."

GENERAL INFO

Activities: Choral groups, concert band, dance, drama/theater, jazz band, literary magazine, marching band, music ensembles, musical theater, opera, pep band, radio station, student government, student newspaper, student-run film society, symphony orchestra, television station, yearbook, campus ministries, international student organization. **Organizations:** 330 registered organizations, 26 religious organizations. 14 fraternities, 6 sororities. **Athletics (Intercollegiate):** *Men:* Baseball, basketball, crew/rowing, cross-country, diving, equestrian sports, fencing, football, golf, ice hockey, lacrosse, sailing, skiing (downhill/alpine), skiing (nordic/cross-country), soccer, squash, swimming, tennis, track/field (outdoor), track/field. *Women:* Basketball, crew/rowing, cross-country, diving, equestrian sports, fencing, field hockey, golf, ice hockey, lacrosse, sailing, skiing (downhill/alpine), skiing (nordic/cross-country), soccer, softball, squash, swimming, tennis, track/field (outdoor), track/ fi. **On-Campus Highlights:** Hopkins Center for Creative and Performing Arts, Hood Museum of Art, Murals by Jose Clemente Orozco, Ten library system, all open to visitors, Ledyard Canoe Club, oldest in the country.

BOTTOM LINE

To enjoy an Ivy League education with a nod to the New England collegiate experience, incoming freshmen at Dartmouth can expect to pay about $42,000 in tuition and roughly another $1,500 in required fees. On-campus room and board totals more than $12,000. Almost half of Dartmouth students receive scholarships to help defray these costs, as the school maintains the philosophy that no one should hesitate to apply for fear they won't be able to afford it. A recent graduate shares her experience: "The administration is great to work with. Opportunities for funding to travel and do research, internships, volunteer, etc. are AMAZING.

SELECTIVITY

Admissions Rating	**96**
# of applicants	18,778
% of applicants accepted	12
% of acceptees attending	52
# accepting a place on wait list	1,027
% admitted from wait list	23

FRESHMAN PROFILE

Range SAT Critical Reading	**670–780**
Range SAT Math	**690–790**
Range SAT Writing	**690–790**
Range ACT Composite	**30–34**
% graduated top 10% of class	**79**
% graduated top 25% of class	**90**
% graduated top 50% of class	**100**

DEADLINES

Regular Deadline	**1/1**
Normal registration	**no**

FACILITIES

Housing: Coed dorms, special housing for international students, fraternity/sorority housing, apartments for married students, cooperative housing, apartments for single students. *Special Academic Facilities/Equipment:* Hood Museum of Art, Hopkins Center for Performing Arts, Tucker Foundation for volunteer services. *Computers:* 100% of classrooms, 100% of dorms, 100% of libraries, 100% of dining areas, 100% of student union, 100% of common outdoor areas have wireless network access.

FINANCIAL FACTS

Financial Aid Rating	**96**
Annual in-state tuition	$41,736
Room and board	$12,369
Required fees	$1,540
Books and supplies	$1,851
% frosh rec. need-based scholarship or grant aid	48
% UG rec. need-based scholarship or grant aid	51
% frosh rec. need-based self-help aid	40
% UG rec. need-based self-help aid	47
% frosh rec. any financial aid	50
% UG rec. any financial aid	52
% UG borrow to pay for school	48
Average cumulative indebtedness	$19,051

Davidson College

PO Box 7156, Davidson, NC 28035-7156 • Admissions: 704-894-2230 • Fax: 704-894-2016

CAMPUS LIFE

Quality of life Rating	99
Fire Safety Rating	60*
Green rating	60*
Type of School	Private
Environment	Village

STUDENTS

Total undergrad enrolllment	1,738
% Male to Female	50/50
% From out of state	74
% From public high school	51
% Live on Campus	91
# of Fraternities	8
% African American	7
% Asian	5
% Caucasian	72
% Hispanic	5
% International	4
# Of Countries Represented	36

ACADEMICS

Academic Rating	98
% Of students graduating within 4 years	89
% Of students graduating within 6 years	91
Calendar	semester
Profs interesting rating	96
Profs accessible rating	99
Most common reg class size	10–19 students
Most common lab size	10–19 students

MOST POPULAR MAJORS

Biology, English language and literature, history

SPECIAL STUDY OPTIONS

Cross-registration, double major, exchange student program (domestic), honors program, independent study, student-designed major, study abroad, teacher certification program. Special programs offered to physically disabled students include note-taking services, reader services, voice recorders, tutors.

ABOUT THE SCHOOL

Davidson is a place where serious students can thrive and really throw themselves into the world of academia, all while surrounded by similarly energetic, curious, and quirky students. At this small, "really beautiful" school north of Charlotte, North Carolina, students come from nearly every state in the union and from dozens of foreign countries to immerse themselves in the "intellectually challenging, academically rigorous" cocoon that Davidson provides. The school offers a classic liberal arts education, encouraging students to take classes in all areas, and "all of these people come out smarter than they came in." Classes are small and intensive, with significant contact between students and faculty both in and out of the classroom, and faculty, while emphasizing teaching, involve students in significant research projects. There is a lot of work, but it "is accompanied by even more resources with which it can be successfully managed." "I have never witnessed people so eager to come do their job every day. [Professors] are almost too willing to help," says a student. The honor code also helps contribute "to having a safe and reliable environment."

Why Students love Davidson College

"Everyone has a unique passion, a unique story and is interested in your uniqueness."

BANG FOR YOUR BUCK

Davidson is consistently regarded as one of the top liberal arts colleges in the country, and its small size (and 20-person class limits) give students access to a level of academic guidance and greatness that most college students can only dream of, at a price that students can afford. The school has just 1,700 undergraduates, but offers $17 million a year in financial aid. On top of the holy triumvirate of financial aid, Davidson offers merit scholarships ranging from $1,000 to the full cost of education. The school is also need-blind to life experience: Need and merit aid can go with students on approved study-abroad programs, thereby eliminating a potential barrier to having an international experience.

STUDENTS

1,738 undergrad enrollment

50% Male ♂♂♂♂♂♂♂

50% Female ♀♀♀♀♀♀♀♀

ADMISSIONS

4,088 applicants → 29% admitted — 41% enrolled

EARLY ADMISSIONS → NR applicants — NR accepted

4.00 avg. high school gpa

ACT range (0–36): 28–32

SAT range (200–800): reading 630–720, math 630–710, writing 620–720

GRADUATION RATES

89% of students graduating within 4 yrs

91% of students graduating within 6 yrs

E-MAIL: ADMISSION@DAVIDSON.EDU • WEBSITE: WWW.DAVIDSON.EDU

STUDENT BODY

Davidson is "an amalgamation of all types of people, religiously, ethnically, politically, economically, etc.," all "united under the umbrella of intellectual curiosity" and their devotion to the school as a community. The typical Davidson student is "probably white," but in the past few years, admissions has been making progress in racially diversifying the campus, which students agree upon as necessary. Though there are plenty of Southern, preppy, athletic types to fit the brochure examples, there are many niches for every type of "atypical" student. "There are enough people that one can find a similar group to connect with, and there are few enough people that one ends up connecting with dissimilar [people] anyway," says a student. Everyone here is smart and well-rounded; admissions "does a good job...so if you're in you'll probably make the cut all the way through the four years." Most students have several extracurriculars to round out their free time, and they have a healthy desire to enjoy themselves when the books shut. "During the week we work hard. On the weekends we play hard. We don't do anything halfway," says a senior. Though the majority of students lean to the left, there's a strong conservative contingent, and there are no real problems between the two.

WHY STUDENTS LOVE DAVIDSON COLLEGE

"If I could spend twenty years being educated by this administration and these professors, I would," says a very happy junior. The school handles the small stuff and provides structure with autonomy, letting the students concentrate on their studies. "Davidson is all about enabling the student to focus on their schoolwork by doing everything else for them," says a student. The availability of professors "is no joke. They love to be visited and have conversations not only about academics, but also personal matters." An idyllic atmosphere and small size "allows for constant interaction with peers and professors," and "everyone has a unique passion, a unique story and is interested in your uniqueness." The people at Davidson "make it a platform from which to develop as a scholar, a leader, and a productive community member."

GENERAL INFO

Activities: Choral groups, concert band, dance, drama/theater, jazz band, literary magazine, music ensembles, musical theater, pep band, radio station, student government, student newspaper, symphony orchestra, yearbook, campus ministries, international student organization. **Organizations:** 151 registered organizations, 15 honor societies, 16 religious organizations. 8 fraternities. **Athletics (Intercollegiate):** *Men:* Baseball, basketball, cross-country, diving, football, golf, soccer, swimming, tennis, track/field (outdoor), wrestling. *Women:* Basketball, cross-country, diving, field hockey, lacrosse, soccer, swimming, tennis, track/field (outdoor), volleyball. **On-Campus Highlights:** Belk Visual Arts Center, Baker-Watt Science Complex, Baker Sports Complex, Campus Center, Lake Campus.

BOTTOM LINE

Tuition runs about $39,000, with an additional $11,000 or so needed for room and board. However, the school hits the three major financial aid points: it admits domestic students on a need-blind basis, meets 100% of all students' calculated need, and does so with grant and work funds only, not requiring students to utilize loans to have their need met. Aid is also guaranteed throughout the four years, if a family's financial circumstances stay the same.

SELECTIVITY

Admissions Rating	**98**
# of applicants	4,088
% of applicants accepted	29
% of acceptees attending	41

FRESHMAN PROFILE

Range SAT Critical Reading	**630–720**
Range SAT Math	**630–710**
Range SAT Writing	**620–720**
Range ACT Composite	**28–32**
Average HS GPA	**4.00**
% graduated top 10% of class	**78**
% graduated top 25% of class	**95**
% graduated top 50% of class	**100**

DEADLINES

Regular Deadline	**1/2**
Normal registration	**no**

FACILITIES

Housing: Coed dorms, cooperative housing, apartments for single students, wellness housing, theme housing. *Special Academic Facilities/Equipment:* Art gallery, scanning electron microscopes, UV-visible spectrometer, laser systems, Baker sports complex, Visual Arts building. *Computers:* Students can register for classes online.

FINANCIAL FACTS

Financial Aid Rating	**98**
Annual tuition	$38,481
Room and Board	$10,857
Required Fees	$385
Books and supplies	$1,000
% frosh rec. need-based scholarship or grant aid	42
% UG rec.need-based scholarship or grant aid	41
% frosh rec. non-need-based scholarship or grant aid	18
% UG rec. non-need-based scholarship or grant aid	17
% frosh rec. need-based self-help aid	23
% UG rec. need-based self-help aid	21
% frosh rec. any financial aid	35
% UG rec. any financial aid	35
% UG borrow to pay for school	32
Average cumulative indebtedness	$23,233

DePauw University

101 E. Seminary, Greencastle, IN 46135 • Admissions: 765-658-4006 • Fax: 765-658-4007

CAMPUS LIFE

Quality of life Rating	77
Fire Safety Rating	66
Green rating	61
Type of School	Private
Environment	Village

STUDENTS

Total undergrad enrolllment	2,362
% Male to Female	43/57
% From out of state	57
% From public high school	83
% Live on Campus	98
# of Fraternities	13
# of Sororities	11
% African American	7
% Asian	3
% Caucasian	72
% Hispanic	4
% International	10
# Of Countries Represented	34

ACADEMICS

Academic Rating	93
% Of students graduating within 4 years	82
% Of students graduating within 6 years	85
Calendar	semester
Profs interesting rating	88
Profs accessible rating	97
Most common reg class size	10–19 students
Most common lab size	10–19 students

MOST POPULAR MAJORS

Economics, speech communication and rhetoric

HONORS PROGRAMS

Honor Scholar Program. Special programs offered to physically disabled students include note-taking services, reader services, voice recorders, tutors.

SPECIAL STUDY OPTIONS

Double major, dual enrollment, exchange student program (domestic), honors program, independent study, internships, student-designed major, study abroad, teacher certification program.

ABOUT THE SCHOOL

Serious-minded students are drawn to DePauw University for its "small classes," "encouraging" professors, and the "individual academic attention" they can expect to receive. Academically, DePauw is "demanding but rewarding," and "requires a lot of outside studying and discipline" in order to keep up. Professors lead small, discussion-based classes and hold their students firmly to high academic standards. Professors' "expectations are very high," which means "you can't slack off and get good grades." Be prepared to pull your "fair share of all-nighters.".

Beyond stellar professors, DePauw's other academic draws include "extraordinary" study abroad opportunities and a "wonderful" alumni network great for "connections and networking opportunities." Alums also "keep our endowment pretty high, making it easy for the school to give out merit scholarships," which undergraduates appreciate. DePauw emphasizes life outside the classroom, too. The school operates several fellowships to support independent projects by high-achieving students, and four out of five DePauw students will complete a professional internship during college. The Winter Program, a month-long inter-term, sends many students abroad while allowing others to undertake research or creative projects. Arts and culture are at the forefront of campus life; a huge new performing arts center is under construction, and the school's annual ArtsFest allows students and invited artists to exhibit or perform for the campus and community.

BANG FOR YOUR BUCK

Small class sizes, close community, athletic opportunities, alumni network, great scholarships, and campus involvement make DePauw a good value. Need-based aid is available, and DePauw is also strong in the area of merit-based awards. All first-year applicants are automatically considered for scholarships, and awards are determined based on a student's GPA, course load, class rank, and standardized test scores. Almost 80 percent of the school's scholarship assistance comes from institutional funds rather than state or federal sources. Once a student is enrolled at DePauw, the only scholarships available come through individual academic departments. In addition to these general scholarships, the school operates several scholarship programs for students that meet specific criteria. To apply for need-based aid, students must submit the FAFSA, as well as the DePauw application for need-based assistance. More than half of DePauw's student body receives some form of need-based financial aid through grants, loans, and work-study. The average financial aid package totals $28,000. Students who aren't eligible for work-study may still apply for campus jobs through the financial aid office.

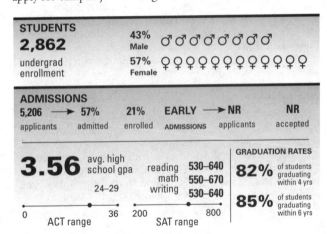

STUDENTS

2,862 undergrad enrollment

43% Male ♂♂♂♂♂♂♂♂

57% Female ♀♀♀♀♀♀♀♀♀♀♀

ADMISSIONS

5,206 applicants → 57% admitted | 21% enrolled | EARLY ADMISSIONS → NR applicants | NR accepted

3.56 avg. high school gpa

ACT range: 0–36; 24–29

SAT range: 200–800; reading 530–640; math 550–670; writing 530–640

GRADUATION RATES

82% of students graduating within 4 yrs

85% of students graduating within 6 yrs

DePauw University

FINANCIAL AID: 765-658-4030 • E-MAIL: ADMISSION@DEPAUW.EDU • WEBSITE: WWW.DEPAUW.EDU

STUDENT BODY

The typical DePauw student is "upper-middle-class," "a little preppy, a little athletic," and "hardworking;" "parties hard on weekend," and "usually become involved with the Greek system." Students describe their peers as "driven" and wearing "polos and pearls." They "have all had multiple internships, international experience, and [have held] some type of leadership position." Though these folks may seem "overcommitted," they "always get their work done." For those who don't fit this mold, don't fret; most students seem to be "accepting of the different types" of people on campus. Diversity on campus is augmented through the school's partnership with the Posse Foundation, which brings in urban (though not necessarily minority) "students from Chicago and NYC every year." These students are described as "leaders on campus" and "take real initiative to hold their communities together."

WHY STUDENTS LOVE DEPAUW UNIVERSITY

A current student describes DePauw as, "A close-knit community of intelligent, extremely hardworking people who know how to let loose and enjoy the best of both the academic and social scenes." "DePauw University has a prestigious reputation among liberal arts colleges" says an undergrad, "and DePauw also offers a small learning environment so that students get maximum exposure to professors one on one." "What I appreciate is the faculty-student ratio–my professors know my name! I know this was the perfect fit for me."

When asked about campus life, a student comments that "clubs and activities are also strengths of DePauw life. You can bet that DePauw offers a club for your particular interest, whether it is political or social."

Why Students love DePauw University

"A close-knit community of intelligent, extremely hardworking people who know how to let loose and enjoy the best of both the academic and social scenes."

GENERAL INFO

Activities: Choral groups, concert band, dance, drama/theater, jazz band, literary magazine, music ensembles, musical theater, opera, pep band, radio station, student government, student newspaper, student-run film society, symphony orchestra, television station, campus ministries, international student organization. **Organizations:** 119 registered organizations, 13 honor societies, 10 religious organizations. 13 fraternities, 11 sorority. **Athletics (Intercollegiate):** *Men:* Baseball, basketball, cross-country, diving, football, golf, soccer, swimming, tennis, track/field (outdoor), track/field (indoor). *Women:* Basketball, cross-country, diving, field hockey, golf, soccer, softball, swimming, tennis, track/field (outdoor), track/field (indoor), volleyball.

BOTTOM LINE

DePauw tuition and fees are about $36,000, with an additional $10,000 for room and board. Incoming students are also required to purchase a laptop. Families have the option of paying their college costs monthly (with no deferred payment charge) or each semester. Although DePauw does not guarantee meeting full demonstrated need for each student, the school's track record is good, with many students receiving all the funding they need.

SELECTIVITY

Admissions Rating	**92**
# of applicants	5,206
% of applicants accepted	57
% of acceptees attending	21
# accepting a place on wait list	39
% admitted from wait list	15

FRESHMAN PROFILE

Range SAT Critical Reading	**530–640**
Range SAT Math	**550–670**
Range SAT Writing	**530–640**
Range ACT Composite	**24–29**
Average HS GPA	**3.56**
% graduated top 10% of class	**53**
% graduated top 25% of class	**83**
% graduated top 50% of class	**97**

DEADLINES

Regular Deadline	**2/1**
Normal registration	**yes**

FACILITIES

Housing: Coed dorms, special housing for disabled students, special housing for international students, fraternity/sorority housing, apartments for single students *Special Academic Facilities/Equipment:* Recently opened Peeler Art Center housing gallery and studio space, Center for Contemporary Media, Performing Arts Center, Anthropology Museum, Shidzuo Iikudo Museum. *Computers:* Students can register for classes online.

FINANCIAL FACTS

Financial Aid Rating	**89**
Annual in-state tuition	$36,500
Room and Board	$9,730
Required Fees	$470
Books and supplies	$750
% frosh rec. need-based scholarship or grant aid	57
% UG rec.need-based scholarship or grant aid	53
% frosh rec. non-need-based scholarship or grant aid	13
% UG rec. non-need-based scholarship or grant aid	11
% frosh rec. need-based self-help aid	43
% UG rec. need-based self-help aid	41
% UG borrow to pay for school	48
Average cumulative indebtedness	$24,210

Duke University

2138 Campus Drive, Box 90586, Durham, NC 27708-0586 • Admissions: 919-684-3214

CAMPUS LIFE

Quality of life Rating	70
Fire Safety Rating	60*
Green rating	94
Type of School	Private
Environment	City

STUDENTS

Total undergrad enrollment	6,066
% Male to Female	52/48
% From out of state	85
% From public high school	65
% Live on Campus	82
# of Fraternities	21
# of Sororities	14
% African American	11
% Asian	15
% Caucasian	58
% Hispanic	7
% International	5
# Of Countries Represented	89

ACADEMICS

Academic Rating	95
% Of students graduating within 4 years	86
% Of students graduating within 6 years	92
Calendar	semester
Profs interesting rating	82
Profs accessible rating	78
Most common reg class size	10–19 students
Most common lab size	20–29 students

MOST POPULAR MAJORS

Economics, psychology, public policy analysis

SPECIAL STUDY OPTIONS

Accelerated program, cross-registration, distance learning, double major, exchange student program (domestic), honors program, independent study, internships, student-designed major, study abroad, teacher certification program, undergrads may take grad level classes. Off-Campus Study: New York Arts Program.

ABOUT THE SCHOOL

Duke University offers students a word-class education and freedom in choosing the academic path that best meets their needs. The school's research expenditures rank in the top ten nationally, the library system is extensive, and the school's Division I sports teams are legendary. Still, the undergraduate experience is the heart and soul of the school. Students are required to live on campus for three years. First-year students live together on East Campus, where about a quarter of them participate in FOCUS, a living/learning program organized around academic themes, which gives them access to faculty mentoring and a smaller community of students they get to know well.

Maybe it's the mild North Carolina climate, but the students say their campus is way more laid-back than what you'd find at any of the other Ivy League schools. It's also breathtakingly beautiful, featuring soaring Gothic buildings, modern teaching and research facilities, accessible athletic fields and recreational spaces, and a lush botanical garden. It's true that Duke Students are focused on academics, but they are just as enthusiastic about attending campus events, participating in Greek functions, or cheering on the teams at Duke sporting events, especially when it's the school's top-ranked basketball team that's playing.

BANG FOR YOUR BUCK

Duke is dedicated to making its outstanding education affordable. More than half of undergraduates receive some sort of financial assistance, including need-based aid, and merit or athletic scholarships. Students are evaluated for admission without regard to their ability to pay. If admitted, Duke pledges to meet 100 percent of need. There are no loans or parental contributions required for families with incomes under $40,000. Families with incomes under $60,000 are not required to make a parental contribution, and the school offers capped loans for eligible families with incomes of more than $100,000.

The biggest value is the academic experience. One student explains, "Every single one of my professors actually knows me very well. They know where I'm from; they know what I actually find funny in class; they know when I'm sick and are incredibly parental in making sure that I get all of my work done and stay healthy; they know *ME*. How many other students can say that in any university?" Another student adds, "I wanted a medium college that was not too large but had research opportunities. I liked the culture at Duke and the choice was easy because they also gave me the best financial package."

STUDENTS

6,066 undergrad enrollment

52% Male ♂♂♂♂♂♂♂♂♂♂♂

48% Female ♀♀♀♀♀♀♀♀♀♀♀

ADMISSIONS

18,090 applicants → 22% admitted | 43% enrolled | EARLY ADMISSIONS → NR applicants | NR accepted

4.09 avg. high school gpa

ACT range (0–36): 29 – 34

SAT range (200–800): reading 690 – 770; math 690 – 800

GRADUATION RATES

86% of students graduating within 4 yrs

92% of students graduating within 6 yrs

Duke University

Financial Aid: 919-684-6225 • E-mail: undergrad-admissions@duke.edu • Website: www.duke.eduwww.duke.edu

STUDENT BODY

The typical Duke student "is someone who cares a lot about his or her education but at the same time won't sacrifice a social life for it." Life involves "getting a ton of work done first and then finding time to play and have fun." The typical student here is studious but social, athletic but can never be seen in the gym, job hunting but not worrying, and so on and so forth." Everyone is "incredibly focused," but "That includes social success as well." Students tend to be "focused on graduating and obtaining a lucrative and prosperous career," and although they "go out two to three times a week," they're "always looking polished." An "overwhelming number" are athletes, "not just varsity athletes...but athletes in high school or generally active people. Duke's athletic pride attracts this kind of person."

Why Students love Duke University

"Not only is Duke an incredible institution academically, but it is also a community of which I am proud to be a part."

WHY STUDENTS LOVE DUKE UNIVERSITY

Overall, the people make the difference at Duke. A student in his fourth year shares, "I have enjoyed all of my professors; I have had many engaging discussions in class. There are a few who make me want to stay at Duke forever. I am so incredibly grateful for this." Another positive aspect that students appreciate is that Duke offers a chance to get a great education while still having an active social life. One current student comments, "Work hard, play harder: Duke provides a balance of social life and academics. It is the best of both worlds."

GENERAL INFO

Activities: Choral groups, concert band, dance, drama/theater, jazz band, literary magazine, marching band, music ensembles, musical theater, opera, pep band, radio station, student government, student newspaper, student-run film society, symphony orchestra, television station, yearbook. **Organizations:** 200 registered organizations, 10 honor societies, 25 religious organizations. 21 fraternities, 14 sororities. **Athletics (Intercollegiate):** *Men:* Baseball, basketball, cross-country, diving, fencing, football, golf, lacrosse, soccer, swimming, tennis, track/field (outdoor), track/field (indoor), volleyball, wrestling. *Women:* Basketball, crew/rowing, cross-country, diving, fencing, field hockey, golf, lacrosse, soccer, swimming, tennis, track/field (outdoor), track/ field (indoor), volleyball. On-Campus Highlights: Primate Center, Sarah P. Duke Gardens, Duke Forest, Levine Science Research Center.

BOTTOM LINE

With a moderately-sized campus of 6,000 undergraduates, students have the opportunity to work closely with the school's accomplished faculty. Academics are challenging, especially in the quantitative majors like science and mathematics. However, there are plentiful student resources, including a writing center and a peer-tutoring program, not to mention the constant support from the school's teaching staff. Innovation and independence are encouraged; the school offers grants for undergraduate research projects, as well as travel grants and awards for artistic endeavors.

SELECTIVITY

Admissions Rating	**97**
# of applicants	18,090
% of applicants accepted	22
% of acceptees attending	43
# accepting a place on wait list	1,026
% admitted from wait list	10

FRESHMAN PROFILE

Range SAT Critical Reading	**690–770**
Range SAT Math	**690–800**
Range ACT Composite	**29–34**
% graduated top 10% of class	**90**
% graduated top 25% of class	**98**
% graduated top 50% of class	**100**

DEADLINES

Regular Deadline	**1/2**
Normal registration	**no**

FACILITIES

Housing: Coed dorms, men's dorms, women's dorms, fraternity/sorority housing, apartments for single students, theme houses. *Special Academic Facilities/Equipment:* Art museum, language lab, university forest, primate center, phytotron, electron laser, nuclear magnetic resonance machine, nuclear lab.

FINANCIAL FACTS

Financial Aid Rating	**94**
Annual in-state tuition	$40,575
Room and Board	$11,830
Books and supplies	$970
% frosh rec. need-based scholarship or grant aid	38
% UG rec.need-based scholarship or grant aid	37
% frosh rec. non-need-based scholarship or grant aid	1
% UG rec. non-need-based scholarship or grant aid	1
% frosh rec. need-based self-help aid	35
% UG rec. need-based self-help aid	35
% UG borrow to pay for school	40
Average cumulative indebtedness	$16,502

Emory University

Boiseuillet Jones Ctr, Atlanta, GA 30322 • Admissions: 404-727-6036 • Fax: 404-727-6039

CAMPUS LIFE

Quality of life Rating	98
Fire Safety Rating	70
Green rating	94
Type of School	Private
Environment	Town

STUDENTS

Total undergrad enrolllment	7,140
% Male to Female	44/55
% From out of state	73
% From public high school	62
% Live on Campus	68
# of Fraternities	14
# of Sororities	12
% African American	10
% Asian	16
% Caucasian	47
% Hispanic	4
% International	13
# Of Countries Represented	101

ACADEMICS

Academic Rating	94
% Of students graduating within 4 years	82
% Of students graduating within 6 years	88
Calendar	semester
Profs interesting rating	89
Profs accessible rating	88
Most common reg class size	10–19 students
Most common lab size	fewer than 10 students

MOST POPULAR MAJORS
Business, economics
biology, psychology

SPECIAL STUDY OPTIONS

Cooperative education program, cross-registration, double major, dual enrollment, English as a Second Language (ESL), honors program, independent study, internships, liberal arts/ career combination, study abroad, teacher certification program, qualified undergraduates may take a semester of off-campus study in Washington, D.C.

ABOUT THE SCHOOL

Emory University is known for demanding academics, highly ranked professional schools, and state-of-the-art research facilities. One student insightfully defines Emory as a place that "seeks to bring together intelligent, well-rounded students and prepare them to positively impact the world around them." Students are taught by Emory's distinguished faculty, which includes President Jimmy Carter, Salman Rushdie, and the Dalai Lama. "The professors are very accessible and open to students, and the classes are small enough that I cannot really go unnoticed" writes one sophomore. At Emory, students take learning seriously but also have the time for extracurricular pursuits as athletes, leaders of clubs and organizations, and community service participants. Campus traditions help create a close-kit community all the way up to graduation, when Dooley, "the spirit of Emory" appears for students' final send-off. As one student puts it: "everywhere I go, I see people I know, but I am constantly meeting new people as well." Students that decide to remain on campus have access to "several academic advisors" throughout the school year and that kind of attention will definitely appeal to undecided academics. Downtown Atlanta is just a few miles from campus, and students head there to catch a concert at Philips Arena or toss a frisbee in Centennial Olympic Park. Research opportunities are available to undergraduates in all fields.

BANG FOR YOUR BUCK

Need-blind admission is a cornerstone of Emory's financial aid philosophy. A family's ability to pay is not considered in the admission process. Emory further enhances access and affordability with special financial aid initiatives such as Emory Advantage. Emory Advantage provides additional need-based grant assistance to eligible families with total annual incomes of $100,000 or less. Emory Advantage funding is designed to reduce a student's dependence on educational borrowing normally required to attain an undergraduate degree. Competitive merit-based scholarships are also offered to incoming first-year students. Through the Emory and Goizueta Scholars Programs, which can cover up to the full cost of tuition and fees, students receive enriched intellectual, cultural, and social programs throughout their college years. Recipients of these competitive awards represent an impressive range of academic, cultural, and extracurricular interests and achievements themselves. Most of the students have been National Merit finalists or semifinalists, and almost all have won distinction beyond the classroom. In addition, some merit scholarships are available to continuing Emory students on a competitive basis after their first or second year of study at Emory.

STUDENTS
7,140 undergrad enrollment
45% Male ♂♂♂♂♂♂♂♂♂
55% Female ♀♀♀♀♀♀♀♀♀♀♀

ADMISSIONS
15,550 applicants → **30%** admitted **3%** enrolled
EARLY ADMISSIONS → **NR** applicants **NR** accepted

3.84 avg. high school gpa

ACT range: 30–34 (0–36)

SAT range (200–800):
reading 640–740
math 670–760
writing 650–750

GRADUATION RATES
85% of students graduating within 4 yrs
93% of students graduating within 6 yrs

FINANCIAL AID: 404-727-6039 • E-MAIL: ADMISS@EMORY.EDU • WEBSITE: WWW.EMORY.EDU

STUDENT BODY

Emory undergrads are a "hardworking" lot, and the typical student is "extremely committed to their academics." Most have "high aspirations" and a "large chunk of the student body is very pre-professional (premed, pre-law, business, etc.)." Luckily, they're "not afraid to have fun," and many are "involved in extracurricular activities and do some community service." Importantly, they also view their peers as "friendly, outgoing, and personable." To some students, it seems as though Emory attracts a large number of "white, wealthy, Northeastern, prep-school kids." And it sometimes feels like "every other person you meet is from Long Island." However, others insist that the university is rather diverse, proclaiming that there are "people from all types of lifestyles, cultures, and backgrounds." As one satisfied international studies undergrad boasts, "All students bring unique perspectives."

Why Students love Emory University

"Emory is excellent at preparing students for professional life after college, particularly pre-professional or graduate school."

WHY STUDENTS LOVE EMORY

An undergraduate notes that "Emory is excellent at preparing students for professional life after college, particularly pre-professional or graduate school." The "small feel...suburban" campus is equipped with "large-school resources" that offers a multitude of "diverse pre-career" instructional programs for students interested in pre-med, pre-business or pre-law schooling. Some students feel that the Emory experience is not for everyone as Emory can sometimes feel "like a marathon; it's a lot of hard work, but you get what you put into it." Once you've made it into this "highly selective liberal arts college," Emory becomes "a place where one can experience diversity in many ways." Some students will be certain to find this through the bustling Greek social strata; while others, not inclined to "hit up frat row" will feel more at home exploring the shifting vicissitudes of Georgia's capital. Emory "sponsors weekly shuttles" to "concerts...malls" and "museums".

GENERAL INFO

Activities: Choral groups, concert band, dance, drama/theater, jazz band, literary magazine, marching band, music ensembles, musical theater, opera, pep band, radio station, student government, student newspaper, student-run film society, symphony orchestra, television station, campus ministries, international student organization. **Organizations:** 51 registered organizations, 30 honor societies, 27 religious organizations. 14 fraternities, 12 sororities. **Athletics (Intercollegiate):** *Men:* Baseball, basketball, cross-country, diving, golf, soccer, swimming, tennis, track/field (outdoor). *Women:* Basketball, cross-country, diving, soccer, softball, swimming, tennis, track/field (outdoor), volleyball. **On-Campus Highlights:** Michael C. Carlos Museum, Lullwater Park.

BOTTOM LINE

The sticker price for tuition, room and board, and fees at Emory is more than $50,000 a year. Financial aid is generous though, so don't let the numbers scare you away from applying.

SELECTIVITY

Admissions Rating	**98**
# of applicants	15,550
% of applicants accepted	30
% of acceptees attending	3
# accepting a place on wait list	1,091
% admitted from wait list	6

FRESHMAN PROFILE

Range SAT Critical Reading	**640–740**
Range SAT Math	**670–760**
Range SAT Writing	**650–750**
Range ACT Composite	**30–33**
Average HS GPA	**3.84**
% graduated top 10% of class	**84**
% graduated top 25% of class	**98**
% graduated top 50% of class	**100**

DEADLINES

Regular Deadline	**1/15**
Normal registration	**no**

FACILITIES

Housing: Coed dorms, special housing for disabled students, special housing for international students, women's dorms, fraternity/sorority housing, apartments for married students, apartments for single students, theme housing.

FINANCIAL FACTS

Financial Aid Rating	**93**
Annual tuition	$40,600
Room and Board	$11,628
Required Fees	$564
Books and supplies	$1,100
% frosh rec. need-based scholarship or grant aid	47
% UG rec.need-based scholarship or grant aid	47
% frosh rec. non-need-based scholarship or grant aid	5
% UG rec. non-need-based scholarship or grant aid	4
% frosh rec. need-based self-help aid	43
% UG rec. need-based self-help aid	42
% frosh rec. any financial aid	55
% UG rec. any financial aid	54
% UG borrow to pay for school	43
Average cumulative indebtedness	$26,311

Franklin W. Olin College of Engineering

OLIN WAY, NEEDHAM, MA 02492-1245 • ADMISSIONS: 781-292-2222 • FAX: 781-292-2210

CAMPUS LIFE

Quality of life Rating	98
Fire Safety Rating	87
Green rating	67
Type of School	Private
Environment	Town

STUDENTS

Total undergrad enrolllment	346
% Male to Female	55/45
% From out of state	88
% Live on Campus	99
% African American	1
% Asian	17
% Caucasian	57
% Hispanic	3
% International	8
# Of Countries Represented	14

ACADEMICS

Academic Rating	99
% Of students graduating within 4 years	83
% Of students graduating within 6 years	90
Calendar	semester
Profs interesting rating	99
Profs accessible rating	95
Most common reg class size	20–29 students

MOST POPULAR MAJORS

Electrical and electronics engineering, engineering, mechanical engineering

SPECIAL STUDY OPTIONS

Accelerated program, cross-registration, double major, exchange student program (domestic), honors program, independent study, internships, student-designed major, study abroad, teacher certification program.

ABOUT THE SCHOOL

Olin College offers a rigorous engineering curriculum that prepares students to be "twenty-first century engineers." At Olin, which only opened in 2002, the spirit of hands-on collaboration transcends the classroom. Though the school's history is short, the vision has long been evolving, and this "tight-knit community of eager learners and tinkerers" thrives on a sense of "innovation and initiative." Located 14 miles outside of Boston, the school is "small, quirky, and somewhat in a bubble," but "full of amazing adventures and opportunities." A typical day includes everything from "watching a movie" to a "midnight bike expedition," not to mention "experimental baking, pickup soccer, zombie video games, auditorium movie screenings, [and] midnight dump raids."

Professors are "one of the best–if not the best–part of Olin," and are frequently described as "always available, always knowledgeable, [and] always approachable." The school's curriculum is designed to create "engineers who understand the entire development process with a deep understanding of engineering's business impact." Programs emphasize inquiry-based learning and team-based projects in a community of self-directed learners, and the focus on "experiential education" and "entrepreneurial implementation" pro¬vides students with "the ability to help design the curriculum and the school culture." All Olin students receive real-world experience through the senior year capstone experience, when they complete a project for a company or organization. In addition, the Office of PostGraduate Planning is very active in helping students find internships. Combined with an extraordinary level of financial aid for all students, Olin provides an unusual opportunity for talented engineering students.

BANG FOR YOUR BUCK

Though a 50 percent tuition scholarship is nothing to sneeze at, this number once stood at 100%, but the economic downturn forced a reduction. The school hopes to return to full scholarship as soon as the financial situation allows. In the meantime, the school still offers quite the bargain, especially considering its reputation among employers. The senior-year capstone project is quite a foot in the door for young engineers entering the workforce, and many students convert their experience into a job. In addition to institutional grants, National Merit Finalists who win a scholarship or corporate sponsorship can use their scholarship at Olin; finalists who designate Olin College as their first choice college but do not receive a NMSC or corporate-sponsored scholarship will be designated as Olin National Merit Scholars, and will be awarded a $1,000 scholarship, renewable for three years, funded by Olin College.

STUDENTS

346 undergrad enrollment

55% Male ♂♂♂♂♂♂♂♂♂♂♂

45% Female ♀♀♀♀♀♀♀♀♀

ADMISSIONS

567 applicants	→ 30% admitted	53% enrolled	EARLY ADMISSIONS →	NR applicants	NR accepted

3.90 avg. high school gpa

ACT range (0–36): 33 – 35

SAT range (200–800): reading 670 – 750; math 710 – 780; writing 650 – 730

GRADUATION RATES

83% of students graduating within 4 yrs

90% of students graduating within 6 yrs

Franklin W. Olin College of Engineering

FINANCIAL AID: 781-292-2343 • E-MAIL: INFO@OLIN.EDU • WEBSITE: WWW.OLIN.EDU

STUDENT BODY

"Take the nation's top engineering students, mix with awesome personalities, add a dash of amazing resources, and shake vigorously." When it comes to describing the typical student, there is no status quo. "There are all sorts of people at Olin. Some of us avoid homework by discussing meta-physics and ethics. Others watch old episodes of Firefly...Some people read books in their spare time." The commonality? "Students care about their educations," and "everyone takes their own paths." Though students say they "may make geeky jokes," "People don't act like socially stunted nerds." "Passionate, intelligent, witty, [and] exceedingly interesting," "The typical student at Olin is atypical, whether that means having a hidden talent in unicycle fire juggling, a passion for writing musicals, an obsession with velociraptors, or a tendency to make pancakes at three in the morning every Thursday."

Why Students love Olin

"Take the nation's top engineering students, mix with awesome personalities, add a dash of amazing resources, and shake vigorously."

WHY STUDENTS LOVE OLIN

There's a whole lot to love at Olin, where "innovation, entrepreneurship, [and] prestige" all come together for a handful of lucky people. "Olin is a place where intelligent, motivated students can explore their interests both in engineering and in life as a whole." "People work hard, but they also know how to play hard, take breaks, and have fun." A love and mutual respect for the abilities of fellow students permeates every classroom, dorm, and dining hall, and students say, "Every student at Olin is interesting enough that you want to sit down and talk to them for hours." Students note that even the higher-ups go by a first name basis: "You can regularly chat with the president at lunch."

GENERAL INFO

Activities: Choral groups, concert band, dance, drama/theater, jazz band, literary magazine, marching band, music ensembles, musical theater, opera, pep band, radio station, student government, **Organizations:** 393 registered organizations, 1 honor societies, 28 religious organizations. **Athletics (Intercollegiate):** *Men:* Baseball, basketball, crew/rowing, cross-country, diving, fencing, football, golf, ice hockey, lacrosse, sailing, skiing (downhill/ alpine), skiing (nordic & cross-country), soccer, squash, swimming, tennis, track/ field (outdoor), track/field (indoor), volleyball. *Women:* Basketball, crew/ rowing, cross-country, diving, fencing, field hockey, golf, ice hockey, lacrosse, sailing, skiing (downhill/alpine), skiing (nordic & cross-country), soccer, softball, squash, swimming, tennis, track/ field, volleyball.

BOTTOM LINE

Olin was founded on the premise that financial considerations should not stand in the way of an excellent engineering education, and hence all enrolled students receive a 50% tuition scholarship, making tuition $19,500 a year, with an additional estimated $20,000 in additional expenses and fees.

SELECTIVITY

Admissions Rating	**99**
# of applicants	567
% of applicants accepted	30
% of acceptees attending	53
# accepting a place on wait list	35
% admitted from wait list	0

FRESHMAN PROFILE

Range SAT Critical Reading	**670–750**
Range SAT Math	**710–780**
Range SAT Writing	**650–730**
Range ACT Composite	**33–35**
Average HS GPA	**3.90**
% graduated top 10% of class	**95**
% graduated top 25% of class	**99**
% graduated top 50% of class	**100**

DEADLINES

Regular Deadline	**1/1**
Normal registration	**no**

FACILITIES

Housing: Coed dorms, special housing for disabled students, apartments for married students, cooperative housing. *Special Academic Facilities/Equipment:* Museums (University Arts Museums, Museums of Cultural History. *Computers:* 98% of classrooms, 100% of dorms, 100% of libraries, have wireless network access.

FINANCIAL FACTS

Financial Aid Rating	**99**
Annual tuition	$39,000
Room and Board	$14,000
Required Fees	$450
Books and supplies	$750
% frosh rec. need-based scholarship or grant aid	40
% UG rec.need-based scholarship or grant aid	18
% frosh rec. non-need-based scholarship or grant aid	100
% UG rec. non-need-based scholarship or grant aid	100
% frosh rec. need-based self-help aid	65
% UG rec. need-based self-help aid	34
% frosh rec. any financial aid	100
% UG rec. any financial aid	100
% UG borrow to pay for school	17
Average cumulative indebtedness	$13,200

Georgetown University

37TH AND O STREETS, NW, 103 WHITE-GRAVEN, WASHINGTON, D.C. 20057 • ADMISSIONS: 202-687-3600

CAMPUS LIFE

Quality of life Rating	80
Fire Safety Rating	82
Green rating	87
Type of School	Private
Environment	Metropolis

STUDENTS

Total undergrad enrolllment	7,092
% Male to Female	43/55
% From out of state	99
% From public high school	40
% Live on Campus	70
% African American	7
% Asian	9
% Caucasian	65
% Hispanic	6
% International	7
# Of Countries Represented	138

ACADEMICS

Academic Rating	87
% Of students graduating within 4 years	85
% Of students graduating within 6 years	93
Calendar	semester
Profs interesting rating	84
Profs accessible rating	81
Most common reg class size	10–19 students
Most common lab size	20–29 students

MOST POPULAR MAJORS

English language and literature, international relations, political science

HONORS PROGRAMS

John Carroll Programs

SPECIAL STUDY OPTIONS

Cross-registration, double major, English as a Second Language (ESL), honors program, independent study, internships, student-designed major, study abroad

ABOUT THE SCHOOL

Georgetown was founded in 1789 by John Carroll, who concurred with his contemporaries Benjamin Franklin and Thomas Jefferson in believing that the success of the young democracy depended upon an educated and virtuous citizenry. Carroll founded the school with the dynamic Jesuit tradition of education, characterized by humanism and committed to the assumption of responsibility and action. Georgetown is a national and international university, enrolling students from all fifty states and more than 100 foreign countries. Undergraduate students are enrolled in one of four undergraduate schools: the College of Arts and Sciences, School of Foreign Service, Georgetown School of Business, and Georgetown School of Nursing and Health Studies. All students share a common liberal arts core and have access to the entire university curriculum.

This moderately sized elite academic establishment stays true to its Jesuit foundations by educating its students with the idea of "cura personalis," or "care for the whole person." The "well-informed" student body perpetuates upon itself, creating an atmosphere full of vibrant intellectual life, that is "also balanced with extracurricular learning and development." "Georgetown is…a place where people work very, very hard without feeling like they are in direct competition," says an international politics major.

BANG FOR YOUR BUCK

Professors tend to be "fantastic scholars and teachers" and are "generally available to students," as well as often being "interested in getting to know you as a person (if you put forth the effort to talk to them and go to office hours)." Though Georgetown has a policy of grade deflation, meaning "A's are hard to come by," there are "a ton of interesting courses available," and TAs are used only for optional discussion sessions and help with grading. The academics "can be challenging or they can be not so much (not that they are ever really easy, just easier);" it all depends on the courses you choose and how much you actually do the work. Internship opportunities in the DC area are valuable, and often take place "in the heart of the nation's capital." People know the importance of connections and spend time making sure they get to know the people here. One student is very enthusiastic about these opportunities. "The location in DC and the pragmatism of people who come here make for people that are fun to be around but are serious about their ambitions. There's a reason that Georgetown tends to draw political junkies. It's because there's no better place in the United States to get involved with politics on a national level."

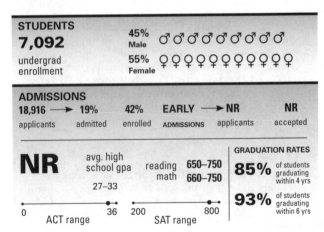

STUDENTS

7,092 undergrad enrollment

45% Male ♂♂♂♂♂♂♂♂♂

55% Female ♀♀♀♀♀♀♀♀♀♀♀

ADMISSIONS

18,916 applicants → 19% admitted — 42% enrolled

EARLY ADMISSIONS → NR applicants — NR accepted

NR avg. high school gpa

ACT range (0–36): 27–33

SAT range (200–800): reading 650–750; math 660–750

GRADUATION RATES

85% of students graduating within 4 yrs

93% of students graduating within 6 yrs

Georgetown University

FINANCIAL AID: 202-687-4547 • FAX: 202-687-5084 • E-MAIL: GUADMISS@GEORGETOWN.EDU • WEBSITE: WWW.GEORGETOWN.EDU

STUDENT BODY

There are "a lot of wealthy students on campus," and preppy-casual is the fashion de rigueur; this is "definitely not a 'granola' school," but students from diverse backgrounds are typically welcomed by people wanting to learn about different experiences. Indeed, everyone here is well-traveled and well-educated, and there are "a ton of international students." "You better have at least some interest in politics or you will feel out-of-place," says a student. The school can also be "a bit cliquish, with athletes at the top," but there are "plenty of groups for everybody to fit into and find their niche," and "there is much crossover between groups."

Why Students love Georgetown University

"Georgetown is a place that challenges your mind in order to develop your soul."

WHY STUDENTS LOVE GEORGETOWN

Students are "extremely well aware of the world around them," from government to environment, social to economic, and "Georgetown is the only place where an argument over politics, history, or philosophy is preceded by a keg stand." Hoyas like to have a good time on weekends, and parties at campus and off-campus apartments and townhouses "are generally open to all comers and tend to have a somewhat networking atmosphere; meeting people you don't know is a constant theme." Whatever your interest is, Georgetown definitely has an organization for you to be involved in. Because there are no fraternities or sororities, "social life is very focused on the clubs a person joins. It provides a great feeling of community and makes social groups flexible and non-cliquey," one undergrad enthuses.

GENERAL INFO

Activities: Choral groups, concert band, dance, drama/theater, jazz band, literary magazine, music ensembles, musical theater, pep band, radio station, student government, student newspaper, student-run film society, symphony orchestra, television station, yearbook. **Organizations:** 139 registered organizations, 14 honor societies, 20 religious organizations. **Athletics (Intercollegiate):** *Men:* Baseball, basketball, crew/rowing, cross-country, diving, football, golf, lacrosse, sailing, soccer, swimming, tennis, track/field (outdoor), track/field (indoor). *Women:* Basketball, crew/rowing, cross-country, diving, field hockey, golf, lacrosse, sailing, soccer, softball, swimming, tennis, track/field (outdoor), track/field (indoor), volleyball. **On-Campus Highlights:** Yates Field House, Uncommon Grounds, The Observatory, The Quadrangle, Healy Hall.

BOTTOM LINE

Georgetown University has a well-deserved reputation for the outstanding quality of its curriculum and the fantastic overall educational experience it provides. Of course, the cost of tuition reflects that to a great extent, amounting to nearly $40,000 with books, supplies, and fees. Room and board tacks on another $13,000. At the same time, Georgetown meets 100 percent of student need; with an average financial aid package of $35,000, it is easy to see that a Georgetown education is still accessible to a large segment of potential students. Total need-based gift aid to freshmen tends to be approximately $28,000, providing even more support for needy undergrads. Students can envision a loan debt of about $23,000 once they graduate from the university.

SELECTIVITY

Admissions Rating	**95**
# of applicants	18,916
% of applicants accepted	19
% of acceptees attending	42
# accepting a place on wait list	1,362
% admitted from wait list	12

FRESHMAN PROFILE

Range SAT Critical Reading	**650–750**
Range SAT Math	**660–750**
Range ACT Composite	**27–33**

DEADLINES

Regular Deadline	**1/10**
Normal registration	**no**

FACILITIES

Housing: Coed dorms, special housing for disabled students, apartments for single students, freshmen and sophomores are required to live on campus. *Special Academic Facilities/Equipment:* Language lab, seismological observatory. *Computers:* Students can register for classes online. Administrative functions (other than registration) can be performed online.

FINANCIAL FACTS

Financial Aid Rating	**95**
Annual tuition	$38,616
Room and Board	$13,125
Required Fees	$420
Books and supplies	$1,060
% frosh rec. need-based scholarship or grant aid	40
% UG rec.need-based scholarship or grant aid	37
% frosh rec. non-need-based scholarship or grant aid	8
% UG rec. non-need-based scholarship or grant aid	7
% frosh rec. need-based self-help aid	38
% UG rec. need-based self-help aid	36
% UG borrow to pay for school	44
Average cumulative indebtedness	$23,333

Gettysburg College

Admissions Office, Eisenhower House, Gettysburg, PA 17325-1484 • Admissions: 717-337-6100 • Fax: 717-337-6145

CAMPUS LIFE

Quality of life Rating	85
Fire Safety Rating	88
Green rating	83
Type of School	Private
Environment	Village

STUDENTS

Total undergrad enrolllment	2,489
% Male to Female	47/53
% From out of state	75
% From public high school	70
% Live on Campus	94
# of Fraternities	12
# of Sororities	6
% African American	4
% Asian	2
% Caucasian	81
% Hispanic	4
% International	2
# Of Countries Represented	38

ACADEMICS

Academic Rating	95
% Of students graduating within 4 years	82
% Of students graduating within 6 years	85
Calendar	semester
Profs interesting rating	91
Profs accessible rating	94
Most common reg class size	10–19 students
Most common lab size	10–19 students

MOST POPULAR MAJORS

Business/commerce, political science, psychology

SPECIAL STUDY OPTIONS

Double major, independent study, internships, student-designed major, study abroad, teacher certification program.

ABOUT THE SCHOOL

Gettysburg is a national college of liberal arts and sciences located in Gettysburg, Pennsylvania. Gettysburg's 2,600 students are actively involved in an academically rigorous and personally challenging educational experience; offered through a wonderful "combination of small student-body and world-class faculty and administrative" members. "The small class sizes are a huge benefit for students, as they get individual attention [something] so hard to find at most other institutions." With an average class size of 18 and a student-to-faculty ratio of 11:1, there are no passive learners here–personal interactions and supports are part of the educational process. Don't be surprised if professors here know you by first name. One visiting, prospective undergraduate explains: "I met a biology professor in the college parking lot [who] took two hours out of his day to show us around the Science Center, the labs and classrooms and even introduce me to the Chair of the Biology Department."

At Gettysburg, all first-years participate in the First-Year Seminar, in which students analyze, investigate, research, discuss, and debate a diverse range of topics and themes. "The small environment provides the best conditions for participating in class, getting to know professors on a personal basis, and having a voice on campus," all while brazenly engaging whatever academic pursuits the student desires. "There is something for everyone," a Sophomore expresses, "from trumpet performance to Latin studies to globalization to health sciences." Gettysburg's world-famous Sunderman Conservatory of Music attracts many artists to its campus and enables students to "seriously study music while allowing [them] to explore other areas of study as well." Research opportunities are copious, and students graduate from Gettysburg with hands-on learning experiences attractive to employers and graduate schools alike. "The Center for Career Development does a great job of helping students of all class years find internships, externships and job-shadowing opportunities."

BANG FOR YOUR BUCK

Gettysburg College awards about $38 million in scholarships and grants each year. Both need-based and merit-based awards are available. Merit-based scholarships range from $7,000 to $25,000 per year. A separate application is not required; decisions on merit scholarship recipients are made as part of the admissions process. Talent scholarships are also available. Gettysburg College grants vary from $500 to $38,690, based on financial need. The average freshman grant is $28,000.

STUDENTS

2,489 undergrad enrollment

47% Male ♂♂♂♂♂♂♂♂♂♂

53% Female ♀♀♀♀♀♀♀♀♀♀♀

ADMISSIONS

5,392 →	40%	33%	EARLY ADMISSIONS →	NR	NR
applicants	admitted	enrolled		applicants	accepted

NR avg. high school gpa

reading 610–690

math 620–680

NR

0 — 36 ACT range

200 — 800 SAT range

GRADUATION RATES

82% of students graduating within 4 yrs

85% of students graduating within 6 yrs

FINANCIAL AID: 717-337-6611 • E-MAIL: ADMISS@GETTYSBURG.EDU • WEBSITE: WWW.GETTYSBURG.EDU

STUDENT BODY

Academics come first at Gettysburg, where "The student body is extremely intelligent and motivated and serious about their work." When they're not studying, "Gettysburg's student body is very involved" in the school and local community, and "Volunteering is very popular." "Each student–in one way or another–takes part in community service during their time at Gettysburg." Demographically, "Most of the student body is...middle-class, white, and from the Northeast." And, lest we forget, the Gettysburg student body is also well known for its uniform "tendency to wear preppy clothes." A current student elaborates, "Open up a J. Crew magazine and find the most attractive models in it and you have a typical Gettysburg College student." While some say the student body has a "cookie-cutter" feel to it, others remind us that "while Gettysburg has a reputation for being mostly white, upper-class students, there is diversity all around if you are willing to open up your eyes and see it."

Why Students love Gettysburg College

"The small environment provides the best conditions for participating in class, getting to know professors on a personal basis, and having a voice on campus."

WHY STUDENTS LOVE GETTYSBERG COLLEGE

"The campus offers countless opportunities for leadership, self-discovery and the like, and where a student isn't just another number, but recognized for their contributions to the campus community," writes one undergraduate. Certain students have a very different take on Gettysburg, describing it as "very 'Hemingway-esque'...habitually drunk, but brilliant nonetheless." Gettysburg prides itself, however, on its "sense of community," being "a small school with a strong Greek program leads to little rivalry" and offers a place where students can "ultimately strike a balance between academics and a social life."

GENERAL INFO

Activities: Choral groups, concert band, dance, drama/ theater, jazz band, literary magazine, marching band, music ensembles, radio station, student government, student newspaper, student-run film society, symphony orchestra, television station, yearbook, campus ministries, international student organization. **Organizations:** 120 registered organizations, 16 honor societies, 7 religious organizations. 10 fraternities, 6 sororities. **Athletics (Intercollegiate):** *Men:* Baseball, basketball, cheerleading, cross-country, football, golf, lacrosse, soccer, swimming, tennis, track/ field (outdoor), track/ field (indoor), wrestling. *Women:* Basketball, cheerleading, cross-country, field hockey, golf, lacrosse, soccer, softball, swimming, tennis, track/field (outdoor), track/field

BOTTOM LINE

At Gettysburg College, tuition and fees cost about $41,000 per year. Room and board on campus costs about $10,000. Prospective students should also factor in the annual cost of books, supplies, transportation, and personal expenses. Overall, about 70 percent of Gettysburg students receive some sort of funding from their "irresistible...and generous financial aid program."

SELECTIVITY

Admissions Rating	**93**
# of applicants	5,392
% of applicants accepted	40
% of acceptees attending	33
# accepting a place on wait list	588
% admitted from wait list	0

FRESHMAN PROFILE

Range SAT Critical Reading	**610–690**
Range SAT Math	**620–680**
% graduated top 10% of class	**68**
% graduated top 25% of class	**86**
% graduated top 50% of class	**99**

DEADLINES

Regular Deadline	**2/1**
Normal registration	**yes**

FACILITIES

Housing: Coed dorms, women's dorms, fraternity/sorority housing, apartments for single students, theme housing, special interest and theme housing. *Special Academic Facilities/Equipment:* Art gallery, Child Study lab, Majestic Theatre, Sunderman Conservatory, planetarium, observatory, electron microscopes, NMR spectrometer, greenhouse, digital classrooms, wireless network, Plasma Physics labs. *Computers:* 100% of classrooms, 100% of dorms, 100% of libraries, 100% of dining areas, 100% of student union, 90% of common outdoor areas have wireless network access.

Financial Aid Rating	**95**
Annual tuition	$41,070
Room and Board	$9,810
Books and supplies	$1,100
% frosh rec. need-based scholarship or grant aid	55
% UG rec.need-based scholarship or grant aid	53
% frosh rec. non-need-based scholarship or grant aid	31
% UG rec. non-need-based scholarship or grant aid	27
% frosh rec. need-based self-help aid	51
% UG rec. need-based self-help aid	50
% frosh rec. any financial aid	70
% UG rec. any financial aid	68
% UG borrow to pay for school	60
Average cumulative indebtedness	$24,987

Grinnell College

1103 Park Street, Grinnell, IA 50112-1690 • Admissions: 641-269-3600 • Fax: 641-269-4800

CAMPUS LIFE

Quality of life Rating	82
Fire Safety Rating	83
Green rating	83
Type of School	Private
Environment	Village

STUDENTS

Total undergrad enrollment	1,603
% Male to Female	45/55
% From out of state	87
% From public high school	70
% Live on Campus	88
% African American	5
% Asian	6
% Caucasian	59
% Hispanic	7
% International	12
# Of Countries Represented	54

ACADEMICS

Academic Rating	96
% Of students graduating within 4 years	84
% Of students graduating within 6 years	87
Calendar	semester
Profs interesting rating	92
Profs accessible rating	95
Most common reg class size	10–19 students
Most common lab size	10–19 students

MOST POPULAR MAJORS

Economics, English, psychology

SPECIAL STUDY OPTIONS

Accelerated program, double major, independent study, internships, liberal arts/career combination, student-designed major, study abroad, teacher certification program; study abroad available in 32 countries, including Grinnell-in-London, Grinnell-in-Washington program, 3-2 programs available in engineering, architecture, and law.

ABOUT THE SCHOOL

Grinnell College is a smorgasbord of intellectual delights in a tiny, quintessential Iowa town that is surrounded by cornfields. The arts and sciences facilities here are world-class. The academic atmosphere is extremely challenging and stressful. Classes are hard and demanding. The ability to handle a lot of reading and writing is vital. Even though Grinnell boasts of an "open curriculum [and] low faculty-to-student ratio," the setting demands that students "work hard [and] play hard." Undergrads here often complete work that would be considered graduate-level at other institutions. At the same time, there isn't much in the way of competition; students bring the pressure on themselves. Classes are small and intimate. Professors are crazy accessible. The curriculum is completely open except for a freshman tutorial–a writing-intensive course that introduces academic thinking and research. Beyond that, there are no subject matter requirements for obtaining a degree from Grinnell, as the school "encourages liberal arts academic exploration." Students are free to design their own paths to graduation. Mentored Advanced Projects provide a chance to work closely with a faculty member on scholarly research or the creation of a work of art. Fifty to sixty percent of every graduating class is accepted onto a wide range of off-campus study programs both domestic and abroad. On the other hand, Scholars' Convocation enriches the college's academic community by bringing notable speakers to campus.

BANG FOR YOUR BUCK

Grinnell was founded by a group of Iowa pioneers in 1843, and that pioneering spirit still informs the college's approach to education. Grinnell's endowment these days is in the range of a billion dollars. That's billion, with a "b," so admission here is in no way contingent on your economic situation. If you can get admitted here (no small feat), Grinnell will meet 100 percent of your financial need. The college is even moving to meet the full demonstrated institutional need of select international students. In a typical year, Grinnell awards more than 10 times more in grants than in loans. As part of the culture of alumni support, the college also raises specific funds from alumni to reduce, at the time of graduation, the indebtedness of seniors who have demonstrated a solid work ethic both academically and co-curricularly. Eligible students may designate one summer devoted to either an approved Grinnell College sponsored internship or summer research at Grinnell College. In return, the expected summer earnings contribution of $2,500 will be eliminated for that one summer only. One student notes that "on-campus employment is virtually guaranteed."

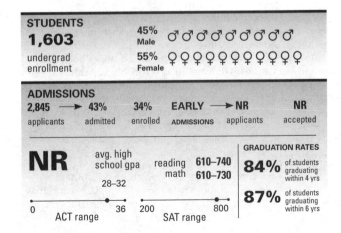

STUDENTS

1,603 undergrad enrollment

45% Male ♂♂♂♂♂♂♂♂♂

55% Female ♀♀♀♀♀♀♀♀♀♀♀

ADMISSIONS

2,845 applicants → 43% admitted | 34% enrolled | EARLY ADMISSIONS → NR applicants | NR accepted

NR avg. high school gpa

reading 610–740
math 610–730

28–32

0 — 36 ACT range

200 — 800 SAT range

GRADUATION RATES

84% of students graduating within 4 yrs

87% of students graduating within 6 yrs

Financial Aid: 641-269-3250 • E-mail: askgrin@grinnell.edu • Website: www.grinnell.edu

STUDENT BODY

Grinnell undergrads describe themselves and their classmates as "students interested in social justice and having a good time." They tend to be "highly intelligent, motivated, and inquisitive" students who constantly challenge one another "to examine topics from different perspectives. This constant thinking outside of the box is a primary aspect of a true liberal arts education." Grinnellians "are frequently left-leaning, but there's not a typical Grinnell student. All the students are different, so there are few issues with fitting in." Intellect and intensity are the most frequent common denominators; as one student explains, "I've heard that every single student is a nerd about something. Perhaps that is what unites us–our passion, whether that be for a sport, academic subject, Joss Whedon, foam-sword fighting, or politics. We all respect that we have different interests but bond because we are interested rather than apathetic."

Why Students love Grinnell College

"I've heard that every single student is a nerd about something. Perhaps that is what unites us–our passion, whether that be for a sport, academic subject, Joss Whedon, foam-sword fighting, or politics."

WHY STUDENTS LOVE GRINNEL COLLEGE

"Grinnell is a challenging, academic school in small-town Iowa with a fairly relaxed and open environment." The school's "academic reputation, small class size, small town, and freedom of class choice" appears custom-tailored to a very specific kind of student. This student looks for a school with an "academic reputation, a social scene and a politically active" climate that is situated in the Midwest and far away from the grit and noise of an urban city-center. The school's unconventional self-governance policy is one of the many peculiarities which exemplifies the idea that "Grinnell is about becoming an independent person...learning how to take responsibility for one's actions and studies and finding out and pursuing one's passions in and outside of the classroom." "Self-governance is a great strength here. Without stringent rules about how to live our lives and what choices to make, students feel at home here because we are independent."

GENERAL INFO

Activities: Choral groups, concert band, dance, drama/theater, jazz band, literary magazine, music ensembles, musical theater, pep band, radio station, student government, student newspaper, student-run film society, symphony orchestra, yearbook, campus ministries, international student organization. **Organizations:** 240 registered organizations, 2 honor societies, 12 religious organizations. **Athletics (Intercollegiate):** *Men:* Baseball, basketball, cross-country, diving, football, golf, soccer, swimming, tennis, track/field (outdoor), track/field (indoor). *Women:* Basketball, cross-country, diving, golf, soccer, softball, swimming, tennis, track/field (outdoor), track/field (indoor), volleyball.

BOTTOM LINE

The tab for tuition, fees, room and board, and everything else at Grinnell comes to about $47,000 per year. About 85 percent of Grinnell's students receive some form of financial aid, though. Financial aid packages for freshman include a $19,500 grant on average.

SELECTIVITY

Admissions Rating	**93**
# of applicants	2,845
% of applicants accepted	43
% of acceptees attending	34
# accepting a place on wait list	356
% admitted from wait list	4

FRESHMAN PROFILE

Range SAT Critical Reading	**610–740**
Range SAT Math	**610–730**
Range ACT Composite	**28–32**
% graduated top 10% of class	**62**
% graduated top 25% of class	**88**
% graduated top 50% of class	**98**

DEADLINES

Regular Deadline	**1/15**
Normal registration	**no**

FACILITIES

Housing: Coed dorms, special housing for disabled students, cooperative housing, wellness housing, theme housing. *Special Academic Facilities/Equipment:* Art galleries, language lab, nuclear magnetic resonance spectrometer, electron microscope, 24-inch reflecting telescope, 365-acre environmental research area. *Computers:* 100% of classrooms, 100% of dorms, 100% of libraries, 100% of dining areas, 100% of student union, 100% of common outdoor areas have wireless network access.

FINANCIAL FACTS

Financial Aid Rating	**98**
Annual tuition	$39,250
Room and Board	$9,334
Required Fees	$560
Books and supplies	$900
% frosh rec. need-based scholarship or grant aid	72
% UG rec.need-based scholarship or grant aid	67
% frosh rec. non-need-based scholarship or grant aid	14
% UG rec. non-need-based scholarship or grant aid	19
% frosh rec. need-based self-help aid	65
% UG rec. need-based self-help aid	60
% frosh rec. any financial aid	90
% UG rec. any financial aid	87
% UG borrow to pay for school	53
Average cumulative indebtedness	$18,578

Hanover College

P.O. Box 108, Hanover, IN 47243-0108 • Admissions: 812-213-2178 • Fax: 812-866-7098

CAMPUS LIFE

Quality of life Rating	69
Fire Safety Rating	78
Green rating	75
Type of School	Private
Environment	Rural

STUDENTS

Total undergrad enrolllment	1,004
% Male to Female	44/56
% From out of state	34
% From public high school	82
% Live on Campus	95
# of Fraternities	5
# of Sororities	5
% African American	9
% Asian	1
% Caucasian	85
% Hispanic	2
% International	3
# Of Countries Represented	13

ACADEMICS

Academic Rating	92
% Of students graduating within 4 years	62
% Of students graduating within 6 years	66
Calendar	4-4-1
Profs interesting rating	93
Profs accessible rating	90
Most common reg class size	10–19 students

MOST POPULAR MAJORS

Biology, history, speech communication and rhetoric

SPECIAL STUDY OPTIONS

Double major, dual enrollment, independent study, internships, student-designed major, study abroad, teacher certification program, CBP (Center for Business Preparation) Business Scholar Program, Philadelphia Center and Washington Center Internship Programs. Special programs offered to physically disabled students include note-taking services, tutors.

ABOUT THE SCHOOL

Overlooking the Ohio River, Hanover College offers the Midwest "an outstanding reputation for providing a quality liberal arts education," with a focus on "small classes and intense discussions." Both qualities–intimacy and a high level of challenge–are mentioned frequently by Hanover students. This is a school devoted to "providing a challenging environment for motivated students" through its "intense classes." The goal is "creating students who are ready to be an active and productive member of the real world" and who will "become successful contributors to society." That doesn't just come from students, either. Hanover officials say students here "are challenged academically and encouraged to continue their research in off-campus and independent study."

Despite the tough education before them, students have plenty of support to help get them through those challenges, thanks to both the class sizes and faculty. The "caring and prestigious faculty" here are marked by "professors that really care." The "intimate classrooms" and are "challenging," but the small class sizes here–the average class size at Hanover is just 14 students–mean students get a chance to know their professors. "You know everyone and everyone knows you," one student points out. Students will receive their education in "small, discussion-based classes that prepare you for success in graduate training and the workforce." Those classes are led by professors who are "intelligent, extremely supportive and helpful."

There are "many extracurricular opportunities" to be had thanks to the school's 165 student organizations. Hanover is "one big, slightly dysfunctional family," and it's a family that enjoys good times together. Those good times include intramural sports, hiking, a student-run restaurant, and drinking–though Hanover students are known for responsibility, and its Greek scene, though strong, does not have a reputation for wildness.

BANG FOR YOUR BUCK

Nearly 100 percent of freshmen receive financial aid of some sort (70 percent of them need-based grants or scholarships), and 98 percent of undergraduates enjoy the same (77 percent of them need-based). These include Federal Pell, SEOG, and state scholarships/grants, along with private scholarships, school scholarship or grant aid from institutional funds. Loan aid is also offered from institutional funds.

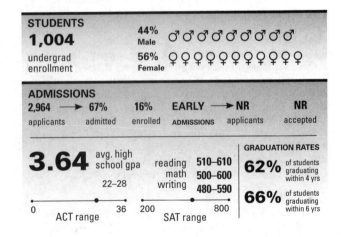

STUDENTS

1,004 undergrad enrollment

44% Male ♂♂♂♂♂♂♂♂♂

56% Female ♀♀♀♀♀♀♀♀♀♀♀

ADMISSIONS

2,964 applicants →	67% admitted	16% enrolled	EARLY ADMISSIONS →	NR applicants	NR accepted

3.64 avg. high school gpa

ACT range (0–36): 22–28

SAT range (200–800): reading 510–610, math 500–600, writing 480–590

GRADUATION RATES

62% of students graduating within 4 yrs

66% of students graduating within 6 yrs

Hanover College

FINANCIAL AID: : 812-866-7029 • E-MAIL: ADMISSION@HANOVER.EDU • WEBSITE: WWW.HANOVER.EDU

STUDENT BODY

At Hanover College, "The typical student is studious, is involved in campus activities, and enjoys spending free time with friends." Among the school's 1,000 undergraduates, "The majority of students are white, but there are many other ethnic groups," as well as "a variety of people of different religious backgrounds, sexualities, political views, and personality types." "Students are split about evenly from large suburban high schools and smaller rural schools," though most come from "Indiana, Kentucky, Illinois, or Ohio." There are "definitely social divisions at Hanover," which tend to form around certain clubs and social groups. If you aren't interested in going Greek, "There is an active 'geek' population that is waiting to be tapped if you search for it (Sci-fi Club, Anime Club)." "Most people are friendly and don't mind crossing-over into a variety of circles of friends."

Why Students love Hanover College

"A welcoming place to come spend four years learning."

WHY STUDENTS LOVE HANOVER COLLEGE

Hanover has a lot to offer, and students' reasons for wanting to be here vary. One is the "beautiful and immaculate campus" which features plenty of open space. The school boasts 650 acres of outdoor environmental labs and easy access to Big Oaks National Wildlife Refuge and Clifty Falls State Park. Though others acknowledge that "the campus is beautiful," they find that "the small campus size really appealed to me." Students enjoy having professors who "call you by name rather than assigning you a number." It is "a welcoming place to come spend four years learning."Some students like "the Presbyterian Church USA affiliation," others like that it is "a close-knit community which demands critical thinking in an exciting and friendly environment." Still others like "athletics and Greek life," or the "campus beauty," or the fact that "you can be a name here and make a name for yourself if you try hard enough."

GENERAL INFO

Activities: Choral groups, concert band, dance, drama/theater, jazz band, literary magazine, music ensembles, musical theater, pep band, radio station, student government, student newspaper, student-run film society, symphony orchestra, television station, yearbook, campus ministries, international student organization. **Organizations:** 60 registered organizations, 8 honor societies, 4 religious organizations. 4 fraternities, 4 sororities. **Athletics (Intercollegiate):** *Men:* Baseball, basketball, cross-country, football, golf, lacrosse, soccer, tennis, track/field (outdoor). *Women:* Basketball, cross-country, golf, soccer, softball, tennis, track/field (outdoor), volleyball. **On-Campus Highlights:** Science Center, Horner Health and Recreation Center (Collier Arena),

BOTTOM LINE

An education at Hanover will cost students $26,950 in annual tuition, plus $8,300 for room and board, $550 for required fees, and $900 for books and supplies. Students graduate with an average accumulated debt of $28,185. Some 98 percent of Hanover students are either employed or enrolled in graduate school within seven months of graduation.

SELECTIVITY

Admissions Rating	**87**
# of applicants	2,964
% of applicants accepted	67
% of acceptees attending	16
# accepting a place on wait list	0

FRESHMAN PROFILE

Range SAT Critical Reading	**510–610**
Range SAT Math	**500–600**
Range SAT Writing	**480–590**
Range ACT Composite	**22–28**
Average HS GPA	**3.64**
% graduated top 10% of class	**31**
% graduated top 25% of class	**65**
% graduated top 50% of class	**92**

DEADLINES

Regular Deadline	**3/1**
Normal registration	**yes**

FACILITIES

Housing: Coed dorms, men's dorms, women's dorms, fraternity/sorority housing, apartments for single students, wellness housing, theme housing. *Special Academic Facilities/Equipment:* Cadaver lab, geological museum, electronic language lab, observatory. *Computers:* 80% of classrooms, 100% of dorms, 50% of libraries, 100% of dining areas, 100% of student union, 20% of common outdoor areas have wireless network access.

FINANCIAL FACTS

Financial Aid Rating	**87**
Annual tuition	$28,250
Room and Board	$8,650
Required Fees	$600
Books and supplies	$900
% frosh rec. need-based scholarship or grant aid	70
% UG rec.need-based scholarship or grant aid	77
% frosh rec. non-need-based scholarship or grant aid	12
% UG rec. non-need-based scholarship or grant aid	11
% frosh rec. need-based self-help aid	58
% UG rec. need-based self-help aid	66
% frosh rec. any financial aid	99
% UG rec. any financial aid	98
% UG borrow to pay for school	66
Average cumulative indebtedness	$28,185

Harvey Mudd College

301 Platt Boulevard, 301 Platt Blvd, Claremont, CA 91711-5990 • Admissions: 909-621-8011 • Fax: 909-621-8360

CAMPUS LIFE

Quality of life Rating	90
Fire Safety Rating	77
Green rating	78
Type of School	Private
Environment	Town

STUDENTS

Total undergrad enrolllment	773
% Male to Female	59/41
% From out of state	60
% From public high school	69
% Live on Campus	99
% African American	1
% Asian	19
% Caucasian	58
% Hispanic	7
% International	5
# Of Countries Represented	23

ACADEMICS

Academic Rating	96
% Of students graduating within 4 years	80
% Of students graduating within 6 years	87
Calendar	semester
Profs interesting rating	98
Profs accessible rating	98
Most common reg class size	10–19 students
Most common lab size	10–19 students

MOST POPULAR MAJORS

Business/commerce, economics
international relations

SPECIAL STUDY OPTIONS

Cross-registration, double major, dual enrollment, exchange student program (domestic), independent study, internships, liberal arts/career combination, student-designed major, study abroad, Innovative client-sponsored design projects.

ABOUT THE SCHOOL

A member of the Claremont Consortium, Harvey Mudd shares resources with Pitzer, Scripps, Claremont McKenna, and Pomona Colleges. It is the "techie" school of the bunch, and focuses on educating future scientists, engineers, and mathematicians–"Mudd is a place where everyone is literate in every branch of science." The college offers four-year degrees in chemistry, mathematics, physics, computer science, biology, and engineering, as well as interdisciplinary degrees in mathematical biology, and a few joint majors for really hard-core types. Harvey Mudd is "small, friendly, and tough. Professors and other students are very accessible. The Honor Code is an integral part of the college." The Honor Code is so entrenched in campus culture that the college entrusts the students to 24-hour per day access to all buildings, including labs, and permits take-home exams, specified either as open-book or closed-book, timed or un-timed. "Our Honor Code really means something," insists one student, "it isn't just a stray sentence or two that got put into the student handbook; it's something that the students are really passionate about." Academics at Harvey Mudd may seem "excessive [and] soul-crushing," but a "great people and community," nonetheless. In order to ensure that all students receive a well-rounded education, students enrolled at Harvey Mudd are required to take a core component of humanities courses. Research opportunities are literally limitless. Engineering majors participate in "Clinic" where they collaborate with other Mudders to satisfy the requests of an actual company. Best of all, these opportunities are available without the cutthroat competition of other similar schools.

BANG FOR YOUR BUCK

Harvey Mudd believes that college choice is more about "fit" than "finances." That's why the college offers a robust program of need-based and merit-based awards to help insure that an HMC education is accessible to all who qualify. Eighty-two percent of students receive financial aid, and 40 percent qualify for merit-based awards. In determining who will receive merit-based awards, the Office of Admission looks primarily at academic achievement–financial need is not considered. While these awards are granted independent of financial need, students who receive a merit-based award and are also eligible for need-based aid. Standout programs include the Harvey S. Mudd Merit Award in which students receive a $40,000 scholarship distributed annually in the amount of $10,000 per year. The President's Scholars Program is a renewable, four-year full-tuition scholarship promotes excellence and diversity at HMC by recognizing outstanding young men and women from populations that are traditionally underrepresented at HMC.

STUDENTS
773 undergrad enrollment
59% Male
41% Female

ADMISSIONS
2,508 applicants → 25% admitted — 31% enrolled
EARLY ADMISSIONS → NR applicants — NR accepted

NR avg. high school gpa

ACT range (0–36): 32–35

SAT range (200–800): reading 670–760; math 740–800; writing 668–760

GRADUATION RATES
80% of students graduating within 4 yrs
87% of students graduating within 6 yrs

Harvey Mudd College

FINANCIAL AID: 909-621-8055 • E-MAIL: ADMISSION@HMC.EDU • WEBSITE: WWW.HMC.EDU

STUDENT BODY

"We are nerds," Mudders tell us, "and we embrace it." They also describe themselves as "outgoing, quirky, and fun but very studious." Students are united by "a brimming passion for science and a love of knowledge for its own sake." "All students are exceptionally intelligent and are able to perform their work in a professional manner." Beyond that, there's "a really diverse group of personalities" at Mudd, who are "not afraid to show their true colors" and who all have "a unique sense of humor." Students say they "are all friendly, smart, and talented, which brings us together. Upperclassmen look out for underclassmen, and students tend to bond together easily over difficult homework." In such a welcoming community, "students primarily fit in by not fitting in–wearing pink pirate hats or skateboarding while playing harmonica or practicing unicycle jousting are all good ways to fit in perfectly."

Why Students love Harvey Mudd College

"I feel that something unique and amazing about Mudd is that...if you can do the work, you can do whatever you want."

WHY STUDENTS LOVE HARVEY MUDD COLLEGE

The mission statement at Harvey Mudd College seeks to "educate engineers, scientists, and mathematicians" but, one student argues, "to be a mathematician, scientist, or engineer in today's world you have to know more than just math, science and engineering." Harvey Mudd is "hard–everyone here was a top student in high school, and due to the unforgiving grading curve it can be difficult to get a good GPA. So it's definitely not a good academic experience for those hoping to breeze through their college classes earning all A's. But for hardworking students who are passionate about science, and who don't mind getting a few bad grades every once in a while, Mudd is a really great place." "With upwards of 30 hours of homework each week," Harvey Mudd can challenge even the brightest striving academic but "the sheer amount you learn from the core classes [alone] is incredible."

GENERAL INFO

Activities: Choral groups, concert band, dance, drama/theater, jazz band, literary magazine, music ensembles, musical theater, pep band, radio station, student government, student newspaper, student-run film society, symphony orchestra, yearbook, campus ministries, international student organization. **Organizations:** 109 registered organizations, 4 honor societies, 6 religious organizations. **Athletics (Intercollegiate):** *Men:* Baseball, basketball, cross-country, diving, football, golf, soccer, swimming, tennis, track/ field (outdoor), water polo. *Women:* Basketball, cross-country, diving, golf, lacrosse, soccer, softball, swimming, tennis, track/field (outdoor), volleyball, water polo. **On-Campus Highlights:** Dorm Lounges, Platt Campus Center Living Room, Liquidamber mall, Jay's Pizza Place., Linde Student Activities Center.

BOTTOM LINE

The retail price for tuition, room and board, and fees at Harvey Mudd ends up being a little more than $55,000 a year. Financial aid is plentiful here though, so please don't let cost scare you away from applying. The average freshman grant is $25,000, but some students do successfully receive "excellent financial aid packages," including a "full tuition scholarship."

SELECTIVITY

Admissions Rating	**97**
# of applicants	2,508
% of applicants accepted	25
% of acceptees attending	31
# accepting a place on wait list	272
% admitted from wait list	0

FRESHMAN PROFILE

Range SAT Critical Reading	**670–760**
Range SAT Math	**790–800**
Range SAT Writing	**660–760**
Range ACT Composite	**32–35**
% graduated top 10% of class	**89**
% graduated top 25% of class	**99**
% graduated top 50% of class	**100**

DEADLINES

Regular Deadline	**1/2**
Normal registration	**no**

FACILITIES

Housing: Coed dorms, apartments for married students, apartments for single students, housing exchange program with Pomona College, Pitzer College, Scripps College, and Claremont McKenna College. *Computers:* 100% of classrooms, 100% of dorms, 100% of libraries, 100% of dining areas, 100% of student union, 75% of common outdoor areas have wireless network access.

FINANCIAL FACTS

Financial Aid Rating	**97**
Annual tuition	$42,410
Room and Board	$13,858
Required Fees	$257
Books and supplies	$800
% frosh rec. need-based scholarship or grant aid	49
% UG rec.need-based scholarship or grant aid	52
% frosh rec. non-need-based scholarship or grant aid	18
% UG rec. non-need-based scholarship or grant aid	24
% frosh rec. need-based self-help aid	34
% UG rec. need-based self-help aid	39
% frosh rec. any financial aid	77
% UG rec. any financial aid	82
% UG borrow to pay for school	57
Average cumulative indebtedness	$19,169

Haverford College

370 Lancaster Avenue, Haverford, PA 19041 • Admissions: 610-896-1350 • Financial Aid: 610-896-1350

CAMPUS LIFE

Quality of life Rating	93
Fire Safety Rating	80
Green rating	88
Type of School	Private
Environment	Town

STUDENTS

Total undergrad enrolllment	1,177
% Male to Female	47/53
% From out of state	86
% From public high school	57
% Live on Campus	99
% African American	7
% Asian	8
% Caucasian	59
% Hispanic	8
% International	3
# Of Countries Represented	33

ACADEMICS

Academic Rating	97
% Of students graduating within 4 years	87
% Of students graduating within 6 years	92
Calendar	semester
Profs interesting rating	93
Profs accessible rating	95
Most common reg class size	fewer than 10 students
Most common lab size	fewer than 10 students

MOST POPULAR MAJORS
Boilogy, history, political science

SPECIAL STUDY OPTIONS

Cross-registration, double major, exchange student program (domestic), independent study, internships, liberal arts/career combination, student-designed major, study abroad, teacher certification program.

ABOUT THE SCHOOL

Haverford College prides itself on the type of student that it draws. Academically minded and socially conscious are two words that often describe the typical Haverford student. Many are drawn to the college due to the accessibility of the professors and attention each student receives in the classroom. They don't have to fight for attention in a large lecture hall since the most common class size is around ten students and most professors live around campus and regularly invite students over for a lively talk over dinner or tea. There is also a larger since of community on campus that is proliferated by the much-lauded honor code, which, according to one surprised student, "really works, and we actually do have things like closed-book, timed, take-home tests." Many find that the honor code (which includes proctor-less exams) brings a certain type of student looking for a mature academic experience that helps prepare students by treating them as intellectual equals. In fact, even comparing grades with other students is discouraged which tends to limit competitiveness and creates a greater sense of community. This sense of togetherness is prevalent throughout campus. Students are actively involved in student government since they have Plenary twice a year, where at least 50 percent of students must be present to make any changes to documents such as the student constitution and the honor code.

BANG FOR YOUR BUCK

Haverford has recently adopted a policy that helps replace loans in the typical financial aid package with grants that helps alleviate the debt students have upon graduating. Though they don't offer any merit-based aid, the school does meet the demonstrated need of all students who were deemed eligible according to the college. The cost of living is low in the city and many students are able to find on campus jobs to help support themselves. Haverford also encourages students to take internships through one of its many programs. The Center for Peace and Global Citizenship helps Haverfordians find fields that are simpatico with the college's ideals of trust and creating civically minded adults. The College and Career Development organizations also has numerous programs that coordinate with alumni and help students expand their networking abilities and create job opportunities for when they graduate.

STUDENTS
1,177 undergrad enrollment
47% Male ♂♂♂♂♂♂♂♂♂♂♂♂♂
53% Female ♀♀♀♀♀♀♀♀♀♀

ADMISSIONS

3,312 →	26%	38%	EARLY →	NR	NR
applicants	admitted	enrolled	ADMISSIONS	applicants	accepted

NR avg. high school gpa NR

ACT range 0–36

reading	650–740
math	650–750
writing	660–750

SAT range 200–800

GRADUATION RATES
87% of students graduating within 4 yrs
92% of students graduating within 6 yrs

Haverford College

E-MAIL: ADMITME@HAVERFORD.EDU • FAX: 610-896-1338 • WEBSITE: WWW.HAVERFORD.EDU

STUDENT BODY

Many students describe themselves as a little "nerdy" or "quirky," but in the best possible way. "For the most part, Haverfordians are socially awkward, open to new friends, and looking for moral, political, [or] scholarly debate." The honor code draws a particular type of student–"don't choose to go here if you're not dedicated to the ideas of trust, concern, and respect and to making sure we are a well-run community." Most are "liberal-minded" and "intellectual" and "want to save the world after they graduate."

WHY STUDENTS LOVE HAVERFORD COLLEGE

Students tell us they are "very active on campus," with "classes, work, on-campus jobs, volunteering, running clubs, and acting on administrative committees." There are nearly 150 campus organizations for students to choose from, certainly offering a little bit of something for everyone, and the Gardner Athletic Center provides students with a variety of sports and fitness options. There is a fine Natural Sciences Center at Haverford, as well as an arboretum and an observatory. One undergrad enthuses, Haverford is "an incredible place where I have been intellectually pushed beyond what I believed possible."

Why Students love Haverford College

"An incredible place where I have been intellectually pushed beyond what I believed possible."

GENERAL INFO

Activities: Choral groups, dance, drama/theater, literary magazine, music ensembles, musical theater, student government, student newspaper, yearbook, campus ministries, international student organization. **Organizations:** 144 registered organizations, 1 honor societies, 6 religious organizations. **Athletics (Intercollegiate):** *Men:* Baseball, basketball, cross-country, fencing, lacrosse, soccer, squash, tennis, track/field (outdoor), track/field (indoor). *Women:* Basketball, cross-country, fencing, field hockey, lacrosse, soccer, softball, squash, tennis, track/field (outdoor), track/field (indoor), volleyball. **On-Campus Highlights:** Integrated Natural Sciences Center, John Whitehead Campus Center, Cantor Fitzgerald Gallery, Arboreteum, Douglas B. Gardner Athletic Center. **Environmental Initiatives:** Our athletic center is the first gold LEED-certified recreation center in the United States (opened in 2005). We have reached 75–85% for grounds recycling. We have completed a master plan to identify utility and powerhouse improvements, and will commence work on these improvements immediately.

BOTTOM LINE

Though the annual tuition is around $42,000 per year, Haverford offers the majority of its student's financial aid. The average cumulative indebtedness is around $16,000, despite the room and board being around $13,000 and the cost of books estimated around $1,000. The price may seem high on paper, but Haverford helps its students afford the education.

SELECTIVITY

Admissions Rating	**97**
# of applicants	3,312
% of applicants accepted	26
% of acceptees attending	38
# accepting a place on wait list	375
% admitted from wait list	0

FRESHMAN PROFILE

Range SAT Critical Reading	**650–740**
Range SAT Math	**650–750**
Range SAT Writing	**660–750**
% graduated top 10% of class	**94**
% graduated top 25% of class	**99**
% graduated top 50% of class	**100**

DEADLINES

Regular Deadline	**1/15**
Normal registration	**no**

FACILITIES

Housing: Coed dorms, men's dorms, women's dorms, apartments for single students, theme housingTheme houses. 60% of campus accessible to physically disabled. *Special Academic Facilities/Equipment:* Art gallery, center for cross-cultural study of religion, arboretum, observatory, foundry. *Computers:* 75% of classrooms, 75% of libraries, 100% of dining areas, 100% of student union, 80% of common outdoor areas have wireless network access.

FINANCIAL FACTS

Financial Aid Rating	**95**
Annual tuition	$41,830
Room and Board	$12,842
Required Fees	$578
Books and supplies	$1,194
% frosh rec. need-based scholarship or grant aid	51
% UG rec.need-based scholarship or grant aid	50
% frosh rec. need-based self-help aid	48
% UG rec. need-based self-help aid	48
% frosh rec. any financial aid	61
% UG rec. any financial aid	60
% UG borrow to pay for school	34
Average cumulative indebtedness	$16,238

Hillsdale College

33 East College Street, Hillsdale, MI 49242 • Admissions: 517-607-2327 • Financial Aid: 517-607-2350

CAMPUS LIFE

Quality of life Rating	84
Fire Safety Rating	87
Green rating	60*
Type of School	Private
Environment	Village

STUDENTS

Total undergrad enrolllment	1,326
% Male to Female	48/52
% From out of state	60
% From public high school	48
% Live on Campus	88
# of Fraternities	4
# of Sororities	3
% International	2
# Of Countries Represented	8

ACADEMICS

Academic Rating	95
% Of students graduating within 4 years	72
% Of students graduating within 6 years	76
Calendar	semester
Profs interesting rating	98
Profs accessible rating	95
Most common reg class size	10–19 students
Most common lab size	20–29 students

MOST POPULAR MAJORS

Biology, business adminstration and management education, history, politics, English

HONOR PROGRAMS

Honor programs available.

SPECIAL STUDY OPTIONS

Double major, dual enrollment, honors program, independent study, internships, student-designed major, study abroad, teacher certification program.

ABOUT THE SCHOOL

Hillsdale College is all about serious academics. The acceptance rate may seem high, but that's because only students who are academically apt apply, knowing the full measure of Hillsdale's reputation. "Writing skills are heavily addressed," reports one student, and another mentions that there "aren't any fluff classes at Hillsdale." The college offers a core curriculum that many students love and the class size is small enough so that many professors know each student. The normal class size stays between 10 and 20 students so that each attendee can get personal attention. The college also lauds its classes, which include mandatory courses on such topics as the Constitution and Western Civilization. Incoming freshman find that there aren't many fluff classes, but that's just the reason they came to Hillsdale in the first place. The college, and the majority of the student body, is fairly conservative in its beliefs. Many are drawn to its somewhat conservative culture and ideals it touts, such as the advantages to a free-market system. While not all students are from Judeo-Christian backgrounds, the "majority of our campus calls itself Christian" and "hold strong moral values," attending religious services regularly. The school is "deeply rooted in our country's Greco-Roman and Christian Heritage."

Why Students love Hillsdale College

"There a general feeling of respect and friendship between all students."

BANG FOR YOUR BUCK

Hillsdale holds true to its conservative beliefs and does not accept any government money for funding; however, its loyal alumni usually dedicate large amounts of money leaving the average aid package around $12,000. There is also a work-study program and quite a few off-campus job opportunities for students looking to boost their income or help pay for supplies. Hillsdale also greatly encourages students to get more experience interning through its Career Services Office, which reaches out to alumni and creates exclusive opportunities for its students. The Washington-Hillsdale Internship Program (WHIP) is a professional sales internship program through the school that offers national placements to help students expand their networks.

STUDENTS

1,326 undergrad enrollment

48% Male ♂♂♂♂♂♂♂♂♂♂

52% Female ♀♀♀♀♀♀♀♀♀♀

ADMISSIONS

1,865 applicants → 57% admitted — 39% enrolled

EARLY ADMISSIONS → NR applicants — NR accepted

3.75 avg. high school gpa

ACT range (0–36): 26-31

SAT range (200–800): reading 630–740, math 570–700, writing 590–700

GRADUATION RATES

72% of students graduating within 4 yrs

76% of students graduating within 6 yrs

Hillsdale College

E-MAIL: ADMISSIONS@HILLSDALE.EDU • FAX: 517-607-2223 • WEBSITE: WWW.HILLSDALE.EDU

STUDENT BODY

"Hillsdale prides itself on being one of the first colleges to openly accept anyone irrespective of nation, color, or sex." All the same, the population here is almost entirely composed of "white, upper-middle-class" students, and "most of our 'minority' students are actually from other countries." There are "leftish students" and plenty of people who don't go to church, but the "majority of our campus calls itself Christian" and "hold strong moral values." "There's a good libertarian crowd," too. However, Christianity, and right-wing politics dominate. "The typical student is religious and conservative," relates a sophomore. "That's the nature of the college." Students describe themselves as "well-mannered" "hard workers" who "are passionate about learning." Ten to twelve percent of students are home-schooled, so it's not hard to find "your homeschoolers who spend Friday night swing-dancing in the dorm." Greeks, athletes, and thespians constitute the other main cliques; though all of these groups may appear dramatically different on the surface, "There a general feeling of respect and friendship between all students."

WHY STUDENTS LOVE HILLSDALE COLLEGE

Members of the student body tell us that "beautiful" campus here "is the hub of social life." Christianity, and right-wing politics dominate. "The typical student is religious and conservative," relates a sophomore. "That's the nature of the college." Students describe themselves as "well-mannered" "hard workers" who "are passionate about learning."

GENERAL INFO

Environment: Village. **Activities:** Choral groups, concert band, dance, drama/theater, jazz band, literary magazine, music ensembles, musical theater, pep band, student government, student newspaper, symphony orchestra, yearbook, campus ministries, international student organization. **Organizations:** 50 registered organizations, 26 honor societies, 4 religious organizations. 3 fraternities, 3 sororities. **Athletics (Intercollegiate):** *Men:* Baseball, basketball, cheerleading, cross-country, football, track/field (outdoor), track/field (indoor). *Women:* Basketball, cheerleading, cross-country, diving, equestrian sports, softball, swimming, track/field (outdoor), track/field (indoor), volleyball. **On-Campus Highlights:** Student Union, Quad (outdoor quadrangle), Sage Center for the Arts, Howard Music Hall, Sports Complex. **Environmental Initiatives:** Central heating and cooling efficiency plan, high efficiency lighting in all new facilities; environmental controls in all buildings for energy management.

BOTTOM LINE

Since it is a private college, there are no additional fees for those coming from out of state. Tuition is just under $21,000 with room and board being an additional $8,000 and the estimated costs of books being $1,000. However, with 93% of incoming freshman receiving financial aid, the cumulative indebtedness is only around $15,500. The average aid package is high, thanks to what one student calls "an expansive and highly dedicated donor base."

SELECTIVITY

Admissions Rating	**93**
# of applicants	1,865
% of applicants accepted	57
% of acceptees attending	39
# accepting a place on wait list	50
% admitted from wait list	10

FRESHMAN PROFILE

Range SAT Critical Reading	**630–740**
Range SAT Math	**570–700**
Range SAT Writing	**590–720**
Range ACT Composite	**26–31**
Average HS GPA	**3.75**
% graduated top 10% of class	**48**
% graduated top 25% of class	**77**
% graduated top 50% of class	**98**

DEADLINES

Regular Deadline	**2/15**
Normal registration	**yes**

FACILITIES

Housing: Men's dorms, women's dorms, fraternity/sorority housing, apartments for single students. *Special Academic Facilities/Equipment:* Early childhood education lab, media center, K–8 private academy, Slayton Arboretum, rare books library. *Computers:* 100% of classrooms, 85% of dorms, 100% of libraries, 100% of dining areas, 100% of student union, 100% of common outdoor areas have wireless network access.

FINANCIAL FACTS

Financial Aid Rating	**84**
Annual tuition	$20,760
Room and Board	$8,310
Required Fees	540
Books and supplies	850
% frosh rec. need-based scholarship or grant aid	27
% UG rec.need-based scholarship or grant aid	29
% frosh rec. non-need-based scholarship or grant aid	76
% UG rec. non-need-based scholarship or grant aid	87
% frosh rec. need-based self-help aid	34
% UG rec. need-based self-help aid	33
% frosh rec. any financial aid	93
% UG rec. any financial aid	95
% UG borrow to pay for school	42
Average cumulative indebtedness	$15,570

Johns Hopkins University

Office of Undergraduate Admissions, Mason Hall, 3400 N. Charles Street, Baltimore, MD 21218 • Admissions: 410-516-8171

CAMPUS LIFE

Quality of life Rating	78
Fire Safety Rating	81
Green rating	95
Type of School	Private
Environment	Metropolis

STUDENTS

Total undergrad enrolllment	4,980
% Male to Female	52/48
% From out of state	87
% From public high school	69
% Live on Campus	55
# of Fraternities	13
# of Sororities	9
% African American	5
% Asian	21
% Caucasian	52
% Hispanic	8
% International	8
# Of Countries Represented	71

ACADEMICS

Academic Rating	86
% Of students graduating within 4 years	84
% Of students graduating within 6 years	92
Calendar	4-1-4
Profs interesting rating	72
Profs accessible rating	75
Most common reg class size	10–19 students
Most common lab size	20–29 students

MOST POPULAR MAJORS

International studies, biomedical engineering, public health

SPECIAL STUDY OPTIONS

Cross-registration, double major, dual enrollment, independent study, internships, student-designed major, study abroad, combined bachelor's/master's programs.

ABOUT THE SCHOOL

Without a doubt, Johns Hopkins University's reputation for academic rigor and its wide array of programs in the sciences and humanities make it a magnet for its top-notch students. In addition to its highly ranked pre-med, biochemical engineering, and international studies programs, this research university also offers opportunities for its students to study at its other divisions, including the Peabody Conservatory, the Nitze School of Advanced International Studies, the Carey Business School, and the Bloomberg School of Public Health. Students appreciate the school's lack of a core curriculum, small class size, and emphasis on academic exploration and hands-on learning. Around two thirds of the students are involved in some kind of research opportunity and an equal amount of students end up with internships. Many of the distinguished professors at Johns Hopkins often serve as mentors and collaborators on these research projects. According to one student, "Johns Hopkins puts you shoulder-to-shoulder with some of the greatest minds in the world while promoting a work ethic that forces you to push yourself to your intellectual limits."

Although heavily focused on academic achievement and research, the school manages to balance this out with a vibrant social scene that can satisfy its diverse and well-rounded student population. With more than 350 student groups including community service groups, outdoor clubs, its Division I lacrosse team and an actual Quidditch team, there are plenty of ways for students to find their own niche. The school's beautiful campus inspires its students with its "brick walkways lined with trees and marble staircases" and its convenient location in historic Baltimore and proximity to Washington D.C. provide access to an exciting nightlife, numerous restaurants, and all the other amenities of a bustling and quirky city.

BANG FOR YOUR BUCK

To apply for financial aid, students must submit the FAFSA. Johns Hopkins distributes more than 90 percent of its financial aid awards on the basis of need and also provides need- and merit-based scholarships including the Hodson Trust Scholarships as well as Bloomberg Scholarships. Along with financial aid, students receive a lot of support from the school's Career Center and Office of Pre-Professional Programs and Advising as well as the extensive and loyal alumni network to help them tackle their career development and post-graduation goals.

STUDENTS

4,980 undergrad enrollment

52% Male ♂♂♂♂♂♂♂♂♂♂

48% Female ♀♀♀♀♀♀♀♀♀♀

ADMISSIONS

18,459 applicants → 21% admitted — 33% enrolled — EARLY ADMISSIONS → NR applicants — NR accepted

3.72 avg. high school gpa

ACT range (0–36): 29–33

SAT range (200–800): reading 630–740, math 660–770, writing 640–740

GRADUATION RATES

84% of students graduating within 4 yrs

92% of students graduating within 6 yrs

Johns Hopkins University

FAX: 410-516-6025 • FINANCIAL AID: 410-516-8028 • E-MAIL: GOTOJHU@JHU.EDU • WEBSITE: WWW.JHU.EDU

STUDENT BODY

While it might be difficult to define the typical Hopkins undergrad, the vast majority are "hardworking and care about their GPAs, and will do what they can to get the grades they want." Thankfully, many are also "balance artists; they are able to balance schoolwork, extracurricular activities, jobs, and a social life without getting too bogged down or stressed." Though students "are competitive in the sense that they all want to do well," that competitiveness is never adversarial.

Why Students love Johns Hopkins

> "Hopkins is a university of action, the type of place where you can study all you want."

WHY STUDENTS LOVE JOHNS HOPKINS

While students may flock to Johns Hopkins for the academic street cred, they quickly learn that the school offers the complete package. One student observes the following: "Competitive and accommodating, top-notch and humble, modern and traditional, Hopkins has it all, better than the others." The school's approach to hands-on learning and experimentation is another of its assets. According to one student, "Hopkins is a university of action, the type of place where you can study all you want, but if you're not doing, you're not learning." Perhaps as a result of this, students seem to come out of the university with some serious critical thinking skills. "If it's a good university it will make you reconsider everything you have learned previously–whether from high school teachers or your parents–and will constantly have you question everything you learn from then on," says one reflective student.

GENERAL INFO

Activities: Choral groups, concert band, dance, drama/theater, jazz band, literary magazine, music ensembles, musical theater, pep band, radio station, student government, student newspaper, student-run film society, symphony orchestra, yearbook, campus ministries. **Organizations:** 250 registered organizations, 17 honor societies, 20 religious organizations. 12 fraternities, 7 sororities. **Athletics (Intercollegiate):** *Men:* Baseball, basketball, cross-country, diving, fencing, football, lacrosse, soccer, swimming, tennis, track/field (outdoor), track/field (indoor), water polo, wrestling. *Women:* Basketball, cross-country, diving, fencing, field hockey, lacrosse, soccer, swimming, tennis, track/field (outdoor), track/field (indoor), volleyball. **On-Campus Highlights:** Mason Hall–new Visitor's Center, Mattin Student Arts Center, Homewood House Museum, Lacrosse Hall of Fame and Museum, Ralph S. O'Connor Recreation Center, Also, Charles Commons, a new building that houses 618 upperclassmen, as well as a new dining facility and retail spaces, opened in the fall of 2007. **Environmental Initiatives:** Commitment to reduce greenhouse gas emissions by 51 percent by 2025.

BOTTOM LINE

Johns Hopkins tuition fees hover at the $42,280 mark with an additional $13,000 for room and board. This does not include books, supplies, personal expenses, or transportation. More than 50 percent of freshmen receive some form of financial aid.

SELECTIVITY

Admissions Rating	**99**
# of applicants	18,459
% of applicants accepted	21
% of acceptees attending	33
# accepting a place on wait list	3,256
% admitted from wait list	1

FRESHMAN PROFILE

Range SAT Critical Reading	**630–740**
Range SAT Math	**660–770**
Range SAT Writing	**640–740**
Range ACT Composite	**29–33**
Average HS GPA	**3.72**
% graduated top 10% of class	**87**
% graduated top 25% of class	**98**
% graduated top 50% of class	**99**

DEADLINES

Regular Deadline	**1/1**
Normal registration	**no**

FACILITIES

Housing: Coed dorms, men's dorms, women's dorms, fraternity/sorority housing, apartments for single students. *Special Academic Facilities/Equipment:* Baltimore Museum of Art, on-campus Digital Media Center, art gallery, electron microscope, Space Telescope Science Institute. *Computers:* 95% of classrooms, 100% of dorms, 100% of libraries, 90% of dining areas, 100% of student union, 50% of common outdoor areas have wireless network access.

FINANCIAL FACTS

Financial Aid Rating	**94**
Annual tuition	$42,280
Room and Board	$12,962
Required Fees	$500
Books and supplies	$1,200
% frosh rec. need-based scholarship or grant aid	44
% UG rec.need-based scholarship or grant aid	41
% frosh rec. non-need-based scholarship or grant aid	6
% UG rec. non-need-based scholarship or grant aid	5
% frosh rec. need-based self-help aid	44
% UG rec. need-based self-help aid	42
% frosh rec. any financial aid	52
% UG rec. any financial aid	49
% UG borrow to pay for school	48
Average cumulative indebtedness	$25,307

Lafayette College

118 Markle Hall, Easton, PA 18042 • Admissions: 610-330-5100 • Fax: 610-330-5355

CAMPUS LIFE

Quality of life Rating	82
Fire Safety Rating	60*
Green rating	95
Type of School	Private
Environment	Village

STUDENTS

Total undergrad enrolllment	2,375
% Male to Female	53/47
% From out of state	77
% From public high school	68
% Live on Campus	94
# of Fraternities	7
# of Sororities	6
% African American	5
% Asian	4
% Caucasian	66
% Hispanic	5
% International	6
# Of Countries Represented	46

ACADEMICS

Academic Rating	92
% Of students graduating within 4 years	87
% Of students graduating within 6 years	89
Calendar	semester
Profs interesting rating	82
Profs accessible rating	78
Most common reg class size	10–19 students
Most common lab size	10–19 students

SPECIAL STUDY OPTIONS

Cross-registration, double major, dual enrollment, exchange student program (domestic), honors program, independent study, internships, student-designed major, study abroad, interim sessions here and abroad. Special programs offered to physically disabled students include tutors.

ABOUT LAFAYETTE COLLEGE

Thinking across disciplinary has defined the Lafayette College experience since its founding in 1826. With a total student body of just under 2,500, the focus is squarely on undergraduates at this top liberal arts college. Lafayette graduates are well-trained in cross-disciplinary thinking and practical application. Here's what that looks like in real terms: computer science, art, biology, and neuroscience students might work together on brain research. A team of engineering, economics, psychology, and English students might take on a consulting project to redesign a new arts and cultural center in New Orleans. Lafayette sees the world through this interdisciplinary lens, and an ability to pursue those intersections in a practical way is a big reason Lafayette students land top research, academic, and employment opportunities. Students love that "even though the school is a small liberal arts college, it's strengths in math, science, and engineering give it a very practical feel," and students also "think our greatest strength is our academic diversity."

Undergrads are quite pleased to discover that "classes are mostly small and even our lecture classes don't get bigger than roughly 75 students." The small student to teacher ratio allows students to build a relationship with their professors, and according to a contented undergrad, "creates a spectacular class dynamic and sense of trust." Robust internship offerings (many with alumni), provide real-world experience.

BANG FOR YOUR BUCK

Lafayette College is part of a very small group of colleges and universities throughout the United States, that provide reduced-loan or no-loan financial aid awards to lower- and middle-income students who gain admission and seek financial assistance. In addition, Lafayette offers merit and need-based scholarships to the top students in its applicant pool. There is no additional application required to be considered for these merit-based awards. The scholarship is renewable all four years and provides a minimum award of $80,000 over the four years, special mentoring activities with faculty and other campus scholars, and an additional $4,000 scholarship for an off-campus course during the interim period (in winter or summer.) The Marquis Scholarship is based on superior academic performance, and evidence of leadership and major contribution to school or community activities. Said one thankful student, "I was lucky enough to be chosen as a Marquis Scholar, giving me ample opportunity to study abroad."

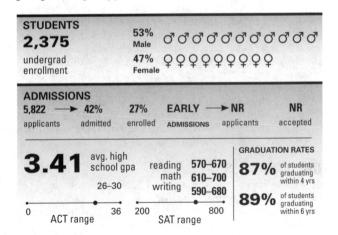

STUDENTS

2,375 undergrad enrollment

53% Male ♂♂♂♂♂♂♂♂♂♂♂

47% Female ♀♀♀♀♀♀♀♀♀♀

ADMISSIONS

5,822 applicants	→ 42% admitted	27% enrolled	EARLY ADMISSIONS → NR applicants	NR accepted

3.41 avg. high school gpa

ACT range (0–36): 26–30

SAT range (200–800): reading 570–670; math 610–700; writing 590–680

GRADUATION RATES

87% of students graduating within 4 yrs

89% of students graduating within 6 yrs

Lafayette College

Financial Aid: 610-330-5055 • E-mail: admissions@lafayette.edu • Website: www.lafayette.edu

STUDENT BODY

Lafayette students are "passionate and driven" and "tend to be athletic, very preppy, and serious about their education." A sophomore says, "The vast majority of students here are middle-to-upper class Caucasians from the tri-state area," but another adds, "Every kind of crowd imaginable is present on campus; whether you're a hipster or a prepster, you'll find a group you're comfortable in." Regardless, some students wish for "better integration of the different cultures represented at school." Many students are "involved with Greek life," and some feel that those "not involved in Greek life or sports can be isolated"; however, an economics major notes, "There are definitely cliques, but nothing even close to the high school scale." On weekends, most students stay on campus, and it's commonly held that "there is quite a bit of drinking," even though "campus safety is very strict and off-campus housing is limited to seniors so the party scene is limited."

Why Students love Lafayette College

"Every kind of crowd imaginable is present on campus; whether you're a hipster or a prepster, you'll find a group you're comfortable in."

WHY STUDENTS LOVE LAFAYETTE COLLEGE

"Deciding to go to Lafayette is the best decision I have ever made." Students praise the "gorgeous" campus, the "impressive," "first rate" facilities, and the surrounding area of Easton. "It's not quite a hectic city but it's not in the middle of nowhere either." "Walking around campus you always see many familiar faces," and "the small community feel is fantastic." "The family atmosphere adds to the education and makes Lafayette feel more like home than school." Student life is marked by enthusiastic support for Lafayette's 23 Division I athletic teams, including a top-ranked football program noted for a long-running and always entertaining rivalry with nearby Lehigh University. In addition to the amenities of the athletic programs, there are vast amounts of other extracurricular activities, including tremendous amounts of leadership opportunities in 250 student clubs and organizations–enabling endless opportunities for growth and exploration.

GENERAL INFO

Activities: Choral groups, concert band, dance, drama/theater, jazz band, literary magazine, music ensembles, musical theater, pep band, radio station, student government, student newspaper, student-run film society, symphony orchestra, yearbook, campus ministries, international student organization. **Organizations:** 250 registered organizations, 14 honor societies, 7 religious organizations. 7 fraternities, 6 sororities.

BOTTOM LINE

The tab for tuition, fees, and room and board at Lafayette College comes to about $51,000 per year. Fortunately, Lafayette's strong endowment enables the college to aggressively offset costs for students. Financial aid packages are generous and include an average freshman grant of about $20,500. Students thoroughly understand and appreciate the value of a Lafayette College education. "It's no secret that the education is expensive, but I feel like I'm really getting my money's worth from Lafayette."

SELECTIVITY

Admissions Rating	**95**
# of applicants	5,822
% of applicants accepted	42
% of acceptees attending	27
# accepting a place on wait list	534
% admitted from wait list	5

FRESHMAN PROFILE

Range SAT Critical Reading	**570–670**
Range SAT Math	**610–700**
Range SAT Writing	**590–680**
Range ACT Composite	**26–30**
Average HS GPA	**3.41**
% graduated top 10% of class	**57**
% graduated top 25% of class	**86**
% graduated top 50% of class	**99**

DEADLINES

Regular Deadline	**1/1**
Normal registration	**yes**

FACILITIES

Housing: Coed dorms, special housing for disabled students, men's dorms, women's dorms, fraternity/sorority housing, apartments for single students, wellness housing, theme housing, scholars houses, Hillel House, arts houses. *Special Academic Facilities/ Equipment:* Art and geological museums, center for the arts, engineering labs, INSTRON materials testing machine, electron microscopes, transform nuclear magnetic resonance spectrometer, computerized gas chromatograph/mass spectrometer.

FINANCIAL FACTS

Financial Aid Rating	**93**
Annual in-state tuition	$40,340
Room and Board	$12,362
Required Fees	$1,018
Books and supplies	$1,000
% frosh rec. need-based scholarship or grant aid	37
% UG rec.need-based scholarship or grant aid	43
% frosh rec. non-need-based scholarship or grant aid	11
% UG rec. non-need-based scholarship or grant aid	12
% frosh rec. need-based self-help aid	34
% UG rec. need-based self-help aid	39
% UG borrow to pay for school	52
Average cumulative indebtedness	$20,687

Macalester College

1600 Grand Avenue, St. Paul, MN 55105 • Admissions: 651-696-6357 • Fax: 651-696-6724

CAMPUS LIFE

Quality of life Rating	99
Fire Safety Rating	98
Green rating	90
Type of School	Private
Environment	Metropolis

STUDENTS

Total undergrad enrolllment	2,005
% Male to Female	42/58
% From out of state	73
% From public high school	66
% Live on Campus	66
% African American	4
% Asian	6
% Caucasian	69
% Hispanic	6
% International	11
# Of Countries Represented	94

ACADEMICS

Academic Rating	95
% Of students graduating within 4 years	86
% Of students graduating within 6 years	88
Calendar	semester
Profs interesting rating	89
Profs accessible rating	91
Most common reg class size	10–19 students
Most common lab size	10–19 students

MOST POPULAR MAJORS

Biology, economics, political science

SPECIAL STUDY OPTIONS

Cross-registration, double major, honors program, independent study, internships, student-designed major, study abroad,

ABOUT THE SCHOOL

Macalester College has been preparing its students for world citizenship and providing a rigorous, integrated international education for over six decades. (Kofi Annan is an alumnus.) With a total campus size of just fewer than 3,000 undergraduates, students benefit from a curriculum designed to include international perspectives, a multitude of semester-long study abroad programs, faculty with worldwide experience, and a community engaged in issues that matter. With more than 90 countries represented on campus, Macalester has one of the highest percentages of international student enrollment of any U.S. college. Students affirm that the school's "commitment to internationalism is unmatched by any other institution." As a result, Macalester immerses students in a microcosm of the global world from the day each moves into a dorm room, walks into the first classroom, and begins to make friends over global cuisine in Café Mac. One student notes that the student body is "diverse and interesting; some of my best friends are from countries I had hardly heard of before I got here." A fifth of students on campus are people of color, further contributing to diverse perspectives in the classroom.

Macalester's location in a major metropolitan city offers students a wealth of research and internship opportunities in business, finance, medicine, science, government, law, the arts and more. The internship program and career development center help students gain experience and connections that frequently lead to employment opportunities in the United States and around the world. Students say that "one of Macalester's greatest strengths is its commitment to providing students with opportunities to apply their learning in real settings. Most students do an internship and/or participate in some kind of civic engagement during their time here, and the school is great about supporting that." In addition to teaching, Macalester's science and math faculty are very active in research. The college ranks number one among U.S. liberal arts colleges for active National Science Foundation (NSF) grants relative to faculty size. This results in incredible opportunities for students to work with their professors on cutting-edge, real-world research projects.

BANG FOR YOUR BUCK

Macalester meets the full demonstrated financial need of every admitted student in order to ensure that classes are filled with talented, high-achieving students from a broad variety of backgrounds. The comprehensive fee at Macalester covers only about 75 percent of the cost of attending the college; the remainder comes from the college's endowment and gifts to the college, which remains fiscally strong. Every student benefits both academically and financially from this support.

STUDENTS

2,005 undergrad enrollment

42% Male ♂♂♂♂♂♂♂♂

58% Female ♀♀♀♀♀♀♀♀♀♀♀

ADMISSIONS

4,317 applicants → 43% admitted — 28% enrolled

EARLY ADMISSIONS → NR applicants — NR accepted

NR avg. high school gpa

ACT range (0–36): 28–32

SAT range (200–800): reading 640–740, math 620–720, writing 630–730

GRADUATION RATES

86% of students graduating within 4 yrs

88% of students graduating within 6 yrs

Macalester College

FINANCIAL AID: 651-696-6214 • E-MAIL: ADMISSIONS@MACALESTER.EDU • WEBSITE: WWW.MACALESTER.EDU

STUDENT BODY

Macalester "has a very diverse population as far as ethnicity and origin go, but as a whole it is very politically liberal." It's "very easy to fall into a niche at Mac," and while there are the usual cliques– "hipsters, jocks, nerds, hippies"–many students "have the same interests and passions, regardless of their social groups." Undergrads tend to be "fairly relaxed and easy going," "free-thinking," "high-achieving, hardworking, and unpretentious," and most of all, "bizarrely unique." Many describe themselves as "awkward," adding, "We are nerds and proud of it." "I never feel threatened or unwanted here, even when I'm at my oddest," says one student. Jocks that are "only interested in playing football and partying" are atypical, "but they seem to have fun among themselves, too."

Why Students love Macalester College

"Some of my best friends are from countries I had hardly heard of before I got here."

WHY STUDENTS LOVE MACALESTER COLLEGE

Students come to Macalester for "the community of diverse and collaborative students and professors" and its "dedication to political awareness, diversity, internationalism, and environmental sustainability." The students and faculty here "are not shy about how deeply they care for the world around them," and it shows in the "atmosphere of excitement and passion on campus about tons of different interests." The student body as a whole is socially conscious and politically aware; they describe themselves as "engaged, interesting and quirky," and say that Macalester is "the perfect college for high-achieving but unpretentious students who love to discuss, explore, and philosophize just for the fun of it." Small class sizes and "lots of individual attention from professors" allow students to achieve and succeed in a positive, supportive environment.

GENERAL INFO

Activities: Choral groups, concert band, dance, drama/theater, jazz band, literary magazine, music ensembles, radio station, student government, student newspaper, symphony orchestra, campus ministries, international student organization. **Organizations:** 80 registered organizations, 15 honor societies, 10 religious organizations. **Athletics (Intercollegiate):** *Men:* Baseball, basketball, cross-country, diving, football, golf, soccer, swimming, tennis, track/field (outdoor), track/field (indoor). *Women:* Basketball, cross-country, diving, golf, soccer, softball, swimming, tennis, track/field (outdoor), track/field (indoor), volleyball, water polo. **On-Campus Highlights:** Second Floor Campus Center, Bateman Plaza (our front patio), The Quad (our front yard), Shaw Field, Smail Gallery in the Science Center.

BOTTOM LINE

The cost of tuition for a year at Macalester is about $42,000. Room and board is approximately $9,000. Daunting though that may seem, the college is committed to helping. The average financial aid package for grant includes a grant of almost $30,000. Not to mention additional aid offered through scholarships and loans.

SELECTIVITY

Admissions Rating	**94**
# of applicants	4,317
% of applicants accepted	43
% of acceptees attending	28
# accepting a place on wait list	243
% admitted from wait list	0

FRESHMAN PROFILE

Range SAT Critical Reading	**640–740**
Range SAT Math	**620–720**
Range SAT Writing	**680–730**
Range ACT Composite	**28–32**
% graduated top 10% of class	**69**
% graduated top 25% of class	**92**
% graduated top 50% of class	**100**

DEADLINES

Regular Deadline	**1/15**
Normal registration	**no**

FACILITIES

Housing: Coed dorms, cooperative housing, apartments for single students, theme housing, language houses, Kosher Residence, EcoHouse. *Special Academic Facilities/Equipment:* Humanities learning center, econometrics lab, cartography lab, 250–acre nature preserve, observatory and planetarium, two electron microscopes, nuclear magnetic resonance spectrometer, laser spectroscopy lab, X-ray diffractometer, International Center,. *Computers:* 100% of classrooms, 98% of dorms, 100% of libraries, 100% of dining areas, 100% of student union, 90% of common outdoor areas have wireless network access.

FINANCIAL FACTS

Financial Aid Rating	**98**
Annual tuition	$41,800
Room and Board	$9,396
Required Fees	$221
Books and supplies	$1,010
% frosh rec. need-based scholarship or grant aid	75
% UG rec.need-based scholarship or grant aid	69
% frosh rec. non-need-based scholarship or grant aid	7
% UG rec. non-need-based scholarship or grant aid	4
% frosh rec. need-based self-help aid	67
% UG rec. need-based self-help aid	65
% frosh rec. any financial aid	80
% UG rec. any financial aid	73

Massachusetts Institute of Technology

77 Massachusetts Avenue, Room 3-108, Cambridge, MA 02139 • Admissions: 617-253-3400 • Fax: 617-258-8304

CAMPUS LIFE

Quality of life Rating	81
Fire Safety Rating	78
Green rating	91
Type of School	Private
Environment	City

STUDENTS

Total undergrad enrolllment	4,285
% Male to Female	55/45
% From out of state	90
% From public high school	65
% Live on Campus	93
# of Fraternities	27
# of Sororities	6
% African American	8
% Asian	24
% Caucasian	37
% Hispanic	13
% Native American	1
% International	9
# Of Countries Represented	92

ACADEMICS

Academic Rating	97
% Of students graduating within 4 years	84
% Of students graduating within 6 years	93
Calendar	4-1-4
Profs interesting rating	70
Profs accessible rating	76
Most common reg class size	fewer than 10 students
Most common lab size	10–19 students

MOST POPULAR MAJORS

Computer science, mathematics mechanical engineering

SPECIAL STUDY OPTIONS

Cooperative education program, cross-registration, double major, internships, study abroad, teacher certification program, Undergraduate Research Opportunities Program (UROP); Independent Activities Period (IAP); freshman learning communities.

ABOUT THE SCHOOL

The essence of Massachusetts Institute of Technology is its appetite for problems. Students here tend to be game-changers, capable of finding creative solutions to the world's big, intractable, complicated problems. A chemical engineering major says that "MIT is different from many schools in that its goal is not to teach you specific facts in each subject. MIT teaches you how to think, not about opinions but about problem solving. Facts and memori¬zation are useless unless you know how to approach a tough problem." While MIT is a research university committed to world-class inquiry in math, science, and engineering, MIT has equally distinguished programs in architecture, the humanities, management, and the social sciences. No matter what their field, almost all MIT students get involved in research during their undergraduate career, making contributions in fields as diverse as biochemistry, artificial intelligence, and urban planning. "Research opportunities for undergrads with some of the nation's leading profes¬sors" is a real highlight for students here. The school also operates an annual Independent Activities Period during the month of January, during which MIT faculty offer hundreds of non-credit activities and short for-credit classes, from lecture and film series to courses like Ballroom Dance or Introduction to Weather Forecasting (students may also use this period to work on research or independent projects.)

Students are frequently encouraged to unite MIT's science and engineering excellence with public service. Recent years have focused on projects using alternative forms of energy, and machines that could be used for sustainable agriculture. MIT's D-Lab, Poverty Action Lab, and Public Service Center all support students and professors in the research and implementation of culturally-sensitive and environmentally-responsible technologies and programs that alleviate poverty.

BANG FOR YOUR BUCK

Aid from all sources totals more than $115.6 million, and 72 percent of that total is provided by MIT Scholarships. Sixty-two percent of undergraduates qualify for need-based MIT Scholarships, and the average scholarship award exceeds $32,000. MIT is one of only a few number of institutions that have remained wholly committed to need-blind admissions and need-based aid. (There are no purely merit-based scholarships.) What truly sets MIT apart, however, is the percentage of students from lower-income households. Twenty-eight percent of MIT undergraduates are from families earning less than $75,000 a year, and 19 percent qualify for a federal Pell Grant. MIT also educates a high proportion of first-generation college students, including 16 percent of the current freshman class.

STUDENTS

4,285 undergrad enrollment

55% Male ♂♂♂♂♂♂♂♂♂♂♂

45% Female ♀♀♀♀♀♀♀♀♀

ADMISSIONS

16,632 applicants → 10% admitted | 64% enrolled | EARLY ADMISSIONS → NR applicants | NR accepted

NR avg. high school gpa

32-35 ACT range (0–36)

reading	670–760
math	740–800
writing	670–770

SAT range (200–800)

GRADUATION RATES

84% of students graduating within 4 yrs

93% of students graduating within 6 yrs

Massachusetts Institute of Technology

FINANCIAL AID: 617-253-4971 • E-MAIL: ADMISSIONS@MIT.EDU • WEBSITE: WEB.MIT.EDU

STUDENT BODY

"There actually isn't one typical student at MIT," students here assure us, explaining that "hobbies range from building robots and hacking to getting wasted and partying every weekend. The one thing students all have in com- mon is that they are insanely smart and love to learn. Pretty much anyone can find the perfect group of friends to hang out with at MIT." "Most students do have some form of 'nerdiness'" (like telling nerdy jokes, being an avid fan of Star Wars, etc.), but "Contrary to MIT's stereotype, most MIT students are not geeks who study all the time and have no social skills. The majority of the students here are actually quite 'normal.'" The "stereotypical student [who] looks techy and unkempt...only represents about twenty-five percent of the school." The rest include "multiple-sport standouts, political activists, fraternity and sorority members, hippies, clean-cut business types, LARPers, hackers, musicians, and artisans.

Why Students love MIT

"The one thing students all have in common is that they are insanely smart and love to learn."

WHY STUDENTS LOVE MIT

Simply put, students love MIT because "academically, MIT is the best," but also "tries to balance education with sports and social activities." Though MIT is admittedly challenging, students say that "the administration knows that it's hard and tries to help in any way." There are "tons of study breaks to help break the stress," and students with good time-management skills can enjoy "great frat parties" on the weekends, as well as "movies, shopping, museums, and plays" in nearby Cambridge and Boston. "The one thing students all have in common is that they are insanely smart and love to learn." MIT makes it possible for such students to thrive by providing great financial aid packages and giving their students plenty of choices. With one mathematics major calls MIT the "best school and had the best financial package."

GENERAL INFO

Activities: Choral groups, concert band, dance, drama/theater, jazz band, literary magazine, marching band, music ensembles, musical theater, radio station, student government, student newspaper. **Organizations:** 400 registered organizations, 10 honor societies, 29 religious organizations. 27 fraternities, 6 sororities. **Athletics (Intercollegiate):** *Men:* Baseball, basketball, crew/rowing, cross-country, diving, fencing, football, golf, gymnastics, lacrosse, pistol, riflery, sailing, skiing, soccer, squash, swimming, tennis, track/field. *Women:* Basketball, crew/rowing, cross-country, diving, fencing, field hockey, gymnastics, ice hockey, lacrosse, pistol, riflery, sailing, skiing, soccer, softball, swimming, tennis, track/field.

BOTTOM LINE

For the fall and spring terms, MIT tuition is about $40,000. Room and board averages about $12,000 per academic year, though those costs vary depending on a student's living situation. Books run about $1,000. MIT admits students without regard to their family's circumstances and awards financial aid to students solely on the basis of need.

SELECTIVITY

Admissions Rating	**99**
# of applicants	16,632
% of applicants accepted	10
% of acceptees attending	64
# accepting a place on wait list	573
% admitted from wait list	11

FRESHMAN PROFILE

Range SAT Critical Reading	**670–760**
Range SAT Math	**740–800**
Range SAT Writing	**670–770**
Range ACT Composite	**32–35**
% graduated top 10% of class	**98**
% graduated top 25% of class	**100**
% graduated top 50% of class	**100**

DEADLINES

Regular Deadline	**1/1**
Normal registration	**no**

FACILITIES

Housing: Coed dorms, special housing for disabled students, women's dorms, fraternity/sorority housing. *Special Academic Facilities/Equipment:* List Visual Arts Center; MIT Museum; Ray and Maria Stata Center for Computer, Information and Intelligence Sciences; numerous labs and centers. *Computers:* 100% of classrooms, 100% of dorms, 100% of libraries, 100% of dining areas, 100% of student union, 80–98% of common outdoor areas have wireless network access.

FINANCIAL FACTS

Financial Aid Rating	**93**
Annual tuition	$40,460
Room and Board	$11,775
Required Fees	$272
Books and supplies	$1,050
% frosh rec. need-based scholarship or grant aid	65
% UG rec.need-based scholarship or grant aid	63
% frosh rec. non-need-based scholarship or grant aid	5
% UG rec. non-need-based scholarship or grant aid	2
% frosh rec. need-based self-help aid	39
% UG rec. need-based self-help aid	43
% frosh rec. any financial aid	88
% UG rec. any financial aid	87
% UG borrow to pay for school	44
Average cumulative indebtedness	$15,228

Middlebury College

The Emma Willard House, Middlebury, VT 05753-6002 • Admissions: 802-443-3000 • Fax: 802-443-2056

CAMPUS LIFE

Quality of life Rating	96
Fire Safety Rating	89
Green rating	98
Type of School	Private
Environment	Village

STUDENTS

Total undergrad enrolllment	2,502
% Male to Female	50/50
% From out of state	95
% From public high school	52
% Live on Campus	97
% African American	2
% Asian	6
% Caucasian	61
% Hispanic	6
% International	10
# Of Countries Represented	64

ACADEMICS

Academic Rating	99
% Of students graduating within 4 years	84
% Of students graduating within 6 years	91
Calendar	4-1-4
Profs interesting rating	99
Profs accessible rating	97
Most common reg class size	10–19 students

MOST POPULAR MAJORS

Economics, English language and literature, psychology

SPECIAL STUDY OPTIONS

Accelerated program, double major, exchange student program (domestic), honors program, independent study, internships, student-designed major, study abroad, teacher certification program, Williams College-Mystic Seaport Program in American Maritime Studies, Oxford University summer Program,independent scholar programs with Berea College and Swarthmore College, 3-year international major. Special programs offered to physically disabled students include note-taking services, reader services, voice recorders, tutors.

ABOUT THE SCHOOL

Home to "smart people who enjoy Aristotelian ethics and quantum physics, but aren't too stuck up to go sledding in front of Mead Chapel at midnight," Middlebury College is a small, exclusive liberal arts school with "excellent foreign language programs" as well as standout offerings in environmental studies, the sciences, theater, and writing. The successful Middlebury candidate excels in a variety of areas including academics, athletics, the arts, leadership, and service to others. These strengths and interests permit students to grow beyond their traditional comfort zones and conventional limits. The classrooms are as varied as the Green Mountains, the Metropolitan Museum of Art, or the great cities of Russia and Japan. Outside the classroom, students informally interact with professors in activities such as intramural basketball games and community service. At Middlebury, students develop critical-thinking skills, enduring bonds of friendship, and the ability to challenge themselves. Middlebury offers majors and programs in forty-five different fields, with particular strengths in languages, international studies, environmental studies, literature and creative writing, and the sciences. Opportunities for engaging in individual research with faculty abound at Middlebury.

BANG FOR YOUR BUCK

Distribution requirements and other general requirements ensure that a Middlebury education "is all about providing students with a complete college experience including excellent teaching, exposure to many other cultures, endless opportunities for growth and success, and a challenging (yet relaxed) environment." Its "small class size and friendly yet competitive atmosphere make for the perfect college experience," as do "the best facilities of a small liberal arts college in the country. The new library, science center, athletic complex, arts center, and a number of the dining halls and dorms have been built in the past ten years." Students are grateful for the stellar advantages the school is able to provide them with. "I think that even if I didn't have classes or homework, I wouldn't be able to take advantage of all of the opportunities available on campus on a day-to-day basis." The academics here are unbeatable. I'd come here over an Ivy League school any day."

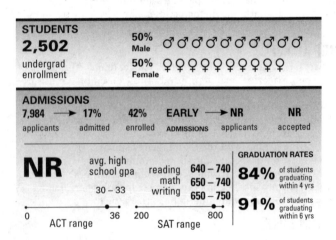

STUDENTS
2,502 undergrad enrollment
50% Male ♂♂♂♂♂♂♂♂♂♂
50% Female ♀♀♀♀♀♀♀♀♀♀

ADMISSIONS

7,984 applicants → 17% admitted	42% enrolled
EARLY ADMISSIONS → NR applicants	NR accepted

NR avg. high school gpa

ACT range (0–36): 30 – 33

SAT range (200–800): reading 640 – 740; math 650 – 740; writing 650 – 750

GRADUATION RATES
84% of students graduating within 4 yrs
91% of students graduating within 6 yrs

E-MAIL: ADMISSIONS@MIDDLEBURY.EDU • WEBSITE: WWW.MIDDLEBURY.EDU

STUDENT BODY

"The typical [Middlebury] student is athletic, outdoorsy, and very intelligent." The two most prominent demographics are "very preppy students (popped collars)" and "extreme hippies." One undergrad explains: "The typical students are one of two types: either 'Polo, Nantucket red, pearls, and summers on the Cape,' or 'Birks, wool socks, granola, and suspicious smells about them.' A lot of people break these two molds, but they often fall somewhere on the spectrum between them." There's also "a huge international student population, which is awesome," but some international students, "tend to separate out and end up living in language houses." There's also "a really strong theater/artsy community here." One student notes, "Other than a few groups, everyone mingles pretty well."

Why Students love Middlebury College

"Smart people who enjoy Aristotelian ethics and quantum physics, but aren't too stuck up to go sledding in front of Mead Chapel at midnight."

WHY STUDENTS LOVE MIDDLEBURY COLLEGE

Expect to work hard; "It's tough, but this is a mini-Ivy, so what should one expect? There is plenty of time to socialize, and due to the collaborative atmosphere here, studying and socializing can often come hand in hand. The goal of many students here is not to get high grades" but rather "learning in its purest form, and that is perhaps this college's most brightly shining aspect." The collaborative atmosphere is abetted by the fact that "admissions doesn't just bring in geniuses, they bring in people who are leaders and community servants. Think of the guy or girl in your high school whom everybody describes as 'so nice'...that's your typical Middlebury student." A high level of involvement in everything translates into an amazing campus atmosphere at Middlebury, where "most people are very involved.

GENERAL INFO

Activities: Choral groups, dance, drama/theater, jazz band, literary magazine, music ensembles, musical theater, radio station, student government, student newspaper, student-run film society, symphony orchestra, yearbook. **Organizations:** 100 registered organizations, **Athletics (Intercollegiate):** *Men:* Baseball, basketball, cross-country, diving, football, golf, ice hockey, lacrosse, skiing (downhill/alpine), skiing (nordic/cross-country), soccer, swimming, tennis, track/field (outdoor), track/field (indoor). *Women:* Basketball, cross-country, diving, field hockey, golf, ice hockey, lacrosse, skiing (downhill/alpine), skiing (nordic/cross-country), soccer, softball, squash, swimming, tennis, track/field (outdoor), track/field (indoor), volleyball.

BOTTOM LINE

Middlebury College is not the most expensive institution in the country, but it is a substantial investment. Fortunately, the opportunity for financial aid and other support is provided for needy students. Comprehensive tuition is over $50,000 per year. Almost half of all enrollees at the school are recipients of need-based scholarship or grant aid. Over 40% of students borrow to help offset the cost of their education, and upon graduating, are looking at a total loan debt of over $20,000; extremely reasonable for an education of the caliber provided by Middlebury.

SELECTIVITY

Admissions Rating	**97**
# of applicants	7,984
% of applicants accepted	17
% of acceptees attending	42
# accepting a place on wait list	865
% admitted from wait list	15

FRESHMAN PROFILE

Range SAT Critical Reading	**640-740**
Range SAT Math	**650-740**
Range SAT Writing	**650-750**
Range ACT Composite	**30-33**
% graduated top 10% of class	**86**
% graduated top 25% of class	**90**
% graduated top 50% of class	**100**

DEADLINES

Regular Deadline	**1/1**
Normal registration	**yes**

FACILITIES

Housing: Coed dorms, special housing for disabled students, apartments for single students, multi-cultural house, environmental house, foreign language house, 5 co-ed social houses. Commons System organizes residence halls into 5 groups,each with its own budget, government, faculty, and staff associates. *Special Academic Facilities/ Equipment:* Art museum, theatres, language lab, observatory, electron microscope, mountain campus, downhill and cross-country ski areas, golf course, Franklin Environmental Center, organic garden.

FINANCIAL FACTS

Financial Aid Rating	**95**
Annual comprehensive tuition	$53,800
Books and supplies	$1,000
% frosh rec. need-based scholarship or grant aid	41
% UG rec.need-based scholarship or grant aid	47
% frosh rec. need-based self-help aid	36
% UG rec. need-based self-help aid	43
% frosh rec. any financial aid	41
% UG rec. any financial aid	47
% UG borrow to pay for school	42
Average cumulative indebtedness	$21,520

Mount Holyoke College

Newhall Conter, 50 College Street, South Hadley, MA 01075 • Admissions: 413-538-2023 • Fax: 413-538-2409

CAMPUS LIFE

Quality of life Rating	91
Fire Safety Rating	79
Green rating	76
Type of School	Private
Environment	Town

STUDENTS

Total undergrad enrollment	2,287
% Male to Female	0/100
% From out of state	74
% From public high school	58
% Live on Campus	94
% African American	4
% Asian	7
% Caucasian	48
% Hispanic	7
% International	21
# Of Countries Represented	74

ACADEMICS

Academic Rating	98
% Of students graduating within 4 years	74
% Of students graduating within 6 years	82
Calendar	semester
Profs interesting rating	97
Profs accessible rating	96
Most common reg class size	10–19 students
Most common lab size	10–19 students

MOST POPULAR MAJORS

Biology, international relations
political science

SPECIAL STUDY OPTIONS

Cooperative education program, cross-registration, double major, exchange student program (domestic), independent study, internships, liberal arts/career combination, student-designed major, study abroad, teacher certification program, Community-based learning courses and First-Year seminars. Special programs offered to physically disabled students include note-taking services, reader services, voice recorders, tutors.

ABOUT THE SCHOOL

From its outstanding academic program and facilities to its accomplished students to the formidable faculty that love teaching as much as research, Mount Holyoke provides a first-rate experience. The academic experience is phenomenal. So is the library. The dorms are luxurious, too. This small, elite, all-female school also boasts extremely approachable professors. Students say that they are "beyond accessible, and always more than willing to make the effort to meet with you outside of class." They pile on the homework, though. Students here have to work very hard to make good grades, but many maintain that they have "never had a better classroom experience." Undergraduate research is remarkably commonplace, and the college offers over one-half million dollars every summer for students to conduct unpaid internship and research projects. Membership in the Five College Consortium is another perk. Mount Holyoke students can benefit from more than 5,000 courses, all manner of cultural events, and tons of the resources of four other prominent schools within a 12-mile radius: Amherst, Hampshire, Smith, and University of Massachusetts–Amherst.

Despite its impressive legacy, Mount Holyoke is anything but an ivory tower: students are encouraged to develop a meaningful connection to the world through community-based learning courses; a Speaking, Arguing and Writing Center; and by developing their own networks from among the student body. According to students, Mount Holyoke is focused on "empowering women to pursue leadership positions in fields about which they are passionate." Mount Holyoke's Nexus: Curriculum to Career program enables students to link their liberal arts education with their career goals through internships, research projects, and summer employment.

BANG FOR YOUR BUCK

Mount Holyoke College makes an extraordinary and extraordinarily successful effort to support an economically diverse student population. Almost three-quarters of students receive some sort of financial aid, and Mount Holyoke College is one of the rare schools that is always able to meet 100 percent of your financial need (if you can just get accepted). In addition to all the need-based aid, Mount Holyoke offers a decent number of merit-based scholarships. The 21st Century Scholars program includes a scholarship of $25,000 per year for four years, funding for a summer internship program, and participation in a first-year tutorial. The Mount Holyoke Leadership Award is also on offer, and consists of merit-based scholarships ranging between $10,000 and $20,000 per year. One other perk is the Laurel Fellowship, an award designed to ensure that students on need-based financial aid can study abroad.

STUDENTS

2,287 undergrad enrollment

0% Male

100% Female ♀♀♀♀♀♀♀♀♀♀

ADMISSIONS

3,359 applicants →	52% admitted	31% enrolled	EARLY ADMISSIONS →	NR applicants	NR accepted

3.70 avg. high school gpa

ACT range (0–36)	27–31
SAT reading	610–700
SAT math	580–690
SAT writing	620–710

SAT range: 200–800

GRADUATION RATES

74% of students graduating within 4 yrs

82% of students graduating within 6 yrs

Mount Holyoke College

Financial Aid: 413-538-2291 • E-mail: admission@mtholyoke.edu • Website: www.mtholyoke.edu

STUDENT BODY

At Mount Holyoke, "The students are happy, intelligent women dedicated to making a real difference in the world." Typical students are "poised, eloquent, passionate, and doing interesting things both inside and outside the classroom" and "down-to-earth and laid-back but also willing to have complex conversations over breakfast." It's clear most are "very into being left-wing and excited about political awareness," and a sophomore says, "Mt. Holyoke is full of geeky feminists," who are "at least socially engaged if not activists." There is "a very strong gay community and much of the party scene is queer-based social networks," and students say, "Sexual orientation is often flexible."

Why Students love Mount Holyoke College

"The students are happy, intelligent women dedicated to making a real difference in the world."

WHY STUDENTS LOVE MOUNT HOLYOKE COLLEGE

Though Mount Holyoke College has many strengths, including a beautiful campus and top-notch academics, the one the students appreciate the most is the close-knit community and the "strong sense of sisterhood" that women develop at here. The social atmosphere is "warm and accepting", and the students are "diverse, strong, passionate, friendly and fun". This strong support system is important to Mount Holyoke students, who come here to receive a first-class education in a highly academic environment, which is "both challenging and supportive at the same time." Support comes from many places other than your peers at Mount Holyoke. Professors here are "beyond accessible," an administration that "listens to the students and does its best to provide for us," and an "incredible" Alumnae Association.

GENERAL INFO

Activities: Choral groups, dance, drama/theater, jazz band, literary magazine, music ensembles, musical theater, radio station, student government, student newspaper, student-run film society, symphony orchestra, yearbook, campus ministries, international student organization. **Organizations:** 150 registered organizations, 4 honor societies, 12 religious organizations. **Athletics (Intercollegiate):** *Women:* Basketball, crew/ rowing, cross-country, diving, equestrian sports, field hockey, golf, horseback riding, lacrosse, soccer, squash, swimming, tennis, track/field (outdoor), track/ field (indoor), volleyball.

BOTTOM LINE

Tuition is more than $40,000. This school does a tremendous job of making itself affordable for everyone, though, regardless of income. If you can get admitted here, you'll almost certainly find a way to pay for it while borrowing very little money.

SELECTIVITY

Admissions Rating	**95**
# of applicants	3,359
% of applicants accepted	52
% of acceptees attending	31
# accepting a place on wait list	515
% admitted from wait list	15

FRESHMAN PROFILE

Range SAT Critical Reading	**610–700**
Range SAT Math	**580–690**
Range SAT Writing	**620–710**
Range ACT Composite	**27–31**
Average HS GPA	**3.70**
% graduated top 10% of class	**58**
% graduated top 25% of class	**82**
% graduated top 50% of class	**98**

DEADLINES

Regular Deadline	**1/15**
Normal registration	**yes**

FACILITIES

Housing: Special housing for disabled students, women's dorms, apartments for single students, special housing arrangements are available upon request. *Special Academic Facilities/ Equipment:* Art and historical museums, bronze-casting foundry, child study center, audio-visual center. *Computers:* 20% of classrooms, 100% of dorms, 100% of libraries, 100% of dining areas, 100% of student union, 4% of common outdoor areas have wireless network access.

FINANCIAL FACTS

Financial Aid Rating	**96**
Annual tuition	$41,270
Room and Board	$12,140
Required Fees	$186
Books and supplies	$950
% frosh rec. need-based scholarship or grant aid	70
% UG rec.need-based scholarship or grant aid	68
% frosh rec. non-need-based scholarship or grant aid	12
% UG rec. non-need-based scholarship or grant aid	9
% frosh rec. need-based self-help aid	62
% UG rec. need-based self-help aid	67
% frosh rec. any financial aid	82
% UG rec. any financial aid	79
% UG borrow to pay for school	66
Average cumulative indebtedness	$22,499

Northwestern University

PO Box 3060, 1801 Hinman Avenue, Evanston, IL 60204-3060 • Admissions: : 847-491-7271

CAMPUS LIFE

Quality of life Rating	73
Fire Safety Rating	73
Green rating	78
Type of School	Private
Environment	Town

STUDENTS

Total undergrad enrolllment	8,364
% Male to Female	48/52
% From out of state	75
% From public high school	65
% Live on Campus	65
# of Fraternities	17
# of Sororities	19
% African American	5
% Asian	18
% Caucasian	58
% Hispanic	7
% International	5
# Of Countries Represented	42

ACADEMICS

Academic Rating	89
% Of students graduating within 4 years	86
% Of students graduating within 6 years	93
Calendar	quarter
Profs interesting rating	75
Profs accessible rating	76
Most common reg class size	fewer than 10 students
Most common lab size	10–19 students

MOST POPULAR MAJORS

Economics, engineering journalism

SPECIAL STUDY OPTIONS

Accelerated program, cooperative education program, double major, honors program, independent study, internships, liberal arts/career combination, student-designed major, study abroad, teacher certification program. Honors programs: Honors Program in Medical Education, Integrated Science Program, MENU, MMSS.

ABOUT THE SCHOOL

One student relates that Northwestern University "is all about balance–academically it excels across the academic spectrum, its location is just the right balance between urban and suburban and its student body while not incredibly ethnically diverse still has a range of people." The total undergraduate enrollment is more than 8,000 students; adding to the school's diversity, nearly three-quarters of kids come from out-of-state. Northwestern University is a school built on communities, be it socially, politically, or academically. A rigorous, "very challenging" multidisciplinary school that is pre-professional and stimulating, students are pleased by the fact that "Northwestern is not an easy school. It takes hard work to be average here." Northwestern not only has a varied curriculum, but "everything is given fairly equal weight." Northwestern students and faculty "do not show a considerable bias" toward specific fields. As well, excellences in competencies that transcend any particular field of study are highly valued.

BANG FOR YOUR BUCK

Northwestern University works hard to empower students to become leaders in their professions and communities. People are goal-oriented and care about their academic success, and are pleased that Northwestern helps provide "so many connections and opportunities during and after graduation." Numerous resources established by administrators and professors, including tutoring programs such as Northwestern's Gateway Science Workshop, provide needy students with all of the support they desire.

STUDENTS

8,364 undergrad enrollment

48% Male ♂♂♂♂♂♂♂♂♂♂

52% Female ♀♀♀♀♀♀♀♀♀♀

ADMISSIONS

25,013 applicants → **26%** admitted | **32%** enrolled | **EARLY** ADMISSIONS → **NR** applicants | **NR** accepted

NR avg. high school gpa

ACT range (0–36): 30–33

SAT range (200–800): reading 670–750; math 690–780; writing 670–750

GRADUATION RATES

85% of students graduating within 4 yrs

93% of students graduating within 6 yrs

STUDENT BODY

The typical Northwestern student "was high school class president with a 4.0, swim team captain, and on the chess team." So it makes sense everyone here "is an excellent student who works hard" and "has a leadership position in at least two clubs, plus an on-campus job." Students also tell us "there's [a] great separation between North Campus (think: fraternities, engineering, state school mentality) and South Campus (think: closer to Chicago and its culture, arts and letters, liberal arts school mentality). Students segregate themselves depending on background and interests, and it's rare for these two groups to interact beyond a superficial level." The student body here includes sizeable Jewish, Indian, and East-Asian populations.

Northwestern University

FINANCIAL AID: : 847-491-7400 • E-MAIL: UG-ADMISSION@NORTHWESTERN.EDU • WEBSITE: WWW.NORTHWESTERN.EDU

Why Students love Northwestern University

"Extracurricular activities are incredible here."

WHY STUDENTS LOVE NORTHWESTERN UNIVERSITY

Two-thirds of students live on a beautiful campus, which is buzzing with activity of all sorts. The Greek community is very predominant at the school; fraternities and sororities dominate the social scene, with more than 35 in total. One student raves that "extracurriculars are incredible here. There is a group for every interest, and the groups are amazingly well-managed by students alone." Activism is also very popular, with many involved in political groups, human-rights activism, and volunteering. One student describes the school as having "Ivy League academics with Big 10 sensibilities." There are also two campuses; students tell us "there's great separa¬tion between North Campus (fraternities, engineering, state school mentality) and South Campus (closer to Chicago and its culture, arts and letters, liberal arts school mentality). North campus is more "fratty," with a lot of the "cool kids" living up there. South campus feels more like a liberal arts college, with a strong theater and arts component...we are able to go downtown and explore the city; having Chicago 40 minutes away by train is also a huge plus."

GENERAL INFO

Activities: Choral groups, concert band, dance, drama/theater, jazz band, literary magazine, marching band, music ensembles, musical theater, opera, pep band, radio station, student government, student newspaper, student-run film society, symphony orchestra, television station, yearbook, campus ministries, international student organization. **Organizations:** 415 registered organizations, 23 honor societies, 29 religious organizations. 17 fraternities, 19 sororities. **Athletics (Intercollegiate):** *Men:* Baseball, basketball, cheerleading, diving, football, golf, soccer, swimming, tennis, wrestling. *Women:* Basketball, cheerleading, cross-country, diving, fencing, field hockey, golf, lacrosse, soccer, softball, swimming, tennis, volleyball. **On-Campus Highlights:** Shakespeare Garden, Dearborn Observatory, Norris Student Center, Henry Crown Sports Pavilion and Aquatic Center, the lakefill on Lake Michigan. **Environmental Initiatives:** Commitment to purchase of renewable energy credits for 20% of the University's usage. Commitment to LEED certifications awarded (LEED NC Silver and LEED CI Gold).

BOTTOM LINE

Northwestern is among the nation's most expensive undergraduate institutions, a fact that sometimes discourages some qualified students from applying. The school is increasing its efforts to attract more low-income applicants by increasing the number of full scholarships available for students whose family income is less than $45,000. Low-income students who score well on the ACT may receive a letter from the school encouraging them to apply. With tuition more than $40,000 a year, any and all support is greatly appreciated by undergrads and their parents.

SELECTIVITY

Admissions Rating	**97**
# of applicants	25,013
% of applicants accepted	26
% of acceptees attending	32
# accepting a place on wait list	1,037
% admitted from wait list	12

FRESHMAN PROFILE

Range SAT Critical Reading	**670–750**
Range SAT Math	**690–780**
Range SAT Writing	**670–750**
Range ACT Composite	**30–33**
% graduated top 10% of class	**85**
% graduated top 25% of class	**96**
% graduated top 50% of class	**99**

DEADLINES

Regular Deadline	**1/1**
Normal registration	**yes**

FACILITIES

Housing: Coed dorms, men's dorms, women's dorms, fraternity/sorority housing, wellness house, theme housing. *Special Academic Facilities/Equipment:* Art gallery, learning sciences institute, communicative disorders and materials and life sciences buildings, catalysis center, astronomical research center. *Computers:* 100% of classrooms, 100% of dorms, 100% of libraries, 100% of dining areas, 100% of student union, 100% of common outdoor areas have wireless network access.

FINANCIAL FACTS

Financial Aid Rating	**93**
Annual in-state tuition	$38,088
Room and Board	$11,703
Required Fees	$373
Books and supplies	$1,686
% frosh rec. need-based scholarship or grant aid	38
% UG rec.need-based scholarship or grant aid	40
% frosh rec. need-based self-help aid	34
% UG rec. need-based self-help aid	36
% frosh rec. any financial aid	60
% UG rec. any financial aid	60
% UG borrow to pay for school	49
Average cumulative indebtedness	$19,908

Occidental College

1600 Campus Road, Office of Admission, Los Angeles, CA 90041-3314 • Admissions: 323-259-2700 • Fax: 323-341-4875

CAMPUS LIFE

Quality of life Rating	82
Fire Safety Rating	72
Green rating	80
Type of School	Private
Environment	Metropolis

STUDENTS

Total undergrad enrollment	2,073
% Male to Female	44/56
% From out of state	54
% From public high school	58
% Live on Campus	80
# of Fraternities	3
# of Sororities	4
% African American	6
% Asian	16
% Caucasian	57
% Hispanic	19
% Native American	2
% International	3
# Of Countries Represented	26

ACADEMICS

Academic Rating	90
% Of students graduating within 4 years	80
% Of students graduating within 6 years	85
Calendar	semester
Profs interesting rating	84
Profs accessible rating	84
Most common reg class size	10–19 students
Most common lab size	10–19 students

MOST POPULAR MAJORS

Economics, international relations, English language and literature

SPECIAL STUDY OPTIONS

Cross-registration, double major, exchange student program (domestic), honors program, independent study, internships, student-designed major, study abroad, Richter fellowships for international research; summer undergraduate research program; endowment investment management program (Blyth Fund).

ABOUT THE SCHOOL

Although the curriculum is reportedly difficult, students actually appreciate it. A "very prestigious school," and "tough academically," "the benefits of getting an education here are worth all the work." Professors really care about their students and desperately want them to be successful. Undergrads are pleased that profs here don't exist to "publish or perish;" "they actually are at Oxy to teach–and not to teach so they can research." Students say it is "really easy" to get "independent study, internships, and grants" that would "not be offered anywhere else to undergraduates." "I've been working with postdoctoral researchers as an undergraduate. It's very rewarding." There is also the highly respected Center for Academic Excellence, which provides free tutoring. With a total student body of only 2000 or so students–women being more highly represented–individual attention is a wonderful advantage for all undergrads.

Occidental offers a semester-long, residential United Nations program, one of the few programs of its kind; the country's only Campaign Semester program, which every two years offers students the opportunity to earn academic credit while working on House, Senate, and presidential campaigns; one of the few opportunities to pursue fully funded undergraduate research overseas (almost 50 percent of Occidental students study overseas); and one of the country's best undergraduate research programs that has sent more than 170 students to the National Conference on Undergraduate Research over the past six years.

BANG FOR YOUR BUCK

Internships for academic credit are available for sophomores, juniors, and seniors through the Career Development Center; the CDC also offers a limited number of paid summer internships through its Community Arts and Public Service program. The CDC also offers a career shadowing program with alumni professionals (the Walk in My Shoes program) Occidental emphasizes experiential learning. "I've gotten a broader sense of self and have been able to fulfill my learning goals," said one student appreciatively. The admissions team at Occidental is adamant about not adhering to formulas. They rely heavily on essays and recommendations in their mission to create a talented and diverse incoming class. The college attracts some excellent students, so a demanding course load in high school is essential for the most competitive candidates. Successful applicants tend to be creative and academically motivated. A stellar total of 80% of students graduate within four years.

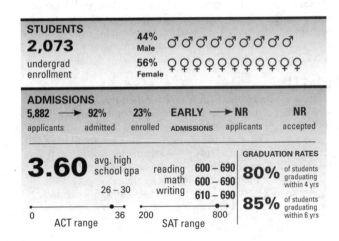

STUDENTS

2,073 undergrad enrollment

44% Male

56% Female

ADMISSIONS

5,882 applicants → 92% admitted; 23% enrolled

EARLY ADMISSIONS → NR applicants; NR accepted

3.60 avg. high school gpa

ACT range (0–36): 26 – 30

SAT range (200–800): reading 600 – 690; math 600 – 690; writing 610 – 690

GRADUATION RATES

80% of students graduating within 4 yrs

85% of students graduating within 6 yrs

Occidental College

FINANCIAL AID: 323-259-2548 • E-MAIL: ADMISSION@OXY.EDU • WEBSITE: WWW.OXY.EDU

STUDENT BODY

The typical Oxy undergrad "is politically and globally aware, is passionate about more than one interest, and loves to speak up about any and every issue (both related to the school and outside of it)." Most are "very liberal, studious, hardworking, and playful." Atypical students "are usually conservative or party animals. The conservative students have a bit of a hard time since the college and its students are typically very left-winged, yet they manage. The party animals fit in very well, although [they are] not necessarily liked in all situations, such as group projects, since they are a bit less hardworking." In terms of personality types, "we range from kids who are proud of being hicks to the artsy hipsters to some Goth kids to just your average run-of-the-mill sandwich-eating college kid." Common threads are "intelligence and desire to discuss issues, whatever they may be" and "the laid-back groove of California," which most here embody.

Why Students love Occidental College

"We range from kids who are proud of being hicks to the artsy hipsters to some Goth kids to just your average run-of-the-mill sandwich-eating college kid."

WHY STUDENTS LOVE OCCIDENTAL COLLEGE

Common threads are "intelligence and desire to discuss issues, whatever they may be" and "the laid-back groove of California," according to a few student body members. Most students stay on campus over the weekends, but the school does clear out somewhat during the day, as trips to Santa Monica or into downtown LA are popular. "Every week the school offers trips around Southern California." Extracurricular diversions are copious; "Chinatown, Disneyland, the beach, the movies, plays, museums, the Glendale Galleria, [and] the Santa Monica Promenade. The loca¬tion definitely has advantages," one student relates; and, so does the Oxy campus.

GENERAL INFO

Activities: Choral groups, concert band, dance, drama/theater, jazz band, literary magazine, music ensembles, musical theater, radio station, student government, student newspaper, student-run film society, symphony orchestra, yearbook, international student organization. **Organizations:** 8 honor societies, 5 religious organizations. 4 fraternities, 4 sororities. **Athletics (Intercollegiate):** *Men:* Baseball, basketball, cross-country, diving, football, golf, soccer, swimming, tennis, track/field (outdoor), water polo. *Women:* Basketball, cross-country, diving, golf, lacrosse, soccer, softball, swimming, tennis, track/field (outdoor), volleyball, water polo.

BOTTOM LINE

About three out of four Occidental students receive some form of financial aid, including need-based aid and merit scholarships. The average financial aid package is $34,140. Oxy actively seeks out talented students from all backgrounds: 24 percent of Oxy students are Pell Grant recipients, and 19 percent are the first in their family to attend college. There are well more than 300 student scholarships available. "They gave me gave me extraordinary financial aid," says one undergrad.

SELECTIVITY

Admissions Rating	**95**
# of applicants	5,882
% of applicants accepted	42
% of acceptees attending	23
# accepting a place on wait list	352
% admitted from wait list	8

FRESHMAN PROFILE

Range SAT Critical Reading	**600–690**
Range SAT Math	**600–690**
Range SAT Writing	**610–690**
Range ACT Composite	**26–30**
Average HS GPA	**3.60**
% graduated top 10% of class	**62**
% graduated top 25% of class	**93**
% graduated top 50% of class	**100**

DEADLINES

Regular Deadline	**1/10**
Normal registration	**no**

FACILITIES

Housing: Coed dorms, women's dorms, fraternity/sorority housing, theme housing. *Special Academic Facilities/Equipment:* Keck Theater; Mullin Studio and Art Gallery; Moore Ornithology Collection; Smiley Geological Collection; Morse Collection of Astronomical Instruments; superconducting magnet; vivarium; greenhouses. *Computers:* 100% of classrooms, 100% of dorms, 90% of libraries, 100% of dining areas, 80% of student union, 50% of common outdoor areas have wireless network access.

FINANCIAL FACTS

Financial Aid Rating	**97**
Annual tuition	$41,860
Room and Board	$11,990
Required Fees	$1,100
Books and supplies	$1,180
% frosh rec. need-based scholarship or grant aid	59
% UG rec.need-based scholarship or grant aid	54
% frosh rec. non-need-based scholarship or grant aid	9
% UG rec. non-need-based scholarship or grant aid	3
% frosh rec. need-based self-help aid	49
% UG rec. need-based self-help aid	50
% frosh rec. any financial aid	77
% UG rec. any financial aid	79
% UG borrow to pay for school	67
Average cumulative indebtedness	$17,561

Randolph College

2500 Rivermont Avenue, Lynchburg, VA 24503-1555 • Admissions: 434-947-8100 • Fax: 434-947-8996

CAMPUS LIFE

Quality of life Rating	84
Fire Safety Rating	89
Green rating	70
Type of School	Private
Environment	City

STUDENTS

Total undergrad enrollment	517
% Male to Female	34/66
% From out of state	42
% From public high school	75
% Live on Campus	91
% African American	10
% Asian	2
% Caucasian	66
% Hispanic	5
% International	13
# Of Countries Represented	34

ACADEMICS

Academic Rating	92
% Of students graduating within 4 years	64
% Of students graduating within 6 years	66
Calendar	semester
Profs interesting rating	98
Profs accessible rating	96
Most common reg class size	fewer than 10 students
Most common lab size	fewer than 10 students

MOST POPULAR MAJORS

Biology, political science psychology

SPECIAL STUDY OPTIONS

Accelerated program, cross-registration, double major, dual enrollment, exchange student program (domestic), honors program, independent study, internships, liberal arts/career combination, student-designed major, study abroad, teacher certification program, 7-college exchange with Washington and Lee University, Hollins University, Hampden-Sydney College, Mary Baldwin College, Sweet Briar College, and Randolph-Macon College. Study abroad is encouraged and facilitated.

ABOUT THE SCHOOL

In the heart of Virginia near the Blue Ridge Mountains, Randolph College's campus is part of the grow¬ing town of Lynchburg. The college's motto "Vita Abundantior" ("Live Abundantly") expresses its historical emphasis on the importance of quality education to a full, rich life. Its slogan, "Be an Original," expresses the value of distinction and difference. A combination of great academics, cultural integrity, individuality and traditions, with a broad range of students from different backgrounds and ethnicities, assists in helping make these words ring true. "I love that our college is so international. We have students coming from many different countries and we have many study abroad opportunities." "Study abroad programs enable students to see and live through the eyes of another culture," and "develop critical skills to learn, adapt, and succeed in a rapidly changing global environment." Students are very impressed by the academic experience at Randolph, as well. "The school has a great academic program, much better than most schools of this size." "The level of expectation for scholarly performance is high on both sides of the desk (student and professor)." Career-oriented experiential learning is touted highly, and "the college's strong emphasis on writing enables students to communicate clearly and persuasively." "My life at school is usually stressful but rewarding," says one undergrad.

BANG FOR YOUR BUCK

Randolph College is part of CAREER15, a unique resource of the Virginia Foundation for Independent Colleges that connects students and graduates of 15 independent Virginia colleges with more than 140 companies seeking interns and employees including Fortune 500 companies, government agencies and non-profit organizations. The Experiential Learning Center prepares students for networking with employers. Student government is very visible and active. Required internships are part of the College's curriculum and many students take advantage of multiple internship or service learning opportunities. There's no minimum GPA or standardized test score requirements, but be aware that most successful candidates have impressive classroom credentials. Many students over breaks or in the summer have internships or study abroad. One student tells us that "it is also a very small school with most of my classes having 10 students or less, this was an important factor in picking a school." 90% of students live on campus, and more than 40 percent of enrollees come from another state originally. Women outnumber men 2:1, and there are only 500 or so students in total at the school.

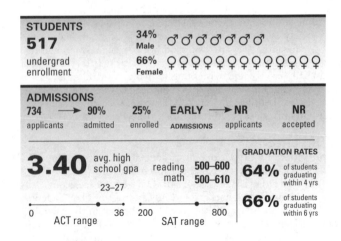

STUDENTS

517 undergrad enrollment

34% Male ♂♂♂♂♂♂♂

66% Female ♀♀♀♀♀♀♀♀♀♀♀♀♀

ADMISSIONS

734 applicants	→ 90% admitted	25% enrolled	EARLY ADMISSIONS	→ NR applicants	NR accepted

3.40 avg. high school gpa

ACT range (0–36): 23–27

SAT range (200–800): reading 500–600, math 500–610

GRADUATION RATES

64% of students graduating within 4 yrs

66% of students graduating within 6 yrs

Financial Aid: 434-947-8128 • E-mail: admissions@randolphcollege.edu • Website: www.randolphcollege.edu

STUDENT BODY

As a rule, students at Randolph "are academically motivated and open to other ideas and cultures." In line with that, "Those that are not serious about academics or that are very close minded will most likely quickly find that this school is not the correct fit for them." This is due to the "great diversity of students" on campus that makes for some "extraordinarily unique" individuals who, despite differences, manage to "fit together perfectly." "There's enough diversity here for everyone to be different," says one undergrad, "but enough conformity for groups of friends to develop and interact with each other." Students are "serious but not very nerdy," "liberal," and "more informed than most." Despite academics being "the number one priority for students," most here are "very involved in a number of clubs and extracurricular activities." There are also "very few cliques," though "a few do exist."

Why Students love Randolph College

"A place where everybody really does know your name and everyone smiles at each other."

WHY STUDENTS LOVE RANDOLPH COLLEGE

Values and traditions are the things this school holds important. RC carries over several traditions from its time as a women's college, like Skellar Sings, Ring Night, Pumpkin Parade, Stomps, Greek Play, plus many more. "One such tradition is class rivalry. You are designated an "even" or an "odd" depending on when you graduate, and you have sing-offs and even/odd day, etc. These traditions are so much fun and allow students to blow off steam." Walking distance to the Blackwater Creek Trails, where it is great to go for a run, a hike, ride bikes or just take a stroll. The environmental club has a bike sharing program, where you can borrow a donated bike and helmet in return for being good to the environment.

GENERAL INFO

Activities: Choral groups, dance, drama/theater, literary magazine, music ensembles, pep band, radio station, student government, student newspaper, student-run film society, yearbook, international student organization. **Organizations:** 40 registered organizations, 7 honor societies, 6 religious organizations. **Athletics (Intercollegiate):** *Men:* Basketball, cross-country, equestrian sports, horseback riding, lacrosse, soccer, tennis. *Women:* Basketball, cross-country, equestrian sports, horseback riding, lacrosse, soccer, softball, swimming, tennis, volleyball. **On-Campus Highlights:** The Maier Museum of Art, Macon Bookshop (on Rivermont Avenue), The Whiteside Amphitheater, Botanical Gardens, Randolph College Riding Center Skeller.

BOTTOM LINE

Randolph College offers a comprehensive program of financial assistance, including need-based grants, merit scholarships, and a variety of loan options. Annual tuition is somewhat steep at almost $30,000; room and board adds another $10,000. Fortunately, support is prevalent. An incredible 99 percent of undergrads receive financial aid, putting an educational experience of high caliber accessible to many people who would not be able to come here otherwise.

SELECTIVITY

Admissions Rating	**79**
# of applicants	734
% of applicants accepted	90
% of acceptees attending	25

FRESHMAN PROFILE

Range SAT Critical Reading	**500–600**
Range SAT Math	**500–610**
Range ACT Composite	**23–27**
Average HS GPA	**3.40**
% graduated top 10% of class	**20**
% graduated top 25% of class	**60**
% graduated top 50% of class	**90**

DEADLINES

Regular Deadline	**2/1**
Normal registration	**yes**

FACILITIES

Housing: Coed dorms, women's dorms, special housing for non-traditional age students. *Special Academic Facilities/Equipment:* Maier Museum of American Art, 100-acre equestrian center, language lab, science and math resource center, learning resources center, writing lab, nursery school, nature preserves, observatory, electron microscope. *Computers:* 100% of classrooms, 100% of dorms, 100% of libraries, 100% of dining areas, 100% of student union, 100% of common outdoor areas have wireless network access.

FINANCIAL FACTS

Financial Aid Rating	**85**
Annual in-state tuition	$29,866
Room and Board	$10,386
Required Fees	510
Books and supplies	$1,000
% frosh rec. need-based scholarship or grant aid	74
% UG rec.need-based scholarship or grant aid	66
% frosh rec. non-need-based scholarship or grant aid	22
% UG rec. non-need-based scholarship or grant aid	18
% frosh rec. need-based self-help aid	66
% UG rec. need-based self-help aid	58
% frosh rec. any financial aid	99
% UG rec. any financial aid	96
% UG borrow to pay for school	75
Average cumulative indebtedness	$27,218

Reed College

3203 SE Woodstock Boulevard, Portland, OR 97202-8199 • Admissions: 503-777-7511 • Fax: 503-777-7553

CAMPUS LIFE

Quality of life Rating	94
Fire Safety Rating	92
Green rating	82
Type of School	Private
Environment	City

STUDENTS

Total undergrad enrollment	1,418
% Male to Female	44/56
% From out of state	87
% From public high school	59
% Live on Campus	69
% African American	2
% Asian	6
% Caucasian	56
% Hispanic	4
% International	5
# Of Countries Represented	46

ACADEMICS

Academic Rating	99
% Of students graduating within 4 years	59
% Of students graduating within 6 years	79
Calendar	semester
Profs interesting rating	99
Profs accessible rating	88
Most common reg class size	10–19 students
Most common lab size	10–19 students

MOST POPULAR MAJORS

Anthropology, English language and literature, psychology

SPECIAL STUDY OPTIONS

Cross-registration, double major, dual enrollment, exchange student program (domestic), independent study, internships, liberal arts/career combination, study abroad, Computer Science By arrangement with the University of Washington, a student may obtain a bachelor of arts degree from Reed and a bachelor of science degree in computer science from the University of Washington. A joint five-year program is also available with the Pacific Northwest College of Art. These programs are described in more detail in the art department section of the catalog.

ABOUT THE SCHOOL

Students greatly enjoy the non-traditional aspects of a Reed educational experience. The "unique and quirky atmosphere," in a "beautiful" part of the country with a "gorgeous" campus, provides students with a "traditional, classical, highly structured curriculum–yet, at the same time, a progressive, free-thinking, decidedly unstructured commu¬nity culture." Reed students tend to be "smart, intellectually curious, and a little quirky." Politics tilt strongly to the left. Though the academics are incredibly intense, students are still playful and funky. Members of the student body here tell us that "Reed met my every desire with characteristic zeal; I received the financial aid I needed, I was able to sign up for challenging classes, and the living situation is ideal." Also, Reed doesn't "pad your ego." "Getting an A is a hard fought battle here, but it means more because of it." Reed exalts the individual and the self-thinker. Even if a student doesn't start off with these qualities, he or she will likely develop them. Although the workload is intense, Reed enrollees are fiercely intellectual and more concerned with academic pursuits for their own sake than for any financial rewards their educations will produce. "I wanted to challenge myself and what I believed. I didn't want that passive undergraduate experience I see so much in other college students." "I was intrigued by the idea of an environment where people study because they care and participate in class because they feel that education is a worthwhile endeavor." It's a place where one comes to learn for the sake of learning, not to earn good grades, in a supportive environment. It is a place that is genuinely dedicated to the life of the mind, and teaches the student to approach all aspects of life with a scholarly attitude.

BANG FOR YOUR BUCK

Of fundamental importance at Reed is how you contribute to the intellectual life of the college. "I am challenged to work hard and I strive to meet the very high expectations for Reed students." Students seek out an "academic rigor that definitely prepares us for graduate school and scholarly work." High-level research and scholarship at the cutting edge of each academic discipline is important to the school. With outstanding professors, and a healthy social environment, "For students who are interested both in exploring great ideas and in developing personal autonomy, it makes very good sense." Aptly put by another undergrad, "I wanted a challenge–if college isn't hard, you're doing something wrong."

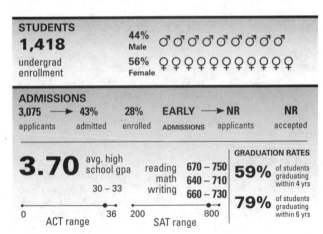

STUDENTS

1,418 undergrad enrollment

44% Male ♂♂♂♂♂♂♂♂♂

56% Female ♀♀♀♀♀♀♀♀♀♀♀

ADMISSIONS

3,075 applicants → 43% admitted; 28% enrolled

EARLY ADMISSIONS → NR applicants; NR accepted

3.70 avg. high school gpa

ACT range (0–36): 30 – 33

SAT range (200–800): reading 670 – 750; math 640 – 710; writing 660 – 730

GRADUATION RATES

59% of students graduating within 4 yrs

79% of students graduating within 6 yrs

Reed College

FINANCIAL AID: 503-777-7223 • E-MAIL: ADMISSION@REED.EDU • WEBSITE: WWW.REED.EDU

STUDENT BODY

Reed students tend to be "smart, intellectually curious, and a little quirky." Politics tilt strongly to the left. One student reports, "There is virtually no political dialogue. The student body is so liberal the only dialogue is really between socialists and communists. For students who regard themselves as liberal and, consequentially, open-minded, there is very little acceptance of people who don't identify themselves as liberal or who simply like political dialogue." Students note there is "a growing population of minority students (minority in various senses), and they are making efforts constantly to establish themselves as a social presence on campus. Student groups like the Latino, Asian, and Black and African Student Unions and places like the Multicultural Resource Center offer places for support."

Why Students love Reed College

"The dorms are divided, so even within a large dorm, you mainly live with ten to twenty other people focused around a common room."

WHY STUDENTS LOVE REED COLLEGE

There are lots of things to do for fun in Portland. There are plentiful and unique shopping options, and the beach isn't too far away from the college. There is also the ski cabin, which is open for student use on Mt. Hood. Hawthorne, a trendy neighborhood nearby campus, is nearby, or students can take a short bus ride to downtown Portland. Reed has an enormous endowment for student activities, and undergrads get to decide where this money is best spent. Also, the "extremely nice" dorms result in the homey feel on campus, and there are a large number of themed dorms. "The dorms are divided, so even within a large dorm, you mainly live with ten to twenty other people focused around a common room." As one student sums up best, "All in a lively, young city with beautiful trees and delicious food."

GENERAL INFO

Activities: Choral groups, dance, drama/theater, literary magazine, music ensembles, radio station, student government, student newspaper, student-run film society, symphony orchestra, campus ministries, international student organization. **Organizations:** 130 registered organizations, 1 honor societies, 5 religious organizations. **On-Campus Highlights:** Thesis Tower, Nuclear Research Reactor, Crystal Springs Canyon, Cerf Amphitheatre, The Paradox Cafe. **Environmental Initiatives:** LEED construction recycling installation for energy efficiency across campus, i.e., lighting, windows, heating.

BOTTOM LINE

Annual tuition is over $40,000; with books, room, board, and fees, you can tack another $10,000 onto that total. However, about half of Reed students are recipients of need-based scholarship or grant assistance; as is commonly heard on campus, "I received generous financial aid." And not only in-state students benefit from these advantages. "Reed was really generous with my financial aid package, and made it possible for me to go out of state to college."

SELECTIVITY

Admissions Rating	**98**
# of applicants	3,075
% of applicants accepted	43
% of acceptees attending	28
# accepting a place on wait list	616
% admitted from wait list	1

FRESHMAN PROFILE

Range SAT Critical Reading	**670–750**
Range SAT Math	**640–710**
Range SAT Writing	**660–730**
Range ACT Composite	**30–33**
Average HS GPA	**3.70**
% graduated top 10% of class	**63**
% graduated top 25% of class	**90**
% graduated top 50% of class	**99**

DEADLINES

Regular Deadline	**1/15**
Normal registration	**no**

FACILITIES

Housing: Coed dorms, special housing for disabled students, women's dorms, cooperative housing, apartments for single students, wellness house, theme housing. Reed language houses accommodate upper-division students studying Chinese, French, German, Russian, and Spanish. First-year students required to live on campus; exceptions granted for unusual situations. *Special Academic Facilities/Equipment:* Art gallery, studio art building, language labs, computerized music listening lab, nuclear research reactor, 20 music practice rooms and midi lab.

FINANCIAL FACTS

Financial Aid Rating	**96**
Annual tuition	$42,540
Room and Board	$11,050
Required Fees	$260
Books and supplies	$950
% frosh rec. need-based scholarship or grant aid	46
% UG rec.need-based scholarship or grant aid	48
% frosh rec. need-based self-help aid	49
% UG rec. need-based self-help aid	50
% frosh rec. any financial aid	53
% UG rec. any financial aid	54
% UG borrow to pay for school	53
Average cumulative indebtedness	$16,910

Scripps College

1030 Columbia Avenue, Claremont, CA 91711 • Admissions: 909-621-8149 • Fax: 909-607-7508

CAMPUS LIFE

Quality of life Rating	89
Fire Safety Rating	77
Green rating	81
Type of School	Private
Environment	Town

STUDENTS

Total undergrad enrolllment	946
% Male to Female	0/100
% From out of state	55
% From public high school	60
% Live on Campus	91
% African American	4
% Asian	9
% Caucasian	60
% Hispanic	10
% International	3
# Of Countries Represented	15

ACADEMICS

Academic Rating	97
% Of students graduating within 4 years	80
% Of students graduating within 6 years	82
Calendar	semester
Profs interesting rating	93
Profs accessible rating	92
Most common reg class size	10–19 students
Most common lab size	10–19 students

MOST POPULAR MAJORS

Fine/studio arts, political science psychology

HONORS PROGRAMS

Honors programs in all academic majors available.

SPECIAL STUDY OPTIONS

Accelerated program, cross-registration, double major, dual enrollment, exchange student program (domestic), independent study, internships, student-designed major, study abroad.

ABOUT THE SCHOOL

As the women's college within a consortium of four other co-ed colleges all within walking distance of one another, Scripps offers the intimacy and intense focus of a small college campus with the academic and co-curricular offerings of a larger university. You can use all the facilities at the other four schools in the Claremont Consortium and cross-register for all manner of courses. Students find this system "very beneficial because it offers opportunities and resources that a small school would not otherwise have access too, and makes for interesting class discussions with people from very diverse academic backgrounds." Scripps' innovative Money Wise Women program includes a financial literary course that covers everything from buying a first home to signing a prenuptial agreement. Professors at Scripps are always accessible and consistently excellent. There's a demanding, three-semester, interdisciplinary core program that sets the academic tone when you arrive. Students say they appreciate how the Core program "strengthens your understanding of Western thought in ways you'd never imagined." Every student also completes a thesis or senior project prior to graduation. Most students here also participate in a couple of internships before graduating, and there are 8 to 12 competitive internship grants available for students annually.

BANG FOR YOUR BUCK

Scripps College meets 100 percent of an eligible student's demonstrated financial need with the combination of grants, scholarships, part-time employment, and loans. Additionally, merit funds ranging from $10,000 a year to $20,000 a year are available to students who apply for admission by the required deadline. No separate application is required in order to be considered for these merit awards. The pick of the litter is the New Generation Award. It's renewable, and it's a full ride in the truest sense. In addition to tuition, fees, and room and board, you get three round-trip airfares home annually, and a $3,000 one-time summer research stipend. The James E. Scripps Award is a half-tuition, renewable scholarship. There are 25–30 of them available. New Trustee and Presidential Scholarships offers students whose "strong academic performance and school or community involvement indicate that they will add vitality and intellectual value to the campus" a four-year renewable award worth $15,000 and $10,000 respectively. A biology major says that she chose Scripps College "because of the fantastic merit scholarships. Not only did they defray the expense of attending a private college, but they convinced me I could be a big fish in a small pond here."

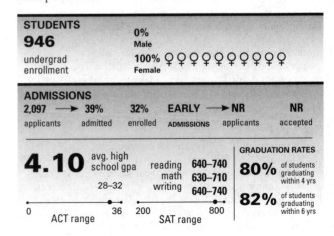

STUDENTS

946 undergrad enrollment

0% Male

100% Female ♀♀♀♀♀♀♀♀♀♀

ADMISSIONS

2,097 applicants → **39%** admitted **32%** enrolled

EARLY ADMISSIONS → **NR** applicants **NR** accepted

4.10 avg. high school gpa

ACT range (0–36): 28–32

SAT range (200–800): reading 640–740, math 630–710, writing 640–740

GRADUATION RATES

80% of students graduating within 4 yrs

82% of students graduating within 6 yrs

FINANCIAL AID: : 909-621-8275 • E-MAIL: ADMISSION@SCRIPPSCOLLEGE.EDU • WEBSITE: WWW.SCRIPPSCOLLEGE.EDU

STUDENT BODY

"Inspiring, strong women out to change the world" who are united by curiosity and intellect, all Scripps students "are intelligent and have a passion." Scripps students are "feminist liberals who will go on to change the world with their elite education, but [they] will do so with fun and style." Though the "'typical' student is upper-middle-class, overachiever, from SoCal, the pacific northwest, or the East Coast," "there are many exceptions to this." The stereotypes at Scripps' tends to be 'Militant Feminist' or 'Daddy's Girl.' We all sort of laugh at that because neither of those are a majority here." Though the average student is "politically liberal [and] somewhat idealistic [and] enjoys obscure music and literature," "there are all kinds of women–outspoken lesbians, very outdoorsy types, girls who love to party, extreme intellects, etc." The bottom line is at Scripps "women support women." "I didn't intend on going to a women's college, but I am really glad that I did. It's been a great experience; it's helped me to build confidence in a world that is still male-dominated."

Why Students love Scripps College

"The traditions at Scripps are amazing."

WHY STUDENTS LOVE SCRIPPS COLLEGE

Students love Scripps College because of its comfortable and flexible position within the Claremont Consortium. Scripps is a "small community of women within a larger, co-ed community," which means that the college can be "as big or small as you want it to be," as well as "as much or as little of a women's college as the students wish." In short, Scripps provides young women the opportunity to customize their academic and social experiences to their specifications. Some say that Scripps is "the ideal way to receive all the benefits of a woman's education in a basically coed environment," while others enjoy the quiet and beautiful atmosphere of the campus, with the option of a lively nightlife across the street at any of the other colleges in the Consortium. One student says she "liked the idea that I could party when I wanted at the other 5-C's, but whenever I wanted to relax and be quiet I could come back to my campus." For those not interested in the party scene, "residence halls often host evening soirees and there are numerous art openings.

GENERAL INFO

Activities: Choral groups, dance, drama/theater, literary magazine, music ensembles, radio station, student government, student newspaper, symphony orchestra, yearbook, campus ministries, international student organization. **Organizations:** 200 registered organizations, 5 honor societies, 7 religious organizations. **Athletics (Intercollegiate):** *Women:* Basketball, cross-country, diving, golf, lacrosse, soccer, softball, swimming, tennis, track/field (outdoor), volleyball, water polo. **On-Campus Highlights:** Williamson Gallery, Rare book room, Denison Library, Margaret Fowler Garden, Malott Commons, Graffiti Wall, Sallie Tiernan Field House.

BOTTOM LINE

The retail price for tuition, room and board, and fees at Scripps is a little more than $53,000 a year. Financial aid is superabundant here, though, so please don't let cost keep you from applying. Also worth noting: The average total need-based indebtedness for Scripps graduates is less than $10,000–well below the national average at private colleges and universities.

SELECTIVITY

Admissions Rating	**76**
# of applicants	2,097
% of applicants accepted	39
% of acceptees attending	32
# accepting a place on wait list	139
% admitted from wait list	6

FRESHMAN PROFILE

Range SAT Critical Reading	**640–740**
Range SAT Math	**630–710**
Range SAT Writing	**640–740**
Range ACT Composite	**28–32**
Average HS GPA	**4.10**
% graduated top 10% of class	**37**
% graduated top 25% of class	**62**
% graduated top 50% of class	**78**

DEADLINES

Regular Deadline	**1/2**
Normal registration	**yes**

FACILITIES

Housing: special housing for disabled students, women's dorms, apartments for single students, small college-owned houses. *Special Academic Facilities/Equipment:* Art center, music complex, dance studio, humanities museum and institute, science center, biological field station, field house. *Computers:* 100% of classrooms, 100% of dorms, 100% of libraries, 100% of dining areas, 100% of common outdoor areas have wireless network access.

FINANCIAL FACTS

Financial Aid Rating	**95**
Annual tuition	$41,736
Room and Board	$12,950
Required Fees	$214
Books and supplies	$800
% frosh rec. need-based scholarship or grant aid	44
% UG rec.need-based scholarship or grant aid	37
% frosh rec. non-need-based scholarship or grant aid	4
% UG rec. non-need-based scholarship or grant aid	3
% frosh rec. need-based self-help aid	39
% UG rec. need-based self-help aid	37
% frosh rec. any financial aid	49
% UG rec. any financial aid	54
% UG borrow to pay for school	36
Average cumulative indebtedness	$9,435

Sewanee–The University of the South

735 University Avenue, Sewanee, TN 37383-1000 • Admissions: 931-598-1238 • Financial Aid: 800-522-2234

CAMPUS LIFE

Quality of life Rating	81
Fire Safety Rating	90
Green rating	93
Type of School	Private
Environment	Rural

STUDENTS

Total undergrad enrolllment	1,455
% Male to Female	47/53
% From out of state	76
% Live on Campus	93
% From public high school	50
# of Fraternities	12
# of Sororities	9
% African American	4
% Asian	2
% Caucasian	54
% Hispanic	3
% International	2
# Of Countries Represented	23

ACADEMICS

Academic Rating	92
Calendar	semester
Profs interesting rating	97
Profs accessible rating	94
Most common reg class size	10–19 students
Most common lab size	20–29 students

MOST POPULAR MAJORS

Economics, English literature, history, environmental studies

SPECIAL STUDY OPTIONS

Double major, independent study, internships, student-designed major, study abroad Special programs offered to physically disabled students include note-taking services, reader services, voice recorders.

ABOUT THE SCHOOL

There are only 1,400 students on The University of the South's (more commonly known as Sewanee) Tennessee campus, but the university's stature–not to mention traditions–loom large. This small and very demanding fortress of the liberal arts and sciences is located on a mountain roughly in the middle of nowhere, and is a place where students still don a jacket and tie to go to class. This place oozes southern tradition, and, according to students, it's everything a college should be. Classes are small. The core curriculum is broad and well rounded. About a third of all your courses here will be general education requirements, and you have to pass a comprehensive exam in your major. Students work incredibly hard, telling us the coursework is "very demanding." And there's no grade inflation here, either. An A at Sewanee is truly earned.

Why Students love Sewanee

"It really is one of the friendliest communities that I have ever seen."

BANG FOR YOUR BUCK

Sewanee's endowment is more than $300 million, and it offers generous financial aid packages, which greatly add to the benefits of attending the school. Some 70 percent of the students receive some kind of aid. In addition to work-study, loans, and grants, the school offers a host of need-based and merit-based scholarships. The school has full confidence in the value of a Sewanee education, alongside the belief of keeping that value within reach of good students and their families. Sewanee scholarships come from more than 200 endowed scholarship funds, annual gifts, remissions of tuition, and additional amounts budgeted from the university's operating funds. As previously mentioned, many of these scholarships are awarded on the basis of calculated need-based eligibility, and applicants are automatically considered for these scholarships as part of the normal need-based financial aid award process.

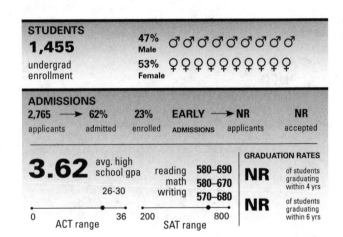

STUDENTS

1,455 undergrad enrollment

47% Male ♂♂♂♂♂♂♂♂♂

53% Female ♀♀♀♀♀♀♀♀♀♀

ADMISSIONS

2,765 →	62%	23%	EARLY →	NR	NR
applicants	admitted	enrolled	ADMISSIONS	applicants	accepted

3.62 avg. high school gpa

ACT range (0–36): 26-30

SAT range (200–800):

reading	580–690
math	580–670
writing	570–680

GRADUATION RATES

NR of students graduating within 4 yrs

NR of students graduating within 6 yrs

Sewanee–The University of the South

E-MAIL: ADMISS@SEWANEE.EDU • FAX: 931-538-3248 • WEBSITE: WWW.SEWANEE.EDU

STUDENT BODY

Even though the administration here is "pushing the diversity card to the nth degree," Sewanee is "strikingly homogenous." "A lot more students here are liberal than you would guess," and Yankees are "not viewed as aliens," but "Sewanee is a Southern and conservative school in every sense of the word." During the week, students hit the books. However, they spend their weekends partying. The Greek system is absolutely massive, and virtually everyone is either part of it or spends their weekends reveling at the frats. However, the administration does require all Greek events to be open to the entire campus. Students are typically "laid-back," "rich, conservative, and fun" "children of the Southern aristocracy." Some are "heavily spoiled and coddled." "We have lots of cookie-cutter, preppy, extreme social drinkers, but then again you can also find people who wear only organic hemp, sleep outside, and have dreadlocks," explains a junior. "There are a lot of outdoorsy styles mixed in as well." While "social arrangements are very cliquish," students tell us they are "relatively peacefully coexisting."

WHY STUDENTS LOVE SEWANEE–THE UNIVERSITY OF THE SOUTH

Sewanee's serene and geographically isolated campus is breathtaking. Students tell us that the campus is "absolutely gorgeous." It's a "serene haven" in "an idyllic setting" atop a mountain. Also, the school owns an "incredible amount of land." "Hiking the beautiful perimeter trail" is a favorite pastime, and students can bike, kayak, and "play in the woods" to their hearts' content. Students take the honor code here very seriously. Professors are very accessible, and they are almost always great teachers. "They are leading scholars and researchers with a commitment to teaching," says one freshman, and even wear academic gowns when they teach. Many Sewanee students "follow the tradition of dressing up for class." The "close faculty-student interaction ensures that each student enjoys a rich and personal educational experience," marvels an undergrad. There are also a large number of intercollegiate sporting events every weekend. "It really is one of the friendliest communities that I have ever seen," declares a sophomore.

GENERAL INFO

Activities: Choral groups, concert band, dance, drama/theater, jazz band, literary magazine, music ensembles, musical theater, radio station, student government, student newspaper, student-run film society, symphony orchestra, yearbook, campus ministries, international student organization, Model UN. **Organizations:** 110 registered organizations, 9 honor societies, 11 religious organizations. 12 fraternities, 9 sororities. **Athletics (Intercollegiate):** *Men:* Baseball, basketball, cross-country, diving, equestrian sports, football, golf, lacrosse, soccer, swimming, tennis, track/field. *Women:* Basketball, cheerleading, cross-country, diving, equestrian sports, field hockey, golf, lacrosse, soccer, softball, swimming, tennis, track/field, volleyball. **On-Campus Highlights:** Outdoor recreation on Sewanee's 10,000 a, All Saints' Chapel, Abbo's Alley Ravine Garden, Memorial Cross and University View, University Golf and Tennis Club.

BOTTOM LINE

One academic credit hour at Sewanee costs about $1,200. If you take 36 credits in an academic year, you can expect to cough up approximately $43,000, and that's not including room and board. It's unlikely that you will pay anywhere near that, though, given the profusion of need-based aid and academic scholarships. Seventy percent of students receive some form of financial assistance at Sewanee. Financial aid packages are generous and flexible, and include a $23,000 grant for freshman, on average.

SELECTIVITY

Admissions Rating	**92**
# of applicants	2,765
% of applicants accepted	62
% of acceptees attending	23
# accepting a place on wait list	58
% admitted from wait list	31

FRESHMAN PROFILE

Range SAT Critical Reading	**580–690**
Range SAT Math	**580–670**
Range SAT Writing	**570–680**
Range ACT Composite	**26–30**
Average HS GPA	**3.62**
% graduated top 10% of class	**50**
% graduated top 25% of class	**77**
% graduated top 50% of class	**92**

DEADLINES

Regular Deadline	**2/1**
Normal registration	**no**

FACILITIES

Housing: Coed dorms, special housing for disabled students, fraternity/sorority housing, apartments for married students, cooperative housing, apartments for single students, wellness housing, theme housing, substance-free housing & Living and Learning Communities. *Special Academic Facilities/Equipment:* Art gallery, observatory, keyboard collection, materials analysis lab with electron microscope. *Computers:* 80% of classrooms, 80% of dorms, 100% of libraries, 100% of dining areas, 100% of student union.

FINANCIAL FACTS

Financial Aid Rating	**91**
Annual tuition	$32,020
Room and Board	$9,226
Required Fees	$272
Books and supplies	$800
% frosh rec. need-based scholarship or grant aid	33
% UG rec.need-based scholarship or grant aid	34
% frosh rec. non-need-based scholarship or grant aid	29
% UG rec. non-need-based scholarship or grant aid	17
% frosh rec. need-based self-help aid	25
% UG rec. need-based self-help aid	25
% frosh rec. any financial aid	79
% UG rec. any financial aid	74
% UG borrow to pay for school	39
Average cumulative indebtedness	$19,337

Stanford University

Undergraduate Admission, Montag Hall, Stanford, CA 94305-6106 • Admissions: 650-723-2091

CAMPUS LIFE

Quality of life Rating	95
Fire Safety Rating	85
Green rating	94
Type of School	Private
Environment	City

STUDENTS

Total undergrad enrolllment	6,889
% Male to Female	52/48
% From out of state	55
% From public high school	58
% Live on Campus	91
# of Fraternities	15
#of Sororities	13
% African American	10
% Asian	23
% Caucasian	34
% Hispanic	14
% International	7
# Of Countries Represented	90

ACADEMICS

Academic Rating	99
% Of students graduating within 4 years	78
% Of students graduating within 6 years	95
Calendar	semester
Profs interesting rating	82
Profs accessible rating	78
Most common reg class size	10–19 students
Most common lab size	10–19 students

MOST POPULAR MAJORS

Biology, economics, international relations

SPECIAL STUDY OPTIONS

Distance learning, double major, exchange student program (domestic), honors program, independent study, internships, student-designed major, study abroad, Marine research center, Bing Stanford in Washington program, exchange programs with Dartmouth, Howard, Morehouse and Spelman, undergraduate research opportunities, Bing Honors College, overseas study.

ABOUT THE SCHOOL

Stanford University is widely recognized as one of the nation's most outstanding universities, considered by many to be the West Coast's answer to the Ivy League. Stanford alumni, who can be found in 143 countries, 18 territories, and all 50 states, have distinguished themselves in many fields, from government service to innovation to business to arts and entertainment. Academics are simply top-notch, and despite the fact that this is a research-driven university, professors are seriously interested in getting to know their undergrads. Students say that teachers at Stanford are "wonderful resources for guidance and tutoring," and there is "an opportunity to engage with them on a regular basis." The classroom experience is discussion-oriented and otherwise awesome. There are tons of majors, and, if you don't like any of the ones on offer, it's a breeze to design your own. The dorms are like palaces. The administration runs the school like a finely tuned machine. There's very little not to like about this place. "The classes, campus and faculty are amazing," reports one contended undergrad; another is happy to find that Stanford "has incredible resources, incredible people…and an unrivaled atmosphere of openness and collaboration."

BANG FOR YOUR BUCK

Like a handful of other spectacularly wealthy schools in the United States, Stanford maintains a wholly need-blind admission policy, and it demonstrates a serious commitment to making its world-class education available to talented and well-prepared students regardless of economic circumstances. All of Stanford's scholarship funds are need-based. For parents with total annual income and typical assets below $60,000, Stanford will not expect a parent contribution toward educational costs. For parents with total annual income and typical assets below $100,000, the expected parent contribution will be low enough to ensure that all tuition charges are covered with need-based scholarship, federal and state grants, and/or outside scholarship funds. Families with incomes at higher levels (typically up to $200,000) may also qualify for assistance, especially if more than one family member is enrolled in college. The hard part is getting admitted. If you can do that, the school will make sure you have a way to pay. The vast majority of successful applicants will be among the strongest students (academically) in their secondary schools.

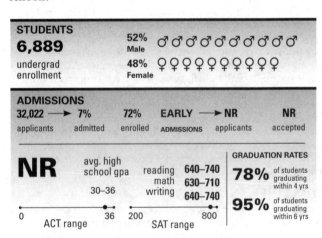

STUDENTS

6,889 undergrad enrollment

52% Male ♂♂♂♂♂♂♂♂♂♂

48% Female ♀♀♀♀♀♀♀♀♀♀

ADMISSIONS

32,022 applicants → 7% admitted — 72% enrolled

EARLY ADMISSIONS → NR applicants — NR accepted

NR avg. high school gpa

ACT range (0–36): 30–36

SAT range (200–800): reading 640–740, math 630–710, writing 640–740

GRADUATION RATES

78% of students graduating within 4 yrs

95% of students graduating within 6 yrs

Stanford University

FINANCIAL AID: 650-723-3058 • E-MAIL: ADMISSION@STANFORD.EDU • FAX: 650-725-2846 • WEBSITE: WWW.STANFORD.EDU

STUDENT BODY

"It's easy to find your own niche" here. "There isn't a typical student." The university offers "immense diversity of race, religion, and sexual orientation," and most find their peers "incredibly accepting." While students are "driven," they're fortunately "not that competitive or intense." Indeed, the "preppy button-down [types]...are replaced with chilled-out" students in "shorts and flip-flops." Undergrads are "smart yet unassuming" and typically "committed to a million different things." Additionally, they're "generally pretty social and athletic," as well as "service-minded and focused on their future careers." One junior adds, "The jock is doing better than you in chemistry, [and] the cute party animal is double-majoring and president of an activist group." He concludes by saying, "I guess the thing that unites us is that we're all nerds, even if it's not the first thing you see."

Why Students love Stanford University

"You can drive forty-five minutes west to the coast, take the train forty-five minutes south to San Francisco, or you can drive a few hours east to Lake Tahoe."

WHY STUDENTS LOVE STANFORD UNIVERSITY

The student body is unanimous in its praise for Stanford University. "Stanford is a rigorous and cutting-edge institution filled with curious, intelligent, friendly and down-to-earth students." "It is the best university in the world. Academics are engaging and challenging." While students are "driven," they're fortunately "not that competitive or intense." Guidance and support are plentiful, and Stanford Alumni Mentoring connects students with alumni in ongoing one-on-one mentoring relationships for career planning and goals. Endless options for entertainment and recreation are everywhere, both on and off campus.

GENERAL INFO

Activities: Choral groups, concert band, dance, drama/theater, jazz band, literary magazine, marching band, music ensembles, musical theater, opera, pep band, radio station, student government, student newspaper, student-run film society, symphony orchestra, television station, yearbook, cam pus ministries, international student organization. **Organizations:** 600 registered organizations, 40 religious organizations. 17 fraternities, 11 sororities. **Athletics (Intercollegiate):** *Men:* Baseball, basketball, crew/rowing, cross-country, diving, fencing, football, golf, gymnastics, sailing, soccer, swimming, tennis, track/field (outdoor), volleyball, water polo, wrestling. *Women:* Basketball, crew/rowing, cross-country, diving, fencing, field hockey, golf, gymnastics, lacrosse, sailing, soccer, softball, squash, swimming, synchronized swimming, tennis, track/field (outdoor), volleyball, water polo.

BOTTOM LINE

A year of tuition, fees, room and board, and basic expenses at Stanford costs about $51,000. While that figure is staggering, you have to keep in mind that few students pay anywhere near that amount. Financial packages here are very generous. Most aid comes with no strings attached. The average newly minted Stanford alum walks away with about $16,000 in loan debt.

SELECTIVITY

Admissions Rating	**99**
# of applicants	32,022
% of applicants accepted	7
% of acceptees attending	72

FRESHMAN PROFILE

Range SAT Critical Reading	**670–760**
Range SAT Math	**690–790**
Range SAT Writing	**680–780**
Range ACT Composite	**30–36**
% graduated top 10% of class	**90**

DEADLINES

Regular Deadline	**1/1**
Normal registration	**no**

FACILITIES

Housing: Coed dorms, special housing for disabled students, women's dorms, fraternity/sorority housing, apartments for married students, cooperative hous ing, apartments for single students, theme *Housing:* Academic, cross-cultural, language theme and ethnic theme houses. 98% of campus accessible to physically disabled. *Special Academic Facilities/Equipment:* Art museum, marine station, observatory, biological preserve, linear accelerator. *Computers:* 100% of classrooms, 100% of dorms, 100% of libraries, 100% of dining areas, 100% of student union, 75% of common outdoor areas have wireless network access.

FINANCIAL FACTS

Financial Aid Rating	**96**
Annual tuition	$40,050
Room and Board	$12,291
Required Fees	$519
Books and supplies	$1,485
% frosh rec. need-based scholarship or grant aid	53
% UG rec.need-based scholarship or grant aid	51
% frosh rec. non-need-based scholarship or grant aid	5
% UG rec. non-need-based scholarship or grant aid	8
% frosh rec. need-based self-help aid	30
% UG rec. need-based self-help aid	32
% UG rec. any financial aid	80
% UG borrow to pay for school	35
Average cumulative indebtedness	$14,058

Thomas Aquinas College

10000 North Ojai Road, Santa Paula, CA 93060 • Admissions: 805-525-4417 • Fax: 805-421-5905

CAMPUS LIFE

Quality of life Rating	96
Fire Safety Rating	90
Green rating	60*
Type of School	Private
Environment	Rural

STUDENTS

Total undergrad enrolllment	355
% Male to Female	46/54
% From out of state	60
% From public high school	14
% Live on Campus	100
% Asian	1
% Caucasian	73
% Hispanic	11
% International	6
# Of Countries Represented	7

ACADEMICS

Academic Rating	99
% Of students graduating within 4 years	72
% Of students graduating within 6 years	73
Calendar	semester
Profs interesting rating	97
Profs accessible rating	91
Most common reg class size	14–19 students
Most common lab size	14–19 students

MOST POPULAR MAJORS

Biology, business, English/language arts teacher education

SPECIAL STUDY OPTIONS

The sole academic program offered: a "cross-disciplinary" curriculum of liberal education through reading and analyzing the "Great Books," with special emphasis on philosophy, theology, mathematics, science, and literature.

ABOUT THE SCHOOL

Everything about this cozy college is permeated by traditional Catholic faith, and though the rules that guide students' lives may be stricter than at other colleges (campus dress is more formal, for instance), students here are happy to oblige. The student morale is indeed great, and "there is a positive and peaceful atmosphere that comes with knowing you are seeking the truth in the best way possible."

The Great Books and the ensuing "fascinating classical curriculum" provide an endless fountain of discussion–four whole years of it–and "each student comes out well-rounded, and well-versed in the thoughts of yesterday and today." Professors (called "tutors" here) "are more than happy to continue the discussion outside class," and all are required to take an Oath of Fidelity and make the Profession of Faith. Students all graduate with the same liberal arts degree, and there is no competition for grades, as there is no valedictorian or "rank-in-class." "We are all here to seek truth and to help others to do the same," says a student.

The close-knittedness of the community here is palpable; students spend a great deal of time together in class, on weekends, in the single-sex residence halls, at three daily meals, and in mass. Hiking in the nearby national forest, intramural sports, choir, and a variety of extracurricular activities further the bonds: "Your friendships with students will develop into family relationships."

BANG FOR YOUR BUCK

Not having to buy textbooks has never felt so sweet. The Great Books curriculum means that all of the books can be found online cheap, or in the school's majestic 70,000-book strong library. The broad education found here brings together students who are heading out into all walks of life and church, so you won't see piles of students jockeying for the same internships come spring: every student emerges with the same degree, and the same quality of education.

The school is committed to making its Catholic liberal education available to all accepted students, regardless of financial need, yet remain autonomous in its teaching. Rather than accepting church or state subsidies, it relies on contributions from individuals and charitable foundations to make up the difference between what students are able to pay and the actual cost of their education. Transfer students are just as eligible for financial aid as incoming freshmen.

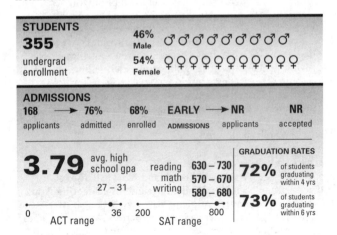

STUDENTS

355 undergrad enrollment

46% Male ♂♂♂♂♂♂♂♂♂♂

54% Female ♀♀♀♀♀♀♀♀♀♀♀

ADMISSIONS

168 applicants → 76% admitted | 68% enrolled | EARLY ADMISSIONS → NR applicants | NR accepted

3.79 avg. high school gpa

reading	630 – 730
math	570 – 670
writing	580 – 680

ACT range (0–36): 27 – 31

SAT range (200–800)

GRADUATION RATES

72% of students graduating within 4 yrs

73% of students graduating within 6 yrs

Thomas Aquinas College

FINANCIAL AID: 800-634-9797 • E-MAIL: ADMISSIONS@THOMASAQUINAS.EDU • WEBSITE: WWW.THOMASAQUINAS.EDU

STUDENT BODY

With just 350 students, the student body "is big enough to avoid people but small enough to get to know most people." The vast majority of students "are Catholic," "devoted to learning and their faith," and politically "conservative." That being said, a senior assures us, "Any student with any interest can usually find a group that shares his or her passion." Importantly, many agree that their peers are "very kind and inclusive" as well as "joyful and inviting." One junior elaborates saying, "You walk down the hallways and sidewalks and are personally greeted by freshmen and seniors alike." An overwhelming number of undergrads here declare their fellow students "intellectually curious" and "somewhat obsessed with philosophy." Indeed, the typical student "is a thinker [who] will never hesitate to get into a philosophical argument."

Why Students love Thomas Aquinas College

"Your friendships with students will develop into familyrelationships."

WHY STUDENTS LOVE THOMAS AQUINAS COLLEGE

Students who have lived a Catholic life all come together in the gorgeous southern California environs to explore the thoughts and works of the masters. For those that want to go to a school "that takes learning seriously for its own sake, not just as preparation for a job," the "unapologetically Catholic" Thomas Aquinas is the dream. "I often find myself grateful to the classmate who understands the text and is able to explain it to me as well." Students are in awe of their tutors, who sometimes dine with them in the Commons, so "it's easy to catch them with a question, or just to soak up their wisdom."

Everyone lives on campus unless they are married, providing an intimacy not found at a lot of other colleges, and the College's intellectual life is essentially bound up with its community life. "The Catholic/small college setting creates an atmosphere of trust and faith that makes it easier to study, live, and grow at school," says a student.

GENERAL INFO

Activities: Choral groups, dance, drama/theater, music ensembles, musical theater **Organizations:** 2 registered organizations, 4 religious organizations. **On-Campus Highlights:** St. Joseph Commons, The Dumb Ox Coffee Shop, Dorm Commons, St. Bernardine Library, Student Lounge.

BOTTOM LINE

The school avoids tacking on fees at every turn, and instead sets out a very straightforward financial plan: tuition runs $22,850, and since all students must live on campus (unless married), room and board is a non-negotiable additional $7,550. Beyond that, students need only pay for books (about $450 a year, or cheaper if found online, which is easily done) and pocket money. Admissions here are need-blind, there is no application fee, and though students and their parents are expected to contribute the maximum amount possible, there is plenty of financial aid to cover the rest. Students may request a preliminary estimate for how much aid they would receive should they gain acceptance here.

SELECTIVITY

Admissions Rating	**91**
# of applicants	168
% of applicants accepted	76
% of acceptees attending	68
# accepting a place on wait list	5
% admitted from wait list	40

FRESHMAN PROFILE

Range SAT Critical Reading	**630–730**
Range SAT Math	**570–670**
Range SAT Writing	**580–680**
Range ACT Composite	**27–31**
Average HS GPA	**3.79**
% graduated top 10% of class	**44**
% graduated top 25% of class	**78**
% graduated top 50% of class	**89**

DEADLINES

Regular Deadline	**10/1**
Normal registration	**no**

FACILITIES

Housing: Men's dorms, women's dorms, students living with their families may live off campus. 100% of campus accessible to physically disabled. *Special Academic Facilities/Equipment:* St. Bernardine Library.

FINANCIAL FACTS

Financial Aid Rating	**99**
Annual out-of-state tuition	$22,850
Room and Board	$7,550
Required Fees	$0
Books and supplies	$450
% frosh rec. need-based scholarship or grant aid	75
% UG rec.need-based scholarship or grant aid	69
% frosh rec. need-based self-help aid	82
% UG rec. need-based self-help aid	77
% frosh rec. any financial aid	86
% UG rec. any financial aid	81
% UG borrow to pay for school	82
Average cumulative indebtedness	$16,311

University of Chicago

1101 E 58th Street, Rosenwald Hall Suite 105, Chicago, IL 60637 • Admissions: 773-702-8650 • Fax: 773-702-4199

CAMPUS LIFE

Quality of life Rating	77
Fire Safety Rating	82
Green rating	86
Type of School	Private
Environment	Metropolis

STUDENTS

Total undergrad enrollment	5,225
% Male to Female	51/49
% From out of state	78
% From public high school	64
# of Fraternities	10
# of Sororities	3
% African American	5
% Asian	16
% Caucasian	43
% Hispanic	8
% International	9
# Of Countries Represented	71

ACADEMICS

Academic Rating	98
% Of students graduating within 4 years	87
% Of students graduating within 6 years	92
Calendar	quarter
Profs interesting rating	83
Profs accessible rating	81
Most common reg class size	fewer than 10 students
Most common lab size	10–19 students

MOST POPULAR MAJORS

Economics, biology
political science

SPECIAL STUDY OPTIONS

Accelerated program, cross-registration, double major, dual enrollment, English as a Second Language (ESL), exchange student program (domestic), honors program, independent study, internships, student-designed major, study abroad, teacher certification program.

ABOUT THE SCHOOL

The University of Chicago has a reputation as a favorite destination of the true intellectual: students here are interested in learning for learning's sake and they aren't afraid to express their opinions. A rigorous, intellectually challenging, and world-renowned research university, the University of Chicago continues to offer a community where students thrive and ideas matter. Here, an attitude of sharp questioning seems to be the focus, rather than the more relaxed inquiry and rumination approach at some schools of equal intellectual repute. Many find welcome challenges in the debates and discussions that define the campus atmosphere; the typical Chicago student is task-oriented, intellectually driven, sharp, vocal, and curious. As one student surveyed said, "There is nothing more exciting, challenging, and rewarding than the pursuit of knowledge in all of its forms." The undergraduate program at Chicago emphasizes critical thinking through a broad-based liberal arts curriculum. At the heart of the experience is the Common Core: a series of distribution requirements in the humanities, science, and mathematics. No lecture courses here–Core courses are discussion-based, and enrollment is limited to 20. Chicago's numerous major programs range from early Christian literature to media studies, history, linguistics, and math.

BANG FOR YOUR BUCK

The University of Chicago operates a completely need-blind admissions process, admitting qualified students regardless of their financial situation. Once admitted, the school guarantees to meet 100 percent of a student's demonstrated financial need. The school is also committed to limiting debt from student loans. Students graduate with only $24,000 in loan debt on average. Highly qualified freshman candidates may also be considered for Chicago's competitive merit scholarships, some of which cover the entire cost of tuition. University Scholarships are awarded to about 100 students annually; these scholarships cover about a third of student's tuition ($10,000) and are guaranteed for four years of study. Scholarships are awarded to applicants on the basis of outstanding academic and extracurricular achievement, demonstrated leadership, and commitment to their communities. To be considered for any of Chicago's merit scholarships, simply check the box on the Common Application that reads "Do you intend to apply for merit-based scholarship?" All first-year applicants are eligible.

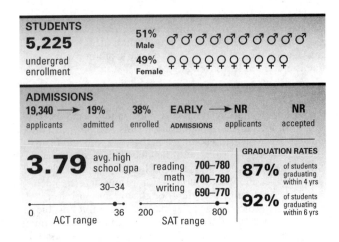

STUDENTS
5,225 undergrad enrollment

51% Male ♂♂♂♂♂♂♂♂♂♂
49% Female ♀♀♀♀♀♀♀♀♀♀

ADMISSIONS

19,340 applicants →	19% admitted	38% enrolled	EARLY ADMISSIONS →	NR applicants	NR accepted

3.79 avg. high school gpa

ACT range (0–36): 30–34

SAT range (200–800):

reading	700–780
math	700–780
writing	690–770

GRADUATION RATES

87% of students graduating within 4 yrs

92% of students graduating within 6 yrs

University of Chicago

FINANCIAL AID: 773-702-8655 • E-MAIL: COLLEGEADMISSIONS@UCHICAGO.EDU• WEBSITE: WWW.UCHICAGO.EDU

STUDENT BODY

Students at UChicago are "intense," "opinionated," "engaged with the world around them," and "somewhat zany." "Most everyone has a quirk," a senior reports. Without question, "the popular stereotype" of the UChicago student is "a nerdy, socially awkward person." Living up to the hype are an abundance of students "religiously dedicated to academic performance" and "a bunch of strange people," "usually clutching some fantastic book." However, "there aren't as many extremely strange and nerdy students as there have been in the past," and many say the stereotype is increasingly inaccurate. "There are loads of people who are fascinating," a sophomore writes, including many who are "cool and attractive." There are "artists, communists, fashionistas, activists." "Everyone who is at the University of Chicago considers themselves at the best possible university," concludes one student.

Why Students love the University of Chicago

"Learning more than you ever wanted to and loving it."

WHY STUDENTS LOVE THE UNIVERSITY OF CHICAGO

At the University of Chicago, students aren't afraid to be intellectuals. That's because the rigorous pursuit of academic excellence is woven into the culture–and that's just how students like it.While students appreciate the school's close proximity to areas like Hyde Park and downtown Chicago, the main draw is the challenging yet rewarding academics that give the university its lovingly adopted, tongue-in-cheek unofficial slogan, "Where fun goes to die." They don't mean it, of course. The slogan is merely way of pointing out that student culture here takes education very seriously. "I chose the University of Chicago for its reputation of being an academic power house. There is no room for the fluff you get at many other colleges...You will be challenged to the limits of your mental and emotional capacity."

GENERAL INFO

Activities: Choral groups, concert band, dance, drama/theater, jazz band, literary magazine, music ensembles, musical theater, pep band, radio station, student government, student newspaper, student-run film society, symphony orchestra, yearbook, campus ministries, international student organization. **Organizations:** 400 registered organizations, 5 honor societies, 36 religious organizations. 10 fraternities, 3 sororities. **Athletics (Intercollegiate):** *Men:* Baseball, basketball, cross-country, diving, football, soccer, swimming, tennis, track/field (outdoor), track/field (indoor), volleyball, wrestling. *Women:* Basketball, cross-country, diving, soccer, softball, swimming, tennis, track/field, volleyball.

BOTTOM LINE

Yearly tuition to University of Chicago is a little more than $40,000, plus an additional $2,000 in mandatory fees. For campus residents, room and board is about $12,000 per year. Once you factor in personal expenses, transportation, books, and supplies, an education at University of Chicago costs about $56,000 per year. At University of Chicago, all demonstrated financial need is met through financial aid packages.

SELECTIVITY

Admissions Rating	**99**
# of applicants	19,340
% of applicants accepted	19
% of acceptees attending	38
# accepting a place on wait list	2,892
% admitted from wait list	3

FRESHMAN PROFILE

Range SAT Critical Reading	**700–780**
Range SAT Math	**700–780**
Range SAT Writing	**690–770**
Range ACT Composite	**30–34**
Average HS GPA	**3.79**
% graduated top 10% of class	**89**
% graduated top 25% of class	**98**
% graduated top 50% of class	**100**

DEADLINES

Regular Deadline	**1/3**
Normal registration	**no**

FACILITIES

Housing: Coed dorms, special housing for disabled students, special housing for international students, fraternity/sorority housing, apartments for married students, cooperative housing. *Special Academic Facilities/Equipment:* Smart Museum, Renaissance Society, Oriental Institute, Business and Economics Resource Center, D'Angelo Law Library, Echhart Library, John Crerar Library, Joseph Regenstein Library. *Computers:* 100% of classrooms, 100% of dorms, 100% of libraries, 100% of dining areas, 100% of student union, 100% of common outdoor areas have wireless network access.

FINANCIAL FACTS

Financial Aid Rating	**94**
Annual in-state tuition	$41,853
Room and Board	$12,633
Required Fees	$1,927
Books and supplies	$1,350
% frosh rec. need-based scholarship or grant aid	46
% UG rec.need-based scholarship or grant aid	47
% frosh rec. need-based self-help aid	35
% UG rec. need-based self-help aid	39
% frosh rec. any financial aid	48
% UG rec. any financial aid	46
% UG borrow to pay for school	50
Average cumulative indebtedness	$22,359

University of Notre Dame

220 Main Building, Notre Dame, IN 46556 • Admissions: 574-631-7505 • Fax: 574-631-8865

CAMPUS LIFE

Quality of life Rating	81
Fire Safety Rating	88
Green rating	88
Type of School	Private
Environment	City

STUDENTS

Total undergrad enrolllment	8,367
% Male to Female	54/46
% From out of state	92
% From public high school	50
% Live on Campus	81
% African American	4
% Asian	7
% Caucasian	76
% Hispanic	1
% Native American	1
% International	3
# Of Countries Represented	89

ACADEMICS

Academic Rating	87
Calendar	semester
Profs interesting rating	86
Profs accessible rating	96
Most common reg class size	10–19 students
Most common lab size	20–29 students

MOST POPULAR MAJORS

Finance, political science, psychology

SPECIAL STUDY OPTIONS

Accelerated program, cross-registration, double major, dual enrollment, exchange student program (domestic), honors program, independent study, internships, liberal arts/career combination, student-de signed major, study abroad, teacher certification program, Teacher Certification only available through Cross Registration with St. Mary's College.

ABOUT THE SCHOOL

As a private school with traditions of excellence in academics, athletics and service, and with a vast, faithful alumni base that provides ample resources, the University of Notre Dame draws on its Catholic values to provide a well-rounded, world class education. One student is thrilled that being "raised as an Irish Catholic, Notre Dame is basically the equivalent of Harvard. I've always viewed the school as an institution with rigorous academics as well as rich tradition and history–and a symbol of pride for my heritage." Not all are Catholic here, although it seems that most undergrads "have some sort of spirituality present in their daily lives," and have a "vibrant social and religious life."

Total undergraduate enrollment is just more than 8,000 students. ND is reportedly improving in diversity concerning eco¬nomic backgrounds, according to members of the student body here. An incredible 90 percent are from out-of-state, and 90 countries are now represented throughout the campus. Undergrads say they enjoy "a college experience that is truly unique," "combining athletics and academics in an environment of faith." "It's necessary to study hard and often, [but] there's also time to do other things." Academics are widely praised, and one new student is excited that even "large lectures are broken down into smaller discussion groups once a week to help with class material and…give the class a personal touch."

BANG FOR YOUR BUCK

Notre Dame is one of the most selective colleges in the country. Almost every¬one who enrolls is in the top ten percent of their graduating class and pos¬sesses test scores in the highest percentiles. But, as the student respondents suggest, strong academic ability isn't enough to get you in here. The school looks for students with other talents, and seems to have a predilection for ath¬letic achievement. Each residence hall is home to students from all classes; most will live in the same hall for all their years on campus. An average of ninety-three percent of entering students will graduate within five years. Students report that "the administration tries its best to stay on top of the students' wants and needs." The school is also extremely community-oriented, and Notre Dame has some of the strongest alumni support nationwide.

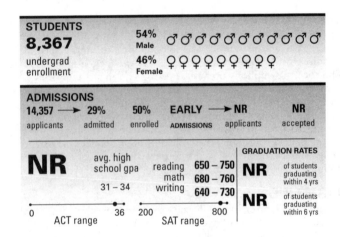

STUDENTS

8,367 undergrad enrollment

54% Male ♂♂♂♂♂♂♂♂♂♂♂

46% Female ♀♀♀♀♀♀♀♀♀

ADMISSIONS

14,357 applicants → **29%** admitted — **50%** enrolled

EARLY ADMISSIONS → **NR** applicants — **NR** accepted

NR avg. high school gpa

31 – 34 — ACT range (0–36)

reading 650 – 750
math 680 – 760
writing 640 – 730

SAT range (200–800)

GRADUATION RATES

NR of students graduating within 4 yrs

NR of students graduating within 6 yrs

University of Notre Dame

FINANCIAL AID: 574-631-6436 • E-MAIL: ADMISSIONS@ND.EDU • WEBSITE: WWW.ND.EDU

STUDENT BODY

Undergrads at Notre Dame report "the vast majority" of their peers are "very smart" "white kids from upper to middle-class backgrounds from all over the country, especially the Midwest and Northeast." The typical student "is a type-A personality that studies a lot, yet is athletic and involved in the community. They are usually the outstanding seniors in their high schools," the "sort of people who can talk about the BCS rankings and Derrida in the same breath." Additionally, something like "eighty-five percent of Notre Dame students earned a varsity letter in high school." "Not all are Catholic" here, though most are, and it seems that most undergrads "have some sort of spirituality present in their daily lives." "ND is slowly improving in diversity concerning eco nomic backgrounds, with the university's policy to meet all demonstrated financial need."

Why Students love University of Notre Dame

> "The amount of school spirit and atmosphere on football game days is amazing."

WHY STUDENTS LOVE UNIVERSITY OF NOTRE DAME

Sports dominate the social scene. Students like that the "great aspect of ND is that it is a top 20 school where you get tier 1 academics with a Division 1 football team–which makes the fall semester every year that much more exciting;" "The amount of school spirit and atmosphere on football game days is amazing." Another undergrad tells us that "students at ND are extremely athletic. It's rare to find someone who wasn't on some varsity team in high school." As a result, intramural sports are popular, and virtually every stu¬dent plays some kind of sport. "If someone is not interested in sports upon arrival, he or she will be by the time he or she leaves." Beyond residential life and sports, religious activities, volunteering, campus publications, student government, and academic clubs round out the rest of ND life.

GENERAL INFO

Activities: Choral groups, concert band, dance, drama/theater, jazz band, literary magazine, marching band, music ensembles, musical theater, opera, pep band, radio station, student government, student newspaper, student-run film society, symphony orchestra, yearbook, campus ministries, international student organization. **Organizations:** 299 registered organizations, 10 honor societies, 11 religious organizations. **Athletics (Intercollegiate):** *Men:* Baseball, basketball, cross-country, diving, fencing, football, golf, ice hockey, lacrosse, soccer, swimming, tennis, track/field (outdoor). *Women:* Basketball, crew/rowing, cross-country, diving, fencing, golf, lacrosse, soccer, softball, swimming, tennis, track/field (outdoor), volleyball.

BOTTOM LINE

Notre Dame, while certainly providing a wonderful academic environment and superb education, does reflect this in the cost of attending the college. Annual tuition is more than $40,000. With room, board, and books, students are looking at close to $55,000 a year. Fortunately, over half of incoming freshmen are provided with need-based scholarship or grant aid. Almost 60 percent of undergrads borrow to pay for their education here, and leave Notre Dame being on the hook for $30,000 in cumulative indebtedness.

SELECTIVITY

Admissions Rating	**95**
# of applicants	14,357
% of applicants accepted	29
% of acceptees attending	50
# accepting a place on wait list	1,060
% admitted from wait list	24

FRESHMAN PROFILE

Range SAT Critical Reading	**650–750**
Range SAT Math	**680–760**
Range SAT Writing	**640–730**
Range ACT Composite	**31–34**

DEADLINES

Regular Deadline	**12/21**
Normal registration	**no**

FACILITIES

Housing: Men's dorms, women's dorms.
Special Academic Facilities/Equipment: Art museum, theater, germ-free research facility, radiation laboratory.

FINANCIAL FACTS

Financial Aid Rating	**92**
Annual tuition	$40,910
Room and Board	$11,388
Required Fees	$507
Books and supplies	$950
% frosh rec. need-based scholarship or grant aid	51
% UG rec.need-based scholarship or grant aid	47
% frosh rec. non-need-based scholarship or grant aid	34
% UG rec. non-need-based scholarship or grant aid	29
% frosh rec. need-based self-help aid	41
% UG rec. need-based self-help aid	42
% UG borrow to pay for school	51
Average cumulative indebtedness	$28,371

University of Pennsylvania

1 College Hall, Philadelphia, PA 19104 • Admissions: 215-898-7507 • Fax: 215-898-9670

CAMPUS LIFE

Quality of life Rating	87
Fire Safety Rating	73
Green rating	89
Type of School	Private
Environment	Metropolis

STUDENTS

Total undergrad enrolllment	9,865
% Male to Female	49/51
% From out of state	81
% From public high school	59
% Live on Campus	62
# of Fraternities	36
# of Sororities	13
% African American	7
% Asian	19
% Caucasian	46
% Hispanic	7
% International	11
# Of Countries Represented	126

ACADEMICS

Academic Rating	95
% Of students graduating within 4 years	88
% Of students graduating within 6 years	96
Calendar	semester
Profs interesting rating	73
Profs accessible rating	79
Most common reg class size	fewer than 10 students
Most common lab size	20–29 students

MOST POPULAR MAJORS
Economics,
finance, nursing

HONORS PROGRAMS

Wharton Scholars. Fisher Program in Management and Technology, the Huntsman Program in International Studies and Business, the Vagelos Scholars Program in Molecular Life Sciences, and the Civic Scholars Program.

SPECIAL STUDY OPTIONS

Accelerated program, cross-registration, double major, dual enrollment, exchange student program (domestic), honors program. independent study, internships, liberal arts/career combination, student-designed major, study abroad, teacher certification program, Joint degree programs among schools.

ABOUT THE SCHOOL

The University of Pennsylvania (commonly referred to as Penn), as one of the eight members of the Ivy League, gives you all of the advantages of an internationally recognized degree with none of the attitude. Founded by Benjamin Franklin, Penn is the fourth-oldest institution of higher learning in the United States. The university is composed of four undergraduate schools, and students tend to focus on what they'll do with their degree pretty early on. The Wharton School of Business is home to Penn's well-known and intense undergraduate business program. This, along with other career-focused offerings, contributes to a pre-professional atmosphere on campus. That comes with an element of competition, especially when grades are on the line. Penn students love the opportunity to take classes with professors who are setting the bar for research in his or her. Professors are praised for being "enthusiastic and incredibly well-versed in their subject," a group who is "passionate about teaching" and who will "go out of their way to help you understand the material."

Penn students don't mind getting into intellectual conversations during dinner, but "partying is a much higher priority here than it is at other Ivy League schools." Students here can have intellectual conversations during dinner, and *Animal House*-like interactions at the frat houses later that night. Weekend trips to New York and Philadelphia are common, and students have plenty of access to restaurants, shopping, concerts, and sports games around campus.

BANG FOR YOUR BUCK

Transparency is embedded in Penn's financial aid process. Its website provides a chart of the percent of applicants offered aid and median award amounts for family income levels ranging from $0–$190,000. For 2010–2011, Penn committed more than $130 million of its resources for grant aid to undergraduate students. Approximately 80 percent of freshman who applied for aid received an award. Penn's financial aid packages meet 100 percent of students' demonstrated need. University Named Scholarships are provided through direct gifts to the university and privately endowed funds and enable Penn to continue to admit students solely on the basis of academic merit. Mayor's Scholarships are available to outstanding high school seniors who are Philadelphia residents and who attend schools in Philadelphia or contiguous Pennsylvania counties. The scholarship amount varies according to financial need. Staff at Penn provide strong support for applicants, with one student noting, "It was the only school to call me during the admissions process instead of just e-mailing me extra information."

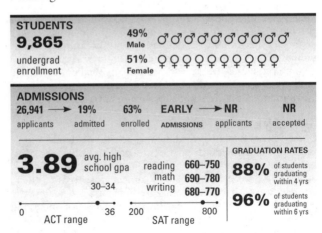

STUDENTS
9,865 undergrad enrollment
49% Male ♂♂♂♂♂♂♂♂♂♂
51% Female ♀♀♀♀♀♀♀♀♀♀

ADMISSIONS
26,941 applicants → **19%** admitted — **63%** enrolled
EARLY ADMISSIONS → **NR** applicants — **NR** accepted

3.89 avg. high school gpa

30–34 ACT range (0–36)

reading **660–750**
math **690–780**
writing **680–770**
SAT range (200–800)

GRADUATION RATES
88% of students graduating within 4 yrs
96% of students graduating within 6 yrs

University of Pennsylvania

FINANCIAL AID: 909-621-8205 • E-MAIL: INFO@ADMISSIONS.UGAO.UPENN.EDU • WEBSITE: WWW.UPENN.EDU

STUDENT BODY

This "determined" bunch "is either focused on one specific interest, or very well-rounded." Pretty much everyone "was an overachiever ('that kid') in high school," and some students "are off-the-charts brilliant," making everyone here "sort of fascinated by everyone else." Everyone has "a strong sense of personal style and his or her own credo," but no group deviates too far from the more mainstream stereotypes. There's a definite lack of "emos" and hip- pies. There's "the career-driven Wharton kid who will stab you in the back to get your interview slot" and "the nursing kid who's practically nonexistent," but on the whole, there's tremendous school diversity, with "people from all over the world of all kinds of experiences of all perspectives."

Why Students love Penn

"It was the only school to call me during the admissions process instead of just e-mailing me extra information."

WHY STUDENTS LOVE THE UNIVERSITY OF PENNSYLVANIA

Sweeping diversity in thought, culture, and intellectual pursuits is at the core of what makes Penn special to students. The community "allows me the opportunity to grow into the person that I want to be" and guarantees students will "meet different people from all over the world." Maybe that's why students call Penn "the social Ivy." This is a school that "thrives on fostering of student individuality and creating a versatile mind that can handle any challenge." When students call it the "ugly stepsister" of the other Ivy League schools, they're paying Penn a compliment, celebrating a campus that encourages putting just as much energy into a diverse, active social life as it does academic excellence. Speaking of the campus, students at Penn offer almost universal praise. Located in Philadelphia, Penn manages to be a "perfect mix between an urban setting and a traditional college campus." This "beautiful" campus is "green but not in the middle of nowhere," offering easy access to the bustling night life of downtown Philadelphia.

GENERAL INFO

Activities: Choral groups, concert band, dance, drama/theater, jazz band, literary magazine, marching band, music ensembles, student government, student newspaper, symphony orchestra. **Organizations:** 350 registered organizations, 9 honor societies, 29 religious organizations. 35 fraternities, 13 sororities. **Athletics (Intercollegiate):** *Men:* Baseball, basketball, crew/rowing, cross-country, diving, fencing, football, golf, lacrosse, light weight football, soccer, squash, swimming, tennis, track/field (outdoor), track/field (indoor), wrestling. *Women:* Basketball, crew/rowing, cross-country, diving, fencing, field hockey, golf, gymnastics, lacrosse, soccer, softball, squash, swimming, tennis, track/field (outdoor), track/field (indoor), volleyball.

BOTTOM LINE

A year's tuition is more than $37,000. You'll pay another $11,900 in room and board. Don't be alarmed: Penn offers loan-free packages to all dependent students who are eligible for financial aid, regardless of the family's income level. The average student indebtedness upon graduation is just $17,000. Students have noted the school's "generous aid program" as being "phenomenal."

SELECTIVITY

Admissions Rating	**99**
# of applicants	26,941
% of applicants accepted	19
% of acceptees attending	63
# accepting a place on wait list	1,760
% admitted from wait list	3

FRESHMAN PROFILE

Range SAT Critical Reading	**660–750**
Range SAT Math	**690–780**
Range SAT Writing	**680–770**
Range ACT Composite	**30–34**
Average HS GPA	**3.89**
% graduated top 10% of class	**96**
% graduated top 25% of class	**99**
% graduated top 50% of class	**100**

DEADLINES

Regular Deadline	**1/1**
Normal registration	**no**

FACILITIES

Housing: Coed dorms, special housing for disabled students, fraternity/sorority housing, apartments for married students, apartments for single students, wellness housing, private off-campus. *Computers:* 85% of classrooms, 100% of dorms, 100% of libraries, 85% of dining areas, 100% of student union, 25% of common outdoor areas have wireless network access. Students can register for classes online. Administrative functions (other than registration) can be performed online.

FINANCIAL FACTS

Financial Aid Rating	**97**
Annual tuition	$37,620
Room and Board	$11,878
Required Fees	$4,478
Books and supplies	$1,160
% frosh rec. need-based scholarship or grant aid	45
% UG rec.need-based scholarship or grant aid	44
% frosh rec. need-based self-help aid	46
% UG rec. need-based self-help aid	46
% frosh rec. any financial aid	47
% UG rec. any financial aid	45
% UG borrow to pay for school	43
Average cumulative indebtedness	$17,013

University of Redlands

1200 E. Colton Avenue, Redlands, CA 92373 • Admissions: 909-335-4074 • Fax: 909-335-4089

CAMPUS LIFE

Quality of life Rating	87
Fire Safety Rating	81
Green rating	79
Type of School	Private
Environment	Town

STUDENTS

Total undergrad enrolllment	2,335
% Male to Female	44/56
% From out of state	29
% Live on Campus	66
# of Fraternities	5
# of Sororities	5
% African American	2
% Asian	4
% Caucasian	55
% Hispanic	17
% Native American	1
% International	1
# Of Countries Represented	6

ACADEMICS

Academic Rating	89
% Of students graduating within 4 years	58
% Of students graduating within 6 years	64
Calendar	semester
Profs interesting rating	88
Profs accessible rating	91
Most common reg class size	10–19 students

MOST POPULAR MAJORS

Business/commerce, liberal arts and sciences, psychology

HONORS PROGRAMS

The Johnston Center for Integrative Studies. Special programs offered to physically disabled students include note-taking services, reader services, tutors.

SPECIAL STUDY OPTIONS

Cross-registration, double major, dual enrollment, exchange student program (domestic), honors program, independent study, internships, liberal arts/career combination, student-designed major, study abroad, teacher certification program.

ABOUT THE SCHOOL

Private and intimate, The University of Redlands is a prestigious school with an enrollment of approximately 2,500 students. The campus "has that small community feeling, so you feel appreciated and you are not just a number," says a freshman. Redlands is also attractive due to The Johnston Center for Integrative Studies, valued by one student for providing him with "unprecedented control over my education and future," while being prized by another for "the freedom it allows to explore my interests." The Johnson Center also enables students to create their own majors. "Redlands really tries to make sure you get the education you want," and develop "the ability to gain meaningful employment," according to a few other pleased undergrads. Another student is impressed by the school's efforts in "striving to keep a strong, politically and socially aware community while providing the tools for success after graduation."

The University takes student safety and diversity seriously, and provides a fine support system. "There should never be any reason for someone to feel left out or out of place on this campus with all of the effort that is put into making it open, inviting, and accepting," one student says. "Stressing understanding with sensitivity to cross-cultural issues" gives one student great pride in the school, while another states happily that "even if on the surface I am 'one of a kind' in my classes, I don't feel as if I am alone." The institution is extremely committed to the pursuit of international learning, with a "prestigious" and "phenomenal" study abroad program; impressively, almost 50% of all students participate.

BANG FOR YOUR BUCK

The financial support is said by students to be "well above average" and "unbeatable." For another grateful undergrad, "the scholarship money sealed the deal." University Merit and Talent Scholarships are awarded to students regardless of financial need. Achievement Awards are awarded to incoming students who have superior academic records and have demonstrated an unusual degree of leadership and accomplishment. Talent Awards in the areas of Art, Creative Writing, Music and Theatre are also available. Graduates place very strongly among liberal arts colleges in regard to future earning potential, making them very competitive when seeking employment after graduation. Government and industry professionals mention that they "value students because they possess excellent problem solving abilities, write well, and learn very quickly." Academic advisers are in frequent contact with students, tutoring options are readily accessible, and both the Career Center and Alumni Association continue to work with and support graduates throughout their careers.

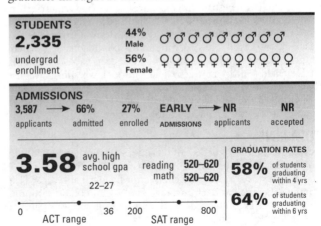

STUDENTS

2,335 undergrad enrollment

44% Male ♂♂♂♂♂♂♂♂♂

56% Female ♀♀♀♀♀♀♀♀♀♀♀♀

ADMISSIONS

3,587 applicants → 66% admitted — 27% enrolled

EARLY ADMISSIONS → NR applicants — NR accepted

3.58 avg. high school gpa

reading 520–620
math 520–620

ACT range (0–36): 22–27

SAT range (200–800)

GRADUATION RATES

58% of students graduating within 4 yrs

64% of students graduating within 6 yrs

University of Redlands

FINANCIAL AID: 909-748-8047 • E-MAIL: ADMISSIONS@REDLANDS.EDU • WEBSITE: WWW.REDLANDS.EDU

STUDENT BODY

Students at Redlands are "passionate." They have a "sense of wonder and enthusiasm" and "a huge variety of interests." As a whole, students are "quite liberal" politically. Most students are "fairly involved in many aspects of school," and they promise that "everyone can find a niche somewhere on campus." The undergraduate population melds pretty well. There's "no separation of athletes, geeks, Greeks, etc."

Why Students love University of Redlands

"There should never be any reason for someone to feel left out or out of place on this campus with all of the effort that is put into making it open, inviting, and accepting."

WHY STUDENTS LOVE THE UNIVERSITY OF REDLANDS

Redlands has "one of the strongest community service programs in Southern California," according to one student, but facts bear that out: every year students contribute more than 100,000 hours. Examples of student involvement abound, and undergrads work for the benefit of others throughout the greater Redlands community. Many students are involved in research, and find that the school "offers tons of on campus jobs," and "with our active student government and the large number of clubs, it makes it very easy to get involved and become a student leader." Redlands greatly values all input; the school "is constantly looking for feedback," with deans and administrators who "are here to seek out student's best interests, and are always willing to lend a hand," say a few students. A surprised undergrad likes that "the president will often stop by the cafeteria to have lunch with students and chat."

GENERAL INFO

Activities: Choral groups, concert band, dance, drama/theater, jazz band, literary magazine, music ensembles, musical theater, opera, radio station, student government, student newspaper, student-run film society,symphony orchestra, yearbook. **Organizations:** 105 registered organizations, 8 honor societies, 8 religious organizations. 5 fraternities, 5 sororities. **Athletics (Intercollegiate):** *Men:* Baseball, basketball, cross-country, diving, football, golf, soccer, swimming, tennis, track/field (outdoor), water polo. *Women:* Basketball, cross-country, diving, golf, lacrosse, soccer, softball, swimming, tennis, track/field (outdoor), volleyball, water polo. **On-Campus Highlights:** Armacost Library, Peppers Art Center, Currier Gymnasium/Fitness Center, Chapel, Post Office, Other popular places on campus: Math and Physics Building, Aquatic Center, Football Stadium, Jasper's Corner, and Plaza Cafe.

BOTTOM LINE

Annual tuition at the university comes to about $37,000. Room and board will add another $11,000, and you can expect to spend $2,000 on required fees, books, and supplies. While this brings the total cost to nearly $50,000 per year, it's unlikely you will anything close to that figure; Redlands does an admirable job of making itself affordable for everyone. For many students, the decision to attend is sealed because they "received a great financial aid package." A few need-based scholarships and grants are available.

SELECTIVITY

Admissions Rating	**90**
# of applicants	3,587
% of applicants accepted	66
% of acceptees attending	27

FRESHMAN PROFILE

Range SAT Critical Reading	**520–620**
Range SAT Math	**520–620**
Range ACT Composite	**22–27**
Average HS GPA	**3.58**
% graduated top 10% of class	**30**
% graduated top 25% of class	**67**
% graduated top 50% of class	**93**

DEADLINES

Regular Deadline	**12/15**
Normal registration	**yes**

FACILITIES

Housing: Coed dorms, special housing for disabled students, men's dorms, women's dorms, fraternity/sorority housing, apartments for single students, abroad programming, apartments for students with dependent children. *Special Academic Facilities/Equipment:* Art gallery, Far East art collection, Southwest collection, center for communicative disorders. *Computers:* 100% of classrooms, 100% of dorms, 100% of libraries, 100% of dining areas, 100% of student union, 100% of common outdoor areas have wireless network access.

FINANCIAL FACTS

Financial Aid Rating	**85**
Annual in-state tuition	$37,002
Room and Board	$11,196
Required Fees	$300
Books and supplies	$1,650
% frosh rec. need-based scholarship or grant aid	79
% UG rec.need-based scholarship or grant aid	74
% frosh rec. non-need-based scholarship or grant aid	15
% UG rec. non-need-based scholarship or grant aid	8
% frosh rec. need-based self-help aid	61
% UG rec. need-based self-help aid	61
% frosh rec. any financial aid	82
% UG rec. any financial aid	81
% UG borrow to pay for school	67
Average cumulative indebtedness	$20,364

University of Richmond

28 Westhampton Way, University of Richmond, VA 23173 • Admissions: 804-289-8640

CAMPUS LIFE

Quality of life Rating	87
Fire Safety Rating	82
Green rating	95
Type of School	Private
Environment	City

STUDENTS

Total undergrad enrolllment	2,945
% Male to Female	46/59
% From out of state	79
% From public high school	60
% Live on Campus	91
# of Fraternities	8
# of Sororities	8
% African American	7
% Asian	5
% Caucasian	63
% Hispanic	5
% International	6
# Of Countries Represented	67

ACADEMICS

Academic Rating	92
% Of students graduating within 4 years	81
% Of students graduating within 6 years	87
Calendar	semester
Profs interesting rating	91
Profs accessible rating	91
Most common reg class size	10–19 students
Most common lab size	10–19 students

MOST POPULAR MAJORS

Business adminstration and management, English language and literature, social sciences

SPECIAL STUDY OPTIONS

Accelerated program, cross registration, distance learning, double major, English as a Second Language (ESL), exchange student program (domestic), honors program, independent study, internships, student-designed major, study abroad, teacher certification program, Notes on above: Summer English Language Institute is for accepted International Students only. Distance Learning offered through School of Continuing Studies.

ABOUT THE SCHOOL

While the University of Richmond offers the academic opportunities of a larger research university, it maintains the advantages of a small liberal arts college. The average class size is 17; 99 percent of classes have fewer than 30 students; and no class is larger than 40. No classes are taught by teaching assistants. A top-ranked undergraduate business program and the nation's first school of leadership studies are among the highlights here. Richmond's new first-year seminar program includes courses taught by professors from all five of its schools, as well as by the university president and provost.

This large and lush suburban campus is located a few miles from downtown Richmond and about 90 miles from Washington, D.C. Greek row is central to social life. The fraternities and sororities pretty much run the party scene. Sports are also big, and a great many students are involved in intercollegiate and club teams or intramurals. If none of that appeals to you, there are also tons of organizations and campus events.

BANG FOR YOUR BUCK

The University of Richmond prides itself on its practice of need-blind admission, and this school invests a tremendous amount of time and money in making it possible for lower and middle-income students to come here. Nearly half of students receive need-based financial aid, with an average award of more than $35,000. Virginians who qualify for financial aid and have a family income below $40,000 receive an aid package equal to full tuition and room and board (without loans). The university also offers generous merit-based scholarships. Full-tuition scholarships are awarded to Richmond Scholars. Presidential and Trustee scholarships are available for up to $15,000, and National Merit Scholarships, National Achievement Finalists and National Hispanic Scholarships are awarded. Qualified students may be eligible for full-tuition Army ROTC scholarships and scholarships through the Yellow Ribbon Program. Through the Bonner Scholars Program, students make a four-year commitment to sustained community engagement and social justice education. Bonner Scholars commit 10 hours per week of community engagement in exchange for a monetary award of up to $2,500 per academic year.

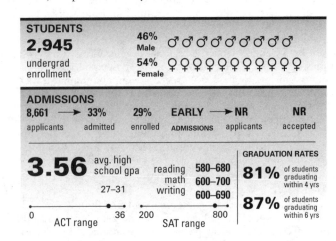

STUDENTS

2,945 undergrad enrollment

46% Male ♂♂♂♂♂♂♂♂♂

54% Female ♀♀♀♀♀♀♀♀♀♀♀

ADMISSIONS

8,661 applicants → 33% admitted — 29% enrolled

EARLY ADMISSIONS → NR applicants — NR accepted

3.56 avg. high school gpa

ACT range (0–36): 27–31

SAT range (200–800): reading 580–680, math 600–700, writing 600–690

GRADUATION RATES

81% of students graduating within 4 yrs

87% of students graduating within 6 yrs

University of Richmond

E-MAIL: WWW.RICHMOND.EDU/ADMISSION/INDEX. • FAX: 804-287-6003 • WEBSITE: WWW.RICHMOND.EDU

STUDENT BODY

Nearly eighty percent of the students at Richmond come from out of state. "A large percentage of the students here are attending on scholarship or with a very generous financial aid package." There's also a "growing number of" international students. Nevertheless, "Richmond is pretty homogenous." The typical student is "from 'outs ide Philly' or 'outside Boston'" or is a "Mid-Atlantic prep school kid" "who probably owns several pairs of Sperrys." Many students "dress well" and "obviously care about their physical appearance." There are "lots of Polos, button-downs, and sundresses." Otherwise, these "clean cut," and (if they don't mind saying so themselves) "good looking" students are "ambitious," "friendly," "outgoing," "overcommitted, and usually a little stressed." There's also "a great mixture of nerds and athletes," and "Everyone brings their own sense of individuality."

WHY STUDENTS LOVE RICHMOND

The University of Richmond provides "the resources of a large university with the personal attention of a small college" and just "a hint of Southern charm." Financial aid is "generous." Facilities are "outstanding." "Students have access to state-of-the-art technologies and research labs that normally only graduate students would be able to work with." Among the sixty or so undergraduate majors, students call our attention to the "great business program" and the "excellent premed program." "Another of Richmond's strengths is its study abroad programs." Every year, a few hundred Richmond students take classes in more than thirty countries or complete a summer internship in one of six countries.

Why Students love University of Richmond

"Everyone brings their own sense of individuality."

GENERAL INFO

Activities: Choral groups, concert band, dance, drama/theater, jazz band, literary magazine, music ensembles, musical theater, pep band, radio station, student government, student newspaper, student-run film society, symphony orchestra, campus ministries, international student organization, Model UN. **Organizations:** 208 registered organizations, 28 honor societies, 17 religious organizations. 6 fraternities, 8 sororities. **Athletics (Intercollegiate):** *Men:* Baseball, basketball, cross-country, football, golf, soccer, tennis, track/field (outdoor), track/field (indoor). *Women:* Basketball, cross country, diving, field hockey, golf, lacrosse, soccer, swimming, tennis, track/field (outdoor), track/field (indoor). **On-Campus Highlights:** Tyler Haynes Commons, Robins Center (Athletic Center), Boatwright Memorial Library and Coffee Shop, Stern Plaza (Weinstein Hall, Jepson Hall, etc.), Westhampton Green (Modlin Center for the Arts). **Environmental Initiatives:** Signing the ACUPCC and subsequent creation of the Climate Action Plan (in process); waste diversion initiatives; energy conservation and efficiency projects.

BOTTOM LINE

The total cost for tuition, room and board, and everything else exceeds $50,000 per year at the University of Richmond. You'll get help though: A family's finances are never considered in the admission decision. Need-based financial aid and large scholarships are profuse.

SELECTIVITY

Admissions Rating	**92**
# of applicants	8,661
% of applicants accepted	33
% of acceptees attending	29
# accepting a place on wait list	984
% admitted from wait list	8

FRESHMAN PROFILE

Range SAT Critical Reading	**580–680**
Range SAT Math	**600–700**
Range SAT Writing	**600–690**
Range ACT Composite	**27–31**
% graduated top 10% of class	**54**
% graduated top 25% of class	**86**
% graduated top 50% of class	**99**

DEADLINES

Regular Deadline	**1/15**
Normal registration	**no**

FACILITIES

Housing: Coed dorms, special housing for disabled students, men's dorms, women's dorms, apartments for single students, theme housing*Global House, Outdoor House, and Civic Engagement represent co-ed housing. *Special Academic Facilities/Equipment:* Art gallery, mineral museum, Virginia Baptist archives, language lab, Neuroscience lab, Speech Center, Music Technology lab, Jepson School of Leadership, Center for Civic Engagement. *Computers:* 100% of classrooms, 100% of dorms, 100% of libraries, 100% of dining areas, 100% of student union, 100% of common outdoor areas have wireless network access.

FINANCIAL FACTS

Financial Aid Rating	**97**
Annual tuition	$43,170
Room and Board	$9,250
Books and supplies	$1,050
% frosh rec. need-based scholarship or grant aid	47
% UG rec.need-based scholarship or grant aid	47
% frosh rec. non-need-based scholarship or grant aid	11
% UG rec. non-need-based scholarship or grant aid	18
% frosh rec. need-based self-help aid	39
% UG rec. need-based self-help aid	40
% frosh rec. any financial aid	63
% UG rec. any financial aid	70
% UG borrow to pay for school	42
Average cumulative indebtedness	$23,070

Vanderbilt University

2305 West End Avenue, Nashville, TN 37203 • Admissions: 615-322-2561 • Fax: 615-343-7765

CAMPUS LIFE

Quality of life Rating	98
Fire Safety Rating	91
Green rating	96
Type of School	Private
Environment	Metropolos

STUDENTS

Total undergrad enrollment	6,879
% Male to Female	49/51
% From out of state	84
% From public high school	57
% Live on Campus	85
# of Fraternities	20
# of Sororities	15
% African American	8
% Asian	7
% Caucasian	64
% Hispanic	7
% Native American	<1
% International	7
# Of Countries Represented	111

ACADEMICS

Academic Rating	91
% Of students graduating within 4 years	85
% Of students graduating within 6 years	91
Calendar	semester
Profs interesting rating	86
Profs accessible rating	85
Most common reg class size	10–19 students
Most common lab size	10–19 students

MOST POPULAR MAJORS

Human and organizational development, economics, political science, engineering

HONORS PROGRAMS

Psychology, Child Development, Cognitive Studies, and Child Studies, Biomedical Engineering, Biological Sciences.

SPECIAL STUDY OPTIONS

Accelerated program, cooperative education program, cross-registration, distance learning, double major, dual enrollment, honors program, independent study, internships.

ABOUT THE SCHOOL

Vanderbilt offers its 6,700 undergraduate students a heady blend of superior academic offerings, an exceptional urban environment, and a community at once steeped in tradition and enmeshed in state-of-the-art research. Students are engaged in learning at all times, whether as part of the interdisciplinary curriculum, the Commons first-year living and learning residential community, conducting research through one of the university's 120 research centers, exploring global cultures through study abroad, or participating in one of more than 300 student-led organizations. A campus-wide Honor System ensures that Vanderbilt students navigate the university's tough academics with integrity.

Students from the 70 degree programs in Vanderbilt's four undergraduate schools participate in research aside world-renowned professors in fields ranging from neuroscience to child psychology, from music education to nanotechnology. During their four years as an undergraduate, approximately three quarters of Vanderbilt students take advantage of internships, research positions, and service projects on campus, in Nashville, and abroad, and/or study abroad programs, which enhance their academic experiences, building valuable skills important to future careers. Vanderbilt's ethos of service permeates campus and students routinely engage in projects designed to make a difference in their communities.

BANG FOR YOUR BUCK

Talent isn't the special property of the privileged and pedigreed, and Vanderbilt goes above and beyond to ensure that promising students can have access to a Vanderbilt education no matter what their financial situation may be. Vanderbilt's financial aid program does not use income bands or cutoffs; there is no specific income level that automatically disqualifies a family from receiving need-based financial aid, benefiting middle-class as well as low-income families. In addition to need-based financial assistance, Vanderbilt offers merit scholarships to a highly selective group of the most talented applicants. Applicants for these merit scholarships must demonstrate exceptional academic records and leadership in their communities. The majority of merit scholarships are awarded as part of three signature scholarship programs: the Ingram Scholarship Program, the Cornelius Vanderbilt Scholarship Program, and the Chancellor's Scholarship Program. All three signature awards include full tuition for four years, plus summer stipends for study.

STUDENTS

6,879 undergrad enrollment

49% Male ♂♂♂♂♂♂♂♂♂♂

51% Female ♀♀♀♀♀♀♀♀♀♀

ADMISSIONS

21,811 →	18%	41%	EARLY →	NR	NR
applicants	admitted	enrolled	ADMISSIONS	applicants	accepted

3.70 avg. high school gpa

ACT range (0–36): 30–34

SAT range (200–800): reading 670–760, math 690–770, writing 660–750

GRADUATION RATES

85% of students graduating within 4 yrs

91% of students graduating within 6 yrs

Vanderbilt University

FINANCIAL AID: 800-288-0204 • E-MAIL: ADMISSIONS@VANDERBILT.EDU • WEBSITE: WWW.VANDERBILT.EDU

STUDENT BODY

A sophomore admits, "The stereotype of a typical Vandy student used to be wealthy, conservative, white, Southern, etc." However, he continues, "While some still fit the stereotype there is much more diversity on campus. At Vanderbilt, you'll find an undergraduate population that's "hardworking, sociable, and enjoys having fun." Indeed, many Vanderbilt students "definitely fit the 'work hard, play hard' personality type." An "overachieving" and "accomplished" lot, undergrads at Vanderbilt are "very involved in something, be it a sorority or fraternity, dance group, [or] religious group." "This is not a school where students lock themselves in the room to study 24/7. It's rare to find a student who is involved in only one club or not involved in anything."

Why Students love Vanderbilt University

"The commitment to community service at Vanderbilt is incredible. The amount of time, effort, and innovation my fellow students put into serving others truly astounds me."

WHY STUDENTS LOVE VANDERBILT UNIVERSITY

If there is a buzzword at Vanderbilt it is "community." Student after student tout the close ties and sense of belonging fostered at the school, which is located in the heart of legendary Nashville, Tennessee. The biggest draw, students say, are the students themselves. Rather than nurture an air of fierce competition, those at the University "embrace an attitude that we are all in the same boat." Because of this, Vanderbilt has "all the charm and intimacy of a smaller school" while offering "the excitement of the city of Nashville." Students visiting "really connected with the professors, the students, and the campus," making it an "ideal place to do research and study."Nashville and all it offers proves to be a big draw for students, who enjoy the "beautiful campus and prime location in a lively city."

GENERAL INFO

Activities: Choral groups, concert band, dance, drama/theater, jazz band, literary magazine, marching band, music ensembles, musical theater, opera, pep band, radio station, student government, **Organizations:** 329 registered organizations, 20 honor societies, 18 religious organizations. 19 fraternities, 12 sororities. **Athletics (Intercollegiate):** *Men:* Baseball, basketball, cross-country, football, golf, tennis. *Women:* Basketball, cross-country, golf, lacrosse, soccer, tennis, track/field (outdoor).

BOTTOM LINE

In addition to being need-blind in the admissions process, Vanderbilt meets 100 percent of a family's demonstrated financial need through its Expanded Aid Program. Best of all, need-based financial aid packages for eligible students have been loan-free since 2009.

SELECTIVITY

Admissions Rating	**99**
# of applicants	21,811
% of applicants accepted	18
% of acceptees attending	41
# accepting a place on wait list	1,733
% admitted from wait list	19

FRESHMAN PROFILE

Range SAT Critical Reading	**670–760**
Range SAT Math	**690–770**
Range ACT Composite	**30–34**
Average HS GPA	**3.70**
% graduated top 10% of class	**85**
% graduated top 25% of class	**96**
% graduated top 50% of class	**100**

DEADLINES

Regular Deadline	**1/3**
Normal registration	**no**

FACILITIES

Housing: Coed dorms, special housing for disabled students, men's dorms, special housing for international students, women's dorms, apartments for married students, apartments for single students, theme housing. The Commons is a community of first-year students, residential faculty, and professional staff. *Special Academic Facilities/Equipment:* Art galleries, center for research on education and human development, multimedia classrooms. *Computers:* 100% of classrooms, 100% of dorms, 100% of libraries, 100% of dining areas, 100% of student union, 100% of common outdoor areas have wireless network access.

FINANCIAL FACTS

Financial Aid Rating	**96**
Annual tuition	$40,320
Room and Board	$13,560
Required Fees	$1,676
Books and supplies	$1,344
% frosh rec. need-based scholarship or grant aid	44
% UG rec.need-based scholarship or grant aid	43
% frosh rec. non-need-based scholarship or grant aid	29
% UG rec. non-need-based scholarship or grant aid	22
% frosh rec. need-based self-help aid	25
% UG rec. need-based self-help aid	28
% frosh rec. any financial aid	64
% UG rec. any financial aid	63
% UG borrow to pay for school	37
Average cumulative indebtedness	$18,605

Vassar College

124 Raymond Avenue, Poughkeepsie, NY 12604 • Admissions: 845-437-7300 • Fax: 845-437-7063

CAMPUS LIFE

Quality of life Rating	74
Fire Safety Rating	80
Green rating	86
Type of School	Private
Environment	Public

STUDENTS

Total undergrad enrolllment	2,408
% Male to Female	42/58
% From out of state	73
% From public high school	63
% Live on Campus	95
% African American	5
% Asian	9
% Caucasian	67
% Hispanic	9
% International	6
# Of Countries Represented	53

ACADEMICS

Academic Rating	97
% Of students graduating within 4 years	90
% Of students graduating within 6 years	93
Calendar	semester
Profs interesting rating	91
Profs accessible rating	89
Most common reg class size	10–19 students
Most common lab size	10–19 students

MOST POPULAR MAJORS

English language and literature, political science, psychology

HONORS PROGRAMS

For highly qualified students, a series of interdisciplinary honors courses are offered. Additionally, for students especially talented in individual areas of study, most departments in the College offer special studies leading to graduation with honors in a particular discipline.

SPECIAL STUDY OPTIONS

Cross-registration, double major, dual enrollment, honors program, independent study, internships, study abroad, teacher certification program.

ABOUT THE COLLEGE

A co-ed institution since 1969, Vassar was founded in 1861 as the first of the Seven Sister Colleges. Located in Poughkeepsie, New York, Vassar is a private, liberal arts school where there is very little in the way of a core curriculum, which allows students the freedom to design their own courses of study. This approach, students agree, "really encourages students to think creatively and pursue whatever they're passionate about, whether medieval tapestries, neuroscience, or unicycles. Not having a core curriculum is great because it gives students the opportunity to delve into many different interests."

Vassar is a comfortable respite for indie types who revel in their obscure tastes, some socially awkward high school archetypes, and some popped-collar prep schoolers. There are a lot more females here than males. Student life is campus-centered, in large part because hometown Poughkeepsie does not offer much in the way of entertainment. It's a very self-contained social scene; virtually everyone lives on Vassar's beautiful campus. A vibrant oasis in the middle of nowhere, it's easy for students here to get caught in the "Vassar Bubble." There are clubs and organizations aplenty, and the school provides interesting lectures, theater productions, and a wide array of activities pretty much every weeknight. Weekends, on the other hand, are more about small parties and gatherings. More adventurous students make the relatively easy trek to New York to shake up the routine.

BANG FOR YOUR BUCK

Vassar has a need-blind admissions policy. Vassar is able to meet 100 percent of the demonstrated need of everyone who is admitted for all four years. Each year Vassar awards more than $34 million dollars in scholarships. Funds come from Vassar's endowment, money raised by Vassar clubs, and gifts from friends of the college and all are need-based. No merit-based awards are available.

STUDENTS

2,408 undergrad enrollment

42% Male ♂♂♂♂♂♂♂♂

58% Female ♀♀♀♀♀♀♀♀♀♀♀

ADMISSIONS

7,822 applicants → 24% admitted | 36% enrolled | EARLY ADMISSIONS → NR applicants | NR accepted

3.77 avg. high school gpa

ACT range (0–36): 29–32

SAT range (200–800): reading 670–740, math 640–720, writing 660–750

GRADUATION RATES

90% of students graduating within 4 yrs

93% of students graduating within 6 yrs

STUDENT BODY

There are "lots of hipsters" at Vassar including kids who are "very left-wing politically" and "very into the music scene." The school is "not entirely dominated by hipsters," however; there are "lots of different groups" on campus. "Walking around you'll see students who walked out of a thrift store next to students who walked out of a J. Crew catalog," one student tells us. Another adds that Vassar is a comfortable respite for "indie-chic students who revel in obscurity, some socially awkward archetypes, and some prep school pin-ups with their collars popped. But the majority of kids on campus are a mix of these people, which is why we mesh pretty well despite the cliques that inevitably form."

FINANCIAL AID: 845-437-5320 • E-MAIL: ADMISSIONS@VASSAR.EDU • WEBSITE: WWW.VASSAR.EDU

Why Students love Vassar

"Vassar admissions works tremendously hard to ensure every student at Vassar is unique and mold-breaking."

WHY STUDENTS LOVE VASSAR

Vassar is for off-beat students who relish their off-beat nature and who shun the stereotypical life of the college student; "smart and passionate hipsters" out to prove they have something to offer the world. Greek life does not exist on the Vassar campus. When social events aren't centering around small gatherings of quirky, eccentric people, "lots of parties are awesome, school-sponsored, theme events." There isn't much to do off-campus, but students don't attend Vassar for the thriving nightlife. Rather, they attend, in the words of one student, because they're "given the chance to experiment with your life in an encouraging and stimulating environment." The pursuit of individuality is encouraged here, something exemplified in the student-driven entertainment provided on campus every night. There may not be a wild downtown or bustling city nearby, but on campus students will find a myriad of theater groups, music, comedy troupes, and more.

Vassar thrives on a lenient disciplinary system and self-governance, a good match for its small class sizes and focus on the arts and independent research. This also means Vassar may not be a good fit for students who desire a more structured environment–something exacerbated by a close-knit campus life that doesn't provide much escape for students who don't mesh with the general student population–but those who desire a loose, independent approach love Vassar's "amazing academics and world-class professors." The lack of a core curriculum is a major draw for Vassar students, who enjoy being about to pursue interests as varied as "medieval tapestries, neuroscience, or unicycles." Those who revel in their individuality will find that Vassar welcomes them with open arms.

GENERAL INFO

Activities: Choral groups, concert band, dance, drama/theater, jazz band, literary magazine, marching band, music ensembles. **Organizations:** 105 registered organizations, 2 honor societies, 11 religious organizations. **Athletics (Intercollegiate):** *Men:* Baseball, basketball, crew/rowing, cross-country, diving, fencing, lacrosse, soccer, squash, swimming, tennis, track/field (outdoor), volleyball. *Women:* Basketball, crew/rowing, cross-country, diving, fencing, field hockey, golf, lacrosse, soccer, squash, swimming, tennis, track/field (outdoor), volleyball. **On-Campus Highlights:** Library, Shakespeare Garden, Class of 1951 Observatory, Frances Lehman Loeb Art Center, Center for Drama and Film. **Environmental Initiatives:** composting nearly. 100% of food waste on site purchasing local food.

BOTTOM LINE

The sticker price at Vassar for tuition, fees, and room and board runs about $55,000 for a year. That said, Vassar has a need-blind admission policy, and financial aid is extremely generous. It's probably harder to get admitted here than it is to afford going here. Meeting financial standards is less important than exceedingly high academic standards and intellectual pursuits that venture far outside the classroom.

SELECTIVITY

Admissions Rating	**98**
# of applicants	7,822
% of applicants accepted	24
% of acceptees attending	36
# accepting a place on wait list	568
% admitted from wait list	0

FRESHMAN PROFILE

Range SAT Critical Reading	**670–740**
Range SAT Math	**670–720**
Range SAT Writing	**660–750**
Range ACT Composite	**29–32**
Average HS GPA	**3.77**
% graduated top 10% of class	**65**
% graduated top 25% of class	**96**
% graduated top 50% of class	**100**

DEADLINES

Regular Deadline	**1/1**
Normal registration	**no**

FACILITIES

Housing: Coed dorms, fraternity/sorority housing, apartments for single students, wellness housing, theme housing, Wellness = Substance Free. *Special Academic Facilities/Equipment:* Museum of Anthropology, Charlotte and Philip Hanes Art Gallery, Scales Fine Arts Center. *Computers:* 100% of classrooms, 100% of dorms, 100% of libraries, 100% of dining areas, 100% of student union, 5% of common outdoor areas have wireless network access.

FINANCIAL FACTS

Financial Aid Rating	**99**
Annual tuition	$44,050
Room and Board	$10,430
Required Fees	$655
Books and supplies	$860
% frosh rec. need-based scholarship or grant aid	64
% UG rec.need-based scholarship or grant aid	62
% frosh rec. need-based self-help aid	64
% UG rec. need-based self-help aid	63
% frosh rec. any financial aid	64
% UG rec. any financial aid	63
% UG borrow to pay for school	49
Average cumulative indebtedness	$18,153

Wabash College

PO Box 352, 301 W. Wabash Av, Crawfordsville, IN 47933 • Admissions: 765-361-6225

CAMPUS LIFE

Quality of life Rating	85
Fire Safety Rating	87
Green rating	68
Type of School	Private
Environment	Village

STUDENTS

Total undergrad enrolllment	872
% Male to Female	100/0
% From out of state	25
% From public high school	91
% Live on Campus	84
# of Fraternities	9
% African American	5
% Asian	2
% Caucasian	77
% Hispanic	5
% Native American	1
% International	6
# Of Countries Represented	18

ACADEMICS

Academic Rating	96
% Of students graduating within 4 years	71
% Of students graduating within 6 years	77
Calendar	semester
Profs interesting rating	98
Profs accessible rating	98
Most common reg class size	10–19 students
Most common lab size	fewer than 10 students

MOST POPULAR MAJORS
History, psychology, religion

SPECIAL STUDY OPTIONS

Double major, independent study, internships, liberal arts/career combination, study abroad, teacher certification program, Student designed majors, minors, or areas of concentration. Immersion Learning courses are offered, which involve travel domestically and abroad.

ABOUT THE SCHOOL

There are still all-male liberal arts colleges out there, and Wabash College is among the last and the best of them. Wabash College is one of just three remaining men's liberal arts colleges in the nation. Even so, Wabash's solid reputation and even more solid endowment ensure that the tradition of quality, single-sex education will continue into the foreseeable future. Academically, a flexible curriculum and rigorous academic programs define the Wabash experience. With a student body of fewer than 1,000 students, the school boasts an excellent student-to-teacher ratio of 11:1. First-rate professors and a hands-on administration enhance the Wabash experience, along with special programs designed to complement classroom learning with real-world experience. For example, the school's Immersion Learning Courses allow students to link their classroom work to a 7–10 day trip within the United States or overseas, at no additional cost to the student.

Wabash students adhere to the elegant Gentleman's Rule, which simply requires them to behave as responsible students both on and off campus. Though the student body has grown more diverse in recent years, Wabash men are typically very bright, very ambitious, and very conservative. Not all are religious, but those who are take their faith very seriously. Weeknights at Wabash are all about academics, while weekends are filled with parties. Life at Wabash is very Greek-oriented–half of students belong to a fraternity. Purdue, Ball State, Butler, and Indiana University are all nearby, should students crave the occasional getaway, and women from neighboring schools often travel to the Wabash campus on the weekends. Hometown Crawford is small–home to only 15,000 permanent residents–but Indianapolis is less than 50 miles to the southeast.

BANG FOR YOUR BUCK

The school can afford to distribute aid generously. Admissions are based on academic ability, not ability to pay. At Wabash, 100 percent of student financial need is met. Merit-based aid is also plentiful. Wabash's Top-10 Scholarship Program provides four-year, renewable, merit-based scholarships to students who rank in the top 10 percent of their high school class. Famously, the school offers $2.5 million worth of competitive academic scholarships on its Honor Scholarship Weekend, during which students travel to the school to take a series competitive exams with other prospective students. There are also merit-based scholarships for students who demonstrate exceptional character and excellence in leadership, such as the Lilly Award, which covers the full cost of tuition, and room and board.

STUDENTS
872 undergrad enrollment

100% Male ♂♂♂♂♂♂♂♂♂♂
0% Female

ADMISSIONS

1,535 applicants	→ 56% admitted	29% enrolled	EARLY ADMISSIONS	→ NR applicants	NR accepted

3.58 avg. high school gpa

ACT range (0–36): 22–28

SAT range (200–800):

reading	510–615
math	540–660
writing	490–610

GRADUATION RATES

71% of students graduating within 4 yrs

77% of students graduating within 6 yrs

Wabash College

E-MAIL: ADMISSIONS@WABASH.EDU • FAX: 765-361-6437 • WEBSITE: WWW.WABASH.EDU

STUDENT BODY

A typical Wabash student "is an athlete who is willing to work long hours to get good grades." "Studious, eager to learn and to get work done, [and] serious about school," students here are "almost treated like peers by professors." "Everyone at Wabash works very hard and benefits from the rigorous academic requirements." "Lower-class to upper class backgrounds allow for a variety of perspectives and previous educations." Regardless of where they hail from, "Students embrace the backgrounds of their classmates and work together to learn." Others say, "It's an all-male college, but that's where the universal attributes end." "There could stand to be some more ethnic diversity"; however, others say, "I think that's got more to with self-selection than anything else." "The library is packed Sunday through Thursday evening."

Why Students Love Wabash

"After four years at Wabash College, any man can be transformed into a gentleman and a scholar and be more prepared for life after college than any other student."

WHY STUDENTS LOVE WABASH

"It is a powerful, small school that changes lives." So says one alumni. It's an oft-repeated theme among students there, who tout Wabash as a place that turns boys into refined, thoughtful, and intelligent gentlemen. Students like that Wabash is a "prestigious college with a very intellectually stimulating environment." Wabash students take their academics seriously, and the school meets them head-on with challenging academics –but students don't fear failure. "The professors are helpful and teach very well," one polled student said. "The courses are tough, but the amount of help the professors provide makes them passable." Students appreciate that Wabash has "the best academic atmosphere of any place that I visited for college" and "the best professors in the nation," a sentiment aired repeatedly by alumni.

GENERAL INFO

Activities: Choral groups, concert band, drama/theater, jazz band, literary magazine, music ensembles, pep band, radio station, student government, student newspaper, student-run film society, **Organizations:** 65 registered organizations, 7 honor societies, 5 religious organizations. 9 fraternities. **Athletics (Intercollegiate):** *Men:* Baseball, basketball, cross-country, diving, football, golf, soccer, swimming, tennis, track/field (outdoor), track/field (indoor), wrestling. **On-Campus Highlights:** Allen Athletics and Recreation Center, Wabash Chapel, New Science Building, Hays Hall, Trippet Hall, Lilly Library, Malcolm X Institute of Black Studies.

BOTTOM LINE

Few students pay the full cost of attendance at Wabash. Most students receive generous aid packages in the form of loans and scholarships, drastically offsetting the price. Therefore, most undergraduates pay just a fraction of the estimated $40,000 cost to attend (which includes $31,800 tuition and $8,50 for room and board, plus other expenses.)

SELECTIVITY

Admissions Rating	**89**
# of applicants	1,535
% of applicants accepted	56
% of acceptees attending	29
# accepting a place on wait list	98
% admitted from wait list	17

FRESHMAN PROFILE

Range SAT Critical Reading	**510–615**
Range SAT Math	**540–660**
Range SAT Writing	**490–610**
Range ACT Composite	**22–28**
Average HS GPA	**3.58**
% graduated top 10% of class	**43**
% graduated top 25% of class	**67**
% graduated top 50% of class	**93**

DEADLINES

Regular Deadline	**12/1**
Normal registration	**yes**

Facilities

Housing: Special housing for disabled students, men's dorms, fraternity/sorority housing, college-owned houses and apartments. *Special Academic Facilities/Equipment:* Malcolm X Institute of Black Studies, two art galleries, language lab, electron microscope. *Computers:* 100% of classrooms, 100% of dorms, 100% of libraries, 100% of dining areas, 100% of student union, 100% of common outdoor areas have wireless network access.

FINANCIAL FACTS

Financial Aid Rating	**95**
Annual tuition	$31,800
Room and Board	$8,500
Required Fees	$650
Books and supplies	$800
% frosh rec. need-based scholarship or grant aid	82
% UG rec.need-based scholarship or grant aid	77
% frosh rec. non-need-based scholarship or grant aid	12
% UG rec. non-need-based scholarship or grant aid	10
% frosh rec. need-based self-help aid	73
% UG rec. need-based self-help aid	68
% frosh rec. any financial aid	86
% UG rec. any financial aid	79
% UG borrow to pay for school	81
Average cumulative indebtedness	$29,897

Wake Forest College

P.O. Box 7305, Reynolda Station, Winston Salem, NC 27109 • Admissions: 336-758-5201 • Fax: 336-758-4324

CAMPUS LIFE

Quality of life Rating	74
Fire Safety Rating	87
Green rating	83
Type of School	Private
Environment	City

STUDENTS

Total undergrad enrollment	4,560
% Male to Female	49/51
% From out of state	74
% From public high school	65
% Live on Campus	70
# of Fraternities	19
# of Sororities	9
% African American	7
% Asian	6
% Caucasian	80
% Hispanic	4
% International	2

ACADEMICS

Academic Rating	89
% Of students graduating within 4 years	85
% Of students graduating within 6 years	90
Calendar	semester
Profs interesting rating	85
Profs accessible rating	85
Most common reg class size	10–19 students
Most common lab size	10–19 students

MOST POPULAR MAJORS

Business/commerce, political science, psychology

HONORS PROGRAMS

For highly qualified students, a series of interdisciplinary honors courses are offered. Additionally, for students especially talented in individual areas of study, most departments in the College offer special studies leading to graduation with honors in a particular discipline.

SPECIAL STUDY OPTIONS

Cross-registration, double major, dual enrollment, honors program, independent study, internships, study abroad.

ABOUT THE SCHOOL

Wake Forest combines the best tradition of a small liberal arts college with the resources of a national research university. Founded in 1834, the University believes deeply in its responsibility to educate the whole person, mind, body, and spirit. One students says, "I was very impressed with the quality of the facilities and professors." To help assist with their studies, Wake Forest students receive a laptop upon entering. They certainly need all the help they can get, as Wake Forest academics are rigorous. Wake has a nurturing environment with professors and faculty that care about the well-being and personal growth of its students. "Small classes with a lot of discussion are common." Small class sizes create opportunities for intense discussion, and though the workload may be heavy at time, professors are extremely accessible outside of class for additional help or questions. Professors, not graduate assistants, are the primary instructors. Students have access to top-flight scholars from the very first day of their college career. Wake Forest also offers extraordinary opportunities for undergraduate students to get involved in faculty research projects.

BANG FOR YOUR BUCK

"Wake Forest's generous financial aid program allows deserving students to enroll regardless of their financial circumstances." Wake Forest is one of a small group of private institutions that agrees to meet 100 percent of each regularly admitted student's demonstrated financial need. Nearly two-thirds of the students here receive some form of financial aid. In addition, each year Wake Forest awards merit-based scholarships to less than three percent of its first-year applicants. These scholarships are renewable through four years, subject to satisfactory academic, extracurricular, and civic performance. Though criteria differ slightly, the programs all recognize extraordinary achievement, leadership, and talent. Most scholarships do not require a separate merit-based scholarship application. The Committee on Scholarships and Student Aid annually recognizes up to ten students as Thomas E. and Ruth Mullen Scholars of the Upper-class Carswell Scholarships. Applicants must have completed at least one year of coursework at Wake Forest and are judged on the basis of academic and extracurricular leadership while here. The competition is steep, with recipients generally standing at least in the top 10 percent of the class. "Wake Forest's Reynolds and Carswell merit-based scholarships cover tuition, room board and summer grants for individually-designed study projects. Gordon Scholarships are awarded to up to seven students each year to students among constituencies historically underrepresented at Wake Forest."

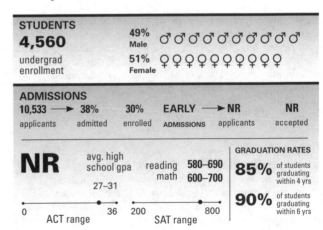

STUDENTS
4,560 undergrad enrollment
49% Male ♂♂♂♂♂♂♂♂♂♂
51% Female ♀♀♀♀♀♀♀♀♀♀

ADMISSIONS
10,533 applicants → 38% admitted — 30% enrolled — EARLY ADMISSIONS → NR applicants — NR accepted

NR avg. high school gpa

27–31 ACT range (0–36)

reading 580–690
math 600–700
SAT range (200–800)

GRADUATION RATES
85% of students graduating within 4 yrs
90% of students graduating within 6 yrs

Wake Forest College

FINANCIAL AID: 336-758-5154 • E-MAIL: ADMISSIONS@WFU.EDU • WEBSITE: WWW.WFU.EDU

STUDENT BODY

"There is a lot of Southern prep at Wake Forest" and "a slight air of materialism." "Most people fit into the preppy white kid stereotype," observes a first-year student, "even the non-white students." The typical undergrad is basically "your all-American" kid. Many students come from "well-to-do" families. "Pearl-wearing, North Face jacket-owning, Kate Spade-toting, Greek letter-wearing" types are quite common. Students tell us they range from "really friendly" to "exceedingly perky." They also tend to be athletic. "Politically, most kids are moderates–perhaps a bit right of center, but not drastically so," and "rightwing and leftwing groups tend to be vocal about their views." Some students suggest that Wake "could do with more diversity," and the school has been listening: last year, Wake Forest enrolled its most diverse freshman class ever.

Why Students love Wake Forest

"Ample opportunities for students to get involved and meet other students outside of the classroom"

WHY STUDENTS LOVE WAKE FOREST

Life at Wake is largely confined to on-campus events, although there is also the appeal of hometown Winston-Salem. Plus, other state universities and bigger cities are close enough to travel to. "Greek life is "massive, and "very popular" at Wake Forest; "a large portion of the student body is a member of a fraternity or sorority." However, non-Greeks are equally accepted and have a wide variety of other groups to choose from. Intramural sports are popular, providing "ample opportunities for students to get involved and meet other students outside of the classroom."

GENERAL INFO

Activities: Choral groups, concert band, dance, drama/theater, jazz band, literary magazine, marching band, music ensembles, pep band, radio station, student government, student newspaper, student-run film society, symphony orchestra, television station, yearbook, campus ministries, international student organization. **Organizations:** 168 registered organizations, 16 honor societies, 16 religious organizations. 14 fraternities, 9 sororities. **Athletics (Intercollegiate):** *Men:* Baseball, basketball, cheerleading, cross-country, football, golf, soccer, tennis, track/field (outdoor), track/field (indoor). *Women:* Basketball, cheerleading, cross-country, field hockey, golf, soccer, tennis, track/field (outdoor), track/field (indoor), volleyball. **On-Campus Highlights:** Charlotte and Philip Hanes Art Gallery, Museum of Anthropology, The Z. Smith Reynolds Library, Wait Chapel, Benson University Center. **Environmental Initiatives:** Campus Master Plan: plan for sustainable design (e.g., LEED) as well as stormwater management and biohabitat protection. Conserve energy during normal operating periods and to cycle down energy use to minimal levels during low- or no-occupancy periods. Recycling: Approximately 30 percent of the WFU waste stream is diverted from the landfill as either recycled or reused.

BOTTOM LINE

At Wake Forest College, the total cost for tuition and fees, room and board, books, travel, and personal expenses comes to about $56,000. Fortunately, the average financial aid package for freshman includes a grant totaling $22,000. Additional aid is available in the form of scholarships, work-study, and loans.

SELECTIVITY

Admissions Rating	**94**
# of applicants	10,553
% of applicants accepted	38
% of acceptees attending	30

FRESHMAN PROFILE

Range SAT Critical Reading	**580–690**
Range SAT Math	**600–700**
Range ACT Composite	**27–31**
% graduated top 10% of class	**75**
% graduated top 25% of class	**89**
% graduated top 50% of class	**99**

DEADLINES

Regular Deadline	**1/1**
Normal registration	**no**

FACILITIES

Housing: Coed dorms, fraternity/sorority housing, apartments for single students, wellness housing, theme housing, Wellness = Substance Free. *Special Academic Facilities/Equipment:* Museum of Anthropology; Charlotte and Philip Hanes Art Gallery; Scales Fine Arts Center; Reynolda House, Museum of American Art; Laser and Electron Microscope Labs. *Computers:* 100% of classrooms, 100% of dorms, 100% of libraries, 100% of dining areas, 100% of student union, 5% of common outdoor areas have wireless network access.

FINANCIAL FACTS

Financial Aid Rating	**90**
Annual in-state tuition	$41,100
Room and Board	$11,410
Required Fees	$476
Books and supplies	$1,025
% frosh rec. need-based scholarship or grant aid	28
% UG rec.need-based scholarship or grant aid	35
% frosh rec. non-need-based scholarship or grant aid	17
% UG rec. non-need-based scholarship or grant aid	25
% frosh rec. need-based self-help aid	24
% UG rec. need-based self-help aid	32
% frosh rec. any financial aid	39
% UG rec. any financial aid	39
% UG borrow to pay for school	38
Average cumulative indebtedness	$24,561

Wellesley College

BOARD OF ADMISSION, 106 CENTRAL STREET, WELLESLEY, MA 02481-8203 • PHONE: 781-283-2270

CAMPUS LIFE

Quality of life Rating	95
Fire Safety Rating	85
Green rating	89
Type of School	Private
Environment	Town

STUDENTS

Total undergrad enrollment	2,296
% Male to Female	0/100
% From out of state	84
% From public high school	62
% Live on Campus	97
% African American	6
% Asian	22
% Caucasian	46
% Hispanic	9
% International	10
# Of Countries Represented	70

ACADEMICS

Academic Rating	98
% Of students graduating within 4 years	84
% Of students graduating within 6 years	87
Calendar	semester
Profs interesting rating	99
Profs accessible rating	98
Most common reg class size	10–19 students
Most common lab size	10–19 students

MOST POPULAR MAJORS

Economics, political science, psychology

SPECIAL STUDY OPTIONS

Cross-registration, double major, dual enrollment, exchange student program (domestic), honors program, independent study, internships, student-designed major, study abroad, teacher certification program Combined degree programs: BA/MA, Brandeis MA IEF (International Economics and Finance). Special programs offered to physically disabled students include note-taking services, reader services, voice recorders, tutors.

ABOUT THE SCHOOL

Students spend a tremendous amount of time reading and writing papers at Wellesley. Spending part of junior year abroad is a staple of a Wellesley education. The Wellesley College Center for Work and Service (CWS) offers grants and stipends, which allow students to pursue what would otherwise be unpaid research and internship opportunities. When they get their diplomas, Wellesley graduates are able to take advantage of a tenaciously loyal network of more than 20,000 alums who are ready to help students with everything from arranging an interview to finding a place to live. Wellesley's close-knit student population collectively spends large segments of its weekdays in stressed-out study mode. Students don't spend all of their weekdays this way, though, because there is a ton of extracurricular activities available on this beautiful, state-of-the-art campus. Wellesley is home to more than 150 student organizations. Lectures, performances, and cultural events are endless. Wellesley is in a suburb of Boston and access to cultural, academic, social, business, and medical institutions is a powerful draw. On the weekends, many students head to Boston to hit the bars or to parties on nearby campuses. While enrolling just 2,300 undergraduates, Wellesley offers a remarkable array of more than 1,000 courses and fifty-four major programs; plus, "You can cross-register at MIT (and to a limited extent at Brandeis, Babson, and Olin.)" From research to internships to overseas studies, Wellesley "provides great resources and opportunities to all its students."

BANG FOR YOUR BUCK

With an endowment worth more than $1 billion, Wellesley is rolling in the riches. Admission is completely need-blind. If you get admitted (no easy task), Wellesley will meet 100 percent of your demonstrated financial need. Most financial aid comes in the form of a scholarship; it's free money and you'll never have to pay it back. Packaged student loan amounts are correlated to family income. No student will graduate with more than $12,825 in packaged student loans. Students from families with a calculated income between $60,000-$100,000 will graduate with no more than $8,600 in packaged student loans. And students from families with the greatest need, with a calculated income of $60,000 or less, will graduate with $0 in packaged student loans.

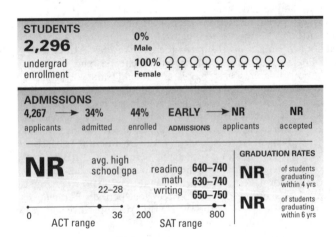

STUDENTS

2,296 undergrad enrollment

0% Male

100% Female ♀♀♀♀♀♀♀♀♀♀

ADMISSIONS

4,267 applicants → 34% admitted — 44% enrolled

EARLY ADMISSIONS → NR applicants — NR accepted

NR avg. high school gpa

ACT range: 22–28 (0–36)

SAT range (200–800): reading 640–740, math 630–740, writing 650–750

GRADUATION RATES

NR of students graduating within 4 yrs

NR of students graduating within 6 yrs

Wellesley College

FINANCIAL AID PHONE: 781-283-2360 • E-MAIL: ADMISSION@WELLESLEY.EDU • FAX: 781-283-3678 • WEBSITE: WWW.WELLESLEY.EDU

STUDENT BODY

While many students describe Wellesley as an "ethnically and financially diverse campus," a typical Wellesley undergraduate is "white, very liberal, very intelligent, [and] politically active, does a lot of community service, and has fashion sense like you wouldn't believe." Others describe their classmates as "intelligent, engaged, curious, quick-witted, articulate, politically aware, outspoken, thoughtful, passionate, ambitious, and poised." Wellesley women come in a "variety of packages, from women who brag about showering in the Science Library to those who party [in] Cambridge every weekend to rugby players and Shakespearean actors to sorority-girlesque 'society' members." Students tend to be very driven academically. Fortunately, no matter how busy they are, "People always try to make time for friends."

Why Students love Wellesley College

"It is a very friendly, respectful, intellectual environment where professors believe in your ability to do great things and the whole world seems to open up to you."

WHY STUDENTS LOVE WELLESLEY COLLEGE

Widely considered to be the top women's college in the nation, "Wellesley grooms its students to be strong leaders" through rigorous academic programs, "an intense intellectual environment," and "fierce commitment to social change." As a small college, Wellesley offers ample "personal attention" and a "comfortable environment;" however, choice and opportunity separate Wellesley from other similar institutions. Attracting "fiercely driven and deeply passionate women," a Wellesley education "can be stressful and intense." At the same time, "It is a very friendly, respectful, intellectual environment where professors believe in your ability to do great things and the whole world seems to open up to you."

GENERAL INFO

Activities: Choral groups, dance, drama/theater, jazz band, literary magazine, music ensembles, radio station, student government, student newspaper, student-run film society, symphony orchestra, yearbook, campus ministries, international student organization. **Organizations:** 160 registered organizations, 7 honor societies, 30 religious organizations. **Athletics (Intercollegiate):** *Women:* Basketball, crew/rowing, cross-country, diving, fencing, field hockey, golf, lacrosse, soccer, softball, squash, swimming, tennis, track/field, volleyball. **On-Campus Highlights:** Wang Campus Center, Davis Museum and Cultural Center, Clapp Library and Knapp Media Center, Science Center, Lake Waban.

BOTTOM LINE

The total cost for a year of tuition, fees, and room and board at Wellesley is over $51,000. However, this school has the financial resources to provide a tremendous amount of financial aid. Your aid package is likely to be quite extensive, and students leave with just $12,000 in loan debt on average. That's chump change for an education worth more than $200,000.

SELECTIVITY

Admissions Rating	**96**
# of applicants	4,267
% of applicants accepted	34
% of acceptees attending	44
# accepting a place on wait list	495
% admitted from wait list	0

FRESHMAN PROFILE

Range SAT Critical Reading	**640–740**
Range SAT Math	**630–740**
Range SAT Writing	**650–750**
Range ACT Composite	**28–31**
% graduated top 10% of class	**78**
% graduated top 25% of class	**45**
% graduated top 50% of class	**99**

DEADLINES

Regular Deadline	**1/15**
Normal registration	**no**

FACILITIES

Housing: Women's dorms, cooperative housing, apartments for single students, wellness housing, theme housing. *Special Academic Facilities/Equipment:* Clapp Library Davis Museum and Cultural Center Harambee House Houghton Memorial Chapel Hunnewell Arboretum, Keohane Sports Center Knapp Media and Technology Center Knapp Social Science Center Lake Waban Pforzheimer Learning and Teaching Center Ruth Nagel Jones Theatre Science Center. *Computers:* 100% of classrooms, 100% of dorms, 100% of libraries, 100% of dining areas, 100% of student union, 5% of common outdoor areas have wireless network access.

FINANCIAL FACTS

Financial Aid Rating	**98**
Annual tuition	$39,420
Room and Board	$12,284
Required Fees	$246
Books and supplies	$800
% frosh rec. need-based scholarship or grant aid	60
% UG rec.need-based scholarship or grant aid	61
% frosh rec. need-based self-help aid	53
% UG rec. need-based self-help aid	58
% frosh rec. any financial aid	61
% UG rec. any financial aid	63
% UG borrow to pay for school	58
Average cumulative indebtedness	$12,495

Wesleyan College

4760 Forsyth Road, Macon, GA 31210-4462 • Admissions: 478-477-1110 • Fax: 478-757-4030

CAMPUS LIFE

Quality of life Rating	85
Fire Safety Rating	60*
Green rating	78
Type of School	Private
Environment	City

STUDENTS

Total undergrad enrolllment	630
% Male to Female	0/100
% From out of state	7
% From public high school	81
% Live on Campus	82
% African American	28
% Asian	1
% Caucasian	45
% Hispanic	2
% International	20
# Of Countries Represented	21

ACADEMICS

Academic Rating	90
% Of students graduating within 4 years	51
% Of students graduating within 6 years	52
Calendar	semester
Profs interesting rating	95
Profs accessible rating	85
Most common reg class size	fewer than 10 students

MOST POPULAR MAJORS

Business, international business
psychology

HONORS PROGRAMS

Honors Program. Special programs offered to physically disabled students include note-taking services, tutors.

SPECIAL STUDY OPTIONS

Accelerated program, cross-registration, double major, dual enrollment, exchange student program (domestic), honors program, independent study, internships, liberal arts/career combination, student-designed major, study abroad, teacher certification program, weekend college, dual-degree engineering (3/2) with Georgia Tech, Auburn University and Mercer University.

ABOUT THE SCHOOL

Chartered in 1836, Wesleyan College was the first college in the world to grant degrees to women. "It is the first and best, and I wouldn't want my degree from anywhere else," exclaims one junior. Every year since then, Wesleyan women have been making history. "I chose Wesleyan College because it is a fantastic school and wonderfully known. I really enjoy going to a college with such a rich history." "There is a wonderful education program at this institution" with more than 30 majors and almost 30 minors on offer here. There are pre-professional programs galore as well. Dentistry, medicine, veterinary medicine, engineering, pharmacy, seminary–you name it, really. If you don't like any of the programs on offer, you can feel free to design your own. Being a small campus is a big advantage for Wesleyan students, fostering a climate for students to "[see] the world in a grain of sand." An exceptional faculty teaches small, seminar-style classes where there is plenty of opportunity for one-on-one interaction with professors. "Wesleyan faculty is one of the greatest strengths at the school."

Wesleyan's academic atmosphere is rigorous, and academic expectations are high. Students love it, though: "life is good at Wesleyan. We study, but we have social lives [too]." Wesleyan is a "small campus," and has an "intimate classroom setting [with] approachable professors." Before graduating, all seniors are required to have an internship. Upon graduation, a high percentage of Wesleyan's newly minted degree holders go on to graduate and professional school.

BANG FOR YOUR BUCK

On average, Wesleyan's tuition is about 50 percent less than the national average for private colleges. In addition, the university spends $4 million annually for student scholarships, grants, and campus jobs. Every year, Wesleyan awards nearly 100 scholarships, which are based on need. The average scholarship is more than $6,000. Scholarships recognize not only academic achievement but also leadership and artistic talent. Prospective students do not have to apply for individual scholarships. Wesleyan automatically matches prospective students with scholarships during the admissions process. One student maintains that the reason she chose Wesleyan was "the amount of money I was offered in scholarships. Wesleyan gave me the most merit-based scholarship money." Georgia residents with a 3.0 GPA or better qualify for the $3,000 HOPE scholarship and receive an additional $1,000 from the Georgia Tuition Equalization Program.

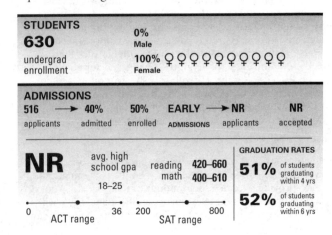

STUDENTS
630 undergrad enrollment

0% Male
100% Female ♀♀♀♀♀♀♀♀♀♀

ADMISSIONS

516	→ 40%	50%	EARLY ADMISSIONS	→ NR	NR
applicants	admitted	enrolled		applicants	accepted

NR avg. high school gpa

ACT range: 18–25 (scale 0–36)

SAT range (scale 200–800): reading 420–660; math 400–610

GRADUATION RATES

51% of students graduating within 4 yrs

52% of students graduating within 6 yrs

Wesleyan College

Financial Aid: : 478-757-5205 • E-mail: admissions@wesleyancollege.edu • Website: www.wesleyancollege.edu

STUDENT BODY

There are just 600 undergraduates at Wesleyan College, yet "Wesleyan students come from all kinds of backgrounds, countries, ethnic groups, and religions." Within the Wesleyan community, you'll meet "artsy kids, hippies, science geeks, religious girls, political activists." "Wesleyan truly embraces how you are, no matter who you are." A junior attests, "Everybody is different here, but since diversity is so celebrated, there are very few people who just don't fit in." "The top students are strong-willed [and] outspoken and passionately love the work they do." At the same time, the average student "maintains a balance between their academics, extracurricular activities, and community service." On that note, most students are involved in their school and community, as the student body's small size "allows for you to be involved in student activities as much as you want."

Why Students love Wesleyan College

"The college itself is beautiful, and the majority of students on campus are very lively and active."

WHY STUDENTS LOVE WESLEYAN COLLEGE

The students attending this school are focused first and foremost on "sisterhood." One student says that "life [at Wesleyan] is that of a normal college student: testing the limits that are set upon you while getting a good education." "There is always something to do on campus (meetings, athletic games, theater shows, art exhibits, and much more)." But keep in mind that "Wesleyan is all about promoting education for women through sisterhood, intimate education allowing women to reach their potential." It's an "underrated school with an awesome, supportive environment no matter who you are." Although some students maintain that "sometimes there isn't much to do on campus;" Macon is always nearby: it's a "fun town and there is a lot to do if you just put yourself out there and make some friends." However, in keeping with the rigorous schedule of the sisterhood, there is typically "never any down time for any student at Wesleyan. If you're bored, you're not doing something right."

GENERAL INFO

Activities: Choral groups, dance, drama/theater, literary magazine, music ensembles, student government, student newspaper, yearbook, campus ministries, international student organization. **Organizations:** 40 registered organizations, 10 honor societies, 5 religious organizations. **Athletics (Intercollegiate):** *Women:* Basketball, cross-country, equestrian sports, soccer, softball, tennis, volleyball. **On-Campus Highlights:** Historic quad of buildings Georgian brick design, Equestrian and Fitness Centers, Lake, Residence Halls, Art Galleries. **Environmental Initiatives:** Energy Star purchasing policy in accordance with the President's Climate Commitment. Campus-wide recycling program.

BOTTOM LINE

At Wesleyan College, the total cost for tuition and fees and room and board comes to about $27,500 each year. That's certainly not chump change, but if you look around you'll find that it's much less than the average private school, especially when you add in the generous financial aid available here.

SELECTIVITY

Admissions Rating	**85**
# of applicants	516
% of applicants accepted	40
% of acceptees attending	50
# accepting a place on wait list	0

FRESHMAN PROFILE

Range SAT Critical Reading	**420–660**
Range SAT Math	**400–610**
Range ACT Composite	**18–25**

DEADLINES

Regular Deadline	**3/1**
Normal registration	**yes**

FACILITIES

Housing: Special housing for disabled students, women's dorms, apartments for single students. Students required to live on campus unless married or living with family in the local area. *Special Academic Facilities/Equipment:* Art and history museums, special collection of Georgiana and Americana, on-campus equestrian center. *Computers:* 80% of classrooms, 100% of libraries, 100% of dining areas, 100% of student union, 50% of common outdoor areas have wireless network access.

FINANCIAL FACTS

Financial Aid Rating	**86**
Annual tuition	$18,500
Room and Board	$8,200
Books and supplies	$1,500
% frosh rec. need-based scholarship or grant aid	70
% UG rec.need-based scholarship or grant aid	61
% frosh rec. non-need-based scholarship or grant aid	22
% UG rec. non-need-based scholarship or grant aid	15
% frosh rec. need-based self-help aid	48
% UG rec. need-based self-help aid	46
% frosh rec. any financial aid	96
% UG rec. any financial aid	91
% UG borrow to pay for school	62
Average cumulative indebtedness	$20,896

Wesleyan University

70 Wyllys Avenue, Middletown, CT 06459-0265 • Admissions: 860-685-3000 • Fax: 860-685-3001

CAMPUS LIFE

Quality of life Rating	87
Fire Safety Rating	84
Green rating	85
Type of School	Private
Environment	Town

STUDENTS

Total undergrad enrolllment	2,837
% Male to Female	49/51
% From out of state	92
% From public high school	53
% Live on Campus	98
# of Fraternities	9
# of Sororities	4
% African American	6
% Asian	7
% Caucasian	56
% Hispanic	9
% International	7
# Of Countries Represented	42

ACADEMICS

Academic Rating	98
% Of students graduating within 4 years	88
% Of students graduating within 6 years	93
Calendar	semester
Profs interesting rating	88
Profs accessible rating	94
Most common reg class size	10–19 students
Most common lab size	10–19 students

MOST POPULAR MAJORS
Economics, psychology

SPECIAL STUDY OPTIONS

Cross-registration, double major, dual enrollment, exchange student program (domestic), honors program, independent study, student-designed major, study abroad Combined degree programs:

ABOUT THE COLLEGE

Wesleyan University is a member of the historic Little Three colleges along with Amherst and Williams Colleges, and has long been known as one of the "Little Ivies." Just like an Ivy League school, Wesleyan is home to exceptional academics, fantastic resources, and brilliant students. "Wesleyan was a clear fit for me based on the artistic and diverse environment and the academic possibilities offered," says one junior. There are no required core courses at Wesleyan, giving each student the opportunity to chart their own intellectual path. "Academically, the university is in ranks with the most elite American universities, but it has a special social quirkiness that really sets it apart." As a result, the university attracts students with a high level of intellectual interest and curiosity. "I knew it would allow me to grow," says one student, "[and] become someone that I would look up to. At other schools, I just would have been comfortable and would have stayed the same." Professors are passionate about their work, and are always available to meet with students outside of class. Breaking bread at a professor's home is not uncommon for students. "Whether in a class of seven, or a class of 100, my professors have always gone out of their way to help me in whatever I was struggling with; or sometimes just to get to know me," tells one senior. Wesleyan's rigorous academics produce the goods: the university produces more history doctorates per undergraduate history major than any other college or university in the United States and medical school acceptances historically have averaged above 90 percent.

Wesleyan students are nothing if not eclectic, and the many ways in which they entertain themselves outside of class reflects their diverse interests and passions. "Wesleyan is [about] staying up all night in the library studying with friends, loving it, and sledding down hills on cafeteria trays while quoting Hegel and Homer Simpson." Whether engaging in deep intellectual conversations or gathering at traditional frat party, Wesleyan students know how to kick back and have fun. The campus is home to dozens of student-

BANG FOR YOUR BUCK

There's a Wesleyan wherever you go, and a Wesleyan degree will open doors for you for the rest of your life. The university started a Military Veterans Endowed Scholarship Fund in the fall of 2008. Recipients will have no loans in the financial aid package and may graduate with $0 loan indebtedness for the time they are enrolled at Wesleyan. A student reveals that she "received a very good financial aid packet." The average freshman grant is $27,000.

STUDENTS
2,837 undergrad enrollment
49% Male ♂♂♂♂♂♂♂♂♂♂
51% Female ♀♀♀♀♀♀♀♀♀♀

ADMISSIONS
10,657 applicants → **21%** admitted — **34%** enrolled
EARLY ADMISSIONS → **NR** applicants — **NR** accepted

3.77 avg. high school gpa

ACT range (0–36): 30–33

SAT range (200–800): reading 635–740, math 660–740, writing 650–750

GRADUATION RATES
88% of students graduating within 4 yrs
93% of students graduating within 6 yrs

Wesleyan University

Financial Aid: 860-685-2800 • E-mail: admissions@wesleyan.edu • Website: www.wesleyan.edu

STUDENT BODY

Undergrads at Wesleyan are fairly adamant about the fact that they cannot "be pigeon-holed." While many insist "there are no typical students," others concede that there "are a few traits that often connect [everyone]." Most people "are interested in engaging with the world around them, often in hopes of improving it." Indeed this is a "passionate" group who are very "socially conscious, politically aware, and [into] activism." Moreover, Wesleyan students are "driven," "intellectually curious" and "eager to learn and experience new things." These are kids who are "serious about academics" but also know how to "relax and have fun." They are also "very proud to be part of a diverse community" and are always excited to "meet new people."

Why Students love Wesleyan University

"Academically, the university is in ranks with the most elite American universities, but it has a special social quirkiness that really sets it apart."

WHY STUDENTS LOVE WESLEYAN UNIVERSITY

"The greatest strengths of my school are the openness, the ubiquitous intellectual curiosity, and the unending desire to change the world," says an incoming freshman. Another student mentions that Wesleyan "personifies the cliché of 'love what you do and do what you love.'" One student describes how great Wesleyan faculty is: "I have had incredibly brilliant professors. They are clearly well-versed in their respective areas. But what has impressed me most is how down to earth they are. They are understanding, accessible, and truly care about you and your studies. The vast majority of the time the lectures and discussions are extremely intellectually stimulating." One student says that "when we look at something that we cannot describe because it's outrageously creative, intellectual, and riveting, we say merely 'It's Wesleyan.'"

GENERAL INFO

Activities: Choral groups, concert band, dance, drama/theater, jazz band, literary magazine, music ensembles, musical theater, pep band, radio station, student government, student newspaper, student-run film society, symphony orchestra, yearbook, campus ministries. **Organizations:** 220 registered organizations, 2 honor societies, 10 religious organizations. 9 fraternities, 4 sororities. **Athletics (Intercollegiate):** *Men:* Baseball, basketball, crew/rowing, cross-country, diving, football, golf, ice hockey, lacrosse, soccer, squash, swimming, tennis, track/field (outdoor), track/field (indoor), wrestling. *Women:* Basketball, crew/rowing, cross-country, diving, field hockey, ice hockey, lacrosse, soccer, softball, squash, swimming, tennis, track/field (outdoor), track/field (indoor), volleyball. **On-Campus Highlights:** Center for the Arts, Freeman Athletic Center, Center for Film Studies, Olin Memorial Library, Van Vleck Observatory, Freeman East Asian Studies Center.

BOTTOM LINE

The total retail price here for tuition, room and board, and everything else comes to about $55,000 per year. Financial aid here is beyond generous, though, and the full financial need of all undergraduate students, is met with a combination of loans, part-time employment, and grants.

SELECTIVITY

Admissions Rating	**98**
# of applicants	10,657
% of applicants accepted	21
% of acceptees attending	34
# accepting a place on wait list	645
% admitted from wait list	14

FRESHMAN PROFILE

Range SAT Critical Reading	**635–740**
Range SAT Math	**660–740**
Range SAT Writing	**650–750**
Range ACT Composite	**30–33**
Average HS GPA	**3.77**
% graduated top 10% of class	**68**
% graduated top 25% of class	**91**
% graduated top 50% of class	**99**

DEADLINES

Regular Deadline	**1/1**
Normal registration	**no**

FACILITIES

Housing: Coed dorms, special housing for disabled students, fraternity/sorority housing, apartments for married students, apartments for single students, wellness housing, theme housing. *Special Academic Facilities/Equipment:* Art center, art galleries, Center for Afro-American studies, East Asian Studies Center, Cinema Archives, concert hall, public affairs center, language lab, electron microscope, observatory, nuclear magnetic resonance spectrometers. *Computers:* 90% of classrooms, 100% of dorms, 90% of libraries, 90% of dining areas, 100% of student union, 90% of common outdoor areas have wireless network access.

FINANCIAL FACTS

Financial Aid Rating	**98**
Annual tuition	$43,404
Room and Board	$12,032
Required Fees	$300
% frosh rec. need-based scholarship or grant aid	44
% UG rec.need-based scholarship or grant aid	43
% frosh rec. need-based self-help aid	47
% UG rec. need-based self-help aid	48
% frosh rec. any financial aid	47
% UG rec. any financial aid	48
% UG borrow to pay for school	39
Average cumulative indebtedness	$29,227

Wheaton College

501 College Avenue, Wheaton, IL 60187 • Admissions: 630-752-5005 • Fax: 630-752-5285

CAMPUS LIFE

Quality of life Rating	97
Fire Safety Rating	88
Green rating	76
Type of School	Private
Environment	Town

STUDENTS

Total undergrad enrolllment	2,406
% Male to Female	49/51
% From out of state	76
% From public high school	57
% Live on Campus	90
% African American	3
% Asian	8
% Caucasian	83
% Hispanic	4
% International	1
# Of Countries Represented	26

ACADEMICS

Academic Rating	89
% Of students graduating within 4 years	79
% Of students graduating within 6 years	88
Calendar	semester
Profs interesting rating	90
Profs accessible rating	91
Most common reg class size	10–19 students
Most common lab size	10–19 students

MOST POPULAR MAJORS

Business/managerial, economics, english language and literature, health services

HONORS PROGRAMS

Some departments offer qualified students to submit an honors project.

SPECIAL STUDY OPTIONS

Cross-registration, double major, exchange student program (domestic), independent study, internships, liberal arts/career combination, student-designed major, study abroad, teacher certification program.

ABOUT THE SCHOOL

A private, non-denominational college, with rigorous academics taught from a Christian perspective, Wheaton is "a prestigious academic institution that is respected for the positive impact that its graduates have on the world," according to one student. Undergrads say they enjoy the "academically challenging Christian liberal lrts school with good athletics and a fun environment," and that Wheaton provides all of these things with a "remarkable and unique effectiveness." "Wheaton is serious about both the Christian life and academics, while most schools are one or the other," states another student. Undergrads are further impressed that "it is the only Christian college that I felt was academically credible," and that Wheaton is "a place where my faith would be buoyed, not stifled."

"For Christ and His Kingdom" is Wheaton's motto. "Excelling academically in a way that is up to par with the top secular universities while upholding core Christian values," with "specific and intentional focus on personal development," according to members of the student body, Wheaton helps students explore issues concerning what it means to be a citizen of an increasingly global society while "teaching students to think critically and live morally in America today." Wheaton draws students from over 50 countries, "which creates a rich and challenging learning and growing atmosphere." The school makes a "serious push for true diversity, and not just diverse representation," marvels another undergrad. Programs like HNGR (Human Needs and Global Resources), focus on internship experiences in developing nations. Students love that travel abroad opportunities are numerous, providing "many valuable resources for those interested in or considering pursuing world missions," and that Bible and Theology faculty are at "the top of the field." Instructors are "definitely demanding. You have to show up and do the work;" "even general education classes can be challenging."

BANG FOR YOUR BUCK

Wheaton is committed to making education accessible for all students regardless of their socio-economic status and offers substantial grant aid. Merit awards include a number of scholarship opportunities for academically successful students, minority students, music majors and international students. Wheaton also has a debt (loan) forgiveness program (Bennett Fund) for anyone planning to serve for a minimum of four years in overseas missions. The number of students receiving need-based scholarship or grant aid is right around 50%. Non-need-based scholarship or grant aid is under 20%.

STUDENTS

2,406 undergrad enrollment

49% Male ♂♂♂♂♂♂♂♂♂♂

51% Female ♀♀♀♀♀♀♀♀♀♀

ADMISSIONS

2,010 applicants	→ 66% admitted	45% enrolled	EARLY ADMISSIONS →	NR applicants	NR accepted

3.73 avg. high school gpa

26–32 — ACT range (0–36)

reading 600–730
math 610–700
writing 590–710
SAT range (200–800)

GRADUATION RATES

79% of students graduating within 4 yrs

88% of students graduating within 6 yrs

Wheaton College

FINANCIAL AID: 630-752-5021 • E-MAIL: ADMISSIONS@WHEATON.EDU • WEBSITE: WWW.WHEATON.EDU

STUDENT BODY

Pretty much the entirety of Wheaton is composed of "academically strong, driven, and Christian students," and the phrase "type-A personality" is oft-used. The school draws students from all over the country (including "quite a lot of homeschooled and international students"), and the diversity isn't as strong as some students would like, though "they are making a lot of efforts to change that in the admissions office." Students at Wheaton "take their studies extremely seriously and work very hard to keep high grades," but most still get involved with student activities, ministries, and sports, and enjoy the groups of friends that form when people share a "common identity." In their downtime, people "have a respectful and creative sense of fun and do not waste their time." All in all, "Most students find some way to fit in."

Why Students love Wheaton College

"A place where my faith would be buoyed, not stifled."

WHY STUDENTS LOVE WHEATON COLLEGE

"The freshman experience, including Passage at Honey Rock and Residence Life, is excellently put together," says one undergrad. "Pursuing academic excellence influenced by our faith in God in an environment of grace–but we still have fun," says another happy resident. Still others add that Wheaton "prepares Christians of today for being a light in the world of tomorrow;" and feel that "everyone has a certain glow around them." The school has nationally respected varsity and club sports programs; the weight room even "has a verse to remind us what we are doing is for a greater purpose." Built on the foundation of the Community Covenant, "they hold people accountable for their actions" at Wheaton. There is a strong commitment to sustainable practices, and with a no-alcohol/drug policy, the college maintains a very positive atmosphere for learning and creativity.

GENERAL INFO

Activities: Choral groups, concert band, dance, drama/theater, jazz band, literary magazine, music ensembles, musical theater, opera, pep band, radio station, student government, student newspaper, student-run film society, symphony orchestra, television station, yearbook, campus ministries, international student organization. **Organizations:** 85 registered organizations, 13 honor societies, 12 religious organizations. **Athletics (Intercollegiate):** *Men:* Baseball, basketball, cross-country, football, golf, soccer, swimming, tennis, track/field (outdoor), track/field (indoor), wrestling. *Women:* Basketball, cross-country, golf, soccer, softball, swimming, tennis, track/ field (outdoor), track/field (indoor), volleyball, water polo.

BOTTOM LINE

Through the generous support of alumni and friends who subsidize a large portion of the actual educational costs, Wheaton is able to stay below the national average for a top tier liberal arts institution. Annual tuition is $27,316; room and board will add another $7,900. Books and supplies will run about $800. One student notes, "The thing that really decided it for me, however, was the amount of financial aid they were willing to give me." Another undergrad mentioned, "I will be graduating with NO debt thanks to Wheaton's generous financial aid package." The average cumulative indebtedness is $21,241.

SELECTIVITY

Admissions Rating	**94**
# of applicants	2,010
% of applicants accepted	66
% of acceptees attending	45
# accepting a place on wait list	126
% admitted from wait list	46

FRESHMAN PROFILE

Range SAT Critical Reading	**600–730**
Range SAT Math	**610–700**
Range SAT Writing	**590–710**
Range ACT Composite	**26–32**
Average HS GPA	**3.73**
% graduated top 10% of class	**58**
% graduated top 25% of class	**82**
% graduated top 50% of class	**98**

DEADLINES

Regular Deadline	**1/10**
Normal registration	**no**

FACILITIES

Housing: Coed dorms, men's dorms, women's dorms, apartments for married students, cooperative housing, apartments for single students, housing for disabled provided as needed. *Special Academic Facilities/ Equipment:* World evangelism museum, language lab, observatory, *Computers:* 10% of classrooms, 100% of dorms, 100% of libraries, 100% of dining areas, 100% of student union, 75% of common outdoor areas have wireless network access.

FINANCIAL FACTS

Financial Aid Rating	**81**
Annual tuition $28,960	
Room and Board	$8,220
Books and supplies	$816
% frosh rec. need-based scholarship or grant aid	52
% UG rec.need-based scholarship or grant aid	51
% frosh rec. non-need-based scholarship or grant aid	18
% UG rec. non-need-based scholarship or grant aid	16
% frosh rec. need-based self-help aid	51
% UG rec. need-based self-help aid	50
% frosh rec. any financial aid	76
% UG rec. any financial aid	71
% UG borrow to pay for school	50
Average cumulative indebtedness	$21,241

Whitman College

345 Boyer Ave, Walla Walla, WA 99362 • Admissions: 509-527-5176 • Fax: 509-527-4967

CAMPUS LIFE

Quality of life Rating	97
Fire Safety Rating	74
Green rating	82
Type of School	Private
Environment	Town

STUDENTS

Total undergrad enrolllment	1,535
% Male to Female	42/58
% From out of state	62
% From public high school	75
% Live on Campus	67
# of Fraternities	4
# of Sororities	3
% African American	1
% Asian	7
% Caucasian	68
% Hispanic	6
% International	3
# Of Countries Represented	29

ACADEMICS

Academic Rating	98
% Of students graduating within 4 years	80
% Of students graduating within 6 years	85
Calendar	semester
Profs interesting rating	99
Profs accessible rating	99
Most common reg class size	10–19 students
Most common lab size	20–29 students

MOST POPULAR MAJORS

Biology, English language and literature, political science

SPECIAL STUDY OPTIONS

Accelerated program, cooperative education program, cross-registration, double major, dual enrollment, exchange student program (domestic), honors program, independent study, liberal arts/career combination, student-designed major, study abroad, undergraduate research conference.

ABOUT THE SCHOOL

Whitman College attracts students who represent the Whitman mosaic: down-to-earth, high achievers with diverse interests. One student says, "I wanted to attend a college where I would be intellectually challenged and stimulated. Now that I'm a second semester senior, I can say that what I've learned in my classes at Whitman will benefit me for the rest of my life." The college is known for combining academic excellence with an unpretentious, collaborative culture, which includes "professors who take the time to chat with students, invite them to dinner in their homes, organize field trips, [and] enlist students to help them in their research projects." For a real-life example, look no further than Whitman's tradition of awarding summer, annual, and per-semester grants for student-faculty research collaboration, aimed at turning students into a "whole, intelligent, [and] interesting person, to the best possible extent of your ability." "Internships, study abroad, work, research opportunities (in and out of the sciences) are abundant at Whitman. Grants are easily accessible for those who have valid reason to seek them." The recently established Whitman Internship Grant program provides a stipend of approximately $2,000 to students completing non-paid summer internships that are relevant to their educational goals and career interests. It allows them to get creative with internships and to take part in opportunities that best match their academic or career interests. "Whitman has so many strengths, but I think the most important is that the students and faculty at Whitman promote and maintain a great, collaborative, and intellectually active atmosphere for academics," says one student.

BANG FOR YOUR BUCK

A full suite of scholarships are on offer here, covering up to the full cost of tuition and fees for four years. Highlights include the Whitman awards, which are renewable, four-year merit-based scholarships, ranging from $8000 to $12,000 to entering students who have excelled academically. Whitman's Paul Garrett and Claire Sherwood Memorial Scholarships range from $2,500 to $45,000 depending on demonstrated financial need. The scholarship includes a trip to NYC to visit corporate headquarters and graduate schools on the East Coast. The Eells Scholarship covers the full cost of tuition for four years, and includes a research grant. Whitman's outside scholarship policy allows students to add scholarships they receive from non-Whitman sources on top of the college's awarded scholarship.

STUDENTS

1,535 undergrad enrollment

42% Male ♂♂♂♂♂♂♂♂

58% Female ♀♀♀♀♀♀♀♀♀♀♀♀

ADMISSIONS

3,164 applicants → 47% admitted; 28% enrolled

EARLY ADMISSIONS: NR applicants → NR accepted

3.80 avg. high school gpa

NR — ACT range (0–36)

SAT range (200–800): reading 610–720; math 610–720; writing 610–719

GRADUATION RATES

80% of students graduating within 4 yrs

85% of students graduating within 6 yrs

FINANCIAL AID: 509-527-5178 • E-MAIL: ADMISSION@WHITMAN.EDU • WEBSITE: WWW.WHITMAN.EDU

STUDENT BODY

It's a sociable bunch at Whitman, where most students "are interested in trying new things and meeting new people" and "everyone seems to have a weird interest or talent or passion." The quirky Whitties "usually have a strong opinion about something," and one freshman refers to her classmates as ""cool nerds." Diversity has risen steadily over the past several years, as the school has made an effort to recruit beyond the typical "mid- to upper-class and white" contingent. Everyone here is pretty outdoorsy and environmentally aware ("to the point where you almost feel guilty for printing an assignment"), and a significant number of students have won fellowships and scholarships such as the Fulbright, Watson, Truman, and Udall."

Why Students love Whitman College

"Whitman has so many strengths, but I think the most important is that the students and faculty at Whitman promote and maintain a great, collaborative, and intellectually active atmosphere for academics."

WHY STUDENTS LOVEWHITMAN COLLEGE

One student confesses that "Whitman is my secret garden: all the things I love about school (awesome professors and interesting classes) and all the fun stuff I want in a college experience tucked away in the naturally beautiful Walla Walla valley." "Whitman creates an intimate community of learners who strive to not only learn about the world around them, but also do good for what surrounds them." Another student says that "I feel at home when I'm at Whitman. The professors are people I can talk to about school, life, and any difficulties I may be having." In regards to faculty, one senior confides that "generally, Whitman professors are... really caring: I've had tea and dinner outside of class with [them]." "Whitman feels like summer camp, but somehow I am working harder and learning more than I have in my life," says one student.

GENERAL INFO

Activities: Choral groups, concert band, dance, drama/theater, jazz band, literary magazine, music ensembles, musical theater, radio station, student government, student newspaper, student-run film society, symphony orchestra, campus ministries, international student organization. **Organizations:** 80 registered organizations, 3 honor societies, 7 religious organizations. 4 fraternities, 3 sororities. **Athletics (Intercollegiate):** *Men:* Baseball, basketball, cross-country, golf, soccer, swimming, tennis. *Women:* Basketball, cross-country, golf, soccer, swimming, tennis, volleyball. **On-Campus Highlights:** Reid Campus Center, Penrose Library.

BOTTOM LINE

Whitman College is one of the nation's top liberal arts colleges. The total cost of tuition, room and board, and everything else adds up to about $48,500 per year. Both need-based and merit aid is available to help offset costs. Every spring, Whitman offers a financial planning night that addresses not only loans but also financial issues for graduating students to be aware of. Whitman offers internships during the summer that allows the students to work in the same area as their degree and hopefully helps with employment when they graduate. Whitman also meets 100% of the student's need with the Garrett/Sherwood scholarships and the President's scholarships.

SELECTIVITY

Admissions Rating	**96**
# of applicants	3,164
% of applicants accepted	47
% of acceptees attending	28
# accepting a place on wait list	188
% admitted from wait list	1

FRESHMAN PROFILE

Range SAT Critical Reading	**610–720**
Range SAT Math	**610–720**
Range SAT Writing	**610–710**
Average HS GPA	**3.80**
% graduated top 10% of class	**62**
% graduated top 25% of class	**99**
% graduated top 50% of class	**100**

DEADLINES

Regular Deadline	**1/15**
Normal registration	**yes**

FACILITIES

Housing: Coed dorms, special housing for international students, women's dorms, fraternity/sorority housing, apartments for single students, theme housing. Interest houses. *Special Academic Facilities/ Equipment:* Art gallery, planetarium, outdoor observatory, outdoor sculpture walk, technology/video-conferencing center, indoor and outdoor rock-climbing walls, organic garden. *Computers:* 100% of classrooms, 100% of dorms, 100% of libraries, 100% of dining areas, 100% of student union, 40% of common outdoor areas have wireless network access.

FINANCIAL FACTS

Financial Aid Rating	**92**
Annual tuition	$40,180
Room and Board	$10,160
Required Fees	$316
Books and supplies	$1,400
% frosh rec. need-based scholarship or grant aid	43
% UG rec.need-based scholarship or grant aid	40
% frosh rec. non-need-based scholarship or grant aid	54
% UG rec. non-need-based scholarship or grant aid	47
% frosh rec. need-based self-help aid	25
% UG rec. need-based self-help aid	17
% frosh rec. any financial aid	76
% UG rec. any financial aid	78
% UG borrow to pay for school	50
Average cumulative indebtedness	$14,285

Wofford College

429 North Church Street, Spartanburg, SC 29303-3663 • Admissions: 864-597-4130 • Fax: 864-597-4147

CAMPUS LIFE

Quality of life Rating	56
Fire Safety Rating	78
Green rating	82
Type of School	Private
Environment	City

STUDENTS

Total undergrad enrollment	1,525
% Male to Female	52/48
% From out of state	40
% From public high school	67
% Live on Campus	94
# of Fraternities	8
# of Sororities	4
% African American	7
% Asian	3
% Caucasian	82
% Hispanic	2
% International	1
# Of Countries Represented	16

ACADEMICS

Academic Rating	93
% Of students graduating within 4 years	78
% Of students graduating within 6 years	82
Calendar	4-1-4
Profs interesting rating	97
Profs accessible rating	96
Most common reg class size	10–19 students
Most common lab size	20–29 students

MOST POPULAR MAJORS

Biology, business.managerial economics, finance

SPECIAL STUDY OPTIONS

Accelerated program, cross-registration, double major, dual enrollment, independent study, internships, student-designed major, study abroad, teacher certification program, Presidential International Scholar program; "Success Initiative, Bonner Scholars, Community of Scholars, Learning Communities and Creative Writing Concentration.

ABOUT THE SCHOOL

Wofford College, a small liberal arts school in South Carolina, offers beauty, brains and brawn. Its stunning campus, which is designated as an arboretum, serves as an idyllic backdrop to an academic powerhouse with standout programs in biology, pre-med, and pre-law. One of Wofford's unique assets is the January Interim, a four-week term during which students get a chance to explore a non-traditional class on topics that vary from knitting to fencing to Chinese calligraphy to scuba diving. The school also strongly encourages its students to study abroad and offers support such as funding to pay for students to travel and advice on how to design a program that works with their areas of study. The student body is highly active and forms close relationships with the administration and teaching faculty. One student observes, "The student government on campus does a really great job of voicing student complaints or ideas for improvement to the administration. The professors are excellent and my academic experience has been challenging but rewarding."

Outside of the classroom, Greek life dominates the social scene with many of Wofford's students enjoying continuous parties held on fraternity row (The Row). For those who seek stimulation outside of the Greek party scene, the school is chock full of activities such as dances, Division I athletics, hot air balloon rides, theater productions, paintball, and concerts which are presented as part of the Troubador Series. Wofford students take their football games very seriously and traditionally dress up for the events although casual attire is becoming more popular. With so many activities to choose from, students tend to socialize on campus on the weekends, which helps to build a close-knit community. For those who want to explore life off campus, they can easily travel to Charlotte, Charleston, and Atlanta to find numerous options for dining, shopping, and nightlife.

BANG FOR YOUR BUCK

Close to 90 percent of the students at Wofford receive some form of financial aid, which includes federal loans, state and private scholarships, institutional grants, and work-study options. The school also offers the Bonner Scholars program, which provides students with four-year scholarships and engages them in service work. Additional services provided by school include The Success Initiative, a four-year scholarship program focused on creative problem-solving skills as well as The Institute for Professional Development's five-week summer program to help students prepare for the professional workplace. The college also works to ensure that a high percentage of its students can study internationally.

STUDENTS
1,525 undergrad enrollment
52% Male ♂♂♂♂♂♂♂♂♂♂
48% Female ♀♀♀♀♀♀♀♀♀♀

ADMISSIONS
2,595 applicants → 62% admitted — 27% enrolled
EARLY ADMISSIONS → NR applicants — NR accepted

3.56 avg. high school gpa

ACT range (0–36): 22–28

SAT range (200–800):
reading 560–675
math 590–680
writing 545–650

GRADUATION RATES
78% of students graduating within 4 yrs
82% of students graduating within 6 yrs

Wofford College

FINANCIAL AID: 864-597-4160 • E-MAIL: ADMISSION@WOFFORD.EDU • WEBSITE: WWW.WOFFORD.EDU

STUDENT BODY

Easily characterized with their "polo and pearls," Wofford undergrads admit the typical student is "Southern, Protestant, rich," and heavily "involved in Greek life." However, fret not if you don't find any of those adjectives applicable. A junior assures us "everyone interacts together, and there are no exclusive groups on campus." Indeed, most people are "friendly...and outgoing," and even atypical students will find it "easy to fit in...and get involved." Regardless of background, Wofford undergrads are an intellectual and curious lot. By and large, they tend to be academically "driven... and hardworking" and "motivated to do well" both in and out of the classroom. A few students bemoan the fact that Wofford seems to lack diversity, citing that most of their peers are "Caucasian" and "conservative." While others concede to this fact, they are quick to highlight this is slowly changing.

Why Students love Wofford College

"We work and play as a community and we, with pleasure and humility, devote all of our energies to the pursuit of knowledge."

WHY STUDENTS LOVE WOFFORD COLLEGE

Students at Wofford are not shy about extolling the virtues of their school. One student describes Wofford as "The utopia of academic, social and personal interaction for Southern ladies and gentlemen–deeply rooted in tradition." Another student raves that it is "the best way to achieve a quintessential education while achieving the highest level of academics, traveling the world, and making the friends of a lifetime."Students also place a high premium on the sense of community that develops at their school. One student observes, "We work and play as a community and we, with pleasure and humility, devote all of our energies to the pursuit of knowledge." This sentiment is echoed by another student who effuses, "Wofford is about relationships: relationships between you and other students, between the professors and their students, even the faculty and staff and the students; everyone knows each other and is willing to help each other all the time."

GENERAL INFO

Activities: Choral groups, concert band, dance, drama/theater, literary magazine, music ensembles, pep band, student government, student newspaper, yearbook, campus ministries. **Organizations:** 105 registered organizations, 10 honor societies, 8 religious organizations. 8 fraternities, 4 sororities. **Athletics (Intercollegiate):** *Men:* Baseball, basketball, cross-country, football, golf, riflery, soccer, tennis, track/field (outdoor), track/field (indoor). *Women:* Basketball, cross-country, golf, riflery, soccer, tennis, track/field (outdoor), track/field (indoor), volleyball. **On-Campus Highlights:** The Roger Milliken Arboretum, Roger Milliken Science Center/Great Oaks, Main Building/Leonard Auditorium, Franklin W. Olin Building.

BOTTOM LINE

For tuition and room and board, the price tag of an education at Wofford comes out to about $42,000, and students will need a little more than $1,200 to cover the cost of books and supplies. But as we said earlier: almost 9 out of 10 students receive some form of student aid.

SELECTIVITY

Admissions Rating	**93**
# of applicants	2,595
% of applicants accepted	62
% of acceptees attending	27
# accepting a place on wait list	49
% admitted from wait list	16

FRESHMAN PROFILE

Range SAT Critical Reading	**560–675**
Range SAT Math	**590–680**
Range SAT Writing	**545–650**
Range ACT Composite	**22–28**
Average HS GPA	**3.56**
% graduated top 10% of class	**56**
% graduated top 25% of class	**80**
% graduated top 50% of class	**98**

DEADLINES

Regular Deadline	**2/1**
Normal registration	**yes**

FACILITIES

Housing: Coed dorms, apartments for single students, wellness housing. *Special Academic Facilities/Equipment:* Campus is an Arboretum, Art galleries, Franklin W. Olin Building (teaching technology center), Milliken Science Center. *Computers:* 100% of classrooms, 10% of dorms, 100% of libraries, 100% of dining areas, 100% of student union, 40% of common outdoor areas have wireless network access.

FINANCIAL FACTS

Financial Aid Rating	**89**
Annual tuition	$33,190
Room and Board	$9,375
Books and supplies	$1,200
% frosh rec. need-based scholarship or grant aid	57
% UG rec.need-based scholarship or grant aid	55
% frosh rec. non-need-based scholarship or grant aid	20
% UG rec. non-need-based scholarship or grant aid	19
% frosh rec. need-based self-help aid	30
% UG rec. need-based self-help aid	29
% frosh rec. any financial aid	91
% UG rec. any financial aid	88
% UG borrow to pay for school	47
Average cumulative indebtedness	$23,103

Best Value Public Schools

Appalachian State University

Office of Admissions, ASU Box 32004, Boone, NC 28608-2004 • Admissions: 828-262-2120 • Fax: 828-262-3296

CAMPUS LIFE

Quality of life Rating	88
Fire Safety Rating	86
Green rating	98
Type of School	Public
Environment	Village

STUDENTS

Total undergrad enrolllment	15,137
% Male to Female	48/52
% From out of state	8
% Live on Campus	34
# of Fraternities	18
# of Sororities	11
% African American	3
% Asian	1
% Caucasian	87
% Hispanic	3
% International	1
# Of Countries Represented	47

ACADEMICS

Academic Rating	76
% Of students graduating within 4 years	37
% Of students graduating within 6 years	65
Calendar	semester
Most common reg class size	20–29 students
Most common lab size	20–29 students

MOST POPULAR MAJORS

Business administration and management, general elementary education and teaching

HONORS PROGRAMS

Heltzer Honors Program offers promising and highly motivated students opportunities by providing honors classes in many fields.

SPECIAL STUDY OPTIONS

Special programs offered to physically disabled students include note-taking services, reader services, voice recorders, tutors.

ABOUT THE SCHOOL

Appalachian State University prepares students for the future through high-quality programs that teach students to adapt to new environments, to integrate knowledge from diverse sources, and to continue learning throughout their lives. A senior says, "I was originally here for the chemistry program, but then I switched my focus to English and anthropology. This school is a great place to be for both of these fields of study." Students say that the school is "small enough [that] you can make a difference through clubs, legislation, or any other way you would like." One student shares her experience: "I fell in love with the beautiful atmosphere and the friendly community." AppState's international experiences include study-abroad opportunities on nearly every continent: "The study abroad program is very impressive as are the global studies and sustainable development programs. The food services, cafes, and stores are all self-sustaining and self-owned. Also, we can rent out books as opposed to spending hundreds of dollars each semester."

At AppState there is an emphasis on community service, hands-on learning, undergraduate research, internships, campus involvement, and cultural and recreational activities to provide a well-rounded educational experience that prepares students for a competitive job market. One junior says, "This school is such a brilliant paradox; it is a big school housed in a tiny institution. Here at Appalachian there is a gigantic sense of amazing student life in academics, athletics, foreign studies, etc., that bewitches you into thinking it is a bigger university."

BANG FOR YOUR BUCK

Each year, Appalachian State awards thousands of leadership and merit-based scholarships from 150 different programs across campus. Totaling more than $2 million each year, these scholarship awards help Appalachian students offset tuition and fees. Top scholarships include the Chancellor's Scholarship, a four-year scholarship covering full tuition and fees for the top 15 freshmen in the Heltzer Honors College; the W.H. Plemmons Leader Fellows Scholarship, a four-year scholarship for students with outstanding leadership experiences; the Diversity Scholarship, a four-year scholarship for students interested in promoting and enhancing diversity; and the ACCESS Scholarship, a four-year, full tuition and fees scholarship to help students with the highest financial need graduate debt-free. Additional support includes a textbook rental program, which saves students hundreds of dollars over the course of four years.

STUDENTS

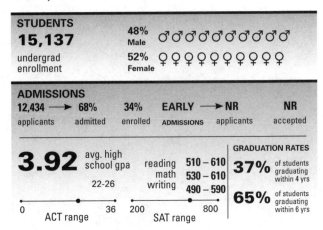

15,137 undergrad enrollment

48% Male ♂♂♂♂♂♂♂♂♂♂

52% Female ♀♀♀♀♀♀♀♀♀♀

ADMISSIONS

12,434 applicants → 68% admitted — 34% enrolled

EARLY ADMISSIONS → NR applicants — NR accepted

3.92 avg. high school gpa

reading	510 – 610
math	530 – 610
writing	490 – 590

ACT range (0–36): 22-26

SAT range (200–800)

GRADUATION RATES

37% of students graduating within 4 yrs

65% of students graduating within 6 yrs

Appalachian State University

FINANCIAL AID: 828-262-2190 • E-MAIL: ADMISSIONS@APPSTATE.EDU • WEBSITE: WWW.APPSTATE.EDU

STUDENT BODY

There are a lot of people that are very outdoorsy at ASU; they're attracted by the school's remote mountain setting, which is ideal for hiking, fishing, hunting, skiing, and whitewater rafting. The school tends to attract a lot of "environmentally and globally conscious kids who let their opinions be known." At Jamestown, "many organizations promote weekend activities such as dances, game nights, and Wii parties to get students to stay on campus." Students find plenty of fun things to do in addition to organized events such as "chalk art, baking, movies, and Taco Bell." Jamestown is "a community, everyone knows each other," and "the students are all close, both studying together and spending recreational times together."

Why Students love Appalachian State University

"I suppose Appalachian State, at 3,333 feet above sea level, really does redefine 'higher education.'"

WHY STUDENTS LOVE APPALACHIAN STATE UNIVERSITY

"People assume the college is surrounded by only mountains and never-ending forests. When you visit Appalachian State University, you will soon see that it is located in a small but very busy town. Boone's main attraction, besides the school, is the small shops located on King Street. There are a variety of restaurants," and, another student explains, since "Appalachian is in the heart of the mountains, so much of the student life is spent outdoors." The students that attend ASU are always buzzing about outside: "Snow sports, hiking, swimming, and cookouts are constant. Downtown Boone is a good location because of the convenient bus system. Also, Boone is small enough that you can pretty much walk everywhere.

GENERAL INFO

Activities: Choral groups, concert band, dance, drama/theater, jazz band, literary magazine, marching band, music ensembles, musical theater, opera, pep band, radio station, student government, student newspaper, student-run film society, symphony orchestra, campus ministries, international student organization. **Organizations**: 270 registered organizations, 20 honor societies, 25 religious organizations. 18 fraternities, 11 sororities. **Athletics (Intercollegiate)**: Baseball, basketball, cross-country, football, golf, soccer, tennis, track/field (outdoor), track/field (indoor), wrestling. **Athletics (Intramural)**: Basketball, cross-country, field hockey, golf, soccer, softball, tennis, track/field (outdoor), track/field (indoor), volleyball. **On-Campus Highlights**: Student Union, Central Dining Hall, Belk Library, Student Recreation Center, Holmes Convocation Center.

BOTTOM LINE

In-state residents attending AppState full-time can expect to pay approximately $3,000 in annual tuition–that barely covers the cost of required fees at some other colleges. Out-of-state students pay about $14,000 in annual tuition (still quite low, comparatively), and students who live on campus can expect to pay an additional $6,600 (low cost of living in hometown Boone, t is another perk.) Students graduate with about $16,000 in debt on average.

SELECTIVITY

Admissions Rating	**85**
# of applicants	12,434
% of applicants accepted	68
% of acceptees attending	34

FRESHMAN PROFILE

Range SAT Critical Reading	**510–610**
Range SAT Math	**530–610**
Range SAT Writing	**490–590**
Range ACT Composite	**22–26**
Average HS GPA	**3.92**
% graduated top 10% of class	**19**
% graduated top 25% of class	**57**
% graduated top 50% of class	**92**

DEADLINES

Regular Deadline	**3/15**
Normal registration	**yes**

FACILITIES

Housing: Coed dorms, special housing for disabled students, men's dorms, special housing for international students, women's dorms, apartments for married students, apartments for single students, wellness housing, theme housing. Sorority housing. *Special Academic Facilities/Equipment:* Language lab, Dark Sky Observatory, meteorological reporting station, art gallery, and geology museum. *Computers:* 95% of classrooms, 70% of dorms, 90% of libraries, 90% of dining areas, 85% of student union, 5% of common outdoor areas have wireless network access.

FINANCIAL FACTS

Financial Aid Rating	**63**
Annual in-state tuition	$2,961
Annual out-of-state tuition	$14,273
Room and Board	$6,600
Required Fees	$2,290
Books and supplies	$700
% frosh rec. need-based scholarship or grant aid	12
% UG rec.need-based scholarship or grant aid	32
% frosh rec. non-need-based scholarship or grant aid	12
% UG rec. non-need-based scholarship or grant aid	8
% frosh rec. need-based self-help aid	22
% UG rec. need-based self-help aid	29
% frosh rec. any financial aid	66
% UG rec. any financial aid	65
% UG borrow to pay for school	52
Average cumulative indebtedness	$16,130

California Polytechnic State University, San Luis Obispo

Admissions Office, Cal Poly, San Luis Obispo, CA 93407-0031 • Admissions: 805-756-2311

CAMPUS LIFE

Quality of life Rating	60 *
Fire Safety Rating	61
Green rating	60 *
Type of School	Public
Environment	Town

STUDENTS

Total undergrad enrollment	17,332
% Male to Female	55/45
% From out of state	6
% From public high school	74
% Live on Campus	36
# of Fraternities	23
# of Sororities	14
% African American	1
% Asian	10
% Caucasian	65
% Hispanic	12
% Native American	1
% International	1
# Of Countries Represented	73

ACADEMICS

% Of students graduating within 4 years	26
% Of students graduating within 6 years	73
Calendar	quarter
Most common reg class size	20–29 students
Most common lab size	20–29 students

ABOUT THE SCHOOL

California Polytechnic State University, San Luis Obispo is located halfway between San Francisco and Los Angeles, and it offers students a hands-on educational experience that prepares them for today's scientific and technical world. "Cal Poly says it's really hands on, and it is," attests a student. The school (which runs on a quarterly schedule) has more than 140,000 alumni living and working worldwide, which is not a bad network to have at graduation. Because students must declare a major when they apply–there are plenty to choose from, including more traditional liberal arts subjects–students come to Cal Poly with a certain level of focus that is not always found at other schools, and are able to get right down to gaining real-world experience; the university certainly encourages students to pursue co-op and internship opportunities as soon as they're ready. "Cal Poly grads get the job first because they know how to do it."

Why Students love San Luis Obispo

"Gathering of people that get excited about very specific topics and delve deep into learning about them."

BANG FOR YOUR BUCK

A Cal Poly graduate can expect a great return on their investment in their education. In a 2008–2009, self-reported survey conducted by Career Services, 81 percent of graduates reported they are working full time or attending graduate school (56 percent reported job offers before graduation). Science and tech-oriented grads are in high demand in the job market, and so once you get the degree it's a relatively easy sell, especially since Cal Poly hosts from 300 to 600 different employers each year through its on-campus recruiting program and job fair events.

STUDENTS
17,332 undergrad enrollment

55% Male ♂♂♂♂♂♂♂♂♂♂♂
45% Female ♀♀♀♀♀♀♀♀♀

ADMISSIONS
33,627 applicants → 3% admitted | 32% enrolled
EARLY ADMISSIONS → NR applicants | NR accepted

3.89 avg. high school gpa

ACT range (0–36): 24-29

SAT range (200–800): reading 540–640, math 580–680, writing NR

GRADUATION RATES
26% of students graduating within 4 yrs
9% of students graduating within 6 yrs

California Polytechnic State University, San Luis Obispo

FINANCIAL AID: 805-756-2927 • E-MAIL: ADMISSIONS@CALPOLY.EDU • FAX: 805-756-5400 • WEBSITE: WWW.CALPOLY.EDU

STUDENT BODY

More than 80 percent of Cal Poly students live off campus, which means that students don't get to know each other. "You must join a club or an organization" if you want to make friends, according to one student. And students tend to befriend other students in their respective majors. Cal Poly students are very laid back and some are apathetic as regards the classroom. They're always smiling and easy to get along with." People are "very respectful of differences."

WHY STUDENTS LOVE CAL POLY

With the rolling mountains and valleys surrounding the giant campus, it's hard not for students to fall in love at first sight. "I felt like I fit in," says a student of his first visit. Entertainment options are varied: "On campus and in the surrounding area, you can go to the movies, go kayaking, go to the beach, build a computer, go clubbing, go camping, or shear some sheep." The beaches are definitely tempting–"I've learned how to surf only after studying, which was the 'hardest' lesson at Cal Poly" says a student–and the "really friendly and fun student body" seems like a "gathering of people that get excited about very specific topics and delve deep into learning about them. Faculty are equally accessible and welcoming. "Most of the professors are here because they want to teach you," one student says.

GENERAL INFO

Activities: Choral groups, concert band, dance, drama/theater, jazz band, literary magazine, marching band, music ensembles, musical theater, opera, pep band, radio station, student government, student newspaper, symphony orchestra, television station, campus ministries, international student organization. **Organizations:** 400 registered organizations, 14 religious organizations. 25 fraternities, 14 sororities. **Athletics (Intercollegiate):** *Men:* Baseball, basketball, cross-country, football, golf, soccer, swimming, tennis, track/field (outdoor), wrestling. *Women:* Basketball, cross-country, golf, soccer, softball, swimming, tennis, track/field (outdoor), track/field (indoor), volleyball. **On-Campus Highlights:** Performing Arts Center, Recreation Center, Julian's Coffee Shop, Spanos Stadium, University Union, El Corral Bookstore.

Why Students love San Luis Obispo

"I felt like I fit in."

BOTTOM LINE

As part of the CSU system, tuition runs a mere $7,921, with an additional $15,567 in additional fees and room and board. Non-resident students pay fees plus $248 per unit non-resident tuition. Cal Poly has almost 800 named scholarships in every college and almost every major, including more than 100 scholarships to students in the College of Agriculture, Food, and Environmental Science. Students may also apply for federal aid, work study, and grants (including Cal Grants).

SELECTIVITY

Admissions Rating	**94**
# of applicants	33,627
% of applicants accepted	33
% of acceptees attending	32

FRESHMAN PROFILE

Range SAT Critical Reading	**540–640**
Range SAT Math	**580–680**
Range ACT Composite	**24–29**
Average HS GPA	**3.84**
% graduated top 10% of class	**52**
% graduated top 25% of class	**86**

DEADLINES

Regular Deadline	**1/30**
Normal registration	**no**

FACILITIES

Housing: Coed dorms, special housing for disabled students, special housing for international students, apartments for single students, theme housing. *Special Academic Facilities/Equipment:* Dairy, veterinary clinic, printing museum, art gallery. *Computers:* 100% of classrooms, 5% of dorms, 100% of libraries, 100% of dining areas, 100% of student union, 5% of common outdoor areas have wireless network access.

FINANCIAL FACTS

Financial Aid Rating	**60***
Annual tuition	$5,602
Room and Board	$10,444
Required Fees	$2,319
Books and supplies	1,698
% frosh rec. need-based scholarship or grant aid	25
% UG rec.need-based scholarship or grant aid	24
% frosh rec. non-need-based scholarship or grant aid	2
% UG rec. non-need-based scholarship or grant aid	1
% frosh rec. need-based self-help aid	20
% UG rec. need-based self-help aid	23
Average cumulative indebtedness	$16,130

California State University–Long Beach

1250 Bellflower Boulevard, Long Beach, CA 90840 • Admissions: 562-985-5471 • Fax: 562-985-4973

CAMPUS LIFE

Quality of life Rating	89
Fire Safety Rating	62
Green rating	60*
Type of School	Public
Environment	City

STUDENTS

Total undergrad enrolllment	27,436
% Male to Female	59/41
% From out of state	1
% Live on Campus	7
# of Fraternities	16
# of Sororities	15
% African American	4
% Asian	19
% Caucasian	27
% Hispanic	31
% International	5
# Of Countries Represented	136

ACADEMICS

Academic Rating	73
% Of students graduating within 4 years	12
% Of students graduating within 6 years	41
Calendar	semester
Most common reg class size	20–29 students
Most common lab size	20–29 students

MOST POPULAR MAJORS

Corrections and criminal justice, management information systems, general psychology

SPECIAL STUDY OPTIONS

Accelerated program, cross-registration, distance learning, double major, dual enrollment, English as a Second Language (ESL), honors program, independent study, internships, student-designed major, study abroad, teacher certification program. Special programs offered to physically disabled students include note-taking services, reader services. Career services: Alumni services, career assessment, internships.

ABOUT THE SCHOOL

Lots of excellent, career-oriented academic options and a fabulous location are a few of the features that make California State University–Long Beach an attractive destination. There are eight colleges and tons of majors, but some students say "CSULB is about experiencing college, not just the classroom." There's a strong arts education presence here, which students believe makes the campus "diverse and environmentally beautiful." Engineering is particularly strong, and the nursing program has an excellent reputation. "The school has flexible academic options, as minoring and double majoring opportunities are in abundance," says one student. "There are few courses and disciplines that are not offered [and] probably the greatest strengths are affordability and location; there is substantial bang for the buck and we never have bad weather." The faculty gets stellar reviews from students, especially relative to other schools of CSULB's size. CSULB is predominantly a commuter school with an incredibly diverse and mostly tolerant student population. One student details that "people enjoy eating on campus during classes, and partying off campus on weekends. They do not participate in extreme partying, but enjoy going out." Students are friendly, but CSULB's transient nature makes it difficult to meet people outside of academic and social cliques. People are trying, though; the garden-like campus is bursting with activities.

BANG FOR YOUR BUCK

An optimist would say that tuition is free at CSULB for state residents. A pessimist would observe that CSULB may not have tuition but it does have fees, which look exactly like tuition. Either way, you can't deny that it's cheap to go here. The combination of low cost and a high level of financial aid availability make this school an affordable option regardless of your economic means. And the secret's out: CSULB had received almost 80,000 applications for the 2010-2011 academic year–the highest in the nation. About 60 percent of all undergrads receive some kind of financial aid and the administration tries to give as much aid as possible in the form of free money. CSULB also provides "valuable information to parents and students while most universities refuse to make such information available." This information includes: "average student debt upon graduation compared to state and national averages; average starting salaries of graduates; average mid-career salaries of graduates; etc," according to the office of Cal State President, F. King Alexander. Grants cover much of the cost of attending for low-income California residents (and pretty much everyone here is a Golden State resident). Scholarships are ample.

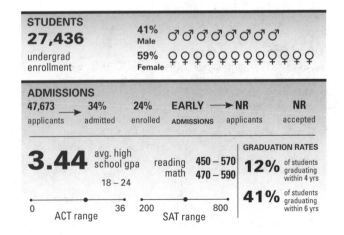

STUDENTS
27,436 undergrad enrollment
41% Male ♂♂♂♂♂♂♂♂
59% Female ♀♀♀♀♀♀♀♀♀♀♀♀

ADMISSIONS
47,673 applicants → 34% admitted 24% enrolled
EARLY ADMISSIONS → NR applicants NR accepted

3.44 avg. high school gpa

reading 450 – 570
math 470 – 590

ACT range: 18 – 24 (0–36)
SAT range: (200–800)

GRADUATION RATES
12% of students graduating within 4 yrs
41% of students graduating within 6 yrs

California State University–Long Beach

FINANCIAL AID: 562-985-8403 • E-MAIL: ESLB@CSULB.EDU • WEBSITE: WWW.CSULB.EDU

STUDENT BODY

"At Cal State–Long Beach, "everyone is very different." "You can be yourself, and no one will mind," says one student. It's a "very relaxed" and "mellow" crowd. "Our school has one of the most diverse student bodies of any school in the nation," gloats a junior. "Think of any social/religious/ethnic archetype and we've got 'em in droves–liberals, conservatives, religious zealots (Western and Eastern), adamant atheists, and a greater variety of skin color than a 1990s diversity promotion." Many students are "working part-time or full-time." "There are students here that are attending school solely for the social interaction and just happen to receive an education," relates a senior. "There are also those here solely for the education and interact socially only through their classes. Every student has a place where they can feel welcome and enjoy themselves."

Why Students love CSULB

"Cal State Long Beach is about helping students acquire a quality education without breaking the bank."

WHY STUDENTS LOVE CSULB

CSULB has been nationally ranked as the "top university for students hoping not to acquire student loan debt upon graduation." According to one student, CSULB is a "nice campus with great instructors," that is "also close to home so I wouldn't have to live on campus." Although some students prefer to cut costs by opting to not live on-campus, others, like this one Senior, maintain that CSULB's "strengths would be what the campus offers: from our Career Development office, to a Passport office [or] to a Union that has handfuls of services...they cater to students." Others feel that the financial aid offered by the school is adequate: "Cal State Long Beach is about helping students acquire a quality education without breaking the bank." One top-ranking Cal State Salsa dancer dotes on the overall experience at the school: "We [Salsa Team] promote dancing often, and when we're not dancing, odds are we are in front of a Playstation playing games or discussing domestic policy.

GENERAL INFO

Activities: Choral groups, concert band, dance, drama/theater, jazz band, literary magazine, music ensembles, musical theater, opera, radio station, student government, student newspaper, student-run film society, symphony orchestra, television station, yearbook. **Organizations:** 300 registered organizations, 25 honor societies, 20 religious organizations. 16 fraternities, 15 sororities. **Athletics (Intercollegiate):** Baseball, basketball, cross-country, golf, track/field (outdoor), volleyball, water polo Basketball, cross-country, golf, soccer, softball, tennis, track/field (outdoor), volleyball, water polo.

BOTTOM LINE

Attending classes for a year costs Californians about $4,800 (in fees, not tuition). If you can't claim California residency, you'll have to cough up more than twice that amount. On-campus room and board costs an addition $11,000 or so. Keep in mind that grants and scholarships flow like water here, especially if you come from a lower-income California family. According to F. King Alexander, President of CSULB, "33 percent of the collected State University tuition and fees" are redirected to "the neediest Cal State University students" and "few parents or students know about this redirection."

SELECTIVITY

Admissions Rating	**90**
# of applicants	47,673
% of applicants accepted	34
% of acceptees attending	24

FRESHMAN PROFILE

Range SAT Critical Reading	**450–570**
Range SAT Math	**470–590**
Range ACT Composite	**18–24**
Average HS GPA	**3.44**
% graduated top 25% of class	**84**
% graduated top 50% of class	**100**

DEADLINES

Regular Deadline	**11/30**

FACILITIES

Housing: Coed dorms, special housing for international students. *Special Academic Facilities/Equipment:* Art and science museums, Japanese garden, special events arena with meeting facilities.

FINANCIAL FACTS

Financial Aid Rating	**82**
Annual in-state tuition	$0
Annual out-of-state tuition	$11,160
Room and Board	$11,294
Required Fees	$5,464
Books and supplies	$1,858
% frosh rec. need-based scholarship or grant aid	49
% UG rec.need-based scholarship or grant aid	49
% frosh rec. non-need-based scholarship or grant aid	7
% UG rec. non-need-based scholarship or grant aid	9
% frosh rec. need-based self-help aid	41
% UG rec. need-based self-help aid	58
% UG borrow to pay for school	36
Average cumulative indebtedness	$10,787

Christopher Newport University

1 University Place, Newport News, VA 23606-2998 • Admissions: 757-594-7015 • Fax: 757-594-7333

CAMPUS LIFE

Quality of life Rating	81
Fire Safety Rating	87
Green rating	80
Type of School	Public
Environment	City

STUDENTS

Total undergrad enrolllment	4,768
% Male to Female	43/57
% From out of state	7
% Live on Campus	61
# of Fraternities	7
# of Sororities	7
% African American	9
% Asian	3
% Caucasian	79
% Hispanic	4
# Of Countries Represented	40

ACADEMICS

Academic Rating	79
% Of students graduating within 4 years	42
% Of students graduating within 6 years	60
Calendar	semester
Profs interesting rating	86
Profs accessible rating	88
Most common reg class size	20–29 students
Most common lab size	23 students

MOST POPULAR MAJORS

Biology, business administration and management, psychology

HONORS PROGRAMS

CNU Honors Program provides enriched educational experience for academically talented students motivated to participate in challenging courses and cultural and intellectual activities. Special programs offered to physically disabled students include note-taking services, voice recorders.

SPECIAL STUDY OPTIONS

Cross-registration, double major, dual enrollment, honors program, independent study, internships, student-designed major, study abroad, Member of the Virginia Tidewater Consortium, Freshman Learning Communities.

ABOUT THE SCHOOL

Named for an English seaman, Christopher Newport University (located in the Hamptons Roads area of Virginia) is a liberal arts college that runs on a "determination for student success." The small school's "modern outlook on education" is matched by its modern facilities (CNU is averaging one new building every year through 2015), and "It does not lack any of the resources of larger schools." Coupled with a well-run honors program, CNU's "growing prestige" means that "the future holds great things for this little school."

There's a palpable excitement for this relatively new school among its students, and though "it isn't well known across the nation, perhaps not even in Virginia...this allows currently associated (students, faculty, administration, etc.) to help put CNU on the map for generations to come." Academics are high-quality, and extracurriculars are abundant at the school. "The teachers take a personal interest in their students and there are many opportunities for students to take the lead on projects, shape their education, and become campus and community leaders." Much like the academic buildings, the residential halls and campus are "breathtaking." "I feel like I am living in a luxury hotel," says one student.

BANG FOR YOUR BUCK

The admis¬sions department pays close attention to the academic success of students in high school, especially the strength of the curriculum and any honors or AP courses. The school looks for leaders, and students with diverse histories. The undergraduate experience–one that combines cutting-edge academics, stellar leadership opportunities, and high-impact service initiatives strives to shape hearts and minds for a lifetime of service. This small school's "modern outlook on education" is matched by its contemporary, state-of-the-art residential facilities, and wins rave reviews from students and parents alike. Undergraduates will study alongside distinguished professors, and team with faculty on research. Many classes are structured like workshops, and even the lecture hall classes are capped at seventy-five students, so "you'll never find yourself drowning in a 500-person classroom here at CNU," according to one relieved undergraduate. Outside the classroom, students gain hands-on experience through internships with top organizations like NASA and the Thomas Jefferson National Laboratory. There are innumerable opportunities to develop leadership skills; undergrads can make an impact through the President's Leadership Program or design their own curriculum.

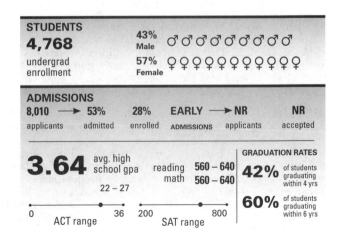

STUDENTS

4,768 undergrad enrollment

43% Male ♂♂♂♂♂♂♂♂♂

57% Female ♀♀♀♀♀♀♀♀♀♀♀

ADMISSIONS

8,010 applicants → 53% admitted | 28% enrolled | EARLY ADMISSIONS → NR applicants | NR accepted

3.64 avg. high school gpa

reading 560 – 640

math 560 – 640

ACT range (0–36): 22 – 27

SAT range (200–800)

GRADUATION RATES

42% of students graduating within 4 yrs

60% of students graduating within 6 yrs

Christopher Newport University

FINANCIAL AID: 757-594-7170 • E-MAIL: ADMIT@CNU.EDU • WEBSITE: WWW.CNU.EDU

STUDENT BODY

CNU prides itself on its sense of community, and the students within band together to create "a family-like atmosphere." This "incredibly friendly" group is typically the "middle-class, nice," "healthy, all-American sort." Everyone is open-minded and fairly outgoing, and "just a few weeks into classes...you feel like you know half the student body." "We pride ourselves on being a community of 'door holders,'" says a student. There are "very few socially deviant individuals, such as gang members, hardcore punks, goths, skinheads, etc.," but "nobody, regardless of race or background, sticks out like a sore thumb." Though there's a certain devotion to academics, the average student "is able to balance school work and play."

Why Students love CNU

"The majority of my professors bring both a sense of expertise and uniqueness to their teaching styles."

WHY STUDENTS LOVE CNU

While teaching methods of the "absolutely fabulous" faculty may vary, quality rarely does, and most professors "make even my least favorite subjects at least interesting." "The majority of my professors bring both a sense of expertise and uniqueness to their teaching styles...keeping a sense of personality in their teaching to keep students involved," says a student. Many classes are structured like workshops, and even the "few" lecture hall classes are capped at seventy-five students, so "you'll never find yourself drowning in a 500-person classroom here at CNU." The administration (especially the well-liked president) "cares to listen to students' concerns," and the "free tutoring is amazing here." Also, as a few students astutely observe, The possibilities for distinguishing oneself at a school in its first stages is much greater than at a long-established institution." "There is a chance to actively have a hand in the university's traditions and student life."

GENERAL INFO

Activities: Choral groups, concert band, dance, drama/theater, jazz band, literary magazine, marching band, music ensembles, musical theater, opera, pep band, radio station, student government, student newspaper, student-run film society, symphony orchestra, television station, campus ministries, international student organization. **Organizations:** 139 registered organizations, 23 honor societies, 12 religious organizations. 7 fraternities, 7 sororities. **Athletics (Intercollegiate):** *Men:* Baseball, basketball, cheerleading, cross-country, football, golf, lacrosse, sailing, soccer, tennis, track/field (outdoor), track/field (indoor). *Women:* Basketball, cheerleading, cross-country, field hockey, lacrosse, sailing, soccer, softball, tennis, track/field (outdoor), track/field (indoor), volleyball. **On-Campus Highlights:** Trible Library, Freeman Athletic Center, Ferguson Center for the Arts, McMurran Classroom Building, David Student Union, CNU Village for upper class students.

BOTTOM LINE

In-state tuition is a mere $6,000; out-of-state students can expect that figure to rise a bit, to right around $15,000 a year. There is plenty of financial support provided to those enrolling at Christopher Newport, though–75% of freshman receive financial aid packages averaging more than $8,000. The school also meets 70 percent of a students' annual need, and the average freshman need-based gift aid amounts to more than $5,000. The school "gave me the greatest scholarship," a thrilled student body member told us.

SELECTIVITY

Admissions Rating	**84**
# of applicants	8,010
% of applicants accepted	53
% of acceptees attending	28
# accepting a place on wait list	260
% admitted from wait list	32

FRESHMAN PROFILE

Range SAT Critical Reading	**560–640**
Range SAT Math	**560–640**
Range ACT Composite	**22–27**
Average HS GPA	**3.64**
% graduated top 10% of class	**19**
% graduated top 25% of class	**57**
% graduated top 50% of class	**99**

DEADLINES

Regular Deadline	**2/1**
Normal registration	**yes**

FACILITIES

Housing: Coed dorms, fraternity/sorority housing, apartments for single students, theme housing. *Special Academic Facilities/Equipment:* Falk Art Gallery, The Freeman Center, The Ferguson Center for the Arts, Trible Library houses the Mariners Museum Collection. *Computers:* 10% of classrooms, 10% of dorms, 100% of libraries, 100% of dining areas, 100% of student union, 100% of common outdoor areas have wireless network access.

FINANCIAL FACTS

Financial Aid Rating	**72**
Annual in-state tuition	$5,914
Annual out-of-state tuition	$14,776
Room and Board	$9,528
Required Fees	$4,170
Books and supplies	$1,005
% frosh rec. need-based scholarship or grant aid	35
% UG rec.need-based scholarship or grant aid	32
% frosh rec. non-need-based scholarship or grant aid	22
% UG rec. non-need-based scholarship or grant aid	11
% frosh rec. need-based self-help aid	38
% UG rec. need-based self-help aid	37
% frosh rec. any financial aid	75
% UG rec. any financial aid	70
% UG borrow to pay for school	51
Average cumulative indebtedness	$20,879

City University of New York—Brooklyn College

2900 Bedford Avenue, Brooklyn, NY 11210 • Admissions: 718-951-5001 • Fax: 718-951-4506

CAMPUS LIFE

Quality of life Rating	69
Fire Safety Rating	60*
Green rating	91
Type of School	Public
Environment	Metropolis

STUDENTS

Total undergrad enrolllment	11,790
% Male to Female	40/60
% From out of state	2
% From public high school	80
# of Fraternities	7
# of Sororities	9
% African American	24
% Asian	17
% Caucasian	41
% Hispanic	12
% International	5

ACADEMICS

Academic Rating	65
% Of students graduating within 4 years	23
% Of students graduating within 6 years	48
Calendar	semester
Profs interesting rating	68
Profs accessible rating	67
Most common reg class size	20–29 students
Most common lab size	20–29 students

MOST POPULAR MAJORS

Accounting, business administration and management, psychology, film, TV/radio

SPECIAL STUDY OPTIONS

Distance learning, double major, dual enrollment, English as a Second Language (ESL), honors program, independent study, internships, study abroad, teacher certification program, weekend college.

ABOUT THE SCHOOL

Respected nationally for its rigorous academic standards, the college takes pride in such innovative programs as its award-winning Freshman Year College; the Honors Academy, which houses six programs for high achievers; and its nationally recognized core curriculum. Its School of Education is ranked among the top twenty in the country for graduates who go on to be considered among the best teachers in New York City. Brooklyn College's strong academic reputation has attracted an outstanding faculty of nationally renowned teachers and scholars. Among the awards they have won are Pulitzers, Guggenheims, Fulbrights, and many National Institutes of Health grants. The Brooklyn College campus, considered to be among the most beautiful in the nation, is in the midst of an ambitious program of expansion and renewal.

Education at the college is taken seriously and the curriculum is challenging. Students mention that "the material is engaging and interesting while the professors are first rate;" "I find myself learning beyond the course description." There is respect for the opinions of their students, and "each professor allows students to have free reign of their thoughts and ideas," one student says admiringly. Another satisfied undergrad tells us that "it is hard to estimate my academic gains but they have been substantial." Additionally, each student is assigned a peer mentor and a counseling class that "helps us adapt to college life. I think that it helped me to be a more active student."

BANG FOR YOUR BUCK

Brooklyn College enables students with less-than-stellar high school records to have a chance to prove themselves here. Once they get in, though, they need to be prepared to work hard–it's easier to get in than to stay in. "An academically challenging and rigorous school" that "feels a lot more competitive than one would anticipate," students tell us. Students are especially sanguine about special programs here, such as the various honors programs, in which "you will meet tons of highly intelligent people. Honors classes boast strong in-class discussions and highly vibrant, enthusiastic students. "I am in the honors program and the professors are welcoming, encouraging and challenging," raves one student. The library is up to date and one of the largest in all the CUNY campuses, and there are numerous resources that students can access for additional academic help. The school also works hard to provide "constant and innumerable job opportunities available to students and the Magner Center, which helps students find jobs and internships, and [to] help them prepare for the real world through resume writing workshops [and] job interview workshops."

STUDENTS

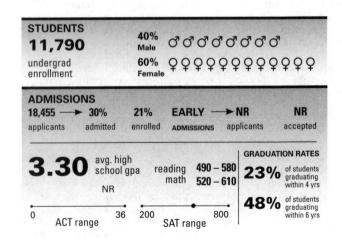

11,790 undergrad enrollment

40% Male ♂♂♂♂♂♂♂♂

60% Female ♀♀♀♀♀♀♀♀♀♀♀♀

ADMISSIONS

18,455 applicants → 30% admitted | 21% enrolled | EARLY ADMISSIONS → NR applicants | NR accepted

3.30 avg. high school gpa

reading 490 – 580
math 520 – 610

NR
0 — 36 ACT range

200 — 800 SAT range

GRADUATION RATES

23% of students graduating within 4 yrs

48% of students graduating within 6 yrs

FINANCIAL AID: 718-951-5045 • WEBSITE: WWW.BROOKLYN.CUNY.EDU

STUDENT BODY

"The typical student at Brooklyn College is hardworking, from the New York metro area, and a commuter." Many "hold part-time jobs and pay at least part of their own tuition, so they are usually in a rush because they have a lot more responsibility on their shoulders than the average college student." Like Brooklyn itself, "The student body is very diversified," with everyone from "an aspiring opera singer to quirky film majors to single mothers looking for a better life for their children," and so "no student can be described as being typical. Everyone blends in as normal, and little segregation is noticed (if it exists)." Students here represent more than 100 nations and speak nearly as many languages. There are even students "that come from Long Island to North Carolina, from Connecticut to even Hong Kong." The college's accessibility by subway or bus allows students to further enrich their educational experience through New York City's many cultural events and institutions.

Why Students love Brooklyn College

"There are a lot of student organizations and a lot of activities done to help enhance student life on campus."

WHY STUDENTS LOVE BROOKLYN COLLEGE

Brooklyn College "is the perfect representative of Brooklyn as a borough and [of] success in the community," an institution that, like its home borough, "educates its students in an environment that reflects diversity, opportunity (study abroad, research, athletics, employment), and support." "Lauded as one of the best senior colleges in CUNY" and boasting "a beautiful campus," Brooklyn College entices a lot of bright students looking for an affordable, quality, undergraduate experience as well as some attracted by the school's relatively charitable admissions standards. Professors "are fabulous" and "really passionate about the subjects that they teach and their students' career paths."

GENERAL INFO

Activities: dance, drama/theater, literary magazine, music ensembles, musical theater, radio station, student government, student newspaper, television station, yearbook, international student organization. **Organizations:** 171 registered organizations, 7 honor societies, 7 fraternities, 9 sororities. **Athletics (Intercollegiate):** *Men:* Basketball, cross-country, soccer, tennis, track/field (outdoor), track/field (indoor), volleyball. *Women:* Basketball, cross-country, softball, tennis, track/field (outdoor), track/field (indoor), volleyball. **On-Campus Highlights:** Library, Student Center, Lily Pond, Library Cafe, Cafeteria, Dining Hall, Magner Center, James Hall. **Environmental Initiatives:** Reduce consumption; awareness.

BOTTOM LINE

Brooklyn College provides students with an excellent education for a cost that will not break any banks—piggy or otherwise. Fortunately, in-state tuition runs only $5,000 or so; out-of-state credit hours are around $450 each. Perhaps most importantly, the institution is able to meet 99 percent of all need. Undergraduates average nearly $4,000 in need-based gift aid; financial aid packages generally come to about $7,500.

SELECTIVITY

Admissions Rating	**88**
# of applicants	18,455
% of applicants accepted	30
% of acceptees attending	21
# accepting a place on wait list	2,112
% admitted from wait list	14

FRESHMAN PROFILE

Range SAT Critical Reading	**490–580**
Range SAT Math	**520–610**
Average HS GPA	**3.30**
% graduated top 10% of class	**18**
% graduated top 25% of class	**52**
% graduated top 50% of class	**83**

DEADLINES

Regular Deadline	**2/1**
Normal registration	**no**

FACILITIES

Housing: 100% of campus accessible to physically disabled. *Special Academic Facilities/Equipment:* Art museum. language lab, TV studios, speech clinic, research centers and institutes, particle accelerator. *Computers:* 2% of classrooms, 90% of libraries, 100% of dining areas, 75% of student union, 75% of common outdoor areas have wireless network access. .

FINANCIAL FACTS

Financial Aid Rating	**94**
Annual in-state tuition	$4,830
Annual out-of-state tuition	$435 per credit
Required Fees	$454
Books and supplies	$1,146
% frosh rec. need-based scholarship or grant aid	61
% UG rec.need-based scholarship or grant aid	67
% frosh rec. non-need-based scholarship or grant aid	25
% UG rec. non-need-based scholarship or grant aid	24
% frosh rec. need-based self-help aid	52
% UG rec. need-based self-help aid	66
% frosh rec. any financial aid	77
% UG borrow to pay for school	48
Average cumulative indebtedness	$9,500

City University of New York—Hunter College

695 Park Ave, Room N203, New York, NY 10065 • Admissions: 212-772-4490 • Fax: 212-650-3472

CAMPUS LIFE

Quality of life Rating	75
Fire Safety Rating	88
Green rating	84
Type of School	Public
Environment	Metropolis

STUDENTS

Total undergrad enrolllment	14,609
% Male to Female	33/67
% From out of state	4
% From public high school	70
# of Fraternities	2
# of Sororities	2
% African American	11
% Asian	22
% Caucasian	39
% Hispanic	19
% International	8

ACADEMICS

Academic Rating	64
% Of students graduating within 4 years	17
% Of students graduating within 6 years	46
Calendar	semester
Profs interesting rating	66
Profs accessible rating	84
Most common reg class size	20–29 students

MOST POPULAR MAJORS

Accounting, psychology

SPECIAL STUDY OPTIONS

Accelerated program, cross-registration, distance learning, double major, dual enrollment, exchange student program (domestic), honors program, independent study, internships, liberal arts/career combination, student-designed major, study abroad, teacher certification program.

ABOUT THE SCHOOL

The City University of New York–Hunter College has a lot to offer beyond its miniscule tuition. For many New Yorkers seeking a top-notch college degree, Hunter offers the best, most affordable option available. Hunter's 15,000-plus students choose from more than 70 undergraduate programs. Regardless of their area of concentration, all Hunter students are encouraged to have broad exposure to the liberal arts: "Hunter is all about bringing people from all different parts of the world together in one place to learn from one another and to be exposed to almost every subject imaginable to help one find their true calling in life," says one sophomore. Though a Hunter College education doesn't come with a lot of frills, the school's faculty is a huge asset. Professors are very often experts in their fields, and they work hard to accommodate undergraduates. One student says, "Many of the professors teach at other, more expensive universities. Throughout my Hunter career, I have had professors who also teach at NYU, Hofstra, Cooper Union, and Yale! So it really is quite the bargain," and continues: "I am not missing out on a challenging, intellectual educational process by attending a public school."

BANG FOR YOUR BUCK

Extraordinarily low tuition makes Hunter affordable, and more than 1,000 scholarships, awards, and special program opportunities offered throughout the CUNY campuses complements that affordability. The usual combination of work-study jobs, need-based grants, scholarships, and credit-bearing internships help students fund their educations. Need-based grants from the state of New York are available. Hunter offers a variety of scholarship programs for entering freshman who have maintained a high level of academic achievement while in high school and who demonstrate potential for superior scholarship at the college level. Institutional scholarships [at Hunter College] are offered to more than 50 percent of the aid-eligible population. The Macaulay Honors College is definitely one of the highlights. Accepted students receive a full-ride scholarship (except for fees), a laptop computer, and additional funds to pursue research, internships, or service activities. One student boasts: "The Macaulay Honors College allows me access to the best Hunter and CUNY has to offer, and to the wide resources of New York City itself [all] while paying no tuition." Also, financial sessions are offered at Hunter to incoming students and cover topics such as loans, credit cards and budgeting. All new students are considered for Hunter College sponsored scholarships automatically–no separate application is required.

STUDENTS

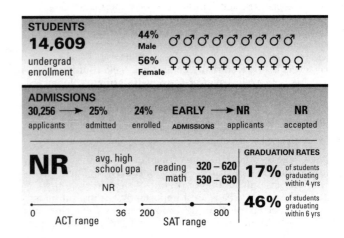

14,609 undergrad enrollment

44% Male ♂♂♂♂♂♂♂♂♂

56% Female ♀♀♀♀♀♀♀♀♀♀♀

ADMISSIONS

30,256 →	25%	24%	EARLY →	NR	NR
applicants	admitted	enrolled	ADMISSIONS	applicants	accepted

NR avg. high school gpa

reading 320 – 620
math 530 – 630

NR
0 — 36 ACT range
200 — 800 SAT range

GRADUATION RATES

17% of students graduating within 4 yrs

46% of students graduating within 6 yrs

City University of New York—Hunter College

Financial Aid: 212-772-4820 • E-mail: admissions@hunter.cuny.edu • Website: www.hunter.cuny.edu

STUDENT BODY

Hunter College is "extremely diverse in almost every sense of the word." Ethnic, religious, gender preference, and political diversity are all in evidence. "Our population is as diverse as New York," one student aptly observes. Undergraduates are even diverse in age; as one undergraduate observes, "The average age for a Hunter student is, I believe, twenty-five. That alone opens up the spectrum of atypical students." What they share in common is that so many have "something to contribute, an experience that can be shared somewhere where others can learn from it. Everyone exchanges their experiences, allowing Hunter students to be some of the most open-minded, understanding people I believe New York City, and even the rest of the country, has to offer." Students tend to be "very liberal and outspoken."

Why Students love Hunter College

"In teaching you how to think independently, how to remain intellectually flexible, and how to apply knowledge to local circumstances, Hunter educates its students to live actively in the world."

WHY STUDENTS LOVE HUNTER COLLEGE

"Hunter's school of education has a wonderful reputation," says one student. Another student relates their preference for Hunter because "the greatest strengths at [this] school is the diversity, the value, the professors, and the library." One senior relays, "in teaching you how to think independently, how to remain intellectually flexible, and how to apply knowledge to local circumstances, Hunter educates its students to live actively in the world." "Hunter is great at accommodating students. I work full time, as do many of my peers, and I have never had trouble getting a class I wanted and having it work with my schedule. Also of course, New York can't be beat, nor can my fellow students," says one student.

GENERAL INFO

Activities: Choral groups, concert band, dance, drama/theater, jazz band, literary magazine, music ensembles, musical theater, radio station, student government, student newspaper, student-run film society, symphony orchestra, television station, yearbook. **Organizations:** 150 registered organizations, 20 honor societies, 2 fraternities, 2 sororities. **Athletics (Intercollegiate):** *Men:* Basketball, cross-country, fencing, soccer, tennis, track/field (outdoor), track/field (indoor), volleyball, wrestling. *Women:* Basketball, cross-country, diving, fencing, softball, swimming, tennis, track/field (outdoor), track/field (indoor), volleyball. **On-Campus Highlights:** More than 100 campus clubs, CARSI Geography Lab, Television Studio, Learning Center and Computer Lab, Sports Complex.

BOTTOM LINE

Full-time tuition for New York residents ranges between approximately $194–$220 per credit hour. That's ridiculously cheap. If you can't claim state residency, you'll pay about three times that amount. Also, as you know if you are a New Yorker and probably have heard if you aren't, New York City can be a painfully expensive place to live. But that shouldn't dissuade prospective student since about 80 percent of students receive aid.

SELECTIVITY

Admissions Rating	**72**
# of applicants	30,256
% of applicants accepted	25
% of acceptees attending	24

FRESHMAN PROFILE

Range SAT Critical Reading	**520–620**
Range SAT Math	**530–630**

DEADLINES

Regular Deadline	**2/1**
Normal registration	**yes**

FACILITIES

Housing: Coed dorms. 100% of campus accessible to physically disabled. *Special Academic Facilities/Equipment:* Art Gallery, theatre, geology club, on-campus elementary and secondary schools. *Computers:* 70% of classrooms, have wireless network access. Students can register for classes online.

FINANCIAL FACTS

Financial Aid Rating	**85**
Annual in-state tuition	$4,830
Annual out-of-state tuition	$13,050
Room	$3,726
Required Fees	$399
Books and supplies	$1,179
% frosh rec. need-based scholarship or grant aid	52
% UG rec.need-based scholarship or grant aid	54
% frosh rec. non-need-based scholarship or grant aid	43
% UG rec. non-need-based scholarship or grant aid	20
% frosh rec. need-based self-help aid	7
% UG rec. need-based self-help aid	17
% frosh rec. any financial aid	91
% UG rec. any financial aid	94
% UG borrow to pay for school	53
Average cumulative indebtedness	$7,500

Clemson University

105 Sikes Hall, Box 345124, Clemson, SC 29634-5124 • Admissions: 864-656-2287 • Financial Aid: 864-656-2280

CAMPUS LIFE

Quality of life Rating	96
Fire Safety Rating	93
Green rating	86
Type of School	Public
Environment	Village

STUDENTS

Total undergrad enrolllment	15,459
% Male to Female	54/46
% From out of state	29
% From public high school	89
% Live on Campus	41
# of Fraternities	26
# of Sororities	17
% African American	7
% Asian	2
% Caucasian	84
% Hispanic	2
% International	1
# Of Countries Represented	84

ACADEMICS

Academic Rating	77
% Of students graduating within 4 years	50
% Of students graduating within 6 years	76
Calendar	semester
Profs interesting rating	82
Profs accessible rating	89
Most common reg class size	10–19 students
Most common lab size	10–19 students

MOST POPULAR MAJORS

Business/commerce, biology, engineering

HONOR PROGRAMS

The National Scholars Program.

SPECIAL STUDY OPTIONS

Cooperative education program, distance learning, double major, exchange student program (domestic), honors program, independent study, internships, study abroad, teacher certification program, We have an RN to BSN program located in Greenville, South Carolina. This is an off-campus degree program for students that have a two-year degree in nursing and an RN.

ABOUT THE SCHOOL

Located in sunny South Carolina, Clemson University is "the total package: chal¬lenging academics, beautiful campus, sports, a thriving Greek life, Southern edge, and that extra something that just makes me excited to be here every morning when I wake up," according to one happy undergrad. The atmosphere is laid-back yet competitive; learning is fostered often for its own sake, and financial aid, alumni connections, and relationships within the community help put the learning within reach for all. Clemson is also very flexible in allowing its motivated students to achieve dual degrees, double majors, and five-year Master's degree options.

Professors at Clemson strike an amazing balance between their lives as researchers and teachers. They manage to make themselves fully accessible to students while still engaging in valuable research, which provides great opportunities for undergraduates. One student tells us, "Overall, my professors at Clemson have been engaging, encouraging students to not only learn the information being presented, but also to apply it. Many of my courses have been solely discussion based, and those with predominately lectures encourage class participation. I truly enjoy attending class at Clemson because the professors make the topics interesting." Overall, students feel that the value is unbeatable. "The scholarship money was great, the location picture perfect, the atmosphere friendly, and the quality of education among the best in the nation," according to a current freshman. "I have been challenged throughout my college career," another student informs us.

BANG FOR YOUR BUCK

Clemson University works to engage students and provide them with advantages in the workforce that begin with their undergraduate experience. Students have worked at more than 375 companies through cooperative education, providing them with the ability to apply what is learned in class to real-life situations, while making invaluable contacts in the field they have chosen to pursue. Subsequently, this makes them strong contenders in today's job market. As one student relates, "Being able to research as an undergraduate has been exceedingly helpful in obtaining a job after graduation." One junior reports, "At Clemson, I'm earning a respected degree working alongside the leading researcher in my field, gaining valuable leadership experience while serving the community, and having the time of my life with my best friends. What's not to love?" Yet another student adds, "Clemson has put a large emphasis on recruiting the best faculty over the past ten years, and it shows."

STUDENTS

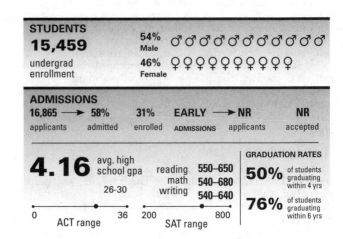

15,459 undergrad enrollment

54% Male ♂♂♂♂♂♂♂♂♂♂

46% Female ♀♀♀♀♀♀♀♀♀

ADMISSIONS

16,865 →	58%	31%	EARLY →	NR	NR
applicants	admitted	enrolled	ADMISSIONS	applicants	accepted

4.16 avg. high school gpa

26-30 — ACT range (0–36)

reading 550–650
math 540–680
writing 540–640
SAT range (200–800)

GRADUATION RATES

50% of students graduating within 4 yrs

76% of students graduating within 6 yrs

E-MAIL: CUADMISSIONS@CLEMSON.EDU • FAX: 864-656-2464 • WEBSITE: WWW.CLEMSON.EDU

STUDENT BODY

"Clemson students have a bond," a happy student notes. "I have made so many connections with others because we both attended Clemson." Clemson is "not a hot spot of diversity by any means," and "your typical student is Southern, Christian, and somewhat preppy." That doesn't mean that students from different backgrounds can't fit in. "Although Clemson is a 'jock school' with a some what homogeneous student body, most people are pleasant, and you can easily enjoy your college experience." Another student relates that, while most students are Southern and religiously conservative, "as a non-religious student from the North, I've felt welcome here and have loved every minute of my experience."

Why Students love Clemson University

"Nowhere else feels more like home."

WHY STUDENTS LOVE CLEMSON UNIVERSITY

Students have a determined spirit in reference to all aspects of student life, including but not limited to academic excellence, service to the campus and community, an appreciation of the arts, and athletic pursuits. The school spirit and tradition found throughout campus make the experience one of family, and more than one student lists "happiness" as a valuable asset of Clemson life. One student says, "Clemson is all about pride, pride in ourselves, in each other, and in Clemson itself." A current sophomore adds to that sentiment, saying, "You hear a lot about the 'Clemson Family' as a prospective student. It's not just talk: it's an attitude you can feel the minute you set foot on campus, and makes for a fantastic college experience." "Nowhere else feels more like home," mentions another student.

GENERAL INFO

Activities: Choral groups, concert band, dance, drama/theater, jazz band, literary magazine, marching band, music ensembles, pep band, radio station, student government, student newspaper, television station, yearbook. **Organizations:** 292 registered organizations, 23 honor societies, 24 religious organizations. 26 fraternities, 17 sororities. **Athletics (Intercollegiate):** *Men:* Baseball, basketball, cheerleading, cross-country, diving, football, golf, soccer, swimming, tennis, track/field (outdoor), track/field (indoor). *Women:* Basketball, cheerleading, crew/rowing, cross-country, diving, soccer, swimming, tennis, track/field (outdoor), track/field (indoor), volleyball. **On-Campus Highlights:** SC Botanical Garden/Discovery Center/Geology Muse, Hendrix Student Center–Clemson Ice Cream, Conference Center and Inn at Clemson/Walker Golf Course, Fort Hill–John C. Calhoun House, Lee Art Gallery.

BOTTOM LINE

Clemson University provides a diverse, yet comprehensive educational experience, at an affordable cost. One satisfied student shares, "I wanted to be a part of the Clemson family, and the price was right. I received full scholarship and stipend, and thus Clemson became the best value for an education." Yearly tuition is just more than $12,000 for students from in-state. Undergraduates from elsewhere will be looking at an increase to more than $27,000; nonetheless, 30 percent of students do come from out-of-state. Another $8,000 or so will cover room and board, as well as books and required fees for all students.

SELECTIVITY

Admissions Rating	**89**
# of applicants	16,865
% of applicants accepted	58
% of acceptees attending	31
# accepting a place on wait list	638
% admitted from wait list	17

FRESHMAN PROFILE

Range SAT Critical Reading	**550–650**
Range SAT Math	**590–680**
Range SAT Writing	**540–640**
Range ACT Composite	**26-30**
Average HS GPA	**4.16**
% graduated top 10% of class	**51**
% graduated top 25% of class	**83**
% graduated top 50% of class	**98**

DEADLINES

Regular Deadline	**12/1**
Normal registration	**yes**

FACILITIES

Housing: Coed dorms, men's dorms, special housing for international students, women's dorms, fraternity/sorority housing, apartments for single students, wellness housing, theme housing, learning-living communities. *Special Academic Facilities/Equipment:* The South Carolina Botanical Gardens, the Campbell Geology Museum, the Brooks Center for the Performing Arts, the Rudolph Lee Art Gallery, the Garrison Livestock Arena, the John C. Calhoun Home. *Computers:* 75% of classrooms, 25% of dorms, 100% of libraries, 100% of dining areas, 100% of student union, 40% of common outdoor areas have wireless network access.

FINANCIAL FACTS

Financial Aid Rating	**70**
Annual in-state tuition	$12,668
Annual out-of-state tuition	$28,826
Room and Board	$7,228
Books and supplies	$1,090
% frosh rec. need-based scholarship or grant aid	15
% UG rec.need-based scholarship or grant aid	18
% frosh rec. non-need-based scholarship or grant aid	77
% UG rec. non-need-based scholarship or grant aid	59
% frosh rec. need-based self-help aid	24
% UG rec. need-based self-help aid	28
% frosh rec. any financial aid	87
% UG rec. any financial aid	71
% UG borrow to pay for school	44
Average cumulative indebtedness	$17,882

College of Charleston

66 George Street, Charleston, SC 29424 • Admissions: 843-953-5670 • Fax: 843-953-6322

CAMPUS LIFE

Quality of life Rating	89
Fire Safety Rating	95
Green rating	85
Type of School	Public
Environment	City

STUDENTS

Total undergrad enrollment	9,771
% Male to Female	37/63
% From out of state	36
% From public high school	80
# of Fraternities	14
# of Sororities	13
% African American	6
% Asian	2
% Caucasian	84
% Hispanic	3
% International	1
# Of Countries Represented	62

ACADEMICS

Academic Rating	79
% Of students graduating within 4 years	54
% Of students graduating within 6 years	66
Calendar	semester
Profs interesting rating	83
Profs accessible rating	86
Most common reg class size	20–29 students
Most common lab size	20–29 students

MOST POPULAR MAJORS

Biology, business administration and management, speech communication and rhetoric

HONORS PROGRAMS

Honors College at the College of Charleston.

SPECIAL STUDY OPTIONS

Accelerated program, cooperative education program, cross-registration, distance learning, double major, dual enrollment, exchange student program (domestic), independent study, internships, liberal arts/career combination, study abroad, Semester at Sea.

ABOUT THE SCHOOL

South Carolina's College of Charleston is a moderately sized school that manages to make itself feel like a small school, a "Southern secret" that is "extremely diverse" and offers "many great fields of study." The college manages to maintain relatively small class sizes, which "allows professors to pay individualized attention to students and to make time to advise their students outside of class." Charleston offers a "perfect balance of a full liberal arts education with a bustling, charming city." The student body is "a mix of funky, hip students who love the beach and the city." Students are "intelligent," but "not overly intellectual." It is not an easy school, students report, "nor is it extremely difficult." Yet don't be lulled into a false sense of security, because "it's a tougher school academically than people think it is." For those who do want to tackle a more rigorous program, there is an Honors College at Charleston, which provides students with "a wealth of opportunities and challenges." Students say many professors are "leaders in their respective fields" and that "few disappoint." They are "engaging" and "markedly passionate" about teaching; "I've never had a professor that didn't absolutely love what he or she taught." Another notes that across the board faculty here "make a strong effort to cater to the needs of the students," and more than a few suggest this school is staffed by "amazing professors who know how to teach and teach well."

Why Students love College of Charleston

"Perfect balance of a full liberal arts education with a bustling, charming city."

BANG FOR YOUR BUCK

The College of Charleston is affordable for most students, most notably for those in state, who pay less than half what out-of-state students pay. Some students can expect "a large amount of scholarships," again, especially if they are in state. Further, those who show academic excellence can expect financial assistance. According to the administration, "The majority of students in the Honors College at the College of Charleston receive some form of academic scholarship."

STUDENTS

9,771 undergrad enrollment

37% Male ♂♂♂♂♂♂♂

63% Female ♀♀♀♀♀♀♀♀♀♀♀♀♀

ADMISSIONS

11,280 applicants	→ 70% admitted	25% enrolled	EARLY ADMISSIONS → NR applicants	NR accepted

3.87 avg. high school gpa

ACT range (0–36): 23 – 27

SAT range (200–800): reading 570 – 650; math 570 – 640

GRADUATION RATES

54% of students graduating within 4 yrs

66% of students graduating within 6 yrs

College of Charleston

FINANCIAL AID: 843-953-5540 • E-MAIL: ADMISSIONS@COFC.EDU • WEBSITE: WWW.COFC.EDU

STUDENT BODY

The student body is more than sixty percent female–a fact that some love while others wish for "a better girl-to-guy ratio" as well as "more ethnic diversity." "The typical student is Caucasian, female, and wealthy," and "very preppy/Southern. Not too many Northerners." That doesn't mean that the students aren't "friendly" and "accepting." "Students fit in pretty well because there are many groups and clubs on campus where you can meet people." Although an out-of-state student cautions that "it can be difficult for students from out of state to fit in because [a lot] of the students are either local or in-state and already know each other." "There are three types of students at this school," one student claims. "1) Preppy Southerners clad in Vera Bradley and Ralph Lauren. 2) Disaffected hipsters/artists who clearly are not the starving type seeing as their entire wardrobe comes from Urban Outfitters and American Apparel. 3) Everyone else." "Most are the 'prep' or 'hipster' type," another student confirms. However, others see a wider variety in the student body. "There are hippies, sorority girls, fraternity guys, feminists, surfers, preppy Southern gentlemen, people from the Jersey shore, international students, Christians, atheists, pagans, vegans, Republicans, Democrats, Libertarians...it is hard to sum up just one 'typical' student here."

WHY STUDENTS LOVE COLLEGE OF CHARLESTON

Location, location, location. If there is a primary reason why students love the College of Charleston, it is its perfect blend of "the urban environment but small-town feel." When confronted with a school that is "on the beach in a beautiful Southern city," one student asks the obvious question: "How do you say no to that?" Mother Nature does her part to help that atmosphere. "The weather is a million times better than the North." The night life here is strong and boasts a thriving music scene. The beach is a short 20-minute drive away, and an active Greek culture provides plenty of off-campus partying opportunities whether or not you are actually involved with Greek life.

GENERAL INFO

Activities: Choral groups, dance, drama/theater, jazz band, literary magazine, music ensembles, musical theater, pep band, radio station, student government, student newspaper, symphony orchestra, yearbook, campus ministries, international student organization. **Organizations:** 120 registered organizations, 19 honor societies, 16 religious organizations. 13 fraternities, 12 sororities. **Athletics (Intercollegiate):** *Men:* Baseball, basketball, cross-country, diving, golf, sailing, soccer, swimming, tennis. *Women:* Basketball, cross-country, diving, equestrian sports, golf, sailing, soccer, softball, swimming, tennis, track/field (outdoor), track/field (indoor), volleyball.

BOTTOM LINE

In-state tuition falls below the $10,000 mark, while out-of-state tuition is still a manageable $23,000. Add to that about $9,800 in room and board costs and an additional $1,200 in books and supplies, and those in state can expect to pay $21,000 a year while those out of state will put out about $34,000 a year. Some 31 percent of freshmen receive need-based grants or scholarships, and 33 percent receive non-need-based grants or scholarships. Students graduate with an average debt of about $19,800.

SELECTIVITY

Admissions Rating	**88**
# of applicants	11,280
% of applicants accepted	70
% of acceptees attending	25

FRESHMAN PROFILE

Range SAT Critical Reading	**570–650**
Range SAT Math	**570–640**
Range ACT Composite	**23–27**
Average HS GPA	**3.87**
% graduated top 10% of class	**31**
% graduated top 25% of class	**68**
% graduated top 50% of class	**94**

DEADLINES

Regular Deadline	**2/1**
Normal registration	**yes**

FACILITIES

Housing: Coed dorms, men's dorms, women's dorms, fraternity/sorority housing, apartments for single students, theme housing. *Special Academic Facilities/Equipment:* Halsey Institute of Contemporary Art, sculpture facility, Rivers Communications Museum, Miles Early Childhood Development Center, Avery Institute for African-American History and Culture, Patriots Point Athletics Complex (includes softball, baseball, tennis, soccer and sailing).

FINANCIAL FACTS

Financial Aid Rating	**77**
Annual in-state tuition	$9,616
Annual out-of-state tuition	$24,330
Room and Board	$10,179
Books and supplies	$1,224
% frosh rec. need-based scholarship or grant aid	31
% UG rec.need-based scholarship or grant aid	28
% frosh rec. non-need-based scholarship or grant aid	33
% UG rec. non-need-based scholarship or grant aid	19
% frosh rec. need-based self-help aid	33
% UG rec. need-based self-help aid	35
% frosh rec. any financial aid	43
% UG rec. any financial aid	42
% UG borrow to pay for school	44
Average cumulative indebtedness	$19,875

The College of New Jersey

PO Box 7718, Ewing, NJ 08628-0718 Admissions: 609-771-2131 • Financial Aid: 609-771-2211

CAMPUS LIFE

Quality of life Rating	90
Fire Safety Rating	95
Green rating	85
Type of School	Public
Environment	Village

STUDENTS

Total undergrad enrolllment	6,410
% Male to Female	42/58
% From out of state	6
% From public high school	70
% Live on Campus	62
# of Fraternities	13
# of Sororities	13
% African American	6
% Asian	6
% Caucasian	66
% Hispanic	9
# Of Countries Represented	30

ACADEMICS

Academic Rating	89
% Of students graduating within 4 years	71
% Of students graduating within 6 years	86
Calendar	semester
Profs interesting rating	90
Profs accessible rating	90
Most common reg class size	20–29 students
Most common lab size	20–29 students

MOST POPULAR MAJORS

Biology, business adminstration and management, psychology

HONOR PROGRAMS

The National Scholars Program.

SPECIAL STUDY OPTIONS

Accelerated program, double major, dual enrollment, exchange student program (domestic), honors program, independent study, internships, liberal arts/career combination, student-designed major, study abroad, teacher certification program, 7-year medical program with UMDNJ, 7-year BS/OD program with SUNY, mentored undergraduate summer research program.

ABOUT THE SCHOOL

The College of New Jersey is situated on 289-acre in Ewing. The small, state run public school starts incoming freshmen off on the right foot with a strong foundation of core requirements, which eventually leads to a final capstone courses their senior year. Students who signup for the First Year Experience will participate in the program for the duration of the year and receive support related to their transition from high school to college. The group is required to sign up for a First Seminar course where they will discuss issues that may arise while adjusting, and be housed on the same floor in their dorm.

No courses are complete without outstanding professors, and students at TCNJ say theirs are the best. "I think the personal attention is the greatest strength," a student shared. "I loved that all of my professors knew my name. The classes are small and you really get to know both your professor and the other students in the class." The faculty goes above and beyond, even inviting their students in on the hiring process. "Whenever a position opens up in a department, the students are encouraged to attend lectures by prospective candidates and offer their input," one student writes. They also "find no cake-walk when it comes to classes."

BANG FOR YOUR BUCK

Close to 50 percent of full-time undergraduates benefit from financial aid, which can come in the form of merit-based scholarships, work-study programs, loans, or government or institutional grants. Title IV students may compete for the College's merit scholarships, which are funded by the state government as well as private donors. These awards are offered to those applicants with top SAT scores and class rankings. Over the last six years, TCNJ has given scholarships totaling more than $12 million. Almost three-quarters of students graduate within 4 years, and over a third pursue graduate studies. In addition to "top-notch faculty and the newest technology," students have the opportunity to develop their own special interest learning communities on campus. Also, commitment to sustainability has been incorporated into the curriculum at TCNJ. The college's Municipal Land Use Center is authoring the State's sustainability and climate neutrality plans, and the school has committed to offsetting greenhouse gas produced by faculty and staff travel on an annual basis through the purchase of carbon offsets

STUDENTS

6,410 undergrad enrollment

42% Male ♂♂♂♂♂♂♂♂

58% Female ♀♀♀♀♀♀♀♀♀♀♀♀

ADMISSIONS

9,956 applicants → 47% admitted — 30% enrolled

EARLY ADMISSIONS → NR applicants — NR accepted

NR ACT range (0–36)

avg. high school gpa NR

SAT range (200–800): reading 560–670, math 590–680, writing 560–670

GRADUATION RATES

71% of students graduating within 4 yrs

86% of students graduating within 6 yrs

The College of New Jersey

E-MAIL: TCNJINFO@TCNJ.EDU • FAX: 609-637-5174 • WEBSITE: WWW.TCNJ.EDU

STUDENT BODY

"You can find any personality type at TCNJ," students tell us, from "your typical jocks who love to party," to "extremely conservative kids who haven't missed a Sunday mass since getting here," and "a few hippie types and everything in between. Whatever your social circle, you're bound to fit in." What they share in common is that most are "smart, dedicated people who care about their education very much," "were in the top fifteen percent of their high school class," and "are willing to push themselves to do better in school."

WHY STUDENTS LOVE THE COLLEGE OF NEW JERSEY

TCNJ students, or "Lions," are a diverse bunch who are nonetheless all "smart, dedicated people who care about their education very much," students say. Many "different faiths and ethnicities" are represented here and accepted. "You can find any personality type at TCNJ," students tell us, from "your typical jocks who love to party," to "extremely conservative kids who haven't missed a Sunday mass since getting here," and "a few hippie types and everything in between. Whatever your social circle, you're bound to fit in." While "everyone has different interests," "this is a great place for everyone to be able to find a niche."

GENERAL INFO

Environment: Village. **Activities:** Choral groups, concert band, dance, drama/theater, jazz band, literary magazine, music ensembles, musical theater, opera, pep band, radio station, student government, student newspaper, symphony orchestra, television station, yearbook, campus ministries, international student organization, Model UN. **Organizations:** 205 registered organizations, 16 honor societies, 11 religious organizations. 12 fraternities, 16 sororities. **Athletics (Intercollegiate):** *Men:* Baseball, basketball, cross-country, diving, football, soccer, swimming, tennis, track/field (outdoor), track/field (indoor). *Women:* Basketball, cross-country, diving, field hockey, lacrosse, soccer, softball, swimming, tennis, track/field (outdoor), track/field (indoor).

Why Students love TCNJ

"It's low cost and provides a ton of opportunities to try new things."

BOTTOM LINE

"A smaller school that is a bargain for its quality of education," according to one happy undergrad, The College of New Jersey lives up to these words. With in-state tuition and fees amounting to just more than $12,000, and plenty of aid available, the school makes college a possibility for most every budget. More than 80 percent of freshmen receive financial aid, with the average total package being more than $10,000. Out-of-state students are looking at a bit more than $20,000 per year; room and board for all students is less than $10,000. The college meets just less than 50 percent of all need, and the average need-based gift aid is more than $11,000. "Many of my friends... got into very prestigious schools...but chose TCNJ because of its unbeatable cost," reports one undergrad. There is also a respectable 13:1 student-to-faculty ratio, within such a large campus; there are 6,500 students in all, 1,400 of whom are incoming freshman.

SELECTIVITY

Admissions Rating	**90**
# of applicants	9,956
% of applicants accepted	47
% of acceptees attending	30
# accepting a place on wait list	549
% admitted from wait list	21

FRESHMAN PROFILE

Range SAT Critical Reading	**560–670**
Range SAT Math	**590–680**
Range SAT Writing	**560–670**
% graduated top 10% of class	**60**
% graduated top 25% of class	**91**
% graduated top 50% of class	**100**

DEADLINES

Regular Deadline	**1/15**
Normal registration	**yes**

FACILITIES

Housing: Coed dorms, special housing for disabled students, special housing for international students, women's dorms, apartments for single students, wellness housing. Faculty and students have the opportunity to develop their own special interest learning communities on campus. *Special Academic Facilities/Equipment:* Art gallery, concert hall, greenhouse, observatory, planetarium, nuclear magnetic resonance lab, optical spectroscopy lab, scanning and transmission electron microscopes. *Computers:* 22% of classrooms, 5% of dorms, 100% of libraries, 85% of dining areas, 70% of student union, 5% of common outdoor areas have wireless network access.

FINANCIAL FACTS

Financial Aid Rating	**66**
Annual in-state tuition	$9,760
Annual out-of-state tuition	$19,569
Room and Board	$10,677
Required Fees	$4,127
Room and Board	$1000
% frosh rec. need-based scholarship or grant aid	23
% UG rec.need-based scholarship or grant aid	20
% frosh rec. non-need-based scholarship or grant aid	38
% UG rec. non-need-based scholarship or grant aid	22
% frosh rec. need-based self-help aid	34
% UG rec. need-based self-help aid	36
% frosh rec. any financial aid	80
% UG rec. any financial aid	70
% UG borrow to pay for school	56
Average cumulative indebtedness	$27,057

The Evergreen State College

2700 Evergreen Pkwy NW, Olympia, WA 98505 • Admissions: 360-867-6170 • Fax: 360-867-5114

CAMPUS LIFE

Quality of life Rating	75
Fire Safety Rating	84
Green rating	86
Type of School	Public
Environment	City

STUDENTS

Total undergrad enrolllment	4,314
% Male to Female	46/54
% From out of state	27
% Live on Campus	21
% African American	4
% Asian	3
% Caucasian	70
% Hispanic	5
% Native American	3
# Of Countries Represented	15

ACADEMICS

Academic Rating	76
% Of students graduating within 4 years	39
% Of students graduating within 6 years	50
Calendar	semester
Profs interesting rating	88
Profs accessible rating	77
Most common reg class size	20–29 students

MOST POPULAR MAJORS

Humanities, interdisciplinary studies, social sciences

SPECIAL STUDY OPTIONS

Accelerated program, double major, exchange student program (domestic), independent study, internships, student-designed major, study abroad, teacher certification program, weekend college, Learning disabilities services, summer session for credit, off-campus study.

ABOUT THE SCHOOL

"A small, quirky, liberal college in the Pacific Northwest," Evergreen is located in Olympia, Washington's state capital. The school is perfect for self-motivated students, with one saying, "Evergreen is about active and participatory education, not passive absorption." Providing an alternative education with innovative academic programs and a strong focus on social justice issues, Evergreen is prized by students for allowing them "to truly take your learning in your own hands" and be responsible for their own education, with opportunities to "create your own learning structure, to explore uncharted academic waters." One undergrad likes that ESC "prepares students for life rather than herding people into some career." TESC is strongly supportive of independent endeavors, allowing students to write independent learning contracts. "If you want to learn something, you most likely can do it and get credit for it." Creative thinking is highly encouraged, and the faculty has great enthusiasm for originality. Plenty of opportunities for special projects and internships are evident, and the school has an extremely active student government. There is a strong emphasis on community work and interacting with other cultures, and a sense of awareness about racial and social issues. Non-traditional students of all ages are welcomed, and there is a decidedly non-competitive vibe on campus. "Evergreen offers an open-minded environment that promotes ecological and social awareness and responsibility," one student informs us.

BANG FOR YOUR BUCK

Evergreen is an extremely affordable and cost-effective public school–especially for in-state students. "Our school is one of the only schools offering such an alternative approach to higher education, and might be the only one that does it at state tuition," says one resident. Others are pleased to discover "the cost of attending this school was a lot lower than I thought," and that ESC is "the best education for my money." "I wanted to choose what I was going to spend my time and money on studying, instead of have it chosen for me through pre-requisites." Most Evergreen students are very active in the community, and internships are usually required. "Since we are so close to the state capital I was given the opportunity to be a student lobbyist for my school and make a difference for access to higher education." Independent studies and study abroad are features included in many upper-division programs, affording students invaluable real-life experiences.

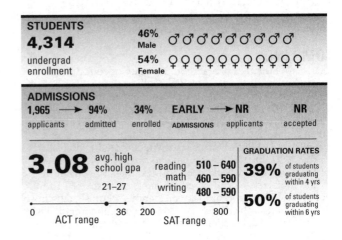

STUDENTS

4,314 undergrad enrollment

46% Male ♂♂♂♂♂♂♂♂♂

54% Female ♀♀♀♀♀♀♀♀♀♀♀

ADMISSIONS

1,965 applicants → 94% admitted | 34% enrolled | EARLY ADMISSIONS → NR applicants | NR accepted

3.08 avg. high school gpa

ACT range (0–36): 21–27

SAT range (200–800): reading 510 – 640; math 460 – 590; writing 480 – 590

GRADUATION RATES

39% of students graduating within 4 yrs

50% of students graduating within 6 yrs

The Evergreen State College

FINANCIAL AID: 360-867-6205 • E-MAIL: ADMISSIONS@EVERGREEN.EDU • WEBSITE: WWW.EVERGREEN.EDU

STUDENT BODY

Evergreen is a "quirky" college, and, as such, it tends to attract students looking for something other than the classic undergraduate experience. There is "no typical student" at Evergreen, but you'll definitely meet your share of "hipster, coffee-shop types" and "Earth-friendly, artsy types" at this alternative school. A sophomore jokes, "I'm not sure what you would have to wear to not fit in at Evergreen–maybe a suit and tie?" Politically and socially, "the student body definitely swings left, with a large portion of students interested in environmental conservation, organic farming, LGBT rights, and Eastern philosophy and religion."

WHY STUDENTS LOVE THE EVERGREEN STATE COLLEGE

"If you got bored here, you are doing something wrong," notes an incredulous undergrad. Others tell us that "there is an amazing amount of environmental, political and nutritional awareness on campus," including administration, faculty, and the student body. "People think and talk about politics and world events quite a lot;" "it seems almost everyone has a passion for some cause." Everyday conversation is often an intellectual discussion. Students at ESC want to "learn how to change the world, realistically, responsibly, and effectively." Evergreen has a fine reputation for promoting sustainability and working to be environmentally friendly, having a student body, which is very progressive and "green."

Why Students love The Evergreen State College

"There is an amazing amount of environmental, political and nutritional awareness on campus."

GENERAL INFO

Activities: Choral groups, dance, drama/theater, literary magazine, music ensembles, pep band, radio station, student government, student newspaper, student-run film society, television station, campus ministries, Model UN. **Organizations:** 61 registered organizations, 3 religious organizations. **Athletics (Intercollegiate):** *Men:* Basketball, cross-country, soccer, track/field (outdoor), track/field (indoor). *Women:* Basketball, cross-country, soccer, track/field (outdoor), track/field (indoor), volleyball. **On-Campus Highlights:** Longhouse Cultural and Education Center, Organic Farm, College Library, College Activities Building, New Seminar II Building, The Flaming Eggplant, a student-run cafe featuring organic, local, and vegan food.

BOTTOM LINE

Evergreen State College has an enrollment of approximately 4500 students, 75% being native to the state. The in-state tuition will run just over $6000 per year, and out-of-state students will be responsible for slightly more than $17,000 per year. Room and board is $8500; required fees, $550, and supplies, $1000.

SELECTIVITY

Admissions Rating	**72**
# of applicants	1,965
% of applicants accepted	94
% of acceptees attending	34

FRESHMAN PROFILE

Range SAT Critical Reading	**510–640**
Range SAT Math	**460–590**
Range SAT Writing	**480–590**
Range ACT Composite	**21–27**
Average HS GPA	**3.08**
% graduated top 10% of class	**12**
% graduated top 25% of class	**27**
% graduated top 50% of class	**62**

DEADLINES

Regular Deadline	**11/1**
Normal registration	**yes**

FACILITIES

Housing: Coed dorms, special housing for disabled students, special housing for international students, apartments for married students, apartments for single students, wellness housing, theme housing. *Special Academic Facilities/Equipment*: Longhouse Cultural Center, 4 computer music labs, 3 digital studio production studios, organic farm. *Computers*:100% of classrooms, 95% of dorms, 100% of libraries, 100% of dining areas, 100% of student union, 80% of common outdoor areas have wireless network access.

FINANCIAL FACTS

Financial Aid Rating	**72**
Annual in-state tuition	$6,909
Annual out-of-state tuition	$18,090
Room and Board	$9,000
Required Fees	$577
Books and supplies	$972
% frosh rec. need-based scholarship or grant aid	36
% UG rec.need-based scholarship or grant aid	46
% frosh rec. non-need-based scholarship or grant aid	29
% UG rec. non-need-based scholarship or grant aid	11
% frosh rec. need-based self-help aid	34
% UG rec. need-based self-help aid	42
% frosh rec. any financial aid	50
% UG rec. any financial aid	57
% UG borrow to pay for school	48
Average cumulative indebtedness	$16,065

Florida State University

PO Box 3062400, Tallahassee, FL 32306-2400 • Admissions: 850-644-6200 • Fax: 850-644-0197

CAMPUS LIFE

Quality of life Rating	86
Fire Safety Rating	80
Green rating	90
Type of School	Public
Environment	City

STUDENTS

Total undergrad enrolllment	30,830
% Male to Female	45/55
% From out of state	9
% From public high school	84
% Live on Campus	20
# of Fraternities	31
# of Sororities	27
% African American	11
% Asian	4
% Caucasian	69
% Hispanic	14
% Native American	1
# Of Countries Represented	132

ACADEMICS

Academic Rating	68
% Of students graduating within 4 years	69
% Of students graduating within 6 years	74
Calendar	semester
Profs interesting rating	79
Profs accessible rating	81
Most common reg class size	20–29 students

MOST POPULAR MAJORS

Criminal justice/safety studies, finance, political science

HONORS PROGRAMS

Florida State University Honors Program

SPECIAL STUDY OPTIONS

Accelerated program, cooperative education program, cross-registration, distance learning, double major, dual enrollment, English as a Second Language (ESL), honors program, independent study, internships, study abroad, teacher certification program

ABOUT THE SCHOOL

Opportunity, diversity, and choice: These terms define the undergraduate experience at Florida State University. One student says, "I chose FSU because it is affordable, the campus is beautiful, I received excellent scholarships and it's in a perfect location for gaining internship experience." In addition to intense academic competition at FSU, "the professors at Florida State are very interested in the success of their students and are available for office hours and outside help for a wide spectrum of times convenient for you." FSU also awards research fellowships to promising undergraduates, with numerous grants available to help offset the costs of studying overseas. "The Student Government Association is very active on campus. There are great student organizations to get involved in." When they aren't studying, many FSU undergrads will tell you that lots of students equals lots of fun. Football games, kegs, bonfires, and Greek parties are all a big part of life at FSU. "The Greek Life here at FSU has a strong influence that challenges students to better their campus and college experience." "Aside from having a great football team and incredible academics, FSU also has a top-notch international program." One junior says that "a lot of people don't know about FSU's great international programs. I spent a semester abroad at FSU's campus in central London which is one of the best decisions I've made in college." A research giant, the school's faculty includes Nobel Laureates, members of the National Academy of Sciences, Guggenheim Fellows, and Pulitzer Prize winners. "All of my professors continuously push our mental abilities to ensure that students are thinking outside of the box and improving our problem solving capabilities." Opportunities abound. "The professors are very learned individuals that support the growth of their students in and out of the classroom. Overall, the academic experience is a challenging course through a wide array of studies."

BANG FOR YOUR BUCK

For a low in-state tuition, FSU offers unmatched resources, diverse academic opportunities, access to major research facilities, and a bustling campus environment. All things considered, this school is a steal for Florida residents. In addition to the low price tag, students may submit the FAFSA to apply for need-based loans, grants, and work-study. Students with AP course credit can receive an FSU degree within just three years of study, thereby saving a year's tuition and expenses. The school awards numerous scholarships for academic merit, as well as for athletics and the arts. The top admitted students are offered the University Scholarship, a $9,600 gift distributed over four years. All applicants to Florida State University are automatically considered for merit scholarships.

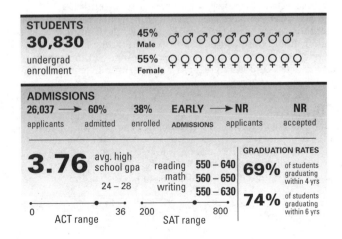

STUDENTS
30,830 undergrad enrollment
45% Male
55% Female

ADMISSIONS
26,037 applicants → 60% admitted; 38% enrolled
EARLY ADMISSIONS → NR applicants; NR accepted

3.76 avg. high school gpa

ACT range (0–36): 24 – 28

SAT range (200–800): reading 550 – 640; math 560 – 650; writing 550 – 630

GRADUATION RATES
69% of students graduating within 4 yrs
74% of students graduating within 6 yrs

Florida State University

FINANCIAL AID: 850-644-5716 • E-MAIL: ADMISSIONS@ADMIN.FSU.EDU • WEBSITE: WWW.FSU.EDU

STUDENT BODY

Your average FSU student is a "football fan, partier, into academics and community service, [and] passionate." Students tend to be "extremely involved," whether it's in athletics, "Greek life or community service, or one of the other hundreds of groups and clubs here at FSU." "Greek is a huge part of campus, but you are fine if you are not in one." Although "the majority of students are Caucasians," "students of all races and religions work together here to make FSU an enjoyable environment," and "the school continues to become more diverse each year." No matter what their background, every FSU student has "a colossal amount of school spirit and loves to go out and support the team."

Why Students love Florida State University

"Some of the greatest strengths of FSU is the support it has from alumni and the immediate Tallahassee area, the large amount of faculty, and the wide variety of involvement opportunities around campus."

WHY STUDENTS LOVE FLORIDA STATE UNIVERSITY

One thing about FSU that students love is "having a large student body, thus, having a magnanimous amount of organizations and opportunities." One student writes that "[FSU] doesn't force some sort of warped school patriotism. People are very artistic and thoughtful and we enjoy learning from each other's experiences." Another positive aspect of FSU is location: "Florida State is in the heart of the capital of Florida. It offers thousands of opportunities for students to participate hands-on in the workings of our state government."

GENERAL INFO

Activities: Choral groups, concert band, dance, drama/theater, jazz band, literary magazine, marching band, music ensembles, musical theater, opera, pep band, radio station, student government, student newspaper, student-run film society, symphony orchestra, television station, yearbook, campus ministries, international student organization. **Organizations:** 520 registered organizations, 23 honor societies, 30 religious organizations. 32 fraternities, 28 sororities. **Athletics (Intercollegiate):** *Men:* Baseball, basketball, cheerleading, cross-country, diving, football, golf, swimming, tennis, track/field (outdoor), track/field (indoor). *Women:* Basketball, cheerleading, cross-country, diving, golf, soccer, softball, swimming, tennis, track/field (outdoor), track/field (indoor), volleyball.

BOTTOM LINE

FSU is affordable. For state residents, annual tuition and fees run a little more than $5,000. The school estimates that students will spend another $8,000 or so on room and board. Non-residents pay $19,600 in tuition and fees, a significant increase from the in-state rate, yet still cheaper than many private institutions. One student explains details "how inexpensive FSU is. FSU offered me a scholarship on top of my bright future's and prepaid. I actually have enough money leftover each semester to pay for my sorority." To secure the best aid package and scholarships, the school recommends that prospective students apply as early as possible.

SELECTIVITY

Admissions Rating	**89**
# of applicants	26,037
% of applicants accepted	60
% of acceptees attending	38

FRESHMAN PROFILE

Range SAT Critical Reading	**550–640**
Range SAT Math	**560–650**
Range SAT Writing	**550–630**
Range ACT Composite	**24–28**
Average HS GPA	**3.76**
% graduated top 10% of class	**39**
% graduated top 25% of class	**76**
% graduated top 50% of class	**97**

DEADLINES

Regular Deadline	**1/25**
Normal registration	**yes**

FACILITIES

Housing: Coed dorms, special housing for disabled students, women's dorms, fraternity/sorority housing, apartments for married students, apartments for single students. *Special Academic Facilities/Equipment:* Art gallery, museum, developmental research school, marine lab, oceanographic institute, tandem Van de Graaff accelerator, national high magnetic field lab.

FINANCIAL FACTS

Financial Aid Rating	**91**
Annual in-state tuition	$3,397
Annual out-of-state tuition	$18,564
Room and Board	$9,412
Required Fees	$2,428
Books and supplies	$1,000
% frosh rec. need-based scholarship or grant aid	23
% UG rec.need-based scholarship or grant aid	23
% frosh rec. non-need-based scholarship or grant aid	36
% UG rec. non-need-based scholarship or grant aid	28
% frosh rec. need-based self-help aid	24
% UG rec. need-based self-help aid	27
% frosh rec. any financial aid	97
% UG rec. any financial aid	86
% UG borrow to pay for school	48
Average cumulative indebtedness	$20,993

Georgia Institute of Technology

Georgia Institute of Technology, Atlanta, GA 30332-0320 • Admissions: 404-894-4154 • Fax: 404-894-9511

CAMPUS LIFE

Quality of life Rating	81
Fire Safety Rating	89
Green rating	99
Type of School	Public
Environment	Metropolis

STUDENTS

Total undergrad enrolllment	13,160
% Male to Female	69/31
% From out of state	26
% From public high school	86
% Live on Campus	59
# of Fraternities	39
# of Sororities	16
% African American	6
% Asian	17
% Caucasian	62
% Hispanic	5
% International	7
# Of Countries Represented	73

ACADEMICS

Academic Rating	72
% Of students graduating within 4 years	33
% Of students graduating within 6 years	80
Calendar	semester
Profs interesting rating	61
Profs accessible rating	63
Most common reg class size	10–19 students
Most common lab size	20–29 students

MOST POPULAR MAJORS

Business administration and management, industrial engineering, mechanical engineering

HONORS PROGRAMS

The Georgia Tech Honors Program.

SPECIAL STUDY OPTIONS

Accelerated program, cooperative education program, cross-registration, distance learning, double major, dual enrollment.

ABOUT THE SCHOOL

The Georgia Institute of Technology is the Southern, public institution for the scholar. "Unlike at high school, no one looks down upon you if you know the entire periodic table, if you can do differential equations, or you can speak three languages; rather, you are respected," one student claims. Firmly rooted in research, Georgia Tech teaches its students to be independent learners who are able to recognize when it's time to ask for help. "If you're organized and get help when you need it, you'll be okay, because we have tons of free tutoring on campus…If you need help with anything, there are countless different places that offer tutoring. The best resource is usually fellow students. The school "is extremely challenging, academically," a student tells us. Because everyone knows how tough of a school it is, there is a spirit of camara¬derie here that you don't find anywhere else," one student says.

Why Students love Georgia Tech

"Because everyone knows how tough of a school it is, there is a spirit of camaraderie here that you don't find anywhere else."

BANG FOR YOUR BUCK

Almost 95 percent of freshman students return for their sophomore year–always an encouraging sign. Popular programs on the Atlanta campus include engineering, computing, management, architecture, and the sciences. Graduates of Georgia Tech often find themselves well prepared once they embark upon the workforce. Undergraduates are offered countless opportunities to earn valuable work experience through the institution's co-op and internship programs early research that can be started as soon as their freshman year. For those with international interests, immersions are available through study abroad, work abroad, or the international plan. The Career Services department is said by students to be "outstanding, "and Georgia Tech is "one of the only schools in the country that offers the BS distinction for liberal arts majors because we [get] such a rigorous grounding in math and science." There are also more than 20 different honor societies.

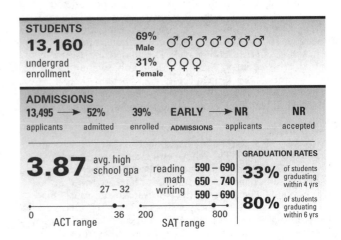

STUDENTS

13,160 undergrad enrollment

69% Male ♂♂♂♂♂♂♂

31% Female ♀♀♀

ADMISSIONS

13,495 applicants → 52% admitted; 39% enrolled

EARLY ADMISSIONS → NR applicants; NR accepted

3.87 avg. high school gpa

ACT range (0–36): 27 – 32

SAT range (200–800): reading 590 – 690; math 650 – 740; writing 590 – 690

GRADUATION RATES

33% of students graduating within 4 yrs

80% of students graduating within 6 yrs

Georgia Institute of Technology

FINANCIAL AID: 404-894-4160 • E-MAIL: ADMISSION@GATECH.EDU • WEBSITE: WWW.GATECH.EDU

STUDENT BODY

"The greatest strength of Georgia Tech is its diversity," undergrads report. "Students, activities, opportunities, teachers–all are diverse." One observes that the school hosts "the full range of stereotypes, from the fraternity boys with their croackies and boat shoes to the socially challenged nerds who stay in their rooms 24/7 programming computers. But no matter what, you know everyone is highly intelligent." One student explains, "Unlike at high school, no one looks down upon you if you know the entire periodic table, if you can do differential equations, or you can speak three languages; rather, you are respected." One sore spot: Men outnumber women here by greater than a two to one ratio. The situation is most pronounced in engineering (three to one) and computer (more than four to one) disciplines. Women actually outnumber men in the liberal arts and science colleges.

WHY STUDENTS LOVE GEORGIA TECH

According to students, this campus has a place for everyone but "but no matter what, you know everyone is highly intelligent." It's not all about the books though; the average Georgia Tech student (or "Yellow Jacket") is knows how to let loose with the best of them. There is a healthy Greek presence on campus, with over 50 fraternities and sororities, and an urban playground easily accessible by school run transportation. Situated on more than 400 acres, The Georgia Institute of Technology offers hundreds of activities and clubs as well, ranging from a salsa club on weekends, musical groups, intra-mural sports and a skydiving club.

GENERAL INFO

Activities: Choral groups, concert band, dance, drama/theater, jazz band, literary magazine, marching band, music ensembles, musical theater, pep band, radio station, student government, student newspaper, student-run film society, symphony orchestra, television station, yearbook, campus ministries, international student organization. **Organizations:** 429 registered organizations, 24 honor societies, 39 religious organizations. 38 fraternities, 14 sororities. **Athletics (Intercollegiate):** *Men:* Baseball, basketball, cheerleading, cross-country, diving, football, golf, swimming, tennis, track/field (outdoor), track/field (indoor). *Women:* Basketball, cheerleading, cross-country, diving, softball, swimming, tennis, track/field (outdoor), track/ field (indoor), volleyball.

BOTTOM LINE

In-State Tuition is extremely affordable, at approximately $7,300 per year. While out-of-state tuition is substantially higher at more than $25,000 eac h year, there are a variety of ways to reduce that total through various financial aid and scholarship opportunities. Nearly 75 percent of all undergraduates receive some form of need-based financial aid, and the average package for freshman is just more than $11,000. On-campus room and board is just under $9,000, with required fees, books, and supplies running in the neighborhood of $3,400.

SELECTIVITY

Admissions Rating	**96**
# of applicants	13,495
% of applicants accepted	52
% of acceptees attending	39
# accepting a place on wait list	621
% admitted from wait list	42

FRESHMAN PROFILE

Range SAT Critical Reading	**590–690**
Range SAT Math	**650–740**
Range SAT Writing	**590–690**
Range ACT Composite	**27–32**
Average HS GPA	**3.87**
% graduated top 10% of class	**89**
% graduated top 25% of class	**98**
% graduated top 50% of class	**100**

DEADLINES

Regular Deadline	**1/15**
Normal registration	**yes**

FACILITIES

Housing: Coed dorms, special housing for disabled students, men's dorms, special housing for international students, women's dorms, fraternity/sorority housing, apartments for married students, apartments for single students, theme housing. *Special Academic Facilities/Equipment:* Nuclear Magnetic Resonance Spectroscopy Center, Georgia Tech Research Institute, Ovarian Cancer Institute, Paper Museum.

FINANCIAL FACTS

Financial Aid Rating	**80**
Annual in-state tuition	$7,282
Annual out-of-state tuition	$25,492
Room and Board	$8,826
Required Fees	$2,370
Books and supplies	$1,000
% frosh rec. need-based scholarship or grant aid	36
% UG rec.need-based scholarship or grant aid	32
% frosh rec. non-need-based scholarship or grant aid	25
% UG rec. non-need-based scholarship or grant aid	19
% frosh rec. need-based self-help aid	19
% UG rec. need-based self-help aid	24
% frosh rec. any financial aid	79
% UG rec. any financial aid	73
% UG borrow to pay for school	51
Average cumulative indebtedness	$21,838

Indiana University–Bloomington

300 North Jordan Avenue, Bloomington, IN 47405-1106 • Admissions: 812-855-0661 • Fax: 812-855-5102

CAMPUS LIFE

Quality of life Rating	90
Fire Safety Rating	83
Green rating	96
Type of School	Public
Environment	City

STUDENTS

Total undergrad enrolllment	31,892
% Male to Female	50/50
% From out of state	31
% Live on Campus	36
# of Fraternities	38
# of Sororities	25
% African American	4
% Asian	4
% Caucasian	78
% Hispanic	3
% International	7
# Of Countries Represented	137

ACADEMICS

Academic Rating	73
% Of students graduating within 4 years	49
% Of students graduating within 6 years	71
Calendar	semester
Profs interesting rating	78
Profs accessible rating	83
Most common reg class size	20–29 students
Most common lab size	20–29 students

MOST POPULAR MAJORS

Business, exploratory biology, journalism, psychology

HONORS PROGRAMS

Hutton Honors College and the Hudson/Holland Scholar Programs.

SPECIAL STUDY OPTIONS

Accelerated program, cooperative education program, distance learning, double major, dual enrollment, external degree program, honors program, independent study, internships, liberal arts/career combination, student-designed major, study abroad, teacher certification program

ABOUT THE SCHOOL

Indiana University–Bloomington offers a quintes¬sential college town, campus, and overall academic experience. Students enjoy all of the advantages, opportunities, and resources that a larger school can offer, while still receiving personal attention and support. Indiana is a "Big Ten research university that offers a huge variety of classes and majors…within a surprisingly diverse student body," says one student. Quite accurate, and exemplified by undergrads from 140 different countries being represented throughout the campus. Indiana offers more than 5,000 courses and nearly 200 undergraduate majors, of which many are known nationally and internationally. Students can tailor academic programs to meet their needs, and enjoy research opportunities and state-of-the-art technology throughout all university departments. Students love the curriculum at IU. "The best combination of academics and extracurriculars one could ask for in a school." Many majors require students to hold an internship before graduating, so "you really have to be self-motivated."

Why Students love IU–Bloomington

"Big Ten research university that offers a huge variety of classes and majors…within a surprisingly diverse student body."

BANG FOR YOUR BUCK

Above-average high school performers traditionally meet little resistance from the IU admissions office. Providing tradition and complete academic excellence in one package, one undergraduate is pleased that "the best part is that IU prepares you for a well-rounded go at life but focuses on giving you a solid academic foundation." The school's "international and minority student populations are growing, and there are a lot of services available to help minority students feel comfortable on campus." About 140 different countries are represented throughout the increasingly diverse student body. Also, IU's music program is highly competitive; a successful audition is imperative. Representatives from businesses, government agencies, and not-for-profit organizations come to cam¬pus frequently to recruit IU students.

STUDENTS

31,892 undergrad enrollment

50% Male ♂♂♂♂♂♂♂♂♂♂

50% Female ♀♀♀♀♀♀♀♀♀♀

ADMISSIONS

36,719 →	69%	28%	EARLY →	NR	NR
applicants	admitted	enrolled	ADMISSIONS	applicants	accepted

3.61 avg. high school gpa

reading	520 – 630
math	540 – 650

ACT range (0–36): 24 – 29

SAT range (200–800)

GRADUATION RATES

49% of students graduating within 4 yrs

71% of students graduating within 6 yrs

Indiana University–Bloomington

FINANCIAL AID: 812-855-0321 • E-MAIL: IUADMIT@INDIANA.EDU • WEBSITE: WWW.INDIANA.EDU

STUDENT BODY

While "most IU students are white and come from a middle-class background," the school's "international and minority student populations are growing, and there are a lot of services available to help minority students feel comfortable on campus." Those who aren't native Hoosiers are most often Chicagoans or East Coasters from New York and New Jersey, although IU attracts students from all 50 states and 137 countries. The school is big enough to accommodate many personality types: "some Greeks, some who are academically oriented, some who enjoy and actively pursue the arts, and others who enjoy sports such as IU basketball...small cultures exist within the larger IU culture."

WHY STUDENTS LOVE IU–BLOOMINGTON

Undergraduates are very fond of the Bloomington area. "A great city to live in," with "amazing cultural events." The campus is alive with lectures, art exhibits, theatrical and musical shows, and the school's beloved inter collegiate athletics. "We spend a lot of time thinking about basketball and football, depending obviously on the season," reports one student. The ability to mix a great education with a fun college atmosphere is often cited as a prime reason for enrolling here; school spirit is "huge," and there are almost 60 fraternities and sororities. While a lot of people talk about partying and Greek organizations, it is not necessary to take part of these activities to be accepted. Intercollegiate sports are also a major part of life at IU. One student wraps all of these things up well by stating, "Indiana is one of the greatest places to be a college student.

GENERAL INFO

Activities: Choral groups, concert band, dance, drama/theater, jazz band, literary magazine, marching band, music ensembles, musical theater, opera, radio station, student government, student newspaper, symphony orchestra, television station, yearbook, campus ministries, international student organization. **Organizations:** 9 religious organizations. **Athletics (Intercollegiate):** *Men:* Baseball, basketball, cheerleading, cross-country, diving, football, golf, soccer, swimming, tennis, track/field (outdoor), wrestling. *Women:* Basketball, cheerleading, cross-country, diving, field hockey, golf, soccer, softball, swimming, tennis, track/field (outdoor), volleyball, water polo.

BOTTOM LINE

A very large institution, Indiana University has a total undergraduate enrollment of well more than 30,000 students; almost one-third of students are originally from another part of the country. In-state tuition will come to a bit more than $8,000; for out-of-state this total more than triples to $27,000. Room, board, fees, and supplies will add an extra $10,000. One student was excited that although "my financial resources were limited, I was in-state...IU was a great deal." There is also plenty of financial assistance available; freshman receiving some form of need-based scholarship or grant aid is nearly 40%. Upon graduation, enrollees can expect to have in the area of $28,000 in cumulative indebtedness.

SELECTIVITY

Admissions Rating	**88**
# of applicants	36,719
% of applicants accepted	69
% of acceptees attending	28
# accepting a place on wait list	0

FRESHMAN PROFILE

Range SAT Critical Reading	**520–630**
Range SAT Math	**540–650**
Range ACT Composite	**28–32**
Average HS GPA	**3.61**
% graduated top 10% of class	**38**
% graduated top 25% of class	**74**
% graduated top 50% of class	**97**

DEADLINES

Regular Deadline	**4/1**
Normal registration	**yes**

FACILITIES

Housing: Coed dorms, special housing for disabled students, men's dorms, special housing for international students, women's dorms, fraternity/sorority housing, apartments for married students, cooperative housing, apartments for single students, apartments for students with dependent children, residential language houses and living/learning centers available, wellness center, African-American living/learning. Honor College floors, First-Year Academic Interest Group Housing; suites for 2–3 students. *Special Academic Facilities/Equipment:* Art Gallery, folklore, radio station, natural history museum.

FINANCIAL FACTS

Financial Aid Rating	**80**
Annual in-state tuition	$8,124
Annual out-of-state tuition	$26,785
Room and Board	$7,918
Required Fees	$909
Books and supplies	$812
% frosh rec. need-based scholarship or grant aid	37
% UG rec.need-based scholarship or grant aid	32
% frosh rec. non-need-based scholarship or grant aid	7
% UG rec. non-need-based scholarship or grant aid	4
% frosh rec. need-based self-help aid	27
% UG rec. need-based self-help aid	3
% UG borrow to pay for school	55
Average cumulative indebtedness	$27,752

Iowa State University

100 Enrollment Services Center, Ames, IA 50011-2011 • Admissions: 515-294-5836 • Fax: 515-294-2592

CAMPUS LIFE

Quality of life Rating	91
Fire Safety Rating	80
Green rating	88
Type of School	Public
Environment	Town

STUDENTS

Total undergrad enrollment	23,104
% Male to Female	56/44
% From out of state	25
% From public high school	91
% Live on Campus	46
# of Fraternities	33
# of Sororities	19
% African American	2
% Asian	3
% Caucasian	79
% Hispanic	3
% International	8
# Of Countries Represented	103

ACADEMICS

Academic Rating	71
% Of students graduating within 4 years	39
% Of students graduating within 6 years	70
Calendar	semester
Profs interesting rating	69
Profs accessible rating	72
Most common reg class size	20–29 students
Most common lab size	20–29 students

MOST POPULAR MAJORS

Finance, marketing, mechanical engineering

HONORS PROGRAMS

ISU offers both a University Honors Program and a Freshman Honors Program.

SPECIAL STUDY OPTIONS

Accelerated program, cooperative education program, cross-registration, distance learning, double major, dual enrollment, exchange student program (domestic), external degree program, honors program.

ABOUT THE SCHOOL

Iowa State University has the reputation of being a "large university with a small-town feel." With more than 100 undergraduate programs to choose from, many students are drawn to the ISU campus due to interests in agriculture, food science, pre-veterinary studies or architecture. Not to be overlooked is the university's engineering program, which students boast is exceptionally supportive of its female engineering students. Undergraduates at Iowa State, known as Cyclones, say they always feel like they have full support of faculty and professors. Though accomplished, holding accolades such as Rhodes Scholars, Fulbright Scholars, and National Academy of Sciences and National Academy of Engineering members, the majority of Iowa State's 1,700 faculty members are easily accessible.

"There are so many services on campus to help students, it is almost unreal. From tutoring to study sessions and counseling to mock interviews and resume building, ISU offers a wide variety of services to stu¬dents." This superior support is not limited to the classroom though, "there are a lot of opportunities for student research and 'hands on' learning;" some students insist that ISU is "the best 'outside of class' university in the nation." ISU offers a Freshman Honors Program, which promotes an enhanced academic environment for students of high ability. Benefits include unique courses, small class sizes, research opportunities and funding, access to graduate-level courses, and priority registration.
The University is heavily focused on the environment, too. The Commitment to Sustainable Operations, highlighted by a joint contract with the City of Ames, and Campus Green Teams dedicated to increasing sustainability efforts, being two of the most noteworthy.

BANG FOR YOUR BUCK

With an enrollment of more than 23,000 students, 4,500 of those being freshman, Iowa State University "holds true to its initial mission of providing affordable, practical education with a special focus on agriculture." As would befit an agricultural school, the campus encompasses 1800 acres. Nearly 60% of students are male; full-time students account for 95% of the enrollees at the university, although distance education undergraduate degree programs are also offered. Iowa State employs 1,600 full-time faculty members, and there is a comfortable 17:1 Student-to-Faculty ratio – excellent for such a large school. Additionally, nearly a quarter of all students continue on to pursue graduate school studies.

STUDENTS

23,104 undergrad enrollment

56% Male ♂♂♂♂♂♂♂♂♂♂♂

44% Female ♀♀♀♀♀♀♀♀♀

ADMISSIONS

15,066 applicants → 81% admitted — 38% enrolled

EARLY ADMISSIONS → NR applicants — NR accepted

3.54 avg. high school gpa

reading	460 – 640
math	530 – 670

ACT range: 22 – 28 (0–36)

SAT range (200–800)

GRADUATION RATES

39% of students graduating within 4 yrs

70% of students graduating within 6 yrs

Iowa State University

FINANCIAL AID: 515-294-2223 • E-MAIL: ADMISSIONS@IASTATE.EDU • WEBSITE: WWW.IASTATE.EDU

STUDENT BODY

As at many big schools, "It is hard to describe a typical student at Iowa State because there are many styles of students." "Every stereotype is here; sorority girl/frat boy, farmer kid, international student, nerd, computer geek, socially awkward, [and] goth. Iowa State has every kind of person." Iowa is a conservative state, and ISU has a large agricultural student population. The "population of out-of-state students seems to be growing," and "there is a diversity of international students" filling out the ranks as well, so most students can find a niche at ISU, and fortunately "Everyone here is laid-back and easygoing," so the overall vibe is live-and-let-live.

Why Students love Iowa State University

"There are so many services on campus to help students, it is almost unreal."

WHY STUDENTS LOVE IOWA STATE UNIVERSITY

The campus makes up around half of the town of Ames, Iowa; the population "doubles with students around, and the city has adapted to this increase," one student reports. Another loves that "Cyride (the bus system that is operated by the city and university) offers students free transportation to mostly everywhere in Ames." But those that live on school grounds assure that there are no shortages of activities and entertainment closer to campus. There are many ways to "get involved in leadership positions," and Army, Navy, and Air Force ROTC are well established at the school. Most would agree, though, that football is king among the 800 student organizations and clubs, sixty intramural sports, arts, and recreational activities.

GENERAL INFO

Activities: Choral groups, concert band, dance, drama/theater, jazz band, literary magazine, marching band, music ensembles, musical theater, opera, pep band, radio station, student government, student newspaper, student-run film society, symphony orchestra, television station **Organizations:** 799 registered organizations, 43 honor societies, 34 religious organizations. 34 fraternities, 19 sororities. **Athletics (Intercollegiate):** *Men:* Basketball, cross-country, football, golf, track/field (outdoor), track/field (indoor), wrestling. *Women:* Basketball, cross-country, diving, golf, gymnastics, soccer, softball, swimming, tennis, track/field (outdoor), track/field (indoor), volleyball.

BOTTOM LINE

Tuition at Iowa State University is an excellent value for in-state students, with in-state credit hours being just $267. Room and board will come to about $8,000; books, supplies, and required fees will add another $2000. Students from out-of-state can expect to pay $762 per credit hour, with overall tuition being just upwards of $18,000–still a very affordable total for a school providing such a wealth of educational opportunities. Plus, almost 90 percent of freshmen receive some manner of financial support, with nearly 80 percent receiving some form of need-based aid. Financial aid packages average between $11,000 to $12,000; for most freshman, the total need-based gift aid approaches $7,500, with the average amount of loan debt per graduate at about $30,000.

SELECTIVITY

Admissions Rating	**83**
# of applicants	15,066
% of applicants accepted	81
% of acceptees attending	38

FRESHMAN PROFILE

Range SAT Critical Reading	**460–640**
Range SAT Math	**530–670**
Range ACT Composite	**22–28**
Average HS GPA	**3.54**
% graduated top 10% of class	**29**
% graduated top 25% of class	**61**
% graduated top 50% of class	**92**

DEADLINES

Regular Deadline	**7/1 rolling**
Normal registration	**yes**

FACILITIES

Housing: Coed dorms, special housing for disabled students, men's dorms, special housing for international students, women's dorms, fraternity/sorority housing, apartments for married students, apartments for single students, theme housing. *Special Academic Facilities/Equipment:* Brunnier art museum, Farm House museum, observatory, numerous institutes, research centers, College of Design Gallery, Virtual Reality Application Center, Pappajohn Center for Entrepreneurship. *Computers:* 100% of classrooms, 75% of dorms, 100% of libraries, 100% of dining areas, 100% of student union, 40% of common outdoor areas have wireless network access.

FINANCIAL FACTS

Financial Aid Rating	**82**
Annual in-state tuition	$6,408
Annual out-of-state tuition	$18,208
Room and Board	$7,982
Required Fees	$1,078
Books and supplies	$1,044
% frosh rec. need-based scholarship or grant aid	54
% UG rec.need-based scholarship or grant aid	54
% frosh rec. non-need-based scholarship or grant aid	27
% UG rec. non-need-based scholarship or grant aid	26
% frosh rec. need-based self-help aid	40
% UG rec. need-based self-help aid	45
% frosh rec. any financial aid	87
% UG rec. any financial aid	79
% UG borrow to pay for school	69
Average cumulative indebtedness	$30,062

James Madison University

Sonner Hall, MSC 0101, Harrisonburg, VA 22807 • Admissions: 540-568-5681 • Fax: 540-568-3332

CAMPUS LIFE

Quality of life Rating	91
Fire Safety Rating	71
Green rating	89
Type of School	Public
Environment	Town

STUDENTS

Total undergrad enrolllment	17,306
% Male to Female	41/59
% From out of state	28
% Live on Campus	35
# of Fraternities	15
# of Sororities	9
% African American	4
% Asian	5
% Caucasian	80
% Hispanic	3
% International	1
# Of Countries Represented	69

ACADEMICS

Academic Rating	78
% Of students graduating within 4 years	67
% Of students graduating within 6 years	82
Calendar	semester
Profs interesting rating	84
Profs accessible rating	84
Most common reg class size	20–29 students
Most common lab size	20–29 students

MOST POPULAR MAJORS

Community health services/liason/counseling, marketing, psychology

HONORS PROGRAMS

Academic honors program, honors scholars (3.25 or above), honors courses, and senior honors project (3.25).

SPECIAL STUDY OPTIONS

Accelerated program, distance learning, double major, English as a Second Language (ESL), honors program, independent study, internships, study abroad, teacher certification program, continuing education programs offered on campus.

ABOUT THE SCHOOL

James Madison University is located on 700 acres in Virginia's breathtaking Shenandoah Valley. "The moment I walked on campus I was captured by the student spirit and how beautiful it is," one student says. The university itself, however, offers its students much more than the "benefits of walking in the mountains." There is an impressive balance of educational, social, and extracurricular activities to enrich students' experience, including more than 100 majors to choose from including everything from musical theater, business, to an innovative information security program.

Both students and professors alike contribute to the feeling of community on campus. Students love the "positive, enriching, and supportive learning environment." Most who take classes here can agree that the faculty is always "available to help" and constantly proving they're "interested in student achievement." While most of the programs offered at JMU are rigorous teachers "are very down to earth, approachable and huge supporters of discussion based classes." In fact most go the extra mile and are "willing to facilitate your education in any way possible;" one student believes that "the greatest strengths of the school is the ability to get any sort of assistance when needed." JMU offers extensive academic and co-curricular experiences that allow students hands-on exploration of sustainability. JMU's President formed a Commission on Environmental Stewardship and Sustainability to coordinate campus environmental stewardship efforts.

Why Students love James Madison University

> "The greatest strengths of the school is the ability to get any sort of assistance when needed."

BANG FOR YOUR BUCK

Having an enrollment of 4,000 freshman, and nearly 18,000 students overall, James Madison University includes representation from more than 80 countries. 95% of students are full-time, with 60% being female and almost 30% from out-of-state. With almost 1,400 faculty on campus, students are pleased to find two-thirds having PhDs. Impressively, 9 out of every 10 students return to the university for sophomore year. Additionally, nearly half of all undergrads go on to pursue graduate work at James Madison.

STUDENTS

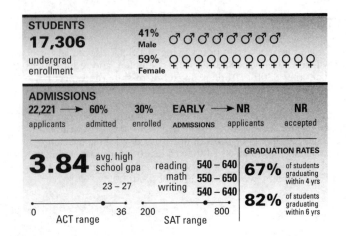

17,306 undergrad enrollment

41% Male ♂♂♂♂♂♂♂♂

59% Female ♀♀♀♀♀♀♀♀♀♀♀♀

ADMISSIONS

22,221 applicants → 60% admitted — 30% enrolled

EARLY ADMISSIONS → NR applicants — NR accepted

3.84 avg. high school gpa

ACT range: 23 – 27 (0–36)

SAT range (200–800): reading 540 – 640; math 550 – 650; writing 540 – 640

GRADUATION RATES

67% of students graduating within 4 yrs

82% of students graduating within 6 yrs

James Madison University

Financial Aid: 540-568-7820 • E-mail: admissions@jmu.edu • Website: www.jmu.edu

STUDENT BODY

At JMU, "The typical student is friendly, smart, open-minded, and fun." Students describe themselves as "excellent [at] maintaining a round, balanced life," and say, "everyone seems relaxed and knows how to have fun but keep their school work a priority." One student jokes that the typical student is "probably a girl considering our ratio seems like eighty to twenty at times," and another concurs, "more males would be nice." Students tend to be "white from the upper to middle class," and an International Affairs major says, "Although we do have all types here, most people consist of your typical prep wearing Uggs and a North Face." Others note, however, "Greek life is small," and parties "are usually open to everyone," adding that partying isn't "all students here think about."

Why Students love James Madison University

"Everyone seems relaxed and knows how to have fun but keep their school work a priority."

WHY STUDENTS LOVE JAMES MADISON UNIVERSITY

Undergrads find that "classrooms and facilities are always well kept and very up-to-date with all the best teaching technology," and with a Student-to-Faculty ratio of 16:1, enrollees find an environment at the university that is "comfortable and conducive to learning." Among other resources, the school has more than 300 on-campus organizations, 28 honor societies, 28 religious organizations, and nearly 25 fraternities and sororities. Students at JMU pride themselves on keeping their lives balanced. They recognize the importance of knowing when to study and when to let loose. The "sheer number of student activities is stellar. "With access to more than 350 student clubs and organizations, and a cutting edge, 147,000-square-foot recreation center this is not a difficult task.

GENERAL INFO

Activities: Choral groups, concert band, dance, drama/theater, jazz band, literary magazine, marching band, music ensembles, musical theater, opera, pep band, radio station, student government, student newspaper, student-run film society, symphony orchestra, yearbook, campus ministries, international student organization. **Organizations:** 298 registered organizations, 28 honor societies, 28 religious organizations. 15 fraternities, 9 sororities. **Athletics (Intercollegiate):** *Men:* Baseball, basketball, cheerleading, football, golf, soccer, tennis. *Women:* Basketball, cheerleading, cross-country, diving,field hockey, golf, lacrosse, soccer, softball, swimming, tennis, track/field (outdoor), volleyball.

BOTTOM LINE

With in-state tuition being just over $4,000 per year, James Madison University is an exceptionally affordable school. Another $8000 will provide students with full room and board; books and educational supplies will increase this figure by about $900, and required school fees are about $3,600. Out-of-state tuition is just less than $17,000. Almost 60% of undergrads receive need-based financial aid, with the average need-based gift aid being in the neighborhood of $7,000. Financial aid packages will generally provide freshman with over $8,000 in support.

SELECTIVITY

Admissions Rating	**89**
# of applicants	22,221
% of applicants accepted	60
% of acceptees attending	30
# accepting a place on wait list	1,200
% admitted from wait list	38

FRESHMAN PROFILE

Range SAT Critical Reading	**540–640**
Range SAT Math	**550–650**
Range SAT Writing	**540–640**
Range ACT Composite	**23–27**
Average HS GPA	**3.84**
% graduated top 10% of class	**27**
% graduated top 25% of class	**72**
% graduated top 50% of class	**98**

DEADLINES

Regular Deadline	**11/1**
Normal registration	**no**

FACILITIES

Housing: Coed dorms, special housing for disabled students, fraternity/sorority housing, apartments for single students, wellness housing, theme housing.
Computers: 25% of classrooms, 100% of dorms, 100% of libraries, 50% of dining areas, 100% of student union, 25% of common outdoor areas have wireless network access.

FINANCIAL FACTS

Financial Aid Rating	**75**
Annual in-state tuition	$4,182
Annual out-of-state tuition	$16,946
Room and Board	$8,020
Required Fees	$3,678
Books and supplies	$876
% frosh rec. need-based scholarship or grant aid	22
% UG rec.need-based scholarship or grant aid	18
% frosh rec. non-need-based scholarship or grant aid	80
% UG rec. non-need-based scholarship or grant aid	27
% frosh rec. need-based self-help aid	36
% UG rec. need-based self-help aid	30
% frosh rec. any financial aid	61
% UG rec. any financial aid	57
% UG borrow to pay for school	50
Average cumulative indebtedness	$20,417

Kansas State University

119 Anderson Hall, Manhattan, KS 66506 • Admissions: 785-532-6250 • Fax: 785-532-6393

CAMPUS LIFE

Quality of life Rating	98
Fire Safety Rating	65
Green rating	83
Type of School	Public
Environment	Town

STUDENTS

Total undergrad enrolllment	18,753
% Male to Female	52/48
% From out of state	15
% From public high school	81
% Live on Campus	17
# of Fraternities	28
# of Sororities	16
% African American	4
% Asian	1
% Caucasian	82
% Hispanic	5
% International	5
# Of Countries Represented	102

ACADEMICS

Academic Rating	77
% Of students graduating within 4 years	26
% Of students graduating within 6 years	60
Calendar	semester
Profs interesting rating	74
Profs accessible rating	76
Most common reg class size	10–19 students

MOST POPULAR MAJORS

Animal sciences, business administration and management, elementary education and teaching

HONORS PROGRAMS

The University Honors Program is an opportunity for undergraduate students from all colleges to enhance their education with special classes and opportunities for personal growth.

SPECIAL STUDY OPTIONS

Accelerated program, cooperative education program, distance learning, double major, English as a Second Language (ESL), exchange student program (domestic), honors program, independent study, internships, study abroad, teacher certification program, Minors.

ABOUT THE SCHOOL

Kansas State University may seem like the typical large Midwestern state university in a college town, however, the programs and the professors really make this school stand out. Agricultural studies are quite prevalent here with research facilities such its Konza Prairie, which is the world's largest tall grass prairie preserve. The school also has its acclaimed Biosecurity Research Institute, which studies infectious diseases that can be carried from farms to the grocery store and works to address those threats. However with more than 250 majors within the university's 9 colleges, incoming freshmen really have their pick of numerous programs, with excellent engineering and architecture majors as well. A lot of students find that the classes in their first year tend to be a little crowded, but that goes away once they move further in to their field of study. In fact, most laud the fact that they get to foster relationships with their professors later in their college careers. Kansas State University's sheer number of Rhodes, Marshall, g, Goldwater and Udall scholars rank first in the nation among state universities. The University Honors Program is an opportunity for undergraduate students from all colleges to enhance their education with special classes and opportunities for personal growth. The university also offers its contest, The Next Big Thing, which is open to all majors. Students enter the contest with an entrepreneurial idea and for a chance to win money to further explore their concept. They also offer a series of seminars on how to perform research and create a financial analysis that focuses on the feasibility of their project.

BANG FOR YOUR BUCK

Kansas State University helps its students with more than $16 million in scholarships awarded each year and ninety percent of those are awarded based on merit. Each incoming freshman is assigned a personal assistance financial advisor, an upperclassmen at Kansas State that has been trained to answer any question regarding financial assistance, that way the student feels like they don't have to go through the bureaucracy that can often be involved with paying for school. KSU also has numerous programs to help out its graduating seniors like its Career Employment Services which have events such as on-campus interviews and career fairs as well as workshops on resume formatting. The school's Academic and Career Information Services group also helps students figure out their various career options and what might be best suited to each individual. A university-wide task force was recently created, for long-term planning in all areas of the university, including campus operations, curriculum, research, and external relations/outreach. Development of a new 10,000 square foot recycling facility on campus has been undertaken, as well.

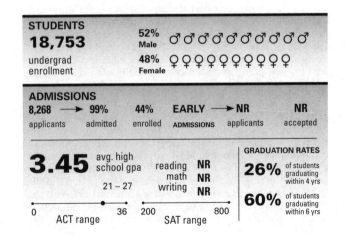

STUDENTS

18,753 undergrad enrollment

52% Male ♂♂♂♂♂♂♂♂♂♂

48% Female ♀♀♀♀♀♀♀♀♀♀

ADMISSIONS

8,268 →	99%	44%	EARLY →	NR	NR
applicants	admitted	enrolled	ADMISSIONS	applicants	accepted

3.45 avg. high school gpa

ACT range: 21 – 27 (0–36)

SAT range (200–800): reading NR, math NR, writing NR

GRADUATION RATES

26% of students graduating within 4 yrs

60% of students graduating within 6 yrs

Kansas State University

FINANCIAL AID: 785-532-6420 • E-MAIL: K-STATE@K-STATE.EDU • WEBSITE: WWW.K-STATE.EDU

STUDENT BODY

The "hardworking and honest" students at K-State tell us they bask in "country hospitality." "The students are the friendliest in the country," asserts a senior. "You cannot walk through campus without people smiling or acknowledging you"–"not in that creepy, stalker way, but the way that makes you feel warm and fuzzy inside." The "typical Midwestern" population here mostly comes in two varieties. There are the "yokels" and "farm boys from small towns in Kansas." There are also the kids from "suburban white neighborhoods" in Kansas City and Wichita. You'll see "punk rock kids," "cowboys in Wranglers," and "the occasional hippie," but "they form their own weird groups," but "the vast majority of the students look, dress, and act the same." Politically, K-State "tends towards conservatism." On the whole, though, these students "generally represent the middle of the road in nearly every American way of thought."

Why Students love Kansas State University

"The students are the friendliest in the country."

WHY STUDENTS LOVE KANSAS STATE UNIVERSITY

The majority of the students also find the campus to be quite easy to navigate and gorgeous any time of year. Many find the campus to be ideal and love to spend time there. The library is "amazing." In upper level courses, "it becomes easier to cultivate a relationship with your professor." Administratively, "the school is a pretty well-oiled machine." Management is full of "gifted people who genuinely love K-State;" and "students have a large say in everything the university does." Also, the top brass is ultra-accessible for such a large institution. Since it is a state university the majority of students hail from Kansas, but with more than 400 student organizations there will be something for almost anyone.

GENERAL INFO

Activities: Choral groups, concert band, dance, drama/theater, jazz band, marching band, music ensembles, musical theater, pep band, radio station, student government, student newspaper, symphony orchestra, television station, yearbook, campus ministries, international student organization, Model UN. **Organizations:** 594 registered organizations, 36 honor societies, 37 religious organizations. 28 fraternities, 16 sororities. **Athletics (Intercollegiate):** *Men:* Baseball, basketball, cheerleading, cross-country, football, golf, track/field (outdoor), track/field (indoor). *Women:* Basketball, cheerleading, crew/rowing, cross-country, equestrian sports, golf, tennis, track/field (outdoor), track/field (indoor), volleyball.

BOTTOM LINE

Many of Kansas State's students, including 3,500 freshman, are from Kansas because of the great deal for in-state tuition; residents pay only about $6,600. Tuition for out-of-state students is quite different at almost $18,000. Room and board runs almost $7,000 and books are averaged at about $1,000 per year. Seven out of ten receive financial aid of some sort and the average student graduates with about $22,600 in cumulative indebtedness. The preponderance of classes are taught by PhD-level instructors; nearly 900 of 1,100 faculty members possess these degrees.

SELECTIVITY

Admissions Rating	**79**
# of applicants	8,268
% of applicants accepted	99
% of acceptees attending	44

FRESHMAN PROFILE

Range ACT Composite	**21–27**
Average HS GPA	**3.45**
% graduated top 10% of class	**20**
% graduated top 25% of class	**45**
% graduated top 50% of class	**76**

DEADLINES

Regular Deadline	**11/1**
Normal registration	**yes**

FACILITIES

Housing: Coed dorms, men's dorms, women's dorms, fraternity/sorority housing, apartments for married students, cooperative housing, apartments for single students. *Special Academic Facilities/Equipment:* South Asian area study center, education communications center, center for cancer research, planetarium, nuclear reactor/accelerator, Beach Art museum. *Computers:* 85% of classrooms, 100% of dorms, 100% of libraries, 100% of dining areas, 100% of student union, 10% of common outdoor areas have wireless network access.

FINANCIAL FACTS

Financial Aid Rating	**79**
Annual in-state tuition	$6,936
Annual out-of-state tuition	$18,402
Room and Board	$7,198
Required Fees	$721
Books and supplies	$1,100
% frosh rec. need-based scholarship or grant aid	33
% UG rec.need-based scholarship or grant aid	31
% frosh rec. non-need-based scholarship or grant aid	37
% UG rec. non-need-based scholarship or grant aid	24
% frosh rec. need-based self-help aid	38
% UG rec. need-based self-help aid	42
% frosh rec. any financial aid	47
% UG rec. any financial aid	49
% UG borrow to pay for school	54
Average cumulative indebtedness	$22,633

Longwood University

Admissions Office, 201 High Street, Farmville, VA 23909 • Admissions: 434-395-2060 • Fax: 434-395-2332

CAMPUS LIFE

Quality of life Rating	67
Fire Safety Rating	84
Green rating	80
Type of School	Public
Environment	Village

STUDENTS

Total undergrad enrolllment	4,125
% Male to Female	34/66
% From out of state	4
% From public high school	74
% Live on Campus	74
# of Fraternities	9
# of Sororities	12
% African American	6
% Asian	1
% Caucasian	83
% Hispanic	3
% Native American	1
% International	1
# Of Countries Represented	46

ACADEMICS

Academic Rating	74
% Of students graduating within 4 years	39
% Of students graduating within 6 years	56
Calendar	semester
Most common reg class size	20–29 students
Most common lab size	20–29 students

MOST POPULAR MAJORS

Business/commerce, general elementary education and teaching psychology

HONORS PROGRAMS

The Honors Program focuses on the exchange of ideas and the enrichment of students' educational and cultural experiences. Learning takes place not only in the classroom, but also through cultural events, conferences, field trips, and study abroad.

SPECIAL STUDY OPTIONS

Accelerated program, cross-registration, distance learning, double major, dual enrollment, English as a Second Language (ESL), honors program, independent study, internships, study abroad, teacher certification program.

ABOUT THE SCHOOL

Longwood University is a public institution that displays diversity, tradition, sustainability, and leadership. The school emphasizes the importance of honor, integrity, and conducting yourself in a professional manner. Also, Longwood provides all the perks of a large university in a country setting that is "relatively safe and worry free," and "not afraid to grow and change to adapt to the students who attend." Longwood is a community with immense history and tradition that treats each student as a valued individual; a "school where you can be yourself and not have to worry about finding a place to fit in." Well-known for educating good teachers, "the closed campus helps to create a sense of togetherness and helps you focus on your academics." Also, conducting research is highly important at Longwood. This prepares the students for graduate school, expands learning, and heightens professionalism. "If you are looking for a rigorous academic career, you will be challenged with one."

There is a Peer Mentor program for incoming freshmen that helps them get better acquainted to college; students can easily get the classes they want, even as a freshman. "My professors have challenged me and raised my level of confidence in my ability to succeed." Longwood is a place with a lot of opportunity not only in the classroom but also in the community. Most students are involved in community service, and almost everything on campus is in some way ecologically friendly. "It's a small school on a beautiful campus where I can be well known and feel like I can make an impact in my school."

BANG FOR YOUR BUCK

Longwood University is a "school with friendly people and a wonderful atmosphere." Most feel that "Longwood University takes pride in setting students up for success by creating a positive campus" and that it's a "beautiful environment [with] good facilities." Longwood has one of the highest job placement rates among public institutions in Virginia. "Longwood also requires an internship, which is very important in finding a job." The internship not only will benefit you on your resume, but help you better understand your field of interest. "I feel Longwood is giving me all the tools I need to become a great teacher." "Everything any parent or student would want for their child or themselves, is portrayed beautifully at this university."

STUDENTS

4,125 undergrad enrollment

34% Male ♂♂♂♂♂♂♂

66% Female ♀♀♀♀♀♀♀♀♀♀♀

ADMISSIONS

4,402 applicants → 67% admitted | 32% enrolled | EARLY ADMISSIONS → NR applicants | NR accepted

3.34 avg. high school gpa

ACT range (0–36): 20 – 23

SAT range (200–800): reading 480 – 560; math 470 – 510

GRADUATION RATES

39% of students graduating within 4 yrs

56% of students graduating within 6 yrs

Longwood University

Financial Aid: 800-281-4677 • E-mail: admissions@longwood.edu • Website: www.whylongwood.com

STUDENT BODY

At Longwood University "students are happy, polite, and eager to be on campus" as well as "motivated and hardworking." The student body is predominately female, and most say the typical students are "female majors in education" who "spend a lot of time socializing." Students say they "fit in well with others and balance time between school work and extracurricular activities," adding, "A typical student is someone who likes to go and party, but they know when they need to buckle down." Overall, there's a "jeans and hoodie vibe" among students," and students say they are "down-to-earth, focused on their major, and having a wild college experience."

Why Students love Longwood University

"Longwood University takes pride in setting students up for success by creating a positive campus."

WHY STUDENTS LOVE POMONA COLLEGE

Longwood University offers "small class sizes and one-on-one time with professors" in an "intimate atmosphere" that "gives you the best chance to succeed in your field of choice." A senior says, "If you are looking for a rigorous academic career, you will be challenged with one," and all agree that "Longwood has an excellent education program." A mathematics education major says, "At Longwood, all my professors know me by name and genuinely care about my education," and students feel that "smaller classes help make connections with the professors," which "lead to a comfortable and open learning environment." Professors are "passionate," "qualified, and challenging but provide a positive interaction" and are known to "facilitate discussion rather than just lecture."

GENERAL INFO

Environment: Village. **Activities:** Choral groups, concert band, dance, drama/theater, jazz band, literary magazine, music ensembles, pep band, radio station, student government, student newspaper, yearbook, campus ministries, international student organization. **Organizations:** 129 registered organizations, 17 honor societies, 11 religious organizations. 9 fraternities, 12 sororities. **Athletics (Intercollegiate):** *Men:* Baseball, basketball, cheerleading, cross-country, golf, soccer, tennis. *Women:* Basketball, cheerleading, cross-country, field hockey, golf, lacrosse, soccer, softball, tennis. **On-Campus Highlights:** Brock Commons, Lankford Student Union, Health and Fitness Center, Greenwood Library, Dorrill Dining Hall, Science Building.

BOTTOM LINE

Longwood has a small private college feel for a public school price. In-state tuition is just less than $6,000, although out-of-state students are looking at more than $17,000. Room, board, books, and fees add up to another $12,000. The school offers great financial aid and scholarships services, however. The school is able to meet more than 80 percent of average need, and 60 percent of freshmen get financial aid. With an average FA package of more than $11,000, many enrollees find that these monies allow them to take advantage of the excellent learning opportunities at the school they would not have been able to afford otherwise. The approximate amount of loan debt upon leaving school after graduation is around $22,000. One undergraduate described the academic experience here by saying, "Longwood provides a private school education at a public school price.

SELECTIVITY

Admissions Rating	**75**
# of applicants	4,402
% of applicants accepted	67
% of acceptees attending	32

FRESHMAN PROFILE

Range SAT Critical Reading	**480–560**
Range SAT Math	**470–510**
Range ACT Composite	**20–23**
Average HS GPA	**3.34**
% graduated top 10% of class	**11**
% graduated top 25% of class	**38**
% graduated top 50% of class	**82**

DEADLINES

Regular Deadline	**3/1**
Normal registration	**no**

FACILITIES

Housing: Coed dorms, special housing for disabled students, women's dorms, fraternity/sorority housing, apartments for single students, Honor Student Housing.
Special Academic Facilities/Equipment: Longwood Center for the Visual Arts
Computers: 100% of classrooms, 100% of libraries, 100% of dining areas, 100% of student union, have wireless network access.

FINANCIAL FACTS

Financial Aid Rating	**88**
Annual in-state tuition	$5,880
Annual out-of-state tuition	$17,070
Room and Board	$8,114
Required Fees	$4,650
Books and supplies	$800
% frosh rec. need-based scholarship or grant aid	42
% UG rec.need-based scholarship or grant aid	40
% frosh rec. non-need-based scholarship or grant aid	1
% UG rec. non-need-based scholarship or grant aid	1
% frosh rec. need-based self-help aid	83
% UG rec. need-based self-help aid	35
% frosh rec. any financial aid	60
% UG borrow to pay for school	62
Average cumulative indebtedness	$22,665

Missouri University of Science and Technology

300 W. 13th Street; 106 Parker Hall, Rolla, MO 65409-1060 • Admissions: 573-341-4165 • Fax: 573-341-4082

CAMPUS LIFE

Quality of life Rating	67
Fire Safety Rating	80
Green rating	71
Type of School	Public
Environment	Village

STUDENTS

Total undergrad enrolllment	5,195
% Male to Female	78/22
% From out of state	19
% From public high school	85
% Live on Campus	51
# of Fraternities	21
# of Sororities	9
% African American	5
% Asian	2
% Caucasian	82
% Hispanic	2
% International	3
# Of Countries Represented	49

ACADEMICS

Academic Rating	72
% Of students graduating within 4 years	25
% Of students graduating within 6 years	63
Calendar	semester
Profs interesting rating	71
Profs accessible rating	78
Most common reg class size	20–29 students
Most common lab size	20–29 students

MOST POPULAR MAJORS

Civil engineering, electrical and electronics engineering, mechanical engineering

HONORS PROGRAMS

Honors Academy and Master Student Fellowship Programs .

SPECIAL STUDY OPTIONS

Distance learning, double major, dual enrollment, English as a Second Language (ESL), honors program, independent study, internships, liberal arts/career combination, study abroad, teacher certification program.

ABOUT THE SCHOOL

Missouri University of Science and Technology, located in the city of Rolla, may not have a lot to offer off-campus, but the academics and price more than make up for it. Most students find their time occupied with studying one of the 65 disciplines offered through MS&T. The classes are considered quite tough and fairly time-consuming, though they pay off since the school has a 90 percent job placement rate. The professors also make things quite a bit easier as many students find that their teachers are available whenever they may need assistance. Out of all of their disciplines, Missouri University's Engineering and Science programs are "extensive," and are the school's "biggest strength," according to students. One of the schools more unique majors includes its Explosives emphasis, which the school founded in 1997 and focuses on uses such as mining and demolitions.

The undergraduate population keeps itself busy with more than 200 student organizations. With 29 honor societies, 13 religious organizations, and "fraternities and sororities being a very prominent part of residential life," one is never at a lack for something to do. The semi-annual Etiquette Dinner offers a five-course dinner and tips to business dining. Intramural sports are also fairly popular as are engineering college staples like creating potato cannons and siege machines, though most students tend to stay busy in their dorms studying, playing video games or watching movies with their friends. A lot of students also take slight issue that the gender gap is quite prevalent with the majority of its students being male, but many are happy that the gap is narrowing. For those looking to leave campus, Mizzou and other colleges are only a drive away. Although with the Castleman Performing Arts Center, an observatory, and an explosives testing lab, fascinating and entertaining things to do are easily within reach.

BANG FOR YOUR BUCK

Though the school is slightly more expensive for non-residents, more than 80 percent of the students receive some form of financial aid and they offer combinations of federal, state and institutional need-based aid to assist with costs. They also offer career advice to incoming freshman about resumes and cover letters, helping them get in the mindset of finding a job when they graduate. The Missouri Career Opportunities and Employer Relations group also offers students an Opening Week Mini-Career Fair so they can start networking as soon as possible. The average starting salary of a graduate of MS&T is more than $57,000 and that's quite a number considering the previously mentioned 90 percent job placement rate.

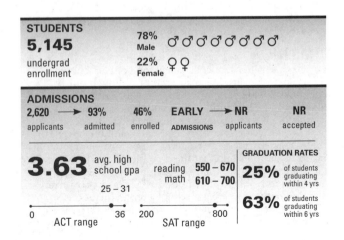

STUDENTS

5,145 undergrad enrollment

78% Male ♂♂♂♂♂♂♂♂

22% Female ♀♀

ADMISSIONS

2,620 applicants → 93% admitted | 46% enrolled | EARLY ADMISSIONS → NR applicants | NR accepted

3.63 avg. high school gpa

reading 550 – 670
math 610 – 700

25 – 31

0 – 36 ACT range

200 – 800 SAT range

GRADUATION RATES

25% of students graduating within 4 yrs

63% of students graduating within 6 yrs

Missouri University of Science and Technology

FINANCIAL AID: 573-341-4282 • E-MAIL: ADMISSIONS@MST.EDU • WEBSITE: WWW.MST.EDU

STUDENT BODY

The typical student here is described as "a Midwestern white boy" or, as one student puts it, "a white male, nerdy, who never sees the sun." Either way, one thing is clear, women are "very much in the minority" here. This is reflected on both sides of the gender coin, with guys noting "there aren't many girls here, which stinks," and girls sometimes feeling that they're being "treated differently" by their peers. That said, some say "what once was a huge gap in gender population is now becoming a more respectable margin" and "the ethnic makeup of the student population is quite diverse." Fundamentally, students here are "smart," "welcoming," and "open-minded." They "make their own fun," and a good deal of bonding is done with video games: *Rock Band*, *Guitar Hero*, and *World of Warcraft* are "hugely popular" here.

Why Students love Missouri University of Science & Technology

"Reputation for academic excellence."

WHY STUDENTS LOVE MISSOURI UNIVERSITY OF SCIENCE & TECHNOLOGY

Formerly known as University of Missouri–Rolla, Missouri University of Science and Technology has undergone a name change, but its "reputation for academic excellence" has remained the same. Its focus on "challenging" academics ensures "the classes are tough," so "don't expect to walk right on through, but be glad that you aren't able to." Luckily, the school offers a "large number of assets" to students, including "lots of opportunities for students to lead" and professors who "really want the students to understand the material." Most students describe the professors as "very knowledgeable" and "willing to help students whenever they are in need of assistance."

GENERAL INFO

Environment: Village. **Activities:** Choral groups, concert band, dance, drama/theater, jazz band, literary magazine, marching band, music ensembles, musical theater, pep band, radio station, student government, student newspaper, symphony orchestra, yearbook, campus ministries, international student organization. **Organizations:** 202 registered organizations, 29 honor societies, 13 religious organizations. 21 fraternity, 4 sororities. **Athletics (Intercollegiate):** *Men:* Baseball, basketball, cross-country, football, soccer, swimming, track/field (outdoor), track/field (indoor). *Women:* Basketball, cross-country, soccer, softball, track/field (outdoor), track/field (indoor), volleyball.

BOTTOM LINE

Missouri residents pay the fairly low rate of almost $8,000, whereas non-residents pay around $20,000. Room and board is around $8,000 as well and books are estimated to run a little under $1,000. The average financial aid package is almost $11,000, and the average amount of loan debt per graduate is just over $21,000. Students (and parents) appreciate Missouri S&T's "cheaper cost" than comparable colleges, as well as the fact their "tuition goes toward academics, not athletics."

SELECTIVITY

Admissions Rating	**86**
# of applicants	2,620
% of applicants accepted	93
% of acceptees attending	46

FRESHMAN PROFILE

Range SAT Critical Reading	**550–670**
Range SAT Math	**610–700**
Range ACT Composite	**25–31**
Average HS GPA	**3.63**
% graduated top 10% of class	**43**
% graduated top 25% of class	**71**
% graduated top 50% of class	**94**

DEADLINES

Regular Deadline	**12/1**
Normal registration	**no**

FACILITIES

Housing: Coed dorms, special housing for disabled students, fraternity/sorority housing, apartments for married students, cooperative housing, apartments for single students, wellness house, theme housing. *Special Academic Facilities/Equipment:* Writing Center; Student Design Center; nuclear reactor; observatory; explosives testing lab; underground mine; Museum of Rocks, Minerals, and Gemstones; Centers for Environmental Research, Water Resources, Industrial Research, and Rock Mechanics Research.

FINANCIAL FACTS

Financial Aid Rating	**80**
Annual in-state tuition	$7,848
Annual out-of-state tuition	$20,643
Room and Board	$8,520
Required Fees	$1,345
Books and supplies	$948
% frosh rec. need-based scholarship or grant aid	42
% UG rec.need-based scholarship or grant aid	42
% frosh rec. non-need-based scholarship or grant aid	60
% UG rec. non-need-based scholarship or grant aid	57
% frosh rec. need-based self-help aid	46
% UG rec. need-based self-help aid	45
% frosh rec. any financial aid	70
% UG rec. any financial aid	83
% UG borrow to pay for school	81
Average cumulative indebtedness	$24,235

New Mexico Institute of Mining and Technology

CAMPUS STATION, 801 LEROY PLACE, SOCORRO, NM 87801 • ADMISSIONS: 575-835-5424 • FAX: 575-835-5989

CAMPUS LIFE

Quality of life Rating	69
Fire Safety Rating	60
Green rating	65
Type of School	Public
Environment	Village

STUDENTS

Total undergrad enrolllment	1,385
% Male to Female	68/32
% From out of state	16
# of Fraternities	0
# of Sororities	0
% African American	1
% Asian	3
% Caucasian	82
% Hispanic	26
% International	1
# Of Countries Represented	30

ACADEMICS

Academic Rating	79
% Of students graduating within 4 years	17
% Of students graduating within 6 years	45
Calendar	semester
Most common reg class size	2–9 students
Most common lab size	2–9 students

MOST POPULAR MAJORS

Computer and information sciences, general electrical, electronics and communications engineering, mechanical engineering

SPECIAL STUDY OPTIONS

Accelerated program, cooperative education program, distance learning, double major, dual enrollment, exchange student program (domestic), independent study, internships, student-designed major, teacher certification program.

ABOUT THE SCHOOL

Just an hour outside of Albuquerque, The New Mexico Institute of Mining and Technology is a small school for the hardworking student. The science and engineering-focused institution offers more than 30 bachelors of Science degrees in rigorous fields including technology, the sciences, engineering, management, and technical communication. Though most students agree that the curriculum in most departments is intense, there are plenty of opportunities to take advantage of free tutoring for every subject and professors are always happy to help. With less than 2,000 students on campus one-on-one attention is readily available for those who need it. "Small class sizes and help resources make success totally possible. People band together and look out for one another and you really get to know one another at such a small school," one student reports. Like with most good things, there's always a flipside. A different student warns: "NMT is a small enough school that I get personal attention from all of my professors. It's a gift and a curse; your profs all know who you are and what you're capable of, but then they also know when you ditched class." All in all, the good outweighs the bad when students think about the additional opportunities that are afforded to them due to the intimate setting. The school is also proud to offer Living/Learning Communities, composed of freshmen in the same residence hall who take the same three courses together as a group. These courses, which include a freshman year research course, are linked together through a common theme, which creates a more engaging, realistic and exciting atmosphere.

BANG FOR YOUR BUCK

New Mexico Tech offers outstanding preparation in science, engineering, and technology related fields. Undergrads may have opportunities to assist professors with research projects; there are also many opportunities to gain experience while working on campus. With only 1400 total students, and just more than 300 freshmen becoming a part of the Institute every year, the school is able to provide an excellent faculty-to-student ratio of 11:1. This allows close relationships with professors, enabling students to make the most of time spent in the classroom. And fortunately for all undergrads, 99 percent of Tech's full-time faculty has earned doctoral degrees. All of these points certainly help lead to the following fact: the annual salary of NMT graduates ranks in the top 15 percent of more than 599 universities in the nation. New Mexico Institute tries to stay ahead of the curve in many ways; for instance, The Institute for Complex Additive Systems Analysis (ICASA) opened in the late 1990s to study, research and combat cyber-terrorism and computer-based crime.

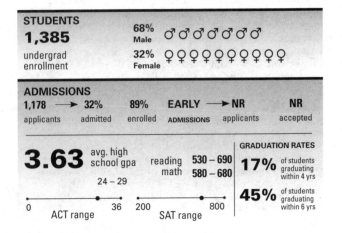

STUDENTS

1,385 undergrad enrollment

68% Male ♂♂♂♂♂♂♂

32% Female ♀♀♀♀♀♀♀♀♀

ADMISSIONS

1,178 →	32%	89%	EARLY ADMISSIONS →	NR	NR
applicants	admitted	enrolled		applicants	accepted

3.63 avg. high school gpa

ACT range (0–36): 24 – 29

SAT range (200–800): reading 530 – 690; math 580 – 680

GRADUATION RATES

17% of students graduating within 4 yrs

45% of students graduating within 6 yrs

New Mexico Institute of Mining and Technology

FINANCIAL AID: 575-835-5333 • E-MAIL: ADMISSION@ADMIN.NMT.EDU • WEBSITE: WWW.NMT.EDU

STUDENT BODY

At a typical school, you see people listening to music because it's popular, not really because they think it sounds good, one Techie explains. "The clothes they wear, the way they talk, everything is done to try to impress others and try to be as 'cool' as possible. Here however, this is not the concern. No one wears the most expensive 'cool' brand-name clothing, no one listens to the music that's popular. Individuality is absolutely held onto tightly here because no one cares what anyone else thinks of them. I know people who only shower three times a week because they think that's all they need. They're wrong, but they don't care whether you think they're wrong or not. They do because they want." Another student adds that "high school 'popular kids' will probably feel very out of place here. On the other hand, gamers, nerds, geeks, and students who just never fit the mold will find a friendly home."

Why Students love New Mexico Institute of Mining and Technology

"NMT is a small enough school that I get personal attention from all of my professors."

WHY STUDENTS LOVE NEW MEXICO INSTITUTE OF MINING AND TECHNOLOGY

Located in the colorful and historic Rio Grande valley, and founded in 1899, New Mexico Tech has a beautifully landscaped green campus, with easy access to rock-climbing, mountain biking, hiking, camping, stargazing, scuba diving, golf, and many more outdoor activities in the sunny town of Socorro. Indoor options are plentiful, too: student government, ballroom dance, poetry and creative writing, music, fine arts, martial arts, Celtic dance, yoga, aerobics, and much more. Math and science are king at NMT; the average student enjoys the academic challenge and strives to excel, leaving little room for wild parties. "We work really hard here, but you only get out of Tech what you put in. School is always on our minds, and to have fun we generally party or just hang out with friends." However, the Institute is within reach of Albuquerque, about 75 miles south for when students, or "Pygmies," want a taste of city life.

GENERAL INFO

Environment: Village. **Activities:** Choral groups, concert band, dance, drama/theater, jazz band, music ensembles, musical theater, radio station, student government, student newspaper. **Organizations:** 60 registered organizations, 7 honor societies, 3 religious organizations. **On-Campus Highlights:** Fidel Student Center, Skeen Library, Workman Center.

BOTTOM LINE

New Mexico Institute strives hard to provide students with an affordable, quality education. Almost 40 percent of undergrads receive need-based financial aid, and an amazing 90 percent of students' average need is able to be met. In-state credit hours will run $200 or so; out-of-state enrollees are looking at a yearly tuition rate of over $15,000. Room, board, books, supplies, and all required fees will total approximately $8000 for all students. As mentioned above, financial aid is generous; the total package will be nearly $12,000 per student, with need-based gift aid of almost $7,000. Upon graduation, undergrads normally owe a bit more than $15,000; very reasonable in these times, especially for the quality of education provided by the institute.

SELECTIVITY

Admissions Rating	**88**
# of applicants	1,178
% of applicants accepted	32
% of acceptees attending	87

FRESHMAN PROFILE

Range SAT Critical Reading	**530–690**
Range SAT Math	**580–680**
Range ACT Composite	**24–29**
Average HS GPA	**3.63**
% graduated top 10% of class	**33**
% graduated top 25% of class	**65**
% graduated top 50% of class	**89**

DEADLINES

Regular Deadline	**8/1**
Normal registration	**no**

FACILITIES

Housing: Coed dorms, men's dorms, women's dorms, apartments for married students, apartments for single students. *Special Academic Facilities/Equipment:* Mineral museum, observatory, radio telescope, seismic observatory and library, explosives labs.

FINANCIAL FACTS

Financial Aid Rating	**88**
Annual in-state tuition	$8,356
Annual out-of-state tuition	$15,075
Room and Board	$6,108
Required Fees	$658
Books and supplies	$1,010
% frosh rec. need-based scholarship or grant aid	15
% UG rec.need-based scholarship or grant aid	27
% frosh rec. non-need-based scholarship or grant aid	30
% UG rec. non-need-based scholarship or grant aid	29
% frosh rec. need-based self-help aid	17
% UG rec. need-based self-help aid	29
% frosh rec. any financial aid	34
% UG rec. any financial aid	39
% UG borrow to pay for school	33
Average cumulative indebtedness	$15,964

North Carolina State University

Box 7103, Raleigh, NC 27695 • Admissions: 919-515-2434 • Fax: 919-515-5039

CAMPUS LIFE

Quality of life Rating	95
Fire Safety Rating	98
Green rating	97
Type of School	Public
Environment	Metropolis

STUDENTS

Total undergrad enrollment	23,500
% Male to Female	57/43
% From out of state	7
% From public high school	80
% Live on Campus	32
# of Fraternities	32
# of Sororities	17
% African American	8
% Asian	5
% Caucasian	77
% Hispanic	3
% International	1
# Of Countries Represented	117

ACADEMICS

Academic Rating	77
Calendar	semester
Profs interesting rating	83
Profs accessible rating	84
Most common reg class size	20–29 students
Most common lab size	20–29 students

MOST POPULAR MAJORS

Biology, business administration and management, mechanical engineering

HONORS PROGRAMS

The University Honors Program, University Scholars program, or more than 30 honors programs located in the colleges or departments that include honors sections of courses, honors seminars, and honors research. Some programs require a senior honor thesis.

SPECIAL STUDY OPTIONS

Accelerated program, cooperative education program, cross-registration, distance learning, double major, dual enrollment, exchange student program (domestic), honors program, independent study, internships, liberal arts/career combination, student-designed major, study abroad.

ABOUT THE SCHOOL

Science and technology are big at North Carolina State University, a major research university and the largest four-year institution in its state. While the College of Engineering and the College of Agriculture and Life Sciences form the backbone of the academic program, the school also boasts nationally-reputable majors in architecture, design, textiles, management, agriculture, humanities and social sciences, education, physical and mathematical sciences, natural resources, and veterinary medicine, providing "big-school opportunity with a small-school feel." The "vicinity to top of the line research" is palpable, as more than 70 percent of NC State's faculty is involved in sponsored research, and the school is "an incubator for outstanding engineering and scientific research." For undergraduates, many of whom grew up wanting to attend the school, this opportunity to participate in important research is a major advantage. It makes sense, given that NCSU "is all about developing skills in school that will help you throughout your professional career." In addition, an education at NC State includes many opportunities for students to get a head start on real-world job, and the school also has "a great First Year College for students…who aren't sure what major they want to go into." The university's co-op program is one of the largest in the nation, with more than 1,000 work rotations a year, all due to the school's excellent reputation. "I want my degree to pack a punch when people see it, without having to be ridiculously rich or a prodigy of some sort," says a student of his decision to go to NCSU.

Despite the school's size, students are a very open and tight-knit group, and create a "very friendly atmosphere." Atlantic Coast Conference sports are a major part of campus life. On-campus food and dorms aren't exactly posh, but a majority of NC State students live off campus, and almost all of the students find fun things to do in surrounding Raleigh.
The bars on Hillsborough Street are very popular, and "Raleigh is a hoppin' and bop¬pin' place, and there [are] always shows and

BANG FOR YOUR BUCK

NC State continues to be a bargain for North Carolina residents. Offering financial assistance to qualified students is an integral part of NC State's history. In fact, this school was one of the first universities in the nation to create a scholarship program for students with the greatest financial need. The school's program, Pack Promise, guarantees that North Carolina's most disadvantaged students will receive 100 percent of their financial aid needs met through scholarships, grants, federal work-study employment and need-based loans. In addition, this program includes academic counseling to ensure that students will graduate in four years.

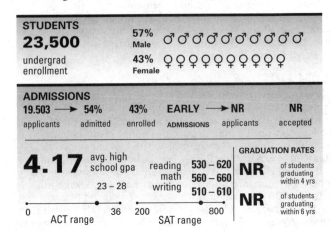

STUDENTS

23,500 undergrad enrollment

57% Male ♂♂♂♂♂♂♂♂♂♂

43% Female ♀♀♀♀♀♀♀♀♀♀

ADMISSIONS

19.503 → 54% → 43%; EARLY ADMISSIONS → NR → NR

19.503	54%	43%	EARLY ADMISSIONS	NR	NR
applicants	admitted	enrolled		applicants	accepted

4.17 avg. high school gpa

ACT range (0–36): 23 – 28

SAT range (200–800): reading 530 – 620, math 560 – 660, writing 510 – 610

GRADUATION RATES

NR of students graduating within 4 yrs

NR of students graduating within 6 yrs

Financial Aid: 919-515-2421 • E-mail: undergrad_admissions@ncsu.edu • Website: www.ncsu.edu

STUDENT BODY

NCSU "students have a reputation for being very practical," and most are "very driven" academically. "The students [on campus] vary from Southern-born-and-raised crop science majors, to devout Muslims, to 4.0 Columbia-bound premeds, to partying fraternity boys...and sometimes all of these are combined into one." "The city student is typically a Democrat, not particularly religious, [and] very friendly. The smaller-town student is typically a religious Republican and is also very friendly." Fortunately, "people of all ethnicities and backgrounds interact seamlessly," though on the whole, "The student body is somewhat conservative compared to other schools in the area." If there's any uniting factor on campus, it's that "Everyone loves the Wolfpack...everyone is very loyal and very passionate about the school's athletic program, no matter how successful or unsuccessful it might be that year."

Why Students love NC State

"This school has the most school spirit I have ever seen, with a majority of the students wearing NCSU attire and colors everyday!"

WHY STUDENTS LOVE NC STATE

It's pretty simple why NCSU gets such top talent: the school's strength in so many programs (particularly the sciences) is a huge draw. "The great engineering program coupled with in-state tuition made it a no-brainer," says a student. "[The decision to come here] had a lot to do with what my family could afford at first, but once I was able to visit the school, I loved everything I saw," says another. "The education provided here is comparable to any private institution around," and professors "are always willing to help when needed." Not having to worry about academics or price tag takes a load off students, and "the campus environment is extremely friendly." One student says: "This school has the most school spirit I have ever seen, with a majority of the students wearing NCSU attire and colors everyday!

GENERAL INFO

Activities: Choral groups, concert band, dance, drama/theater, jazz band, literary magazine, marching band, music ensembles, musical theater, pep band, radio station, student government, student newspaper, symphony orchestra, yearbook, campus ministries, international student organization. **Organizations:** 560 registered organizations, 26 honor societies, 25 religious organizations. 33 fraternities, 17 sororities. **Athletics (Intercollegiate):** *Men:* Baseball, basketball, cheerleading, cross-country, diving, football, golf, riflery, soccer, swimming, tennis, track/field (outdoor), track/field (indoor), wrestling. *Women:* Basketball, cheerleading, cross-country, diving, golf, gymnastics, riflery, soccer, softball, swimming, tennis, track/field (outdoor), track/field (indoor), volleyball.
On-Campus Highlights: RBC Center–Sports Arena, Gallery of

BOTTOM LINE

Annual tuition and fees for North Carolina residents are roughly $4,800. For non-residents, tuition and fees reach $17,000. For both residents and non-residents, room and board runs about $8,000 per year, while books and supplies average about $1,000 annually. Around half of all NC State students take out loans–students who borrow money graduate with an average loan debt of roughly $19,000.

SELECTIVITY

Admissions Rating	**92**
# of applicants	19,503
% of applicants accepted	54
% of acceptees attending	43
# accepting a place on wait list	0

FRESHMAN PROFILE

Range SAT Critical Reading	**530–620**
Range SAT Math	**560–660**
Range SAT Writing	**510–610**
Range ACT Composite	**23–28**
Average HS GPA	**4.17**
% graduated top 10% of class	**42**
% graduated top 25% of class	**81**
% graduated top 50% of class	**99**

DEADLINES

Regular Deadline	**2/1**
Normal registration	**yes**

FACILITIES

Housing: Coed dorms, special housing for disabled students, men's dorms, special housing for international students, women's dorms, fraternity/sorority housing, apartments for married students, apartments for single students, theme housing, living/learning dormitories. *Special Academic Facilities/Equipment:* Art and arts/crafts galleries, research farms and forest, phytophotron with controlled atmosphere growth chambers.

FINANCIAL FACTS

Financial Aid Rating	**87**
Annual in-state tuition	$5,153
Annual out-of-state tuition	$17,988
Room and Board	$8,536
Required Fees	$1,865
Books and supplies	$1,250
% frosh rec. need-based scholarship or grant aid	49
% UG rec.need-based scholarship or grant aid	45
% frosh rec. non-need-based scholarship or grant aid	4
% frosh rec. need-based self-help aid	37
% UG rec. need-based self-help aid	38
% frosh rec. any financial aid	72
% UG rec. any financial aid	67
% UG borrow to pay for school	47
Average cumulative indebtedness	$19,988

The Ohio State University–Columbus

Undergraduate Admissions 110 Enarson Hall, 154 W. 12th Avenue, Columbus, OH 43210 • Admissions: 614-292-3980

CAMPUS LIFE

Quality of life Rating	85
Fire Safety Rating	80
Green rating	95
Type of School	Public
Environment	Metropolis

STUDENTS

Total undergrad enrolllment	40,851
% Male to Female	53/47
% From out of state	11
% From public high school	87
% Live on Campus	25
# of Fraternities	42
# of Sororities	25
% African American	6
% Asian	5
% Caucasian	78
% Hispanic	3
% International	5
# Of Countries Represented	106

ACADEMICS

Academic Rating	70
% Of students graduating within 4 years	49
% Of students graduating within 6 years	78
Calendar	semester
Profs interesting rating	65
Profs accessible rating	70
Most common reg class size	20–29 students
Most common lab size	20–29 students

MOST POPULAR MAJORS

Biology, finance, psychology

HONORS PROGRAMS

The University Honors Program, the University Scholars Program.

SPECIAL STUDY OPTIONS

Accelerated program, cooperative education program, cross-registration, distance learning, double major, dual enrollment.

ABOUT THE SCHOOL

One of the largest universities in the country with more than 40,000 undergraduates on campus, Ohio State University is a big school with big opportunities. "The size of campus can be in some ways intimidating," though. For students who thrive in this sort of environment, the payoff is tremendous. Academics can be rigorous, and the university's Honors Program is dedicated to promoting the intellectual and personal development of high-performing students. The program enables motivated students to be part of smaller, selective communities within the larger university environment. Each of the 14 honors programs focuses on a common theme, and scholars live together, attend classes together, and experience diverse opportunities outside the classroom.

All students benefit from Ohio State's Undergraduate Research Office, which provides undergrads with opportunities and funding to work hands-on in faculty-guided research projects. Faculty generally receives high marks across the board, and is surprisingly accessible to students who show just a little bit of initiative. Be warned, however: OSU is not a school which holds your hand though planning and logistical matters. The general education curriculum is unpopular with many students, but Ohio State is on a quarter system and coursework moves pretty fast. Any class you don't like will be over relatively quickly.

BANG FOR YOUR BUCK

Ohio State offers a number of merit-based scholarship opportunities to qualified students. Honors students may compete for the Presidential and Medalist Scholarships, valued at the full cost of tuition (Presidential) and the full cost of in-state tuition (Medalist). Other awards of note include the Maximus Scholarship, worth $12,000 over four years, and the Provost's Scholarship, worth $9,600 over four years. The Morrill Scholars Program intended to promote diversity, multiculturalism, and leadership, offers awards with values ranging from full tuition to the full cost of attendance (i.e. books, transportation, room and board, etc). Qualified students from outside of Ohio who are required to pay a non-resident surcharge may earn the National Buckeye Scholarship, worth $34,800 over four years.

STUDENTS

40,851 undergrad enrollment

53% Male ♂♂♂♂♂♂♂♂♂♂

47% Female ♀♀♀♀♀♀♀♀♀

ADMISSIONS

24,302 applicants → 68% admitted | 40% enrolled

EARLY ADMISSIONS → NR applicants | NR accepted

NR avg. high school gpa

26 – 30 ACT range (0–36)

SAT range (200–800)	
reading	540 – 650
math	590 – 700
writing	540 – 640

GRADUATION RATES

49% of students graduating within 4 yrs

78% of students graduating within 6 yrs

The Ohio State University–Columbus

FAX: 614-292-4818 • FINANCIAL AID: 614-292-0300 • E-MAIL: ASKABUCKEYE@OSU.EDU • WEBSITE: WWW.OSU.EDU

STUDENT BODY

It's hard to categorize students here, says a sophomore. The vibe is "middle class" and "very Midwestern," and just about everyone is either "from small Ohio towns" or from "from a suburban-type setting" around Columbus, Toledo, Cincinnati, or Cleveland. Otherwise, "Ohio State is a melting pot," and "it easy to blend into the crowd." "There is no real homogenous, average student." Several ethnic minorities are solidly represented. Many students dress "like they shopped in a department store, albeit a nice department store," observes a senior. "There is a lot of style and fashion walking around campus," too. There are also hordes of students clad in "OSU clothing." A huge contingent of students is "smart, outgoing, athletic, and involved," but "the stereotypical weird kids at other universities have several hundred like-minded classmates at OSU."

Why Students love The Ohio State University

"A great blend of academics, opportunity, and fun."

WHY STUDENTS LOVE THE OHIO STATE UNIVERSITY–COLUMBUS

The Ohio State University in Columbus is "a great blend of academics, opportunity, and fun." This is one of the largest universities in the country, and as such, you'll find "every resource you could possibly need" and "unlimited" academic opportunities. "Everything from music to biochemical engineering and anything and everything in between" is available. "You name it and we've got it," guarantees an English major. Professors are "incredibly eager to work with students" and are "as interesting and entertaining as they can be when lecturing." The entire campus is filled up with "a ton of Buckeye spirit." "Attending the varsity sports events is popular." "Everyone is obsessed with Buckeye football." It's a little bit "like a religion," and the team is "idolized." The "great" recreation center here is absolutely gargantuan. "There is always an interesting event, conference, or performance," and OSU brings in plenty of "big entertainment acts."

GENERAL INFO

Activities: Choral groups, dance, drama/theater, jazz band, literary magazine, marching band, music ensembles, musical theater, opera, pep band, radio station, student government, student newspaper, student-run film society, symphony orchestra, television station, yearbook, international student organization. **Organizations:** 950 registered organizations, 39 honor societies, 93 religious organizations. 42 fraternities, 25 sororities. **Athletics (Intercollegiate):** *Men:* Baseball, basketball, cheerleading, cross-country, diving, fencing, football, golf, gymnastics, ice hockey, lacrosse, pistol, riflery, soccer, swimming, tennis, track/field, volleyball, wrestling. *Women:* Baseball, basketball, cheerleading, crew/rowing, cross-country, diving, fencing, field hockey, golf, gymnastics, ice hockey, lacrosse, pistol, riflery, soccer, softball, swimming, synchronized swimming, tennis, track/field.

BOTTOM LINE

The cost of attending Ohio State is below the national average for four-year public universities. Annual tuition and fees hover around $9,500, while campus room and board will run you another $9,000. Out-of-state undergraduates pay almost $14,000 more in tuition and fees.

SELECTIVITY

Admissions Rating	**84**
# of applicants	24,302
% of applicants accepted	68
% of acceptees attending	40
# accepting a place on wait list	247
% admitted from wait list	83

FRESHMAN PROFILE

Range SAT Critical Reading	**540–650**
Range SAT Math	**590–700**
Range SAT Writing	**540–640**
Range ACT Composite	**26–30**
% graduated top 10% of class	**54**
% graduated top 25% of class	**89**
% graduated top 50% of class	**98**

DEADLINES

Regular Deadline	**2/1**
Normal registration	**yes**

FACILITIES

Housing: Coed dorms, special housing for disabled students, special housing for international students, women's dorms, fraternity/sorority housing, apartments for married students, cooperative housing, apartments for single students, wellness housing, theme housing. *Special Academic Facilities/Equipment:* Wexner center for the Arts, zoology museum, geology museum, art and photography galleries, nuclear research reactor.

FINANCIAL FACTS

Financial Aid Rating	**70**
Annual in-state tuition	$9,309
Annual out-of-state tuition	$24,204
Room and Board	$9,180
Required Fees	$426
Books and supplies	$1,554
% frosh rec. need-based scholarship or grant aid	46
% UG rec.need-based scholarship or grant aid	40
% frosh rec. non-need-based scholarship or grant aid	3
% UG rec. non-need-based scholarship or grant aid	1
% frosh rec. need-based self-help aid	47
% UG rec. need-based self-help aid	51
% frosh rec. any financial aid	98
% UG rec. any financial aid	53
% UG borrow to pay for school	59
Average cumulative indebtedness	$22,830

Purdue University–West Lafayette

1080 Schleman Hall, West Lafayette, IN 47907-2050 • Admissions: 765-494-1776 • Fax: 765-494-0544

CAMPUS LIFE

Quality of life Rating	86
Fire Safety Rating	84
Green rating	85
Type of School	Public
Environment	Town

STUDENTS

Total undergrad enrolllment	30,836
% Male to Female	58/42
% From out of state	37
% Live on Campus	30
# of Fraternities	48
# of Sororities	33
% African American	3
% Asian	5
% Caucasian	74
% Hispanic	3
% International	11
# Of Countries Represented	127

ACADEMICS

Academic Rating	71
% Of students graduating within 4 years	40
% Of students graduating within 6 years	70
Calendar	semester
Profs interesting rating	73
Profs accessible rating	80
Most common reg class size	20–29 students
Most common lab size	20–29 students

MOST POPULAR MAJORS

Mechanical engineering, biology, management, consumer science retail, civil engineering

HONORS PROGRAMS

University Honors Program. Special programs offered to physically disabled students include note-taking services, reader services, voice recorders, tutors.

SPECIAL STUDY OPTIONS

Accelerated program, cooperative education program, cross-registration, distance learning, double major, dual enrollment, exchange student program (domestic), honors program, independent study, internships, liberal arts/career combination, study abroad, teacher certification program, weekend college.

ABOUT THE SCHOOL

Though it is wedged between the cornfields of rural Indiana, Purdue, having over 30,000 students, is one of the most educationally and ethnically diverse universities in the United States. Purdue has rich tradition and the oldest College of Agriculture in the nation. "An institution filled with brain power and immense achievement, yet at the same time exceedingly humble and saturated with the warm-hearted hospitality of the Midwest," a contented undergrad tells us. Academics are taken seriously here. Purdue is research-intensive, but retains great faculty-student interaction inside and outside of the classroom. "It allows undergraduates to enter laboratory research very early in their college career," says one student excitedly. Purdue has excellent research opportunities that are open to almost anyone who shows interest and dedication, and prides itself on being strong in STEM (science, technology, engineering and math) education, with heavy emphasis on real-world practical research and knowledge. When combined with an emphasis on innovation and creative thinking, Purdue becomes a great choice for anyone looking to have a successful future. A well-networked university, that is incorporated into the surrounding town through collaborative learning, field experiences, and service opportunities, allows students to learn in and out of the classroom.

BANG FOR YOUR BUCK

One student perhaps describes the value of a Purdue education by saying, "I considered the problem mathematically. Math + Science + social skills = Engineering. Engineering + Midwest = Purdue." Others add, "I knew that I would be receiving an excellent education and that I would be prepared for my chosen career field." "A great education that will prepare you for a career and it won't break the bank." "Tries it's hardest to ensure everyone comes out of college with a job lined up." Purdue also draws a lot of employers for internships and full time positions at many of their career fairs; the school produces marketable graduates who are in high demand by a number of top employers. Students are not hesitant with their praise. "I love Purdue and all of the doors it has opened for me in terms of engineering jobs and opportunities." "Emphasis on real-world practical research and knowledge, combined with an emphasis on innovation and creative thinking make Purdue a great choice for anyone looking to have a successful future." High expectations ensure that the students at Purdue are well prepared for the future. "Nurturing a strong work ethic and high moral accountability" is important at Purdue, one student tells us. "It's been extremely tough, and a lot of work, but I feel like a much better engineer than I would have been, had I gone anywhere else," says another appreciative enrollee.

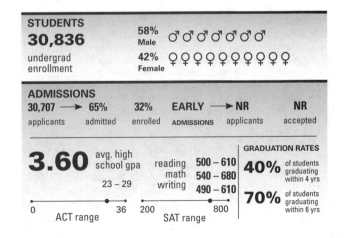

STUDENTS

30,836 undergrad enrollment

58% Male ♂♂♂♂♂♂♂

42% Female ♀♀♀♀♀♀♀♀♀

ADMISSIONS

30,707 →	65%	32%	EARLY →	NR	NR
applicants	admitted	enrolled	ADMISSIONS	applicants	accepted

3.60 avg. high school gpa

reading	500 – 610
math	540 – 680
writing	490 – 610

ACT range: 23 – 29 (0 – 36)

SAT range (200 – 800)

GRADUATION RATES

40% of students graduating within 4 yrs

70% of students graduating within 6 yrs

Purdue University–West Lafayette

FINANCIAL AID: 765-494-0998 • E-MAIL: ADMISSIONS@PURDUE.EDU • WEBSITE: WWW.PURDUE.EDU

STUDENT BODY

Students are "very relaxed and friendly," despite always being "aware of their obligations, be it for school or one of the student organizations that they may be involved with." The majority of students come from Indiana, and are "conservative, but not radically conservative. They are what you expect from twenty-somethings in the Midwest." Happily, students think Purdue's size means "that no matter who you are or where your interests may lie, you will be able to find another group of students that share similar interests." "The Greek System is pretty big here, but by no means is that necessary for someone to fit in," and the same goes for sports. Some say that "it is true that science and engineering majors sometimes look down on other students," a growing number of others say "The technical majors do not think that other majors are less intelligent. Campus life affords a mutual respect, and though there is joking around, everyone understands that having a Purdue degree is prestigious, no matter what their major is titled."

Why Students love Purdue University–West

"Big Ten sports are huge...but not so huge that those who are uninterested in sports feel left out."

WHY STUDENTS LOVE PURDUE UNIVERSITY–WEST LAFAYETTE

A Big Ten school with all the accompanying sports and heritage, "Purdue had everything I was looking for in a college: strong academic programs, a top-tier research university, Big Ten athletics, a vibrant Greek community, and a friendly and welcoming student body." Students love the food, and many other amenities here, too. "They have the best dining courts of any of the colleges I've visited." "The athletics are great, and they are completely self-sufficient and not funded by academic fees etc., which shows Purdue...has its priorities correct." "At Purdue, you can try anything–we have more than 800 organizations, hundreds of research labs, great internship opportunities." "The facilities are state of the art and the traditions are priceless."

GENERAL INFO

Activities: Choral groups, concert band, dance, drama/theater, jazz band, literary magazine, marching band, music ensembles, musical theater, opera, pep band, radio station, student government, student newspaper, student-run film society, symphony orchestra, television station, yearbook, campus ministries, international student organization. **Organizations:** 850 registered organizations, 25 honor societies, 66 religious organizations. 48 fraternities, 32 sororities. **Athletics (Intercollegiate):** *Men:* Baseball, basketball, cross-country, diving, football, golf, swimming, tennis, track/field (outdoor), track/field (indoor), wrestling. *Women:* Basketball, cross-country, diving, golf, soccer, softball, swimming, tennis, track/field (outdoor), track/field (indoor), volleyball.

BOTTOM LINE

Tuition is a bit north of $8,000 for in-state students, with those from other states looking at a substantial increase to over $27,000. Room, board, books, and fees will increase this amount by another $11,000. "The financial aid package was the best offered to me along with a very good scholarship." "Cheaper than a private school but it is a world renowned engineering school at the same time." "Gave me a very generous scholarship package."

SELECTIVITY

Admissions Rating	**88**
# of applicants	30,707
% of applicants accepted	65
% of acceptees attending	32
# accepting a place on wait list	250
% admitted from wait list	0

FRESHMAN PROFILE

Range SAT Critical Reading	**500–610**
Range SAT Math	**540–680**
Range SAT Writing	**490–610**
Range ACT Composite	**23–29**
Average HS GPA	**3.60**
% graduated top 10% of class	**37**
% graduated top 25% of class	**71**
% graduated top 50% of class	**95**

DEADLINES

Regular Deadline	**3/1**
Normal registration	**yes**

FACILITIES

Housing: Coed dorms, special housing for disabled students, men's dorms, women's dorms. *Special Academic Facilities/Equipment:* Hall of music, child development lab, speech and hearing clinic, small animal veterinary clinic, horticulture park, linear accelerator, tornado simulator, nuclear accelerator. *Computers:* 95% of classrooms, 5% of dorms, 95% of libraries, 90% of dining areas, 95% of student union.

FINANCIAL FACTS

Financial Aid Rating	**86**
Annual in-state tuition	$8,893
Annual out-of-state tuition	$27,061
Room and Board	$9,896
Required Fees	$585
Books and supplies	$1,330
% frosh rec. need-based scholarship or grant aid	39
% UG rec.need-based scholarship or grant aid	35
% frosh rec. non-need-based scholarship or grant aid	29
% UG rec. non-need-based scholarship or grant aid	17
% frosh rec. need-based self-help aid	46
% UG rec. need-based self-help aid	44
% frosh rec. any financial aid	53
% UG rec. any financial aid	46
% UG borrow to pay for school	52
Average cumulative indebtedness	$26,360

Southern Utah University

Southern Utah University, Admissions Off, 351 West University, Cedar City, UT 84720 • Website: www.suu.edu

CAMPUS LIFE

Quality of life Rating	94
Fire Safety Rating	60*
Green rating	60*
Type of School	Public
Environment	Village

STUDENTS

Total undergrad enrollment	7,236
% Male to Female	42/58
% From public high school	74
% African American	1
% Asian	1
% Caucasian	86
% Hispanic	9
% Native American	2
% International	2
# Of Countries Represented	7

ACADEMICS

Academic Rating	81
% Of students graduating within 4 years	15
% Of students graduating within 6 years	28
Calendar	semester
Most common reg class size	20–29 students
Most common lab size	20–29 students

MOST POPULAR MAJORS

Business/commerce, economics international relations

SPECIAL STUDY OPTIONS

Cooperative education program, distance learning, double major, English as a Second Language (ESL), honors program, independent study, internships, liberal arts/career combination, teacher certification program, weekend college. Special programs offered to physically disabled students include reader services, voice recorders, tutors.

ABOUT THE SCHOOL

Southern Utah University is known for a lot of things; primary among them is the approachability of the students, professors, and pretty much everyone else on campus. Students rave about their ability to access professors for any question and the professors' enthusiasm to help them at just about anything from meeting a student at a library to help them on a paper to getting them assistant jobs in their fields. The professors in every discipline are known for demonstrating "passion for the subjects they teach, but are more concerned about the student and his or her potential," according to one undergrad, and the small class size makes every student feel like it truly is an individual experience. Some of the strongest programs of the school include their business, nursing and theater programs; the latter being especially popular due to the annual four-month-long Utah Shakespearean Festival that is renowned nation-wide. There is also a popular Neil Simon Festival that theater students can participate in as well.

BANG FOR YOUR BUCK

Any incoming freshman (whether they're a resident or non-resident) who applies for admission before the December 1 deadline is automatically considered for academic scholarships without having to fill out additional paperwork. These programs include aid packets that range from two to four years like the President's, Founders', Dean's, and Centurium scholarships. Southern Utah University also looks to prepare their graduates for the real world with systems like their Experiential Education program that requires students to get experience outside of the classroom and can include jobs and internships. Their Career and Professional Development Coordinator can help students find interning opportunities as well. The Experiential Education program also offers a resource called "Optimal Resume," which helps students create and format their resumes and portfolios. Each person must also write a short proposal for a project they wish to do and include a budget plan that they will get feedback on.

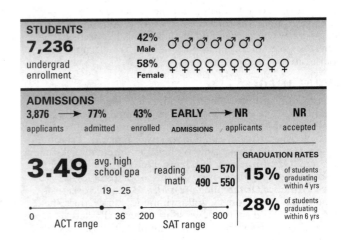

STUDENTS

7,236 undergrad enrollment

42% Male ♂♂♂♂♂♂♂

58% Female ♀♀♀♀♀♀♀♀♀♀

ADMISSIONS

3,876 →	77%	43%	EARLY ADMISSIONS →	NR	NR
applicants	admitted	enrolled		applicants	accepted

3.49 avg. high school gpa

ACT range (0–36): 19 – 25

SAT range (200–800): reading 450 – 570; math 490 – 550

GRADUATION RATES

15% of students graduating within 4 yrs

28% of students graduating within 6 yrs

Southern Utah University

ADMISSIONS: 435-586-7740 • FAX: 435-865-8223 FINANCIAL AID: 909-621-8205 • E-MAIL: ADMINFO@SUU.EDU

STUDENT BODY

"Students tell us that the "typical T-bird" has "an eagerness for learning, a passion for involvement, and a contagious friendliness" that combine to put other students at ease. "It is fairly easy to strike up a conversation with a random student on campus." Students are heavily "into [the] outdoors," and proximity to the Utah Shakespearean Festival also attracts "many theater" types. In addition, "a large majority of the students belong to the LDS faith." This homogeneity has its fans and detractors: one student enjoys having his fellow "Mormons...among the student body, because their morals are so high." There are two non-LDS Christian groups and six multicultural organizations on campus. Students are "accepting."

Why Students love Southern Utah University

"It is fairly easy to strike up a conversation with a random student on campus."

WHY STUDENTS LOVE SOUTHERN UTAH UNIVERSITY

The students are known for being quite eager and passionate themselves, as well as incredibly friendly. Many incoming freshman seem to find this cheerfulness comforting as it tends to be quite easy to strike up a random conversation. A majority of the students also belong to the LDS faith and, though many enjoy it, quite a few find the school to be lacking in diversity. Everyone, however, agrees that each student is treated with respect. The campus provides a small town atmosphere and, while the campus grounds are beautiful, many students trek outside to the mountains that are adjacent to the school. "Students are heavily into [the] outdoors," says an undergrad, and love to explore the incredible western landscape. Students say that "everyone is treated with respect" and "fits in."

GENERAL INFO

Environment: Village. **Activities:** Choral groups, concert band, dance, drama/theater, jazz band, literary magazine, marching band, music ensembles, musical theater, opera, pep band, radio station, student government, student newspaper, symphony orchestra, television station, yearbook. **Organizations: Athletics (Intercollegiate):** *Men:* Baseball, basketball, cross-country, football, golf, track/field (outdoor). *Women:* Basketball, cross-country, gymnastics, softball, tennis, track/field (outdoor).

BOTTOM LINE

Southern Utah has more than 7,000 students on campus, of which over three-quarters are full-time, and enrolled about 1,300 freshmen last year. Each student pays $540 in student fees, with books and supplies around $1,600, but the resident and non-resident tuition amounts differ. Incoming freshmen who are residents can expect to pay just less than $5,000 in tuition, while non-residents can expect something just a little north of $15,000. Room and board ranges between $2,000 and $6,000 depending on which dorm the student lives in. The average financial aid package is nearly $8,000.

SELECTIVITY

Admissions Rating	**77**
# of applicants	3,876
% of applicants accepted	77
% of acceptees attending	43

FRESHMAN PROFILE

Range SAT Critical Reading	**450–570**
Range SAT Math	**440–550**
Range ACT Composite	**19–25**
Average HS GPA	**3.49**
% graduated top 10% of class	**31**
% graduated top 25% of class	**56**
% graduated top 50% of class	**83**

DEADLINES

Regular Deadline	**5/1**
Normal registration	**no**

FACILITIES

Housing: Coed dorms, special housing for disabled students, men's dorms, special housing for international students, women's dorms, fraternity/sorority housing, apartments for single students.

FINANCIAL FACTS

Financial Aid Rating	**73**
Annual in-state tuition	$4,658
Annual out-of-state tuition	$15,370
Room and Board	$5,496
Required Fees	$540
Books and supplies	$1,600
% frosh rec. need-based scholarship or grant aid	51
% UG rec.need-based scholarship or grant aid	59
% frosh rec. non-need-based scholarship or grant aid	34
% UG rec. non-need-based scholarship or grant aid	19
% frosh rec. need-based self-help aid	26
% UG rec. need-based self-help aid	35
% UG borrow to pay for school	45
Average cumulative indebtedness	$11,170

St. Mary's College of Maryland

Admissions Office 18952 E. Fisher Rd, St. Mary's City, MD 20686-3001 • Admissions: 240-895-5000 • Fax: 240-895-500

CAMPUS LIFE

Quality of life Rating	90
Fire Safety Rating	81
Green rating	90
Type of School	Public
Environment	Rural

STUDENTS

Total undergrad enrollment	1,943
% Male to Female	41/59
% From out of state	15
% From public high school	60
% Live on Campus	86
% African American	8
% Asian	3
% Caucasian	81
% Hispanic	3
% International	2
# Of Countries Represented	33

ACADEMICS

Academic Rating	89
% Of students graduating within 4 years	72
% Of students graduating within 6 years	77
Calendar	semester
Profs interesting rating	93
Profs accessible rating	93
Most common reg class size	10–19 students
Most common lab size	10–19 students

MOST POPULAR MAJORS

Psychology, English, biology, economics, political science

HONORS PROGRAMS

Nitze Scholars Program Special programs offered to physically disabled students include note-taking services, reader services, voice recorders, tutors.

SPECIAL STUDY OPTIONS

Double major, dual enrollment, exchange student program (domestic), honors program, independent study, internships, student-designed major, study abroad, teacher certification program

ABOUT THE SCHOOL

Maryland's St. Mary's College is one of the country's two public honors colleges. This draws students from all over to the campus, in search for an affordable yet prestigious education. Students also take pride in the school's "small and intimate learning environment and inclusive community environment." Classes on campus are "engaging," and they "tend to have a great combination of lecture, discussion, and experiential learning." This, students say, leads to "a challenging and altogether high-quality academic experience." St. Mary's professors are the icing on the cake, "always available for discussion and clarification." Most offer office hours and make themselves available outside of the classroom, even giving out their personal cell phone numbers. "At St. Mary's, you are not just a number in the classroom, but an essential part of the classroom experience," says one student. Students continue to be a driving force behind the College's sustainability initiatives. In addition to various larger projects, smaller in-house renovations and energy conservation programs have yielded big dividends for the campus and environment.

BANG FOR YOUR BUCK

St. Mary's College believes that qualified students should have an opportunity for a college education. as a public institution, the school offers a variety of programs designed to assist in meeting college expenses. These programs include scholarships, grants, loans, work opportunities, and a tuition payment plan. Every accepted student is automatically reviewed by the Scholarship Review Committee. There are only 2000 students enrolled at St. Mary's, with just over 400 freshman added to the enrollment each year; virtually everyone is full-time. There is also a stellar 11:1 Student-to-Faculty ratio, which obviously helps just about 90% return for their sophomore year, and aiding in three-quarters of freshman being able to graduate within four years. There are a variety of different housing options at SMCM. Townhouses for upper-class students as well as suites are offered. There is also special interest housing, such as SAFE house, which is substance and alcohol free housing, as well as living learning centers, like the International, Women in Science, and Eco houses. There are many opportunities to get involved on campus, "whether by participating in club activities or taking a student position in campus affairs, or just becoming a student tutor."

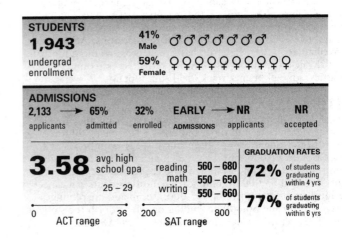

STUDENTS

1,943 undergrad enrollment

41% Male ♂♂♂♂♂♂♂

59% Female ♀♀♀♀♀♀♀♀♀♀

ADMISSIONS

2,133 applicants → 65% admitted — 32% enrolled

EARLY ADMISSIONS → NR applicants — NR accepted

3.58 avg. high school gpa

ACT range (0–36): 25 – 29

SAT range (200–800): reading 560 – 680; math 550 – 650; writing 550 – 660

GRADUATION RATES

72% of students graduating within 4 yrs

77% of students graduating within 6 yrs

St. Mary's College of Maryland

FINANCIAL AID: 240-895-3000 • E-MAIL: ADMISSIONS@SMCM.EDU • WEBSITE: WWW.SMCM.EDU

STUDENT BODY

"Friendliness" is the hallmark of the typical St. Mary's undergrad, and many are quick to assert that there's "a very welcoming student body." Indeed, as this junior gushes, "You could sit down and have dinner with someone you have never seen before, and be completely comfortable." The average "Seahawk" is also "focused on their studies" and "involved in all sorts of activities." Students here tend to be "politically aware and left-leaning, and very concerned with the environment." While many St. Mary's undergrads do often share these attributes, another junior assures us, "There are many different types of students [here]: some preppy kids, jocks, the artsy kids, bookworms, hippies, country kids, city kids. Everyone finds their niche, but then mixes up with other people."

Why Students love SMCM

"You could sit down and have dinner with someone you have never seen before, and be completely comfortable."

WHY STUDENTS LOVE SMCM

Most students can't help but notice how welcoming the spirit on campus is. "You could sit down and have dinner with someone you have never seen before, and be completely comfortable." Those that are "politically aware and left-leaning, and very concerned with the environment," will feel at home at St. Mary's. However, "there are many different types of students [here]: some preppy kids, jocks, the artsy kids, bookworms, hippies, country kids, city kids. Everyone finds their niche, but then mixes up with other people," one junior assures. "When it's nice out, everyone is outside, and on the weekends, the docks are crowded by 11:00 a.m. People throw Frisbees, footballs, run around barefoot, grill, and chill." Complimentary access to sail boats or kayaks are a big hit as well. Campus life is nearly as abundant as the academic life.

GENERAL INFO

Activities: Choral groups, dance, drama/theater, jazz band, literary magazine, music ensembles, musical theater, radio station, student government, student newspaper, symphony orchestra, television station, yearbook, campus ministries, international student organization. **Organizations:** 117 registered organizations, 8 honor societies, 4 religious organizations. **Athletics (Intercollegiate):** *Men:* Baseball, basketball, cross-country, lacrosse, sailing, soccer, swimming, tennis. *Women:* Basketball, cross-country, field hockey, lacrosse, sailing, soccer, swimming, tennis, volleyball.

BOTTOM LINE

As "a public honors college," St. Mary's is able to provide "a rigorous academic curriculum" at an affordable price. Yearly in-state tuition comes to just more than $12,000, with out-of-state being twice that figure. Room and board will run just under $11,000; books, supplies, and fees will add another $3,500. Financial aid is plentiful, with almost 60 percent of students receiving some manner of need-based assistance. Nearly 50% of a students' average need is able to be met. The total financial aid package will normally amount to $13,000, with the average need-based loan being $13,000, and total loan debt per grad about $8,000.

SELECTIVITY

Admissions Rating	**90**
# of applicants	2,133
% of applicants accepted	65
% of acceptees attending	32
# accepting a place on wait list	95
% admitted from wait list	36

FRESHMAN PROFILE

Range SAT Critical Reading	**560–680**
Range SAT Math	**550–650**
Range SAT Writing	**550–660**
Range ACT Composite	**25–29**
Average HS GPA	**3.58**
% graduated top 10% of class	**33**
% graduated top 25% of class	**71**
% graduated top 50% of class	**93**

DEADLINES

Regular Deadline	**1/1**
Normal registration	**yes**

FACILITIES

Housing: Coed dorms, special housing for disabled students, men's dorms, women's dorms, apartments for single students, wellness housing, theme housing. There are a variety of different housing options at SMCM. Townhouses for upper-class students as well as suites are offered. *Special Academic Facilities/Equipment:* Art gallery, archaeological sites, Historic St. Mary's City

FINANCIAL FACTS

Financial Aid Rating	**81**
Annual in-state tuition	$12,005
Annual out-of-state tuition	$24,082
Room and Board	$10,915
Required Fees	$2,440
Books and supplies	$1,000
% frosh rec. need-based scholarship or grant aid	40
% UG rec.need-based scholarship or grant aid	42
% frosh rec. non-need-based scholarship or grant aid	26
% UG rec. non-need-based scholarship or grant aid	25
% frosh rec. need-based self-help aid	41
% UG rec. need-based self-help aid	42
% frosh rec. any financial aid	66
% UG rec. any financial aid	66
% UG borrow to pay for school	50
Average cumulative indebtedness	$17,505

State University of New York at Geneseo

1 College Circle, Geneseo, NY 14454-1401 • Admissions: 585-245-5571 • Financial Aid: 585-245-5731

CAMPUS LIFE

Quality of life Rating	80
Fire Safety Rating	89
Green rating	87
Type of School	Public
Environment	Village

STUDENTS

Total undergrad enrolllment	5,488
% Male to Female	43/57
% From out of state	2
% From a public high school	81
% Live on Campus	47
# of Fraternities	8
# of Sororities	11
% African American	2
% Asian	6
% Caucasian	75
% Native American	3
% Hispanic	5
# Of Countries Represented	39

ACADEMICS

Academic Rating	84
% Of students graduating within 4 years	62
% Of students graduating within 6 years	77
Calendar	semester
Profs interesting rating	77
Profs accessible rating	83
Most common reg class size	20–29 students
Most common lab size	10–19 students

MOST POPULAR MAJORS

Biology, business adminstration, psychology

SPECIAL STUDY OPTIONS

Cross-registration, double major, dual enrollment, English as a Second Language (ESL), honors program, independent study, internships, study abroad, teacher certification program, Albany semester, Washington semester, 3/2 Engineering, 3-3 Engineering, 4/1 MBA, 3/4 Dentistry, 3/4 Optometry, 3/4 Osteopathic Medicine, 3/2 or 3/1 nursing, 3/3 physical therapy, pre-med and pre-law advisory program.

ABOUT THE SCHOOL

The State University of New York at Geneseo sits in a small town in the Finger Lakes region of upstate New York. Proudly sporting the title of the "Ivy of the SUNYs," this university is the place for students looking for all the prestige of a posh private school on a public-school budget. Small classes and enthusiastic professors make it easy to excel at SUNY Geneseo. "I truly feel that Geneseo's greatest strength is its sense of community. This is true when it comes to Professor-student interactions, student-student interactions and all others. Everyone is very receptive to new ideas and to learning from each other," one student shares. Professors "seek to challenge" their students, and the "course load is tough," according to members of the student body.

Why Students love Geneseo

"Geneseo has a great atmosphere, challenging classes, a wonderful student population, and the best price!"

BANG FOR YOUR BUCK

Students are thrilled that SUNY Geneseo provides them with "an outstanding education [at] an affordable price;" also, two-thirds of faculty at the school have PhDs. An intimate environment, which promotes close student-teacher interaction, provides students with the chance to explore the varied curriculum in an in-depth and comprehensive manner. With nearly 1,000 freshman enrolling last year, virtually everyone is a full-time student and lives on campus; there are only 6,000 students in all. "Geneseo has a great atmosphere, challenging classes, a wonderful student population, and the best price!"

STUDENTS

5,488 undergrad enrollment

43% Male ♂♂♂♂♂♂♂♂♂

57% Female ♀♀♀♀♀♀♀♀♀♀♀

ADMISSIONS

9,885 applicants → **38%** admitted — **27%** enrolled

EARLY ADMISSIONS → **NR** applicants — **NR** accepted

3.75 avg. high school gpa

reading 600–690
math 600–700

27-30 — 0 to 36 ACT range

200 to 800 SAT range

GRADUATION RATES

62% of students graduating within 4 yrs

77% of students graduating within 6 yrs

State University of New York at Geneseo

E-MAIL: ADMISSIONS@GENESEO.EDU • FAX: 585-245-5550 • WEBSITE: WWW.GENESEO.EDU

STUDENT BODY

What is one thing that unites Geneseo undergrads? Students here agree that their peers are "very good at time management." Indeed, "They know how to study, but they also know how to have a good time." Having multitasking down to an art form, "They are able to get their work done and excel in classes while still participating in social events and hanging out with their friends." Fortunately, Geneseo is "not a pressure cooker school," and most students are "pretty relaxed." While some assert that the school is "very diverse," others say that the "typical student is a white, middle-class, well-rounded, high school overachiever." Regardless of stereotype, students are very "open to meeting new people," and "making friends [is] really easy here." As one content freshman elaborates, "The students are very accepting. They come together frequently and support each other, causes, and the community."

WHY STUDENTS LOVE SUNY BUFFALO

While beautiful, the historic, sleepy town of Geneseo is hardly an entertainment Mecca. However, most students don't seem to mind due to the abundance of activities offered. It is easy to find "many on-campus activities for students to get involved in;" "the greatest strengths are the diversity of subjects the school offers. I am able to participate in all sorts of academic programs, clubs, and extra activities that fit all the things I enjoy to do," say students. Campus organizations are widely popular; there are over 175 to select from. The nearly 20 fraternities and sororities are also an option, although "you don't have to go to parties or join a Greek organization to have a good time."

GENERAL INFO

Environment: Village. **Activities:** Choral groups, dance, drama/theater, jazz band, literary magazine, music ensembles, musical theater, pep band, radio station, student government, student newspaper, symphony orchestra, television station, campus ministries, international student organization. **Organizations:** 175 registered organizations, 12 honor societies, 7 religious organizations. 8 fraternities, 11 sororities. **Athletics (Intercollegiate):** *Men:* Basketball, cross-country, diving, ice hockey, lacrosse, soccer, swimming, track/field. *Women:* Basketball, cross-country, diving, equestrian sports, field hockey, lacrosse, soccer, softball, swimming, tennis, track/field (outdoor), track/field (indoor), volleyball. **On-Campus Highlights:** MacVittie College Union, The Gazebo, Milne Library, Alumni Fieldhouse (Workout Center), College Green. **Environmental Initiatives:** Signing of the Presidents Climate Commitment. Currently developing our Climate Action Plan. Establishment of Geneseo's Environmental Impact and Sustainability Task Force. Gold Lecture Series–Live Green Task Force Work/Initiatives.

BOTTOM LINE

SUNY Geneseo provides a comprehensive education while not digging deeply into students' pockets. In-state credit hours are only a bit more than $200, while out-of-state students can expect to pay closer to $600 for each hour. Books and supplies will come to about $1,000. There are plenty of ways to lower costs at the school, however. More than 60 percent of freshmen receive financial assistance, and the school is able to meet 75 percent of total need. The average aid package is over $8,000, and freshman need-based gift aid surpasses $4,000. Undergrads here can expect to graduate with approximately $21,000 in loan debt.

SELECTIVITY

Admissions Rating	**94**
# of applicants	9,885
% of applicants accepted	38
% of acceptees attending	27
# accepting a place on wait list	342
% admitted from wait list	0

FRESHMAN PROFILE

Range SAT Critical Reading	**600–690**
Range SAT Math	**600–700**
Range ACT Composite	**27–30**
Average HS GPA	**3.75**
% graduated top 10% of class	**52**
% graduated top 25% of class	**87**
% graduated top 50% of class	**99**

DEADLINES

Regular Deadline	**1/1**
Normal registration	**yes**

FACILITIES

Housing: Coed dorms, special housing for disabled students, special housing for international students, town houses and special interest housing is available. Some fraternities and sororities have housing independent of college. *Special Academic Facilities/Equipment:* Four theaters, electron microscopes. Integrated Science Center *Computers:* 100% of classrooms, 60% of dorms, 100% of libraries, 100% of dining areas, 100% of student union, 10% of common outdoor areas have wireless network access.

FINANCIAL FACTS

Financial Aid Rating	**88**
Annual in-state tuition	$4,970
Annual out-of-state tuition	$13,380
Room and Board	$10,042
Required Fees	$1,431
Books and supplies	$950
% frosh rec. need-based scholarship or grant aid	19
% UG rec.need-based scholarship or grant aid	44
% frosh rec. non-need-based scholarship or grant aid	19
% UG rec. non-need-based scholarship or grant aid	16
% frosh rec. need-based self-help aid	23
% UG rec. need-based self-help aid	40
% frosh rec. any financial aid	60
% UG rec. any financial aid	70
% UG borrow to pay for school	54
Average cumulative indebtedness	$21,200

State University of New York at New Paltz

100 Hawk Drive, New Paltz, NY 12561-2499 • Admissions: 845-257-3200 • Financial Aid: 845-257-3250

CAMPUS LIFE

Quality of life Rating	60*
Fire Safety Rating	72
Green rating	91
Type of School	Public
Environment	Village

STUDENTS

Total undergrad enrolllment	6,582
% Male to Female	36/64
% From out of state	7
% From a public high school	74
% Live on Campus	32
# of Fraternities	11
# of Sororities	17
% African American	5
% Asian	4
% Caucasian	64
% Hispanic	11
% International	4
# Of Countries Represented	60

ACADEMICS

Academic Rating	85
% Of students graduating within 4 years	42
% Of students graduating within 6 years	65
Calendar	semester
Profs interesting rating	62
Profs accessible rating	67
Most common reg class size	20–29 students
Most common lab size	20–29 students

MOST POPULAR MAJORS

Elementary Education and teaching, Psychology, general visual and performing arts.

HONOR PROGRAM

The Honors Programs available.

SPECIAL STUDY OPTIONS

Cooperative education program, cross-registration, distance learning, double major, dual enrollment, English as a Second Language (ESL), exchange student program (domestic), honors program, independent study, internships, liberal arts/career combination, student-designed major, study abroad, teacher certification program.

ABOUT THE SCHOOL

Quirky, artsy liberal arts school SUNY New Paltz is located in the historic village of New Paltz, nestled between the Hudson and the Shawangunk Mountains ("a rural town among many cities"). Surrounded by such beauty, the school offers "a beautiful, fun, and friendly environment with cool people and terrific professors." As the largest cultural institution in the Hudson Valley, the school provides its students (and the surrounding town) with plenty of lectures, conferences, concerts, gallery shows, theatrical performances and other opportunities for life-long learning. "New Paltz is a vibrant community that is both intellectually and culturally rich," says a student. These offerings complement the school's "strong academics" and "helpful professors" to make for "a variety of opportunities to pursue any sort of career." New Paltz also has active internship opportunities for students in all five of its academic schools (some students receive credit and others do not), and over 400 students participate in credit-bearing internships during the spring, fall, and summer semesters. The Career Resource Center staff is there to assist students with all phases of career planning.

Why Students love New Paltz

"New Paltz is a vibrant community that is both intellectually and culturally rich."

BANG FOR YOUR BUCK

With such a strong internship program (more than 550 students took internships last year), the school has a great reputation among employers, and 98% of internship employers said they would rehire or take another New Paltz intern. New Paltz also offers a CAS Internship Stipend Program (a highly selective and competitive program) to provide a certain number of students with the opportunity to gain valuable experiential education without sacrificing needed income.

STUDENTS
6,582 undergrad enrollment

36% Male ♂♂♂♂
64% Female ♀♀♀♀♀♀

ADMISSIONS

15,204 applicants	→ 37% admitted	19% enrolled	EARLY ADMISSIONS → NR applicants	NR accepted

3.50 avg. high school gpa

ACT range (0–36): 23-27

SAT range (200–800): reading 520–610; math 520–610; writing NR

GRADUATION RATES
42% of students graduating within 4 yrs
65% of students graduating within 6 yrs

State University of New York at New Paltz

E-MAIL: ADMISSIONS@NEWPALTZ.EDU • FAX: 845-257-3209 • WEBSITE: WWW.NEWPALTZ.EDU

STUDENT BODY

Undergrads here believe that the student body is very diverse in terms of ethnicity and also in terms of personality type; one student observes, "There is a sizable group of atypical students who hang out with the other atypical students like themselves.' Their ranks include "the free-spirited hippies, the metal heads, the guys who just like sports but don't play, and the people who are actually here to study." Geographically, the school is less diverse. Nearly everyone is a New York State resident, with many coming from "downstate New York"–Long Island, New York City, and Westchester County. There's a fair amount of upstate kids as well. One students says, "I think people from anywhere get along pretty well." And a fellow classmate adds, "It's really hard to find anyone who doesn't fit in with at least one group on campus because there are so many with so many different interests."

WHY STUDENTS LOVE STATE UNIVERSITY OF NEW YORK AT NEW PALTZ

With so many arts and theater majors, the school's "proximity to New York City" is a huge plus (not to mention a 90-minute bus ride away), and the town itself offers an outstanding quality of life. The "variety of smart and creative people" here "love music, partying, and learning," and there is "lots of interaction with theater and going to the small town." The student body "supports its diverse range of students." Other strengths of New Paltz include "the great dining system, the exciting surrounding time, and the friendly atmosphere." For students looking to get away on weekends, the city of Rochester is under an hour away, packed with shopping, dining, and nightlife options.

GENERAL INFO

Activities: Choral groups, concert band, dance, drama/theater, jazz band, literary magazine, music ensembles, musical theater, radio station, student government, student newspaper, symphony orchestra, television station, campus ministries, international student organization. **Organizations:** 196 registered organizations, 12 honor societies, 10 religious organizations. 11 fraternities, 17 sororities. **Athletics (Intercollegiate):** *Men:* Baseball, basketball, cross-country, diving, soccer, swimming, tennis, volleyball. *Women:* Basketball, cross-country, diving, field hockey, lacrosse, soccer, softball, swimming, tennis, volleyball. **On-Campus Highlights:** Samuel Dorsky Museum of Art, Lenape and Esopus Residence Halls, Athletic and Wellness Center, Student Union, Hasbrouck Dining Hall.

BOTTOM LINE

SUNY Geneseo provides a comprehensive education while not digging deeply into students' pockets. In-state credit hours are only a bit more than $200, while out-of-state students can expect to pay closer to $600 for each hour. Books and supplies will come to about $1,000. There are plenty of ways to lower costs at the school, however. More than 60 percent of freshmen receive financial assistance, and the school is able to meet 75 percent of total need. The average aid package is over $8,000, and freshman need-based gift aid surpasses $4,000. Undergrads here can expect to graduate with approximately $21,000 in loan debt.

SELECTIVITY

Admissions Rating	**83**
# of applicants	15,204
% of applicants accepted	37
% of acceptees attending	19

FRESHMAN PROFILE

Range SAT Critical Reading	**520–610**
Range SAT Math	**520–610**
Range ACT Composite	**23–27**
Average HS GPA	**3.50**
% graduated top 10% of class	**26**
% graduated top 25% of class	**66**
% graduated top 50% of class	**95**

DEADLINES

Regular Deadline	**4/1**
Normal registration	**no**

FACILITIES

Housing: Coed dorms, special housing for disabled students, men's dorms, special housing for international students, women's dorms, The First-Year Initiative, Honors Housing, Art Program Housing. 9*Special Academic Facilities/Equipment:* Samuel Dorsky Museum of Art, Resnick Engineering Hall, Coykendall Media Center, Communication Disorders Training Center and Clinic; Music Therapy Training Center and Clinic; Shepherd Recital Hall, Honors Center; Martin Luther King, Jr. Study Center; Fournier Mass Spectrometer;Raymond Kurdt Theatre Collection. *Computers:* 70% of classrooms, 45% of dorms, 100% of libraries, 90% of dining areas, 90% of student union, 10% of common outdoor areas have wireless network access.

FINANCIAL FACTS

Financial Aid Rating	**60***
Annual in-state tuition	$5,270
Annual out-of-state tuition	$14,320
Room and Board	$9,950
Required Fees	$1,288
Books and supplies	$1,200
% frosh rec. need-based scholarship or grant aid	27
% UG rec.need-based scholarship or grant aid	26
% frosh rec. non-need-based scholarship or grant aid	6
% UG rec. non-need-based scholarship or grant aid	3
% frosh rec. need-based self-help aid	49
% UG rec. need-based self-help aid	45
% frosh rec. any financial aid	73
% UG rec. any financial aid	67
% UG borrow to pay for school	61
Average cumulative indebtedness	$25,732

State University of New York–College of Environmental Science and Forestry University

Office of Undergraduate Admissions, SUNY-ESF, Syracuse, NY 13210 • Admissions: 315-470-6600

CAMPUS LIFE

Quality of life Rating	79
Fire Safety Rating	96
Green rating	97
Type of School	Public
Environment	City

STUDENTS

Total undergrad enrolllment	1,725
% Male to Female	58/42
% From out of state	16
% From a public high school	74
% Live on Campus	33
# of Fraternities	26
# of Sororities	21
% African American	1
% Asian	84
% Caucasian	3
% Hispanic	1
% International	1
# Of Countries Represented	37

ACADEMICS

Academic Rating	75
% Of students graduating within 4 years	51
% Of students graduating within 6 years	53
Calendar	semester
Most common reg class size	10–19 students
Most common lab size	10–19 students

MOST POPULAR MAJORS

Enivornmental biology, environmental science, landscape architecture

HONOR PROGRAM

Lower Division Honors Program, Upper Division Thesis Honors Program, Honors Thesis/Project course.

SPECIAL STUDY OPTIONS

Cooperative education program, cross-registration, distance learning, double major, honors program, independent study, internships, study abroad, teacher certification program, Associate degrees in forest technology & land surveying technology are offered at The Ranger School campus. Graduates of these degrees may then continue their studies at the Syracuse campus to complete bachelor degrees.

ABOUT THE SCHOOL

Located in Syracuse, SUNY's nationally-renowned College of Environmental Science and Forestry offers 22 unique programs, including a variety of specialties in addition to the obvious two within its name; fisheries science, landscape architecture, construction management, paper engineering, and wildlife sciences are just a few of them. Students are often involved in research projects, and field trips are prominent in most classes. Undergraduates tell us SUNY–ESF is "a small, personal school" with "tough" coursework. "Challenging but alsotvery interesting and real." "They connect real-life problems to all the coursework." Professors are a wonderful resource, "fantastic" and "brilliant in their fields," as well as "supportive and easy to find and speak to." Students are impressed by faculty members who "can back up their teaching with real experiences;" professors and undergrads have an excellent relationship. Discipline is a prized trait at SUNY-ESF, as students find that "class schedules are very rigid," and that the "academic program is very specialized, so there is not a lot of flexibility with general studies and choosing minors." Students who put in a concerted effort regarding their studies and involvement in class will find SUNY-ESF to be a fine match for them.

Why Students love SUNY–ESF

"No one here ever says no to going out for a hike."

BANG FOR YOUR BUCK

SUNY–ESF awards approximately half of its total institutional scholarships based on academic merit, with the other half based on financial need. There are many special scholarships available for students who live outside New York State to help them cover tuition costs. All students in the bioprocess engineering program, and the paper science and engineering programs, are required to complete a summer internship in a related industry. They are also encouraged to complete a semester-long paid internship. More than 95% of students in these programs are placed in a related job or graduate study within nine months of graduation.

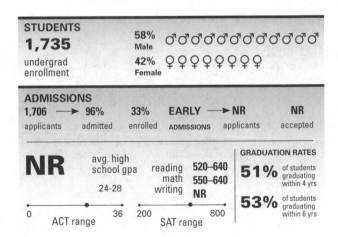

STUDENTS

1,735 undergrad enrollment

58% Male ♂♂♂♂♂♂♂♂♂♂♂♂

42% Female ♀♀♀♀♀♀♀♀

ADMISSIONS

1,706 applicants → 96% admitted — 33% enrolled

EARLY ADMISSIONS → NR applicants — NR accepted

NR avg. high school gpa

reading 520–640
math 550–640
writing NR

24-28

ACT range 0–36

SAT range 200–800

GRADUATION RATES

51% of students graduating within 4 yrs

53% of students graduating within 6 yrs

State University of New York–College of Environmental Science and Forestry University

FINANCIAL AID: 315-470-6706 • E-MAIL: ESFINFO@ESF.EDU • FAX: 315-470-6933 • WEBSITE: WWW.ESF.EDU

STUDENT BODY

Ethnic diversity at ESF is seriously lacking. It's an overwhelming white group of people from the state of New York. "Students generally don't put a lot of time into dressing for school and are generally very laidback" here. People universally "love the outdoors." To grossly generalize, "there are two loose groups at ESF." The "more populous" group is the "vegan, save-the-world" "tree huggers." For them, "tie-dye and green are the preferred colors to wear." "We're always taking the stairs instead of the elevators (even up to the eighth floor), using Tupperware instead of Styrofoam or plastic, and we love plants," explains a first-year hippie. Not surprisingly, these students "lean more toward the left." The other, smaller group is "fairly conservative" "hunters" and "rednecks" who have "a management view of the environment." "They "often major in forestry resources management, construction management, paper science engineering, or some such thing." "Somehow," members of both groups manage to get along pretty well.

WHY STUDENTS LOVE SUNY–ESF

The school motto at SUNY is "Improve your world." Academic excellence, the close sense of community, and a commitment to sustainability are all important to the student body. The beautiful Adirondack Mountains are nearby, and "no one here ever says no to going out for a hike." Winter might be "brutal because our campus is on a huge hill," notes one student. However, the environment also contributes to some unique pastimes, such as woodsmen's teams. These groups compete using old-fashioned lumberjack techniques with other schools in the Northeast and Canada. Most of the other, less unusual activities are focuses around the main quad at ESF. Off-campus is also very nice, with downtown offering "lots of culture."

GENERAL INFO

Environment: City. **Activities:** Choral groups, concert band, dance, drama/theater, jazz band, literary magazine, marching band, music ensembles, musical theater, pep band, radio station, student government, student newspaper, student-run film society, symphony orchestra, television station, yearbook, campus ministries, international student organization. **Organizations:** 300 registered organizations, 1 honor societies, 13 religious organizations. 26 fraternities, 21 sororities. **Athletics (Intercollegiate):** *Men:* Cross-country, golf, soccer. *Women:* Cross-country, golf, soccer **On-Campus Highlights:** Library, green houses, wildlife collection, Laboratories & Studios, student lounge, snack bar, student store.

BOTTOM LINE

SUNY–ESF is highly specialized and selective; it is the oldest and largest environmental college in the country. The school enjoys a unique partnership with Syracuse University that gives ESF students special access to Syracuse University classes, academic facilities, student clubs and organizations and other services, while paying low state-supported tuition. SUNY's in-state and out-of-state tuition rates are among the lowest in the Northeast for public colleges.

SELECTIVITY

Admissions Rating	**80**
# of applicants	1,706
% of applicants accepted	96
% of acceptees attending	33

FRESHMAN PROFILE

Range SAT Critical Reading	**520–640**
Range SAT Math	**550–640**
Range ACT Composite	**24–28**
% graduated top 10% of class	**29**
% graduated top 25% of class	**63**
% graduated top 50% of class	**97**

DEADLINES

Regular Deadline	**12/1**
Normal registration	**no**

FACILITIES

Housing: Coed dorms, special housing for disabled students, special housing for international students, fraternity/sorority housing, apartments for married students, apartments for single students, theme housing. 100% of campus accessible to physically disabled. *Special Academic Facilities/Equipment:* Museums, art galleries, plant growth and animal environmental simulation chambers, wildlife collection, electron microscope, paper making facility, photogrammetric and geodetic facilities, hydrology flumes. *Computers:* 50% of classrooms, 100% of dorms, 100% of libraries, 100% of dining areas, 100% of student union, 10% of common outdoor areas have wireless network access.

FINANCIAL FACTS

Financial Aid Rating	**93**
Annual in-state tuition	$4,070
Annual out-of-state tuition	$13,380
Room and Board	$14,032
Required Fees	$971
Books and supplies	$1,200
% frosh rec. need-based scholarship or grant aid	63
% UG rec.need-based scholarship or grant aid	59
% frosh rec. non-need-based scholarship or grant aid	41
% UG rec. non-need-based scholarship or grant aid	16
% frosh rec. need-based self-help aid	63
% UG rec. need-based self-help aid	59
% frosh rec. any financial aid	89
% UG rec. any financial aid	72
% UG borrow to pay for school	80
Average cumulative indebtedness	$27,000

State University of New York–Oswego

229 Sheldon Hall, Oswego, NY 13126-3599 • Admissions: 315-312-2250 • Financial Aid: 315-312-2248

CAMPUS LIFE

Quality of life Rating	79
Fire Safety Rating	69
Green rating	74
Type of School	Public
Environment	Village

STUDENTS

Total undergrad enrolllment	7,377
% Male to Female	48/52
% Live on Campus	58
# of Fraternities	13
# of Sororities	10
% African American	4
% Asian	2
% Caucasian	83
% Hispanic	6
% International	1
# Of Countries Represented	15

ACADEMICS

Academic Rating	72
% Of students graduating within 4 years	39
% Of students graduating within 6 years	60
Calendar	semester
Most common reg class size	10–19 students
Most common lab size	10–19 students

MOST POPULAR MAJORS

Elementary education and teaching

HONOR PROGRAM

The Honors Programs is available.

SPECIAL STUDY OPTIONS

Accelerated program, cross-registration, distance learning, double major, dual enrollment, English as a Second Language (ESL), exchange student program (domestic), external degree program, honors program, independent study, internships, liberal arts/career combination, study abroad, teacher certification program

ABOUT THE SCHOOL

The State University of New York–Oswego, located in a picturesque, natural setting on the banks of Lake Ontario, offers a variety of opportunities for students seeking an affordable public education. Strong business, teaching, and honors programs, as well as excellent study-abroad options, highlight the academic offerings of the school. The student body "consists mostly of middle-class to lower-middle-class students from upstate New York," according to one undergrad, although folks from the city and its surrounding areas are also well-represented on the campus.

Why Students love Oswego

"In the summer and spring people will spread out beach towels and get some sun on the lakeside of campus."

BANG FOR YOUR BUCK

The university offers more than $80 million a year in need-based financial aid, and more than $2.7 million a year in merit-based scholarships. Almost $750 million in capital improvements have been completed or are in progress. There are more than 1,000 internships and service learning opportunities, and the Career Services office provides exceptional assistance to students preparing for life after graduation. The Financial Aid office is a valuable resource to both students and graduates, assisting them in managing student loans and personal finances, and there is a wonderful connection to alumni at the university. A strong 5-year accounting program designed around new CPA requirements is a popular choice for students, too. One undergrad raved, "5 years to get my Masters sounds like an awesome idea."

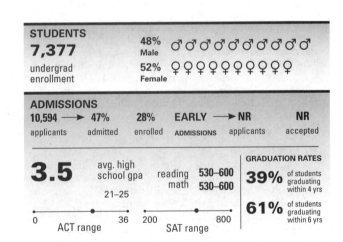

STUDENTS

7,377 undergrad enrollment

48% Male ♂♂♂♂♂♂♂♂♂♂

52% Female ♀♀♀♀♀♀♀♀♀♀

ADMISSIONS

10,594 applicants → **47%** admitted — **28%** enrolled

EARLY ADMISSIONS → **NR** applicants — **NR** accepted

3.5 avg. high school gpa

reading 530–600

math 530–600

ACT range: 21–25 (0–36)

SAT range (200–800)

GRADUATION RATES

39% of students graduating within 4 yrs

61% of students graduating within 6 yrs

State University of New York–Oswego

E-MAIL: ADMISS@OSWEGO.EDU • FAX: 315-312-3260 • WEBSITE: WWW.OSWEGO.EDU

STUDENT BODY

SUNY–Oswego's student body "consists mostly of middle-class to lower-middle-class students from upstate New York." That said, there are also many "from downstate like NYC and Long Island." How do you tell the difference between upstaters and downstaters? Word on campus is that upstaters aren't afraid to occasionally wear their flip-flops outside in the winter, while downstaters keep their Uggs on. In addition to permanent residence somewhere in the Empire State, "the majority of students are white." Temperamentally, "the typical student is usually someone who is studious from Sunday to Wednesday, and parties on weekends. "There are some students who don't go to class, and those who don't party," explains an undergrad. "They are all accepted by the community and will have friends in different social cliques." "They normally fit in by finding a club that they enjoy," agrees another.

WHY STUDENTS LOVE STATE UNIVERSITY OF NEW YORK AT NEW PALTZ

Students say there is a "friendly" and "helpful" social atmosphere, "devoted to promoting multiculturalism," with a "gorgeous" lakeside campus. There is a niche to be found for everyone at Oswego, and undergrads "are all accepted by the community and will have friends in different social cliques." A happy resident states, "The greatest strengths are the extracurricular activities around campus. Very diverse and popular." There are nearly 200 clubs and organizations, great for socializing and networking, and offering activities and involvement opportunities of all kinds. Students with a fondness for recreational pursuits will find no shortage of options at Oswego, especially for cold-weather sports.

GENERAL INFO

Environment: Village. **Activities:** Choral groups, concert band, dance, drama/theater, jazz band, literary magazine, music ensembles, musical theater, radio station, student government, student newspaper, student-run film society, sym phony orchestra, television station, yearbook, international student organization. **Organizations:** 148 registered organizations, 21 honor societies, 6 religious organizations. 13 fraternities, 10 sororities. **Athletics (Intercollegiate):** *Men:* Baseball, basketball, cross-country, diving, golf, ice hockey, lacrosse, soccer, swimming, tennis, track/field (outdoor), track/field (indoor), wrestling. *Women:* Basketball, cross-country, diving, field hockey, ice hockey, lacrosse, soccer, softball, swimming, tennis, track/field (outdoor), track/field (indoor), volleyball.

BOTTOM LINE

Affordability is often the primary factor for students who choose to attend SUNY–Oswego. The university provides "a great education for the money," says a thankful student. Additionally, the Oswego Guarantee assures students their on-campus room and board charges will not increase while at the college. Providing a high-quality education, as well as preparing undergraduates for the job market and a life of continued learning, are paramount at Oswego.Upon graduation, enrollees can expect to have a cumulated indebtedness of a bit more than $17,000. Nearly 90 percent of the student body receives some manner of financial aid. More than 40 percent of students borrow in some way to pay for school, and can envision a cumulative indebtedness once graduating from the institution of more than $17,000. Clemson students are especially thrilled by the incredible support the univer¬sity offers. "The value is unbeatable." "I have found the scholarships amazing, financial aid and assistance has been all-inclusive, and high-quality." "The deciding factor for me attending Clemson was the full scholarship the University provided."

SELECTIVITY

Admissions Rating	**84**
# of applicants	10,544
% of applicants accepted	47
% of acceptees attending	28

FRESHMAN PROFILE

Range SAT Critical Reading	**530–600**
Range SAT Math	**530–600**
Range ACT Composite	**21–25**
Average HS GPA	**3.50**
% graduated top 10% of class	**13**
% graduated top 25% of class	**54**
% graduated top 50% of class	**85**

DEADLINES

Regular Deadline	**1/1**
Normal registration	**yes**

FACILITIES

Housing: Coed dorms, wellness housing, theme housing Global living and learning center, suites for upperclassmen, nontraditional student housing, first-year experience residence hall for incoming freshmen only, housing for 21 and over single suites, several rooms equipped with special equipment to meet needs of disabled students available. *Special Academic Facilities/Equipment:* Tyler Hall Art Galleries, Rice Creek Biological Field Station, curriculum materials center, electron microscopy lab, planetarium. *Computers:* 80% of classrooms, 10% of dorms, 100% of libraries, 100% of dining areas, 100% of student union, have wireless network access.

FINANCIAL FACTS

Financial Aid Rating	**83**
Annual in-state tuition	$5,270
Annual out-of-state tuition	$14,320
Room and Board	$12,310
Required Fees	$1,240
Books and supplies	$800
% frosh rec. need-based scholarship or grant aid	50
% UG rec.need-based scholarship or grant aid	56
% frosh rec. non-need-based scholarship or grant aid	10
% UG rec. non-need-based scholarship or grant aid	5
% frosh rec. need-based self-help aid	56
% UG rec. need-based self-help aid	56
% frosh rec. any financial aid	84
% UG rec. any financial aid	85
% UG borrow to pay for school	86
Average cumulative indebtedness	$25,488

State University of New York–Stony Brook University

Office of Admissions, Stony Brook, NY 11794-1901 • Admissions: 631-632-6868 • Financial Aid: 631-632-6840

CAMPUS LIFE

Quality of life Rating	68
Fire Safety Rating	73
Green rating	93
Type of School	Public
Environment	Town

STUDENTS

Total undergrad enrolllment	16,045
% Male to Female	52/48
% From out of state	7
% From a public high school	90
% Live on Campus	59
# of Fraternities	15
# of Sororities	14
% African American	6
% Asian	23
% Caucasian	38
% Hispanic	9
% International	7
# Of Countries Represented	111

ACADEMICS

Academic Rating	63
% Of students graduating within 4 years	43
% Of students graduating within 6 years	65
Calendar	semester
Profs interesting rating	67
Profs accessible rating	66
Most common reg class size	20–29 students
Most common lab size	20–29 students

MOST POPULAR MAJORS

Biology, business/commerce, psychology

SPECIAL STUDY OPTIONS

Cross-registration, distance learning, double major, exchange student program (domestic), honors program, independent study, internships, student-designed major, study abroad, teacher certification program. Albany Semester, Undergrads may take grad level courses BS/MS programs, BE/MS, BS/MA–Living Learning Centers in residence halls, Honors College, undergraduate research and creative activities program where undergraduates work with faculty on research projects, university learning communities and (WISE) Women in Science and Engineering.

ABOUT THE SCHOOL

The State University of New York at Stony Brook houses more than 24,000 students on 1,000 acres of woodlands in the North Shore of Long Island. The Research and Development Campus encompasses 246 acres adjacent to the main campus; there are also Southampton and Manhattan locations. The university boasts more than 150 undergraduate majors, minors, and joint-degree pro¬grams, including rich research opportunities and a Fast Track MBA program. This creates an unparalleled first-year experience program for incoming freshman. "The breadth of the school's curriculum" is impressive," says one contented undergrad.

Why Students love Stony Brook

"I feel that the balance between independence and assistance has prepared me well for entering a profession."

BANG FOR YOUR BUCK

Stony Brook "combines affordability and excellence with academic prestige," where students can learn from "world-renowned professors for a great price." There is a highly-respected Honors College, an opportunity for a semester of study in Albany, and undergrads may take grad level courses as well. Students can also work with faculty on interesting projects; "it is relatively easy to find internships and research opportunities" as an undergraduate," especially with over 1500 faculty members. First-year resident members of each college are housed together in the same residential Quadrangle, and there are also new undergraduate apartments. "I feel that the balance between independence and assistance has prepared me well," one student relates.

STUDENTS

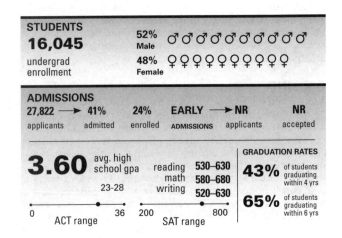

16,045 undergrad enrollment

52% Male ♂♂♂♂♂♂♂♂♂♂

48% Female ♀♀♀♀♀♀♀♀♀♀

ADMISSIONS

27,822 applicants ➔ 41% admitted — 24% enrolled

EARLY ADMISSIONS ➔ NR applicants — NR accepted

3.60 avg. high school gpa

ACT range: 23-28 (0–36)

SAT range (200–800): reading 530–630, math 580–680, writing 520–630

GRADUATION RATES

43% of students graduating within 4 yrs

65% of students graduating within 6 yrs

State University of New York–Stony Brook

E-MAIL: ENROLL@STONYBROOK.EDU • FAX: 631-632-9898 • WEBSITE: WWW.STONYBROOK.EDU

STUDENT BODY

Drawing a large crowd from the state of New York and a smattering of international students, Stony Brook University "combines the diversity of New York City with academic excellence to create a truly unique experience." At this large school, "Every personality type is represented...and it is easy to find a group to fit in with." Politically, "there are both strong right-wing and left-wing school newspapers," though "many more people support the liberal side." No matter what your persuasion, the community is generally open and accepting of different backgrounds, opinions, and interests. A current student elaborates, "I've never seen such a heterogeneous mixture of individuals in my life. And yet, despite the vast differences amongst students, everyone seems to get along." Across the board, academics are a priority, but most students strike a balance between work and play. At Stony Brook, "A typical student will go to class, spend a lot of their time studying, and try to have some fun on Thursday nights and the weekends."

WHY STUDENTS LOVE STATE UNIVERSITY OF NEW YORK–STONY BROOK

Students at Stony Brook University rave about their professors despite the challenges the curriculum presents, calling them "approachable and interested in their sub¬ject, making them good educators." Though classes are often large, many students assure that the faculty often keeps "reasonable office hours," and make themselves "very accessible" to students that need a little extra help. More independent learners will do especially well here. "Professors and staff are more than willing to help, but you have to ask for it...I feel that the balance between independence and assistance has prepared me well for entering a profession," one student says.

GENERAL INFO

Activities: Choral groups, concert band, dance, drama/theater, jazz band, literary magazine, marching band, music ensembles, musical theater, opera, pep band, radio station, student government, student newspaper, student-run film society, symphony orchestra, yearbook, campus ministries. **Organizations:** 292 registered organizations, 6 honor societies, 25 religious organizations. 17 fraternities, 16 sororities. **Athletics (Intercollegiate):** *Men:* Baseball, basketball, cross-country, diving, football, lacrosse, soccer, swimming, tennis, track/field (outdoor), track/field (indoor). *Women:* Basketball, cross-country, diving, lacrosse, soccer, softball, swimming, tennis, track/field (outdoor), track/field (indoor), volleyball. **On-Campus Highlights:** Staller Center for the Arts, Sports Complex and Stadium, Student Activities Center, University Hospital, The Charles B. Wang Center.

BOTTOM LINE

There are nearly 16,000 students at the school, with 3000 or so freshman enrolling each year. In-state credit hours are very reasonable, at just over $200; out-of-state students can expect that figure to rise to just under $600. On-campus room and board is approximately $10,000; out-of-state tuition is upwards of $13,000. Books, supplies, and required fees will add another $3000. However, options for aid are prevalent. Nearly 75% of undergrads receive some manner of financial support, with the same percentage of average need being met. In general, aid packages tend to be about $11,000 per student; need-based gift aid averages $7,500. Students can expect to graduate with about $20,000 in loan debt.

SELECTIVITY

Admissions Rating	**92**
# of applicants	27,822
% of applicants accepted	41
% of acceptees attending	24
# accepting a place on wait list	704
% admitted from wait list	5

FRESHMAN PROFILE

Range SAT Critical Reading	**530–630**
Range SAT Math	**580–680**
Range SAT Writing	**520–630**
Range ACT Composite	**25–29**
Average HS GPA	**3.60**
% graduated top 10% of class	**38**
% graduated top 25% of class	**72**
% graduated top 50% of class	**95**

DEADLINES

Regular Deadline	**1/15**
Normal registration	**yes**

FACILITIES

Housing: Coed dorms, special housing for disabled students, apartments for married students, apartments for single students, single sex floors in coed dorms. Living Learning Centers, first year resident members of each college are housed together in the same residential Quadrangle. *Special Academic Facilities/Equipment:* SAC Gallery, Staller Gallery, Wang Center, Tabler Center for the Arts. *Computers:* 50% of classrooms, 50% of dorms, 50% of libraries, 50% of dining areas, 50% of student union, 50% of common outdoor areas have wireless network access.

FINANCIAL FACTS

Financial Aid Rating	**73**
Annual in-state tuition	$4,970
Annual out-of-state tuition	$13,380
Room and Board	$10,574
Required Fees	$1,850
Books and supplies	$900
% frosh rec. need-based scholarship or grant aid	51
% UG rec.need-based scholarship or grant aid	49
% frosh rec. non-need-based scholarship or grant aid	31
% UG rec. non-need-based scholarship or grant aid	16
% frosh rec. need-based self-help aid	54
% UG rec. need-based self-help aid	53
% frosh rec. any financial aid	75
% UG rec. any financial aid	66
% UG borrow to pay for school	59
Average cumulative indebtedness	$19,770

State University of New York–University at Buffalo

12 Capen Hall, Buffalo, NY 14260-1660 • Admissions: 716-645-6900 • Financial Aid: 716-645-2450

CAMPUS LIFE

Quality of life Rating	72
Fire Safety Rating	60*
Green rating	65
Type of School	Public
Environment	City

STUDENTS

Total undergrad enrolllment	19,199
% Male to Female	54/46
% From out of state	4
% Live on Campus	34
# of Fraternities	22
# of Sororities	17
% African American	7
% Asian	10
% Caucasian	57
% Hispanic	4
% International	15
# Of Countries Represented	108

ACADEMICS

Academic Rating	66
% Of students graduating within 4 years	43
% Of students graduating within 6 years	67
Calendar	semester
Profs interesting rating	62
Profs accessible rating	67
Most common reg class size	20–29 students
Most common lab size	20–29 students

MOST POPULAR MAJORS

Business/commerce, engineering, social sciences

HONOR PROGRAMS

There is a University Honors College as well as honors programs within the majors.

SPECIAL STUDY OPTIONS

Accelerated program, cooperative education program, cross-registration, distance learning, double major, dual enrollment, exchange student program (domestic), honors program, independent study, internships, study abroad, teacher certification program, Certificate programs, Early Assurance Program with School of Medicine & Dentistry, Honors College & Learning Communities.

ABOUT THE SCHOOL

Offering more than 400 undergraduate, graduate and professional degree programs, SUNY–Buffalo is one of the nation's premier public research universities. UB is divided into three campuses. South Campus in Northeast Buffalo North Campus," which is located in the suburban enclave of Amherst. The school also has a downtown campus. A school with this much to offer is bound to be large, making it "easy not to attend class and fall through the cracks, so one must be self-motivated to do well." "If you're not serious about what you're doing you will get left behind." It puts a lot of emphasis on research, and there are labs that are open 24 hours a day. There really isn't an extreme concerning politics, but it mostly seems to be a pretty moderate campus. You have your liberal groups and your right-wingers, but no one is really outspoken. They have grown in their environmental awareness and are clearly trying to become more environmentally sound.

Why Students love SUNY Buffalo

"Between all of the clubs and organizations, the Office of Student Life, athletics, and the Student Association, there is always something to do."

BANG FOR YOUR BUCK

New freshmen are considered each year for Provost Scholarships, starting at $2,500, depending on academic achievement, talent in the performing and creative arts, and the cost of attendance. Acker Scholarships are renewable for up to four years, may cover up to the full cost of tuition, and are awarded to students who will participate in the Daniel Acker Scholars Program. Consideration is given to students with financial need, first-generation college students, and students who have demonstrated their ability to contribute to the cultural diversity of UB. The University at Buffalo has a variety of internship and experiential education programs, which allow students to gain an advantage in the marketplace upon graduation. One student relates that "programs are all of the highest quality, translating [into] a best-value education for students."

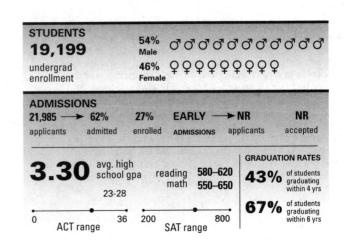

STUDENTS

19,199 undergrad enrollment

54% Male ♂♂♂♂♂♂♂♂♂♂♂

46% Female ♀♀♀♀♀♀♀♀♀♀

ADMISSIONS

21,985 applicants → 62% admitted | 27% enrolled | EARLY ADMISSIONS → NR applicants | NR accepted

3.30 avg. high school gpa

reading 580–620
math 550–650

23-28 — ACT range (0–36)

SAT range (200–800)

GRADUATION RATES

43% of students graduating within 4 yrs

67% of students graduating within 6 yrs

State University of New York–University at Buffalo

E-MAIL: UB-ADMISSIONS@BUFFALO.EDU • FAX: 716-645-6411 • WEBSITE: WWW.BUFFALO.EDU

STUDENT BODY

Because of UB's size, "You can find just about every kind of person there is here. Everyone has a place in this large and diverse student population." As one student notes, "Although the typical student is of traditional college age, there really isn't a 'typical' student–the student body is very diverse in terms of religion, ethnicity, nationality, age, gender, and orientation. 'Atypical' students fit in well because of the diversity of the student population." Another student adds, "There are a lot of foreign and minority students, to the point that the actual 'majority' is the minority here at UB." Geographically, UB draws "from urban areas, rural areas, NYC, Long Island, and most every country in the world." As a state school, "a lot of the students are from New York State, but with differing areas of the state, there are many different types of students."

WHY STUDENTS LOVE SUNY BUFFALO

Students tell us that "between all of the clubs and organizations, the Office of Student Life, athletics, and the Student Association, there is always something to do" on campus. The school's Division I sports teams "are a big hit around here. Even if we are the worst in the division, we still cheer hard and go crazy for our guys and girls." Those who explore Buffalo extol its "amazing art and music scene." Offering "more academic programs per dollar than any other university in the state," SUNY Buffalo (UB for short) "is about choices. You can choose many different...combinations of academics and social activities with the support in place." Students brag that UB's "programs are all of the highest quality, translating [into] a best-value education for students." The School of Engineering and Applied Science in particular "is well respected" and "works with corporate partners in a variety of ways that range from joint-research ventures to continuing education to co-op work arrangements for our students."

GENERAL INFO

Activities: Choral groups, concert band, dance, drama/theater, jazz band, literary magazine, marching band, music ensembles, musical theater, pep band, radio station, student government, student newspaper, student-run film society, symphony orchestra, television station, campus ministries, international student organization. **Organizations:** 215 registered organizations, 29 honor societies, 35 religious organizations. 22 fraternities, 17 sororities. **Athletics (Intercollegiate):** *Men:* Baseball, basketball, cross-country, football, soccer, swimming, tennis, track/field (outdoor), wrestling. *Women:* Basketball, crew/rowing, cross-country, soccer, softball, swimming, tennis, track/field (outdoor), volleyball. **On-Campus Highlights:** Center for the Arts, Alumni Arena and Athletic Stadium, Center for Computational Research, Apartment-style student housing, The Commons (on-campus shopping).

BOTTOM LINE

Offering "more academic programs per dollar than any other university in the state," according to one student, SUNY–Buffalo is able to provide great education at a low price. And at a fraction of the cost of comparable private colleges and universities, a UB education is also an exceptional value. Tuition for in-state students is only a bit over $5,000; for those from out-of-state, $15,000 per year is the total to be expected. Room and board will add another $10,000 or so. Half of all students here utilize financial aid, with the average package being over $7,000; the school is also able to meet over 60% of student need.

SELECTIVITY

Admissions Rating	**87**
# of applicants	21,985
% of applicants accepted	51
% of acceptees attending	28
# accepting a place on wait list	415
% admitted from wait list	64

FRESHMAN PROFILE

Range SAT Critical Reading	**500–610**
Range SAT Math	**550–650**
Range ACT Composite	**23–28**
Average HS GPA	**3.30**
% graduated top 10% of class	**28**
% graduated top 25% of class	**65**
% graduated top 50% of class	**93**

DEADLINES

Regular Deadline	**11/1**
Normal registration	**yes**

FACILITIES

Housing: Coed dorms, special housing for disabled students, special housing for international students, apartments for married students, apartments for single students, theme housing Honors Housing, Academic Interest Housing, Freshman Housing. *Special Academic Facilities/Equipment:* UB Center for the Arts, Slee Concert Hall, Anthropology Research Museum, Multidisciplinary Center for Earthquake Engineering Research (MCEER), New York State Center of Excellence in Bioinformatics and Life Sciences, Center for Computational Research (CCR), New York State Center for Engineering Design and Industrial Innovation.

FINANCIAL FACTS

Financial Aid Rating	**80**
Annual in-state tuition	$5,270
Annual out-of-state tuition	$14,320
Room and Board	$10,728
Required Fees	$2,212
Books and supplies	$1,004
% frosh rec. need-based scholarship or grant aid	41
% UG rec.need-based scholarship or grant aid	32
% frosh rec. non-need-based scholarship or grant aid	28
% UG rec. non-need-based scholarship or grant aid	8
% frosh rec. need-based self-help aid	43
% UG rec. need-based self-help aid	40
% frosh rec. any financial aid	50
% UG rec. any financial aid	52
% UG borrow to pay for school	37
Average cumulative indebtedness	$17,406

Truman State University

100 E. Normal, Kirksville, MO 63501 • Admissions: 660-785-4114 • Fax: 660-785-7456

CAMPUS LIFE

Quality of life Rating	80
Fire Safety Rating	64
Green rating	73
Type of School	Public
Environment	Village

STUDENTS

Total undergrad enrollment	5,675
% Male to Female	41/59
% From out of state	21
% From public high school	85
% Live on Campus	49
# of Fraternities	18
# of Sororities	11
% African American	4
% Asian	2
% Caucasian	81
% Hispanic	3
% Native American	1
% International	5
# Of Countries Represented	49

ACADEMICS

Academic Rating	87
% Of students graduating within 4 years	43
% Of students graduating within 6 years	70
Calendar	semester
Profs interesting rating	83
Profs accessible rating	87
Most common reg class size	20–29 students
Most common lab size	10–19 students

MOST POPULAR MAJORS

Biology, business, English language and literature

HONORS PROGRAMS

General Honors Program. Departmental honors are also available for some disciplines.

SPECIAL STUDY OPTIONS

Double major, dual enrollment, honors program, independent study, internships, student-designed major, study abroad, teacher certification program.

ABOUT THE SCHOOL

Truman students aren't shy about discussing their school's "extremely well-deserved academic reputation," nor should they be: the school is Missouri's only highly selective public university, and students are here due to hard work, in order to work hard. The "grade-conscious" students here at the "Harvard of the Midwest" receive an education grounded in the liberal arts and sciences, and the school keeps a constant eye on its applicability to their futures, incorporating critical thinking, writing, and leadership skill-building opportunities along the way to a degree. Many experiential learning opportunities exist all across campus, in which students can gain practical knowledge that will be relevant to future schooling and careers; the Career Center sets up a yearly Career Expo and Non-Profit Fair in order to expose students to employers, and give them the chance to hone their interviewing, resume, and professional skills. The classes are difficult, but "serve to develop the students into well-prepared graduates ready to face post-college life." Students are also able to diversify their studies across multiple subjects and throughout multiple countries by taking advantage of the numerous study abroad options, many of which can be covered by financial aid.

Kirksville, Missouri may not be a buzzing metropolis, but "part of the fun of Truman is to find non-orthodox things to do." Students make life at Truman interesting by finding their own niches, whether in Greek life, sports, or the abundance of student organizations. "You can be a huge political advocate, involved in protests on the quad; you can become involved in community service locally and nation-wide; or you can work in a lab to make discoveries." The school also offers a lot of events, such as comedians, concerts, and movies.

BANG FOR YOUR BUCK

Truman offers a private school education at a public price; students and their families can even set up a flexible payment plan through the Financial Aid Office. The school offers four separate types of loans for students, covering everything from tuition to a new computer to study abroad, and there are numerous federal and state aid options also available. Automatic scholarships are offered to incoming freshmen based on academic merit, and additional opportunities to apply for endowed Foundation scholarships occur each spring. The school understands that everything costs money (except the application–it's free!), and their comprehensive financial aid programs can be used to make sure that students are able to focus on their studies. Basically, if a student wants to attend Truman, then numbers can be crunched.

STUDENTS

5,675 undergrad enrollment

41% Male ♂♂♂♂♂♂♂♂

59% Female ♀♀♀♀♀♀♀♀♀♀♀♀

ADMISSIONS

4,702 applicants → 74% admitted | 41% enrolled | EARLY ADMISSIONS → NR applicants | NR accepted

3.76 avg. high school gpa

ACT range (0–36): 25 – 30

SAT range (200–800): reading 570 – 710; math 560 – 680

GRADUATION RATES

43% of students graduating within 4 yrs

70% of students graduating within 6 yrs

Truman State University

FINANCIAL AID: 660-785-4310 • E-MAIL: ADMISSIONS@TRUMAN.EDU • WEBSITE: WWW.TRUMAN.EDU

STUDENT BODY

All of the students at Truman are bonded by one thing; their respect for other students' academic abilities, and all students are here to study. "People here love learning and enjoy the educational process," says a student. Therefore, "It is easy to get to know other classmates and have study groups or friends to lean on in times of need." "Most people strive to excel here, so there is a healthy focus on academics within friends," and the "typical student is an over-achiever with big dreams and goals." Also, many are "from Missouri, specifically St. Louis, and a high proportion are from Catholic, private schools." As one student tells us, "The typical student can be described as the typical American…there is no distinct description to identify the typical person."

Why Students love Truman State University

"Most people strive to excel here, so there is a healthy focus on academics within friends."

WHY STUDENTS LOVE TRUMAN STATE UNIVERSITY

Students almost unanimously love life at Truman State. "The campus is beauti¬ful, and the atmosphere is very welcoming." The school is about an all-around college experience, and "the classes, the activities, the professors, the friends, everyone and everything work together well and are what makes Truman such a wonderful school." Other schools of this caliber are generally much more expensive, and "the focus is on school and applying perspectives to find solutions and keep the world going," which is easy enough to do in "an atmosphere where intelligence is credited and clear ideas are applauded." Students are well-supported in whatever they choose, and "there is stuff to do and opportunities to take advantage of if you keep your eyes open."

GENERAL INFO

Activities: Choral groups, concert band, dance, drama/theater, jazz band, literary magazine, marching band, music ensembles, musical theater, opera, pep band, radio station, student government, student newspaper, student-run film society, symphony orchestra, television station, campus ministries, international student organization. **Organizations:** 282 registered organizations, 18 honor societies, 16 religious organizations. 16 fraternities, 11 sororities. **Athletics (Intercollegiate):** *Men:* Baseball,basketball, cross-country, football, golf, soccer, swimming, tennis, track/field (outdoor), track/field (indoor), wrestling. *Women:* Basketball, cross-country, golf, soccer, softball, swimming, tennis, track/field (outdoor), track/field (indoor), volleyball.

BOTTOM LINE

Residents of Missouri pay $6,772 in tuition; non-residents pay just $12,316, which is still a bargain. Ninety-six percent of Truman students receive some form of aid, whether in scholarships or federal grants. There are two full-ride awards offered to incoming freshmen: the Truman Leadership Award, which offers continuing leadership programming throughout undergrad, and the John J. Pershing Scholarship includes an additional stipend for a future study abroad experience. Financial aid programs to help fund undergraduate research and study abroad experiences are also available.

SELECTIVITY

Admissions Rating	**91**
# of applicants	4,702
% of applicants accepted	74
% of acceptees attending	41

FRESHMAN PROFILE

Range SAT Critical Reading	**570–710**
Range SAT Math	**560–680**
Range ACT Composite	**25–30**
Average HS GPA	**3.76**
% graduated top 10% of class	**47**
% graduated top 25% of class	**77**
% graduated top 50% of class	**98**

DEADLINES

Regular Deadline	**12/1**
Normal registration	**yes**

FACILITIES

Housing: Coed dorms, special housing for disabled students, special housing for international students, apartments for married students, apartments for single students, theme housing, sorority housing, French language housing, and Spanish language housing. *Special Academic Facilities/Equipment:* Art gallery, local history and artifacts museum, human performance lab, greenhouse, observatory. *Computers:* 100% of classrooms, 100% of dorms, 100% of libraries, 75% of dining areas, 100% of student union, 90% of common outdoor areas have wireless network access.

FINANCIAL FACTS

Financial Aid Rating	**84**
Annual in-state tuition	$6,772
Annual out-of-state tuition	$12,316
Room and Board	$7,254
Required Fees	$240
Books and supplies	$1,000

University of California–Berkeley

110 Sproul Hall, #5800, Berkeley, CA 94720-5800 • Admissions: 510-642-3175 • Fax: 510-642-7333

CAMPUS LIFE

Quality of life Rating	71
Fire Safety Rating	77
Green rating	96
Type of School	Public
Environment	City

STUDENTS

Total undergrad enrollment	35,838
% Male to Female	53/47
% From out of state	7
% Live on Campus	35
# of Fraternities	38
# of Sororities	19
% African American	3
% Asian	40
% Caucasian	30
% Hispanic	11
% Native American	1
% International	7
# Of Countries Represented	79

ACADEMICS

Academic Rating	86
% Of students graduating within 4 years	69
% Of students graduating within 6 years	96
Calendar	semester
Profs interesting rating	78
Profs accessible rating	67
Most common reg class size	fewer than 10 students

MOST POPULAR MAJORS

Computer engineering,
English language and literature,
political science

SPECIAL STUDY OPTIONS

Accelerated program, cross-registration, double major, dual enrollment, English as a Second Language (ESL), exchange student program (domestic), honors program, inde pendent study, internships, student-designed major, study abroad, teacher certi fication program

ABOUT THE SCHOOL

University of California–Berkeley enjoys a reputation for quality and value that few other colleges can match. Large, diverse, and highly regarded, Berkeley is often ranked among the top public institutions in the world. Berkeley offers around 300 undergraduate and graduate degree programs in a wide range of disciplines. Best known for research, the school counts Nobel Laureates, MacArthur Fellowship recipients, Pulitzer Prize, and Academy Award winners among its faculty. With an "all-star faculty and resources," professors here are "intelligent, accessible," with many departments boasting "the best [academics] in their field." Needless to say, undergraduate education is first-rate. The school maintains a low student-to-teacher ratio and opportunities to get in on cutting-edge research at Berkeley abound. In fact, approximately half of the school's undergraduates assist faculty in creative or research projects during their time here. As some students note, "you don't get the coddling that the private universities show. You don't have a billion counselors catering to your every need." Though students note that survey classes here can sometimes be "enormous," professors "make themselves very accessible via e-mail and office hours." Berkeley maintains an incredibly high number of nationally ranked programs; however, engineering, computer science, molecular and cell biology, and political science are the most popular majors for undergraduates.

BANG FOR YOUR BUCK

Berkeley's Undergraduate Scholarships, Prizes and Honors unit of the Financial Aid Office administers three different scholarship programs. Twenty-five Berkeley Undergraduate Scholarships are awarded each year. The Regent's and Chancellor's Scholarship is Berkeley's most prestigious scholarship, and is awarded annually to approximately 200 incoming undergraduates. The by-invitation-only Cal Opportunity Scholarship is designed to attract high-achieving students who have overcome challenging socio-economic circumstances. Award amounts vary for each of these scholarship programs, and is often based on financial need. All applicants to Berkeley are automatically considered for these scholarship programs.

As a public institution, UC Berkeley's low in-state tuition makes this school very affordable. With a low cost and an active financial aid program, Berkeley is an ideal choice for high-achieving students from low-income families. According to its website, Berkeley serves more economically disadvantaged students than all the Ivy League universities combined. More than 30 percent of Berkeley undergraduates are eligible for Pell Grants.

STUDENTS

35,838 undergrad enrollment

53% Male ♂♂♂♂♂♂♂♂♂♂♂

47% Female ♀♀♀♀♀♀♀♀♀

ADMISSIONS

52,995 →	NR	NR	EARLY →	NR	NR
applicants	admitted	enrolled	ADMISSIONS	applicants	accepted

3.88 avg. high school gpa

reading	620 – 740
math	660 – 770
writing	660 – 750

NR

0 — 36 ACT range

200 — 800 SAT range

GRADUATION RATES

69% of students graduating within 4 yrs

96% of students graduating within 6 yrs

University of California–Berkeley

FINANCIAL AID: 510-642-6642 • WEBSITE: WWW.BERKELEY.EDU

STUDENT BODY

To simply label this school as "diverse" seems like a simplification. Here, people "think about everything." It's a place where "it's not uncommon to hear conversations vary from the wicked party last night…turn into debates about the roles of women in Hindu mythology to the specifics behind DNA replication." Students here are a self-motivated lot. Students here "are ambitious, but fun to be around." For the most part, "Students fit in just fine, but the experience they have is what they make of it." Full of their signature optimism, students here say that "life at Berkeley has no limits;" we "study and hear obscure languages, meet famous scientists, engage with brilliant students, eat delicious food, and just relax with friends daily." The general consensus is that "everyone here is not afraid to express themselves, and the opportunity to make a fresh start in college is amazingly liberating."

Why Students love UC Berkeley

"The amount of fun you'll have depends on your course load, though there are always events on campus, whether they are concerts, circus performances, club-sponsored activities, or events in the dorms."

WHY STUDENTS LOVE UC BERKELEY

The University of California–Berkeley is a large public university where students feel that their "professors [are] all warm, open, and inviting." In fact, many students choose UC Berkeley because they feel "it's the best public university in the world." Students are quick to point out, "There are some amazing and inspiring minds at Berkeley." Academics here are "on par with the best in the nation." For those students seeking a first-class education, UC Berkeley is "a place of incredible academic opportunity." In addition, students find individual attention within "upper-division classes." In general, UC Berkeley features the opportunity to work with "amazing professors from every department. Challenging, yet stimulating."

GENERAL INFO

Activities: Choral groups, concert band, dance, drama/theater, jazz band, literary magazine, marching band, music ensembles, musical theater, pep band, radio station, student government, student newspaper, student-run film society, symphony orchestra, television station, yearbook, international student organization. **Organizations:** 300 registered organizations, 6 honor societies, 28 religious organizations. 38 fraternities, 19 sororities. **Athletics (Intercollegiate):** *Men:* Baseball, basketball, crew/rowing, cross-country, diving, football, golf, gymnastics, rugby, sailing, soccer, swimming, tennis, track/field (outdoor), water polo. *Women:* Basketball, crew/rowing, cross-country, diving, field hockey, golf, gymnastics, lacrosse, sailing, soccer, softball, swimming, tennis, track/field (outdoor), volleyball, water polo.

BOTTOM LINE

For California residents, Berkeley is a great deal, ringing in at roughly $11,000 annually for tuition and fees. In addition to tuition, the school estimates expenditures of $1,300 for books and supplies, though these costs vary by major. Non-resident tuition alone is more than $32,000 annually.

SELECTIVITY

Admissions Rating	**97**
# of applicants	52,995
# accepting a place on wait list	197
% admitted from wait list	0

FRESHMAN PROFILE

Range SAT Critical Reading	**620–740**
Range SAT Math	**660–770**
Range SAT Writing	**650–750**
Average HS GPA	**3.88**

DEADLINES

Regular Deadline	**11/30**
Normal registration	**yes**

FACILITIES

Housing: Coed dorms, special housing for disabled students, men's dorms, special housing for international students, women's dorms, fraternity/sorority housing, apartments for married students, cooperative housing, apartments for single students, theme housing. *Special Academic Facilities/Equipment:* Lawrence Berkeley National Lab; Pacific Film Archive; Earthquake Data Center; Museums of art, anthro pology, natural history, paleontology; Botanical Garden.

FINANCIAL FACTS

Financial Aid Rating	**78**
Annual in-state tuition	$9,402
Annual out-of-state tuition	$32,281
Room and Board	$15,308
Required Fees	$1,538
Books and supplies	$1,314

University of California–Davis

178 Mrak Hall, One Shields Ave, Davis, CA 95616 • Admissions: 530-752-2971 • Fax: 530-752-1280

CAMPUS LIFE

Quality of life Rating	93
Fire Safety Rating	75
Green rating	93
Type of School	Public
Environment	Town

STUDENTS

Total undergrad enrollment	24,497
% Male to Female	45/55
% From out of state	2
% From public high school	84
% Live on Campus	25
# of Fraternities	28
# of Sororities	21
% African American	3
% Asian	39
% Caucasian	34
% Hispanic	15
% Native American	1
% International	3
# Of Countries Represented	121

ACADEMICS

Academic Rating	74
% Of students graduating within 4 years	57
% Of students graduating within 6 years	82
Calendar	quarter
Profs interesting rating	73
Profs accessible rating	73
Most common reg class size	20–29 students
Most common lab size	20–29 students

MOST POPULAR MAJORS

Biology, economics, psychology

HONORS PROGRAMS

The Davis Honors Challenge (DHC).
Integrated Studies Honors Program (ISHP).

SPECIAL STUDY OPTIONS

Accelerated program, cross-registration, double major, dual enrollment, English as a Second Language (ESL), honors program, independent study, internships, student-designed major, study abroad, teacher certification program, Washington, DC, Center.

ABOUT THE SCHOOL

The University of California–Davis is a large, public university that has come a long way from its agrarian roots. Today, its rigorous academics, vibrant campus community, and location near the state capitol draw students from all over the world. UC Davis is known as a world-class research university, offering more than 100 interdisciplinary majors, as well as 90 graduate programs and advanced degrees from six professional schools. More than half of Davis's undergraduates work on research projects with a faculty member during college. Many students (upwards of 6,000) also participate in real-world internships during their undergraduate career, including the school's 11-week internship in Washington, D.C., open to students in any discipline. Davis's life sciences division receives top marks–in fact, the school claims to have more biology majors than any other campus in America. Science students also have access to Davis's multitude of world-class facilities, such as the Bodega Bay Laboratory and the Lake Tahoe Environmental Research Center. The school boasts top programs in engineering, enology and viticulture, and animal science, as well as the first Native American studies program in the country. UC Davis's quarter system affords "no time to fool around." "It is not really a school for a slacker."

BANG FOR YOUR BUCK

Davis offers many excellent scholarship opportunities. Besides awarding over $6 million in campus-based merit scholarship aid, the Undergraduate and Prestigious Scholarship Office also assists students in preparing for and applying to national and international competitive awards, such as the Rhodes, Marshall, Truman and Goldwater Scholarships. The University of California's financial aid programs are designed to make a UC education accessible to students at every income level. In addition, UC has established the Blue and Gold Opportunity Plan to help low and middle-income families. The program ensures that California undergraduates who are in their first four years of attendance at Davis (or two years for transfer students) will receive enough scholarship and grant assistance to at least fully cover their system-wide UC fees. For 2011-12, students qualify if they have incomes below the median for California households ($80,000) and they meet other basic eligibility requirements for need-based financial aid. Many students receive grants to help cover costs in addition to tuition and fees, and many students with parent incomes above $80,000 will qualify for financial aid.

STUDENTS

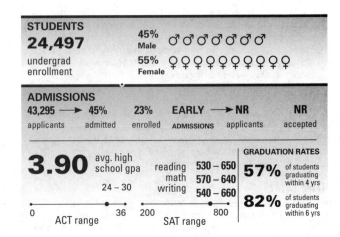

24,497 undergrad enrollment

45% Male ♂♂♂♂♂♂♂

55% Female ♀♀♀♀♀♀♀♀♀

ADMISSIONS

43,295 applicants →	45% admitted	23% enrolled	EARLY ADMISSIONS →	NR applicants	NR accepted

3.90 avg. high school gpa

ACT range (0–36): 24 – 30

SAT range (200–800): reading 530 – 650; math 570 – 640; writing 540 – 660

GRADUATION RATES

57% of students graduating within 4 yrs

82% of students graduating within 6 yrs

University of California–Davis

FINANCIAL AID: 530-752-2396 • E-MAIL: UNDERGRADUATEADMISSIONS@UCDAVIS.EDU • WEBSITE: WWW.UCDAVIS.EDU

STUDENT BODY

Students here are the hardworking, studious, responsible kids, says a sophomore. "The student body is mostly made up of white and Asian students," but "Davis is a melting pot." "Many different cultures, ethnicities, and religions are present," and "everybody is really accepting." Students here describe themselves as "goal-oriented," "down-to-earth, well-rounded, balanced, amiable, and intelligent." "Some seem shy and timid." "There are some atypical students who care more about their looks and having fun than just studying, but I feel like they are a minority," says a sophomore. There are "the uber-serious premed students who spend all of their waking time in class or in the library having an aneurism." There's "the sorority girl; the band geek, the jock; the crazy, outspoken chick;" and "a lot of hippies," too.

Why Students love UC–Davis

"I have consistently found my professors to be wonderful teachers who care deeply about their students."

WHY STUDENTS LOVE UC–DAVIS

UC Davis is a huge research university with the atmosphere of an intimate community. The agricultural and food sciences programs are excellent. There are more than 100 majors. Research opportunities for undergraduates are abundant. Study abroad and internship programs are "fantastic." "Things seem to work magically around here." "The administration is like Atlantis," offers a linguistics major; "it's rumored to exist, but you've never actually seen it." "As for your academic experience, 90 percent of it is dependent upon who your professor is, and 100 percent is dependent upon your personal interest," explains an international relations major. "I know that adds up to 190 percent. You can blame my statistics professor."

GENERAL INFO

Activities: Choral groups, concert band, dance, drama/theater, jazz band, literary magazine, marching band, music ensembles, musical theater, pep band, radio station, student government, student newspaper, student-run film society, symphony orchestra, television station, yearbook, campus ministries, international student organization. **Organizations:** 364 registered organizations, 1 honor societies, 50 religious organizations. 28 fraternities, 21 sororities. **Athletics (Intercollegiate):** *Men:* Baseball, basket- ball, cross-country, diving, football, golf, soccer, swimming, tennis, track/field (outdoor), track/field (indoor), water polo, wrestling. *Women:* Basketball, crew/ rowing, cross-country, diving, field hockey, golf, gymnastics, lacrosse, soccer, softball, swimming, tennis, track/field (outdoor), track/field (indoor), volleyball, water polo.

BOTTOM LINE

In-state tuition for California residents is about $10,000 annually, while nonresidents are responsible for a total of $33,000 in tuition each year. All students need to add an additional $12,500 for room and board if they intend to live on campus. Once you factor in books and supplies and required fees, California residents and nonresidents can expect to pay about $28,000 and $49,000, respectively. The school's comprehensive aid packages can drastically offset the price, though if you aren't a California resident, that additional $23,000 in tuition makes the deal a wee bit less palatable.

SELECTIVITY

Admissions Rating	**96**
# of applicants	43,295
% of applicants accepted	45
% of acceptees attending	23
# accepting a place on wait list	1,510
% admitted from wait list	39

FRESHMAN PROFILE

Range SAT Critical Reading	**530–650**
Range SAT Math	**570–640**
Range SAT Writing	**540–660**
Range ACT Composite	**24–30**
Average HS GPA	**3.90**

DEADLINES

Regular Deadline	**11/30**
Normal registration	**no**

FACILITIES

Housing: Coed dorms, special housing for disabled students, women's dorms, apartments for married students, cooperative housing, apartments for single students, wellness housing, theme housing. Special Interest Communities: Da- vis Honors Challenge, Hammar-skold, International Relations, Integrated Studies, Multiethnic Program, Music, Arts & Performance, Quiet Program, RainbowHouse, Women's Community. *Special Academic Facilities/ Equipment:* Art galleries, 150–acre university arboretum, equestrian center, craft center, student experimental farm, nuclear lab, human performance lab, natural reserves, early childhood lab, raptor center, primate research center.

FINANCIAL FACTS

Financial Aid Rating	**70**
Annual in-state tuition	$11,220
Annual out-of-state tuition	$34,098
Room and Board	$12,697
Required Fees	$2,640
Books and supplies	$1,589
% frosh rec. need-based scholarship or grant aid	63
% UG rec.need-based scholarship or grant aid	60
% frosh rec. need-based self-help aid	45
% UG rec. need-based self-help aid	43
% frosh rec. any financial aid	65
% UG rec. any financial aid	62
% UG borrow to pay for school	60
Average cumulative indebtedness	$16,659

University of California–Irvine

Office of Admissions & Relations with Schools, 204 Aldrich Hall, Irvine, CA 92697-1075 • Admissions: 949-824-6703

CAMPUS LIFE

Quality of life Rating	86
Fire Safety Rating	60*
Green rating	98
Type of School	Public
Environment	City

STUDENTS

Total undergrad enrolllment	21,976
% Male to Female	47/53
% From out of state	1
% From public high school	74
% Live on Campus	41
# of Fraternities	21
# of Sororities	25
% African American	2
% Asian	51
% Caucasian	22
% Hispanic	15
% International	3
# Of Countries Represented	97

ACADEMICS

Academic Rating	71
% Of students graduating within 4 years	59
% Of students graduating within 6 years	80
Calendar	quarter
Most common reg class size	2–9 students
Most common lab size	2–9 students

MOST POPULAR MAJORS

Business/managerial, economics, political science and government

HONORS PROGRAMS

Campus-wide Honors Program (CHP). Combined degree programs: 3-2 MBA. Special programs offered to physically disabled students include note-taking services, reader services, voice recorders.

SPECIAL STUDY OPTIONS

Accelerated program, distance learning, double major, dual enrollment, English as a Second Language (ESL), honors program, independent study, internships, liberal arts/career combination, study abroad, teacher certification program.

ABOUT THE SCHOOL

There are 20,000 or so undergrads at the University of California–Irvine. The campus is situated in the warm, suburban town of Irvine, California. Many concur that on-campus life "revolves around academics" at UC Irvine. Students tell us that the school is an ideal place to study, as "it's quiet, almost pastoral, with Aldrich Park in the middle of the campus." Students here are able to choose from a slew of academic programs–many of them nationally renowned–and a vast number of courses. UCI is consistently ranked among the nation's best universities, with more than 40 top-ranked academic programs. As you would expect from a large, well-funded, public research institution, cutting-edge research is the norm here. Three of UCI's researchers have won Nobel Prizes, and in 2010, one faculty member won the prestigious Templeton Prize. Big lecture courses are part of the deal, too, especially in your first year or two. Fortunately, many professors are at the top of their fields, and the faculty generally gets high praise from students. Upper-level classes get smaller.

One of the campus's unique strengths lies in the way it combines the advantages of a large dynamic research university with the friendly feel of a small college. The undergraduate experience extends beyond the classroom to participation in campus organizations, multicultural campus and community events, volunteer service projects, internships, study abroad, entrepreneurial ventures and much more. UCI's quiet, sprawling, suburban campus is located in sunny Southern California. The suburban environment often means lights-out relatively early for most undergrads. Even so, Irvine's location in dreamy southern California leaves open the possibility for stimulating alternatives.

BANG FOR YOUR BUCK

UCI tends to attract the third-largest applicant pool in the University of California system (behind UC Berkeley and UCLA). With all the stellar resources available here and the plethora of nationally recognized programs, admission to UCI is a fabulous consolation prize. If you can get admitted, UCI offers generous financial aid assistance in the form of scholarships, loans, and grants. In addition to federal and state aid programs, UC Irvine offers a robust grant program for needy students. The Blue and Gold Opportunity Plan covers educational and student services fees for California residents whose families earn less than $80,000 a year and qualify for financial aid. Blue and Gold students often qualify for additional grant aid to further help reduce the cost of attendance.

STUDENTS

21,976 undergrad enrollment

47% Male ♂♂♂♂♂♂♂♂♂

53% Female ♀♀♀♀♀♀♀♀♀♀

ADMISSIONS

45,742 applicants	→ 95% admitted	21% enrolled	EARLY ADMISSIONS	→ NR applicants	NR accepted

3.88 avg. high school gpa

reading	520 – 640
math	570 – 680
writing	530 – 640

NR

0 — 36 ACT range

200 — 800 SAT range

GRADUATION RATES

59% of students graduating within 4 yrs

80% of students graduating within 6 yrs

University of California–Irvine

FAX: 949-824-2951 • FINANCIAL AID: 909-621-8205 • E-MAIL: ADMISSIONS@POMONA.EDU • WEBSITE: WWW.POMONA.EDU

STUDENT BODY

While they are overwhelmingly from California, they are otherwise a radically diverse group. "UC Irvine has a very diverse group of students, and we all generally get along." While you'll find plenty of athletic people, you won't find the distractions of big-time athletics here. It's not much of a party school, either. This place is pretty cerebral for the most part. Students tend to be either career-oriented or grad-school-oriented. Getting good grades is the focal point of life for many. Because the school attracts the best and the brightest, students at UC Irvine "can say hello to a Nobel Laureate on the way to class, and then see an Olympic gold medalist practicing with the women's volleyball team in the same afternoon." A freshman further details, "Over half the students at UCI are Asian American, but it doesn't really seem to matter a whole lot for most people. People seem to be more concerned with doing well in classes than

Why Students love UC Irvine

"We're all here to succeed in college and beyond."

WHY STUDENTS LOVE UC IRVINE

A serious public school in sunny Orange County, UC Irvine is a good fit for studious undergrads looking to benefit from the University of California's famous faculty and ample research opportunities. Because the school has more than 24,000 students, freshmen inevitably find themselves in many big lecture courses. Even so, a sophomore reassures, "I never felt like I was just a number or a nobody." Indeed, students agree that most UC Irvine professors "honestly care about our education and the expansion of our minds," and students are quick to praise "the commitment of the faculty to helping undergraduate students." Nonetheless, the school's demanding academic programs keep students "very busy studying and keeping up with lectures."

GENERAL INFO

Activities: Choral groups, concert band, dance, drama/theater, jazz band, literary magazine, music ensembles, musical theater, opera, pep band, radio station, student government, student newspaper, student-run film society, symphony orchestra, yearbook, international student organization. **Organizations:** 484 registered organizations, 18 honor societies, 51 religious organizations. 21 fraternities, 23 sororities. **Athletics (Intercollegiate):** *Men:* Baseball, basketball, cross-country, golf, sailing, soccer, tennis, track/field (outdoor), volleyball, water polo. *Women:* Basketball, cross-country, golf, sailing, soccer, tennis, track/field (outdoor), volleyball, water polo. On-Campus Highlights: Anteater Recreation Center, Bren Events Center, Cross-Cultural Center, Beall Center for Art and Technology, Arts Plaza.

BOTTOM LINE

Tuition, room and board, and everything else costs about $25,000 a year at UCI. (It's considerably less if you commute.) With all the sources of need-based and merit-based aid available here, most students don't pay anywhere near that amount. UCI is a truly a bargain if you can meet California's residency standards. On the other hand, if you are branded as a nonresident, the costs here approach those of a private school.

SELECTIVITY

Admissions Rating	**96**
# of applicants	22,124
% of applicants accepted	33
% of acceptees attending	45

FRESHMAN PROFILE

Range SAT Critical Reading	**520–640**
Range SAT Math	**570–680**
Range SAT Writing	**530–640**
Average HS GPA	**3.88**
% graduated top 10% of class	**96**
% graduated top 25% of class	**100**

DEADLINES

Regular Deadline	**11/3**
Normal registration	**no**

FACILITIES

Housing: Coed dorms, special housing for disabled students, men's dorms, special housing for international students, women's dorms, fraternity/sorority housing, apartments for married students, cooperative housing, apartments for single students, theme housing. *Special Academic Facilities/Equipment:* Museum of systemic biology, freshwater marsh reserve, electron microscope, nuclear reactor, laser institute, research facilities. *Computers:* 90% of classrooms, 100% of libraries, 100% of dining areas, 100% of student union, have wireless network access.

FINANCIAL FACTS

Financial Aid Rating	**77**
Annual in-state tuition	$10,152
Annual out-of-state tuition	$33,030
Room and Board	$11,611
Required Fees	$2,750
Books and supplies	$1,553
% frosh rec. need-based scholarship or grant aid	46
% UG rec.need-based scholarship or grant aid	45
% frosh rec. non-need-based scholarship or grant aid	1
% UG rec. non-need-based scholarship or grant aid	1
% frosh rec. need-based self-help aid	36
% UG rec. need-based self-help aid	33
% UG borrow to pay for school	46
Average cumulative indebtedness	$16,878

University of California–Los Angeles

1147 Murphy Hall, Box 951436, Los Angeles, CA 90095-1436 • Admissions: 310-825-3101 • Fax: 310-206-1206

CAMPUS LIFE

Quality of life Rating	89
Fire Safety Rating	85
Green rating	97
Type of School	Public
Environment	Metropolis

STUDENTS

Total undergrad enrolllment	26,162
% Male to Female	45/55
% From out of state	7
% From public high school	76
% Live on Campus	36
# of Fraternities	30
# of Sororities	28
% African American	4
% Asian	37
% Caucasian	32
% Hispanic	16
% Native American	<1
% International	6
# Of Countries Represented	72

ACADEMICS

Academic Rating	82
% Of students graduating within 4 years	70
% Of students graduating within 6 years	90
Calendar	quarter
Profs interesting rating	69
Profs accessible rating	67
Most common reg class size	10–19 students
Most common lab size	10–19 students

MOST POPULAR MAJORS

Political science, psychology, biology

HONORS PROGRAMS

The College Honors Program Special programs offered to physically disabled students include note-taking services, reader services, voice recorders, tutors.

SPECIAL STUDY OPTIONS

Accelerated program, double major, English as a Second Language (ESL), honors program, independent study, internships, liberal arts/career combination, student-designed major, study abroad.

ABOUT THE SCHOOL

In a word, the University of California–Los Angeles is about diversity–in what you can study, in what you can do with your free time, in ethnicity, in genre and sexuality, in everything. With over 300 undergraduate and graduate degree programs on offer for its 26,000 students, there truly is something for everyone. The technology and research resources here are dreamy. There is comprehensive quality across the broad range of disciplines. There are more than 3,000 courses. You can take classes here in pretty much any academic endeavor, and you will likely run across some of the best and brightest professors in the world. Brushes with fame are common here–with a location near Hollywood and a world-famous film and television school, the UCLA campus has attracted film productions for decades. That being said, you should be aware that bigness and breadth have their limitations (i.e. lots of teaching assistants, big classes, anonymity). But if you don't mind being a small fish in a big pond, chances are you'll have a great experience here. And with just a little bit of initiative you might even make a splash. Perhaps more notable, "UCLA is the kind of school that pushes you to work hard academically but reminds you that interaction with people outside of the classroom is just as important."

Just as with academics, social life at UCLA is whatever you want it to be. Students here have a lot of things going on that are in no way related to what they are studying. Most people get involved in a club, an organization, or the Greek system. UCLA is home to more than 800 student organizations, and more than 60 Greek-letter organizations. Most students study quite a bit, and their future careers are never far from their minds. However, the party scene is formidable on the weekends. Sporting events are also a huge part of the overall culture here.

BANG FOR YOUR BUCK

Even in a time of rising fees, UCLA remains far below most of the other top research universities in total costs for undergraduate study. A little less than half of the student population here receives need-based financial aid. This school prizes its diversity, and that definitely includes economic diversity. UCLA ranks second in the country among major research universities in the percentage of its students that receive Pell Grants (which is free government money for low-income students). The university also offers the prestigious Regents Scholarship, intended to reward extraordinary academic excellence and exemplary leadership and community service accomplishments. Also, the career-planning operation here is first-rate, and there are extensive opportunities for internships with local employers.

STUDENTS

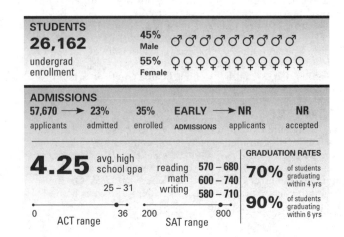

26,162 undergrad enrollment

45% Male ♂♂♂♂♂♂♂♂♂

55% Female ♀♀♀♀♀♀♀♀♀♀♀

ADMISSIONS

57,670 applicants	→ 23% admitted	35% enrolled	EARLY ADMISSIONS	→ NR applicants	NR accepted

4.25 avg. high school gpa

ACT range (0–36): 25 – 31

SAT range (200–800): reading 570 – 680; math 600 – 740; writing 580 – 710

GRADUATION RATES

70% of students graduating within 4 yrs

90% of students graduating within 6 yrs

University of California–Los Angeles

FINANCIAL AID: 310-206-0400 • E-MAIL: UGADM@SAONET.UCLA.EDU • WEBSITE: WWW.UCLA.EDU

STUDENT BODY

UCLA "is the mold that fits you." Indeed, "26,000 students and more than 950 student groups," virtually assures that "there is no 'typical' student" to be found at UCLA. This wide range of individuals and activities guarantees that "everyone has their niche." Certainly, the Bruin community is a "vibrant" one, and "the unmatched diversity broadens students' horizons culturally and socially." Of course, undergrads here do tread some common ground. Many define their peers as "very hardworking and ambitious," and they typically "strive for success and to do their absolute best." They "know how to have a good time, but they also know when it is time to study." Further, it's an active student body, and it often "seems like everyone is in at least one club or organization."

Why Students love UCLA

"UCLA is the campus. The people, the weather, the academics, the sports; it has absolutely everything I could ever want."

WHY STUDENTS LOVE UCLA

Undergrads at this esteemed university don't mince words when boasting about all that UCLA has to offer. As a geography and environmental science double-major proudly declares, "There's nothing that can't be accomplished at UCLA. The possibilities are endless, and the resources are unparalleled." Moreover, students appreciate the "ideal" location as well as the "pride of going to a Division I school with more NCAA championships than any other college/university." Students are continually impressed by their professors who are "leaders in their field." Indeed, most consider it "a privilege to study under them." "Most professors care about their students." A political science major interjects, saying that professors "are willing to work extra hours with students and help us with anything we need." And an English major concurs, sharing, "I have never had a professor that I did not feel comfortable approaching, which has made my academic experience incredibly more beneficial."

GENERAL INFO

Activities: Choral groups, concert band, dance, drama/theater, jazz band, literary magazine, marching band, music ensembles, musical theater, opera, pep band, radio station, student government, student newspaper, student-run film society, symphony orchestra, television station, yearbook, campus ministries, international student organization. **Organizations:** 870 registered organizations, 21 honor societies, 38 religious organizations. 36 fraternities, 28 sororities. **Athletics (Intercollegiate):** *Men:* Baseball, basketball, cross-country, football, golf, soccer, tennis, track/field (out door), track/field (indoor), volleyball, water polo. *Women:* Basketball, crew/row ing, cross-country, diving, golf, gymnastics, soccer, softball, swimming, tennis, track/field (outdoor), track/field (indoor), volleyball, water polo.

BOTTOM LINE

For Californians, the cumulative price tag to attend UCLA for a year when you add up fees, room and board, and basic expenses is somewhere between $22,000–$30,000 each year. Your living arrangements can make a noticeable difference. If you can't claim residency in the Golden State, the cost ranges from $45,000–$53,000.

SELECTIVITY

Admissions Rating	**98**
# of applicants	57,670
% of applicants accepted	23
% of acceptees attending	35

FRESHMAN PROFILE

Range SAT Critical Reading	**570–680**
Range SAT Math	**600–740**
Range SAT Writing	**580–710**
Range ACT Composite	**25–31**
Average HS GPA	**4.25**
% graduated top 10% of class	**97**
% graduated top 25% of class	**100**
% graduated top 50% of class	**100**

DEADLINES

Regular Deadline	**11/30**
Normal registration	**no**

FACILITIES

Housing: Coed dorms, special housing for disabled students, fraternity/sorority housing, apartments for married students, apartments for single students, well ness housing, theme housing. *Special Academic Facilities/Equipment:* Art gallery, cultural history mu seum, sculpture garden, graphic arts center, numerous study centers, research institutes, UCLA Armand Hammer Museum of Art and Cultural Center, Murphy Sculpture Garden, Fowler Museum of Cultural History.

FINANCIAL FACTS

Financial Aid Rating	**82**
Annual in-state tuition	$11,618
Annual out-of-state tuition	$34,496
Room and Board	$13,652
Books and supplies	$1,509
% frosh rec. need-based scholarship or grant aid	54
% UG rec.need-based scholarship or grant aid	52
% frosh rec. non-need-based scholarship or grant aid	1
% UG rec. non-need-based scholarship or grant aid	1
% frosh rec. need-based self-help aid	37
% UG rec. need-based self-help aid	38
% frosh rec. any financial aid	56
% UG rec. any financial aid	55
% UG borrow to pay for school	44
Average cumulative indebtedness	$18,203

University of California–Riverside

3106 Student Services Building, Riverside, CA 92521 • Admissions: 951-827-3411 • Fax: 951-827-6344

CAMPUS LIFE

Quality of life Rating	61
Fire Safety Rating	88
Green rating	95
Type of School	Public
Environment	City

STUDENTS

Total undergrad enrolllment	18,242
% Male to Female	48/52
% From out of state	1
% From public high school	91
% Live on Campus	32
# of Fraternities	20
# of Sororities	20
% African American	8
% Asian	40
% Caucasian	16
% Hispanic	31
% International	1
# Of Countries Represented	102

ACADEMICS

Academic Rating	70
% Of students graduating within 4 years	39
% Of students graduating within 6 years	67
Calendar	quarter
Profs interesting rating	62
Profs accessible rating	64
Most common reg class size	20–29 students
Most common lab size	20–29 students

MOST POPULAR MAJORS

Biology, business administration and management, psychology

SPECIAL STUDY OPTIONS

Accelerated program, cross-registration, double major, English as a Second Language (ESL), honors program, independent study, internships, student-designed major, study abroad, teacher certification program. Special programs offered to physically disabled students include note-taking services, reader services, voice recorders, tutors.

ABOUT THE SCHOOL

Although perhaps not as famous as some of the other schools in the UC system, The University of California–Riverside (UCR) has much to boast about. For starters, this research university offers state-of-the-art facilities in genomics and nanotechnology. Its top-ranked entomology department draws insect-loving students like the proverbial moths to a flame. For those not inclined towards the sciences, UCR provides the largest undergraduate business program in the UC system as well as the only undergraduate creative writing program among the UC schools. The school's "fantastic" Honors Program is another highly praised asset. With an emphasis on ethnic diversity and social consciousness, the school attracts a student population that stands out among other campuses across the country. As a commuter school, UCR faces the challenge of keeping the social scene on campus lively and interesting despite having many of its students gone on the weekends. With more than 400 student organizations, the school strives to have a steady stream of events on and off campus including concerts and movie screenings.

Why Students love UC–Riverside

"Most of the students seem serious about being in college and are here for the right reasons."

BANG FOR YOUR BUCK

More than 70% of undergrads at UCR receive some form of financial aid and the school also offers a Blue & Gold Program for California applicants with a family income of up to $80,000 which covers the full cost of tuition through a combination of grants and scholarships. Merit-based scholarships are also offered to freshmen with excellent academic qualifications regardless of financial need. In addition to various forms of financial aid, UCR also provides additional services through its Internship Program which places many students in paid positions with Fortune 100 companies as well as through its Student On-Campus Employment Program (SCOEP).

STUDENTS

18,242 undergrad enrollment

48% Male ♂♂♂♂♂♂♂♂♂♂

52% Female ♀♀♀♀♀♀♀♀♀♀

ADMISSIONS

26,478 applicants →	78% admitted	22% enrolled	EARLY ADMISSIONS →	NR applicants	NR accepted

3.50 avg. high school gpa

ACT range (0–36): 19 – 24

SAT range (200–800): reading 450 – 560; math 480 – 610; writing 460 – 570

GRADUATION RATES

39% of students graduating within 4 yrs

67% of students graduating within 6 yrs

University of California–Riverside

FINANCIAL AID: 951-827-3878 • E-MAIL: ADMIN@UCR.EDU • WEBSITE: WWW.UCR.EDU

STUDENT BODY

UCR is "one of the most diverse of all the UC campuses." "It's hard to describe the typical student, because there are so many different types of people." There are "the fraternity freaks, the overachievers, the geeks, the recluses, the trendy people," and many other subgroups. At the same time, UCR is mostly full of "average college students." "Everybody is pretty relaxed and friendly." Sure, there "weirdoes here and there, "maybe a few people with green hair," but "no one is out of the ordinary." Just about everyone here is from California. Some seventy percent of all students receive financial aid. "Most of the students seem serious about being in college and are here for the right reasons," though not all of them. "There are the extremely bright students who spend all day studying," relates a sophomore. "There are also students who barely got in and do nothing at all."

WHY STUDENTS LOVE UC–RIVERSIDE

The student population at UCR recognizes that its ethnic diversity is a major strength of the school. One proud student proclaims, "My school has the best diversity in the state." Actually, that student would be underselling UCR since it ranks as one of the most diverse schools in the entire nation. Students are also appreciative of the school's approach to preparing their students for more than just academic life. According to a student, "The school for UCR is all about making sure the students are prepared for life after college." Although many students do not seem to be particularly excited about their school's social scene, they do acknowledge that there are opportunities out there to get involved in campus life. Says one student, "What I do know is that there is an attempt by many clubs and organizations to always have events on and off campus." UCR students are also able to carve out their own niche and find enjoyment in various ways. One busy student explains, "For fun I like to do random things, anything from bowling, to community service, to going into workshops or watching dvds. Riverside is not too far from LA and Fullerton and Long Beach so I hang out there when I can."

GENERAL INFO

Activities: Choral groups, concert band, dance, drama/theater, jazz band, literary magazine, music ensembles, musical theater, pep band, radio station, student government, student newspaper, student-run film society, international student organization. **Organizations:** 264 registered organizations, 9 honor societies, 27 religious organizations. 20 fraternities, 20 sororities. **Athletics (Intercollegiate):** *Men*: Baseball, basketball, cross-country, golf, soccer, tennis, track/field (outdoor), track/field (indoor). *Women:* Basketball, cross-country, golf, soccer, softball, tennis, track/field (outdoor), track/field (indoor), volleyball. **On-Campus Highlights:** Basketball games, Student Recreation Center and intramural sports, The Barn (music and comedy acts), Coffee Bean and Tea Leaf. The Highlander Union Building (HUB).

BOTTOM LINE

For students who are California residents, the cost of tuition is about $12,000, which makes the school a good value for the price. For any out-of-state students, it is a different story. The tuition reaches up to around $34,560 plus another $12,100 for room and board. Whether you're an in-state or out-of-state student, do not forget to factor in the additional required fees and cost of books and supplies, which add up to a little bit over $4,000.

SELECTIVITY

Admissions Rating	**92**
# of applicants	26,478
% of applicants accepted	78
% of acceptees attending	22

FRESHMAN PROFILE

Range SAT Critical Reading	**450–560**
Range SAT Math	**480–610**
Range SAT Writing	**460–570**
Range ACT Composite	**19–24**
Average HS GPA	**3.50**
% graduated top 10% of class	**94**
% graduated top 25% of class	**100**
% graduated top 50% of class	**100**

DEADLINES

Regular Deadline	**11/30**
Normal registration	**no**

FACILITIES

Housing: Coed dorms, special housing for disabled students, special housing for international students, apartments for married students, apartments for single students, theme housing. *Special Academic Facilities/Equipment:* Art gallery, photography museum, botanical gardens, audio-visual resource center/studios, media resource center, statistical consulting center, citrus research center and agricultural experiment station.

FINANCIAL FACTS

Financial Aid Rating	**82**
Annual in-state tuition	$11,850
Annual out-of-state tuition	$34,562
Room and Board	$12,100
Required Fees	$2,281
Books and supplies	$1,800
% frosh rec. need-based scholarship or grant aid	74
% UG rec.need-based scholarship or grant aid	69
% frosh rec. non-need-based scholarship or grant aid	2
% UG rec. non-need-based scholarship or grant aid	1
% frosh rec. need-based self-help aid	65
% UG rec. need-based self-help aid	57
% frosh rec. any financial aid	81
% UG rec. any financial aid	73
% UG borrow to pay for school	64
Average cumulative indebtedness	$18,094

University of California–San Diego

9500 Gilman Drive, 0021, La Jolla, CA 92093-0021 • Admissions: 858-534-4831 • Fax: 858-534-5723

CAMPUS LIFE

Quality of life Rating	74
Fire Safety Rating	80
Green rating	97
Type of School	Public
Environment	Metropolis

STUDENTS

Total undergrad enrolllment	23,663
% Male to Female	49/51
% From out of state	3
% Live on Campus	34
# of Fraternities	19
# of Sororities	14
% African American	2
% Asian	44
% Caucasian	24
% Hispanic	13
% International	7
# Of Countries Represented	70

ACADEMICS

Academic Rating	80
% Of students graduating within 4 years	57
% Of students graduating within 6 years	82
Calendar	quarter
Profs interesting rating	68
Profs accessible rating	68
Most common reg class size	10–19 students
Most common lab size	20–29 students

MOST POPULAR MAJORS

Biology, economics

SPECIAL STUDY OPTIONS

Accelerated program, cooperative education program, cross-registration, double major, English as a Second Language (ESL), exchange student program (domestic), honors program, independent study, internships, liberal arts/career combination, student-designed major, study abroad, teacher certification program, Summer sessions for credit; special services for students with learning disabilities; Research programs, freshman honors program, in-depth academic assignments working in small groups or one-to-one with faculty.

ABOUT THE SCHOOL

Mathematics and the sciences reign supreme at the University of California–San Diego, and the school has an excellent reputation, huge research budgets, and an idyllic climate that have helped it attract eight Nobel Laureates to its faculty. While research and graduate study garner most of the attention, undergraduates still receive a solid education that results in an impressive degree. The division of the undergraduate program into six smaller colleges helps take some of the edge off UC San Diego's big-school vibe (roughly 22,000 undergraduates) and allows students easier access to administrators. A quarterly academic calendar also keeps things moving.

Campus life is generally pretty quiet. Students are divided on whether this school in scenic but sleepy La Jolla has a boring social scene or that one simply has to look hard to find recreation. "There is always something to do on campus, and it is always changing! I never get bored!" But one thing is certain: Some students work way too hard to afford the luxury of a social life. Students are often too busy with schoolwork to spend a lot of time partying, and when they have free time, they find hometown La Jolla a little too tiny for most college students. The town won't sanction a frat row so Greek life doesn't include raucous parties, but the new 1,000-bed Village at Torrey Pines, built especially for transfer students, is one of the most environmentally sustainable student housing structures in the nation. Students also spend a lot of time at the beach or in competition, enjoying the school's intramural sports programs. One student summed up the dichotomy perfectly: "My school is all about science and the beach." Trying to study the hard sciences despite the distraction of the Pacific only a few blocks away is a mammoth task. And a fine public transit system makes downtown San Diego very accessible.

BANG FOR YOUR BUCK

The financial aid program here is exceedingly generous and goes More than half of UC San Diego's undergraduate students receive need-based support. The University of California's Blue and Gold Opportunity Plan (B&G) will cover students' UC fees if they are California residents and their families earn $80,000 or less and the student also qualifies for UC financial aid. For needy middle-class families earning up to $120,000, UC offers additional grant money that offsets half of any UC fee increase. In response to California's current economic climate, UC San Diego launched the $50 million Invent the Future student support fundraising campaign that will help fund scholarships and fellowships for all who need them.

STUDENTS

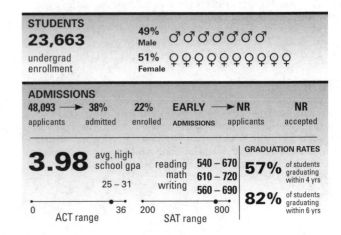

23,663 undergrad enrollment

49% Male ♂♂♂♂♂♂♂

51% Female ♀♀♀♀♀♀♀♀♀♀♀

ADMISSIONS

48,093 applicants →	38% admitted	22% enrolled	EARLY ADMISSIONS →	NR applicants	NR accepted

3.98 avg. high school gpa

ACT range (0–36): 25 – 31

SAT range (200–800):

reading	540 – 670
math	610 – 720
writing	560 – 690

GRADUATION RATES

57% of students graduating within 4 yrs

82% of students graduating within 6 yrs

University of California–San Diego

FINANCIAL AID: 858-534-4480 • E-MAIL: ADMISSIONSINFO@UCSD.EDU • WEBSITE: WWW.UCSD.EDU

STUDENT BODY

The typical UC San Diego undergrad is hardworking, maybe a little antisocial, but extremely bright. These students populate the premed and engineering programs, and, when not working, like to relax with a computer game. The typical student at our school is Asian American and studious, one student reports. "Great professors and nice, dorky kids," is how one student sums up the demographic. "UCSD has very smart people doing really incredible things." They can "surf and dance and loads of other things, so it just goes to show that intelligence comes in all kinds of packages." As has been established, some view the nightlife as a dead zone, but many find kindred spirits through sports teams, whether it's university-sponsored or intramural.

Why Students love UC San Diego

"My professors have been phenomenal; always accessible, enthusiastic, and encouraging."

WHY STUDENTS LOVE UC SAN DIEGO

UCSD is one of the world's premier research institutions, and the economic downturn hasn't diminished its importance or vitality. What began as an oceanography school that expanded into a university in the early 1960s has grown into a haven for neurosciences, chemistry, medicine, engineering, ocean studies, and even theater and dance. The faculty, filled with Nobel laureates, earns across-the-board praise from students for their knowledge and dedication. "My professors are amazing and truly want to teach every student," one says. "My professors have been phenomenal; always accessible, enthusiastic, and encouraging" adds another. Others say their classes got smaller and the instruction better as they progressed in their degree programs. "It's especially cool when you take a class on poli-sci immigration from the leader in the field, or take a physics class taught by (astronaut) Sally Ride." Libraries and research facilities get high marks. Best of all, students say, the school has a sterling reputation, so "I know my degree won't be meaningless."

GENERAL INFO

Activities: Choral groups, concert band, dance, drama/theater, jazz band, literary magazine, marching band, music ensembles, musical theater, opera, pep band, radio station, student government, student newspaper, student-run film society, symphony orchestra, television station, yearbook, campus ministries, international student organization. **Organizations:** 406 registered organizations, 5 honor societies, 46 religious organizations. 19 fraternities, 14 sororities. **Athletics (Intercollegiate):** *Men:* Baseball, basketball, crew/rowing, cross-country, diving, fencing, golf, soccer, swimming, tennis, track/field (outdoor), volleyball, water polo. *Women:* Bas ketball, crew/rowing, cross-country, diving, fencing, soccer, softball, swimming, tennis, track/field (outdoor), volleyball, water polo.

BOTTOM LINE

California residents attending UC San Diego full time pay roughly a little more than $9,000 in fees. Room and board costs come close to $12,000, not to mention additional costs for transportation, books, and personal expenses. Nonresidents pay more than $32,000 in tuition alone.

SELECTIVITY

Admissions Rating	**97**
# of applicants	48,093
% of applicants accepted	38
% of acceptees attending	22

FRESHMAN PROFILE

Range SAT Critical Reading	**540–670**
Range SAT Math	**610–720**
Range SAT Writing	**560–690**
Range ACT Composite	**25–31**
Average HS GPA	**3.98**

DEADLINES

Regular Deadline	**11/30**
Normal registration	**yes**

FACILITIES

Housing: Coed dorms, special housing for disabled students, men's dorms, special housing for international students, women's dorms, fraternity/sorority housing, apartments for married students, cooperative housing, apartments for single students, International House for international students and others interested in international living. *Special Academic Facilities/Equipment:* Art galleries, center for U.S.-Mexican studies, music recording studio, audiovisual center, center for music experimentation, aquarium, structural lab, San Diego supercomputer center, electron microscopes lab.

FINANCIAL FACTS

Financial Aid Rating	**76**
Annual in-state tuition	$10,152
Annual out-of-state tuition	$33,030
Room and Board	$11,684
Required Fees	$1,976
Books and supplies	$1,456
% frosh rec. need-based scholarship or grant aid	62
% UG rec.need-based scholarship or grant aid	57
% frosh rec. non-need-based scholarship or grant aid	1
% frosh rec. need-based self-help aid	55
% UG rec. need-based self-help aid	49
% frosh rec. any financial aid	77
% UG rec. any financial aid	63
% UG borrow to pay for school	51
Average cumulative indebtedness	$17,689

University of California–Santa Barbara

Office of Admissions, 1210 Cheadle Hall, Santa Barbara, CA 93106-2014 • Admissions: 805-893-2881 • Fax: 805-893-267

CAMPUS LIFE

Quality of life Rating	99
Fire Safety Rating	91
Green rating	97
Type of School	Public
Environment	Metropolis

STUDENTS

Total undergrad enrolllment	19,184
% Male to Female	47/53
% From out of state	3
% From public high school	87
% Live on Campus	33
# of Fraternities	17
# of Sororities	18
% African American	3
% Asian	14
% Caucasian	39
% Hispanic	18
% Native American	1
% International	1
# Of Countries Represented	72

ACADEMICS

Academic Rating	74
% Of students graduating within 4 years	63
% Of students graduating within 6 years	80
Calendar	quarter
Profs interesting rating	79
Profs accessible rating	86
Most common reg class size	20–29 students
Most common lab size	20–29 students

MOST POPULAR MAJORS

Biology, economics

HONORS PROGRAMS

The College Honors Program.

SPECIAL STUDY OPTIONS

Accelerated program, cross-registration, double major, dual enrollment, English as a Second Language (ESL), exchange student program (domestic), honors program, independent study, internships, student-designed major, study abroad.

ABOUT THE SCHOOL

UCSB's beautiful campus is located 100 miles north of Los Angeles, with views of the ocean and the mountains, and typically benevolent Southern California weather. Perched above the Pacific coast, the University of California–Santa Barbara is a top-ranked public university with a multitude of world-class academic, extracurricular, and social opportunities. University of California–Santa Barbara is "a beautiful, laid-back learning institute on the beach," yet students say it's much more than a great place to get a tan. This prestigious public school is "one of the best research universities in the country," which "attracts many excellent professors" as well as a cadre of dedicated students. Maybe it's the sunny weather, but "professors here are more accessible than [at] other universities," and they are "genuinely interested in helping the students learn." This large university offers more than 200 major programs, of which business, economics, biology, communications, psychology, and engineering are among the most popular. Students agree that the competent and enthusiastic faculty is one of the school's greatest assets. Teaching assistants are also noted for being dedicated and helpful, especially in leading small discussion sessions to accompany large lecture courses. There are five Nobel Laureates on the UCSB faculty, and the school offers many opportunities for undergraduates to participate in research.

BANG FOR YOUR BUCK

As a part of the prestigious University of California system, UCSB fuses good value and strong academics. It is a state school with over 19,000 students enrolled, so and many classes are large. But with all the resources of a major research school at your fingertips, it's a definite bargain. The University of California operates the Blue and Gold Opportunity Plan. For in-state students with household incomes of less than the state median of $60,000, the Blue and Gold Opportunity plan will fully cover the mandatory UC fees for four years. California residents are also eligible for Cal Grants, a grant program administered by the state and open to college students that meet certain minimum GPA requirements. In addition to state and federal aid, there are a number of scholarships available to UCSB undergraduates. New freshmen and transfer students with outstanding academic and personal achievement may be awarded the prestigious Regents Scholarship. There are additional merit awards offered through each of the university's four colleges, as well as through the alumni association.

STUDENTS

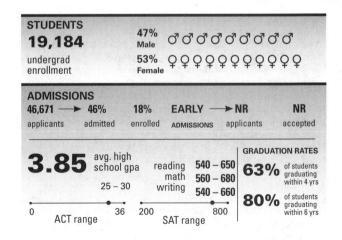

19,184 undergrad enrollment

47% Male ♂♂♂♂♂♂♂♂♂

53% Female ♀♀♀♀♀♀♀♀♀♀♀

ADMISSIONS

46,671 →	46%	18%	EARLY ADMISSIONS →	NR	NR
applicants	admitted	enrolled		applicants	accepted

3.85 avg. high school gpa

ACT range (0–36): 25 – 30

SAT range (200–800): reading 540 – 650; math 560 – 680; writing 540 – 660

GRADUATION RATES

63% of students graduating within 4 yrs

80% of students graduating within 6 yrs

University of California–Santa Barbara

FINANCIAL AID: 805-893-2118 • E-MAIL: ADMISSIONS@SA.UCSB.EDU • WEBSITE: WWW.UCSB.EDU

STUDENT BODY

At this beautiful, beachfront school, the typical undergraduate is a "white kid from California that likes to have fun, go out on the weekends, but knows when to take his or her studies seriously." Many students (especially those in the College of Creative Studies) "are highly driven toward the field that they choose for their major." UCSB does not have the diversity you might find at University of California's urban campuses. Nonetheless, "there are people from all sorts of backgrounds, levels of income, and religions," and "Almost everybody here at UCSB is extremely friendly. Nobody is judgmental or discriminatory." Given the school's spectacular surroundings, it's not surprising that "a general commonality among many people seems to be a love of the beach or at least an appreciation for the beautiful surroundings."

Why Students love UCSB

"Almost everybody here at UCSB is extremely friendly. Nobody is judgmental or discriminatory."

WHY STUDENTS LOVE UCSB

"Bordered by the mountains to the north, the ocean to the south, and the college town to the west," UCSB is a veritable paradise. Here, students have the luxury of deciding, "whether they want to go surf or spend the day playing volleyball in the park." When describing the campus environment, the word "idyllic" comes to mind. A resident student details, "I step out of my door and am only a few steps away from Carrillo, one of the three on-campus dining halls. Directly next to Carrillo is a swimming pool, and right across the way there is a community center with a piano, televisions, a pool and ping-pong table, and comfortable chairs." In addition to nightlife, students love "exploring downtown Santa Barbara–which is so much more than just State Street–hiking around campus, kayaking in the ocean, or simply spending quality time with friends."

GENERAL INFO

Activities: Choral groups, concert band, dance, drama/theater, jazz band, literary magazine, music ensembles, musical theater, opera, pep band, radio station, student government, student newspaper, student run film society, symphony orchestra, television station, yearbook, campus ministries, international student organization. **Organizations:** 508 registered organizations, 5 honor societies, 19 religious organizations. 17 fraternities, 18 sororities. **Athletics (Intercollegiate):** *Men:* Baseball, basketball, cross-country, diving, golf, gymnastics, soccer, swimming, tennis, track/field (outdoor), volleyball, water polo. *Women:* Basketball, cross-country, diving, gymnastics, soccer, softball, swimming, tennis, track/field (outdoor), volleyball, water polo.

BOTTOM LINE

Depending on where you live and what you study, the cost of attending UC Santa Barbara fluctuates. For California residents, the school estimates that total expenses range between $22,000 and $31,000 annually. For out-of-state residents, the estimated annual cost ranges between $48,000–$54,000.

SELECTIVITY

Admissions Rating	**83**
# of applicants	46,671
% of applicants accepted	46
% of acceptees attending	18
# accepting a place on wait list	1,276
% admitted from wait list	99

FRESHMAN PROFILE

Range SAT Critical Reading	**540–650**
Range SAT Math	**560–680**
Range SAT Writing	**540–660**
Range ACT Composite	**25–30**
Average HS GPA	**3.85**

DEADLINES

Regular Deadline	**11/30**
Normal registration	**no**

FACILITIES

Housing: Coed dorms, fraternity/sorority housing, apartments for married students, cooperative housing, apartments for single students, wellness housing, theme housing. *Special Academic Facilities/Equipment:* Art museum, centers for black studies, Chicano studies, and study of developing nations, institutes for applied behavioral sciences, community/organizational research, marine science, and theoretical physics, Channel Islands field station. *Computers:* 100% of dorms, 100% of dining areas, 100% of student union, have wireless network access.

FINANCIAL FACTS

Financial Aid Rating	**77**
Annual in-state tuition	$10,152
Annual out-of-state tuition	$33,030
Room and Board	$13,110
Required Fees	$2,356
Books and supplies	$1,414
% frosh rec. need-based scholarship or grant aid	51
% UG rec.need-based scholarship or grant aid	45
% frosh rec. non-need-based scholarship or grant aid	1
% frosh rec. need-based self-help aid	43
% UG rec. need-based self-help aid	38
% frosh rec. any financial aid	55
% UG rec. any financial aid	66
% UG borrow to pay for school	47
Average cumulative indebtedness	$17,768

University of California–Santa Cruz

Office of Admissions, Cook House, 1156 High Street, Santa Cruz, CA 95064 • Admissions: 831-459-4008

CAMPUS LIFE

Quality of life Rating	84
Fire Safety Rating	76
Green rating	99
Type of School	Public
Environment	City

STUDENTS

Total undergrad enrolllment	15,666
% Male to Female	47/53
% From out of state	3
% From public high school	87
% Live on Campus	48
# of Fraternities	6
# of Sororities	11
% African American	3
% Asian	23
% Caucasian	45
% Hispanic	20
% Native American	1
% International	1
# Of Countries Represented	87

ACADEMICS

Academic Rating	85
% Of students graduating within 4 years	50
% Of students graduating within 6 years	74
Calendar	quarter
Profs interesting rating	74
Profs accessible rating	77
Most common reg class size	10–19 students
Most common lab size	10–19 students

MOST POPULAR MAJORS

Business/commerce, art studies

SPECIAL STUDY OPTIONS

Cooperative education program, cross registration, double major, exchange student program (domestic), independent study, internships, student-designed major, study abroad, teacher certification program

ABOUT THE SCHOOL

UCSC is a world-class research and teaching university, featuring interdisciplinary learning and a distinctive residential college system that provides a small college environment within the larger research institution. Tucked within "a friendly and diverse community full of lovely scenery," a student observes how easy it is to "focus on scholastic endeavors in a beautiful forest setting." The university combines a multicultural, open community with a high-quality education, and the campus is very politically aware. Students enjoy the "medium-size school, where it is possible to get a university experience but the professors also want to learn your name." Undergraduates are provided with significant access to faculty and have a valuable opportunity to incorporate creative activities into their studies; they conduct and publish research, and work closely with faculty on leading-edge projects. What sets instructors apart from those at a typical research-driven university is that "they are very passionate about their subject even when teaching undergrads," according to a surprised student.

BANG FOR YOUR BUCK

Scholarships are sponsored by the UCSC Alumni Association, honoring high-achieving students who have compelling financial need. Student Organization Advising and Resources (SOAR) sponsor internships which help students gain skills in leadership, networking, program planning, and outreach. Under The Blue and Gold Opportunity Plan, undergraduates who are California residents in their first four years of attendance (or two for transfer students) will receive enough scholarship and grant assistance to at least fully cover their system-wide fees. Alternative Spring Break is an opportunity for students to immerse themselves in a service project such as building homes in Mexico and assisting with the rebuilding efforts in New Orleans. The Health Science major requires an internship in the health field in a Spanish speaking community, where students can volunteer in a hospital, spend time shadowing a physician, or assist in providing health services to underserved populations.

STUDENTS

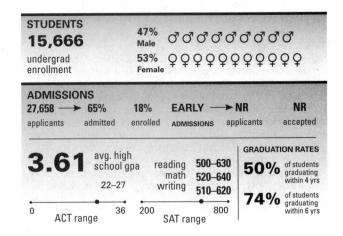

15,666 undergrad enrollment

47% Male ♂♂♂♂♂♂♂♂♂

53% Female ♀♀♀♀♀♀♀♀♀♀♀

ADMISSIONS

27,658 applicants	→ 65% admitted	18% enrolled	EARLY ADMISSIONS	→ NR applicants	NR accepted

3.61 avg. high school gpa

ACT range (0–36): 22–27

SAT range (200–800): reading 500–630, math 520–640, writing 510–620

GRADUATION RATES

50% of students graduating within 4 yrs

74% of students graduating within 6 yrs

University of California–Santa Cruz

FINANCIAL AID: 831-459-2963 • E-MAIL: ADMISSIONS@UCSC.EDU • FAX: 831-459-4452 • WEBSITE: WWW.UCSC.EDU

STUDENT BODY

"The 'stereotypical' Santa Cruz student is a hippie," and the school certainly has its fair share of those "The typical student is very hardworking until about 9:00 p.m., when hikes to the forest are common practice and returning to your room smelling like reefer is acceptable," one undergrad explains–but "there are many different types who attend UCSC." "It seems that almost every student here has a personal passion, whether it be an activism or cause of some sort, etc.," one student writes. "Everyone is so...alive." "Most are liberal," and there's a definite propensity for earnestness; it's the sort of place where students declare without irony that they "not only possess a great respect for one another but the world and life in general. The world to an average UCSC student is a sacred and beautiful place to be shared and enjoyed by all its inhabitants."

Why Students love UCSC

"I love that it is extremely vegetarian/vegan friendly, and being healthy is a lifestyle among students."

WHY STUDENTS LOVE UCSC

The liberal environment helps cultivate politically aware individuals who are "committed to advancing social justice." "Participating in activist rallies or protests" is common, one student says. The Student Environmental Center collaborates with the university to find ways to implement environmentally sound practices on campus. Students can "propose ideas to create beneficial changes," and find the administration to be responsive. The party scene consists of "mostly decentral¬ized, smaller parties, due to the near-absence of fraternities and sororities." KZSC, the university radio station, enables students to host their own radio shows. "I love that it is extremely vegetarian/vegan friendly, and being healthy is a lifestyle among students." Students marvel at "how easy it is to get where you need to go," and greatly enjoy the city of Santa Cruz. "Downtown is lively and usually has something fun going on such

GENERAL INFO

Activities: Choral groups, dance, drama/theater, jazz band, literary magazine, music ensembles, musical theater, opera, radio station, student government, student newspaper, student-run film society, symphony orchestra, television station, campus ministries, international student organization. **Organizations:** 138 registered organizations, 3 honor societies, 19 religious organizations. 9 fraternities, 11 sororities. **Athletics (Intercollegiate):** *Men:* Basketball, diving, soccer, swimming, tennis, volleyball. *Women:* Basketball, cross-country, diving, golf, soccer, swimming, tennis, volleyball. **On-Campus Highlights:** Arboretum, Farm and Garden, East Field House, Bay Tree Bookstore/Grad Student Commons, Pogonip Open Area Reserve.

BOTTOM LINE

Nearly 16,000 students are enrolled at the university, with almost everyone originally from California, and the student population is split evenly between residents and commuters. Room and board is $14,500 per year. Required fees are $12,500; books and supplies will come to an additional $1400. Out-of-state tuition is approximately $23,000.

SELECTIVITY

Admissions Rating	**95**
# of applicants	27,658
% of applicants accepted	65
% of acceptees attending	18
# accepting a place on wait list	592
% admitted from wait list	0

FRESHMAN PROFILE

Range SAT Critical Reading	**500–630**
Range SAT Math	**520–640**
Range SAT Writing	**510–620**
Range ACT Composite	**22–27**
Average HS GPA	**3.61**
% graduated top 10% of class	**96**
% graduated top 25% of class	**100**
% graduated top 50% of class	**100**

DEADLINES

Regular Deadline	**11/30**
Normal registration	**yes**

FACILITIES

Housing: Coed dorms, men's dorms, special housing for international students, women's dorms, apartments for married students, apartments for single students, theme housing. *Special Academic Facilities/ Equipment:* Eloise Pickard Smith Gallery Mary Porter Sesnon Gallery Center for Agroecology Wellness Center Long Marine Laboratory. *Computers:* 100% of classrooms, 100% of dorms, 100% of libraries, 100% of dining areas, 100% of student union, have wireless network access.

FINANCIAL FACTS

Financial Aid Rating	**78**
Annual in-state tuition	$13,417
Annual out-of-state tuition	$22,878
Room and Board	$14,727
Required Fees	$12,366
Books and supplies	$1,401
% frosh rec. need-based scholarship or grant aid	53
% UG rec.need-based scholarship or grant aid	49
% frosh rec. need-based self-help aid	52
% UG rec. need-based self-help aid	48
% frosh rec. any financial aid	59
% UG rec. any financial aid	56
% UG borrow to pay for school	53
Average cumulative indebtedness	$16,024

University of Central Florida

P.O. Box 160111, Orlando, FL 32816-0111 • Admissions: 407-823-3000 • Financial Aid: 407-823-2827

CAMPUS LIFE

Quality of life Rating	91
Fire Safety Rating	83
Green rating	92
Type of School	Public
Environment	City

STUDENTS

Total undergrad enrolllment	47,652
% Male to Female	46/54
% From out of state	5
% From public high school	82
% Live on Campus	15
# of Fraternities	11
# of Sororities	9
% African American	10
% Asian	6
% Caucasian	64
% Hispanic	17
% International	1
# Of Countries Represented	167

ACADEMICS

Academic Rating	70
% Of students graduating within 4 years	34
% Of students graduating within 6 years	63
Calendar	semester
Profs interesting rating	69
Profs accessible rating	71
Most common reg class size	20–29 students
Most common lab size	20–29 students

MOST POPULAR MAJORS

Engineering, business, hospitality management

HONOR PROGRAMS

The Burnett Honors College offers two main tracks, University Honors, Honors in the Major, and there is also a special accelerated Medical School program in partnership with University of South Florida. Honors English Composition. Honors Symposium. Honors in the Major.

SPECIAL STUDY OPTIONS

Cooperative education program, distance learning, double major, dual enrollment, internships, study abroad, teacher certification program.

ABOUT THE SCHOOL

With a student body of mind-boggling proportions (more than 40,000 undergraduates!) and a campus located in one of America's entertainment capitals, the University of Central Florida in Orlando boasts diversity in every experience it has to offer. When it comes to academics, students find themselves driven to excel–thanks to a career-driven yet laid-back environment that places an emphasis on the future without forgoing the fun. To help ensure students' success, UCF has implemented resources for free tutoring. A new Veteran Academic Resource Center provides services to military students and families, and the university's nationally-recognized Transfer and Transition Services Office and Sophomore and Second Year Center–one of only a few in the country–focuses on helping undeclared sophomores and students change their majors.

The school maintains strong ties to the booming community to give its undergraduates in business, computer science, education, engineering, hospitality managementtt, and mass communications hands-on experience in their fields before they graduate. UCF connects students with internships, co-op experiences, and service-learning work that ultimately results in high-wage jobs post-graduation. A new 25,000 square-foot building dedicated specifically to career services and experiential learning, features state-of-the-art resources such as a practice interview room with recording capabilities that provides students with an immediate assessment of their skills through the production of a personal DVD. Interested in energy? Defense? Space? Technology? You've come to the right place.

BANG FOR YOUR BUCK

UCF offers an array of merit and need-based financial awards. Several merit scholarship awards are available to freshmen based upon strong academic credentials in high school and solid test scores. As a bonus, all incoming freshmen are automatically considered for a merit scholarship. Students should be quick to contact their academic departments too, as they also offer awards that require a separate application. Other awards are available to those who excel in academics, athletics, leadership, music, or drama, and for those who have an alumni affiliation. Minority scholarships and ROTC scholarships are also available.

STUDENTS

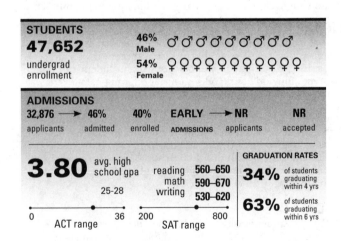

47,652 undergrad enrollment

46% Male

54% Female

ADMISSIONS

32,876 applicants	→ 46% admitted	40% enrolled	EARLY ADMISSIONS	→ NR applicants	NR accepted

3.80 avg. high school gpa

ACT range (0–36): 25-28

SAT range (200–800): reading 560–650; math 590–670; writing 530–620

GRADUATION RATES

34% of students graduating within 4 yrs

63% of students graduating within 6 yrs

University of Central Florida

E-MAIL: ADMISSION@MAIL.UCF.EDU • FAX: 407-823-5625 • WEBSITE: WWW.UCF.EDU

STUDENT BODY

With such a sizeable student body, there is hardly a typical student, and certainly no limit to the amount of campus associations and activities you can join to meet like-minded folks. Between the school and Orlando at large, there is something to do every night of the week. "The only real thing that many students share in common is sandals," observes a business major. "At a given time, seventy-five percent of the campus is probably wearing sandals." UCF students hail overwhelmingly from in-state, too. And "the girls are insanely pretty." Otherwise, "it is difficult to generalize" about some 42,000 undergrads. "There is no possible way to describe a typical student." Students tend to have "their own set of friends, activities, and experiences at UCF." "This is a melting pot of culture."

WHY STUDENTS LOVE UCF

The University of Central Florida is "a growing school with a solid academic image." "Its reputation needs to catch up with how it actually is," urges a junior. The engineering and science programs are renowned, and students laud the hospitality, management, and business programs. UCF undergrads also benefit from "awesome technology" all over campus. UCF boasts a "very scenic," "comfortable" campus. Socially, if you're bored here, you just aren't trying very hard. "The campus organizes a wide variety of social events." "We have a ridiculous number of clubs and organizations," boasts a sophomore. "There are about a million events going on at any given time." There is almost every imaginable intramural sport. There is "a huge three story gym" that features "every kind of workout machine."

Why Students love UCF

"Walking around campus you see a little bit of every culture, every race, and every ethnicity."

GENERAL INFO

Activities: Choral groups, concert band, drama/theater, jazz band, literary magazine, marching band, music ensembles, musical theater, pep band, radio station, student government, student newspaper, student-run film society, symphony orchestra, campus ministries, international student organization. **Organizations:** 361 registered organizations, 36 honor societies, 29 religious organizations. 21 fraternities, 18 sororities. **Athletics (Intercollegiate):** *Men:* Baseball, basketball, cheerleading, cross-country, football, golf, soccer, tennis. *Women:* Basketball, cheerleading, crew/rowing, cross-country, golf, soccer, softball, tennis, track/field (outdoor), track/field (indoor), volleyball. **On-Campus Highlights:** Student Union, Recreation and Wellness Center, bookstore (Barnes and Noble cafe), Reflecting Pond, new Arena and Football Stadium.

BOTTOM LINE

State residency has its privileges–an academic year of tuition, room and board, and fees at UCF for a Florida resident is just under $14,000, while nonresidents will find themselves paying closer to $30,000. Of the 40 percent of students who borrow to pay for their education, most leave the school with about $19,000 in cumulative debt.Upon graduation, enrollees can expect to have a cumulated indebtedness of a bit more than $17,000.Nearly 90 percent of the student body receives some manner of financial aid.

SELECTIVITY

Admissions Rating	**90**
# of applicants	32,876
% of applicants accepted	46
% of acceptees attending	40
# accepting a place on wait list	367
% admitted from wait list	28

FRESHMAN PROFILE

Range SAT Critical Reading	**560–650**
Range SAT Math	**590–670**
Range SAT Writing	**530–620**
Range ACT Composite	**25–28**
Average HS GPA	**3.80**
% graduated top 10% of class	**33**
% graduated top 25% of class	**72**
% graduated top 50% of class	**96**

DEADLINES

Regular Deadline	**2/1**
Normal registration	**yes**

FACILITIES

Housing: Coed dorms, men's dorms, women's dorms, fraternity/sorority housing, apartments for single students, wellness housing, theme housing, affiliated student residences available across street from campus with university resident assistants. On-campus: Honors Center; Living Learning Communities, Lead Scholars Center. *Special Academic Facilities/Equipment:* Center for research and education in optics and lasers, arboretum, observatory, new student union, student recreation center. *Computers:* 100% of classrooms, 100% of dorms, 100% of libraries, 90% of dining areas, 100% of student union, 90% of common outdoor areas have wireless network access.

FINANCIAL FACTS

Financial Aid Rating	**70**
Annual in-state tuition	$5,020
Annual out-of-state tutition	$20,500
Room and Board	$8,765
Required Fees	$0
Books and supplies	$1,200
% frosh rec. need-based scholarship or grant aid	29
% UG rec.need-based scholarship or grant aid	31
% frosh rec. non-need-based scholarship or grant aid	59
% UG rec. non-need-based scholarship or grant aid	38
% frosh rec. need-based self-help aid	21
% UG rec. need-based self-help aid	29
% frosh rec. any financial aid	95
% UG rec. any financial aid	81
% UG borrow to pay for school	41
Average cumulative indebtedness	$17,044

University of Colorado–Boulder

552 UCB, Boulder, CO 80309-0552 • Admissions: 303-492-6301 • Fax: 303-492-7115

CAMPUS LIFE

Quality of life Rating	79
Fire Safety Rating	87
Green rating	91
Type of School	Public
Environment	City

STUDENTS

Total undergrad enrolllment	25,782
% Male to Female	54/47
% From out of state	33
% Live on Campus	24
# of Fraternities	19
# of Sororities	15
% African American	2
% Asian	6
% Caucasian	77
% Hispanic	7
% N.A.	1
% International	2
# Of Countries Represented	98

ACADEMICS

Academic Rating	74
% Of students graduating within 4 years	41
% Of students graduating within 6 years	68
Calendar	semester
Profs interesting rating	67
Profs accessible rating	71
Most common reg class size	10–19 students
Most common lab size	20–29 students

MOST POPULAR MAJORS

International/global studies, physiology, psychology

HONORS PROGRAMS

The CU Honors Program. The Honors Residential Academic Program (HRAP) is a residential academic program within the general Honors Program. The Norlin Scholars Program. The Presidents Leadership Class.

SPECIAL STUDY OPTIONS

Accelerated program, cooperative education program, cross-registration, distance learning, double major, dual enrollment, Presidents Leadership Class.

ABOUT THE SCHOOL

A large research institution of more than 27,000 students, The University of Colorado offers more than 150 fields of study in its nine colleges. The school operates particularly strong programs in engineering and the sciences; students also hold the architecture, journalism, mass communications, and aerospace programs in high esteem. (The university is the country's number one recipient of NASA funding.) Since the school is large, there are many available academic choices, but the diverse faculty reflects that, among them 4 Nobel Prize winner, 19 Rhodes Scholars and 7 MacArthur Genius Grant Fellowships. "Being in a class taught by a Nobel laureate is not something everyone gets to experience." It is not uncommon at all for students to be on a five or six-year plan as a result of the extensive amount of academic choices. When they do finish, CU graduates are likely to find themselves well-prepared for the real world. The career services office offers counseling, job and internship listings, and on-campus recruiting to the general student population; in addition, the college has numerous online tools to help students prepare for the job market, as well as having the innovative multi-disciplinary Information Technology center.

Campus commitment to environmental education and research has helped CU–Boulder become one of the nation's top environmental research universities. The school's reputation and performance as a national leader in environmental issues and sustainability enhances an already respected environmental studies department. CU–Boulder students have a decades-long legacy of leadership in these areas, and are very "environmentally motivated." On Earth Day 1970, students founded the Environmental Center, now the nation's oldest, largest, and most accomplished student-led center of its kind.

BANG FOR YOUR BUCK

For Colorado residents, scholarship opportunities include the CU Promise Program for freshman and transfers, and the First Generation Scholarship, for students whose parents do not have college degrees. For out-of-state students, CU offers this enticing guarantee: There will be no tuition increases during your four years of study. In addition, the top 25 percent of out-of-state admissions are eligible to receive the Chancellor's Achievement Scholarship. With 5,000 new freshman "Buffaloes" on campus each year, the school nonetheless provides an incredible array of resources. "CU is an amazing place because you can find an array of challenges and opportunities whether your drive is research, the arts, sports, a job, or tough classwork." I am able to research in one of my professor's labs while receiving a great education."

STUDENTS

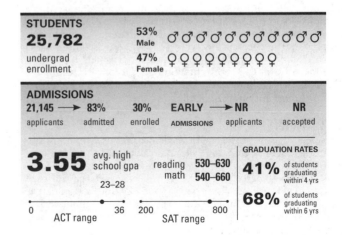

25,782 undergrad enrollment

53% Male ♂♂♂♂♂♂♂♂♂♂♂

47% Female ♀♀♀♀♀♀♀♀♀

ADMISSIONS

21,145 →	83%	30%	EARLY →	NR	NR
applicants	admitted	enrolled	ADMISSIONS	applicants	accepted

3.55 avg. high school gpa

reading	530–630
math	540–660

ACT range: 23–28 (0–36)

SAT range (200–800)

GRADUATION RATES

41% of students graduating within 4 yrs

68% of students graduating within 6 yrs

University of Colorado–Boulder

FINANCIAL AID: 303-492-5091 • WEBSITE: WWW.COLORADO.EDU

WHY STUDENTS LOVE UNIVERSITY OF COLORADO–BOULDER

The university's student government has an autonomy agreement with the university's administration and oversees an annual budget of more than $30 million dollars, making it the most financially powerful student government in the nation. Students also love the campus and the amount of extracurricular groups that the university provides. The school "really encourages students to get involved with the ceaseless amounts of activities, groups, and clubs." Along with clubs and intramural sports, intercollegiate football remains huge among undergraduates. Off campus, students can head to the mountains to ski or snowboard, catch a concert at one of the many local music venues, visit Denver (for free with a student pass), go camping, hang out on Pearl Street, or just sit in one of the many coffee shops in the city of Boulder.

GENERAL INFO

Activities: Choral groups, concert band, dance, drama/theater, jazz band, literary magazine, marching band, music ensembles, musical theater, opera, pep band, radio station, student government, student newspaper, student-run film society, symphony orchestra, television station, campus ministries, international student organization. **Organizations:** 300 registered organizations, 26 honor societies, 35 religious organizations. 20 fraternities, 19 sororities. **Athletics (Intercollegiate):** *Men:* Basketball, cross-country, football, golf, skiing (downhill/alpine), skiing (nordic/cross-country), track/field (outdoor), track/field (indoor). *Women:* Basketball, cross-country, golf, skiing (downhill/alpine), skiing (nordic/cross-country), soccer, tennis, track/field (outdoor), track/field (indoor), volleyball. **On-Campus Highlights:** University Memorial Center (UMC), Student Recreation Center, Norlin Library, ATLAS Building, Farrand Field, CU–Boulder's Outdoor Program, at the Recreation Center.

Why Students love University of Colorado–Boulder

"CU provides students with plenty of resources to enjoy their college lives (whether that is skiing, music, partying, or just about any outdoor activity imaginable) while also receiving a first-class education."

THE BOTTOM LINE

CU's reasonable tuition is one of the school's major selling points. Tuition (including mandatory fees) for Colorado residents averages just about $8,500 annually. For nonresidents, tuition and fees average about $30,000. Room and board is an additional $11,000 annually. Books average $2,000 per year. Each year, more than half of CU's undergraduates apply for and receive financial aid through a combination of loans, work-study programs, and scholarships. Nearly 9 of every 10 students receive financial aid, with the average amounting to over $14,000. Total need-based gift aid to freshman is approximately $8000.

SELECTIVITY

Admissions Rating	**83**
# of applicants	21,145
% of applicants accepted	83
% of acceptees attending	30
# accepting a place on wait list	232
% admitted from a waitlist	33

FRESHMAN PROFILE

Range SAT Critical Reading	**530–630**
Range SAT Math	**540–660**
Range ACT Composite	**23–28**
Average HS GPA	**3.55**
% graduated top 10% of class	**26**
% graduated top 25% of class	**59**
% graduated top 50% of class	**93**

DEADLINES

Regular Deadline	**1/15**
Normal registration	**yes**

FACILITIES

Housing: Coed dorms, special housing for disabled students, fraternity/sorority housing, apartments for married students. *Special Academic Facilities/Equipment:* Art galleries, natural history museum, heritage center, observatory, planetarium. *Computers:* 100% of classrooms, 65% of dorms, 100% of libraries, 100% of dining areas, 100% of student union, 50% of common outdoor areas have wireless network access.

FINANCIAL FACTS

Financial Aid Rating	**87**
Annual in-state tuition	$7,672
Annual out-of-state tuition	$28,850
Room and Board	$11,278
Required Fees	$1,480
Books and supplies	$1,992
% frosh rec. need-based scholarship or grant aid	36
% UG rec. need-based scholarship or grant aid	30
% frosh rec. non-need-based scholarship or grant aid	1
% UG rec. non-need-based scholarship or grant aid	1
% frosh rec. need-based self-help aid	36
% UG rec. need-based self-help aid	32
% frosh rec. any financial aid	86
% UG rec. any financial aid	64
% UG borrow to pay for school	93
Average cumulative indebtedness	$19,758

University of Delaware

210 South College Ave, Newark, DE 19716-6210 • Admissions: 302-831-8123 • Fax: 302-831-6905

CAMPUS LIFE

Quality of life Rating	77
Fire Safety Rating	99
Green rating	89
Type of School	Public
Environment	Town

STUDENTS

Total undergrad enrolllment	15,757
% Male to Female	42/58
% From out of state	64
% From public high school	80
% Live on Campus	46
# of Fraternities	22
# of Sororities	15
% African American	5
% Asian	5
% Caucasian	4
% Hispanic	6
% International	2
# Of Countries Represented	91

ACADEMICS

Academic Rating	76
% Of students graduating within 4 years	61
% Of students graduating within 6 years	75
Calendar	4-1-4
Profs interesting rating	77
Profs accessible rating	80
Most common reg class size	20–29 students
Most common lab size	10–19 students

MOST POPULAR MAJORS
Biology, psychology

HONORS PROGRAMS
University Honors Program

SPECIAL STUDY OPTIONS
Combined degree programs: 4+1 BS Hotel Restaurant and Inst. Mgmt./MBA. Accelerated program, cooperative education program, distance learning, double major, dual enrollment, honors program, independent study, internships, liberal arts/career combination, student-designed major, study abroad, teacher certification program.

ABOUT THE SCHOOL
The University of Delaware is the largest university in the state. Delaware students benefit from a series of signature academic programs, where students rave about the "challenging classes and friendly professors." Other programs include service-learning, study abroad, and undergraduate research opportunities. Every freshman participates in First Year Experience, a program that allows them to meet other students in their major, learn about the school's resources, and generally feel more at home on campus. The school has renowned engineering, science, business, education, and chemical engineering programs. It is also one of only handful of schools in North America with a major in art conservation; the Animal Science program is esteemed as well, with a farm that's campus-adjacent for hands-on experience. Service learning at UD allows students to heighten their academic experience, and destinations run the gamut: from Newark to Vietnam, New York to Costa Rica. The University Honors Program (UHP) is the intellectual pearl of the university.

Why Students love University of Delaware

"The perfect balance of academic intensity and excellent social life."

BANG FOR YOUR BUCK
Part of the billion-dollar endowment club, the University of Delaware can afford to award more than $100 million annually in federal, state, and institutional aid. Every manner of scholarship is available, including awards for merit, art, athletics, and music. Some require a separate application or audition, so it's best to contact UD's financial aid office for more information. The University of Delaware awards more than $100 million annually in aid. Our commitment to making a University of Delaware education affordable is seen in our reasonable tuition for in-state and out-of-state students and in our variety of scholarships, financial aid programs, and financing plans.

STUDENTS
15,757 undergrad enrollment
42% Male ♂♂♂♂♂♂♂♂
58% Female ♀♀♀♀♀♀♀♀♀♀♀♀

ADMISSIONS
24,744 applicants → 57% admitted — 30% enrolled
EARLY ADMISSIONS → NR applicants — NR accepted

3.50 avg. high school gpa

24–28 — ACT range (0–36)

reading 520–630
math 540–650
writing 520–640
SAT range (200–800)

GRADUATION RATES
61% of students graduating within 4 yrs
75% of students graduating within 6 yrs

FINANCIAL AID: 302-831-8761 • E-MAIL: ADMISSIONS@UDEL.EDU • WEBSITE: WWW.UDEL.EDU

STUDENT BODY

It's a largely East Coast crowd at University of Delaware, drawing the vast majority of its undergraduates from "around NYC, Philly, or Baltimore." Within that demographic, "Preppy sorority kids are probably the most common, but no matter who you are or what your into, the school population is big enough [that] you're bound to find a group that shares your interest." At UD, "You'll have your jocks and frat boys, but you'll also find skaters, rockers, artsy types, and everything else in between." However, most UD students share an incredible enthusiasm for their school community, and "A typical student is engaged in coursework and a multitude of various extracurricular [activities]." Despite its long-standing repute as a party school, "students here have become more focused on academics. Most students here really do have a passion for learning and study really hard in order to get those grades and graduate." Even so, UD's reputation for revelry isn't lost on undergraduates: "The typical UD student cares about their school work but loves to have fun on the weekends."

WHY STUDENTS LOVE UNIVERSITY OF DELAWARE

Most "Fightin' Blue Hens" share an incredible enthusiasm for their school community, and "a typical student is engaged in coursework and a multitude of various extracurricular [activities]." The University of Delaware manages to keep each student contented with programs like the Undergraduate Research Program, which gives talented, motivated students the chance to work closely with faculty; there are more than 40 research centers and institutes, and about 700 students take advantage of this opportunity each year. UD's extensive study abroad program, the first in the United States and "one of the best in the nation," offers students more than 80 programs in more than 45 countries around the world, and almost 40 percent of all UD students take part.

GENERAL INFO

Activities: Choral groups, concert band, dance, drama/theater, jazz band, literary magazine, marching band, music ensembles, musical theater, opera, pep band, radio station, student government, student newspaper, student-run film society, symphony orchestra, television station, campus ministries, international student organization. **Organizations:** 250 registered organizations, 23 honor societies, 24 religious organizations. 22 fraternities, 15 sororities. **Athletics (Intercollegiate):** *Men:* Baseball, basketball, cross-country, diving, football, golf, lacrosse, soccer, swimming, tennis, track/field (outdoor). *Women:* Basketball, crew/rowing, cross-country, diving, field hockey, lacrosse, soccer, softball, swimming, tennis, track/field (outdoor), track/field (indoor), volleyball.

THE BOTTOM LINE

The cost of attending the University of Delaware is comparatively cheap, especially if you're from Delaware. Annual tuition and fees hover around $11,000, while campus room and board will run you another $10,000. Out-of-state undergraduates pay almost $25,000 more in tuition. As part of its UD Commitment, the university works to make a UD education affordable to all qualified state residents, and has pledged to meet their full demonstrated financial need (up to the cost of in-state tuition and fees). Over half of freshmen are recipients of financial aid packages averaging almost $14,000 per enrollee. The average amount of loan debt upon graduation is a relatively low $17,000.

SELECTIVITY

Admissions Rating	**91**
# of applicants	24,744
% of applicants accepted	57
% of acceptees attending	30
% accepting a place on wait list	669
% admitted from wait list	29

FRESHMAN PROFILE

Range SAT Critical Reading	**520–630**
Range SAT Math	**540–650**
Range SAT Writing	**520–640**
Range ACT Composite	**24–28**
Average HS GPA	**3.50**
% graduated top 10% of class	**37**
% graduated top 25% of class	**74**
% graduated top 50% of class	**96**

DEADLINES

Regular Deadline	**1/15**
Normal registration	**yes**

FACILITIES

Housing: Coed dorms, special housing for disabled students, women's dorms, fraternity/sorority housing, apartments for married students, apartments for single students, theme housing, special interest housing. *Special Academic Facilities/Equipment:* Lammont du Pont Laboratory, Biotechnology Center, Fischer Greenhouse 35-acre Woodlot harboring numerous wild species of animals and birds, 28 micro-computing sites, 6-acre Morris Library.

FINANCIAL FACTS

Financial Aid Rating	**80**
Annual in-state tuition	$9,670
Annual out-of-state tuition	$25,940
Room and Board	$10,470
Required Fees	$1,522
Books and supplies	$800
% frosh rec. need-based scholarship or grant aid	36
% UG rec. need-based scholarship or grant aid	39
% frosh rec. non-need-based scholarship or grant aid	22
% UG rec. non-need-based scholarship or grant aid	16
% frosh rec. need-based self-help aid	39
% UG rec. need-based self-help aid	48
% frosh rec. any financial aid	57
% UG rec. any financial aid	55
% UG borrow to pay for school	44
Average cumulative indebtedness	$17,200

University of Houston

P.O. Box 160111, Orlando, FL 32816-0111 • Admissions: 407-823-3000 • Financial Aid: 407-823-2827

CAMPUS LIFE

Quality of life Rating	75
Fire Safety Rating	88
Green rating	87
Type of School	Public
Environment	Metropolis

STUDENTS

Total undergrad enrollment	29,378
% Male to Female	50/50
% From out of state	1
% From public high school	92
% Live on Campus	15
# of Fraternities	29
# of Sororities	19
% African American	14
% Asian	21
% Caucasian	31
% Hispanic	23
% International	4
# Of Countries Represented	127

ACADEMICS

Academic Rating	67
% Of students graduating within 4 years	15
% Of students graduating within 6 years	46
Calendar	semester
Profs interesting rating	73
Profs accessible rating	70
Most common reg class size	20–29 students
Most common lab size	20–29 students

MOST POPULAR MAJORS

Biology, business adminstration and manadement, psychology

HONOR PROGRAMS

The Honors College at the University of Houston.

SPECIAL STUDY OPTIONS

Accelerated program, cooperative education program, cross-registration, distance learning, double major, dual enrollment, exchange student program (domestic), honors program, independent study, internships, study abroad, teacher certification program, weekend college, Academic Enrichment programs, certification programs, affiliated studies, and continuing education.

ABOUT THE SCHOOL

Situated in the heart of the 4th largest city in the United States, The University of Houston is a growing, up-and-coming research university located in an urban setting. The school is one of the most ethnically diverse colleges in the country, having "a thriving multicultural mix" within one of the nation's most international cities also known as "the energy capital of the world." One undergraduate here loves the fact that "you meet people from different social/economic backgrounds every day and it's humbling and amazing!" Students communicate, share ideas, and build relationships with people from all over the world, enabling "political discussion and religious awareness to flow freely throughout the university." Despite the metropolitan environment, there is still a close-knit feel to the campus. With a great balance of residents and commuters, Houston is also non-traditional, "so you'll meet lots of people who are coming back to school after serving our country, having kids, or trying a few classes at a community college first." The location also makes it convenient for students who wish to work while attending, and Houston tries hard to accommodate them by providing evening, distance learning, internet, and Saturday classes. Enthused one satisfied beneficiary of these services, "commuters can still have school spirit!"

BANG FOR YOUR BUCK

Students tell us that the school's financial aid packages are "considerably higher than other institutions," and are instrumental in "helping bright kids from low-middle income households build an optimistic future." Also, "tuition rates are quite low compared to its competitors." These and other accolades from students (and parents!) are quite common. "Such a great value." "Amazingly affordable." "A quality education that will be long lasting and nationally recognized." Described as "amazing," "generous," and "substantial" by students, there are an abundance of scholarships available at Houston. "I got an all-expenses paid scholarship for being a National Merit Scholar!" The TierOne Scholarship program offers a distinguished, high-profile award intended to attract highly qualified students. Awarded to first-time-in-college freshmen, they cover tuition and mandatory fees for up to five years of undergraduate study. Selection is based on merit and consideration of a students need for financial assistance.

TierOne Scholars also receive stipends for undergraduate research and for study-abroad programs. Also highly respected is the

STUDENTS

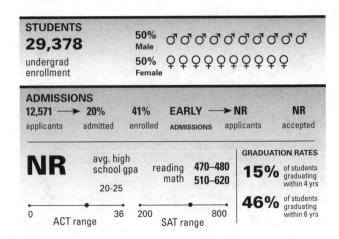

29,378 undergrad enrollment

50% Male ♂♂♂♂♂♂♂♂♂♂

50% Female ♀♀♀♀♀♀♀♀♀♀

ADMISSIONS

12,571 →	20%	41%	EARLY →	NR	NR
applicants	admitted	enrolled	ADMISSIONS	applicants	accepted

NR avg. high school gpa

ACT range: 0 — 36; 20-25

SAT range: 200 — 800; reading 470–480; math 510–620

GRADUATION RATES

15% of students graduating within 4 yrs

46% of students graduating within 6 yrs

University of Houston

E-MAIL: ADMISSION@MAIL.UCF.EDU • FAX: 407-823-5625 • WEBSITE: WWW.UCF.EDU

STUDENT BODY

This is one heckuva "multicultural campus," with "all ages, races, religions, and...varying languages." This diversity is a beloved aspect of the school, and "Everyone, no matter who they are or where they're from, seems to fit in." "You meet so many different people with different cultures, which helps you grow and expand your world views," adds a student. Texas being Texas, this "loud and friendly" group goes about it their own way: "It's easy to fit in. You just start talking to someone." Still, common threads do run throughout, and the "majority of the students are commuters," with many holding down full-time jobs and families. People most often fit in immediately with their similar races and social groups, but "Over time, almost everyone breaks through that initial shell."
and "Most networking and meeting people is done through clubs

WHY STUDENTS LOVE UNIVERSITY OF HOUSTON

"Enthusiasm, optimism, and determination" contribute to the academic, social, and cultural atmosphere at Houston. Known as "a hidden treasure" with "southern charm" by the student body, the President and the Deans of the colleges all care immensely about their students. The school motto is "You are the Pride," and "Pride is at the forefront of everything cougars do!" Participation in extra-curricular activities and organizations is rampant, with more than 400 clubs, fraternities, sororities and leadership programs. The first-class M.D. Anderson library with 24-hour access is impressive, and the campus is constantly looking to improve its facilities.

Why Students love University of Houston

> "Walking around campus you see a little bit of every culture, every race, and every ethnicity."

GENERAL INFO

Activities: Choral groups, concert band, dance, drama/theater, jazz band, literary magazine, marching band, music ensembles, musical theater, opera, pep band, radio station, student government, student newspaper, student-run film society, symphony orchestra, television station, yearbook, campus ministries, international student organization. **Organizations:** 518 registered organizations, 25 honor societies, 39 religious organizations. 23 social fraternities, 20 social sororities. **Athletics (Intercollegiate):** *Men:* Baseball, basketball, cross-country, football, golf, track/field (outdoor), track/field (indoor). *Women:* Basketball, cross-country, diving, soccer, softball, swimming, tennis, track/field (outdoor), track/field (indoor), volleyball. **On Campus Highlights:** University Center, Campus Recreation and Wellness Center, University Center Satellite, Blaffer Gallery, Campus Activities.

BOTTOM LINE

In-state tuition is around $6,500 per year; for out-of-state students, the cost is just over $15,000. Room and board will come to $8,300; required fees, $2,700; books and supplies, $1,100. More than 40 percent of students borrow in some way to pay for school, and can envision a cumulative indebtedness once graduating from the institution of more than $17,000. Clemson students are especially thrilled by the incredible support the university offers. "The value is unbeatable."

SELECTIVITY

Admissions Rating	**72**
# of applicants	12,571
% of applicants accepted	70
% of acceptees attending	41

FRESHMAN PROFILE

Range SAT Critical Reading	**470–580**
Range SAT Math	**510–620**
Range ACT Composite	**20–25**
% graduated top 10% of class	**27**
% graduated top 25% of class	**59**
% graduated top 50% of class	**86**

DEADLINES

Regular Deadline	**12/1**
Normal registration	**yes**

FACILITIES

Housing: Coed dorms, special housing for disabled students, fraternity/soror ity housing, apartments for married students, apartments for single students, special housing for honors students, upper level and graduate students. Calhoun Loft, Cambridge Oaks and Cullen Apartment. *Special Academic Facilities/Equipment:* Art gallery, language lab, human development lab school, University Hilton (staffed in part by students in Coll. of Hotel and Restaurant Management), opera studio. *Computers:* 100% of classrooms, 25% of dorms, 100% of libraries, 25% of dining areas, 100% of student union, 25% of common outdoor areas have wireless network access.

FINANCIAL FACTS

Financial Aid Rating	**79**
Annual in-state tuition	$6,466
Annual out-of-state tutition	$15,856
Room and Board	$8,318
Required Fees	$2,745
Books and supplies	$1,100
% frosh rec. need-based scholarship or grant aid	57
% UG rec.need-based scholarship or grant aid	51
% frosh rec. non-need-based scholarship or grant aid	3
% UG rec. non-need-based scholarship or grant aid	1
% frosh rec. need-based self-help aid	44
% UG rec. need-based self-help aid	49
% frosh rec. any financial aid	85
% UG rec. any financial aid	68
% UG borrow to pay for school	44
Average cumulative indebtedness	$14,922

University of Illinois at Urbana Champaign

901 West Illinois Street, Urbana, IL 61801 • Admissions: 217-333-0302 • Fax: 217-244-0903

CAMPUS LIFE

Quality of life Rating	79
Fire Safety Rating	66
Green rating	95
Type of School	Public
Environment	City

STUDENTS

Total undergrad enrolllment	31,540
% Male to Female	53/47
% From public high school	75
% Live on Campus	50
# of Fraternities	60
# of Sororities	36
% African American	5
% Asian	11
% Caucasian	68
% Hispanic	6
% International	17
# Of Countries Represented	123

ACADEMICS

Academic Rating	66
% Of students graduating within 4 years	65
% Of students graduating within 6 years	84
Calendar	semester
Profs interesting rating	63
Profs accessible rating	68
Most common reg class size	20–29 students
Most common lab size	20–29 students

MOST POPULAR MAJORS

Engineering, business, communication, psychology

HONORS PROGRAMS

Campus Honors Program, James Scholars Program. Combined degree programs: BA/MEng, MD/Ph.D.

SPECIAL STUDY OPTIONS

Accelerated program, cooperative education program, cross-registration, distance learning, double major, dual enrollment.

ABOUT THE SCHOOL

In many ways, the flagship campus of the University of Illinois at Urbana-Champaign is the prototypical large, state-funded research university. It's hard to get admitted, but not too hard, however, it does stand apart. The admissions office reviews every candidate individually, which is rare. The library is stellar, and the amazing research resources are practically endless. With 17 colleges and about 150 undergraduate programs to offer, students have a wide-range of options, but even the best professors aren't going to hold your hand, and lower-level class sizes are mostly lectures filled with students. Despite this, many students agree that the professors are incredibly passionate and intelligent. Incredibly, nearly all faculty have PhDs. The engineering and business schools are the most prestigious and, therefore, offer the most competition. Agriculture, architecture, and psychology are also quite well-respected.

University of Illinois is a magnet for engineering and sciences research. The research resources are amazing," one pleased undergrad enthuses. Another student relates that "the library has almost any resource an undergraduate or even an advanced researcher would ever need." The university has been a leader in computer-based education and hosted the PLATO project, which was a precursor to the internet and resulted in the development of the plasma display. That legacy of leading computer-based education and research continues today–Microsoft hires more graduates from the University of Illinois than from any other university in the world. The University of Illinois media organization (the Illini Media Co.) is also quite extensive featuring a student newspaper that isn't censored by the administration since it receives no direct funding from it.

BANG FOR YOUR BUCK

The University of Illinois provides an incredibly wide array of undergraduate programs at a great price. A large percentage of the student population receives some form of financial assistance. The usual set of work-study, loans, and need-based grants is available, of course, along with a bounty of private and institutional scholarships. The school confers more than 1,500 individual merit-based scholarships each year. These awards vary considerably in value, and they are available to students who excel in academics, art, athletics, drama, leadership, music, and pretty much anything else. Alumni scholarships are available, too, if someone in your family is a graduate of U of I. There's an online scholarship database at Illinois's website that is definitely worth perusing. Application procedures vary, and so do the deadline dates.

STUDENTS

31,540 undergrad enrollment

53% Male ♂♂♂♂♂♂♂♂♂♂♂

47% Female ♀♀♀♀♀♀♀♀♀

ADMISSIONS

27,273 applicants → 67% admitted; 38% enrolled

EARLY ADMISSIONS → NR applicants; NR accepted

3.98 avg. high school gpa

30 – 34 ACT range (0–36)

reading 530–660
math 680–770
SAT range (200–800)

GRADUATION RATES

65% of students graduating within 4 yrs

84% of students graduating within 6 yrs

University of Illinois at Urbana Champaign

FINANCIAL AID: 217-333-0100 • E-MAIL: UGRADADMISSIONS@UIUC.EDU • WEBSITE: WWW.ILLINOIS.EDU

STUDENT BODY

The U of I has a decidedly Midwestern feel, and "Midwestern hospitality" is abundant. "Kids from out-of-state and small-town farm students" definitely have a presence, but, sometimes, it seems like "practically everyone is from the northwest suburbs of Chicago." There's a lot of ethnic diversity "visible on campus." On the whole, the majority of students are "very smart kids who like to party." "They really study fairly hard, and when you ask, it turns out that they're majoring in something like rocket science." "There is a niche for everyone."

WHY STUDENTS LOVE UNIVERSITY OF ILLINOIS AT URBANA-CHAMPAIGN

At the University of Illinois, there is "never a dull moment, despite the surrounding cornfields." Social life on this huge but easy-to-navigate campus is whatever you want it to be. "The typical student is involved and really good at balancing schoolwork, clubs and organizations, and a social life." "Anything that you are interested in, you can do," gloats an engineering major. "It's a huge campus, but it's not too spread out," says a Spanish major. "You can get around anywhere by bike or bus, and you don't need a car." Out-of-state students will find it easy to commute back and forth to campus: the University of Illinois is one of the few educational institutions to own an airport. "Overall, I am very pleased with my academic experience at UIUC."

Why Students love University of Illinois at Urbana-Champaign

"Anything that you are interested in, you can do."

GENERAL INFO

Activities: Choral groups, concert band, dance, drama/theater, jazz band, literary magazine, marching band, music ensembles, musical theater, opera, pep band, radio station, student government, student newspaper, student-run film society, symphony orchestra, television station, yearbook, campus ministries, international student organization. **Organizations:** 1000 registered organizations, 30 honor societies, 95 religious organizations. 60 fraternities, 36 sororities. **Athletics (Intercollegiate):** *Men:* Baseball, basketball, cheerleading, cross-country, football, golf, gymnastics, tennis, track/field (outdoor), wrestling. *Women:* Basketball, cheerleading, cross-country, diving, golf, gymnastics, soccer, softball, swimming, tennis, track/field (outdoor), volleyball. **On-Campus Highlights:** Campus Town restaurants and shops, Krannert Center for Performing Arts, Assembly Hall, Multiple Campus Recreation Centers, Illini Student Union, on-campus Arboretum; The Japan House; extensive athletic facilities; historic round barns; Siebel Computer Science Center; spacious green space at the Central and Bardeen Quads; Papa Dels Pizza and Za's Italian Cafe.

THE BOTTOM LINE

The University of Illinois requires all first-year undergraduate students (who do not commute) to stay on campus. The cost for a year of tuition, fees, room and board, and basic expenses averages about $20,000 for Illinois residents. For nonresidents, the average is about $33,000. The average student indebtedness upon graduation is $17,000. Around three-quarters of students are recipients of financial aid; the average is a very generous $13,000. Also, the average need-based gift aid comes to nearly $12,000.

SELECTIVITY

Admissions Rating	**85**
# of applicants	27,273
% of applicants accepted	67
% of acceptees attending	38
% accepting a place on wait list	192
% admitted from wait list	89

FRESHMAN PROFILE

Range SAT Critical Reading	**530–660**
Range SAT Math	**680–770**
% graduated top 10% of class	**56**
% graduated top 25% of class	**93**
% graduated top 50% of class	**99**

DEADLINES

Regular Deadline	**1/2**
Normal registration	**no**

FACILITIES

Housing: Coed dorms, special housing for disabled students, men's dorms, women's dorms, fraternity/sorority housing. *Special Academic Facilities/Equipment:* Art, cultural and natural history museums, performing arts center, National Center for Supercomputing Applications, Beckman Institute. *Computers:* 85% of classrooms, 100% of dorms, 100% of libraries, 100% of dining areas, 100% of student union, 1% of common outdoor areas have wireless network access.

FINANCIAL FACTS

Financial Aid Rating	**81**
Annual in-state tuition	$11,104
Annual out-of-state tuition	$25,246
Room and Board	$10,680
Required Fees	$3,310
Books and supplies	$1,200
% frosh rec. need-based scholarship or grant aid	38
% UG rec. need-based scholarship or grant aid	34
% frosh rec. non-need-based scholarship or grant aid	13
% UG rec. non-need-based scholarship or grant aid	12
% frosh rec. need-based self-help aid	39
% UG rec. need-based self-help aid	39
% frosh rec. any financial aid	54
% UG rec. any financial aid	56
% UG borrow to pay for school	57
Average cumulative indebtedness	$16,866

University of Kansas

OFFICE OF ADMISSIONS AND SCHOLARSHIPS, 1502 IOWA STREET, LAWRENCE, KS 66045-7576 • ADMISSIONS: 785-864-3911

CAMPUS LIFE

Quality of life Rating	96
Fire Safety Rating	82
Green rating	83
Type of School	Public
Environment	City

STUDENTS

Total undergrad enrolllment	19,983
% Male to Female	51/49
% From out of state	21
% Live on Campus	22
# of Fraternities	22
# of Sororities	13
% African American	3
% Asian	4
% Caucasian	79
% Hispanic	5
% Native American	1
% International	5
# Of Countries Represented	112

ACADEMICS

Academic Rating	70
% Of students graduating within 4 years	32
% Of students graduating within 6 years	61
Calendar	semester
Profs interesting rating	81
Profs accessible rating	83
Most common reg class size	20–29 students
Most common lab size	10–19 students

MOST POPULAR MAJORS

Business/commerce, biology, psychology

HONORS PROGRAMS

The University Honors Program

SPECIAL STUDY OPTIONS

Accelerated program, cooperative education program, distance learning, double major, dual enrollment, honors program, independent study, internships, liberal arts/career combination. Off Campus Study: Washington D.C. semester, study abroad in more than 60 countries.

ABOUT THE SCHOOL

A large research university set in our nation's heartland, University of Kansas still manages to foster "a sense of community" for its students. Indeed, despite its size, KU offers "plenty of opportunities for students to connect with each other and with faculty." Importantly, the academics here are top-notch. From biology and engineering to art and architecture, undergrads can study whatever they fancy. Practical experience is coupled with classroom learning, allowing students to sharpen their skill-sets. For example, business students have the opportunity to help manage a fund valued at $1 million and architecture students design and build environmentally friendly houses. Additionally, service learning is large component of the university ethos with KU undergrads logging roughly 15,000 volunteer hours over the last year. Finally, students and faculty alike are quick to taut the challenging Honors Program, an "unbelievable resource" that offers "fabulous classes." KU's bustling campus also offers a good deal outside of academics. An active student body, undergrads can partake in more than 600 student-run clubs and organizations. From marching band to international celebrations, students are never at a loss for things to do. Greek life is fairly popular at Kansas and fraternity and sorority parties often form the crux of weekend social activities. Of course, the "fantastic" Division I athletics also bring the campus together and students pack the stands for basketball and football games. When undergrads are itching to escape for a bit, hometown Lawrence provides some great restaurants, cafés and bars. For those looking to get a little further away, Kansas City, Topeka, Wichita and Omaha are all within reach.

BANG FOR YOUR BUCK

KU is definitely a leader when it comes to providing an affordable undergraduate education. Impressively, the university offers a four-year, fixed tuition rate meaning your tuition will never increase during your tenure. Additionally, KU proudly trumpets renewable four-year merit scholarships. These aid packages can range anywhere from $4,000 to $40,000. And, of course, undergraduates might also be eligible for state, federal or institutional scholarships and grants as well as private scholarships. When combined, these options total $62 million devoted to aid each year. With all of these sources, it's no wonder that more than half of KU's students graduate debt-free! KU doesn't simply stop with an affordable price tag. The university also strives to ensure that its students are financially savvy. To that end, the school offers Student Money Management Services. Providing one-on-one sessions, class presentations and outreach, the program helps students learn how to better manage money, create a budget and reduce debt.

STUDENTS

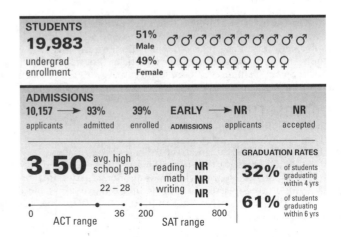

19,983 undergrad enrollment

51% Male ♂♂♂♂♂♂♂♂♂♂

49% Female ♀♀♀♀♀♀♀♀♀♀

ADMISSIONS

10,157 →	93%	39%	EARLY →	NR	NR
applicants	admitted	enrolled	ADMISSIONS	applicants	accepted

3.50 avg. high school gpa

22 – 28
ACT range 0–36

reading NR
math NR
writing NR
SAT range 200–800

GRADUATION RATES

32% of students graduating within 4 yrs

61% of students graduating within 6 yrs

University of Kansas

FAX: 785-864-5017 • FINANCIAL AID: 785-864-4700 • E-MAIL: ADM@KU.EDU • WEBSITE: WWW.KU.EDU

STUDENT BODY

The typical KU student "would be from one of the big suburbs in Kansas such as Overland Park, Topeka, or Wichita," but "because the university is so big with many different colleges, there is a place for everyone." On this campus you'll find everything "from international students from across the globe to white Republicans to gays and lesbians." The student body divides into "two distinct categories: the Greeks and everyone else. There is no animosity between the two groups but they don't intermingle very much." They are also divided by their devotion to academics. As one student explains, "There are those who come to KU, take large lecture classes (which they sleep through), party on the weekend, and catch every basketball game. Then there are those who have three separate majors, two internships, four jobs, and no sleep. The rest of us fall somewhere between those two extremes."

Why Students love University of Kansas

"The KU campus and surrounding area is a unique microcosm of existence where no personality ceases to fit in."

WHY STUDENTS LOVE UNIVERSITY OF KANSAS

Bursting with school pride, students here are quick to proclaim themselves "loyal Jayhawks." Undergrads truly appreciate that KU manages to provide an "unbelievable education" along with the "quintessential college sports and party scene." Students are quick to laud the university's "diverse and challenging" course offerings and highlight their "dedicated professors [who] are very willing to work with students." Beyond academics, undergrads can't speak highly enough about their peers. As one ecstatic mechanical engineering gushes, "The KU campus and surrounding area is a unique microcosm of existence where no personality ceases to fit in; hippies, nerds, partiers, music junkies, sports fanatics, and a little mix of everything else; yep, we got it all.

GENERAL INFO

Activities: Choral groups, concert band, dance, drama/theater, jazz band, literary magazine, marching band, music ensembles, musical theater, opera, pep band, radio station, student government, student newspaper, symphony orchestra, television station, international student organization. **Organizations:** 476 registered organizations, 14 honor societies, 39 religious organizations. 27 fraternities, 16 sororities. **Athletics (Intercollegiate):** *Men:* Baseball, basketball, cross-country, football, golf, track/field (outdoor), track/field (indoor). *Women:* Basketball, crew/rowing, cross-country, diving, golf, soccer, softball, swimming, tennis, track/field (outdoor), track/field (indoor), volleyball. **On-Campus Highlights:** Spencer Museum of Art, Kansas Union and Bookstore, Natural History Museum, Athletic Hall of Fame, Robert J. Dole Institute of Politics, beautiful campus to walk around.

BOTTOM LINE

Kansas' tuition fees run almost $8,300 for in-state students. Out-of-state students face a slightly heftier bill of $21,750. Further, room and board will run you $7,000 with required fees and books and supplies costing $858 and $850 respectively. However, it is important to note that the KU Pell advantage program will cover tuition and fees for Kansas residents who qualify. The program extends through four years. Further, KU is a partner in the Midwest Exchange.

SELECTIVITY

Admissions Rating	**79**
# of applicants	10,157
% of applicants accepted	93
% of acceptees attending	39

FRESHMAN PROFILE

Range ACT Composite	**22–28**
Average HS GPA	**3.50**
% graduated top 10% of class	**2**
% graduated top 25% of class	**55**
% graduated top 50% of class	**89**

DEADLINES

Regular Deadline	**4/1**
Normal registration	**yes**

FACILITIES

Housing: Coed dorms, women's dorms, fraternity/sorority housing, apartments for married students, cooperative housing, apartments for single students *Special Academic Facilities/Equipment:* 12 libraries (including art and architecture, engineering, law, medical, music and dance, rare research materials.

FINANCIAL FACTS

Financial Aid Rating	**75**
Annual in-state tuition	$8,364
Annual out-of-state tuition	$21,750
Room and Board	$7,080
Required Fees	$858
Books and supplies	$850
% frosh rec. need-based scholarship or grant aid	31
% UG rec.need-based scholarship or grant aid	30
% frosh rec. non-need-based scholarship or grant aid	19
% UG rec. non-need-based scholarship or grant aid	12
% frosh rec. need-based self-help aid	38
% UG rec. need-based self-help aid	35
% frosh rec. any financial aid	65
% UG rec. any financial aid	66
% UG borrow to pay for school	48
Average cumulative indebtedness	$23,319

University of Mary Washington

1301 College Avenue, Fredericksburg, VA 22401 • Admissions: 540-654-2000 • Fax: 540-654-1857

CAMPUS LIFE

Quality of life Rating	77
Fire Safety Rating	86
Green rating	78
Type of School	Public
Environment	City

STUDENTS

Total undergrad enrolllment	4,271
% Male to Female	36/64
% From out of state	20
% From public high school	78
% Live on Campus	57
% African American	5
% Asian	5
% Caucasian	58
% Hispanic	4
# Of Countries Represented	23

ACADEMICS

Academic Rating	74
% Of students graduating within 4 years	65
% Of students graduating within 6 years	72
Calendar	semester
Profs interesting rating	90
Profs accessible rating	75
Most common reg class size	20–29 students
Most common lab size	20–29 students

MOST POPULAR MAJORS

Business administration and management,
English language and literature

SPECIAL STUDY OPTIONS

Accelerated program, distance learning, double major, independent study, internships, student-designed major, study abroad, teacher certification program.

ABOUT THE SCHOOL

Boasting a student population that hovers around 5,000, University of Mary Washington is a modest sized university that manages to offer a private school education at state school prices. With a school of education, business and arts and sciences, UMW maintains a rigorous and diverse academic catalogue. Top departments include a leading program in historic preservation, political science and international affairs, biology, economics and a stellar concentration in creative writing. The English, environmental science and visual arts programs are also highly lauded along with UMW's top-ranked debate team. Additionally, opportunities abound for both undergraduate research and service learning. Outside of the classroom, students are involved in more than 100 clubs and organizations as well as multiple DIII championship teams. Further, both students and the university at large love to take advantage of UMW's location, smack in between Richmond and Washington D.C. The cities serve as a fantastic resource for recreational, educational and professional opportunities. Many undergrads are quick to advantage of cultural offerings and head off to explore the museums, national monuments and restaurants Richmond and DC provide. And perhaps more importantly, UMW students and grads alike frequently land internships and jobs in both cities.

BANG FOR YOUR BUCK

The University of Mary Washington provides students with a number of options to help off-set the costs of their education. Through the Office of Financial Aid, undergrads are privy to a comprehensive program of loans, grants, scholarships and work-study opportunities. This funding comes from a variety of state, federal and private resources. UMW also maintains their own institutional merit scholarships. For example, each year they award the Washington Scholarship to eight in-state students with stellar academic credentials. This scholarship covers the full cost of tuition. Not to be left the behind, the Alvey Scholarship is awarded to two out-of-state academic all-stars. Further, the UMW Friends of the Orchestra offers a full-tuition scholarship every academic year to a freshman who participates in the UMW Philharmonic Orchestra. Of course, there are plenty of merit-based scholarships available to the broader student population as well. Indeed, the school doles out a handful of renewable awards in amounts of up to $5,000 annually. Finally, in total, UMW administers more than $26 million in financial assistance, including education loans totaling $19 million.

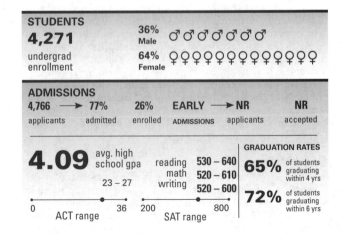

STUDENTS

4,271 undergrad enrollment

36% Male ♂♂♂♂♂♂♂

64% Female ♀♀♀♀♀♀♀♀♀♀♀♀♀

ADMISSIONS

4,766 applicants	→ 77% admitted	26% enrolled	EARLY ADMISSIONS	→ NR applicants	NR accepted

4.09 avg. high school gpa

ACT range (0–36): 23 – 27

SAT range (200–800):

reading	530 – 640
math	520 – 610
writing	520 – 600

GRADUATION RATES

65% of students graduating within 4 yrs

72% of students graduating within 6 yrs

University of Mary Washington

Financial Aid: 540-654-2468 • E-mail: admit@umw.edu • Website: www.umw.edu

STUDENT BODY

UMW students describe their fellow classmates as "typically bright, fairly hardworking but easygoing for the most part," and say, "Most students fit in very well." An anthropology major says, "There are prepsters with pearls and Ralph Lauren, athletes sporting sweats, punks with gauges and flannel, and everyone in between." However, one student notes, "We have lots of diversity in terms of religious background, sexual orientation, and the gender ratio, but the school needs to work on becoming more racially balanced." "As with anywhere, groups tend to form," but students say, "There isn't a feeling of exclusivity," and they assert that "students have a lot of opportunity to connect...through the mandatory two years they need to live on campus." A common freshman complaint is that "there is nothing to do on the weekends," but upperclassmen insist that "below the surface, Mary Wash is a hotspot of activity" and rave about programs like "Cheap Seats," which sponsors dollar movies on campus.

Why Students love U of Mary Washington

"The atmosphere is incredibly friendly."

WHY STUDENTS LOVE U OF MARY WASHINGTON

Undergrads here really appreciate their time at Mary Washington and are quick to highlight the strong "sense of community among the student body and the university [as a whole]." As a content anthropology major points out, "The population size and the layout of the campus make it impossible to not bump into someone you know. The atmosphere is incredibly friendly." Notably, students are also full of praise for the "excellent" faculty. As one biology major brags, "Professors are awesome. They're always available to help and are always friendly! I still have professors from three years ago that still say hi to me on campus. I've loved all my classes at Mary Washington." Outside of academics, undergrads love the campus which is "beautiful during every season of the year." Further, they enjoy the fact that "there is always something to do socially [or an event being sponsored by] various organizations."

GENERAL INFO

Activities: Choral groups, concert band, dance, drama/theater, jazz band, literary magazine, music ensembles, musical theater, opera, radio station, student government, student newspaper, student-run film society, symphony orchestra, yearbook, campus ministries, international student organization. **Organizations**: 120 registered organizations, 23 honor societies, 10 religious organizations. **Athletics (Intercollegiate):** *Men:* Baseball, basketball, crew/rowing, cross-country, equestrian sports, lacrosse, soccer, swimming, tennis, track/field (outdoor), track/field (indoor). *Women:* Basketball, crew/rowing, cross-country, equestrian sports, field hockey, lacrosse, soccer, softball, swimming, tennis, track/field (outdoor), track/field (indoor), volleyball. **On-Campus Highlights:** Woodard Campus Center, Battleground Athletic facilities/Fitness Center, Palmieri Plaza Fountain, Ball Circle, Lee Hall.

BOTTOM LINE

A public institution, University of Mary Washington boasts a modest $4,460 price tag for in-state students. Of course, out-of-state undergrads will have to dig a little deeper into their pockets to foot their $16,190 tuition bill. Additionally, room and board will run you roughly $9,800. The university also charges another $4,340 for various required fees. Finally, they recommend you set aside an additional $1,000 for books and supplies.

SELECTIVITY

Admissions Rating	**76**
# of applicants	4,766
% of applicants accepted	77
% of acceptees attending	26
# accepting a place on wait list	165
% admitted from wait list	50

FRESHMAN PROFILE

Range SAT Critical Reading	**530–640**
Range SAT Math	**520–610**
Range SAT Writing	**520–620**
Range ACT Composite	**23–27**
Average HS GPA	**3.58**

DEADLINES

Regular Deadline	**2/1**
Normal registration	**yes**

FACILITIES

Housing: Coed dorms, special housing for disabled students, men's dorms, special housing for international students, women's dorms, apartments for single students, wellness housing, theme housing, substance-free. *Special Academic Facilities/Equipment:* Two art galleries, Center for Historic Preservation, language labs, Leidecker Center for Asian Studies, cartography lab, greenhouse. *Computers:* 100% of classrooms, 100% of dorms, 100% of libraries, 100% of dining areas, 100% of student union, 5% of common outdoor areas have wireless network access.

FINANCIAL FACTS

Financial Aid Rating	**67**
Annual in-state tuition	$4,462
Annual out-of-state tuition	$16,190
Room and Board	$9,840
Required Fees	$9,344
Books and supplies	$1,000
% frosh rec. need-based scholarship or grant aid	18
% UG rec.need-based scholarship or grant aid	15
% frosh rec. non-need-based scholarship or grant aid	17
% UG rec. non-need-based scholarship or grant aid	9
% frosh rec. need-based self-help aid	23
% UG rec. need-based self-help aid	18
% frosh rec. any financial aid	56
% UG rec. any financial aid	58
% UG borrow to pay for school	44
Average cumulative indebtedness	$15,630

University of Maryland–College Park

MITCHELL BUILDING, COLLEGE PARK, MD 20742-5235 • ADMISSIONS: 301-314-8385 • FAX: 301-314-9693

CAMPUS LIFE

Quality of life Rating	65
Fire Safety Rating	79
Green rating	97
Type of School	Public
Environment	Metropolis

STUDENTS

Total undergrad enrollment	26,194
% Male to Female	53/47
% From out of state	23
% Live on Campus	42
# of Fraternities	36
# of Sororities	27
% African American	12
% Asian	15
% Caucasian	58
% Hispanic	7
% International	2
# Of Countries Represented	128

ACADEMICS

Academic Rating	77
% Of students graduating within 4 years	62
% Of students graduating within 6 years	81
Calendar	semester
Profs interesting rating	71
Profs accessible rating	67
Most common reg class size	20–29 students
Most common lab size	20–29 students

MOST POPULAR MAJORS

Criminology, economics, psychology

HONORS PROGRAMS

Gemstones, Honors, Honors Humanities.

SPECIAL STUDY OPTIONS

Accelerated program, cooperative education program, cross-registration, distance learning, double major, dual enrollment, external degree program, honors program, internships, liberal arts/career combination, student-designed major, study abroad, teacher certification program, Living-Learning programs including Gemstone Program, Jiminez-Porter Writers House, Civicus, College Park Scholars, and others.

ABOUT THE SCHOOL

The University of Maryland–College Park is a big school. There are many different people from various backgrounds, as well as numerous student organizations on-campus. Some incoming freshman might find this intimidating, but thanks to the university's system of living and learning communities, which allows students with similar academic interests to live in the same residential community, take specialized courses, and perform research; this campus of almost 27,000 can feel a lot smaller and more intimate than it actually is. UMD offers a "top-notch honors program" for academically talented students, which offers special access and opportunities with a community of intellectually-gifted peers. More than 100 undergraduate degrees are on offer here, and the university's location near Washington, D.C. means that top-notch research and internship opportunities are literally in your backyard. The university recently received funding from the Department of Homeland Security to create a new research center to study the behavioral and social foundations of terrorism. It's no surprise then that UMD's political science program is strong. A well-respected business program, top-ranked criminology program, and solid engineering school are also available. The school is also extremely invested in promoting sustainability across the University curriculum, and developing a sustainability ethic in campus culture.

BANG FOR YOUR BUCK

University of Maryland–College Park offers a comprehensive aid program for students who demonstrate financial need. But it's the university's full suite of merit-based scholarships that make a UMD degree an exceptional value. Highlights include the Banneker/Key Scholarship, the university's most prestigious merit scholarship, which may cover up to the full the cost of tuition, mandatory fees, room and board, and a book allowance each year for four years. The President's Scholarship provides four-year awards of up to $12,000 per year for four years to exceptional entering freshmen. Maryland Pathways is a new financial assistance program set up by the university to assist low-income families by reducing the debt component and increasing grants to those who receive it. National Merit, creative and performing arts, and departmental scholarships are also available. To be considered for most merit scholarships, entering freshmen applying for the fall semester must submit their complete application for undergraduate admission by the priority deadline of November 1. The eligibility requirements for each scholarship vary. Award notifications begin in early March.

STUDENTS

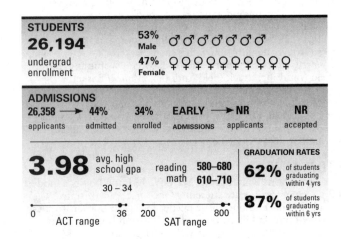

26,194 undergrad enrollment

53% Male ♂♂♂♂♂♂♂

47% Female ♀♀♀♀♀♀♀♀♀♀

ADMISSIONS

26,358 applicants → 44% admitted — 34% enrolled

EARLY ADMISSIONS → NR applicants — NR accepted

3.98 avg. high school gpa

ACT range (0–36): 30 – 34

SAT range (200–800): reading 580–680, math 610–710

GRADUATION RATES

62% of students graduating within 4 yrs

87% of students graduating within 6 yrs

University of Maryland–College Park

FINANCIAL AID: 301-314-9000 • E-MAIL: UM-ADMIT@UGA.UMD.EDU • WEBSITE: WWW.MARYLAND.EDU

STUDENT BODY

"The University of Maryland is a very large school," so "there is no 'typical' student here. Everyone will find that they can fit in somewhere." UMD is "an especially diverse school," and this makes people "more tolerant and accepting of people from different backgrounds and cultures." A student from New Jersey explains it this way: "Coming from a very diverse area, I thought it was going to be hard to find a school that had that same representation of minority and atypical students until I found Maryland. I don't think I have ever learned so much about different religions, cultures, orientations, or lifestyles. All of them are accepted and even celebrated" at UMD.

Why Students love University of Maryland–College Park

"UMD provides a great environment for students to meet people they would normally not know and helps to provide great connections with these people."

WHY STUDENTS LOVE UNIVERSITY OF MARYLAND–COLLEGE PARK

Hometown College Park offers a great setting for college students, with its 1250-acre campus, and a slew of fun activities are routinely available both on and off campus. The student union has an arcade and a bowling alley, in addition to the typical free movie nights. Also, there's a "new campus recreation center that has virtually everything you could wish for." UMD's Frat Row is a favorite destination for students looking to unwind, while those looking for more laid-back fun simply head to the quad to toss around a Frisbee or two. School spirit is really in the air when UMD basketball is in season.

GENERAL INFO

Activities: Choral groups, concert band, dance, drama/theater, jazz band, literary magazine, marching band, music ensembles, musical theater, opera, pep band, radio station, student government. **Organizations:** 574 registered organizations, 53 honor societies, 55 religious organizations. 36 fraternities, 27 sororities. **Athletics (Intercollegiate):** *Men:* Baseball, basketball, cross-country, football, golf, lacrosse, soccer, swimming, tennis, track/field (outdoor), track/field (indoor), wrestling. *Women:* Basketball, cheerleading, cross-country, field hockey, golf, gymnastics, lacrosse, soccer, softball, swimming, tennis, track/field (outdoor), track/field (indoor), volleyball, water polo.

THE BOTTOM LINE

College costs may be on the upswing, but the cost of an education at the University of Maryland–College Park is still a very good deal. Tuition and fees for Maryland residents is just $8,400 drawing in many from around the area; though nonresidents can expect to pay three times as much. All students who decide to live on campus can expect to pay an additional $9,000-plus in room and board. When you factor in the cost of books and supplies, transportation, and incidentals, the total cost of a UMD degree is $22,000 for all those who hail from the state, and $38,000 for those who don't.

SELECTIVITY

Admissions Rating	**95**
# of applicants	26,358
% of applicants accepted	44
% of acceptees attending	34

FRESHMAN PROFILE

Range SAT Critical Reading	**580–680**
Range SAT Math	**610–710**
Average HS GPA	**3.98**
% graduated top 10% of class	**71**
% graduated top 25% of class	**91**
% graduated top 50% of class	**100**

DEADLINES

Regular Deadline	**1/20**
Normal registration	**yes**

FACILITIES

Housing: Coed dorms, special housing for disabled students, special housing for international students, women's dorms, fraternity/sorority housing, cooperative housing, apartments for single students, wellness housing, theme housing. *Special Academic Facilities/Equipment:* Aerospace buoyancy lab, art gallery, international piano archives, center for architectural design and research, model nuclear reactor, wind tunnel. *Computers:* 100% of classrooms, 100% of dorms, 100% of libraries, 100% of dining areas, 100% of student union, 100% of common outdoor areas have wireless network access.

FINANCIAL FACTS

Financial Aid Rating	**65**
Annual in-state tuition	$6,966
Annual out-of-state tuition	$24,337
Room and Board	$9,742
Required Fees	$1,689
Books and supplies	$1,076
% frosh rec. need-based scholarship or grant aid	21
% UG rec. need-based scholarship or grant aid	26
% frosh rec. non-need-based scholarship or grant aid	23
% UG rec. non-need-based scholarship or grant aid	16
% frosh rec. need-based self-help aid	24
% UG rec. need-based self-help aid	27
% frosh rec. any financial aid	72
% UG rec. any financial aid	63
% UG borrow to pay for school	43
Average cumulative indebtedness	$22,696

University of Massachusetts Boston

100 Morrissey Boulevard, Boston, MA 02125-3393 • Admissions: 617-287-6000 • Fax: 617-287-5999

CAMPUS LIFE

Quality of life Rating	68
Fire Safety Rating	60*
Green rating	93
Type of School	Public
Environment	Metropolis

STUDENTS

Total undergrad enrollment	11,568
% Male to Female	44/56
% From out of state	5
# of Fraternities	0
# of Sororities	0
% African American	15
% Asian	12
% Caucasian	45
% Hispanic	8
% International	3
# Of Countries Represented	133

ACADEMICS

Academic Rating	71
% Of students graduating within 4 years	11
% Of students graduating within 6 years	39
Calendar	semester
Most common reg class size	20–29 students
Most common lab size	20–29 students

MOST POPULAR MAJORS

Management science, general

HONORS PROGRAMS

The University Honors Program seeks to meet the needs of students who thrive on intellectual challenge by offering special interdisciplinary academic opportunities outside the major.

SPECIAL STUDY OPTIONS

Cooperative education program, cross-registration, distance learning, double major, dual enrollment, English as a Second Language (ESL), exchange student program (domestic), honors program, in- dependent study, internships, liberal arts/career combination, student-designed major, study abroad, teacher certification program.

ABOUT THE SCHOOL

The University of Massachusetts Boston is a "culturally diverse institution that fosters growth while maintaining high academic standards." It boasts "one of the top nursing programs in the state," and offers "an excellent education in a supportive environment." UMB is largely a commuter school, and students say, "You need to make an effort to get involved," but they add, "It's a very supportive and understanding place for students who work and have other obligations outside of school." Being heavily populated with commuters, there is an absence of dorms on campus, although some semblance of "dorm life" can be found at Harbor Point and Peninsula Apartments, located right off the campus. Some feel that "no dorms = no distractions" is a benefit, and are happy that UMB "lacks a fraternity lifestyle" and "caters to adult learners. Most students work at least part time," and are "ambitious and self-motivated." Students agree that, "there is enormous diversity on campus and in the classroom. It makes for a great learning environment."

BANG FOR YOUR BUCK

"For a public university where one year costs the fraction of one semester at a private university, the quality of the education is excellent," reports one student. Another raves that at UMass, "a first rate education from world-renowned faculty without leaving you to pay off school loans for a significant part of your life." Combining affordability and diversity in an urban setting provides undergrads with great access to rewarding employment opportunities. As a heavy commuter school, UMass also caters to the "unconventional" student as much as the regular one. Many students at UMB balance work and school, and one student remarks that the university "offered me the flexibility to keep my job and get my degree." Says another excited non-traditional undergrad, "I am an older student and UMass has a large number of things I was looking for in a school. It offers a large number of courses during the summer and online so I can get my degree faster." Finally, one student was pleased that UMass Boston is "on the rise and I wanted to join an up and coming, thriving campus."

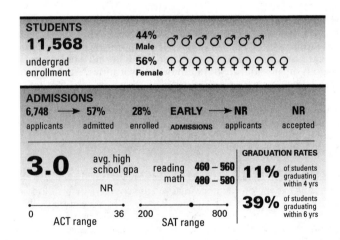

STUDENTS

11,568 undergrad enrollment

44% Male ♂♂♂♂♂♂♂

56% Female ♀♀♀♀♀♀♀♀♀♀

ADMISSIONS

6,748 applicants → **57%** admitted | **28%** enrolled | **EARLY ADMISSIONS** → **NR** applicants | **NR** accepted

3.0 avg. high school gpa

NR

0–36 ACT range

reading **460 – 560**
math **480 – 580**

200–800 SAT range

GRADUATION RATES

11% of students graduating within 4 yrs

39% of students graduating within 6 yrs

University of Massachusetts Boston

FINANCIAL AID: 617-287-6300 • E-MAIL: ENROLLMENT.INFO@UMB.EDU • WEBSITE: WWW.UMB.EDU

STUDENT BODY

There is no argument that "UMass Boston prides itself on being one of the most diverse universities around, and it shows. Students from all walks of life are welcome and fit in well with one another." Students agree that, "there is enormous diversity on campus and in the classroom. It makes for a great learning environment." The student population is a mix of "average right out of high school students...and older adults wanting to continue their college educations." However it's commonly held that "The two groups mesh well," because "Most people aren't at UMB for the college experience; they're there to get their degree and continue on with their lives."

Why Students love UMB

"It's a very supportive and understanding place for students who work and have other obligations outside of school."

WHY STUDENTS LOVE UNIVERSITY OF MASSACHUSETTS BOSTON

Many students at UMB balance work and school, and one student remarks that the university "offered me the flexibility to keep my job and get my degree." A philosophy major says, "UMass Boston is cheap, the classes are interesting, and the professors are deeply committed to the students." In fact many students describe UMB as a "diamond in the rough" that offers "an excellent education in a supportive environment." Professors are generally held to be "engaging and active" individuals who "bring a lot of real-world experience to their classes." Most students say, "The ratio of tuition cost to quality of instruction cannot be beat." UMB is largely a commuter school, and students say, "It's a very supportive and understanding place for students who work and have other obligations outside of school."

GENERAL INFO

Activities: Choral groups, concert band, dance, drama/theater, jazz band, literary magazine, music ensembles, radio station, student government. **Organizations:** 75 registered organizations, 1 honor societies. **Athletics (Intercollegiate):** *Men:* Baseball, basketball, cross-country, ice hockey, lacrosse, soccer, tennis, track/field (outdoor), track/field (indoor). *Women:* Basketball, cross-country, ice hockey, soccer, softball, tennis, track/field (outdoor), track/field (indoor), volleyball.

BOTTOM LINE

The University of Massachusetts at Boston provides an incredible in-state tuition of just less than $2,000 a year...for those from out-of-state, still an affordable $10,000 or so. "It's affordable, providing generous scholarship packages to hard-working students," one enrollee tells us. Another amazing figure is the school being able to meet well more than 90 percent of all student need, and the total financial aid package is normally about $14,000. The average need-based loan is about $6,500.

SELECTIVITY

Admissions Rating	**74**
# of applicants	6,748
% of applicants accepted	57
% of acceptees attending	28

FRESHMAN PROFILE

Range SAT Critical Reading	**460–560**
Range SAT Math	**480–580**
Average HS GPA	**3.0**

DEADLINES

Regular Deadline	**6/1**
Normal registration	**yes**

FACILITIES

Housing: University housing referral service. *Special Academic Facilities/Equipment:* Art gallery, tropical greenhouse, observatory, adaptive computer lab. *Computers:* 100% of classrooms, 100% of libraries, 100% of dining areas, 100% of student union, have wireless network access.

FINANCIAL FACTS

Financial Aid Rating	**79**
Annual in-state tuition	1,714
Annual out-of-state tuition	$9,758
Room and Board	$11,100
Required Fees	$9,693
% frosh rec. need-based scholarship or grant aid	58
% UG rec.need-based scholarship or grant aid	52
% frosh rec. non-need-based scholarship or grant aid	3
% UG rec. non-need-based scholarship or grant aid	2
% frosh rec. need-based self-help aid	57
% UG rec. need-based self-help aid	58
% UG borrow to pay for school	66
Average cumulative indebtedness	$22,387

University of Michigan–Ann Arbor

1220 Student Activities Building, Ann Arbor, MI 48109-1316 • Admissions: 734-764-7433 • Fax: 734-936-0740

CAMPUS LIFE

Quality of life Rating	90
Fire Safety Rating	91
Green rating	84
Type of School	Public
Environment	City

STUDENTS

Total undergrad enrolllment	26,830
% Male to Female	51/49
% From out of state	32
% Live on Campus	37
# of Fraternities	40
# of Sororities	28
% African American	5
% Asian	12
% Caucasian	67
% Hispanic	4
% International	6
# Of Countries Represented	118

ACADEMICS

Academic Rating	82
Calendar	semester
Profs interesting rating	65
Profs accessible rating	71
Most common reg class size	10–19 students
Most common lab size	20–29 students

MOST POPULAR MAJORS

Business administration and management, economics psychology

HONORS PROGRAMS

LSA Honors Program; departmental honors programs.

SPECIAL STUDY OPTIONS

Accelerated program, cooperative education program, cross-registration, distance learning, double major, dual enrollment, English as a Second Language (ESL), exchange student program (domestic), external degree program, honors program, independent study, internships, liberal arts/career combination, student-designed major, study abroad, teacher certification program, weekend college.

ABOUT THE SCHOOL

The University of Michigan–Ann Arbor is a big school with big opportunities, and we do mean big. The university has a multibillion dollar endowment and one of the largest research expenditures of any American university, also in the billions. Its physical campus includes more than 30 million square feet of building space, and its football stadium is the largest college football stadium in the country. With more than 26,000 undergraduates, the scale of the University of Minnesota's stellar offerings truly is overwhelming. But for those students who can handle the "First-class education in a friendly, competitive atmosphere," there's a lot of advantages to attending a university of this size and stature, and they will find "a great environment both academically and socially." You get an amazing breadth of classes, excellent professors, a "wide range of travel abroad opportunities," unparalleled research opportunities, and inroads into an alumni network that can offer you entry into any number of post-graduate opportunities. The school "provides every kind of opportunity at all times to all people," and students here get "it the opportunity to go far within their respective concentrations."

With more than 1,200 registered student organizations on campus, "if you seek it out, you can find organizations for any interest." Students here have a reputation for political activism.
A University of Michigan student movement which contributed to the establishment of the Peace Corps was initiated on this campus following a speech given by President John F. Kennedy. Students here also know how to let loose and unwind, and the school's location offers the perfect "mix of city and college."

BANG FOR YOUR BUCK

UM spent $300 million dollars in 2010 on total undergraduate need-based and merit-aid. That is truly staggering and reflects an amount more than the total endowment of many schools. Students who are Pell-grant eligible may benefit from UM's debt elimination programs. All students can expect to have 100 percent of their demonstrated need met. There are plenty of merit-based scholarships on offer here.

The university's schools, colleges, and departments administer their own scholarship programs so you should feel free to check with them directly. UM's Office of Financial Aid also administers a variety of scholarship programs that recognize superior academic achievement, leadership qualities, and potential contribution to the scholarly community. Some are based on need and others emphasize diversity. The majority of these scholarships are awarded automatically to eligible students. A full list of UM scholarships is available on the university's website.

STUDENTS

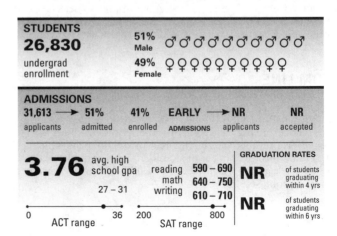

26,830 undergrad enrollment

51% Male ♂♂♂♂♂♂♂♂♂♂

49% Female ♀♀♀♀♀♀♀♀♀♀

ADMISSIONS

31,613 applicants	→ 51% admitted	41% enrolled	EARLY ADMISSIONS	→ NR applicants	NR accepted

3.76 avg. high school gpa

ACT range (0–36)	27 – 31
SAT reading (200–800)	590 – 690
SAT math	640 – 750
SAT writing	610 – 710

GRADUATION RATES

NR of students graduating within 4 yrs

NR of students graduating within 6 yrs

University of Michigan–Ann Arbor

FINANCIAL AID: 734-763-6600 • WEBSITE: WWW.UMICH.EDU

STUDENT BODY

The Michigan student body "is hugely diverse," which "is one of the things Michigan prides itself on." "If you participate in extracurricular activities and make an effort to get to know other students in class and elsewhere, you'll definitely end up with a pretty diverse group of friends," undergrads assure us. Although varied, students tend to be similar in that they "are social but very academically driven." A number of students "are on the cutting edge of both research and progressive thinking," and there is a decided liberal tilt to campus politics. Even so, there's a place for everyone here, because "there are hundreds of mini-communities within the campus, made of everything from service fraternities to political organizations to dance groups. If you have an interest, you can find a group of people who enjoy the same thing."

Why Students love UM—Ann Arbor

"It's great to be at a place where there is always something to do, but your friends completely understand when you have to stay in and get work done."

WHY STUDENTS LOVE UNIVERSITY OF MICHIGAN–ANN ARBOR

It has the social, fun atmosphere of any Big Ten university, but "people are still incredibly focused on their studies. It's great to be at a place where there is always something to do, but your friends completely understand when you have to stay in and get work done." There is a robust party scene, as well as a vigorous social scene for the non-drinking crowd, with "great programs like UMix...phenomenal cultural opportunities in Ann Arbor especially music and movies." The sense of school spirit here is "impressive," and one student says "I fell in love with the campus atmosphere from the first second I was there." "The people around me are all great people, and it is very easy to make quality relationships," says another.

GENERAL INFO

Activities: Choral groups, concert band, dance, drama/theater, jazz band, literary magazine, marching band, music ensembles, musical theater, opera, pep band, radio station, student government. **Organizations:** 1000 registered organizations, 13 honor societies, 67 religious organizations. 39 fraternities, 27 sororities. **Athletics (Intercollegiate):** *Men:* Baseball, basketball, cheerleading, cross-country, diving, football, golf, gymnastics, ice hockey, swimming, tennis, track/field (outdoor), track/field (indoor), wrestling. *Women:* Basketball, cheerleading, crew/rowing, cross-country, diving, field hockey, golf, gymnastics, soccer, softball, swimming, tennis, track/field (outdoor), track/field (indoor), volleyball, water polo.

BOTTOM LINE

UM's top-of-the-line education and comparatively low tuition make this school the definition of a best value. For Michigan residents, the estimated total cost of attendance for one year is about $25,000, including tuition, fees, and room and board, books and supplies, and personal expenses. For nonresidents, the price is almost exactly double the in-state rate. The good news is that the average financial aid package for freshman includes a $58,000 grant—you do the math and see for yourself how easy it is to come out on top here.

SELECTIVITY

Admissions Rating	**97**
# of applicants	31,613
% of applicants accepted	51
% of acceptees attending	41
# accepting a place on wait list	3,724
% admitted from wait list	2

FRESHMAN PROFILE

Range SAT Critical Reading	**590–690**
Range SAT Math	**640–750**
Range SAT Writing	**610–710**
Range ACT Composite	**27–31**
Average HS GPA	**3.76**
% graduated top 10% of class	**84**
% graduated top 25% of class	**97**
% graduated top 50% of class	**100**

DEADLINES

Regular Deadline	**1/31**
Normal registration	**yes**

FACILITIES

Housing: Coed dorms, special housing for disabled students, women's dorms, fraternity/sorority housing, apartments for married students, cooperative housing, apartments for single students, wellness housing, theme housing. *Special Academic Facilities/Equipment:* Anthropology, archaeology, art, natural science, paleontology, and zoology museums; audiovisual center, planetarium.

FINANCIAL FACTS

Financial Aid Rating	**91**
Annual in-state tuition	$12,440
Annual out-of-state tuition	$37,588
Room and Board	$9,468
Required Fees	$194
Books and supplies	$1,048
% frosh rec. need-based scholarship or grant aid	48
% UG rec.need-based scholarship or grant aid	48
% frosh rec. non-need-based scholarship or grant aid	39
% UG rec. non-need-based scholarship or grant aid	33
% frosh rec. need-based self-help aid	51
% UG rec. need-based self-help aid	53
% frosh rec. any financial aid	89
% UG rec. any financial aid	87
% UG borrow to pay for school	46
Average cumulative indebtedness	$27,828

University of Minnesota–Crookston

2900 University Avenue, Crookston, MN 56716-5001 • Admissions: 218-281-8569 • Fax: 218-281-8575

CAMPUS LIFE

Quality of life Rating	80
Fire Safety Rating	98
Green rating	67
Type of School	Public
Environment	Village

STUDENTS

Total undergrad enrollment	2,528
% Male to Female	40/52
% From out of state	26
% Live on Campus	40
# of Fraternities	1
# of Sororities	1
% African American	3
% Asian	1
% Caucasian	60
% Hispanic	1
% International	5
# Of Countries Represented	29

ACADEMICS

Academic Rating	75
% Of students graduating within 4 years	21
% Of students graduating within 6 years	35
Calendar	semester
Most common reg class size	10–19 students
Most common lab size	10–19 students

MOST POPULAR MAJORS

Animal sciences, general business administration and management, general natural resources, general conservation

HONORS PROGRAMS

University of Minnesota–Crookston Honor's Program. Special programs offered to physically disabled students include note-taking services, reader services, voice recorders, tutors.

SPECIAL STUDY OPTIONS

Cross-registration, distance learning, double major, dual enrollment, English as a Second Language (ESL), honors program, independent study, internships, student-designed major, study abroad, teacher certification program.

ABOUT THE SCHOOL

The University of Minnesota–Crookston prides itself on being a "small campus with a big degree." Though it was initially viewed an agricultural school, in recent years UMC has really ratcheted up its other departments. Indeed, the school now boasts stellar programs in biology, pre-vet studies, business technology, animal science, early childhood education and communications. Importantly, the university places a huge emphasis on practical and hands-on learning. To that end, all undergraduates are required to complete an internship in their chosen field.

Beyond the classroom, UMC students are involved in over 30 clubs and are extremely proactive when it comes to logging volunteer hours. Though hometown Crookston doesn't offer much in the way of entertainment, undergrads are often content with making their own fun. Many like to take advantage of opportunities for outdoor activities such as fishing and hunting. And when students are itching to get a little farther away, they join a campus-sponsored trip to a regional attraction.

BANG FOR YOUR BUCK

The financial aid program here is exceedingly generous and goes beyond just covering tuition, room and board, and fees, for which Pomona can, and does meet, 100 percent of students' demonstrated financial need. The financial aid packages consist wholly of grants and scholarships, probably along with a campus job that you work maybe 10 hours a week. Believe it or not, it gets even better. For students on financial aid who wish to participate in study abroad, Pomona ensures that cost is not a barrier. All programs carry academic credit and no extra cost for tuition or room and board. To ensure that all Pomona students are able to participate in the college's internship program, funding is provided in the form of an hourly wage for semester-long internships, making it possible for students to take unpaid positions. The Career Development Office (CDO) also subsidizes transportation to and from internships. In addition, the college offers funding, based on need, to students with job interviews on the East Coast during Winter Break Recruiting Days program.

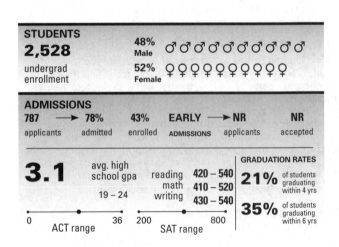

STUDENTS

2,528 undergrad enrollment

48% Male ♂♂♂♂♂♂♂♂♂♂

52% Female ♀♀♀♀♀♀♀♀♀♀

ADMISSIONS

787 applicants → 78% admitted | 43% enrolled | EARLY ADMISSIONS → NR applicants | NR accepted

3.1 avg. high school gpa

ACT range (0–36): 19 – 24

SAT range (200–800): reading 420 – 540, math 410 – 520, writing 430 – 540

GRADUATION RATES

21% of students graduating within 4 yrs

35% of students graduating within 6 yrs

University of Minnesota–Crookston

FINANCIAL AID: 218-281-8563 • E-MAIL: UMCINFO@UMN.EDU • WEBSITE: WWW.CRK.UMN.EDU

STUDENT BODY

"The agricultural focus of UMC has historically been reflected in its student body. While farm and small-town kids are still the norm here, there has been a steady increase in campus diversity over the past few years. In particular, many note that there's a "growing population of international students…UMC is becoming more diverse and I like that." However, others point out that the number of these students has increased to the extent that "they are creating their own communities" "instead of integrating with the campus," "which defeats the purpose of studying abroad." There are "a lot of athletes" at UMC and a growing population of students from states like Florida, Illinois, and California. On this small campus, it's easy to make friends, and "Most everyone is laid-back and friendly."

Why Students love UM–Crookston

"The friendly staff works with you when you need help."

WHY STUDENTS LOVE UM–CROOKSTON

Undergrads here happily report that UMC is a "great place to learn, meet great people, and get the private school deal at a public school [price]." The university does a wonderful job of making students feel as if they are part of a "small-knit family" and there are "many opportunities to learn, grow [and] achieve." Indeed, undergrads truly appreciate the school's "personal approach" and note that "the friendly staff works with you when you need help." Additionally, "small class sizes" virtually guarantee that "professors are easily accessible." As one satisfied student sums up, UMC is simply "about creating leaders and providing an excellent education."

GENERAL INFO

Activities: Choral groups, drama/theater, pep band, radio station, student government, campus ministries, international student organization. **Organizations:** 38 registered organizations, 1 honor societies, 2 religious organizations. 1 fraternity, 1 sorority. **Athletics (Intercollegiate):** *Men:* Baseball, basketball, football, golf, ice hockey. *Women:* Basketball, equestrian sports, golf, soccer, softball, tennis, volleyball. **On-Campus Highlights:** Sargeant Student Center, University Teaching and Outreach Center, Sports Center, Bergland Laboratory, Centennial Hall Student Apartments, Campus Mall Dairy Barns Kiehle Auditorium.

BOTTOM LINE

University of Minnesota–Crookston is a unique force within the field of higher education. This is because, despite being a state institution, U of M–Crookston maintains a flat rate tuition fee regardless of residence. All undergraduates can expect to pay about $12,000 in tuition and fees. Additionally, room and board will cost roughly $6,500. Students should also anticipate spending $1,000 on books and supplies. There is, however, one exception. U of M–Crookston does maintain a reciprocity agreement with North Dakota, South Dakota, Wisconsin and Manitoba. Residents of the aforementioned states may attend UMC under specially designated tuition rates.

SELECTIVITY

Admissions Rating	**68**
# of applicants	787
% of applicants accepted	78
% of acceptees attending	43

FRESHMAN PROFILE

Range SAT Critical Reading	**420–540**
Range SAT Math	**410–520**
Range SAT Writing	**430–540**
Range ACT Composite	**19–24**
Average HS GPA	**3.1**
% graduated top 10% of class	**11**
% graduated top 25% of class	**34**
% graduated top 50% of class	**62**

DEADLINES

Regular Deadline	**2/15**
Normal registration	**yes**

FACILITIES

Housing: Coed dorms, special housing for disabled students, apartments for single students, theme housing. *Special Academic Facilities/Equipment:* Red River Valley Natural History Area; Northwest Research and Outreach Center; UMC Horse Riding Arena; Valley Technology Park. *Computers:* 20% of classrooms, 100% of dorms, 100% of libraries, 75% of dining areas, 100% of student union, 25% of common outdoor areas have wireless network access.

FINANCIAL FACTS

Financial Aid Rating	**80**
Annual tuition	$9,629
Room and Board	$6,465
Required Fees	$1,436
Books and supplies	$1,100
% frosh rec. need-based scholarship or grant aid	64
% UG rec.need-based scholarship or grant aid	60
% frosh rec. non-need-based scholarship or grant aid	21
% UG rec. non-need-based scholarship or grant aid	13
% frosh rec. need-based self-help aid	55
% UG rec. need-based self-help aid	57
% frosh rec. any financial aid	66
% UG rec. any financial aid	64
% UG borrow to pay for school	81
Average cumulative indebtedness	$25,852

University of Minnesota—Twin Cities

240 Williamson Hall, 231 Pillsbury Drive SE, Minneapolis, MN 55455-0213 • Admissions: 612-625-2008

CAMPUS LIFE

Quality of life Rating	88
Fire Safety Rating	82
Green rating	85
Type of School	Public
Environment	Metropolis

STUDENTS

Total undergrad enrolllment	33,607
% Male to Female	48/52
% From out of state	25
% Live on Campus	21
# of Fraternities	24
# of Sororities	12
% African American	5
% Asian	9
% Caucasian	72
% Hispanic	3
% N.A.	1
% International	6
# Of Countries Represented	130

ACADEMICS

Academic Rating	69
% Of students graduating within 4 years	50
% Of students graduating within 6 years	70
Calendar	semester
Profs interesting rating	70
Profs accessible rating	69
Most common reg class size	20–29 students
Most common lab size	10–19 students

MOST POPULAR MAJORS

Journalism, psychology, business, education, biology, engineering, kinesiology, nutrition

HONORS PROGRAMS

Honors, Undergraduate Research Opportunities Program.

SPECIAL STUDY OPTIONS

Accelerated program, cooperative education program, cross-registration, distance learning, double major, dual enrollment, English as a Second Language (ESL), exchange student program (domestic).

ABOUT THE COLLEGE

The University of Minnesota–Twin Cities offers more than 140 degree programs to its undergraduate student body of over 33,000. That equals a whole lot of opportunity. The university's top ranked College of Pharmacy is complemented by exceptional programs in business and engineering. Off-the-beaten track majors are also available, as UM has enough academic offerings to cover almost every esoteric interest you can imagine. This is a big research university, so some professors won't have teaching undergraduates at the top of their list of priorities–but even those who don't are appreciated by students for their knowledge and brilliance. Instructors "enjoy teaching the material and getting to know the students personally." Qualified undergraduates may take graduate level classes, too. It's a large school, so lower-level courses can get crowded–though freshman seminars are usually capped at 15-20 students. Study abroad opportunities here are expansive and a good proportion of students take advantage.

The campus itself is located in Minneapolis, which a lot of students love for its great art museums and bars. The downtown area is only a short bus ride away from campus. It's great to be close to everything Minneapolis has to offer because winters seem perennial there. Okay, perennial might be an exaggeration, but it's true that they're really, really, long. As such, campus activities often center around snow culture. Sledding, ice skating, and hockey games are favorite pastimes on campus, as well as the campus-wide snowball fights in the winter. For those adventurous folks who can handle a little bit of frostbite, house parties, keggers, and fratastic blowouts are all readily available, come snow or sunshine.

BANG FOR YOUR BUCK

University of Minnesota offers a comprehensive program of need-based and merit-based aid. Each year, the incoming freshmen class receives over $9 million in academic scholarships to be used over the course of their college careers. Some scholarships last one or two years, and range from $1,000-$3,000 each year. Other awards last four years, and range from $1,000-$12,000 each year. UM offers a national scholarship program for non-resident freshmen ranging up to $11,000 per year for four years. Additionally, the University of Minnesota's Job Center makes it convenient for incoming students to find a job to help defray costs: the first 500 incoming freshman who respond to a Center mailing receive a campus job guarantee. There are eight conventional residence halls, plus three new apartment style facilities.

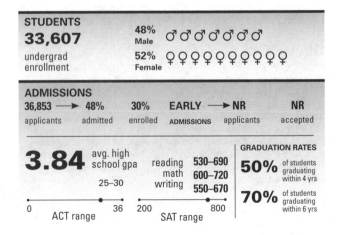

STUDENTS
33,607 undergrad enrollment
48% Male ♂♂♂♂♂♂♂
52% Female ♀♀♀♀♀♀♀♀♀♀

ADMISSIONS
36,853 applicants → 48% admitted | 30% enrolled
EARLY ADMISSIONS NR applicants → NR accepted

3.84 avg. high school gpa

ACT range: 25–30 (0–36)

SAT range (200–800):
reading 530–690
math 600–720
writing 550–670

GRADUATION RATES
50% of students graduating within 4 yrs
70% of students graduating within 6 yrs

University of Minnesota—Twin Cities

FAX: 612-626-1693 • FINANCIAL AID: 612-624-1111 • WEBSITE: WWW.UMN.EDU

STUDENT BODY

Students are generally from the Midwest somewhere. More often than not, they are "right out of suburbia" or from "small to medium-sized towns" in "Minnesota or Wisconsin." There are a lot of "tall," "blond," people who "are 'Minnesota Nice'" but students assure that the U of M "is a human zoo." "It's a school that embraces diversity." Also, "there is a microcosm for just about every subculture imaginable." There are "the math nerds," the "frat boys," and "lots of hippies and artsy people." There's "a huge gay population." "Preppy, athletic, emo," and nontraditional students are also visible. Politically, "the conservatives add a good balance to the grand scheme of things," but the campus leans left. Some students are "very politically aware." "There always seems to be some group protesting or trying to convince me of something," notes one student.

WHY STUDENTS LOVE UNIVERSITY OF MINNESOTA – TWIN CITIES

The "beautiful," "very environmentally friendly" campus here is "spread over two cities and a river." There are over 600 campus organizations. "There's a group for just about every interest," and "there is always something to do, even on a random Tuesday night." 10 different religious organizations are available to partake in; one student is pleased that "it's a school that embraces diversity." Minnesota has over 30 fraternities and sororities, but there's also a lot happening off campus. According to students here, "Minneapolis is one of the greatest places in the country." "The music scene is unreal." Shopping at the Mall of America is another popular pastime. The neighborhoods near campus are generally "very young and energetic" and public transportation is "readily available and cheap."

GENERAL INFO

Activities: Choral groups, concert band, dance, drama/theater, jazz band, literary magazine, marching band, music ensembles, musical theater, opera, pep band, radio station, student government, student newspaper, student-run film society, symphony orchestra, television station, international student organization. **Organizations:** 600 registered organizations, 10 religious organizations. 22 fraternities, 12 sororities. **Athletics (Intercollegiate):** *Men:* Baseball, basketball, cross-country, diving, football, golf, gymnastics, ice hockey, swimming, tennis, track/field (outdoor), track/field (indoor), wrestling. *Women:* Basketball, cheerleading, cross-country, diving, golf, gymnastics, ice hockey, soccer, softball, swimming, tennis, track/field (outdoor), track/field (indoor), volleyball. **On-Campus Highlights:** Weisman Art Museum, McNamara Alumni Center, TCF Bank Stadium, Goldstein Gallery, Northrup Memorial Auditorium, Coffman Memorial Union, Mariucci Arena, University Theater, Rarig Center.

THE BOTTOM LINE

Tuition and fees at the University of Minnesota–Twin Cities runs about $12,000 per year for Minnesota, North Dakota, South Dakota, and Manitoba, Wisconsin residents. Nonresidents get a pretty good deal also: they can expect to pay in the range of $16,000 a year. Room and board is an additional $7,500, bringing the total cost of attendance to $19,500 for residents and $23,500 for nonresidents. University of Minnesota also fosters both learning and frugality with its unique 13th-credit tuition incentive in which every credit after 13 is free of charge, keeping costs down for families and helping students achieve graduation in four years. (Students typically take 15-16 credits each semester or 120 credits over four years).

SELECTIVITY

Admissions Rating	**87**
# of applicants	36,853
% of applicants accepted	48
% of acceptees attending	30
# accepting a place on wait list	0

FRESHMAN PROFILE

Range SAT Critical Reading	**530–690**
Range SAT Math	**600–720**
Range SAT Writing	**550–670**
Range ACT Composite	**25–30**
% graduated top 10% of class	**43**
% graduated top 25% of class	**83**
% graduated top 50% of class	**99**

DEADLINES

Regular Deadline	**12/15**
Normal registration	**yes**

FACILITIES

Housing: Coed dorms, special housing for disabled students, special housing for international students, fraternity/sorority housing, apartments for married students, cooperative housing, apartments for single students, Honors housing, residential college (academic programs in residence). Eight conventional residence halls, plus three new apartment style residence halls. *Special Academic Facilities/Equipment:* Frederick R. Weisman Art Museum, Bell Museum of Natural History.

FINANCIAL FACTS

Financial Aid Rating	**82**
Annual in-state tuition	$11,650
Annual out-of-state tuition	$16,650
Room and Board	$7,834
Required Fees	$1,348
Books and supplies	$1,000
% frosh rec. need-based scholarship or grant aid	55
% UG rec. need-based scholarship or grant aid	53
% frosh rec. non-need-based scholarship or grant aid	8
% UG rec. non-need-based scholarship or grant aid	6
% frosh rec. need-based self-help aid	50
% UG rec. need-based self-help aid	47
% frosh rec. any financial aid	56
% UG rec. any financial aid	55
% UG borrow to pay for school	63
Average cumulative indebtedness	$27,578

University of Missouri—Kansas City

5100 Rockhill Road, 101 AC, Kansas City, MO 64114 • Admissions: 816-235-1111 • Fax: 816-235-5544

CAMPUS LIFE

Quality of life Rating	74
Fire Safety Rating	72
Green rating	70
Type of School	Public
Environment	Metropolis

STUDENTS

Total undergrad enrolllment	9,863
% Male to Female	92/58
% From out of state	26
% Live on Campus	11
# of Fraternities	6
# of Sororities	7
% African American	14
% Asian	5
% Caucasian	60
% Hispanic	5
% International	3
# Of Countries Represented	66

ACADEMICS

Academic Rating	75
% Of students graduating within 4 years	19
% Of students graduating within 6 years	44
Calendar	semester
Most common reg class size	10–19 students
Most common lab size	10–19 students

MOST POPULAR MAJORS

Business/commerce, economics international relations

HONORS PROGRAMS

UMKC Honors Program

SPECIAL STUDY OPTIONS

Accelerated program, distance learning, double major, dual enrollment, English as a Second Language (ESL), honors program, independent study, internships, liberal arts/career combination, student-designed major, study abroad, teacher certification program.

ABOUT THE SCHOOL

The University of Missouri–Kansas City is a reputable state school that tends to attract a lot of students from the surrounding area. Offering a wide array of academic programs, undergrads appreciate that they can run from an organic chemistry class to ballet at the renown Conservatory of Music and Dance. The highest praise is typically reserved for the "outstanding" business school and, in particular, the entrepreneurship program. This includes the Institute for Entrepreneurship and Innovation, which has helped students launch numerous ventures. Also of note, UMKC's fast-track medical program, allowing outstanding students to earn a combined BA/MD in six years. Hometown Kansas City certainly adds some appeal as undergrads are able to take advantage of a myriad of service learning and internship opportunities around the city. Additionally, it's a highly affordable place to live and provides many entertainment options.

Why Students love UMKC

"UMKC's network building efforts and job placements before and after graduation."

BANG FOR YOUR BUCK

University of Missouri–Kansas City strives to help all undergraduates meet their financial needs. Through a combination of grants, scholarships, loans and work-study opportunities, UMKC ensures that all qualified students will be able to attend. The university maintains three types of scholarship: automatic, competitive and academic. Automatic scholarships are awarded based upon information included on the regular application. No further paperwork is necessary. To be awarded a competitive scholarship, prospective students must submit an additional application. Academic scholarships are granted by an individual school or program. The application process for academic scholarships varies. Additionally, University of Missouri offers the UMKC Advantage Grant to resident freshmen and transfer students who are Pell eligible. This grant helps to bridge the gap between the rest of a student's aid package and the remaining tuition. Students must be enrolled full-time and maintain a minimum 2.5 GPA. Finally, UMKC has implemented a financial literacy program, teaching students how to make the right financial decisions.

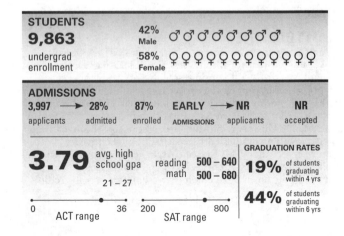

STUDENTS

9,863 undergrad enrollment

42% Male ♂♂♂♂♂♂♂♂

58% Female ♀♀♀♀♀♀♀♀♀♀♀

ADMISSIONS

3,997 applicants → **28%** admitted | **87%** enrolled | **EARLY** ADMISSIONS → **NR** applicants | **NR** accepted

3.79 avg. high school gpa

21 – 27 ACT range (0–36)

reading 500 – 640
math 500 – 680
SAT range (200–800)

GRADUATION RATES

19% of students graduating within 4 yrs

44% of students graduating within 6 yrs

University of Missouri—Kansas City

FINANCIAL AID: 816-235-1154 • E-MAIL: ADMIT@UMKC.EDU • WEBSITE: WWW.UMKC.EDU

STUDENT BODY

For many students here, UMKC is their choice because it is "nearby and cost effective." Students tend to hail "from Kansas City or the surrounding areas." At the same time, this campus is "extremely diverse." Ethnic minorities make up an ample contingent of the undergraduate population. There are students from all across the country. "There are many international students" as well. While UMKC is home to plenty of newly-minted high school graduates, "there are quite a few students in their thirties and forties," and "it is not strange to see nontraditional students in every class." At UMKC, you'll find "focused" business students, art students who "drink expensive coffee," and pretty much any other kind of student you seek. By and large, students are "serious, committed to making good grades, and very busy trying to fit everything into their schedule," "but not so driven that they don't have time to relax and enjoy life."

WHY STUDENTS LOVE UMKC

Undergrads at UMKC stress that, from the moment they enrolled, they could discern that the university "really cared about its students." Indeed, a welcoming campus and a friendly vibe make the school a great "place to grow." Beyond the openness, undergrads note that UMKC truly helps students "to reach their full potential as intellectuals." Professors push students to develop their "logical, critical and creative thinking skills." Perhaps more importantly, they are "very dedicated to helping you succeed." Students also greatly appreciate "UMKC's network building efforts and job placements before and after graduation."Though UMKC has a fair number of commuter students, undergrads assure us that the campus is "extremely diverse." Indeed, students hail from across the country and "there are many international students" as well.

GENERAL INFO

Activities: Choral groups, concert band, dance, drama/theater, jazz band, literary magazine, music ensembles, musical theater, opera, pep band, student government, student newspaper, symphony orchestra, campus ministries, international student organization. **Organizations:** 200 registered organizations, 32 honor societies, 13 religious organizations. 6 fraternities, 7 sororities. **Athletics (Intercollegiate):** *Men:* Basketball, cheerleading, cross-country, golf, riflery, soccer, tennis, track/field (outdoor). *Women:* Basketball, cheerleading, cross-country, golf, riflery, softball, tennis, track/field (outdoor), volleyball. **On-Campus Highlights:** Muddy's Coffee Shop, Nelson Atkins Museum, Sweeney Recreation Center, Minsky's restaurant, Planet Sub restaurant. **Environmental Initiatives:** Recycling, energy management, building design.

BOTTOM LINE

The University of Missouri–Kansas City tallies its tuition based upon credit hours. The fee goes toward everything from your actual classroom education to the Student Union and transportation costs. Naturally, non-residents are responsible for meeting higher payments. UMKC also participates in the Midwest Exchange Program, meaning residents of designated surrounding states may attend at a reduced rate. Undergraduates who fall within this category are expected to pay $480.36 for one credit hour to $6,448.95 for 15 credit hours. Further, UMKC posits that room and board on campus will cost $10,131 and roughly $8,670 for off-campus housing. The university also estimates that students will likely need $6,140 to cover personal expenses.

SELECTIVITY

Admissions Rating	**88**
# of applicants	3,997
% of applicants accepted	28
% of acceptees attending	87

FRESHMAN PROFILE

Range SAT Critical Reading	**500–640**
Range SAT Math	**500–650**
Range ACT Composite	**21–27**
Average HS GPA	**3.29**
% graduated top 10% of class	**27**
% graduated top 25% of class	**57**
% graduated top 50% of class	**81**

DEADLINES

Regular Deadline	**2/1**
Normal registration	**yes**

FACILITIES

Housing: Coed dorms, special housing for disabled students, fraternity/sorority housing, apartments for married students, apartments for single students, University owned houses. *Special Academic Facilities/ Equipment:* Art gallery, professional theater, geosciences museums, language lab, observatory. *Computers:* 90% of classrooms, 100% of dorms, 100% of libraries, 100% of dining areas, 100% of student union, have wireless network access.

FINANCIAL FACTS

Financial Aid Rating	**73**
Annual tuition	$7,737
Annual out-of-state tuition	$19,905
Room and Board	$10,798
Required Fees	$1,161
Books and supplies	$1,376
% frosh rec. need-based scholarship or grant aid	63
% UG rec.need-based scholarship or grant aid	53
% frosh rec. non-need-based scholarship or grant aid	3
% UG rec. non-need-based scholarship or grant aid	1
% frosh rec. need-based self-help aid	46
% UG rec. need-based self-help aid	54
% frosh rec. any financial aid	63
% UG rec. any financial aid	62
% UG borrow to pay for school	60
Average cumulative indebtedness	$22,374

University of North Carolina at Asheville

CPO #1320, One University Heights, Asheville, NC 28804-8502 • Admissions: 828-251-6481 • Fax: 828-251-6482

CAMPUS LIFE

Quality of life Rating	92
Fire Safety Rating	83
Green rating	83
Type of School	Public
Environment	Town

STUDENTS

Total undergrad enrolllment	3,418
% Male to Female	44/56
% From out of state	12
% From public high school	87
% Live on Campus	33
# of Fraternities	1
# of Sororities	2
% African American	2
% Asian	1
% Caucasian	87
% Hispanic	4
% International	1
# Of Countries Represented	20

ACADEMICS

Academic Rating	85
% Of students graduating within 4 years	30
% Of students graduating within 6 years	56
Calendar	semester
Profs interesting rating	92
Profs accessible rating	86
Most common reg class size	10–19 students
Most common lab size	20–29 students

MOST POPULAR MAJORS

Business management, English language and literature, psychology

HONORS PROGRAMS

University Honors Program, Undergraduate Research Program, University Research Scholars. Special programs offered to physically disabled students include note-taking services, reader services, voice recorders, tutors.

SPECIAL STUDY OPTIONS

Cross-registration, distance learning, double major, dual enrollment, exchange student program (domestic), honors program, independent study, internships, liberal arts/career combination, student-designed major, study abroad, teacher certification program.

ABOUT THE SCHOOL

The liberal arts tradition is alive and well at UNC Asheville, where students are encouraged to question, to discuss, and that education "is used to expand the minds of every student, facility member, and guest that graces its campus." Focusing on undergraduate studies, the school helps students dig into learning, providing opportunities for faculty-mentored research projects, career-related internships, study abroad, and service projects; the school even had Michelle Obama come speak recently, an impressive achievement for one of its size. More than half of students complete original research in their field of study through the University's nationally recognized Undergraduate Research Program, and tutoring sessions are free and plentiful for those undergrads who feel that they require more assistance. "The small class sizes gave me a chance to stand out while still feeling like I lived in a university setting," says a student. Faculty are overwhelming supportive of the students, and "for better or worse, they know our names, and know when we don't come to class." Even if there is not a set major for what you want, "the Interdisciplinary Studies dean will do her best to personalize a major for you."

The school's small, personal feel makes the transition to college an easy one, and UNC Asheville alumni, faculty and staff welcome new and returning students in August by helping them move into the residence halls. The school contains about 3,700 undergraduate students, most of whom are "very politically aware as well as environmentally conscious"; freshmen are required to live on campus their first year, but most move off campus (but nearby) after that. Downtown Asheville offers a wide variety of shops, restaurants, and bars, and the mountains offer hiking and camping, so "you are never bored." While there is a Greek system, "partying does not define the school," and the school's student-athletes have one of the highest graduation rates in the NCAA.

BANG FOR YOUR BUCK

UNC Asheville is an inexpensive way to achieve an excellent education, at a school that may be less intimidating than a larger institution. The myriad research opportunities help flesh out a resume, and the stress on real world application gets students job-ready before they even set foot outside the mountains. Students (especially those in-state) have access to the small class sizes and familial relationships of a small private school, at a state school price.

STUDENTS

3,418 undergrad enrollment

44% Male ♂♂♂♂♂♂♂♂♂

56% Female ♀♀♀♀♀♀♀♀♀♀♀

ADMISSIONS

2,362 applicants → 77% admitted — 33% enrolled

EARLY ADMISSIONS → NR applicants — NR accepted

3.91 avg. high school gpa

ACT range (0–36): 22 – 27

SAT range (200–800): reading 540 – 650; math 520 – 620; writing 510 – 620

GRADUATION RATES

30% of students graduating within 4 yrs

56% of students graduating within 6 yrs

University of North Carolina at Asheville

FINANCIAL AID: 828-251-6535 • E-MAIL: ADMISSIONS@UNCA.EDU • WEBSITE: WWW.UNCA.EDU

STUDENT BODY

UNC Asheville seems to hold appeal for self-described "hippies." One sophomore says, "This school attracts the sort of people who get excited about local, organic, dairy-free muffins and sandals made from recycled flax." Indeed many undergrads "care about the environment, [are] liberal-leaning, enjoy the outdoors, [and are] pretty sociable." Happily, the university "fosters the idea that individuality is essential," and students assure us that everyone "is easily accepted here" regardless of political affiliation. Perhaps this acceptance stems from the fact that the campus welcomes students from a variety of "economic backgrounds, religious backgrounds and sexual orientations." Asheville does manage to attract both a large number of "commuter students" as well as "a lot of nontraditional students."

Why Students love UNC Asheville

"This school attracts the sort of people who get excited about local, organic, dairy-free muffins and sandals made from recycled flax."

WHY STUDENTS LOVE UNC ASHEVILLE

"UNCA is a school that promotes the growth of its students with an emphasis on a personal approach to undergraduate education," says a student. The "opportunity for undergraduate research on campus is immense, and in any department," and students love "all learning a little bit about everything instead of everything about one thing." Smaller class sizes make for "more diverse interactions and more vibrant class discussions."

The school is "a lot of fun to live at," and the "amazing and quirky city" of Asheville is "the Western North Carolina hub of liberalism, art, and fabulous scenery." A favorite Asheville activity for many students is "the drum circle," where "people gather every Friday evening (in warm weather), circulating, dancing, thrumming, and drumming."

GENERAL INFO

Activities: Choral groups, concert band, dance, drama/theater, jazz band, literary magazine, music ensembles, musical theater, pep band, radio station, student government, student newspaper, campus ministries, international student organization. **Organizations:** 82 registered organizations, 14 honor societies, 10 religious organizations, 1 fraternity, 2 sororities. **Athletics (Intercollegiate):** *Men:* Baseball, basketball, cheerleading, cross-country, soccer, tennis, track/field (outdoor). *Women:* Basketball, cheerleading, cross-country, soccer, tennis, track/field (outdoor), volleyball.

BOTTOM LINE

The already low in-state tuition of $5,393 can be subsidized by financial aid in the form of federal, state, local and institutional grants and scholarships; more than half of students receive some form of aid. In the past year, 85 percent of students' financial need was met. Additionally, the university's prestigious merit-based scholarship, the Laurels Scholarship, also provides a variety of awards, including full tuition and fees. The scholarship, which is funded by the generosity of donors, is awarded to entering freshmen who demonstrate high academic achievements.

SELECTIVITY

Admissions Rating	**84**
# of applicants	2,362
% of applicants accepted	77
% of acceptees attending	33

FRESHMAN PROFILE

Range SAT Critical Reading	**540–650**
Range SAT Math	**520–620**
Range SAT Writing	**510–620**
Range ACT Composite	**22–27**
Average HS GPA	**3.91**
% graduated top 10% of class	**22**
% graduated top 25% of class	**58**
% graduated top 50% of class	**95**

DEADLINES

Regular Deadline	**2/15**
Normal registration	**yes**

FACILITIES

Housing: Coed dorms, special housing for disabled students, men's dorms, women's dorms, substance-free dorms, 24 hour quiet dorms. *Special Academic Facilities/ Equipment:* Undergraduate Research Center, Steelcase Teleconference Center, Music Recording Center, Asheville Botanical Gardens, NC Arboretum, Center for Creative Retirement. *Computers:* 1% of classrooms, 100% of libraries, 100% of dining areas, 90% of student union, have wireless network access.

FINANCIAL FACTS

Financial Aid Rating	**86**
Annual in-state tuition	$3,166
Annual out-of-state tuition	$16,798
Room and Board	$7,302
Required Fees	$2,227
Books and supplies	$950
% frosh rec. need-based scholarship or grant aid	44
% UG rec.need-based scholarship or grant aid	46
% frosh rec. non-need-based scholarship or grant aid	8
% UG rec. non-need-based scholarship or grant aid	6
% frosh rec. need-based self-help aid	27
% UG rec. need-based self-help aid	32
% frosh rec. any financial aid	71
% UG rec. any financial aid	66
% UG borrow to pay for school	48
Average cumulative indebtedness	$15,443

University of North Carolina—Wilmington

601 South College Rd, Wilmington, NC 28403-5904 • Admissions: 910-962-3243 • Fax: 910-962-3038

CAMPUS LIFE

Quality of life Rating	93
Fire Safety Rating	89
Green rating	77
Type of School	Public
Environment	City

STUDENTS

Total undergrad enrolllment	11,770
% Male to Female	41/59
% From out of state	87
% Live on Campus	36
# of Fraternities	11
# of Sororities	11
% African American	4
% Asian	2
% Caucasian	83
% Hispanic	5
% N.A.	1
% International	1
# Of Countries Represented	73

ACADEMICS

Academic Rating	67
Calendar	semester
Most common reg class size	20–29 students
Most common lab size	20–29 students

MOST POPULAR MAJORS

Business management, economics, elementary education and teaching, psychology, general

HONORS PROGRAMS

The Honors Scholars Program.

SPECIAL STUDY OPTIONS

Accelerated program, cooperative education program, cross-registration, distance learning, double major, dual enrollment, English as a Second Language (ESL), exchange student program (domestic), program, independent study, internships, study abroad, teacher certification program, 2+2 Pre-Engineering Program.

ABOUT THE SCHOOL

The University of North Carolina–Wilmington offers all of the opportunities and diversity that come with being a modern, state-supported university of 13,000, but remains true to its small school roots; most classes have less than 30 students, although there are 2,000 new freshman coming to the school each year. UNCW boasts a solid faculty, two-thirds of whom have PhD's. Teachers ensure that students know they are more than just a number by making time to help them outside of class, and the teachers aren't afraid to show passion for the subject at hand. "There have been several classes that I wasn't expecting to get much out of that I've just loved because of the professor," one student told us. Ambitious students should shoot for entry into the Honors Program, which opens up avenues of education and opportunities that are otherwise unavailable to the general college.

At UNCW, students earn real-world experience through internships, research initiatives, international travel opportunities, and service-learning activities. In fact, every academic area on campus requires applied learning as a part of the undergraduate curriculum covering everything from a nursing program at a rural health clinic in Peru, to a sociology program with a public housing community in Wilmington, to hands-on marine science research with leading faculty from the university's internationally-recognized Center for Marine Science, with resources such as its new 11,000 square foot oyster hatchery. The Career Center and Cameron School of Business also hold several networking receptions with prospective employers to help their students get a leg up on finding a job when they graduate.

BANG FOR YOUR BUCK

The UNC system boasts one of the lower in-state tuitions in the country, which is a real bargain when coupled with the relatively high quality of instruction throughout the system. The school offers both need and merit-based aid, with the majority of funds allocated to the needy. Need-based aid comes in the form of fede ral work-study, institutional employment, scholarships, grants, and loans. UNCW's financial aid offerings emphasize student-centered service, a hallmark of the UNCW experience. The university's financial aid application process begins by connecting students and their families to individual financial aid counselor

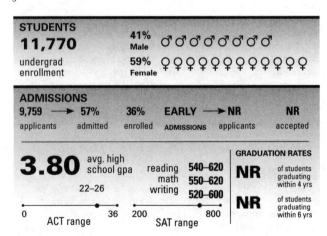

s

STUDENTS

11,770 undergrad enrollment

41% Male ♂♂♂♂♂♂♂♂♂

59% Female ♀♀♀♀♀♀♀♀♀♀♀♀♀

ADMISSIONS

9,759 applicants → 57% admitted | 36% enrolled | EARLY ADMISSIONS → NR applicants | NR accepted

3.80 avg. high school gpa

ACT range (0–36): 22–26

SAT range (200–800): reading 540–620, math 550–620, writing 520–600

GRADUATION RATES

NR of students graduating within 4 yrs

NR of students graduating within 6 yrs

University of North Carolina—Wilmington

FINANCIAL AID: 910-962-3177 • E-MAIL: ADMISSIONS@UNCW.EDU • WEBSITE: WWW.UNCW.EDU

STUDENT BODY

The University of North Carolina–Wilmington, "has a laid-back atmosphere and a close-knit student body" on a "beautiful" campus. One student says, "It's awesome: beautiful weather, beautiful beaches, fantastic people, great atmosphere...basically everything you could ask for in a college experience." Clubs on campus are described as "numerous" and "accessible," and students say the "staff and administrators are dedicated to students' development as learners, leaders, and engaged citizens." However, there is disagreement about the level of enthusiasm on campus, with some saying, "You 'feel the teal' wherever you go" and others lamenting the lack of a football team and feeling that "If you're looking for school spirit, UNCW may not be quite the place for you."

WHY STUDENTS LOVE UNIVERSITY OF NORTH CAROLINA–WILMINGTON

The school "has a laid-back atmosphere and a close-knit student body" on a "beautiful" campus. One student says, "It's awesome: beautiful weather, beautiful beaches, fantastic people, great atmosphere...basically everything you could ask for in a college experience." Clubs on campus are described as "numerous" and "accessible," and students say the "staff and administrators are dedicated to students' development as learners, leaders, and engaged citizens."

Why Students love University of North Carolina–Wilmington

"It's awesome: beautiful weather, beautiful beaches, fantastic people, great atmosphere...basically everything you could ask for in a

GENERAL INFO

Activities: Choral groups, concert band, dance, drama/theater, jazz band, literary magazine, music ensembles, pep band, radio station, student government, student newspaper, student-run film society, symphony orchestra, television station, campus ministries, international student organization. Organizations: 173 registered organizations, 8 honor societies, 14 religious organizations. 11 fraternities, 11 sororities. Athletics (Intercollegiate): Men: Baseball, basketball, cheerleading, cross-country, diving, golf, soccer, swimming, tennis, track/field (outdoor). Women: Basketball, cheerleading, cross-country, diving, golf, soccer, softball, swimming, tennis, track/field (outdoor), volleyball. On-Campus Highlights: Fisher Student Center, William Randall Library, UNCW Student Recreation Center, Trask Coliseum, Cultural Arts Building.

THE BOTTOM LINE

The average out-of-pocket cost of attending UNCW for an in-state student is roughly $14,000 annually; out-of-state students can expect to spend $24,000 per year. The cost of attendance at UNCW is reasonable but does include loans for most (54 percent of students borrow). Tuition only for an in-state resident is $3,000; out-of-state, $14,000. Room and board, about $7,500. Nearly half of all freshman receive financial aid, with the total package being more than $9,000. Graduates can expect to have approximately $19,000 in loan debt when they leave school.

SELECTIVITY

Admissions Rating	**88**
# of applicants	9,759
% of applicants accepted	57
% of acceptees attending	36

FRESHMAN PROFILE

Range SAT Critical Reading	**540–620**
Range SAT Math	**550–620**
Range SAT Writing	**520–600**
Range ACT Composite	**22–26**
Average HS GPA	**3.80**
% graduated top 10% of class	**23**
% graduated top 25% of class	**64**
% graduated top 50% of class	**94**

DEADLINES

Regular Deadline	**2/1**
Normal registration	**yes**

FACILITIES

Housing: Coed dorms, special housing for international students, women's dorms, apartments for single students, wellness housing, theme housing. *Special Academic Facilities/Equipment*: Upperman African American Cultural Arts Center, N.C. Teachers Legacy Hall, Ev-Henwood Nature Preserve, Center for Marine Science. *Computers*: 100% of classrooms, 100% of dorms, 100% of libraries, 100% of dining areas, 100% of student union, 50% of common outdoor areas have wireless network access.

FINANCIAL FACTS

Financial Aid Rating	**81**
Annual in-state tuition	$3,028
Annual out-of-state tuition	$14,127
Room and Board	$7,608
Required Fees	$2,387
Books and supplies	$985
% frosh rec. need-based scholarship or grant aid	38
% UG rec. need-based scholarship or grant aid	39
% frosh rec. non-need-based scholarship or grant aid	19
% UG rec. non-need-based scholarship or grant aid	16
% frosh rec. need-based self-help aid	26
% UG rec. need-based self-help aid	31
% frosh rec. any financial aid	43
% UG rec. any financial aid	43
% UG borrow to pay for school	54
Average cumulative indebtedness	$16,115

University of North Florida

1 UNF Drive, Jacksonville, FL 32224-7699 • Admissions: 904-620-5555 • Fax: 904-620-2414

CAMPUS LIFE

Quality of life Rating	79
Fire Safety Rating	73
Green rating	83
Type of School	Public
Environment	Metropolis

STUDENTS

Total undergrad enrollment	19,258
% Male to Female	45/55
% Live on Campus	19
# of Fraternities	14
# of Sororities	10
% African American	10
% Asian	5
% Caucasian	73
% Hispanic	7
% International	2
# Of Countries Represented	116

ACADEMICS

Academic Rating	69
Calendar	semester
Most common reg class size	20–29 students
Most common lab size	20–29 students

MOST POPULAR MAJORS

Business administration and management, mass communication/ media studies

HONORS PROGRAMS

The Honors Program at the University of North Florida. Special programs offered to physically disabled students include note-taking services, reader services, voice recorders.

SPECIAL STUDY OPTIONS

Accelerated program, cooperative education program, distance learning, double major, dual enrollment, English as a Second Language (ESL), exchange student program (domestic), honors program, independent study, internships, student-designed major, study abroad, teacher certification program, weekend college, Learning Communities.

ABOUT THE SCHOOL

The University of North Florida enrolls more than 16,000 students, but here students aren't just a number. Expect one-on-one personalized attention from professors in smaller classroom settings. UNF has five colleges: the Coggin College of Business, Brooks College of Health, College of Arts and Sciences, College of Computing, Engineering and Construction, and the College of Education and Human Services. The Brooks College of Health boasts a 100 percent first-time pass rate for physical therapy and nurse practitioner students, while the Coggin College of Business boasts a state-of-the-art logistics information technology solutions laboratory, one of only ten of its kind in the country. The Biology faculty is on the cutting edge of research, having received millions of dollars in funding from the National Science Foundation, National Institute of Health, the Department of Defense, and the Florida Institute of Oceanography. UNF biologists have played a pivotal role in studying the effects of the BP oil spill in the Gulf of Mexico, working to understand the effects of the spill on marine animals such as sharks and turtles as well as on sensitive coastal ecosystems and habitats such as coral reefs and seagrass beds. Three UNF electrical engineering students helped develop a prototype wristwatch capable of monitoring every beat of a patient's heart and alerting paramedics in an emergency.Internships are required in the program of study for many academic programs. Career Services manages the Cooperative Education Program which enables students in any of the colleges to set up a co-op assignment for academic credit. Transformational Learning Opportunities (TLOs) broaden and deepen students' intellectual and worldviews through study abroad experiences; service-learning experiences; research experiences with a faculty member; internships, practicum, field and co-op experiences. For example, the College of Arts and Sciences will soon open a

BANG FOR YOUR BUCK

UNF rewards academically talented high school students with several merit-based scholarships. The 2011 incoming class was awarded $3.3 million in scholarships, including a $10,000 Presidential Scholarship, which is given to freshmen who meet minimum test score and GPA requirements, a $20,000 Academic Scholarship is given to freshmen who are National Merit, National Achievement, and National Hispanic Finalists. In addition to merit-based scholarships, UNF also provides many awards on the basis of demonstrated financial need. The Pathways to Success scholarship program was established to help students achieve higher education despite financial barriers and requires a separate application. UNF also has Career Wings, an online job posting site, which gives students access to jobs and internships posted by employers.

STUDENTS

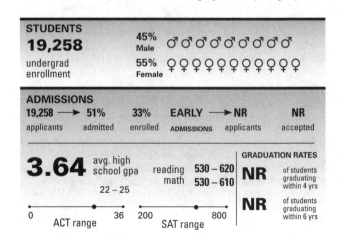

19,258 undergrad enrollment

45% Male ♂♂♂♂♂♂♂♂♂

55% Female ♀♀♀♀♀♀♀♀♀♀♀

ADMISSIONS

19,258 →	51%	33%	EARLY ADMISSIONS →	NR	NR
applicants	admitted	enrolled		applicants	accepted

3.64 avg. high school gpa

ACT range (0–36): 22 – 25

SAT range (200–800): reading 530 – 620; math 530 – 610

GRADUATION RATES

NR of students graduating within 4 yrs

NR of students graduating within 6 yrs

University of North Florida

FINANCIAL AID: 904-620-2698 • E-MAIL: ADMISSIONS@UNF.EDU • WEBSITE: WWW.UNF.EDU

STUDENT BODY

Students at UNF are an active bunch, and life on campus is described as "filled with studying and extra-curricular activities." With "many clubs and organizations that fit the life or interests of any student," most students are "involved in a campus activity, either frats or student government, or have a part time job." The "beautiful" campus is largely conducive to outdoor activities, with "nature trails great for hiking, mountain biking, or trail running" and "lakes where students can rent canoes and paddle around." For those not interested in the great outdoors, UNF is located in the city of Jacksonville, where students can partake in everything from sporting events to the beach and dance clubs.

Why Students love University of North Florida

"Nature trails great for hiking, mountain biking, or trail running."

WHY STUDENTS LOVE UNIVERSITY OF NORTH FLORIDA

"There is no typical student at UNF." Filled with "friendly" people who are mostly "from Florida," UNF students "love to learn and are actively involved in making a real difference." Possessing "all the aspects of a huge state college with a much more laid back feel," "everyone is very friendly, and there are many organizations to be a part of." Professors are described as "knowledgeable" with a "working knowledge of real business practices." "What they teach is applicable to the real world," so students feel prepared "for opportunities in the professional world." Many students rave about the "personal experience" at UNF, where "small size and scholarship offers make me feel like I really matter," and "you're not a number, you're a person."

GENERAL INFO

Activities: Choral groups, concert band, dance, drama/theater, jazz band, literary magazine, music ensembles, pep band, radio station, student government, student newspaper, television station, campus ministries, international student organization. **Organizations:** 140 registered organizations, 8 honor societies, 29 religious organizations. 14 fraternities, 10 sororities. **Athletics (Intercollegiate):** *Men:* Baseball, basketball, cheerleading, cross-country, golf, soccer, tennis, track/field (outdoor), track/field (indoor). *Women:* Basketball, cheerleading, cross-country, diving, soccer, softball, swimming, tennis, track/field (outdoor), track/field (indoor), volleyball. **On-Campus Highlights:** Student Union, Bookstore, Art Gallery, Nature Trails, Campus skate park, Greek Affairs, Earth Music Festival, Athletics NCAA I, free movies on Campus, Jazz Program (nationally recognized), Division I sports.

BOTTOM LINE

The cost of attending UNF is below the national average for four-year public universities. Tuition for in-state students is about $3,700, while out-of-state students pay about $18,000. Campus room and board will run you another $8,400. Students graduate with about $15,000 in debt on average.

SELECTIVITY

Admissions Rating	**83**
# of applicants	11,743
% of applicants accepted	51
% of acceptees attending	32

FRESHMAN PROFILE

Range SAT Critical Reading	**530–620**
Range SAT Math	**530–610**
Range ACT Composite	**22–25**
Average HS GPA	**3.64**
% graduated top 10% of class	**22**
% graduated top 25% of class	**52**
% graduated top 50% of class	**83**

DEADLINES

Regular Deadline	**6/6**
Normal registration	**no**

FACILITIES

Housing: Coed dorms, special housing for disabled students, apartments for single students, suite style housing. *Special Academic Facilities/Equipment:* Art gallery, bird sanctuary, Fine Arts Center. *Computers:* 100% of classrooms, 50% of dorms, 100% of libraries, 50% of dining areas, 100% of student union, 100% of common outdoor areas have wireless network access.

FINANCIAL FACTS

Financial Aid Rating	**89**
Annual in-state tuition	$3,742
Annual out-of-state tuition	$18,002
Room and Board	$8,452
Required Fees	$1,707
Books and supplies	$1,000
% frosh rec. need-based scholarship or grant aid	33
% UG rec.need-based scholarship or grant aid	29
% frosh rec. non-need-based scholarship or grant aid	41
% UG rec. non-need-based scholarship or grant aid	26
% frosh rec. need-based self-help aid	20
% UG rec. need-based self-help aid	26
% frosh rec. any financial aid	94
% UG rec. any financial aid	76
% UG borrow to pay for school	37
Average cumulative indebtedness	$15,300

University of Oklahoma

1000 Asp Avenue, Norman, OK 73019-4076 • Admissions: 405-325-2252 • Fax: 405-325-7124

CAMPUS LIFE

Quality of life Rating	87
Fire Safety Rating	91
Green rating	90
Type of School	Public
Environment	City

STUDENTS

Total undergrad enrolllment	20,498
% Male to Female	48/52
% From out of state	29
% Live on Campus	33
# of Fraternities	31
# of Sororities	20
% African American	5
% Asian	6
% Caucasian	65
% Hispanic	4
% Native American	6
% International	2
# Of Countries Represented	85

ACADEMICS

Academic Rating	71
% Of students graduating within 4 years	33
Calendar	semester
Profs interesting rating	76
Profs accessible rating	77
Most common reg class size	20–29 students
Most common lab size	20–29 students

MOST POPULAR MAJORS

Interdisciplinary studies, journalism, organization and behavior studies

HONORS PROGRAMS

Honors at Oxford. Honors in Italy. Honors in Germany. Honors Undergraduate Research Assistant Program. Medical Humanities Scholars Program. Honors Undergraduate Writing Assistant Program. Honors Undergraduate Research Opportunities Program. Undergraduate Research Day. Conversations with the Dean. Honors College Reading Groups. The Honors Undergraduate Research Journal.

SPECIAL STUDY OPTIONS

Accelerated program, cooperative education program, distance learning, double major, dual enrollment.

ABOUT THE SCHOOL

Pomona College is the founding member of the Claremont Colleges The University of Oklahoma combines a unique mixture of academic excellence, varied social cultures, and a variety of campus activities to make your educational experi¬ence complete. At OU, comprehensive learning is our goal for your life. OU students receive a valuable classroom learning experience, but OU is considered by many students to be one of the finest research institutions in the United States. They appreciate the opportunity to be a part of technology in progress. There are tons of organizations on OU's campus, and "There's no way you could possibly be bored." "From the Indonesian Student Association to the Bocce Ball League of Excellence, there's a group for" you. "The programming board here brings in a lot of great acts and keeps us very entertained in the middle of Oklahoma," adds one student. "School spirit is rampant," and intercollegiate athletics are insanely popular–particularly football. "Not everyone likes Sooner football," but it sure seems that way. Students at OU "live and breathe football" "to the point of near-frightening cultism." Game days in the fall are "an unforgettable experience," because "the campus goes into a frenzy." Fraternities and sororities are also "a large part of social life." Some students insist that the Greek system isn't a dominant feature of the OU landscape. "You hardly notice their presence" if you're not involved, they say, and "The majority of students aren't involved." The "friendly and cute little town" of Norman is reportedly an ideal place to spend a day when not in class. Right next to campus is an area "full of" boutique shops and "a fine selection of bars and restaurants." "Norman is such a great town," gushes one student. "It's not too little to be boring but not too big to be impersonal."

BANG FOR YOUR BUCK

The University of Oklahoma's tuition and fees remain perennially low when compared to its peer institutions in the Big 12 athletic conference, and OU is mighty proud of its dedication to providing financial assistance to students who want to attend. Alumni are loyal and the fundraising machine is epic. In fact, OU's Campaign for Scholarships recently passed the $130 million mark, allowing the university to double new scholarships for students in just four years. As far as scholarships go, OU offers several merit and need-based aid programs to students. Funds cover up to the full cost of tuition, and are available to Oklahoma residents and nonresidents.

STUDENTS

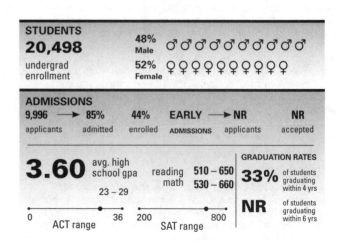

20,498 undergrad enrollment

48% Male ♂♂♂♂♂♂♂♂♂♂

52% Female ♀♀♀♀♀♀♀♀♀♀

ADMISSIONS

9,996 →	85%	44%	EARLY →	NR	NR
applicants	admitted	enrolled	ADMISSIONS	applicants	accepted

3.60 avg. high school gpa

ACT range (0–36): 23 – 29

SAT range (200–800): reading 510 – 650; math 530 – 660

GRADUATION RATES

33% of students graduating within 4 yrs

NR of students graduating within 6 yrs

University of Oklahoma

FINANCIAL AID: 405-325-5505 • E-MAIL: ADMREC@OU.EDU • WEBSITE: WWW.OU.EDU

STUDENT BODY

The typical student here is "pretty laid-back," "very good at prioritizing," "in some sort of organization or club," and "from Oklahoma or Texas." That student also "loves football," has "a penchant for fun," and has "no outrageous features." OU is home to "a wide variety of students with different political, religious, and economic backgrounds" though, and "There are plenty of options for every major and lifestyle." A lot of students come from a "suburban background" while "many come from small towns." There's also a "quite impressive" contingent of international students. Many students are "vaguely to devoutly Christian." Politically, "The atmosphere on campus tends to be conservative," but the left is well-represented. "We have a ton of liberals," relates one student, "and they are very much liberal." "There are the fraternity dudes and sorority girls" dressed in "North Face apparel and Nike shorts." "You have your partiers, hardcore studiers, and those in between who may lean one way or the other."

Why Students love University of Oklahoma

"School spirit is rampant."

WHY STUDENTS LOVE UNIVERSITY OF OKLAHOMA

Students "just swell with school pride" when they talk about the University of Oklahoma. They note, for example, that this "dynamic," "affordable," and "very research-oriented" institution reels in a slew of national merit scholars. They extol the "extensive" study abroad program. The meteorology program is "outstanding." "The engineering facilities are fantastic," and the campus as a whole is "gorgeous" and "well-kept." "The library is beautiful," reports a journalism major. "I could live in there." Like at any similar "big-time university," "The education here is what you make of it." "Anyone who truly wants to learn and achieve can find all sorts of opportunities." "Most professors are great," relates an industrial engineering major. They "know what they are talking about," and they're "approachable." Professors "usually lecture more than they promote discussions." "The best can keep you riveted until the very end of the class period," promises an economics major.

GENERAL INFO

Environment: City. **Activities:** Choral groups, concert band, dance, drama/theater, jazz band, literary magazine, marching band, music ensembles, musical theater, opera, pep band, radio station, student government, student newspaper, student-run film society, symphony orchestra, television station, yearbook, campus ministries, international student organization. **Organizations:** 388 registered organizations, 17 honor societies, 39 religious organizations. 30 fraternities, 20 sororities. **Athletics (Intercollegiate):** *Men:* Baseball, basketball, cross-country, football, golf, gymnastics, tennis, track/field (outdoor), track/field (indoor), wrestling. *Women:* Basketball, crew/rowing, cross-country, golf, gymnastics, soccer, softball, tennis, track/field (outdoor), track/field (in door), volleyball.

BOTTOM LINE

Tuition, fees, and room and board at OU run about $16,000 per year for Oklahoma residents. Nonresidents can expect to pay in the range of $27,000 a year. About 90 percent of undergrads here receive some type of financial assistance in the form of scholarships, grants, loans, work-study, and tuition waivers totaling close to $200 million.

SELECTIVITY

Admissions Rating	**84**
# of applicants	9,996
% of applicants accepted	85
% of acceptees attending	44
# accepting a place on wait list	1,545
% admitted from wait list	73

FRESHMAN PROFILE

Range SAT Critical Reading	**510–650**
Range SAT Math	**530–660**
Range ACT Composite	**23–29**
Average HS GPA	**3.60**
% graduated top 10% of class	**35**
% graduated top 25% of class	**67**
% graduated top 50% of class	**93**

DEADLINES

Regular Deadline	**4/1**
Normal registration	**yes**

FACILITIES

Housing: Coed dorms, special housing for disabled students, men's dorms, special housing for international students, women's dorms, fraternity/sorority housing, apartments for married students, apartments for single students, Honors House, Cultural Housing, National Merit, and Scholastics floors. *Special Academic Facilities/ Equipment:* Fred Jones Museum of Art, Sam Noble Museum of Natural His tory, National Weather Center, National Severe Storms Library.

FINANCIAL FACTS

Financial Aid Rating	**86**
Annual in-state tuition	$3,079
Annual out-of-state tuition	$11,841
Room and Board	$8,060
Required Fees	$3,631
Books and supplies	$1,043
% frosh rec. need-based scholarship or grant aid	27
% UG rec.need-based scholarship or grant aid	28
% frosh rec. non-need-based scholarship or grant aid	34
% UG rec. non-need-based scholarship or grant aid	24
% frosh rec. need-based self-help aid	31
% UG rec. need-based self-help aid	35
% frosh rec. any financial aid	83
% UG rec. any financial aid	90
% UG borrow to pay for school	57
Average cumulative indebtedness	$23,671

University of Pittsburgh at Bradford

Office of Admissions: Hanley Library, 300 Campus Drive, Bradford, PA 16701 • Admissions: 814-362-7555

CAMPUS LIFE

Quality of life Rating	71
Fire Safety Rating	85
Green rating	75
Type of School	Public
Environment	Village

STUDENTS

Total undergrad enrolllment	1,627
% Male to Female	48/52
% From out of state	16
% From public high school	74
% Live on Campus	55
# of Fraternities	5
# of Sororities	3
% African American	7
% Asian	2
% Caucasian	84
% Hispanic	2
% International	1
# Of Countries Represented	10

ACADEMICS

Academic Rating	71
% Of students graduating within 4 years	24
% Of students graduating within 6 years	38
Calendar	semester
Most common reg class size	20–29 students
Most common lab size	20–29 students

MOST POPULAR MAJORS

Business, commerce, general elemtary education and teaching

HONOR PROGRAMS

The University of Pittsburgh at Bradford offers the Scholars Program which is designed to create a learning community for outstanding students at Pitt Bradford. Special programs offered to physically disabled students include note-taking services, reader services, voice recorders, tutors.

SPECIAL STUDY OPTIONS

Cross-registration, distance learning, double major, dual enrollment, external degree program, honors program, independent study, internships, study abroad, teacher certification program.

ABOUT THE SCHOOL

The University of Pittsburgh at Bradford takes students beyond: beyond the classroom by offering internships and research opportunities; beyond the degree by providing a robust Career Services Office and an informal alumni network; beyond 9 to 5 by offering an active student life, a friendly residence life environment, excellent athletic and cultural facilities, and a wide range of recreational opportunities; beyond place by providing a liberal arts education that exposes students to the world and offering students many study-abroad opportunities; and beyond students' expectations by giving them a college experience that will transform them.

Pitt-Bradford is nestled in the foothills of the Allegheny Mountains and only steps away from the Allegheny National Forest. Students at Pitt Bradford live and learn on a safe, intimate campus, where they receive individual and personalized attention from committed professors who work side by side with them. And, they earn a degree from the University of Pittsburgh, which commands respect around the world. Because Pitt-Bradford is a personalized campus, opportunities for leadership abound. Many students become campus leaders as early as their sophomore year.

Why Students love Pitt at Bradford

"I love how it has that out-in-the-country feel."

BANG FOR YOUR BUCK

The school wants to make college education affordable, and the numerous need- and merit-based scholarships in place are good evidence of this (not to mention the entirely reasonable tuition). Factoring in the financial aid most students receive, the cost of attending Pitt-Bradford is much less than you might expect, and the university's growing reputation means the degree is increasingly more valuable. Merit Scholarships (called Panther Scholarships) are determined using only GPA and the Math and Critical Reading portion of the SATs, so a good student can get $5,500 knocked off their tuition bill each year.

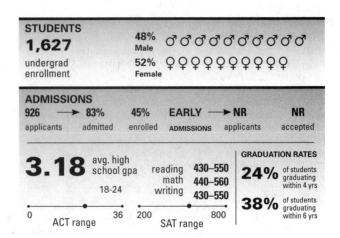

STUDENTS

1,627 undergrad enrollment

48% Male ♂♂♂♂♂♂♂♂♂♂

52% Female ♀♀♀♀♀♀♀♀♀♀

ADMISSIONS

926 applicants → 83% admitted — 45% enrolled

EARLY ADMISSIONS → NR applicants — NR accepted

3.18 avg. high school gpa

ACT range (0–36): 18-24

SAT range (200–800): reading 430–550; math 440–560; writing 430–550

GRADUATION RATES

24% of students graduating within 4 yrs

38% of students graduating within 6 yrs

University of Pittsburgh at Bradford

FINANCIAL AID: 814-362-7550 • E-MAIL: ADMISSIONS@UPB.PITT.EDU • FAX: 814-362-5150 • WEBSITE: WWW.UPB.PITT.EDU

STUDENT BODY

The typical undergrad is either "from a small town or from Pittsburgh." "There are a lot of commuter and adult learners" as well. Students describe themselves as "down-to-earth people" "who are easily approachable." The "friendly hello" is common here. "If you run short of money while doing laundry, don't be surprised if somebody throws you a dollar to help you get your laundry done," predicts a senior. "There are a handful of weird" students but nobody really strays too far in any direction away from the social median. "Everyone has friends." "Everyone fits in everywhere" and, "for the most part, everyone gets along with everybody else." says one student. "Walking around campus you see a little bit of every culture, every race, and every ethnicity." "There are strong subcultures for the minorities" and ages, ranging from students "right out of high school" and those "older in years [who] are looking to further their careers."

WHY STUDENTS LOVE PITT-BRADFORD

The University of Pittsburgh at Bradford is "a cozy gem in the middle of nowhere" that offers "small classes with individualized attention, professors who are always available, and a generally student-friendly atmosphere." The curriculum is largely career-oriented. Popular majors include business, education, and nursing. The athletic training major is reportedly excellent and "this school excels in the criminal justice area" as well. "Some professors are amazing," says a biology major. Overall, faculty members are "personable" and they "have real-life experiences to bring back to the classrooms." "Professors learn your name," adds an elementary education major, "and you are yourself instead of just a number." The administration is "very friendly and helpful."

GENERAL INFO

Activities: Choral groups, dance, drama/theater, literary magazine, radio station, student government, student newspaper, campus ministries. **Organizations:** 54 registered organizations, 8 honor societies, 1 religious organizations. 3 fraternities, 3 sororities. **Athletics (Intercollegiate):** *Men:* Baseball, basketball, cross-country, golf, soccer, swimming, tennis. *Women:* Basketball, cross-country, golf, soccer, softball, swimming, tennis, volleyball. **On-Campus Highlights:** Sport and Fitness Center, The Commons, student apartments, Blaisdell Hall (Fine Arts Building), smart classrooms. **Environmental Initiatives:** Development of an Alternative Energy Institute. Partner ship in a consortium that includes the University of Pittsburgh, Penn State, and others for development of an alternative energy university consortium. **Environmental Initiatives:** In-House Building Commissioning Team; full-time Sustainability Marketing and Outreach; retrofitting water conservation devices on campus.

BOTTOM LINE

Tuition for in-state students is $11,736, and out-of-state students pay $21,928, with an additional $8564 going toward room, board, and additional fees. Ninety-two percent of students receive some form of financial aid through grants, loans, work study, or scholarships, with the average award for in-state students at $16,490, and for out-of-state students, about $19,250.More than 40 percent of students borrow in some way to pay for school, and can envision a cumulative indebtedness once graduating from the institution of more than $17,000. Clemson students are especially thrilled by the incredible support the university offers. "The value is unbeatable."

SELECTIVITY

Admissions Rating	**70**
# of applicants	926
% of applicants accepted	83
% of acceptees attending	45

FRESHMAN PROFILE

Range SAT Critical Reading	**430–550**
Range SAT Math	**440–560**
Range SAT Writing	**420–550**
Range ACT Composite	**18–24**
Average HS GPA	**3.18**
% graduated top 10% of class	**4**
% graduated top 25% of class	**28**
% graduated top 50% of class	**66**

DEADLINES

Regular Deadline	**1/1**
Normal registration	**no**

FACILITIES

Housing: Coed dorms, special housing for disabled students, apartments for single students. 99% of campus accessible to physically disabled. *Special Academic Facilities/Equipment:* Ceramics Studio, Biodiesal Lab, Television and Radio Broadcast Labs. *Computers:* 100% of classrooms, 100% of dorms, 90% of libraries, 90% of dining areas, 100% of student union, 50% of common outdoor areas have wireless network access.

FINANCIAL FACTS

Financial Aid Rating	**89**
Annual in-state tuition	$11,736
Annual out-of-state tuition	$21,928
Room and Board	$7,804
Required Fees	$760
Books and supplies	$1,110
% frosh rec. need-based scholarship or grant aid	56
% UG rec.need-based scholarship or grant aid	36
% frosh rec. non-need-based scholarship or grant aid	61
% UG rec. non-need-based scholarship or grant aid	31
% frosh rec. need-based self-help aid	86
% UG rec. need-based self-help aid	57
% frosh rec. any financial aid	86
% UG rec. any financial aid	83
% UG borrow to pay for school	80
Average cumulative indebtedness	$21,695

University of Pittsburgh

4227 Fifth Avenue, First Floor Alumni Hall, Pittsburgh, PA 15260 • Admissions: 9412-624-7488 • Fax: 412-648-8815

CAMPUS LIFE

Quality of life Rating	98
Fire Safety Rating	81
Green rating	92
Type of School	Public
Environment	Metropolis

STUDENTS

Total undergrad enrolllment	17,994
% Male to Female	49/51
% From out of state	22
% Live on Campus	45
# of Fraternities	20
# of Sororities	16
% African American	7
% Asian	5
% Caucasian	79
% Hispanic	2
% International	2
# Of Countries Represented	48

ACADEMICS

Academic Rating	78
% Of students graduating within 4 years	61
% Of students graduating within 6 years	78
Calendar	semester
Profs interesting rating	81
Profs accessible rating	83
Most common reg class size	10–19 students
Most common lab size	20–29 students

MOST POPULAR MAJORS

Psychology, rhetoric and composition, marketing

HONORS PROGRAMS

University Honors College.

SPECIAL STUDY OPTIONS

Accelerated program, cooperative education program, cross-registration, distance learning, double major, dual enrollment, English as a Second Language (ESL), exchange student program (domestic), external degree program, honors program, independent study, internships, liberal arts/career combination, student-designed major, study abroad, teacher certification program, weekend college.

ABOUT THE SCHOOL

An academic powerhouse, University of Pittsburgh is one of Pennsylvania's premiere institutions. With 107 degree programs spread throughout 10 undergraduate schools, students can study virtually any topic they desire. Impressively, strong prospective freshmen can be considered for guaranteed-admission to 15 graduate/professional schools including dentistry, medicine and law. Additionally, Pitt has established a number of fantastic programs that enhance (and encourage) learning beyond the classroom. For example, the Outside the Classroom Curriculum (OCC) assists undergrads in finding internship, research and volunteer opportunities where students gain practical experience (and a resume boost). The Engineering Co-Op Program also helps students pair their education with a professional setting. And the stellar Honors Program (offering a unique BPhil degree), maintains several prestigious programs including the Brackenridge Summer Research Fellowships and the Yellowstone Field Program. Finally, hometown Pittsburgh provides students with a number of educational and cultural opportunities. Recently voted one of the most livable cities in the country, students frequently take advantage of the city's myriad bars, restaurants, museums and theaters (even getting a discount through PITTARTS).

Why Students love Pitt

"Being in the middle of everything with the greatest people you can find."

BANG FOR YOUR BUCK

Pitt endeavors to help all students with financial need and limited resources. To begin with, all prospective freshmen who present an outstanding academic record (and complete an application by January 15) will automatically be considered for merit scholarships. These awards range from $2,000 to full coverage for tuition, room and board. Importantly, these scholarships are renewable up to three years, provided recipients meet pre-determined GPA and progress requirements.

STUDENTS

17,994 undergrad enrollment

49% Male ♂♂♂♂♂♂♂♂♂♂

51% Female ♀♀♀♀♀♀♀♀♀♀

ADMISSIONS

22,616	58%	29%	EARLY ADMISSIONS → NR	NR
applicants	admitted	enrolled	applicants	accepted

3.91 avg. high school gpa

ACT range (0–36): 25 – 30

SAT range (200–800):

reading	570 – 680
math	600 – 690
writing	560 – 660

GRADUATION RATES

61% of students graduating within 4 yrs

78% of students graduating within 6 yrs

University of Pittsburgh

FINANCIAL AID: 412-624-7488 • E-MAIL: OAFA@PITT.EDU • WEBSITE: WWW.PITT.EDU

STUDENT BODY

Roughly three-quarters of Pitt students are from Pennsylvania, and overall, students are "middle-class" and "personable and accepting." "You're going to find slackers at every school, but the majority of people [here] work very hard and have heavy workloads." Going to Pitt is about "being in the middle of everything with the greatest people you can find." Beyond that, "We're big enough that there's a group for everyone" and that students "can develop a group of friends" while still being "accepted with open arms" by the larger student community. Says one Pitt student, "There are many atypical students when considering backgrounds, ethnicity, and beliefs, but a common interest in positive academic pursuits and community development brings us all together."

WHY STUDENTS LOVE PITT

The University of Pittsburgh has done quite a job amassing a group of highly content students. Undergrads here frequently assert how at home they felt from the minute they stepped onto campus. "A haven in a large, urban city" Pitt manages to foster a "friendly" atmosphere that often feels "truly electric." Indeed, despite being a large school, Pitt still "values each individual student and makes everyone feel welcome and accepted." Moreover, undergrads note Pitt's great reputation and say that it is most definitely warranted. While the university maintains a number of excellent majors, students especially highlight the "strong" pre-med, nursing, pharmacy and engineering programs. They are also full of praise for their professors, citing that they are "brilliant" and "caring." Additionally, undergrads love Pittsburgh and the fact that "the whole city revolves around the university." For example, "With my Pitt ID, I can do virtually anything. I can walk to the Carnegie Museum, I can hop a (free!) bus to another museum, like the Mattress Factory or Andy Warhol. I can get discounts to movies." The city truly is their metaphorical oyster. As one pleased student happily sums up, "I've had nothing but great experiences here and I would never go anywhere else."

GENERAL INFO

Activities: Choral groups, concert band, dance, drama/theater, jazz band, literary magazine, marching band, music ensembles, pep band, radio station, student government, student newspaper, student-run film society, television station, yearbook, campus ministries, international student organization. **Organizations:** 395 registered organizations, 17 honor societies, 20 fraternities, 16 sororities. **Athletics (Intercollegiate):** *Men:* Baseball, basketball, cross-country, diving, football, soccer, swimming, track/field (outdoor), wrestling. *Women:* Basketball, cross-country, diving, gymnastics, soccer, softball, swimming, tennis, track/field (outdoor), volleyball. **On-Campus Highlights:** Cathedral of Learning, William Pitt Union, Heinz Chapel, Peterson Event Center, Sennott Square.

BOTTOM LINE

Pennsylvania residents should expect to pay $14,076 per academic year. Out-of-state undergraduates will need to shell out $23,732 annually. There are also additional, required fees totaling $860. Of course, the university offers a variety of grants, loans and work-study opportunities.

SELECTIVITY

Admissions Rating	**93**
# of applicants	22,616
% of applicants accepted	58
% of acceptees attending	29
# accepting a place on wait list	234
% admitted from wait list	6

FRESHMAN PROFILE

Range SAT Critical Reading	**570–680**
Range SAT Math	**600–690**
Range SAT Writing	**560–660**
Range ACT Composite	**25–30**
Average HS GPA	**3.91**
% graduated top 10% of class	**51**
% graduated top 25% of class	**85**
% graduated top 50% of class	**99**

DEADLINES

Regular Deadline	**10/1**
Normal registration	**yes**

FACILITIES

Housing: Coed dorms, special housing for disabled students, women's dorms, fraternity/sorority housing, apartments for single students, wellness housing, theme housing. *Special Academic Facilities/Equipment:* Stephen Foster Memorial, observatory. *Computers:* 100% of classrooms, 25% of dorms, 100% of libraries, 100% of dining areas, 100% of student union, 50% of common outdoor areas have wireless network access.

FINANCIAL FACTS

Financial Aid Rating	**81**
Annual in-state tuition	$15,272
Annual out-of-state tuition	$24,680
Room and Board	$9,430
Required Fees	$860
Books and supplies	$1,110
% frosh rec. need-based scholarship or grant aid	41
% UG rec.need-based scholarship or grant aid	39
% frosh rec. non-need-based scholarship or grant aid	23
% UG rec. non-need-based scholarship or grant aid	16
% frosh rec. need-based self-help aid	44
% UG rec. need-based self-help aid	45
% frosh rec. any financial aid	63
% UG rec. any financial aid	62
% UG borrow to pay for school	63
Average cumulative indebtedness	$26,612

University of South Carolina—Columbia

Office of Undergraduate Admissions, University of South Carolina, Columbia, SC 29208 • Admissions: 803-777-7700

CAMPUS LIFE

Quality of life Rating	85
Fire Safety Rating	86
Green rating	97
Type of School	Public
Environment	City

STUDENTS

Total undergrad enrolllment	21,031
% Male to Female	47/53
% From out of state	28
% Live on Campus	36
# of Fraternities	20
# of Sororities	14
% African American	11
% Asian	3
% Caucasian	78
% Hispanic	3
% International	1
# Of Countries Represented	120

ACADEMICS

Academic Rating	71
% Of students graduating within 4 years	53
% Of students graduating within 6 years	68
Calendar	semester
Profs interesting rating	76
Profs accessible rating	81
Most common reg class size	20–29 students
Most common lab size	20–29 students

MOST POPULAR MAJORS

Business administration and management, experimental psychology, sport and fitness administration/ management

HONORS PROGRAMS

The Honors College is a small college of about 1,000 students, all of whom excel in academics.

SPECIAL STUDY OPTIONS

Accelerated program, cooperative education program, cross-registration, distance learning, double major, dual enrollment, exchange student program (domestic), external degree program, independent study, internships, student-designed major, study abroad.

ABOUT THE SCHOOL

The University of South Carolina offers 350-plus programs of study in its fourteen colleges and schools. The campus is home to an Honors College that offers a few select undergraduates a small, liberal arts college experience on USC's campus, including a selection of courses offered exclusively to Honors College students. Small, discussion-based classes are the norm, and students in the Honors College receive lots of personalized attention from professors. Academic offerings for regular students are just as good. USC boasts respected programs in business, nursing, journalism, chemistry, and hospitality management. Across the board, professors are approachable and knowledgeable in their fields, though, as at any large university, some are more concerned about their research than teaching. USC's campus is steeped in Southern tradition and all that it entails. School spirit is off the charts, and attending a home game is an experience like none other. 2010 was a very good year for USC's sports programs: the university won the national championship for Division-I baseball, and beat the Florida Gators to cinch the SEC East title. If sports don't interest you, chances are you'll find distraction in one of USC's 300-plus registered student organizations. Greek life also beckons. Hometown Columbia is a great college town, close to Charlotte, Atlanta, and Charleston. And here's an interesting fact: USC houses the largest collection of Robert Burns and Scottish literature materials outside of Scotland.

BANG FOR YOUR BUCK

The University of South Carolina awards more than 1,000 need-based and merit-based scholarships to entering freshman each year. If you have a strong academic record and are a leader in your high school and community, you may qualify for a Carolina Scholars Scholarship worth up to $40,000 over four years. Lieber Scholarships award National Merit Finalists, National Achievement Finalists, and National Hispanic Recognition Program Scholars scholarships worth up to $40,000 over four years. Smaller scholarship awards ranging from $2,000–$20,000 over four years are also available. Nonresidents are also eligible for scholarships. Forty out-of-state students with strong academic records who are leaders in their high schools and communities will be selected as McNair Scholar Finalists and receive awards ranging up to $60,000 for four years.

STUDENTS

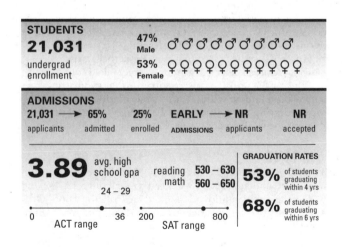

21,031 undergrad enrollment

47% Male

53% Female

ADMISSIONS

21,031 applicants → 65% admitted | 25% enrolled | EARLY ADMISSIONS → NR applicants | NR accepted

3.89 avg. high school gpa

ACT range (0–36): 24 – 29

SAT range (200–800): reading 530 – 630, math 560 – 650

GRADUATION RATES

53% of students graduating within 4 yrs

68% of students graduating within 6 yrs

University of South Carolina—Columbia

FAX: 803-777-0101 • FINANCIAL AID: 803-777-8134 • E-MAIL: ADMISSIONS@SC.EDU • WEBSITE: WWW.SC.EDU

STUDENT BODY

Archetypal students at USC are "politically conservative, openly religious (mostly Christian), and traditionally Southern." The atmosphere "can be intimidating to non-Southerners at times." "If you are from a different part of the country," counsels a first-year student, "it's a culture shock." Students here are also "very involved on campus" and exceedingly proud of their school. "We all have Gamecock pride," explains a sophomore. Otherwise, this place is "a huge melting pot," with "a wide range" of students and organizations. Students who pledge fraternities and sororities constitute the most visible bloc. "A lot of the girls are the classic blond Southern girl and many of the guys are preppy" types. "There is a different group for everyone down here," though. "Good old boys and some more progressive types," "artsy" kids, "gothic" kids, "theater kids, ROTC kids," and "self-proclaimed honors college nerds" all have their respective niches. "Every type of person goes to this school," says a sophomore.

Why Students love USC—Columbia

"The school spirit is crazy."

WHY STUDENTS LOVE USC—COLUMBIA

At the University of South Carolina's flagship campus, you'll find "a mixture of deep South tradition and an increasingly progressive education." You can get "a good degree in just about any field" here. The nationally recognized business school is "definitely a strength." There's a "great nursing program" as well. USC also excels in journalism, chemistry, and hospitality management. In most majors, the academic atmosphere is "not impossible, but a good amount of time goes into studying outside of class." "It is just the right amount of work to still have a good social life," opines a broadcast journalism major. Students in the "fantastic" honors college enjoy "small, discussion-based classes and a lot of personal attention." Meanwhile, for the run of USC-ers, classes are much bigger, teaching assistants are common, and the professors "vary vastly." A lot of professors are "very well-prepared," "very approachable," and "passionate about their subjects." "Most of the teachers I have had here have been outstanding,"

GENERAL INFO

Activities: Choral groups, concert band, dance, drama/theater, jazz band, literary magazine, marching band, music ensembles, musical theater, opera, pep band, radio station, student government, student newspaper, symphony orchestra. **Organizations:** 300 registered organizations, 25 honor societies, 32 religious organizations. 20 fraternities, 14 sororities. **Athletics (Intercollegiate):** *Men:* Baseball, basketball, diving, football, golf, racquetball, soccer, softball, swimming, tennis, track/field (outdoor). *Women:* Basketball, cross-country, diving, equestrian sports, golf, racquetball, soccer, softball, swimming, tennis, track/field (outdoor), volleyball. **On-Campus Highlights:** Strom Thurmond Wellness & Fitness Center, Russell House, Greek Village, Williams Brice Stadium, Historic Horseshoe. **Environmental Initiatives:** Operation of biomass plant producing

BOTTOM LINE

The cost of attending the University of South Carolina is extremely affordable. Annual tuition and fees hover around $9,300, while campus room and board will run you another $7,700. Out-of-state undergraduates pay almost $15,000 more in tuition and fees.

SELECTIVITY

Admissions Rating	**87**
# of applicants	18,485
% of applicants accepted	65
% of acceptees attending	35
# accepting a place on wait list	0

FRESHMAN PROFILE

Range SAT Critical Reading	**530–630**
Range SAT Math	**560–650**
Range ACT Composite	**24–29**
Average HS GPA	**3.89**
% graduated top 10% of class	**28**
% graduated top 25% of class	**60**
% graduated top 50% of class	**90**

DEADLINES

Regular Deadline	**12/1**
Normal registration	**yes**

FACILITIES

Housing: Coed dorms, special housing for disabled students, men's dorms, special housing for international students, women's dorms, fraternity/sorority housing, apartments for married students, apartments for single students, wellness housing, Honors housing (first year freshman and upperclass).

FINANCIAL FACTS

Financial Aid Rating	**79**
Annual in-state tuition	$9,768
Annual out-of-state tuition	$25,952
Room and Board	$8,026
Required Fees	$400
Books and supplies	$950
% frosh rec. need-based scholarship or grant aid	21
% UG rec.need-based scholarship or grant aid	25
% frosh rec. non-need-based scholarship or grant aid	40
% UG rec. non-need-based scholarship or grant aid	29
% frosh rec. need-based self-help aid	32
% UG rec. need-based self-help aid	38
% frosh rec. any financial aid	82
% UG rec. any financial aid	72
% UG borrow to pay for school	49
Average cumulative indebtedness	$21,811

University of South Dakota

414 East Clark, Vermillion, SD 57069 • Admissions: 605-677-5434 • Fax: 605-677-6323

CAMPUS LIFE

Quality of life Rating	65
Fire Safety Rating	93
Green rating	78
Type of School	Public
Environment	Village

STUDENTS

Total undergrad enrolllment	6,103
% Male to Female	38/62
% From out of state	29
% From public high school	91
% Live on Campus	29
# of Fraternities	8
# of Sororities	3
% African American	2
% Asian	1
% Caucasian	88
% Hispanic	2
% Native American	2
% International	1
# Of Countries Represented	33

ACADEMICS

Academic Rating	70
% Of students graduating within 4 years	25
% Of students graduating within 6 years	49
Calendar	semester
Profs interesting rating	74
Profs accessible rating	74
Most common reg class size	10–19 students
Most common lab size	20–29 students

MOST POPULAR MAJORS

Business/commerce, education, psychology

HONORS PROGRAMS

University Honors Program. Thesis Scholars Program, Alumni Student Scholars Program, Law Honors Scholars Program.

SPECIAL STUDY OPTIONS

Accelerated program, cross-registration, distance learning, double major, dual enrollment.

ABOUT THE SCHOOL

USD is South Dakota's only designated liberal arts university, and the school awards scholarships to more than 800 first-year students, and more than eighty percent of USD students receive some form of financial aid through grants, loans, and work-study jobs. USD students earn the nation's most prestigious scholarships. The quality of teaching and research prepares students to pursue their passions all over the world, at institutions such as Columbia, Johns Hopkins, The University of Chicago, and beyond. Fifty-nine students have been awarded prestigious Fulbright, Rhodes, National Science Foundation, Boren, Truman, Udall, Gilman, and Goldwater scholarships and grants for graduate study. As the flagship liberal arts institution in South Dakota, USD–founded in 1862–has long been regarded as a leader in the state and the region.

"Vermillion is located within an hour of Yankton, Sioux City, and Sioux Falls. They are bigger cities and offer everything a person would want to do. "Many of the upperclassmen live in the larger cities to the north and south." "The smaller community gives me a chance to work with teachers more easily and helps build stronger bonds between academic advisers. I chose the University of South Dakota, because it is a small, public, liberal arts school that gives plenty of options for academic and social growth." Students tell us, "The campus is up-to-date and is constantly changing for the better. I also feel the professors are a higher quality than those in the same department at other schools." The attention to undergraduate research is apparently phenomenal. "They pay for every conference I want to attend," and the school has summer research programs that pay students a very descent salary, and "faculty acceptance for undergraduate researchers is amazing."

BANG FOR YOUR BUCK

The University of South Dakota offers a "great student to faculty communicative experience at a reasonable price." "The perfect fit for students looking for a smart educational investment." For students willing to throw themselves into their studies "the odds of getting into a professional or graduate program are good." Annually, USD awards scholarships to more than 800 first-year students; very impressive, with a total enrollment of only 6,000 students. "The people are extremely welcoming and if I had to go back a year and look at colleges without financial limits, I would have still chosen USD."

STUDENTS

6,103 undergrad enrollment

38% Male ♂♂♂♂♂♂♂♂

62% Female ♀♀♀♀♀♀♀♀♀♀♀♀♀

ADMISSIONS

3,452 applicants → 85% admitted — 30% enrolled — EARLY ADMISSIONS → NR applicants — NR accepted

3.25 avg. high school gpa

ACT range (0–36): 20 – 25

SAT range (200–800): reading 440 – 630; math 450 – 610; writing

GRADUATION RATES

25% of students graduating within 4 yrs

49% of students graduating within 6 yrs

University of South Dakota

FINANCIAL AID: 605-677-5446 • E-MAIL: ADMISSIONS@USD.EDU • WEBSITE: WWW.USD.EDU

STUDENT BODY

A typical USD student "would be a conservative Midwesterner. He or she would be Caucasian" and would most likely have originated in "small towns in South Dakota, Iowa, and Nebraska." "Many people join a Greek system or are athletes or musicians. Those who do not fit into these three main groups seem to focus on their academics" and "[fit] in fine with the majority because of the open mindedness of most students." For example, "Gay students are able to get along with the rest of student population." There's no denying that "partying is a definite part of the culture, though many of the 'smart' kids both party and work hard." Student organizations call out to many, and "it seems like every person on campus is part of at least one of them. It is a great way to meet new people and [to participate in] activities."

Why Students love University of South Dakota

"The perfect fit for students looking for a smart educational investment."

WHY STUDENTS LOVE UNIVERSITY OF SOUTH DAKOTA

With an honors program that is "the best-kept secret in the country" and professors who are "nearly always willing to go the extra mile for students," the University of South Dakota offers a "great student to faculty communicative experience at a reasonable price." Numerous departments garner praise from students. While the nursing school is the most frequently praised, the "business, biology, premed, law, and psychology classes are very solid," and the "dental hygiene, music, and journalism schools" also stand out, with the most copious laurels heaped on the music department's professors who are "some of the best." All told, the wide selection of quality academics "gives students many options as far as majors go," and for students willing to throw themselves into their studies "the odds of getting into a professional or graduate program are good."

GENERAL INFO

Activities: Choral groups, concert band, dance, drama/theater, jazz band, literary magazine, marching band, music ensembles, musical theater, opera, pep band, radio station, student government, student newspaper, symphony orchestra, television station, campus ministries, international student organization. **Organizations:** 120 registered organizations, 6 honor societies, 6 religious organizations. 8 fraternities, 3 sororities. **Athletics (Intercollegiate):** *Men:* Basketball, cross-country, diving, football, golf, swimming, track/field (outdoor), track/field (indoor). *Women:* Basketball, cross-country, diving, golf, soccer, softball, swimming, tennis, track/field (outdoor), track/field (indoor), volleyball.

BOTTOM LINE

The University of South Dakota provides students with an extremely affordable tuition rate, making a quality education available to most anyone who seeks it. Yearly tuition is a mere $3,500 for those from the state; and out-of-state students actually only pay a bit more, at just more than $5,000. Another $10,000 will cover all room, board, books, supplies, and fees. 45 percent of freshmen receive a form of non-need based scholarship or grant aid, and more than 90 percent of all students get financial aid packages in one form or another. As one student tells us, "I chose USD because I knew I could get a quality undergraduate education with little to no debt."

SELECTIVITY

Admissions Rating	**74**
# of applicants	3,452
% of applicants accepted	85
% of acceptees attending	30

FRESHMAN PROFILE

Range SAT Critical Reading	**440–630**
Range SAT Math	**450–610**
Range ACT Composite	**20–25**
Average HS GPA	**3.25**
% graduated top 10% of class	**13**
% graduated top 25% of class	**34**
% graduated top 50% of class	**64**

DEADLINES

Regular Deadline	**9/20**
Normal registration	**yes**

FACILITIES

Housing: Coed dorms, special housing for disabled students, fraternity/sorority housing, apartments for married students, apartments for single students, apartments for students with dependent children. *Special Academic Facilities/Equipment:* W.H. Over Museum, The National Music Museum, Oscar Howe Art Gallery, Center for Instructional Design and Delivery, Institute of American Indian Studies, Native American Cultural Center. *Computers:* 60% of classrooms, 100% of libraries, 100% of dining areas, 100% of student union, have wireless network access.

FINANCIAL FACTS

Financial Aid Rating	**88**
Annual in-state tuition	$3,429
Annual out-of-state tuition	$5,143.50
Room and Board	$6,543
Required Fees	$3,780
Books and supplies	$1,100
% frosh rec. need-based scholarship or grant aid	32
% UG rec.need-based scholarship or grant aid	32
% frosh rec. non-need-based scholarship or grant aid	45
% UG rec. non-need-based scholarship or grant aid	30
% frosh rec. need-based self-help aid	54
% UG rec. need-based self-help aid	58
% frosh rec. any financial aid	94
% UG rec. any financial aid	91

University of Tennessee–Knoxville

320 Student Service Building, Circle Park Drive, Knoxville, TN 37996-0230 • Admissions: 865-974-2184

CAMPUS LIFE

Quality of life Rating	74
Fire Safety Rating	83
Green rating	88
Type of School	Public
Environment	City

STUDENTS

Total undergrad enrolllment	20,849
% Male to Female	51/49
% From out of state	13
% Live on Campus	26
# of Fraternities	23
# of Sororities	18
% African American	8
% Asian	3
% Caucasian	84
% Hispanic	2
% Native American	1
% International	1
# Of Countries Represented	115

ACADEMICS

Academic Rating	71
% Of students graduating within 4 years	31
% Of students graduating within 6 years	61
Calendar	semester
Profs interesting rating	70
Profs accessible rating	75
Most common reg class size	20–29 students
Most common lab size	20–29 students

MOST POPULAR MAJORS

Business administration and management, journalism, psychology

HONORS PROGRAMS

1. Chancellor's Honors Program 2. Haslam Scholars Program 3. College Scholars Program 4. Global Leadership Scholars Program 5. College of Engineering Honors Pro gram 6. College of Agricultural and Natural Resources Honors Program 7. College of Social Work Honors Program 8. Howard H. Baker Jr. Center for Public Policy's Baker Scholars Program 9. The Math Honors Program 10. Additional departmental honors programs.

ABOUT THE SCHOOL

The University of Tennessee, Knoxville, offers students the great program diversity of a major university, opportunities for research or original creative work in every degree program, and a welcoming campus environment. UT blends more than 200 years of history, tradition, and 'Volunteer Spirit' with the latest technology and innovation. Life at UT is all "about education, community, and becoming a true Tennessee volunteer." "There's a great sense of unity." The faculty "tries extremely hard to encourage acceptance of several kinds of diversity." A "LGBTQ Resource Center [recently] opened on campus." "There is also a large 'Stop Bias' program that is promoted." In general, there are "tons of clubs and organizations to get involved with if you are passionate about something." Nine colleges offer more than 170 undergraduate majors and concentrations to students from all fifty states and 100 foreign countries, and UT students can make the world their campus through study abroad programs. More than 400 clubs and organizations on campus allow students to further individualize their college experience in service, recreation, academics, and professional development. The typical UT student "loves all aspects of the university's life from its sports to its long-standing traditions." Students flock here for "family history, athletics, and to sing 'Rocky Top.'" "We love football just about as much as academics." However, academics here are just as intense as athletics, "Being a larger university, I have had many more opportunities than people I know at smaller schools in education as well as extracurriculars." "The University of Tennessee combines the best of all worlds: great education for a great price, sports, social life, and a ton of extracurriculars to choose from."

BANG FOR YOUR BUCK

UTK offers students the standard docket of work-study and state and federal grants and loans. Scholarships are plentiful. More than $23 million in scholarship funds are awarded annually, with four-year, one-year, and renewable scholarships available. A few highlights include: Bonham Scholarships are four-year awards based on academic merit. They provide six new recipients with $5,000 per year for four years. The Manning Scholarship honors Peyton Manning, a 1998 alumnus, who was the protoypical scholar-athlete. The scholarship awards recipients $6,000 per year for four years. The University of Tennessee Achieve the Dream Grant recognizes high-achieving students from lower-middle-income families. Awards are based on academic achievement and financial need. Awards come in the form of four-year grants with a maximum amount of $3,000 per year, when combined with the UT Volunteer or University Scholarships.

STUDENTS

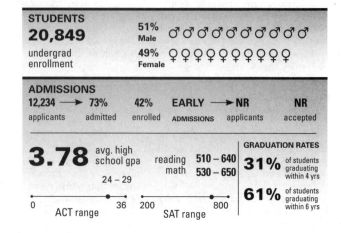

20,849 undergrad enrollment

51% Male ♂♂♂♂♂♂♂♂♂♂

49% Female ♀♀♀♀♀♀♀♀♀♀

ADMISSIONS

12,234 applicants → 73% admitted — 42% enrolled

EARLY ADMISSIONS → NR applicants — NR accepted

3.78 avg. high school gpa

reading	510 – 640
math	530 – 650

ACT range (0–36): 24 – 29

SAT range (200–800)

GRADUATION RATES

31% of students graduating within 4 yrs

61% of students graduating within 6 yrs

University of Tennessee–Knoxville

FINANCIAL AID: 865-974-3131 • E-MAIL: ADMISSIONS@UTK.EDU • WEBSITE: WWW.UTK.EDU

STUDENT BODY

"There is not one 'popular' group of students. We have athletes, artists, musicians, dancers, religious students, scientists, Greeks, volunteers, etc." In general a live-and-let-live atmosphere pervades this "friendly" "energetic," "personable" campus; "All students fit in extremely well." The Greek community here "is especially prevalent." Some wonder "how non-Greeks fit in." "The conservative, upper-class attitude is definitely the one with the strongest voice." However, others counter this stalwart image. "The best thing about being an average student here? If you don't want to conform, you don't have to." "Once you go beyond the surface and away from the jocks and sorority girls, there are all types of students at UT." Others enthusiastically concede, "The literary snob crowd is small, but it's here, they do cool stuff, and they welcome new folks all the time with open arms."

Why Students love University of Tennessee–Knoxville

"The University of Tennessee combines the best of all worlds: great education for a great price, sports, social life, and a ton of extracurriculars to choose from."

WHY STUDENTS LOVE UNIVERSITY OF TENNESSEE–KNOXVILLE

The University of Tennessee "provides a family-like atmosphere full of opportunity and support!" Life at UT is all about "atmosphere, affordability, and school spirit." Many here tout "the school spirit and sense of community." In addition, the "in-state tuition and scholarship money" make "Tennessee a good deal for the amount you pay. I have fabulous teachers, great friends, fun activities to participate in, nice housing, a decent meal plan, and I pay $2,000 for all of it." "Although [UT is] a large school, you're not just a number; you're a face, a person, and a name." In general, "Professors greatly appreciate an appetite to learn, and they welcome challenges that help us learn and grow as students." Most are "very intelligent, open to debate, well-versed on their topics, and willing to meet with students outside of class for any reason."

GENERAL INFO

Environment: City. **Activities:** Choral groups, concert band, dance, drama/theater, jazz band, literary magazine, marching band, music ensembles, musical theater, opera, pep band, radio station, student government, student newspaper, student-run film society, symphony orchestra, television station, yearbook, campus ministries, international student organization, Model UN. **Organizations:** 450 registered organizations, 90 honor societies, 30 religious organizations. 23 fraternities, 18 sororities. **Athletics (Intercollegiate):** *Men:* Baseball, basketball, cheerleading, cross-country, diving, football, golf, swimming, tennis, track/field (outdoor), track/field (indoor). *Women:* Basketball, cheerleading, crew/rowing, cross-country, diving, golf, soccer, softball, swimming, tennis, track/field (outdoor), track/field (indoor), volleyball.

BOTTOM LINE

A year of tuition for a full load of courses at the University of Tennessee–Knoxville costs about $7,000 if you are a resident of Tennessee. If you are from another state, you'll pay about $21,000. The estimated cost for room and board is about $7,000.

SELECTIVITY

Admissions Rating	**88**
# of applicants	12,234
% of applicants accepted	73
% of acceptees attending	42

FRESHMAN PROFILE

Range SAT Critical Reading	**510–640**
Range SAT Math	**530–650**
Range ACT Composite	**24–29**
Average HS GPA	**3.78**
% graduated top 10% of class	**39**
% graduated top 25% of class	**70**
% graduated top 50% of class	**92**

DEADLINES

Regular Deadline	**12/1**
Normal registration	**yes**

FACILITIES

Housing: Coed dorms, special housing for disabled students, men's dorms, special housing for international students, women's dorms, fraternity/sorority housing, apartments for married students, apartments for single students, theme housing, transfer student floors. *Special Academic Facilities/Equipment:* Comprehensive museum of anthropology, archaeology, art, geology, natural history, and medicine, theatre-in-the-round, livestock farms, robotics research center, electron microscope, McClung Museum. *Computers:* 100% of classrooms, 100% of dorms, 100% of libraries, 100% of dining areas, 100% of student union, 25% of common outdoor areas have wireless network access.

FINANCIAL FACTS

Financial Aid Rating	**80**
Annual in-state tuition	$5,918
Annual out-of-state tuition	$19,714
Room and Board	$6,652
Required Fees	$932
Books and supplies	$1,366
% frosh rec. need-based scholarship or grant aid	51
% UG rec.need-based scholarship or grant aid	44
% frosh rec. need-based self-help aid	26
% UG rec. need-based self-help aid	31
% frosh rec. any financial aid	53
% UG rec. any financial aid	50
% UG borrow to pay for school	47
Average cumulative indebtedness	$24,593

University of Tennessee at Martin

200 Hall-Moody, Administrative Building, Martin, TN 38238 • Admissions: 731-881-7020 • Fax: 731-881-7029

CAMPUS LIFE

Quality of life Rating	79
Fire Safety Rating	75
Green rating	77
Type of School	Public
Environment	Village

STUDENTS

Total undergrad enrolllment	7,947
% Male to Female	43/57
% From out of state	4
% Live on Campus	27
# of Fraternities	12
# of Sororities	8
% African American	14
% Asian	1
% Caucasian	67
% Hispanic	1
% International	2
# Of Countries Represented	21

ACADEMICS

Academic Rating	72
% Of students graduating within 4 years	23
% Of students graduating within 6 years	34
Calendar	semester
Most common reg class size	10–19 students
Most common lab size	10–19 students

MOST POPULAR MAJORS

Business/commerce, economics international relations

HONORS PROGRAMS

University Scholars Honors Seminar.

SPECIAL STUDY OPTIONS

Accelerated program, cooperative education program, cross-registration, distance learning, double major, dual enrollment, English as a Second Language (ESL), exchange student program (domestic), honors program, independent study, internships, student-designed major, study abroad, teacher certification program, 3-1 programs in pharmacy, veterinary medicine, dentistry, medicine, optometry, podiatry and chiropractory.

ABOUT THE SCHOOL

A Land Grant school based on agriculture, founded in 1900 and possessing a quaint, rural atmosphere with southern charm, the University of Tennessee at Martin is said by one undergrad to be "Small Town USA! We love to make Martin a very 'homey' place!" There are plenty of opportunities to be involved on campus and in the community, and doing so is highly encouraged. The freshman retention rate is high, and students love that the "helpful, friendly staff made the transition painless." "You will be helped along the way. They make sure each student knows what to do so you don't feel lost."

Courses at Martin are "challenging, but rewarding;" "this allows for one-on-one learning so all of my questions get full detailed answers," report students. Undergrads say, "It's big enough to be lively and fun, but small enough to get individual attention in even the largest classes." "I feel lucky to have had great teachers who make comprehending the material a breeze. They are all very likable and made my first semester in school a great experience." Another student is pleased that the school "offers a good amount of class sections to better help with registration and minimize class conflicts."

BANG FOR YOUR BUCK

UT Martin offers financial assistance to students based on need, academic achievement, character, and leadership ability. Those with top academic credentials can compete for Honors Programs Scholarships, and others who meet established academic criteria are eligible to receive the Tennessee Education Lottery HOPE Scholarship. There is also the respected University Scholars Program for qualified students. The administration is respected, and "takes student opinion into account when making campus changes." The student employment office is now part of the Office of Financial Aid and Scholarships. This organizational change has created a new emphasis in counseling students to choose work over taking out student loans, to help students decrease debt upon graduation. "Friendly staff, they are prompt when doing things and taking care of problems," a student reports. "Everyone knows how to do things in an organized and efficient manner." Martin takes the advancement of its students seriously; students are quite cognizant of the value of a UT degree, and the school is known to prepare you for professional school. "Close relationships with professors have gotten me so much farther by making me aware of internship opportunities," says a grateful student.

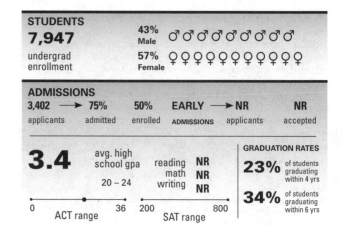

STUDENTS

7,947 undergrad enrollment

43% Male ♂♂♂♂♂♂♂♂♂♂

57% Female ♀♀♀♀♀♀♀♀♀♀♀

ADMISSIONS

3,402 →	75%	50%	EARLY →	NR	NR
applicants	admitted	enrolled	ADMISSIONS	applicants	accepted

3.4 avg. high school gpa

20 – 24 ACT range (0–36)

SAT range (200–800): reading NR, math NR, writing NR

GRADUATION RATES

23% of students graduating within 4 yrs

34% of students graduating within 6 yrs

University of Tennessee at Martin

Financial Aid: 731-881-7040 • E-mail: admitme@utm.edu • Website: www.utm.edu

STUDENT BODY

UT Martin is "very welcoming to students from any background and nationality" including "clusters of minority groups," numerous nontraditional students, and a respectable smattering of international students. Decent contingents of students come from both Nashville and Memphis as well. Indeed, "to say that everyone fits in one demographic is pushing it." Nevertheless, the undergrads hail overwhelmingly from the state of Tennessee, and a high percentage chooses UTM because it is "close to home." "Most of the students who attend this school are from surrounding smaller towns." A typical student here comes from a decidedly "middle-class" background and is an "average small-town person." Students describe themselves as "busy," "hardworking," "upbeat, friendly," and "not highly political."

Why Students love UT at Martin

"It's big enough to be lively and fun, but small enough to get individual attention in even the largest classes."

WHY STUDENTS LOVE UT AT MARTIN

UTM has a solid Greek Life system; while not a "party school," there are many social, professional and honorary organizations. "All of the sororities and fraternities on campus try to participate in extracurricular activities and make up a large portion of the student body." With 140 registered groups, students are likely to find something of interest. The school also presents artists, poets, musicians, and other speakers. The campus is clean and well-maintained, and UTM provides the "ultimate leisure, educational, and research facilities beginning with the two-story Paul Meek Library up to the state-of-the-art recreational center. Our new recreation facilities are phenomenal and our library is very organized and learning-conducive," raves an undergrad.

GENERAL INFO

Activities: Choral groups, concert band, dance, drama/theater, jazz band, literary magazine, marching band, music ensembles, opera, pep band, radio station, student government, student newspaper, television station, yearbook, campus ministries, international student organization. **Organizations:** 100 registered organizations, 27 honor societies, 11 religious organizations. 12 fraternities, 8 sororities. **Athletics (Intercollegiate):** *Men:* Baseball, basketball, cross-country, football, golf, riflery, rodeo. *Women:* Basketball, cheerleading, cross-country, equestrian sports, riflery, rodeo, soccer, softball, tennis, volleyball. **On-Campus Highlights:** Boling University Center, PaulMeek Library, Fitness Center, Elam Center and Intramural facilities, Quad, Captain's Coffee in Paul Meek Library Student Life Center.

BOTTOM LINE

The University of Tennessee at Martin takes great pride in its reasonably priced, yet high-quality education. "I chose UT martin because it is affordable;" "I was offered more money to go here than anywhere else;" frequently heard reasons for students choosing to attend the University of Tennessee, with "I received a full scholarship to attend" being not far behind in popularity. In-state tuition is only $5,640, with out-of-state costs running a student $18,050. Room and board will be $5,424.

SELECTIVITY

Admissions Rating	**76**
# of applicants	3,402
% of applicants accepted	75
% of acceptees attending	50

FRESHMAN PROFILE

Range ACT Composite	**20–24**
Average HS GPA	**3.4**
% graduated top 10% of class	**23**
% graduated top 25% of class	**53**
% graduated top 50% of class	**87**

DEADLINES

Regular Deadline	**8/1**
Normal registration	**no**

FACILITIES

Housing: Coed dorms, special housing for disabled students, men's dorms, special housing for international students, women's dorms, fraternity/sorority housing, apartments for married students, apartments for single students, theme housing. *Special Academic Facilities/Equipment:* Paul Meek Library contains Houston Gordon University Museum. *Computers:* 100% of classrooms, 50% of dorms, 100% of libraries, 100% of dining areas, 100% of student union, 100% of common outdoor areas have wireless network access.

FINANCIAL FACTS

Financial Aid Rating	**80**
Annual in-state tuition	$5,640
Annual out-of-state tuition	$18,050
Room and Board	$5,424
Required Fees	$1,078
Books and supplies	$1,500
% frosh rec. need-based scholarship or grant aid	47
% UG rec.need-based scholarship or grant aid	46
% frosh rec. non-need-based scholarship or grant aid	63
% UG rec. non-need-based scholarship or grant aid	40
% frosh rec. need-based self-help aid	34
% UG rec. need-based self-help aid	43
% frosh rec. any financial aid	94
% UG rec. any financial aid	75
% UG borrow to pay for school	60
Average cumulative indebtedness	$19,048

University of Wisconsin–Eau Claire

105 Garfield Avenue, Schofield 112, Eau Claire, WI 54701 • Admissions: 715-836-5415 • Fax: 715-836-2409

CAMPUS LIFE

Quality of life Rating	79
Fire Safety Rating	75
Green rating	77
Type of School	Public
Environment	Village

STUDENTS

Total undergrad enrolllment	7,947
% Male to Female	43/57
% From out of state	4
% Live on Campus	27
# of Fraternities	12
# of Sororities	8
% African American	14
% Asian	1
% Caucasian	67
% Hispanic	1
% International	2
# Of Countries Represented	21

ACADEMICS

Academic Rating	72
% Of students graduating within 4 years	23
% Of students graduating within 6 years	44
Calendar	semester
Most common reg class size	10–19 students
Most common lab size	10–19 students

MOST POPULAR MAJORS

Agriculture, general biology/ biological studies, general multi/interdisciplinary studies

SPECIAL STUDY OPTIONS

Accelerated program, cooperative education program, cross-registration, distance learning, double major, dual enrollment, English as a Second Language (ESL), exchange student program (domestic), external degree program, honors program, independent study, internships, student-designed major, study abroad, teacher certification program, collaborative programs in Early Childhood Education. Special programs offered to physically disabled students include note-taking services, reader services, tutors.

ABOUT THE SCHOOL

Located in the scenic Chippewa Valley, The University of Wisconsin–Eau Claire was founded in 1916, as a public institution. With almost 11,000 students now enrolled, and only 2100 being freshman, undergrads enjoy a "close-knit campus with a sense of community, while still offering unique opportunities in education and lifestyles." "While it is in the UW system, it truly feels like a private school setting," mentions one student, and the school has much flexibility in degree programs. UW–Eau Claire is well-known for its music, education, business, nursing and science departments. Also offering accredited programs in communication, journalism, computer science, and chemistry, as well as many others, one undergrad is truly amazed at "the array of classes to choose from!"

There are always plenty of opportunities outside of the classroom on campus, and for building relationships with the community. Various internships and service learning choices are available to enhance student learning, and "astounding graduate level research that is available to undergraduates," a student tells us. Another finds Wisconsin to be a "great environment for learning, living, and expanding your skill set as a student leader because of all of the hands-on academic practices."

BANG FOR YOUR BUCK

Educational value is first and foremost on the minds of most everyone attending the University of Wisconsin, and they are not disappointed with what they find. Students say the university is "a great all around school while still being affordable." "It's a very good education for a very reasonable price." "It makes a high quality education accessible to those who could not typically afford one." Scholarships and grants are numerous, and often considerable, too. "Scholarships offered secured my decision to attend," a thankful student told us. One of the most prestigious scholarships is the Blugold Fellowship. Each year, 20 new freshmen are selected for a two-year award that is part scholarship, part research stipend. Students are paired with a faculty mentor on a collaborative undergraduate research project. Additionally, the university offers the Diversity Scholar award, given to outstanding students from diverse backgrounds. The University of Wisconsin–Eau Claire awards more than $250,000 to new freshmen each year. Many undergrads participate in the Midwest Student Exchange, enabling students from neighboring states to enroll in certain programs at a reduced tuition.

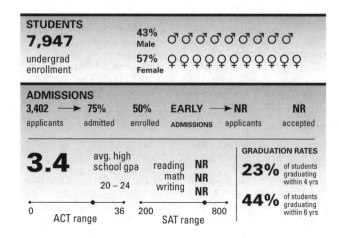

STUDENTS

7,947 undergrad enrollment

43% Male ♂♂♂♂♂♂♂♂♂

57% Female ♀♀♀♀♀♀♀♀♀♀♀

ADMISSIONS

3,402 applicants	→ 75% admitted	50% enrolled	EARLY ADMISSIONS	→ NR applicants	NR accepted

3.4 avg. high school gpa

ACT range (0–36): 20 – 24

SAT range (200–800): reading NR, math NR, writing NR

GRADUATION RATES

23% of students graduating within 4 yrs

44% of students graduating within 6 yrs

University of Wisconsin–Eau Claire

FINANCIAL AID: 715-836-3373 • E-MAIL: ADMISSIONS@UWEC.EDU • WEBSITE: WWW.UWEC.EDU

STUDENT BODY

UW–Eau Claire is located in "the beautiful Chippewa Valley." "It truly feels like a private school setting," guarantees a junior, "because [the] campus is so enclosed and is surrounded by the woods and the river that cuts right through the middle of it." Also, surrounding Eau Claire is by most accounts "a great college town." Students regularly frequent the bar and cheap restaurants nearby. "Campus life is awesome." "It's not a huge school so people know each other and acknowledge one another." "You can go to sporting events, concerts in the student union, or view the campus movie, all of which are free." "A lot of people do intramural sports." Residence halls are centers of much activity. "The dorm life here is amazing and very community-based," explains a senior. "Each hall kind of has its own theme, so you get to meet people of similar majors and get advice from seniors on which classes to take, how to plan out your years at college, etc."

Why Students love UW–Eau Claire

"The dorm life here is amazing and very community-based."

WHY STUDENTS LOVE UW–EAU CLAIRE

Students tell us that the school has a "gorgeous" campus; 333 acres, in fact, surrounded by woods, and having a river which "cuts right through the middle." During the summer, people go tubing, rafting, swimming, cliff diving, sightseeing, for walks, shoot hoops, play sand volleyball, go to the outdoor movie theater, the dance clubs on campus, and bonfires. Undergrads are certainly never bored, saying, "I think that the greatest strength of my school is how active all the students are;" "the opportunities are endless for fun things to do." "I have become friends with people who are completely different than me," exclaims a thrilled and happy student.

GENERAL INFO

Activities: Choral groups, concert band, dance, drama/theater, jazz band, literary magazine, marching band, music ensembles, musical theater, opera, pep band, radio station, student government, student newspaper, student-run film society, symphony orchestra, television station, campus ministries, international student organization, Model UN. **Organizations:** 240 registered organizations, 30 honor societies, 16 religious organizations. 2 fraternities, 3 sororities. **Athletics (Intercollegiate):** *Men:* Basketball, cross-country, diving, football, golf, ice hockey, swimming, tennis, track/field (outdoor), track/field (indoor), wrestling. Women: Basketball, cross-country, diving, golf, gymnastics, ice hockey, soccer, softball, swimming, tennis, track/field (outdoor), track/field (indoor), volleyball. **On-Campus Highlights:** Chippewa River Footbridge, Davies Center (Student Center/Union), McPhee Center (Athletic Facility), Hass Fine Arts Center, Higher Ground (Recreational Facility).

BOTTOM LINE

One of the more impressive aspects of the university is its inexpensiveness in relation to the quality of education being offered. Tuition for in-state students is only $5,640 per year. For an out-of-state student, that figure is $18,050. Room and board will come to $5,424. The school is very committed to making quality education available to most every student; 90% of the total average need is met, with more than 70% of undergraduates receiving at least some manner of need-based financial aid. The average financial support package is $8,500.

SELECTIVITY

Admissions Rating	**76**
# of applicants	3,402
% of applicants accepted	75
% of acceptees attending	50

FRESHMAN PROFILE

Range ACT Composite	**20–32**
Average HS GPA	**3.4**
% graduated top 10% of class	**23**
% graduated top 25% of class	**53**
% graduated top 50% of class	**87**

DEADLINES

Regular Deadline	**8/1**
Normal registration	**no**

FACILITIES

Housing: Coed dorms, men's dorms, women's dorms, apartments for single students. *Special Academic Facilities/Equipment:* Art gallery, human development center, bird museum, field station, planetarium. *Computers:* 50% of classrooms, 10% of dorms, 100% of libraries, 100% of dining areas, 100% of student union, 100% of common outdoor areas have wireless network access.

FINANCIAL FACTS

Financial Aid Rating	**80**
Annual in-state tuition	$5,640
Annual out-of-state tuition	$18,050
Room and Board	$5,424
Required Fees	$1,078
Books and supplies	$1,500
% frosh rec. need-based scholarship or grant aid	26
% UG rec.need-based scholarship or grant aid	26
% frosh rec. non-need-based scholarship or grant aid	23
% UG rec. non-need-based scholarship or grant aid	44
% frosh rec. need-based self-help aid	72
% UG rec. need-based self-help aid	69
% frosh rec. any financial aid	94
% UG rec. any financial aid	75
% UG borrow to pay for school	60
Average cumulative indebtedness	$19,048

Utah State University

0160 Old Main Hill, Logan, UT 84322-0160 • Admissions: 435-797-1079 • Fax: 435-797-3708

CAMPUS LIFE

Quality of life Rating	84
Fire Safety Rating	75
Green rating	85
Type of School	Public
Environment	Town

STUDENTS

Total undergrad enrollment	14,646
% Male to Female	51/49
% From out of state	21
# of Fraternities	5
# of Sororities	3
% African American	1
% Asian	1
% Caucasian	86
% Hispanic	3
% Native American	1
% International	4
# Of Countries Represented	78

ACADEMICS

Academic Rating	70
Calendar	semester
Most common reg class size	20–29 students

MOST POPULAR MAJORS

Accounting, information science/studies, marketing/marketing management, general

HONORS PROGRAMS

The Honors Pro gram offers undergraduate students intensive seminars, experimental and interdisciplinary courses, writing projects, leadership opportunities, artistic and social activities. Other advantages include priority registration, an Honors-only computer lab, the Honors lounge and study areas. Special programs offered to physically disabled students include reader services, voice recorders.

SPECIAL STUDY OPTIONS

Accelerated program, cooperative education program, cross-registration, distance learning, double major, dual enrollment, English as a Second Language (ESL), exchange student program (domestic), honors program, independent study, internships, liberal arts/career combination, student-designed major, study abroad, teacher certification program, weekend college.

ABOUT THE SCHOOL

Utah State University is a large, affordable, research-oriented school that offers an amazing number of majors to choose from. The surrounding town of Logan is small, and religion is a huge part of campus. The Church of Latter-Day Saints has "a strong influence" here. "The LDS community at USU is very devout but at the same time very accepting." One of the greatest strengths of the school is its Undergraduate Research Program. "This program is amazing because it gives students the opportunity to learn about and conduct research with faculty members as well as complete original research." There's a decent-sized contingent of international students on campus but there is "only a small percentage of minority students." "The administration's main focus is on the students," lauds a speech communication major, "and that is apparent from the amount of effort that they put toward student services and functions." "An incredibly beautiful and inspiring place to live and learn."

BANG FOR YOUR BUCK

USU's undergraduate research program is the second oldest in the country, after MIT's. More than a fourth of all undergrads perform their own research, and well over a thousand undergrads are employed in paid research positions each year. A variety of programs encourage students from all backgrounds to get involved internationally as well. With nationally ranked programs, award-winning faculty, and a close-knit family of illustrious alumni, USU students are fully equipped to succeed in anything.

STUDENT BODY

"Everyone is pretty laid back and conservative" at USU. Students describe themselves as "studious," "very motivated to achieve," and "nothing but welcoming and nice." There's a decent-sized contingent of international students on campus but there is "only a small percentage of minority students." "This is northern Utah," says a sophomore. "Most of the students are white and Mormon." The Church of Latter-Day Saints has "a strong influence" here. Scores of students "do not drink, smoke, or have sex before marriage." "Many are married" already and "have a part-time job." Some students say that "it's tough fitting in as a non-Mormon." Others say that the "the LDS community at USU is very devout but at the same time very accepting." There are "some overzealous Mormons" who are "pretty nearly intolerant and look down on other faiths," they say, but "you get those nut jobs with every religion."

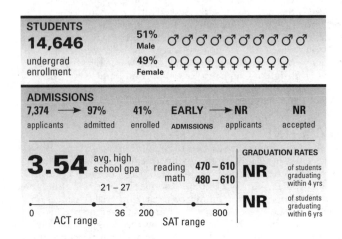

STUDENTS
14,646 undergrad enrollment

51% Male ♂♂♂♂♂♂♂♂♂♂
49% Female ♀♀♀♀♀♀♀♀♀♀

ADMISSIONS

7,374 applicants → 97% admitted — 41% enrolled

EARLY ADMISSIONS → NR applicants — NR accepted

3.54 avg. high school gpa

ACT range: 0 — 21 – 27 — 36

SAT range: 200 — 800; reading 470 – 610; math 480 – 610

GRADUATION RATES

NR of students graduating within 4 yrs

NR of students graduating within 6 yrs

FINANCIAL AID: 909-621-8205 • E-MAIL: ADMIT@USU.EDU • WEBSITE: WWW.USU.EDU

Why Students love Utah State University

"The administration's main focus is on the students."

WHY STUDENTS LOVE UTAH STATE UNIVERSITY

Utah State University is a large, affordable, research-oriented school that offers more than 200 majors and "one hell of an engineering program." The College of Education is "top notch" as well and there are strong programs in agriculture and business. Overall, "the academic experience is superb." "The professors are saints as far as I'm concerned," declares a civil engineering major. "They are here because they love teaching and seeing their students succeed." "You can find a club or organization for just about anything" at USU. Sports are reportedly "quite popular." "Aggie Basketball is huge." However, other teams are "sickeningly terrible." There is a smattering of Greek life, however, nobody really comes here for the party scene. This is "Mormonville." "Dinner and a movie" and a lot of good old-fashioned dating are far more common than drinking. The surrounding town of Logan is "small" and "in the middle of the mountains." It's "pretty steep" around here but it's "an incredibly beautiful and inspiring place to live and learn" and "a great place for the outdoors." "Everyone goes sledding on Old Main Hill in the winter." For serious skiers and snowboarders, there is a resort "really close" and "the snow in the canyon is awesome." "A lot of people miss class after a good snowstorm to hit the slopes," observes a junior.

GENERAL INFO

Activities: Choral groups, concert band, dance, drama/theater, jazz band, marching band, music ensembles, musical theater, opera, pep band, radio station, student government, student newspaper, student-run film society, symphony orchestra, television station, campus ministries, international student organization. **Organizations:** 194 registered organizations, 32 honor societies, 8 religious organizations. 5 fraternities, 3 sororities. Athletics (Intercollegiate): ***Men:*** Basketball, cross-country, football, golf, tennis, track/field (outdoor), track/field (indoor). ***Women:*** Basketball, cross-country, gymnastics, soccer, softball, tennis, track/field (outdoor), track/field (indoor), volleyball. **On-Campus Highlights:** Outdoor Recreation Center, Nora Eccles Jones Art Museum, Fieldhouse athletic facility, Taggart Student Center, The quad. **Environmental Initiatives:** Increased energy efficiency in buildings, recycling, Aggie Blue Bikes.

BOTTOM LINE

Room and board at the University is only a bit over $5,000 per year. While out-of-state tuition is more than $15,000 a year, more than 60 percent of undergrads receive need-based financial aid, both for freshman as well as for the rest of the school's population, and the school meets more than 60 percent of average need. The average total financial aid package is around $9000. Undergrads can look to be having an approximate loan debt upon graduation of more than $15,000. As just one example from a thankful student, "I received a great scholarship that allowed me to complete Undergraduate Research."

SELECTIVITY

Admissions Rating	**76**
# of applicants	7,374
% of applicants accepted	97
% of acceptees attending	41

FRESHMAN PROFILE

Range SAT Critical Reading	**470–610**
Range SAT Math	**480–610**
Range ACT Composite	**21–27**
Average HS GPA	**3.54**
% graduated top 10% of class	**24**
% graduated top 25% of class	**50**
% graduated top 50% of class	**80**

DEADLINES

Regular Deadline	**4/1**
Normal registration	**no**

FACILITIES

Housing: Coed dorms, special housing for disabled students, men's dorms, special housing for international students, women's dorms, fraternity/sorority housing, apartments for married students, apartments for single students, theme housing. *Special Academic Facilities/Equipment:* Art gallery, agricultural and engineering experiment station, water research lab. *Computers:* 99% of classrooms, 95% of dorms, 99% of libraries, 99% of dining areas, 99% of student union, 50% of common outdoor areas have wireless network access.

FINANCIAL FACTS

Financial Aid Rating	**72**
Annual tuition	$15,252
Room and Board	$5,280
Required Fees	$825
Books and supplies	$1,190
% frosh rec. need-based scholarship or grant aid	17
% UG rec.need-based scholarship or grant aid	30
% frosh rec. non-need-based scholarship or grant aid	18
% UG rec. non-need-based scholarship or grant aid	19
% frosh rec. need-based self-help aid	22
% UG rec. need-based self-help aid	31
% frosh rec. any financial aid	61
% UG rec. any financial aid	63
% UG borrow to pay for school	46
Average cumulative indebtedness	$15,194

Virginia Polytechnic Institute

UNDERGRADUATE ADMISSIONS, 201 BURRUSS HALL, BLACKSBURG, VA 24061 • ADMISSIONS: 540-231-6267

CAMPUS LIFE

Quality of life Rating	98
Fire Safety Rating	76
Green rating	99
Type of School	Public
Environment	Town

STUDENTS

Total undergrad enrolllment	23,600
% Male to Female	58/42
% From out of state	25
% Live on Campus	37
# of Fraternities	31
# of Sororities	12
% African American	4
% Asian	8
% Caucasian	76
% Hispanic	4
% International	2
# Of Countries Represented	113

ACADEMICS

Academic Rating	71
Calendar	semester
Profs interesting rating	75
Profs accessible rating	79
Most common reg class size	20–29 students
Most common lab size	20–29 students

MOST POPULAR MAJORS

Biology, engineering

SPECIAL STUDY OPTIONS

Accelerated program, cooperative education program, distance learning, double major, dual enrollment, English as a Second Language (ESL), honors program, independent study, internships, study abroad, teacher certification program.

ABOUT THE SCHOOL

Virginia Polytechnic University (Virginia Tech) is one of only two senior military colleges within a larger state university. (Texas A&M is the other.) This affords students a unique learning experience while benefiting from opportunities in a university with 174 undergraduate degree options. Unlike at your typical tech school, students at Virginia Tech happily discover that they don't have to forfeit a variety of exciting extracurricular activities in order to achieve an excellent education. VT's programs in engineering, architecture, agricultural science, and forestry are all national leaders, while the outstanding business program offers top-notch access to occupations in the field. Significant research is being conducted in each of the school's nine colleges. Nonetheless, undergrads are continually surprised by the genuine interest the school's first-rate faculty takes in students and their educations. At Virginia Tech, professors are dedicated to their students, a fact that is continually demonstrated by their open office doors, frequent e-mail communication, and willingness to accept undergraduates as researchers.

BANG FOR YOUR BUCK

Sixty percent of Virginia Tech students receive some form of financial aid. Students can receive funds from federal, state, private, and university scholarships, as well as Stafford and Perkins loans, work-study, and federal Pell Grants. Some scholarships consider a student's financial need, while others are awarded independently, based on a student's academic or athletic achievement. Students can browse the numerous scholarship opportunities online through the school's scholarship database.

Membership in the Virginia Tech Corps of Cadets offers excellent opportunities for supplemental scholarships. About 650 cadets receive $1.5 million in Emerging Leaders Scholarships. In addition, 429 cadets garnered $7.8 million in Army, Navy, and Air Force ROTC scholarships. The cadets, of course, have access to other scholarships and financial aid. But the Emerging Leaders and ROTC scholarships provide more than $9 million in total aid to members of the 857 student corps.

STUDENTS

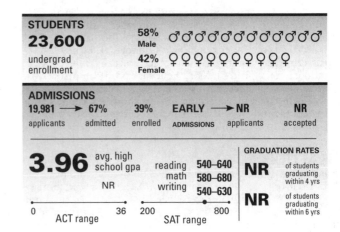

23,600 undergrad enrollment

58% Male ♂♂♂♂♂♂♂♂♂♂♂♂

42% Female ♀♀♀♀♀♀♀♀♀♀

ADMISSIONS

19,981 applicants → 67% admitted — 39% enrolled

EARLY ADMISSIONS → NR applicants — NR accepted

3.96 avg. high school gpa

NR — ACT range 0–36

reading 540–640
math 580–680
writing 540–630
SAT range 200–800

GRADUATION RATES

NR of students graduating within 4 yrs

NR of students graduating within 6 yrs

FINANCIAL AID: 540-231-5179 • E-MAIL: VTADMISS@VT.EDU FAX: 540-231-3242 • WEBSITE: WWW.VT.EDU

STUDENT BODY

School spirit is strong at Virginia Tech, where students "are typically clad head to toe in maroon and orange with a Virginia Tech/HokieBird logo at least somewhere on their outfit." Students regard themselves as "well-rounded and friendly," the sort of people who "enjoy going out and partying but also know when to study and get their work done." There are lots of folks who fit the description: "Caucasian; middle class; and from the Northern Virginia, Richmond, or Virginia Beach areas," but the school is "very open to student diversity. That's actually an aspect that is being pushed in the student population," where you'll also find "a lot of students from other countries like India and China." With more than 23,000 undergraduates, Virginia Tech's "large student body makes it easy to find many people that have the same interests and are able to become good friends."

WHY STUDENTS LOVE VIRGINIA TECH

Students at tech schools don't typically brag about their quality of life, but then again, Virginia Polytechnic Institute and State University, otherwise known as Virginia Tech, is not your typical tech school. Here, students happily discover that they can enjoy "a diverse community," "an accepting atmosphere," "a football program that takes priority for all but the most dedicated students," and the opportunity "to have a blast in college while still staying focused on their education." Without losing access to "a great science program" (in which "undergraduate research is huge"), strong engineering programs, and outstanding offerings in architecture, agricultural science, forestry, and business.

Why Students love Virginia Tech

"It's hard not to be excited about football when you are tailgating with friends and seeing 60,000 people pack the stadium."

GENERAL INFO

Environment: Town. **Activities:** Choral groups, concert band, dance, drama/theater, jazz band, literary magazine, marching band, music ensembles, musical theater, pep band, radio station, student government, student newspaper, year book. **Organizations:** 600 registered organizations, 32 honor societies, 53 religious organizations. 31 fraternities, 12 sororities. **Athletics (Intercollegiate):** *Men:* Baseball, basketball, cheerleading, cross-country, diving, football, golf, soccer, swimming, tennis, track/field (outdoor), track/field (indoor), ultimate Frisbee, water polo. *Women:* Basketball, cheerleading, cross-country, diving, lacrosse, soccer, softball, swimming, tennis, track/field (outdoor), track/field (indoor), ultimate Frisbee, volleyball, water polo. **Environmental Initiatives:** The Virginia Tech Climate Action Commitment Resolution and Sustainability Plan.

BOTTOM LINE

Virginia Tech's high-quality education and low tuition make this school an excellent investment. For Virginia residents, the estimated total cost of attendance for one year is just $14,600, including tuition, fees, and room and board. For nonresidents, the price is a little less than double the in-state rate. In the popular school of engineering, the cost per credit hour is a bit higher than other major fields.

SELECTIVITY

Admissions Rating	**91**
# of applicants	19,981
% of applicants accepted	67
% of acceptees attending	39
# accepting a place on wait list	1,349
% admitted from wait list	0

FRESHMAN PROFILE

Range SAT Critical Reading	**540–640**
Range SAT Math	**580–680**
Range SAT Writing	**540–630**
Average HS GPA	**3.96**
% graduated top 10% of class	**45**
% graduated top 25% of class	**85**
% graduated top 50% of class	**99**

DEADLINES

Regular Deadline	**1/15**
Normal registration	**yes**

FACILITIES

Housing: Coed dorms, special housing for disabled students, men's dorms, special housing for international students, women's dorms, fraternity/sorority housing, wellness housing, theme housing, Housing for Corps of Cadets and athletes. *Special Academic Facilities/Equipment:* Art gallery, digital music facilities, multimedia labs, Black Cultural Center, television studio, anaerobic lab, CAD-CAM labs, observatory, wind tunnel, farms, Math Emporium, the CAVE (virtual reality learning facility). Virtual Reality Cave.

FINANCIAL FACTS

Financial Aid Rating	**73**
Annual in-state tuition	$7,309
Annual out-of-state tuition	$20,498
Room and Board	$6,290
Required Fees	$2,150
Books and supplies	$1,100
% frosh rec. need-based scholarship or grant aid	28
% UG rec.need-based scholarship or grant aid	30
% frosh rec. non-need-based scholarship or grant aid	36
% UG rec. non-need-based scholarship or grant aid	34
% frosh rec. need-based self-help aid	30
% UG rec. need-based self-help aid	32
% frosh rec. any financial aid	62
% UG rec. any financial aid	69
% UG borrow to pay for school	52
Average cumulative indebtedness	$23,100

INDEX OF SCHOOLS

A
Agnes Scott College 236
Amherst College 238
Appalachian State University 368

B
Barnard College 240
Bates College 242
Beloit College 244
Berea College 214
Boston College 246
Bowdoin College 248
Brandeis University 250
Brown University 252
Bryn Mawr College 254
Bucknell University 256

C
California Institute of Technology 162
California Polytechnic State University, San Luis Obispo 370
California State University—Long Beach 372
Carleton College 258
Centenary College of Louisiana 260
Centre College 262
Christopher Newport University 374
City University of New York—Brooklyn College 376
City University of New York—Hunter College 378
Claremont McKenna College 264
Clemson University 380
Colby College 266
Colgate University 268
College of Charleston 382
College of New Jersey, The 384
College of the Atlantic 270
College of Holy Cross 272
College of the Ozarks 216
College of William & Mary, The 192
Colorado College 274
Columbia University 276
Cooper Union for the Advancement of Science and Art, The 218
Cornell College 278
Cornell University 280

D
Dartmouth University 282
Davidson College 284
Deep Springs College 220
DePauw University 286
Duke University 288

E
Emory University 290
Evergreen State College, The 386

F
Florida State University 388
Franklin W. Olin College of Engineering 292

G
Georgetown University 294
Georgia Institute of Technology 390
Gettysburg College 296
Grinnell College 298

H
Hamilton College 166
Hanover College 300
Harvard College 142
Harvey Mudd College 302
Haverford College 304
Hillsdale College 306

I
Indiana University—Bloomington 392
Iowa State University 394

J
James Madison University 396
Johns Hopkins University 308

K
Kansas State University 398

L
Lafayette College 310
Longwood University 400

M
Macalester College 312
Massachusetts Institute of Technology 314
Middlebury College 316
Missouri University of Science and Technology 402
Mount Holyoke College 318

N
New College of Florida 180
New Mexico Institute of Mining & Technology 404
North Carolina State University 406
Northwestern University 320

O
Occidental College 322
Ohio State University—Columbus, The 408

P
Pomona College 150
Princeton University 138
Purdue University—West Lafayette 410

R
Randolph College 324
Reed College 326
Rice University 146

S
Scripps College 328
Sewanee—The University of the South 330
Southern Utah University 412
St. Mary's College of Maryland 414
Stanford University 332
State University of New York at Geneseo 416
State University of New York—Binghamton University 184
State University of New York—College of Environmental Science and Forestry 420
State University of New York—New Paltz 418

State University of New York—Oswego 422
State University of New York—Stony Brook University 424
State University of New York—University at Buffalo 426
Swarthmore College 134

T

Thomas Aquinas College 334
Truman State University 428

U

United States Air Force Academy 222
United States Coast Guard Academy 224
United States Merchant Marine Academy 226
United States Military Academy 228
United States Naval Academy 230
University of California—Berkeley 430
University of California—Davis 432
University of California—Irvine 434
University of California—Los Angeles 436
University of California—Riverside 438
University of California—San Diego 440
University of California—Santa Barbara 442
University of California—Santa Cruz 444
University of Central Florida 446
University of Chicago, The 336
University of Colorado—Boulder 448
University of Delaware 450
University of Florida 196
University of Georgia 200
University of Houston 452
University of Illinois at Urbana-Champaign 454
University of Kansas 456
University of Mary Washington 458
University of Maryland—College Park 460
University of Massachusetts—Boston 462
University of Michigan—Ann Arbor 464
University of Minnesota—Twin Cities 468
University of Minnesota—Crookston 466
University of Missouri—Kansas City 470
University of North Carolina at Asheville, The 472
University of North Carolina at Chapel Hill, The 172
University of North Carolina at Wilmington, The 474
University of North Florida 476
University of Notre Dame 338
University of Oklahoma 478
University of Pennsylvania 340
University of Pittsburgh—Pittsburgh Campus 482
University of Pittsburgh at Bradford 480
University of Redlands 342
University of Richmond 344
University of South Carolina—Columbia 484
University of South Dakota, The 486
University of Tennessee at Martin 490
University of Tennessee—Knoxville 488
University of Texas at Austin, The 208
University of Virginia 176
University of Washington 204
University of Wisconsin—Eau Claire 492
University of Wisconsin—Madison 188
Utah State University 494

V

Vanderbilt University 346
Vassar College 348
Virginia Polytechnic Institute 496

W

Wabash College 350
Wake Forest University 352
Washington University in St. Louis 154
Webb Institute 232
Wellesley College 354
Wesleyan College 356
Wesleyan University 358
Wheaton College (IL) 360
Whitman College 362
Williams College 130
Wofford College 364

Y

Yale University 158

INDEX OF SCHOOLS BY STATE

CALIFORNIA

California Institute of Technology (Pasadena) 162
California Polytechnic State University, San Luis Obispo (San Luis Obispo) 370
California State University—Long Beach (Long Beach) 372
Claremont McKenna College (Claremont) 264
Harvey Mudd College (Claremont) 302
Occidental College (Los Angeles) 322
Pomona College (Claremont) 150
Scripps College (Claremont) 328
Stanford University (Stanford) 332
Thomas Aquinas College (Santa Paula) 334
University of California--Berkeley (Berkeley) 430
University of California--Davis (Davis) 432
University of California--Irvine (Irvine) 434
University of California--Los Angeles (Los Angeles) 436
University of California--Riverside (Riverside) 438
University of California--San Diego (La Jolla) 440
University of California--Santa Barbara (Santa Barbara) 442
University of California--Santa Cruz (Santa Cruz) 444
University of Redlands (Redlands) 342

COLORADO

Colorado College (Colorado Springs) 274
United States Air Force Academy (Colorado Springs) 222
University of Colorado--Boulder (Boulder) 448

CONNECTICUT

United States Coast Guard Academy (New London) 224
Wesleyan University (Middletown) 356
Yale University (New Haven) 158

DELAWARE

University of Delaware (Newark) 450

FLORIDA

Florida State University (Tallahassee) 388
New College of Florida (Sarasota) 180
University of Central Florida (Orlando) 446
University of Florida (Gainesville) 196
University of North Florida (Jacksonville) 476

GEORGIA

Agnes Scott College (Atlanta/Decatur) 236
Emory University (Atlanta) 290
Georgia Institute of Technology (Atlanta) 390
University of Georgia (Athens) 200
Wesleyan College (Macon) 356

IOWA

Cornell College (Mount Vernon) 278
Grinnell College (Grinnell) 298
Iowa State University (Ames) 394

ILLINOIS

Northwestern University (Evanston) 320
University of Chicago (Chicago) 336
University of Illinois at Urbana-Champaign (Urbana) 454
Wheaton College (Wheaton) 360

INDIANA

DePauw University (Greencastle) 286
Hanover College (Hanover) 300
Indiana University—Bloomington (Bloomington) 392
Purdue University—West Lafayette (West Lafayette) 410
University of Notre Dame (South Bend) 338
Wabash College (Crawfordsville) 350

KANSAS

Kansas State University (Manhattan) 398
University of Kansas (Lawrence) 456

KENTUCKY

Berea College (Berea) 214
Centre College (Danville) 262

LOUISIANA

Centenary College of Louisiana (Shreveport) 260

MASSACHUSSETTS

Amherst College (Amherst) 238
Boston College (Boston) 246
Brandeis University (Waltham) 250
College of the Holy Cross (Worcester) 272
Franklin W. Olin College of Engineering (Needham) 292
Harvard College (Cambridge) 142
Massachusetts Institute of Technology (Cambridge) 314
Mount Holyoke College (South Hadley) 318
University of Massachusetts Boston (Boston) 462
Wellesley College (Wellesley) 354
Williams College (Williamstown) 130

MARYLAND

Johns Hopkins University (Baltimore) 308
St. Mary's College of Maryland (St. Mary's City) 414
United States Naval Academy (Annapolis) 230
University of Maryland-College Park (College Park) 460

MAINE

Bates College (Lewiston) 242
Bowdoin College (Brunswick) 248
Colby College (Waterville) 266
College of the Atlantic (Bar Harbor) 270

MICHIGAN

Hillsdale College (Hillsdale) 306
University of Michigan--Ann Arbor (Ann Arbor) 464

MINNESOTA

Carleton College (Northfield) 258
Macalester College (St. Paul) 312
University of Minnesota--Twin Cities (Twin Cities) 468
University of Minnesota, Crookston (Crookston) 466

MISSOURI

College of the Ozarks (Point Lookout) 216

Missouri University of Science and Technology (Rolla) 402
Truman State University (Kirksville) 428
University of Missouri-Kansas City (Kansas City) 470
Washington University in St. Louis (St. Louis) 154

NORTH CAROLINA

Appalachian State University (Boone) 368
Davidson College (Davidson) 284
Duke University (Durham) 288
North Carolina State University (Raleigh) 406
University of North Carolina at Asheville (Asheville) 472
University of North Carolina at Chapel Hill (Chapel Hill) 172
University of North Carolina at Wilmington (Wilmington) 474
Wake Forest University (Winston-Salem) 251

NEW HAMPSHIRE

Dartmouth University (Hanover) 282

NEW JERSEY

College of New Jersey, The (Ewing) 384
Princeton University (Princeton) 138

NEW MEXICO

New Mexico Institute of Mining & Technology (Socorro) 404

NEVADA

Deep Springs College (Dyer) 220

NEW YORK

Barnard College (New York) 240
City University of New York-Brooklyn College (Brooklyn) 376
City University of New York-Hunter College (New York) 378
Colgate University (Hamilton) 268
Columbia University (New York) 276
Cooper Union for the Advancement of Science and Art (New York) 218
Cornell University (Ithaca) 280
Hamilton College (Clinton) 166
State University of New York at Geneseo (Geneseo) 416
State University of New York at New Paltz (New Paltz) 418
State University of New York at Oswego (Oswego) 422
State University of New York--College of Environmental Science and Forestry (Syracuse) 420
State University of New York-Binghamton University (Binghamton) 184
State University of New York-Stony Brook University (Stony Brook) 424
State University of New York-University at Buffalo (Buffalo) 426
United States Merchant Marine Academy (Kings Point) 226
United States Military Academy (West Point) 228
Vassar College (Poughkeepsie) 348
Webb Institute (Glen Cove) 232

OHIO

Ohio State University—Columbus, The (Columbus) 408

OKLAHOMA

University of Oklahoma (Norman) 478

OREGON

Reed College (Portland) 326

PENNSYLVANIA

Bryn Mawr College (Bryn Mawr) 254
Bucknell University (Lewisburg) 256
Gettysburg College (Gettysburg) 296
Haverford College (Haverford) 304
Lafayette College (Easton) 310
Swarthmore College (Swarthmore) 134
University of Pennsylvania (Philadelphia) 340
University of Pittsburgh (Pittsburgh) 482
University of Pittsburgh at Bradford (Bradford) 480

RHODE ISLAND

Brown University (Providence) 252

SOUTH CAROLINA

Clemson University (Clemson) 380
College of Charleston (Charleston) 382
University of South Carolina—Columbia (Columbia) 484
Wofford College (Spartanburg) 364

SOUTH DAKOTA

University of South Dakota, The (Vermillion) 486

TENNESSEE

Sewanee—The University of the South (Sewanee) 330
University of Tennessee at Martin (Martin) 490
University of Tennessee—Knoxville (Knoxville) 488
Vanderbilt University (Nashville) 346

TEXAS

Rice University (Houston) 146
University of Houston (Houston) 452
University of Texas at Austin, The (Austin) 208

UTAH

Southern Utah University (Cedar City) 412
Utah State University (Logan) 494

VIRGINIA

Christopher Newport University (Newport News) 374
College of William & Mary, The (Williamsburg) 192
James Madison University (Harrisonburg) 396
Longwood University (Farmville) 400
Randolph College (Lynchburg) 324
University of Mary Washington (Fredericksburg) 458
University of Richmond (Richmond) 344
University of Virginia (Charlottesville) 176
Virginia Polytechnic Institute (Blacksburg) 496

VERMONT

Middlebury College (Middlebury) 316

WASHINGTON

Evergreen State College, The (Olympia) 386
University of Washington (Seattle) 204
Whitman College (Walla Walla) 362

WASHINGTON, D.C.

Georgetown University (Washington, D.C.) 294

WISCONSIN

Beloit College (Beloit)	244
University of Wisconsin-Eau Claire (Eau Claire)	492
University of Wisconsin-Madison (Madison)	188

Acknowledgments

My sincere thanks go to the many who contributed to this tremendous project. I would first like to thank all of the colleges who participated in this project. The students who completed our surveys and USA TODAY made this project possible. A special thank you goes to our authors, Jen Adams, Eric Owens, Andrea Kornstein, Calvin Cato, Nick LaQualia, Ann Weil, Jennifer Zbrizher, Brandi Tape, Eric San Juan, Jen Clark, and Eric Ginsberg. Evan Schreier deserves many thanks for his incredible dedication to working with thousands of student quotes and school surveys to produce the school profiles. Very special thanks go to Robert Franek and Seamus Mullarkey for their editorial commitment to and vision for our editorial endeavors. My continued thanks go to our data collection team, David Soto, Courtney Richter, Lyle Friedman, and Stephen Koch for their successful efforts in collecting and accurately representing the statistical data that appear with each college profile. The enormousness of this project and its deadline constraints could not have been realized without the calm presence of our production designers John Wujcik, Ryan Tozzi, Aaron DeLand, and Vanessa Han for their dedication and focus. Special thanks also go to Jeanne Krier, our Random House publicist, for the dedicated work she continues to do for all of our books. I would also like to make special mention of Tom Russell, Nicole Benhabib, Alison Stoltzfus, and Ellen Reed, our Random House publishing team, for their continuous investment and faith in our ideas. We are so lucky to have the USA TODAY team as partners. Last, I thank my TPR Partner Team, Scott Kirkpatrick, Michael Bleyhl, Paul Kanarek, Brian Healy, and Lev Kaye for their confidence in me and my content team and for their commitment to providing students the resources they need to find the right fit school for them. Again, to all who contributed so much to this publication, thank you for your efforts; they do not go unnoticed.

Laura Braswell
Senior Editor
The Princeton Review